ENCYCLOPEDIA OF AMERICAN LIVES

The SCRIBNER ENCYCLOPEDIA *of*
AMERICAN LIVES

The SCRIBNER ENCYCLOPEDIA *of*

AMERICAN LIVES

SPORTS FIGURES

VOLUME ONE

A–K

ARNOLD MARKOE
VOLUME EDITOR

KENNETH T. JACKSON
SERIES EDITOR IN CHIEF

CHARLES SCRIBNER'S SONS

GALE GROUP
THOMSON LEARNING
New York • Detroit • San Diego • San Francisco
Boston • New Haven, Conn. • Waterville, Maine
London • Munich

Charles Scribner's Sons
An imprint of The Gale Group
300 Park Avenue South, 9th floor
New York, NY 10010

Library of Congress Cataloging-in-Publication Data

The Scribner encyclopedia of American lives. Sports figures / edited by Arnold
    Markoe.
        p.   cm.
    Includes bibliographical references and index.
        ISBN 0-684-80665-7 (set : alk. paper)—ISBN 0-684-31224-7 (vol. 1)—ISBN
    0-684-31225-5 (vol. 2)
        1. Athletes—United States—Biography—Dictionaries. 2. Sports—United
    States—Encyclopedias.   I. Markoe, Arnie.
GV697.A1   S42   2002
796'.092'2—dc21   201049603
                                                                  CIP

1 3 5 7 9 11 13 15 17 19 20 18 16 14 12 10 8 6 4 2
PRINTED IN THE UNITED STATES OF AMERICA

Preface

The *Scribner Encyclopedia of American Lives (SEAL) Sports Figures* set is published in two alphabetically arranged volumes containing the biographies of 614 notable figures in the history of American sports. Biographies include family background, formative influences, and achievements outside the realm of sport as well as the significance of subjects' athletic accomplishments. It is the first in a projected series of *SEAL* thematic volumes dedicated to discrete topics in United States history.

We have followed the successful format of previous *SEAL* volumes. Entries are headed by an opening paragraph that highlights some of the subject's most important achievements and are accompanied by a photograph of the subject. Articles are signed by their authors and the back matter in Volume 2 identifies authors by institutional or occupational affiliation in addition to listing all entries by sport or category.

Many of the 205 academics, journalists, and archivists who have written biographies in these two volumes have previously written for *SEAL* and, before that, for the *Dictionary of American Biography*, also published by Scribners. Contributors include authors who have written full-length biographies of their subjects, sports reporters, and historians, as well as present and former staff members of sports halls of fame. We are gratified that many authors who have worked with us in the past have chosen to stay on board for this project; this Scribner endeavor, however, is an entirely new venture with all entries written specifically for the *Sports Figures* volumes. In addition to thorough reviews of source material, authors have often interviewed their subjects and subjects' family members. Both the *Dictionary of American Biography* and previous *SEAL* volumes limited entries to notable Americans who were deceased. *SEAL Sports Figures* comprises both the living and the dead, both active and retired athletes, media personalities, coaches, and administrators who have contributed to the American sports mosaic.

Choosing approximately 600 subjects from the entire history of American sports for inclusion was a challenge met, but we are aware that thoughtful readers might suggest additional significant figures left beyond the covers of our two volumes. Weighing the relative merits of figures from different sports is more difficult than comparing figures in the same sport, which itself is often cause for controversy, as evidenced by long-standing heated debates about elections to the various halls of fame. *SEAL*'s biographical focus is American, but also included are athletes of other nationalities, exemplified by Sammy Sosa and Bobby Orr, who played for American teams. Although there are many entries of amateur sports figures, we have concentrated on professional athletes, who perhaps best provide a national perspective to these volumes. Statistical rankings were important to our selection process, but we also sought biographies that told a story or illuminated less-known aspects of sports history. We have conferred with numerous experts and also received suggestions from a wide sampling of fans. The final responsibility for selection, however, rests entirely with the editors.

After the Civil War the American sporting scene, previously unorganized, was shaped by the increase of leisure time, the growth of cities, and entrepreneurs who pursued opportunities for profit in spectator sports. Although there are many biographies of nineteenth-century sports personalities, such as heavyweight champion John L. Sullivan and baseball pioneer Albert Spalding, twentieth-century figures dominate these two volumes. With the advent of radio and increased press coverage, America embraced athletes as never before during the 1920s, the era dubbed the Golden Age of sports. Athletes from different economic strata and ethnic backgrounds were honored. Excluded from male sporting preserves in the nineteenth century, increasing numbers of women athletes gained prominence. Color barriers remained rigid, but sports in the African-American community flourished. Many Americans began to read the sports page before the front page. By the end of the twentieth century, with television a prime player, spectator sports had become a national obsession or, for the less passionate, at least a respite from the concerns of the evening news.

We have represented sports from auto racing to wrestling. Many of the athletes chosen would be on anyone's list. Among the most noteworthy entries are: in baseball, Babe Ruth, Ty Cobb, Joe DiMaggio, Ted Williams, and Jackie Robinson; auto racing, Bill France, Sr., and Richard Petty; basketball, Kareem Abdul-Jabbar, Magic Johnson, Larry Bird, John Wooden, and Michael Jordan; golf, Ben Hogan and Babe Didrikson Zaharias; football, Jim Thorpe, Walter Payton, and Vince Lombardi; swimming, Johnny Weissmuller and Mark Spitz; tennis, Martina Navratilova and Pete Sampras; hockey, Wayne Gretzky and Gordie Howe; track, Jesse Owens and Wilma Rudolph; and boxing, Jack Johnson, Jack Dempsey, and Muhammad Ali.

Others celebrated are Junior Johnson, moonshine runner who became a race car legend; peerless players Shoeless Joe Jackson and Pete Rose, both banned from baseball; pitcher Lefty Gomez, nicknamed "El Goofy," who stopped a World Series game to watch a plane fly over Yankee Stadium; Lynette Woodard, first woman to play for the Harlem Globetrotters; Tiger Woods, all-time top money winning golfer; Dick Fosbury, whose "Fosbury flop" revolutionized high jump technique; and Trudy Ederle, first woman to swim the English Channel, in the process setting a new world record for women *and* men. As one life borders the next in these pages, we hope readers will be enticed to review entries across the range of American sports history.

There are many to acknowledge in an undertaking of this dimension. At the heart of these volumes are dedicated photo researchers and copy editors and hundreds of talented writers. Richard H. Gentile, a valued colleague from the inception of this project, provided insight and expert guidance on research materials. Scribner staff members Anthony Aiello and Kelly Baiseley were superb editorial assistants. We have benefited immensely from the resourcefulness of Sarah Feehan and Jan Klisz, project editors at Scribners, who kept us on track. And we are especially indebted to Timothy J. DeWerff, Associate Publisher, the guiding spirit of *SEAL*, for his patience, good cheer, professional judgment, and friendship.

Arnold Markoe, Volume Editor
Kenneth T. Jackson, Series Editor in Chief

CONTENTS

VOLUME 1

VOLUME 2

The SCRIBNER ENCYCLOPEDIA *of*
AMERICAN LIVES

A

AARON, Henry Louis ("Hank") (*b.* 5 February 1934 in Mobile, Alabama), possibly the greatest hitter in Major League Baseball history and the holder of the all-time home run and runs batted in records.

Aaron was the third of eight children of Herbert and Estella Aaron. His father was a boilermaker's helper with the Alabama Dry-Dock and Ship Building Company in Mobile. One of Aaron's younger brothers, Tommie, also played professional baseball; his major-league career included a stint as Hank Aaron's teammate with the Braves in Milwaukee.

Aaron played softball in recreational leagues in Mobile because his high school, the Josephine Allen Institute, did not have a baseball team. He was discovered by the Mobile Black Bears, a semiprofessional African-American team, and played with them during his high school years, especially when strong traveling teams came to town. Upon Aaron's graduation in 1951, the Negro Leagues' Indianapolis Clowns signed him for the 1952 season. Halfway through the season Aaron's skills caught the attention of scouts for Major League Baseball as they signed African-American players in the early 1950s. The New York Giants and the Milwaukee Braves each pursued Aaron, but the Giants felt they had a star in Willie Mays, so they did not work as hard to sign Aaron as the Braves did. The Braves signed Aaron on 14 June 1952 and sent him to Eau Claire, Wisconsin, of the Northern League, where he won the Rookie of the Year and was second in hitting with a .336 average. In 1953 Aaron went to Jacksonville, Florida, and had an excellent season, leading the South Atlantic (Sally) League with a .362 average and 125 runs batted in (RBI). Despite his success on the field, Aaron experienced racial discrimination beyond that which he had as a child in Mobile.

Aaron married Barbara Lucas on 3 October 1953; they had five children. The couple divorced in 1971, and Aaron married Billy Suber Williams on 12 November 1973.

Aaron made his debut with the Braves in 1954 and had a strong rookie season. In 122 games he hit 13 home runs and batted .280. After solid seasons for the Braves in 1955 and 1956, Aaron broke through in 1957. He batted .322, led the league with 44 home runs and 132 RBI, and was selected the National League's (NL) most valuable player (MVP) while leading the Braves to the National League pennant. In the 1957 World Series Aaron batted .393 in the Braves' 7-game victory over the New York Yankees, with 3 home runs and 7 RBI. The Braves won the AL pennant again in 1958, but lost to the Yankees in seven games.

Aaron established himself in the late 1950s and early 1960s as one of the best hitters in the game, leading the league in home runs three more times. In 1963, still in Milwaukee (the Braves moved to Atlanta in 1966), he hit 44 home runs to tie with Willie McCovey. In the first two years at Atlanta, Aaron again led the league in home runs, hitting 44 in 1966 and 39 in 1967. Aaron also led the league in RBI in 1963 (130) and 1966 (127). He compiled tremendous career numbers during his twenty-three years in professional baseball by staying healthy and by consistently hitting for power. While Aaron never hit 50 home runs, a mark often used to distinguish the best power hitters in baseball, he recorded 30 home runs 15 times, including 8 seasons with over 40. Similarly, he drove in over 100 runs 11 times and scored 100 runs 15 times (including every season from 1955 to 1967).

Aaron recorded his 3,000th hit on 17 May 1970, in only his seventeenth season. It was not until the early 1970s that reporters and fans started thinking that Aaron had a chance at Babe Ruth's all-time home run record of 714. By the end of the 1970 season Aaron had 592 homers, third behind Ruth and Willie Mays (who had 628 homers at that time). While Mays saw his production drop significantly over the next three seasons and ended his career with 660 home runs, Aaron defied his age and proceeded to have three outstanding seasons that placed him on the verge of Ruth's record. In the three seasons starting in 1971, Aaron hit 47, 34, and 40 home runs. Aaron passed Mays with his 649th home run on 10 June 1972, and his 40 home runs in 1973 gave him 713, 1 behind Ruth. Aaron never savored media attention, but as he got closer to Ruth's record he had to play under great media and public scrutiny. He said at the time, "I can't recall a day this year or last when I did not hear the name of Babe Ruth." Although Aaron became a national hero in his home-run chase, he was also subject to numerous threats and hate letters from bigots upset that an African American was about to break one of the most sacred records of baseball. Aaron hired bodyguards, and the Federal Bureau of Investigation was involved in protecting his safety.

The Braves were scheduled to open the 1974 season with a series in Cincinnati against the Dodgers, then head down to Atlanta for their first home game. Braves management planned to keep Aaron out of the Cincinnati games to focus the public's attention on him tying and breaking Ruth's record in Atlanta, but commissioner Bowie Kuhn interceded and forced the Braves to play their superstar. Aaron hit his 714th homer on opening day and tied Babe Ruth, but he played poorly in the rest of the series. On 8 April 1974 in Atlanta, Aaron hit home run 715 off the Dodgers Al Downing. He was congratulated by the Dodgers' players as he rounded the bases and greeted by fans who ran onto the field as he reached home.

After the excitement of setting the new record, Aaron's production dropped off. He ended the season in 1974 with 20 home runs in 112 games and was traded to the Milwaukee Brewers, returning to the city where his pro career began. He played primarily as a designated hitter and was able to contribute to the team. Over his two seasons with the Brewers, Aaron played in 222 games, batted .232, drove in 95 runs, and hit 22 home runs, giving him a career total

Hank Aaron. ARCHIVE PHOTOS, INC.

of 755. The *New York Times* recorded every home run that he hit with a special graphic to denote the new record.

When Aaron retired from playing in 1976, he became the vice president and director of player development for the Atlanta Braves under their new owner, Ted Turner of the Turner Broadcasting System (TBS-TV) in Atlanta. Aaron was one of the first African Americans to hold an executive role with a major league team, following Frank Robinson's breakthrough as the first African-American manager. Throughout his twenty-five–year tenure as an executive with the Braves, Aaron was a vocal advocate of opening the doors of baseball management to African Americans.

Aaron was elected to the National Baseball Hall of Fame in 1982, his first year of eligibility. He received 97.8 percent of the vote, the second-highest percentage ever received (behind Ty Cobb). As well as the home-run crown, Aaron holds the career record for RBI (2,297) and is third in hits (3,771). He summed up his feeling about his achievements this way: "I'm hoping someday that some kid, black or white, will hit more home runs than myself. Whoever it is, I'd be pulling for him."

★

Aaron wrote numerous books, including *Aaron* (1974), with Furman Bisher; *I Had a Hammer* (1991), with Lonnie Wheeler;

and *Home Run: My Life in Pictures* (1999), with Dick Schaap. Books about Aaron include George Plimpton, *One for the Record: The Inside Story of Hank Aaron's Chase for the Home-Run Record* (1974), and Peter Golenbock, *Hank Aaron: Brave in Every Way* (2001). Information on Aaron is also available at the National Baseball Hall of Fame Library.

COREY SEEMAN

ABBOTT, Senda Berenson. *See* Berenson Abbott, Senda.

ABDUL-JABBAR, Kareem (*b.* 16 April 1947 in New York City), Hall of Fame basketball player who was one of the most dominant centers in the sport's history.

Abdul-Jabbar was born Ferdinand Lewis "Lew" Alcindor, Jr., in Harlem, the only child of Lewis Alcindor, Sr., a transit police officer, and Cora Alcindor, a homemaker. Height ran in the family. Abdul-Jabbar's mother was nearly six feet tall, and his father was six feet, two inches. Abdul-Jabbar's parents told him that his grandfather, who had

Kareem Abdul-Jabbar (*right*). AP/WIDE WORLD PHOTOS

come from Alcindor Trace, a section of the Balandra district of Trinidad, was over six feet, eight inches in height, and Abdul-Jabbar was over twenty-two inches long at birth.

Abdul-Jabbar's mother read to him constantly, hence he learned to love books at an early age. His father, who played the trombone, often took Abdul-Jabbar to the Elks Club at 5th Avenue and 126th Street, where the senior Alcindor joined other musicians for long jam sessions. From his father, who graduated from the Juilliard School of Music in 1952, Abdul-Jabbar gained a lasting love of jazz music.

When Abdul-Jabbar was three, his father thought the area around Seventh Avenue and 111th Street was becoming too dirty and dangerous, so in 1950 he moved his family to the Dyckman Housing Project in Inwood, a section of northern Manhattan. Between the first and second grades at P.S. 52, Abdul-Jabbar first picked up a basketball and tried unsuccessfully to put it through the hoop. When he was eight years old his parents, devout Catholics, transferred him to Saint Jude's, a private Catholic boy's school nearby, where he was one of only two blacks.

When Abdul-Jabbar was ready to enter fourth grade, his parents were both working, so they enrolled him in Holy Providence, a Catholic school in Pennsylvania. The five-foot, four-inch boy was teased for his height, shyness, and bookish habits. He participated in swimming, track, baseball, and basketball and soon learned to love the last sport. Most of the other students at Holy Providence spoke and behaved in a rough manner. After one year his parents withdrew Abdul-Jabbar, returning him to Saint Jude's in the fall of 1957. He joined the basketball team and, although he was six feet tall, spent most of the season on the bench. Farrell Hopkins, his coach, helped him improve his skills, allowing the eager youngster to continue practice after regular hours.

When Abdul-Jabbar was in seventh grade, Hopkins got the team new uniforms. Abdul-Jabbar's new number was 33, the number he wore for the remainder of his basketball career. Encountering racial prejudice from whites, he concentrated on his studies and basketball. By the eighth grade, when he was fourteen, he was six feet, eight inches tall and could dunk. In one game he scored thirty-three points, more than the entire team usually scored.

Abdul-Jabbar's friend and neighbor Arthur Kenny, a freshman at Power Memorial Academy, a Catholic high school for boys in Manhattan, took Abdul-Jabbar to practice at the high school, where the coach, Jack Donohue, offered Abdul-Jabbar a full scholarship. Donohue ran a summer camp at Friendship Farm in Saugerties, New York, and he invited Abdul-Jabbar to spend the summer before his freshman year there. The only black player at the camp, Abdul-Jabbar was shunned by the other boys, and he returned home after only three weeks.

Abdul-Jabbar played on the varsity team at Power Memorial Academy in his freshman year, and by his sopho-more year he had become a great player, leading the school to the New York City Catholic high school championship. He was named to numerous All-America high school teams and had his picture in national magazines. By his junior year the sixteen year old was seven feet, one-and-a-half inches tall and almost unstoppable on the basketball court. During halftime of a game against Saint Helena's in the Bronx, Coach Donohue scolded his team for a lackadaisical performance and hurled a racial epithet at his star center. Abdul-Jabbar was stunned. He eventually led Power Me-morial to another city championship, but he refused to work during the summer at Friendship Farm. During his senior year Abdul-Jabbar broke the New York City high school basketball records for career points (2,076) and total rebounds (2,002). He graduated in 1965 and won a New York State Regents' scholarship. Heavily recruited, Abdul-Jabbar enrolled at the University of California at Los Angeles (UCLA).

Abdul-Jabbar liked the UCLA coach John Wooden im-mediately. He spent most of his time with black friends, like Lucius Allen, his roommate and teammate on the freshman basketball team, and J. J. Johnson, who intro-duced him to black literature. Reading Malcolm X's *The Autobiography of Malcolm X* (1965), Abdul-Jabbar became interested in black nationalism and the religion of Islam.

Shunned by many whites, Abdul-Jabbar devoted himself to basketball. In his first season he broke the previous UCLA freshman records for total points (696), total re-bounds (425), and single game total points (48). Off the court he was not so successful. Because he refused to give interviews, reporters described him as moody and surly. The white girl he was dating received threatening calls, forcing the couple to break off the relationship.

As a sophomore Abdul-Jabbar set a school single game scoring record (56 points) in his first varsity game. UCLA won all twenty-six games that season, and its star center was chosen Player of the Year by a United Press Interna-tional poll. In the summer of 1967 Abdul-Jabbar found rewarding work teaching basketball in the ghetto areas of New York City in a program called Operation Sports Res-cue, run by the New York City Housing Authority.

In his junior year Abdul-Jabbar led UCLA to another championship season. Because he could stuff the ball so easily, the National Collegiate Athletic Association (NCAA) banned the dunk shot. To compensate, Coach Wooden helped Abdul-Jabbar develop a hook shot, which over the years developed into the famous skyhook, a mod-ification of the traditional hook shot in which the ball trav-els downward from the peak of an arch. Joining other black athletes, he boycotted the 1968 Olympics because of the discrimination that black athletes who had won medals in the 1964 Olympics faced at home. As a result he received

a great deal of hate mail. He took refuge again in Operation Sports Rescue over the summer. At the same time he con-verted to Islam. His new name became Kareem (noble and generous) Abdul (servant) Jabbar (powerful).

Abdul-Jabbar's senior year capped a significant college career. He became the first player to receive the NCAA Tournament Most Valuable Player (MVP) award three times. When he left UCLA he had won a record eighty-eight games, losing only to Houston and the University of Southern California. He had scored a total of 2,325 points (26.4 per game average) and had grabbed 1,367 rebounds (15.5 per game average). Writing his senior thesis on Islam in North America, he graduated in 1969 with a B.A. degree in history.

In 1969, signing a five-year, $1.4 million contract, Abdul-Jabbar began his pro basketball career with the last-place Milwaukee Bucks of the National Basketball Asso-ciation (NBA). By the end of his first season he had earned NBA Rookie of the Year honors for the 1969–1970 season and had carried the Bucks to the Eastern Division playoffs. In his second season Abdul-Jabbar teamed up with the leg-endary Oscar Robertson, recently traded to Milwaukee from the Cincinnati Royals, and the Bucks won the 1971 NBA championship. Abdul-Jabbar was named MVP of the NBA finals.

On 28 May 1971 Abdul-Jabbar married Janice Brown, a schoolteacher, in Washington, D.C. Shortly thereafter he changed his name legally to Kareem Abdul-Jabbar. His wife also changed her name, taking the Islamic name of Habiba. They had one daughter. In 1972 Abdul-Jabbar won the league's MVP award. In December 1974, after suf-fering an eye injury while going for a loose ball, he began to wear goggles when he played. That season Abdul-Jabbar was again named the league MVP.

By the end of the 1974–1975 season, Abdul-Jabbar's marriage had soured. Habiba, beleaguered from the pres-sures of being a pro basketball wife, took their three-year-old daughter and moved back to Washington, D.C. Abdul-Jabbar had never liked Milwaukee and asked to be traded. In 1975 he signed a five-year contract with the Los Angeles Lakers and moved into a ranch house in Stone Canyon, above the UCLA campus. Although the Lakers' new team did not make the playoffs that year, Abdul-Jabbar won his fourth MVP award in six years as a pro basketball player. In 1976 the American Basketball Association merged into the National Basketball Association, bringing to the Lakers many new players and a new coach, Jerry West, who guided Abdul-Jabbar to his fifth MVP award.

The Lakers had their star center, and all they needed was a playmaker. They found that person in the 1979–1980 season, when they added a rookie, Earvin "Magic" John-son. The Jabbar-Johnson combination helped the Lakers win the NBA championship that season, and Abdul-Jabbar won an unprecedented sixth MVP title. Taking over as head coach in 1981, Pat Riley developed a running game based on the fast break known as "show time," which won the Lakers their second NBA title in three years in 1982. On 5 April 1984 Abdul-Jabbar surpassed Wilt Chamberlain to become the league's all-time leading scorer with 31,420 total career points. According to Abdul-Jabbar, the best moment in his career was in 1985, when the Lakers beat the Boston Celtics for the NBA title.

By 1986 the offensive leadership of the Lakers had passed to Magic Johnson, and while the team continued to win NBA titles, Abdul-Jabbar struggled for points. In 1989 his streak of 787 consecutive games in which he scored in double figures came to an end. By this time he was averaging only eight points and four rebounds per game. He was still suffering financially from a 1983 fire that had destroyed his Bel-Air home and ruined his beloved, valuable jazz record collection. In addition he had lost millions of dollars in bad business investments. In 1989, at age forty-two, Abdul-Jabbar decided to retire. He had won six world championships and six MVP awards. In 1995 he was inducted into the Basketball Hall of Fame.

Frustrated by retirement and devastated by the death of his mother, Abdul-Jabbar sought work. In 1999 he coached the high school basketball team at White Mountain Apache Reservation in Whiteriver, Arizona. He was an assistant coach for the Los Angeles Clippers from February to May 2000. He made many movie and television appearances, including memorable Hollywood roles as the copilot named Flying High in *Airplane!* (1980) and the Monster Shouter in Stephen King's *The Stand* (1994). He had two sons in relationships after Habiba left (they divorced in 1993), and he has spent most of his retirement time with his three children, traveling between his homes in Los Angeles and Maui, Hawaii. Most of his earnings have come from speaking engagements, signing autographs at trading card shows, and product endorsements.

Abdul-Jabbar's pro basketball career statistics are staggering. His regular-season numbers averaged 24.6 points, 11.2 rebounds, and 3.6 blocked shots per game. He had a lifetime shooting percentage of .559, and he was first-team all-league ten times and second-team five times. He established NBA records for most seasons of 1,000 or more points (19), most minutes played (57,446), most field goals (15,837), most field goal attempts (28,307), most points (38,387), and most personal fouls (4,657) as well as several NBA All-Star Game records.

★

Abdul-Jabbar authored three autobiographical memoirs, *Giant Steps* (1983), *Kareem* (1991), and *A Season on the Reservation* (2000), along with a chronicle of the lives of famous African Americans, *Profiles in Black Courage* (1996). James Haskins, *From Lew*

Alcindor to Kareem Abdul-Jabbar (1972), gives detailed information about Abdul-Jabbar's early life. Thomas R. Cobourn, *Kareem Abdul-Jabbar* (1995), is the most recent biography and contains an extensive bibliography.

JOHN J. BYRNE

ABEL, Sid(ney) Gerald (*b.* 22 February 1918 in Saskatchewan, Canada; *d.* 8 February 2000 in Farmington Hills, Michigan), hockey player who was the center in the famed Detroit Red Wing "Production Line" with Gordie Howe and Ted Lindsay during the late 1940s and early 1950s.

Abel made his debut with the Red Wings in 1938. He played only thirty-nine games over the next two seasons but emerged as a regular in 1940, recording eleven goals and twenty-two assists in forty-seven games. For the 1942–1943 season Abel, though only twenty-four years old, was named team captain and led the Red Wings to a four-game sweep of the Boston Bruins in the Stanley Cup finals. Tallying forty-two points on eighteen goals and twenty-four assists in forty-nine regular season games, Abel excelled in the playoffs, collecting thirteen points in ten games (five goals, eight assists). Yet after winning the Stanley Cup, Abel left the NHL for nearly three years.

Like many players, Abel joined the military during World War II, fighting with the Canadian armed forces. However, Abel did not completely forget about hockey; from 1943 until 1945 he managed to play a few games with the Montreal Royal Canadian Air Force team, the Montreal

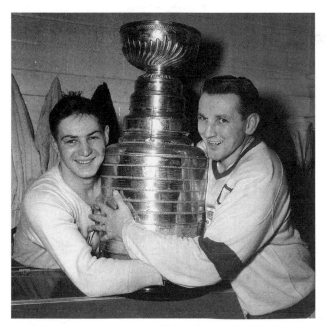

Sid Abel (*right*) and goalie Terry Sawchuck after winning the 1952 Stanley Cup. AP PHOTO/PRESTON STROUP

Canada Car, and the Lachine Rapides. Abel returned to the Red Wings late in 1946, playing in only seven regular-season and three playoff games, as the Bruins eliminated Detroit in the semifinals. Back with the club full-time in the 1946–1947 season, Abel could not prevent a disappointing fourth-place finish and another early exit from the playoffs. Given their lackluster performances during the 1945–1946 and 1946–1947 seasons, no one could have predicted that the Red Wings were about to make hockey history.

Following the 1946–1947 season, Red Wings coach Jack Adams resigned after twenty-one years to concentrate on his duties as general manager. One of the first decisions new coach Tommy Ivan made was to put Abel on a line with a rugged left winger named Ted Lindsay and a promising right winger named Gordie Howe, who had just completed his rookie season. The trio meshed effortlessly from the outset. By the end of their first season together (1947–1948), the press had christened them the "Production Line," an epithet inspired as much by their blue-collar work ethic as by their prolific scoring.

Although less celebrated, Abel was arguably the most important member of the line. His unmatched talent, savvy, and creativity propelled the Red Wings to Stanley Cup championships in 1950 and 1952. Hockey historian Ed Fitkin maintained that Abel "will go down in the Red Wings' history as the greatest competitor and inspirational force the Red Wings ever had." Certainly Lindsay and Howe relied on him for guidance and leadership.

Abel savored his role as mentor. On the ice, Howe said, it was Abel who controlled the pace and action of the game, orchestrating his wingers' heroics. "Sid gave Ted and I [sic] a lot of room to work with. . . . He was the leader, that's why he wore the 'C.'" Abel contributed at least as much to the development and maturity of Howe and Lindsay away from the rink. "Sid taught us so much," Howe declared. "We used to sit up in the trains for hours after the game, and he'd go over everything. He'd take us through the whole game, pointing out what we did right and what we did wrong. I think I learned more on the trains than I did on the ice."

In the 1949–1950 season, Lindsay (23 goals, 55 assists, 78 points), Abel (34–35–69), and Howe (35–33–68) led the NHL in scoring and brought the Red Wings a Stanley Cup championship, at last avenging the heartbreaking defeat that the Toronto Maple Leafs had administered in 1942. The Production Line stayed together for two more seasons, winning another Stanley Cup in 1952, before Abel asked to be released from his contract to become player-coach of the Chicago Blackhawks. Abel played only thirty-nine games for the Hawks in the 1952–1953 season and only three in the 1953–1954 season, retiring to concentrate solely on coaching. Returning to Detroit as an analyst on Red Wings television broadcasts, Abel replaced Jimmy Skinner

as Red Wings coach midway through the 1957–1958 season, when Skinner had to resign because of ill health.

Abel coached the Red Wings until 1968, compiling a record of 340 wins, 339 losses, and 132 ties. He also served as general manager between 1962 and 1971. During Abel's tenure as coach, the Red Wings, although no longer the most talented team in the NHL, reached the Stanley Cup finals in 1961, 1963, 1964, and 1966, but never won. Almost universally admired, Abel, according to Wings defenseman Bill Gadsby, "treated players like men. He never singled out anybody in the dressing room. The guys respected that."

Inducted into the Hockey Hall of Fame in 1969, Abel finished his career with 189 goals and 283 assists in 612 regular season games, all but 42 of them in a Red Wings uniform. He added 28 goals and 30 assists in 98 playoff contests. Twice during his illustrious career, in 1949 and 1950, Abel was First Team All-Star, and twice, in 1942 and 1951, he was a member of the Second Team. He became the first player in the history of the NHL to attain All-Star status at two positions, having been selected as a left-wing in 1942 and as a center in 1949. Abel also won the Hart Trophy in 1949 as the league's Most Valuable Player.

Between 1976 and 1986 Abel again provided expert commentary on Red Wings radio and television broadcasts. "Old Bootnose," as Abel was known after Maurice Richard broke his nose in a fight, died just before his eighty-second birthday following a long battle with heart disease and cancer. His wife Gloria survived him, along with his two children. Abel is buried at Glen Edan Memorial Park in Livronia, Michigan.

Despite having played for and coached the Blackhawks, as well as briefly coaching the St. Louis Blues (1971–1972) and the Kansas City Scouts (1975–1976), Abel always thought of himself as "a Red Wing through and through." The Red Wings organization honored that commitment in 1995, retiring Abel's number 12 jersey to the rafters of Joe Louis Arena. Appropriately, it hangs between Gordie Howe's number 9 and Ted Lindsay's number 7.

★

For full-length works on Abel and the Red Wings, see Stan Fischler, *Motor City Muscle: Gordie Howe, Terry Sawchuk, and the Championship Detroit Red Wings* (1995); Paul R. Greenland, *Wings of Fire: The History of the Detroit Red Wings* (1997); Richard Bak, *The Detroit Red Wings: The Illustrated History* (1998); and Brian McFarlane, *The Detroit Red Wings* (1999). For specific team information, see Bob Duff, "Franchise Histories: Detroit Red Wings," in *Total Hockey: The Official Encyclopedia of the National Hockey League* (1998). Chuck Carlton, "Production Line Center Was Ready, Willing, and Abel," *Hockey News* 53, no. 24 (2000), is an obituary that provides insight on Abel's role in the famous line.

MARK G. MALVASI

ADDIE, Pauline May Betz. *See* Betz, Pauline May.

AGASSI, Andre Kirk (*b.* 29 April 1970 in Las Vegas, Nevada), tennis player and winner of seven Grand Slam events from 1992 to 2001.

Agassi was born to Emmanuel "Mike" Agassi and his wife, Elizabeth. He was groomed to play professional tennis literally from the day he was born. His father was an Iranian immigrant and a former Olympic boxer who became infatuated with the game of tennis as a young man. As his personal opportunities to pursue an athletic career dwindled, Mike Agassi turned his attention to raising his children to be sports champions, specifically tennis superstars. Because he was only marginally successful in training his three older children, he resorted to extreme measures by the time his youngest child was born. So determined was Mike Agassi to raise young Agassi to be a champion that he spared no effort in providing the newborn with a head start in the sport. The elder Agassi went so far as to hang a tennis ball over the infant's cradle in order to accustom the boy to watching the ball. The baby Agassi was encouraged to swat balloons with a Ping-Pong paddle and was given a full-size racket before he could walk so he could

Andre Agassi. AP/WIDE WORLD PHOTOS

become accustomed to the weight. Agassi's father also established connections in professional tennis and arranged a practice match between his toddler son and Jimmy Connors. Agassi was barely of school age the first time he played against Ilie Nastase and still in grade school when he first practiced with Bjorn Borg.

Given his father's overwhelming influence, Agassi's career in tennis was an assumption rather than an option. In pursuit of this goal, Mike Agassi held down two casino jobs and donated much of his remaining time to working as a tennis coach for local children, including his own. When Agassi was six years old his father purchased a Las Vegas property with a large grounds and built a family home complete with tennis court. At his father's insistence, Agassi maintained a practice regimen in grade school that involved hitting about 3,000 balls daily. The balls were served to Agassi by means of three makeshift ball machines that operated simultaneously, pitching serves at speeds as high as 110 miles per hour. This practice setup was enhanced by powerful industrial fans rigged to send the balls on erratic trajectories.

Agassi competed in local amateur tournaments from the age of seven, winning nine events in the ten-and-under category during his first season of competition. After junior high, he enrolled in the Nick Bollettieri Tennis Academy in Bradenton, Florida. An above-average student, Agassi also spent his mornings in a traditional curriculum at the Bradenton Academy. This rigorous course of academic study and athletic training left young Agassi with an urgent need to succeed. While still competing at the junior level he won five national titles, including four doubles and one singles. In 1982 and 1984 Agassi was the fourth-ranked junior player in the United States and qualified for the United States Tennis Association (USTA) tour at age fifteen.

When Agassi became a professional in May 1986, shortly after his sixteenth birthday, he embarked on an impressive, albeit erratic, career. After a series of final-round losses in Grand Slam events, Agassi won his first Grand Slam title at Wimbledon in 1992. The following year he underwent wrist surgery to correct an injury and withdrew from the professional circuit while recuperating. He returned to active play in February 1994. Although Agassi was ranked twentieth and unseeded, he won the U.S. Open that year and registered winnings in excess of $2.4 million by the year's end. In 1995 he won the Australian Open and became the top-ranked men's player. Also that year Agassi's earnings approached $3 million, and he was recognized as a major force in bringing the Davis Cup competition to Las Vegas, although he dropped out of the competition on the third day due to an injury. In 1996 he represented the United States at the Olympic games in Atlanta, winning a gold medal.

Despite his innate shyness, Agassi adopted a flamboyant

persona early in his career. He displayed a trademark fashion sense on the court, wearing earrings, brightly colored clothes, and keeping his hair dyed and long. He incurred fines for his unsportsmanlike gesturing and occasional temper tantrums. In 1996 he was assessed a huge fine of $50,000 for shunning certain mandatory functions in conjunction with the Association of Tennis Professionals (ATP) Tour World Championship in Hanover, Germany. His personal life proved equally sensational. He married actress Brooke Shields on 19 April 1997.

Agassi receded from the public spotlight for a time following his marriage to Shields; he reemerged professionally after their divorce in 1999 to win the French and U.S. Opens that year and the Australian Open in 2000. With another Australian title in 2001, Agassi had captured seven Grand Slam wins and was again ranked number one. Later that year, on 22 October 2001, he married retired German tennis player Steffi Graf; days later Graf gave birth to the couple's son, Jaden Gil.

★

Paul Bauman's (unauthorized) biography, *Agassi and Ecstasy: The Turbulent Life of Andre Agassi*, was published in 1997; an in-depth profile appears in *Sports Stars,* Series 1–4 (1994–1998). For an assessment of Agassi's career, see also Jon L. Wertheim, "One for the Aged," *Sports Illustrated* (9 Apr. 2001).

GLORIA COOKSEY

AIKMAN, Troy Kenneth (*b.* 21 November 1966 in West Covina, California), football player who led the Dallas Cowboys to three Super Bowl titles.

Aikman was the youngest of three children of Kenneth Aikman, an oil-field worker and rancher, and Charlyn Aikman, a homemaker. Aikman spent his early years in California until his family moved to Henryetta, Oklahoma, when he was twelve years old. As a small child, Aikman had problems with his feet that were treated with casts and orthopedic shoes. As a teenager, he endured the culture shock of moving from suburban Southern California to a ranch in Henryetta (population 6,000), where his father raised cattle, pigs, and chickens. "I hated it," Aikman later told *Sports Illustrated.* "I just couldn't understand why we moved there. All my friends were in California, and I was already doing well in sports there." He overcame it by playing baseball and football (quarterback) at Henryetta High School. Although Aikman excelled in both sports, he passed up the opportunity to play professional baseball after graduating, and instead accepted a scholarship to play football for coach Barry Switzer at the University of Oklahoma.

Troy Aikman. AP/WIDE WORLD PHOTOS

Unfortunately, as a strong-armed, six-foot-four quarterback, Aikman was not a good fit for Switzer's run-oriented wishbone offense. A broken ankle shortened his sophomore season, and freshman Jamelle Holieway stepped in as quarterback. After Holieway led Oklahoma to the 1985 national championship, Aikman realized he would have little opportunity to play for Switzer and decided to transfer to University of California, Los Angeles (UCLA). Readjusting to Southern California was difficult for him. His teammates thought of him as a cowboy, because he chewed tobacco and liked country music. But Aikman became an All-American at UCLA, leading the Bruins to a pair of 10–2 campaigns and to victories in the Aloha and Cotton Bowls.

It was at the Cotton Bowl in Dallas that the NFL's Dallas Cowboys scouted Aikman. The Cowboys had the first pick in the upcoming college draft and coveted Aikman. In his last game with UCLA, Aikman was named Most Valuable Player (MVP) of the Cotton Bowl, as he guided the Bruins to a 17–3 win over Arkansas. By the time the draft took place in April 1989, the Cowboys had a new owner and head coach, but Aikman was their selection nonetheless. Ironically, the new Cowboys coach was former Oklahoma State University (OSU) and University of Miami coach Jimmy Johnson, who had recruited Aikman at

OSU and prompted Aikman to consider transferring to Miami before he ultimately chose UCLA.

Life in Dallas did not start smoothly for Aikman. During a special supplemental draft in the summer of 1989, the Cowboys also selected Johnson's heralded quarterback from Miami, Steve Walsh. As the two rookies battled for playing time, Dallas finished with a record of 1–15 that year. The lone win occurred when Aikman was sidelined with a broken finger and Walsh was in the lineup. "It was a painful, painful year," Aikman later recalled. "But I learned some very, very valuable lessons."

In 1990 Aikman and the Cowboys began to turn things around. The team picked running back Emmitt Smith in the first round of the college draft, and when Walsh was traded to the New Orleans Saints soon afterward, it provided the opportunity for Aikman, Smith, and wide receiver Michael Irvin to form an explosive offensive trio known as "The Triplets." Dallas improved to 7–9 in 1990 and 11–5 in 1991. Although Aikman missed five games at the end of 1991 with a knee injury, the Cowboys made the playoffs for the first time since 1985.

Aikman enjoyed an exceptional season in 1992, passing for 3,445 yards and 23 touchdowns. Dallas finished 13–3 that year and advanced to Super Bowl XXVII with a 30–20 victory against the San Francisco 49ers in the conference championship. On 31 January 1993 Aikman passed for four touchdowns and was named Super Bowl MVP following a 52–17 rout of the Buffalo Bills. (Aikman gave the car he won to his sister.) The following season, the Cowboys went 12–4 and repeated their feat, beating the 49ers 38–21 for the conference crown, and the Bills 30–13 in Super Bowl XXVIII on 30 January 1994.

Surprisingly, Johnson's tenure as coach of the Cowboys ended shortly thereafter, and in a twist of fate, Switzer was hired as his replacement. Dallas compiled another 12–4 record in 1994, but this time lost the conference title game to San Francisco. However, the Cowboys rebounded in 1995. They again finished 12–4, then defeated the Green Bay Packers 38–27 to advance to Super Bowl XXX. Once there, they beat the Pittsburgh Steelers 27–17 on 28 January 1996. "After having done this three times in four years, certainly this team has made a place in history," reflected Aikman on the trio of championships.

Unlike previous Cowboys quarterback Roger Staubach, Aikman was not famous for thrilling come-from-behind victories. In fact, when Aikman rallied Dallas from a twenty-one-point fourth quarter deficit to a 41–35 overtime win against the Washington Redskins on 12 September 1999 as his career was winding down, there was little precedent. Rather, Aikman developed a reputation for precision passing and efficiency that helped the Cowboys dominate opponents during their Super Bowl years. Only when the careers of his primary receivers ended—Jay Novacek

after the 1995 season and Irvin during the 1999 campaign—did his efficiency and the team's dominance begin to wane.

On 8 April 2000 Aikman married Rhonda Worthey, a former public relations aide for the Cowboys, at his home in Plano, Texas. A year later, on 9 April 2001, Aikman retired from football at age thirty-four. The Cowboys had released him a month earlier, and though he did consider joining another team, he ultimately decided to stop playing altogether. He had suffered a series of concussions and numerous other injuries over the years, and with new wife Rhonda expecting their second child, he concluded it was not in their best interests to continue playing. "It was 12 of the best years of my life," said Aikman at his farewell press conference.

By posting ninety regular-season victories during the 1990s, Aikman achieved an unparalleled starting quarterback record for any decade in NFL history. He led Dallas to six division titles and was selected to the Pro Bowl six times. Known for his extensive community involvement and charitable endeavors, Aikman had a street named after him in Henryetta and was honored as 1997's "NFL Man of the Year." In 1998 he was treated for skin cancer. Upon his retirement, he became a television football analyst with the Fox network.

★

For more information about Aikman's career, see *Beckett Great Sports Heroes: Troy Aikman* (1996), and the "Troy Aikman Roundup" and "Ultimate Aikman" retirement specials at *DallasCowboys.com* and *DallasNews.com*, respectively. Aikman's personal story, written with Greg Brown, is in a best-selling children's book, *Troy Aikman: Things Change* (1995), as well as in Aikman's *Troy Aikman: Mind, Body, and Soul* (1998). Also see a biography by Bill Gutman, *Troy Aikman: Super Quarterback* (1999).

Jack Styczynski

AKERS, Michelle Anne (*b.* 1 February 1966 in Santa Clara, California), soccer player who was the most prolific woman scorer in U.S. soccer history, with 136 goals in 153 international contests, and was a key player in U.S. World Cup and Olympic competitions.

Akers was the elder of two children of Robert D. Akers, a family counselor, and Anne Falaschi, a firefighter. Akers began to play soccer at age eight. Her initial experience in the sport was less than pleasant. She hated losing, and being the goalie on a team that frequently lost did not help. That experience did not last long. In the summer of 1975 the family moved to Seattle and Akers's mother signed her up for a local soccer club. Playing as a midfielder, Akers

Michelle Akers. AP/WIDE WORLD PHOTOS

soon discovered her own talent and began to enjoy the game. At age fourteen she was invited to join the Union Bay Flyers, one of the strongest under-nineteen club teams in the Pacific Northwest. At Shorecrest High School in Seattle she was a three-time high-school All-American (1982–1984) and led the team to the state championship her senior year.

Akers earned an athletic scholarship to the University of Central Florida (UCF) in Orlando, where she was a four-time National Collegiate Athletic Association (NCAA) All-American (1985–1988). In 1988 she received the Hermann Trophy for being the best female collegiate soccer player. Akers graduated from UCF in 1989 with a B.S. in liberal studies and health. After graduation, Akers accepted an assistant coaching job with the women's soccer team at UCF. In spring 1990 she married the former professional soccer player Roby Stahl. Shortly after their honeymoon, Akers went to Sweden to play for the Tyreso Football Club, a semiprofessional soccer team. She also played for Tyreso in 1992 and 1994.

Back in spring 1985, during her first year at UCF, Akers joined the first U.S. national women's soccer team in history. In August 1985, at an international tournament in Italy, Akers scored the first-ever U.S. women's national team goal against Denmark's national team. Six years later,

Akers ensured her place in the annals of women's soccer history. At the inaugural Women's World Championship in 1991 in China, Akers scored ten goals in six games, winning the tournament's Golden Boot award. In the title game against Norway, with the score tied 1–1 and fewer than five minutes to play, Akers drove home the game-winning goal to give the United States the championship.

In 1991 Akers scored thirty-nine goals in twenty-six international games. Representing the Fédération Internationale Football Association (FIFA), she traveled around the world promoting women's soccer. She also wrote a regular column in *Soccer Junior* magazine. But her health began to decline. In 1992 she was diagnosed with a severe case of mononucleosis, and became very ill in 1993. "Just surviving through the day seemed like an accomplishment," recalled Akers. Finally in 1994 she tested positive for Epstein-Barr virus, commonly known as chronic fatigue dysfunction syndrome, a more serious form of mononucleosis. The disease was like a thief, wrote Akers, that was "stealing everything that had been important to me. My health. My physical strength. My soccer career. My independence. My identity." In the course of her playing career, she had thirteen knee surgeries, five shoulder surgeries, and repeated concussions. Also contributing to her physical decline was the unhappiness of her failing marriage.

In the summer of 1994 Akers retreated to her family's mountain cabin in the Cascades outside of Seattle. The summer hiatus did not mend her health, but it did renew her spirit. Returning to her home in Oviedo, Florida, that autumn, Akers began to work out with her new training partner, Steve Slain. Also, under Slain's influence, she began to attend church services and a Bible study fellowship program.

In January 1995 Akers and Stahl were divorced, marking the first step of her comeback. Soccer had consumed her life, and it also had been the focal point of her marriage. Everything else—her relationships with her family, friends, and religion—had been relegated to the sideline. Attending church services helped to change her perspective. By the time of the 1995 Women's World Cup, Akers had regained much of her health. Injuries, however, kept her out of much of the competition. The U.S. team was eliminated by Norway in the semifinals, and Norway went on to win the championship. After the disappointing finish at the World Cup, the U.S. team set their sights on the first-ever Olympic soccer tournament in 1996, where they defeated the world champion Norway team 2–1 in the semifinals. They also defeated China in the final by the same score, capturing the first-ever women's soccer Olympic gold medal.

After the Olympics, Akers became more actively involved in missionary work, using soccer as a tool. In 1998 she founded Soccer Outreach International, an evangelistic Christian ministry. By early 1999 Akers had recovered significantly from the Epstein-Barr virus. She was convinced that God's plan for her life included one more World Cup. At age thirty-three, Akers was the oldest player on her team and the heart and soul of U.S. women's soccer. She led the team to a championship match against China in the Rose Bowl. After 120 minutes of scoreless regulation time and two overtimes, with the field temperature at 100 degrees Fahrenheit, and in front of 95,000 spectators, the game had to be decided by penalty kicks. The United States won by a score of 5–4. After the medal award ceremony, the crowd at the Rose Bowl spontaneously gave Akers a special tribute acknowledging her contributions to U.S. women's soccer.

On 24 August 2000 Akers announced her retirement, and her plans to devote her time to the work of Soccer Outreach International. She attributed her achievements to God. "I can't make it through life by myself. I need God's help and strength." Soccer, to Akers, had become more than just a game. "I've got a new game plan now. On and off the field, I want to play, work, and live for His glory."

★

Akers has written, with Gregg Lewis, *The Game and the Glory: An Autobiography* (2000). See also Kelly Whiteside, "World Beater: Michelle Akers, Soccer's Top Female, Is Ready to Lead the U.S. to Another Title," *Sports Illustrated* (5 June 1995); M. Bamberger, "Dream Come True: Michelle Akers and the Nineteen Other Members of the World Cup–Winning U.S. Soccer Team Gave America a Summer to Savor Forever," *Sports Illustrated* (20 Dec. 1999); *FIFA Women's World Cup USA 1999 Official Program* (1999); and *Michelle Akers: The Most Decorated Woman in Soccer* (2001).

YING WUSHANLEY

ALBRIGHT, Tenley Emma (*b.* 18 July 1935 in Boston, Massachusetts), figure skater and surgeon who was the first American woman figure skater to win the World Championship and a gold medal in the Olympics.

Albright, the daughter of Hollis L. Albright, a general surgeon and teacher, and Elin M. Peterson Albright, a homemaker, grew up in Newton Centre, Massachusetts. Her only brother, Niles Albright, also became a champion skater and a surgeon. When she was eight, Albright attended an ice show. Enthralled by the performance of Gretchen Merrill, a former national figure skating champion, Albright asked her parents for a pair of ice skates. She got the skates that Christmas, but they were the tubular type, fine for ice hockey but not for figure skating. Albright skated on a flooded rink in the backyard. Her next pair of skates had the proper notched blades, and at age nine she began taking lessons at the Skating Club of Boston. There she attracted the attention of Maribel Vinson (married name Owen), a

Tenley Albright. AP/WIDE WORLD PHOTOS

nine-time U.S. champion and a noted coach. Vinson saw that Albright had promise but, like many young skaters, had no desire to practice the basic figures and was chiefly interested in free skating. Albright loved to spin and jump to music, but Vinson stressed the importance of mastering the compulsory figures since they counted more in competitive skating. Characteristic of Albright's need for perfection, she began to practice the figures, finding their precision fascinating.

In September 1946 Albright contracted polio. At first it was uncertain whether or not she would walk again, but fortunately the disease was the nonparalytic type. After three weeks in the hospital, Albright emerged with weakened muscles in her lower back. The doctors recommended she return to skating to strengthen the muscles and told her parents that other children would not be allowed to play with Albright because of their parents' fears of the disease. Skating was something she could do alone and was an activity she enjoyed before she was stricken with the disease. Skating Club instructor Willie Frick remarked on Albright's determination, "She'd fall, get up and go right on." In a 1991 interview Albright remarked, "If you don't fall down, you aren't trying hard enough."

In early 1947 Albright decided she wanted to travel to Philadelphia to watch the Eastern Figure Skating Championships. Vinson, who had become her coach, stated that if she went it would be as a competitor. At Philadelphia, Albright won her first title, for juveniles under twelve. She won the national novice title in 1949, then the national junior championship in 1950. In 1952, at age sixteen, she won the first of her five consecutive U.S. Women's Singles titles and a silver medal at the Winter Olympics in Oslo, Norway.

Such accomplishments came with effort. Albright had two dreams, to be a champion figure skater and to become a doctor. Aware of the importance of study and discipline to make the most of her time, Albright practiced four hours a day, two hours on compulsory figures and two hours for free skating. A student at Manter Hall in Cambridge, Massachusetts, she regularly practiced early, from four to six in the morning, at the Boston Arena. During the summers she traveled to Lake Placid, New York; Denver, Colorado; and places in California, anywhere with an indoor rink.

Her silver medal at Oslo in February 1952 was unexpected. No American woman figure skater had placed higher than second since Beatrix Loughran did so in 1924. After the compulsory figures, Albright was second. Her difficult free skating program included three splits in a row and a double flip. Following the Olympics, she worked on her free skating for six weeks under the direction of Gene Turner, a Chicago professional. A year later, on 13 February 1953, she skated a nearly perfect performance to win America's first Women's World Figure Skating Championship at Davos, Switzerland. Skating at an altitude of 4,500 feet in subzero cold that caused some skaters to faint, her free skating program included double axels, double loops, and double solchows. At age seventeen Albright was the youngest woman to win the Worlds to that date. Following this victory she won the North American Championship and a second national title. Albright was the first American to accomplish this feat: the triple crown of skating.

In the fall of 1953 Albright entered Radcliffe College on her way to becoming a doctor. She continued skating practices from four to six in the morning, attended classes, took ballet lessons, and studied. Early in 1954 she returned to Oslo to defend her World Championship, but she fell attempting a difficult double loop jump and placed second. In 1955 she regained the championship in Vienna, Austria, giving a flawless performance. Her next goal was the Olympics.

While Albright was training in Cortina D'Ampezzo, Italy, on 19 January 1956, her skate caught in a rut in the ice, and she fell. The blade of the right skate tore through the boot of her left skate, cutting deeply into her ankle. She could hardly walk. Her father flew to Italy to make some emergency repairs, but Albright could not practice her jumps. No one knew about her injury except her coach and her teammates, and she was not able to practice her full free skating routine until the morning of the competition. During the competition, as her music, "Barcarolle" from Jacques Offenbach's *The Tales of Hoffman,* began, the audience started humming and singing along. Albright later told reporters, "It made me forget my injury." She skated a nearly perfect program, receiving a number of 5.8s out of a perfect 6, and won her gold medal on 2 February 1956, the first American woman to do so in figure skating.

Albright traveled to Garmisch, Germany, for the World Championship, but the injury to her ankle hampered her skating. She lost to Carol Heiss of the United States. Albright retired from competition and focused on her other goal, becoming a doctor. After only three years of study, she graduated from Radcliffe in 1957 and that year entered Harvard Medical School, one of 6 women in a class of 130. Albright received her M.D. in 1961 and continued to study in residency programs, specializing in surgery. On 31 December 1962 she married Tudor Gardiner, a lawyer. They had three daughters before they divorced in 1976. On 1 December 1981 Albright married real estate developer Gerald W. Blakeley. As of 1999 she resided in Brookline, Massachusetts.

In addition to her medical practice, Albright has devoted time to sports medicine and skating, participating in skating exhibitions to raise money for skating and skaters. She has supported the Figure Skating Association Memorial Fund, established to honor the victims of an air crash in 1961 that killed eighteen members of the U.S. national skating team. Vinson, Albright's former coach, was one of the victims. A member of the Sports Medicine Committee of the U.S. Olympic Committee, she in 1979 became the first woman officer of the U.S. Olympic Committee. She was named to the International Women's Sports Hall of Fame in 1983 and the Olympic Hall of Fame in 1988.

As a skater Albright's great strength was her ability to blend her aesthetic and athletic skills. Her studied precision in the compulsory figures gave her an advantage, but her innovative free skating and her soaring jumps made her a champion. Albright's success initiated the emergence of U.S. women as major powers in international figure skating competitions.

★

Essays on Albright are Larry Bortstein, *After Olympic Glory: The Lives of Ten Outstanding Medalists* (1978), and Janet Woolum, *Outstanding Women Athletes: Who They Are and How They Influenced Sports in America* (1998). Periodical articles include "Formula for Titles," *Newsweek* (6 Apr. 1953), which focuses on the world championship at Davos; and "Olympic Bulletin," *Boston Globe* (2 Feb. 1956), front page coverage of her victory at Cortina. Articles by her father and her coach that provide additional insight are Hollis Albright, "Tenley Almost Misses Shot at Olympic Title," *Boston Globe* (3 Feb. 1956); and Maribel Vinson, "Tenley Couldn't 'Feel' Ice in Triumphant Windup," *Boston Globe* (3 Feb. 1956). Albright's life after the Olympics is described in Barbara La Fontaine, "There Is a Doctor on the Ice," *Sports Illustrated* (8 Feb. 1967). See also W. Bingham, "Guts and Gold," *Sports Illustrated* (19 Oct. 1987); and Barbara Matson, "Albright Was First, Foremost," *Boston Globe* (25 Sept. 1999).

MARCIA B. DINNEEN

ALEXANDER, Grover Cleveland (*b.* 26 February 1887 in Elba, Nebraska; *d.* 4 November 1950 in Saint Paul, Nebraska), pitcher for Philadelphia Phillies, Chicago Cubs, and St. Louis Cardinals, winner of 373 games, and 1938 National Baseball Hall of Fame inductee.

Alexander was one of eight children born to William Alexander and Margaret Cootey, farmers in Elba, Nebraska. Following graduation from high school in Saint Paul, Nebraska, Alexander worked as a telephone lineman and pitched semiprofessional baseball.

In 1909 Alexander was signed to a professional contract with Galesburg, Illinois, of the Illinois-Missouri League. However, his baseball career was sidetracked when he was knocked unconscious by a thrown baseball as he attempted to break up a double play at second base. Suffering from double vision, Alexander was sold to the Indianapolis Indians, who, in turn, dealt him to the Syracuse Chiefs of the New York State League. Recovering his vision before the 1910 season, Alexander won twenty-nine games for the Chiefs, leading the Philadelphia Phillies to draft him that same year.

Alexander's rookie performance in Philadelphia was outstanding. Standing six feet, one inch tall and weighing 185 pounds, the right-handed pitcher with exceptional control won twenty-eight games (still the rookie record), including seven shutouts. In September 1911 Alexander mastered a 1–0 victory over baseball immortal Cy Young, who was playing his final season.

By 1915 Alexander was one of the dominant pitchers in the National League, achieving 31 victories, 241 strikeouts, and a stingy earned run average of 1.22. He led the Phillies to their first pennant, but Philadelphia was defeated in the World Series by the Boston Red Sox and Babe Ruth. In 1916 Alexander won thirty-three games, including sixteen shutouts, followed by another thirty-win season the following year.

From 1911 to 1917 Alexander posted 190 victories for the Phillies, one-third of the total games they won during that time. However, anticipating that he would be drafted for military service in 1918, the Phillies traded him to the Chicago Cubs. In May 1918 Alexander married Aimee Marie Arrants before departing for France as a sergeant in a U.S. Army artillery unit, the 342d Battalion of the 89th Division.

In 1919, when Alexander returned to the Cubs, he was suffering from epileptic seizures. In addition he had a severe hearing loss caused by frontline artillery fire. These problems appeared to exacerbate Alexander's alcohol dependency. Nevertheless, he was an effective pitcher for the Cubs. Between 1918 and 1926 Alexander won 128 games for the Chicago franchise, including a league-leading twenty-seven games in 1920.

Early in the 1926 season the new Cubs manager Joe McCarthy, seeking to curb his club's drinking, allowed the St. Louis Cardinals to claim Alexander on waivers. Manager Rogers Hornsby made little effort to reform Alexander, and the right-hander contributed nine victories to the Cardinals' pennant drive. Perhaps the most memorable moment of Alexander's career occurred during the 1926 World Series between the Cardinals and the New York Yankees. After victories in Games 2 and 6, Alexander was taking a well-deserved rest in the Cardinal bullpen when he was summoned to the mound in the seventh inning of Game 7 to face Tony Lazzeri with two out, the bases loaded, and St. Louis leading 3–2. Many speculate that Alexander was still intoxicated from celebrating his victory in Game 6. Despite an unsteady appearance, Alexander retired Lazzeri on four pitches and held the Yankees scoreless over the last two innings, assuring the Cardinals their first world championship.

Indicating that his World Series performance was no fluke, Alexander, or Old Pete, as he was often called, won twenty-one games for St. Louis in 1927, followed by sixteen victories in 1928. However, in 1929 Alexander's skills began to slip, and his victory total fell to nine games. He was traded back to the Phillies in 1930, appearing in nine games

Grover Cleveland Alexander. © UNDERWOOD & UNDERWOOD/CORBIS

for them before finishing the season with Dallas of the Texas League.

Although he continued to pitch with semiprofessional teams and in exhibition contests, Alexander's major league career was over in 1930. In twenty big-league seasons he won 373 games, pitched 5,190 innings, struck out 2,198 batters, and averaged only 1.65 walks per nine innings. His lifetime achievements were recognized with his election to the National Baseball Hall of Fame in 1938.

Alexander's years after baseball were difficult. He pitched briefly for the barnstorming House of David sect from Benton Harbor, Michigan. His problems with alcohol were pronounced, and he struggled to maintain employment, working at a race track, laboring in a factory, and even serving as a sideshow attraction for a penny arcade in New York City. He divorced, remarried, and again divorced his wife, Aimee.

Although few recognized him, Alexander was invited to the 1950 World Series between the Phillies and the Yankees. In 1952 he was the subject of a biopic film, *The Winning Team,* starring Ronald Reagan and Doris Day. But he was unable to enjoy this fame. Surviving on a small pension from baseball and the military, he lived in a boardinghouse in Saint Paul, Nebraska, and was found dead there, apparently from a heart attack. He is buried in Elmwood Cemetery in Saint Paul.

Although Alexander's personal life was troubled, there is no denying his attributes on the baseball diamond. His pitching exploits rank him among the greatest right-handed pitchers in National League history, alongside his rival, the New York Giants' "Christian Gentleman" Christy Mathewson.

★

A player file on Alexander is available in the National Baseball Hall of Fame in Cooperstown, New York. Useful biographies include Jerry E. Clark and Martha Ellen Webb, *Alexander the Great* (1993), and Jack Kavanagh, *Ol' Pete: The Grover Cleveland Alexander Story* (1996). Alexander is also profiled in Lee Allen and Tom Meany, *Kings of the Diamond* (1965); Lawrence Ritter, *The Glory of Their Times* (1966); and Bob Broeg, "Incredible Alex— The Mound Master," *Sporting News* (14 June 1969). An obituary is in the *New York Times* (5 Nov. 1950).

RON BRILEY

ALI, Muhammad (*b.* 17 January 1942 in Louisville, Kentucky), three-time heavyweight boxing champion, and showman extraordinaire; one of the finest and most controversial athletes of all time.

Ali was born Cassius Marcellus Clay, Jr. His father, Cassius Marcellus Clay, Sr., a sign painter, and his mother, Odessa Lee Grady, had one other son, Rudolph Valentino Clay (later known as Rahaman Ali; he also had a career as a boxer).

Clay took up boxing at the age of twelve under the tutelage of a white Louisville police officer, Joe Martin. Clay, who had little interest in academic or intellectual pursuits—in 1960 he barely graduated from Central High School in Louisville—devoted himself with almost monk-like austerity to learning the art and science of boxing. He became one of the country's most impressive amateurs, winning National Amateur Athletic Union (AAU) championships in 1959 and 1960. He won a gold medal as a light-heavyweight in the 1960 Rome Olympics, where he made a name for himself by reciting poetry, bragging about his abilities, and reassuring the foreign press that the American race problem was being properly handled. While Clay's demeanor enraged fight traditionalists as much as his unorthodox boxing style (he held his hands low, jabbed in retreat, and in general boxed like a heavyweight version of his idol, the middleweight champion Sugar Ray Robinson), many found him refreshing, winning, and utterly charming in a boyish way. Like Motown Records, established in 1959, and students conducting sit-in protests at African-American colleges, Clay represented a new African-American youth culture; these were young men and women who were unwilling to do things as their parents and grandparents had.

Upon his return from Rome to the United States, and under the management of a consortium of white Louisville businessmen, Clay turned professional. Guided by veteran trainer Angelo Dundee, who did little to change his style, Clay accumulated a string of victories largely against mediocre opposition. Tall, rangy, with astonishing hand and foot speed, Clay's constant patter and poetry, predictions of the outcome of his fights, and clowning garnered much attention but also produced a cadre of sports fans who found him insufferable. Most people came to the fights hoping to see him get beaten, although younger fans tended to like him. He also drew many new fans to boxing, purely on the basis of the beauty of his fighting style and the brashness of his personality. On the whole, Clay's influence was good for the sport, which had been in the doldrums for most of the 1950s. It had been diminished by revelations of fixed fights, riddled by the presence of gangsters, investigated by a Senate subcommittee, and fronted by two champions—Floyd Patterson and Sonny Liston—who were skilled boxers but moody and unappealing men. Clay brought a great deal of showmanship and youth appeal to boxing.

In February 1964 Clay won the heavyweight title in Miami by beating the former convict Sonny Liston in an oddly inconclusive fight, when the champion failed to come out for the seventh round. Clay was a seven-to-one underdog;

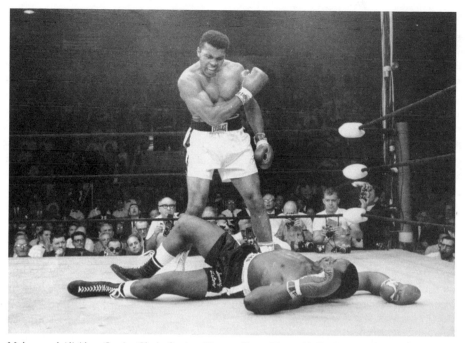

Muhammad Ali (then Cassius Clay) after knocking out Sonny Liston, 1965. AP/WIDE WORLD PHOTOS

some even thought he would not show up to fight the mighty Liston, who had effortlessly knocked out Floyd Patterson in one round in 1962 and repeated the feat in 1963. Clay stunned the world when he beat Liston, convincing many, despite the strangeness of the fight, of his courage and his enormous skills.

Clay evoked strong feelings but was not perceived as a villain by a large number of whites until after the Liston fight, when he announced his membership in the Nation of Islam, a small but influential religious sect in the African-American community that practiced self-empowerment, avoided politics, and believed that white people were devils and African-American people a superior race. The group denounced racial integration as a political and social goal of the leaders of the civil rights movement. The most impressive spokesperson for the Nation of Islam was the fiery, highly articulate, and logical Malcolm X, who had been in Clay's training camp before the Liston fight. The Nation of Islam was seen by the white press and by some African Americans as a hate group, an extremist group, and Clay was roundly denounced for becoming a member. He further outraged the white American public by taking the name Cassius X, reflecting the group's belief that African-American surnames derive from those of the slaves' white masters. Nearly all the publications in the United States refused to call Clay by his new name. A short time later, the group's leader, the Honorable Elijah Muhammad, gave him the name Muhammad Ali. Malcolm X had left the Nation of Islam shortly after the Liston fight to form his

own group, and he and others suggested that Elijah Muhammad wished to prevent Clay from leaving as well. To be sure, the Nation of Islam officially did not lionize Clay until after he won the Liston fight of 1964; few in the higher circles of the sect thought that he would win.

A few months later Clay adopted the Muslim name Muhammad Ali and toured Ghana, Nigeria, and the United Arab Republic (UAR; the brief political union of Egypt and Syria). Everywhere he was met by huge numbers of people, many of whom held signs proclaiming him King of the World. Even newspapers of these countries, which gave Ali extraordinary coverage, referred to him by this title, as if he were a form of royalty, an Islamic prince, or a head of state. Ali enjoyed audiences with heads of state such as Kwame Nkrumah of Ghana and Gamal Abdel Nasser of the UAR, an honor unheard of for a foreign athlete, especially a boxer, with utterly no native connection to the country.

In a sense, the press and the crowds were right. Ali was the king of a certain portion of the world, a large segment of what was referred to as the colored or Bandung world, so called after the site of the famous 1954 Afro-Asian Unity conference. Certainly, no heavyweight champion before Ali had ever had such a following in the Third World. No champion boxer had ever toured these countries before, particularly no American.

But Ali was different, and his rise reflected changing racial politics in the ideologically charged cold war universe, where African and Asian independence and anti-colonial movements found common ground with the

American civil rights movement and growing African-American political militancy. Unexpectedly, this young African American from the South, who combined the antics of Dizzy Dean, the Pan-Africanist rhetoric of Malcolm X, the narrow-minded fervor of a cult zealot, the good looks of a Hollywood star, the heart and abilities of a superbly gifted athlete, and the moral sensibilities of Jack Armstrong, the fictional "all-American boy" of radio, came to dominate American sports and personalize dissident American politics.

Malcolm X was assassinated in February 1965, and tension was high between his followers and the Nation of Islam, which allegedly was responsible for the murder. In Lewiston, Maine, on 25 May 1965, Ali knocked out Liston in one round, apparently with a single punch that many, to this day, have been unable to discern. Because of his unpopularity in the United States, Ali defended his title abroad in several fights, including wins over Canadian George Chuvalo, Englishman Henry Cooper, and German Karl Mildenberger.

White public disapproval of Ali intensified when he spoke against the military draft. He had been initially classified as 1-Y, which meant that he was unfit to serve because of his low score on the army intelligence tests. After the Liston fight of 1964 he was retested, failing again, much to his embarrassment. ("I always said I was the greatest. I never said I was the smartest.") But in 1966, as a result of the Gulf of Tonkin incident and the escalation of the Vietnam War (which resulted in a recalibration of the intelligence tests) Ali was reclassified 1-A (fit to serve). In a panic, when told this by reporters, he said that he did not want to go Vietnam and "had no quarrel with those Viet Cong," of whom he never heard until a reporter mentioned them. The public took this as a far more self-consciously political statement than it truly was. Ali fought the draft, but on religious, not political or racial, grounds. (Elijah Muhammad, whom Ali saw as a father figure, had gone to prison for draft dodging and sedition in October 1942, as did his son Wallace D. Muhammad in 1961.)

In 1967 Ali was convicted in federal court of violation of the Selective Service Act and sentenced to five years in prison. He was also stripped of his titles, denied a license to fight in the United States, and denied a passport to fight abroad. He did not fight again until October 1970, when public opinion had turned against the war and public respect for Ali had grown in light of the sincerity, tenacity, and earnestness with which he held his beliefs. Ali eventually won his case on 28 June 1971, when the Supreme Court unanimously reversed Ali's conviction on a technicality.

Although Ali's skills were somewhat diminished by his three-and-a-half-year layoff, he returned to the ring a

dominating presence. In the 1970s he proved himself against several highly skilled opponents, including the relentless Joe Frazier, to whom Ali, in the eyes of the public, lost his title in March 1971 on a fifteen-round decision; the awkward Ken Norton, whom he never completely mastered; and the powerful George Foreman, from whom he regained the title in dramatic fashion in Kinshasa, Zaire, in 1974 at the age of thirty-two, when everyone thought he was washed up. In 1964 Ali had promised many Ghanaians and Nigerians that he would build a house in Africa and live there, but he never did so; he never liked Africa very much. He left Zaire immediately after his fight with Foreman, thoroughly wearied by the place.

In the 1970s Ali was worshipped by a huge international audience. He was arguably the most famous man on the planet. He appeared in commercials, in a film about his life (based on an autobiography edited by Toni Morrison), even in a comic book where he beat up Superman. He had a huge entourage and, to support it, continued to fight although he was past his prime. He had difficult, draining fights against Frazier, Norton, Jimmy Young, and Earnie Shavers. He defeated Frazier on 28 January 1974, in ten rounds, and 1 October 1975 in Manila, the Philippines, in thirteen rounds. Ali went on to defeat Norton in their third and final meeting on 28 September 1976, in a close fifteen-round decision.

Ali became almost unbearably egotistical during this period. He had always insulted opponents, sometimes playfully, as when he called Liston "the Bear," and sometimes more viciously, as when he called Patterson a girl, and a rabbit. (Patterson, to some degree, had this coming. He had embarked on a personal crusade to bring the heavyweight title "back to America" when Ali announced his membership in the Nation of Islam. Later in the 1960s, however, Patterson was the only boxer to publicly defend Ali.) In the 1970s, in an attempt to add more political drama and tension to his fights, Ali's insults became shriller, sometimes tasteless.

In the late 1960s and the 1970s certain Nation of Islam mosques became associated with crime and drugs in the African-American community, and Ali, for a time, was associated with a charismatic underworld figure named Major Coxson, who was mysteriously executed along with his entire family. Also, the blood feud between the Nation of Islam and other sects of African American Muslims continued unabated into the 1970s.

On 15 February 1978 a fat, lethargic Ali lost his title to Leon Spinks, an ex-Marine and native of the notorious Pruitt-Igoe housing project in North St. Louis, Missouri, who had had only eight previous professional fights. Ali, however, got himself in shape and won the rematch on 15

September convincingly, becoming the first heavyweight to win the title three times.

In 1979, with his reflexes gone, his taste for competition dulled, and his body battered from numerous ring wars, Ali retired. Unfortunately, like many others, he did not stay retired. Unwisely, he returned to the ring on 2 October 1980 and fought his former sparring partner, and current heavyweight champion, Larry Holmes. Ali was savagely and shockingly beaten over ten rounds. He fought yet again on 11 December 1981 against journeyman heavyweight Trevor Berbick. Again, Ali lost in a ten-round decision. This was Ali's last fight. His final ring record was fifty-six wins (thirty-seven knockouts) and five losses. He was elected to the International Boxing Hall of Fame in 1987.

Ali's personal life was perennially disordered. He married Sonji Roi on 14 August 1964; they divorced in 1966 and had no children. His second marriage to Belinda Boyd on 17 August 1967 lasted until 1976; they had four children. The following year, on 19 June 1977 he married Veronica Porche; they divorced in 1986 after having had two children, one of whom, a daughter Laila, became a boxer. Later that year, on 19 November, he married Lonnie Williams and they adopted a son. Altogether, Ali had nine children: seven among his four marriages and two by mistresses.

As early as the 1970s, as Ali's skills deteriorated and he absorbed more and more punishment in the ring, many noticed that his speech was becoming progressively more slurred. After his retirement, this slurring became worse, and his body movements became slower. He also began to suffer attacks of palsy. Most doctors diagnosed Ali's condition not as Parkinson's disease but as Parkinson's syndrome, largely induced by the punishment he endured in the ring. Eventually Ali began to move more like an aged man, and he rarely speaks in public. However, he still makes numerous public appearances and loves to be around people. A devout Muslim, Ali now follows Wallace D. Muhammad's more traditional Islamic organization.

Ali, without question, represented a kind of African-American athlete who was strikingly different from previous heroes such as Joe Louis, Jack Johnson, and Jackie Robinson, although he adopted aspects of their demeanor. His inchoate African-American nationalism and Pan-Africanism fashioned him for the times when youth and nationalism were the hallmarks of the African-American political movement in the United States after 1965. To be sure, Ali was virtually the sole inspiration of the Olympic boycott movement of 1968 (the boycott, aimed at getting South Africa removed from international athletic competition because of its apartheid policy, was not actually carried out). Harry Edwards, John Carlos, Tommie Smith, and the new cadre of militant African-American athletes saw Ali as a hero not only for his brilliance as an athlete

who met all challengers in the ring, but also because he stood up for his beliefs. Many may not have agreed with his beliefs but they respected them and Ali's right to hold them.

Moreover, Ali arose at the time when sports were emerging as a big media business in the United States. This greatly benefited Ali; in his heyday he was probably the most photographed and the most televised African-American athlete, perhaps African-American person, in the United States. On the other hand, Ali almost single-handedly made televised boxing a marketable enterprise and made closed-circuit matches the bonanza they became.

Finally, Ali emerged in the era of the assertive athlete who would not accept the traditional lines of authority in sports: the coach/trainer/manager as father figure, the owner/promoter as dictator of the athlete's career path and pay. In this context, it is probably useful to compare the careers of Ali and Joe Namath, the stylish NFL quarterback, who also ducked the draft. Ali did not invent the independent athlete as much as he represented it. In retrospect, it is no surprise that it was during the Ali era that free agency came into organized team sports. After all, at least in the public's eye, if probably not in actual fact, Ali seemed so much a free agent himself.

Rarely was an international audience so moved as when the middle-aged Muhammad Ali, palsied and rendered virtually speechless by boxing-induced Parkinson's syndrome, tremblingly lit the flame that officially opened the 1996 Summer Olympic Games in Atlanta. The man who had, many years earlier, been demonized as an African-American racist, an unpatriotic bum, a coward, a fool, and a disgrace to his profession, who was, in effect, unwelcome in his native land, was now the subject of elegiac accolades. Many viewers openly wept at the sight of this proud but injured man. He had become a grand American hero.

★

Many books discuss Ali as either a primary subject or a significant actor in someone else's story. Muhammad Ali, with Richard Durham, *The Greatest: My Own Story* (1975); Gerald Early *The Muhammad Ali Reader* (1998); George Foreman, *By George: The Autobiography of George Foreman* (2000); Joe Frazier, with Phil Berger, *Smokin' Joe: The Autobiography of a Heavyweight Champion of the World* (1996); Elliott Gorn, ed., *Muhammad Ali: The People's Champ* (1995); Thomas Hauser, *Muhammad Ali: His Life and Times* (1991); Larry Holmes, *Larry Holmes: Against the Odds* (1998); Ken Norton, with Marshall Terrill and Mike Fitzgerald, *Going the Distance: The Ken Norton Story* (2000); Mark Kram, *The Ghosts of Manila: The Fateful Blood Feud Between Muhammad Ali and Joe Frazier* (2001); Norman Mailer, *The Fight* (1975); Jack Olsen, *Black Is Best: The Riddle of Cassius Clay* (1967); George Plimpton, *Shadow Box* (1977); David Remnick, *King of*

the World: Muhammad Ali and the Rise of the American Hero
(1998); Jeffrey Sammons, *Beyond the Ring: The Role of Boxing in
American Society* (1988); Wilfred Sheed, *Muhammad Ali* (1975);
Jose Torres, *Sting Like a Bee: The Muhammad Ali Story* (1971);
and Nick Tosches, *The Devil and Sonny Liston* (2000).

GERALD EARLY

ALLEN, Forrest Clare ("Phog") (*b.* 18 November 1885
in Jamesport, Missouri; *d.* 16 September 1974 in Lawrence,
Kansas), noted college basketball coach at the University of
Kansas from 1908 to 1909 and from 1920 to 1956 who was
elected to the Naismith Memorial Basketball Hall of Fame in
1959.

Allen was the fourth of six sons born to William T. Allen,
a produce wholesaler, and Mary Elexzene Perry, a homemaker, writer, and lawyer. In 1887 the family moved to
Independence, Missouri, where Allen and his brothers went
to school and participated in all available sports, particularly the new game of basketball. In 1899 Allen's older
brother Pete organized the Independence Young Men's
Christian Association (YMCA) basketball team, and in
March the team played the University of Kansas team from
Lawrence, Kansas, which was coached by the physical education director James Naismith, the inventor of basketball.

Allen did not graduate from Independence High
School. In the summer of 1902 he went to work for the
Kansas City Southern Railroad as an axeman, pounding
stakes on the track. He returned to Independence the following year and joined the Kansas City Athletic Club,
where he became the best basketball player on the team; in
1904 he was named captain. Later that year the Allen brothers formed their own basketball team, which played for five
years through 1908.

In 1904 Naismith took note of Allen and encouraged
him to enroll at the University of Kansas when Allen successfully secured sponsors for an Amateur Athletic Union
(AAU) sanctioned basketball tournament, which pitted Allen's Kansas City Athletic Club team against the Buffalo
Germans from Buffalo, New York, winner of the 1904 AAU
Tournament. The Kansas City Athletic Club soundly defeated the Germans in two out of three games played before
a packed Kansas City audience. Allen's biographer, Blair
Kerkhoff, noted that Allen "had created a basketball event,
promoted it, won it, then cashed in on it."

Allen, whose nickname, Phog, was derived from his fog-
horn voice, enrolled at the University of Kansas in the fall
of 1905, though he had never graduated from high school.
He had played only one season of basketball for Kansas
when officials at Baker University in Baldwin, Kansas, approached him with an offer to coach their team. Naismith

Phog Allen *(left)* with his 1952 NCAA champions, the Kansas Jayhawks. © BETTMANN/CORBIS

dismissed the coaching offer by saying, "You can't coach a game like basketball. You play it." Allen disagreed. He accepted the offer and coached at Baker from 1906 to 1908. He then coached at the University of Kansas from 1908 to 1909 and at Haskell Indian Institute, a Native American institution of higher learning also located in Lawrence, in 1909. At the end of the 1908–1909 season, Allen's college record was 115–23.

On 25 June 1908 Allen took time out of his coaching schedule to marry Bessie Milton, whom he had met in Independence. The couple eventually had six children together. That year Allen decided to take a break from coaching and entered the Central College of Osteopathy in Kansas City. His decision to enroll was motivated in part by a back injury he suffered as a member of the University of Kansas football team when he was a freshman. In 1912 he graduated with a doctor of osteopathy degree and accepted a position as coach and athletic administrator at the Missouri State Normal School (now known as Central Missouri State University) in Warrensburg, Missouri.

Allen coached basketball, baseball, and football for the Normals for seven years, resigning in 1919. As a coach, he posted a 84–31 record in basketball and a 29–17–2 record in football. He briefly practiced osteopathic medicine in Warrensburg before accepting a position as director of athletics at the University of Kansas, joining Naismith once again.

Allen began his long career at the University of Kansas in 1920. Recognized for his flashy on-court dress and his inspirational locker room speeches, Allen, known as Doc to his players, led his team to two Helms Foundation national championship titles in 1922 and 1923. He was promoted to the chairmanship of the Department of Physical Education, a position Naismith had held. In 1924 Allen completed his first book, ghostwritten by his wife, entitled *My Basket-Ball Bible,* one of the first published basketball coaching manuals. The book also explained how to treat sports injuries, always part of Allen's coaching philosophy. In 1937 Allen published *Better Basketball,* an updated version of the 1924 publication.

Throughout his coaching career, Allen was a vocal supporter of college and amateur basketball around the world. In 1927 he was instrumental in forming the National Association of Basketball Coaches (NABC), which implemented changes to collegiate basketball rules, and he served as the organization's first president. In 1936 he led a successful effort to include basketball as a sport in the 1936 Olympic games. Allen was named director of Olympic Basketball but resigned after a dispute with the AAU, which refused to pay the travel costs of team members. In 1939 Allen served on an NABC committee that created the first post-season tournament, the forerunner of the current National Collegiate Athletic Association (NCAA) tournament.

Allen was an outspoken proponent of raising the basketball goal from ten to twelve feet because he believed the area around the basket was congested with smaller players attempting to prevent the penetration of the larger players. Although he was unsuccessful in this effort, he did succeed in another area—focusing attention on the problem of gambling in collegiate basketball. In 1944 he told a reporter for the United Press Associates in Kansas City about point shaving that occurred in games played in New York City's Madison Square Garden. The allegations sent shock waves through the sport, and evidence of gambling was uncovered at other sports venues. Allen's solution, which was outlined in his last book, *Coach Phog Allen's Sports Stories for You and Youth* (1947), was to create a basketball czar who could suspend coaches, athletic directors, and players who violated the rules.

The 1951–1952 season was one of Allen's most memorable. Led by Indiana native Clyde Lovellette, an All-American selection, at center, Kansas won the National Collegiate Athletic Association (NCAA) tournament. It was Allen's first national championship since 1923. The year 1952 was also an Olympic year. Because of its NCAA win, Kansas sent seven players to the Olympic team, and Allen served as the Olympic team's assistant coach. A year later, Allen and his own assistant coach, Dick Harp, instituted a pressure man-to-man defense. Allen's fellow coaches quickly copied the defensive scheme.

The 1955–1956 season was Allen's last as head basketball coach at the University of Kansas because he had reached the mandatory retirement age of seventy. In his forty-eight years of coaching, Allen won 744 games and lost a mere 263 contests, and at retirement he had the most wins as a coach in collegiate basketball history. That record stood until 1968, when Adolph Rupp of the University of Kentucky, Allen's former student, broke it. In 1959 Allen was elected to the Naismith Memorial Basketball Hall of Fame in Springfield, Massachusetts.

During his busy retirement, Allen maintained an active lecture circuit and opened an osteopathic practice in Lawrence specifically to treat sports injuries. He later opened the Phog Allen Health Center in Kansas City, Missouri. The coach, afflicted by arthritis, began to slow in 1968. He died of natural causes when he was eighty-eight years old and is buried in the Oak Hill Cemetery in Lawrence.

Allen was a remarkable fixture on the collegiate basketball landscape. He worked side by side with the game's founder, James Naismith, but, unlike Naismith, who saw basketball primarily as a form of recreation, Allen saw it as a sport to be coached and correctly earned the title "Father of Basketball Coaching." Dean Smith, who played under Allen in the 1950s and later became head basketball coach at the University of North Carolina, remarked on the eve of the 1991 NCAA Final Four tournament games that all four teams were there because they utilized the pressure man-to-man defense invented by coaches Allen and Harp in 1952. Through his example and his books, Allen taught others to coach. He also fostered the growth of basketball in North America when he founded the NABC and internationally through his effort to make the sport an Olympic event.

★

Allen recorded some biographical data in *Coach Phog Allen's Sports Stories for You and Youth* (1947). Blair Kerkhoff, *Phog Allen: The Father of Basketball Coaching* (1996), is the only published biography on Allen. The relationship between Allen and Naismith is detailed in Bernice Larson Webb, *The Basketball Man: James Naismith* (1973). Allen's career coaching data can be found in Gary K. Johnson, comp., *NCAA Men's Basketball's Finest* (1998). An obituary is in the *Kansas City Star* (16 Sept. 1974).

Jon E. Taylor

ALLEN, Marcus LeMarr   (*b.* 26 March 1960 in San Diego, California), Heisman Trophy winner (1981) and professional football player.

Allen was one of six children born to Harold "Red" Allen, a construction worker, and Gwen Allen, a vocational nurse.

Marcus Allen, 1982. © Bettmann/CORBIS

The Allen home provided him with ample opportunity to participate in sports, music, and church-related activities. Allen recalled, "Sports were always a big thing to us." In his grade-school years, he emulated the play of stars from all sports in backyard events. Allen attended elementary and junior-high schools in San Diego and in 1975 he entered Lincoln High School. In his sophomore year Allen played on Lincoln's football team, the Hornets, as a free safety, and during his junior year he continued in the safety position and served as a backup quarterback and wingback on offense. During his senior year he played quarterback on offense and free safety on defense. On offense he scored more than 500 points, a county record, and led the Hornets to a state championship win. Allen was selected to the Parade All-America, Scholastic Coach All-America, and National High School Coaches Squad All-America teams. The *San Diego Tribune* named him the schoolboy athlete of the year.

Allen entered the University of Southern California (USC) in Los Angeles in 1978 and played football with the Trojans, coached by John Robinson. His first year of play as a tailback was unremarkable. During his sophomore year he moved to the fullback position, and as a junior he played tailback again. Between his junior and senior seasons, Allen worked on his skills and perfected what would become his trademark—the cutback, a move that allowed him to cut across to the open field and quickly explode downfield.

At the beginning of his senior year at USC, Allen set an ambitious goal to rush for 2,000 yards. He began his senior season by rushing for 210 yards and scoring four touchdowns against Tennessee. One game later, the top-ranked Trojans took on the second-ranked Oklahoma Sooners and defeated them by a score of 28–24. Allen rushed for more than 200 yards against a superb Sooners defensive line. Later, the Sooners coach Barry Switzer, who was one of the few coaches to recruit Allen out of high school, commented, "He's got my vote for the Heisman." Allen made his 2,000-yard rushing goal in a game played against the Washington Huskies and finished the season against the arch-rival University of California, Los Angeles, by rushing for 213 yards, bringing his total regular season rushing yards to 2,342. At the time, this achievement was an all-time season record. In the Heisman Trophy balloting, Allen won the award over Herschel Walker of Georgia. Allen received numerous other honors, including college player-of-the-year awards from the Walter Camp Foundation, the Maxwell Club, and *Football News*.

In 1982, after graduating from USC, Allen was chosen tenth in the National Football League (NFL) draft, the first-round pick of the Los Angeles Raiders. Allen was excited to play for the Raiders, a team he had admired when he was growing up, but he was somewhat anxious, because the team had a winning tradition and expected him to make an immediate contribution. When Allen arrived at training camp, he found the competition for the running-back position keen as he competed against the veterans Mark van Eeghen and Greg Pruitt. Winning this competition, and with Gregg Pruitt as one of his NFL mentors, Allen experienced immediate success with the Raiders. In his first season (1982–1983), which was cut short by a strike, he rushed for 697 yards and eleven touchdowns in nine games, and led the league in scoring with 84 points. He was named as the NFL's rookie of the year, was picked to be on several All-Pro teams, and was invited to play in the Pro Bowl. His second season (1983–1984) brought everything a professional football player could want. The Raiders finished with a 12–4 record of wins and losses and entered the Super Bowl to play the Washington Redskins. During the contest Allen carried the ball twenty times and ran for 191 yards, including two touchdowns that led the Raiders to a 38–9 victory. Allen's efforts earned him the Most Valuable Player (MVP) award for Super Bowl XVIII.

While Allen's on-field performance was exceptional, it did not seem to impress Raiders owner Al Davis. Allen observed after the 1984–1985 season, in which he rushed for 1,168 yards, that he felt a "growing uneasy relationship with Al Davis." The source of Davis's antagonism remained somewhat of a mystery to Allen, even when the coaching staff told him that Davis thought he was a selfish player. Davis's assessment was hard for Allen to understand because he had excelled on the field. Allen seriously considered the owner's characterization and examined his play, but could not find merit in his charge.

Despite Davis's lukewarm reaction to Allen, the owner did renew his contract in the offseason prior to the start of the 1985–1986 season. Allen demonstrated to Davis that he made the right decision when Allen rushed for over 1,759 yards—a career high and league rushing record. Those rushing yards combined with Allen's 555 receiving yards for the year brought his total combined yardage of the season to 2,314—an NFL single season record. Allen's outstanding performance led to his third Pro Bowl appearance. The Raiders entered the playoffs with a 12–4 record but were defeated by the New England Patriots. In the game, the team failed to mix its offensive passing game with Allen's explosive offensive ground attack. After the game, Al Davis announced, "We're never again going to be so dependent on one guy. This team has become too one-dimensional."

Allen believed Davis's comments were directed at him but was stunned to hear these discouraging words in light of one of his most successful seasons. During the 1986–1987 season the relationship between Allen and Davis degenerated further. Allen fumbled in a regular season game against the Philadelphia Eagles and the Eagles capitalized on Allen's error and scored a game-winning touchdown over the Raiders. After the game, Davis told Allen that he should have been traded. Some sports analysts saw this

game as pivotal, because the Raiders lost their next three regular-season games which took them out of the playoff contention. From 1987 until 1992, his last season with the Raiders, Allen was hampered by injuries and frustrated by reduced playing time. In the 1989–1990 and 1991–1992 seasons Allen played in only eight games each season. His best season during those six years came in 1988 when he amassed 831 rushing yards, and his worst season came in 1991 when he accumulated a total of only 287 rushing yards. In 1993 Allen was traded to the Kansas City Chiefs. His personal life also changed on 26 June 1993, when he married Kathryn Eickstaedt. The couple did not have any children.

Allen arrived in Kansas City the same year Joe Montana joined the Chiefs. At the end of Allen's first season he led the team in rushing, scored twelve touchdowns, and was selected by his teammates as the Chiefs' MVP. *Pro Football Weekly* named him the NFL's comeback player of the year, and he traveled to the Pro Bowl once again after a six-year absence. In 1997 Allen retired from the game, and became a color commentator for CBS Sports. As a Kansas City Chief he had scored more rushing touchdowns than any other back in the history of the franchise. He left the NFL as the first player in its history to lead two teams in rushing touchdowns.

Allen was the first college player to rush for more than 2,000 yards in a single season. As a professional he played in 222 games, scored 123 touchdowns, and caught 587 passes—the most of any NFL running back at the time of his retirement. In 2000 he was inducted into the College Football Hall of Fame. Nonetheless, Allen's professional career will be remembered for his rocky relationship with Davis, even though Allen brought the Raiders and Davis a Super Bowl victory in 1984.

★

The Autobiography of Marcus Allen (1997), with Carlton Stowers, details Allen's life. Information on Allen's career as a Kansas City Chief is in Mark Stallard, *AFL to Arrowhead: Four Decades of Chiefs History and Trivia* (1999). Allen's career accomplishments are highlighted in "Marcus Allen Retires from NFL," *Jet* (27 Apr. 1998).

JON E. TAYLOR

ALWORTH, Lance Dwight (*b.* 3 August 1940 in Houston, Texas), wide receiver for the San Diego Chargers and Dallas Cowboys, who was the American Football League's (AFL) first true superstar.

Alworth was the son of Richard Alworth, an oil field–construction foreman, and Elizabeth Louise Parrish, a schoolteacher. Although Alworth was born in Houston, the family moved to Brookhaven, Mississippi, where Alworth

Lance Alworth, 1970. AP/WIDE WORLD PHOTOS

grew up and attended the public schools. Alworth was an outstanding athlete at Brookhaven High School, earning fifteen varsity letters and recognition as a scholastic All-America football player in 1957. Alworth credited much of his success to his father, who discouraged alcohol consumption and smoking. Although Mississippi was embroiled in violent reactions to the civil rights movement in the late 1950s, Alworth's experience was different. He asserted, "Small towns teach you people are people. I used to pick cotton with black people, and to me a person's a person, color never made any difference."

Alworth graduated from high school in 1958. The New York Yankees offered him a baseball contract, and football scholarships were available from schools such as the University of Arkansas, University of Minnesota, and University of Mississippi. However, the University of Mississippi withdrew its scholarship offer when Alworth married his high school sweetheart, Betty Jean, during his senior year of high school. The couple later had two children. Alworth later explained, "There must have been fifteen married couples in my graduating class. It seemed like the thing to do at the time."

Alworth was impressed by coach Frank Broyles of the University of Arkansas and elected to become a Razorback. The running back enjoyed a distinguished career at Arkansas. During his senior year he led the National Collegiate Athletic Association (NCAA) with sixty-one punt returns and was selected as an All-American. Alworth graduated

from Arkansas in 1962 with a B.A. degree in marketing and enrolled in law school for one semester.

Alworth, however, focused on opportunities in sports rather than in the business world. The exceptional speed of the six-foot, 180-pound Alworth continued to attract baseball scouts. He turned down contracts from the Yankees and Pittsburgh Pirates, casting his lot with football. In 1962 the National Football League (NFL) was in a bidding war for player talent with its upstart rival, the American Football League (AFL). Taking advantage of this situation, Alworth signed a lucrative contract with the San Diego Chargers of the AFL, who had picked him in the second round of the player draft.

Alworth's youthful appearance and leaping, twisting style on the football field earned him the nickname "Bambi." But as a wide receiver for the Chargers, Alworth proved to be a rugged athlete who could take the vicious hits of defensive backs. For example, Alworth played much of the 1966 football season with two broken hands until he was sidelined with a hamstring injury, yet he still led the AFL in all pass-receiving categories. Alworth's accomplishments and stature as a football player helped the AFL in its struggle to achieve parity with the NFL, which culminated in the merger of the two leagues in 1970.

Alworth gained over 1,000 yards receiving each season from 1963 to 1969 and was selected as an All-Pro in those years. Alworth led the AFL in receiving three times and played in two AFL championship games. However, in a 1969 *Look* magazine article, Charger coach Sid Gillman was critical of Alworth's work ethic, long hair, and sideburns. Alworth responded, "A person has to feel like he or she's special. I want to do my own thing. I hate for somebody to get on me in front of people." Following the 1970 season, San Diego traded Alworth to the Dallas Cowboys. Alworth caught thirty-four passes for the Cowboys in 1971, and snagged a touchdown pass in the Super Bowl as the Cowboys defeated the Miami Dolphins.

Following the 1972 season, Alworth retired from professional football at age thirty-two. During 11 seasons, Alworth scored 87 touchdowns (all but 2 via pass receptions) and caught 542 passes for 10,266 total yards to rank fourth on the all-time receiving list at the time of his retirement. Alworth was selected as a member of the All-Time American Football Conference team, and his number 19 was retired by the Chargers. He was inducted into the Professional Football Hall of Fame in 1978. At the induction ceremonies in Canton, Ohio, Al Davis, general manger of the Oakland Raiders and a key figure in the establishment of the AFL, noted that Alworth was the first member of the new league to be elected to the Hall of Fame. Davis proclaimed, "He was the most feared player of our time and deserves to be the standard-bearer for the American Football League."

After he retired Alworth settled in San Diego, where he pursued business interests including real estate development. Alworth's first marriage ended in divorce in 1969; he married Marilyn Joyce Gallo in 1970. Alworth and Gallo had three children, two of whom died in infancy. They divorced in 1979.

Alworth is a successful businessman in San Diego and owner of Space Saver, an industrial real estate company. But Alworth is best remembered for his acrobatic catches for the San Diego Chargers during the early years of the American Football League.

★

Journalistic profiles providing some background information on Alworth's life include Edward Shrake, "They All Go Bang! at Bambi," *Sports Illustrated* (13 Dec. 1965); Herman L. Marin, "Fawn-Loving Rover Boy," *Senior Scholastic* (16 Sept. 1966); G. Brown, "It's Pride that Gets You Up There," *Saturday Evening Post* (14 Dec. 1968); and Gerald Astor, "Lance Alworth: Charger Goes Groovy," *Look* (2 Dec. 1969). For information on Alworth's football career, see Ronald L. Mendell and Timothy B. Phares, *Who's Who in Football* (1974); and *Total Football: The Official Encyclopedia of the National Football League* (1999).

RON BRILEY

ANDERSON, George Lee ("Sparky") (*b.* 22 February 1934 in Bridgewater, South Dakota), one of the most successful managers in major league baseball history and the only manager to win the World Series for both a National League and American League team.

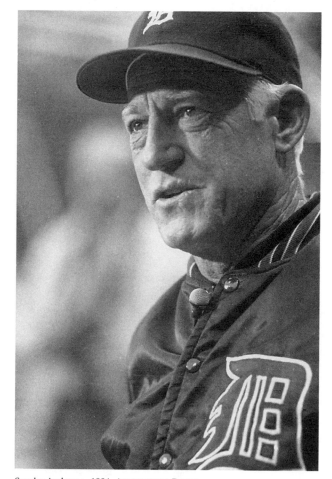

Sparky Anderson, 1984. ASSOCIATED PRESS

Anderson was one of five children. He grew up in a household of nine people, including his father, a painter and postal worker; his mother, a homemaker; his grandparents; three sisters; and a brother. When Anderson was eight, his family moved to the area in Los Angeles later known as Watts, near the University of Southern California (USC). Anderson spent a fair amount of time at the USC baseball field. Eventually, he became a batboy for the university team, coached by Rod Dedeaux, and developed a love for baseball.

After graduating from Dorsey High School in Los Angeles, he signed a contract as an infielder with the Brooklyn Dodgers farm system in 1953. That year, on 3 October, Anderson married his high school sweetheart, Carol Valle, and they eventually had three children. He was sent to Santa Barbara of the California League and began his professional career, primarily playing second base.

Anderson moved up the ranks of the Dodgers' minor league system by virtue of his fielding skills. Over his ten-year minor league career, he led the league four times in double plays but never batted above .300. He played at Pueblo (Western League, 1954), Fort Worth (Texas League, 1955), Montreal (International League, 1956 and 1958), and Los Angeles (Pacific Coast League, 1957) in the Dodgers organization. It was at Fort Worth where he received the nickname "Sparky," because of his explosive arguments with umpires.

In December 1958 Anderson was traded to the Philadelphia Phillies for three players. He started in 1959 for the Phillies and had a modest rookie year. He played in practically every game (152 out of 154), batted .208, scored 42 runs, and stole 6 bases. He had an impressive .984 fielding average at second base for the last-place Phillies, but he was shipped back to the minors the following year.

From 1960 until 1963 Anderson played second base for the Toronto Maple Leafs of the International League. For the 1964 season Anderson retired as a player and became the Maple Leafs' manager. During his first season with Toronto (a co-op team with players from the Milwaukee Braves and the Washington Senators), they went 80–72, fifth in the league.

Anderson then managed in the St. Louis Cardinals organization at Rock Hill (Western Carolinas League) in 1965, and at St. Petersburg (Florida State League) in 1966. In 1967 he began two years of managing in the Cincinnati Reds organization, first for Modesto (California League) and then for Asheville (Southern League). In 1969 he was hired as a coach for the San Diego Padres.

In 1970 Anderson returned to the Cincinnati Reds organization and accepted his first major league managerial position. Anderson immediately made an impact, leading the Reds, third place finishers in 1969, to a 102–60 record. He led the Reds to the World Series for the first time since 1961, losing to the Baltimore Orioles in five games. Beginning with the 1972 season, Anderson's Reds finished no worse than second over seven consecutive seasons. In 1972 the Reds made it to the World Series but lost to the Oakland A's.

In both 1975 and 1976 the team that Anderson had been building finally won World Series championships against the Boston Red Sox and New York Yankees, respectively. These Reds teams were known as the "Big Red Machine" and were led by Hall of Fame players Tony Perez, Johnny Bench, and Joe Morgan, as well as Pete Rose, Don Gullet, and George Foster.

The Reds primarily won with their offense, having a good, but not spectacular, pitching corps. Given the pitchers that he had to work with, Anderson earned the nickname "Captain Hook" for his tendency to replace pitchers with relievers at any point in the game. He knew he was being tough on his pitchers, but he didn't see any other way to handle it. "My mother, I love her," Sparky once said, "but she don't pitch for me." The common school of thought among managers in the 1970s was to let the starting pitchers stay in the game and work themselves out of problems. By going quickly to the bullpen, Anderson helped revolutionize the game. The Reds finished second to the Los Angeles Dodgers in both 1977 and 1978. Despite his success, Anderson was fired after the 1978 season over differences with the club management.

Anderson took off the early part of the 1979 season, but after weighing several offers, decided to accept the managerial position with the Detroit Tigers. He debuted with the Tigers on 14 June in the middle of what became a fifth-place finish. The Tigers were a very young team that had not won their division since 1972, but they already had many of the players who would make up the core of the pennant contenders of the 1980s, including Alan Trammell, Lou Whitaker, Jack Morris, Lance Parrish, and Milt Wilcox.

Under Anderson, the team steadily improved until they finished 92–70 in 1983. They started the 1984 season with a 35–5 record and stayed in first place all season. They finished 104–58, swept Kansas City in the American League Championship Series (ALCS), and defeated the Padres in five games for their first World Series win since 1968. While they remained competitive through the mid-to-late-1980s, they only won the division title in 1987, losing to the Minnesota Twins in the ALCS. In 1984 and 1987 Anderson won the American League Manager of the Year award.

The Tigers fortunes under Anderson began to wane in the late 1980s. In 1989, during a season that saw the Tigers drop from second to seventh in the standings, Anderson took time off, sitting out seventeen games from 19 May to 4 June. Anderson returned to a team that had a combination of aging stars like Trammell and Whitaker and younger players who would never blossom into major league stars.

In 1995, when major league owners pursued replacement players to field teams during the prolonged players' strike, Anderson stood alone among managers by refusing to manage these hastily assembled teams. He was relieved of his duties, but when the strike broke during spring training, Anderson was brought back to manage the Tigers. After another poor finish by the Tigers that year, Anderson retired.

Anderson once said, "The biggest misconception about me is that I'm an extrovert. I'm an introvert. My real name is George, and that's the name I like best, and it's who I am." The upbeat media personality known as "Sparky" was a very different individual. Anderson believed that a large part of his job was showmanship. He patterned himself after Casey Stengel and was never more pleased than when someone compared him to the great manager. *Sports Illustrated* said he "blessed Tiger Stadium with a style and syntax that were all his own."

In his nine years with the Cincinnati Reds and seventeen years with the Detroit Tigers, Anderson was the only manager to win World Series in both the National and American leagues. He compiled a lifetime managerial record of 2194–1834, the third highest win total in baseball history. Anderson was named Manager of the Year four times during his career, and in 2000, during the first year he was eligible, he was elected to the Baseball Hall of Fame.

★

Information on Anderson is available in a players file at the National Baseball Hall of Fame Library. Anderson cowrote several books, including *The Main Spark: Sparky Anderson and the Cincinnati Reds* (1978), with Si Burick; *Bless You Boys: Diary of the Detroit Tigers' 1984 Season* (1984), with Dan Ewald; *Sparky* (1990), with Ewald; and *They Call Me Sparky* (1998), with Dan Ewald. Information about Anderson can also be found in Leonard Koppett, *The Man in the Dugout: Baseball's Top Managers and How They Got That Way* (2000).

COREY SEEMAN

ANDERSON, Paul Edward (*b.* 17 October 1932 in Toccoa, Georgia; *d.* 15 August 1994 in Vidalia, Georgia), amateur weightlifter and professional strongman who, as an Olympic and world champion and a Christian evangelist, captured public attention and was widely regarded in the 1950s and 1960s as the world's strongest man.

Anderson was the younger child of Robert Anderson and Ethel Bennett. His father was a construction foreman who worked on dams and power plants in the southern Appalachians. His mother was a homemaker. Since the family moved frequently, Anderson attended many public schools, and he graduated in 1950. That year he enrolled at Furman University in Greenville, South Carolina, on a football scholarship, but resigned during the first year. At Furman, however, Anderson first realized his extraordinary strength by performing a 400-pound deep knee bend in the gym.

Upon returning home to Elizabethton, Tennessee, he was discovered by the legendary deadlifter Bob Peoples, who witnessed Anderson performing a remarkable 550-pound squat for two repetitions. Although concentrating on hip lifting (with a heavy safe) and lower-body development, he also began practicing overhead movements in order to enter competitions. In the 1952 Tennessee State meet, he broke all heavyweight records with a 275-pound press, a 225-pound snatch, and a 300-pound clean and jerk. Then he executed an astounding 660-pound squat. Hampered by injuries, Anderson did not perform in national or international competitions until 1955, when he set a world record of 436 pounds in the clean and jerk at the national championships in Cleveland. That same year in Moscow, Russia, Anderson won international acclaim by being the first man in history to press over 400 pounds. "U.S. Weightlifter Amazes Russians" was the front-page headline in the *New York Times* for 16 June 1955. The Russians called him *chudo pirody,* a wonder of nature. Anderson set a new standard of performance and became a cold-war symbol of U.S. strength and superiority.

At five feet, nine inches tall and 350 pounds, the Georgia strongman known as "The Dixie Derrick" became the 1955 world heavyweight champion at Munich, Germany, breaking two world records in the process. He was thought to be "surer of winning an Olympic title [in 1956] than any man, from any country, in any sport," predicted America's weightlifting coach Bob Hoffman. But in the days prior to the Melbourne, Australia, games, Anderson suffered from a high fever and severe loss of weight. Trailing after the press and snatch, and missing his first two clean and jerks, it was only through a superhuman effort that he made his final attempt of 413 pounds, setting an Olympic record and thereby winning on lesser bodyweight. He returned to his hill-country home as a conquering hero and quickly became an enduring strength phenomenon.

Anderson's fellow Georgians held him in high esteem. At an appearance at the 1957 North-South football classic in Atlanta, he walked around the stadium and each section stood as he passed; by the time he got all the way around, the whole stadium was standing and applauding. "It was

Paul Anderson, 1956. AP/WIDE WORLD PHOTOS

like a slow motion wave," recalled a fourteen-year-old at the event. "He was just a Georgia country boy out of nowhere who made good, and these were his people. I had goose bumps." Another contemporary recalled Anderson as quiet and laid-back. "A cracker boy with no airs about him." Yet he never doubted his own strength. "Just load the bar and I'll pick it up," was his line. In his training methods Anderson provided strong support for exponents of the squat as the most effective builder of overall strength. He also advocated a protein-rich diet, consuming large quantities of milk and even experimenting with raw beef blood.

By no means the least remarkable aspect of his athletic prowess was his speed. Despite his great size, he was alleged to have sprinted 100 yards in 11.6 seconds and leaped over nine feet in the standing broad jump. A lesser-known fragment of lifting lore is that Anderson was rejected for service in the Korean War because no shirt could be found large enough to accommodate his twenty-two-and-one-half-inch neck. He was the first true super-heavyweight of the modern era, representing a quantum leap in size and strength, but unlike most successors, he made his reputation without the use of steroids.

Having won the highest accolades possible in amateur weightlifting, Anderson entered show business as a professional strongman in 1957, performing feats of strength where he hoisted humans and safes filled with silver dollars at a Reno, Nevada, casino and on the *Ed Sullivan Show*. Whether he unofficially performed a 1,200-pound squat in Nevada and a 6,270-pound backlift in his parents' backyard in Toccoa has been much debated. Although there is no irrefutable evidence for either feat, most iron-game buffs believe he either did them or could have done them. One credible witness saw him perform eight easy squats with 700 pounds. Anderson claimed to have done eight with 800 pounds. For several years he also pursued a successful professional wrestling career and then a brief, less successful fling at boxing, where his strength was less of an advantage.

On 1 September 1959 Anderson married Glenda Garland; their only child, a daughter, was born in 1966. After committing their lives to Christ in 1961, the Andersons established the Paul Anderson Youth Home in Vidalia to raise boys in a wholesome and disciplined environment. Over the next two decades, Anderson traveled an estimated 3 million miles throughout the country, conducting lifting exhibitions and giving Christian witness to raise money for his youth home, sometimes putting on as many as 500 shows a year. His record was fourteen shows in one day during a visit in 1967 to Charlottesville, Virginia.

In 1974 he was inducted into the Georgia Sports Hall of Fame. At the 1992 USA Power and Strength Symposium in Orlando, Florida, Anderson was named the strongest man of the century. After a prolonged kidney illness, he died at age sixty-one and is buried on the grounds of his home for boys.

Anderson was, in many ways, an iron game innovator and icon who blazed his way through American sport and society for a quarter century. He is entitled, perhaps more than any other weightlifter for his respective era, to be called the world's strongest man.

★

Any study of Anderson's life and lifting career should begin with his autobiography, with Jerry B. Jenkins and James R. Adair, *A Greater Strength* (1990). The largest single source of information on Anderson's lifting career is Randall J. Strossen, *Paul Anderson: The Mightiest Minister* (1990). Also see Ed Linn, "Paul Anderson: The Georgia Strong Boy," *Sport* (June 1956); Bob Hise and Steve Neece, "Paul Anderson," *MuscleMag International* (July 1995); and Osmo Kiiha, "Paul Anderson," *The Iron Master* (Jan. 1992).

JOHN D. FAIR

ANDRETTI, (Gabriele) Mario (*b.* 28 February 1940 in Montona, Ítaly), auto racing champion who was winner of the Daytona 500 in 1967, the Indianapolis 500 in 1969, and the Grand Prix driving championship in 1978; was Champ Car National Champion in 1965, 1966, 1969, and 1984 and Phoenix 200 Champ Car Champion in 1993; and became a successful business executive.

Andretti was born in Italy near the Trieste area, to Louis and Rina Andretti. He has a twin brother, Aldo, and an older sister. As part of World War II reparations, Trieste was given to Yugoslavia, forcing the Andrettis to leave in 1948. They spent seven years in a camp for displaced persons in the central Italian province of Lucca. Andretti's father worked building toys. To earn additional money for the family, young Andretti began parking cars at age thirteen. His job allowed him to drive all sorts of vehicles, and, like his twin, he developed a love for fast cars and for racing. His father knew about the twins' passion. The boys' reckless driving habits led him to forbid them from racing or even driving cars. But Andretti was an admirer of the Italian racecar driver Alberto Ascari (whom he had first seen racing at Monza, Italy), and the brothers secretly became racecar drivers, racing formula junior racing cars from 1953 until 1955. In 1954 Andretti watched Ascari race the Mille Miglia, a difficult 1,000-mile course in Italy that made a circuit from Brescia to Rome and back.

The Andretti family immigrated to the United States on 16 June 1955, and settled in Nazareth, Pennsylvania. Because of his poor English skills, the teenaged Andretti was enrolled in the seventh grade later that year. He was much older than most of classmates, and he soon grew bored with his studies and left school. He later finished high school

Mario Andretti. ARCHIVE PHOTOS, INC.

through a correspondence course and received a high school equivalency diploma. In 1959, at age nineteen, Andretti became a naturalized citizen and began his U.S. racing career.

Both Andretti brothers secretly continued to pursue their passion for racing in the United States. They built their version of a Hudson Hornet and began competing on the National Association for Stock Car Auto Racing circuit. Both had won two races each when Aldo Andretti crashed in the fifth race, fracturing his skull. When their father found out, he expressed his disapproval by not speaking to them. Despite his father's disapproval, Aldo continued racing for another ten years until a second accident forced him to retire. Rather than fight with his father or give up what he loved, Mario moved out of the house.

In 1960 and 1961 Andretti won twenty-one of the forty-six stock car races in which he participated. In November 1961 he married Dee Ann Hock, his English tutor, and entered the racing business with Hock's father, who helped sponsor him. The couple has three children: Michael, Jeff, and Barbie. Both Michael and Jeff have pursued careers in racing, at times even competing against their father.

On 3 March 1962, at age twenty-two, racing 1/4 midget racecars, Andretti won his first major victory. Later that year he began racing Offy midget cars for the Mataba brothers. On Labor Day 1963 Andretti won three midget car races, one at Flemington, New Jersey, and the other two at Hatfield, Pennsylvania. The next year he participated in his first United States Auto Club (USAC) race and he formed an association with car manager Clint Braumer and pit manager Jim McGee. In 1965 he signed with Dean Van

Lines, his first racing contract in the USAC. That year he was chosen as Rookie of the Year, placed third in his first Indianapolis 500 race, and won the USAC Championship. In 1966 he won eight of fifteen Champ Car races and another USAC Championship. Andretti also won the Daytona 500 in 1967 and the USAC championship races for 1969, 1984, and 1987. Throughout the 1960s he participated in all versions of car racing—midget, Formula One, sprint, dirt track, and drag racing. In 1968, driving a Ford Mustang, he won his first and only match race and in 1969, on his fifth try, he won the Indianapolis 500. Andretti continued his winning streak through the 1970s and into the 1980s, winning races at Portland and Pocono in 1986 and the Long Beach Grand Prix in 1987 (the third of three such victories between 1983 and 1987), and the Livingwell-Provimi 200 in Elkhart Lake, Wisconsin. He was named Driver of the Year (1967, 1978, and 1984); Driver of the Quarter-Century (1992); and Driver of the Century (1999–2000).

In addition to his many wins and honors, Andretti enjoys racing with his sons. In 1989 he and his son Michael raced as a team in the Champ Car race for that year. On 3 June 1990 Andretti, his sons, and his nephew John competed in the Champ Car race held in Milwaukee, Wisconsin. The following year, the four competed at Indianapolis.

Andretti has had his share of disappointment, as well. In 1981 he narrowly lost to Bobby Unser in a disputed and controversial finish to that year's Indianapolis 500. The dispute centered around Unser passing cars during a yellow caution flag. He was penalized a lap for his illegal move, making Andretti the winner. Unser and Roger Penske, the car's owner, appealed the decision. After four months, the USAC overturned the ruling, fined Unser $40,000 for his illegal move, and declared him the winner. In 1985 Andretti suffered a broken collarbone in a wreck during the Michigan 500, and in 1987 he crashed shortly after the start of the Pocono 500, but was not hurt.

Still, by 1987 Andretti had won forty-nine races, earning $5.7 million in prize money. Until 1989 he held the record for winning both a Formula One World Championship and an Indianapolis Car National Title. His record as of mid-2001 stood at more than 100 major wins, fifty-two Indianapolis career victories, four national championships, the distinction of earning more pole positions (sixty-seven) than anyone else in auto racing, and earning $12.5 million in prize money.

In late 1993 Andretti announced that 1994 would be his last year to participate in the Champ Car races. Although he has bowed out of this competition, he has not retired from racing entirely. He continues to compete in the Le Mans endurance race. In 1995 he placed second. When he is not racing, Andretti is occupied with his business interests, having invested the winnings from his many races in a variety of lucrative enterprises. As of July 2001 Andretti's corporation, Andretti International, owned a winery, a gasoline distributorship (Andretti Petroleum), a Toyota dealership, and Andretti Hanna Carwashes. The company also produced video games and car care products. The man who says that if he were not a driver he would be a fighter pilot is thought by many to deserve the title Driver of the Century.

★

Andretti is the author of an autobiography, *What's It Like Out There?* (1970). Biographies include Alan Johnson, *Driving in Competition* (1972), Hal Higdon, *Finding the Groove* (1973), and Gordon Kirby, *Mario Andretti: A Driving Passion* (2001). For additional biographical material, see *Biographical Dictionary of American Sports: Outdoor Sports* (1988). Relevant articles are in *Sports Illustrated:* "Bob Ottum, A Reckless Dash to Disaster" (13 June 1966), "Gentlemen, Junk Your Engines" (12 June 1967), and Kim Chapin, "La Dolce Indy" (7 June 1971). See also "Auto Racing: What Is This Danger?" *Time* (21 Apr. 1966), and "Andretti: Vroom at the Top," *Newsweek* (29 May 1967). Useful websites include the Motorsports Hall of Fame at <http://www.mshf.com/hof/>, and the Andretti family site at <http://www.andretti.com>.

BRIAN B. CARPENTER

ANSON, Adrian Constantine ("Cap"; "Pop") (*b.* 17 April 1852 in Marshalltown, Iowa; *d.* 18 April 1922 in Chicago, Illinois), major league baseball's first true superstar as a great hitter, manager, and innovator with the Chicago White Stockings.

Anson was the younger of two sons of Henry Anson, a homesteader and hotel operator who helped found Marshalltown, and Jeannette Rice, a homemaker who died when Anson was seven years old. Anson attended Marshalltown public schools, spent two years at the Notre Dame boarding school, and studied for one year at the University of Iowa, from 1869 to 1870. Between 1866 and 1870 he played with his father and uncle on the Marshalltown Stars baseball club, winners of the 1867 state championship.

In 1871 Anson signed for $66 a month as a third baseman with the Forest City Club of Rockford, Illinois, in the National Association. He led Rockford with a .325 batting average and led the league with 11 doubles. After Rockford disbanded, Anson played for the Philadelphia Athletics primarily at first base from 1872 through 1875. He batted .415 with 50 runs batted in (RBI) and paced the National Association with a .455 on-base percentage in 1872. He hit .398 in 1873. In five National Association seasons he compiled a .360 batting average with 423 hits and 197 RBI.

In 1876 Anson married Virginia Fiegal; they had seven children. William Hulbert, the owner of the Chicago White Stockings in the National League, secretly signed Anson

Cap Anson. ASSOCIATED PRESS AP

for the 1876 season for $2,000. Hulbert had violated league rules by conducting negotiations with Anson and other players while the season was in progress, and in order to forestall expulsion from the National Association, he formed the National League. Anson unsuccessfully sought to be released from that contract when the Athletics offered him $500 more and his new wife opposed moving west.

Anson played first base with the Chicago White Stockings from 1876 to 1897, setting a major league longevity record. He planned originally to rejoin Philadelphia in 1877, but following the 1876 season the National League expelled the Athletics for failing to complete the 1876 road schedule. A right-hander at six feet, one inch and 220 pounds, Anson batted .329 with 2,995 hits and 1,879 RBI in twenty-two seasons for Chicago and hit over .300 in twenty seasons. He led the National League in RBI eight times (1880–1882, 1884–1886, 1888, 1891), recording a career-high 147 in 1886. Anson won four National League batting titles, hitting .317 in 1879, .399 in 1881, .347 in 1887, and .344 in 1888. He also paced the National League five times in fielding percentage (1877, 1880–1881, 1888–1889), three times in on-base percentage (1881, 1888, 1890), twice in doubles (1877–1885), and once each in hits (1881) and walks (1890).

Anson also was notable for his other hitting achievements. A booming line-drive hitter with power in the "dead ball era," he recorded five or more hits in ten games, and in July 1883 he became the first player to double four times in a major league game. On 6 August 1884 he became the first player to belt three consecutive home runs in a major league game. He had clouted two home runs the previous day, making him the first player to hit five home runs in consecutive major league games. He then tied a major league record with six runs scored on 24 August 1886.

The premier nineteenth-century manager, Anson piloted the Chicago White Stockings from 1879 to 1897. His clubs won 1,296 games, giving him a .578 career win-loss percentage. During his first eight managerial seasons, Anson directed Chicago to National League pennants in 1880, 1881, 1882, 1885, and 1886. He hit .423 to help the White Stockings defeat the St. Louis Browns of the American Association in the 1885 World Championship Series, but St. Louis defeated Chicago 4–2 in the 1886 World Championship Series.

Anson managed numerous star players, including Larry Corcoran, Jim McCormick, Clark Griffith, Michael Kelly, Ed Williamson, and Bill Lange. A strong disciplinarian, Anson did not allow his players to drink alcoholic beverages, smoke cigarettes or cigars, or use drugs. He helped introduce the practice of spring training in 1886, when he took the White Stockings to Hot Springs, Arkansas. Anson pioneered the use of hit-and-run plays, signaling, base stealing, player platooning, coaching boxes, and pitcher rotation. He also participated on American All-Star teams

visiting England in 1874 and touring the world in 1888 and 1889.

Anson, reflecting the racial prejudices of that era, opposed allowing African Americans to play major league baseball. In 1883 he threatened to withdraw the White Stockings from an exhibition game with the Toledo Mudhens because Toledo catcher Moses Fleetwood Walker was African-American. Anson relented, however, when Toledo threatened to withhold Chicago's financial guarantee. Four years later his club refused to play an exhibition game with Newark of the International League because of their outstanding African-American pitcher, George Washington Stovey. The incident dissuaded the New York Giants from promoting Stovey to the major leagues. The color barrier lasted in major league baseball until 1947, when Jackie Robinson integrated the Brooklyn Dodgers.

In 1888 Anson signed a ten-year contract to manage Chicago. The White Stockings did not capture any more National League pennants and experienced several losing seasons. From 1891 to 1897 the new Chicago co-owner, James Hart, clashed with Anson over the latter's managerial strategies. In 1897, when Chicago finished in ninth place, thirty-four games behind, Anson was dismissed as manager. He piloted the New York Giants for two months in 1898.

In *A Ball Player's Career* (1900), Anson recounted his professional baseball career and international goodwill tours. He criticized the National League as a gigantic monopoly and in 1900 helped establish a rival American Association. Anson was named American Association president, but he dissolved the league when it proved difficult to launch; it became instead a minor league. He established billiard and bowling businesses in Chicago and managed a semiprofessional baseball team, but these enterprises floundered financially. He was elected city clerk of Chicago in 1905 but was defeated for reelection in 1907.

Anson toured the vaudeville circuit with two of his daughters to earn additional income, performing an act titled "Cap Anson and Daughters" that was partly devoted to baseball. Shortly after, he declared bankruptcy and saw his home foreclosed. When the National League attempted to establish a pension fund for him, he rejected the financial assistance. Anson, who had hoped to become baseball's first commissioner in 1921, was managing Chicago's Dixmoor Club when he died of a heart attack. The National League paid for his funeral, and he is buried at the Oakwood Cemetery in Chicago.

Anson died thinking he was the first player with 3,000 National League hits, but he actually fell five hits short. He had been credited erroneously with twenty more hits than he earned in the 1879 season. In 1939 the Veterans Committee elected him to the National Baseball Hall of Fame. His hitting, managerial skills, innovative leadership, and aggressive style helped transform a sandlot sport into the national pastime.

★

Anson's files are in the National Baseball Library in Cooperstown, New York, and in the Chicago Historical Society. His autobiography, *A Ball Player's Career* (1900), features his international tours. Bill James, *The Baseball Book* (1990); Jerry E. Clark, *Anson to Zuber* (1992); Brad Herzog, *The Sports 100* (1995); and Frederick Ivor-Campbell et al., *Baseball's First Stars* (1996) contain brief career summaries. For Anson's role with Chicago, see Warren Brown, *The Chicago Cubs* (1946); Arthur Bartlett, *Baseball and Mr. Spalding* (1951); Eddie Gold and Art Ahrens, *The Golden Era Cubs, 1876–1940* (1985); Peter Levine, *A. G. Spalding and the Rise of Baseball* (1985); and Warren Wilbert and William Hageman, *Chicago Cubs: Seasons at the Summit* (1997). Pertinent articles include Roger H. Van Bolt, "'Cap' Anson's First Contract," *Annals of Iowa* (Apr. 1953); George S. May, "Major League Baseball Players from Iowa," *Palimpsest* (Apr. 1955); David L. Porter, "Cap Anson of Marshalltown: Baseball's First Superstar," *Palimpsest* (July/Aug. 1980); and Tom Nawroki, "Captain Anson's Platoon," *National Pastime* (1995). Obituaries are in the *Chicago Tribune* (22 Apr. 1922), *New York Times* (22 Apr. 1922), and "Baseball's Grand Old Man," *Literary Digest* (6 May 1922).

DAVID L. PORTER

Eddie Arcaro, 1951. ASSOCIATED PRESS AP

ARCARO, George Edward ("Eddie") (*b.* 19 February 1916 in Cincinnati, Ohio; *d.* 14 November 1997 in Miami, Florida), hard-riding jockey who rode two thoroughbreds to the Triple Crown and was inducted into the Racing Hall of Fame in 1958.

Arcaro was the son of Pasquale Arcaro, an Italian fruit vendor, and Josephine Giancola. At school his flyweight proportions prevented him from making any headway in traditional athletics. In an April 1956 interview with *Look* magazine, Arcaro observed, "I remember the only thing I really hungered for as a kid was [to be] the size to play baseball. When the other kids would choose up sides for a game, I was always left over, and I think that's why I went for racing." Arcaro's size made him a promising jockey, and his considerable assets of courage, intelligence, and horse craft saw him emerge as one of the top five U.S. jockeys in the twentieth century. At five feet, two inches tall and 114 pounds he was cast in an ideal mold for a prospective jockey.

Like many jockeys, Arcaro had been around horses from a very young age. He quit the Cincinnati school system at age thirteen and started working at the Latonia Race Track. If it was a good day he could earn fifty cents per ride working as an exercise rider with various racing stables. He was a boy who enjoyed taking risks and had the capacity to

recover from major falls and tumbles. He once hit a tree while snow sledding, and "the inside of his right thigh was ripped to the bone and forty stitches were required. After three months the doctor allowed Eddie to get back on his feet. He did not know Arcaro had been walking on his own for a month previous."

Horse racing has always been a highly dangerous sport. Like other great jockeys, Arcaro bounced back from fearful accidents and rode through the pain of injury. For example, in 1933 Arcaro was thrown at Washington Park Raceway in Chicago. After being unconscious for three days, he had to spend three months in the hospital with a fractured skull, a punctured lung, and a broken nose. On another occasion he fell under a horse on a muddy track and would have drowned if not saved by an observant track photographer.

The California trainer Clarence Davidson eventually took Arcaro under his wing and became his mentor. An apocryphal story in the fables of horse racing had Arcaro as an ill-starred rider, having not one victory in 250 starts. In fact, Arcaro rode his first winner after forty-five races; his mount was Eagle Bird and the date was 14 January 1932. At the start of his racing career with Davidson he earned $20 per month as part of a fixed three-year contract. By the time he retired, Arcaro was enjoying the lifestyle of a celebrity millionaire.

Following his training with Davidson, Arcaro joined the more lucrative Calumet Farm syndicate and rode for Warren Wright. Arcaro had an avalanche of victories—132 in the 1933 season—and never eschewed his feisty persona. Throughout his career he was a "scrapping rider" and "as gladiatorial as a hornet." In the 1930s Arcaro graduated from being a nobody to a nonpareil. He went from "nags and bags that were just one step short of pulling milk carts to riding some of the finest thoroughbreds in the game." By the late 1930s Arcaro was the premier jockey for Mrs. Payne Whitney's prestigious Greentree Stable. In 1937 he married a former model, Ruth; they had two children.

In the 1940s Arcaro became the only jockey to ride two thoroughbreds to the Triple Crown: Whirlaway in 1941 and Citation in 1948. Winning the Triple Crown, the Kentucky Derby, Preakness, and Belmont Stakes races all in the same year, is the ultimate achievement in the sport. Arcaro won the Belmont Stakes six times, the Preakness six times, and the Suburban Handicap eight times. He received the Jockey Club Gold Cup on ten occasions and earned numerous Horse of the Year rides, including those on Whirlaway (1941 and 1942), Citation (1948), Nashua (1955), Bold Ruler (1957), Sword Dancer (1959), and Kelso (1960 and 1961).

Toward the end of his racing career, Arcaro authored a colorful biography of his life and times, *I Ride to Win* (1951). In it, he told of being suspended for a year after driving a Cuban rival jockey into the rail of the racetrack. He also discussed the trials and tribulations of jockeys trying to make weight: "Some riders will all but saw their legs off to get within the . . . limit." He believed courage and mental toughness had to be shown in race after race, because, "If a jockey showed even the slightest trace of cowardice it could get awfully rough out there."

When Arcaro retired in 1961 he was the top money-winning jockey of his time with $39 million of purse money. He had been the leading money winner in the years 1940, 1942, 1948, 1950, 1952, and 1958. Arcaro combined his successful career as a jockey with an entrepreneurial flair for business. He invested in oil, bought into a number of West Coast eateries, and especially enjoyed owning and managing a wholesale saddlery business. With Johnny Longden and Sam Resnick, he also founded and was the president of the Jockey's Guild. Arcaro liked being a color commentator for televised horse races and unashamedly embraced his roles as a fashion plate and celebrity. Not surprisingly Arcaro's favorite home was situated in Garden City on Long Island, New York, a mere twenty minutes from one of his favorite stomping grounds, Belmont Park.

In *The Sports 100 Ranking the Greatest Athletes of All Time* (1995), Bert Randolph Sugar listed Arcaro in fifty-sixth place and described him as having the "sensitive touch of a piano player." A good case can be made that in his relatively short career, the man nicknamed "Banana Nose" and "The Master" was the most successful of all jockeys. While his grand total of 4,779 winners was impressive, his ratio of rides-to-stakes monies was epoch shattering. Of his 24,921 races between 1931 and his retirement in 1961, he finished "in the money" (first, second, or third) on more than half of these mounts during a career that went from 1949 until his retirement in 1961.

Arcaro was inducted into the Racing Hall of Fame in 1958. A plaque in the National Museum of Racing's Hall of Fame at Saratoga Springs, New York, wonderfully captures the magic and mastery of this great jockey: "He had great hands and seat, was unexcelled in switching the whip, possessed a sure sense of pace, and for two decades won the important races with casual excellence. . . . His superb talent was sought for all good ones." Bill Shoemaker, the doyen of U.S. jockeys, said of Arcaro, "He could do everything. The way he rides he looks part of the horse."

★

Frank J. Cavaioli has written a short profile on Arcaro in the *Encyclopedia of Ethnicity and Sports in the United States* (2000). There is an extensive narrative on Arcaro in *Current Biography* (1958), and *Current Biography Yearbook* (1998) has a concise obituary. Tom Gilcoyne, archival assistant at the National Museum of Racing and Hall of Fame, Saratoga Springs, New York, provides a useful Hall of Fame minibiography of Arcaro. Bert Randolph Sugar, *The Sports 100 Ranking of Greatest Athletes of All Time* (1995), has a lively and detailed summary of Arcaro's life. For a truly memorable social history of racing, see Laura Hillenbrand, *Seabiscuit: An American Legend* (2000), which contains telling fragments about Arcaro. There are nine wonderful black-and-white photographs of Arcaro in *Horse Racing: The Golden Age of the Track* (2001). An obituary is in the *New York Times* (15 Nov. 1997).

SCOTT A. G. M. CRAWFORD

ARCHIBALD, Nathaniel ("Nate"; "Tiny") (b. 2 September 1948 in the Bronx, New York), professional basketball player who was inducted into the Naismith Memorial Basketball Hall of Fame and named to the list of Fifty Greatest Players in NBA history.

Archibald was the second of six children born to "Big Tiny" Archibald, a construction worker, and Julia Archibald, a department store supervisor. The Archibalds, who had immigrated to the United States in 1946 from the West Indies, settled in the Bronx. From the age of six to eleven, Archibald attended Public School 18. After school he raced to the neighborhood basketball court to shoot baskets. At Clark Junior High School he made the school basketball team, and at night he played basketball at Public School 18 Community Center. In the fall of 1963, the same year

Nate Archibald, 1982. AP/WIDE WORLD PHOTOS

his father left the family, Archibald entered DeWitt Clinton High School. He had thoughts of quitting school, but the former City College of New York star Floyd Layne, his basketball coach at the Public School 18 Community Center, persuaded him to finish his education. As a junior, Archibald made the basketball team but sat on the bench most of the season. He continued to practice his passing and dribbling skills and as a senior became a starting guard for the team. During his outstanding senior season, Archibald was the team's second leading scorer, and his play led the Clinton Governors to a Bronx championship and later to the 1965–1966 Public School Athletic League basketball championship of New York City.

Archibald's play received little attention from local colleges, but Don Haskins, the head basketball coach of Texas Western in El Paso, was interested. Archibald agreed to play for Haskins but spent his freshman year at Arizona Western College in Yuma, where he averaged 29.5 points in twenty-seven games. After his freshman junior college basketball season, Archibald returned home, where he organized a youth basketball team from the Patterson Projects, the same public housing project in the South Bronx

where he grew up. Throughout the remainder of his college and professional life, he continued to return home to sponsor teams and events for the youth in his neighborhood. Organizing youth basketball teams was not Archibald's only off-court accomplishment in 1967. That year he married Shirley Dixon; the couple had five children.

When Archibald arrived on the campus of Texas Western for the 1967–1968 season, the education major found his niche as a guard on the basketball team. Nicknamed "Nate the Skate" by the fans who gathered to watch him play, Archibald dazzled them with his ability to pass the ball and to drive to the hoop and score against much taller opponents. He had good seasons with Texas Western (which changed its name to the University of Texas at El Paso), but the team and Archibald received little notice. In his three years at the University of Texas he played in seventy-three games and averaged twenty points a game. After his senior year, Archibald entered the National Basketball Association (NBA) draft without finishing his college degree and was selected in the second round by the Cincinnati Royals. Archibald, who had grown to six foot, one inch in stature and added about fifteen pounds to his high school weight of 145 pounds, had a solid inaugural season (1970–1971) with the Royals, averaging sixteen points a game.

In 1972 the owners of the Cincinnati Royals sold the franchise to a group of investors from Kansas City, Missouri, and Omaha, Nebraska, and the team changed its name to the Kansas City/Omaha Kings. The coach, Bob Cousy, decided to build the team around Archibald. At the end of the 1972–1973 season, Archibald had posted 910 assists and averaged thirty-four points a game, which set an NBA record. Archibald's outstanding on-court performance led to his first of six All-Star appearances as a player. In the first game of the 1973–1974 season he injured his Achilles tendon and appeared in only thirty-five games. His injury allowed him time to complete his B.A. in education at the University of Texas at El Paso in 1974. Archibald had two more productive seasons with the Kansas City Kings and then was traded to the New York Nets for the 1976–1977 season. That year he broke a bone in his foot after stepping on another player's instep and played in just thirty-four games. He was traded to the Buffalo Braves for the 1977–1978 season, but he saw no playing time, still recovering from the foot injury. The following season he was traded to the Boston Celtics.

During his 1978–1979 season as a Boston Celtic, Archibald was an important bench player who contributed 324 assists to the team. In the 1979–1980 season he started as a Celtic guard and boosted his number of assists to 671 — the highest number of his career since the 1972–1973 season record. During the 1980–1981 season Archibald continued as a starter registering 618 assists and, in the words of one analyst, "quarterbacked" the team, along with Larry

Bird, to an NBA championship title. In 1981 he was named Most Valuable Player for the NBA All-Star game. The 1982–1983 season was Archibald's last in a Celtic uniform. He was traded to the Milwaukee Bucks, with whom he played the 1983–1984 season, his last as a professional.

Over the course of Archibald's fourteen-year NBA career, he appeared in 876 games, posted 6,476 assists, scored 16,481 points, and averaged almost nineteen points a game. His on-court efforts earned him induction into the Naismith Memorial Basketball Hall of Fame (1991) and selection as one of the Fifty Greatest Players in NBA history (1996). From 1984 to 1989 Archibald served as an assistant basketball coach at the University of Georgia and then at his alma mater, the University of Texas at El Paso. He returned to New York in 1989 and in 1993 earned an M.A. from Fordham University in adult education and human resources development, and later began to pursue a Ph.D. He began teaching health and physical education at Public School 175/Independent School 275 in Harlem. In 1999 he continued to organize youth basketball in New York City by teaming up with the Washington Wizards star Rod Strickland to create the Rod Strickland–Tiny Archibald Summer League for boys. In January 2001 Archibald accepted a coaching position with the Fayetteville (N.C.) Patriots, one of eight teams in the newly organized National Basketball Development Team League. The League, which served as a "minor league" for the NBA, was designed to provide playing opportunities for American players over the age of twenty so they would not have to leave the United States to gain playing experience in overseas basketball leagues.

Archibald will be remembered for his unique style of play, explosive drives, and the remarkable 1972–1973 season in which he led the league in the most assists and points scored. He also will be remembered for his commitment to the youth of New York City.

★

A chronicle of Archibald's life through 1977 is in John Devaney, *Tiny!: The Story of Nate Archibald* (1977). Archibald's post-basketball pursuits are covered in John O'Keefe, "Tiny Archibald, Basketball Hall of Famer," *Time* (9 Nov. 1998), Chuck O'Donnell, "Summer Basketball Remains Part of the New York Culture," *New York Amsterdam News* (22 July 1999), Brett Friedlander, "Archibald eager to get started as Fayetteville coach," *Fayetteville Observer* (1 Feb. 2001), and Brian Holloway, "Community programs important to patriots coach Archibald," *Fayetteville Observer* (14 Aug. 2001). Archibald's college statistics are in Michael V. Earle, ed., *NCAA: Men's Basketball's Finest,* (1998), and his professional career totals are recorded in Zander Hollander and Alex Sachare, eds., *The Official NBA Basketball Encyclopedia: The Complete History and Statistics of Professional Basketball* (2000).

JON E. TAYLOR

ARIZIN, Paul Joseph (*b.* 9 April 1928 in Philadelphia, Pennsylvania), basketball player who excelled at both the college and professional levels and was one of the pioneers of the jump shot.

Arizin was one of two children of Roger Arizin, a mechanic for the Pennsylvania Railroad, and Anna Galen, a homemaker. He was raised as a Roman Catholic and his parish was Saint Monica's in South Philadelphia. Arizin received a half scholarship to attend LaSalle, a Catholic preparatory school. He was a good student and played intramural baseball, football, and basketball. When he tried out for the varsity basketball team in his senior year, he played sparingly for about five games and then he and the other senior nonstarters were cut from the team. Arizin graduated from high school in 1946.

Arizin decided to attend college at Villanova University, west of Philadelphia, living at home and commuting by train and bus. He had tried for one of three available academic scholarships, but finished thirteenth out of 275 applicants. Arizin played in several intramural, church, and independent basketball leagues, and in his freshman year one of the teams he was on, Hastings Club, made it to the finals of the Fraternal Order of Eagles citywide tournament. His team lost to the Main Liners (Villanova's team in the off-season), but Arizin was named the tournament's Most Valuable Player (MVP) and caught the eye of the Villanova coach Al Severance, who offered him a scholarship. Before the next season, Arizin also played summer basketball and was the athletic coordinator at the Nevele Country Club hotel in the Catskills.

In the next three years Arizin proved to be an outstanding collegiate player. Although he mostly had a deadly one-hand set shot from about twenty-five feet and drove forcefully to the basket for a fluid hook shot, his claim to fame was the jump shot—a rarity in those days. Although he did not invent it, he became its craftsman. He later explained that the shot came to him almost by accident. Because the floors at the Philadelphia gyms where he played were often waxed for dances, his foot often slipped while taking the hook shot. Therefore, he decided to use the jump shot. He could jump high and stay in the air a bit longer than most, so he used it when he wanted to force his way to the basket. His shots also had a low trajectory, because some of those gyms had low ceilings.

Arizin eventually moved on-campus, and did well in his studies, graduating in 1950 with a B.S. degree in accounting. Although bothered by a sinus condition plus nearsightedness (he did not wear glasses while playing), Arizin led Villanova in scoring and was its MVP during his three varsity seasons, scoring a then-record 1,648 points for a 20.1 points per game average. In his junior year (1948–1949) he made honorable mention for the Associated Press All-

Paul Arizin, 1952. AP/WIDE WORLD PHOTOS

America team and was chosen as the MVP in the Philadelphia district by the city's basketball writers. That was also the season he scored eighty-five points in one game, including thirty-five field goals, both of which were records at that time for major colleges. Ironically, the high school coach who cut him refereed that game. Villanova finished third in the National Collegiate Athletic Association tournament that year.

Arizin's senior year of 1950 was a standout. He won the national scoring title with his 735 points, five short of the record. His 25.3 points per game scoring average was the second all-time highest average, and his 49.3 field goal percentage was fourth in the nation. (Villanova led the nation in team offense.) He was a unanimous All-American on teams of the Associated Press, United Press International, Catholic All-America, *Sporting News,* and Helms Foundation, and the latter two each named him the player of the year. He was again voted the MVP in the Philadelphia district and was voted the MVP of the Globetrotters Tour. He sent a telegram of thanks to the *Sporting News,* and received a letter back saying that in its nine years of selecting All-Americans in football and basketball, he was only the third person ever to thank them.

When *Sport* magazine named its all-time, All-America team, Arizin was selected for the third team. His 1,648

career points were a record at that time for Villanova, and when the school became the thirty-second program to record 1,000 victories in 1984, the three living coaches were asked to select their all-era teams. Needless to say, Severance put Arizin on his. Arizin's "11" jersey was retired.

In 1950 Arizin was the territorial draft pick of the Philadelphia Warriors of the National Basketball Association (NBA) and signed with them for $9,000. After averaging 17.2 points per game in his first season, he averaged twenty or more points per game thereafter, leading the league in scoring in 1952 and 1957. He was selected to ten All-Star games and played in nine (he was injured for one), and was selected as the MVP in the 1952 game, in which he scored twenty-six points (he also led his East team in scoring in the 1958 and 1959 games). After the brilliant 1952 season, he enlisted in the U.S. Marine Corps for the next two years and earned the rank of sergeant. He married Maureen McAdams on 18 October 1952; they had five children.

After completing his military service in 1954, Pitchin' Paul resumed his NBA career without missing a beat. He averaged 22.8 points per game in his career, was named to the NBA first team three times and the second team twice, and was the third-leading scorer in league history with 16,266 points when he retired. When the league picked its Silver Anniversary Team in 1970 (1946–1971), Arizin was one of the four forwards selected. Despite these individual accomplishments, he most cherished the 1956 NBA championship won by the Warriors. That year he averaged 24.2 points per game during the regular season and 28.9 for the playoffs.

Arizin chose to retire in 1962 when the Warriors relocated to San Francisco. He played three seasons with the Camden Bullets of the Eastern League; they won the regular season title his first two years and the championship his third year, and he was voted the league's MVP in 1963. He was selected for the National Basketball Hall of Fame (1978), Helms Foundation Hall of Fame, Villanova's Athletic Hall of Fame, and Pennsylvania's Hall of Fame. He was among the first seven inductees in the Philadelphia Basketball Hall of Fame and in 1988 was named a Philadelphia Living Sports Legend by the Philadelphia Sportswriters Association.

When Arizin left basketball in 1965 he became a senior account manager for the IBM Corporation; he retired in 1985. He and his wife reside in Springfield, Pennsylvania. He has coached Catholic Youth Organization teams, has been involved with the Lions Club, and was the chairman of the Multiple Sclerosis Liberty Bell Classic in 1973. He enjoys reading, gardening, and spending time with his many grandchildren.

Above all, Arizin was a team player in his basketball career. He exhibited skills in all areas of the game, exemplified sportsmanship, was unselfish, and thoroughly deserved all the honors that came his way.

★

The bulk of the material about Arizin may be found in the Villanova University Sports Information Office. In addition, see Phil Pepe, *Greatest Stars of the NBA* (1970). For a review of Arizin's career after his selection to the National Basketball Hall of Fame, see the *Philadelphia Inquirer* (4 Apr. 1978 and 2 May 1978); *Boston Evening Globe* (28 Apr. 1978); and *Christian Science Monitor* (5 May 1978).

ROBERT W. LANGRAN

ARLEDGE, Roone Pinckney, Jr. (*b.* 8 July 1931 in New York City), television executive and producer known for innovative ABC sports programming, as well as for making ABC the most popular source for television news.

Born to Roone Arledge, Sr., a lawyer, and Gertrude Stritmater, a homemaker, Arledge was raised in the Forest Hills section of Queens in New York City. He graduated from Mepham High School in Merrick, New York, in 1948, and then attended Columbia University, graduating with a B.A. degree in 1952. That year he found a job with the DuMont network, where he learned the technical and economic nuts and bolts of the emerging television industry. Moving to

Roone Arledge, 1972. ASSOCIATED PRESS AP

NBC in 1954, he became an in-house producer assigned to news stories, special events (including sports), and even a puppet show, for which he won the first of his many Emmy Awards. He made another career move in 1960, arguably a risky one, leaving the powerful NBC to become a sports producer at ABC, which was then the perennial "third network" in a field of three.

It proved a wise decision. Lacking the entrenched corporate power structure of its older and richer rivals, ABC provided Arledge with the opportunity to be creative in what was then one of television's least creative programming genres. Before Arledge, television network sports coverage was typically little more than a radio broadcast with a camera following the ball. Announcers were restricted by the networks to colorless play-by-play descriptions and quick interviews with star players. Prevailing wisdom was that sportscasters' lack of personality would reassure viewers of the network's fairness and objectivity in the presentation of the game.

Within a year of his arrival at ABC, Arledge created and produced *ABC's Wide World of Sports* (1961), an anthology showcase that presented an eclectic array of events, including track and field, auto racing, ice skating, swimming and diving, and dozens of other sports, many of them ignored by the other networks. The show's signature credits sequence featured the voice of the anchor Jim McKay announcing to viewers that the show was "spanning the globe" to bring them "the thrill of athletic competition . . . the glory of victory and the agony of defeat," accompanied by an appropriate visual montage of highlights and lowlights. The sequence was soon familiar to every sports fan in the country.

Another Arledge production, *ABC's American Sportsman* (1965), provided an umbrella for various types of hunting, fishing, and outdoor photography expeditions. The series, which featured guest athletes and other celebrities each week, was a solid indication of the direction that Arledge would take ABC Sports and televised sports in general: the synthesis of sports and showmanship, with sports integrated into the general mix of entertainment. As with *Wide World of Sports,* Arledge's insistence on making the ABC imprimatur part of the title of the sports production helped to create a brand identity for the network, a tactic he continued to use successfully throughout his career in sports, and later in news.

Football became another growth area for ABC under Arledge. During the 1950s CBS had achieved a lock on broadcasts of the professional sport by signing an exclusive contract with the National Football League (NFL). Unable to compete for NFL games, ABC signed a similarly structured contract in 1960 to carry the games of the new American Football League (AFL), although few insiders held out hope for the AFL's long-term survival. Arledge was instrumental in promoting the new league, which became so successful that eventually the NFL was forced to merge with it. In 1964 Arledge was named the vice president of ABC Sports, and in 1968 the president of the division.

One of Arledge's greatest innovative successes was *ABC's Monday Night Football,* which premiered in 1969. Although ABC had been instrumental in the AFL's birth and survival, in 1964 its rival NBC outbid the network and came away with most of the profits as the new league reached parity with the NFL. Shut out of professional football coverage once again, Arledge made a characteristically bold proposal that the NFL restructure its entire schedule so that a single game be played each Monday night to be shown on ABC during prime time, the most watched and most lucrative period of the broadcast day. Understanding the special need for showmanship in prime time, Arledge put together a broadcast team consisting of the former New York Giants flankerback Frank Gifford, an articulate, even-toned student of the game; Don Meredith, the former Dallas Cowboys quarterback with a good old boy's drawl and easygoing personality; and Howard Cosell, a loudmouthed former lawyer whose abrasive personality played off dramatically against those of the two star athletes.

Coverage of the Olympic Games was another area in which Arledge forged changes in television, sports, and televised sports. In 1968, at a time when ABC was still striving to reach parity with its rivals, Arledge convinced the network to go out on a financial limb to obtain the broadcast rights to the games. Once again, he brought showmanship to what had been pious, ritualistic reportage. Punctuating live coverage of the Olympic events with "up close and personal" taped interviews, he made television stars of ice skaters, gymnasts, pole vaulters, and platform divers who were previously unknown to the general public. In 1972, when Palestinian terrorists killed eleven Israeli athletes and coaches at the Munich games in Germany, Arledge personally produced eighteen hours of live coverage as well as a filmed documentary, which he completed in less than twenty-four hours after the murders. ABC won twenty-nine Emmy Awards for the coverage.

In 1977 the chief executive officer Leonard Goldenson broadened Arledge's responsibilities dramatically, making him the president of ABC News as well as the president of ABC Sports. He was the first nonjournalist ever to head a network news operation. Although news purists were scandalized, Arledge went about the business of doing for the news division what he had done for the sports division. Introducing innovative series (including *Nightline* and *20/20*), attractive personalities, eye-catching graphics, and savvy promotion, he was instrumental in bringing ABC News to the top of the list in ratings and profits. Arledge gave up his leadership of ABC Sports in 1985 when the network's new owner, Capital Cities Communication, asked him to

focus exclusively on news. On 21 May 1994 Arledge married his third wife, Gigi Shaw, after having been married to Joan Heise and Anne Arledge. In 1998, having lost most of his day-to-day power at ABC, he became chairman of ABC News, a ceremonial role given to him in fulfillment of a lifetime contract.

Over the course of his career, Arledge won virtually every honor available to a broadcast executive, including thirty-six Emmy Awards, four Peabodys, and two Christophers. He was the first broadcaster to receive a Medal of the Olympic Order, and was inducted into the U.S. Olympic Hall of Fame in 1992. According to a 1997 *Time* magazine article, Arledge "virtually invented the world of big-time sports television, [by] giving fans *Wide World of Sports,* the instant replay, and Howard Cosell." There are some, however, who associated Arledge's achievements with the subjugation of contemporary sports, and especially the Olympics, to the needs of commercial television. Charges of this kind, whether true or not, come hand-in-hand with success in television.

★

Marc Gunther, *The House That Roone Built* (1994), although primarily concerned with his career as the head of the ABC News division, reveals much about Arledge's personality and ideas. Marc Gunther with Bill Carter, *Monday Night Madness* (1988), specifically focuses on what is probably his most enduring creation. Extensive interviews with the television executive were conducted by *Broadcasting* (2 Dec. 1985) and the renamed *Broadcasting and Cable* (10 Oct. 1994); the earlier article contains more sports information.

DAVID MARC

ARMOUR, Thomas Dickson ("Tommy") (*b.* 24 September 1895 in Edinburgh, Scotland; *d.* 11 September 1968 in Larchmont, New York), major championship golfer who was known as the "Silver Scot" and was one of the game's most respected and most quoted teachers and authors.

Armour was the son of a confectioner who had a consuming interest in golf (his parents' names are unknown). He spent much of his youth in the company of his older brother, an accomplished golfer who was a Scottish Open champion. The two became friends with Bobby Cruickshank, from whom Armour learned to use long irons and woods, later a defining characteristic of his game.

It is remarkable that Armour's career ever began. He enlisted in the British Army in 1914 and was a machine gunner with the Black Watch Highland Regiment in World War I. He lost the use of his left eye in a gas attack at the Battle of Ypres, in Belgium. In another battle, his tank was hit by a shell. The explosion injured Armour's head and shattered his left arm. As a result, metal plates were inserted in his head and arm.

Tommy Armour, 2000. AP PHOTO/CHUCK STOODY

Armour had been a student at Edinburgh University before the war, but decided to concentrate on golf. He married Consuelo Carrera in 1919; they had two children. Supported by his wife's wealth and practicing against several of Britain's top professionals, Armour began his amateur career in 1919, placing second in the Irish Amateur Open and winning the Dispatch Trophy. In 1920 he won four tournaments, including the Scottish and French Opens, and won his match in a pre–Walker Cup international tournament.

The popularity of golf in the United States convinced Armour to emigrate in 1921. He became an American citizen in 1922 and won three minor tournaments that year. In 1924, Armour represented the United States in a match against Britain, the only golfer to have competed on national teams from both countries.

Armour turned professional in 1924. He had a flair for strong finishes. His five pars and a birdie on the last six holes of the 1927 U.S. Open put him in a playoff with "Light-Horse" Harry Cooper. In the playoff Armour shot seventy-six to Cooper's seventy-nine. Armour won five other tournaments in 1927, including the Canadian Open,

his first of three titles in that event. In 1928 he won four more titles, and in 1929 set a 72-hole record of 273 to win the Western Open.

An affinity for aphorisms and carefully delivered critiques—along with his glibness—helped put Armour in demand as a speaker in the years between world wars. Armour was on a speaking tour in 1929 when he met Estelle Andrews. Later that year Armour divorced his first wife, married Andrews, and adopted her son.

In the 1930 PGA Championship at Fresh Meadows on Long Island, New York, Armour began the quarterfinal by losing five of the first six holes to Johnny Farrell. Armour beat Farrell, won his semifinal match, and faced Gene Sarazen in the final. On Sarazen's home course on the thirty-sixth and final hole, Armour won with a par.

By 1931 Armour had become only the third player to have won three major tournaments in his career: the 1927 U.S. Open at Oakmont, New York; the 1930 Professional Golfers Association (PGA) championships at Fresh Meadows on Long Island; and the 1931 British Open at Carnoustie, Scotland. Armour's final-round score of seventy-one at Carnoustie gave him the victory. Among his tournament appearances between 1931 and 1935 were two victories in the Miami Open, and a victory in the Canadian Open in 1927. He retired from golf in 1935, having won fourteen PGA tour tournaments.

Armour was in great demand as a teacher. Bobby Jones came to him for help in 1926; later that year Jones won both the U.S. Open and the British Open. Armour's students included Julius Boros, Lawson Little, Babe Didrikson Zaharias—and Richard Nixon. Armour charged $50 a lesson, a steep fee at the time, but there was always a line waiting. A session would begin with Armour watching the player hit twenty balls, then delivering a concise, brutal assessment. After that came another twenty balls and more of Armour's honesty. Armour also wrote several instructional books about golf: *How to Play Your Best Golf All the Time* (1953), which made the *New York Times* best-seller list and remained a steady seller for years; *A Round of Golf with Tommy Armour* (1959); and *Tommy Armour's ABC's of Golf* (1967).

Woods and long irons were the strength of Armour's game. His long waggle before a shot grew out of necessity—an adjustment to his war wounds. His power and finesse began with a pair of hands that Grantland Rice, the prominent sportswriter of the 1920s and 1930s, described as "two stalks of bananas." In *How to Play Your Best Golf All the Time* Armour wrote, "The basic factor in all good golf is the grip. Get it right, and all other progress follows."

Armour died in 1968 in Larchmont, New York. He has a posthumous connection to the golf club manufacturing company that bears his name. The Burke-Victor golf company, whose clubs Armour once endorsed, changed its name in 1985 to Tommy Armour Golf Company.

Armour's legend extends well beyond his twelve years as a professional golfer. His postcompetitive career was a blend of his own competitive enthusiasm and his passion for improving the game of golf. Ross Goodner wrote, "Nothing was small about Tommy Armour's reputation. At one time or another, he was known as the greatest iron player, the greatest raconteur, the greatest drinker, and most expensive teacher in golf."

★

For information about Armour's career, see Ross Goodner, *Golf's Greatest* (1978); George Peper, *Golf in America: The First One Hundred Years* (1988); and Herbert Warren Wind, *The Story of American Golf* (1948). Obituaries are in the *New York Times* (14 Sept. 1968), *Time* (20 Sept. 1968), and *Newsweek* (23 Sept. 1968).

TED BROCK

ARMSTRONG, Henry Jackson, Jr. (*b*. 12 December 1912 in Columbus, Mississippi; *d*. 24 October 1988 in Los Angeles, California), simultaneously held the featherweight, lightweight, and welterweight championship titles in the late 1930s and earned respect as one of the greatest boxers in the modern history of the sport.

Henry Armstrong. AP/WIDE WORLD PHOTOS

Jackson, the eleventh of fifteen children born to Henry Jackson and America Armstrong, spent his first years in Columbus, Mississippi, where his parents grew cotton as sharecroppers. In 1917, when Jackson was four, the family joined the Great Migration of thousands of African Americans who moved north to escape the poverty and humiliation that sharecropping life imposed. The Jacksons eventually settled on the south side of St. Louis, Missouri, where the elder Jackson had already relocated with the family's two oldest sons. Although the family continued to endure hardships throughout his youth, Jackson flourished as a student at Vashon High School, where he was elected student body president and was honored as the graduating class's poet laureate in 1929. Without the resources to go on to college, Jackson took a job as a section hand for the Missouri Pacific Railroad after graduation.

Although he had been a standout student in high school, Jackson also drew attention for his fighting skills, honed on the rough streets of the south side. Impressed by the large purses awarded in professional boxing matches, Jackson began to train at the segregated Young Men's Christian Association (YMCA) and in January 1930 won the featherweight championship in a tournament held by the Amateur Athletic Union. The fact that there was only one other fighter in the weight class made little difference to Jackson,

who was determined to forge ahead in the sport. Fighting a series of matches around the Pittsburgh, Pennsylvania, area, Jackson adopted the surname Armstrong in tribute to his best friend, Harry Armstrong, and to relaunch his amateur career in California under a new name. Together, the two made their way to Los Angeles by hopping a series of freight trains in 1932.

Resuming his amateur career in Los Angeles, Armstrong secured eighty-five wins in a row as he made a living from operating a series of shoe-shine stands. He also concentrated on making the United States team for the 1932 Olympics. Armstrong was bitterly disappointed in losing a qualification match for the featherweight division and lost in another attempt to qualify in the bantamweight division. Turning professional, he became known as "Homicide Hank" for his tenacity as a fighter and power as a puncher. He used his perpetual-motion style of constant punches to win a series of fights leading up to his first title bout against Baby Arizmendi for the California–Mexico world featherweight title on 4 August 1936. Armstrong won the match in a ten-round decision and went on to claim the world featherweight title against Petey Sarron in New York City on 29 October 1937. This time, Armstrong won by a knockout in the sixth round.

By then Armstrong had a contract with Al Jolson and

George Raft, and a new manager, Eddie Mead. As successful as his 1937 bouts had been—he won all of his twenty seven matches, all but one by a knockout—the following year earned Armstrong a special distinction in the history of boxing. After winning the featherweight title in the 126-pound division, a heavier Armstrong fought against Barney Ross in the 147-pound welterweight division. In a fifteen-round decision, Armstrong won the fight and on 31 May 1938 claimed titles in two weight divisions. In August, a leaner Armstrong fought for the 135-pound lightweight division title against Lou Ambers. In a brutal match that went fifteen rounds, Armstrong suffered a cut over his left eye and a cut on the lip that bled so much that the fighter took out his mouth guard in order to swallow the blood and keep on fighting. Barely outlasting his opponent, Armstrong took the title in a close decision.

Armstrong retained all three titles only briefly; he gave up his featherweight title in November 1938 and subsequently lost his lightweight title to Ambers in a brutal rematch in August 1939. On 4 October of the following year, Armstrong fought to retain his welterweight crown against Fritzie Zivic at Madison Square Garden. Relentlessly attacking the spot above Armstrong's left eye, where he had been injured in his first title fight against Ambers, Zivic knocked down the titleholder in the fifteenth round and took the fight by decision. In a rematch the following year, Zivic won again after the referee ended the match in the twelfth round. The adversaries met a third time in 1942 in a match that Armstrong won, although Zivic had already lost the welterweight title to another fighter.

With Eddie Mead's death in 1942 Armstrong found that his finances had been seriously mismanaged, with over $250,000 owed in back taxes. Returning to the ring, Armstrong attempted a comeback and continued to fight until 1945, when the numerous injuries that he sustained to his eyes prevented him from boxing. His personal life in disarray from his excessive drinking, Armstrong bottomed out in 1949 when he was arrested and put into the Los Angeles drunk tank. The former fighter battled back, however; he gave up drinking and eventually became an ordained Baptist minister in 1951. Unfortunately, his first marriage to Willa Mae Shondy (also documented as "Shony"), which had produced a daughter in 1935, ended during this period. In 1960 Armstrong married longtime acquaintance Velma Tartt, and the couple raised their two children in St. Louis. After Tartt's death, Armstrong had a brief third marriage before marrying for a final time in 1978, to Gussie Henry. Armstrong also kept busy with the Henry Armstrong Youth Foundation, an outreach program to combat juvenile delinquency.

Armstrong's final years were marked by failing health and financial hardship; a 1979 mugging in St. Louis also contributed to Armstrong's decline. Although he earned over $1 million in prize money during his career, his extravagance and mismanagement had long ago dissipated the fighter's earnings. At the time of his death from heart failure, Armstrong's only income was a monthly $800 Social Security check. Yet with his amazing run of victories that resulted in three simultaneous championship titles in separate weight divisions, Armstrong is remembered as one of the most talented fighters in the sport's history. As a measure of his stature, during his first year of eligibility for the Boxing Hall of Fame in 1954, Armstrong was inducted along with Jack Dempsey and Joe Louis. Armstrong was also assured that his remarkable feat would go unmatched, since in the 1940s the sport banned boxers from holding multiple titles.

★

After his retirement from boxing, Armstrong published *Gloves, Glory, and God: An Autobiography* (1956). An interview with Armstrong is in Peter Heller, *In This Corner . . . ! Forty-two World Champions Tell Their Stories* (1994). A full account of Armstrong's record as a professional fighter appears in *The Boxing Register: International Hall of Fame Official Record Book* (1999). *People* (21 Nov. 1988) published a lengthy tribute to Armstrong after his death. Obituaries are in the *Los Angeles Times* (24 Oct. 1988) and *New York Times* (25 Oct. 1988).

TIMOTHY BORDEN

ARMSTRONG, Lance (*b.* 18 September 1971 in Plano, Texas), endurance events prodigy and cycling wunderkind who overcame testicular cancer and returned to athletics stronger than ever, winning three consecutive Tours de France.

Armstrong was born tenacious. His mother, Linda Walling, was just seventeen years old when Lance, her only child, was born. She was married and divorced twice before she turned twenty, and her struggle for personal and financial independence became one of the major influences in Armstrong's life. "My mother taught me to be a fighter," he has said.

Walling, who took the name in 1992 when she married technical recruiter John Walling, worked her way up from fast food to real estate. She became Armstrong's closest friend as well as his inspiration. At her urging, Armstrong translated his anger ("I was a kid with about four chips on his shoulder") into fuel for athletic accomplishment. He began running in fifth grade, and showed a prodigious aptitude for all endurance events, competing in cycling, swimming, and running.

By fourteen, he was participating in triathlons and gaining a measure of local celebrity. He dazzled the press with confidence and ambition, matched by exceptional ability

Lance Armstrong. ARCHIVE PHOTOS, INC.

and dedication. By sixteen, he earned national recognition as a triathlete. At seventeen, he won the United States sprint triathlon championship, a race that includes a 1,000-meter swim, a fifteen-mile bike ride, and a three-mile run. His favorite element of the triathlon was the bicycle—it was his strongest as well, and he wasn't the only one who noticed. When he repeated as sprint champion the following year, Armstrong was invited to train with the junior national cycling team.

After graduating from high school in 1989, he moved to Austin, Texas, and committed himself full-time to cycling. The results were immediate. He qualified for the world junior team, and placed eleventh in the 1990 amateur world championships. In 1991 he won the U.S. National Amateur Championships and raced in the Tour du Pont, the longest and most difficult stage race in the United States. He continued to burnish his reputation as talented and brash. When compared to American cycling's brightest light, three-time Tour de France winner Greg LeMond, by *New York Times* writer Frank Litsky, Armstrong quipped to Litsky, "I'm not the next Greg LeMond; I'm the first me."

By 1993 Armstrong had turned professional, signing with the Motorola racing system. He placed second overall in the Tour du Pont and won that year's Triple Crown, a much-publicized racing series with a $1 million grand prize. He also won a stage at the Tour de France (he is thought to be the youngest rider ever to do so).

His potential seemed unlimited. In August 1993 Armstrong went to Oslo, Norway, and became the youngest ever world road-racing champion at just twenty-one years of age. Despite a slippery course that caused him to crash twice, Armstrong came back from fourth position at the beginning of the last lap to win by a startling nineteen seconds over some of the greatest cyclists in the world. He covered the final 700 meters of the course while blowing kisses to the crowd, bowing, and punching his fists in the air. This was consistent with Armstrong's cowboy image in America, but his behavior did not translate well in Europe. He also showed up King Harald V of Norway by bringing his mother to their meeting, against protocol. "I probably came on pretty strong, but man, I don't check my Mom at the door. I don't care who it is," Armstrong confided to a friend. The Italian newspaper *La Gazzetta* summed up the European reaction, calling him an "irascible, capricious, occasionally surly champion" who was "disrespectful of the great riders in the field."

Throughout the next two years, Armstrong continued to win big races. In 1995 Armstrong won the Tour du Pont and Spain's San Sebastian Classic, in the process becoming the first American to win a World Cup road race. In 1996 Armstrong won the Fleche Wallone in Belgium and defended his title at the San Sebastian Classic.

By the time he arrived back in the United States for the 1996 Tour du Pont, Armstrong, who dated fashion models and drove sports cars, was something of a rock star in the staid cycling community. The crowds included a row of bikini-clad women with Armstrong's name painted on their bellies. Alan Shipnuck of *Sports Illustrated* described the scene: "Armstrong's bionic legs, savvy in the saddle, and steel will may have dazzled his competitors, but it is his charisma and matinee-idol good looks that charmed the two-million plus fans" in attendance. He won the race and was on top of the world, a leading contender for the 1997 Tour de France.

During that time, Armstrong signed a $2 million contract with the French cycling team Cofidis. He also signed an endorsement deal with Nike and moved into a million-dollar Mediterranean-style villa on Lake Austin, named *Casa Linda* after his mother. "Twenty-five and entering the peak of my career," Armstrong later said. "I felt bullet-proof."

He soon found out he was not invulnerable. On 2 October 1996 Armstrong was diagnosed with an advanced case of testicular cancer. He had experienced pain in his testicles before, but attributed it to irritation from the bicycle seat. After coughing up blood that morning, he saw a doctor immediately for a comprehensive exam. An ultrasound revealed a malignancy, and the testicle was removed the following day.

The news did not improve. A few days later doctors discovered the cancer had spread to his lungs. Shortly after that, he was told the cancer had spread to his brain. The prognosis for survival was pegged at 40 percent. Things looked so grim that Armstrong began selling off prized possessions, including his $125,000 Porsche 911. "I thought I'd never make another dime the rest of my life," he said. Though he was at first concerned only about his ability to compete again, Armstrong later became persuaded that he was fighting for his life. "I just wanted to make it to my twenty-sixth birthday," said Armstrong.

After further surgeries to remove lesions from his brain and tumors from his lungs, he faced twelve grueling weeks of chemotherapy. His regimen was divided into four cycles: a week of treatment followed by two weeks of recovery. With each cycle, the nausea grew worse. He lost over fifteen pounds, all of it muscle—he had entered chemotherapy with less than 2 percent body fat. Through it all, Armstrong stayed on his bike. He rode in Austin during the recovery time. Though he struggled to finish ten miles, he was happy just to ride. "I wasn't training," he said. "Cycling is what I enjoy, and that's why I did it."

Doctors believe that Armstrong's extraordinary physical conditioning allowed him to withstand the grueling chemotherapy sessions better than the average person. He came out of the experience with newfound maturity, focus, and sense of purpose. He established the Lance Armstrong Foundation to raise public awareness of testicular cancer. He married Kristin Richard, a former public relations executive, in May 1998.

Before long, his stamina returned. By December 1997 Armstrong was riding 500 to 700 miles a week. He began to notice that not only was he back, he was better than ever. The experience had left him with a lighter, leaner body, more suited to the brutal climbs of the French Alps. Armstrong set his sights on the Tour de France, and signed with a new team sponsored by the United States Postal Service.

As he did when he was younger, Armstrong used his anger as motivation. He felt that various sponsors and teams had abandoned him on the road to recovery. He told one writer, "I keep a list, a mental list." He rode for vindication, and received it quickly. In 1999, after winning the first stage of the Tour, he pedaled past members of Cofidis, the French team that had dropped him. "That was for you," he said.

But Armstrong was there for more than vindication, he was there to win. Remarkably, less than three years after his initial cancer diagnosis, he was in position to do just that. On a mountain stage, he made a climb so dramatic it produced an audible gasp in the pressroom, and gave him a six-minute lead. As Armstrong surged towards victory down the Champs Elysées, Richard Hoffer wrote in *Sports Illustrated* that the performance was "so remarkable that everything we thought we knew about human athletic achievement needs to be reconsidered."

Indeed, the heroic feat left many speculating that Armstrong had engaged in some form of performance enhancement. Such talk was not surprising; cycling is notoriously rife with drugs and blood-doping. The 1998 Tour had been marred by arrests and suspensions after vast quantities of the blood-doping agent Erythropoetin (EPO) were found in a team car. The French daily *L'Equipe* alleged that a minimum of 90 percent of the cycling elite was using EPO between 1994 and 1998. Five-time winner Jacques Anquetil once said, "You can't ride the Tour de France on mineral water."

Although Armstrong had never tested positive for any banned substance or procedure, he could not escape suspicion. The reason, he felt, was jealousy. Cycling is the national obsession of France, with 40 million watching on television and 10 million lining the roads. Yet it had been fourteen years since a Frenchman had won the Tour—and Armstrong knew his Texas bravura ran counter to French sensibilities. For his part, Armstrong insisted his secret weapon was preparation. For months his team had practiced over key portions of the racecourse, especially the grueling climbs and breakneck turns. "We rode twelve of the stages in training," he says. "Nobody else can say they rode two."

Armstrong bristled at the speculation, but life went on. Seven months after his wedding, his wife began in vitro fertilization (with sperm put in storage by Armstrong before undergoing chemotherapy). Their son was born on 12 October 1999.

Going into 2000, Armstrong had one goal: to prove that his 1999 Tour de France victory was not a fluke. He began conservatively, and was in sixteenth place beginning the tenth stage, almost six minutes behind Albert Elli of Italy. The day promised to be difficult; it turned out to be historic. The tenth stage was the first mountain climb, and the weather was frigid and rainy, with cold winds lashing at the riders like knives. "To me it was like a sunny day at the beach," Armstrong said later. He rode patiently with the *peloton*, or pack, before making an astonishing breakaway through the rain, up the Pyrenees. With his rivals behind him, standing and pumping furiously to keep pace, Armstrong calmly remained in the saddle, accelerated, and pulled away.

The breakaway gained Armstrong a large chunk of time and, perhaps more importantly, it devastated his competitors psychologically. "I had the impression I was watching someone descending a hill I was trying to scale," said French rider Stephane Heulot. The peak in question, Mount Hautacam, is rated for cycling purposes as *hors de catégorie,* so steep that it exceeds categorization. Legendary French climber Raymond Poulidor called Armstrong's ascent "unprecedented in the annals of cycling." The 2,254-mile, twenty-three-day race was, for all intents and purposes, over. Armstrong held on to win with ease.

By all accounts, Armstrong followed the same strategy again in 2001, holding steady until the mountains, then pulling away in a devastating surge, this time up Alpe d'Huez. He won his third consecutive Tour de France in a performance that Joel Stein of *Time* magazine called "his most dominant yet."

With three consecutive victories, Armstrong surely surpasses Greg LeMond as the greatest American cyclist ever. The record for career Tour victories is five, shared by a number of cyclists. Armstrong is halfway to a new record, and at this pace he may win six or more consecutively. Yet for all the natural talent he displays, Armstrong continues to say, "If I'd never had cancer, I never would have won the Tour de France."

It remains open to debate whether the larger part of Armstrong's growing legend is his nearly superhuman cycling ability or his phenomenal comeback from testicular cancer. To the average fan, it matters little. His racing and his recovery are inextricably linked in the public consciousness. He is the author of the greatest comeback in sports history, and is well on his way to becoming the greatest cyclist of all time.

★

A number of books about Armstrong have emerged from his extraordinary cycling career and cancer comeback, but the most worthwhile is his own, *It's Not About The Bike: My Journey Back to Life* (2000), a personal history and part inspirational manual in which Armstrong tells his story with an unflinching eye, an impressive attention to detail, both medical and athletic, and a special affection for his extraordinary mother.

TIMOTHY KRINGEN

ASHE, Arthur Robert, Jr. (*b.* 10 July 1943 in Richmond, Virginia; *d.* 6 February 1993 in New York City), tennis star, teacher, author, and social activist who was the first black man to win the Wimbledon tournament. Ashe was instrumental in combating racial discrimination and broadening awareness about AIDS.

Ashe was the older of two sons of Arthur Robert Ashe, Sr., a parks superintendent, and Mattie Cordell Cunningham, a homemaker. Ashe, who was of Native American, Mexican, and black heritage, grew up in a segregated area of Richmond. The Ashe family lived in a caretaker's cottage in the park supervised by his father, where as a child Ashe spent many hours engaged in athletic pursuits. At the age of seven he started playing tennis on the segregated courts near his home. His mother died when Ashe was six years old. Five years after her death, his father married Lorraine Kimbrough.

At the age of ten Ashe began taking tennis instruction from Robert Walter Johnson, a black physician who also had taught Althea Gibson, the first African American to

Arthur Ashe at the 1975 Wimbledon tournament. © HULTON-DEUTSCH COLLECTION/CORBIS

break the color barrier in tennis, winning both Wimbledon and the U.S. Open. Ashe spent the next several summers in Lynchburg, Virginia, training for tennis. Despite his small size and slender physique, he took readily to tennis and, under Johnson's influence, developed an unswerving commitment and a cool approach to the many challenges that would face him on and off the court. At the age of seventeen Ashe was ranked among the top junior players in the country, but he could not compete in white tournaments in Virginia. In the summer of 1960 Ashe moved to St. Louis, Missouri, and lived with Richard Hudlin, a tennis instructor. He transferred from Maggie Walker High School to attend Sumner High School while continuing his tennis education. By the time he graduated he was the fifth-ranked junior tennis player nationwide and had won the American Tennis Association Junior Indoor Singles title two times.

In 1961 Ashe's outstanding academic achievements and tennis skills earned him a scholarship to the University of California, Los Angeles (UCLA), the first ever granted to an African-American tennis player. During his sophomore year, Ashe was named to the Junior Davis Cup team to represent the United States internationally. By 1963 Ashe was ranked sixth nationally among amateurs, and in 1965 he ranked second. At twenty-one, he won the U.S. Intercollegiate Singles championship. In 1966 he graduated from UCLA with a B.S. in business administration and, in 1967, was commissioned as a second lieutenant in the Reserve Officers Training Corps (ROTC) of the U.S. Army. Ashe continued to advance his tennis career while serving in the army, and in 1968 he won the U.S. Amateur title in Boston. Ashe came into prominence during the civil rights controversy but did not identify with the violent confrontations of the era. When he was invited to the U.S. Open tournament, Ashe waged a "refined revolution" and quietly and politely resolved to fight for racial equality at home and in South Africa. In his first Grand Slam, he defeated Tom Okker in the U.S. Open at Forest Hills, New York, in 1968. Ashe was the top player in the world and became the only amateur ever to win the U.S. Amateur and the U.S. Open titles in the same year. He concluded his collegiate career in 1968 when he led the U.S. team to its first Davis Cup victory in five years.

In 1969, after an honorable discharge with the rank of first lieutenant, Ashe turned professional and remained among the top five players internationally until 1975. Ashe was the first African-American man ever to play professional tennis. In 1970, under the sponsorship of the U.S. Department of State, Ashe made a goodwill tennis tour of South Africa. The trip gave him a new understanding of racial problems facing Africa. He won his second Grand Slam title in 1970 when he captured the Australian Open singles title. In 1972 he became a cofounder of the Association of Tennis Professionals. In 1973 Ashe became the first black athlete to play in a major tournament in South Africa.

In 1975 Ashe defeated Jimmy Connors 6–1, 6–1, 5–7, 6–4 for the Wimbledon singles championship, becoming the first African-American man ever to win that title. He also won the World Championship Tennis Singles and attained the top tennis ranking in the United States. According to the sportswriter Frank Deford, it was the cap to Ashe's career and the most brilliantly orchestrated match ever played in the sport. Ashe also won at the Australian Open in 1977. In 1976 Ashe met the New York City photographer Jeanne-Marie Moutoussamy. They were married on 20 February 1977 and had one child. In 1979, when he was ranked seventh in the world, Ashe's tennis career was disrupted when he had the first of three heart attacks and underwent quadruple heart bypass surgery. In 1980 he retired from professional tennis but continued with his contributions to social causes. Ashe served as a nonplaying captain of the U.S. Davis Cup team until 1985, leading the United States to two championships. He later became a tennis commentator for Home Box Office (HBO) and the American Broadcasting Company (ABC), and in 1988 he started establishing tennis programs for underprivileged inner-city children. Ashe's greatest fight came in 1988, after he underwent brain surgery that revealed he had contracted AIDS from an unscreened blood transfusion during his second open-heart surgery in 1983.

In April 1992 Ashe made public his illness after *USA Today* threatened to announce that he had the disease. That same year, *Sports Illustrated* named Ashe the Sportsman of the Year, honoring him as much for his conscience, commitment, and integrity as for his tennis achievements. He became a leading spokesperson for AIDS, creating the Arthur Ashe Foundation for the Defeat of AIDS. Before his death Ashe wrote an acclaimed three-volume book, *A Hard Road to Glory: A History of the African-American Athlete* (1988). During the last five years of his life, he devoted himself to the fight against AIDS and to active opposition to South Africa's apartheid. A few months before he died, Ashe was arrested in Washington, D.C., while protesting U.S. policy toward Haitian refugees seeking asylum.

In Manayunk, Pennsylvania, a tennis club was named in Ashe's honor, and in Richmond, Virginia, a center was named the Ashe Athletic Center. Ashe also received several honorary doctorates from various institutions. He served on the board of Aetna Life and Casualty and the United States Tennis Association, and as chairman of the Black Tennis sports foundation, the American Heart Association, and the National Foundation for Infectious Diseases. He held corporate posts in several businesses and wrote occasional newspaper columns. As a tennis star he won thirty-three championship titles and was inducted into the International Tennis Hall of Fame in 1985. In New York the National Tennis Center at Flushing Meadows, site of the U.S. Open, named their stadium for Ashe. At the age of forty-nine, Ashe died from AIDS-related pneumonia at New York Hospital. He is buried in Woodland Cemetery in Richmond.

As the only black man competing in a sport dominated by white players, Ashe was known for the composure he displayed while battling racism as well as tennis opponents. During his struggle with racism and disease, he remained a model of grace.

★

Arthur Ashe: Portrait in Motion (1975), which Ashe wrote with Frank Deford, is a diary of one year in tennis that covers his first trip to South Africa. *Days of Grace: A Memoir* (1993) was written in collaboration with Arnold Rampersad. Biographies include Ted Weissberg, *Arthur Ashe: Tennis Great* (1991), and David K. Wright, *Arthur Ashe: Breaking the Color Barrier in Tennis* (1996). *Bud Collins' Tennis Encyclopedia,* 3d ed. (1997), gives a summary of Ashe's career. In "The Sportsman of the Year: The Eternal Example," *Sports Illustrated* (21 Dec. 1992), Kenny Moore provides the most comprehensive information about Ashe's life after AIDS. Obituaries are in the *New York Times* (8 Feb. 1993) and *Tennis* (28 Apr. 1993). An HBO documentary, *Arthur Ashe: Citizen of the World* (1994), discusses Ashe the person instead of the tennis star.

NJOKI-WA-KINYATTI

ASHFORD, Evelyn   (*b.* 15 April 1957 in Shreveport, Louisiana), track and field short-distance runner who won five Olympic medals and was known at her peak as the "World's Fastest Woman."

Ashford was born into a military family. Her father, Samuel, a U.S. Air Force sergeant, and her mother, Vietta, frequently moved their family around the country, which made young Evelyn shy and reserved. She began to run track at Roseville High School in California; her school did not have a girls' track team, so Ashford ran on the boys' team until she graduated in 1974. Nevertheless, she won respect (she co-captained the team her senior year), races, and ultimately garnered enough attention to be given an athletic scholarship in track and field to the University of California at Los Angeles (UCLA) in 1975, one of the first women to receive such a scholarship. She received All-American honors in 1977 and 1978 and won the 1977 Association for Intercollegiate Athletics for Women national championships.

Outside the collegiate arena, Ashford made an immediate impact on the competitive racing world. Virtually unknown beyond California, she gained a spot on the U.S. Olympic team in 1976 and finished fifth in the finals of the 100-meter competition. She continued her winning streak in the 1979 Montreal World Cup competition by beating Marlies Gohr, who was Ashford's consistent rival throughout her career. In this first meeting, Ashford beat Gohr, won the 100 meter, and looked toward the 1980 Olympics to claim her title as the fastest woman in the world. But politics nearly dashed her dreams when she and her coach, Pat Connolly, heard President Jimmy Carter's announcement of the U.S. boycott of the 1980 Olympics in Moscow. The boycott affected Ashford deeply: She dropped out of UCLA in 1978 and began to work for a Nike shoe store, but then enrolled in California State, Los Angeles, to study fashion design.

She continued to train for the 1984 Olympics, to be held in Los Angeles, proving to her colleagues that she deserved to be on the world stage by winning the 100 meter and the 200 meter, and anchored the second-place 4×100-meter relay in the 1981 World Cup. Two years later, she competed against her rival Gohr, who held the record in the 100 meter; Ashford beat her again, but in the World Championships in Helsinki, Finland, Ashford pulled her right hamstring muscle and fell onto the track in the finals. She did not withdraw from the 1984 Olympic trials, however, and won a place on the team. Ashford was seen as the leading hope for a gold medal; between 1981 and 1984, *Track and Field News* consistently ranked Ashford as the best American woman sprinter.

In the 1984 Olympics, Ashford's legendary 100-meter run made her the first woman to run the race in the Olympics in under eleven seconds. Some were not positive she would make it; her injury-prone history caused her to miss key races, and there was speculation that her right leg, which she had pulled in the 1983 World Championships and in the 1984 U.S. trials, would again cause her to sit out her meet. She even withdrew from the 200-meter race to protect her chances in the 400 meter. Ashford ran in the fourth lane, between Angela Bailey and Heather Oakes, but she saw neither of them as she broke the Olympic record. As she stood on the victory stand, Ashford cried, remembering how far she had come since the 1980 boycott. Six days later, she won her second gold medal as the anchor leg in the 4×400-meter relay.

Ashford continued to drill herself on the track and off. In Zurich in 1984, she posted a new world record for the 100 meter with a time of 10.76. The following year, she and her husband had a baby daughter. Though some urged her to give up running to spend more time with her infant, Ashford demurred, saying, "Motherhood made me a better runner. My endurance was better. I could run a mile, two miles, or four miles and have fantastic times." Indeed, in 1986, a year after giving birth, Ashford placed first in the 100 meter in the World Championships with a time of 10.88 seconds. For that achievement, she was called the

Evelyn Ashford. AP/WIDE WORLD PHOTOS

World's Fastest Woman. In the 1988 Olympics in Seoul, South Korea, Ashford returned to the victory stand twice, again winning gold in the 4×400-meter relay and taking a silver medal in the 100-meter dash. Though her time of 10.83 seconds was exceptional, Florence "Flo-Jo" Griffith-Joyner won the race, beating Ashford by three-tenths of a second. In 1989 the Women's Sports Foundation awarded Ashford the Flo Hyman Trophy. But her career was not yet over; Ashford competed in the 1992 Olympics, again winning a gold medal in the 4×100-meter relay. Her teammates affectionately called her "the grand old lady of track" at the ripe old age of thirty-five.

Ashford and her husband, Herbert "Ray" Washington, live in Walnut Creek, California, with their daughter. Ashford, who considers herself a full-time mom, still runs two to three miles each day.

Evelyn Ashford won a career nineteen national titles and is one of the greatest women sprinters in track and field history. She was a member of five U.S. Olympic teams, thus giving her one of the longest and most successful careers of any sprinter. She won four gold medals and one silver medal. In 2000, when the Los Angeles Invitational ranked the greatest forty runners to compete in the meet over forty years, Ashford was the first unanimous selection. A poll conducted by the International Amateur Athletic Federation ranked Ashford the all-time women's 100-meter best performer. She was inducted into the National Track and Field Hall of Fame in 1997.

★

Michael D. Davis, *Black American Women in Olympic Track and Field* (1992), does a good job of placing Ashford in context with her fellow athletes, but unfortunately the analysis of her career ends with the 1988 Olympics. Ashford was also profiled in running magazines after her induction into the Track and Field Hall of Fame.

JUDITH A. PARKER

AUERBACH, Arnold ("Red") (*b.* 20 September 1917 in Brooklyn, New York), longtime coach and general manager of the Boston Celtics whose team accumulated more championships than any previous team in the history of professional team sports.

Auerbach was the second of four children of Hyman Auerbach, who came to the United States as a teen from Minsk in Russia and operated a cleaning and drying plant, and Marie Thompson, a cashier. As a teen, steering clear of neighborhood gangs, Auerbach earned money by pressing pants and cleaning cab windows, and he helped out at home.

Auerbach showed athletic ability in elementary school, then he played varsity handball and basketball at Eastern District High School. He also was elected class president and was named to the All-Brooklyn second team. After

Red Auerbach, 1966. © BETTMANN/CORBIS

graduating in 1935, he enrolled at Seth Lo Junior College, a Brooklyn branch of Columbia University, but was encouraged to transfer to George Washington University in Washington, D.C., by its basketball coach William J. Reinhardt. Auerbach played guard, and in his three years at George Washington his team went 38–19. Auerbach credited Reinhardt with inventing the fast break, in which the ball is rapidly passed back and forth without dribbling as the offensive players rush downcourt toward the basket. At George Washington, Auerbach met Dorothy Lewis, an education major, whom he married on 5 June 1941. They had two daughters.

In the spring of 1940 Auerbach was awarded a B.A. degree in physical education and then, in 1941, an M.A. degree. He joined the faculty of Roosevelt High School in Washington, D.C., where he taught history and hygiene and coached basketball and baseball. In the summer he officiated in playground basketball games. In May 1943 he joined the U.S. Navy. During his service he set up intramural sports programs for sailors and did rehabilitation work for the wounded in the Bethesda Hospital in Washington, D.C.

Upon his discharge in 1946 with the rank of ensign, Auerbach took interest in the newly formed Basketball Association of America and was hired, at a one-year salary of $5,000, to coach the Washington Capitals. A tactic he began using there and retained later was keeping one of the top

five players on his team out of the starting lineup. He inserted that player at a strategic point when the opposing players were tiring. In the first season the Capitals finished 49–11 but were eliminated in the playoffs. In Auerbach's third season the Capitals started 15–0. Auerbach's three-year record with the Capitals was 115–63, but he quit when the owner Mike Uline refused to give him a three-year contract at the end of the period. After a brief stint as an assistant coach at Duke University, Auerbach took a two-year head coach position with the Moline Blackhawks of the National Basketball Association (NBA), the new name of the athletic association. Auerbach quit after one year when the owner Ben Kerner made a deal without consulting him.

Auerbach then began his long association with the Boston Celtics. When he was appointed head coach on 27 April 1950, the Celtics were a struggling franchise, but Auerbach drafted shrewdly. He selected the guard Bob Cousy from Holy Cross College in Worcester, Massachusetts, in 1950 and the center Bill Russell, an intimidating defensive and rebounding genius, from the University of San Francisco in 1956. The acquisition of Russell was instrumental in turning the team around. Beginning with the 1956–1957 season, the Celtics won eight consecutive NBA championships and eleven in thirteen seasons.

So he could concentrate fully on basketball, Auerbach resided in the Lenox Hotel in Boston during the season, while his family lived in Washington, D.C. He kept total control; he had no assistant coaches. As a bench coach he missed only one game, to attend his father's funeral. He promoted a family-like atmosphere but treated the players as individuals. He used the forward Tommy Heinsohn as the whipping boy because he could take it, but he handled Russell with kid gloves. Scoring was spread evenly, so the Celtics never had a player among the league leaders in scoring. In practice Auerbach ran his team harder than the other coaches did theirs. Though often boorish in his own behavior, he demanded neatness in his players' attire off the court. On the court he insisted on low-cut dark sneakers in contrast to the high white ones favored by the rest of the league. A notorious referee baiter, Auerbach sometimes had himself ejected to motivate his team. When a win was assured in a game, he characteristically lit up his "victory" cigar. Altogether, including playoffs, Auerbach coached 1,585 NBA games, winning 1,037 of them. The Celtics became regarded as the elite NBA franchise.

In February 1966 Auerbach gave up his position as bench coach to become general manager. Russell succeeded him as coach and also played on two more championship teams. In his new position Auerbach took charge of acquiring new players and releasing others. Used to dealing directly with players, he was uncomfortable with the agents and demanding lawyers who were beginning to represent players. But in his appraisal of talent, Auerbach had no peer. When, because of mass retirements, the Celtics fell out of contention for the 1969–1970 season, he rebuilt the franchise by drafting the center and forward Dave Cowens. With Heinsohn as coach, the Celtics won titles in 1974 and 1976. After another dip, Auerbach again set up championships in 1981, 1984, and 1986 through the acquisition of one of the strongest forecourts ever assembled, consisting of the forwards Larry Bird and Kevin McHale and the center Robert Parish. Altogether, as coach and general manager, Auerbach won an unprecedented sixteen championships.

Auerbach was instrumental in advancing the placement of black players. In April 1950 he drafted the NBA's first black player, Chuck Cooper from Duquesne University, and in 1965–1966 his Celtics featured the NBA's first all-black starting five. His skill in leadership apparently rubbed off, as his players went on to become coaches of the Celtics and other NBA teams. Besides Russell and Heinsohn, K. C. Jones, Cowens, Don Chaney, and Tom "Satch" Sanders coached the Celtics; Cousy coached the Cincinnati Royals; Larry Siegfried coached the Houston Rockets; Bill Sharman coached the Los Angeles Lakers; Don Nelson coached the Golden State Warriors; and Larry Bird coached the Indiana Pacers. Other players coached college teams.

Auerbach had a long career, achieved a remarkable winning record, displayed a colorful personality, and conducted clinics abroad for the State Department. He was the single person most responsible for spreading the fame of the NBA throughout the world during the first five decades of its existence.

★

Arnold "Red" Auerbach, *Basketball for the Player, the Fan, and the Coach* (1952), contains various ploys on how to increase the chances of winning, such as telling an opposing player he or she was lucky upon the completion of a good play. Dan Shaughnessy, *The Red Auerbach Story: Seeing Red* (1994), is valuable for its verbatim accounts of Cousy, Russell, Bird, Auerbach's daughter Randy, and others. See also Frank Deford, "A Man for All Seasons," *Sports Illustrated* (15 Feb. 1982).

ABRAHAM A. DAVIDSON

B

BABASHOFF, Shirley (*b*. 31 January 1957 in Whittier, California), versatile swimmer who broke many U.S. and world long- and short-distance records and was the all-time Olympic medal leader among U.S. women until 2000.

Babashoff was one of four children of Jack Babashoff, a machinist, and Vera Slivkoff, a homemaker. Her father, a second-generation Russian immigrant, had been a swimming instructor in Hawaii and always wanted his own children to become Olympians. Although he may have laid out the blueprint for the future of his children, his wife carried out the plan by driving her kids to and from training sessions and taking care of almost everything else. "It was through my mom's saving everything that we afforded swimming," recalled Babashoff. All four Babashoff kids began swimming training at an early age, and every one became an excellent swimmer. Jack Babashoff, Jr., the oldest, won the silver medal in the 100-meter freestyle race at the 1976 Montreal Olympics. Billy swam on the University of California, Los Angeles (UCLA), team. Babashoff's younger sister, Debbie, was a national 1,500-meter freestyle champion in 1986.

Babashoff started swimming competitively at age nine but did not show signs of future greatness until she was thirteen, when she began setting age-group records under Flip Darr, her coach at the Huntington Beach Aquatic Club. Later Babashoff made a major career move by joining the Mission Viejo Nadadores Swim Club, where she blos-

somed under coach Mark Schubert, meeting his most demanding challenges. It was Schubert who made Babashoff into one of the most versatile swimmers in the world, capable of competing at the highest level in both distances and sprints as well as in individual medleys. By age fifteen, when Babashoff made the 1972 U.S. Olympic team, she was already one of the best women's freestyle swimmers in the United States.

The 1972 Olympic Games in Munich provided the venue in which Babashoff began to establish her international dominance. When she entered the Games, she already held both the 200-meter freestyle and the 4 × 100-meter freestyle relay world records. Her pursuit of individual gold medals failed, however. In the 200-meter freestyle race, Babashoff broke her own world record but came in second to another fifteen-year-old phenomenon, Shane Gould of Australia. In the 100-meter freestyle race Babashoff beat Gould, the world record – holder, but lost the event to her teammate Sandra Neilson. Babashoff's first Olympic gold medal came when she anchored the winning U.S. team in the 4 × 100-meter freestyle relay.

Returning home without an individual gold medal was a disappointment, but Babashoff was not discouraged. In addition to attending Fountain Valley (California) High School (she graduated in 1974), she resumed her training with Mark Schubert, setting even higher goals for the 1976 Olympics. In addition to freestyle, Babashoff devoted substantial time to the other three strokes and to strength training. The results were phenomenal. Between the two Olympics, Babashoff developed into an all-around world-class swimmer. In May 1975, at the Western Olympic Development Meet, Babashoff easily swept the 100-, 200-, 400-, and 800-meter freestyle races and the 200- and 400-meter individual medleys. During this period, she also broke the world records for the 200-, 400-, and 800-meter freestyle and won in both 200- and 400-meter freestyle competitions at the 1973 and 1975 World Swimming Championships.

The U.S. Olympic women's swimming team entered the 1976 Montreal Olympics as favorites only to see their dreams shattered. In world-record time, Babashoff slammed into final wall after final wall and found larger, more muscular athletes of the German Democratic Republic (GDR) already there. Female swimmers of the GDR had never before won Olympic golds, yet in Montreal they rolled over the rest of the world, taking eleven gold medals in the first twelve events and setting eight world records. The U.S. women redeemed some dignity by winning the 4 x 100-meter freestyle relay, the last women's swimming event, barely averting their first Olympic gold medal shutout in a quarter-century. As in 1972 Babashoff anchored the relay team. In addition to the relay gold medal, she brought home four silver medals in the 200-, 400-, and 800-meter freestyle competitions and in the 4 x 100-meter medley relay.

Babashoff did become the center of attention at the Games, at least for a few moments. Before the Montreal Olympics, many suspected that the East German swimmers were using steroids, but Babashoff was the only one who expressed this opinion publicly. After winning the freestyle relay, Babashoff refused to accept the congratulations of the GDR swimmers on the victory stand on this basis, drawing criticism from the public and the media. As a result, a large segment of the press called her "Surly Shirley." She was, however, later vindicated by the revelation that thousands of GDR athletes, including Olympic swimmers, were trained on steroids.

Steroids, if they were in fact used, were not the worst problem Babashoff encountered in Montreal. "Three weeks before the most important meet of your life, the [U.S.] Olympic staff takes your personal coach away and gives you another one," said Babashoff. "I was given some ridiculous practices, like 5 x 1,500 [meters] when I was to race the sprints." She believed that she could have won more gold medals had she kept her personal coach, Mark Schubert. "I feel worse about that than about the drugs. I could've beaten the East Germans anyway with Mark."

Babashoff's Olympic career ended with the conclusion of the Montreal Games. She enrolled at UCLA in the fall of 1976 but left school after her freshman year. Not bound by any eligibility rules to compete as an amateur, Babashoff was free to accept a four-year endorsement contract of $20,000 a year from Arena, a swimsuit manufacturer. Babashoff got married in 1978 but was divorced in 1980. She never remarried. Babashoff taught and coached swimming in various places in the Los Angeles area and in South Korea. After the birth of her son, Adam, in 1986, she took a job as a mail carrier in Huntington Beach, California.

During her competitive career, Babashoff managed to set eleven world records (six individuals and five relays) and thirty-nine U.S. records (seventeen individuals and twenty-two relays). She also accumulated two gold and six silver Olympics medals. For these achievements, Babashoff was inducted into the International Swimming Hall of Fame in 1982 and into the U.S. Olympic Hall of Fame in 1987.

★

Notable articles on Babashoff include Kenny Moore, "Babashoff and Ender," *Sports Illustrated* (13 July 1992), and Mark Merfeld, "Babashoff: One Hamburger, French Fries, and a Couple World Records . . .To Go," *Swimming World* 16 (July 1975). For an overview of her Olympic swimming career, see David Wallechinsky, *The Complete Book of the Olympics* (1984). Additional information about Babashoff is available at the International Swimming Hall of Fame website at http://www.ishof.org. See also "Babashoff Swims to Fourth Berth," *New York Times* (21 June 1976).

YING WUSHANLEY

BAKER, Hobart Amory Hare ("Hobey") (*b.* 15 January 1892 in Wissahickon, Pennsylvania; *d.* 21 December 1918 in Toul, France), hockey and football player who was not only the first American elected to the Hockey Hall of Fame but also the sole athlete ever enshrined both there and in the College Football Hall of Fame.

Baker was the second son of Alfred Thornton Baker, an aristocratic Philadelphian who manufactured upholstery, and Mary Augusta Pemberton, a Philadelphia socialite. The Bakers belonged to many prominent clubs and enjoyed considerable wealth. Thus, Hobey and his elder brother, Thornton, lived a privileged childhood. In 1903, at ages ten and eleven, respectively, the Baker boys entered the prestigious Saint Paul's School in Concord, New Hampshire. Thornton was a respected athlete there, and after graduating, he moved directly into a successful career at his father's manufacturing company. For Hobey, Saint Paul's marked the beginning of a legendary athletic life.

Even though he mastered every sport the school offered, Baker especially loved football and hockey. He routinely skated on the frozen pond at night learning to handle the puck in darkness. By his senior year, Baker's prep-school

football game against Yale. He became one of the most versatile and popular college football players of the early 1900s. Excelling as punter, kicker, quarterback, halfback, and punt-returner, Baker set Princeton's single-season record for scoring in 1912 with a mark that lasted more than half a century. Although he was only five feet, nine inches tall and 160 pounds, his chiseled and handsome appearance drew attention to him on the field, where he was called "the blond Adonis of the gridiron." The Princeton Tigers achieved a 20–3–4 record over Baker's three varsity seasons and reached the nation's top ranking in 1911.

While an All-America selection in football, Baker dominated college hockey to an even greater extent. In the era of seven-man hockey, he played the rover position, allowing him to control games from any part of the ice. Lawrence Perry, a *New York Post* sportswriter, commented, "Men and women went hysterical when Baker flashed down the ice on one of his brilliant runs with the puck. I have never heard such spontaneous cheering for an athlete as greeted him a hundred times a night and never expect to again." More impressive than his appearance or even his 27–7 record at Princeton was Baker's ability to play so successfully while strictly adhering to his code of good sportsmanship. He was penalized only once in college, and always individually thanked the opposition for "a good game."

Moreover, Baker epitomized the well-rounded gentleman off the ice as well. He was a solid B student who participated on the Senior Council, organized his class prom, socialized at the exclusive Ivy Club, and treated everyone with kindness. Devoting his vacations to social work at the YMCA, Baker represented a rapidly dwindling breed of selfless athletes. His fellow Princetonian F. Scott Fitzgerald described him as "an ideal worthy of everything in my enthusiastic admiration, yet consummated and expressed in a human being who stood within ten feet of me." Fitzgerald found Baker's Princeton legacy so fascinating that he based the character Allenby in *This Side of Paradise* on him. Baker's legend also permeated the fiction of writers John Tunis, George Frazier, Mark Goodman, and Geoffrey Wolff.

Joining the J. P. Morgan banking firm in New York after his 1914 Princeton graduation, and soon moving on to his father's business, Baker remained nostalgic for his college days of glory. He told his friend James M. Beck, "I realize that my life is finished. No matter how long I live, I will never equal the excitement of playing on the football fields." He did find some enjoyment in playing for a talented amateur hockey team called Saint Nick's as well as in dating the attractive New York socialite Mimi Scott. Nevertheless, for all the attention he received in these activities, Baker craved the action of collegiate competition. In May 1917 he happily accepted the rank of lieutenant in

Hobey Baker. PRINCETON UNIVERSITY LIBRARY

hockey team trounced powerful college squads. Still, Baker's legacy at Saint Paul's transcended mere success, as noted by his coach Malcolm Gordon, also a future member of the Hockey Hall of Fame. "[Baker] set a new standard for amateur sportsmanship and the game is better because of his leadership. No one could play with or against Hobey without being influenced by his spirit of fair play." Following in the footsteps of his father and grandfather, Baker proceeded to Princeton University, whose fields showcased not only his unique talent but also his exemplary conduct and grace.

As if it were scripted, soon after Baker entered Princeton in 1910 he scored the winning touchdown in a freshman

the U.S. Army, hoping World War I would restore his enthusiasm for living.

By the end of 1917 Baker had earned distinction in marksmanship and later won the French croix de guerre and the American Distinguished Service Award. He loved to fly his Spad, a lightweight single-propeller aircraft, and used the same coordination skills that he had displayed as an athlete to shoot down three enemy airplanes. When the war ended and it was time for him to return to his less exhilarating life in America, Baker stubbornly decided to take "one last flight in the old Spad." On 21 December 1917, showing his usual audacity, sense of responsibility, and determination, Baker insisted that he be the pilot to test a previously faulty plane. Against the wishes of his worried friends, he took off for the test run. After a quarter of a mile the engine died, and the plane nosedived into the ground. Baker died in an ambulance shortly thereafter. He is buried in the West Laurel Hill Cemetery in Bala Cynwyd, Pennsylvania.

Amid the sorrow and praise that followed Baker's death, some felt that the crash might not have been an accident. Perhaps he wished to die with drama and avoid returning to the business world that bored him. Others believed that by testing the plane himself, he simply died, daringly, in another man's place. In either case, Baker's death bears the marks of a classical tragedy, for his fearless spirit was partially responsible for his demise.

The death of this romantic American hero paralleled a post–World War I decline in American optimism and idealism. And yet, although Baker's life was lost and his chivalrous and nonchalant style fell out of fashion, his accomplishments were immortalized. Princeton dedicated the Hobey Baker Rink in 1923. The Hockey Hall of Fame elected him to charter membership in 1945, also making him its first American player. The College Football Hall of Fame enshrined him in 1977, giving him unique status as an athlete in both halls. The United States Hockey Hall of Fame made him a charter member in 1973. Appropriately, since 1981 the top player in American college hockey receives the Hobey Baker Award. Baker's greatest legacy, however, lies in the impression he left on his contemporaries, such as Lawrence Perry, in whose eyes "he was qualified to stand alone as the ultimate product of all that is worthy, not alone in American college athletics, but in American college life."

★

The Hobart A. H. Baker Papers are at the Seeley Mudd Manuscript Library, Princeton University. Other valuable Baker papers and data are available in the Saint Paul's School Library. The definitive biography of Baker is John Davies, *The Legend of Hobey Baker* (1966). Mark Goodman explores Baker's legacy in his novel *Hurrah for the Next Man Who Dies* (1985), while *St. Paul's School*

in the Great War (1926), provides an interesting perspective on Baker's earlier life and its significance. Ron Fimrite wrote an illuminating essay on Baker, "A Flame That Burned Too Brightly," *Sports Illustrated* (18 Mar. 1991). Baker's legendary hockey coach, Malcolm Gordon, considered the father of American hockey, wrote a tribute titled "Hobey" for the *St. Paul's School Alumni Horae* (1940).

CHARLES SCRIBNER IV

BANKS, Ernest ("Ernie") (*b.* 31 January 1931 in Dallas, Texas), Hall of Fame shortstop; first baseman, power hitter, and flawless fielder; and the most popular baseball player ever to play for the Chicago Cubs.

Banks was born to poor but devoted African-American parents in Dallas. His father, Eddie Banks, picked cotton, worked for the Works Project Administration, and stocked for the Texas Wholesale Grocery Corporation. His mother, Essie Banks, was a domestic worker. Banks hoped his father would help him get a job with the grocery wholesaler, but Eddie told him to aim higher.

Eddie pitched and caught for two semiprofessional baseball teams, and Banks and his brother enjoyed being batboys for them. Banks excelled in high school basketball, football, and track, but he didn't play varsity baseball. In 1948, the summer before his junior year, a scout for the Detroit Colts, a semipro team from Texas, spotted Banks playing for a church softball team. After agreeing to his

Ernie Banks (*in Cubs hat*). AP/WIDE WORLD PHOTOS

mother's condition—that her son's education wouldn't be compromised by playing baseball—Banks and a friend tried out in Amarillo, Texas. After hitting a home run in his first game, Banks was instructed to pass his cap among the fans, who rewarded him with about $6. During his second season with the Colts, Banks met the legendary "Cool Papa" Bell of the Negro Leagues' Kansas City Monarchs.

Before Banks completed high school, Bell persuaded Dizzy Dismukes to sign him with the Monarchs, promising him $300 per month. After a successful season, Banks, at age nineteen, toured with Jackie Robinson's Major League All-Stars in the fall of 1950. There he was mentored by future Hall of Famers Roy Campanella, Larry Doby, and Robinson. Banks spoke of his debt to each of these men, who helped integrate Negro League players with the all-white Major League Baseball teams.

Banks served in the U.S. Army from 1951 to 1953, but before shipping overseas he played basketball briefly for the Harlem Globetrotters. Coach Abe Saperstein told Banks to sit beside him on the bench and learn the Globetrotters' routines, but Banks didn't know how to respond. He had never before sat next to a white person.

After serving in Germany, where a softball mishap caused his knee to lock up (an injury that prefigured knee problems that would plague his career), Banks rejoined the Monarchs. In 1953 Monarchs manager Buck O'Neil accompanied twenty-two-year-old shortstop and pitcher Bill Dickey to meet Chicago Cub officials at Wrigley Field. The Cubs planned to call up shortstop Gene Baker from their Los Angeles minor league affiliate as their first African-American player, but Baker was injured. So they offered Banks a contract at $800 per month. Because the Negro Leagues weren't affiliated with Major League Baseball, players had to be released by their Negro League team before signing with any major league organization. O'Neil, who was aware that integration would mean the end of the Negro Leagues, actively sought to place his best players in good major or minor league situations. He later joined the Cubs as a scout, and Banks never forgot his debt to "a role model, a father, a mentor, a teacher, a sensei, a hero, a gentleman, a man. Who do you think I got my let's-play-two attitude from?"

After joining the Cubs, Phillies outfielder Richie Ashburn told Banks that he was played as a "punch-and-judy" hitter in his first season, so Banks learned to accelerate his wrists through the swing and quickly developed one of the smoothest right-handed power strokes the game has ever seen. In 1955 he set a record for shortstops by hitting forty-four home runs, five of which came with the bases loaded, then broke it with forty-seven in 1958. This record stood until 23 September 2001, when Alex Rodriguez of the Texas Rangers hit his forty-eighth. Banks called Rodriguez to con-

gratulate him, saying, "I'm just so proud of you. I wish you were my son."

Between 1955 and 1960 Banks hit more homers than any other major leaguer—including Mickey Mantle, Willie Mays, Roger Maris, and Hank Aaron. Before his career ended, he surpassed the threshold of 500 career home runs (512), with five seasons at 40 or more, and played eight seasons with more than 100 runs batted in.

After the 1958 season, Banks's life changed dramatically. Arriving at a meeting to discuss a business matter, he was smitten by the receptionist, a Texas native named Eloyce Johnson. Before the end of the year, they had eloped, and the following fall their family expanded by twin sons.

His fielding was almost as impressive as his batting. In 1959 Banks set a National League shortstop record of .985. He led National League shortstops in fielding percentage in three of his eight seasons at that position. In 1958 and again in 1959 he was named the National League's Most Valuable Player, an honor usually reserved for stars of contending teams. The Cubs had finished in fifth place both years.

In addition to being steady in the field and dangerous with the bat, Banks was durable in a position noted for causing injury. He set a league record by playing shortstop in 424 consecutive games from the day he joined the Cubs, then after being sidelined for 15 days, began another string of 717 straight games before a knee injury sent him to the bench. Banks moved to left field for 23 games starting in 1961, when his arthritic knees prevented his returning to shortstop. He then moved to first base for the rest of his career, leading the league in fielding with a .997 percentage (four errors in 1,506 chances) in 1969, the year Cubs fans voted him the best player in franchise history.

Banks's fondest memory as a Cub exemplifies his team spirit. On 2 July 1967 the Cubs took sole possession of first place for the first time in his career. It was his proudest moment, although he was sidelined by an injury resulting from a collision the previous day. The team finished second in 1969 and 1970. It was as close to the World Series as Banks ever came. When his knees gave out in 1971 and forced him to retire from the game, Banks held franchise records in games played, base hits, total bases, runs batted in, and home runs. The most popular Cub ever, he was the first member of the team to have his number retired and the eighth player elected to the Baseball Hall of Fame in his first year of eligibility. A Chicago city councilman proposed in 1967 that a five-story statue of Banks be erected instead of Pablo Picasso's abstract piece. Although Mayor Richard Daley accepted the Picasso sculpture, he considered Banks "a veritable incarnation of the Chicago spirit."

Since his retirement, Banks has brought his optimism and versatility to many commercial and philanthropic projects. He served on the Chicago Transit Authority Board of

Directors and held positions in commercial banking and corporate insurance. His charitable interests have included the World Children's Baseball Fair, the Children's Miracle Network, the Children's Hospital Los Angeles, and the Ernie Banks International Live Above and Beyond Foundation. In 1997, Banks married again, to the former Liz Ellzey of Chicago. The best man at the Barbados wedding was home run king Hank Aaron.

Banks was one of the finest baseball players of his time and a model of the citizen-athlete. In an era when pitchers intentionally threw the ball to hit black batters, Banks viewed the antagonism in a positive way: "I just thought it was part of the game. I felt they were basically paying me a compliment because they thought I was a threat to win the game." The late umpire Tom Gorman recalled that "in 1957 Banks was knocked down four times by four different pitchers . . . . And each time he was knocked down, [he] hit [the] next pitch out of the park."

Banks's love for the game, its players, fans, coaches, and even sportswriters, resonate in his comment about the only thing wrong with doubleheaders: "You don't get to play three games."

★

Banks's 1971 autobiography is titled *Mr. Cub.* For information about Banks's relationship with Jackie Robinson, see Jules Tygiel, *Baseball's Great Experiment: Jackie Robinson and His Legacy* (1983). For general comments about Banks and the Cubs, see Mitchell LeBlanc, ed., *Baseball: Professional Sports Team Histories* (1994). Steve Wulf comments on the early years, and Banks's relationship with Monarchs manager Buck O'Neil, in "The Guiding Light," *Sports Illustrated* (19 Sept. 1994). Information on Banks's later years, including his charity efforts, is in Thomas Bonk, "He Says You're Never Too Old to Play Two . . . A Hall of Famer on the Charity Circuit," *Los Angeles Times* (31 Jan. 1992).

DAVID DOUGHERTY

BARBER, Walter Lanier ("Red") (*b.* 17 February 1908 in Columbus, Mississippi; *d.* 22 October 1992 in Tallahassee, Florida), pioneering radio and television sportscaster who endeared himself to listeners for more than fifty years with his extensive vocabulary and colorful figures of speech that became known as "Barberisms."

Barber was one of three children of William L. Barber, a raconteur railroad conductor, and Selena Martin, an English teacher. Barber grew up in a home filled with expressive language. Although his original career ambition was to sing, dance, and tell jokes in minstrel shows, when vaudeville began to wane in the late 1920s, Barber decided to attend the University of Florida at Gainesville in 1928, planning to become an English teacher.

Red Barber, 1943. ASSOCIATED PRESS AP

One day on campus, Barber encountered a desperate university radio announcer on the verge of reading three agricultural academic papers on a farm report show. (The professor scheduled to read the reports had forgotten to show up for his air time.) The announcer asked Barber to read a paper on bovine obstetrics, and Barber grudgingly agreed. After the station manager heard Barber's reading, he decided that anyone capable of vitalizing cattle procreation tastefully for the radio listener deserved a job.

On 4 March 1930 Barber signed his first radio contract with WRUF at the University of Florida at Gainesville, earning a starting salary of $50 per month. Soon the star of the college airwaves, Barber worked his salary up to $50 per week and then left WRUF in 1934 to take over as the radio voice of the Cincinnati Reds baseball team. Barber's father told him he was making a mistake to take a 50 percent pay cut to go to Cincinnati, but the young broadcaster replied, "I want the chance," recognizing an opportunity at that stage in his career meant more than money. While still in college, Barber was in a car accident and became friends with a nurse who cared for him, Lylah Scarborough. They were married on 28 March 1931; the couple had one daughter.

The twenty-six-year-old Barber had never even seen a Major League baseball game before calling opening day for the 1934 Reds, and he didn't "see" many that first year in

Cincinnati. The Reds vice president Larry MacPhail's initial media strategy consisted of broadcasting very few home games from Crosley Field (only twenty in 1934), focusing primarily on having Barber re-create road games as Western Union wired the basic game facts into his studio. The young broadcaster then used his substantial imagination and knowledge of the players' mannerisms to transform the telegraph ticker tape into a vivid picture of action.

By the end of the 1935 season Barber had earned a national reputation as a sportscaster. The recently formed Mutual Broadcasting System chose him to team with Chicago's Bob Elson and Quin Ryan to broadcast the World Series, and Barber continued to get the nod each year in October for the remainder of his tenure at Cincinnati. In 1938 MacPhail left Cincinnati to run the Brooklyn Dodgers. At that time, all three New York Major League teams (Yankees, Giants, and Dodgers) had agreed to a radio blackout, fearing a drop in attendance if games were broadcast. Knowing how Barber's commentating had increased attendance for the Cincinnati Reds games, MacPhail refused to renew the blackout agreement, and hired his favorite sportscaster to come to Brooklyn for the 1939 season.

In no time at all, Barber's unique accounts of Brooklyn Dodgers games became the talk of the town. He saw his role as being that of a game reporter, not a fan, and it was his full-blown reporting that allowed him to use the language skills he had gained from his parents. From his mother, Barber gained an appreciation for a broad vocabulary. When a hitter singled and got to second because an outfielder misplayed the ball, Barber explained the runner's advancing on the fielder's "concomitant" error. When a player erred on a play, becoming the goat of the game, he stood at his position suffering in "ignominy." From his colorful father, Barber learned to use figures of speech. A team didn't put together a scoring rally; it "tore up the pea patch." A runner didn't knock down an infielder to break up a double play; he "swung the gate on him."

The broadcaster's greatest challenge came in connection with Jackie Robinson's entry into the Major Leagues in 1947. Although initially averse to the racial integration of the game, thinking Branch Rickey's "great experiment" would most likely turn into a social circus, through the continuing influence of his wife, Barber overcame his prejudice and called Dodger games in 1947 without once mentioning that Robinson was an African American. His broadcasts deserved much of the credit for Brooklyn's early and unwavering acceptance of the Great Jackie as a player and a man.

Barber left the Dodgers after the 1953 season and moved across town to team with Mel Allen, broadcasting Yankee games through 1966, when he was fired for reporting that only 413 people had attended a Yankee game. After leaving the press box, he wrote his autobiography and three other books, covering topics as diverse as the history of broadcasting, the strength of the human spirit, and spiritual preparation for death. During those years, Barber also narrated films, wrote newspaper columns, and preached frequently as a lay minister in the Episcopal Church. In 1978 Barber and Allen became the first recipients of the National Baseball Hall of Fame's Ford C. Frick Award for their outstanding broadcasting contributions to baseball.

From 1981 until shortly before his death, Barber returned to the radio, teaming with Bob Edwards of National Public Radio's *Morning Edition* program. Every Friday morning, Edwards presented four minutes with Barber in his spontaneous glory, endearing the Ol' Redhead to a new audience, for whom he became America's grandfather figure on the air. Barber died of kidney complications following surgery for an intestinal blockage in October 1992; his remains were cremated

Barber's goal in life was to conduct himself in such a way that he could always "sleep with himself." Throughout his amazing life, sleep came easily to the man who adhered to the highest broadcasting and personal standards, played a key role in the racial integration of professional baseball, committed his knowledge and wisdom to multiple books on a wide variety of subjects, and ended his life sharing his insights for a new generation of radio listeners. For all of this, he is regarded by many as the most important sportscaster of the twentieth century.

★

Barber teamed with Robert Creamer on his superb autobiography, *Rhubarb in the Catbird Seat* (1968). Curt Smith, *Voices of the Game* (1987), provides the history of sportscasting, with Barber's contributions put in their proper context. Finally, see Bob Edwards, *Fridays with Red: A Radio Friendship* (1993), a moving tribute by Barber's National Public Radio partner and a good biography.

TALMAGE BOSTON

BARKLEY, Charles Wade (*b.* 20 February 1963 in Leeds, Alabama), basketball player and member of the first "Dream Team" (the 1992 U.S. Olympic basketball team) who is known for his rebounding skills and for his outspokenness and wit.

Barkley, the only child of Frank and Charcey Glenn Barkley, was born weighing only six pounds and suffering from anemia, which required a complete blood transfusion when he was six weeks old. Barkley's parents were very young when he was born, separating and divorcing when he was a baby. His mother, a domestic worker, remarried, but his stepfather died in an automobile accident when Barkley was in grade school. He grew up with his mother and

Charles Barkley. AP/WIDE WORLD PHOTOS

grandmother, and the family saw difficult times, emotionally and financially.

Barkley resolved early to make his way out of his impoverished background by playing basketball, practicing shots seven nights a week and leaping back and forth over a chain-link fence to improve his jumping. His mother reported, "He said he was gonna make it in the NBA, nothin' was gonna stop him, and he meant it." As a junior at Leeds High School, Barkley was a chubby five feet, ten inches tall and did not even start for the varsity basketball team; but in the summer before his senior year, he grew to six feet, four inches, which enabled him to star for the Leeds team and go on to Auburn University in 1981.

Barkley may have been tall by ordinary standards, but he had an unusual build for a basketball player and was far shorter than many of those he battled for rebounds; nevertheless, he excelled in that area of the game. He also weighed 270 pounds and became known as the "Round Mound of Rebound." In the 1983–1984 season, he was named Southeastern Conference Player of the Year, averaging 14.1 points and clearing 9.4 rebounds per game. Auburn's record was 20–11 that season, their second-best in twenty-five years. Barkley was invited to the tryouts for the

1984 U.S. Olympic team, but Coach Bob Knight disliked his flashy playing style. Barkley didn't make the final cut.

Barkley majored in business management at Auburn but made a decision to leave school a year early to apply for the 1984 National Basketball Association (NBA) draft. In the same year that such stellar players as Michael Jordan and Hakeem Olajuwon were available, he was selected fifth by the Philadelphia 76ers, despite questions about his weight and his attitude—the latter due to his battles with Knight at the Olympic tryouts. Joining such stars as Julius Erving and Moses Malone, Barkley played only part time in the 1984–1985 season but averaged 14 points and 8.6 rebounds a game. In his second year he averaged 20 points and was second in the league in rebounding, a statistic he led the league in for the first time in 1986–1987. Though he had been known primarily as a rebounder in college, he improved his scoring as well, usually averaging over 20 points a game. In 1989 he married Maureen Blumhardt, and in that same year their daughter, Christiana, was born.

Despite Barkley's play, the 76ers began to slip in the late 1980s, and Barkley himself became even more controversial, publicly complaining about his teammates. In 1987 he called the 76ers "a bad team that has to play perfect to win" and was fined $3,000 by the team. Barkley continued to work on his game, however, and the 76ers made the playoffs in 1988 and 1989. In the 1991–1992 season he attempted to spit on a fan who had been heckling him and hit a little girl instead. He apologized and bought season tickets for her family, but he was fined again. Still, sports experts recognized his ability. Mike Lupica of *Esquire* said, "There will always be a lot of mouth to Charles Barkley. But there is also a lot of talent, the kind of talent only a handful of players ever have."

By 1992 the Olympic rules had changed, allowing professionals to compete in basketball for the first time. The United States put together the "Dream Team," made up of twelve of the top pros. Barkley was one of the stars, though he was criticized for his rough play, particularly when he elbowed a skinny Angolan player aside. The "Dream Team" did win the gold medal, but Barkley, along with Michael Jordan, almost refused to attend the ceremony because the team's uniforms were made by Reebok, and he and Jordan represented Nike.

Though his career was at its peak, he had worn out his welcome in Philadelphia, and after the 1991–1992 season he was traded to the Phoenix Suns for three players. He continued to flourish there, averaging 25.6 points and 12.2 rebounds per game and being voted the league's Most Valuable Player for 1992–1993. The Suns reached the NBA championship series but were beaten in six games by Jordan and the Chicago Bulls. Barkley injured his back in the 1993–1994 season, and his scoring average dropped; he considered retirement. However, he remained with the Suns through 1995–1996, continuing to star.

In 1994 Rick Reilly assembled a selection of Barkley's "wit and wisdom," entitled *Sir Charles.* Some of his remarks caused controversy, such as his statement that athletes should not be role models. He also became known for his Nike commercials, particularly one in which he played one-on-one against Godzilla, then asked the giant saurian, "Ever think of wearing shoes?" In 1996 the league named Barkley as one of the fifty greatest players of all time. But he was traded again, this time to the Houston Rockets for four players. There he continued to play well, but the championship eluded him and he struggled with injuries. In 1999 he reached a plateau of over 23,000 points, 12,000 rebounds, and 4,000 assists for his career, a combination previously attained only by Wilt Chamberlain.

He announced before the 1999–2000 season that it would be his last one. But in December his farewell tour was interrupted when he tore the quadriceps tendon in his left leg during a game against the 76ers. Still, he was able to return on 19 April 2000, the last game of the regular season, for a cameo appearance in which he notched two more rebounds and a final field goal. After the game, with characteristic wit, he noted his retirement by saying, "Just what the country needs: another unemployed black man." Having once said, "If push came to shove, I could lose all self-respect and become a reporter," he moved up to the broadcast booth, doing the *Inside the NBA* show with Kenny Smith and Ernie Johnson on the TNT network. Unsurprisingly, he proved to be an outspoken and witty commentator, never hesitating to criticize sharply but also recognizing good play.

In the summer of 2001 Michael Jordan announced that he was considering returning to basketball. Barkley practiced with Jordan and stated that he too was thinking of coming back. Barkley finally decided he was through as an active player, but he continued to ponder another stated goal—running for governor of Alabama as a Republican.

Barkley had a long and successful basketball career through hard work, courage, and determination. Although he was shorter than most, he excelled as a rebounder. His willingness to openly voice his opinions has gained him public notoriety as well as admiration. But despite his own words on the subject, one could do much worse than to take him as a role model.

★

Biographical information on Barkley can be found in his autobiography, *Outrageous! The Fine Life and Flagrant Good Times of Basketball's Irresistible Force* (1992), written with Roy Johnson, Jr., a typically no-holds-barred performance. Frank Deford's excellent article, "Barkley's Last Shot," appeared in *Vanity Fair* (Feb. 1995). Barkley's final game was reported by Michael Murphy in the *Houston Chronicle* (20 Apr. 2000).

ARTHUR D. HLAVATY

BARROW, Joseph Louis. *See* Louis, Joe.

BARRY, Richard Francis, III ("Rick") (*b.* 28 March 1944 in Elizabeth, New Jersey), basketball Hall of Famer who led the National Collegiate Athletic Association (NCAA), the National Basketball Association (NBA), and the American Basketball Association (ABA) in scoring; often remembered more for his difficult temperament than his basketball skills.

The younger of two sons of a perfectionist father, Barry learned to push hard for what he wanted at an early age. His mother, Alpha Stephanovich, was a homemaker. Barry grew up in Elizabeth, New Jersey, and by fifth grade was playing on a basketball team with seventh- and eighth-graders. His father was the coach and his brother was his teammate. "My father was very demanding of me," Barry told George Diaz of the *Orlando Sentinel,* "teaching me the fundamentals, taking me out of a game if I made a mistake. So I became very demanding of myself, and I was very demanding of my teammates."

After graduating from Roselle Park High School, Barry accepted a scholarship to play for the University of Miami. In his senior year at Miami, 1964–1965, Barry was an All-American and led the NCAA Division I in scoring with 37.4 points per game. In June 1965 he married Pam Hale, the daughter of his Miami coach, when he was twenty-one. They had four sons, all of whom went on to play professional basketball, and an adopted daughter.

The San Francisco Warriors (later the Golden State Warriors) signed Barry out of college, and he made a name for himself immediately. In his first professional season, 1965–1966, Barry averaged 25.7 points per game, made the NBA All-Star team, was the Most Valuable Player (MVP)

Rick Barry *(right),* 1974. ASSOCIATED PRESS AP

in that year's All-Star game, and was named NBA Rookie of the Year. Only Wilt Chamberlain, Walt Bellamy, and Oscar Robertson had scored more in their rookie seasons.

In his second season, Barry led the league in scoring, averaging 35.6 points per game, and hit a career-high of 2,775 points for the year. (The only player to beat his record in the following twenty-five years was Michael Jordan.) Barry returned to the NBA All-Star game (in the second of eight appearances) and won the game's MVP award in 1967. The Warriors won the Western Division and took the great Chamberlain-led Philadelphia 76ers to six games in the finals before losing. His record 40.8 scoring average for the series held until Jordan's 41 per game in 1993.

Taking an opportunity that was unheard of at the time, Barry jumped leagues and signed with the Oakland Oaks of the ABA, a fledgling rival to the NBA. His contract was unprecedented for 1967—$500,000 for three years, including ownership of 15 percent of the team's stock, plus a percentage of ticket sales. With the NBA's Warriors, he had received only $30,000 per year. Barry also wanted to change teams because his father-in-law, Bruce Hale, was the Oakland Oaks' coach. The move to change leagues landed Barry in a court dispute that sidelined him for the entire 1967–1968 season. With the 1968–1969 season, Barry established himself as the undisputed star of the ABA. He averaged 34 points per game and accomplished what no other player had done in the history of the game: he led the NCAA, the NBA, and the ABA in scoring.

Over his next four years with the ABA, Barry's team moved from Washington, D.C., to Virginia to New York City. When the Oaks were initially sold in 1969, Barry signed a new five-year contract with the NBA's Warriors, hoping to stay in San Francisco. Instead, he was back in court, with the two leagues battling over him again. In the end, Barry was required to honor his contract with the ABA. Despite having been on three teams in four cities in the ABA, Barry produced four All-Star selections, a championship, and an ABA scoring title. Still, it was not over.

Barry grew to like playing in New York City and decided to stay. But once again his contractual obligations took precedence. In 1972 the Warriors won a court case forcing him to fulfill his earlier contract with them. Although initially hesitant to return to his old team, once there, Barry experienced his longest period of stability while in their camp over the next six years. His non-scoring skills had improved while in the ABA and the twenty extra pounds he had gained gave him muscle to use against other NBA players.

In his six seasons with the Warriors, Barry always delivered. He was an All-Star every season, led the team to its first NBA championship in 1975, and was voted MVP in the championship game. Between 1972 and 1978 Barry earned six NBA free throw percentage titles, using his sig-

nature style, bending his knees and shooting the ball underhand with two hands. He scored his career high of sixty-four points on 26 March 1974. He ranked among the NBA's top ten in assists with 6.1 per game. In 1975 the Warriors swept the Washington Bullets in four games, winning the championship. Barry made 90 percent of his free throws. At the time, he was the most accurate free throw shooter in NBA history.

Although he was a superior athlete, Barry was his own worst enemy throughout his career, and was widely disliked for his abrasive personality. Bruce Schoenfeld of the *New York Times* described him as possessing "a competitiveness that verged on fury." He was outspoken (some said arrogant) and driven by his need for perfection. Because he was critical of referees, teammates, and opponents alike, he eventually lost their support. Despite his incredible year, he was left out of the running for 1974–1975 postseason honors, and his reputation cost him all future chances at getting a head coaching job in the NBA.

Signing a contract with the Houston Rockets in 1978 put Barry at odds with Warriors fans once again. He was accused of having no loyalty to any team. He played two years as a Houston reserve forward before retiring on 12 September 1980 at age thirty-six.

Barry's private life mirrored some of the rockiness of his professional life. As his career waned, Barry left his wife, Pam Hale, and became embroiled in a contentious divorce, which became final in 1979. During his second marriage to Pam Stenesen, whom he married the following year, Barry had little contact with his children. He pursued a career in broadcasting and married his third wife, Lynn Norenberg, on 31 August 1991. They had one son.

In 1987 Barry was elected to the Naismith Memorial Basketball Hall of Fame. He worked as a minor league basketball coach in the 1990s, turning to radio broadcasting at San Francisco's KNBR in August 2001.

Barry's basketball legacy was tarnished by his demanding personality; nevertheless he was named by the NBA as one of the fifty greatest players in NBA history in 1996. Barry's talent was indisputable, his contentious disposition undeniable, and his place in basketball history secure.

★

The NBA website, <http://global.nba.com>, has an excellent history of Barry's career, including career statistics. Two revealing articles about Barry's personal life and his relationship with his basketball-playing sons are Bruce Newman, "Daddy Dearest," *Sports Illustrated* (2 Dec. 1991), and Bruce Schoenfeld, "Hoop Is Thicker Than Water," *New York Times* magazine (3 Mar. 1996). Barry's post-basketball-playing struggles are discussed in George Diaz, "Barry Shoots from the Lip," *Orlando Sentinel* (18 June 2000).

JANET INGRAM

BAUGH, Samuel Adrian ("Sammy") (*b.* 17 March 1914 in Temple, Texas), football player generally credited with popularizing the forward pass in pro football who led the Washington Redskins to the National Football League (NFL) championship as a rookie in 1937 and only added to this reputation for the next fifteen seasons.

Baugh was born to James Baugh and Katherine Baugh, who were farmers. Baugh's father gave up farming and moved the family to Sweetwater, Texas, where the elder Baugh became a checker for the Atchison, Topeka & Santa Fe railroad that ran through the town. Like many Texas youngsters before and since, Baugh began playing football early, in fourth grade to be precise. Because he was tall and lanky, eventually reaching six feet, two inches and weighing 180 pounds, he began his career as an end. By the time Baugh got to Sweetwater High School, he played in the backfield as an end. Before long the coach noticed that Baugh could throw better than those who threw to him.

Baugh was a fine all-around athlete in high school and was an outstanding pro baseball prospect. In football he led Sweetwater to the quarterfinals and semifinals in the Texas state high school playoffs as a junior and as a senior (he graduated in 1933). Baugh developed his uncanny passing skills by spending long hours throwing a football through an old tire, swinging pendulum-like, suspended by a rope from a tree branch in his backyard. He enrolled at the University of Texas but could not find a job in Austin to finance his tuition. The Texas baseball coach "Uncle Billy" Disch, who did not think the lanky Baugh was sturdy enough to play Southwest Conference (SWC) football, lent him money to enroll at the rival Texas Christian University (TCU). Freshmen were not eligible for varsity competition at that time, so not until his sophomore season did the rest of the Southwest Conference notice Baugh.

Baugh was good in 1934 with nearly a thousand yards of total offense (997), but his next two seasons were exponentially better. He was an All-American in 1935 and consensus All-American in 1936. Baugh and his TCU Horned Frogs, coached by Leo R. "Dutch" Meyer, are credited with promoting the SWC as an "aerial circus," throwing the ball close to twenty times a game when the rest of the country was plodding and plunging into the middle of the line. While leading TCU to bowl games after his junior and senior seasons, Baugh also took part in some memorable games. The 1935 loss to the nearby rival Southern Methodist University (SMU) is considered a college classic. Although the SMU Mustangs won 20–14, Baugh's passes were eating up chunks of yardage deep in SMU territory when the game ended. That game drew a huge crowd of 42,000 fans and was the focus of the national press. Another storied game was the 1936 Sugar Bowl, a 3–2 victory over Louisiana State University (LSU). The field and the ball were wet, which limited Baugh's passing, but his punting (44.6-yard average) and defensive work (many key tackles and 2 interceptions) allowed TCU to stay in the game and win on a late field goal. At the end of his senior season Baugh led the Horned Frogs to a Cotton Bowl victory (16–6) over Marquette University. When Baugh left Fort Worth, his marks for most passes (587), most completions (270), most touchdown passes (39), and most passing yards (3,384) set SWC records.

When the NFL owners met after the 1936 season to draft for the next year, the Redskins owner George Preston Marshall was in the process of moving his franchise from Boston to Washington, D.C. Even though his team won

Sammy Baugh (*far left*), 1942. ASSOCIATED PRESS AP

the NFL Eastern Division in 1936, Marshall felt the city of Boston and its fans did not appreciate him or his team. He felt insulted when the Boston newspapers crowded his Redskins off the sports pages to write up a girls' high school field hockey game. Marshall, ever the promoter, thought that, if he drafted a player from Texas to lead his new-kid-in-town Redskins, the player should look like a Texan or at least like the easterner's perception of a Texan. Marshall told Baugh that when he arrived in Washington he should be wearing a ten-gallon hat and high-heeled boots. Baugh replied that not only did he not own that gear, he had never worn such garb. Marshall said, "Well, buy some and send me the bill." Baugh did as he was told, and surviving photos prove his dutiful acceptance of Marshall's request. Less than thrilled about the photo op, he said, "Those damn pointy-toed boots cramped my feet."

Before playing for the Redskins, Baugh was voted to the College All-Star team that played the defending NFL champion Green Bay Packers in the *Chicago Tribune* Charities Game on 1 September 1937. Baugh entered the game on the second play and promptly threw a forty-seven-yard scoring pass to Gaynell Tinsley of LSU. It was the game's only score, and the collegians shocked the pro champs 6–0. Baugh had also played a summer of minor league baseball in the St. Louis Cardinals' system. A confident Baugh reported to the Redskins training camp and showed his confidence to Coach Ray Flaherty. Explaining a pass pattern, the coach said, "And I want you to hit him in the eye with the ball. OK?" Baugh replied, "Which eye?"

In his first official pro game, Baugh was sensational against the New York Giants, completing 11 of 16 passes in a 13–3 victory. Later he clinched a spot in the NFL title game for his team by going 11 for 15 in a 49–14 rout of the Giants at New York City's Polo Grounds. In the championship game Baugh propelled the Redskins to a 28–21 triumph over the Chicago Bears on the frozen turf of Wrigley Field. He threw 3 touchdown passes, 2 to Wayne Millner (55 and 78 yards) and 1 to Ed Justice (35 yards). Baugh opened the game by throwing from his end zone, which was nearly unheard of at the time, for a 42-yard gain. His record 354 yards passing (18 of 36 passes) was astounding considering the weather conditions in the Windy City. For his year-long stellar performance Baugh was named to the official All-League team. On 12 April 1938 Baugh married Edmonia Gary Smith, who also attended TCU. They had two sons, Todd and Davey, both named after Baugh's teammates—Dick Todd of the Redskins and Davey O'Brien of TCU.

For the next eight years Baugh directed the Redskins to winning records, usually a first- or second-place finish. He appeared in four more championship games, winning again in 1942. Baugh almost had another NFL title to his credit in 1945, playing on frozen turf in Cleveland, when a pass from his end zone struck a goal post. Under the rules of the day it was a safety and two points for Cleveland, giving Cleveland the championship game at 15–14.

Baugh is most often called a quarterback, but in truth his sixteen-year career was split evenly as a single-wing tailback and as a T-formation quarterback. The tall, lean Texan was an extremely versatile performer. He was the acknowledged pass master of his time or any other time according to many observers. One historian said, "Baugh was to passing what Babe Ruth was to home run hitting." He could also run, kick (especially quick kick), block, tackle, and defend against opponents' passes.

A half-century after he retired he was still the NFL's all-time career punt leader, averaging 45.10 yards per punt over 16 seasons. In 1940 he averaged 51.40 yards per kick. He set a record for leading the league four times in punting average and four years consecutively. Only Steve Young of the San Francisco 49ers equaled Baugh at becoming the league's leading passer six times. Only Dan Marino of the Miami Dolphins led the league more often in pass completions, six to Baugh's five. Only the Kansas City Chiefs quarterback Len Dawson bettered Baugh for the most years leading in pass completion percentage, eight to Baugh's seven. Only Ken Anderson of the Cincinnati Bengals bettered Baugh for a season's pass completion percentage, 70.55 percent to Baugh's 70.33 percent (128 of 182 in 1945).

Slingin' Sammy was also part of an unprecedented rout in NFL championship game history when the machine-like Bears soundly thrashed the Redskins 73–0 in 1940. Baugh showed a realistic sense of humor after the lopsided loss. When the game was still scoreless, the usually reliable Charley Malone dropped a sure touchdown pass from Baugh. After the game a sportswriter asked Baugh if he thought the final score would have been different if Malone had made the catch. "Yeah," replied Baugh, "seventy-three to six."

Baugh was truly "Mr. Redskin" and, many thought, "Mr. NFL." For most of his sixteen-year career he was the NFL's brightest star. He was also the highest-paid player of his time. His teammates did not mind, though; they knew he was their meal ticket. Baugh, who used his salary to buy a large ranch near Rotan, Texas, showed his wit again when he said, "Half my salary goes to taxes and half goes to Texas." Perhaps the best way to illustrate Baugh's versatility is to cite his 1945 performance. Baugh led the NFL in passing, interceptions, and punting, representing all three phases of the game—offense, defense, and special teams. When Baugh left the Redskins after the 1952 season, much like when he left TCU, he held a host of passing records.

Baugh coached on the college and pro levels after retiring but spent most of his time at his ranch. His weathered face and salty-but-not-offensive language is on various

NFL films and videos. He is a charter member of the Professional Football Hall of Fame and a member of the College Football Hall of Fame.

When Dick McCann, the Redskins' general manager for much of Baugh's tenure, was asked to prepare a profile of Baugh for an anthology of quarterbacks, he began: "Pay no attention to anything else you'll read in this book. Slingin' Sammy Baugh was the best. Never mind what other fellows have written about other quarterbacks. Sam Baugh, by any test, in any tense, was the best, is the best, and will still be the best, long after the last pass has been thrown by some yet unborn boy in some distant decade." Baugh's teammate and fellow Texan Hugh "Bones" Taylor, perhaps with less of a literary flair, echoed McCann, saying, "There are passers, and there are throwers, and then there's Sammy Baugh." It has been said Baugh's impact on the pro game is felt every time a quarterback throws downfield, and few who saw him play would argue.

★

There is no biography of Baugh, but his life and career are discussed in Arthur Daley, *Pro Football Hall of Fame* (1963); Don Smith, *The Quarterbacks* (1963); George Sullivan, *Pro Football's All-Time Greats* (1968); Myron Cope, *The Game That Was* (1970); and George Allen with Ben Olan, *Pro Football's 100 Greatest Players* (1982).

JIM CAMPBELL

BAYLOR, Elgin (*b.* 16 September 1934 in Washington, D.C.), basketball forward and offensive powerhouse for the Los Angeles Lakers and one of the National Basketball Association's fifty greatest players.

John and Uzziel Baylor named their son "Elgin," after the brand of pocket watch John carried. Baylor grew up in the poor Southeast section of Washington, D.C. Segregation laws in the nation's capital barred black children from most of the city's playgrounds by day, which meant that there were few options for recreation. Thus Baylor wasn't introduced to basketball until his early teens, when he was living at the Southeast Settlement House. According to Baylor, his preference for basketball was one of necessity: "We couldn't play any other sport. We only got on the playground when it closed. And the only thing you could do was try to shoot baskets."

Baylor attended all-black Spingarn High School in Northeast Washington, D.C., from 1948 to 1952. Spingarn's basketball team already had a reputation for excellence, and Elgin quickly added to the growing legend. As a senior he became the first black player named to the all-metropolitan squad in the Washington, D.C., area. Although a number of schools scouted the promising player, though

Baylor's academic record was insufficient for a major school deal. Finally, a high school friend brought Baylor to the attention of the football coach at the College of Idaho. Although Baylor had not even played football in high school, Idaho offered him a scholarship.

Once at Idaho, Baylor returned to basketball, averaging 31.3 points per game during his freshman year. His outstanding play drew more attention, and Baylor transferred to Seattle University in 1954 to play for the Chieftains after his freshmen year. In accordance with National Collegiate Athletic Association (NCAA) rules, Baylor sat out the following season but returned the next year and, after averaging 29.7 points per game, was named second team All-American. The next year, Baylor was first team All-American; he also was second in the nation in scoring (32.5 points per game) and third in rebounding (19.3 per game). Baylor's play led the Chieftains all the way to the finals of the NCAA Tournament. Though Baylor played dismally in the final game against Adolph Rupp's Kentucky squad, going 9 for 32 from the field, he showed enough skill to be named the most outstanding player in the Final Four.

After his second season playing for the Chieftains, Baylor opted to turn professional. He drew the eye of Bob Short, owner of the Minneapolis Lakers. The Lakers had been dominant in the early years of the National Basketball Association (NBA) but had fallen on difficult times both on the court and at the gate. In 1958 Short gambled the future of his franchise on the rookie forward, paying him a then-impressive salary of $20,000 to help rebuild it. Short said, "If he had turned me down then, I'd have been out of business. The club would have been bankrupt."

Baylor made an immediate positive impact. His dynamic play led the Lakers as far as the NBA finals in his first year, although the team lost to the Boston Celtics. For his part, Baylor garnered Rookie of the Year honors for 1959. He quickly became a fixture in the Lakers lineup as the team made the transition from Minnesota to Los Angeles in 1960. He and guard Jerry West became the most feared offensive duo in the circuit.

In 1961 Baylor was drafted for military service but continued with the Lakers when he could get free from his post at Fort Lewis, Washington. Although he appeared in fewer than fifty games, The Big E, as he was now known, made his appearances count, averaging 38.3 points per game. Baylor displayed explosive scoring power, and on any given night seemed to bury opponents single-handedly.

Baylor broke the single-game scoring mark in 1960, lighting up the New York Knicks for seventy-one. He also set a record for points in a playoff game (sixty-one) in the 1962 finals against the Celtics. Though Michael Jordan later scored sixty-three in a playoff game, that record included overtime play. With West directing the offense on the floor and with Baylor as the team's emotional leader

Elgin Baylor *(right)*, 1965. Associated Press FILES

on and off the court, the duo seemed poised to earn a championship. Although the team dominated the Western Division throughout the 1960s, it could not seem to get past its nemesis, the Celtics, losing a total of seven NBA finals to Boston.

In 1965, in the midst of yet another playoff run, disaster struck. During a game against the Baltimore Bullets, Baylor's knee gave out, ending his season and nearly his career. Though he returned the following season, the injury had robbed Baylor of much of his trademark quickness, and his per-game average dropped by more than fifteen points. But what had been lost in speed and fluidity was replaced with determination and strength. Baylor rebuilt his game and brought his average back up over twenty-four points per game the next year and for the remainder of his career. Baylor and the Lakers continued to dominate the West but still could not defeat the Celtics.

By the end of the 1960s Baylor's knee problems began to curtail his playing time, but he continued to contribute when on the floor. At the end of the 1969–1970 season, the Lakers faced the New York Knicks in the finals, having finally outlasted the Celtics' dynasty. However, the game-seven heroics of the injured Willis Reed gave the championship to the Knicks, denying Baylor's Lakers for the eighth time. Two games into the following season, Baylor's ailing knee again gave out, sidelining him for the season. Rather than continue on as a diminished player, he retired early in 1971. A cruel irony saw the 1971–1972 Lakers go

on to a record thirty-three-game winning streak and to the franchise's first championship in Los Angeles.

His playing days over, Baylor turned to coaching, first as an assistant for the expansion New Orleans Jazz team in its 1974–1975 inaugural season. He became the Jazz's head coach in 1976, the same year he was inducted into the Basketball Hall of Fame. Baylor remained skipper of the Jazz until 1979, although the team never made the playoffs. In 1986 he was named vice president of basketball operations for the ailing Los Angeles Clippers franchise, and in 1992 he helped guide it to its first playoff appearance since the team's days in Buffalo, New York, during the 1970s.

During his twenty-two-year playing career, Baylor was named an All-Star eleven times, made the all-NBA First Team ten times, and amassed 23,149 points and 11,463 rebounds. Because his playing days overlapped those of the game's greatest offensive player, Wilt Chamberlain, Baylor never won an individual scoring title, despite averaging more than thirty points per game three times.

Called "the man of a thousand moves," Baylor seemed able to score at will from any angle, evading his defenders with strength and grace. Bill Sharman, who played against and later coached Baylor, said that "Elgin Baylor is the greatest cornerman who ever played pro basketball."

★

Baylor is discussed at length in Phil Pepe, *Winners Never Quit* (1968), and in Merv Harris's history of the Lakers franchise, *The*

Fabulous Lakers (1972). He is also mentioned in autobiographies by teammates, in particular, Wilt Chamberlain, *A View from Above* (1991), and Jerry West, *Mr. Clutch: The Jerry West Story* (1969), cowritten with Bill Libby.

MATTHEW TAYLOR RAFFETY

BEAMON, Robert Alfred ("Bob") (*b.* 29 August 1946 in Jamaica, New York), track and field athlete and Olympic champion whose world long-jump record of 29 feet, 2½ inches stood from 1968 to 1991 and is considered one of history's greatest athletic achievements.

Beamon was the son of Naomi Brown Beamon and an unnamed physician, whom his mother met when she worked as a nurse's aide at a hospital in Queens, New York. Her husband, James Beamon, was serving a prison sentence at the New York state penitentiary in Ossining at the time. Beamon's mother died of tuberculosis when he was eleven months old, and he was raised by his paternal grandmother. Throughout his life, Beamon believed that his grandmother was the only person who really cared about him as a child. Unwanted by his mother's husband, Beamon lived at his Aunt Carly's rooming house. In addition to her paying tenants, she provided rooms for abandoned children. An older boarder known as Mr. Moore often beat young Beamon with his blackjack, saying "this is how they treat bad people." One night Beamon, then age five, slipped into Mr. Moore's room, found the blackjack and began beating him as he slept, repeating the words said to him. Mr. Moore woke up and threatened to strangle Beamon, until Aunt Carly intervened. The next day, Beamon's grandmother took him home.

Beamon, known as a troublemaker throughout elementary and junior high school for fighting, shoplifting, and drug dealing, recalled that people "predicted I would be in prison by the time I was fourteen."

Beamon did not go to prison by age fourteen, but rather to Public School 622, one of New York City's reform schools for juvenile delinquents. More than anything else, success in basketball and track and field changed his life. Beamon, who stood six feet tall at age fifteen, outrebounded and outscored other youngsters his size and age because of his great leaping ability. A year later, he longjumped 24 feet to win the local Junior Olympic title. Beamon wanted to leave the reform school after two years and asked Larry Ellis, the dean of boys and track and field coach at Jamaica High School, if he could transfer there to "better himself." Ellis approved Beamon's transfer.

At Jamaica High School, Beamon developed into a good basketball player and a superstar in track and field. He earned a varsity basketball position in 1964 and quickly gained acclaim for his rebounding and shot-blocking skills. "Beamon," observed one reporter, "was above the basket

Bob Beamon jumping to a new world record at the 1968 Olympics in Mexico City. ASSOCIATED PRESS AP

as often as he was under it." In 1965 he averaged fifteen points and eleven rebounds a game and scored over twenty points in an All-Star game. Between 1964 and 1965 Beamon improved his national ranking in the long jump from tenth to second, and his ranking in the triple jump from sixteenth to first. In 1965 he long jumped 25 feet, 3½ inches, just one and a quarter inch behind the national high school record set that year by Californian John Johnson. On 12 June 1965 Beamon exceeded Johnson's standard by one inch, but an aiding tailwind disqualified the performance from record status. His triple of 50 feet, 3¾ inches, however, marked a national high school record. After Beamon finished fourth in the long jump at the 1965 Amateur Athletic Union (AAU) championships, Ralph Boston, the national champion, predicted that he would "put the world record out of sight" one day.

Beamon, who graduated from Jamaica High School in 1965, earned an athletic scholarship to North Carolina Agricultural and Technical University, a predominantly black institution in Greensboro, North Carolina. Despite achieving personal bests of 25 feet, 7 inches in the long jump, 55 feet, 8 inches in the triple jump, and 9.5 seconds in the 100-yard dash while at that school, in 1967 he transferred to the Texas Western University in El Paso, Texas, where Coach Wayne Vandenburg had assembled a crack cohort of track and field talent. That year, Beamon captured the AAU indoor championship and established an American record of 26 feet, 11½ inches in the long jump. A third place in the 1967 AAU outdoor championships preceded a silver medal–winning performance in the long jump at the Pan American Games. Beamon set indoor world records of 27 feet, 1 inch, and 27 feet, 2¾ inches in winning the 1968 National Association of Intercollegiate Athletics (NAIA) title and the 1968 National Collegiate Athletic Association (NCAA) championship, respectively. At the NCAA championship, he also won the triple jump title. Asked for the secret of his success by a *Time* reporter, Beamon replied, "There's nothing to it, really, I just jump."

For Beamon, the rest of 1968 was marred by controversy. In April he and seven other Texas Western athletes boycotted a track and field meet against Brigham Young University in Provo, Utah, to protest Mormon views "that blacks are inferior to whites and are disciples of the devil." Beamon lost his scholarship because Vandenburg ruled that the boycott participants "voluntarily removed themselves from the team."

Although sympathetic to a movement among black athletes to boycott the 1968 Olympic Games at Mexico City to protest American racism, Beamon participated in the games anyway because, as he said, "I had worked very hard for many, many years" to be an Olympian. At the Olympics, his years of hard work came together in one remarkable long jump of 29 feet, 2½ inches. Upon learning what

he had done, Beamon fell to his knees, held his face in his hands, and mumbled, "It's not possible, I can't believe it. Tell me I am not dreaming." Although experts debated the effect of Mexico City's elevation of 7,575 feet on Beamon's performance, U.S. Olympic official Dan Ferris, who had attended every Olympics since 1912, praised it as "the greatest single achievement I've ever seen."

Beamon, who suffered a hip injury after the 1968 Olympics, never equaled his Olympic feat. His best subsequent performance came in the 1969 AAU championship with a winning long jump of 26 feet, 11 inches. Track and field meet directors nevertheless wanted the Olympic champion to appear at their competitions, even if only to jog around the track and wave at the crowd. Beamon received bitter criticism from the press for "going around the track circuit, not jumping, just making appearances."

In 1972, after failing to qualify for the U.S. Olympic trials, he retired from track and field. That year Beamon graduated from Adelphi College in Garden City, New York, earning a B.A. in both anthropology and physical education. In 1973 he toured with the Professional International Track Association and tried out for the San Diego Conquistadors of the American Basketball Association. Beamon earned an M.A. in psychology at San Diego State University and operated a center for inner-city youths. Since 1982 he has worked in the sports development office of the Metro-Dade County Parks and Recreation Department in Miami, Florida. He is married to the former Milana Walter and has two children from previous marriages. At the 1991 world championships at Tokyo, Japan, Michael Powell surpassed Beamon's world record with a long jump of 29 feet, 4½ inches.

★

Bob Beamon and Milana Walter Beamon, *The Man Who Could Fly: The Bob Beamon Story* (2000), is an autobiographical work emphasizing triumph over personal struggle. See also Dick Schaap, *The Perfect Jump* (1976), and David L. Porter, ed., *Biographical Dictionary of American Sports: Outdoor Sports* (1989).

ADAM R. HORNBUCKLE

BECKMAN, John (*b.* 22 October 1892 [or 1895] in New York City; *d.* 22 June 1968 in Miami, Florida), professional basketball player who was the most prolific scorer of the 1920s, particularly on the Original Celtics, the dominant team of the era.

Beckman was born and raised just north of the Chelsea district of New York City. His birth year was either 1892 or 1895, with the former being most likely. Beckman had one brother.

Beckman, called "Johnny," began playing basketball at

Johnny Beckman, 1921. © Bettmann/CORBIS

a young age and, never attending high school, by age fourteen or fifteen was a star on the Christ Church Five, his first organized team. In 1910 Beckman was one of the stars of the Saint Gabriel's team of New York that won the lightweight (or middleweight) national title that year. Basketball was played on a weight-class basis with either two or three weights; little import was given to great height, in contrast to later decades. Beckman, who was a solid 156 pounds on a five foot, eight-and-a-half-inch frame, had a strong build and also had competed as an amateur boxer and runner in his youth. His teammates on the Saint Gabriel's team included Chris Leonard and Ernie Reich, future teammates on the Original Celtics, and Jack Murray, another future professional player and later a basketball writer. The team remained together until about 1914.

Beckman joined his first professional team, the Opals of the Hudson County League, around 1911. By 1913 he was playing for a number of professional teams in and around New York City. The next year (1914–1915) he also played for a team in the Connecticut State League. In 1915 to 1916 he made his first appearance with an Eastern League team, De Neri of Philadelphia, for whom he was the leading scorer and finished seventh in the league. Beckman also played for Paterson of the Interstate League and was their leading scorer in the so-called World Championship series against Greystock and Wilkes-Barre.

Professional basketball players of the day were essentially independent contractors, and therefore played on many teams within the same year. Beckman had become highly sought after by 1916 because of his great shooting and all-around play, and in that year he played for Reading of the Eastern League, Bridgeport and Danbury of the Interstate League, and the Newark Turners. He ranked near the top of the Eastern League in scoring and assists while playing for Reading. In 1917 to 1918 he returned to De Neri, played for Norwalk, the Newark Turners, the Blue Ribbons of the Connecticut League, and for Nanticoke of the Penn State League. He set incredible scoring marks with Nanticoke. In twenty-six games for them that year (1917–1918), Beckman averaged just under eleven points per game, an amazing total at a time when teams routinely scored less than twenty points per game.

The start of World War I and the subsequent takeover of the railroads by the U.S. government caused many leagues to shut down in 1918 to 1919, but Beckman still played on at least three different teams in the New York City area. In addition, he played for the Standard Shipyard team of Staten Island, for whom he ostensibly worked during the war. After the war Beckman returned to Nanticoke, where he led the Penn State League in both the 1919–1920 and 1920–1921 seasons in scoring. In the latter year he scored more than 100 points more than the second-leading scorer and led his team to the Penn State League championship. Again Beckman played on at least two other squads during that year.

The next year Beckman made his first appearance for the Original Celtics and, after signing an exclusive contract with them for more than $12,000 per year, played only with the Celtics until January 1927, when he was sold to the Baltimore Orioles of the American Basketball League. During this period the Celtics won the championship of the Eastern League (1921–1922) and went undefeated in the Metropolitan League (1922–1923) before rejoining the Eastern League. Unfortunately their success drove the league toward financial insolvency and it folded in early 1923. The Celtics toured the country, compiling the finest record in basketball and earning acclaim as the game's greatest team.

In February 1922 the Celtic captain Ernie Reich died and Beckman became the team captain, a position he held until he was traded. Teams at that time had managers, but no coach, and Beckman was essentially the Celtic player-coach. In 1925 the American Basketball League (ABL) was formed, but the Celtics chose not to join because they could make more money playing independently. The next year the ABL refused to allow its member squads to play non-league teams, and the Celtics joined the league in December, taking over the Brooklyn franchise. The Celtics proceeded to win consecutive league titles (1926–1927 and

1927–1928) before the team was disbanded because of pressure from the league and the conviction of its owner, who was incarcerated for embezzlement. The success of the Celtics affected attendance at games involving other teams. By disbanding the Celtics and redistributing their players, the owners hoped to draw more fans to all of the league games rather than to just those of the Celtics.

By this time Beckman had joined first the Orioles of the ABL and then Chicago and Detroit (1927–1928). The following two seasons he played for Rochester, Cleveland, and Fort Wayne, all of the ABL, until the league folded after the 1930 season. Beckman then joined many of his old mates on a new version of the Original Celtics and barnstormed—traveled throughout the region to play non-league games against local teams or other barnstorming squads—from 1930 to 1941.

Beckman finally retired from basketball at the age of forty-six (or forty-nine). He was offered a number of coaching positions, but declined them all. According to his only son, Beckman felt he did not have the patience and personality to coach and could no longer lead by example. In 1957 Beckman moved to Miami and died in Florida in 1968 of Alzheimer's disease. In 1972 he was posthumously inducted in the James Naismith Memorial Basketball Hall of Fame.

There is little question that Beckman was one of the two greatest players of the 1920s, along with Nat Holman. He was recognized for his shooting, his toughness, and for being an all-around player. Beckman was able to dominate at every level at which he played, partly because of talent, but also because of his great work ethic and basketball acumen.

★

No biography or autobiography of Beckman exists. An in-depth discussion of Beckman's career can be found in Murry Nelson, *The Originals: The New York Celtics Invent Modern Basketball* (1999). An obituary is in the *New York Times* (24 June 1968). Both the New York Celtics file and the John Beckman file at the James Naismith Basketball Hall of Fame have clippings and letters about Beckman, but these are incomplete.

MURRY R. NELSON

BEDNARIK, Charles Philip ("Chuck") (*b.* 1 May 1925 in Bethlehem, Pennsylvania), professional football player who, despite other considerable accomplishments, is most famous for his performance during the 1960 championship season as "the last of the sixty-minute men."

Bednarik grew up in a blue-collar section of Bethlehem, a community in the Lehigh Valley whose economy depended

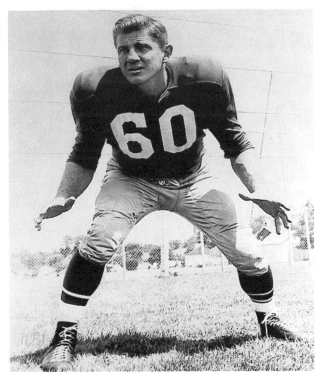

Chuck Bednarik. ASSOCIATED PRESS AP

heavily on the huge steel mill named for the town. His Slovak immigrant parents, Charles Albert Bednarik, a millwright at "the Steel," as the locals referred to the sprawling mill, and Mary Pivovarnicek, a homemaker, provided sufficiently for "Chuck" and his two siblings. Bednarik, a sturdy youngster, was a fine all-around athlete. Ironically at Bethlehem Catholic and Liberty High Schools he was a good football player but an excellent basketball and baseball player. As World War II raged, Bednarik was drafted into the U.S. Army Air Corps when he turned eighteen in May 1943. Like others of "the Greatest Generation," the teenage Bednarik had many harrowing experiences as a waist gunner in a B-24 bomber over Europe. He survived thirty bombing missions and was awarded the Air Medal with five battle stars and four oak leaf clusters. Bednarik recalled his last mission of 23 April 1945: "It was our thirtieth, the required number. When we got back to England, I jumped out and kissed the plane, kissed the ground, and vowed I would never fly again. Never! Of course, I was wrong. You couldn't play in the National Football League [NFL] and not fly."

When Bednarik enrolled at the University of Pennsylvania in 1945, choosing the Ivy League school over Pennsylvania State University, he had grown from a six-foot, 180-pound high school senior to a six-foot, three-inch, 230-pound returning war veteran. His Penn career was a storied one. He was consensus All-America his final two seasons, and he won the Maxwell Award, second only to the Heisman Trophy in prestige. Bednarik played twenty-seven games at Penn, and the Quakers won twenty-four of those games. Before his last collegiate season, on 5 June 1948 Bednarik married Emma Margetich. They had five daughters. Soon after his graduation, with a B.S. degree in physical education, Bednarik was the first player taken in the National Football League (NFL) draft for 1949 by the Philadelphia Eagles.

The professional team Bednarik joined was destined to become NFL champions in 1949. It was a cliquish team on which a rookie, especially a highly touted, local, outspoken one, had a hard time fitting in. But Bednarik's talent and desire could not be denied. He backed up the offensive center Vic Lindskog in 1949 and in 1950 began a run as one of the best linebackers, both outside and middle. Nicknamed "the Clutch" because once he got his large, strong hands on a ball carrier the play was usually over, Bednarik played in every Pro Bowl from 1951 to 1958 with the exception of 1956. He was for many years one of the few points of light on Eagles teams that were quite dismal.

With a trade for the quarterback Norm Van Brocklin in 1958 and a runner-up finish in 1959, the Eagles and Bednarik were set for the storybook season of 1960. The season did not begin well as the Browns bashed the Eagles 41–24. Two close wins over Dallas and St. Louis and a solid victory against Detroit placed the Eagles in a rematch with the Browns in Cleveland. Bob Pelligrini, an outside linebacker, was injured early in the game, and Coach Buck Shaw asked Bednarik, playing center, to play Pelligrini's position in addition to his own. "Concrete Charlie," another nickname acquired during his days as an off-season cement salesman, played a then unheard-of fifty-two minutes, and the Eagles won, 31–29, on a long, late field goal by Bobby Walston. The Eagles did not taste defeat again until the last game of the season, when many regulars, but not Bednarik, were rested. Coming into that final game Bednarik averaged fifty-eight minutes of action over a stretch of crucial games.

On 20 November 1960 in New York City, Bednarik made "the tackle heard round the world." Late in the game, with the Eagles ahead 17–10, the Giants drove for the tying score. Frank Gifford, the Giants Hall of Fame halfback, caught a pass and dodged and darted dangerously close to scoring territory. He instinctively cut back without looking and ran right into the pursuing Bednarik. Gifford went down as if shot. The ball came loose and was recovered by the Eagles, assuring victory for Philadelphia. An elated Bednarik danced a Slovak version of an Irish jig. The Giants and their fans misinterpreted this as disrespectful of the fallen Gifford, who suffered a concussion, but the always emotional Bednarik simply was celebrating an im-

portant victory. In a scheduling oddity, the Giants played the Eagles the next Sunday in Philadelphia. During the week, especially in New York City, much talk focused on getting Bednarik. It never happened. With Bednarik "going both ways," the Eagles won the grudge match 31–23. Gifford sat out the entire 1961 season as a result of the deep concussion. When Gifford married Kathie Lee, he told her, "A name you'll hear often is Chuck Bednarik—get used to it." He then explained the connection. Lee once said, "When I first heard Chuck Bednarik, I thought it was a pasta dish."

By winning the Eastern Division the Eagles were pitted against Vince Lombardi's Green Bay Packers in the NFL title game. After Green Bay went ahead 13–10, the Eagles used a long kickoff return to set up their own go-ahead touchdown. But the Packers drove as the clock ran down. With only seconds left Jimmy Taylor caught a pass from Bart Starr, and the powerhouse fullback rumbled toward a touchdown. He pinballed past several Eagles, but finally "the Clutch" grabbed him. The Packers had no timeouts, and Bednarik continued to hold Taylor until the Franklin Field clock showed 0:00. The Eagles were world champions, the only team that ever defeated Lombardi in a championship game. Bednarik recalled, "I said, 'Okay, Taylor, you can get up now—it's over.'"

Bednarik, thirty-five years old at the time of his iron man performances, had planned to call it a career after the 1960 season, but he was persuaded to play another two years. When asked how he prepared for his sixty-minute role, Bednarik said: "I practiced with the offense all during the week, and would stay out afterwards with [defensive coordinator] Jerry Williams and work on the defenses. Physically, I was in good enough shape to go both ways, although at times I felt a little silly standing out there in the middle of the field by myself as forty-two other guys ran on and off."

Bednarik was elected to the Pro Football Hall of Fame in 1967 after the mandatory five-year wait. He was a College Football Hall of Fame inductee in 1969. He settled in Coopersburg, Pennsylvania, not far from his native Bethlehem. A vocal critic of the modern NFL, he became an advocate for better pensions for the pro pioneers of his day and before.

Bednarik was an outstanding player who at thirty-five became a throwback to twenty or more years before, when all players "went both ways." His contributions to his team in the 1960 championship season became one of the enduring legends of pro football history. Any legitimate all-time team, college or pro, would have to give serious consideration to Bednarik. In 1994, at age sixty-nine, Bednarik wrote a friend, "I guess I'm a dreamer, but I feel like I could still snap the ball [for punts, extra points, and field goals] in the NFL today."

★

Jack McCallum wrote a biography of Bednarik, *Chuck Bednarik: The Last of the Sixty-Minute Men* (1977). Bednarik's life and career are discussed in George Sullivan, *Pro Football's All-Time Greats* (1968); Murray Olderman, *The Defenders* (1973); and George Allen with Ben Olan, *Pro Football's 100 Greatest Players* (1982).

JIM CAMPBELL

BELL, DeBenneville ("Bert")   (*b.* 25 February 1894 in Philadelphia, Pennsylvania; *d.* 11 October 1959 in Philadelphia, Pennsylvania), football player, coach, and team owner best known as commissioner of the National Football League (NFL), which he provided with strong leadership throughout the 1940s and 1950s, establishing policies that prepared the league for its subsequent success.

Bell was born into a Philadelphia main line family. He was the son of John Cromwell Bell, a lawyer who served as district attorney of Philadelphia and attorney general of Pennsylvania, and Fleurette de Benneville Myers. Bell's brother John was lieutenant governor and governor of Pennsylvania before his election to the United States Senate.

The family's affluence allowed Bell to attend several prestigious preparatory schools, including Haverford, from which he graduated in 1915. Bell then entered the University of Pennsylvania, where he majored in English and played quarterback on the football team. At five feet, eight inches, Bell was a good but not great player. He did guide Penn to its only Rose Bowl appearance at the end of the 1916 season. Bell quit school in 1918 to join the military, most notably serving in a field hospital in France during World War I. In 1919 Bell returned home for one more year at Penn before leaving the college without a degree.

Bell served as an assistant coach for the Penn football team from 1920 to 1928. He held a similar position at Temple University in 1930 and 1931. During these years, Bell spent much of his time gambling, drinking, and generally squandering the money allotted to him by his father. After losing a considerable amount of cash at the horse track, Bell's father stopped giving him money in 1932 and forced him to work as a manager at one of the family's hotels, the Ritz-Carlton in Philadelphia. It was there that Bell met Frances Upton, a popular entertainer with the Ziegfeld Follies. In 1934 the two wed, but only after Bell promised to give up alcohol. Their marriage produced three children.

In 1933 Bell and several other investors purchased the Frankford (Pennsylvania) Yellow Jackets, a franchise that had ceased operations during the 1931 season of the still relatively young National Football League (NFL). Bell renamed the squad the Philadelphia Eagles, inspired by the

Bert Bell *(center)* with George Halas *(left)* and Charles Bidwell. ASSOCIATED PRESS AP

symbol of the New Deal's National Recovery Administration. With the nation still mired in the Great Depression, the Eagles reportedly lost $80,000 over the next four seasons. The players were paid so little that many of them roomed at Bell's Philadelphia mansion. The franchise was put up for public auction in 1936. Bell, as the only bidder, paid $4,500 for sole ownership of the Philadelphia team. He immediately named himself head coach and general manager, while also assuming public relations and ticket sales duties. Between 1936 and 1940 the Eagles won only ten of fifty-six games and suffered terribly at the gate.

As owner of the Eagles, Bell suggested the creation of a college draft, whereby NFL teams would select collegiate players and gain negotiating rights to them. Under Bell's scheme, the team with the poorest record from the previous season would select first. While clearly an attempt to boost Bell's struggling Eagles, the draft was also supported by George Halas of the Chicago Bears and other prosperous owners. They, along with Bell, saw the broad advantages to creating competitive balance within the league. Ironically, despite getting the first pick in the inaugural NFL draft, Bell was unable to sign any of his choices in 1936. Other major sports leagues eventually adopted Bell's model, creating similar systems of drafting collegiate and amateur players.

In a complicated deal after the 1940 NFL season, Bell sold the Eagles to businessman Alexis Thompson and purchased a half-interest in the Pittsburgh Steelers, becoming co-owner with friend Art Rooney. Bell served as president and general manager of the Steelers and coached the team briefly in 1941. In 1946 Bell sold his interests in the Pittsburgh franchise when he was selected to replace Elmer Layden as NFL commissioner.

Bell and the NFL immediately faced fierce competition from the newly created All-America Football Conference (AAFC). During the expensive four-year "war," Bell steadfastly refused to cooperate with the new league. In 1949 the NFL finally merged with the AAFC. Three financially stable AAFC franchises (Cleveland, Los Angeles, and Baltimore) were absorbed into the older circuit, while the rest of the AAFC teams folded. After league owners were unable to agree on a plan for the fair distribution of former AAFC players to NFL teams, Bell stepped in and reassigned the players himself.

Bell also dealt swiftly with the influence of gamblers who, he felt, threatened the integrity of the sport. Prior to the 1946 NFL championship game between the Chicago Bears and the New York Giants, rumors circulated about players being approached to fix the results of the contest. As such contact with gamblers violated New York state law, Bell immediately investigated and suspended two members of the Giants—Merle Hapes and Frank Filchock. Both suspensions lasted nearly a decade. Bell then pushed successfully for the passage of sports antibribery laws in other states.

Bell's experiences as an owner of losing teams made him sympathetic to underdog franchises and guided his efforts in several areas. Starting in 1948 Bell determined the league's schedule of games. Previously, the strong teams scheduled weak teams early in the season to ensure a winning record for themselves and to maintain fan interest throughout the entirety of the season. This left the poorer clubs to close out the year by playing each other in meaningless contests before small crowds. Bell altered the schedule to guarantee that divisional races would remain competitive late into the season.

As television became increasingly prominent, Bell negotiated league contracts with the Dumont and CBS networks in the 1950s. Again, his concern for competitive balance and sympathy for the weaker teams led to a policy of sharing television revenues equally among NFL teams. This policy was one of the foundations of NFL prosperity and stability throughout the remainder of the twentieth century. Bell also showed an acute understanding of the medium's potentially harmful effects on the still-developing NFL by insisting that games not be televised in home markets. The gravel-voiced commissioner reasoned, "You can't give a game to the public for free on television and expect them to pay to go to the ball park for the same game." Expanded television exposure, anchored by Bell's blackout policy, brought a mass audience to professional football in the 1950s and beyond.

In 1959, while attending a game between the Eagles and Steelers at Philadelphia's Franklin Field, Bell, who had been in ill health, suffered a heart attack and died shortly thereafter.

While assuming almost dictatorial powers as commissioner of the NFL, Bell made strong but fair decisions. In the process, the NFL attracted a greater following and became the most successful sports enterprise in the United States. In recognition of his vital role, Bell was admitted to the Pro Football Hall of Fame in 1963.

★

Materials concerning Bell are on file at the NFL office in New York City; a newspaper clippings collection is housed at the Pro Football Hall of Fame in Canton, Ohio. W. C. Heinz, "Boss of the Behemoths," *Saturday Evening Post* (3 Dec. 1955), presents a good overview of Bell's activities through the mid-1950s. Pro Football Hall of Fame, "Bert Bell: The Commissioner," *Coffin Corner* 18, no. 3 (1996), is a good summary of Bell's career. Upton Bell and David Chanoff, "Any Given Sunday," *Philadelphia Magazine* (Sept. 2000), cowritten by Bell's son, provides interesting anecdotes and insights into Bell's personality. An obituary is in the *New York Times* (12 Oct. 1959).

MARC S. MALTBY

BELL, James Thomas ("Cool Papa") (*b.* 17 May 1903 in Starkville, Mississippi; *d.* 7 March 1991 in St. Louis, Missouri), Negro League outfielder enshrined in the National Baseball Hall of Fame who may have been the fastest player in baseball history.

Bell was one of five sons and two daughters of Jonas Bell, a Mississippi farmer, and Mary Nichols. He began playing baseball as a young boy on local sandlots. There was no high school for black youth in Starkville, so in 1920 he went to St. Louis, Missouri, where he could live with his four older brothers and go to school. Bell attended high school for two years while working part-time for the Independent Packing Company and pitching for the semiprofessional Compton Hill Cubs and East St. Louis Cubs.

In 1922 Bell got a contract to play for a professional team, the St. Louis Stars, for a salary of $90 a month. A lefthander, Bell earned his colorful nickname, "Cool Papa," when he was a rookie by striking out the famous Oscar Charleston in the clutch. A teammate complimented him by calling him Cool. Manager Bill Gatewood thought the name sounded incomplete and added the Papa.

"Cool Papa" Bell, shortly after his induction in the Baseball Hall of Fame, 1974. ASSOCIATED PRESS AP

While still a young pitcher, Bell injured his arm and was moved to the outfield in 1924. To make the most of his speed, he learned to switch-hit. A rail-thin five-foot, eleven-inch speedster, he had little power but accumulated high totals of doubles and triples because of his speed. He often went from first to third on a sacrifice bunt.

In a game against a major league all-star team, Bell drew attention by continuing home when he saw that nobody was covering the plate. St. Louis *Post-Dispatch* sports editor Bob Broeg later explained how the extraordinary play happened: "He did it in a post-season black-versus-white series in which Murray Dickson pitched and Roy Partee caught for the major leaguers. On first base, Bell was off and running when the batter, Satchel Paige, laid one down. The third baseman charged in, which prompted Bell to zoom past second to third. And when Bell noted that Partee was running down the line to cover third, [he] dashed home ahead of the return throw. The year was 1948 and Bell was 45 years old."

Bell claimed to have circled the bases in twelve seconds in a timed test. Satchel Paige, a noted raconteur, said that when he roomed with Bell, the latter could turn off the light switch and jump into bed before the light went out. Bell said later that it was a true story; the switch was defective and didn't douse the light instantly.

Bell was an excellent hitter despite his lack of power and 150-pound frame. His published batting averages during his ten years with the St. Louis Stars varied from .312 to .362. (The Stars won Negro National League championships in 1928, 1930, and 1931.) He played for the Pittsburgh Crawfords from 1933 to 1936, for whom he batted between .317 and .362. In 1937 Bell joined Paige and other Crawfords in the Dominican Republic where the dictator Rafael Trujillo built a powerhouse baseball team to enhance his popularity. He was with Trujillo's team that year when it won the Denver *Post* tournament for independent teams. He hit .450 and had five extra base hits and eleven stolen bases in thirteen games.

Bell rejoined the Crawfords in 1938 but was soon lured to Mexico, playing with integrated teams in Tampico, Torreon, Veracruz, and Monterrey and earning $450 a month, his top salary in a twenty-four-year playing career. In the 1940 season, he led the Mexican League in runs (119), hits (167), triples (15), home runs (12), and runs batted in (79).

In 1942, at the age of thirty-nine, Bell returned to the United States and joined the Chicago American Giants. He went to the Homestead (Pennsylvania) Grays the following season. There he teamed up with power hitters Josh Gibson, Buck Leonard, Jud Wilson, Sam Bankhead, Vic Harris, and Jerry Benjamin to win three straight National Negro League titles and two Negro World Series.

When he was forty-three years old, Bell retired from professional baseball and joined the semipro Detroit Senators. He returned to the pros in 1948 when Tom Baird and J. L. Wilkinson of the Kansas City Monarchs hired him to manage their second team. When the team played in Monarchs territory, it was called the Kansas City Stars or Travelers. Outside the Midwest, the team used the Kansas City Monarchs name. In his three seasons as a manager, Bell tutored Ernie Banks and Elston Howard, among other future major leaguers.

After retiring from baseball for a second time, in 1951, Bell became a part-time scout for the St. Louis Browns (now the Baltimore Orioles). He also took a job as custodian and night security man at St. Louis City Hall and worked there until 1973. The street where he lived was renamed James "Cool Papa" Bell Avenue in the late 1970s, when Bell began to be recognized, belatedly, for his contributions to baseball.

Bell was inducted into the National Baseball Hall of Fame in 1974. With considerable understatement, his plaque reads: "Contemporaries rated him the fastest man on the basepaths." In fact, contemporaries had trouble believing their eyes when they saw him run. Bill Yancey of New York's Lincoln Giants remembered: "The first time Cool Papa came to New York with the St. Louis Stars, he hit a ball into right field. . . . I went out to get the throw, and I looked up as Cool Papa was slowing up going into third. And I said to myself, 'That sonofagun didn't touch second.' Next time up he hit another ball about the same place. I watched this guy run. Well, he came across second base and it looked like his feet weren't touching the ground!"

Bell and Clarabelle Thompson Bell had married on 8 September 1920. They had no children but were extraordinarily close. Clarabelle died on 20 January 1991, and just over a month later, Bell suffered a heart attack. He died on 7 March 1991 at St. Louis University Hospital and was buried in Saint Peter's Cemetery in St. Louis.

★

As a Hall of Fame ballplayer, Bell had a career worthy of discussion in numerous sports columns and articles. Overviews of his career are in Dick Clark and Larry Lester, eds., *The Negro Leagues Book* (1994), and James A. Riley, *The Biographical Encyclopedia of the Negro Baseball Leagues* (1994). Robert W. Peterson, *Only the Ball Was White* (1970), contains information about Bell, including recollections of his contemporaries. Among the best articles about Bell is James Bankes, "Flying Feet: The Life and Times of Cool Papa Bell, the Fastest Runner Baseball Has," *Baseball History* (Fall 1996).

ROBERT W. PETERSON

BENCH, Johnny Lee (*b.* 7 December 1947 in Oklahoma City, Oklahoma), catcher known for controlling the game on both sides of the plate, a distinction that made him the standard by which catchers are judged.

Bench, a Native American, was the third of four children of Ted and Katy Bench. Ted, a truck driver, played semi-professional baseball in Oklahoma and realized his own dream of becoming a major leaguer through his youngest son. At Binger (Oklahoma) High School, Bench was All-State in both basketball and baseball as well as the valedictorian of his graduating class.

Selected during the 1965 amateur draft by the Cincinnati Reds, Bench spent the next few seasons in the minors. As an eighteen-year-old backstop for Peninsula of the Carolina league in 1966, he hit twenty-two home runs in ninety-eight games and was labeled a "can't miss" prospect. The following season he spent four months at Buffalo before taking over the catching duties for the Cincinnati Reds in August 1967.

In 1968, his rookie year, the six-foot, one-inch, 210-pound Bench set records for number of games caught by a rookie (154) and doubles by a catcher (40) and became the first backstop to win the National League's Rookie of the Year Award. The following year, he collected twenty-six home runs and 90 RBI, and became the cleanup hitter for a Reds team that finished in third place, behind Atlanta and San Francisco in the National League's Western Division. Bench became the most feared power hitter on the dominant team of the 1970s.

Bench batted fourth or fifth for Cincinnati's Big Red

Johnny Bench, c. 1976. © BETTMANN/CORBIS

Machine, which boosted a lineup of stars like Pete Rose, Joe Morgan, Tony Perez, George Foster, and Dave Concepcion. With Bench's leadership behind the plate and his big bat in the lineup, the Reds won six division titles, four pennants, and two World Series between 1970 and 1977. The first of his two Most Valuable Player (MVP) awards came in 1970 when he hit a league-leading 45 homers and 148 RBI, both of which were all-time records for catchers. His second MVP award came in 1972 when he led the league again in homers (40) and RBI (125). But Bench, always one to give credit where it was due, attributed the success of the Big Red Machine to first baseman Tony Perez. "We were able to capture back-to-back world championships in 1975 and 1976 with the game we played best; power, speed, and defense," he said. "But mostly we were steady, and nobody gave us that sense of equilibrium more than Tony Perez. We were winners with him, for so many reasons people not close to the club would never see. Tony's 'stay-with-'em' attitude allowed us to block out all the other pressures of playing the game to concentrate on what really mattered."

Playing with conditions that included broken bones in his feet, numerous knee problems, and what turned out to be a benign lesion on one of his lungs, the native Oklahoman redefined the catching position with his one-handed style, his sweep tag, his catlike quickness and his powerful arm. His oversized, hinged mitt would later become an essential part of every catcher's equipment. He set an endurance record by catching a hundred or more games for thirteen consecutive seasons between 1968 and 1980. By the end of his seventeen-year career, Bench's defensive prowess earned him thirteen consecutive All-Star appearances as well as National League records for catchers, with 9,260 putouts and 10,110 total chances, while also compiling ten Gold Gloves and a .990 fielding average.

Offensively, Bench was just as outstanding, with a career .267 batting average, 389 home runs, and 1,376 RBI. From 1970 to 1980 he averaged 31 home runs and 108 RBI, remarkable statistics for a catcher given the physical abuse endured behind the plate. "Johnny Bench is the greatest athlete who has ever played the game," said Reds manager Sparky Anderson. "It's almost pitiful that one man should have so much talent."

By 1981 Bench was worn out from catching and repeatedly asked to shift to another position. The Reds complied, moving him to first base and later to third before he retired from the game in 1983. He spent nine years with CBS Radio, broadcasting the National Game of the Week, the All-Star Game, the League Championship Series, and the World Series. He has also called Reds baseball games on both television and radio.

During his playing career, Bench dated several women but was very discreet in his relationships. In 1975 he was briefly married to Vicki Chesser, a model from South Carolina, but has since sworn himself to bachelorhood.

Throughout his professional career, the star catcher used his celebrity status to aid worthy causes, including the American Heart Association, the American Cancer Society, the Kidney Foundation, and the Muscular Dystrophy Association. He spent many off seasons appearing in the "Bob Hope Christmas Show." He also actively supports the Cincinnati Orchestra, the Museum of Science and Industry, and his own Johnny Bench Scholarship Fund, which grants financial aid to Greater Cincinnati–area college students.

"People who are sick and less fortunate are wild about their sports heroes," Bench said. "I became sensitive to that after surgeons found a lesion on one of my lungs [after the 1972 season]. That operation had made me well aware of how vulnerable and how mortal I am, that we all are." Bench often avoided the publicity attached to his community service because of a concern that the press would misinterpret his intentions. "When you're in the business I am in, most people see you the way they want to; not for who you really are," he once explained.

Bench was elected to the Baseball Hall of Fame in 1989, and in 1998 *Sporting News* named him the greatest catcher ever and the sixteenth-greatest player of all time. A year later he was selected by fans to the All-Century team.

Today Bench serves as a special consultant to the general manager of the Cincinnati Reds and plays on the Senior Professional Golf tour. He lives with his twelve-year-old son in Cincinnati, Ohio.

★

Bench's autobiography was written with William Brashler and is titled *Catch You Later: The Autobiography of Johnny Bench* (1979). For more information on his career, see Johnny Bench with John Sammis, *Catching and Power Hitting* (1975).

WILLIAM KASHATUS

BERENSON ABBOTT, Senda (*b*. 19 March 1868 in Vilna, Lithuania; *d*. 16 February 1954 in Santa Barbara, California), physical educator who introduced basketball to women at Smith College and published the first rule book for women's basketball.

Berenson was born Senda Valvrojenski in a small town in Lithuania. Her father, Albert, wanted a different life for his children and immigrated to the United States in 1874. A year later, she, her mother, and her two brothers joined her father in Boston, where he changed the family name to Berenson and became a peddler of pots and pans. Her mother, Julia Mieliszanski, sewed and cooked to earn money, and two more daughters joined the family. Berenson attended Boston Girls' Latin School but did not finish due to poor health. Her father, a well-read man, and her older brother Bernard, who later graduated from Harvard University and became a noted art historian and critic, tutored her at home. Her love of music led her to study piano at the Boston Conservatory of Music, but poor health again disrupted her studies.

After much prodding, Berenson enrolled at the Boston Normal School of Gymnastics in 1890 to try to improve her frail health. At first she hated it. "Gymnastic work did not interest me and the simplest exercises made me ache all over. After five minutes of standing erect I had to lie flat on three stools," she once said in an interview. However, with time her body and her attitude changed. "after three months, I began to feel that I was better and at the end of the year was doing all the gymnastics required." This experience was a turning point for Berenson, leading to her life's work. "I had changed an aching body to a free and strong mechanism, ready and eager for whatever might come. My indifference had changed to deep conviction and I wanted to work only in physical education so that I might help others as I had been helped."

In January 1892 Berenson left the Boston Normal School and was hired as the director of physical education at Smith College, a women's college in Northampton, Massachusetts. Berenson, a petite woman standing five feet tall with long, dark, wavy hair, enthusiastically developed the physical-education program for the female students. During her first month on the job, she read the monthly newsletter published by the Young Men's Christian Association (YMCA) in nearby Springfield, Massachusetts. The newsletter described a new sport called "basket ball" that had been invented by James Naismith, one of the YMCA instructors. Berenson introduced the new game to the students at Smith and it quickly became very popular. A March 1893 game between members of the first-year class of 1896 and the sophomore class of 1895 was considered the first official women's basketball game in history. The sophomores won 5–4 with Berenson serving as both the coach and referee.

The idea of teams of women competing against one another was not widely accepted at the time. Women did solo activities such as swimming, ice skating, and walking or one-on-one games such as tennis, but not team sports like basketball. To make basketball seem more "womanly," Berenson modified Naismith's original rules. The most notable modification was that Berenson divided the court into three equal sections to encourage team play and avoid overexertion. Players could not leave their designated section. The "guards" defended their own basket while the "homes" (later called "forwards") tried to score. The "centers" occupied the middle section and either passed or blocked the ball going from one section to the other. Berenson also placed a three-bounce limit on dribbling and a three-second limit on holding the ball. At first these rules were only applied to games at Smith College.

As basketball quickly spread across the country, each team adopted its own rules. Some schools played by the original boys' rules, but more often the rules were modified in some way for women. As a result, there were dozens of versions of rules across the country, which made interscholastic competition difficult. This problem of multiple rules was discussed at an 1899 physical-education conference in Springfield. A four-woman committee, including Berenson, was formed and established a set of rules for women's basketball. These rules were first published in 1901 with Berenson serving as the editor, a role she continued until 1917. Her influence on the game lasted for decades. Her idea of a divided court remained the standard in women's basketball through the late 1960s. It wasn't until the early 1970s that women in the United States routinely played full-court basketball.

Berenson served as the director of physical education at Smith College for nineteen years, resigning in 1911 when, at the age of forty-three, she married Smith English professor Herbert V. Abbott on 15 June of that year. Berenson continued teaching physical education at the Mary A. Burnham School, a private girls' school in Northampton. She was active in the community, appearing in local theater productions, participating in women's clubs, and teaching gymnastics at what was then called the Northampton Lunatic Hospital. She gave numerous lectures and published many articles about women's basketball and physical education. While she discouraged interscholastic competition for women in favor of intramural play, Berenson continually promoted the importance of physical activity for women, once writing that "any girl who plays basketball becomes awake to her studies and the world."

Berenson traveled to Europe several times, visiting her brother Bernard in Italy and studying music, art, and literature. In 1929 her husband died at age sixty-four. Five years later she moved to Santa Barbara, California, to live with one of her sisters. Berenson died there in 1954 at age eighty-five.

Berenson's contributions to women's sports, particularly basketball, were widely recognized in the decades after her death. She was inducted into the Naismith Memorial Basketball Hall of Fame (1985), International Jewish Sports Hall of Fame (1987), and Women's Basketball Hall of Fame (1991). Her longtime commitment to women's basketball also earned her a spot on the *Sports Illustrated* list of the greatest sports figures of the twentieth century.

★

One chapter in Joan Hult and Marianna Trekell, eds., *A Century of Women's Basketball: From Frailty to Final Four* (1991), is devoted to Berenson's role in the development of women's basketball. A more in-depth account of her contributions to women's physical education can be found in Agnes Stillman, "Senda Berenson Abbott: Her Life and Contributions to Smith College and to the Physical Education Profession," master's thesis, Smith College (1971).

KELLY NELSON

BERG, Patricia Jane ("Patty") (*b.* 13 February 1918 in Minneapolis, Minnesota), one of the greatest women golfers of all time and a founding member of the Ladies Professional Golf Association (LPGA).

Berg was the daughter of Herman L. Berg, a semiprofessional baseball player, and Teresa Berg, who died in 1939. A natural athlete, Berg played sandlot football when she was eleven, quarterbacking for the Fiftieth Street Tigers, a team on which her lifelong friend, future football great Bud Wilkinson, played right tackle. Berg plunged into golf at age fourteen with the same unbridled enthusiasm she showed for football. Her father was her first golf teacher, coaching her through her years at Washburn High School in Minneapolis. It was Lester Bolstad, however, her trainer at the University of Minnesota, who honed Berg's skills and remained her coach and mentor for the next forty years.

At sixteen, only three years after taking up the game,

Patty Berg. ARCHIVE PHOTOS, INC.

she won the 1934 Minneapolis City Championship, the Minnesota State Championship, and was the runner-up in the U.S. Amateur Championship. She repeated as state champion in 1936, and the following year again placed second in the U.S. Amateur. Berg's 1938 golf season was perhaps the most successful, in percentage terms, of any golfer in history, male or female. She won ten out of the thirteen tournaments that she entered, including the Western Amateur, National Amateur, Western Derby, Trans-Mississippi, Helen Lee Doherty, and her third Minnesota State Championship. In all, she won twenty-eight amateur titles.

Before 1948, professional women's golf blurred the distinction between amateur and professional victories. When Berg turned professional in 1940, she was among the first ten women to do so. This did little to improve her financial situation, however. Purses for women golfers at the time were so small that Berg earned most of her income giving exhibitions and clinics for the Wilson Sporting Goods Company, which sponsored her. She became one of the company's most successful touring pros, as charming and enthusiastic as she was skillful. So apparent and superior were her abilities that golfing enthusiasts were anxious to learn from her.

Her first major professional victory was in the Western Open, which she won in 1941 (and again in 1943, 1948, 1951, 1955, 1957, and 1958). She also won the All-American Open five times (1943, 1945, 1953, 1955, and 1957). During her career she amassed eighty-two tournament victories, fifty-one of them as a professional, giving her the record for the most career victories.

Berg joined the U.S. Marines during World War II, where she became a lieutenant and served as a recruiting officer. Fortunately her time away from the professional circuit did not diminish her abilities because she continued to play while in the military. After returning to civilian life in 1946 she won the first U.S. Women's Open.

In 1948 Berg was one of the principal founders and charter members of the Ladies Professional Golf Association (LPGA), which grew out of the Women's Professional Golf Association. The Wilson Golf Company covered the group's administrative costs for the first several years and Fred Corcoran booked its events. Berg served as its first president (from 1950 to 1952) and in 1951 was among the four original inductees into the LPGA Hall of Fame.

Back on the links, Berg won the Eastern Open in 1950, four World Championships (1953, 1954, 1955, and 1957), the American Women's Open (1958 and 1960), and the Titleholders Championship seven times—three as an amateur (1937, 1938, and 1939) and four as a pro (1948, 1953, 1955, and 1957). In 1952 she shot a sixty-four at the Richmond California Open, an LPGA record that she held for twelve years. She won the first Vare Trophy in 1953, with subsequent wins in 1955 and 1956, and was the LPGA's highest-grossing player in 1954, 1955, and 1957. In 1962, at age forty-four, Berg won her last professional victory in the Muskogee (Oklahoma) Civitan Open but continued to play until 1980, when a hip replacement and other health concerns brought her professional playing career to an end.

Berg has been inducted into at least ten halls of fame, including the LPGA and the Professional Golf Association (PGA)/World Golf Hall of Fame. She received the 1963 Bob Jones Award, one of the highest honors bestowed by the United States Golf Association (USGA). In 1976 the Golf Writers Association presented her with the Ben Hogan Award. Her other honors include the Associated Press Woman Athlete of the Year (1938, 1943, and 1955), *Los Angeles Times* Award (1948 and 1955), Serbin Trophy, Babe Zaharias Trophy, Golf Digest Performance Average Award (1955, 1956, and 1957), William Richardson Award, and the Women's Golf Personality of the Year Award (1959). She was also the first woman admitted to the Minnesota Sports Hall of Fame (1958).

Berg was not only a superb golfer but a tireless advocate of the game, traveling around the world and giving more clinics and exhibitions, according to the Wilson Sporting Goods in 1962, than any man or woman in the history of golf. Her engaging personality, red hair and blue eyes, enthusiasm for golf, and diplomatic style made her one of the sport's most successful ambassadors. Since 1946 she has lived in Fort Meyers, Florida, during the winter. At age seventy-three she made a hole-in-one.

★

Berg's writings include *Golf* (1941), with Otis Dypwick, and *Golf Illustrated* (1950). She is the subject of a biography for young readers by James Hahn and Lynn Hahn entitled *Patty! The Sports Career of Patty Berg* (1981). An informative brief biography is posted on the LPGA website, <http.//www.lpga.com>.

MARTIN J. SHERWIN

BERNSTEIN, Kenneth Dale ("Kenny") (*b.* 6 September 1944 in Clovis, New Mexico), businessman and record-setting drag racer who became the first National Hot Rod Association driver to surpass 300 miles per hour in the quarter mile.

Bernstein is one of two sons born to Bert Bernstein, a retailer and B-29 pilot, and Pat Bernstein, a homemaker. He was raised in Lubbock, Texas, where his father managed Levine's Department Store and instilled a positive work ethic and a sense of the value of money in his children.

At age nine, a charismatic Bernstein stepped into his business future by selling merchandise at Levine's. He became a workaholic as a teenager and held many part-time jobs. He also applied this determination to other endeavors.

At Monterey High School in Lubbock, where he graduated in 1963, he was a five-foot, seven-inch, 180-pound linebacker who fearlessly tackled opposing football players.

Bernstein's future also held fast cars. In high school, muscle cars such as Chevrolet 409s and Pontiac 421s lured him. As a hobby, he would purchase them and turn them into hot rods that satisfied his passion for speed. Racing continued to be a big part of Bernstein's life at Arlington (Texas) State College, where he was a student from 1963 to 1966 and majored in business administration. By the late 1960s he was driving top-fuel dragsters and eventually drove for the Anderson brothers, Vance Hunt, Prentiss Cunningham, and the Carroll brothers.

Bernstein left college in 1966 before graduating, to combine real-world business skills with racing as a sideline. He sold women's fashions during the week to finance weekend racing at tracks along his five-state-area sales route. Bernstein started a successful Dallas wrecker service in 1971, also to fund his racing. At about this time he married Donna Easom. They had a son but divorced in 1974.

Unable to challenge top race teams, Bernstein left racing in 1973 intending to never return. He also sold his wrecker service and used the proceeds to open a restaurant in Lubbock with Randy Pumphrey. By 1978 the Chelsea Street Pub had opened restaurants in five states and employed 2,700 people.

In 1978 Gene Beaver asked Bernstein to drive his car at the National Hot Rod Association (NHRA) U.S. Nationals. Surprised, Bernstein agreed and became permanently hooked on racing. In his own Chelsea King funny car, named for his restaurants' distinctive sandwich, Bernstein began to beat top race teams. In 1979, with crew chief Leroy Goldstein, Bernstein won his first national event, the NHRA's Cajun Nationals, and the International Hot Rod Association (IHRA) Winston Championship. More important, that same year, in a savvy business maneuver that illustrated his skill at fostering and maintaining financial support, Bernstein turned a rain-delayed NHRA event into a Budweiser sponsorship beginning in 1980. Subsequently, he sold his chain of restaurants and began racing full time, unveiling the first Budweiser King funny car in 1980.

In 1981, with crew chief Ray Alley, Bernstein won national events in the NHRA, IHRA, and the American Hot Rod Association (AHRA). Dale Armstrong became crew chief for the Budweiser King race team in 1982. With Armstrong's mechanical acumen and a large research and development budget, the team scorched opponents with clutch-management, aerodynamic, and fuel-system innovations. Bernstein won the NHRA Funny Car Division four consecutive times from 1985 to 1988. In the mid-1980s he formed a National Association for Stock Car Automobile Racing (NASCAR) team, a company to distribute onboard computers to gather race car data, a public-relations business, and an Indy Car team.

In 1988 driver Ricky Rudd won Bernstein his first NASCAR race. Two years later, in 1990, Bernstein switched from funny car to top fuel and in 1996 won the NHRA Top Fuel World Championship. In 1994 driver Scott Goodyear won Bernstein his first Indy Car race, making him the first car owner to win races in Indy Car, NASCAR, and NHRA. In 1997 Lee Beard replaced Armstrong as crew chief and helped Bernstein continue his winning streak. On 8 November 2000 Bernstein married longtime girlfriend Sheryl Johnson. The next year, Tim Richards replaced Beard as crew chief.

Bernstein has won six world championships and over seventy national events, mostly in NHRA Top Fuel and Funny Car Divisions. He has also attained many racing firsts. He became the first driver to win national events and set national records in the NHRA, IHRA, and AHRA in one season (1981). In the Bud King funny car, he was the first driver to win the Big Bud Shootout and the NHRA U.S. Nationals in the same weekend (1983). In March 1984 and August 1986, Bernstein became the first funny car driver to exceed 260 miles per hour and 270 miles per hour in the quarter-mile, respectively. He also became the first driver to break the 5.5-second and 5.4-second quarter-mile barriers, in September 1986 and April 1987, respectively. On 20 March 1992 Bernstein drove his top-fuel dragster to 301.7 miles per hour, becoming the first driver to exceed 300 in the quarter-mile, a speed he doubted was possible three years earlier. Bernstein was also first to exceed 310 miles per hour and to win NHRA championships in both Top Fuel and Funny Car divisions. On 8 April 2001, he and his son became the NHRA's first father-and-son pair to win classes at the same national event. Bernstein set a new NHRA top-fuel national record of 4.477 seconds at 330.88 miles per hour on 2 June 2001.

The cars that set such records are astonishing. They usually have supercharged 500-cubic-inch V-8 engines that produce approximately 6,000 horsepower using ninety percent nitromethane fuel. They accelerate from zero to one hundred miles per hour in eight-tenths of a second. During races, Bernstein experiences a force of roughly five Gs during acceleration and negative five Gs when parachutes open to slow his car. These forces have caused stars such as Don Garlits and Joe Amato to experience detached retinas, which forced them to quit driving.

Bernstein is a superb driver whose starting-line presence intimidates opponents. He plans to retire after the 2002 race season, when his son will become driver of the Bud King dragster. "I think there's two things that I want to be remembered for," Bernstein said. "One was obviously the 300 mile-per-hour barrier. . . . I also hope the business side is remembered for us bringing in [Budweiser as a sponsor]."

As in his youth, fast cars and successful sales continue to exhilarate King Kenny.

★

Highlights of Bernstein's career can be found in Tony Sakkis, *Drag Racing Legends* (1996); Robert C. Post, *High Performance: The Culture and Technology of Drag Racing 1950–2000* (2001); and in Terry Spohn, ed., *The Fast Lane: The History of NHRA Drag Racing* (2001). Articles about Bernstein include "Budweiser's Beasts: Strong Brew for the '80s," *Car Craft* (July 1980); "Kenny Bernstein 'Bud' Bound for 1981 Season," *National Dragster* (5 Dec. 1980); Leonard Emanuelson, "Kenny Bernstein's Chelsea King Funny Car," *Popular Hot Rodding Yearbook* (1980); Sam Moses, "Three for the Money," *Sports Illustrated* (18 Apr. 1988); Michael Lutfy, "Innerview: Kenny Bernstein," *Drag Racing Magazine* (June 1989); and Michael Lutfy, "Innerview: Kenny Bernstein," *Drag Racing Magazine* (July 1989). The latter two articles comprise an interesting two-part interview with Bernstein. Videos include *Kenny Bernstein: 20 Years Bud King,* by Diamond P. Sports, and *King of Speed.* Additional highlights and statistics of Bernstein's career can be found at <http://www.kennybernstein.com>.

GARY MASON CHURCH

BERRA, Lawrence Peter ("Yogi") (*b*. 12 May 1925 in St. Louis, Missouri), Hall of Fame baseball player, coach, and manager who epitomized the winning tradition of the New York Yankees from the late 1940s to the mid-1960s.

Berra was the youngest son and one of five children born to Pietro Berra, a factory worker, and Paulina Longoni, a homemaker, who were first-generation immigrants from northern Italy. Joe Garagiola, the future major league catcher and sportscaster, lived across the street from Berra on "the Hill," an Italian neighborhood in St. Louis. Berra quit school after the eighth grade and in 1942 signed with the New York Yankees for a $500 bonus and $90 a month. He was assigned to the Norfolk (Virginia) Tars of the Class B Piedmont League. When he turned eighteen in 1943, he enlisted in the U.S. Navy and participated in the invasion of Normandy at Omaha Beach on D-Day, 6 June 1944. Berra received a distinguished unit citation and two battle stars for his military service. After the war he played for the minor league team in New London, Connecticut, and in 1946 he was promoted to the Newark (New Jersey) Bears of the Triple A International League. He joined the Yankees at the close of the 1946 season and played with them until 1963.

On 26 January 1949 Berra married Carmen Short. Berra and his wife had three sons; the youngest, Dale, enjoyed a ten-year major league career with the Pittsburgh Pirates and New York Yankees. Berra and his wife are longtime residents of Montclair, New Jersey.

Yogi Berra, 1958. © BETTMANN/CORBIS

Berra was initially a platoon catcher and outfielder, but after Casey Stengel joined the Yankees as manager in 1949, Berra blossomed into a star. Former Yankees catcher Bill Dickey took him under his wing, as Berra famously said later, to "learn me all his experience." Under Dickey's tutelage, he became an excellent defensive catcher. In fact, Berra was selected the Most Valuable Player in the American League in 1951, 1954, and 1955 and was a fifteen-time All-Star. He caught an average of 143 of the 154 regular season games for the Yankees from 1950 to 1955, and he called Don Larsen's no-hit perfect game from behind the plate in game five of the 1956 World Series—twenty-seven consecutive outs—against the Brooklyn Dodgers. He played 148 consecutive games without an error between July 1957 and May 1959. He was the only player who remained on the Yankees roster during Stengel's entire tenure as manager (1949 to 1960). Stengel referred to Berra as "my assistant manager," declared that except for Joe DiMaggio he was "the greatest player I ever had to manage," and recalled in his autobiography that Berra "has got a sports mind. And he did a beautiful job for me for many years."

Berra was also a formidable batter. He hit the first pinch-hit homer in World Series history in 1947. Though a notorious "bad ball" hitter, he was exceptionally difficult to strike out. In 1950, for example, he struck out only twelve times in 597 at-bats, and he struck out only 414 times in over 7,500 at-bats during his career. He hit thirty home runs in 1952, the major league record for catchers at the time. His best year was probably 1956, when he hit .298 with 30 home runs and 105 runs batted in (RBI) in 140 games. In 1961, Berra's last constructive season as a player, he hit twenty-two home runs for the team that set a major league record for team home runs in a season (240). By 1963 Berra was a part-time player and first-base coach. Though he played four games with the New York Mets in 1965, he effectively retired as a player after the 1963 season with 358 career home runs, a .285 career batting average, and 1,430 career RBI. He held records for most World Series played (fourteen), most Series games (seventy-five), most Series games by a catcher (sixty-three), most Series at-bats (259), most Series hits (seventy-one), most times on a world championship team (ten), and he held several Series fielding records. In addition, he hit twelve Series home runs.

He was also a successful major league manager, winning pennants with both the Yankees in the American League (1964) and the Mets in the National League (1973). "The first time I managed in the major leagues was in 1964," he reminisced. "I took a cut in pay to get the job. I would do it again." Though the Yankees finished in first place, Berra was fired after they lost to St. Louis in the World Series. In a public relations coup, he was hired as a coach by the New York Mets in 1965 when Stengel was still manager and succeeded Gil Hodges as manager of the Mets in 1972. He led the "Miracle" Mets in 1973 from last place the year before to the National League pennant. Berra was again fired after the 1975 season. He returned to the Yankees as a coach from 1976 through 1978, and the team won the pennant all three years. Though he managed the Yankees in 1984 to a third-place finish, he was fired early in the 1985 season. He joined the Houston Astros as a coach in 1986 and retired after the 1989 season but remained as an adviser to the team until 1992.

Berra was elected to the Baseball Hall of Fame in January 1972 with over 85 percent of the votes of the Baseball Writers of America. "Getting into the Hall of Fame was my biggest thrill," he recalled in his autobiography. "Second? I guess the perfect game." The Yankees retired his uniform number 8 later that summer and dedicated a plaque to him in center field of Yankee Stadium in 1988. The late commissioner of baseball, A. Bartlett Giamatti, once praised him: "Talking with Yogi Berra about baseball is like talking with Homer about the Gods." Though famous for his "Yogi-isms" (for example, "No one goes there anymore; it's too crowded," "It ain't over 'til it's over,"

"Never answer an anonymous letter," and "When you come to a fork in the road, take it"), Berra was an astute teacher of the game and regarded Don Mattingly, the Yankee first-baseman and captain, as his favorite player to manage.

★

While still an active player, Berra collaborated with Ed Fitzgerald on *Yogi: The Autobiography of a Professional Baseball Player* (1961). After his retirement from active coaching, Berra collaborated with Tom Horton on a second autobiography, *Yogi: It Ain't Over* (1989). Martin Appel, *Yogi Berra* (1992), is an illustrated, straightforward account of Berra's life for young adult readers. See also Joseph J. Bannan, et al., eds., *Yogi Berra: An American Original* (1998).

GARY SCHARNHORST

BERRY, Raymond Emmett (*b.* 27 February 1993 in Corpus Christi, Texas), football player who raised catching a football to nearly an art form, his scientific approach enabled him to retire from the Baltimore Colts as the National Football League's (NFL) all-time leader in pass receptions.

Berry was one of two children born to Mark Raymond Berry, a teacher and football coach, and Bess Ermine

Raymond Berry, 1964. ASSOCIATED PRESS AP

Hudgins, a homemaker. Berry played football for his father at Paris High School in Paris, Texas, but Berry was not a first-string player until his senior year. After graduation from high school in 1950, the 153-pound Berry enrolled as a two-way end at Schreiner Institute, a junior college in Kerrville, Texas. At Schreiner, he began to develop as a receiver—thirty-two catches for eight touchdowns in his only year there. After Schreiner, Berry enrolled at Southern Methodist University (SMU) on a football scholarship in 1951. At SMU, Berry, who was six foot, one inch tall, and never weighed more than 180 pounds, was known as much for his defensive as offensive work. Although his final two seasons at SMU saw Berry catch only twenty-eight passes and score just one touchdown, he was co-captain as a senior.

Because of the year he spent at Schreiner, Berry was eligible as an NFL "future" draft pick as a junior at SMU; he was taken in the twentieth round by the Baltimore Colts. When Berry reported to the Colts training camp in 1956, he was not assured of making the team. Berry and another unheralded rookie, Johnny Unitas (who had been cut by the Pittsburgh Steelers in training camp the year before) stayed after practice and worked together. Very soon the Unitas-to-Berry pass/catch combination would strike fear in the heart of many NFL defenders. Colts lineman Gino Marchetti said, "What allowed Raymond to make the team was the fact that we didn't have many good offensive ends. He didn't look like a seven-alarm fire himself, but he hustled all the time." Berry's hustle also caught the eye of Colts coach Weeb Ewbank.

Berry's long hours after practice working with Unitas paid off. By 1957 both receiver and quarterback were established as vital parts of the Colts' offense. Berry flourished in 1958 when he led the NFL in receptions, a feat he repeated in 1959 and 1960, and the Colts won the championship in both 1958 and 1959. The 1958 NFL championship game against the New York Giants, a sudden-death overtime game (the first in championship game history) is frequently called "The Greatest Game Ever Played." The 23–17 Colts victory, which was televised coast-to coast, is credited with lighting the fuse that caused the professional football explosion in the 1960s and beyond. Berry could not have had a bigger game. He put the Colts up 14–3 with an early 15-yard touchdown catch, but the Giants were ahead 17–14 with 2 minutes to play. With the ball 79 yards from the end zone—Berry said, "It looked like seventy-nine miles"—Berry and Unitas went to work. Three times on the critical drive, Unitas looked for Berry. Three times Berry got free of double coverage and made crucial catches, tacking on valuable additional yardage when needed—gains of twenty-five, fifteen, and twenty-two yards. The third catch was carried to the thirteen-yard line as time was ticking down, and Steve Myra kicked the tying field goal as time ran out. In overtime, it was Unitas to Berry again. Berry made a critical twenty-yard catch-and-run on a third-and-fifteen situation at the Colts' thirty-seven–yard line. And then another, a twelve-yard gain that carried to the Giants' eight-yard line and all but assured the victory. Alan Ameche scored the title-winning touchdown two plays later. For the day, Berry made 12 catches for 178 yards and 1 touchdown.

Berry further refined his scientific approach to receiving by having his wife (Sally Anne Crook, whom he married on 20 August 1960; they had three children) throw to him. The couple found a nearby park with a soccer goal that served as a backstop. This was important, because Berry never wanted easy throws to catch—he wanted errant throws that he had to leap for, dive for, dig for, to extend himself. Sally, lacking football experience and skill, dutifully provided these kinds of throws. Berry also watched literally miles of film, studying opposition defenses and defensive personnel.

A certain mythology surrounded Berry, especially after he reached stardom in the NFL. Supposedly he wore a back brace, had one leg shorter than the other, was extremely slow, and had impaired vision. Though somewhat limited physically, Berry was no near invalid. He was, however, one of the first NFL players to wear contact lenses on the field. When the Colts played late-season games on the West Coast, as they did each year, Berry fashioned a pair of "sunglasses"—the California sun hit at an annoying angle late in the game—from a pair of underwater goggles with tinted lenses.

Berry retired from the Colts after the 1967 season with 631 catches for 9,275 yards (both NFL career records) and became an assistant coach with the Dallas Cowboys. While working with Cowboy receivers in training camp, Berry felt something was amiss. As he ran a sideline pattern, instead of catching the ball at the sideline just before going out of bounds, he was going out of bounds just before the catch. Berry questioned the width of the field but was told, "It has to be right, we've been playing on it for years." However, when the field was measured it was a foot short of regulation.

Berry took over as head coach of the New England Patriots eight games into the 1984 season. In 1985, with an 11–5 record, Berry had the Patriots in contention for a spot in the Super Bowl. With three victories away from their home field, the underdog, wild-card Patriots gained a berth in Super Bowl XX. Unfortunately, though they scored first, they were no match for the Chicago Bears, who won 46–10. Berry's success as head coach somewhat surprised even his closest friends and teammates, many of whom thought he was simply "too nice a guy" to enforce the discipline needed for a winning team. But as he did for much of his life as a player, Berry proved the doubters wrong. He ended

his NFL head coaching career in 1989 with a 51–41 record. His last coaching stint was as an assistant with the Denver Broncos in 1992. Berry and his wife settled in Golden, Colorado, where Berry continues to work on special projects, including those with youth ministries.

Berry was one of those rare athletes, like Michael Jordan and Jim Brown, who had to be seen in person to be believed. There was something about Berry's genius—the concentration and purpose—that did not come through on television. One example of Berry's attention to detail is the way he practiced falling on fumbles. Although he perfected the skill, it was never really necessary. Only once in his 13-year career did Berry fumble away any of his 631 catches. His hands, generally considered the game's best, were strengthened by daily exercises with Silly Putty.

Berry reportedly had "by his own count, eighty-eight different moves to get past a defender," but he denied this by saying, "I never counted the moves; I don't see how anyone could have many." Such myths were part of the Berry mystique. According to former Cowboy coach Tom Landry, Berry "perfected his moves to the extent that man-to-man coverage wasn't effective. He brought about what became 'zone' coverage." In 1982 Berry wrote *Complete Guide for Pass Receivers,* not to make money, but to share his vast knowledge and insight with young, aspiring pass-catchers.

Through dedication and innovation, Berry took a modest natural ability and turned it into a record-setting career. He was not imposing physically and did not have the blazing speed that many great offensive ends of his era had. In fact, he remained so unassuming in appearance throughout his life that he once stumped the panel of the television show *What's My Line?* because they could not believe he was a football player. What Berry did have was a desire to succeed and the knowledge and inquisitiveness to make it happen. Berry once summed himself up by saying, "My whole life and ambition could be summarized in one sentence—I just had to play football."

★

There is no biography of Berry. His life and career are discussed in Berry Stainback, *The Specialist in Pro Football* (1966); Dave Klein, *The Game of Their Lives* (1976); and George Allen and Ben Olan, *Pro Football's 100 Greatest Players* (1982).

Jim Campbell

BETZ, Pauline May (*b.* 6 August 1919 in Dayton, Ohio), renowned tennis star during World War II who won the U.S. Championship in 1942, 1943, 1944, and 1946 and the 1946 Wimbledon Championship.

Betz's family moved from Dayton to Los Angeles when she was eight years old, and she grew up in a climate that

Pauline Betz. AP/WIDE WORLD PHOTOS

enabled her to play sports year-round. It was her mother, a high school physical education teacher, who introduced her to the game of tennis. An energetic tomboy and athlete, Betz attended championship matches in California and later claimed that the American tennis great Don Budge inspired her backhand. At the age of fifteen she began formal tennis lessons; however, due to the family's limited financial resources, Betz was not able to play East Coast tennis matches such as the National Junior Championships. She resigned herself to playing, and often winning, statewide tournaments.

In 1939 Betz received a tennis scholarship to Rollins College in Florida, where she studied economics. There, her tennis career ascended when she made it to the finals in the 1941 U.S. Lawn Tennis Association (USLTA) Championships, losing the match to Sarah Palfrey Cooke. While still an undergraduate, Betz won her first U.S. Championship (now called the U.S. Open) singles title at Forest Hills, New York, defeating Louise Brough in 1942. She repeated her performance in 1943, once again overcoming Brough. That same year Betz began graduate school at Columbia University, balancing her tennis career with her studies.

In 1944 Betz defeated Margaret Osborne for her third U.S. Championship singles title. Although Betz's streak came to an end 2 September 1945, when she lost in three

sets to Cooke, she reclaimed the title of National Champion in 1946 when she defeated Patricia Canning. From 1942 to 1945 Betz, along with her tennis partner Doris Hart, also made it to the finals of the U.S. Championship women's doubles, each time defeated by the team of Brough and Osborne.

During World War II only the United States continued top-level competitive play. With the enlistment of many male tennis players into the armed forces, women players took center court. Betz was one of a host of female players who gained international recognition for their game. In 1946 she was a member of the Wightman Cup team that traveled to England for championship play, along with Brough, Osborne, and Hart. Soon deemed the "Betz club" because of Betz's outstanding performances (she won both her singles and doubles championships), the Wightman team defeated Great Britain by a score of 7–0. That same year, at the age of twenty-six, Betz won the prestigious All England Club singles championship at Wimbledon, again beating Brough. But the formidable team of Brough and Osborne defeated Betz and Hart in the final round of the Wimbledon women's doubles.

After winning another U.S. Championship in 1946, Betz considered ending her amateur status and turning professional. Unfortunately, the decision was made for her when the USLTA got word that Betz and Cooke were considering organizing a professional tour for themselves. In 1947 the association suspended both Betz and Cooke from amateur play, forcing them to turn professional. The suspension highlighted a double standard for women's tennis: when Don Budge decided to turn professional in 1938, he was allowed to finish the season by competing both at Wimbledon and in the Davis Cup matches.

Although Betz was disappointed, she did not challenge the USLTA's decision. Instead, she and Cooke embarked on a professional tour in 1947, only the fourth professional tour ever for women. Driving from city to city on the grueling nonstop tour, Betz and Cooke dressed up and staged skits to teach college and high school level players. Betz estimated that they made approximately $10,000 on their one-year tour, a vast improvement from the average $12 a day on the amateur route. From 1947 to 1951 Betz toured America and Europe with well-known tennis stars such as Budge, Bobby Riggs, Jack Kramer, Pancho Segura, and Gertrude "Gussy" Moran.

In 1950 Betz married Bob Addie, a sportswriter for the *Washington Post*. Raising their five children left Betz little time for professional tennis, although she did consider returning to Wimbledon in 1968. She wrote three books on the sport—*Wings on My Tennis Shoes* (1949), *Tennis Is Fun*, and *Tennis for Everyone* (1966)—and started her own tennis club in Stuart, Florida. Later in her career Betz taught tennis at the Cabin John Indoor Tennis Courts in Bethesda, Maryland. In 1965 she was inducted into the International Tennis Hall of Fame.

Betz, along with the many great women players of the period, inspired a generation of up-and-coming female players. Her stunning backhand, her amazing agility, and her quick ground strokes were admired by her fans and peers alike. Out of thirty-seven matches played at Forest Hills, Betz won thirty-three. She held nineteen U.S. singles titles and, along with Billie Jean King, was one of the only women to win two triple sweeps at the Indoor Championship, winning singles, doubles, and mixed doubles (1941 and 1943). In 1946, the year she won her Wimbledon championship, Betz appeared on the cover of *Time,* having become an American tennis sensation.

Betz was one of the women who kept tennis alive during World War II, when sports became a much-needed diversion for Americans and male athletes were scarce. Along with the other members of the Wightman team, she demonstrated the talent of American women athletes. Her strong will and determination marked her as one of the sport's greatest female athletes. Although her competitive career spanned only a few years, Betz's character, athletic ability, and speed on the court assured her a place in tennis history.

★

There is no full-length biography on Betz, but she is often included in general surveys of tennis history. Owen Davidson and C. M. Jones, *Great Women Tennis Players* (1971), contains a chapter that serves as a collective biography of Betz, Osborne, Brough, and Hart, a grouping that is often used to exemplify the women players of the World War II period. Angela Lumpkin, *Women's Tennis: A Historical Documentary of the Players and Their Game* (1981), and Billie Jean King, *We Have Come a Long Way: The Story of Women's Tennis* (1988), offer some of the best biographical information on Betz. Stan Hart, *Once a Champion: Legendary Tennis Stars Revisited* (1985), has an account of the author's tennis match with Betz in her later years.

STEFANIE DECKER

BING, David ("Dave") (*b.* 29 November 1943 in Washington, D.C.), professional basketball player, voted one of the fifty best players in National Basketball Association (NBA) history, who became a successful Detroit businessman after his retirement.

The son of Hasker Bing, a bricklayer, and Juanita Bing, a domestic, Bing accidentally damaged his left eye at age five, leaving him with permanently blurred vision in that eye. He gained early business experience helping his father build apartment houses and churches in Washington's poorer neighborhoods.

Dave Bing. AP/WIDE WORLD PHOTOS

Initially shunned by older boys in playground basketball, Bing grew into a slender, powerful, six-foot, three-inch forward at Spingarn High School under the tutelage of famed coach William Roundtree. After graduating from high school, and influenced by the charismatic football player Ernie Davis from Syracuse University, Bing chose to attend Syracuse, then a lesser collegiate basketball power. With Bing on the team, however, the Orangemen soared. He averaged 24.6 points a game and thrilled spectators with his slashing, graceful drives to the basket and unerring jump shots. Bing earned first-team All-America honors in his senior year and graduated with a degree in economics. While still in college he married his high school sweetheart, Aaris. The couple had three daughters, but later divorced.

Bing was the second overall choice in the 1966 NBA draft, signing a $15,000 first-year contract with the Detroit Pistons. More than earning his money, he averaged just over twenty points a game and was named the NBA's Rookie of the Year. In his sophomore season, Bing improved his scoring average to 27.1, becoming the first guard to notch top-scoring honors in twenty years. For the 1969 season Bing leveraged an offer from the upstart American Basketball Association to raise his Pistons contract to $450,000 for three years.

Bing's natural leadership was admired by his teammates, and in 1971 he was named team captain. That season he averaged twenty-seven points a game with a career high 2,213 points. So impressive were his accomplishments that former player and then-Pistons scout Earl Lloyd told *Sport* magazine: "Maybe some other player does this better, and another player does that better. [But] nobody does as much as Dave does." Teammate Otto Moore concurred, adding, "He can run, dribble, shoot, do everything."

Bing's high-flying career was almost cut short at the beginning of the next season when Happy Hairston of the Los Angeles Lakers inadvertently poked a finger into Bing's right eye. Although he was in intense pain, Bing thought the injury was minor until he awoke a few days later to find his vision almost gone. The doctors discovered a detached retina, which required surgery and kept him on the sidelines for three months. Determined to recover completely, Bing practiced free throws during his convalescence. His diligence paid off; in forty-five games that season, he averaged 22.6 points with a much higher free-throw percentage and improved defensive skills. His greatest skill was disrupting defenses with leaping drives to the basket followed by acrobatic layups or deft passes to open teammates. His steady, intelligent play secured his place on seven All-Star teams.

Even Bing's talents could not lift the struggling Pistons, however. The team made the playoffs only twice during his nine-year tenure; in the 1973–1974 season, they were ousted in the second round by the Chicago Bulls, and the following year they were finished in the first round by the Seattle Supersonics. Frustrated by the team's mediocrity, Bing requested a trade that sent him home to the Washington Bullets for the 1975–1976 season. Although Bing earned Most Valuable Player (MVP) honors in the 1976 NBA All-Star game, his accomplishments with the Bullets were spotty, with his vision becoming an increasing problem. When his scoring average dropped to ten points a game, the team released him after the 1976 season. He rebounded for one last year with the Boston Celtics, during which he averaged 13.6 points a game. He retired at the end of the season with a lifetime scoring average of 20.3 points per game, a record that earned him a selection as one of the fifty best players in NBA history in 1996. His jersey number, 21, was retired by the Pistons.

After retiring, Bing put his drive and leadership to work in the business world. Because he had used his off-seasons learning the ropes at local banks, the Chrysler Corporation, and the Paragon Steel Company, he began his second career with valuable business experience and contacts. Paragon Steel offered him a training position, which allowed him to learn the business from the ground up. Branching out on his own, he used his own capital and a line of credit from banks to establish Bing Steel Company.

Despite his initial discouragement when most clients either talked only basketball or canceled contracts without notice, Bing persevered, taking no salary for six months. His first big order came from General Motor's Fisher Body Plant, and within a few years Bing Steel had found a market finishing steel parts for automobiles. During the mid-1980s he supplemented his income by working as a television commentator for the Pistons. In 1984 he was named National Minority Small Businessperson of the Year.

Using tough personnel methods (trainees were fired for being late four times in the first three months) and promises of equity to managers who stayed more than three years, Bing Steel rose to $61 million in sales by 1990, placing it tenth on the Black Enterprise list of top black-owned companies. In 1991 Bing expanded his empire, acquiring Superb Manufacturing Company ($28.4 million in sales in 1990) and Heritage ($3.6 million). Other acquisitions followed. By 2000 Bing's nine corporations netted $7 million in profits with $300 million in sales. The companies employ 1,500 people, about 78 percent of whom are African-American.

Although Bing still works about sixty hours a week, he devotes a quarter of them to a variety of charities, some of which derive from his businesses. He established an employee training center for minorities in 1999, for example, and located his plants in inner-city Detroit to provide employment opportunities for the city's residents. In 1998 Bing established a joint venture to produce car parts with the Lear Company that he plans to expand into Mexico and South America. He also serves on Standard Federal Bank's board of directors.

★

Biographical material on Bing may be found in several articles, including Ronald C. Modra, "Life Lessons from a Man of Steel," *Sports Illustrated* (19 Aug. 1991), and Tomas Kellner, "Rebound Man," *Forbes* (18 Sept. 2000).

GRAHAM RUSSELL HODGES

BIONDI, Matt(hew) (*b.* 8 October 1965 in Moraga, California), swimmer who won eleven Olympic medals, including eight gold, and who is considered one of America's greatest Olympians and the best male freestyle swimmer ever.

Biondi grew up in an athletic household in southern California, the son of Nicolas Biondi, an ex-football player and coach, and Lucille Biondi. The middle of three children, he began swimming at age five for recreation but waited another ten years before swimming competitively at Campolindo High School in Moraga.

Biondi's feel for the water was apparent at an early age. He was just ten when Stuart Kahn, coach of the Moraga Valley summer team, told the audience at an awards banquet that Biondi was as good as John Naber, an Olympic

Matt Biondi after winning his fourth Olympic gold medal at the 1988 Olympics in Seoul. ASSOCIATED PRESS
AP

medalist who won four golds and a silver at the 1976 Summer Olympics in Montreal. "I had a pretty good view of what the perfect stroke looked like," Kahn said later. "At age ten, Matt was better technically than any college swimmer."

Biondi's parents were careful to help him keep swimming in perspective. They wanted him to enjoy a normal childhood, free from competitive pressures and mindful of good sportsmanship. He recalled how his mother scolded him for throwing his racket in the middle of a tennis match: "She came through the fence, grabbed me by the ear right in the middle of the game and took me home. She never said anything." In addition to tennis, swimming, and water polo, Biondi played basketball and soccer, sang in the choir, and took piano lessons.

Yet Biondi understood he had a natural talent. "I knew. When I swam, I knew there was something special about me in the water, something I hadn't experienced in those other disciplines." When Biondi turned to competitive swimming in high school, he was talented but still years away from the form that would earn him a place in swimming history. He was so tall and lanky that his classmates called him "Spiderman." With his body still growing dramatically (at sixteen he was six feet, one inch tall and weighed 130 pounds), Biondi worked hard to perfect his technique. "I took practice very seriously. I was always conscious in practice—every lap, every stroke I was thinking about what I was doing and how I could make it better."

Stuart Kahn worked with Biondi to use his long body as an advantage, with his kick as a special weapon. As his body matured he eventually reached six feet, seven inches

and 210 pounds, with a wingspan of nearly seven feet. Biondi was able to combine length and strength with finesse and technique to revolutionize freestyle swimming.

When Biondi entered the University of California, Berkeley, in the fall of 1983, he was nearly complete as a swimmer. Berkeley swimming coach Nort Thornton remembers the first time he saw Biondi swim in high school: "I thought he had fins on." Thornton felt he needed only to help fine-tune Biondi's already prodigious technique.

At the 1984 Olympic trials, however, Biondi was still largely unknown, ranked fiftieth in the country in the 50-meter freestyle. To the surprise of the crowd, he finished fourth and earned a spot on the 4 x 100-meter relay. Veteran American swimmer and then–world record holder Rowdy Gaines good-naturedly dubbed Biondi "Matt who?" Together they would triumph at the Summer Olympics in Los Angeles. As Biondi later recalled, "I won a gold medal even though no one had heard of me. Mostly I'd been a water polo player in high school."

But Biondi could not keep his name out of the headlines much longer. He won a record seven medals at the 1986 World Championships, including three golds. Entering the 1988 Olympic Games in Seoul, South Korea, Biondi was at the top of his form, holding the ten fastest times ever in the 100-meter freestyle. He was scheduled to swim seven events—four individual and three relays. The pressure was on Biondi to match Mark Spitz's feat of seven gold medals at the 1972 Olympics in Munich, Germany, but Biondi himself was skeptical.

In his first event, the 200-meter freestyle, Biondi took bronze, losing out to a new world record, but beating the previous record holder. Biondi felt it was a very good performance in his weakest event, though he was angered by the media coverage, which stressed that he would "fail" to match Spitz's record of seven golds.

Biondi took silver in his second competition, the 100-meter butterfly, where he was out-touched at the wall by one one-hundredth of a second. Biondi spoke of his disappointment: "I had been winning the race easily the whole way. It's been eating me up." He translated that frustration into his swimming, reeling off five consecutive gold medals to close the games: in the 4 × 200-meter freestyle relay, the 100-meter freestyle, the 4 × 100-meter freestyle relay, the 50-meter freestyle, and the medley relay. In the end, he reached his goal of seven Olympic medals—five gold, one silver, and one bronze.

Despite his success, the pressure of the spotlight increasingly wore on Biondi, and he sought other outlets beyond swimming. In 1989, building on a lifelong interest in marine biology, he cofounded the Delphys Foundation, a nonprofit organization that supports marine mammal research and education. He kept a diary for *Sports Illustrated* at the 1988 Olympics in which he confided: "If things work out here, and I end up becoming some kind of Olympic star, I'd like to use that platform to talk about how we're destroying our oceans and environment." He made good on that promise, and ultimately graduated from Berkeley with a degree in natural resource conservation.

After the 1992 Olympics, Biondi retired from competitive swimming. He had won another three medals for a total of eleven, but was ready to get on with the rest of his life. In 1995 he married Kirsten Metzger, a former Berkeley swimmer, and embarked on a tour of public appearances and lectures. He found it lucrative but felt that his life "was getting too soft." The couple moved to Portland, Oregon, and Biondi enrolled in a master's degree program in education at Lewis and Clark College. He completed the degree and began teaching social studies in Oregon schools. Their son was born in 1999.

Biondi combined talent and technique to become the greatest freestyle swimmer of all time. The American records he set in the 100- and 200-meter freestyle in 1988 still stood at the end of the twentieth century. Yet he shunned the spotlight and always sought balance in his life. He remains critical of intensive youth swimming programs. "At a meet in Salinas," Biondi recounted for *Life* in 1988, "a man came up to me and said, 'My boy holds a 1,000 yard free-style record for eight-year-olds.' Instead of pounding 15,000 meters a day—which is as much as I swim—that kid should be exploring what's out there. Sure he'll be a national record holder, but he'll burn out. What is that going to teach him?"

★

There is no formal biography of Biondi, nor is there much in the way of a literature of swimming, especially in comparison to track and field or cycling. The best place to read more about Biondi is in the back issues of *Sports Illustrated,* where he and his exploits were profiled on a regular basis between 1985 and 1992.

TIMOTHY KRINGEN

BIRD, Larry Joe (*b.* 7 December 1956 in West Baden, Indiana), college and professional basketball player whose dedication and superlative offensive and defensive skills revitalized professional basketball in the 1980s.

Bird was the fourth of six children of Claude Joseph ("Joe") Bird and Georgia Kerns Bird. His father worked at the Kimball piano factory, while his mother worked as a waitress and cook. The family moved often between West Baden Springs, Indiana, and French Lick, a mile away.

In 1971 Bird entered Springs Valley High School in French Lick, where he played football and made the "B" basketball team. The coach, Jim Jones, taught Bird the basic fundamentals of the game, including how to play left-handed. Bird did not play much basketball his freshman

Larry Bird. AP/WIDE WORLD PHOTOS

year but excelled in baseball as a pitcher and shortstop. Bird missed almost his entire sophomore basketball season because of a broken ankle, which he suffered going for a rebound. Although his leg was in a cast and he was on crutches, he continued to practice, turning his attention to passing, which he soon perfected. In his junior year Bird made the varsity team and began his career as a forward. At the sectionals that year, he sank two foul shots, winning the game almost single-handedly. He had improved his performance at the foul line by shooting 500 free throws every morning before school. By his senior year Bird was six feet, six inches tall and an ambidextrous ball handler. He averaged 31 points, 21 rebounds, and 4 assists per game. He was recruited by colleges from across the nation, but wanting to stay close to home, he accepted a scholarship to Indiana University in Bloomington, whose team was coached by the legendary Bobby Knight. After entering Indiana in the fall of 1974, Bird soon discovered that a school with over 33,000 students was too big for his tastes. He never made it to the official opening of practice. Without saying a word to anyone, he hitchhiked back to French Lick after only twenty-four days at Indiana.

Bird's mother had divorced his father because of his heavy drinking, and when he came back to French Lick, Bird moved in with his grandmother, Lizzie Kerns. He enrolled in Northwood Institute, a junior college in West Baden, but quit after two weeks because of a lack of competition on the basketball team. He decided to work for a year before returning to school and got a job with the French Lick street department picking up trash, mowing grass, removing snow, and fixing roads. He loved the work.

Bill Hodges, a basketball scout from Indiana State University, asked Bird to come to Terre Haute to practice. Larry liked the school and the basketball coach, Bob King, and enrolled in 1975. Although he had to sit out a year due to rules governing the transfer of athletes from one school to another, he continued to practice. On 8 November 1975, shortly after entering Indiana State, Bird married Janet Condra, a girl he had known since first grade. The marriage was an unhappy one, and the couple divorced less than a year later. A brief reconciliation produced a daughter, born in 1977. Bird's greatest personal tragedy occurred in February 1975, when his father, driven by alcoholism and despair because he could not make child support payments, committed suicide. To escape depression, Bird dedicated himself even more intensely to the game of basketball.

In his sophomore year Bird, a six-foot, nine-inch, 220-pound forward, led the Indiana State Sycamores to a 25–3 record and was named third-team All-America. He was eligible for the National Basketball Association (NBA) draft in his junior year but turned down an offer by the Indiana Pacers because he loved playing college ball. At the season's

end, he was named first-team All-America. In Bird's senior year, Indiana State won thirty-three straight games and played in the National Collegiate Athletic Association (NCAA) tournament. In the championship game, the Michigan State Spartans, spearheaded by the brilliant play of Earvin ("Magic") Johnson, defeated the Sycamores 75–64 and kept Bird to just nineteen points. Bird finished his college career as College Player of the Year, winning the John Wooden Award, making first-team All-America, and earning the title of fifth all-time leading NCAA scorer. In June 1979 he received a B.S. in physical education, the first member of his family to earn a college degree.

On 8 June 1979 Bird signed a five-year, $3.25 million contract with the Boston Celtics, making him the highest paid rookie in the history of team sports. He looked forward to playing for player-coach Dave Cowans, but unfamiliar with urban settings, he kept getting lost in Boston, which resulted in his famous remark to the press, "I guess I'm still a hick from French Lick." By the end of his rookie year, the "hick" power forward, under new coach Bill Fitch, had helped the Celtics to a 61–21 record. The 32-win improvement from the year before, when the team was 29–53, was the biggest single-season turnaround in NBA history. Bird was named NBA Rookie of the Year and selected to play in the All-Star game, in which he hit the first three-pointer in the history of the game. In his second season, with the help of new teammates Robert Parish and Kevin McHale, Bird led Boston to the NBA championship, where they defeated Houston in the final.

In 1983 Bill Fitch was replaced by K. C. Jones, a coach who allowed his players freedom to improvise and who organized Bird, Parish, and McHale into what was arguably the greatest frontcourt in the history of the NBA. In the 1983–1984 season the Celtics beat the Los Angeles Lakers for the NBA championship. Bird won both the series' and the regular season's Most Valuable Player (MVP) award and led the NBA in free-throw shooting percentage. In 1984 he re-signed with the Celtics for seven years and $12.6 million, then the highest yearly contract in the NBA. The following season Bird scored sixty points in a game against the Atlanta Hawks, and although the Celtics lost the NBA championship final to the Lakers, Bird was named an NBA All-Star and received the MVP award for the second year in a row.

In 1985–1986 Bird led the league in free throws with an 89.6 percentage while suffering severe back pain. With newly acquired backup center Bill Walton, he helped the Celtics win a third NBA championship, beating Houston in the final. When Bird won the MVP award, he joined Bill Russell and Wilt Chamberlain as the only players to ever receive the award three years in a row. The following season, still in great pain, Bird was again an All-Star and won the NBA long-distance shoot-out contest, a feat he would accomplish two more times in his career. The Celtics lost the 1987 championship to the Lakers, but it was the Eastern Conference finals against Detroit that provided Bird with the most memorable moment of his career. With five seconds left in the game, he made a miraculous steal of Isiah Thomas's inbound pass to give Boston a win in game five of the playoff series.

By 1988 Bird's body showed the wear and tear from so many years of pounding under the boards. After playing six games he had surgery for bone spurs in both feet and could not return to finish the season. Although still experiencing back pain in 1989, he achieved his 5,000th career assist on 5 November. Twenty-five days later he scored his 20,000th career point against the Washington Bullets. During the season he sank seventy-one consecutive free throws, the third best record in NBA history. In June 1991 Bird had surgery on a swollen disc but continued to have back pain. In the 1991–1992 season he played just forty-five games but showed his old form against the Portland Trailblazers in a March contest by scoring forty-nine points, including a three-point goal in the last two seconds that tied the game and led to a Celtic win in double overtime. That summer, Bird served as cocaptain of the original "Dream Team" that won the gold medal at the 1992 Olympics in Barcelona, Spain. He announced his retirement shortly afterward.

Between 1992 and 1997 Bird was a special assistant and consultant to the Celtics but became bored with the job. In May 1997 he was named head coach of the Indiana Pacers. In his first year Bird led the team to a franchise record of fifty-eight victories and was named the NBA Coach of the Year. The Pacers went to the Eastern Conference finals each year he was coach and in 2000 faced Los Angeles in the NBA championship final. Indiana lost in six games, and after the season ended, Bird stepped down as coach.

Bird owns a home in Naples, Florida, and one in French Lick. He lives with his wife, Dinah (Mattingly), whom he married on 30 September 1989, and their two adopted children. He owns a hotel and restaurant in Terre Haute, Larry Bird's Home Court Hotel, and a Ford dealership in Martinsville, Indiana. Bird's statistics are impressive. In his thirteen years and 897 games in the NBA, he had a total of 8,974 rebounds (10.0 average), 5,695 assists (6.3 average), 3,960 free throws (.886 percent average), 1,556 steals, and 21,791 points. He was named an NBA All-Star twelve times. His one-on-one duels with Dominique Wilkins of the Atlanta Hawks, Julius ("Dr. J") Erving of the Philadelphia 76ers, and Magic Johnson of the Los Angeles Lakers helped to make professional basketball a major televised attraction. Bird's concentration on fundamentals and his dedication to hard work inspired countless future players. Above all, he was devoted to the notion of team: "I've never felt the greater purpose of my playing well is to break personal records, but it *is* to help my team win games." Bird was inducted into the Basketball Hall of Fame in 1998.

★

Bird's autobiography with Bob Ryan, *Drive: The Story of My Life* (1989), contains informative items about his childhood days and family life. Lee Daniel Levine, *Bird: The Making of an American Sports Legend* (1988), is a somewhat adulatory but interesting summary of Bird's life and career. Peter May, *The Big Three* (1993), gives autobiographical and career details for Bird, Robert Parish, and Kevin McHale and describes the teamwork they established to create a Celtic dynasty.

JOHN J. BYRNE

BLAIK, Earl Henry ("Red") (*b.* 15 February 1897 in Detroit, Michigan; *d.* 6 May 1989 in Colorado Springs, Colorado), college football coach responsible for bringing the U.S. Military Academy into athletic prominence.

Blaik was one of three children of William Douglas Blaik, a blacksmith and carriage maker who later shifted his interests to real estate development, and Margaret Jane Purcell, a homemaker. When Blaik was four, the family relocated to Dayton, Ohio.

Blaik began his athletic career at Dayton's Steele High School, where he played football and basketball and occasionally appeared in drama productions. He was an indifferent student but did well enough to get by. Following his graduation in 1914, Blaik enrolled in the pre-law program at Miami University in Oxford, Ohio. There he became president of the student body and earned letters in baseball and football. During his junior and senior years, the Miami football team went undefeated, winning two Ohio Conference championships and outscoring their opponents 441–12.

After receiving a B.A. degree from Miami in 1918 and with the United States embroiled in World War I, Blaik won an appointment to the U.S. Military Academy in West Point, New York. He continued to play sports, winning third-team All-America honors from Walter Camp for his work on the gridiron and the Army Athletic Association's Saber Award as the best athlete in his class. Due to wartime exigencies, Blaik's class was pushed through West Point in only two years. He was sent to Fort Riley, Kansas, for cavalry training and in 1921 joined the Eighth Cavalry Regiment at Fort Bliss, Texas, as a first lieutenant. With the war over and his prospects as an officer less exciting, Blaik spent a year at Fort Bliss before resigning his commission in 1922. He returned to Dayton and joined his father's home-construction business. On 20 October 1923 he married Merle McDowell, with whom he had two sons.

Red Blaik, 1953. © BETTMANN/CORBIS

While working in the family business, Blaik volunteered as an assistant coach with the Miami University football team. In 1926 he took time off to become part-time assistant football coach at the University of Wisconsin, before serving in the same capacity at the U.S. Military Academy from 1927 to 1933. In 1934 he left the home-building business after being named head football coach at Dartmouth College in Hanover, New Hampshire.

Blaik turned Dartmouth into a regional power. In his first two years as head coach, the team posted records of 6–3 and 8–2, including their first-ever victory over Yale in 1935. Under Blaik, Dartmouth won twenty-two straight games from 1936 to 1938 and unofficial Ivy League championships in 1936 and 1937. Blaik's most famous Dartmouth victory came in 1940, when a confused referee allowed undefeated Cornell University a fifth down in the last seconds of the season's match between the two schools. Cornell scored a touchdown and appeared to have won 7–3, but when a review of the game films confirmed the

error, Cornell conceded the victory to Dartmouth. Blaik earned a reputation as a cerebral coach who used a variety of tactics to win. He hired a number of outstanding assistant coaches and approached the game with the philosophy that hard work was the only path to victory. From 1934 to 1940 Blaik's Dartmouth record was 45–15–4, including one undefeated season in 1937.

Blaik left Dartmouth in 1941 to become the first civilian head coach in thirty years at the U.S. Military Academy, whose Cadets' 1940 record was a dismal 1–7–1. After being assured of a direct line of communication to the school's superintendent and a loosening of the weight and height restrictions that were in place at the time, Blaik began the challenging process of turning around the team. His efforts resulted in a 5–3–1 record his first year and were further aided by the United States' entrance into World War II, when freshman cadets became eligible to play on varsity teams and more top athletes arrived at West Point. These included halfback Glenn Davis in 1943 and fullback Felix ("Doc") Blanchard in 1944. With Davis and Blanchard carrying the ball, Blaik's teams began a thirty-two-game unbeaten streak. In 1944 Army boasted a 9–0 record, outscoring their opponents 504–35 and beating nemesis Notre Dame and archrival Navy to win the national championship. The Cadets, now nicknamed the Black Knights, repeated their performance in 1945. A 0–0 tie with Notre Dame was the only blemish on their 1946 record and cost them that year's national championship, but Blaik being named Coach of the Year by the American Football Coaches Association softened the blow. A narrow defeat to Columbia University in 1947 ended Army's unbeaten streak, but the next week, they began another undefeated string of twenty-eight games. From 1944 to 1950 Blaik's Army teams compiled a 57–3–4 record and became the dominant college football power in the United States.

Blaik faced a low point in his career in 1951, when ninety West Point cadets, including thirty-seven football players, were accused of academic cheating and dismissed for violating the school's honor code. Blaik believed that the punishment was excessive and that the violation was due more to the way tests were administered than to a moral lapse on the part of the cadets. Because of the large number of football players involved, he questioned whether anti-football sentiment was behind the harsh punishment. In Blaik's first autobiography, he titled the chapter relating to the expulsions "The Ninety Scapegoats." His son Bob, the starting quarterback on the team, was one of those dismissed.

Ironically, the "cribbing scandal" probably encouraged Blaik to extend his coaching career. He had earlier gone on record as saying that coaches should retire at age fifty. Now, his program in shambles and his reputation tarnished, Blaik felt the need to prove himself. By the end of the 1953 season, his rebuilt Army team was ranked four-teenth in the nation with a 7–1–1 record. The Cadets captured the Lambert Trophy, the symbol of Eastern football supremacy, and Blaik received Coach of the Year honors from the Washington Touchdown Club. In 1958 Army went undefeated for the first time in nine years, with just one tie marring their record. The highlight of the season was Blaik's introduction of the "lonely end" offensive formation, a strategy that placed end Bill Carpenter wide of the formation as a "far flanker," never entering the huddle. The strategy's aim, which proved successful, was to weaken the opponent's defensive line because of the need to cover Carpenter. Blaik's innovation improved Army's passing game and allowed halfback Pete Dawkins to rack up yardage with ball carries.

Following the season-ending win over Navy and after compiling a 121–33–10 record during his eighteen years as Army's head coach, Blaik announced his resignation. He said his main reason for leaving coaching was the greater financial reward of private business. He soon became a vice president and director of Avco Corporation, an aerospace company, and later served as chairman of the executive committees of both Avco and Blaik Oil Company. He was elected to the National Football Foundation's College Hall of Fame in 1964 and received the foundation's Gold Medal Award in 1966. He continued his interest in football by contributing articles to magazines and gave the keynote address at the opening of the College Football Hall of Fame's museum at King's Island, Ohio, in 1978. (The museum relocated to South Bend, Indiana, in 1995.)

After a long retirement in Colorado Springs, Colorado, Blaik died at age ninety-two of complications from a broken hip. He is buried in West Point Cemetery in West Point. Blaik's combined Dartmouth and Army career record was 166 wins, 48 losses, and 14 ties. At West Point he coached six undefeated teams, seven Lambert Trophy winners, and two national champions. Three of his Army players (Blanchard, Davis, and Dawkins) won both the Heisman Trophy and the Maxwell Award, and guard Joe Steffy was awarded the Outland Trophy. Sixteen of Blaik's assistant coaches, including Vince Lombardi, Sid Gillman, and Murray Warmath, became head coaches for college or professional teams. More importantly, most of this success was at the U.S. Military Academy. During World War II and the cold war, Americans wanted to believe that their country was protected by the best and the brightest. Army's success on the gridiron suggested that maybe they were. In 1986 President Ronald Reagan presented Blaik with the Presidential Medal of Freedom.

★

Blaik wrote two autobiographies: *You Have to Pay the Price*, with Tim Cohane (1960), and *The Red Blaik Story* (1974). Jack Clary, *Army vs. Navy: Seventy Years of Football Rivalry* (1965),

includes Blaik's tenure as Army's most successful coach. Cohane, *Great College Football Coaches of the Twenties and Thirties* (1973), covers Blaik's Dartmouth career. Henry E. Mattox, *Army Football in 1945: Anatomy of a Championship Season* (1990), gives an account of Blaik's coaching at its best. An obituary is in the *New York Times* (7 May 1989).

HAROLD W. AURAND, JR.

BLAIR, Bonnie (*b.* 18 March 1964 in Cornwall, New York), speed skater who dominated the sport between 1986 and 1995, winning five gold medals in three consecutive Winter Olympics.

Blair was the youngest of six children of Charlie, a civil engineer, and Eleanor Blair, a homemaker. Shortly after Blair's birth, her family moved to Champaign, Illinois. Blair took up speed skating when she was two years old, joining a family of avid speed skaters. She entered her first competition at age four and won her first race at age seven. By the time she was in grade school, speed skating had become her number-one leisure activity.

As a teenager Blair began to take the sport more seriously. In 1979 she began training with Cathy Priestner, a Canadian speed skater who had won a silver medal at the 1976 Winter Olympics. Blair trained every morning before school and her discipline paid off; at age fifteen she qualified for the U.S. Olympic trials, but narrowly missed making the team. The experience strengthened her determination to become an Olympian. Realizing that success required both dedication and sacrifice, she gave up her spot on the Centennial High School cheerleading team to focus on skating and competitions. An excellent student, she was allowed to graduate halfway through her senior year to focus on her training. The Champaign police department sponsored a campaign to support "Champaign Policemen's Favorite Speeder," raising $7,000 for Blair so that she could move to Milwaukee, Wisconsin, and practice there with other competitive skaters.

The results were impressive. Blair made the 1984 U.S. Olympic team and competed in the 500-meter event at the Winter Games in Sarajevo, Yugoslavia. Although she finished eighth in the event, Blair returned to the United States with a renewed dedication to her training and soon began to shine in national competitions. At the 1985 National Sports Festival, Blair swept the gold medals in all four women's short-track skating races, and won another gold as a member of a men's 5,000-meter relay team. This sensational run made Blair the top gold medalist at the festival. A year later she captured her first World Short-Track Championship by winning three of the four events.

To become an Olympic champion, Blair needed further training as well as racing experience on the long track. With the oval in Milwaukee closed in the off-season, the best

Bonnie Blair. AP/WIDE WORLD PHOTOS

places to practice were in Europe. It was an expensive undertaking, but with the help of her family, friends, and money from the Champaign police department, Blair was able to go. She embarked on a whirlwind travel schedule in Europe, taking on the world's best. From 1986 to 1988 at the World Sprint Championships, Blair finished second once and third twice. She also set a world record for the 500-meter event in Heerenveen, Holland, at the end of the 1987 season.

Blair entered the 1988 Olympics in Calgary, Canada, as a veteran of hundreds of races, a world record holder, and the favorite to win the 500-meter event. With family members and dozens of friends, teammates, and fans cheering her on, Blair made her best start ever and zipped through the course in 39.1 seconds, setting a new world record and winning the gold medal. She also captured a bronze medal in the 1,000-meter event, becoming the only U.S. athlete to win more than one medal at Calgary.

The following summer Blair moved to Butte, Montana, where she enrolled at the Montana College of Mineral Science and Technology. She cut back on her skating and took up competitive bicycle racing. Realizing the risk involved in cycling, Blair soon gave up the sport and returned her focus to speed skating. She won the 1989 World Championship, setting a new world record in the overall event; finished second in 1990; and placed fifth in 1991, her worst finish in six years.

In the summer of 1991 Blair resumed full-time training back in Milwaukee under her new coach, Peter Mueller. She soon regained her form and confidence, winning dozens of 500- and 1,000-meter races leading up to the 1992 Olympics. She entered the Winter Games in Albertville, France, as the favorite in both events. Despite unfavorable weather conditions at the outdoor rink, Blair won the 500-meter race. Four days later, she took the gold in the 1,000-meter race, winning by just two one-hundredths of a second. These dramatic accomplishments earned her the 1992 Sullivan Award as the nation's leading amateur athlete and the 1992 U.S. Olympic Committee (USOC) Sportswoman of the Year Award.

In 1986 the International Olympic Committee decided to alternate the Summer and Winter Games every two years, moving the 1996 Winter Games to 1994. For Blair, a skater in the prime of her career, the new schedule was an opportunity to try again for Olympic gold. Serendipitously, Milwaukee opened a new indoor skating rink in 1992, allowing her to train there all year.

At the 1994 Olympics in Lillehammer, Norway, Blair again won both the 500- and 1,000-meter races. Having gained five gold medals and one bronze medal in three Olympic Games, Blair became the most decorated female Winter Olympian in U.S. history. She was named as the Associated Press Female Athlete of the Year and the USOC Sportswoman of the Year. In March 1995, shortly after winning the World Cup and setting a new world record in the 500-meter event, Blair retired from competitive speed skating.

After the 1994 Olympics, Blair received more honors and product endorsement offers. On 23 June 1996 she married Dave Cruikshank, a fellow speed skater on the U.S. Olympic team. They settled in Milwaukee, where Blair has spent much of her time on the Bonnie Blair Charitable Gift Fund and as a celebrity representative for Olympic sponsors. Blair's athletic achievements, combined with her friendly, down-to-earth manner, earned her recognition from journalists as an "All-American girl." Her retirement from the sport, however, created a void in the talent pool of U.S. speed skaters that would be felt in the years to come.

★

A short biography of Blair is Cathy Breitenbucher, *Bonnie Blair: Golden Streak* (1994). See also Alexander Wolff, "Bonnie's Bounty: Unassuming Bonnie Blair Sped to Victory in 1,000 Meters to Become the U.S.'s Most Gilded Woman Olympian Ever," *Sports Illustrated* (7 Mar. 1994); Steve Rushin, "Child of Innocence: Bonnie Blair Grew up with the Ideal That Competing—Not Just Winning—Is Everything," *Sports Illustrated* (19 Dec. 1994); and Steve Rushin, "The Last Lap: After Racing to Another World Title, Bonnie Blair Leaves the U.S. Facing a Big Chill in Her Sport," *Sports Illustrated* (27 Feb. 1995).

YING WUSHANLEY

BLANCHARD, Felix Anthony, Jr. ("Doc") (*b.* 11 December 1924 in McColl, South Carolina), Army football player known as "Mr. Inside" who won the Heisman Trophy in 1945; after graduating from the United States Military Academy he enjoyed a successful career in the U.S. Air Force.

Blanchard was one of two children of Dr. Felix Blanchard, a country physician who settled and practiced in South Carolina, and Mary Elizabeth Tatum Blanchard. Dubbed "Doc" as a boy, the younger Blanchard inherited both a passion and a talent for football, a sport in which his father had excelled at both Saint Stanislaus College preparatory school in Mississippi and at Tulane University in New Orleans. When the younger Blanchard followed his parent to the same prep school, he soon demonstrated the gridiron abilities that would make him famous. In 1942 Blanchard enrolled at the University of North Carolina—partly to be near his family and perhaps partly because Jim Tatum, the football coach there, was related to his mother.

Blanchard excelled on the field as a freshman, but with World War II raging, he tried to enroll in the navy's V-12 training program. Rejected for both less-than-perfect eyesight and his weight, he then enlisted in the army and found himself stationed in Clovis, New Mexico. Having earlier attracted the attention of Earl "Red" Blaik, the football coach at the United States Military Academy at West Point, New York, Blanchard was recruited to join the class reporting to West Point in the summer of 1944. His arrival there coincided with that of a cadet named Glenn Davis, who had been turned out from the previous class because of academic difficulties. Their collaboration marked the beginning of a legendary era in the history of college football.

During the three seasons from 1944 through 1946, Blaik's Army teams—"Blaik's Black Knights," as one New York sportswriter christened them—dominated college football with a won-loss-tied record of 27–0–1. While it is true that the Cadets were able to field superb athletes against college programs depleted by the war's manpower demands, it is also quite arguably true that the success achieved by Blaik's squads was based on more than merely talent differential. Not yet members of the starting team, Blanchard and Davis were part of a second unit consisting mostly of freshman (plebe) players that Blaik alternated freely with the more senior eleven on the first unit. Both made their presence known immediately and received first-team All-America honors at season's end. Blanchard turned in a particularly important performance in the Army–Navy game, carrying the ball seven times for forty-eight yards and a touchdown during a critical fourth-quarter drive. In an era when sportswriters fancied themselves poets, Tim Cohane exploited the dichotomy of Blanchard's status as both West Point plebe and football star in a parody of Rudyard Kipling's "Tommy," noting that despite the treatment accorded plebes by the upperclass cadets, "O it's 'Thank you, Mister Blanchard' when the football whistle blows."

The 1945 season was Blanchard's finest. The Army team went undefeated again and won another national championship while "Mr. Inside"—Blanchard's half of the "Touchdown Twins" to Glenn Davis's "Mr. Outside"—won the Heisman Trophy; he was the first junior ever to do so. He also became the first football player to win the Amateur Athletic Union's James E. Sullivan Award, presented to the nation's best amateur athlete. Moreover, he received both the Maxwell Cup and the Walter Camp Trophy. All these honors derived from a splendid nine-game season that featured a 7.1-yard rushing average and nineteen touchdowns from Blanchard, including three in a season-ending victory over Navy.

The next and final season of 1946 belonged more to Glenn Davis, who won the Heisman that year; but Blanchard's contributions to another unbeaten season were substantial—in spite of a debilitating knee injury incurred in the season's opening game. Several weeks later he scored the game-winning touchdown in a fiercely contested victory over highly ranked Michigan, and he scored twice in a close final victory over Navy. Blanchard concluded his Army football career with 1,666 yards rushing and thirty-eight touchdowns: twenty-six rushing, seven receiving, four returned interceptions, and one kickoff return.

As that scoring variety suggests, what made Blanchard a remarkable athlete was not merely his particular skill as a running back, but his athletic versatility. He was a fine punter and boomed kickoffs deep into enemy territory; he also demonstrated great ability as a pass receiver and played excellent defense. Moreover, he complemented his powerful inside rushing game with speed; he could run the hun-

Felix Blanchard *(left)* with Army coach Earl Blaik and fellow Heisman Trophy winner Glenn Davis. AP PHOTO

dred-yard dash in ten seconds flat. Indeed, he excelled in track and field events as well as football, once winning the IC4A shot-put championship.

Blanchard graduated from West Point in 1947 and was commissioned into the Army Air Corps just as it became the U.S. Air Force. Denied the opportunity to play professional football immediately because of their obligation to military service, Blanchard and Davis spent part of their graduation furlough making a Hollywood film called *Spirit of West Point,* in which they played themselves with much less skill than they played the game. Though Davis would leave the service after a few years and play briefly in the National Football League, Blanchard's military career lasted for twenty-four years. It included service at home and abroad, assignments flying a variety of jet aircraft, squadron and wing commands, and a tour of duty in Southeast Asia that involved 113 combat missions. That career, which culminated in his 1971 retirement as a colonel, also included some assignments coaching football—twice back at West Point, once at the Air Force Academy. After two years as commandant of the New Mexico Military Institute, in 1973 Blanchard retired for good to a series of homes in Texas, where he had met and married his wife, Jody King Blanchard, during flight training in 1948; they had three children.

Blanchard was elected to the National Football Foundation and College Hall of Fame in 1959. His Heisman Trophy, his many other awards and honors, and his remarkable statistical achievements put him in a special category. To some extent his continuing renown emanates from

what he and his famous backfield mate Glenn Davis represent: dominating athletic performance by modest figures in an era when college football was the preeminent form of the sport. That "Mr. Inside" and his teammate played at West Point during World War II was, of course, part of the romance that embellished their reputation. That Blanchard went on to a career of military service in peace and war only enhances his status as one of the most accomplished and celebrated athletes of his generation.

★

Sportswriter Tim Cohane provided a useful contemporaneous view of Blanchard's life and college football career in *Gridiron Grenadiers: The Story of West Point Football* (1948). Much of the same material appears in a book that Cohane later coauthored with Blanchard's legendary coach, Earl H. "Red" Blaik: *You Have to Pay the Price* (1960). Blaik later supplemented that text in *The Red Blaik Story* (1974). Two retrospectives of Blanchard's athletic and, to a lesser extent, military careers appear in Dave Newhouse, *Heismen: After the Glory* (1985), and Henry E. Mattox, *Army Football in 1945: Anatomy of a Championship Season* (1990).

JAMES R. KERIN, JR.

BLANDA, George Frederick (*b.* 17 September 1927 in Youngwood, Pennsylvania), quarterback elected to the Pro Football Hall of Fame in 1981 who is best remembered for his heroic performance during the 1970 and 1971 seasons.

Blanda was one of eleven children born to Michael and Mary Blanda, who were of Czech ancestry. Michael Blanda

George Blanda *(left)*, 1964. ASSOCIATED PRESS

was a Pennsylvania coal miner who labored long hours underground so that his children would have the opportunity to pursue an education. His son George proved to be an outstanding athlete at Youngwood High School, earning varsity letters in football, basketball, and track and field.

Following high school graduation in 1945, Blanda entered the University of Kentucky on a scholarship. At Kentucky, Blanda played for the legendary coach Paul "Bear" Bryant. Coach Bryant was a stern but admired taskmaster. Blanda said, "I owe my longevity in the game to him and his coaching philosophy. Hard work equals success." After playing as a reserve quarterback during his sophomore and junior years, Blanda started during his senior year, leading the Kentucky Wildcats to eight victories in eleven games. During his tenure at Kentucky, Blanda met Betty Harris, and the two were married in 1949. The marriage produced two children.

Graduating in 1949 with a degree in education, Blanda was drafted by the Chicago Bears of the National Football League (NFL). Unfortunately for Blanda, Chicago already had two outstanding quarterbacks—Sid Luckman and Johnny Lujack. Blanda received little playing time and had an acrimonious relationship with George Halas, owner and coach of the Bears. In his early years with the Bears, Blanda saw action mostly as a field-goal kicker and kickoff specialist.

In 1950 Blanda was traded to the Baltimore Colts but

was released and rejoined the Bears later that season. Finally, in 1953, Blanda won the starting quarterback job for Chicago, leading the NFL in passes attempted (362) and completed (169), yet the team compiled a disappointing annual record of three wins, eight losses, and one tie. Blanda again became a reserve quarterback, playing behind Zeke Bratkowski and Ed Brown.

Following the 1958 season, Blanda retired from football, frustrated over lack of playing time and the fact that Halas would not deal him to another team. In ten seasons with the Bears, Blanda played in 115 games, passed for forty-eight touchdowns and 5,936 yards, kicked eighty-eight field goals (scoring 247 out of a possible 250 extra points), and ran for five touchdowns.

However, Blanda still wanted to play football, and the emergence of a new professional league, the American Football League (AFL), in 1960 provided him with the opportunity. That year, Blanda signed with owner Bud Adams of the Houston Oilers for approximately $20,000. The former reserve made the most of his chance to be a starting professional quarterback. In his first three years with Houston, Blanda led the Oilers to three division titles and two league championships. He led the AFL in passing yardage and touchdown passes in 1961. From 1963 to 1965 Blanda was the league's dominant quarterback, completing 672 out of 1,370 passes. He was selected for the AFL All-Star game for the three seasons between 1961 and 1963.

But by the mid-1960s the Oilers were in decline, and

late in the 1966 season Blanda was replaced by Don Trull. In 1967 he was traded to the Oakland Raiders, where he served as the team's place kicker and backup quarterback for starter Daryl Lamonica. Blanda was content with his role and contributed to the team's 1967 AFL championship. In 1968 and 1969 Oakland won Western Division titles but was defeated in the AFL championship game.

In 1970 the AFL and NFL merged, and the AFL became the American Football Conference (AFC) of the NFL. Professional football emerged as the number one televised sport in America, and Blanda's exploits during the 1970 season made the forty-three-year-old athlete an American hero. Blanda's series of "miracle finishes" began on 25 October, when he replaced Lamonica and threw three touchdown passes, leading Oakland to a victory over Pittsburgh. A week later, Blanda kicked a forty-eight-yard field goal with three seconds remaining to tie the Kansas City Chiefs. In November, the heroics continued; during the last ninety seconds of a game against the Cleveland Browns, Blanda tossed a touchdown pass and kicked a field goal for an Oakland victory. The next Sunday, Blanda completed a touchdown pass with two and a half minutes remaining to defeat the Denver Broncos. On 22 November, Blanda kicked a field goal with seven seconds left in the game to give the Raiders a win over the San Diego Chargers. Blanda's series of fantastic finishes led Oakland into the playoffs, where they were defeated by the Baltimore Colts. Blanda's 1970 exploits were recognized by the United Press International and by *Sporting News,* which voted him AFC Player of the Year. The Associated Press named Blanda Male Athlete of the Year.

On 31 October 1971 Blanda surpassed Lou Groza's career point record of 1,609. In the remaining fifty seconds of that record-setting game, Blanda again relieved Lamonica, throwing a touchdown pass and kicking a field goal as the Raiders tied the Chiefs. However, Kansas City edged out Oakland for the 1971 Western Division title.

Blanda remained with Oakland through the 1975 season, although his playing time was limited, with most of his action as a place kicker. At age forty-eight, Blanda retired. He finished his career with 2,002 points scored and 340 games played. As a quarterback, Bland attempted 4,007 passes, completing 1,911, for 26,920 yards and 236 touchdowns. He also kicked 335 field goals and scored 942 extra points. Blanda was voted into the Pro Football Hall of Fame in 1981.

After retirement Blanda worked as an executive with the Railway Express Agency in Chicago and enjoys playing golf and going to the race track. Blanda had a distinguished football career with three teams, but his miracle finishes of the 1970 and 1971 seasons captured the nation's imagination.

★

An authorized biography of Blanda is Wells Twombly, *Blanda: Alive and Kicking: The Exclusive Authorized Biography* (1972). An account of Blanda's role in the early years of the American Football League may be found in Harold Rosenthal, ed., *AFL Official History, 1960–1969* (1970). Journalistic profiles of Blanda include "George Blanda Is Alive and Kicking," *Time* (23 Nov. 1970); and Tom Maule, "Let George Do It and He Does," *Sports Illustrated* (23 Nov. 1970). For Blanda's perspective on his celebrated finishes in the 1970 and 1971 seasons, see George Blanda with Jim Olsen, "Decade of Revenge," *Sports Illustrated* (19 July 1971); "I Keep Getting My Kicks," *Sports Illustrated* (26 July 1971); and "That Impossible Season," *Sports Illustrated* (2 Aug. 1971).

RON BRILEY

BLATNICK, Jeff(rey) (*b.* 26 July 1957 in Schenectady, New York), wrestler celebrated for winning an Olympic gold medal in Greco-Roman wrestling, the second ever won for the United States in this competition, after surviving cancer.

Blatnick began his storied wrestling career in 1973 at Schenectady's Niskayuna High School. During his three years of varsity wrestling, he compiled a record of 62–19–0 and

Jeff Blatnick *(right)* wrestling in the 1984 Olympics in Los Angeles. ASSOCIATED PRESS AP

in 1975 was the New York State Wrestling Champion in the heavyweight division.

Blatnick continued his athletic accomplishments at Springfield College in Massachusetts, where he was a student between 1975 and 1979. He was a starting offensive tackle on the varsity football team and went on to become a two-time Division II national champion and a three-time Division II All-American in the heavyweight wrestling division. As a senior, he also garnered a third-place finish in the 1979 National Collegiate Athletic Association (NCAA) Division I meet, prompting legendary Springfield wrestling coach Doug Parker to deem Blatnick "the best wrestler to compete for the college in any weight class—ever."

It was in Greco-Roman wrestling, however, that Blatnick made his greatest impact. Upon graduating from Springfield with a degree in physical education, Blatnick qualified for the 1980 U.S. Olympic Greco-Roman team but was unable to compete due to the government boycott of the Games in Moscow. Instead, Blatnick competed in and won the 1980 Amateur Athletic Union Championships and then went on to win a World Cup silver medal. He was an Amateur Athletic Union champion again the next year.

In 1982 Blatnick noticed lumps along the right side of his neck. He was diagnosed with Hodgkin's disease in the lymph nodes. "The doctor told me that the tests came up positive," he recalled, "but I never felt like I was going to die."

Doctors removed Blatnick's spleen for precautionary reasons, and he began radiation therapy on his lymph nodes. Only two weeks later, Blatnick resumed working out by pedaling on a stationary bicycle. His workout partners would often ask about the large pink scar on his stomach and about the magic marker scrawls that covered his body. "It was to show the technicians where the radiation treatments were supposed to go and where they were not supposed to go," Blatnick said.

With his treatments complete, Blatnick began training for the 1984 Olympic team. The 248-pound Blatnick qualified and found himself in the gold medal match facing a much larger Swedish wrestler, the 275-pound Thomas Johansson. "The Swede is big," his father told him, "but you've come too far to let anything stop you now." His mother invoked the memory of his brother Dave, who had died seven years earlier in a motorcycle accident. "Do it for Dave," she said.

Blatnick did, winning the 1984 Greco-Roman wrestling gold medal in the super-heavyweight division, defeating Johansson by a score of 2–0. Blatnick became the second U.S. wrestler ever to win a gold medal in the Greco-Roman style. The first, Steve Fraser, won his medal the previous night in the 198-pound division.

In 1985 Blatnick was again diagnosed with Hodgkin's disease. After winning this second bout with cancer, which this time required twenty-eight sessions of chemotherapy in 1985 and 1986, Blatnick officially retired from competition. He nonetheless continued to participate in wrestling and American athletics by acting as an Olympic wrestling commentator from 1988 to 2000. He has served on numerous presidential committees on physical fitness and has taught wrestling at camps across the country. He also became a motivational speaker, lecturing to children of all ages, to corporations, and to cancer patients about his own struggles and how he overcame them.

Blatnick once said, "If you can win in adversity, you can win anywhere." This remark not only exemplifies Jeff Blatnick's life but also explains people's fascination with him. Blatnick was a three-time Greco-Roman national champion, an eight-time Greco-Roman All-American, a two-time World Cup medal winner, a two-time Freestyle All-American, and was inducted into the National Wrestling Hall of Fame in 1999.

Blatnick won both on and off of the mat and did so in the face of extreme adversity. The victories he achieved over seemingly insurmountable conditions have inspired people to believe that anyone can win.

★

For information about Blatnick before his participation in the Olympics, see Dave Anderson, "Ecstatic, Not Embarassed," *New York Times* (6 Aug. 1984). For information on his college years, see Howard M. Davis, "Springfield's Best—Ever," *Springfield College Bulletin* 53, no. 3 (Jan. 1979). For a look at his years fighting cancer, see Eric Levin, "Greco-Roman Wrestling Star," *People Weekly* (5 May 1986).

MATTHEW J. PIERCE

BLAZEJOWSKI, Carol Ann (*b.* 29 September 1956 in Elizabeth, New Jersey), basketball player known for her jump shot and the General Manager for the New York Liberty, one of the original professional teams of the Women's National Basketball Association (WNBA).

During a time when parents usually held their children to strict stereotypical roles, Leon and Grace Blazejowski encouraged their daughter to play sports. By age ten Blazejowski was regularly playing basketball against neighborhood boys. Her hardworking blue-collar parents always knew where they could find their daughter—on the courts. Blazejowski did not play organized basketball until her senior year at Cranford High School, which she attended from 1970 to 1974. She served as team captain and averaged twenty-five points a game, and was primarily known for her classic jump shot, usually taken from fifteen feet. However, Blazejowski's dynamic senior year and incredible

Carol Blazejowski. AP/WIDE WORLD PHOTOS

shooting ability did not earn her one of the few athletic scholarships offered to women in 1975. Blazejowski chose to attend Montclair State College in Upper Montclair, New Jersey, and to pay her own way.

As a five foot, ten inch forward Blazejowski, nicknamed "the Blaze," accumulated an incredible 3,199 points during her college career, more than any other college basketball player, male or female, at the time. The three-time All American (1976, 1977, and 1978) led the nation in scoring with 33.5 points per game her junior year and 38.6 points per game her senior year. Blazejowski also led the Montclair Squaws in rebounds and steals, and had an 87.3 free throw percentage. During college she participated in the World University Games and was named Converse Women's Player of the Year in 1977. The following year Blazejowski helped her team advance to the national semifinals.

Blazejowski had her sights set on making the U.S. Olympic Team in 1976 but was cut in the final rounds of tryouts. When she asked why, she was told her defense was weak. Blazejowski and Montclair coach Maureen Wendelken took the criticism hard. Blazejowski would later play the team of the coach who kept her from making the Olympic team when Montclair traveled to California in 1978 to compete against the University of California, Los Angeles,

in the Association of Intercollegiate Athletics for Women (AIAW) Final Four. However, although Blazejowski scored 38 points, Montclair lost 85–77.

Blazejowski's most memorable game was against Queens College (of Queens, New York) in 1977. The game was played at Madison Square Garden in front of 12,000 spectators. Blazejowski had a sub par first half, scoring only fourteen points and accumulating three fouls. When Blazejowski picked up her fourth foul in the first few minutes of the second half, coach Wendelken kept her in the game but instructed her to only take jump shots. Blazejowski then went on to score 38 points for a record-setting total of 52 points, allowing Montclair to win the game with a score of 102–94.

As team captain, Blazejowski was the Montclair Squaws' emotional leader. She led by example, often pushing players through practice and encouraging them to run or shoot afterwards. No one worked harder on improving her game than Blazejowski. She ended her college career by winning the first Wade Trophy, which Blazejowski said was one of the her proudest moments. The award recognized the nation's women's collegiate basketball player of the year. Blazejowski was also an honor graduate, having earned a 3.6 grade point average from Montclair's physical education program.

After graduation in 1978, Blazejowski refused to turn professional, although the New Jersey Gems took her in the first round of the Women's Basketball League (WBL) draft, because she still had Olympic dreams. Between graduation and the 1980 Olympic tryouts, Blazejowski enrolled in graduate school at Montclair in the physical education department and continued to train and practice. She played internationally on the gold medal-winning 1979 World University Team, and the silver medal-winning 1979 Pan American Team, as well as for the national amateur Crestettes from Allentown, Pennsylvania. However, remaining an amateur also meant she was required to turn down every potentially lucrative endorsement she was offered.

Blazejowski was finally selected for the 1980 Olympic team. The team won the prequalifying tournament in Bulgaria, but did not compete in the Olympics. A U.S. boycott imposed by President Jimmy Carter, protesting the 1979 Soviet invasion of Afghanistan, prevented any of the U.S. teams from traveling to Moscow.

Giving up on her Olympic dreams, Blazejowski accepted a three-year contract for $150,000 with the New Jersey Gems later in 1980, and became the highest paid player in the Womens Basketball League (WBL). Unfortunately, the league went bankrupt in 1981, but Blazejowski made her mark during her one season with the Gems. She was the WBL's leading scorer and most valuable player, and was selected to play on the All-Star team.

With the folding of the WBL, Blazejowski's playing options were exhausted. However, she remained involved in sports by working with the sporting-goods company Adidas to develop and implement marketing programs aimed at women's sports. Blazejowski left Adidas after ten years to join the National Basketball Association (NBA) as Director of Licensing (1990 to 1995) and then as Director of Women's Basketball Programs (1996).

When the Women's National Basketball Association (WNBA) was formed in 1996, Blazejowski was named Director of Basketball Development. She spent only one year in that position before becoming the General Manager and vice president of the New York Liberty basketball team in 1997, where one of her main responsibilities included choosing players. The Liberty's back-to-back Conference Championships and three WNBA Finals appearances have attested to Blazejowski's ability to assemble a winning team.

In recognition of her contribution to basketball, Blazejowski was inducted into the Naismith Memorial Basketball Hall of Fame in 1994, one of only thirteen women to receive that honor. Blazejowski was among the twenty-six honorees inducted into the inaugural class of the Women's Basketball Hall of Fame in 1999.

In May 1999 Blazejowski made history again when the Liberty media guide included the information that Blazejowski lived with her partner, Joyce, and their two children. The Liberty players were not told in advance about Blazejowski's biography, to them it simply did not matter.

Blazejowski's contribution to basketball and women's sport has been lasting and significant. Recognized as the best women's basketball player of her day, Blazejowski demonstrated that women could not only keep pace with men on the court, but also in the executive conference room.

★

Most information on Carol Blazejowski comes from current WNBA material and media coverage of her college career. Two particularly important articles are "Carol Blazejowski: Pro in an Amateur World," *Women's Sports* 1, no. 1 (1979), which covers her struggles as an amateur from 1978 to 1980; and "Profile: Carol Blazejowski," *Coaching Women's Athletics* (Jan./Feb. 1979), by Montclair head coach Maureen Wendelken, which discusses Blazejowski's importance to the team and what it was like to coach her.

LISA A. ENNIS

BLEIBTREY, Ethelda (*b.* 27 February 1902 in Waterford, New York; *d.* 6 May 1978 in West Palm Beach, Florida), swimmer who was the first woman to win three gold medals in the Olympic Games and was hailed in her day as the "world's greatest woman swimmer."

Bleibtrey was the second child of John E. Bleibtrey, a funeral director, and Marguerite Quandt, a sales clerk. Her parents separated early, and her mother supported Ethelda

Ethelda Bleibtrey at the 1920 Olympic games in Antwerp. © BETTMANN/ CORBIS

and her brother John by working behind the counter at Bloomingdale's department store. Bleibtrey grew up in Brooklyn and graduated from Erasmus Hall High School.

Bleibtrey, who suffered as a child from the effects of polio, took up competitive swimming at age sixteen in 1918 to help her regain physical strength. She joined the Women's Swimming Association (WSA), a New York organization founded the previous year by Charlotte Epstein. Under the masterful tutelage of renowned swimming coach, Louis deBreda Handley, Bleibtrey advanced from a novice to a world class competitive swimmer by the spring of 1919, when she set world marks in the 100-yard backstroke and 440-yard freestyle (the latter record was disallowed due to an insufficient number of timers). She also won Amateur Athletic Union (AAU) titles in the 440-yard and 880-yard freestyle events. She came to international prominence in August of that year, when in a 100-yard exhibition race she beat the veteran Australian swimming star, Fanny Durack, who had been presumed to be the best in the world.

Also in 1919, Bleibtrey helped advance the cause of

women swimming, when at Manhattan Beach in Brooklyn, New York, she swam in public without wearing the heavy woolen stockings that women bathers were expected to wear. The police cited her for "nude swimming," but the public sided with Bleibtrey, and it soon became acceptable for women to go to the beaches with legs bared. A year later, she became one of the first women of note to cut her hair in the daring new bob style.

By the indoor season of early 1920, when Bleibtrey captured AAU titles in the 100-yard freestyle and 100-yard backstroke, she had become the star of a WSA team that was filled with future Olympians, notably Charlotte Boyle, Aileen Riggin, and Helen Wainwright. During the summer, Bleibtrey took national AAU outdoor titles in the 100-yard, 880-yard, and one-mile freestyle events, and set world records in the 100-yard, 220-yard, 500-yard, and one-mile freestyle events. Bleibtrey not only swept all her competitors, she beat them by wide margins and in all kinds of conditions.

When the Olympic Games opened in Antwerp, Belgium, in August 1920, Bleibtrey was the strongest competitor of the U.S. inaugural women's swimming team. She probably would have won four medals at the games had there been a backstroke event for women, as she was the world record holder at the time. In the only three events available to her—the 100-meter freestyle, 300-meter freestyle, and 400-meter freestyle relay—she won handily in cold and muddy swimming conditions (Belgium had no indoor or outdoor pool facilities in Antwerp, and swimmers had to compete in a tidal estuary). She also set individual world records in the 100 meters (1:13.6) and 300 meters (4:34.0) and anchored the U.S. relay team to achieve a world record in the 400-meter relay (5:11.6). While Bleibtrey was the first woman to win a gold medal for the United States, she was not the first American woman Olympic champion (champion golfer Margaret Abbott had been awarded a porcelain bowl for first place in the 1900 Olympics).

In early 1921, Bleibtrey went on a tour to promote women's swimming, traveling to New Zealand and Australia, and back through Hawaii. Besides winning all her races on the tour, she participated in a "photo op" in Hawaii, surfing with swimming great Duke Kahanamoku. Returning to the competitive wars during the summer of 1921, Bleibtrey won the AAU outdoor titles in 100-yard, 440-yard, and 880-yard freestyle events. Indoors, she notched another 100-yard championship.

In the spring of 1922, Bleibtrey toured the Canal Zone and gave swimming exhibitions. She then shocked the swimming world in May when she turned professional—at the time she held five world records and had won every race she entered since starting competitive swimming in 1919. She soon discovered, however, that the demand for a professional swimmer giving exhibitions was limited. In the summer of 1922 a spate of world records broken by Sybil Bauer (of the Illinois Athletic Club) in the backstroke and

Gertrude Ederle (of the WSA) in the freestyle events captured the public attention, shifting the focus from Bleibtrey. She eventually found work as a swimming coach and instructor. Early in 1927, Bleibtrey married businessman Frederick MacRobert; the couple had one daughter, Leilah.

In 1928 Bleibtrey signed a fourteen-week contract with the Keith Theater vaudeville circuit to present swimming exhibitions on stage, but the tour was aborted the day before it opened when the canvas tank leaked its contents and ruined all the theater's carpeting. The theater demanded $1,000 from Bleibtrey for damages, but the *New York Daily News,* which was campaigning for more public pools, came to her rescue, paying Bleibtrey $1,000 to be arrested swimming in the Central Park's reservoir, where swimming was barred for health reasons. She spent a night in jail, but the subsequent publicity helped bring about the construction of more public pools in the city.

Bleibtrey divorced her husband by the early 1930s and subsequently supported herself and her daughter on income from teaching swimming to children and providing physiotherapy to cerebral palsy and polio patients. She became a practical nurse in 1959 and used her skills to help elderly people and people with disabilities. Bleibtrey's second husband was Al Schlafke, a sportswriter.

In 1967 Bleibtrey was inducted into the International Swimming Hall of Fame. The following year, she moved from New York to North Palm Beach, Florida, where she continued her work using therapeutic swimming to help elderly people stay limber. She died of cancer in West Palm Beach.

★

As one of the most accomplished women swimmers in the history of the sport, Bleibtrey earned the accolade "the world's greatest" in her day, but she proved to be much more than a champion swimmer. She was also a bold pioneer and advocate for the advancement of women in athletics and the advancement of swimming as a public recreation, as well as a lifelong proponent and practitioner of swimming as a therapeutic tool for the aged and disabled. Among the few biographical profiles on Bleibtrey are Julius J. Heller, "Waterford Girl, Who Made Biggest Splash in the '20 Olympics, Still Is 'in the Swim,'" Albany, N.Y., *Knickerbocker News* (30 July 1952); Russ Ramsey, "The First and Greatest," *Swimming World* (July 1986); Buck Dawson, *Weissmuller to Spitz: An Era to Remember* (1989); and Paula Welch, "Ethelda Bleibtrey," *The Twentieth Century: Great Athletes* (1992). An obituary is in the *New York Times* (9 May 1978).

ROBERT PRUTER

BOITANO, Brian Anthony (*b.* 22 October 1963 in Mountain View, California), figure skater, winner of more than fifty skating titles, and gold medalist at the 1988 Winter Olympics in Calgary, Alberta, Canada.

Boitano was born to Lew Boitano, a banker, and Donna Boitano, a homemaker. He grew up in Sunnyvale, California, the youngest of four children in an upper-middle-class Italian-American family. As a youngster Boitano loved to read. He enjoyed a variety of physical activities, including roller-skating, skiing, tennis, biking, and baseball. He became interested in figure skating when, at the age of eight, his parents took him to see the Ice Follies in San Francisco. From that day on, Boitano wanted nothing else but to take ice-skating lessons.

Boitano's parents sent him to the Sunnyvale Ice Palace, a local rink, for skating lessons. There he met Linda Leaver, who would become his lifelong skating coach. Leaver immediately recognized Boitano's talent and ability on the ice and suggested that he take private lessons with her. Boitano quickly grasped figure-skating techniques under Leaver's tutelage, winning competitions almost from the start, including the "pixie boys" division while still eight years old. In 1988 his coach told David Levine of *Sport* magazine that "at ten he was doing things most twenty-year-olds weren't." Boitano was the only eleven-year-old skater to successfully complete a triple jump (the triple salchow, in which a skater takes off from the back inside edge of one skate and lands on the outside edge of the opposite skate). His other feat included landing a triple axel (a jump taken from the forward outside edge of one skate and, after three revolutions in the air,

landed on the back outside edge of the opposite skate) at the age of seventeen.

Boitano's talent and diligence would eventually take him to the pinnacle of men's figure skating. While in elementary school, he practiced at the rink for five hours a day, from mid-afternoon until late evening. After he entered Peterson High School in Sunnyvale, Boitano was at the rink every morning before dawn, where he practiced until mid-morning before going to school. Although his schedule caused him to miss his first two class periods, he received physical education credits for his skating practice. He continued to practice through the summer.

Despite Boitano's extraordinary jumping ability (in competitions he performed the triple lutz, flip, loop, and toe loop in addition to the triple axel and salchow), his perfect landings did not garner him first place in competitions. In fact, at the 1979 U.S. senior men's competition, he placed eighth. He moved to fifth place the following year, fourth place in 1981 and 1982, and second place in 1983 and 1984. At the 1982 U.S. figure-skating championships, Boitano was the first American to perform and land a triple axel. At the 1983 world championships in Helsinki, Finland, he was the first skater to ever complete six different types of triple jumps in competition. At that event he placed seventh. His second-place finish at the 1987 world championships in Cincinnati, Ohio, changed Boitano's skating career. After losing the championship to his rival, Brian Orser of Canada, Boitano hired Sandra Bezic, a skating choreographer, to add artistic elements to complement his technical expertise.

Bezic, a five-time Canadian pairs champion, added grace and artistic sense to Boitano's freestyle program. She replaced Boitano's pop tunes with classical music. In an interview with the *Washington Post,* Bezic said, "He's just now learned to get into the music, to feel the emotion and skate from his heart. This was the last piece to come together." On 20 February 1988 Boitano's outstanding freestyle routine won him the gold medal in men's figure skating at the Winter Olympics in Calgary. He was finally able to beat his chief competitor, Brian Orser. That same year Boitano captured the crown at the world championships in Budapest, Hungary, and afterward turned professional.

As a professional Boitano competed for the world professional title, winning six times. He created a figure-skating jump, the "Tano Triple," that, as of 2001, no skater other than Boitano had executed successfully. He decided against joining the Ice Capades or the Ice Follies, the popular venues for professional skaters. Instead, he opted for other projects, including the starring role in the 1988 television special *Canvas of Ice*, becoming the first American male athlete to have his own network television program. The show won awards at the International Film and Television Festival of New York and the Chicago International

Brian Boitano. AP/WIDE WORLD PHOTOS

Film Festival. In 1990 Boitano won an Emmy Award for his portrayal of Don José in the movie *Carmen on Ice,* shown on cable television.

Boitano and Katarina Witt, the East German Olympic gold medalist in women's figure skating, were the artistic directors for a series of North American skating tours—*Skating, Skating II,* and *Chrysler Skating '92*—that showcased Olympic and World champion figure skaters. In 1995 Boitano cofounded White Canvas Productions with partners Doug Zeghibe and Franc D'Ambrosio. In the late 1990s and early 2000s the company put together several ice-skating shows for television and live audiences, with Boitano serving as artistic director.

Boitano tried again for the men's figure-skating gold in the 1994 Winter Olympics in Lillehammer, Norway, which was open to professional skaters. However, he was unable to place and came in sixth. Later he began competing in the Ice Wars, professional competitions that team the best U.S. skaters against the best world skaters. As a professional, he has won twenty of the twenty-four competitions he has entered—a record in the world of figure skating.

Boitano is a spokesperson for several nonprofit organizations, including the Starlight Children's Foundation, National Safe Kids Campaign Entertainment Alliance, and the Public Awareness Council of the American Red Cross. In 1998 he founded Brian Boitano's Youth Skate, a program that introduces San Francisco's inner-city youth to the sport of ice-skating. Boitano was inducted into both the World and the Figure Skating Halls of Fame in 1996.

★

Boitano is the author of *Boitano's Edge: Inside the Real World of Figure Skating* (1997), written for young adults and filled with personal anecdotes. Additional information can be found in articles in *Time* (15 Feb. 1988) and *Sports Illustrated* (4 Apr. 1988; 12 Feb. 1990; 24 Feb. 1992; and 2 Oct. 1992).

MARGALIT SUSSER

BONDS, Barry Lamar (*b.* 24 July 1964 in Riverside, California), major league baseball outfielder who hit a record 73 home runs in one season and is the first major league baseball player to both hit 400 home runs and steal 400 bases in his career.

Bonds was the first of three sons of Bobby Lee Bonds, a major league baseball player, and Patricia Ann Howard, a homemaker. He is also the godson of the Hall of Fame outfielder Willie Mays and a cousin on his mother's side of the Hall of Fame slugger Reggie Jackson. Bonds attended high school at Serra High School, an all-boys Catholic school in San Mateo, California, starring not only in baseball but in football and basketball as well. Upon Bonds's graduation in 1982, the San Francisco Giants selected him in the

Barry Bonds. AP/WIDE WORLD PHOTOS

second round of the amateur draft. When the Giants' $70,000 offer to Bonds fell short of what he desired, he decided to attend college at Arizona State University.

Bonds was named to the All–Pacific 10 Conference baseball squad in each of his three years playing for the Arizona State Sun Devils. During his sophomore season he tied an NCAA record with seven consecutive hits in the College World Series. As a junior in 1985 he was chosen to the *Sporting News* All-America Team. Bonds entered the major league draft in 1985 and was chosen as a first-round pick (sixth overall) by the Pittsburgh Pirates.

Bonds began his major league career with the Pirates on 31 May 1986. He soon became known for the same combination of power and speed that had marked the careers of his father and his godfather, averaging more than 20 home runs and 20 stolen bases over his first 4 seasons. In 1988 Bonds married Susann "Sun" Margreth. The couple had two children before divorcing in 1994. On 10 January 1998 Bonds married Elizabeth Watson, with whom he had one daughter.

On 5 July 1989 Bonds, building on his father's success, set a record for the most home runs (408) hit by a father and son combination, breaking the mark formerly held by Gus and Buddy Bell and Yogi and Dale Berra. In 1990 Bonds helped lead the Pirates to the National League East division championship. Although the team lost in the League Championship Series to the Cincinnati Reds, Bonds was named the National League Most Valuable Player for the season, posting a .301 batting average with 33 home runs, 114 runs batted in, and 52 stolen bases. He became only the second man, following Eric Davis of the Cincinnati Reds in 1987, to hit at least 30 home runs and steal at least 50 bases in the same season. However, Bonds's performance in the playoffs was disappointing when he hit .167 with only 1 run batted in.

The following year Bonds finished second to Terry Pendleton of the Atlanta Braves in the National League Most Valuable Player award voting. The Pirates, however, finished first in the National League East again. The team lost in the League Championship Series, this time to Pendleton's Braves. Bonds finished with a .148 batting average in postseason play with no runs batted in.

In 1992 the Pirates again lost to the Braves in the National League Championship Series after winning their third straight division crown. While Bonds finished the postseason with better statistics than in the previous two seasons, his .261 batting average and 2 runs batted in still were disappointing. Nevertheless, for his 1992 season Bonds collected his second National League Most Valuable Player award.

On 8 December 1992 Bonds left Pittsburgh as a free agent and signed a six-year, $43.75 million contract with the San Francisco Giants. At the time of its signing, the contract made Bonds the highest-paid player in baseball. In Bonds's first year with the Giants, the team won 103 games under the first-year manager Dusty Baker. However, an incredible second-half surge by the Atlanta Braves left the Giants one game short of the National League West division crown at the end of the season. Bonds though picked up another National League Most Valuable Player award, his third in four years, to become only the eighth player in major league history to win three Most Valuable Player awards.

Between 1994 and 2000, while with the Giants, Bonds continued to provide both speed and power, averaging more than 30 home runs and almost 30 stolen bases per season. Along the way he achieved some career highlights. In 1996 Bonds became only the second major league player, following Jose Canseco in 1988, to steal 40 or more bases and hit 40 or more home runs in the same season. In 1997 Bonds recorded the fifth season of his career in which he hit at least 30 home runs and stole at least 30 bases, tying his father for the most such seasons in major league history. In 1998 Bonds became the first player in major league his-

tory to steal 400 bases and hit 400 home runs in his career. Only Bonds, his father Bobby, his godfather Willie Mays, and the long-time Expo and Cub player Andre Dawson have stolen more than 300 bases and hit more than 300 home runs in their careers.

In 2001 Bonds had one of the most spectacular seasons in baseball history. In the first month of the season, he became the seventeenth player in major league history to surpass the 500 home run mark for his career. By the All-Star break, Bonds had hit 39 home runs, which broke the previous record of 37 held by Mark McGwire and Reggie Jackson. Bonds continued to hit balls out of the park, tying McGwire's record of 70 for the entire season with a home run on 4 October. The next day, Bonds broke the record with two more home runs before finishing with one more two days later to set a new mark of 73. Bonds's record was made all the more remarkable by the lack of hittable pitches that he received. Unlike McGwire's Cardinals, who were out of playoff contention with plenty of time still left in the season, Bonds's Giants were in a pennant race until the season's final week. That season, Bonds also broke Babe Ruth's 78-year-old record for walks in a season, establishing a new mark of 177, and he was again named MVP of the National League.

Throughout his career Bonds has been criticized by many for being unfriendly toward the media, fans, and other ballplayers. But even his most outspoken critics acknowledge Bonds's accomplishments on the field. In terms of raw statistics, no other player has shown the same combination of power and speed as Bonds.

★

Insight into and information about Bonds's life and career are in Hank Hersch, "30/30 Vision," *Sports Illustrated* (25 June 1990); Richard Hoffer, "The Importance of Being Barry," *Sports Illustrated* (24 May 1993); Johnny Dodd, "Family of Giants," *People Weekly* (4 Oct. 1993); and Bruce Schoenfeld, "Unfinished Business," *Sport* (Apr. 1994).

RAYMOND I. SCHUCK

BOSSY, Michael Dean ("Mike") (*b.* 22 January 1957 in Montreal, Quebec, Canada), professional hockey player who played for the New York Islanders from 1977 to 1987, known for breaking the "fifty-in-fifty" record of Maurice Richard and scoring fifty or more goals in nine consecutive seasons.

Great hockey players come once in a decade; sometimes not even that often. They are so superior in their craftsmanship that it is not at all unreasonable to call them inimitable. In the 1930s it was Howie Morenz, "The Stratford Streak"; in the 1940s, Maurice Richard, "The Rocket"; in the 1950s, Gordie Howe, "Mister Hockey"; in the 1960s, Bobby Hull, "The Golden Jet". In 1977 another brilliant

Mike Bossy, 1981. ASSOCIATED PRESS AP

ray appeared on the hockey horizon—Mike Bossy, "The Goal Machine" and "The Boss."

Bossy's genius was evident from his rookie season, but it was not fully realized until he equaled "Rocket" Richard's accomplishment of scoring fifty goals in fifty games in the 1980–1981 season. Though tradition demanded that Bossy keep his intentions to break Rocket's record to himself, he was not a traditionalist, and he made it clear to all. "Nobody sets out to break records," said Bossy. "You just play, you score, and they happen. But the fifty-in-fifty, that's one I want. Having my name next to Richard would not be too shabby."

The Bossy-Richard connection was not a figment of his imagination. Often, without Bossy's knowledge, the legendary Richard watched young Bossy mature as a kid player on assorted Montreal rinks. In 1968 Bossy was the proud recipient of an award from the Rocket himself, so the Bossy-Richard link was forged early.

Early in the 1980–1981 season, it became apparent that Bossy was carrying an unusually hot stick. While this had happened to extraordinary athletes before, they would usually be struck down by injury or slump. When Bossy underlined the point by stating that obtaining fifty-in-fifty would be his deepest personal achievement, the media responded to his clarion call.

Occasionally, Bossy broke stride and fell behind the goal-a-game pace, but in mid-January he came on strong,

scoring seven goals in two games. After his forty-seventh game, Bossy had forty-eight goals. The Calgary Flames, Detroit Red Wings, and Quebec Nordiques formed the final blockade in games forty-eight, forty-nine, and fifty. "It's a challenge," said Bossy before game forty-eight (against Calgary at the Nassau Coliseum in Uniondale, New York). "I think I owe it to everybody to get the record now, because I sort of announced it—and I owe it to myself too."

The Flames blockade was flawless. They double- and sometimes triple-teamed the Islanders' gifted right wing. New York was able to score (the final was 5–0 for the Islanders), but Bossy was manacled at every turn, especially when the tenacious Eric Vail shadowed him.

Two nights later, Bossy took the ice at Joe Louis Arena in Detroit against the Red Wings. "We're going to do everything we can to see that Mike gets it," said teammate Denis Potvin. "And he's going to get it. I'll be surprised if he doesn't do it against Detroit. But I'll guarantee that he's going to get it." The captain's guarantee looked fragile after the Detroit match. Once again, Bossy was stymied. The final score of game forty-nine was 3–0, but Bossy had zip. "If I didn't get the record," Bossy allowed, "it would have been embarrassing because I had made it such a big thing."

Game fifty was at the Nassau Coliseum. Bossy needed not one, but two goals to tie the mark, yet he had been unable to scrape up even one goal in the past two games. Nordiques coach Michel Bergeron knew Bossy from junior

hockey days, and he did not subdue his admiration for the Islanders' ace, saying straight out that he would not instruct his players to try any dirty tricks. "Calgary and Detroit both lost their games by zeroing in on Mike," said Bergeron. "I'd rather win our game and see him score a pair of goals. He'll get no special attention."

Bergeron's words had a hollow ring once the puck was dropped. Although the Nordiques did not assign one special shadow to follow Bossy, they were no less attentive than the Flames or Red Wings. For most of the game, Bossy was no more productive than he had been in the two previous games. After two periods of play in which Bossy seemed almost invisible, he had nothing to show for it but the look of an anxious young man. "I had never been so frustrated in all my hockey career," he admitted later. "I couldn't do anything right. I felt as if my hands were bound with tape and my stomach was tied in knots."

Still, with twenty minutes of hockey left in the game he took the ice and gave it a good Bossy try. At first he seemed to be on a treadmill to nowhere, but by mid-period some of Bossy's magic became evident, although he still had a goose egg for his efforts. More than anything Bossy needed a break, and then, almost miraculously, it happened. With little more than five minutes left in the game, Quebec was hit with a minor penalty. Bossy was dispatched to the scene for the Islanders' power play.

For forty seconds the pattern of futility continued. The clock relentlessly ticked away "4:15 . . . 4:14 . . . 4:13 . . ." Suddenly, the puck was cradled on Bossy's stick—"4:12 . . . 4:11"—he released a backhander in the direction of crouched goalie Ron Grahame, and "4:10," the red light flashed behind the Nordiques' net. With a little more than four minutes remaining, Bossy was back in the chase. Could he translate forty-nine into fifty? If cheers could help, the 15,000 faithful spectators supported Bossy with lung power. But with three minutes remaining, and then two, he was stuck at forty-nine goals.

Early that afternoon, Charlie Simmer of the Los Angeles Kings also had taken aim at the fifty-in-fifty mark. Simmer came up short by one, although he had scored a hat trick against the Boston Bruins. Unlike Bossy, Simmer had a minimum of pressure. He never was as candid as Bossy about his desire to equal the Rocket's record. "The pressure Mike put on himself to score amazes me," Simmer had said.

That pressure had never been more intense than in the final minute-and-a-half of the Quebec game. Once again, coach Al Arbour signaled Bossy to the ice. Bossy-watchers wondered what he would do if he got the puck in scoring position. Some recalled what he had said about his shot: "About ninety percent of the time I don't aim: I just try to get my shot away as quick as possible as a surprise element. I just try to get the puck on the net."

Again the clock was working against him, "1:36 . . . 1:35 . . . 1:34 . . . 1:33 . . . 1:32 . . . 1:31." The puck came to Bossy, camped near the left face-off circle. Goalie Grahame prepared for the shot. Bossy cracked his wrist, and the puck arched goalward. Grahame never touched the rubber; it hit the twine with 1:29 remaining, and the Coliseum reverberated with a noise rarely heard in an arena. Bossy had challenged himself and triumphed.

Nobody summarized Bossy's accomplishment and his future better than New York *Newsday*'s Joe Gergen: "This particular challenge is ended. There will be others. For Mike Bossy, it is not enough to play the game; he must excel." Bossy's impressive career was recorded on the scoring lists. He scored fifty or more goals in no less than nine consecutive seasons, a record that even "The Great One," Wayne Gretzky, who dominated the 1980s and early 1990s, could not match.

Unfortunately, during the 1986–1987 campaign Bossy was so severely afflicted with back problems that he could only play sixty-three games, and his goal scoring tapered drastically to thirty-eight. Worse yet was his medical outlook. Bossy's chronic back problem became so debilitating that he finally admitted that he could no longer play. In a September 1987 press conference he announced that he would take a season off in the hope that a cure could be found. When none was forthcoming, Bossy called it a career. His name, however, became part of the hockey lexicon. Even today it is not unusual for a coach to tell a potential goal scorer to "shoot the puck like Mike Bossy."

The Bossy who will always be remembered by true fans of the game was the Bossy who reached his peak in the 1981–1982 season, when he led the champion Islanders in scoring with sixty-four goals, eighty-three assists, and 147 points. Despite a debilitating leg injury that clearly cramped his style, he led the Islanders to their third consecutive Stanley Cup victory in May 1982 and was awarded the Conn Smythe Trophy as the most valuable player in the playoffs, as well as right wing All-Star. He was no less effective in the 1982–1983 season, when the Islanders won their fourth consecutive Stanley Cup.

Throughout his career, Bossy, who was inducted into the Hockey Hall of Fame in 1991, remained a champion of clean hockey and frequently went public with his feeling that the "goon" game belonged in the sewer. To his credit, Bossy always backed up his words with an admirably clean brand of play, augmented by his excellence.

★

For further information, see Mike Bossy and Barry Meisel, *Boss: The Mike Bossy Story* (1988). See also Stan Fischler, *Golden Ice: The Greatest Teams in Hockey History* (1990), *Bad Boys: The Legends of Hockey's Toughest, Meanest, Most-Feared Players* (1991), and *Metro Ice: A Century of Hockey in Greater New York Starring Rangers, Islanders, Devils, Etc.* (1999).

STAN FISCHLER

BOSTON, Ralph (*b*. 9 May 1939 in Laurel, Mississippi), world record–setting long jumper and Olympic champion.

Boston was the tenth child of a poor African-American family and grew up in Laurel, a small Mississippi town. Athletic talent seemed to run in his family, as he had two brothers who were All-America football players. At Laurel High School, Boston was known as an exceptional athlete and once won eight first places in the same meet. As this feat indicates, he was an all-around athlete, talented in high jumping, sprinting, and high hurdles.

From 1958 to 1961 Boston attended Tennessee State University, majoring in biochemistry (he would later return in 1968 to earn a master's degree). At the university he was a track and field powerhouse, where he had the opportunity to focus on training. Because of his physique—he was nearly six feet, two inches, and weighed 166 pounds—Boston decided that his best chance to make the 1960 Olympic team was as a long jumper. By 1959 he was the fourth-best long jumper in the world but did not qualify for the U.S. team for that year's world championships. However, Boston was determined to make the cut the following year and to compete in the upcoming Olympic Games in Rome.

Not only did Boston make the team, but in the Olympic trials in California, he set a world record for the long jump with a mark of 26 feet, 11.25 inches, making him the favorite for the gold medal in Rome. The new record beat famed athlete Jesse Owens's 1935 world record of twenty-six feet, eight and one-quarter inches, which had stood for an impressive twenty-five years.

The night before the Olympic long jump competition,

Ralph Boston, 1960. ASSOCIATED PRESS AP

Owens himself visited Boston in his room and encouraged him to do his best. Boston, a little awed, said that he wanted to win but was reluctant to wipe out Owens's Olympic record. "After all you've done for Negroes," Boston told Owens, "It just wouldn't be right." Owens said, "Ralph, my record served its purpose a long time ago. You just go out there tomorrow and fly."

Boston did fly. On his first two jumps he covered more than 26 feet. On his third jump, a friend put a piece of paper at the 27-foot mark and told Boston to try to jump over it. On that jump, Boston sprinted down the runway, then leaped and soared, his feet pedaling through the air, to a new Olympic record of 26 feet, 7.75 inches, beating Owens's Olympic record and earning Boston a gold medal.

Boston competed for the next nine years, and in each of the first eight years was named the best long jumper in the world by *Track and Field News*. On 27 May 1961, in Modesto, California, he became the first man to jump more than 27 feet, with a jump of 27 feet, 0.5 inches, setting a world record; six weeks later he jumped 27 feet, 2 inches. That year he was named World Track and Field Athlete of the Year.

In the 1960s Boston's main rival was the Soviet long jumper Igor Ter-Ovanesyan, who periodically wiped out Boston's records. Their competition was played out against the background of the U.S.-Soviet cold war, which intensified the rivalry. As the decade progressed, however, the two men developed a mutual respect that eventually turned into friendship, and when they saw each other at meets, they exchanged gifts from their home countries. Boston said of Ter-Ovanesyan, "Only one of us could win. And when it was over, the thing was done." After meets, they often celebrated by going out for steak together.

Boston won the silver medal at the Tokyo Olympics in 1964. In May 1965 he jumped 27 feet, 4.75 inches in Modesto, California. Each year from 1961 through 1966 Boston won the American Athletic Union (AAU) outdoor championship. Of 140 competitions, he had 128 wins, and of his 12 defeats, he lost by 3 inches or less in 9 of the events. A versatile athlete, Boston won the AAU indoor hurdles title in 1965. He came in fourth in the high jump at the 1963 Pan-American Games and was the champion U.S. triple jumper in 1963.

Boston injured his knee in 1967, but did not stop competing. He was determined to be the first person to jump farther than 28 feet. At the Olympics held in Mexico City in 1968, he led the qualifying round with a mark of 27 feet, 1.5 inches. However, in the first round of the finals, American competitor Bob Beamon flew through a 29-foot, 2-inch jump, and Boston's hopes for gold were ended when he jumped 26 feet, 9 inches. He won the bronze medal, behind Beamon and the German Klaus Beer, who jumped 26 feet, 10.5 inches.

Boston retired from competition in 1969. "Beamon put

the record out of sight and jumped me right out of the event," Boston said. "Fourteen years of jumping into the sand is a long time, and now I've got to find something else." He became an administrator at his alma mater, Tennessee State University. He has also served as a track and field analyst and commentator for television. In 2001, he was president of ServiceMaster Services, a residential cleaning and restoration company, in Atlanta, Georgia.

Boston was the best long jumper in the world for ten years. He broke the world record five times and tied it once. In three Olympic Games he won three medals—a gold, a silver, and a bronze. He was also a talented all-around track and field athlete. Boston was elected to the U.S.A. Track and Field Hall of Fame in 1974 and to the U.S. Olympic Hall of Fame in 1985.

★

The *Lincoln Library of Sports Champions* (1993), contains an in-depth chapter on Boston and his career. David Baldwin, *Track and Field Record Holders* (1996), discusses the significance of Boston's achievements. Public Broadcasting System (PBS) aired an interview with Boston regarding his rivalry with Igor Ter-Ovanesyan in 1999. This interview, filmed as part of the PBS *Red Files* series, "Sports Wars," can be accessed at <www.pbs.org/redfiles/sports/deep/interv/s_int_ralph_boston.htm>.

KELLY WINTERS

BOUCHER, Frank Xavier (*b.* 7 October 1901 in Ottawa, Ontario, Canada; *d.* 12 February 1977 in Ottawa, Ontario, Canada), hockey player who joined the New York Rangers in their inaugural season, later serving as the team's coach and general manager. Most notably, he was seven-time winner of the Lady Byng Trophy for sportsmanship and fair but skillful play.

Frank Boucher. HOCKEY HALL OF FAME

Boucher was the son of Thomas Boucher, a newspaper linotype operator, who although of French extraction could barely speak the language, and an Irish mother, Annie Carroll, whose father drove a hack for Canadian Prime Minister John MacDonald. Boucher's father played football with the father of King Clancy, later the general manager of the Toronto Maple Leafs. The youngest boy in a family of six boys and two girls, he played hockey in the subzero Ontario winter until nine at night.

In 1914, at age thirteen, he quit school to take a job with the Imperial Ministry of Munitions. After World War I ended, he joined what was then called the Northwest Mounted Police and was assigned first to Lethbridge (Alberta) and later to Banff, Alberta. Meanwhile, Boucher continued to play amateur hockey and was offered a professional spot with the Ottawa Senators of the National Hockey League (NHL).

Boucher briefly hesitated, because accepting a professional offer would forever bar him from amateur events, and there were probably no more than 110 professional players in all of Canada. He decided to accept, however, and played with the Ottawa team that lost the Stanley Cup finals in 1922. The Vancouver Maroons of the Pacific Coast Hockey League claimed Boucher as their own because he had last played hockey in western Canada, where they were located. He played for Vancouver for four years, beginning with the 1922–1923 season. In 1924 he married Agnes Sylvester; they had one son.

In 1926 his contract rights were given to Boston but were quickly sold to a newly organized New York team, the Rangers, which offered him $5,000 for a one-year contract. Tex Richard, the owner of the new Madison Square Garden, needed an attraction to fill the building between prizefights, so Tex's Rangers, as they became known, were formed. It was an interesting era in New York sports; Babe

Ruth and Lou Gehrig, among baseball's all-time greats, were the main attractions of the time, as they hit homers for the Yankees.

Boucher was placed on a line with the Cook brothers, Bill and Bun. Hall of Famer Ching Johnson led the defense with his vibrant checking. This was not only the Rangers first line but practically the only line: Boucher claimed he played forty-five minutes a game. Boucher had a formidable poke check, and his linemates claimed to have invented the drop pass. The hockey broadcaster Foster Hewitt later said that they "always seemed to have the puck on a string," and Boucher was the premier passer on the line. In 1928, while living in the Forrest Hotel with fellow residents "Legs" Diamond and Damon Runyon, Boucher led the American Division of the NHL with twenty-three goals.

In 1928 Boucher scored the winning goal in each of the Stanley Cup final wins against the Montreal Maroons. Lorne Chabot was the star goaltender, but he was injured in the second game of the Cup finals. After Ottawa refused to let the Rangers use their goaltender, Boucher suggested that the Rangers' coach and general manager, Lester Patrick, play the position. (In that era, teams would borrow players from the opposition to cover injuries that arose during the Cup series.) Patrick took several hard shots, but he helped win the game, with Boucher scoring the winning goal. In the 1928–1929, 1929–1930, and 1932–1933 seasons, Boucher lead the NHL in goals. In 1933 the Rangers again won the Cup with essentially the same lineup. This was a turning point, as the original Ranger contingent was aging and its members retired one by one. Boucher retired at the end of the 1937–1938 season.

Boucher's most remarkable feat may have been winning the Lady Byng Trophy for sportsmanship in seven of eight years between 1928 and 1935. The Governer-General's wife, Lady Byng, had decided to create the sportsmanship trophy for professional hockey. Boucher, who had actually played games on the grounds of the Canadian Governor-General's palace in has youth, won the trophy so often he was given it to keep. The NHL now awards a copy of the original.

After his retirement as a player in the 1938–1939 season, Boucher immediately got a job as minor league hockey coach, then was named coach of the NHL Rangers in 1939. With All-Stars Phil Watson, Brian Hextall, and Lynn Patrick on the first line and Dave Kerr at goal and Babe Pratt on defense, this team won the Stanley Cup in 1940. Boucher worked with this team to perfect pressing offensively while shorthanded, and the team developed the box defense method of penalty killing. In 1943 Boucher urged the institution of the center red line, in order to keep the defense from clearing or passing the puck into the offensive end and creating an unfair rush on the opponents; this change defined the modern era of hockey.

On the down side, the Rangers lost players to World War II and suffered as a team from lack of talent. (Boucher returned for fifteen games as player-coach in the war-torn 1943–1944 season.) When Patrick, one of his brothers, and others returned from the war, they had lost their luster. The team floundered. Boucher moved to the general manager position, but the team had difficulty qualifying for the playoffs, usually finishing below fourth in a six-team league. In the 1954–1955 season, the team finished fifteen points out of the playoffs despite help from Andy Bathgate, the only Ranger Hall of Famer from this era. Boucher and the team decided it was time to part ways.

Boucher was named to the Hockey Hall of Fame in 1959. During the off season, he lived on a farm in Kemptville, Ontario. In 1965 his farmhouse burned, destroying the Lady Byng Trophy. On 11 May 1972 his wife Agnes died. Boucher's brother George had a long career with the Ottawa Senators, and another brother, Robert, played forty-eight major league hockey games

Boucher's nickname, rarely heard, was "Raffles." He shot from the left side, was five feet, nine inches tall, and weighed 185 pounds. Boucher played 557 NHL games, scoring 160 goals and 423 points in an era when seasons had forty-eight games. Over his entire professional career he served but 119 NHL penalty minutes. He scored thirty-four points in fifty-five Stanley Cup games and was the leading scorer in the 1927–1928 series.

★

Boucher wrote his own biography, *When the Rangers Were Young* (1973). The book was a reminiscence long after the fact, but it is one of the few autobiographies of hockey players in that early era. John Halligan and Wayne Gretzky, *New York Rangers: Seventy-five Years* (2000) contains pictures and accounts of the early Rangers. A brief treatment is Bruce Cooper, "New York Rangers," in Michael L. LeBlanc (ed.) *Professional Sports Team Histories: Vol. 4 Hockey* (1994). The *New York Times* described the famous Patrick goaltending performance on 8 Apr. 1927 in a 1928 article, and carried Boucher's obituary on 13 Feb. 1977.

John David Healy

BOWDEN, Robert Cleckler ("Bobby") (*b.* 8 November 1929 in Birmingham, Alabama), one of the all-time leading college football coaches, with a career spanning more than forty-five years.

Bowden was one of two children born to Robert Pierce Bowden, a banker, and Sunset Cleckler, a homemaker. Bowden grew up loving athletics, especially football. With his father Bowden attended many of the games played by Woodlawn High School—where he later became an all-star quarterback—and Howard College (now Samford

Bobby Bowden, 1998. ASSOCIATED PRESS AP

University). After his 1949 graduation from high school, Bowden went to the University of Alabama, where he made the football team as a freshman. While he had always dreamed of quarterbacking the Crimson Tide of Alabama, he soon left the university and transferred to Howard College in his hometown. He went home to play for Howard and, more importantly, to marry his childhood sweetheart, Julia Ann Estock. They married in 1950 and had six children.

As Howard's quarterback, Bowden made Little All-American in 1951. He secured his bachelor's degree in education at Howard in 1953 and his master's degree, also in education, from George Peabody College in Nashville, Tennessee. Later in 1953, Bowden returned to Howard as an assistant coach, a post he held until 1955. That year, he became the head football and basketball coach at South Georgia Junior College in Douglas, Georgia, where he compiled a gridiron record of 22–11. In the summers he worked as a lifeguard and was a dockworker for a tobacco warehouse.

Bowden returned to Howard in 1959 as head football coach. In four seasons his record was 31–6. Then, in 1963, respected as a consistent winner, Bowden was hired as a receivers coach by Florida State University (FSU). Three years later he became offensive coordinator at West Virginia University (WVU) under head coach Jim Carlen. Bowden became head coach at WVU when Carlen left to take the head job at Texas Tech University. Remaining at WVU until 1976, Bowden featured a wide-open offense with a balanced running and passing attack. Among his notable achievements at WVU was a 13–10 victory over North Carolina State University in the 1975 Peach Bowl.

In 1976 Bowden returned to FSU as the new head coach. He inherited a team that had won only four games in its last three seasons, but with Bowden in charge, the FSU Seminoles went 5–6 the first year. In the second (1977), the team went 9–2 and made it 10–2 after winning the Tangerine Bowl against Carlen's Texas Tech team. Although observers might not have recognized it, Bowden was building a powerful football powerhouse. He was 8–3 in 1978 and unbeaten in the regular season of 1979, losing only to the University of Oklahoma in the Orange Bowl. In 1980 FSU went 10–1 before again losing to Oklahoma in the Orange Bowl.

An offensive mastermind with a seemingly inexhaustible repertoire of trick plays, Bowden was a great recruiter of players and assistant coaches. He also had environment and geography working for him. Glamorous Florida was itself an attraction, and the climate allowed nearly year-round workouts. Bowden especially recruited for speed, a requirement in his wide-open offense and pursuit defense. He scheduled the top teams in the country—opponents such as the universities of Florida, Miami, and Nebraska, Notre Dame, and Ohio State. This rigorous schedule became yet another recruitment tool. The best high school stars sought programs with a high national profile and the highest level of competition.

Through the 1980s FSU continued to field winning teams. Special intrastate rivalries developed with both Miami and Florida. The 1987 season seemed typical. Bowden's team contended for the national championship before losing a regular-season game to Miami, a 26–25 heartbreaker. FSU bounced back, however, by defeating Nebraska 31–28 in the Fiesta Bowl and closing out the year at 11–1. More winning seasons followed: FSU was 11–1 in 1988, 10–2 in 1989, and 10–2 in 1990. The early seasons of the new decade were much like those of the 1980s; ten- and eleven-win seasons became commonplace. Yet a national championship eluded Bowden, as year after year his great teams were thwarted. FSU was consistently in the top ten but never number one.

Change came in the 1993 season. FSU went 11–1; their only loss was at the hands of Notre Dame, 31–24. Although Notre Dame was then favored to remain unbeaten, they lost to Boston College in their last game. After beating Nebraska in the Orange Bowl, FSU was tabbed the national champion in both polls. In 1994 the Seminoles went 10–1–1 and earned another top-five finish; a 10–2 season came next, with FSU coming from behind to beat Notre Dame in the Orange Bowl. That victory was Bowden's eleventh straight bowl victory. The season was his ninth straight with at least ten wins.

Bowden's success rolled on during the late 1990s. His Seminoles won another national championship in 1999 and finished every season of the decade no lower than fifth in national football polls. In 2000 FSU was again playing for the national championship, but lost to Oklahoma by a score of 13–2. Going into the 2001 season, Bowden had 314 wins and was closing in on Bear Bryant's record number of wins (323) for a college coach. Also indicative of his coaching and recruiting skills, Bowden's bowl record is a remarkable 16–4–1.

Bowden also helped to populate the coaching ranks of college football. Three of his sons—Terry, Tommy, and Jeff—became coaches. His daughter Robyn's husband, Jack Hines, also became a college coach.

Bowden has garnered many awards during his sports career, including induction into the Florida Sports Hall of Fame in 1983 and the Alabama Sports Hall of Fame in 1986. Various polls and organizations have also named him Coach of the Year several times.

★

To study Bowden' coaching talents, read Ben Brown, *Saint Bobby and the Barbarians* (1992); Ben Brown, Bobby Bowden, and Terry Bowden, *Winning Is Only Part of the Game* (1996); and Jim Bettinger, Julie S. Bettinger, and Bobby Bowden, *The Book of Bowden* (2001). Useful articles on Bowden include Mike Lopresti, "Bowden Brought, Instilled New Attitude to Fla. State," *USA Today* (5 Jan. 2000); and Chris Dufreshe, "The Inside Track: Bowden's Mark on Game Is Downright Laughable," *Los Angeles Times* (1 Jan. 2001). Also see the lengthy article by Don Markus, "For Bowdens, Cheers, Tears," *Baltimore Sun* (2 Jan. 1999). An extremely informative article can be accessed online at <www.theledger.com/bowden/day2.htm>.

JAMES M. SMALLWOOD

BRADSHAW, Terry Paxton (*b.* 2 September 1948 in Shreveport, Louisiana), football quarterback who led the National Football League's (NFL) Pittsburgh Steelers to victory in four Super Bowl games and became one of America's best-known sports commentators as cohost of *Fox NFL Sunday*.

Bradshaw, the son of William Bradshaw, a welder, and Novis Bradshaw, a homemaker, moved with his parents from Shreveport to Comanche, Iowa, while Bradshaw was still quite young. While living in Iowa, Bradshaw recalls, he made up his mind that he was going to play professional football. At the age of seven, he approached his father and said, "Pop, I'm going to play in the National Football League." As Bradshaw remembers this decisive moment, his father dismissed him by saying, "That's right, son, move on." But Bradshaw kept up the pressure and eventually persuaded his parents to get him a department-store foot-

Terry Bradshaw. ARCHIVE PHOTOS, INC.

ball, which he used to learn to throw. His father hung a rubber tire from an old swing set in the family's backyard, and Bradshaw practiced throwing the ball through the opening in the tire from ten, twenty, and even thirty yards away. He went through dozens of footballs, but eventually he began to develop a strong throwing arm.

Of his early attempts to play football, Bradshaw has said, "I could always throw. I was clumsy, awkward, skinny, not a great athlete. But every weekend I was throwing that football. I could throw it deep; I could throw it hard. But I wasn't accurate. I hated short passes; I was bored with them."

When the family moved back to the Shreveport area, Bradshaw tried out for the football team at Oak Terrace Junior High School but failed to make the team. He intensified his practice routine and tried once more to make the grade but was again rejected. He had better luck at Woodlawn High School in Shreveport, which he entered in 1962, and where he met Lee Hedges, whom Bradshaw describes as "the greatest high school coach in the history of sports there." It was Hedges who taught Bradshaw how to play quarterback.

After establishing himself in high school as a quarterback with a strong arm, Bradshaw stumbled again when he failed the ACT (American College Test) for admission to Louisiana State University upon his graduation from Woodlawn in 1966. Some have suggested that Bradshaw purposely flunked the test so he could attend the smaller, less competitive Louisiana Tech University at Ruston. Whether or not this is true, what followed is indisputable. After entering Louisiana Tech in September 1966, Bradshaw racked up such an enviable record as Tech's quarterback that in 1970 he was the number-one pick in the NFL college draft. The scramble for his skills surprised even Bradshaw, who said, "I didn't think I'd be a first-rounder, so obviously I didn't know much about my talents."

Drafted by the Pittsburgh Steelers, Bradshaw soon felt the pressure of the hopes the team was pinning on his quarterbacking skills. The Steelers had finished dead last in the NFL the previous season and were counting on Bradshaw to help lead them to victory. Although the situation improved slightly for the Steelers over the first three seasons with Bradshaw as quarterback, his performance failed to live up to the promise of his collegiate career. Adding to the pressure on Bradshaw was the media's characterization of him as a hulking country boy without remarkable intellect. His handling by the press was clearly a no-win situation, he told a *New York Times* reporter. "If we have a bad game, it's because I'm dumb. If we have a good game, it's because everybody else played well and I got caught up in the action."

Bradshaw married for the first time in 1972, to Melissa Babish. The marriage soon faltered, and the couple divorced in 1974, adding to Bradshaw's troubles, which included a shoulder injury. The failure of his marriage and his continuing lackluster performance on the field prompted Bradshaw to reassess his fundamental values, leading to a spiritual reawakening. As he described it in *Man of Steel,* he turned his life over to a higher power, saying, "Here I am, God. I've tried to handle it all by myself, and I just can't get the job done. So I'm placing my life in Your hands. I need some peace of mind, and I know you can give it to me."

Near the midpoint of the 1974 season, Steelers coach Chuck Noll tapped Bradshaw as starting quarterback. Before long Bradshaw began showing signs of the dynamism that had characterized his college play. After leading his team to victory in 1974, he went on to spearhead their win over the Minnesota Vikings in Super Bowl IX. Bradshaw and the Steelers capped the 1975 season with another Super Bowl victory, besting the Dallas Cowboys, 21–17. Although he was sidelined with injuries for half of the 1976 season, Bradshaw turned in a stellar performance in a playoff game against Baltimore, winning high praise from defensive tackle Joe Greene, who said Bradshaw "finally destroyed all that crap that was written about him." In June 1976 Bradshaw married the ice skater JoJo Starbuck.

Bradshaw led the Steelers to Super Bowl victory after the 1978 season, defeating the Cowboys once again (35–31) in football's annual championship game. As well as he was doing on the field, Bradshaw's personal life was gloomy by contrast. His second marriage failed, largely because of career and cultural conflicts. However, his personal problems failed to dampen his playing abilities, for he managed to return to the Super Bowl in January 1980, leading the Steelers to a 31–19 win over the Los Angeles Rams. He continued to play for the Steelers through the 1983 season. Three times in his career—in 1976, 1979, and 1980—Bradshaw was selected to play in the NFL's Pro Bowl.

Bradshaw launched a new career in 1984 when he joined CBS Sports as an NFL game analyst, a job in which he continued until 1990, when he was named studio analyst on CBS Sports *The NFL Today.* He moved to the Fox network in 1994 and continues as studio analyst on *Fox NFL Sunday.* Bradshaw lives with his third wife Charla and their two daughters on his ranch in Westlake, Texas. He was inducted into the Pro Football Hall of Fame in 1989.

Probably one of America's most recognizable former sports stars, Bradshaw's popularity has spread well beyond the realm of professional football. Thanks to his appearance in scores of commercials, he has become known to millions of Americans. And, thankfully, not even Bradshaw's spirited portrayal of the country-boy buffoon in his commercials in any way diminishes the enormity of his contribution to the game of football.

★

Books by Bradshaw that provide biographical information include *No Easy Game* (1973), written with Charles Paul Conn; *Terry Bradshaw: Man of Steel* (1979), written with David Diles; and *Looking Deep* (1989), written with Buddy Martin; and *It's Only a Game* (2001), with David Fisher. Bradshaw also supplied the foreword to *Pro Football's Ten Greatest Games* (1981). Other books that cover aspects of Bradshaw's life and career include Murray Chass, *Power Football* (1973); Bill Gutman, *Football Superstars of the 70s* (1975); Jim Benagh, *Terry Bradshaw: Superarm of Pro Football* (1976); and Bob Rubin, *All-Stars of the NFL* (1976).

DON AMERMAN

BRETT, George Howard (*b.* 15 May 1953 in Glen Dale, West Virginia), baseball player who was one of the best-hitting third basemen in history; he is noted for his performance in clutch situations and his .390 batting average in 1980, the most serious assault in the last half of the twentieth century on the 1941 record of .400.

Brett is the son of Jack Francis Brett, an accountant, and Ethel Hansen, a secretary. He grew up in a competitive, athletic family with three older brothers, all of whom played sports professionally. His brother Ken was a journeyman pitcher for several major league teams.

George Brett, 1989. ASSOCIATED PRESS AP

A shortstop at El Segundo (California) High School, Brett was the second draft pick of the Kansas City Royals in 1971. He switched to third base in the minors, where he had solid though unexceptional seasons, never batting higher than .291. Brett was not happy about being drafted by an expansion team, but he moved up quickly. By 1974 he was a regular with the major league Royals.

The young Brett was far from being a star when Charley Lau, the Royals batting coach, challenged him to become a better hitter. During hours of practice, Lau transformed Brett's technique. Coach and player formed a close bond; Brett described Lau as "a second dad." From his teammate Hal McRae, Brett learned an aggressive, take-no-prisoners style of play.

Brett and the Royals improved quickly. In 1976 the team won the American League (AL) West, while Brett and McRae fought to the final game for the batting title. In his last at bat of the season, Brett hit a routine fly that dropped for a hit. He ended up with an inside-the-park home run and the batting championship. McRae, a black player, angrily charged that the ball should have been caught, hinting that the fielder wanted Brett, a white player, to win. Brett

agreed that the ball was catchable, declaring, "I got a present." Notwithstanding the controversy, Brett had clearly established himself, at age twenty-three, as one of the premier hitters in baseball, leading the league in hits, total bases, and triples. His six consecutive three-hit games was a major league record.

The Royals faced the New York Yankees in the AL play-off. Brett hit a three-run homer to tie the deciding game in the eighth inning, but the Yankees scored once more to win the pennant. It was the beginning of a heated rivalry. The Royals faced the Yankees again in 1977 and 1978, losing both times. Brett was plagued by multiple injuries early in 1980 but seemed unstoppable when he came off the disabled list in July. His average climbed throughout the summer, reaching .407 in late August, raising hopes that he would become the first to hit .400 since Ted Williams in 1941. He did not succeed, but his .390 average was surpassed only by Williams in the last sixty years of the twentieth century. Brett drove in 118 runs in his 117 games, the first player in over thirty years to have more RBI (runs batted in) than games played. He won the league's Most Valuable Player (MVP) award. Though an exceptional season, 1980 was emblematic of Brett's career—stretches of greatness interrupted by injury. No regular player had ever won MVP while missing so many games. Kansas City met New York in the league championship series for the fourth time in five years. Brett's three-run homer off of Richard "Goose" Gossage won the decisive game, giving the Royals their first pennant. They were defeated by the Philadelphia Phillies 4–2 in the World Series.

New York and Kansas City were again contenders on 24 July 1983, when, with two outs in the ninth inning, Brett hit a two-run home run off of Gossage at Yankee Stadium. While the Royals celebrated a possible game-winning homer, the Yankees protested that Brett's bat had more pine tar than the allowable eighteen inches above the handle. The umpires agreed and called Brett out. He charged the home plate umpire in uncontrolled fury and had to be restrained. "I don't remember any of it," he later observed. "It's probably the one time in my life where I got so mad, everything just blanked out." Thanks to countless television replays, Brett's tirade became the shout heard round the world. American League president Lee MacPhail later overruled the umpires and reinstated Brett's home run. The angry reaction of Yankee owner George Steinbrenner added to the theatricality of the event. Relatively insignificant in baseball terms, the "Pine Tar" home run, which set no records and decided no championships, became one of the most famous homers in baseball history.

Brett had his finest overall season in 1985, leading the league in slugging and batting .335, the second highest average of his career. Once an erratic fielder, he won the Gold

Glove as the AL's best-fielding third baseman. The Royals captured their division again but lost the first two games of the league playoff series to the favored Toronto Blue Jays. In the next contest, Brett seemed to will his team to victory, going four for four with two home runs. He stopped a Toronto rally with a brilliant defensive play. Kansas City went on to the World Series, defeating the St. Louis Cardinals in seven games.

By 1990 Brett's best years appeared behind him. Struggling at the plate, he was hitting only .256 as July began. But, rekindling memories of 1980, he hit .388 in the second half of the season after the All-Star game, and captured his third batting title. He thus became the first player to win championships in three different decades. Though partly an accident of the calendar (his span of titles could have easily fit in two decades), it was a notable achievement. Winning multiple championships over a fourteen-year period was a feat matched by Stan Musial and exceeded only by Ted Williams. Only Williams and Honus Wagner were older batting champions than the thirty-seven-year-old Brett.

Brett married Leslie Davenport on 15 February 1992. They had three sons. After retiring in 1993 Brett became a vice president of baseball operations for the Royals. He and his brothers made an unsuccessful attempt to buy the team after the death of longtime owner Ewing Kaufmann.

In his twenty-one-year career, Brett recorded 3,154 hits, 317 home runs, and 665 doubles, the fifth highest number in history. The totals could have been higher had injuries not caused him to miss over 400 games, the equivalent of two and a half seasons.

In an era of free agency, Brett was an anomaly, spending his entire career with one organization. Although he played in one of baseball's smallest markets, his playoff battles with the Yankees, his pursuit of the .400 batting record, and the Pine Tar incident kept him in the national limelight. He was elected to the National Baseball Hall of Fame in 1999.

★

George Brett with Steve Cameron, *George Brett: From Here to Cooperstown* (1999), offers many pictures and limited text. Brett has written a brief account of his relationship with Charley Lau in the foreword to Charley Lau, Jr., *Charley Lau's Laws on Hitting* (2000). Steve Cameron's *George Brett: Last of a Breed* (1993), is an uncritical account. Two invaluable sources for watching Brett's career unfold are *Number 5: George Brett and the Kansas City Royals* (1993), and *George Brett: A Royal Hero* (1999), overlapping collections of articles first published in the *Kansas City Star*. For a Yankee perspective on the Kansas City/New York rivalry, including the Pine Tar incident, consult Richard "Goose" Gossage, *The Goose Is Loose* (2000).

FRED NIELSEN

BRICKHOUSE, John Beasley ("Jack") (*b.* 24 January 1916 in Peoria, Illinois; *d.* 6 August 1998 in Chicago, Illinois), broadcaster best known for covering Chicago Cubs baseball; he also covered several national political party conventions and interviewed four U.S. presidents and Pope Paul VI.

Brickhouse was an only child of John William "Will" Brickhouse, a sideshow barker and booking agent for motion pictures, and Daisy James, a Welsh immigrant who worked as a hotel cashier and hostess. Brickhouse's father died when he was three and his mother married Gilbert Schultze. Brickhouse grew up in a household where every penny was needed. After school at Lincoln Grammar School, Brickhouse would often help his grandmother deliver food trays at Proctor Hospital in order to have access to a little extra food. Brickhouse also demonstrated his entrepreneurial streak as a newspaper vendor and a golf caddie.

While attending Peoria Manual Training High School from 1929 to 1933, the gregarious Brickhouse played basketball, served as a reporter and editor for the school paper, was elected senior-class vice president, qualified for the National Honor Society, and played the lead in the senior class play. In the fall of 1933 Brickhouse enrolled at Bradley Polytechnic Institute (now Bradley University) in Peoria, hoping to become a lawyer. The six-foot, three-inch Brickhouse played on the freshman basketball team, but he had to leave college late in 1933 for financial reasons.

While working at a distillery, Brickhouse entered an announcing contest held by Peoria radio station WMBD. Though he did not win, he accepted a job as a half-time switchboard operator and radio announcer, broadcasting news, weather, barn dances, variety shows, and local sports. Brickhouse became known for his "Man on the Street" interviews, during which he approached pedestrians for comment on issues of the day.

During the 1937–1938 basketball season, Brickhouse convinced WMBD to broadcast Bradley Braves games. The Braves were a national contender compiling a 52–9 record from 1936 to 1939. Brickhouse accompanied the team on the road and broadcast the first two National Invitational Tournaments from New York City's Madison Square Garden. He also covered Big Ten football, minor league baseball, and boxing, and initiated shows of his own such as *Here's How They Did It,* a series of interviews with successful businessmen.

On 7 August 1939 Brickhouse married Nelda Teach; they had two daughters, one of whom died after birth in 1947. Brickhouse and Teach divorced in 1978, and he married Patricia Ettelson on 22 March 1980.

In the spring of 1940 Brickhouse was hired by WGN in Chicago as an assistant to legendary broadcaster Bob Elson.

Jack Brickhouse, 1979. AP/WIDE WORLD PHOTOS

He helped out on Cubs and Chicago White Sox broadcasts, broadcast big band concerts, and continued his "Man on the Street" interviews. That fall he began broadcasting Notre Dame football games. Brickhouse caught a break in midsummer 1942, when Elson joined the navy. Brickhouse finished out the baseball season announcing both Cubs and White Sox games. When neither team was at home, Brickhouse would recreate the away games from ticker-tape accounts, using the updates that came out of a machine on a moment-to-moment basis. Brickhouse himself joined the U.S. Marines after the 1943 baseball season but was discharged two months later due to complications of childhood tuberculosis.

WGN did not cover baseball in 1944, and Brickhouse found himself reporting on the first of many Republican and Democratic national conventions. The next January he was in Washington, D.C., to cover President Franklin D. Roosevelt's inauguration. He covered White Sox games for WJJD in 1945 until Elson returned from the navy. In 1946 Brickhouse journeyed to New York City to broadcast New York Giants baseball on WMCA.

"Anybody who could see beyond his nose knew that television would be important someday," Brickhouse reminisced, and so he returned to Chicago in 1947 to experiment with baseball coverage on television station WBKB. That same year Brickhouse became the radio voice of the Chicago Cardinals professional football team.

Brickhouse rejoined WGN in Chicago in 1948 as sports service manager and broadcaster, on both radio and television. The station covered all Cubs and White Sox home games, with Brickhouse as the broadcaster. According to historian Curt Smith, Brickhouse and WGN "began a continuum—an intimacy between ball club and viewer—that decades later, in the wake of cable and thus, WGN's intrusion into millions of American households, fostered for the Cubs an enormous national sect." WGN played a pioneering role in the radio broadcasting of baseball at a time when team owners worried that broadcasts of games would hurt attendance, and the owners took the same view of the new medium of television.

During the late 1940s Brickhouse continued broadcasting Cubs and White Sox baseball and professional and college football. Still a jack-of-all-trades, he also originated a radio show called *Marriage License Romances,* in which he interviewed couples applying for marriage licenses at City Hall. Beginning in 1948 and continuing for nine years, Brickhouse also broadcast professional wrestling, an assignment he initially disliked but came to see as theatrical entertainment.

In the 1950 baseball season Brickhouse covered his first of five All-Star games, this time as the national announcer for the DuMont network. During that same year, he began publishing the annual "Jack Brickhouse's Major League Record Book" (which he published until 1971), helped to pioneer televised golf, and was on the national broadcast team for the first of four World Series. From 1953 to 1976

Brickhouse was the radio voice of the Chicago Bears National Football League (NFL) franchise.

In 1962 a portion of a Cubs-Phillies game with Brickhouse at the mike was included in the first satellite television broadcast to Europe. In 1963 Brickhouse began several years of writing the "Jack Brickhouse Says" column for the *Chicago's American* newspaper. In 1964 he was elected to the Cubs board of directors, resigning in 1975 to forestall any concerns about his journalistic objectivity. Brickhouse broadcast his last White Sox game in 1967, when the team transferred to another station, and began announcing all Cubs games, both home and away. In 1971 he narrated the successful *Great Moments in Cubs Baseball* record album.

In 1975, with the White Sox in danger of leaving Chicago, Brickhouse helped assemble investors for an ownership group headed by Bill Veeck, which kept the team in town. On 5 August 1979 he broadcast his 5000th baseball game, thought to be many more than any other announcer at the time. He retired from Cubs baseball in 1981, though he remained at WGN in a vice-presidential capacity. The Wrigley Field broadcasting booth was named in his honor in 1982.

Although Brickhouse was eventually named to ten halls of fame, his selection as the 1983 recipient of the Ford C. Frick Award, given by the National Baseball Hall of Fame for career excellence in broadcasting, was a personal pinnacle.

Brickhouse carried the flag for WGN as it established itself as the first cable superstation and televised almost all Cubs games from the 1950s through the 1990s. His voice was well known in Midwestern households from the mid-1930s to the early 1980s, and his famous home run call of "Back, back, back . . . Hey Hey!" is still remembered fondly. The only criticism of Brickhouse is that he was a bit too positive, too cheerful, and too optimistic for some viewers, sugarcoating a parade of terrible Cub teams throughout his career. "I like some Gee-Whiz enthusiasm in broadcasting sports," Brickhouse said. He died at age eighty-two of cardiac arrest at Saint Joseph hospital in Chicago and is buried in Rosehill Cemetery in Lincolnwood, Illinois.

★

The library at the National Baseball Hall of Fame maintains a biographical clipping file on Brickhouse. Brickhouse's autobiography, *Thanks for Listening!* (1986), is a substantial source of information on his career, though it can be criticized for the same reason as his broadcasting style; it contains no "juicy stuff." Janice A. Petterchak, *Jack Brickhouse: A Voice for All Seasons* (1996), is not only a biography but also a history of early Chicago broadcasting, which served as a template for sports broadcasting in general in later decades. Obituaries are in the *New York Times* and *USA Today* (both 7 Aug. 1998).

TIM WILES

BRIMSEK, Francis Charles ("Frank") (*b.* 26 September 1915 in Eveleth, Minnesota; *d.* 11 November 1998 in Virginia, Minnesota), legendary Boston Bruins goalie who became a U.S. Hockey Hall of Fame inductee and the first U.S. professional hockey player elected to the Hockey Hall of Fame.

Brimsek's interest in hockey, oddly enough, was accidental. His older brother John was the second-string goaltender on the Eveleth High School team, but he really wanted to be a defenseman. John moved up to the blue line, and his brother took over in the nets. After playing at Eveleth High, Brimsek goaltended for the 1933–1934 season at Saint Cloud Teachers College in Minnesota, then decided to give the pros a shot. In 1935 he tried out for the Baltimore team of the Eastern Amateur Hockey League. He failed.

Hitchhiking back to Minnesota, depressed and disappointed, Brimsek landed in hockey by accident once more. After running out of cash in Pittsburgh, he stopped at the old Duquesne Arena to see if he could borrow money for food. There he discovered that the Pittsburgh team in the Eastern League, the Yellow Jackets, needed a goaltender. Brimsek got the job, and for two years he was their goalie.

In the fall of 1937 Art Ross, the general manager and coach of the Boston Bruins, signed Brimsek to a pro contract. He had never even seen the young man play. However, the start of Brimsek's professional career hardly presaged his eventual eminence. He was assigned to Boston's American League farm club, the Providence (Rhode Island) Reds. Boston's goaltender was none other than Tiny Thompson, known to the hockey world as "the goalie without a weakness." Thompson was the best in the business, a four-time Vezina Trophy winner. Prospects didn't look good for the American kid buried in the minors.

In November 1938 Brimsek got his first chance to play in a big-league game through yet another accident. Thompson developed an eye infection, and Ross sent for Brimsek. It is tough to fill in for any goalie, but the pressure on Brimsek was colossal, considering he was being asked to fill the nets for the great Tiny Thompson. Brimsek's jitters vanished once the game started, however. At the age of twenty-three, he won his National Hockey League debut, 3–2. Three nights later, with Brimsek in the nets, the Bruins beat the Detroit Red Wings.

Thompson recovered and Brimsek was sent back to Providence, but Ross liked what he had seen of him. Thompson, however, was popular with the fans and had been Boston's solid rock for ten years. At thirty-three, he would have several more good seasons. Trading Thompson would not go over well with most Bruin supporters, especially if his replacement failed. Ross journeyed to Providence to take another look at Brimsek, who turned in a couple of shutouts while Ross scouted him. On 28 November 1938 Thompson was dealt to the Red Wings for

Frankie Brimsek, 1938. AP/WIDE WORLD PHOTOS

$15,000, and Brimsek assumed full goaltending responsibilities.

On 1 December 1938, in a game against the Montreal Canadiens, Brimsek went into the nets—not as a replacement but as the regular Bruins goalie. Although the game was played at the Montreal Forum, Brimsek was aware of critical eyes watching his every move. The evening was a disaster. Montreal, which had won only once in eight previous contests, beat Boston 2–0, while simultaneously in Detroit, the exiled Thompson beat Chicago 4–1. Apparently Ross had made a mistake.

Brimsek was down but not out. It took only seven more games for him to become a hockey legend. Playing the next game against the Chicago Blackhawks, Brimsek recorded his first NHL shutout when Boston beat Chicago, 5–0. However, the fans had not yet warmed to him, and Brimsek did little to improve his image. Idiosyncratically he wore red hockey pants instead of the team's then gold, brown, and white colors, and his footwork left much to be desired. But his glove was quick and his confidence was enormous. Boston fans were in for a pleasant surprise.

Two nights later, Boston and Chicago met again, this time in Boston, in Brimsek's first appearance before hostile Bruins fans. Even though he blanked the Blackhawks again, Brimsek later claimed he could feel the coolness from the crowd.

His next game was against the New York Rangers. Although the Rangers belted him with thirty-three shots on

goal, Brimsek stopped them all, earning his third straight shutout, 3–0. He now had 192 minutes and 40 seconds of scoreless goaltending. Thompson's modern record of 224 minutes and 47 seconds was in reach.

By now, even the formerly disgruntled Boston fans were enthusiastically supporting Brimsek. The Bruins were so confident of his ability that they often sent five men into enemy territory, leaving Brimsek to fend for himself. The next game was against Montreal at the Boston Garden. Boston jumped to a 2–0 lead in the first period. The amazing string of scoreless goaltending ran to 212 minutes and 40 seconds.

At the 12-minute mark of the second period, the tension in the Garden grew. At 12:08 the arena went wild. Brimsek, in his fifth game as the Bruins' regular goalie, had erased Thompson's scoreless record of the 1935–1936 season. However, with less than a minute to go in the second period, four Bruins were caught down ice, and Herb Cain took a pass from George Brown and dumped the puck in the Boston goal. Brimsek's marvelous streak ended at 231 minutes and 54 seconds. Boston went on to win the game, 3–2. Thanks largely to the talents of the young American goalie, Boston was now in first place.

Brimsek next shut out Montreal, 1–0. After that were the Detroit Red Wings and the first face-to-face meeting with Thompson. Both goalies played well, but Boston won, 2–0. Brimsek cut down the New York Americans next, 3–0—his third straight shutout, sixth in seven games. He had done the impossible—he had won over the Boston fans, making them forget Tiny Thompson.

Brimsek finished that spectacular rookie season with a brilliant 1.59 goals-against average and had ten shutouts, yielding only seventy goals in forty-four games. Rightfully he was awarded both the Calder Trophy, awarded to the best newcomer in the league, and the Vezina Trophy, for his outstanding play in the nets, the only American player ever to achieve that double win until Tom Barrasso did it in 1984. He was also voted to the All-Star team. He repeated as the Vezina winner in 1942 and was the All-Star team goalie that year as well. He was named to the All-Star team six times during his Boston career. With Brimsek in the nets, the Bruins won the Stanley Cup twice and three times finished first in the league (in the 1938–1939 season through the 1940–1941 season). His prowess in the nets earned him the nickname "Mr. Zero."

Brimsek became an American legend in a game that had long been dominated by Canadian players. In 1966 he was the first professional U.S. hockey player elected to the Hockey Hall of Fame. He was also inducted into the U.S. Hockey Hall of Fame in 1973.

At the end of the 1942–1943 season, Brimsek enlisted in the U.S. Coast Guard and, for the next two years, served aboard a patrol craft in the Pacific. With the outbreak of World War II, many hockey stars joined the armed forces. Several of them came from Michigan and Minnesota and enlisted in the Coast Guard. A team was organized out of Baltimore, Maryland, the U.S. Coast Guard Cutters, and it played in the Eastern Amateur Hockey League. Once the team was formed, other players who wanted to serve and still play hockey joined the Coast Guard and were assigned to Curtis Base near Baltimore. Brimsek was one of them.

After the war, Brimsek returned to Boston to play for the Bruins for four more seasons, but his comeback was a great disappointment. He had lost his edge. The Bruins kept waiting and hoping for the magic to come back, but it never did. Boston traded Brimsek to the dismal Chicago Blackhawks in 1949. He bombed, then retired after one season at the relatively young age of thirty-four.

Brimsek was one of a kind: an American-born, American-developed goaltender who achieved the acme of hockey success. He played on Stanley Cup–winning teams, broke hockey records, and was acknowledged the finest in his profession. But somehow the war drained him of his on-ice skills, and he had little choice but to retire.

Brimsek settled in Virginia, Minnesota, a small town five miles from Eveleth. He became an engineer for the Canadian National Railroad, guiding freight trains between cities in Canada. Brimsek married and had two daughters, and he died at age eighty-three. He is buried in the town of Virginia.

Brimsek's goaltending for the prewar Boston Bruins will forever be cited by hockey cognoscenti as the definitive work of its time. Brimsek also proved beyond a doubt that an American could make it in what was then an exclusively Canadian realm, the National Hockey League.

★

For further information on Brimsek, see Jim Hunt, *The Men in the Nets* (1967); Clark Booth, *The Boston Bruins: Celebrating 75 Years* (1998); Stan Fischler, *The Greatest Players and Moments of the Boston Bruins* (1999); and James Duplacey, Joseph Romain, Stan Fischler, Morgan Hughes, and Shirley Fischler, *Twentieth-Century Hockey Chronicle* (1999). "Teams Often Came Up Blank vs. Brimsek," *Boston Globe* (1 Oct. 1999), reviews Brimsek's career, and an obituary is in the *New York Times* (13 Nov. 1998).

STAN FISCHLER

BROCK, Lou(is Clark) (*b.* 18 June 1939 in El Dorado, Arkansas), legendary National League base stealer who held single-season (118) and career (938) stolen-base records at the time of his retirement in 1979.

One of nine children born to a family of sharecroppers, Brock did not seem destined to become a baseball star. After his father, Maud Brock, deserted them while Brock was still an infant, his mother, Paralee Brock, moved the family

Lou Brock. AP/WIDE WORLD PHOTOS

to Collinston, Louisiana, where she worked as a domestic and a farm laborer. She instilled in her children a strong religious faith, an uncompromising work ethic, and a love for education.

Brock did not play baseball until his freshman year at Union High School in Mer Rouge, Louisiana, but by his senior year he was hitting .540. The young athlete's performance in the classroom matched his accomplishments on the field, and he graduated third in a class of 105 students in 1957. He entered Southern University in Baton Rouge, Louisiana, on an academic scholarship, majoring in mathematics. Attempting to supplement his financial aid, he tried out for the baseball team as a walk-on, with the aim of obtaining an athletic scholarship. After four weeks of practice, Brock finally got to bat, hitting the first five pitches over the right-field fence. In his sophomore year he hit .545 and helped Southern become the first black college to win the National Association of Intercollegiate Athletes (NAIA) baseball championship.

Brock's heroics as a player led to his selection to the U.S. baseball team for the 1959 Pan American Games in Chicago. There he befriended an American sprinter, Deacon Jones, who taught Brock acceleration techniques that served the ballplayer well when he later became the game's best base stealer. By Brock's junior year at Southern, major league scouts had taken notice of his skills. The Chicago Cubs' Buck O'Neil saw him as having the perfect baseball physique as well as a hunger for excellence. After a tryout Brock signed with the Cubs in 1961 for a $30,000 bonus. He played in the Northern League at Saint Cloud, Minnesota, and performed so well—batting .361 and leading the team in hits, runs, and doubles—that he was called up to Chicago at the end of the 1961 season.

With the Cubs, the game that had always been so easy for Brock suddenly became very difficult. For almost two and a half seasons he struggled to hit .260, fielded poorly because of Wrigley Field's blinding right-field sun, and did not have the green light to run. It appeared that his big-league career would be short and that his failures would cause him to lose what the journalist David Halberstam calls "that most critical of athletic abilities: to relax and just play." Fortunately, the Cardinals of St. Louis, Missouri, saw a potential in Brock that the Cubs did not. Searching in June 1964 to find the missing piece of their underachieving team, the Cardinals traded pitcher Ernie Broglio (18–8 in 1963) to Chicago for outfielder Brock in what would become one of the most lopsided deals in baseball history. Following the trade Broglio won only seven more games before his career in the majors ended.

In 1964 Brock hit .251 for the Cubs through fifty-two games. After being traded to the Cardinals, he hit .348 in 103 games. He explained his change in performance in his autobiography: "With the Cardinals, I knew that *you had*

a right to fail. Failure at one thing was permissible in the interest of letting you succeed at another." He had lost his fear of looking bad, which inspired his classic observation, "Show me a man who's afraid to look bad, and I'll show you a guy you can beat every time." In the last week of the 1964 season Brock drove the surging Cardinals past the collapsing Philadelphia Phillies to win the National League pennant. The Cardinals went up against Mickey Mantle's New York Yankees in that fall's World Series and won the title in seven games.

In the remaining years of Brock's career as baseball's premier speedster, three seasons—the 1967, 1968, and 1974 seasons—were particularly impressive. In 1967 he had 206 hits, 113 runs, twenty-one homers, and seventy-six runs batting lead off, helping the Cardinals blow out the rest of the National League for the pennant. In that year's World Series Brock hit .414 with twelve hits, scoring eight runs and stealing seven bases to lead the Cardinals past the Red Sox in seven games.

Brock maintained his torrid pace in 1968, leading the National League in doubles (forty-six), triples (fourteen), and stolen bases (sixty-two) as the Cardinals outshone their competition, again winning the pennant. In the Fall Classic against the Detroit Tigers, Brock amazingly elevated his game above the previous year's World Series, hitting .464 with thirteen hits, stealing seven bases, and moving the legendary baseball scribe Leonard Koppett to remark, "Lou Brock is the most brilliant Cardinal of this (or any) Series." Unfortunately for St. Louis fans, Detroit defeated the Cardinals in seven games. From the 1968 season through the 1973 season, Brock stole 363 bases, and led the league in stolen bases in 1971, 1972, and 1973. He also shared a World Series record with 14 base steals (tying Eddie Collins), and set one with his .391 batting average in three Series.

Brock's last great season came in 1974, when, at the age of thirty-four, he shattered Maury Wills's single-season stolen-base record of 104 by committing 118 thefts, showcasing for the national media his unparalleled ability to read pitchers' moves and follow with his patented pop-up slide. By the time he retired after the 1979 season, Brock had surpassed Ty Cobb as the major league's all-time stolen-base leader, with a career total of 938. He was also only the fourteenth player to have attained 3,000 career hits. Brock played in six All-Star Games, won eight National League titles for base stealing, and compiled a .391 World Series batting average in twenty-one games, setting a series record. For these accomplishments he was a first-ballot inductee into the Baseball Hall of Fame in 1985.

His first marriage, to his high school sweetheart, produced two children before it ended in divorce in 1974. He and his second wife, the Reverend Jacqueline A. Brock, had three children and live in St. Louis, where they are active in business and charitable ventures, most notably the Lou Brock Scholarship Foundation. His awards, honors, and tributes include the Roberto Clemente Man of the Year Award (1975), a bronze statue in his likeness at Busch Stadium in St. Louis, and the renaming of the annual stolen-base leader award to the Lou Brock Award.

Brock's teammate Bob Gibson once commented, "Lou Brock is the best damn money player I ever saw on the Cardinals," while first baseman Bill White quantified Brock's value more specifically: "Lou Brock is worth one run a game." Both observations accurately reflect why, in 1998, the *Sporting News* ranked Lou Brock fifty-eighth among the hundred greatest baseball players of all time.

★

Brock collaborated with Fran Schulze on his autobiography, *Stealing Is My Game* (1976). William B. Mead, *Two Spectacular Seasons: 1930—The Year the Hitters Ran Wild; 1968—The Year the Pitchers Took Revenge* (1990), devotes considerable attention to Brock, as does David Halberstam, *October 1964* (1994). A great interview with Brock is in *St. Louis Cardinals Gameday Magazine* 5 (1999).

TALMAGE BOSTON

BROOKS, Herb(ert) P. (*b*. 5 August 1937 in Saint Paul, Minnesota), member of the United States Hockey Hall of Fame and the International Ice Hockey Federation Hall of Fame who coached the U.S. hockey team to a gold-medal victory in the 1980 Olympics.

Brooks played hockey for Johnson High School in Saint Paul from 1952 to 1955. He attended the University of Minnesota from 1955 to 1959 and earned three varsity letters playing for the University of Minnesota's hockey team. A fine skater, he played both forward and defense.

After graduating from college in 1959, Brooks tried but failed to win a place on the 1960 U.S. Olympic men's ice hockey team. Intent on staying involved in the game, he played on the U.S. National team in 1961 and 1962. In 1964 he won a spot on the U.S. Olympic team and competed in the Games held that year in Innsbruck, Austria. Brooks rejoined the U.S. National team for the 1965 and 1967 seasons. The following year he was the playing captain of the U.S. hockey team that competed in the 1968 Olympic Games in Grenoble, France. In 1970 Brooks competed on the U.S. National hockey team.

Returning to the University of Minnesota in 1972, Brooks began a seven-season stint as head coach of the school's hockey team and quickly established himself as one of the sport's most innovative coaches. He merged elements of European-style hockey and Canadian-American techniques to develop his own distinctive approach to the game.

A strict disciplinarian, he also showed exceptional talent as a motivator.

Under him the Golden Gophers won the National Collegiate Athletic Association (NCAA) ice hockey championship in 1974, the only time that a team consisting entirely of American-born players has won the NCAA title in this sport. Brooks again led Minnesota to national titles in 1976 and 1979. Overall, he posted a coaching record of 175 wins, 100 losses, and 20 ties at the University of Minnesota. In 1979 Brooks coached the U.S. National team in the World Ice Hockey championships, held that year in Moscow.

In 1980 Brooks achieved his greatest distinction, coaching the U.S. hockey team to its celebrated "Miracle on Ice" triumph at the Winter Olympics in Lake Placid, New York. "You're meant to be here," Brooks told his team at the start of the tournament. "This moment is yours." In its first match, Team USA tied Sweden, 2–2, by scoring a goal in the final 27 seconds of the contest. Then the U.S. team beat Czechoslovakia, 7–3; Norway, 5–1; Romania, 7–2; and West Germany, 4–2, to reach the medal round.

These unexpected victories aroused enormous interest and excitement in the American public. Then, Brooks's young skaters upset the mighty USSR team, 4–3, in a tense, thrilling match. As the game's final seconds ticked away, sportscaster Al Michaels shouted into his microphone, "Do you believe in miracles? Yes!"

Overnight, Brooks and his players became national heroes. They completed their storybook saga by defeating Finland, 4–2, to win the gold medal. *Sports Illustrated* named Brooks Sportsman of the Year in 1980. Twenty years later, the magazine selected the 1980 U.S. Olympic hockey team's gold medal—winning performance as the Greatest Sports Moment of the Century. Nearly everyone involved in American hockey, on both the professional and amateur levels, recognizes the Lake Placid victory as a turning point for the sport in the United States. The triumph created legions of new hockey fans and inspired a generation of future hockey stars.

Brooks briefly coached hockey in Switzerland in the 1980–1981 season, then returned to the United States to begin his National Hockey League (NHL) coaching career. As coach of the New York Rangers he guided the team to a respectable 39–27–14 record and a place in the playoffs during the 1981–1982 season. For this achievement the *Sporting News* named him NHL Coach of the Year. Brooks's Rangers made the playoffs in each of his first four years as their coach. He also achieved 100 victories faster than any other coach in Rangers history.

After leaving the Rangers, Brooks coached the Saint Cloud State College hockey team in the 1986–1987 season. He led this team to third place in the national small-college hockey tournament, whereupon Saint Cloud moved up to Division I status. Brooks himself moved on to a coaching

Herb Brooks, 2000. ASSOCIATED PRESS AP

job with the NHL's Minnesota North Stars. In 1987–1988, his one season with the organization, the North Stars won only nineteen games.

Brooks was elected to the U.S. Hockey Hall of Fame in 1990. He returned to the NHL to coach the New Jersey Devils in the 1992–1993 season. He fashioned a 40–37–7 record during that season, then resigned his post because of a dispute with the team's management. Taking over the reins of the NHL's Pittsburgh Penguins partway through the 1999–2000 season, Brooks directed the team to a 29–23–5 record.

In 1999 Brooks was elected to the International Ice Hockey Federation Hall of Fame. In 2001 he received the USA Hockey Distinguished Achievement Award, presented annually to the American hockey professional who has brought the most credit, on and off the ice, to the sport. Brooks, now a scout for the Pittsburgh Penguins, is slated to coach the U.S. hockey team in the 2002 Winter Olympics in Salt Lake City, Utah.

★

Additional information on Brooks may be found in Lord Killanin and John Rodda, eds., *The Olympic Games, 1980: Moscow and Lake Placid* (1979); Wayne Coffey, *1980 U.S. Hockey Team* (1993); and Kevin Allen, "Brooks Deserves to Coach Team USA Again," *USA Today* (3 Oct. 2000).

IRINA BELENKY

BROWN, James Nathaniel ("Jim") (*b.* 17 February 1936 on Saint Simon Island, Georgia), famed college and pro football running back and all-around outstanding athlete who later became a film actor and social activist.

Brown was the only child of Swinton Brown, a professional boxer and itinerant worker, and Theresa Brown, a domestic. His father deserted the family soon after his birth, and his mother left him when he was two for a job as a housemaid on Long Island, in New York. He was raised by his great-grandmother, Nora Peterson, until he was eight years old. Brown recalled that "even though my mother and father weren't around, I had the undying love of my great-grandmother and lived on a beautiful southern island."

In 1944 Brown joined his mother in Manhasset, Long Island, where he attended public schools. At Manhasset High School, he demonstrated extraordinary athletic ability and found mentors in football coach Ed Walsh and local attorney Kenneth Molloy. Brown earned thirteen varsity letters in football, basketball, lacrosse, and track and maintained a B average in academics. During his senior year, he averaged 14.9 yards per carry as a halfback and earned All-State honors. In basketball he averaged thirty-eight points a game. Brown received more than forty college scholarship offers and chose to attend Syracuse University at the urging of Kenneth Molloy, a Syracuse alumnus. In fact, Brown did not have an athletic scholarship at Syra-

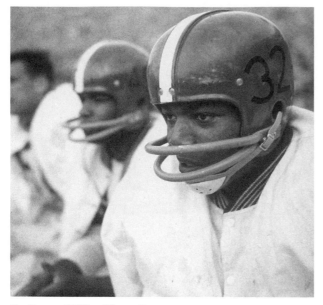

Jim Brown. AP/WIDE WORLD PHOTOS

cuse, but was given a one-year trial period to earn one. Molloy withheld this information from Brown and decided to raise the money for the first year. "Coming from a small town where everyone knew and loved Jim, I passed the hat," said Molloy. "However, that only met half the requirement, so I picked up the rest."

Brown entered Syracuse in 1953 and immediately ran into difficulties on the freshman football team. "The first thing my football coach attacked was my talent. He said I couldn't run the ball and that I wasn't any good. I would fight it every day, but finally I thought, 'Maybe he's right; maybe I can't run.' " Brown decided to quit school, but Raymond Collins, Manhasset's superintendent of schools, drove to Syracuse and convinced Brown to stick it out. After a series of injuries thinned out the Syracuse backfield in 1954, Brown finally got a chance to play. He was a starting halfback for the next two seasons and amassed 2,091 total yards, 25 touchdowns, and 187 points. In his senior year, he set a major college record (which lasted thirty-four years) by scoring forty-three points against Colgate University. Amid racial tension, Brown led Syracuse against Texas Christian University at the 1957 Cotton Bowl in Dallas. Brown dominated the game, scoring three touchdowns and rushing for 132 yards in a narrow Orangemen defeat. Recalling the racial climate of that era, Brown later remarked, "Everyone looks back on my problems because I am well known, but the situation in America at that time hurt all blacks." Brown was selected as an All-American in football and lacrosse in 1956 and earned letters in basketball and track. He is considered among the greatest lacrosse players

to ever play the game and is an inductee of both the Lacrosse Hall of Fame (1983) and the College Football Hall of Fame (1995). Brown also excelled at basketball and was drafted by the Syracuse Nationals of the National Basketball Association. He did not play on the college team during the 1956–1957 season partly because of racial policies enacted by the Syracuse University coaching staff. He graduated in 1957 with a degree in physical education.

The Cleveland Browns selected Brown in the first round of the 1957 National Football League (NFL) draft. After playing in the college All-Star game in Chicago, Brown became the starting fullback for Cleveland under the tutelage of Coach Paul Brown. At six feet, two inches and 228 pounds, Brown immediately showed the power, quickness, and speed that would make him the most dominant back in NFL history. He was named NFL Rookie of the Year in 1957 and led the Browns to the league championship game, which Cleveland lost to the Detroit Lions. Although opposing teams targeted Brown during his nineyear NFL career, he never missed a game because of injury, often playing while hurt. Few NFL players could tackle Brown single-handedly. The San Francisco 49ers coach Red Hickey told how he dealt with the challenge: "I drilled into our guys that Brown was likely to pull away from one, two, or even three tacklers. I told them to figure on being maybe the fourth, fifth, and sixth tacklers, and it worked." Chuck Bednarik, a Pro Football Hall of Fame linebacker, agreed that Brown was the most difficult NFL back to bring down: "I've wrapped my arms around him and locked my hands together. I'm six-three and 235 and have fair strength, but he's broken my hands apart like Samson and run away." Brown married Sue Jones in 1958. They had three children and were divorced in 1972. Brown continued to record remarkable offensive performances during the late 1950s and early 1960s. In 1958 he rushed for 1,527 yards, breaking Hall of Famer Steve Van Buren's 1949 NFL record. Earle ("Greasy") Neale, a pioneer professional player and later the coach of the Philadelphia Eagles, said that Brown was without question the best power runner in the history of professional football. In 1961 Brown carried the ball a league-record 305 times while gaining more than 1,400 yards, including a single-game effort of 237 yards against Philadelphia that tied his own NFL record. Despite Brown's impressive performance, Cleveland failed to win the division title and the chance to compete again for the league championship.

In 1962 Brown had a subpar season. For the first time since entering the NFL, he failed to lead the league in rushing. Despite playing with a painful toe injury, Brown refused to make excuses. "I'm no superman," he said. "I had a good season—not a great one, though. Do I have to lead the league every time for it to be a good year?" During the 1962 season Brown and other Cleveland players were critical of their coach, Paul Brown. They complained that he was too rigid, sending in every offensive play from the bench. He used Brown mainly as a straight-ahead runner between the tackles. Some of the coach's critics thought Brown could be used more effectively by letting him catch more passes and run more sweeps. When Cleveland owner Arthur ("Art") Modell fired Paul Brown in early 1963, many sportswriters accused Brown of orchestrating the move to oust the team's founder and the only coach it had known. Brown was clearly frustrated by Paul Brown's rigid coaching style, but he also admired the man who had displayed confidence in the fullback by putting him in the starting backfield upon his arrival in Cleveland and giving him ample opportunity to display his talent.

Blanton Collier, Paul Brown's assistant, became Cleveland's new head coach. Both the coach and the team got off to a fast start in 1963. Brown gained 787 yards and scored ten touchdowns in the first five games. After being in contention for most of the season, Cleveland failed to win the conference title, but Brown had his best season to date, rushing for 1,863 yards. Everything fell into place in 1964 when the Browns clinched their conference title with a convincing 52–20 victory over their archrival, the New York Giants. In that year's NFL championship game, Cleveland easily defeated the Baltimore Colts 27–0, with Brown's effective rushing allowing Browns quarterback Frank Ryan to mount a formidable passing attack. The following year, Brown scored twenty-one touchdowns, leading Cleveland to another conference title. The Green Bay Packers won the 1965 NFL championship game 23–12, holding Brown to only fifty yards rushing.

In the off-season Brown did public relations for the Pepsi-Cola Company. He initially planned to join the firm full-time when he retired from football. However, after appearing in the film *Rio Conchos* in 1964, Brown decided that he wanted to pursue acting. "I had played all of the football I wanted to and was ready to move on," he said of his decision. "Besides, there was more money in acting." During the summer of 1966, Brown was acting in another movie, *The Dirty Dozen* (1967), in London. When shooting took longer than expected and conflicted with the NFL's preseason training, Brown announced his retirement from professional football. In nine seasons with Cleveland, Brown gained 12,312 rushing yards and 15,459 all-purpose yards. He set NFL records for most average yards per carry (5.2), most seasons leading the league in rushing (eight), and most times leading the league in touchdowns (five). "Football is a whole other world; everyone is out for you," he said. "On the ground, they want to taunt you and knock you out. But they can't knock you out, because you want to win, so it's manhood time." Brown was elected to the Pro Football Hall of Fame in 1971.

Brown founded the Black Economic Union in 1966 in an effort to create more black-owned businesses. He was convinced that economic progress was more important for African Americans than social protest. Brown mobilized financial and moral support among prominent black athletes, such as Kareem Abdul-Jabbar and Muhammad Ali, and borrowed the skills of successful black businessmen. After receiving a Ford Foundation grant in 1968, the organization helped to start more than 400 companies. Meanwhile, Brown was emerging as a major film star and a pioneer in breaking through racial stereotyping in Hollywood. He received top billing over established stars Raquel Welch and Burt Reynolds in *100 Rifles* (1969), played a role originally scripted for a white male in *Ice Station Zebra* (1968), and played Jacqueline Bisset's lover in *The Grasshopper* (1970). In 1968 feminist Gloria Steinem described Brown as "the black John Wayne." "I could play the John Wayne," Brown later agreed. "I could ride horses, shoot guns, rip the blouse off the girl, and mastermind the heist." Interestingly, Wayne began his film career after dropping out of the University of Southern California, where he played tackle on the football team.

In the 1970s Brown's acting career went into a tailspin. The liberal environment in Hollywood began to tighten, and statements Brown made concerning civil rights issues were viewed as controversial. He became an activist for racial equality and was not concerned what the public thought of his activities. "My fight was and is to get racism and inequality off the backs of others," he said. "I will complain strongly about the mistreatment of minorities in this country." Brown was convinced that his views and associations were the cause of his dying film career. He stated simply, "I was blackballed." Events in his personal life may also have tarnished his image. Between 1965 and 1999 Brown faced assault charges on a number of occasions, mostly involving women. In a highly publicized 1968 case, he was accused of throwing his then-girlfriend, Eva Bohn-Chin, from his balcony. "I have done things in my life that are definitely wrong and I'm not going to lie about them, but I never threw Eva out the window or off the balcony," Brown said in 1996. (The charges were subsequently dropped.) In 1999 he was charged with making threats against his wife, Monique Gunthrop, whom he had married in June of that year in Jamaica. He claims he has been the victim of harassment by the Los Angeles Police Department.

In the late 1980s Brown began a comeback as an actor, appearing in about a dozen films in a fifteen-year period. By 2000 he had appeared in more than thirty films altogether. Brown's social activism continued. In 1986 he founded Vital Issues, a project that provided personal growth and life-management skills to gang members. The program became Amer-I-Can in 1988, targeting at-risk youth and gang members in an effort to divert them from lives of crime and violence. Brown has helped establish Amer-I-Can programs in more than a dozen states. In numerous polls conducted at the end of the twentieth century, Brown was almost unanimously selected as the greatest football player of the last 100 years. Not only was he the greatest running back in football history, but he was one of the first truly transcendent black athletes.

★

Materials relating to Brown's career are in the Syracuse University Archives and in the Pro Football Hall of Fame in Canton, Ohio. Brown wrote two autobiographies: *Off My Chest* (1964), with Myron Cope, and *Out of Bounds* (1989), with Steve Delsohn. James P. Terzian and Jim Benagh, *The Jimmy Brown Story* (1964), covers his life and career in sports and Hollywood. Short profiles are in *Current Biography 1964,* and the *Syracuse University Magazine* (spring 1996).

JOHN M. CARROLL

BROWN, Mordecai Peter Centennial   (*b.* 19 October 1876 in Nyesville, Indiana; *d.* 14 February 1948 in Terre Haute, Indiana), Hall of Fame pitcher with the Chicago Cubs during the first two decades of the twentieth century.

Brown, one of five children, received his middle name in celebration of the United States Centennial in 1876, the year he was born. His parents, Peter and Jane, were of Welsh and English descent. As a former mine laborer in

Mordecai "Three Finger" Brown. ASSOCIATED PRESS AP

the western Indiana coal mines of his childhood, Brown was known to his teammates as Miner Brown. His other nickname, Three Finger Brown, was the result of two childhood accidents. First he lost his index finger on his right hand in a corn shredder, leaving only a small stump. Weeks later, with a cast still covering his injured hand, Brown fell while chasing a pig, breaking several of the remaining fingers. This series of mishaps left young Brown short an index finger, with a paralyzed pinky, and with two severely misshapen third and fourth digits.

On 17 July 1898 the star pitcher of the Coxsville, Indiana, baseball team had to be removed due to a freak injury. The call went to the team's third baseman, twenty-one-year-old Brown. From the start of his pitching career Brown turned his handicap into an advantage, throwing a remarkable downward curve using the remaining stump of his index finger. Only one batter during the five innings Brown pitched that day was able to put this unorthodox pitch into play. Brown moved on to Terre Haute of the Three-I League (Indiana-Illinois-Iowa), where he won twenty-three games in 1901, and then to Omaha of the Western League, where he captured twenty-seven victories in 1902. Brown married Sarah Bingham in 1903. They had no children.

Brown's performance with Omaha was enough to attract the attention of the St. Louis Cardinals, who bought his contract for 1903. Brown struggled to a 9–13 record with the last-place Cardinals during his rookie year, but he showed enough promise that the Chicago Cubs manager Frank Selee traded twenty-one-game winner Jack Taylor to the Cardinals for Brown's services for the 1904 season. Brown continued to improve during his first two years with the Cubs, and established himself as one of the premier pitchers in baseball during the 1906 season. Brown finished with a record of 26–6, leading the league with 9 shutouts and a minuscule 1.04 earned run average (ERA).

The Cubs raced through the National League in 1906, winning 116 games while losing only 36 (still a Major League record). That season began what would long be considered one of baseball's great dynasties, a Cubs team that included the famed double play combination of Johnny Evers, Joe Tinker, and Frank Chance, who won four pennants and two World Series titles between 1906 and 1910. Brown led the way for the pitching staff. He won 127 games between 1906 and 1910, while his ERA crept above 1.50 only in 1910. In the days before closers, good starting pitchers were often called upon to finish out games for their weaker teammates, and Brown was very successful in this role. He led the league in saves every year from 1908 to 1911.

Brown's only pitching rival in the league was New York Giants pitcher Christy "Matty" Mathewson, and the two were famous for their pitching duels. Mathewson's plaque at the Baseball Hall of Fame reads, "Matty was master of them all," but one opponent Mathewson could never master was Brown. Brown beat Matty thirteen out of the twenty-four times they squared off, including nine straight wins between 1905 and 1908. The two faced off in many memorable games over the years. On 13 June 1905, Matty beat Brown 1–0 with a no-hitter. The duo's most famous face-off was on 8 October 1908 at New York's Polo Grounds. The game was a play-off for the pennant between the Cubs and the New York Giants forced by the "Merkle's Boner" game of 23 September, where the Giants' first baseman Fred Merkle committed a base-running error that erased a New York victory. Cubs manager Frank Chance chose Jack Pfeister to start the game, but Pfeister allowed one run and retired only two batters. Chance called for Brown to relieve the shaky Pfeister. Brown later recalled, "I had a half-dozen 'black hand' letters in my coat pocket. 'We'll kill you,' these letters said, 'if you pitch and beat the Giants.' " Brown coolly walked to the mound and took over without even warming up. He shut down the Giants, allowing only one run over eight-and-two-thirds innings pitched. Mathewson was not as effective as Brown, allowing four runs in seven innings. Under Brown's leadership, the Cubs won 4–2 and captured their third straight National League Pennant.

Five feet, ten inches in height and weighing 175 pounds, Brown threw right-handed and batted both ways. He was extremely fit as the result of a stringent exercise system he inflicted upon his teammates and himself. Cubs manager Frank Chance called him "the greatest fielding pitcher the game ever had." His unique style can be attributed to the absence of his index finger, which forced Brown to exert extra pressure on the ball with his middle finger. His famous curveball would drop as if rolling off of a table, similar to a modern-day forkball. This "drop-curve" proved to be a constant nemesis to the hitters of his era. Ty Cobb said, "I can't talk about all of baseball, but I can say this: it was the most deceiving, the most devastating pitch I ever faced."

Brown's success in baseball also introduced him to some of the notable figures of early-twentieth-century America. He was on speaking terms with Presidents Theodore Roosevelt and William Howard Taft, and in 1913 John D. Rockefeller paid Brown to tutor his nephew, then a student at Princeton, in the art of pitching.

After his major league career ended, Brown managed and pitched for Indianapolis of the American Association in 1919 and returned to Terre Haute of the Three-I League in 1920. That year he retired and operated a filling station in Terre Haute; he later suffered a stroke and struggled with ill health for three years before his death. Brown is buried at Rose Lawn Cemetery in Terre Haute. He was elected to the National Baseball Hall of Fame in 1949, and

in 1994 a monument was dedicated in his memory near his birthplace in Nyesville, Indiana.

★

The National Baseball Hall of Fame and Museum in Cooperstown, New York, maintains a biographical clipping file of information about Brown. The best resource on the Chicago Cubs dynasty is John J. Evers and Hugh S. Fullerton, *Touching Second; the Science of Baseball, the History of the National Game; Its Development into an Exact Mathematical Sport; Records of Great Plays and Players; Anecdotes and Incidents of Decisive Struggles on the Diamond; Signs and Systems Used by Championship Teams* (1910). Another helpful resource is Peter Golenbock, *Wrigleyville: A Magical History Tour of the Chicago Cubs* (1996). Brown narrates his own story of the 1908 play-off game with the New York Giants in *My Greatest Day in Baseball* (1945). A thrilling account of the amazing 1908 season was compiled by Gordon H. Fleming in *The Unforgettable Season* (1981).

JEREMY JONES

BROWN, Paul Eugene (*b.* 7 September 1908 in Norwalk, Ohio; *d.* 5 August 1991 in Indian Hill, Ohio), successful and innovative football coach at the high school, college, and professional levels.

Brown was one of two children of Lester Brown, a railroad dispatcher, and Ida Sherwood Brown, a homemaker. When he was nine years old, the family moved to Massillon, Ohio, where Brown developed a keen interest in football. Despite his enthusiasm, his father refused to allow the twelve-year-

Paul Brown *(right)* with his star quarterback for the Browns, Otto Graham, 1950. ASSOCIATED PRESS AP

old, ninety-six-pound boy to attend a summer football camp sponsored by the local Washington High School team. Brown remained in bed for three days and refused to eat until his father relented. Later, as a student at Washington High (familiarly known as Massillon), the undersized Brown worked his way up to the starting quarterback position and learned as much about football as he could under his coach, Dave Stewart.

After graduating in 1926, Brown attended Ohio State University, where he hoped to play big-time football. He was too small to compete successfully at Ohio State, so he transferred to Miami University in Oxford, Ohio, when he had completed his freshman year. After sitting out a year because of his transfer, Brown was a capable, but not an extraordinary, quarterback for the Miami Redskins during two successful seasons. In 1929 he married Kathryn Jean Kester, with whom he would have three sons. He received a B.A. in education from Miami the following year and took a job as a teacher and the head football coach at Severn School, a college-prep school in Severn, Maryland.

During the 1930 and 1931 seasons, Brown's Severn Prep teams lost only one game. He was disappointed, however, by what he perceived as the school's lack of total commitment to athletics. He returned to Massillon in 1932 as a teacher and the head football coach, taking over a team that had won only two games the previous season. Brown proceeded to build the most successful high school football program in the nation by the end of the decade. As coach and athletic director (1933), he was a meticulous organizer who managed the athletic program down to the last detail. This would become his trademark wherever he coached. He was also an innovator, introducing the use of the playbook and game films as teaching aids. From 1935 to 1940 Brown's Massillon Tigers compiled a 58-1-1 record, including five 10-0 seasons. Brown continued to innovate, scouting opponents' games to formulate game plans and sending in plays by using hand signals to call plays from the sideline. His teams were so successful that in 1939 the school constructed a 21,000-seat stadium to accommodate their fans. By 1940 Massillon was averaging 18,000 fans for its home games—more than any college in the state except for Ohio State. In 1941, after amassing an 80-8-2 record, including six state championships and four national championships, Brown accepted an offer to become the head football coach at Ohio State, where he had received an M.A. in education the year before.

At age thirty-three Brown became the youngest coach in the Big Ten Conference and inherited a team that had ended the previous season with a 40-0 loss to their archrival, Michigan. Brown recruited effectively, installed his program, and led the team to a 6-1-1 record, including a tie with Michigan. The Ohio Buckeyes finished the 1942 season with a 9-1 record and their first national champi-

onship. Because of a World War II military rule that required army-affiliated schools, such as Ohio State, to disqualify athletes over the age of eighteen, the "Baby" Buckeyes were outmanned in most games in 1943 and posted a 3-6 record. Brown's college coaching career ended with an 18-8-1 record. He was commissioned lieutenant junior-grade in the U.S. Navy in 1944 and assigned to the Great Lakes Naval Training Station in Illinois, where he became head football coach. In two seasons at Great Lakes his teams had a 15-5-2 record, including a highly publicized upset victory over Notre Dame, which was vying for a national championship.

In 1945 the sportswriter Arch Ward of the *Chicago Tribune* organized the All-America Football Conference (AAFC) to challenge the National Football League (NFL). Businessman Arthur McBride hired Brown to coach the Cleveland franchise, which was named the Browns after its coach. At the time of his signing, Brown remarked, "You know me, I'm going to build a football dynasty in Cleveland." When he was discharged from the navy in 1946, Brown put together a powerful team, signing a number of players he had coached at Ohio State and Great Lakes. He made an important contribution to pro football, being the second post–World War II coach to sign African-American players, including Bill Willis, Marion Motley (both 1946), and Horace Gillom (1947). "I wanted to get the best possible players for our team," Brown stated in 1950. "That Motley, Gillom, and Willis are Negroes is incidental. But, honestly now, if people of different colors can fight together to win a war, why shouldn't they play football together?"

The balding, 160-pound coach was an intense, rigid taskmaster and rugged disciplinarian. In his first season with Cleveland, Brown fired tackle Jim Daniell, who had been his team captain at Ohio State, for breaking training. Led by fullback Motley and quarterback Otto Graham, the Browns dominated the AAFC in the four years it existed and won the championship each season, posting a final record of 47-4-3.

Following the demise of the AAFC at the end of the 1949 season, the Browns and two other AAFC teams, the San Francisco 49ers and the Baltimore Colts, joined the NFL. Most commentators considered the former AAFC teams inferior to their NFL counterparts. In an apparent effort to embarrass the Browns, NFL officials scheduled Cleveland against the 1949 champion Philadelphia Eagles to open the 1950 season. Before 71,000 fans in Philadelphia, the Browns defeated the Eagles 35-10 in a stunningly easy upset and went on to win the 1950 NFL championship. Cleveland won two more NFL championships under Brown (1954 and 1955) and was runner-up in four (1951, 1952, 1953, and 1957). Brown's overall NFL record with Cleveland was 120-49-5.

Brown was the most innovative coach in pro football

history, essentially shaping the modern style of training and play in the NFL. He was the first coach to scout colleges for talent, employ his coaching staff year-round, use playbooks, make systematic use of game films, and provide classroom instruction. Brown created the draw play, the four-man defensive line, and the two-minute drill, and he insisted that his players dress and act professionally. After quarterback Otto Graham was hit in the mouth during a game with San Francisco in the 1950s, Brown invented the face mask, receiving royalties for seventeen years for his design. He later recalled, "I made more money from that than from what I was doing in football." When asked in the early 1980s about his many innovations, Brown replied simply, "They just evolved. That's my nature; I watch and look, and things just evolve."

During the late 1950s and early 1960s, Brown continued to produce winning teams in Cleveland but failed to return to the NFL championship game, despite the addition of perennial all-pro fullback Jim Brown. A number of players, including Jim Brown, openly criticized their coach for being too rigid. They focused particularly on the messenger system, another Brown innovation, in which the coach called all offensive plays from the sideline, sending them in with a guard. Two years after buying a controlling interest in the Browns, owner Arthur ("Art") Modell fired Brown as coach amid much controversy. Brown continued as a vice president of the team for a number of years but was effectively out of football for the first time since the 1920s. At the age of fifty-four he tried pursuing a life of leisure in La Jolla, California, but found retirement the "darkest period of my life." His wife, Kathryn, died in 1969, and in 1973 Brown married Mary Taylor Rightsell, a widow with four children.

Brown returned to football in 1968 as the founder, coach, and general manager of the Cincinnati Bengals, a franchise of the American Football League (AFL). The AFL began in 1960 as an alternative to the NFL, eventually giving rise to the Super Bowl. Brown had a voting trust in the Bengals, which gave him complete control over football operations. "It wasn't the money," Brown said of his decision to return to coaching. "Football has been my life. I have a strong desire to become alive again." The AFL and the NFL merged in 1970, forming one league with two conferences, the American Football Conference and the National Football Conference. That year the Bengals won the AFC Central division title in only their third year. Brown also led Cincinnati to postseason berths in 1974 and 1975.

Brown stepped down as head coach of the Bengals in 1976 but continued as the team's vice president and general manager. His autobiography published in 1979 created a controversy charge that in 1962 Art Modell had ordered him

to play Ernie Davis, who was dying of leukemia, in an exhibition game. Modell vehemently denied the accusation.

Brown died of pneumonia at his Indian Hill home at the age of eighty-two and is buried in Rose Hill Memorial Park Cemetery in Massillon. Brown was elected to the Pro Football Hall of Fame in 1967, and both the Massillon Tigers and the Cincinnati Bengals named their stadiums after him. One of Brown's enduring legacies is his excellence as a teacher: more than forty of his former players and assistants went on to coach in the NFL.

★

Materials relating to Brown's career are in the Pro Football Hall of Fame in Canton, Ohio. Brown's autobiography with Jack Clary, *PB: The Paul Brown Story* (1979), provides an in-depth view of his career and innovative approach to the game. Dick Forbes, *The Cincinnati Bengals and the Magic of Paul Brown* (1973), discusses Brown's influence on the team he founded. See also Jack Newcombe, "Paul Brown: Football's Licensed Genius," *Sport* (Dec. 1954), and Lonnie Wheeler, "Father Football," *Ohio* (Sept. 1989). An obituary is in the *New York Times* (6 Aug. 1991).

JOHN M. CARROLL

BRUNDAGE, Avery (*b.* 28 September 1887 in Detroit, Michigan; *d.* 8 May 1975 in Garmisch-Partenkirchen, West Germany), president of the International Olympic Committee from 1952 to 1972 who brought the Soviet Union into the Olympics, tried to unify the East and West German teams, and generally personified the games, which he ceremonially opened and closed for many years.

Brundage was one of three children, one of whom died in infancy, of Charles Brundage, a stonecutter, and Minnie Lloyd, a homemaker, both from upstate New York. In 1892 Charles Brundage left his family (his later whereabouts are unknown), and the family moved to Chicago, where Avery was brought up largely by his uncle Edward, a prominent Illinois lawyer and politician. Brundage excelled in both his studies and in athletics at Chicago's Sherwood Public School (1892–1899) and the R. T. Crane Manual Training School, from which he graduated in 1905. He then entered the University of Illinois at Urbana-Champaign, from which he graduated with a B.S. degree in civil engineering in 1909. At Illinois, Brundage excelled in basketball and track and field, attracting national attention when the university's track team won the intercollegiate conference title.

After graduation, Brundage became a superintendent for the well-known Chicago architectural firm Holabird and Roche. In his spare time Brundage was active in the Chicago Athletic Association, winning numerous track and field contests. In 1912 he successfully qualified in the pentathlon and decathlon for the forthcoming Olympic Games,

Avery Brundage and his wife, Elizabeth Dunlap, 1936. ASSOCIATED PRESS

excelling particularly in the long jump and the javelin throw. At the Stockholm Olympics, Brundage competed in the pentathlon and the decathlon, winning no medals but qualifying for competition in additional events at Helsinki and St. Petersburg. In his unpublished autobiography, Brundage contrasted the fairness of the Olympics with corruption in the construction industry, noting that "my conversion along with many others to [Baron Pierre] de Coubertin's religion, the Olympic Movement, was complete." In 1914 Brundage represented the Chicago Athletic Association in the "all-round" competition in Birmingham, Alabama.

Supplementing his own savings with borrowed money, Brundage founded his own construction firm in Chicago the following year. His victories in other national track and field events in 1916 and 1918 attracted publicity for his construction firm. Despite his repeated attempts in 1917 and 1918 to enlist in the U.S. military, he was always turned down due to poor vision (since childhood he had worn thick glasses). Although as late as 1932 Brundage was ranked as one of America's ten best handball players, with advancing age he turned to sports administration, becoming president of the Amateur Athletic Union (AAU) in 1928. Shortly thereafter he became president of what was then called the American Olympic Committee. By 1930 Brundage had ended the rivalry between the AAU and the National Collegiate Athletic Association over control of U.S. participation in the Olympic Games.

During the 1920s, the Avery Brundage Company constructed major hotels, factories, office buildings, and apartment houses in Chicago, making Brundage a multimillionaire. Expanding into California in 1941, Brundage bought a hotel and country club in Santa Barbara, which he converted into a palatial mansion, housing his by then enormous and famous collection of precious Asian jades and bronzes. On 22 December 1927 he married Elizabeth Dunlap, daughter of Chicago banker Charles Carroll Dunlap. There were no children, but in 1954 the press revealed that Brundage had had two illegitimate children, born earlier that decade, by Lillian Linea Dresden, the daughter of a Finnish gymnast. Brundage supported his two sons financially but did not publicly admit paternity during his lifetime.

In 1931, as a delegate from the AAU to the International Olympic Committee (IOC), Brundage expressed strong support for the continued and expanded participation of women in the Olympics, which resulted in a substantial increase in the number of women's events in the 1932 Olympics. Two years later the American Olympic Commission sent Brundage to Germany to investigate the Nazi regime's assurances of German Jewish participation in the 1936 Berlin Olympics. Notoriously, Brundage accepted these assurances (later violated) and even echoed Nazi propaganda in his public statements, attributing the movement to boycott the 1936 games to "radicals and Communists." In 1936 Brundage was elected to the IOC. The following year he joined the committee's executive board, of which he became vice president in 1946, and finally president in

1952, an office he held for twenty years. When World War II began, Brundage openly sympathized with the Axis powers, opposing American intervention, and blaming the Jews for seeking it. Later, his political views seem to have moderated.

As president of the IOC, Brundage preached amateurism naively, in the opinion of critics. In 1963 he successfully proposed replacing the playing of national anthems with trumpet fanfares. His promotion of amateurism over commercialism or politics led him to oppose athletic scholarships in the same year, and, earlier, to support the participation of Soviet athletes in the 1952 Olympics. He similarly struggled with the problems of a divided Germany and China participating in the games, devising compromise arrangements. By 1962, however, Brundage had expressed strong opposition to South African apartheid in sports, agreeing to that country's exclusion from the 1964 games and trying unsuccessfully to reach a compromise between the IOC and South Africa four years later.

In 1972 Brundage, increasingly criticized as authoritarian and old-fashioned, retired from Olympic administration, expressing disappointment at the election of the Irishman Lord Michael Kilannin as his successor. Visibly shaken by the terrorist attack at the Munich Olympics in that year, Brundage nevertheless stated "the games must go on." A further blow was the death of his wife, in July 1971, but to the surprise of many, on 20 June 1973 Brundage married Princess Mariann Charlotte Katherina Stefanie von Reuss, the daughter of a petty German prince deposed in 1918, who was forty-nine years younger than Brundage. She had been an interpreter for the 1972 Olympic organizing committee. The couple lived in Garmisch-Partenkirchen, West Germany, where Brundage died of heart failure at age eighty-seven. He is buried in Rosehill Cemetery in Chicago.

Attracting controversy for his strong convictions throughout his lengthy career, Brundage was an idealist in the true tradition of Baron de Coubertin, the founder of the modern Olympic Games, in his dedication to the perhaps unrealistic ideal of amateurism.

★

The Avery Brundage Collection, including an unpublished autobiographical work, is in the University of Illinois Archives; other personal papers are in the archives of the International Olympic Committee. The only full-scale biography is Allen Guttmann, *The Games Must Go On: Avery Brundage and the Olympic Movement* (1984). Other works include Alfred Erich Senn, *Power, Politics, and the Olympic Games* (1999); Heinz Schobel, *The Four Dimensions of Avery Brundage* (1968); Richard Espy, *The Politics of the s* (1979); and Christopher R. Hill, *Olympic Politics,* 2d ed. (1996).

STEPHEN A. STERTZ

BRYANT, Kobe (*b.* 23 August 1978 in Philadelphia, Pennsylvania), in 1996 the youngest player in National Basketball Association (NBA) history; in 1998 the youngest All-Star in professional basketball history; guard who with Shaquille O'Neal led the Los Angeles Lakers to consecutive NBA titles in 2000 and 2001.

Bryant's parents named him Kobe after a steak commonly found in Japanese restaurants. His father, Joe Bryant, was a star forward for LaSalle University. Kobe would play Nerf basketball while his father played on television. When Joe went for a towel on the bench to wipe his face, Kobe, at home, would find a towel and do the same. The family, including Bryant's mother, Pamela, a homemaker, his two older sisters, and Bryant himself, then six years old, traveled with Joe to Italy. Joe Bryant was a great success as a professional basketball player in Europe, averaging thirty points per game in the Italian Professional Basketball League.

Kobe Bryant, 2000. ASSOCIATED PRESS AP

When young Bryant was not playing basketball or studying Italian, he watched videotapes of National Basketball Association (NBA) games until his eyes hurt. Then he went outside and spent hours practicing what he had seen on tape. He called this "shadow basketball." His favorite team was the Los Angeles Lakers—he enjoyed watching the charismatic Lakers guard Magic Johnson. He also took every chance he got to practice with his father.

When Bryant was about to enroll in eighth grade, his parents decided it was time for the family to move back to Pennsylvania. His father got a job as an assistant coach at LaSalle University. Word spread swiftly around the Philadelphia area that Kobe Bryant was a name to remember. He was the leading scorer for Lower Merion High School in Ardmore, a Philadelphia suburb, averaging eighteen points a game. He had explosive moves and dazzling basketball skills. He was an especially fine rebounder. His coach, Gregg Downer, told the *Philadelphia Inquirer*, "He's got the total package. He doesn't have a weakness, and we're very excited to work with someone of his caliber." In 1994 Lower Merion went to the district playoffs with a 25–4 record but lost in the second round to Hazleton High School.

In the summer before his senior year, Bryant starred at the elite ABCD Camp in Hackensack, New Jersey, an annual summer stop for the nation's premier high-school players. The camp coaches voted him Most Valuable Player out of the 200 talented athletes. He became a regular visitor to the Philadelphia 76ers practices, running through scrimmages and drills with them. He even played one-on-one with Jerry Stackhouse, the club's number-one draft choice.

In his senior year Bryant had recovered from the last season's playoff loss. He scored a career high of fifty points against Marple Newtown High. A month later, in the district playoffs, Lower Merion defeated Academy Park High and Cedar Cliff High. Lower Merion met Cathedral Prep High in the state AAAA championship game. In a very close game, Bryant dropped in two clutch free throws to tie the score at 41 with just over three minutes to play. The school captured its first state title in more than a half a century, 48–43. Bryant led all scorers with seventeen points—just over half his average but enough to get the job done.

In the spring of 1996 Bryant debated whether to turn professional or enter college. Bryant called Kevin Garnett of the Minnesota Timberwolves, who had faced a similar decision the year before and had decided to turn pro. He also called on legendary Chicago Bulls player Michael Jordan to learn about the demands of playing in the NBA. In a press conference held in the Lower Merion High School gymnasium, Bryant announced that he would skip college to go to the NBA.

A number of teams called Bryant, including the New Jersey Nets, but nobody in the league was more impressed than Hall of Famer Jerry West, the executive vice president of the Los Angeles Lakers. After running Bryant through a workout, West observed, "It was an absolutely incredible workout. He's a potential NBA star. We feel this young man is one of the most exciting young prospects we've seen in a long time." Bryant was picked by the Charlotte Hornets in the first round, but word was that Charlotte had no intention of keeping him. On 11 July 1996 Bryant was traded to the Lakers for Vlade Divac When asked about his future role on the team, Bryant responded, "I just want to be ready to contribute to the basketball team and do whatever it takes to win games. Whether it's sitting on the bench waving a towel, or handing a cup of water or hitting a big-game shot, whatever." Kobe was given Magic Johnson's old locker in the team's home in the Great Western Forum.

In the NBA summer league Bryant drew overflow crowds and averaged twenty-five points in four games. He worked doggedly all summer to hone his game and prepare for his first season. On 3 November 1996, at age eighteen, Bryant became the youngest player in professional basketball history. He was not given much opportunity to display his ability in the early part of his rookie season. He played more in the second half and helped the Lakers win six of their last eight regular-season games. He displayed a rare gift for redirecting the flow of the game and instantly energizing the Lakers with no-look passes, three-point shots, and spectacular dunks.

In 1997 the Lakers played the Portland Trail Blazers in the first round of the playoffs. Bryant saw little time in the first two wins over the Blazers. In the third game, however, he assisted the Lakers in a great comeback game that fell short in the end. One game later, the Lakers closed out the Blazers, taking the series three games to one. In the Western Conference semifinals against the Utah Jazz, the Lakers lost the first two games. Faced with a must-win situation, the Lakers beat the Jazz, 104–84, with Bryant scoring nineteen points. The Jazz defeated the Lakers in the next two games to take the series. Bryant played the series with a lot of confidence but missed some tough shots in the end. Just hours after returning to Los Angeles, he was practicing on the UCLA court.

In the 1997–1998 season Bryant returned with better discipline and consistency. He stopped trying to throw down a play-of-the-day dunk every time he touched the ball. Over a stretch in the first part of the season, he scored in double figures twenty-seven times. That season the Lakers were one of the hottest teams in the NBA.

In just his second year in the NBA, Bryant was voted a starter in the All-Star game; he scored eighteen points and hauled down six rebounds. He went into a slump late in the season, but the team managed to win twenty-two of its last twenty-five regular-season games, enabling them to tie the Seattle Supersonics for first place in the Pacific Division. The Lakers beat the Supersonics in game five to win the series and another chance to play the Utah Jazz. However, the Jazz swept the series and shocked the Lakers with their worst playoff loss in history, 112–77.

Bryant finished the year with more points than any other reserve in the entire league and more than any bench player in club history, and an average of 15.4 points per game. Magic Johnson said of him, "I love him because he works so hard. Kobe and Shaquille [O'Neal] are our hardest workers in practice. He wants to learn, so he asks you a lot of questions. Kobe has had a great impact on the team and the league. Every moment he touches the ball, you don't know what's going to happen. It may be the greatest move you've seen, next to Jordan."

Bryant played a key role in the team's back-to-back championships in the 2000 and 2001 seasons. In the 1999–2000 season he averaged 22.5 points per game, and averaged 28.5 points per game the following season. In the 1999–2000 season he was also selected to the All NBA Second Team as well as the NBA All Defensive First Team. In 2001, Bryant had appeared in twenty NBA playoff games.

Bryant's honors include winning the Nestle Crunch Slam Dunk contest in his rookie year with the Lakers. He set an NBA record by scoring thirty-one points in the Schick rookie game. He was named to the Schick All-Rookie Second Team, averaging 7.6 points in just 15.5 minutes per game. He set the Laker record for the most points scored by a reserve—1,220 points in the 1997–1998 season. At age twenty, the youngest All-Star in professional basketball history, Bryant showed himself the most dynamic young player in the league.

★

For further information on Bryant see Joe Layden, *The "Air" Apparent* (1998); Wayne Coffey, *The Kobe Bryant Story* (1999); Roland Lazenby, *Mad Game* (1999); John Albert Torres, *Kobe Bryant* (2000); Mark Stewart, *Kobe Bryant: Hard to the Hoop* (2000). Phil Taylor, "Together Again," *Sports Illustrated* (25 June 2001) is a cover article.

REED B. MARKHAM

BRYANT, Paul William ("Bear")   (*b.* 11 September 1913 in Kingsland, Arkansas; *d.* 23 January 1983 in Tuscaloosa, Alabama), one of college football's most successful, respected, and beloved coaches.

Born into a farm family living near Fordyce, Arkansas, "Bear" Bryant was one of twelve children of Wilson Monroe Bryant and Ida Kilgore, farmers. Bryant grew up working on the family acreage, a hard job that helped him develop a physique suitable for athletics.

Paul "Bear" Bryant. THE LIBRARY OF CONGRESS

Bryant acquired his nickname in an unusual way. Big for his age, Bryant was thirteen when the Lyric Theater in Fordyce presented a special attraction staged by a traveler who promised a dollar a minute to anyone who would wrestle his bear. Bryant later said he was getting fifty cents a day chopping cotton, and he could not resist the dollar-a-minute prize. He apparently lasted a most limited time before he jumped from the Lyric stage and hid behind a row of seats so the bear could not finish him off. Later Bryant went to collect his money, but the stranger, who had also gambled on the match, had already skipped town with his bear in tow. Of course the stranger also left with all of the attendance money. Bested by both the bear and the felonious promoter, Bryant was forever after known as "Bear."

Bryant attended the Fordyce public schools, where he was an average student. Hardened by strenuous farm work that included brute labor, he became a big, tough boy by the time he entered Fordyce High School, where he played tackle on the football team. Although he later said he was not a good athlete, he made the all-state team as a senior, and after graduating in 1931 Bear was recruited by the University of Alabama. In 1934, while they were both students at the university, Bryant wed Mary Harmon Black.

They had two children. In college Bryant played right end, and his team won the Rose Bowl in 1935, defeating Stanford by a score of 29 to 13.

When his college playing career ended with his graduation that year, Bryant decided to become a football coach. He was an assistant coach at Alabama for four years (1936–1940) and at Vanderbilt for two more years (1940–1941). After serving with distinction in the U.S. Navy during World War II, he became head coach at the University of Maryland in 1945. He coached his team to a superior 6–2–1 season before he resigned in protest because the university president reinstated a player Bryant had dismissed for breaking training rules. Bryant then served as head coach at the University of Kentucky (1946–1953). His teams compiled a 60–23–5 record, and he took his players to four bowl games, winning three. Bryant next coached at Texas A&M, where he gained a reputation as a "brutal" disciplinarian. In 1954, his first year, 115 players on scholarships participated in the opening August practice, but by the time the season began only 27 young survivors remained to take the field. Later in his career, Bryant himself wondered if he was too hard a taskmaster, for despite his efforts to harden his players, his first Aggie team lost nine of its ten games. But Bryant and his boys bounced back, losing only five games in the next three years and producing the Heisman Trophy winner John David Crow, a running back, in 1956. Bryant's discipline had built a winning team after all.

In 1958 the University of Alabama called Bryant home after its football team suffered four disastrous losing seasons in a row. He remained at Tuscaloosa for the rest of his coaching career. With the hard work of both his players and himself, Bryant restored the Alabama Crimson Tide's reputation as a consistent winner and was named the Southeastern Conference Coach of the Year in 1961, an honor he subsequently won seven more times. He was also National Coach of the Year three times, and that award was later named the Paul "Bear" Bryant Award.

Bryant so loved the game and his job that he usually put in fourteen-hour workdays during summer practices and only slightly less strenuous days once the seasons began. During all practices he lodged himself on a high tower to supervise players and assistant coaches on two different practice fields. Under Bryant the Tide fielded scores of good players. The list of those who went on to professional football careers includes "Broadway" Joe Namath (also known as "Willy Joe"), Ken Stabler, Lee Roy Jordan, Steve Sloan, Ray Perkins, and forty-two others. Thirty-nine of his assistant coaches became head coaches elsewhere, including Jack Pardee and Bum Phillips. Bryant's Alabama teams won national championship titles in 1961, 1964, 1973, and 1979, while his 1965 and 1978 teams tied for the title. Bryant's coaching career statistics were phenomenal. In 38 seasons his teams won 323 games, lost only 85, and tied 17.

His overall postseason bowl record included fifteen wins and twelve losses. His favorite bowl was the Sugar Bowl in New Orleans, where his teams won eight games and lost only one.

Bryant also participated in the modern civil rights movement, helping to integrate college football. As early as 1946, when he was at Kentucky, he wanted to recruit black players, but university administrators refused. Bryant faced the same problem at Texas A&M and in his early Alabama years. But in 1971 he was finally allowed to recruit black athletes, the first being Wilbur Jackson, a running back. Of the 128 players on his final team, 54 were African Americans.

By the time he retired after the 1982 season, Bryant was regarded as the nation's premier college football coach. Indeed earlier the National Collegiate Athletic Association (NCAA) named him Coach of the Decade for the 1960s. Certainly the people of Alabama loved him. Bryant died of a heart attack at age sixty-nine. The First Methodist Church in Tuscaloosa held a memorial ceremony. He is buried in Elmwood Cemetery in Birmingham, Alabama.

★

Bryant's autobiography *Bear* (1974) provides an in-depth look at the coach. Mickey Herskowitz's biography *The Legend of Bear Bryant* (1993) is a fascinating look at the legendary coach. Also see Bill Libby, *The Coaches* (1972). Bryant's "brutal" year at Texas A&M is covered in Jim Dent, *The Junction Boys: How Ten Days in Hell with Bear Bryant Forged a Championship Team* (1999). Bryant's career also draws notice in Robert Ours, *The College Football Encyclopedia: The Authoritative Guide to 124 Years of College Football* (1994). Interesting and informative articles include Marty Mule, "Bear on the Bayou," *New Orleans Times-Picayune* (31 Dec. 1996); and Don Freeman, "The Bear Knew How to Motivate Everybody," *San Diego Union-Tribune* (2 Feb. 1994). An obituary is in the *New York Times* (27 Jan. 1983).

JAMES M. SMALLWOOD

BUCHANAN, Junious ("Buck") (*b.* 10 September 1940 in Gainesville, Alabama; *d.* 16 July 1992 in Kansas City, Missouri), professional football player for thirteen seasons with the Kansas City Chiefs and one of the greatest defensive linemen in both the American Football League (AFL) and the National Football League (NFL).

Buchanan, one of four children born to Wallace and Fannie Buchanan, grew up in Gainesville, near Birmingham, Alabama. After winning All-State honors in both basketball and football at A. H. Parker High School in Birmingham, Buchanan became a two-way (offensive and defensive) star and small-college All-American at Grambling State University in Grambling, Louisiana, under coach Eddie Rob-

Buck Buchanan, 1966. ASSOCIATED PRESS AP

inson. From 1959 to 1962, Buchanan played a key role in bringing Grambling and Coach Robinson to national attention as producers of professional football players.

In 1963, following his senior year at Grambling (he completed his degree later, in 1969), Buchanan was the first player drafted by the AFL and the first player ever drafted by the Kansas City Chiefs, a new team that had recently moved from Dallas, where they played for three seasons as the Texans. Buchanan played with the Chiefs in their Super Bowl I loss to the Green Bay Packers in 1967 and in their Super Bowl IV victory over the Minnesota Vikings in 1970. Although first separate leagues, in 1970 the AFL and NFL merged into a single league, and the Chiefs' victory over the Vikings, following the New York Jets' upset of the Baltimore Colts the previous year, fully established the teams of the old AFL as equal partners with the traditional clubs of the NFL.

Each year from 1965 through 1972, Buchanan was named to either the AFL All-Star game or the NFL Pro Bowl. He was named the Chiefs' Most Valuable Player in 1965 and 1967 and was a major reason for the team's dominating defense during its Super Bowl years. Durable as well as talented, he missed only one game in his thirteen seasons with the Chiefs. At six feet, seven inches and 280 pounds, Buchanan was exceptionally quick for his size, a prototype

of the modern defensive tackle. Longtime opponent Gene Upshaw, a guard for the Oakland Raiders, described playing against the huge but elusive Buchanan as being "like hitting a ghost." Although Upshaw was considered too tall for a guard by some scouts, the Raiders drafted him specifically to play against Buchanan. Together the two men raised the standard for future NFL linemen. Raiders coach John Madden once said that Buchanan "revolutionized the game."

After retiring from play in 1975, Buchanan worked for two seasons as an assistant coach for the New Orleans Saints under his former Chiefs coach Hank Stram. He then spent one season with the Cleveland Browns before leaving football permanently and returning to the Kansas City area. He started two businesses, All-Pro Construction Company and All-Pro Advertising, and became deeply involved in local business and civic activities. He was a founder of the Black Chamber of Commerce of Greater Kansas City, serving as its president from 1986 to 1989. He was appointed to the Jackson County Sports Complex Authority in 1987, to the Kansas City Board of Election Commissioners in 1989, and to the board of the Kansas City Downtown Minority Development Corporation in 1991.

For his contributions to the community, Buchanan was the recipient of the first Golden Torch Award in 1990, presented by the University of Missouri–Kansas City to a distinguished citizen who exemplifies how participation in college athletics relates to success in other areas. He received the Kansas City Spirit Award in 1992 and was named among the 100 most influential African Americans in Kansas City by the *Kansas City Globe*. Buchanan died at age fifty-one at his home following a two-year struggle with lung cancer, leaving his wife Georgia and three children from an earlier marriage to Elizabeth Peet, whom he met at Grambling. He is buried in Mount Moriah Cemetery in Kansas City.

As the first player from an all-black college ever drafted in the first round and the first player selected in the entire AFL draft in 1963, Buchanan was a key figure in what might be considered the golden era of black college football. After twelve years of excluding African Americans, the NFL began to sign black players in 1946. That year also saw the appearance of an integrated rival league, the All-America Football Conference. Initially, professional scouts were wary of signing players from black colleges, whose programs were underfunded and isolated from the major universities in the segregated South. A small handful of black-college players nonetheless contributed to the integration of pro football in the 1950s. In the 1960s, following the success of such players as Paul ("Tank") Younger, Roosevelt Brown, Rosey Grier, Willie Galimore, and Willie Davis, black colleges were recognized by pro scouts as a major source of football talent.

By 1965 eighty of the approximately 220 black players in the NFL and AFL were from black colleges, fifteen of them from Grambling alone. By 1970 more than eighty players from Grambling—a number second only to the University of Notre Dame—had gone on to play professional football. Besides Buchanan, defensive starters on the Chiefs' 1970 Super Bowl championship team that came from black colleges included Willie Lanier (Morgan State University), Emmitt Thomas (Bishop State Community College), Jim Marsalis (Tennessee State University), Robert Holmes (Southern University and A&M College, Baton Rouge), and Jim Kearney (Prairie View A&M University). Offensive players included Otis Taylor (Prairie View) and Robert Holmes (Southern). This golden age ended in the 1970s when the remaining universities in the Southeastern Conference and Southwest Conference finally integrated their football teams. As not only one of its greatest linemen but also a major figure in a pioneering generation, Buchanan was an important contributor to the modern NFL during its ascension as the country's number-one sports attraction.

Buchanan was elected to the Pro Football Hall of Fame in 1990 and was named to the halls of fame of the Chiefs, the National Association of Intercollegiate Athletics, the states of Alabama and Louisiana, and Grambling State University.

Don Budge (*left*) with Bobby Riggs, 1947. ASSOCIATED PRESS AP

★

There is no biography or autobiography, either popular or scholarly, of Buchanan, and as a lineman in the 1960s, he was not even the subject of major magazine profiles. His coach at Grambling, Eddie Robinson, comments on Buchanan's importance to his program in his autobiography, written with Richard Lapchick, *Never Before, Never Again: The Stirring Autobiography of Eddie Robinson, the Winningest Coach in the History of College Football* (1999). Two articles in *Ebony* magazine, "Pro Football Stars from Negro Colleges" (Oct. 1965), and A. S. ("Doc") Young, "Pro Football Discovers the Black College" (Sept. 1970), provide a context for Buchanan's role in the greater integration of professional football. For the basic facts of his life and career, see Buchanan's obituary in the *Kansas City Star* (17 July 1992).

MICHAEL ORIARD

BUDGE, (John) Donald ("Don") (*b.* 13 June 1915 in Oakland, California; *d.* 26 January 2000 in Scranton, Pennsylvania), tennis champion best known for winning the first Grand Slam in tennis history: the Australian, French, Wimbledon, and U.S. championships in the same calendar year.

Budge was the son of John Budge, a Scots-Irishman who managed a laundry and had been a member of the Glasgow Rangers soccer team, and Pearl Kincaid. Budge's father's respiratory problems had brought the family to California,

where Budge and his brother grew up competing in as many sports as possible. Budge, who graduated from University High School in Oakland, did not like tennis at first; he preferred baseball, football, and basketball. But in June 1930, as he approached his fifteenth birthday, his older brother jokingly suggested that he enter the California state boys' tennis tournament. Everyone in the room laughed, except for Budge. He practiced for the next two weeks, then proceeded to win the tournament, the first he had ever entered.

After this promising beginning, Budge began to concentrate on tennis exclusively. Budge was a serious, methodical player. Never content with his strokes or his game, he was constantly improving and developed into a steady backcourt player. Not known for his finesse, he drilled his opponents with a strong forehand and a backhand that became like a ferocious weapon.

Budge went East in 1934, where he made his debut at the Seabright Lawn Tennis and Cricket Club in New Jersey. Because he had been raised on the hard courts of California, he took some time getting used to playing on grass. Once he made the adjustment, however, his experience with hard-court tennis became a distinct asset.

Budge had the good fortune to watch Ellsworth Vines, the best American player of that time, on the court and to receive special tutoring and encouragement from British tennis great Fred Perry. Watching these two play convinced

Budge of the importance of a net game; beginning in 1936, he became increasingly an attack player. At the same time, Budge developed a reputation for seriousness on the court, mixed with the manners of a complete and thorough gentleman; he never complained about line calls and was known for humor and sociability off court.

An opportunity to shine came in 1937 at the Davis Cup tournament. Fred Perry had turned professional, leaving the amateur tennis field less crowded than before, and Budge became known as the new American hope. The Davis Cup had been taken by French players in the 1920s and had remained elusive for more than a decade. Now Budge became the centerpiece of the American team, and he played his most memorable match.

The 1937 Davis Cup was played on the grounds of the All England club at Wimbledon. Germany and the United States faced each other in the finals. Budge went up against Gottfried von Cramm in the fifth round. The German was probably the more elegant player; his shotmaking was terrific, and he kept Budge at arm's length during the first half of the match, winning the first two sets, 8–6, 7–5. Budge possessed a relentless competitive instinct, however. He came roaring back to win the next three sets and the match: 6 4, 6–2, 8–6. Those who witnessed the game declared it one of the most intense and hard-fought that they had ever seen. Von Cramm, who had come within one point of winning, was sent to prison on a morals charge when he returned to Germany. He had let down the Nazi cause by losing the tournament and was punished, just as Hitler punished other athletes who failed to win at the 1936 Olympics in Berlin.

Budge's most stellar year was 1938. He won, in succession, the Australian Championships (on grass), the French Championships (on clay), Wimbledon (on grass), and the U.S. Championships at Forest Hills, New York (on grass). No one, not even "Big" Bill Tilden, had ever won all four championships in the same year, and no one would do it again until Rod Laver in 1962. Equally impressive, Budge won Wimbledon without the loss of a single set, and he took the U.S. Championships with the loss of only one.

By this time Budge's game was completely developed. His serve was strong, his volleys crisp, and he reached the net behind many approach shots. Two things made him stand out, however. His backhand was a tremendous weapon; he won many points with outright winners. Second, his height and immaculate appearance gave him the impression of command and control, even if the facts did not always warrant it. Remarkably fit, Budge simply never seemed tired; he went on hitting shot after shot and drove opponents into the ground.

Budge turned professional on 10 November 1938. This decision was a loss to amateur tennis, but his reputation was so great, and he was so well-liked, that the United States Lawn Tennis Association wished him well in his new endeavors. The same generous attitude was not accorded most players who made the move from amateur to professional.

He made his professional debut at Madison Square Garden on 3 January 1939. He was up against Ellsworth Vines, the greatest player between 1930 and 1934, but made a swift adaptation to the indoor play, winning handsomely. He went on to defeat Fred Perry in March and was soon number one on the professional tour.

A new decade dawned, a decade that saw World War II and many societal changes. The new era was not kind to Budge. He spent three years in the Army Air Forces, and when he returned to active tennis play, his formidable game was never the same; some attribute this to a shoulder injury he suffered while in the service. Though he competed gamely, Budge lost the professional match-up of 1946 to Bobby Riggs, a younger American player who had not spent years in the service. It seemed extraordinary that Budge, with his great physique, strength, and attitude, could lose to the much shorter, slighter man, but Riggs was a master of his art.

From that time on, Budge was a dwindling draw on the tennis tour. He continued to compete sporadically, but never again approached his play of the late 1930s, when he had left an indelible imprint on tennis. His decline, while visible, did not matter to his unswerving fans, however. Many of those who saw him at his finest are convinced that Budge was the best tennis player, day in and day out, that the world has ever seen. Even the appearance of notables such as Rod Laver in the 1960s and Pete Sampras in the 1990s could not persuade them otherwise. To his fans, Budge was always "Mister Tennis."

Budge died in Scranton, Pennsylvania, after an automobile accident. He was survived by his second wife, Loriel, and by two sons.

★

Useful references include Jack Kramer, with Frank Deford, *The Game: My Forty Years in Tennis* (1979); Will Grimsley, *Tennis: Its History, People, and Events* (1971); and Budge's own *Budge on Tennis* (1939), with an introduction by Walter L. Pate and a biography by Allison Danzig. An obituary is in the *New York Times* (27 Jan. 2000).

SAMUEL WILLARD CROMPTON

BUNNING, James Paul David ("Jim") (*b.* 23 October 1931 in Southgate, Kentucky), Hall of Fame baseball player who pitched no-hitters in both the American and National Leagues, including the first perfect game in modern National League history for the Philadelphia Phillies against the New York Mets in 1964, and later embarked on a political career as a six-term congressman and a U.S. senator.

Jim Bunning, 1966. ASSOCIATED PRESS FILES

Bunning was one of three children of Louis A. Bunning, Sr., a manager of a ladder manufacturing plant, and Gladys Mae Best, a homemaker. His college years were spent at Xavier University in Cincinnati, Ohio, a Jesuit institution from which he received a B.S. degree in economics in 1953. During his junior year, on 26 January 1952, he married Mary Catherine Theis. The couple had nine children, including two sets of twins.

Bunning, an intense competitor, persevered in the minor leagues before earning a major league job with the Detroit Tigers in 1955. Told early in his career than he would not be successful throwing the way he did—sidearm with a stiff front leg, hurtling off the mound after each pitch—the tall, lanky right-hander proved otherwise by winning twenty games and starting in the All-Star game for the American League in 1957, his first full big league season.

Bunning would switch teams several times in his seventeen-year career. After his ninth season in a Tiger uniform, he spent eight years in the National League, playing in Philadelphia (1964–1967 and 1970–1971), Pittsburgh (1968 and part of 1969), and Los Angeles (1969). Bunning became the second pitcher (Cy Young was the first) to win 100 games and strike out 1,000 batters in each league. When he retired following the 1971 season, Bunning had amassed 224 victories; 184 defeats, mostly for also-ran clubs; and 2,855 strikeouts, at the time second only to Walter Johnson.

As a player Bunning failed to achieve his biggest goal, a chance to pitch in the World Series. In 1964 his Philadelphia Phillies team came close. The team led by six and a half games with twelve games to go, then lost ten in a row. Even though Bunning pitched one of his forty career shutouts on the final day, they finished one game behind the St. Louis Cardinals.

Although he was deprived of the World Series spotlight, Bunning made the most of his All-Star opportunities. In his 1957 start against the National League, he retired nine straight batters in a lineup that included Hank Aaron, Stan Musial, Willie Mays, and Frank Robinson. Four years later, when two All-Star games were played, Bunning retired fifteen batters in a row—six in the first game, nine in the second. In all he pitched eighteen innings in All-Star competition, allowing only seven hits and two earned runs, walking one, and striking out thirteen. It was a record befitting a pitcher who retired Ted Williams to close out his first no-hitter for the Detroit Tigers against the Boston Red Sox at Fenway Park in 1958. Six years later, he celebrated Father's Day at New York City's Shea Stadium by retiring twenty-seven straight Mets batters to pitch the first National League perfect game in eighty-four years.

Those who played with him or against him remembered Bunning best for his fierce competitiveness. Larry Bowa, who played shortstop behind Bunning in the pitcher's last two seasons, recalled making an error once in San Diego. "He turned around and glared at me," Bowa said. "I wanted to find a way to hide. Later he said to me, 'Larry, I didn't mean anything by that.' It's just that he was so intense. I mean this guy battled." Bunning pitched in an era when it was accepted practice to pitch inside, often sending batters sprawling in the dirt. Joe Torre, who played against Bunning in the National League, said: "He was like [Dodger Hall of Famer Don] Drysdale. He gave you the same look—big, came a little sidewinding, and he was mean."

Bunning's serious, all-business approach was evident in his relationship with sportswriters and later with political writers, many of whom found him difficult to interview. He did not tolerate what he considered "dumb questions." His refusal to curry favor with the press was likely a factor in his long wait to make the Hall of Fame. The baseball writers never voted him in, although they once gave him 74.2 percent of the vote, just shy of the 75 percent needed. In 1996, however, Bunning attained baseball's highest honor, voted in by the Hall of Fame Veterans Committee.

Pitching was only part of Bunning's baseball legacy. He was an early leader in the formation of the Major League Baseball Players Association in 1947 and one of the men responsible for choosing Marvin Miller as its first executive director in 1966, a move that angered the owners and ultimately changed the course of the game by shifting the balance of power away from management. In addition Bunning was a driving force in establishing a pension program for big league players that set the standard for pro sports.

When his playing career was over, Bunning became a major league manager. For five years he managed in the Phillies' farm system, but his bluntness and honesty did not always sit well with the organization. The Phillies fired him at the close of his fifth and most successful managerial season. In retrospect, Bunning said, they did him a favor. His baseball career cut short, he surprised everybody, including himself, by turning to politics.

Bunning was hardly the political type. The thought of him shaking hands, making small talk, and kissing babies was laughable to those who knew him. But with a huge assist from his wife, he entered politics. A conservative Republican, he served as city councilman in Fort Thomas, Kentucky (1977–1979), and as Kentucky state senator (1979–1986). In 1983 he made an unsuccessful run for governor. Three years later he was headed to Washington, D.C., elected a congressman from Kentucky's Fourth District. Following his sixth term in the U.S. House of Representatives, he won his biggest prize, a seat in the U.S. Senate (elected in 1998).

Along the way Bunning waged verbal battles with two baseball commissioners, Peter Ueberroth and Bud Selig, and angered the baseball establishment by taking a strong stand against the sport's antitrust exemption. In his Hall of Fame induction speech in the summer of 1996, Bunning pulled no punches, as usual. "For over four years now baseball has been rudderless," he said. "For God's sake and for the game's sake, find a rudder."

Bunning has always said what he thought, not what he thought others wanted to hear. His friends have been intensely loyal. His enemies, whether baseball commissioners, journalists who did not do their homework, or liberal Democrats have often despised him. Through it all, his love for baseball has never disappeared, nor has his disdain for the men running the game.

★

Bunning published an autobiography, as told to Ralph Bernstein, *The Story of Jim Bunning* (1965), aimed primarily at young fans, that includes a play-by-play of his perfect game. The most complete work on Bunning's life as a ballplayer and as a politician is Frank Dolson, *Jim Bunning: Baseball and Beyond* (1998). Bunning's adventures as a minor league manager are covered in Dolson, *Beating the Bushes* (1982). For information on Bunning's work in the formative years of the Major League Baseball Players Association, see Bowie Kuhn, *Hardball: The Education of a Baseball Commissioner* (1987), and Marvin Miller, *A Whole Different Ball Game* (1991). Details of his no-hit games are in Rich Westcott

and Allen Lewis, *No-Hitters* (2000), which includes an exceptionally interesting foreword by Bunning.

FRANK DOLSON

BUTKUS, Richard Marvin ("Dick") (*b.* 9 December 1942 in Chicago, Illinois), football player considered one of the best linebackers of all time; he is a Pro Football Hall of Famer and was a University of Illinois All-American and Chicago Bears All-Pro.

Butkus was the fifth son and seventh child of Lithuanian Americans John Butkus, an electrician, and Emma Goodoff. He came from a family of large people and weighed over thirteen pounds at birth. However, he was small and unathletic as a child, which was a relief to his mother, who did not want him playing football and risking injury the way his brothers did in high school. But Butkus had wanted to be a football player as long as he could remember, and he grew bigger and stronger. At Chicago Vocational High School, he played both fullback and linebacker well enough to be chosen the *Chicago Sun-Times* Player of the Year in 1959 and the 1960 Associated Press Prep-Football Player of the Year.

Dick Butkus. ARCHIVE PHOTOS, INC.

He selected the University of Illinois from all the colleges vying for him. Notre Dame wanted him, but did not want its players to be married, and Butkus already had married his high school sweetheart, Helen Essenberg, with whom he later had three children. At Illinois, Butkus at times played center but was better known for his play at middle linebacker, where he excelled in speed, strength, and toughness. In 1963, his junior year, he was credited with making 145 tackles and causing 10 fumbles. He was chosen All-American, and Illinois was ranked third in the country, winning the Big Ten championship and the Rose Bowl. His senior year, he repeated as All-American and was voted the College Football Player of the Year by the *Sporting News*.

In 1965 the Chicago Bears drafted Butkus, who was also drafted by the American Football League (AFL) Denver Broncos. Butkus was happy to sign with the Bears for $200,000, more than any defensive rookie had ever been paid. The Bears' incumbent middle linebacker, Bill George, had been a star for the team for thirteen years, but he later said that the first time he saw Butkus in practice he realized he was ready to be replaced. In the first game of the Bears' season, the six-foot, three-inch, 245-pound Butkus made eleven unassisted tackles against the San Francisco 49ers. That began a year in which he was chosen All-Pro, and the defense allowed over a hundred fewer points than it had the previous year.

Through 1970 Butkus was the preeminent middle linebacker. Every year he was voted All-Pro and selected to play in the Pro Bowl, and every year he led the Bears in tackles and assists, intercepting a few passes and recovering a few fumbles along the way. In 1969 and 1970 he was chosen Defensive Player of the Year.

Butkus showed his versatility in 1971 with a memorable play. Although he had not played on offense since college, he lined up as a blocking back whenever the team attempted to kick a field goal or extra point. National Football League (NFL) rules at the time stated that the point after touchdown could be kicked through the uprights or run or passed into the end zone, but because the team got one point either way, teams opted for the more certain kick. In a game against the Washington Redskins, however, the snap got away from holder Bobby Douglass. Douglass chased the ball down thirty yards behind the line and heaved a desperation pass to Butkus, who caught it and ran it in for the single point that turned out to be the Bears' margin of victory.

In another game during that season, this one against the Detroit Lions, the television audience saw another side, the human side, of Butkus. After a play, Lions' wide receiver Chuck Hughes collapsed on the way back to the huddle. From across the field, Butkus noticed, ran over to Hughes, and signaled desperately for medical attention. It was too late; Hughes was already dead of a heart attack. The alertness Butkus showed was typical of his play, but his compassion surprised many. For the most part he was accurately portrayed by the media as a fierce, angry linebacker.

It was also in 1971, however, that Butkus suffered the first major injury of his career, damage to the ligaments of his right knee. The surgery was not entirely successful, and for the rest of his career he played in pain. In 1973 Butkus reinjured the knee and retired. He finished his career with 1,020 tackles, 489 assists, 22 interceptions, and 25 recoveries of opposition fumbles. The fumble recoveries were a career record when he retired, but he was later passed by Jim Marshall and Rickey Jackson, both of whom had much longer careers than did Butkus. After his retirement, Butkus sued the Bears on the grounds that his medical treatment was inadequate; the case was settled out of court. In 1995 he had the knee replaced surgically.

Butkus announced Bears' games on the radio from 1985 to 1994 and humorously played off his violent, animalistic image in a series of light beer commercials in which he claimed to be "sensitive" and attended cultural events with fellow behemoth Bubba Smith. He played himself in *Brian's Song*, a 1970 television docudrama about teammate Brian Piccolo, who died of cancer in mid-career. Butkus then went on from that role to a moderate-range acting career, usually portraying athletes. On television, he played Ed Klawicki in the sitcom *My Two Dads* (1987–1989) and high school basketball coach Mike Katowinski in *Hang Time*. He also joined the Internet, lending his name to dickbutkus.com, a successful site offering football news and tips.

In 2001 the World Wrestling Federation attempted to challenge the NFL's hegemony by setting up its own football league, the XFL. Butkus was hired to give the league some credibility as its director of competition (a title created for him), but he could not overcome the league's low quality and resulting low ratings, and the league folded after its first year.

Butkus was elected to the NFL Hall of Fame in 1979, his first year of eligibility. In 1985 the National Collegiate Athletic Association instituted an award for the best college linebacker of the year and named it after him. Butkus was also selected to the NFL's 75th Anniversary All-Time Team. Butkus was among the most skilled in the many categories important to the success of a middle linebacker. He could sense and deduce where the play was going. He was fast enough to catch runners and sometimes to cover potential pass receivers, having the toughness and strength to tackle those he caught. He had the alertness and skill to intercept passes and quickly locate and take advantage of fumbles.

★

The main sources for Butkus's life story are the autobiographies *Stop-Action,* with Robert W. Billings (1972) and *Flesh and Blood: How I Played the Game,* with Pat Smith (1997). George Vass, *George Halas and the Chicago Bears* (1971), tells much about his contributions to the team. Butkus's website, <http://www.dick.butkus.com>, offers further information.

ARTHUR D. HLAVATY

BUTTON, Richard Totten ("Dick") (*b.* 18 July 1929 in Englewood, New Jersey), first American figure skater to win both an Olympic gold medal and the World Championship; he is credited with introducing the modern, athletic style of skating and has been described by many as the best men's figure skater of all time.

Button was the third son of George Button, a businessman, and Evelyn Bunn Totten, a homemaker. A student at the Englewood School for Boys, Button started skating using borrowed skates. At age twelve, he asked for a pair of skates of his own. Assuming he wanted to play hockey, his father bought him hockey skates. When Button told him that he wanted to figure skate, his father promptly traded the hockey skates for figure skates and got his son a teacher. At that time Button was short and overweight. The teacher, confronted with the pudgy boy, stated that he would become a figure skater "when Hell freezes over." Button's father replied that if his son wanted to be a figure skater, so be it, and he would provide the best lessons and opportunities.

The best teacher was Gustav (Gus) Lussi, a skating coach in Lake Placid, New York, and Philadelphia. Button and his mother spent the summer of 1942 in Lake Placid, where he started lessons. At the end of one month, Button failed all his tests, but by the end of the second month, he had passed all three figure skating examinations. Years later, Button remarked, "I was very determined and didn't let defeat discourage me. I made myself into a figure skater with work. I wasn't born to it."

In 1943, Button, now a slender and agile fourteen-year-old, entered his first competition, the Eastern States Novice Championship, and finished second. In his next competition, in April of the same year, he became the Middle Atlantic Novice Champion. In 1944 he won the Eastern States Junior title and the United States Novice Championship title. The following year, he won the United States Junior Championship. At age sixteen, in 1946, he became the United States Senior Champion, the youngest figure skater to hold that title in American skating. Button would win that title for the next six years (1946–1952).

Characteristic of Button's skating was innovation. He and his coach developed moves never before seen in the figure skating community. Some of his jumps and spins were so unusual that judges did not know how to respond to them. A case in point is the response to his performance at the 1947 World Championship in Stockholm. In this

Dick Button at the 1948 Winter Olympics, St. Moritz, Switzerland. AP/WIDE WORLD PHOTOS

competition, Button added a new element to the well-known camel spin by jumping into it. For years afterward, this was called the Button camel. His power-packed free skate program astounded everyone. Sportswriter Oscar Soederlung called Button's skating "something revolutionizing in the art of figure skating—technically the most fantastic performance ever seen here." Button's skating was not only powerful but graceful as well. A Swedish newspaper stated, "Button skated as though he were wearing ballet shoes instead of skates."

Although the crowd and the press loved Button, and he finished with the highest point total, three of the five judges voted Hans Gerschweiler of Switzerland the better skater. Under international rules, Button finished second. Lussi told the press that Button's "stuff" was too new for the judges and claimed that the judges were "so goggle-eyed" watching Button that they forgot to mark their score cards.

In January 1948, just two weeks before the Olympics, Button entered the European Championships and defeated Gerschweiler for the gold medal. Button was the first American to win the European figure skating title—and the last, because the following year Americans were barred from competition. Skating with "boldness and abandon" in his free skate program, Button came from behind in the compulsory figures to win. The crowd, informed by a Prague newspaper that audiences in the United States whistle to show their appreciation, whistled its approval of Button's performance.

Two weeks later, on 5 February, in Saint Moritz, Switzerland, Button won the Olympic gold medal after receiving the highest point total in the history of the event to that time. Although he had a comfortable lead over second-place Gerschweiler, Button did not play it safe in the free skate. Two days earlier, he had successfully landed a double axel, a move that requires two-and-a-half turns in the air and that had never been achieved in competition. Although the ice was not ideal for such a feat, Button performed it successfully. At age eighteen, he was the youngest men's Olympic figure skating champion.

A week later, on 13 February, in Davos, Switzerland, Button won the World Championship in "one of the most brilliant performances ever seen on European ice," according to the *New York Times*. Button was the first American to win the men's World Figure Skating Championship and would win the title the next four years. He was the only skater to capture what could be considered the grand slam of figure skating, winning the United States, North American, European, World, and Olympic championships all in the same year.

While Button competed, he kept up his studies, graduating from the Englewood School for Boys. He was accepted by Yale, but Yale would not allow him to take time off to skate competitively; Harvard would, providing he kept his grades up. Button entered Harvard in fall 1948 and in February 1949 successfully defended his world title in Paris. After his free skate program, which included three successive double axels, the crowd gave him a five-minute ovation. He averaged 5.9 points out of a possible 6, and one judge, as quoted in *Newsweek*, stated, "I've never seen anything like it—and no one else has, either."

In 1949 Button received the prestigious James E. Sullivan Award, which honors the best amateur athlete in the United States. He was the only figure skater to win it. Button receiving the award signified that figure skating was, at last, considered a major sport in the United States.

For the 1952 Olympics, Button treated the audience to a triple loop, the first triple jump performed in competition, and won his second gold medal. After the Olympics, he became a professional skater; he also graduated from Harvard in 1952 and enrolled in Harvard Law School. Button appeared with the Ice Capades, fitting his schedule around his studies until he had earned his law degree in 1956. He married skating coach Slavka Kohout on 10 March 1973, with whom he had two children. They divorced in 1984.

Although Button no longer competes, he has remained involved in skating. Since 1962 he has shared his expertise on figure skating as a commentator on *ABC's Wide World of Sports* and the station's coverage of the Winter Olympics. His work as an expert analyst for televised figure skating competitions earned him an Emmy in 1981. According to author Christine Brennan, through his broadcasts, Button educated the American public about figure skating. "He took the nation by the hand and led it into the sport." Button also has written two books on skating: *Dick Button on Skates* (1955) and *Instant Skating* (1964). Through his company, Candid Productions, Button was the driving force behind a series of new competitions for professional skaters, beginning in 1973 with the World Professional Figure Skating Championship. Other events for professional skaters promoted by Button include the World Challenge of Champions.

Reflecting on Button's skating, Olympic champion figure skater Tenley Albright told *Sports Illustrated,* "Dick showed us how boundless the possibilities were in skating." Button was an innovator who introduced moves that male skaters had never done before. In an effort to explain how Button revolutionized the sport, Olympic silver medalist Paul Wylie said that it was as if "someone had run a four-minute mile five years before someone actually did it."

★

Christine Brennan, *Inside Edge: A Revealing Journey into the Secret World of Figure Skating* (1996), includes material on Button, as does Bill Libby, *Stars of the Olympics* (1975). Regarding the World Championship in Stockholm, see "Swedish Press Hits Award of World Title in Figure Skating to Swiss over U.S. Star,"

New York Times (16 Feb. 1947). Concerning the World Championship in Paris, see "Buttoned Up," *Newsweek* (28 Feb. 1949). William Leggett, "He Was Right on the Button," *Sports Illustrated* (23 Feb. 1976) discusses Button's contributions as a TV commentator, and Jack Craig, "Button an Imperious Sage," *Boston Globe* (10 Feb. 1995), explores his skating and television careers. Good articles include Mark Kram, "U.S. Skating's First Ice-Breaker: Button Has Been a Pioneer First on the Rink, Then Off," *Philadelphia Daily News* (2 Jan. 1998); Philip Hersh, "Fifty Years Later, Dick Button Still a Force," *Chicago Tribune* (31 Mar. 1998), and Mark L. Lund and Lois Elfman, "Dick Button: Man of the Century," *International Figure Skating* 5, no. 6 (Jan./Feb. 2000).

MARCIA B. DINNEEN

BYERS, Walter (*b.* 13 March 1922 in Kansas City, Missouri), athletic association director who guided the National Collegiate Athletic Association (NCAA) to a dominant role in marketing intercollegiate sporting events and regulating competition.

Byers is the son of Ward Byers and Lucille Hebard Byers. He played football for Westport High School in Kansas City, Missouri. In 1939 he entered Rice University in Houston, Texas. In the following year he transferred to the University of Iowa, where he majored in English and journalism. After military service, he was employed as a news reporter for the United Press International (UPI). After short stints in St. Louis and Madison, Wisconsin, he became a sports editor of UPI in Chicago. In 1946 and 1947 he was UPI assistant sports editor in New York City, where he also served as foreign sports editor.

Byers moved quickly from a career as a sports journalist to sports administration. In 1947 Commissioner Kenneth L. "Tug" Wilson hired him as director of the Big Ten Conference Service Bureau in Chicago. At the same time he served as an executive assistant to Wilson, who was also secretary-treasurer of the NCAA. In 1951 Byers was appointed executive director of the NCAA. He served in this position for thirty-six years.

During his tenure, Byers was responsible for administering the rules governing intercollegiate sports. Competition produced both winners and losers; winners were profitable, losers were not. Institutional sponsors adopted rules and regulations to equalize opportunity. Compliance with and enforcement of the rules required organizational supervision. In intercollegiate sports these organizations were conferences composed of similar institutions in a particular region, and associations representing institutional sponsors. The associations included representatives of the professional interests involved in sports. In the United States there were strong traditions of professional cartels, academic amateurism, and institutional autonomy. Undergirding the entire sports structure was the matter of economic viability or financial support.

Founded in 1905, the NCAA was an association of professional athletics administrators, including athletics directors, coaches, institutional presidents, and faculty representatives. It had a long history of conflict and reconciliation with the Amateur Athletic Union (AAU), the United States Olympic Committee (USOC), and other organizations representing amateur sports. Douglas MacArthur, Avery Brundage, and Robert F. Kennedy had each attempted to restore order to amateur intercollegiate sports. The post–World War II emergence of college football and basketball as popular and financially successful sports, and communications technologies that opened mass entertainment markets, strengthened the NCAA's financial position.

Byers's responsibilities at the NCAA included administration, legislation, regulation, enforcement, and financial management. Beginning as a one-man operation in 1947, he secured new staff and consolidated operations. He directed the moving of the headquarters to Kansas City in 1952 and to Shawnee Mission, Kansas, in 1973. In 1969 the headquarters staff included twenty-one people in Kansas City, New York, Washington, and Phoenix. By 1988 the staff at Shawnee Mission included sixty-five people in five departments.

Legislation and litigation accompanied the strengthened NCAA position in amateur athletics and became a standard occurrence in Byers's career. In the 1960s renewed jurisdictional disputes prompted the NCAA to break off relations with the AAU and to withdraw from the USOC. The Amateur Sports Act of 1978, which limited the powers of the AAU and defined the authority of the USOC, indicated the nationwide media and political power of the NCAA. Byers spent about $1 million and twelve years in legal battles with Coach Jerry Tarkanian of the University of Nevada, Las Vegas, which included his 1978 testimony before a congressional committee investigating the NCAA's enforcement process. A 24 June 1984 United States Supreme Court decision held that the NCAA's $283-million football television contract was in violation of the Sherman Antitrust Act. However, it did little to check the NCAA's success in managing sports entertainment programming.

NCAA committees tightened and extended the rules for intercollegiate competition. In 1968 the *Manual* was a 118-page document. By 1988 it was 430 pages long. The annual publication was a detailed code of conduct governing recruiting, eligibility, and rule enforcement in college sports. With continual modification, these rules were shaped to maintain comprehensive and exclusive NCAA control over intercollegiate sports.

Byers was a dedicated believer in compliance and enforcement. He stated, "Intercollegiate athletics is a symbol of the real world because it has true accountability." Rules for the recruitment and eligibility of athletes were major problems in college sports. The Sanity Code of 1948, which required ordinary entrance requirements and "normal progress" for athletes, proved unenforceable. On 8 January 1954 Byers acknowledged, "We are in the enforcement business, apparently to stay." In 1956 the NCAA endorsed grants-in-aid or athletic scholarships, which provided some accountability but had little effect on the need for enforcement. Citing widespread violations in 1984, Byers lamented that violators showed no remorse, coaches didn't cooperate, and presidents had little power or will to act. He estimated that 30 percent of the major sports schools were cheating "in a big way." By 1988 the Compliance and Enforcement Division staff of twenty included fifteen field investigators.

Throughout his tenure, the NCAA's budget ballooned enormously. The NCAA's 1947 budget was $100,000. In 1952 Byers negotiated a football television contract for $1,194,000. The college basketball tournament proceeds were divided fifty-fifty between the participating teams and the NCAA. The NCAA received $87,385 in 1954 and $173,258 in 1961. In 1955 the American Broadcasting Company (ABC) defaulted on a television contract and paid $200,000 to the NCAA. In 1981 the NCAA budget was $22,429,000. In 1988 NCAA surplus television revenue was $13,332,136.

In October 1987 Wayne Duke, the Big Ten commissioner, hailed Byers as the architect of NCAA's football television program, basketball championship tournament, management of the football bowl system, and enforcement program. At Byers's final NCAA convention, ABC television announcer Keith Jackson presided. The University of Michigan's athletic director, Don Canham, characterized Byers as a "great leader," "loyal," "perfectionist," and "tough." In 1988 Byers retired, becoming the director emeritus.

Seven years later Byers published *Unsportsmanlike Conduct: Exploiting College Athletics,* a critique of his former employer. He charged the NCAA with "a psychology of complacency" that emphasized amateurism, added regulations, expanded compliance inspections, centralized eligibility review, emphasized public relations, and established a bureaucracy. His arguments for reform challenged the immensely profitable system that he had created for the NCAA's control of intercollegiate athletic competition. He recalled that he had been "enormously successful" in generating millions of dollars for the colleges but "barely adequate" in enforcing the rules governing intercollegiate athletics. Since 1974 Byers has resided in Mission, Kansas, and served as president of Byers Seven Cross Ranch in Emmett, Kansas.

★

Byers's work is documented in his papers at the NCAA in Indianapolis, the *NCAA Yearbooks,* the *NCAA News,* and the *NCAA Manual.* He discusses his own career in *Unsportsmanlike Conduct: Exploiting College Athletics* (1995). The subject is also addressed in the NCAA's official history, *NCAA: The Voice of College Sports* (1981), by Jack Falla. A critique of the NCAA and its relationships to the media is in Arthur Fleisher, Brian Goff, and Robert Tollison, *The National Collegiate Athletic Association: A Study in Cartel Behavior* (1992). Financial matters are discussed in Gary D. Funk, *Major Violation* (1991). Sources for Byers's 1984 views on enforcement are Jack McCallum, "Why Is This Man Saying the Things He's Saying?" *Sports Illustrated* (17 Sept. 1984), and Peter Alfano, "NCAA Head Asks Assault on Rampant Abuse of Rules," *New York Times* (13 Oct. 1984).

MAYNARD BRICHFORD

C

CALHOUN, Lee Quency (*b.* 23 February 1933 in Laurel, Mississippi; *d.* 21 June 1989 in Erie, Pennsylvania), two-time Olympic gold medalist and world record holder in the high hurdles.

Calhoun was born in Laurel, Mississippi, a community that also produced fellow National Track and Field Hall of Famer Ralph Boston. Calhoun's father was Johnny Jordan. His mother, Erma McMillan, moved north when Calhoun was a toddler and, with his stepfather, the Reverend Cory Calhoun, raised Calhoun in Gary, Indiana. He eventually had fourteen siblings. After he graduated from Roosevelt High School, he attained a scholarship and subsequently enrolled at North Carolina Central University in the fall of 1951, where he was instructed by the Hall of Fame coach Dr. LeRoy Walker, who was later president of the U.S. Olympic Committee.

In 1953 Calhoun entered the U.S. Army for a two-year hitch. When he returned to college, he was more focused and a more complete, committed athlete. In 1956 he won the sixty-yard high hurdles at the New York Athletic Club Indoor and the Amateur Athletic Union (AAU) Senior Indoor championships and the 120-yard high hurdles at the Outdoor National Association of Intercollegiate Athletics, National Collegiate Athletic Association, and AAU championships. His win over the Olympians Jack Davis and Harrison Dillard at the AAU Indoor placed him for the first time in the international spotlight as a hurdler. In 1957,

the year he earned a bachelor's degree, Calhoun repeated the same series of track championships. Before the Melbourne Olympics in 1956, Calhoun's personal best in the 110-yard high hurdles was 14.4 seconds, but at the Olympics he ran 13.5 to win the gold, just edging out his teammate Jack Davis.

In the fall of 1953 Calhoun met Gwen Bannister, a freshman from Stamford, Connecticut, while they were students at North Carolina Central University. On 9 August 1957 his stepfather, the minister of the Evening Star Baptist Church in Gary, performed their marriage ceremony on the national television show *Bride and Groom*. Although the television producers did not know that Calhoun was a runner, the AAU claimed that he had capitalized on his fame as a runner to obtain the gifts given to the show's contestants. Calhoun was suspended from amateur athletics in 1958 for one year, and the AAU threatened to ban him from Olympic competition.

While he was on suspension, Calhoun and his wife worked for the city of Cleveland. In 1959 Calhoun met with Dan Ferris, head of the AAU, to ask that his suspension be lifted. The suspension finally was revoked when John Nagy, chairman of the Lake Erie AAU Association in Cleveland, threatened to withhold nearly $40,000 from the AAU. In 1957, 1959, and 1960 a series of thrilling meets between Calhoun and Hayes Jones at the *Chicago Daily News* Relays, the Cleveland and New York City Knights of Columbus, and elsewhere drew national attention. Cal-

Lee Calhoun with his gold medal for the 100-meter hurdles event at the Melbourne Olympics in 1956. ASSOCIATED PRESS

houn was once again the AAU Outdoor high-hurdles champion in 1959. On 21 August 1960 he tied the world record in the 110-meter high hurdles in Bern, Switzerland, with a time of 13.2. Later that year, at the Rome Olympics, he won gold in the 110-meter high hurdles once more, with a time of 13.4. He was the first man to win consecutive Olympic gold medals in this event.

In 1965 Calhoun earned a master's degree from North Carolina Central University. Shortly thereafter he became the track coach at Grambling University (1967–1970), then at Yale (1971–1980), and finally at Western Illinois University (1980–1989). He was an attentive, committed coach and a role model for his athletes. He truly enjoyed his work, and his athletes frequently took on his persona. Calhoun was made a member of the Olympic Men's Track and Field Committee in 1969. He coached the 1968 and 1976 U.S. Olympic teams and America's 1979 Pan-American Games team.

By all reports Calhoun was a modest family man and an inspiration to his children, both of whom also were outstanding track athletes. Calhoun was named to the Na-

tional Track and Field Hall of Fame (1974), the Western Illinois University Athletic Hall of Fame (1989), the North Carolina Athletic Hall of Fame, and the U.S. Olympic Hall of Fame (1991). A life-size bronze sculpture of him, *Excellence on Winged Feet,* was dedicated at Western Illinois University in 1993. Calhoun experienced a debilitating stroke in February 1989 and was moved to Erie, Pennsylvania, where his sisters could help with his care. He died there of stroke-related complications at age fifty-six. Following his death, the Lee Calhoun Memorial Invitational was instituted in 1989 at Western Illinois University and a scholastic meet in his honor was established at Durham, North Carolina.

★

The best source for the *Bride and Groom* television saga is Lewis H. Carlson and John J. Fogarty, *Tales of Gold* (1987). A helpful source is Hal Bateman, "National Track and Field Hall of Fame Grand Opening and Dedication Reception Booklet" (12 Jan. 1986), available through the Press Information Department, the Athletics Congress/USA. Information about Calhoun's track performances is in Gerald Lawson, *World Record Breakers in Track and Field Athletics* (1997) and the *New York Times* (12 and 19 Feb. 1956 and 17 and 24 Feb. 1957). See also the U.S. Olympic Association, *1960 United States Olympic Book* (1961).

KEITH MCCLELLAN

CAMP, Walter Chauncey (*b.* 7 April 1859 in New Britain, Connecticut; *d.* 14 March 1925 in New York City), football innovator and authority on college athletics who was instrumental in the development of American football rules and is considered the father of American football.

Camp was the only child of schoolmaster-publisher Leverett Lee and Ellen Cornwell Camp, both of New Britain, Connecticut. In 1863 Camp moved with his parents to New Haven, Connecticut. He attended Hopkins Grammar School, a noted institution adjacent to Yale University. After graduating near the top of his class, he entered Yale in 1876, receiving an A.B. in 1880 and going on to Yale Medical School. He had nearly completed medical school when he left because, as he told a close friend, he disliked the sight of blood. In 1882 Camp joined the Manhattan Watch Company in New York City. The next year, he gained employment as a salesman for the New Haven Clock Company. On 30 June 1888 Camp married Alice Graham Sumner, the sister of William Graham Sumner, a noted Yale sociologist. They had two children. At the clock company, he rose to treasurer and general manager (1902), then president (1903), and finally chairman of the board (1923).

Camp's athletic career began in prep school, but he became a star athlete at Yale, particularly in football and baseball. He also participated in crew, golf, swimming, track, and tennis. His prowess as a halfback on the varsity football team from 1877 to 1882 and his participation on the football rules committee, beginning as an undergraduate, brought him great recognition.

As a freshman, in 1876, Camp participated in both the first Harvard-Yale football game, played under Rugby Union rules, and the first Intercollegiate Football Association's Thanksgiving Day game against Princeton. In that contest, Camp was involved in a controversial play that resulted in Princeton's defeat. He had received the ball out of the rugby scrum, proceeded on a long run, and just before being tackled tossed the ball to a teammate who ran for a touch down. Princeton protested, claiming that Camp's pass was forward and therefore illegal. The referee's coin toss ended the dispute in Yale's favor, and Yale went on to win college football's first championship.

Camp's off-the-field football activities, however, were historically more important. He is credited with creating the American version of football that became the dominant college sport. As a Yale sophomore, he attended the 1877 football rules convention, and he continued doing so for the next forty-eight years. While team captain in 1878, 1879, and 1881, Camp proposed a number of rule changes that began the transformation of English rugby into modern American football.

First, he proposed reducing the number of players on each side from fifteen to eleven. Next, he convinced the 1880 student-led rules convention to allow a team to retain possession of the ball after a player was tackled and "down." This changed the unpredictable "scrummage" of rugby to a line of "scrimmage," with a more systematic approach to ball control. Having possession, though, made it possible for one team to keep the ball for an entire half. Camp resolved this issue in 1882 by proposing a system of "downs." A team was given three downs to gain five yards or surrender possession, with the marked five-yard lines creating a gridiron effect on the field. Camp's leadership on the rules committee led to the present point system for touchdowns, extra points, field goals, and safeties. He also proposed that tackling below the waist be permitted, a rule that helped to limit open-field runs and promote greater mass play, but which also brought charges of brutality.

From the 1880s to 1910, Camp achieved acclaim as an unpaid advisory coach for Yale's football team, a kind of coach of coaches. Because he worked at the New Haven Clock Company during the day, he met with Yale's coaches, captains, and key players in the evenings to discuss the team's performance and to offer strategies for improving performance. Yale's greatest player, W. W. "Pudge" Heffelfinger, once told Camp that the Yale football team was "closely tied together . . . with your advice and guidance."

Walter Camp, 1879. AP/WIDE WORLD PHOTOS

During the years that Camp was associated with the team as player and coach, Yale won more than 95 percent of its games. From 1876 through 1909, the team lost only fourteen games, surely the greatest record in intercollegiate football history.

Camp helped to change college football from a relatively insignificant fall pastime into a commercial force and visible sign of college life. He became the paid treasurer of the Yale Financial Union, founded in 1893 to consolidate all athletic teams under one organization. He applied his business skills to college athletics, employing novel promotional methods and innovative playing strategies to create spectator interest. With a $100,000 athletic surplus due in part to Camp's financial acumen, Yale built a 70,000-seat stadium in 1914. Called the Yale Bowl, it was the largest stadium in America.

Camp promoted football to a mass audience through his

prolific writing of numerous newspaper articles and over 200 magazine articles. He was the editor of *Spalding's Official Intercollegiate Football Guide* and the author of more than thirty books, seven of them fiction, including the popular *Jack Hall at Yale: A Football Story* (1909). He coauthored *Football* (1896), an analysis of football playing techniques, with the former Harvard coach Lorin F. Deland. Perhaps Camp's most successful promotional effort was his selection of All-America football teams, which he began in 1889 and continued through 1925, generating much public interest in the star players.

The football brutality crisis of 1905–1906 diminished Camp's role in determining rule changes. Camp was reluctant to change the rules drastically to remove the game's brutality. He opposed the forward pass rule in 1906, but he was an innovator in its use. Camp lost his position as secretary of the football rules committee in 1906, when opponents of his conservative administration formed a new rules committee, the forerunner of the National Collegiate Athletic Association (NCAA). Camp withdrew from most aspects of Yale football after 1910 but remained on the rules committee until his death.

When the United States entered World War I, Camp was asked to direct the U.S. Navy Training Camps' Physical Development Program, out of which came his popular "Daily Dozen" exercises. He continued an active life after the war and resumed his role as secretary of the college football rules committee. While attending the committee's annual meeting in New York City in 1925, Camp died suddenly of a heart attack. He is buried in Grove Street Cemetery in New Haven, Connecticut. Three years after his death, the Walter Camp Memorial Gateway, a massive colonnade, was erected at the entrance to the Yale Bowl. More than 500 colleges and high schools contributed to the memorial.

★

The Walter Camp Papers are housed at Yale University Library, Manuscripts and Archives, and include a carefully indexed guide by Robert O. Anthony and a forty-eight-reel microfilm set. There is no definitive biography of Camp; however, Harford Powel, Jr., *Walter Camp: The Father of American Football, an Authorized Biography* (1926; reprint, 1970), and Kathleen D. Valenzi and Michael W. Hopps, *Champion of Sport: The Life of Walter Camp, 1859–1925* (1990), are informative. Parke H. Davis, *Football: The American Intercollegiate Game* (1911), remains a key volume on early college football, and Ronald A. Smith, *Sports and Freedom: The Rise of Big-Time College Athletics* (1988), contains a good deal on Camp and places him in a larger context, as does John Sayle Watterson, *College Football: History, Spectacle, Controversy* (2000). John S. Martin summarizes Camp's influence in football in "Walter Camp and His Gridiron Game," *American Heritage* 12 (Oct. 1961). See also Richard Borkowski's uncritical

"Life and Contributions of Walter Camp to American Football," Ph.D. dissertation, Temple University (1979). An obituary is in the *New York Times* (15 Mar. 1925).

RONALD A. SMITH

CAMPANELLA, Roy (*b.* 19 November 1921 in Philadelphia, Pennsylvania; *d.* 26 June 1993 in Woodland Hills, California), Baseball Hall of Fame catcher (1969) who was one of the first "Negro Leaguers" to break into the major leagues, winning the Most Valuable Player (MVP) award three times (1951, 1953, and 1955) before his career was cut short by an automobile accident that left him paralyzed.

Campanella was the youngest of five children of market owners John Campanella and Ida Mercer. His father was an Italian immigrant and his mother was African American, and Campanella's first memories of racism were of African Americans teasing him because his father was white. He attended Simon Gratz High School in Philadelphia, but quit after his junior year to play baseball.

In 1938 he joined the Baltimore Elite Giants, then one of the premier Negro League clubs in America. Although the Elite Giants were part of the Negro National League, the Great Depression of the 1930s had ravaged African-American ball clubs, and they played few league-sanctioned games, earning most of their money by barnstorming

Roy Campanella. AP/WIDE WORLD PHOTOS

throughout the United States. It was a tough life—sleeping in cars, dodging segregationist laws, and playing in whatever sandlot was available for a game—but Campanella thrived, partly because his teammates took special care of their young star catcher and partly because Campanella just loved to play. "You have to have a lot of little boy in you to play baseball for a living," he would later say, and he had plenty of little-boy enthusiasm in him in the 1930s and 1940s.

At first Campanella, nicknamed "Campy," was a substitute for one of the best catchers ever, Biz Mackey, but in 1939 he became the Elite Giants' starting catcher. He was an outstanding hitter, a fine handler of pitchers, and he drew the attention of major league scouts, but Kenesaw Mountain Landis, then the commissioner of baseball, was determined to exclude African Americans from "organized baseball." When the Pittsburgh Pirates gave Campanella a tryout, they were discouraged from signing him and other African-American ballplayers by threats of economic sanctions from other team owners. Campanella married his first wife, Bernice Ray, in 1939, and they had two daughters. They were divorced in 1941. That same year Campanella received his draft notice but was granted a deferment to continue playing. After the surprise attack on Pearl Harbor on 7 December 1941, however, he was reclassified and assembled tank parts until the spring of 1942. In 1943 Campanella jumped to the Mexican League for a season; he was, like most Negro League stars who played in Mexico, treated like a visiting prince.

But the major leagues beckoned. In 1945 the general manager Branch Rickey had narrowed to just a few names his list of African-American ballplayers he wanted to sign for the Brooklyn Dodgers, a move that would break baseball's segregation. Among those players was Campanella. Rickey had been emboldened by the new baseball commissioner, Happy Chandler, who declared that there was no official barrier to playing African Americans on major league teams. First, Rickey signed Jackie Robinson, sending Robinson to Brooklyn's minor league franchise in Montreal for one season before bringing him up to play for the Dodgers. Meanwhile, Campanella married his second wife, Ruthe Wills, and adopted her son, David; they later had three children together. Rickey then signed Campanella, sending him to various minor league franchises, where he broke the color barrier. Campanella even managed a team for one game while the regular manager was out sick, thus breaking the color barrier for black managers in previously all-white leagues.

Once with the Dodgers, Campanella was sensational. He was twenty-six years old at the start of his first major league season in 1948 and was already an exceptional catcher. At five feet, nine inches and 190 pounds, he was stocky and solidly built, but he moved with quickness and grace behind the plate, and he was almost without equal at calling pitches and at handling each pitcher he caught.

In 1951 Campanella exploded, hitting .325 and 33 home runs while driving in 108 runs. He was named the National League's MVP. His best year came in 1953, when he hit .312 and 41 home runs (a record for a catcher) and drove in 142 runs (another record for a catcher) while scoring 108 runs. He was again named the league's MVP. In 1954 he injured his wrist, leaving bone splinters in it, and had a poor season. The wrist healed after surgery, though, and he came back in 1955 to hit .312 and 32 home runs, while driving in 107 runs and winning the MVP award for the third time. There was much to enjoy as a Dodger in the 1950s: they took the National League pennant in 1949, 1952, 1953, 1955, and 1957, and won the World Series in 1955. Campanella's leadership and performance were big parts of what propelled the Dodgers to become one of the best teams of the era.

On 28 January 1958, while driving home from the liquor store he owned, Campanella hit the brakes of his car on an icy road on Long Island, and the car skidded and turned over, pinning Campanella under the dashboard. A vertebra in his neck was shattered, and he was paralyzed. The following months were terrible for him. An athlete who had always moved with grace and power, he was frustrated by his inability to even scratch his nose. With the help of his wife, children, and friend and former teammate Don Newcombe, he worked at regaining some movement, and he told his story to Dave Camerer and Joe Reichler, who ghostwrote his autobiography, *It's Good to Be Alive* (1959). The book became a sensation and an inspiration to readers beyond number. The Dodgers had moved to Los Angeles by then, and in 1959 they honored Campanella at an exhibition game in the Coliseum against the Yankees. Over 95,000 fans showed up, a record for attendance at a baseball game. Campanella separated from his wife Ruthe in 1960, and after her death he married his third wife, Roxie Doles, in 1963 and adopted her two children.

By the time *It's Good to Be Alive* aired in its television adaptation in 1974, Campanella could use a wheelchair. Although he was not expected to live long because of complications from his paralysis, he managed to regain more movement over two more decades, and he and his wife Roxie worked for many charities. Campanella lived to be seventy-one before his heart failed. His body was cremated.

"I never want to quit playing ball. They'll have to cut this uniform off of me to get me out of it," Campanella once declared, and in a way his uniform was torn from him. But in the hearts of many Dodgers fans, he will always be a Dodger, the smiling but tough catcher who endured many hardships and still came out ready to swing his bat at whatever was thrown his way. His courage off the field also touched America. Elected to the National Baseball Hall of Fame in 1969, he was one of the best catchers ever.

★

Campanella's autobiography (actually written by Dave Camerer and Joe Reichler), *It's Good to Be Alive,* was published in 1959, only a year after he was paralyzed in an automobile accident. It tells of his rise to stardom and his fight to stay alive after his career's abrupt ending. Its 1974 adaptation as a made-for-television movie drew a large audience. Norman L. Macht, *Roy Campanella: Baseball Star* (1996), explains the social importance of Campanella's baseball career and charitable enterprises. A short but exciting book for young readers is James Tackach et al., *Roy Campanella* (1991). Stewart Wolpin, *Bums No More! The Championship Season of the 1955 Brooklyn Dodgers* (1995), is not only entertaining but offers an account of the ways Campanella was important to the Dodgers' winning seasons.

KIRK H. BEETZ

CAMPBELL, Earl Christian (*b.* 29 March 1955 near Tyler, Texas), powerful football running back who won the Heisman Trophy in 1977 and was inducted into the Pro Football Hall of Fame.

Campbell grew up in poverty, the sixth of eleven children of Burk Campbell, a day laborer, and Ann Collins Camp-

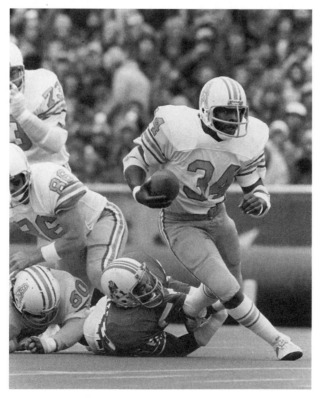

Earl Campbell, 1979. ASSOCIATED PRESS AP

bell in rural east Texas. Earl's father died of a heart attack when Earl was eleven, and the children labored in the area's rose fields to help their mother, a house cleaner. Campbell did not participate in organized sports until junior high school, when he began his football career as a linebacker.

In his senior year at John Tyler High School, a large school classified by size as 4A, Campbell's coach moved him to halfback. He scampered for 2,036 yards and racked up twenty-eight touchdowns as he led his team to the state high school 4A title. After watching Campbell's performance in the championship game, Coach Darrell Royal of the University of Texas at Austin said, "It was a man against boys." Campbell was named to the *Parade* High School All-America team. He decided to attend the University of Texas at Austin despite its reputation as a school where black athletes were not welcome. During his first three years Campbell played fullback under Royal and established a reputation as one of the most devastating runners in the nation. When Fred Akers became head coach in 1977 he converted Campbell to halfback in the "I" formation. As the featured ground-gainer in the high-powered Texas offense, Campbell came into his own as a runner. He piled up 1,744 yards rushing, then a school record, and sped or plowed his way into the end zone for nineteen touchdowns. He led his team to the number-one ranking during the regular season and was awarded the Heisman Trophy as the nation's outstanding football player in 1977. Despite Campbell's heroics, Texas lost to Notre Dame in the Cotton Bowl in January 1978, thus losing the national championship.

Campbell's outstanding running ability made him a coveted choice for professional teams in the 1978 draft. Selected by the Houston Oilers, he was the first college player picked in the entire draft. Campbell made an instant impact on the National Football League (NFL). His powerful running style, which toppled linebackers and safeties with equal ease, helped the Oilers become a winning team under Coach O. A. "Bum" Phillips. During his rookie year Campbell led the league in rushing with 1,450 yards, a performance that earned him Rookie of the Year honors. In the two years that followed Campbell again won rushing titles and was named the NFL Player of the Year. The Oilers did well in the playoffs behind Campbell, but they did not reach their coveted goal of a berth in the Super Bowl.

After this dazzling start, Campbell's performance during the remaining five years of his career was less spectacular. Injuries, coaching changes, and the wear and tear on his body ate away at his skills. In 1985 he was traded to the New Orleans Saints, who were now led by his former coach Bum Phillips, and finished his professional football career there. In eight seasons Campbell racked up 9,407 yards on

2,187 carries and scored seventy-four touchdowns. When he retired, he ranked eighth among the all-time leading rushers in NFL history. Among power backs in the annals of professional football, Campbell was one of the best. He had speed and determination, and broke several long runs after seemingly being stopped at the line of scrimmage. Few who saw him play will forget his ability to turn a short play into a long gain with a twist of his hips or a punishing stiff-arm. Campbell was inducted into the Pro Football Hall of Fame in Canton, Ohio, in 1991, the first year in which he was eligible.

Since his retirement from football, Campbell has been affiliated with the University of Texas both in athletics and student relations. He is currently the special assistant to the athletic director, and informally known as the "Football Ambassador," at that university. In 1980 he married his childhood sweetheart, Reuna Smith; they have two sons, both of whom play football. Campbell has also been involved in several business enterprises in central Texas, including a cattle ranch, a sausage factory, and a restaurant in Austin. These enterprises failed in 2001 and he had to file for bankruptcy. He then became a partner in Earl Campbell Meat Products.

In 1990 Campbell experienced a panic attack while on a drive from Austin to Houston. He was eventually diagnosed with panic disorder. Although he enjoyed being by himself, Campbell faced an imposed solitude and even sleeping with fear. A regimen of therapy and drugs brought the condition under control. In 1999 doctors discovered that Campbell suffers from spinal stenosis, a congenital condition that could have left him paralyzed if he had been hit in the wrong place during his football years. "If I'd ever had a real physical with MRIs and all the stuff you go through now, I probably never would have played football," Campbell observed.

Campbell ranks among the greatest running backs to play football in high school, college, and the pros. He excelled at all levels and defied critics who said that his undergraduate success could not be repeated in the more demanding environment of the NFL. Modest and unassuming, he represented the best that college football could offer in the 1970s, and he performed with equal class as a professional. When Campbell was in his prime, no one could offer a better combination of quickness and power while carrying the football.

★

A biographical file of clippings on Campbell is at the Center for American History, University of Texas at Austin. *The Tyler Rose: The Earl Campbell Story* (1997), written with Paddy Joe Miller, is an autobiographical volume, as is *The Earl Campbell Story: A Football Great's Battle with Panic Disorder* (1999), written with John Ruane. Betty Lou Phillips, *Earl Campbell: Houston Oiler Superstar* (1979), is a book for children, while Sam Blair, *Earl Campbell: The Driving Force* (1979), interprets Campbell at the height of his career. Larry Gerlach, "Earl Campbell," in David L. Porter, ed., *African-American Sports Greats: A Biographical Dictionary* (1995), provides an overview of his life and career. Melissa Ludtke Lincoln, "The Real Earl Campbell Stands Up," *Sport* 69 (1979), and Bruce Newman, "The Roots of Greatness," *Sports Illustrated* (3 Sept. 1979), consider Campbell in his prime. Retrospective accounts of Campbell's life after football include Brian Davis, "Third and Long," *Daily Texan* (9 Oct. 1997); Don McLeese, "Hooking a Heisman," *Austin American-Statesman* (12 Dec. 1999); Andy Clendennen, "Where Have You Gone . . . The Tyler Rose Still Pounds the Ground to Succeed," *Sporting News* (28 June 2001); and Jan Reid, "What Did Football Teach Earl Campbell About Running a Business? Take Your Hits and Keep Moving Forward," *Texas Monthly* (Sept. 2001). "Former Grid Star Learns to Cope," *Parade* (26 Sept. 1999), discusses Campbell's experience with panic disorder.

LEWIS L. GOULD

CAMPBELL, Milton Gray ("Milt") (*b.* 9 December 1933 in Plainfield, New Jersey), Olympic decathlon champion, hurdler, and football player who is considered one of the best athletes of the twentieth century.

Campbell was the second of three children of Thomas Campbell, a construction worker, and Edith Campbell, a homemaker. He attended Emerson Primary School and Plainfield High School, where he was a scholastic All-American in football, swimming, and track. The only time he competed in wrestling, he bested the New Jersey wrestling champion in his weight class. In February 1952 Campbell appeared in his first indoor track meet at the National Amateur Athletic Union (AAU) High School Indoor Track and Field championships at Madison Square Garden in New York City. He won the sixty-yard high hurdles and the high jump in record-setting performances. He also qualified for the National AAU high-hurdles championships held that night and, running as part of the Young Men's Christian Association (YMCA) team, placed third behind the Olympic champion, Harrison Dillard. As one of the three fastest runners in the event, Campbell traveled to London that spring with the AAU national team to participate in a meet that pitted the United States against the United Kingdom.

The Plainfield prodigy did so well in London that his high school track coach, Harold Bruguiere, asked the school's booster club to raise the $1,500 needed to send Campbell to the Olympic trials. Bruguiere's carefully laid plans called for Campbell to try both the 100-meter dash and the high hurdles at the AAU Senior Track and Field

Milt Campbell *(center)* winning the 100-meter hurdles event at the 1952 Olympics in Helsinki. ASSOCIATED PRESS AP

championships held at Long Beach, California, which served as the semifinal tryouts for the Olympic team. Although Campbell had competed in only three of the ten events included in the decathlon, Bruguiere also entered him in the decathlon trials held ten days later in Tulare, California. Campbell qualified for the final tryouts in the high hurdles but missed making the team when he tripped on a hurdle. When Bob Richards passed up the decathlon trials to concentrate on the pole vault for the Olympics in Helsinki, Finland, the eighteen-year-old Campbell took advantage of the opportunity by placing third in the decathlon. He was the only high school athlete to join the 1952 U.S. Olympic track and field team. In Helsinki, Campbell won a silver medal.

In September Campbell returned home to play football on his high school team, declaring, "Football is in my blood." He led the Plainfield team to an unbeaten season, scoring 140 points and winning distinction as an All-State player. Campbell ended his high school athletic career at Madison Square Garden in February 1953 by repeating as the National AAU champion in the high jump and the high hurdles. In July he competed in the National AAU Decathlon championships held in his hometown. Indiana University actively recruited Campbell, offering him a guaranteed four-year scholarship. The school seemed interested in his success, but it had several disadvantages, including the absence of a decathlon coach and a Southern

tradition not wholly accepting of African-American students. He matriculated at Indiana in September 1953. On 20 March 1954, at the Eighteenth Annual *Chicago Daily News* Relays, Campbell placed third in the high hurdles, behind Harrison Dillard and the Big Ten champion Willard Thomson.

The following year, the six-foot, three-inch, 210-pound Campbell was used as a right halfback flanker on the Indiana University varsity football team. His competitive spirit and desire to win were of significant value to the school's football program. In his first punt runback, he sprinted seventy-seven yards for a touchdown. He was an outstanding ground gainer, pass receiver, and defensive back in 1954 and 1955. Road games at schools like the University of Missouri were difficult, however, because he was not allowed to room with the team as the result of local segregation rules. Campbell lettered in track in during 1954 and 1955, but the track coach did not take full advantage of his athletic talents. Nevertheless, he won both the National Collegiate Athletic Association (NCAA) and AAU 120-yard high-hurdles titles in 1955.

After the 1955 football season Campbell dropped out of Indiana University and entered the U.S. Navy, where he was allowed to train full-time for the Olympics, without interference from school studies or the need to earn a living. Campbell expected to earn a place on the Olympic team in the high hurdles but placed fourth in the final trial for that event when he again hit a hurdle. Stunned by his failure in the hurdles, Campbell competed on 13–14 July 1956 at the National AAU Decathlon championships and Olympic trials held at Wabash College in Crawfordsville, Indiana. There, for the second time, he qualified for a spot on the U.S. Olympic team with a second-place finish. At the Melbourne Olympics, the twenty-two-year-old Campbell won a gold medal with 7,937 points (or 7,565 using 1985 tables).

In 1957 Campbell continued to compete in the high hurdles on the indoor track circuit at the *Chicago Daily News* Relays, the Cleveland Knights of Columbus Meet, and elsewhere. He placed second in the sixty-yard high hurdles at the New York Athletic Club Indoor meet and the National AAU Indoor championships. That year, he tied the world record (13.4) in the 120-yard high hurdles. In the fall of 1957 he played professional football as a halfback with the Cleveland Browns, playing the entire nine-game season on a broken ankle. On 25 January 1958 Campbell married Barbara Mount; the couple had three children.

When the Cleveland Brown's training camp opened in 1958, Coach Paul Brown called Campbell into his office to declare his displeasure with Campbell's marriage to a white woman; he expressed his disapproval by using him sparingly during the exhibition season. When he was cut from the team, Campbell asked for, but was never given, an explanation. Campbell played football in the Canadian Football League from 1958 to 1964, for the Hamilton Tiger-Cats and the Toronto Argonauts. After his professional football career, Campbell did community work in Plainfield and was popular as a motivational speaker. He and his wife divorced in 1980.

Campbell had a son, Milton Campbell III, born in 1994. In 2001 he ran as a Republican candidate for the New Jersey State Senate. Campbell is a charter member of the Indiana University Intercollegiate Athletics Hall of Fame (1982) and was inducted into the National Track and Field Hall of Fame in 1989.

Campbell, one of the best athletes of the twentieth century, is one of just twenty-four competitors ever to win the decathlon in the Olympic Games. He was a hurdler and football player who competed in the decathlon five times in his life.

★

Limited biographical information is found in the *Indiana University Football Guide, 1954;* Cecil K. Byrd and Ward W. Moore, *Varsity Sports at Indiana University: A Pictorial History* (1999); and Bob Hammel and Kit Klingelhoffer, *The Glory of Old IU: 100 Years of Indiana Athletics* (1999). The *New York Times* (17 Feb. 1952) and Ed Fried, "Plainfield Proud of Multi-Threat Star," *Newark Sunday News* (28 June 1953) are good sources of information on his high school years. His 1957 placement in the New York Athletic Club and AAU indoor meets can be found in the *New York Times* (17 and 24 Feb. 1957). Bob Carroll et al., eds., *Total Football II: The Official Encyclopedia of the National Football League* (1999), has information about Campbell's National Football League years.

KEITH MCCLELLAN

CARAY, Harry Christopher (*b.* 1 March 1914 in St. Louis, Missouri; *d.* 18 February 1998 in Rancho Mirage, California), beloved Chicago Cubs announcer who developed an enthusiastic national following during more than fifty years of baseball broadcasts with his "Holy Cow!" home-run call and off-key, seventh-inning rendition of "Take Me Out to the Ball Game."

Born Harry Christopher Carabina, Caray was named after his Italian father, Christopher Carabina, whom he never knew. His Romanian mother, Daisy Argint Carabina, remarried, but after her death when Harry was just eight, he went to live with his aunt Doxie at 1909 LaSalle Street in a tough, working-class section of St. Louis inhabited by Italian, Irish, and Syrian families. As a "skinny little kid" he loved playing baseball on its cobblestone streets. Caray's first job was "hawking" the *St. Louis Post-Dispatch* at the corner of Eighteenth and Chouteau Streets to workers coming off the day shift at the International Shoe Factory.

As a teenager Caray "fell deeply, passionately, madly, and irrevocably in love with baseball." He enjoyed nothing more than taking the Grand Avenue streetcar to Sportsman's Park, where for a dime he could get a hot dog outside the ballpark and for fifty cents sit in the bleachers and watch a game. He was a switch-hitting shortstop at Webster Groves High School, southwest of St. Louis, but had to turn down a scholarship to the University of Alabama "when I couldn't swing the room and board." Instead he worked at odd jobs, tending bar, waiting tables, selling newspapers, and being a "flunky" at fight camps, "anything to make a buck." On weekends he played semiprofessional baseball, making $15 a game for the Smith Undertakers and the Webster Groves Birds. He had a minor league tryout with the St. Louis Cardinals, "a dream come true," but lacked the size, speed, and eyesight to make it in the pros.

After high school, Caray made $25 a week as an assistant sales manager with a manufacturer of basketball backboards and gymnastics equipment. He won an audition with the St. Louis radio station KMOX by mailing a "brash" letter marked "personal" to the home of station manager Merle Jones. That led to a job in 1941 as a sports announcer at the 250-Watt WCLS in Joliet, Illinois, where station manager Bob Holt changed his surname from Carabina to Caray. After eighteen months of announcing high

Harry Caray, 1980. © BETTMANN/CORBIS

school and junior college basketball, winter league bowling, and summer softball, Caray became sports director at WKZO in Kalamazoo, Michigan, where he worked beside news director Paul Harvey. Caray produced pregame and postgame shows for Detroit Tigers games and announced a semipro baseball tournament in Battle Creek, Michigan, where he began using his characteristic call of a home run, "It might be . . . it could be . . . It IS . . . a home run," and his signature "Holy Cow!" after particularly exciting plays.

In late 1943 Caray's military status was reclassified 1-A. Anticipating that he would be drafted, he moved his wife, Dorothy, and son, Harry junior (called "Skip"), to his in-laws' home in St. Louis. His poor eyesight, however, kept him out of the service. He became a staff announcer for radio station KXOK in St. Louis, where he "blasted, ripped, praised, and slashed," hoping to become "the Walter Winchell of sports." A crosstown World Series between the Cardinals and Browns in 1944 raised sports fever in St. Louis to an all-time high, persuading Griesedieck Brothers Brewery to broadcast the home games of both teams the following year on station WIL-AM. Caray was hired as their play-by-play man, and former Cardinal manager Gabby Street became the color analyst. By year's end, the two outpaced competing broadcasts of local games, one involving Dizzy Dean. By 1946, the year the Cardinals won their second World Series in three years, Caray's enthusiastic call of each contest helped establish him as a fan favorite. The following year, he was made the exclusive play-by-play announcer for the Cardinals.

Caray's love of the game and respect for the fans brought him wide appeal. He sought out baseball fans in bars and on the street "to find firsthand what they like and what they don't like." He discovered they did not like "being lied to or having their intelligence insulted." Most announcers were reluctant to criticize management or players even over obvious mistakes, but not Caray. He worked for the fan, not the owner, and was "the fan's representative" in the broadcast booth. His bombastic style—his voice was like a breath of beer over gravel—reflected "a fan's excitement and sometimes his despondency." He had heavy jowls and laughing eyes half hidden behind thick, dark glasses, which became his trademark. His delivery made Caray an unparalleled performance artist from a broadcast booth, and it was why many fans felt that hearing Caray's call of a contest was a show more compelling than going to the game.

When August A. ("Gussie") Busch, Jr., the president of Anheuser-Busch, bought the Cardinals in February 1953, fans demanded that he keep Caray as the play-by-play man even though Caray had long been associated with a competing beer company. Joined by future Hall of Fame broadcasters Jack Buck and Joe Garagiola, Caray's description of Cardinals games over the 50,000-Watt KMOX and its ninety-station radio network kept listeners in thirty-eight states from the Rocky Mountains to the Atlantic Coast up past their bedtime.

Caray was seriously injured when struck by a car on 3 November 1968 and received more than a quarter million letters from well-wishers. A dispute with Busch led to his being fired as the Cardinals' broadcaster after the 1969 season. Fans picketed, demanding his return. Caray spent a year away from St. Louis broadcasting the games of the Oakland A's, which led to a breakup with his second wife, Marian. The White Sox lured Caray to Chicago for the 1971 season by agreeing to an attendance clause in his contract. Caray's enthusiasm, plus an improved product on the field, more than doubled attendance to 1.3 million in three years. Caray became as popular with Sox fans as he had been with Cardinals fans. He understood that because of free agency, players came and went, making the sustaining voice of announcers the bond that linked the team to fans. When Bill Veeck, a superb showman, bought the White Sox on 10 December 1975, it opened an era of exploding center-field scoreboards, Caray's fishing nets to catch foul balls, and his memorable bare-chested broadcasts beside fans in the stands with beer in hand.

When Veeck sold the White Sox, Caray went across town and began broadcasting for the Chicago Cubs and their nationwide cable audience of 30 million at the start of the 1982 season. The fans delighted in Caray's ecstatic "Cubs win! Cubs win!" call when the team clinched a postseason berth in 1984 for the first time in thirty-nine years, and his oft-repeated observation, "You can't beat fun at the old ballpark." Even when the Cubs were hopelessly behind, fans stayed just to hear Caray sing "Take Me Out to the Ball Game" during the seventh-inning stretch.

Caray suffered a stroke on 17 February 1987. When he returned to work on 19 May 1987, fans celebrated with "Harry Caray Day," and President Ronald Reagan called him from the White House. On 30 September 1988 President Reagan, himself a former Cubs announcer, joined Caray to broadcast a Cubs game from Wrigley Field. That year, Caray was elected to the National Sportscasters and Sportswriters Hall of Fame. In 1989 he was named the National Baseball Hall of Fame's Ford C. Frick Award winner and thanked "all the fans who are responsible for my being here." In the decade that followed, Caray solidified his reputation as the country's most famous announcer. A fainting spell on the field from heat exhaustion in June 1994 became national news. When he returned from that episode to broadcasting, he began calling Cubs all-star second baseman Ryne Sandberg, "Stein Renburg," and Sammy Sosa, "Sammy Sofa," which further endeared him to his faithful following. Caray opened a highly successful Chicago restaurant and became known as the "Mayor of Rush Street" for his after-hours kibitzing with fans, entertainers, politicians, and sports celebrities.

Caray was married for a third time, to the former Dolores ("Dutchie") Goldmann, on 19 May 1975. One of his five children (all from his previous marriages), Skip, became a widely respected announcer for the Atlanta Braves, and before the 1998 season it was announced that Skip's son Chip would be joining his grandfather in broadcasting Cubs games. Before that could happen, however, Caray died of cardiac arrest and subsequent brain damage at the Eisenhower Medical Center in Rancho Mirage, California, after collapsing at a restaurant in Palm Springs. He is buried in All Saints Cemetery in Des Plaines, Illinois. National

Baseball Hall of Famer Stan Musial mourned the passing of a friend who was "the life of the party, the life of baseball."

Caray predicted that one day, even if it was fifty years in the future, the Cubs would win a World Series and a fan would say, "Gee, I wish Old Harry had lived to see this." That was the only eulogy he wanted. Every day that the Cubs are in town, the fans do him one better. Before entering Wrigley Field, they stop and pose for pictures with a life-size bronze statue of their favorite announcer, dressed in a Cubs warm-up jacket with arms outstretched and mike in hand, as though he were leading them one more time in "Take Me Out to the Ball Game." Caray remains one of baseball's most beloved characters.

★

Biographical files on Caray are in the National Baseball Hall of Fame in Cooperstown, New York, at the Chicago Cubs offices at Wrigley Field, and at WGN-Television in Chicago. Caray covers his years as a baseball announcer in *Holy Cow!* (1989), his autobiography with Bob Verdi. Appreciations include Rich Wolfe and George Castle, *I Remember Harry Caray* (1998), and Steve Stone with Barry Rozner, *Where's Harry?* (1999). A tribute to Caray is in the *Chicago Tribune* (27 Feb. 1998). An obituary is in the *New York Times* (19 Feb. 1998). Caray gave Bob Costas an extensive interview in "When Harry Met Baseball . . . ," a two-hour documentary broadcast on the WGN-TV cable network in 1994 to commemorate Caray's fifty-year anniversary in baseball.

BRUCE J. EVENSEN

CAREW, Rod(ney) Cline (*b.* 1 October 1945 near Gatun, Panama), professional baseball player considered one of the best hitters of his generation, enshrinee of the National Baseball Hall of Fame, and batting coach of the Milwaukee Brewers.

Carew was born on a train near Gatun, Panama, and named in honor of Dr. Rodney Cline, the physician who helped deliver him. His father, Eric Carew, was a painter of ships, bridges, and buoys in the Panama Canal Zone; his mother, Olga Carew, was a domestic. Carew came down with rheumatic fever when he was twelve; the resulting weakness was greeted with contempt by his father who eventually rejected and abandoned his son.

Carew's uncle Joseph French, a Little League coach and recreation official, sought to fill the role of surrogate father by cultivating the boy's interest in baseball. Although his family was poor, his mother ensured that he always had baseball shoes and a glove. Carew's uncle was his first batting coach, exhorting him to practice hitting tape-bound rag balls with a broom handle. Playing with a number of Little League teams in Panama, Carew gradually developed the

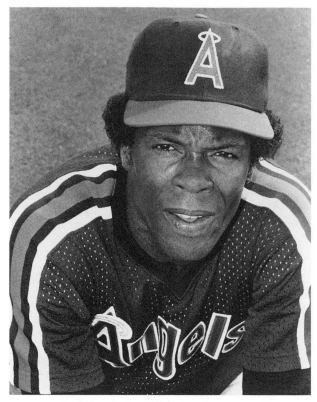

Rod Carew, 1983. ASSOCIATED PRESS AP

full range of skills he needed as a ballplayer. By the time he was thirteen he was playing ball in a senior league and ranked as one of its best hitters. His most prized boyhood possession was a Ted Williams bat, awarded to him for outstanding Little League play. Carew carried the bat with him everywhere he went, even to bed, and dreamed of the day he would play major-league ball in the United States.

Carew's mother, seeking a better life for her two sons, went to the United States in 1960, when Carew was fifteen. After she had a job and located a place for the family to live, she sent for the boys. Carew, the younger son, enrolled at George Washington High School in Upper Manhattan, but he did not participate in high school sports because he worked after school in a neighborhood grocery store. On the weekends, however, he managed to find time to play in sandlot games in a local park. A teammate's father who did some unofficial scouting for the Minnesota Twins alerted team headquarters to Carew's batting skills. A tryout was arranged for Carew when the Twins next visited New York City for a game with the Yankees. Carew was so impressive that Sam Mele, the manager of the Twins, cut short the tryout for fear the Yankees might outbid him for Carew's services. Offered a $5,000 bonus, Carew signed with the Twins about a month later.

Carew spent only three years in the Twins farm system before he was brought up to the big-league club and put in the starting lineup. Playing second base, Carew silenced the critics who claimed he was not ready for the majors by batting .292 his first season out. His stellar debut performance was rewarded with the American League Rookie of the Year Award in 1967. In October 1970 Carew, who is black, married Marilynn Levy, a white woman, setting off a flurry of racist threats and insults.

From 1972 through 1975 Carew won four consecutive batting titles and missed a fifth by only .002 point. His focus on hitting singles rather than home runs meant that he drew less attention from the media than less talented but flashier players. In fact, it was the lack of homers that the Twins' owner, Calvin Griffith, used as an excuse to turn down a 1975 salary increase request from Carew.

Carew's finest year in baseball was 1977, when early in the season it seemed likely that he would become the first player in nearly four decades to bat .400 for the season. Although he faltered late in the season, finishing the year with a batting average of .388, his 100 runs batted in and 100 runs scored were more than enough to win him the American League's Most Valuable Player Award. Carew's long run with the Twins came to an end two years later, when he was traded to the California Angels after he and the Twins were unable to reach agreement on a contract. He played the next seven seasons in Southern California but was abruptly released after the 1985 season. He batted better than .300 five out of his seven seasons with the Angels.

Carew's election to the National Baseball Hall of Fame in 1991 was widely applauded by fans and ballplayers alike. Former manager Sam Mele said of Carew, "You could put him in a tunnel with the lights out and you still know he's going to hit."

Carew has never strayed far from baseball. He spent eight years as the Angels' batting coach before joining the Milwaukee Brewers in the same capacity after the 1999 season. With the Brewers in a batting slump during the 2001 season, Carew came under fire from Brewer fans, particularly on talk radio. In his defense, he told the media, "I can only prepare [the hitters] mentally and physically. When they step up to the plate, there's nothing I can do."

During his career Carew was honored with seven league batting titles, a figure surpassed only by Ty Cobb, Tony Gwynn, and Honus Wagner, and equaled only by Rogers Hornsby and Stan Musial. For fifteen consecutive seasons, playing first with the Minnesota Twins and later with the California Angels, Carew batted over .300. He played on eighteen straight All-Star teams. With more than 3,050 career hits and a lifetime batting average of .328, it is little wonder that Carew was widely described as "the best damn hitter in baseball" for much of the 1970s.

★

An excellent profile of Carew and his baseball career is provided in *Carew* (1979), the baseball player's frank and unblinking autobiography, written with Ira Berkow. Carew shares secrets of his game in *Rod Carew's Art and Science of Hitting* (1986), written with Frank Pace and Armen Keteyian. His life in baseball is among those profiled in *Reflections of the Game: Lives in Baseball* (1998), compiled by Ron C. Modra, the world-famous photographer for *Sports Illustrated*. Ideally suited for younger readers are Bill Libby's *Rod Carew: Master Hitter* (1976), and Marshall Burchard's *Sports Hero: Rod Carew* (1978).

DON AMERMAN

CARLTON, Steven Norman (*b.* 22 December 1944 in Miami, Florida), baseball pitcher who won four Cy Young Awards and achieved a reputation as one of the greatest left-handers in the history of the game.

As a youngster Carlton shied away from organized sports. He was twelve years old when his father signed him up for Little League in Miami, Florida, but he quit after one practice, saying that the game was "no fun." When he finally did start playing baseball at North Miami High School, he excelled at pitching.

After graduating from North Miami, Carlton entered Miami Dade South Community College. He attracted the interest of the St. Louis Cardinals, who signed him in 1964 and promoted him to the majors the following season. Over the next five years the six-foot, five-inch left-hander won

Steve Carlton. ARCHIVE PHOTOS, INC.

seventy-four games for the Cardinals, helping them to two National League pennants and a world championship. In 1969, he set a modern major league record for a nine-inning game by striking out nineteen New York Mets batters.

After the 1971 season Carlton got into a contract dispute with the Cardinals. Unwilling to meet his demands, St. Louis traded him to Philadelphia for Rick Wise, who was embroiled in a similar battle with the Phillies' front office. Wise, who had posted seventeen wins, including a no-hitter the previous season, had been popular with Phillies fans, who were highly critical of the deal. But Carlton quickly won over the Philly faithful in 1972, when he put together one of the greatest seasons in baseball history. Posting a 27–10 record, "Super Steve" was responsible for nearly half of the Phillies' fifty-nine victories that year, the highest ratio in baseball history. He won fifteen consecutive decisions that season and pitched thirty complete games, tops in the majors. Carlton's 1.97 earned run average (ERA) and 310 strikeouts in a staggering 346.5 innings earned him the first of his four Cy Young Awards.

The following season Carlton was hampered by arm trouble and a lingering case of bronchitis, and his record fell to 13–20. When the Philadelphia sportswriters criticized his performance, Carlton, an intensely private individual, gave them the silent treatment, refusing to talk with reporters for the remainder of his Phillies' career. "I found that talking to the press took my focus away," he explained. "I thought about it for more than a year and finally decided I was cheating the fans and myself by allowing myself to be diverted mentally. It was one less obstacle for me, like the hitter."

Carlton also broke with the traditional training routine and became a disciple of Gus Hoefling, a martial arts instructor who taught the young pitcher how to keep his mind and pitching sharp through a Zen-like personal conditioning program. Reunited with his close friend Tim McCarver, who had been his catcher in St. Louis, Carlton recaptured his winning form. He went 20–7 in 1976 and 23–10 with a 2.64 ERA and 198 strikeouts in 1977, when he captured his second Cy Young Award. He and McCarver, who became his personal catcher, were inseparable. "When Steve and I die we're going to be buried sixty feet six inches apart," joked the veteran catcher.

Three times in the 1970s Carlton led the Phillies to the postseason only to lose in the playoffs. In four National League Championship Series (NLCS) starts he was 1–2 with a 5.79 ERA, his regular season brilliance failing him in the postseason. Some began to question whether Carlton had what it took to win the World Series. He removed all doubts in 1980. During the regular season Carlton compiled a 24–9 record, 286 strikeouts, and a 2.34 ERA and earned his third Cy Young Award. He was just as outstanding in the postseason, making two strong starts in the NLCS against Houston (1–0, 2.19 ERA) and winning the second game and the sixth, the deciding game, of the World Series against Kansas City.

Other highlights followed, including a fourth Cy Young Award in 1982, career win number 300 in 1983, and the all-time strikeout lead at 3,522 (later relinquished to Nolan Ryan). His success was due to a pitching repertoire that consisted of an overpowering fastball and a sweeping curve. But Carlton's signature pitch was the slider, which exploded sideways and downward as it crossed the plate. Together with his pinpoint control, this devastating arsenal confounded hitters and made "Lefty" one of the premier pitchers in the game from 1971 to 1983. "Hitting him," according to the Hall of Famer Willie Stargell, "was like trying to drink coffee with a fork."

At the same time Carlton's perfectionism led him to an almost singular preoccupation with the mental aspect of the game. "My job was my performance on the field," he insisted. "I found ways to eliminate any outside influence. . . . Then I go out there and I know I'm going to win." He stuffed cotton in his ears to block out the sound of the crowd. On days he was scheduled to pitch, the tall left-hander rarely spoke with teammates, and of course he never talked to the press. Together with his exceptional intelligence, Carlton's emphasis on the mental part of the game as well as his unorthodox conditioning techniques earned him the reputation of an "eccentric."

A rotator-cuff injury in 1985 limited Carlton to sixteen games that season as his record fell to 1–8. He never returned to the dominant form of his earlier years. The Phillies released their former ace on 25 June 1986. Refusing to admit that his career was over, Carlton, the classic power pitcher, tried to reinvent himself as a junk baller, first with the San Francisco Giants and later with the Chicago White Sox, Cleveland Indians, and Minnesota Twins. By the spring of 1988 even his strong-willed mentality was forced to yield to the reality that his career was over, and he retired with 329 major league victories and 4,136 strike outs. He also withdrew from public life, retreating to a mountain home in Durango, Colorado, to ski, ride horses, and enjoy his privacy.

Carlton did manage to come down from that mountain on at least two occasions. On 29 July 1989 he traveled to Philadelphia's Veterans Stadium to see his number 32 retired by the Phillies, and on 31 July 1994 he attended his Hall of Fame induction at Cooperstown, New York.

★

Carlton's career is discussed in Hal Bodley, *Philadelphia Phillies: The Team That Wouldn't Die* (1981). See also Steve Wulf, "Mastery and Mystery: Steve Carlton of the Phillies," *Sports Illustrated* (21 July 1980); and Jim Stephano, ed., "Steve Carlton: Hall of Famer," *Philadelphia Daily News,* Keepsake Edition (1 Aug. 1994).

WILLIAM C. KASHATUS

CARTER, Cris D. (*b.* 25 November 1964 in Troy, Ohio), All-Pro wide receiver known for his acrobatic catches who has had more than 1,000 receptions and more than 120 touchdowns during his professional career; he ranks second only to Jerry Rice in career 1,000-yard seasons and touchdown receptions.

As a student at Middleton High School in Ohio, Carter caught 80 passes for more than 2,000 yards on the football field and scored over 1,600 points playing basketball. He attended Ohio State University, where he was a two-time Big Ten team pick and a first-team All-America in 1986. That year, Carter set school single-season records with 11 touchdown receptions and 69 catches for 1,127 yards and was the Big Ten's leading receiver. By the time he graduated from Ohio State, he was the Buckeyes' all-time leader in receptions (168 from 1984 to 1986) and touchdown catches (27). Carter ranks second in Buckeye history with 2,725 receiving yards, and as a freshman, he established a Rose Bowl record of 172 receiving yards. He graduated with a B.A. degree.

Carter was chosen in the fourth round of the supplemental National Football League (NFL) draft by the Phila-

Cris Carter, 2001. ASSOCIATED PRESS AP

delphia Eagles in 1986 and was a wide receiver for the team from 1987 to 1989. He and Keith Jackson led the Eagles in touchdown receptions, with six apiece in 1987, but Carter had problems with cocaine and alcohol in Philadelphia and failed three drug tests. Eagles coach Buddy Ryan put him on waivers for $100, complaining that "all he does is catch touchdowns." Minnesota Vikings coach Dennis Green brought him to Minnesota as a wide receiver in September 1990. Carter overcame his addictions and in 1991 had 72 receptions for 962 receiving yards, tying for first in Vikings touchdown catches that season. In 1992 Carter had 53 receptions for 681 yards and six touchdowns, and the next year the totals jumped to 86 receptions for 1,071 yards. He was selected for the Pro Bowl eight consecutive times beginning in 1993.

Carter was named to the *Sporting News*'s NFL All-Pro team in 1994, when he set the NFL single-season record for most pass receptions (122). That year, he and teammate Jake Reed set an NFL record for receptions by a receiving duo (207). Carter caught 122 passes again in 1995 for the most catches in the NFL over a two-year period. He was the second NFL player, after Sterling Sharpe in 1992–1993, to have back-to-back 100-reception seasons. He also set Viking records that year with 17 touchdown receptions and 1,371 yards and became the second NFL player to ever have two or more touchdowns in four straight games.

Carter had no bad years. In 1996 he again led the Vikings in receptions (96) for a sixth consecutive season. He and Reed became the only wide-receiving duo in history to gain 1,000 yards each in three straight seasons. In 1997 Carter ranked first in the NFL with 13 touchdown catches and led the Vikings for a seventh year with 89 receptions for 1,069 yards in regular season play. Carter and Reed each surpassed 1,000 yards in receptions for a fourth year. Carter made 14 catches against Arizona on 2 October 1994 and gained 168 receiving yards against Miami on 10 September 2000.

The Vikings came within a single game of reaching the Super Bowl in 1998, losing to the Atlanta Falcons when Gary Anderson missed a last-minute field goal. Carter made 90 catches for 1,241 yards and 13 touchdowns during regular play in 1999, but the team lost the divisional playoffs to the St. Louis Rams. The next year, Carter caught 96 passes for 1,274 yards and nine touchdowns. Carter and Randy Moss combined for an astounding 2,711 receiving yards in 2000. Carter has never had great speed or separation from pass defenders, but he is sure-handed.

Carter has set nearly every Vikings record for receptions. He has made receptions for at least 100 yards in 39 games for the Vikings and in 41 games during his professional career. He has caught passes for over 1,000 yards in eight consecutive seasons, tying Steve Largent for second place for the most 1,000-yard receiving seasons in NFL history

and trailing only Jerry Rice, who has 12. During the 1990s Carter gained 11,512 yards in the regular season and another 842 yards in the playoffs. Only a Super Bowl championship has eluded him. He made his 1,000th reception, a four-yard touchdown, against the Detroit Lions on 30 November 2000. At the end of the 2000 season, he ranked second in receptions in NFL history with 1,020 catches and had amassed 123 touchdowns. The all-time leader was Rice with 1,281 receptions and 176 touchdowns. Carter, who wears number eighty, is six feet, three inches tall and weighs about 220 pounds. He is famous for his one-handed catches, for receptions while tiptoeing the sidelines or fully extended, and for pointing skyward after each of his touchdowns.

Carter became a Christian in 1994 and was ordained a minister two years later. He and his college roommate, William White of the Falcons, founded the Carter–White Charitable Foundation, which sponsors nonprofit football camps for underprivileged children and funds courses to prepare high school students from low-income families for college-entrance exams. Carter is an activist for "Cris CAUSE" (Christian Athletes United for Spiritual Empowerment) and is involved in the Big Brother–Big Sister program and the Boy Scouts. He often speaks at schools about drug awareness. In September 1994 Carter was given the NFL Extra Effort Award for his outstanding commitment to community service. In 1999 he received the Walter Payton NFL Man of the Year Award in recognition of his charitable work and exemplary character, as well as the NFL Players Association's Byron "Whizzer" White Award.

Carter plays with great intensity. Jim Klobuchar, a Twin Cities sportswriter, has remarked that in the minutes before a game, Carter "is revved to a pitch that you usually see in the face of a high school kid pumping himself for the big game." He is seen as the Vikings team leader ("team warden" by some), even though that job usually goes to the quarterback. He has become part of Coach Green's inner circle—his "adjutant" in the locker room. Carter trains rigorously during the off-season, playing basketball, jogging, or running wind sprints. He practices yoga and, beginning in the spring, works out for six hours a day near his home in Boca Raton, Florida. He is part owner of FAST, a company that designs fitness programs for professional athletes.

Carter's brother Butch, who is eight years older than he, played basketball under Bobby Knight at Indiana University, spent seven years in the National Basketball Association, and coached the Toronto Raptors. Cris Carter and his wife, Melanie, have two children.

Besides being an outstanding receiver, Carter, as a minister, has provided spiritual leadership for players in the NFL. He has been an example of someone who overcame his addictions, and he has remained a tremendous competitor during his long career.

★

With his brother Butch, Carter wrote *Born to Believe: Personal Reflections and Inspiration* (2000). For more information about Carter, see Jim Klobuchar, *Purple Hearts and Golden Memories: 35 Years with the Minnesota Vikings* (1995); Dennis Green with Gene McGivern, *No Room for Crybabies* (1997); Jim Klobuchar, *Knights and Knaves of Autumn: 40 Years of Pro Football and the Minnesota Vikings* (2000); and Jeffri Chadiha, "Time Trial," *Sports Illustrated* (3 July 2000).

JOHN L. SCHERER

CARTER, Don(ald) James   (*b.* 29 July 1926 in St. Louis, Missouri), professional bowler who dominated the sport in the 1950s and 1960s.

Carter was the younger of two sons born to and raised by Gladys Carter in St. Louis. As a child, Carter got his first exposure to bowling while working as a pinsetter. (In those days, the ten pins had to be set by hand.) Carter took up bowling in his early teens after his mother encouraged him to pursue the sport. In 1942 he joined a local bowling club and his fascination with the sport intensified. Although Carter got a charge out of bowling, he participated in other sports as well, playing both baseball and football for Wellston High School. He graduated from Wellston in 1944 and joined the World War II navy effort, spending two years as a radarman before leaving the service in June 1946.

In autumn 1946 Carter signed a contract with the Philadelphia Athletics (later the Oakland A's) to play on one of its baseball farm teams. As a teen, Carter had played American Legion ball with Yogi Berra and Joe Garagiola. The scouts, who had come in hordes to watch Berra and Garagiola, remembered Carter from his youth and offered him a position. During his first (and only) year on a farm team in Red Springs, North Carolina, Carter pitched his way to a dismal 3–7 record and had an earned run average of 4.19. Although he performed better at the plate, compiling a .302 batting average, Carter decided he wasn't major-league material.

Disappointed, Carter returned to St. Louis, moved back in with his mother, and rekindled his passion for bowling. He worked tirelessly to earn enough money to bowl. He found work as a pipe-fitter's helper, a punch-machine operator, and a piston packer. His mother charged him little in rent, so he spent the bulk of his money on practicing at bowling alleys. During the winter of 1947 to 1948, Carter bowled in six leagues. In 1948 he became the general manager of the Golden Eagle Lanes in St. Louis. He was delighted to be spending more time in the bowling alley, but the responsibility of the job didn't leave him much time for

tournament bowling. He finally found a job as an instructor and was able to earn a living and sharpen his skills at the same time.

Carter's reputation in bowling circles soon grew, and he was asked to join a prominent Detroit-based team, the Pfeiffers. In 1951, *Bowlers Journal* named Carter to its All-America team. In 1953 he won the All-Star Championship. This title, coupled with his overall performance as a key player of the Pfeiffer team, earned him the Bowler of the Year honors from the Bowling Writers Association of America, an award he recaptured in 1954, 1957, 1958, 1960, and 1962.

After earning his first bowler-of-the-year title in 1953, Carter was invited to join the St. Louis Budweiser bowling team. For four consecutive years (1956–1959) the team won the National Team Match Game title. In 1958 the Budweiser team rolled the highest score in the history of bowling, setting the five-player team series record at 3,858 points. Their score was thought to be unbeatable and stuck for nearly forty years before it was narrowly broken. The Budweiser company eventually withdrew their sponsorship of the team, and Carter assembled the members into the new Carter Glove team, which won the National Team Match Game title in 1961.

Carter was the first bowler to win all the major bowling titles of his day: the World Invitational (1957, 1959, 1960, 1961, 1962); the Bowling Proprietors Association of America (BPAA) All-Star (later the U.S. Open; 1953, 1954, 1957, 1958); the Professional Bowlers Association (PBA) National (1960); and the American Bowling Congress (ABC) Master's Championship (1961). During his career Carter bowled twenty-three perfect games (twelve strikes in a row for a total of 300 points). He also won the National Men's Doubles championship title in 1958 and 1959, when he teamed with Tom Hennessey. At age fifty Carter retired from professional bowling because an old football knee injury was getting the best of him. Legions of fans had enjoyed watching him bowl, whether on television or in person.

Carter had a unique style. He was no speedballer; instead, he lobbed the ball down the lane in a cold, careful, and calculated manner that ensured accuracy. His concentration skills were unequaled. The six-foot, 200-pound Carter got so wrapped up in his game that he often lost several pounds over the course of a tournament; during matches, he never spoke to an opponent. If he felt a part of his game needed work, he would spend hours practicing that skill. As Carter told the New Jersey *Record*, "To become a great bowler takes temperament and dedication. Bowling is a very difficult game mentally. In golf you see all the hazards. In bowling you don't see the slick boards. Every lane is different. You have to adjust for your mistakes. The best bowlers are the ones who are able to adjust."

While fans relished his style and presence, other profes-

Don Carter. ARCHIVE PHOTOS, INC.

sional bowlers cringed at his unorthodox low-crouched, bent-arm style. Most bowlers thought a professional should crouch only slightly and should keep the arm extended. Fans, however, loved Carter, who single-handedly transformed bowling from a smoke-filled, blue-collar recreational activity to a mainstream television sport. Because of Carter, tournaments were televised and dozens of bowling shows filled the airwaves. Bowling became a favorite pastime.

Along the way, Carter met an amateur bowler named LaVerne Haverly. They married in August 1953 and had a son and a daughter before divorcing. In the mid-1970s he married Paula Sperber, also a bowler. Carter was inducted into the ABC and PBA Halls of Fame in the 1970s. Both of his wives became members of the Women's International Bowling Congress Hall of Fame.

Residents of Miami, Carter and his second wife have raised more than $1 million for abused and neglected children in southern Florida. They also oversee several Florida-based bowling centers named for Carter. Decades after Carter won his last major bowling tournament, fans still referred to him as Mr. Bowling for his tireless promotion of the sport and because no other bowler had so captured the hearts and minds of bowling enthusiasts.

★

There are no full-scale biographies of Carter, although his book with George Kenney, *Bowling the Pro Way* (1975), offers an introduction that touches on his life and accomplishments. Carter

also wrote *Ten Secrets of Bowling* (1958). For articles about Carter's career, see "Mr. and Mrs. Bowling," *Look* (5 Feb. 1957); "Awkward Champion," *Newsweek* (3 Feb. 1958); "Mr. Bowling," *Time* (8 Dec. 1961); *Bowlers Journal* (Jan. 1962); Chuck Pezzano, "Carter Received a Major Salute," New Jersey *Record* (12 Feb. 1995); and Pezzano, "Legendary Don Carter Still Going Strong at Seventy-four," New Jersey *Record* (29 Apr. 2001).

LISA FRICK

CARTER, Vincent Lamar, Jr. ("Vince")   (*b.* 26 January 1977 in Daytona Beach, Florida), basketball player whose spectacular dunks, explosive scoring ability, and mass appeal have drawn comparisons to Michael Jordan.

Carter was the first of two sons born to Michelle and Vince Carter, Sr., of Daytona Beach, Florida. Carter's parents divorced when he was young, and he was raised primarily by his mother and her second husband, Harry Robinson, who were both schoolteachers. His uncle, Oliver Lee, who played college basketball at Marquette University, gave Carter his first ball when he was two years old. By the time Carter was in seventh grade, he could dunk a basketball, despite standing only five feet, eight inches tall. As a teenager, Carter also played other sports. He took up the saxophone and was a drum major at Daytona Beach's Mainland High School, where his stepfather directed the band. When he was a senior, Carter led Mainland to a state basketball championship. Although he received a scholarship

Vince Carter. AP/WIDE WORLD PHOTOS

debut, but when a lockout-shortened season began in February 1999, he was no longer in anyone's shadow. Taking the NBA by storm, the six-foot, six-inch jumping jack was named the league's Rookie of the Year, averaging 18.3 points per game.

Carter's status grew in his second season as a professional. As he improved his scoring average to 25.7 points, it became obvious that Carter ranked with Tim Duncan, Kobe Bryant, Allen Iverson, and a few others among the NBA's hottest young stars. His similarity to the legendary Michael Jordan also became evident when he won the annual slam-dunk contest during All-Star weekend. Carter and his teammate and cousin, Tracy McGrady, led the Raptors to their first appearance in the playoffs, where they fell in the opening round to the New York Knicks, three games to none.

During the 2000 Summer Olympics in Australia, Carter starred on the U.S. gold medal–winning basketball team. Originally not chosen to the squad, Carter was a late addition after Tom Gugliotta was injured. He ended up leading the team in scoring. Although the United States did not dominate the opposition as it had in previous years, Carter provided some memorable moments. A spectacular dunk when he jumped clear over the seven-foot, two-inch Frenchman Frederic Weis and a crucial last-minute basket against Lithuania in the semifinals were among the highlights. His U.S. teammate Jason Kidd called the dunk "probably the greatest play in basketball I've ever seen." Unfortunately, the normally pleasant Carter also was noted for taunting and uncharacteristically boorish behavior during the games. It came at a time when he was dealing with the firing of the Toronto coach Butch Carter (no relation), Tracy McGrady's signing of a free agent contract with the Orlando Magic, and his mother's pending divorce from Robinson.

Carter left all that behind and continued to progress in his third year as a pro. He increased his scoring average for the fifth consecutive season since his freshman year at North Carolina, to 27.6 points per game. For a second straight year the Raptors faced the Knicks in the first round of the playoffs, but this time beat them three games to two after Charles Oakley and other Toronto teammates challenged Carter to step up and take charge. Carter did so against New York and also in the second round against Iverson and the Philadelphia 76ers, when the two stars took turns dominating the action. The series went down to the last shot of the seventh and final contest, when Carter missed a jump shot from the wing, giving Philadelphia 88–87 and four games to three victories. The deciding game took place just hours after Carter had returned from commencement exercises at North Carolina, where he received a B.A. in African-American studies. His decision to attend his graduation was controversial among players and fans,

offer from Bethune-Cookman College for his musical talents, Carter was highly recruited as a basketball player and accepted an athletic scholarship to the University of North Carolina.

At North Carolina, Carter played in the shadow of his teammate Antawn Jamison. As fellow freshmen during the 1995–1996 season, Jamison shined while Carter struggled, averaging only 7.5 points per game. But in their sophomore and junior years, the duo teamed to lead the Tar Heels to consecutive Final Four appearances, losing each time in the national semifinals. Although both became All-Americans, Jamison retained the upper hand by winning National Player of the Year honors for the 1997–1998 season. After that season, both players decided to make themselves available for the National Basketball Association (NBA) draft. Coincidentally, Carter and Jamison were traded for each other immediately after being drafted on 24 June 1998. Jamison was selected fourth overall by the Toronto Raptors, and Carter was picked fifth by the Golden State Warriors; then the two teams swapped, with Golden State adding cash to the deal. A labor dispute delayed Carter's Toronto

but after leaving school early for the NBA, Carter had promised his mother that he would graduate, and he wanted to attend the ceremonies. "It was a wonderful feeling," said Carter, before remembering his team's loss. "It was almost a wonderful day." In addition to the message his graduation sent about the importance of education, in 1998 Carter established the Embassy of Hope foundation to support children's causes and was named a Goodwill Ambassador by Big Brothers/Big Sisters of America. On 1 August 2001, he agreed to a six-year contract extension with Toronto. "I've had three great years here," he announced at a press conference, "Why not six more?"

★

A comprehensive profile of Carter appears in *Sports Illustrated* (29 Jan. 2001), and a profile article appears in *Ebony* (Apr. 2000). Other information can be obtained at the website of the National Basketball Association, www.NBA.com, and the official website of U.S.A. Basketball, www.usabasketball.com.

JACK STYCZYNSKI

CARTWRIGHT, Alexander Joy, Jr. (*b.* 17 April 1820 in New York City; *d.* 12 July 1892 in Honolulu, Hawaii), baseball pioneer, civic leader, and businessman who helped codify baseball's playing rules and establish the game's diamond-shaped field geometry.

Cartwright was the oldest of seven children (three sons and four daughters) of Alexander J. Cartwright, a ship's master and marine surveyor, and Ester Burlock Cartwright. His formal schooling ended in 1836 when his father's fortunes temporarily, but severely, reversed (probably during the early stages of the economically devastating Panic of 1837).

Cartwright held various jobs, including a stint as a clerk at a New York City brokerage before achieving the respected position of teller at the Union Bank. In 1845 he and his brother Alfred opened a bookstore/stationer's shop on Wall Street. In June 1842 he married Eliza Ann Gerrits Van Wie, daughter of a prominent Albany, New York, family. By 1848 they had four children.

Like many young men of his day, Cartwright played "town ball," a primitive version of baseball that had evolved from the British game of "rounders." He and his cronies (properly dubbed "apprentice capitalists" by his biographer) had probably been playing together since 1842. Seemingly at Cartwright's behest, they organized formally on 23 September 1845 as the Knickerbocker Base Ball Club of New York, with a set of playing rules that have served as the foundation of the contemporary game.

These rules are generally attributed to Cartwright and account for his appellation as the "Father of Modern Baseball," although serious questions have been raised about

Alexander Cartwright, 1860. ASSOCIATED PRESS AP

his supposed sole authorship and about just what he proposed. It is clear that the rules called for a regular rotation of batters, allowing each side three outs before the inning was completed, laying out the playing field as a diamond rather than a square, providing for foul lines, and eliminating the practice of retiring a runner by hitting him with a thrown ball. The rules sped up and simplified the game. But the sixth edition of *Total Baseball: The Official Encyclopedia of Major League Baseball* (1999) convincingly maintains that Cartwright "assuredly did NOT do . . . any of the three central things credited to him on his plaque in the Baseball Hall of Fame" (that is, set nine innings as a game, limit a team to nine players on the field, and establish bases ninety feet apart).

Actually, Cartwright did not become widely known for his baseball activities until the late 1930s. In the early years of the twentieth century, a commission had been established at the instigation of sporting goods manufacturer A. G. Spalding to delve into the origins of baseball. The members, like its prime mover, wanted to determine that baseball was a purely American game and reported that it had been invented by Civil War general Abner Doubleday in 1839 and was first played in Cooperstown, New York.

This myth, although challenged almost from the first

moments of its publication, served as the basis for a promotional centennial celebration planned for 1939. The previous year, while plans for that celebration were being finalized, Cartwright's grandson wrote the organizers, sending along a diary, clippings, and other materials detailing his grandfather's activity. The celebration went forward, and the Doubleday myth was allowed for the moment to stand, but Cartwright was acknowledged and elected to the Baseball Hall of Fame (which was conceived in 1935 as part of the centennial promotion, electing its first inductees in 1936).

On learning of the California gold strikes, Cartwright left New York City for the West Coast in March 1849. For some 150 days he and some friends trekked across the country, arriving in San Francisco at the beginning of August. Legend has it that "the extended travel time was created by frequent stopovers devoted to demonstrations" by Cartwright and party of his brand of baseball to fellow travelers and in settlements, large and small, along the way.

The adventuresome Cartwright stayed only briefly in San Francisco, soon shipping out to the Sandwich Islands (as Hawaii was then known). He arrived in Oahu, the most settled of the islands, on 28 August 1849. He made at least two voyages back to California before settling permanently in Honolulu and sending for his wife and children, who, after an arduous voyage around Cape Horn, arrived in 1851.

Cartwright flourished in Hawaii. As he told a correspondent in 1865, "Though by no means rich, I am independent and occupy an excellent position in society." His various enterprises included a general merchandise business, and, while Honolulu was a whaling center, he successfully served as an agent for American companies involved in that industry. For a time he served as Peruvian consul in Honolulu. Cartwright and Company engaged in banking, insurance, ship chandlering, and real estate. Until his death, Cartwright served as a financial advisor to successive generations of Hawaii's ruling royal family.

Within a year of his arrival in Hawaii, the civic-minded Cartwright, a former New York City volunteer fireman, formed Honolulu's first fire department, which he headed for several years. Cartwright was involved in a variety of capacities with different groups, including the Honolulu Library and Reading Room, the Masons, the Queen's Hospital, and such charitable organizations as the Honolulu American Seaman's Institute.

According to his son Bruce, Cartwright "never forgot Base Ball." He maintained an ardent interest in the game as a promoter, player, and rooter. In 1852, well before baseball became the American national pastime, Cartwright laid out a diamond-shaped field in Honolulu's Makiki Park, introducing baseball as the Knickerbocker rules had restructured the game. Over the years he organized clubs,

and the imposing six-foot, two-inch, white-bearded Cartwright would even visit elementary schools, using chalk and blackboard to arouse the children's interest in baseball.

Cartwright died in Honolulu and is buried in Nuuanu (now Oahu) Cemetery in Honolulu. His death went virtually unnoticed in the United States. In 1939, as a result of the rediscovery of Cartwright, baseball immortal Babe Ruth, while on a trip to Hawaii, visited his grave, Makiki Park and a street were renamed in Cartwright's honor, and a plaque describing his activities was placed at City Hall.

Cartwright's contributions to Hawaii are clear and significant. However, his ascribed role in baseball's development has fluctuated dramatically. For a brief moment in time during the 1840s he had some impact. Then he was forgotten. But the game's flawed centennial celebration resulted in his rediscovery. Over the years since 1939 his contribution to baseball has again been somewhat downgraded, but he is accepted and recognized as a seminal figure in the game's early days who helped to codify the rules and field setup that govern the modern sport.

★

An Alexander Cartwright file containing clippings, documents, and copies of articles by and about Cartwright is in the A. Bartlett Giamatti Research Center of the National Baseball Hall of Fame Library. Harold Peterson's interesting biography, *The Man Who Invented Baseball* (1973), spends more time on the trip across the United States than on Cartwright's other ventures. See also Lowell Reidenbaugh, *Baseball's Hall of Fame: Cooperstown, Where Legends Live Forever* (1986).

DANIEL J. LEAB

CHADWICK, Florence May (*b.* 9 November 1918 in San Diego, California; *d.* 15 March 1995 in San Diego, California), persevering long-distance swimmer who became one of the most famous female athletes of the twentieth century.

Chadwick was one of two children of Richard William Chadwick, who, after retiring from a twenty-three-year-long career in the San Diego police department as a detective and narcotics agent, operated a restaurant with his wife, Mary Chadwick.

Chadwick's swimming career began early. She was taught to swim by an uncle but lost her first contest at the age of six, coming in last. "I can still remember the humiliation I felt but it only made me want to win more than ever," she later commented.

Chadwick graduated from Point Loma Junior and Senior High Schools in San Diego in 1936, then attended San Diego State College. She went on to Southwestern University of Law in Los Angeles, California, then to Balboa Law School and Dickenson Business College, both in

Florence Chadwick. ARCHIVE PHOTOS, INC.

San Diego. Chadwick appeared in aquatic shows, was a swimming instructor, gave celebrity endorsements, and in 1944 appeared in the movie musical *Bathing Beauty*.

Years earlier, at the tender age of ten, Chadwick was inspired by the record-setting feats of Gertrude Ederle, the first woman to swim the English Channel. It was this inspiration that led to Chadwick's greatest triumph: swimming the channel on 8 August 1950 in the record time of thirteen hours and twenty minutes—one hour and eleven minutes faster than Ederle had.

The preparation for this triumph had not been easy. After a long and varied swimming career, Chadwick worked for an American oil company in Saudi Arabia, saving the $5,000 needed to enter the contest. She practiced long hours in the Persian Gulf, and when she took to the French waters of Cape Gris-Nez at 2:37 that August morning, the five foot, six inch swimmer weighed in at 141 pounds. As she swam toward England, her father, officials, and friends accompanied her in a fishing boat.

Throughout the swim Chadwick nibbled on sugar cubes and fluctuated her number of strokes per minute to help conserve her energy. For four hours she had to overcome the obstacle of an ebb tide encountered three miles out.

Fortunately for her, British artillery in the area had been suspended. After making it to England, she commented nonchalantly to the reporters on shore, "I feel fine. I am quite prepared to swim back." She did swim back, but not until the next year.

On 10 and 11 September 1951 Chadwick performed the England to France crossing, a much more difficult task, becoming the first woman swimmer to cross the English Channel in both directions. She and her father waited for eleven weeks in a seaside hotel while she strengthened herself with a calorie-rich diet. Finally she decided to brave foggy waters and unfavorable tides and embarked upon her swim, which this time would take her from Dover, England, to Cape Gris-Nez in France. After sixteen hours and twenty-two minutes of arduous swimming (made even worse by the choking fumes from an accompanying motorboat), Chadwick landed at Sangatte, three miles south of the French seaport of Calais. But her conquest of the English Channel did not end there. On 4 September 1953 she again went from England to France, this time in fourteen hours and forty-two minutes. Two years later on 12 October 1955, when she was thirty-six-years-old, she crossed the channel in thirteen hours and fifty-five minutes.

Other aquatic achievements by Chadwick include swimming across the San Diego Bay Channel at age ten, an unprecedented feat by a child of that age; winning the annual 2.5-mile race at La Jolla, California, ten times; breaking a record when she covered the twenty-one miles from Catalina Island to the California mainland in thirteen hours and forty-seven minutes on 21 September 1952; conquering the Strait of Gibraltar between Spain and Africa on 20 September 1953 in five hours and six minutes; completing a round-trip across the Bosporus between Europe and Asia on 7 October 1953 in a little over an hour and fourteen minutes; and setting her fourth record in five weeks on 9 October 1953, crossing the Turkish Dardanelles (a narrow strait also known as Hellespont) in less than two hours. Chadwick received the Helms Athletic Foundation Award as athlete of the month for August 1950; was named to the International Swimming Hall of Fame in 1970; received the Living Legacy Award and induction into the San Diego Hall of Champions, both in 1984; and was inducted into the International Women's Sports Hall of Fame in 1996. Her hometown threw a ticker-tape parade in her honor in 1950, and a white-tipped dahlia was named for her.

For quite a while Chadwick was the world's highest-paid woman athlete. She founded swimming schools named for her in New York, New Jersey, and California and was the aquatic director at Grossinger's, a famous resort in New York State. At the age of fifty, in San Diego, she embarked upon a successful career as a stockbroker, which she pursued for the next two and a half decades.

Chadwick died in San Diego on 15 March 1995 after a long unspecified illness. She was never married and had no children.

Extraordinarily good looking with large, lustrous, dark eyes and a flashing smile, Chadwick was called "the most beautiful woman in sports" by Gypsy Rose Lee, an entertainer and a beauty in her own right. Johnny Weissmuller, an Olympic swimming champion and film star, said she was "the greatest woman swimmer of all time—maybe of either sex—and it's time she got credit for it." But it is in her own words that she is best summed up: "Life seems so much simpler swimming. The experience must be similar to that of a flyer above the clouds by himself. I am also in my own little world out there. . . . If I had a chance to relive my life, I would do it all again because it is trying to do what you badly want to do that counts."

★

Biographical sketches of Chadwick are featured in *Current Biography* (1950, 1995); *Encyclopedia of World Biography* (1998); and *Women in World History* (1999). Entries on Chadwick are also in David L. Porter, *Biographical Dictionary of American Sports: Basketball and Other Indoor Sports* (1989); Ralph Hickok, *A Who's Who of Sports Champions* (1995); Joe Layden, *Women in Sports* (1997); and Janet Woolum, *Outstanding Women Athletes* (1998). Articles on the swimmer's channel crossings include "Channel Challengers," *Newsweek* (21 Aug. 1950), "Two Girls in Swimming," *Time* (21 Aug. 1950), and "Wrong Way Swimmer," *Time* (24 Sept. 1951). Elizabeth Witty, "Chadwick Out of Water but Still 'Swimming,'" *Futures* (Oct. 1986), deals with her post-swimming career. An obituary is in the *New York Times* (19 Mar. 1995).

DOROTHY L. MORAN

CHADWICK, Henry (*b.* 5 October 1824 in Exeter, England; *d.* 20 April 1908 in Brooklyn, New York), known as the "Father of Baseball" because he nurtured the sport in its infancy as its first serious journalist, its first statistician, its first historian, and its leading advocate and innovative rule maker.

Chadwick was the son of James Chadwick of Manchester, England, a journalist and musician, and Therese Coates of Burton-upon-Trent, England. Chadwick's older half brother was Sir Edwin Chadwick (1800–1890), the man responsible for modernizing England's sewage system and improving its drinking water. Chadwick spent the first thirteen years of his life in Plymouth, a small city in Exeter in southwestern England. Like other English children his age, Chadwick played rounders, a game with bats, bases, and a ball. American children also played rounders, which was brought over by British immigrants in the 1600s. On 23 September 1837 Chadwick, his parents, and his younger sister, Rosa, immigrated to the United States. The family took up residence in Brooklyn, where Chadwick lived for the remainder of his life.

Like his father, who was a cellist, Chadwick took up music. He played piano and guitar and throughout the 1840s earned a living as a music teacher. But teaching music was never his true passion. Though he would compose more than one hundred waltzes and sing and play piano for friends and family, he gravitated toward journalism, his father's old profession.

In 1843 Chadwick went to work for the *Long Island Star,* one of three local newspapers in Brooklyn. He wrote news stories but was soon drawn to the burgeoning sports scene in and around New York City. Chadwick, like many immigrants from England, had a passion for the outdoors and a love of ball games, particularly cricket. Cricket was the closest thing to a national pastime in the United States, and its sophistication and scientific approach drew Chadwick not only to play the sport but to eventually become the lead cricket writer for the *New York Times* in the mid-1850s.

If cricket's sophistication attracted Chadwick, baseball's simplicity in the late 1840s initially frustrated him. He had participated in an archaic form of "base ball" in September 1848, when he played shortstop in an amateur game. He found the sport "juvenile and uninspiring." He especially disliked the rule that allowed infielders to throw the ball at the base runners, the only way to put them out. "I remember getting some hard hits in the ribs, occasionally, from an accurately thrown ball," Chadwick recalled. In 1848 Chadwick married Jane Botts, the daughter of Alexander Botts, president of the Virginia State Council. Chadwick and his wife had two daughters.

Ironically, Chadwick's association with cricket led him to rediscover baseball. In 1856, after returning from a cricket match in Hoboken, New Jersey, that he was covering for the *Times,* he witnessed a highly skilled game between the Gotham and Eagle Clubs of New York City. Suddenly he realized baseball's potential: "At once the thought struck me that here was the game that should be the national game of America, as cricket then was and still is the national game of my birth . . . and there and then I decided to do all in my power to make it the national game in word and in truth." Chadwick decided to use his career in journalism as his vehicle to promote the baseball gospel.

Despite Chadwick's belief in the sport's great appeal, only one journalist, William Cauldwell of the *New York Sunday Mercury,* covered baseball in 1856. Believing that publicity would help baseball's growth, Caldwell tried to convince the editors of several dailies to publish the results of all "match" games in an honest effort to sell his own stories and to boost baseball's popularity. Chadwick even offered to send in results of the games for free, but he failed to arouse enthusiasm.

Finally, on 10 July 1856 the *Times* relented and printed

Chadwick's first baseball article summary. It read: "On Tuesday a match of Base Ball was played between the first nine members of the 'Gotham' and nine members of the 'Baltic' Clubs, at their ground at the Red House [in Harlem]. Play commenced at 4 o'clock and ended at 5, the 'Gothams' beating easily, the 'Baltics' making but two aces."

The following summer Chadwick improved baseball's reputation when the weekly sporting journal, the *New York Clipper,* agreed to let him publish game summaries. Chadwick was quickly named baseball and cricket editor. His articles in the *Clipper* helped create an even greater following for the game.

Due to his baseball and cricket expertise, Chadwick was invited to join the Rules Committee of the National Association of Base Ball Players in 1858. His vision of a scientific game, influenced by his own participation in and love for cricket, helped shape baseball as a sport with challenging rules requiring skill. As chairman of the committee he helped to implement the fly catch, which did away with the one-bounce accommodation, and the overhand pitch and to establish the distance between the pitching mound and home plate. Chadwick also invented most of the game's statistics. Besides the box score, which he incorporated from cricket, he invented the batting average and was the first to tabulate home runs, total bases, and hits. He also invented the scoring system.

In 1871 Chadwick created the first professional league, the National Association of Professional Base Ball Players. The professional association evolved into the National League in 1876. In 1881 Chadwick became the official editor of *Spalding's Baseball Guide,* the official guide of the National League.

During his career Chadwick focused on other sports too, writing guidebooks on chess, billiards, and cricket. He even wrote articles on ice skating and the new sport that began to grab the public's attention in the 1890s, football. Football was the favorite sport of Theodore Roosevelt, and though Chadwick disdained football for its excessive violence, he had great admiration for the president, whom he met briefly at the White House. In 1904, in celebration of his eightieth year, Chadwick received a letter from President Roosevelt, whom Chadwick referred to as my young friend Theodore. The letter said: "My Dear Chadwick: I congratulate you on your eightieth year and your fiftieth year in journalism . . . and you are entitled to the good wishes of all for that part you have taken in behalf of decent sport."

Despite his reputation as an expert on the sport and its history, Chadwick became embroiled in the controversy over the origin of baseball that raged for over twenty years. Nationalism and financial motivation led Albert Goodwill Spalding, a former baseball pitching great and a sporting goods manufacturer, to promote the false idea that baseball

was created in the United States without any foreign influence or origin. In 1907 Spalding appointed the Mills commission, which determined that the game had been invented by Abner Doubleday in spite of the fact that Doubleday never mentioned baseball in his voluminous diaries and most likely never even played the sport. To his dying day Chadwick insisted correctly that the game had evolved from rounders.

Chadwick acquired a cold following his attendance at two opening-day matches in early April 1908 and grew progressively weaker as the cold turned into pneumonia. He died at age eighty-three. Several days later he was buried in Green-Wood Cemetery, Brooklyn. His grave is marked by a monument topped by a granite sphere carved to resemble a baseball, and four corners of the lot are marked by stones etched to look like bases.

Chadwick was a visionary. He was an important voice in baseball history whose contribution to the national pastime as the game's greatest advocate cemented his place in both baseball and American history. Perhaps the most touching tribute was delivered by Spalding: "I knew Mr. Chadwick intimately for over forty years. . . . His aid in the upbuilding of baseball has been invaluable and the present great popularity of the game is largely due to his efforts . . . I voice the sentiment of every one interested in baseball and clean sports, when I say that . . . he will for ever be remembered as the 'Father of Baseball.'"

In 1938 Chadwick was elected to the Baseball Hall of Fame in Cooperstown, New York. He is enshrined as the only sportswriter with a plaque in the players' wing of the museum.

★

Chadwick and his contributions to baseball are the subject of a forthcoming biography by Andrew J. Schiff. Chadwick is also discussed in Melvin Adelman, *A Sporting Time: New York City and the Rise of Modern Athletics* (1986); Jeffrey Richman, *Brooklyn's Green-Wood Cemetery: New York's Buried Treasure* (1998); and Jules Tygiel, *Past Time: Baseball as History* (2000). A tribute published shortly after his death is "In Memory of Henry Chadwick, 'Father of Baseball,'" *Baseball Magazine* 1 (June 1908).

ANDREW J. SCHIFF

CHAMBERLAIN, Wilt(on) Norman (*b.* 21 August 1936 in Philadelphia, Pennsylvania; *d.* 12 October 1999 in Los Angeles, California), professional basketball player who was the leading rebounder and one of the most prolific scorers in the history of the National Basketball Association (NBA).

Chamberlain was the sixth of nine surviving children of William Chamberlain, a welder, janitor, and handyman, and Olivia Ruth Johnson, a homemaker and domestic. He

Wilt Chamberlain, 1957. © BETTMANN/CORBIS

attended the Georgia Brooks Elementary School and Overbrook High School in Philadelphia. In high school he competed in the high jump and shot put and ran the 440-yard and 880-yard dash for the local Amateur Athletic Union team. In fact, Chamberlain preferred track and field to basketball, but because of his great height—he was six feet, eleven inches tall by the ninth grade—he was induced by friends to try basketball. Once he started playing, Chamberlain took the game seriously. He improved steadily, playing in the Police Athletic League and the Young Men's Christian Association league. In the summers he worked in New York State as a bellhop at Kutshers Country Club in the Catskills and found time to play on the hotel basketball team with college and professional stars. Chamberlain also played on his high school basketball team for three years and in that span scored 2,252 points (establishing the state scoring record) and led his team to a record of fifty-eight wins and three defeats.

Not surprisingly, the major college basketball programs recruited Chamberlain. After some consideration, he chose the University of Kansas, in part because of his admiration for its legendary coach, Forrest C. ("Phog") Allen. As he had at Overbrook, Chamberlain continued to run track and take part in field events (he was Big Eight high-jump champion). As expected, he excelled at basketball. During his three-year college career, he averaged thirty points and about sixteen rebounds a game. His single biggest disappointment came in his sophomore year, when Kansas lost a triple-overtime, one-point game to the University of North Carolina for the National Collegiate Athletic Association championship. Chamberlain returned for his junior

year but grew progressively discouraged at being double- and triple-teamed and physically abused, and he decided to forgo his senior year. Since at that time a college player could not join the NBA until his college class graduated, Chamberlain signed a one-year contract in 1958 with the Harlem Globetrotters for $65,000, the most generous basketball contract to that date. He enjoyed himself enormously, and when the season ended in 1959 he was ready to play in the NBA.

Chamberlain's professional career lasted fourteen seasons. He spent the first three with the Philadelphia Warriors (1959–1962) and then played for the San Francisco Warriors for three seasons (1962–1965). In 1965 he headed back east, playing for the Philadelphia 76ers (1965–1968), and then finished his career with the Los Angeles Lakers (1968–1972). Overall, he played in 1,045 regular season games plus 160 playoff games. During his career he accumulated 31,419 points (a record broken by Kareem Abdul-Jabbar), led the league in scoring seven times, and averaged 30.1 points a game. In his first year Chamberlain averaged 37.6 points and twenty-seven rebounds and was named Rookie of the Year as well as Most Valuable Player (MVP; an honor accorded him again in 1966, 1967, and 1968). In the 1961–1962 season he averaged 50.4 points (still a record in 2001). His single most memorable performance as a scorer occurred on 2 March 1962 in Hershey, Pennsylvania, when he totaled 100 points against the last-place New York Knicks. By the end of the third quarter he had sixty-nine points, and Eddie Donovan, the Knick coach, ordered his players to foul Chamberlain whenever he had the ball. Chamberlain, a notoriously poor foul shooter, was, in his words, "hot that night," and made twenty-eight of thirty-two free throws. He scored the hundredth point with forty-six seconds remaining. Philadelphia won 169–147.

Although Chamberlain's career scoring was surpassed, the same feat seems unlikely in the case of his rebounding. Chamberlain accumulated 23,928 rebounds, averaging 22.9 per game. (Abdul-Jabbar is in second place with 17,440 rebounds amassed over twenty seasons.) He led the league in rebounding in eleven of his fourteen seasons and never had fewer than ten rebounds per game. In the 1960–1961 season he averaged a record 27.2 rebounds. In 1960 he also grabbed fifty-five rebounds in a game against Bill Russell and the Boston Celtics. That performance no doubt pleased Chamberlain, since in sizing up the two centers, Russell is often judged the better overall player. According to critics, Russell was a "team" player, whereas Chamberlain was a "selfish gunner." Russell was on eleven championship teams and Chamberlain on only two, the 76ers in 1967 and the Lakers in 1972. Furthermore, in head-to-head encounters in the playoffs, Chamberlain prevailed only in 1967. Irritated by the comparison, Chamberlain responded that basketball is a team sport and that Russell was surrounded by superior players such as Bob Cousy, John Havlicek, K. C. Jones, and Sam Jones.

Chamberlain had a point. When Philadelphia won the championship in 1967 and set a record of sixty-eight wins and thirteen losses, his teammates were Hal Greer, Billy Cunningham, and Chet Walker. And when Los Angeles claimed the title in 1972 (and established a new record of sixty-nine wins and thirteen losses), Chamberlain played with Jerry West, Gail Goodrich, Happy Hairston, and Jim McMillan. Chamberlain also has pointed out that he focused on scoring when he was instructed to do so by his coach. When urged to change his approach, he became a passer and led the league in assists in 1968 with 702. Later in his career, when he played for Los Angeles, he was a defensive specialist.

In comparing the two players, one must take into account Chamberlain's physical attributes. Not only was he big (at seven feet, one inch tall and 275 pounds), but he also possessed agility, speed, endurance, leaping ability, and physical strength. Trying to cope with him was a daunting task for any opposing player. Little wonder that the basketball historian Leonard Koppett has concluded that Chamberlain was "clearly the most dominating player who ever played basketball." After fourteen seasons Chamberlain decided to retire, noting: "There was always so much more pain to my losing than ever there was to gain by winning." Not quite ready to quit basketball, he spent the 1973–1974 season coaching the San Diego Conquistadors of the American Basketball Association. He grew progressively weary of the traveling and the long playing season and elected to retire from professional basketball in 1974.

Chamberlain did not retire from the sporting world, however. His earliest athletic interests were in track and field. In retirement he stayed connected to track by sponsoring a women's track team, Wilt's Wonder Women. He took his sponsoring seriously, attending meets and remaining until the last event. He also continued playing basketball. Late in his professional basketball career, he talked about challenging Muhammad Ali to a boxing match. After consulting with his lawyer, Chamberlain, fearing the damage to his image if Ali humiliated him in the ring, backed out of the match.

In retirement Chamberlain found another sport that attracted him: he began playing professional volleyball. He went up against some of the best players on the globe and participated in an All-Star game in which he was selected the MVP. He also assisted in launching the International Volleyball Association (of which he was president). He became a team owner and toured the world with his team, helping bring recognition to the sport. As an athlete, Chamberlain was forced to conduct his life in public view. In his autobiography, *Wilt: Just Like Any Other Seven-Foot Black Millionaire Who Lives Next Door* (1973), he opened the door to the public on his preferences (he loved fast cars and travel) and opinions. For instance, because of his concern for overpopulation, he had decided it would be hypocritical to get married and have children. He also laid bare his sexual exploits, at times in detail, including sexual encounters that took place on airplanes while in flight. Satisfying his "lustful desires" was an inseparable part of Chamberlain's life, as he made patently clear. He claimed to have had sexual liaisons with some 20,000 women, a number that he estimated to be "equal to having sex with 1.2 women a day, every day, since I was fifteen years old."

Chamberlain also discussed criticisms of his "deficiencies" on the basketball court. In effect, if his team won, he received little praise, since victory was expected. When his team lost, though, Chamberlain often was blamed for the outcome. The problem, he concluded in his autobiography, was that he was such a dominating presence on the court that it was virtually impossible for fans, sportswriters, and at times even his teammates to identify with him. Although he came to understand the reason behind the lack of empathy, Chamberlain, who cared deeply what others thought of him, found it difficult to accept.

Chamberlain lived to see his achievements acknowledged officially. In 1978 he was enshrined in the Naismith Memorial Basketball Hall of Fame. In 1996 Chamberlain, who led the league in scoring, rebounding, or assists in every one of his fourteen seasons, was listed among the fifty greatest NBA players of all time. In late October of that year, when the fifty greatest basketball players were announced, Chamberlain attended the ceremony. Three years later he died of congestive heart failure at his home in the

Bel Air section of Los Angeles. His body was cremated, and the ashes were given to family members. Chamberlain left 90 percent of his estate to children's charities, many of which he had supported during his lifetime.

★

The family retains some of Chamberlain's personal effects and papers. The University of Kansas archives also maintains a large bibliographical records file. The fullest account of Chamberlain's life up to 1973 is his autobiography, *Wilt: Just Like Any Other Seven-Foot Black Millionaire Who Lives Next Door* (1973), written with David Shaw. He describes his other book, *A View from Above* (1991), as "a collection of thoughts, my feelings about life and my living of life." Useful articles are in the *New York Post* (15 Oct. 1999), *New York Daily News* (17 Oct. 1999), and *Sports Illustrated* (25 Oct. 1999). An obituary is in the *New York Times* (13 Oct. 1999).

RICHARD P. HARMOND

CHANDLER, Albert Benjamin ("Happy") (*b.* 14 July 1898 in Corydon, Kentucky; *d.* 15 June 1991 in Versailles, Kentucky), successful politician who, as the second Commissioner of Baseball, presided over major changes that secured the sport's national preeminence.

Chandler was one of two sons of Joseph Sephus Chandler, a poor farmer, and Callie Sanders Chandler, a homemaker, who deserted the family when Albert was four years old. Although he had to work to supplement his family's finances, Chandler was valedictorian of his class at Corydon High School, from which he graduated in 1917. Entering Transylvania College with only "a red sweater, a $5 bill and a smile," he starred in four sports (football, baseball, basketball, and track) and won the name "Happy." Chandler served a brief term in the U.S. Army in 1918 before returning to college and earning an A.B. in history and political science in 1921. He then attended Harvard Law School but left after a year to enter the University of Kentucky in 1922. While still in school, Chandler played several summers of semipro baseball as a pitcher-infielder and worked as an assistant football coach and scout at tiny Centre College, in Danville, Kentucky. After obtaining his LL.B. from the University of Kentucky in 1924, Chandler established a practice in Versailles (near Lexington, Kentucky) and married Mildred Lewis Watkins on 12 November 1925, a union that lasted sixty-five years. The couple had four children. In time Chandler received the degree of Doctor of Laws from both Transylvania (1936) and Kentucky (1937).

Chandler, who loved to sing in a passable tenor, was a natural for Democratic politics because of his charismatic folksiness; he was elected to the Kentucky senate in 1929.

"Happy" Chandler, 1946. ASSOCIATED PRESS AP

A gifted speaker, he was lieutenant governor on Ruby Laffoon's ticket in 1931 but broke with the governor over a three percent sales tax imposed during the Great Depression. Although he was ostracized, Chandler used Laffoon's temporary absence from the state in 1935 to obtain legislative enactment of a primary law ending caucus nominations. Party nominations would be made by primary elections, thus putting a stop to cronyism and the control of politics by those in power. Chandler won Kentucky's first primary in the fall of 1935 and was elected governor. He served from 1935 to 1939.

The youngest governor in the nation, Chandler was a strong New Dealer who led a populist administration. Under his administration, the sales tax was repealed and government streamlined, and public works spending built hospitals, schools, and roads—including a four-lane highway to Versailles. Funding for these programs came from Washington, D.C., as well as income, liquor excise, and luxury taxes. In spite of Chandler's achievements as governor, state law prohibited reelection, and Chandler failed in an attempt to unseat the incumbent U.S. senator, Alben Barkley, in 1938. However, the sudden death of Senator Marvell Mills Logan in 1939 allowed Chandler to obtain an interim senatorial appointment. He won a special senatorial election in 1940 and a full six-year term in 1942. As a member of the Military Affairs Committee during World War II, Chandler advocated preparedness, greater emphasis on the Pacific theater of war, and wariness toward Great Britain because he believed they continued to have imperial ambitions. In domestic politics he sanctioned the continuation of major league baseball even though 4,000 of its 5,700 athletes had been inducted into the armed forces.

Chandler's vocal praise for baseball led the baseball executive Larry MacPhail to support him as commissioner. The two men first met when Chandler attended Cincinnati Reds games, and "Loud Larry" convinced other owners that Chandler could replace "Kenesaw Mountain" Landis, the "myth" who had ruled the sport since 1920. Installed as second Commissioner of Baseball on 12 July 1945, Chandler reveled in a seven-year appointment, earning $50,000 per year (five times his senate salary). He retained his senate seat until the war concluded and resigned on 1 November 1945. As baseball commissioner, Chandler was determined not to be a figurehead, and he forced owners to renew their "loyalty oath" to accept his decisions. In 1922, the Supreme Court had decided that baseball was a sport, not a business, and granted it unique exemption from the antimonopoly and antitrust laws. Chandler understood that owners wanted to retain baseball's antitrust exemption and needed his political connections.

Chandler led baseball in historic times. He met a major crisis in April 1946 by suspending eighteen players who had jumped to the Mexican League. Chandler's acceptance of responsibility showed strength, but his insistence on a five-year banishment of the wayward players ultimately cost him support. In June 1945 he successfully opposed player unionization by the American Baseball Guild but was shocked by their paltry salaries. Chandler became the "players commissioner" by endorsing a uniform contract, payment of salary while injured, and weekly spring training allowances; he also suggested higher wages for umpires. Painfully aware of past gambling scandals, Chandler rejected reinstatement for "Buck" Weaver, a member of the Chicago White Sox team (later dubbed the "Black Sox") who had disgraced baseball by throwing the 1919 World Series. Even more dramatically, he suspended the Dodgers manager, Leo Durocher on 9 April 1947 for association with gamblers and "an accumulation of unpleasant incidents . . . detrimental to baseball." As a result of this decision, Chandler was hung in effigy in Brooklyn, and faced down hostile metropolitan fans during Babe Ruth Day later that month. His decisiveness also lost him the support of both MacPhail and the New York media.

Chandler was no backwoods bigot. In May 1945 he called for the desegregation of baseball, but less enlightened owners recorded a 15–1 margin against integration in a still

controversial vote taken in 1946. Chandler nonetheless approved the transfer of the black player Jackie Robinson's contract from the Montreal Royals to the Brooklyn Dodgers and quashed a potentially riotous situation in Philadelphia in 1947. Although the commissioner had no power to enforce integration, Cleveland Indians owner Bill Veeck remembered that Chandler "did what he could to make Robinson's path easier." Chandler also facilitated Larry Doby's integration of the American League that July when Doby was signed to play with the Indians. Chandler's reputation was secured had he done nothing else.

From 1947 to 1950, the commissioner's support among owners eroded. To safeguard baseball's image, he turned down Liebman Brewery's sponsorship of the World Series and accepted Gillette's offer of $1 million annually, 80 percent of which went toward pensions. This arrangement was criticized when Gillette sold the rights for much more. Chandler feuded with the American League over umpire compensation, fined teams for violations of high school signing regulations, located his offices in Cincinnati rather than New York, and even put Robinson "on the carpet" when the Dodger star threatened to "get rough" with those who still opposed integration. Antitrust suits against his Mexican rulings were settled cheaply out of court but troubled the ownership. Most unsettling was Chandler's decision to investigate the owners of the Cardinals and Yankees for questionable conduct. The owner of the St. Louis Cardinals, Fred Saigh, denounced Chandler as a "bluegrass jackass," and the New York Yankees owner Del Webb later said his greatest baseball thrill was ousting Chandler. Tom Yawkey, owner of the Boston Red Sox, said that Chandler was "the player's . . . fan's . . . press' and radio's commissioner, everybody's commissioner but the men who pay." Chandler won nine votes for reappointment in 1951, but lacked the three-quarter margin that owners had imposed in 1945. Accepting the inevitable, he resigned on 15 July 1951. Of his successor, Chandler quipped that the "owners had a vacancy and decided to keep it."

After his resignation, Chandler returned to law and politics, serving as Kentucky's governor from 1955 to 1959 during school-integration struggles. He won votes for U.S. vice president in 1956 and later became something of a perennial national candidate. Honors accumulated. The University of Kentucky Medical Center bears his name (1959), and he is in Kentucky's Sports Hall of Fame. Chandler also was named state Man of the Year and Man of the Century in various polls. His sports reputation won him appointment as commissioner of the short-lived Continental Football League (1965), but baseball ignored him. Conspicuously not invited to World Series and All-Star games, Chandler's vindication came with election to the National Baseball Hall of Fame in Cooperstown, New York (1982). Still happy and contentious, Chandler died of heart disease and is buried in the cemetery of Pisgah Presbyterian Church in Woodford County, near Versailles.

★

Chandler's papers are deposited at the University of Kentucky, with an additional file at the Baseball Hall of Fame in Cooperstown, New York. His autobiography (written with Vance H. Trimble), *Heroes, Plain Folks and Skunks: The Life and Times of Happy Chandler* (1989), is an easy read. More nuanced assessments of his career are in Arthur Mann, *Secret History of the War Between Chandler, Durocher and MacPhail* (1951); Jerome Holtzman, *The Commissioners: Baseball's Midlife Crisis* (1998); and William Marshall, *Baseball's Pivotal Era, 1945–1951* (1999). Jules Tygiel, *Baseball's Great Experiment: Jackie Robinson and His Legacy* (1983) is critical of Chandler, a judgment somewhat modified in a 1997 edition of the book. Obituaries are in the *New York Times* and *Louisville Courier-Journal* (both 16 June 1991).

GEORGE J. LANKEVICH

CHARLESTON, Oscar McKinley ("Charlie") (*b.* 14 October 1896 in Indianapolis, Indiana; *d.* 5 October 1954 in Philadelphia, Pennsylvania), baseball player who was a superstar in African-American baseball during the era of racial separation.

Charleston was the seventh of eleven children born to Tom Charleston and Mary Jeanette Thomas Charleston. His father was a construction worker, but earlier in life had been a jockey, and his mother was a homemaker. Charleston completed the eighth grade at Public School 23 in Indianapolis before leaving to join the army at the age of fifteen. He enlisted on 7 March 1912 at Columbus Barracks, Ohio, and was honorably discharged from Company B of the Twenty-fourth Infantry on 20 March 1915.

During his army stint Charleston was stationed in the Philippines, where he participated in sporting events, including track and baseball. He won the 220-yard dash with a time of 23 seconds, and ran the 120-yard high hurdles in 15.1 seconds. In baseball he was the only African-American player in the Manila League in 1914. During World War I he was recalled to the army and served from 22 August to 3 December 1918, but did not serve overseas during this second stint. Charleston was married twice, first to Helen Grubbs in 1915; the young couple soon divorced. His second marriage was to Jane Blalock, the daughter of a Methodist minister. Their marriage lasted for twenty years before also ending in divorce. Neither marriage produced children.

Charleston was a baseball player and manager for four decades. He was associated with sixteen different teams during this long career, but he was most closely identified with the Indianapolis ABCs, Harrisburg Giants, Home-

Oscar Charleston, c. 1945. © CHARLES "TEENIE" HARRIS/CORBIS

stead Grays, and Pittsburgh Crawfords. Charleston offered a dynamic blend of speed and power—he was a complete player who could run, field, throw, and hit with power. At the plate, he was analogous to a left-handed Rogers Hornsby, consistently hitting over .300 and topping .400 on occasions, while still exhibiting good power. He was also variously compared to Ty Cobb for his baserunning, Tris Speaker for his fielding, and, later in his career, Babe Ruth for his slugging prowess. Charleston was the Willie Mays of his era, and some former Negro Leaguers who saw both players thought that Charleston was the better of the two. Ben Taylor, a longtime player and manager in the Negro Leagues, stated that Charleston was the "greatest outfielder that ever lived . . . greatest of all colors" and James "Cool Papa" Bell, who played both with and against Charleston, called him "the best I ever saw."

Charleston had been a batboy for the Indianapolis ABCs before he entered military service and, after his discharge, he returned to that team in 1915 and thrived under the tutelage of C. I. Taylor. Charleston played seven intermittent seasons with the ABCs, including a championship year in 1916, and established himself as a superstar. Following the 1923 season, he signed with Colonel Strothers as the playing manager for the Harrisburg Giants. Charleston had personal success during his four seasons at the helm, but an Eastern Colored League pennant eluded the team.

When the Harrisburg franchise broke up, Charleston detoured through Hilldale for a couple of years before landing with Cum Posey's Homestead Grays in 1930. By this time he had lost a step in the outfield and moved himself to first base. The Grays defeated the Lincoln Giants in a play-off for the eastern championship that season, and fielded an even stronger team in 1931 that featured Josh Gibson. Most observers felt this was one of the greatest teams in the history of African-American baseball.

A feud between the owners Cum Posey and Gus Greenlee led most of the top Grays stars, including Charleston, to sign with Greenlee's Crawfords. For the next five years, with Charleston at the helm, the Crawfords were the premier team of the era, at times fielding five future Hall of Famers. In addition to Charleston, Satchel Paige, Josh Gibson, Cool Papa Bell, and Judy Johnson were on the team roster for most of these years. The 1935 Crawfords were known as the best team in Negro League history. In 1933 the first annual Negro League East-West All-Star game was played. Although Charleston was a veteran player of almost two decades, he was selected to start the first three games and batted in the third spot in the order the first two years.

Charleston was fearless and well known for his brawls on and off the field. In the heat of action, he frequently fought with umpires and opponents alike. Off-field confrontations included challenging armed Cuban soldiers and snatching the hood off a confrontational Ku Klux Klansman. Yet he was protective of younger players and was idolized by African-American kids everywhere he went. His popularity extended to Cuba, where he played nine winter seasons during his career and compiled a lifetime batting average of .357.

Virtually all of Charleston's adult life was spent in baseball. During World War II he worked as a patrolman in the security and intelligence division of the Philadelphia Quartermaster Depot, but he also played on their baseball team and managed the Philadelphia Stars of the Negro National League. In 1949 Charleston took a sabbatical from the game and worked in the baggage department of the Pennsylvania Railway System in Philadelphia.

Charleston then resumed his career in African-American baseball as a player and manager and pursued it until his death. Later in 1949 he managed the Stars for at least part of the season and continued in that capacity through 1952, when the franchise was disbanded. He then began managing the Indianapolis Clowns in 1954 and had already signed a contract for the impending 1955 season when his heath declined. About a month after checking into Philadelphia General Hospital, Charleston died of a heart attack,

nine days short of his fifty-eighth birthday. He is buried in Floral Park Cemetery in Indianapolis.

Possibly the greatest all-around player in the history of African-American baseball, Charleston received the game's highest honor in 1976 when he was inducted into the National Baseball Hall of Fame at Cooperstown, New York. During his career, his performance on the baseball diamond demonstrated that African Americans could play on a Major League level, and throughout his life he openly challenged the sociopolitical practices that denied African Americans their worth and dignity as individuals.

★

Charleston's entry in the landmark publication James A. Riley, *The Biographical Encyclopedia of the Negro Baseball Leagues* (1994), contains useful information, as does the seminal work Bob Peterson, *Only the Ball Was White* (1970). See also David Porter, ed., *The Biographical Dictionary of American Sports: Baseball* (1987); John Holway, *Blackball Stars* (1988); Mike Shatzkin, ed., *The Ballplayers* (1990); and David Porter, ed., *African-American Sports Greats* (1995).

JAMES A. RILEY

CHELIOS, Chris ("Chel") (*b.* 25 January 1962 in Chicago, Illinois), National Hockey League All-Star defenseman and three-time winner of the James Norris Memorial Trophy.

Chelios grew up in the Chicago suburb of Evergreen Park, Illinois. In 1975 he began attending Mount Carmel High School, where he played varsity ice hockey in both his freshman and sophomore seasons. Mount Carmel was a member of the Chicago Catholic League (the oldest high school hockey league in Illinois), which competed each year for the Kennedy Cup. After winning the 1976–1977 regular-season championship, Mount Carmel squared off against the Brother Rice team in a best-of-three playoff for the Kennedy Cup. With the series tied at one game apiece and the rubber game also knotted at one, Chelios—all 110 pounds of him—scored the cup-winning goal with only ten seconds left in the game. It was the school's first of six consecutive Kennedy Cups, making Chelios's clutch tally one of the biggest goals in Mount Carmel hockey history.

After that magical sophomore season Chelios's family moved to San Diego. Because southern California at the time had little to offer in the way of competitive amateur hockey, Chelios left for Moose Jaw, Canada, and the Saskatchewan Junior Hockey League (SJHL). His superb play in the SJHL was enough to induce the Montreal Canadiens, known as the Habs, to take a chance on the under-age junior as their fifth choice in the second round, fortieth overall, in the National Hockey League's 1981 entry draft.

Chris Chelios, 1999. AP Photo/Duane Burleson

Chelios then moved to the University of Wisconsin–Madison to play under the guidance of Bob Johnson. He was with the Badgers for two seasons, from 1981 to 1983. In 1983 Chelios produced an average of one point per game while playing steady defense to help lead the Badgers to the National Collegiate Athletic Association (NCAA) Championship. He was chosen for the NCAA All-Tournament Team and the Western Collegiate Hockey Association (WCHA) Second All-Star Team. It was a busy year for Chelios, who also played on both the U.S. national and 1984 Olympic teams as well as appearing in twelve games for the Canadiens. He appeared uncertain and unsteady at first in the NHL, but the best was yet to come.

In the 1984–1985 season Chelios became a regular part of the Habs blue-line corps. A year later his name was inscribed on the Stanley Cup. As a valuable addition to a team led by the poised veterans Bob Gainey and Larry Robinson, Chelios pitched in with two goals and nine assists during Montreal's magical 1985–1986 playoff run. In 1988–1989 Chelios's excellent play in the Montreal end and the highest point production of his career earned him the James Norris Memorial Trophy as the league's most outstanding defenseman.

In late June 1990 a trade sent Chelios back to his hometown when the Habs dealt him and a 1991 second-round draft choice to Chicago for Denis Savard. As soon as he arrived back in his hometown, Chelios became one of the most popular Blackhawks. He bought a restaurant—Cheli's Chili Bar—near the United Center where fans could congregate before and after games.

In his second season with the Blackhawks, Chelios anchored the defense in front of the standout goalie Ed Belfour while Jeremy Roenick lit the lamp with goals early and often. This combination led the Blackhawks to an eleven-game winning streak during the first three rounds of the playoffs. The streak, however, was derailed by the surging Pittsburgh Penguins, who swept the Hawks four straight in the finals. While with the Blackhawks, Chelios won two more Norris trophies (1993 and 1996) and played in six All-Star games.

A glorious highlight in Chelios's career came in September 1996, when he was a key part of the Team USA squad that defeated Team Canada in two straight games to win its first World Cup. Chelios was the captain of the U.S. Olympic team at the 1998 games in Nagano, Japan. In 1999 he was dealt to the Detroit Red Wings for Anders Eriksson and draft choices. He also was named the captain of the U.S. team for the 2002 Olympics in Salt Lake City, Utah.

★

For further information on Chelios, see James Duplacey, Joseph Romain, Stan Fischler, Morgan Hughes, and Shirley Fischler, *Twentieth-Century Hockey Chronicle* (1999); Dan Diamond, *Total Hockey: The Official Encyclopedia of the National Hockey League,* 2d ed. (2000); Stan Fischler, *The Ultimate Bad Boys: Hockey's Greatest Fighters* (1998); and Bruce Dowbiggin, *Of Ice and Men: Steve Yzerman, Chris Chelios, Glen Sather, Dominik Hasek: The Craft of Hockey* (1998).

STAN FISCHLER

CHESBRO, John Dwight ("Jack") (*b.* 5 June 1874 in North Adams, Massachusetts; *d.* 6 November 1931 in Conway, Massachusetts), Baseball Hall of Fame pitcher noted for his fastball, spitball, guile, and stamina who holds the twentieth-century major league record for wins in a single season.

Chesbro played sandlot baseball in his hometown of North Adams in the early 1890s. He entered the minor leagues in 1894 and two years later married Mabel Shuttleworth. The minors paid little, and Chesbro took a job as an orderly in a psychiatric hospital, where a patient dubbed him "Happy Jack" because of his dour expression; this name was more commonly shortened to "Happy" when he played in the major leagues.

Chesbro joined the newly formed Atlantic League in 1898, where he won forty games and lost nineteen in the year and a half before the Pittsburgh club of the National League picked him up. He posted a poor record of six wins and nine losses for Pittsburgh and was traded to Louisville,

Jack Chesbro, 1910s. SPORTING NEWS/HULTON|ARCHIVE

but the National League reorganized itself, dropping several unprofitable clubs, including Louisville, and Chesbro found himself back with Pittsburgh.

The Pittsburgh team was led by the hard, tough, immensely talented shortstop Honus Wagner. Wagner's fielding and base-running feats almost overshadowed Chesbro's first great season, 1901, in which he posted twenty-one wins and ten losses, relying on an intimidating fastball. Chesbro's size was not extraordinary at five feet, nine inches tall and 180 pounds, but he had an expression that was a cross between despair and rage, as if he meant to kill each batter. Then in 1902 he added a spitball to his array of pitches, licking his fore- and middle fingers to wet the ball, and became one of the most terrifying pitchers of any age. The spitball, which was legal in Chesbro's era, was an erratic pitch that usually approached home plate like a fastball but then abruptly dropped down. Batters could not be sure whether they were seeing Chesbro's very hard fastball or a pitch that would break, and this kept them off balance. In 1902 Chesbro won twenty-eight games and lost six, for a .824 winning percentage, one of the best seasons any pitcher has had.

Before the 1903 season, the Baltimore franchise of the upstart American League shifted to New York City, becoming the Highlanders (later called the Yankees), because

their park was on a hill. For a raise in pay, Chesbro jumped leagues to the Highlanders. That season he won twenty-one games and lost fifteen. Then in 1904 he had perhaps the greatest season a pitcher has ever had.

As the season began, Chesbro was a respected pitcher whose greatest strength was a dogged determination that never let up. By 1904 pitching rotations had become similar to that of the modern game, with four or five starters forming a team's rotation. There were no relief specialists, and starters were asked to pitch in relief on their off days. New York soon ran into problems; its fine rotation lost three of its members to injuries, leaving Chesbro and Jack Powell to carry nearly the entire burden of pitching games. Powell responded with a 23–19 season, with 390 innings pitched.

Chesbro responded to Powell's record by winning fourteen straight starts, the last on 4 July. The major league ballparks of 1904 had hard dirt that was full of rocks. Every time Chesbro brought his left leg down, his foot slammed into the hardy, stony ground, and by midseason it was jarring him up and down his body. In July his muscles became knotted and he was beset by cramps. In August he hobbled rather than ran. Even so he fielded brilliantly, helping his cause by deftly fielding bunts and throwing out runners. Chesbro's face added the expression of pain to its mixture of despair and rage; yet he started 51 of his team's 151 games and pitched in relief in 4 games. He pitched 48 complete games that season.

The league's pennant race came down to the last weekend of the season and a doubleheader against the Boston Pilgrims (later the Red Sox). New York manager Clark Griffith had advised Chesbro to remain in New York City and rest during the ball club's last road trip, but the team's owner wanted Chesbro to make the trip and to pitch. Ominously, Griffith lost. Going into the last two games of the season on 10 October, New York trailed Boston by one-and-a-half games; New York had to win them both in order to be the league champion. Chesbro pitched the first game; it was a battle against Boston's fine pitcher Bill Dinneen, with the game tied at two runs in the late innings. Chesbro, all knots and pain, made his famous glare at a batter, shortstop Freddy Parent, then uncorked a spitball that moved sharply as it approached the plate. The pitch skipped by journeyman catcher Jack Kleinow, noted for his fine defensive skills; Boston catcher Lou Criger was on third base and scored on the wild pitch. Some journalists at the game thought the pitch should have been ruled a passed ball, and Chesbro's wife later campaigned to have the official ruling changed from "wild pitch," but Chesbro became known as the great pitcher who choked in the big game.

Still, Chesbro won forty-one games and lost only twelve, for a .774 winning percentage and the most wins in a season by any pitcher in the twentieth century. He pitched 454.2 innings and earned the reputation as one of the most valiant pitchers ever. Without Chesbro, New York would not have been anywhere close to Boston in the standings.

Chesbro had only one more twenty-win season, in 1906. He was not the pitcher he had been, and many believe the 1904 season had taken too much out of his arm, but a foot injury from slipping on a stone while delivering a pitch may be more to blame. Chesbro retired after 1909, coached baseball for Amherst College in 1911, and played for some semipro teams. He settled in Conway, Massachusetts, and established a chicken farm. Later he added a sawmill to his assets and proved to be a sharp businessman. At age fifty-seven Chesbro died of a heart attack on his chicken farm in Conway. He is buried there in the Howland Cemetery.

?The Oldtimer's Committee of the National Baseball Hall of Fame eventually chose Chesbro for membership, and he was inducted on 24 April 1946. Since then, some baseball writers have suggested that Chesbro was not good enough for the Hall of Fame, implying he was selected on the basis of one great season. Yet Chesbro had five twenty-win seasons and was not only the best spitball pitcher but also one of the most feared pitchers in the history of baseball.

★

Despite Chesbro's many accomplishments as a pitcher, writers often focus their accounts on his wild pitch at the end of the 1904 season. See, for example, Bill Felber, "Happy Jack's Wild Pitch," in *Baseball History 2: An Annual of Original Baseball Research* (1989), edited by Peter Levine. Pitcher Tom Seaver and journalist Marty Appel weigh in with their opinion about the pitch in "Wild Pitch to Nowhere" in their *Great Moments in Baseball* (1992). As is often the case with pitchers who played before 1920 (most official records were destroyed in a fire), record keepers do not agree about the number of games Chesbro actually won in his career. The official tally is 199 wins, but the most accurate source for baseball records before 1910, the *STATS All-Time Major League Handbook* (1998), puts the tally at 198. Joseph M. Wayman, "Chesbro, 200 Wins!" in *Grandstand Baseball Annual, 1990* (1990), argues that Chesbro should be credited with 200 victories. An obituary is in the *New York Times* (7 Nov. 1931).

KIRK H. BEETZ

CLARKE, Robert Earle ("Bobby") (*b.* 13 August 1949 in Flin Flon, Manitoba, Canada), Hockey Hall of Famer and three-time National Hockey League Most Valuable Player who became the Philadelphia Flyers general manager.

Clarke was born in the mining town of Flin Flon in northern Manitoba. He played for the local junior ice hockey team, the Flin Flon Bombers, in a frontier atmosphere that was rife with brawling and intimidation. He survived these battles and seemed destined for a professional hockey career when word of his diabetic condition circulated through the

Bobby Clarke, 1977. AP/WIDE WORLD PHOTOS

National Hockey League (NHL) scouting grapevine. In addition to diabetes, Clarke also had difficulty with severe myopia. "That means," he once explained, "trouble seeing far away. I never wore lenses in junior hockey. If I was on top of the play, I was okay. It was when the puck was in the air that I had trouble judging it." Fortunately for Clarke, his coach Paddy Ginnell was determined to see that his crack center got a fair chance to reach the top.

Ginnell arranged for Clarke to visit the famed Mayo Clinic in Rochester, Minnesota, and personally escorted him there before the 1968–1969 season. Following a battery of tests, the doctors agreed there was absolutely no reason why Clarke could not play professional hockey, provided he took good care of himself. "What's more, the doctors put it in writing," said Ginnell. "That was all I needed. We went home and when the scouts came around the following season I showed them the letter. I wanted everyone from any NHL team who came to Flin Flon to know about Bobby exactly what the doctors at Mayo Clinic knew."

Skeptical though they were, the Philadelphia Flyers gambled on Clarke, picking him seventeenth overall in the 1969 amateur draft. If anyone had suggested to the Flyers boss Ed Snider that Clarke would, in May 1973, be selected for the Hart Trophy, it is possible that he would have tumbled from his chair laughing. But Clarke made the team on his first try and, from the moment he made his NHL debut, the gap-toothed center was Charlie Hustle on ice. By the 1972–1973 season he had exceeded the 100-point mark.

Clarke's accomplishments were immense during the 1972–1973 season. During a game against the Montreal Canadiens at the Forum, Philadelphia came away with a 7–6 victory. Clarke scored a hat trick, achieving the winning goal with only 3:39 remaining in the game. Even partisan fans from Montreal agreed that the kid from Flin Flon was Most Valuable Player (MVP) material, and the Flyers manager Keith Allan agreed with them. "In Philadelphia," Allan observed, "there was nobody but Clarke to consider. Rick MacLeish had a remarkable year, but I'd hate to think where the Flyers would be without Clarke."

Clarke would have been the All-Canadian Boy, except for one factor: the company he kept. By the middle of the 1972–1973 season, the Flyers had become known as the "Broad Street Bullies" and had established themselves as the toughest swashbucklers of the NHL. Their scorn for the rule book was notorious from Flin Flon to Toronto and a cause for alarm at the NHL headquarters in Montreal. Clarke began to develop a reputation for chippiness.

Still, he never let brawling interfere with scoring. By playoff time in 1973, Clarke had fulfilled the promise of his September press clippings. He finished second in the scoring race, behind the perennial leader Phil Esposito, with 37 goals and 67 assists for 104 points in 78 games. In the 1974–1975 and 1975–1976 seasons, Clarke led the NHL in assists with eighty-nine each time. He also led in play-off assists both years, twelve and fourteen respectively. He was described as "the heart and soul of our club" by Dave Schultz, a Flyers teammate for the 1974 and 1975 Stanley Cup wins.

Clarke's contributions during the 1970s were legion. He was voted the Hart Trophy as the NHL's MVP in 1973, 1975, and 1976. He was First Team All-Star center in 1975 and 1976 and Second Team All-Star in 1973 and 1974. He starred for Team Canada in the eight-game series against the Soviet All-Stars in 1972 and played for the NHL All-Stars against the Soviet Selects in the 1979 Challenge Cup.

By the late 1970s the wear and tear of playing professional hockey for ten years began taking its toll, and Clarke's point production began a downward spiral: 90, 89, 73, 69, and, finally, only 65 points in the 1980–1981 season. The Flyers attempted to relieve Clarke by making him an assistant coach and limiting his playing time, but Clarke's will to play was overwhelming, and in 1981–1982 he helped to invigorate the team's rebuilding process with a gallant show of energy. At the age of thirty-two, he clawed for position with greater zeal than rookies fourteen years his junior.

Clarke retired from the ice in May 1984, and in a natural progression became the Flyers general manager. Although a novice at the demanding job, he soon turned the Flyers into a powerhouse once more. The team reached the Stanley Cup finals in 1985 and again in 1987. The kid from Flin Flon demonstrated that hard work pays off on all levels. He was inducted into the Hockey Hall of Fame in 1987.

Clarke and Snider parted ways for a couple of seasons, but soon Clarke was back as the Flyers general manager, a post he still held in 2001. The hair was gray, glasses were now perched on the nose, but the intensity was still there.

What Pete Rose once meant to baseball and Michael Jordan to basketball, Clarke was to hockey and, more specifically, to the Philadelphia Flyers. Like Rose, Clarke displayed a fervor for his sport that did not diminish with age. His impressive career achievements did not come easily; he lacked the smooth skating skills of Bobby Orr and Mario Lemieux, and his shot was never particularly potent, but he always made the most of what he had. "Guts is what he had in abundance," said the Flyer Larry Zeidel. "Not everybody saw his qualities at first, but after a while they realized he was a winner."

★

For further information on Clarke, see James Duplacey, Joseph Romain, Stan Fischler, Morgan Hughes, and Shirley Fischler, *Twentieth-Century Hockey Chronicle* (1999); Dan Diamond, *Total Hockey: The Official Encyclopedia of the National Hockey League*, 2d ed. (2000); and Stan Fischler, *The Ultimate Bad Boys: Hockey's Greatest Fighters* (1998).

STAN FISCHLER

CLAY, Cassius. *See* Ali, Muhammad.

CLEMENS, (William) Roger (*b.* 4 August 1962 in Dayton, Ohio), baseball pitcher noted for his fastball and superb control who won the Cy Young Award six times.

Clemens was just a baby when his mother Bess Lee Clemens left Bill Clemens, his biological father, a truck driver, taking her family of four with her. Later she married a tool-and-die maker, Woody Booher, the man Clemens considers his actual father even though Booher died when Clemens was nine years old. About that same time, Clemens's eldest brother Randy noticed his younger brother's athletic potential. Randy was a star athlete with numerous awards and boxes full of press clippings, and he encouraged his little brother and arranged for him to play baseball against strong opponents. At one time, Clemens played in four different leagues with as many as ten games a week; he pitched in some and played infield in others.

In 1977, after his freshman year in high school, Clemens moved in with Randy and his wife at Houston, Texas, apparently to take advantage of the superior athletic programs offered by Spring Woods High School. Clemens was not the star of his high school team, but he showed a good

Roger Clemens. AP/WIDE WORLD PHOTOS

fastball, a good curveball, and good control. After high school, Clemens attended San Jacinto Junior College for a year (1980–1981), where he sometimes dominated opposing hitting and caught the eyes of major league scouts. When the University of Texas offered him an athletic scholarship he accepted it happily, and there he became a star. His fastball was almost major league quality, and he had such good control of his pitches that he rarely walked anyone. He pitched the 1981 College World Series championship game, but despite a fine performance his team lost. Scouts complained that Clemens lacked stamina and maybe lacked heart, but Boston Red Sox scout Danny Doyle saw him differently. In 1982 baseball's free agent draft and the College World Series championship game fell on the same day; Clemens won the game against Alabama and was drafted by the Red Sox. The following year, Clemens married Debbie; they had four children.

Clemens moved up through the Red Sox farm system fairly quickly. Although the team management did not want to pressure a pitcher they saw as still growing, they needed help, and Clemens pitched twenty-one games for the major league club in 1984. He was six feet, four inches tall and weighed 220 pounds when he first joined the Red Sox (with his weight rising to 238 pounds by the end of the 2001 season); even though he was a fitness fanatic,

Clemens always looked chubby. He did not exactly take the American League (AL) by storm, posting mediocre results in 1984 and 1985.

The 1986 season, however, was explosive for Clemens. He had one of the best fastballs in history, which he threw at a variety of speeds, as well as a sharp curveball and a split finger that would break abruptly down when it reached home plate. His fastball often zipped across the plate at well over ninety miles per hour (hence his nicknames "Rocket Man" and "Roger the Rocket"), and depending how he gripped it, could break right or left. In the mind game of batter versus pitcher, Clemens had a potent advantage—a batter guessing that he would receive an outside fastball risked being hit by a ninety-mile-an-hour fastball if the ball dodged inside, and this was something else for a hitter to think about while trying to hit the ball. Clemens's 1986 season with the Red Sox was one of the best seasons any pitcher ever had in baseball, resulting in 24 wins against only 4 losses, an .857 winning percentage. Clemens entered the record books by striking out twenty batters in a nine-inning game on 29 April 1986, thus tying a major league record. Clemens received both the AL Cy Young Award and AL Most Valuable Player award for the season. He would win the Cy Young Award twice more while pitching for the Red Sox, for the 1987 and 1991 seasons.

In the seasons from 1992 to 1996, Clemens's performance was worse than mediocre, as nagging injuries made him miss starts and affected his delivery. He had a last hurrah in 1996 in Boston, when he struck out twenty batters in a nine-inning game on 18 September, becoming the only pitcher to accomplish the feat twice. By the end of the 1996 season, Clemens was an unhappy man. He became a free agent in November, and instead of signing again with the Red Sox, he accepted a contract from the Toronto Blue Jays. This led to bitterness from Red Sox management, exacerbated by Clemens's own unpleasant remarks about how he felt he had been improperly treated in Boston.

Clemens was thirty-four years old when he signed with the Blue Jays and apparently losing his athletic skills. Yet he was rejuvenated in Toronto, winning 21 and losing 7 with a tiny earned run average (ERA) of 2.04. He received the AL Cy Young Award for the fourth time that season, and in 1998 won the Cy Young for an unprecedented fifth time, cementing his claim as one of the greatest pitchers in history.

Although in his late thirties, a period in which the careers of even the greatest ballplayers tend to be winding down, Clemens became a hot property when he declared free agency at the end of the 1996 season. The New York Yankees were the wealthiest team in baseball and could afford to sign any free agent they wanted; the Toronto Blue Jays were among the poorest teams in baseball and could not match the money other teams could offer Clemens. Clemens sold his services to the highest bidder, the Yankees, in 1998.

Clemens was plagued by wildness the following year, winning only fourteen and losing ten. In 2000 he recovered his control, throwing his still intimidating fastball and his curve consistently for strikes, but he won only 13 while losing 8 and had an ERA of 3.70, well above his norm. Yet he won some tough games for the Yankees and contributed to their playoff charges toward the World Series. In 2001 the powerhouse Yankee offense gave Clemens the support he needed, and he returned to his spectacular winning form, with twenty wins and only three losses in thirty-three starts. That year he won his sixth Cy Young award.

From his first minor league assignment through the majors, Clemens was always a disciplinary problem because he wanted to prepare himself for games his own way. The Red Sox even suspended him from 26 April through 3 May 1991. But teams had their best results with Clemens when they let him pursue his workouts in the fashion he preferred. His career records, as well as his six Cy Young Awards, make him a surefire Hall of Famer.

★

A number of books about Clemens have been published since the 1980s, most of them for young readers. Of these, Kevin Kernan, *Roger Clemens: Rocket!* (1999); Bill Morgan, *Roger Clemens* (1992); and John Devaney, *Roger Clemens* (1990); are among the most distinguished. *Rocket Man: The Roger Clemens Story* (1987), by Roger Clemens and Peter Gammons, is fascinating for revealing just how much Clemens had accomplished by 1987.

KIRK H. BEETZ

CLEMENTE (WALKER), Roberto (*b.* 18 August 1934 in Carolina, Puerto Rico; *d.* 31 December 1972 in San Juan, Puerto Rico), dynamic and heroic major league outfielder known as "The Great One" who earned posthumous election to the National Baseball Hall of Fame and worldwide acclaim for his humanitarian activities.

The son of sugarcane workers Melchor Clemente and Luisa Walker, Clemente was born into relative poverty during a time of economic depression in Puerto Rico. As the youngest of the large Clemente family, Roberto's love of baseball became obvious to his parents. He soon began an amateur career as a shortstop in youth softball, but his first coach, Roberto Marin, recognized Clemente's superior throwing arm and moved him to the outfield. By the time he reached his teens, Clemente had grown into such an impressive and athletic physical specimen that some observers considered him a major league prospect.

At a tryout camp organized by the Brooklyn Dodgers

Roberto Clemente. TRANSCENDENTAL GRAPHICS

and held at the Sixto Escobar Stadium in Santurce, Puerto Rico, Clemente impressed scout Al Campanis with his speed, bat quickness, and powerful throwing arm. Two years later, on 19 February 1954 Clemente signed a minor league contract with the Dodgers, who paid him a $5,000 salary and a $10,000 bonus. In his only minor league season, Roberto played sporadically for the Montreal Royals. On the advice of scouts Clyde Sukeforth and Howie Haak, the Pittsburgh Pirates drafted the talented but unrefined outfielder. He made his major league debut the next spring, batting a mediocre .255. Clemente improved over his next four seasons, but his overly aggressive baserunning and lack of power made the Pirates wonder whether he would ever become a star.

Clemente also struggled in making the transition to American culture. Still a neophyte English speaker, Clemente experienced difficulties communicating with the media and bristled when newspaper reporters quoted him phonetically. He also became angered when writers criticized him for his tendency to complain about minor injuries. Scarred by what he considered racist treatment, Clemente became a champion for the cause of the Latino athlete.

Clemente's breakout season was 1960. He batted .314 with 94 runs batted in (RBI), helping the Pirates to win the National League pennant. He batted a solid .310 in the

Pirates' stunning seven-game World Series upset of the New York Yankees—a classic game best remembered for Bill Mazeroski's Series-ending home run. Clemente batted safely in each of the World Series games in 1960, but his baserunning helped the Pirates win Game 7. In the eighth inning, a hustling Clemente beat out a routine infield topper, setting the stage for Hal Smith's dramatic three-run homer, which gave the Pirates a short-lived lead. One inning later, Mazeroski concluded one of the unlikeliest upsets in World Series history.

Angered by his eighth-place finish in the 1960 National League Most Valuable Player (MVP) voting, Clemente continued his assault on National League pitchers and baserunners for the rest of the decade. He won his first Gold Glove and the first of four batting titles in 1961 and captured the MVP Award in 1966. Overshadowed at times by fellow Hall of Famers such as Hank Aaron, Mickey Mantle, and Willie Mays, Clemente nonetheless established himself as one of the decade's true greats.

In the mid-1960s, Clemente enjoyed his two best seasons while playing under Pirate manager Harry Walker. In 1966 he won the National League's MVP Award by reaching career highs with 29 home runs and 119 RBIs. The following summer, he batted a career best .357. Even in later seasons, Clemente continued to punish pitchers with his ferocious swing while striking fear in baserunners with his overpowering right arm. Possessing what some scouts have called the greatest throwing arm in baseball history, Clemente played right field like few others and earned twelve consecutive Gold Glove awards.

During the 1971 World Series, Clemente showed a national television audience what Pittsburgh fans had known for years. Clemente tormented the Baltimore Orioles with a parade of line drives, dramatic home runs, dynamic baserunning, and inspiring throws. His MVP performance, which included two home runs and a .414 batting average, lifted the Pirates to an unlikely seven-game victory over the heavily favored Orioles. With this performance, Clemente achieved the international recognition that he felt he long deserved but had previously been denied. He confirmed his greatness the following season, when he became only the eleventh player in history to collect 3,000 hits. Ironically, his 3,000th safety—a double against Jon Matlack of the New York Mets—was the final regular season hit of his legendary career. He finished his eighteen-year tenure in Pittsburgh with a lifetime batting average of .317.

Off the field, Clemente dedicated his time to a variety of humanitarian endeavors. He helped raise money for the Pittsburgh Children's Hospital, one of his favorite charities. During his winters in his native Puerto Rico, Clemente routinely held free baseball clinics for underprivileged children. The events of December 1972 typify his charitable nature. After a strong earthquake struck Nicaragua, Cle-

mente organized a relief effort to assist the victims. On New Year's Eve he boarded a plane filled with emergency supplies. Tragically, the aging plane, overloaded with cargo, crashed off the coast of Puerto Rico. None of the passengers or crew, including the thirty-eight-year-old Clemente, survived the fiery accident. Clemente left behind his wife, the former Vera Cristina Zabala (whom he married 14 November 1964), and their three young sons.

Nearly thirty years after Clemente's induction into the National Baseball Hall of Fame in the summer of 1973, his legacy remains powerful. In Puerto Rico, the "Roberto Clemente Sports City," operated by Clemente's widow and two of their sons, provides underprivileged youngsters with athletic and recreational opportunities. Beneficiaries of this program have included future major league stars such as Roberto Alomar, Sandy Alomar, Jr., Juan Gonzalez, and Ivan Rodriguez.

Since his death, Clemente has been featured on two stamps issued by the U.S. Post Office. In addition, Clemente has been the subject of more books (including several written in Spanish and Japanese) than any Latin American in major league history. His story has proven especially popular as the subject of children's books. Through his outstanding career and philanthropic life, Clemente continues to serve as a role model for today's youth. As former baseball commissioner Bowie Kuhn once said of Clemente, "He had about him the touch of royalty."

★

Among the many books about Clemente are Bruce Markusen, *Roberto Clemente: The Great One* (1998), and Thomas Gilbert, *Roberto Clemente* (1991). Paul Robert Walker, *Pride of Puerto Rico: The Life of Roberto Clemente* (1991) is a children's book about Clemente. Interesting magazine articles include "The Strain of Being Roberto Clemente," *Life* (24 May 1968); "Roberto the Great," *Newsweek* (15 Jan. 1975); and "Roberto Went to Bat for All Latino Ballplayers," *Smithsonian* (Sept. 1993). An obituary is in the *New York Times* (2 Jan. 1973).

BRUCE MARKUSEN

COBB, Ty(rus) Raymond (*b.* 18 December 1886 in The Narrows, Bank County, Georgia; *d.* 17 July 1961 in Atlanta, Georgia), baseball player and manager for the Detroit Tigers who, upon his retirement from the game at the end of the 1928 season, held forty-three major league seasonal and career records.

Cobb was the eldest of the three children of William Herschel Cobb, an educator, newspaper publisher, landholder, and politician, and Amanda Chitwood, a homemaker. Reared in a strict Baptist family of "position and property," in Cobb's words, he grew up and attended schools in Roys-

Ty Cobb. ARCHIVE PHOTOS, INC.

batting. In August 1905 the Detroit Tigers of the American League purchased his contract for $700. For the remaining forty-one games of the season with the Tigers, Cobb hit only .240 and fielded erratically.

Despite this inauspicious beginning, Cobb soon became major league baseball's premier attraction. In his first three full seasons he hit .316, .350, and .324, respectively, thereby helping Detroit win three consecutive American League pennants. In 1907 Cobb, referred to by fans and sportswriters simply as "Ty" or the "Georgia Peach," led the American League in batting average, base hits, runs batted in, and stolen bases. Beginning with that 1907 season Cobb proceeded to dominate the league's offensive statistics as no player had previously in the game's history. Except for 1916, he won every batting title from the 1907 season through the 1919 season. In the same amazing thirteen-season span he led the league in runs scored five times, in hits nine times, in slugging percentage eight times, and in stolen bases six times. Season after season he hit more than a hundred percentage points above the league average. Although Babe Ruth's home run feats stole the limelight from Cobb in the 1920s and other players successfully contested Cobb for the league batting championships, Cobb continued in that decade to be among the league leaders in batting average. Cobb retired from play in 1928. His lifetime batting average was .367, and he won league batting championships twelve times, nine times in succession. Cobb also managed the Tigers from 1921 to 1926, but enjoyed indifferent success. His team posted 479 wins and 444 losses.

Cobb represented far more to baseball than these measurable feats. "Cobb had that terrific fire, that unbelievable drive," recalled Raymond "Rube" Bressler, an American League contemporary. "His determination was fantastic. I never saw anybody like him. It was *his* base. It was *his* game. *Everything* was his." While not blessed with greater natural talent than some of his contemporary players, Cobb drove himself relentlessly to master every facet of the game. "Baseball is not unlike warfare," he said in a remarkably candid autobiography, *My Life in Baseball: The True Record,* published in 1961. "When I played ball, I didn't play for fun. . . . It's no pink tea, and mollycoddles had better stay out. It's a contest and everything that implies, a struggle for supremacy, a survival of the fittest." To subdue adversaries in what was then called "inside" or "scientific" baseball, a strategy that in the face of the powerful pitchers of the day called for trying to score one run at a time, Cobb used every weapon at his disposal, including his bat, fists, speed, spikes, and venomous tongue, to intimidate and defeat his opponents. Fans everywhere came out to see the flamboyant and rampaging Cobb, not just in awe of his ability but to taunt him, to have him taunt back, and in hopes of seeing him stymied by the local club or of seeing a brawl in which Cobb would be the victim.

ton, Georgia, a small town in the Deep South. Distant paternal relatives had been prominent in antebellum North Carolina and Georgia politics, and though not a slaveholder himself, Cobb's paternal grandfather fought with the Confederacy in the Civil War. His maternal grandfather owned substantial cotton lands tilled by African-American tenant farmers. Hard-working and ambitious, Cobb's father taught school; purchased, edited, and did most of the writing for a local newspaper; owned cotton lands; served as Franklin County's first school commissioner; and was elected for one term to the Georgia State Senate.

Living in an age when professional baseball was not a respectable occupation and fearing that the game would lead his son "straight into the devil's arms," Cobb's stern and imperious father sought to dissuade his son from taking up the sport. But when in the end he could not convince his son, he admonished the younger Cobb: "Don't come home a failure." In 1904, at the tender age of seventeen, the left-handed hitting, right-handed throwing, six-foot, one-inch youngster made his professional debut as an outfielder with an Augusta, Georgia, team. Again playing for Augusta in 1905, Cobb led the South Atlantic League in

Cobb was equally truculent off the field. Quick-tempered and prone to try to resolve conflicts physically, he fought with fans, bystanders, service personnel, and members of his own family year after year. On one occasion he even climbed into the stands and assaulted a taunting fan who happened to be physically handicapped. In 1904, pulling the revolver he almost always carried, he demanded an apology from a local Detroit butcher whom he believed had insulted his wife. The butcher complied, but his young assistant challenged Cobb to a fistfight; Cobb beat the boy insensate. He was especially prone to provoke fights with African Americans. On at least two occasions he struck black women whom he thought had not paid him proper deference. He had five children with Charlie Marion Lombard, whom he married in 1908, but his relationship with his wife and his children was distant and tempestuous. After a long separation, the couple divorced in 1947. In 1949 Cobb married Frances Fairburn Cass, but in 1956 that marriage ended in divorce. They had no children.

A set of special circumstances apparently contributed to Cobb's lifelong pugnacity. By his own admission, he desperately hungered for the attention and approval of a demanding father. "I did it [played baseball with a demonic ferocity] for my father, who was an exalted man," he recalled many years later. "They killed him when he was still young. But I knew he was watching me and I never let him down." The mysterious "they" was Cobb's own mother, who, apparently mistaking her husband for an intruder climbing through her bedroom window, fired two shotgun blasts into his stomach. Although his mother was acquitted of voluntary manslaughter charges in late March 1906, locals gossiped that the senior Cobb had been shot while attempting to catch his wife with a lover. Success on the ball field seemed not only to have been for Cobb a source of self-worth but also a means of vindicating his family's tarnished reputation in Georgia.

Having since childhood been shaped by notions of manly honor and finding himself in the North among many Roman Catholic players, Cobb was acutely sensitive about his Southern, Protestant origins. When he was a rookie, the veteran Detroit players hazed him unmercifully. Apart from verbal insults, they nicknamed him "Rebel," hid his clothes, broke his favorite bats, locked him in hotel bathrooms, and shouldered him away from the plate during batting practice. Cobb fought back, both with his fists and with his tongue. His teammates soon wanted nothing to do with him. He roomed alone, usually ate alone, and spent his spare time alone. "I had to fight all my life to survive," he later said, "but I beat the bastards and left them in the ditch." Cobb, like many other white Southerners, felt honor could never be taken for granted; it had to be displayed and asserted in face-to-face encounters. Even the slightest affront had to be rectified, otherwise it carried great shame.

Of anyone who challenged him in what he considered "matters of honor," Cobb demanded an apology, and if it was not forthcoming, he employed physical force to "put the fear of God" into them.

In his retirement Cobb was equally obstreperous. Although he accumulated a substantial fortune from astute investments, including as an early investor in Coca-Cola, he found little satisfaction in money making, family life, playing golf, modest philanthropic projects in Georgia, or remembrances of his past glories. Estranged from family members, living alone, and drinking heavily, he died from cancer at age seventy-four. At the end he remained unloved. Only three people from organized baseball attended his funeral.

Yet as a legendary figure in baseball history, no player except Babe Ruth occupies a larger place than Cobb. He was the quintessential hero of the pre-Ruth age of baseball, when success in the sport, as Cobb himself put it, depended more on "brains rather than brawn," on the "hit-and-run, the steal and the double-steal, the bunt in all its varieties, the squeeze, the ball hit to the opposite field and the ball punched through openings in the defense for the single." The only quality missing from Cobb's list was opportunistic aggressiveness, which he possessed in unalloyed abundance. In recognition of his preeminence in early twentieth-century baseball, Cobb in 1936 received more votes as a charter member of the newly established Hall of Fame than any other player in the game, including the mighty Ruth.

★

Both the National Baseball Library in Cooperstown, New York, and the archives of the *Sporting News* in St. Louis, Missouri, contain substantial clippings files on Cobb. Cobb's posthumously published autobiography with Al Stump, *My Life in Baseball: The True Record* (1961; 1993), is unusually revealing, as is Charles C. Alexander, *Ty Cobb* (1984), a splendid biography. Obituaries are in the *New York Times* (10 Dec. 1965) and *Sporting News* (25 Dec. 1965).

BENJAMIN G. RADER

COCHRANE, Gordon Stanley ("Mickey") (*b.* 6 April 1903 in Bridgewater, Massachusetts; *d.* 28 June 1962 in Lake Forest, Illinois), major-league baseball catcher and manager, who was the best catcher of his era and was the American League Most Valuable Player for 1928 and 1934.

Cochrane used his great athletic ability and quick mind to earn entrance to Boston University in 1920, where he became a sports star. He not only was a running back for the school's football team, he played quarterback and was the kicker. Cochrane also starred in basketball, track, and baseball.

Mickey Cochrane, 1935. ASSOCIATED PRESS AP

After graduating from college in 1923, Cochrane played minor-league baseball in Dover, Delaware. His team demanded $50,000 when the Portland, Oregon, team of the Pacific Coast League tried to buy his contract, but Portland could not afford the price. Connie Mack of the Philadelphia (Pennsylvania) Athletics spotted Cochrane and recognized his talent. Mack bought an interest in the Portland ball club for $150,000 (one account says $132,000) and then bought Cochrane's contract, letting him play as a catcher for Portland before bringing him to the Athletics.

In 1925 Mack was rebuilding his team; he used the rookie Cochrane as a centerpiece for creating one of the best teams in baseball history. Cochrane was smart and was unsurpassed in his ability to motivate pitchers. He was also a true student of the game and learned the strengths and weaknesses of every hitter his team faced. Blessed with a good arm, good foot speed, and outstanding agility, he enhanced his physical gifts with his intelligence and terrific intensity. He was a proponent of a one-handed catching style, often emulated, that helped his throwing hand remain free of injuries.

By 1929 "Black Mike" Cochrane was at the peak of his game. Catchers usually run slowly because of the exceptional strain catching puts on their legs, but Cochrane was fast, sometimes batting in the lead-off spot, although he more usually batted third, a testament to his ability to drive in runs. He also could score, earning more than 100 runs per season four times. For his magnificent leadership, he was voted the league's Most Valuable Player (MVP) in 1928. The following three years he batted .331 (1929), .357 (1930), and .349 (1931). With Cochrane's continued leadership, Philadelphia won three straight American League pennants and the World Series titles in 1929 and 1930. Some baseball historians regard these Athletic teams as better than the 1927 Yankees.

Cochrane had a generous heart, and when other ball players were deeply hurt by the stock market crash of 1929 and the subsequent Great Depression, he helped them by cosigning for loans. In 1931 the stocks of banks declined more than 30 percent in value, and Cochrane's investment in Franklin Trust went belly up. The loans he had cosigned came due, no one had the money to repay them, and Cochrane lost $80,000. The stress this caused may have started the decline in his mental health.

Cochrane's 1932 season, however, was one for the ages—he turned in one of the greatest defensive performances by any catcher in history, with 118 runs scored and 112 RBI (runs batted in). At that time Mack still owned a wonderful team, chock full of future Hall of Famers, but the crowds at home were small. To save the Athletics he began selling the contracts of his best players. After the 1933 season he sold Cochrane's contract to the Detroit Tigers for $100,000.

In 1934 the Tigers made Cochrane the team's manager as well as its starting catcher. In that year he was regarded as the best catcher in baseball for his combination of defense and offense and again was voted the MVP, receiving the award for leading his new team to the American League pennant. The Tigers took the pennant again in 1935. Cochrane had the moment he considered the best of his career when he scored the winning run in Game Six of the 1935 World Series to secure the series victory over the Chicago Cubs.

In 1936 a finger injury cost Cochrane most of his playing time, the first period in his career that he did not catch most of his team's games. He had been made the general manager as well as the manager of the Tigers, a testament to his exceptional knowledge of the players, but the stress he had felt for years was becoming too much to bear. In June 1936 Cochrane checked into a hospital, then visited his ranch in Wyoming, near Billings, Montana, to rest. He returned to the Tigers but had a complete nervous breakdown in July.

Cochrane returned to the Tigers for the 1937 season and played very well; at age thirty-four, he appeared to still be in his prime. Then, on 25 May 1937, in a game versus the Yankees, he was beaned by the pitcher Bump Hadley, perhaps as retaliation for having homered in his previous at bat, and Cochrane nearly died. The second baseman Charlie Gehringer said Cochrane dropped as if he had been hit in the head with an axe. He was in a coma for ten days and never fully recovered. A tough man, Cochrane resumed managing the Tigers later in the season, but by August 1938 it was clear that he needed rest, and he was fired.

Cochrane spent several years at his ranch, the place where he was happiest, before enlisting in the U.S. Navy in 1942 to support the war effort. At nearly thirty-nine years old, he was assigned to the Great Lakes Naval Training Base, where he coached athletics and led a team that beat the Cleveland Indians in an exhibition game. Later he was transferred to the Pacific theater. During World War II, his son was killed in battle in Europe.

After his discharge in 1945, Cochrane returned to his ranch, where he and his wife and their two daughters had happy times. In 1947 he was elected to the Baseball Hall of Fame, the first catcher to be voted in by the Baseball Writers of America. Cochrane's friend and teammate Lefty Grove also was voted in that year.

In 1950 Cochrane was made the general manager of the Athletics, serving only for the year. He became a scout and a coach whose baseball acumen was highly valued. In 1961 he was named as a vice president for the Tigers. This work was cut short by the discovery that Cochrane had lymphosarcoma, a cancerous tumor. He died of the disease on 28 June 1962 and was cremated; his ashes were spread over Lake Michigan.

Cochrane was the prototype for modern catchers. In an era in which catchers were not expected to play in much over half their team's games, he caught at least 120 games in a season for eleven straight seasons, demonstrating the durability expected of catchers of the modern era. His studying of opposition batters and going over them with his pitchers became the standard for all catchers and pitchers, and his perfecting of one-handed catching to protect his throwing hand was imitated by Johnny Bench and many later catchers.

★

Cochrane's book *Baseball: The Fan's Game* (1939), offers his views on the nature and appeal of baseball. For a sensitive, deep account of the catcher's life see Charlie Bevis, *Mickey Cochrane: The Life of a Baseball Hall of Fame Catcher* (1998), which captures the color of Cochrane's era. For a look into Cochrane's career statistics see A. W. Laird, *Ranking Baseball's Elite: An Analysis Derived from Player Statistics, 1893–1987* (1990). Cochrane's career is placed in the context of the history of catching in Milton J. Shapiro, *Heroes Behind the Mask: America's Greatest Catchers* (1968). For a cogent summary of Cochrane's achievements see Donald Honig, *The Greatest Catchers of All Time* (1991). An obituary in the *New York Times* (28 June 1962) summarizes Cochrane's baseball career.

KIRK H. BEETZ

COLLINS, Edward Trowbridge ("Eddie") (*b.* 2 May 1887 in Millerton, New York; *d.* 25 March 1951 in Boston, Massachusetts), Baseball Hall of Fame second baseman who played a remarkable twenty-five seasons; one of the best fielding second basemen and one of the greatest offensive players ever.

Collins was the only child of John Rossman Collins, a railroad freight agent, and his second wife, Mary Meade Trowbridge Collins. Collins graduated from the Irving School, a preparatory school in Tarrytown, New York, in 1903. He entered Columbia University when he was sixteen years old, and at that young age he became quarterback of the school's football team and earned a place on the baseball team. Collins was a very good quarterback, but he was an amazing baseball player. After his junior year he played in six games for the Philadelphia Athletics. He called himself Sullivan while playing for the Athletics to disguise the fact that he had played for money, but Columbia's administration found out and declared him ineligible to play on the school's baseball team because he had lost his amateur standing. Although a major league baseball career beckoned, Collins stayed at Columbia for his senior year, coaching the baseball team and earning his B.A. in 1907. He was

Eddie Collins, 1926. ASSOCIATED PRESS AP

one of the most intelligent men ever to play in the major leagues and often coached while serving as a ballplayer.

Collins was starting at second base for manager Connie Mack's Athletics by 1908. Beginning in 1909, he put together a string of eight straight seasons batting over .300. After two subpar seasons, he had another string of ten straight seasons, from 1919 to 1928, batting over .300. Collins was instrumental in the Athletics American League championships of 1910, 1911, 1913, and 1914, and was a star in each World Series, helping his team to Series victories in 1910, 1911, and 1914. These were the days of the "dead ball," when teams struggled to just score runs one at a time. Collins carried a big fat bat that he choked up on, and he was a line-drive hitter who sprayed hits to all fields. At five feet, nine inches tall, Collins was relatively small for a major leaguer; he used his small size to his advantage by drawing bases on balls, and was often among league leaders in this category.

But Collins's glory on offense was his base running. Getting on base via base hits or bases on balls made Collins a constant irritation to opposing defenses because he was a master at stealing bases and at taking extra-base hits. His blazing speed remained with him throughout his career. He not only led the league in stolen bases with 81 in 1910, but led the league again in 1919, 1923, and 1924.

Collins was part of the Athletics' "$100,000 Infield," with "Stuffy" McInnis at first base, "Home Run" Frank Baker at third, and Jack Barry at shortstop. The quartet was a wonder to watch, making finely timed, perfectly coordinated, balletic moves. As a group, they were perhaps the finest fielding infield that ever played. Collins attributed much of their excellent working relationship to their close friendship off the field, and indeed they all remained friends for life.

Connie Mack introduced Collins to Mabel Harriet Doane, who became his wife on 3 November 1910. They had two sons. In February 1945, two years after Mabel's death, Collins married Emily Jane Mann Hall.

Collins may have been the best fielding second baseman ever. His range was unsurpassed; he would race to the left field side of second base and to foul ground beyond first base to make catches or to scoop up ground balls. As he aged, his arm may have weakened to about average for a major league second baseman, but his marvelous ranginess and gymnast-like physical coordination remained with him until the end of his career.

The worst period of his career, perhaps of his life, came after he was traded to the Chicago White Sox. He had threatened to jump to the upstart Federal League if Connie Mack did not give him a raise, instead, unable to afford to pay Collins and other stars on the Athletics, Mack traded them away. Collins initially played well for the White Sox,

but he had a couple of mediocre years at the plate in 1917 and 1918, and then a rousing year in 1919.

Collins would later say that the 1919 White Sox was the best team he ever played for, in spite of the incessant bickering and hostility among the players. It was also his worst team. Eight players on the White Sox conspired with gangsters to throw the World Series to the Cincinnati Reds, who were considered big underdogs to the White Sox in spite of being a very good team. The White Sox had great pitching and a mighty offense.

Collins and other teammates could tell that something was not right about the play of the conspirators. For instance, Joe Jackson would make uncharacteristically weak throws from the outfield or fail to catch easy fly balls, and Eddie Cicotte would occasionally just lob a ball over the plate. The conspiracy was revealed in 1920, the guilty players were banned from baseball, and Collins never again played in a World Series.

Babe Ruth saved baseball with his titanic home runs, and the ball was given a new more bouncy core, encouraging players to swing for the fences. Collins was no power hitter, but he took advantage of the change by lowering his grip on the bat and hitting streaking line drives past infielders. A brilliant bunter, Collins would sometimes cross up opposing infielders by taking a big swing on a pitch and then laying down a bunt and racing to first base before anyone could pick up the ball. By 1924 the White Sox were paying Collins the princely sum of $40,000 a year, and he also brought in money from commercial endorsements.

Collins managed and played for the White Sox for a few seasons, helping to revive some of the team's former glory by leading it to winning seasons (but fifth-place finishes). He was traded back to the Athletics in 1927, where he excelled as a pinch hitter before retiring as a player after 1929. In 1933, he went from Chicago to the Boston Red Sox in 1933, where he was vice president of the club. Collins was responsible for canny trades and contract purchases that brought the likes of Jimmie Foxx and Lefty Grove to the Red Sox. He was also responsible for signing Ted Williams to the team. Whenever people write about the best players in the history of baseball, Collins is inevitably mentioned as possibly the best of all second basemen.

When Collins died of a cerebral hemorrhage in 1951, he was one of the most loved figures in American sports. He is buried in Linwood Cemetery in Weston, Massachusetts.

★

In *Ranking Baseball's Elite: An Analysis Derived from Player Statistics, 1893–1987* (1990), A. W. Laird makes a strong case for Collins as one of the best offensive and defensive players. Mike Getz offers anecdotes about how Collins accumulated his 3,312 career hits in *Baseball's 3,000-Hit Men* (1982), and Peter C. Bjarkman presents a rousing account of Collins's offensive achievements in *Top Ten Baseball Base Stealers* (1995). Fred McMane, *The 3,000-Hit Club* (2000), recounts the careers of twenty-four baseball players, including Eddie Collins. An obituary is in the *New York Times* (25 Mar. 1951).

KIRK H. BEETZ

COMISKEY, Charles Albert (*b.* 15 August 1859 in Chicago, Illinois; *d.* 26 October 1931 in Eagle River, Wisconsin), baseball player and manager and owner of the Chicago White Sox.

Comiskey was the third of eight children born to John Comiskey, a Chicago politician, and Mary Kearns, a homemaker. Comiskey's love of baseball began early in life despite the fact that his father wished him to be a plumber. He attended Saint Ignatius High School and played baseball throughout Chicago before his father sent him to Saint Mary's College in Dodge City, Kansas, hoping to get baseball out of his life. There Comiskey met Ted Sullivan, who became his mentor in the late 1870s and the early 1880s. Never graduating from Saint Mary's, Comiskey followed Sullivan to teams in Milwaukee, Wisconsin, Elgin, Illinois,

Charles Comiskey. © UNDERWOOD & UNDERWOOD/CORBIS

and Dubuque, Iowa, where he played his first official minor league ball in 1878 and 1879. He continued to play for Dubuque under Sullivan's tutelage until 1882, when Sullivan moved to St. Louis to manage the Browns of the American Association. Comiskey moved to St. Louis with Sullivan.

Comiskey began his professional career as a pitcher, but he injured his arm during his first year in Dubuque and became an outfielder and then a first baseman. Legend has it that he revolutionized first base play by standing off the base and fielding a larger territory, but that is not a verified fact. *Beadles Dime Book* (1867) already advised first basemen to play off first base to increase the range of coverage. In 1882 Comiskey married Nan Kelley; they had one son.

Comiskey's intelligence and knowledge of the game impressed the St. Louis owner Chris Von der Ahe, and when Von der Ahe fired Sullivan in 1883, he named Comiskey the new manager of the Browns. The team subsequently won four consecutive league championships and even defeated the Chicago White Stockings in the World Series in 1886 after having tied them in that series in 1885. Comiskey stayed with the Browns through 1889 but left in 1890 to become player-manager of the Chicago Pirates in the newly organized Players League. That league, organized by the players union called the Brotherhood, lasted only a year, and Comiskey returned to the St. Louis Browns in 1891. In 1892 he joined the Cincinnati franchise in the National League, where he played and managed until 1894. An average hitter and a strong defensive player, Comiskey believed in aggressive base running and intelligent play as the key to winning games.

Comiskey became convinced that baseball would be a profitable business in the 1890s. When his major league playing career ended in 1894, he bought a minor league franchise in what was then the Western League. Ban Johnson, a noted sportswriter from Cincinnati, had taken over the league, and he convinced Comiskey to buy the Sioux City, Iowa, franchise. Johnson and Comiskey intended eventually to challenge the National League with a new organization. Comiskey moved the Sioux City team to Saint Paul, Minnesota, and subsequently moved it to Chicago in 1900 as part of the organization of the American League.

Comiskey's White Sox, as he named his new team, were successful during the first twenty years of existence. They garnered three American League pennants, in 1906, 1917, and 1919, and two World Series championships, in 1906 and 1917. In 1910 Comiskey built a modern steel and concrete stadium at Thirty-fifth Street in the south side working-class section of Chicago, where the Players League team had once played. He purposely kept ticket prices low to attract a cross section of people and to ensure a steady flow of patrons coming to games. In 1918 he contributed part his proceeds to the Red Cross to assist World War I relief activities.

In 1919 a crisis occurred when eight White Sox players conspired with gamblers to purposely lose the World Series to the Cincinnati Reds. While rumors persisted and tensions continued throughout the 1920 season, nothing was proven until newspaper charges came before a grand jury near the end of the season. White Sox players had been paid well below the typical salaries for quality baseball players. Comiskey paid only $3 in meal money compared to the $4 most other teams paid. This team became known as the Black Sox, not only because of the reputation earned in 1919 but because he charged his players twenty-five cents to wash their uniforms after games.

The role of Comiskey throughout the scandal was nebulous and has always been questioned. Reportedly he had heard rumors of the involvement of gamblers, but he neither did anything about it nor reported it to the league president Johnson, with whom he had had a serious falling out earlier in the decade. Comiskey's testimony before the grand jury failed to clarify his role, and because he angered the jurors and judge with his defensiveness, they dismissed him without getting the full story. While the grand jury eventually acquitted the players, controversy remained because some of the testimony and evidence had disappeared only to reappear again in 1924 in the possession of Comiskey's attorney. Judge Kennesaw Mountain Landis, appointed commissioner of baseball in 1920, eventually threw the eight players out of the game, but Comiskey continued to own the White Sox.

Comiskey, who came to be known as "the Old Roman" or "the Noble Roman," had been a highly respected player, manager, and owner up to 1920. His reputation as a penny-pincher and a person who did not back up his players surpassed his previous reputation as a baseball innovator and entrepreneur. His place in history continued to suffer as scholars, players, and politicians of the late twentieth century campaigned for the inclusion of Joe Jackson, the most polished of the eight players implicated in the scandal, into the Baseball Hall of Fame. Former players, most notably Bob Feller, Ted Williams, and Pete Rose, wanted Jackson included and Comiskey, who was elected to the Hall of Fame in 1939, removed.

Comiskey owned the White Sox until his death in 1931, though his son, J. Louis Comiskey, gradually took over the responsibilities for the team. The White Sox tried in vain to return to the luster of the early years, but they made first division only once in the 1920s. Comiskey died at age seventy-two of a heart attack at his retreat in Eagle River, Wisconsin. He is buried at Calvary Catholic Cemetery in Evanston, Illinois.

★

The best sources on Comiskey's life are Johnny Evers, *Baseball in the Big Leagues* (1910); Gustav Axelson, *"Commy": The Life Story of Charles Comiskey* (1919); Warren Brown, *The Chicago White Sox* (1952); Eliot Asinoff, *Eight Men Out: The Black Sox and the 1919 World Series* (1963); and Eugene Murdock, *Ban Johnson: Czar of Baseball* (1982). See also Harry Grayson, "Charles A. Comiskey—Baseball Innovator," *Baseball Digest* (Apr. 1945).

HARRY JEBSEN, JR.

CONN, William David, Jr. ("Billy") (*b.* 8 October 1917 in Pittsburgh, Pennsylvania; *d.* 29 May 1993 in Pittsburgh, Pennsylvania), world light-heavyweight champion who gained lasting fame for his near-upset of heavyweight champion Joe Louis in their legendary 1941 bout.

Conn was one of five children born to William Conn, Sr., a steamfitter at Westinghouse, and the former Marguerite McFarland, a homemaker. Young Conn dropped out of Sacred Heart School in the eighth grade and spent the next three years learning to box in a Pittsburgh gym managed by Harry Pitler, nicknamed "Johnny Ray." A former lightweight fighter, Ray had once trained with Hall of Fame boxer and Pittsburgh legend Harry Greb.

Billy Conn, 1938. AP/WIDE WORLD PHOTOS

Known as "The Pittsburgh Kid," Conn idolized Greb and began fighting as a youth in the alleys and streets of the East Liberty section of Pittsburgh. Conn never boxed as an amateur and made his professional debut as a sixteen-year-old welterweight on 28 June 1934. Conn lost the bout, a four-round decision to twenty-four-year-old Dick Woodward, in Fairmount, West Virginia. One month later, on 20 July, Conn earned his first professional victory with a three-round knockout of Johnny Lewis in Charleston, South Carolina. Conn then embarked on a tour of West Virginia towns, gaining valuable experience by fighting seasoned veterans.

Conn's first big win came on 28 December 1936, when he defeated Fritzie Zivic in a ten-round decision. Zivic was then a top-ten contender and a future member of the International Boxing Hall of Fame. Using speed of hand and masterful boxing skills to disguise his lack of a true knockout punch, Conn rang up an impressive run of victories over various top-ten contenders. On 27 May 1937 Conn survived an eighth-round knockdown to defeat the highly regarded Oscar Rankins. It was Conn's twenty-third straight victory, and by 1938 he had moved into *Ring* magazine's top-ten list of light heavyweight contenders.

Conn was beloved in his native Pittsburgh and celebrated for his Irish good looks and classic boxing style. He even starred in a movie about himself called *The Pittsburgh Kid*. By age twenty-one Conn had defeated nine former or future world champions. After fifty-two fights in and around Pittsburgh and West Virginia, Conn made his Madison Square Garden debut on 6 January 1939 and gained national recognition when he earned a ten-round decision over Freddie Apostoli. Apostoli at the time was regarded by many observers as the finest fighter pound-for-pound in the world. Five weeks later Conn gained a bloody, fifteen-round decision over Apostoli in New York City, and the two fights have been hailed as among the most exciting in Conn's career. Conn later called the Apostoli fights the toughest of his career.

Conn followed with a twelve-round decision win over Solly Krieger, and then signed to fight Melio Bettina for the vacant world light-heavyweight championship. The title had been vacated following the retirement of champion John Henry Lewis, and Conn and Bettina met on 13 July 1939 to decide a new champion. Conn trailed after the first six rounds but dominated the rest of the way to earn a fifteen-round decision. Two months later, Conn retained his title with a fifteen-round decision over Bettina at Pittsburgh's Forbes Field.

Conn defended his crown twice more, both times defeating Gus Lesnevich, then set his sights on heavyweight champion Joe Louis. A fearsome boxer-puncher, Louis at the time was two years into his reign and had embarked on a string of defenses that came to be known as the "Bum of the Month Club." Conn took his first step toward Louis with a thirteenth-round knockout of top-ten heavyweight contender Bob Pastor on 6 September 1940, then earned points verdicts over Al McCoy and Lee Savold. The latter victory came only after Conn was forced to survive a broken nose in the eighth round.

Conn relinquished his light heavyweight title in 1941 to fight Louis, and the bout was held 18 June before 54,486 fans at the Polo Grounds in New York City. Conn was twenty-four years old, Louis twenty-seven, and the two had a history together. Years earlier, Conn had helped work Louis's corner during a bout. Conn weighed in at just 169.5 pounds, and worried promoter Mike Jacobs inflated the challenger's poundage to 174. Louis trained down from his normal 204 pounds to 199 to compensate for Conn's speed, but the lost weight had a negative effect on the champion. Conn started slowly, as was his habit, but began to take the fight to Louis in the middle rounds.

Mindful of Louis's "Bum of the Month" campaign, a grinning Conn told the champion, "Joe, you're in a fight tonight."

"I know it," Louis replied.

With more than 6,000 Pittsburgh fans cheering him on, Conn shook Louis with combinations in the eleventh round, and then brought the huge crowd to it feet when he staggered the champion with a perfect left hook in the twelfth. Conn returned to his corner leading on two of the three ringside judges' cards, and "Conn-fident" that he could knock Louis out. Conn was inspired to go for the knockout rather than the points win to impress his girl-friend, Mary Louise Smith, and his ailing mother, who would soon die of cancer.

"I can take this SOB out," Conn told Johnny Ray in the corner. Instead, it was Conn who was taken out. Rocked by a furious Louis rally, Conn dropped to the canvas and was counted out two minutes and fifty-eight seconds into the thirteenth round, only two seconds away from the sound of the bell.

Afterward, Conn smiled and told reporters, "What's the good of being Irish if you can't be dumb?" Mindful of his mother's condition, Conn said, "I guess I had too much to win for tonight, that's why I wanted to knock him out. Otherwise, I'd a won easy."

Conn married Smith in 1941 and starred in *The Pittsburgh Kid* that same year. He turned down other movie offers, including a role in the classic motion picture *On the Waterfront*.

A proposed rematch with Louis was postponed first because of Conn's family concerns (his mother had passed away), and then by a broken hand suffered in a fight with his father-in-law, "Greenfield" Jimmy Smith. Conn did run off a string of three straight victories, including a win over an up-and-coming Tony Zale in 1942. United States involvement in World War II canceled plans for a Louis-Conn rematch, and Conn joined entertainer Bob Hope and other celebrities on a morale tour for Americans in the service.

Conn and Louis were finally rematched in 1946, but the years away from the ring dulled the abilities of both fighters. In a bout lacking the drama and intrigue of their first epic encounter, Conn was knocked out in the eighth round.

"The Pittsburgh Kid" retired after the bout, and then had a two-bout comeback in 1948. He won both fights, and then retired for good. He and his wife had four children. At age seventy-two Conn was back in the news when he scuffled with a convenience store robber in Pittsburgh. Conn passed away at age seventy-five and is buried in Calvary Cemetery in Pittsburgh. He fought professionally from 1934 to 1948, compiling a record of 63–12–1. The world light heavyweight champion from 1939 to 1941, Conn was elected to the Boxing Hall of Fame in 1990.

While Conn is known by many sports fans chiefly for his near-upset of Louis in 1941, he is remembered by boxing historians as one of the great boxers in ring history, a handsome, skilled boxer who emerged as one of the great light heavyweight champions of all time.

★

Conn and his wife were featured in a lengthy *Sports Illustrated* article, "The Boxer and the Blonde" (17 June 1985), written by Frank Deford. (This issue of *Sports Illustrated* is now considered a collector's edition.) Conn's ring career was well documented in Gilbert Odd, *Boxing: The Great Champions* (1974); Bert Randolph Sugar, *The 100 Greatest Boxers of All Time* (1984); and James B. Roberts and Alex G. Skutt, *The Boxing Register* (1999). Conn is also the subject of an Internet website featuring photos and articles documenting his life and career. The site, named "The Official Site of Boxing Legend Billy Conn," <http://www.billyconn.net/>, is maintained by Ryan Conn, Billy's grandson.

EDWARD GRUVER

CONNER, Bart (*b.* 28 March 1958 in Chicago, Illinois), Olympic gymnastics champion who is the only American gymnast, male or female, to win gold medals at every level of junior, national, and international competition.

Growing up in the Chicago suburb of Morton Grove, Illinois, Conner's introduction to gymnastics occurred at the age of ten, as part of an effort on his parents' part to channel some of their son's energy. Conner immediately took to the sport and began competing in Young Men's Christian Association (YMCA) meets after only a year. While still in his teens, he began to appear in meets on a regional, and then on the national, level.

By the time he was sixteen, in 1974, Conner became the United States Gymnastics Federation's All-Around champion. The following year, while still attending Niles West High School in Skokie, Illinois, Conner tied with gymnast Tom Bench, then a twenty-year-old college student, for first place as the USA Men's All-Around champion; each athlete earned 105.85 points in the competition. Following his high school graduation in 1976, Conner went on to the University of Oklahoma in Norman, Oklahoma, where he joined the gymnastics team. Even as his own talents continued to develop, Conner facilitated the University of Oklahoma's development into a national gymnastics powerhouse on the collegiate level.

In 1978 Conner helped lead his college team to the 1978 National Collegiate Athletic Association (NCAA) team championship, and won the award for All-Around best gymnast. In the following year, he tied for first in the floor exercise championship. In 1979 Conner was a member of the U.S. gymnastics team competing in the World Cup championships. While the team earned the bronze medal, Conner was able to achieve a gold medal for the parallel bars and a bronze medal for the vault. At the age of twenty-one, Conner was also the USA Men's All-Around champion in 1979, earning a total score of 114.25 points. Not only did he win a spot on the U.S. Olympic team for 1980, he was the highest scorer in the trials. Regrettably, due to international political issues, the United States boycotted the 1980 Olympics, which were held in Moscow, then part of the Soviet Union. Nonetheless, Conner continued to train and compete, winning the American Cup Championships in 1981 and 1982. In 1983, however, a torn biceps muscle in his right arm forced him to withdraw from the 1984 national championships. Because this competition contributed 40 percent of the point total in the overall competition for Olympic team membership, this withdrawal normally would have excluded Conner from eligibility for the 1984 U.S. Olympic gymnastics team. The United States Olympic Committee (USOC), however, granted him a waiver and his subsequent success at the Olympic trials earned him a place on the team.

The 1984 Men's U.S. Olympics gymnastics team included Tim Daggert, Mitchell Gaylord, Jim Hartung, Scott Johnson, Jim Mikus, Peter Vidmar, and Conner. Competing in Los Angeles, California, the team managed to capture the gold medal, and Conner earned an individual gold for the parallel bars, and placed fifth—the highest ever placement by an American—in the floor exercises. The highlight of the competition for Conner was the parallel bars event, in which he earned two perfect scores of 10.0. Following this competition, Conner retired from the sport to become a television commentator for ABC, CBS, and ESPN, among others networks. He also began Perfect 10 Productions, Inc., a television production company dedicated to bringing more quality gymnastic meets to television.

Eventually, Conner's interest in gymnastics was such

Bart Conner, 1984. © BETTMANN/CORBIS

that his involvement as a commentator was not enough. He established the Bart Conner Gymnastics Academy, now located at 3206 Bart Conner Drive in Norman, Oklahoma. The facility provides education and training opportunities for gymnasts from around the world; the Bulgarian men's gymnastics team, among others, has trained there. Services and training are available for athletes ranging from ages two through adulthood. Conner's activities also include involvement in a campaign aimed at providing education about, and relief of, the debilitating condition of osteoarthritis. "B.E.A.T. Arthritis: Boost Education of Arthritis Treatment" is the result of Conner's joining with drug manufacturers Pharmacia and Pfizer to advocate the benefits of the drug Celebrex in alleviating this condition. Conner himself has battled the effects of the disease since he was twenty-two years old; the condition was a factor behind his retirement following the 1984 Olympics.

Over the years Conner had known Romanian gymnast Nadia Comaneci, whom he first met on his eighteenth birthday, when they both competed in the America's Cup in New York City. Comaneci, famous for her own spectacular success as a gymnast, had returned to her native country after her performance in the 1976 Olympics. Eventually, despite a relatively privileged lifestyle, Comaneci and several others made a daring exit from Romania in 1989, only months before a revolution toppled the totalitarian regime then governing the country. After a brief stay in Austria, Comaneci was granted political asylum and immigrated to the United States. She began performing in shows with Conner and other gymnasts in 1990, and Conner and Comaneci soon began a personal relationship. The couple was married on 27 April 1996 at a ceremony in Bucharest, Romania, including seven priests and over 2,000 spectators at the Casin Orthodox monastery. Comaneci became an American citizen in June 2000, and the couple resides in Norman, Oklahoma.

Despite a relatively brief career in competition, Conner remains the only gymnast to have won gold medals at all levels of national and international competition ranging from his gold in the Pan American Games to the World Championship Gold, and, of course, his Olympic gold medals. His comprehensive talents, including his skill on the parallel bars, the vault, and the floor exercises, mark Conner as a consistently proficient all-around gymnast, a factor contributing to his success as a trainer and coach. His ongoing involvement as a trainer and coach ensure that his expertise will be passed on to future generations of gymnasts. He and his wife still occasionally appear in gymnastics shows and special events. He was inducted into the USOC Olympic Hall of Fame in 1991, the USA Gymnastics Hall of Fame in 1996, and both the Oklahoma Sports Hall of Fame and the International Gymnastics Hall of Fame in 1997.

★

Conner is the author, with Paul Ziert, of *Winning the Gold* (1985). His story is also told well in Bob Schaller et al., *The Olympic Dream and Spirit,* vol. 3 (1999).

JAMES J. SULLIVAN III

CONNER, Dennis W. (*b.* 16 September 1942 in San Diego, California), professional sailboat racer and motivational speaker, and four-time winner of the America's Cup who is known for his prominent role in that yacht race's growth as an international event.

Conner brought world attention to the America's Cup by losing the three-foot, ornate silver trophy to the Australian challenger in 1983. He was the skipper of the New York Yacht Club's sloop *Liberty*. The loss broke the longest winning streak in sports, twenty-five matches over 132 years, and transformed the America's Cup from a summer endeavor for amateur sportsmen into a corporate-sponsored, professionally crewed show of technology, teamwork, tactics, and lavish budgets.

Conner has asserted throughout his career that there was "no excuse to lose," and used the expression as the title of his first book. Following discouraging defeat, he swept the next America's Cup in 1987 aboard *Stars and Stripes* in four straight races in the turbulent waters of Western Australia. The Cup came back to the United States—to Conner's hometown of San Diego, California, not the traditional East Coast setting. Nevertheless, New York City gave the crew a ticker-tape parade, and President Ronald W. Reagan welcomed them to the White House. Conner became known as "Mr. America's Cup."

Conner has been on winning boats four times in the America's Cup: first as tactician aboard *Courageous* in 1974, and as skipper in 1980, 1987, and 1988. He lost the Cup twice, in 1983 and 1995. In 1992 and 2000 his crew was eliminated before the finals, and he has committed to a challenge in 2003.

No one can win the Cup without first winning the large corporate sponsors whose support is also sought by the other syndicates. The budget for Conner's 1983 defense in *Liberty* was just under $5 million. To win back the Cup in 1987, Conner's budget more than tripled. The money was needed to design, construct, and test a new boat, and to prepare for the unfamiliar venue awaiting the crew halfway around the world. For the 2003 campaign, the goal was set at $40 million. To gain recognition in the business world, Conner became a corporate motivational speaker, using examples from his successes and failures as material.

The America's Cup has often generated heated competition and intrigue off the water as well as on. Normally three to four years elapse between races, but the defeated New Zealanders from 1987 caught San Diego off guard with a 1988 challenge based on the historical documents of the Cup rather than accepted practice. The Mercury Bay Boating Club wanted the Americans to race in the largest single-masted boat permitted and in the minimum time allowed for preparation. The challenging boat was to be over 130 feet long, twice the length of the Twelve-Meter Class boats used for thirty years. San Diego had ten months to field a defender—too short a time to design and build such a boat. Conner countered with a boat half the length, but with two hulls and a fraction of the weight. The catamaran *Stars and Stripes* easily won, yet the legal disputes over the intentions of the original Deed of Gift continued in court. On the final appeal, San Diego Yacht Club retained the Cup. Conner had learned that actions ashore can decide the contest.

After 1992 Conner chose to concentrate his efforts as chairman of Dennis Conner Sports, his sports marketing firm. He picked a younger proven skipper to take the helm of the new 75-foot America's Cup Class entry while he looked for the competitive advantage on shore. In the 1995 defender's series, the other American teams allowed *Stars and Stripes* to continue racing when on the verge of elimination. They allowed a second chance, and were beaten by Team Dennis Conner. However, the New Zealand challenger dominated in the finals and took the Cup down under once again.

Conner's derogatory public comments have tarnished his reputation. He has called certain foreign competition "cheaters" and "losers" in press conferences. After his sensational loss in 1983, he blamed the New York Yacht Club, which had held the Cup since 1851, for not following through with the effort to disqualify the Australian challenger for its innovative winged keel. International measurers had approved the keel, and the Club officials chose not to cancel racing on hearsay that the Australians used a design prohibited by the rules. Even with a slower boat, Conner won three races before Australia took the series.

Conner does not have the persona of a popular hero. He often appears preoccupied or ill at ease in public, yet even the Australians and New Zealanders loved him as the underdog. When he sails, his tanned face is characterized by heavy-lidded eyes, a double chin, and smears of zinc oxide. When the media has disparaged his actions, he has usually ignored the negative publicity. His strength is making winning against the odds look easy by focusing on thorough boat and equipment preparation and a willingness to build a team of specialists who know more than he does. As a result, Conner has excelled in many forms of sailboat racing.

The America's Cup eliminations and finals are a series of match races, one boat against one boat. The skipper needs the mind of a chess master on a fluid board. In other world championships, Conner outmaneuvered dozens of the world's finest skippers in vying for favorable wind and position. In 1971 at the age of twenty-eight, Conner won the Star Class World Championships. The second time he won the Star Worlds, in 1977, he took five firsts in a fleet

Dennis Conner, 1997. ASSOCIATED PRESS AP

of eighty-nine boats, an unequaled record. He won a bronze medal in the Tempest Class in the 1976 Olympic Games. In the 1990s Conner twice fielded competitive entries of the grueling nine-month, 25,000-mile Whitbread Round the World Race, although he sailed the boats only on individual legs of the races.

Conner has written, "To me, luck is work, preparation, ability, attitude, confidence and skill." He hones those elements in himself and in his team. He inspires enduring loyalty, but with sailing as his top priority, his family and his drapery business, which he entered after leaving San Diego State University, have to manage without his day-to-day presence.

★

Conner's account of his early racing career, written with John Rousmaniere, is *No Excuse to Lose: Winning Yacht Races with Dennis Conner* (1978). Conner describes winning back the America's Cup in *Comeback: My Race for the America's Cup* (1987), written with Bruce Stannard. Conner and Michael Levitt share valuable instructional insights in *Sail Like a Champion* (1992), and *Learn to Sail* (1994), and present an overview of America's Cup history in *The America's Cup: The History of Sailing's Greatest Competition in the Twentieth Century* (1998). Conner discusses his business philosophy and management tips in *The Art of Winning* (1998), written with Edward Claflin.

SHEILA MCCURDY

CONNOLLY, Harold V. ("Hal") (*b.* 1 August 1931 in Somerville, Massachusetts), hammer thrower who was an Olympic champion and six-time world record holder.

Connolly was born large, weighing in at 13 pounds, and because of his size, his delivery was complicated by shoulder obstruction and trauma to his left shoulder and arm. He spent much of his childhood wearing shoulder braces and undergoing physical therapy. In spite of the therapy, his left arm remained weak and stunted, three inches shorter than his right arm, and his left hand was only two-thirds the size of his right. As a young man Connolly broke the arm several times while wrestling and playing football.

As a student at Boston College, Connolly discovered the hammer throw when he worked for the track team retrieving thrown hammers from the field. Intrigued by the sport, he took it up with the hope that it would strengthen his weak arm, never suspecting that he would become a world champion and record-holder. Apart from his arm, however, Connolly seemed made for the sport. Six feet tall and weighing 235 pounds, he had the strongly muscular build typical of top athletes in the throwing events. Still, he could not raise his left arm over his head, straighten it, close his fist, or extend his fingers on that side. Because hammer throwers use two hands on the handle of the hammer, this was a huge disadvantage, but Connolly overcame it through determined practice and strength training.

A year after graduation, Connolly traveled to Germany

Hal Connolly practicing the hammer throw, 1964. ASSOCIATED PRESS AP

in 1954 to study the throwing technique of Sepp Christman, a hammer champion, and in 1955 Connolly threw the hammer 201 feet, 5 inches, becoming the first American ever to throw past 200 feet in the event. Connolly was Amateur Athletic Union (AAU) champion from that year through 1961, and in 1964 and 1965.

Connolly first broke the world record on 2 November 1956 with a throw of 224 feet, 10 inches at Los Angeles, three weeks before the Melbourne Olympics, making him the favorite for the gold medal. At the Olympics, he went up against his Soviet rival, the former world record — holder Mikail Krivonosov. Krivonosov led early in the finals, but on his final throw Connolly won the gold medal by setting a new Olympic record of 207 feet, 3.5 inches.

He also won the heart of Olga Fikotova, a Czechoslovakian athlete who was awarded the gold medal in women's discus. Fikotova had to return to Czechoslovakia, but Connolly followed her. At the time, the Soviet Union and its Eastern European satellites were engaged in a cold war with the United States. As a result, the Czechoslovakian government opposed Fikotova's attempt to emigrate to the West in order to marry Connolly. The couple had to fight mountains of Czechoslovakian red tape. They were

determined to marry, however, and made a personal plea to the president of Czechoslovakia for permission. Permission was granted after many weeks of bureaucratic silence, and Connolly married Fikotova in Prague on 27 March 1957. Their best man was Emil Zatopek, the famed Czechoslovakian long-distance runner. Although the location of the wedding was supposedly secret, it leaked out, and 50,000 Czechoslovakians showed up to cheer the couple.

The two went home to California after the wedding, and Connolly became a teacher and administrator when he was not competing. Fikotova, who became a U.S. citizen, went on to compete for the United States in the Olympics of 1960, 1964, 1968, and 1972. She never won any more medals, although she did throw a personal best of 175 feet, 5 inches in 1969. She later developed a career as a writer.

Connolly and Fikotova had four children, one of whom, Jim, became a talented competitor in the decathlon at the University of California, Los Angeles (UCLA); he won the National Collegiate Athletic Association decathlon in 1987. The couple divorced in 1975, and Connolly later married Pat Winslow, a three-time Olympic athlete who had competed in the pentathlon in 1960, 1964, and 1968. At the time of their marriage, Winslow was a track and field coach at UCLA. Their son Adam was ranked number one among high school hammer throwers.

Connolly beat his own world record on 29 May 1958 at Ceres, California, with a throw of 225 feet, 4 inches. In the following year he was the Pan-American hammer champion. He was favored to win in the 1960 Olympics because he had set a new world record of 230 feet, 9 inches shortly before the Games. However, he came in eighth with a disappointing throw of 208 feet, 6 inches. At the same Olympics, the Soviet athlete Vasily Rudenkov beat Connolly's 1956 Olympic record with a toss of 220 feet, 2.25 inches.

On 21 July 1962 Connolly set yet another world record with a toss of 231 feet, 10 inches. However, he came in sixth at the 1964 Olympics in Tokyo with a best throw of 218 feet, 8 inches.

At the 1965 Amateur Athletics Union (AAU) championship, Connolly threw 232 feet, 2 inches, and topped his own world record in that same year with a throw of 233 feet, 9 inches. With this throw, Connolly had made seven of the eight longest throws ever made by any athlete in the sport.

Although Connolly made the team for the 1968 Olympics in Mexico City, he did not make the finals. He attended the trials for the 1972 Olympic team, but did not make the team because he came in fifth and was not among the top three athletes.

Connolly became a teacher and worked as head of the Washington, D.C., Special Olympics program for many years. He also worked as a volunteer coach for Georgetown University. His wife became a track and field coach at Radford University in Virginia in 1997, and in 1999 Connolly retired from the Special Olympics to join her at Radford to work as a volunteer assistant coach.

Connolly once said of the rotational moves inherent to hammer throwing, "You insert yourself into harmonious orbit with the universe in a way you never do without the hammer. You become close to that orbiting universe. The idea is to get the two orbits, yours and the universe, in harmony, in sync. Then you get a good throw."

The California Governor's Committee for Employment of Disabled Americans established the Hal Connolly Scholar-Athlete Awards in 1985, which provides financial assistance for college freshmen with disabilities who have participated in varsity athletics.

In addition to being an Olympic champion and six-time world record—holder, Connolly was ranked number one in the world twice, number two six times, and number three, three times. He won the AAU hammer championship in nine separate years. All these accomplishments would be outstanding for any athlete, and they are even more impressive in light of Connolly's disability.

★

Connolly and Fikotova's romance is discussed in Norman Giller, *The 1984 Olympic Handbook* (1983). Connolly's thoughts on the mystical aspects of hammer throwing, as well as informa-

tion on his arm injury, appeared in William Gildea, "For Georgetown's McMahon, It's Hammer Time," *Washington Post* (31 May 1995). For information on Connolly's coaching career, see *RU (Radford University) Magazine* (May 1999).

KELLY WINTERS

CONNOLLY, Maureen Catherine ("Little Mo") (*b.* 17 September 1934 in San Diego, California; *d.* 21 June 1969 in Dallas, Texas), tennis player who in 1953 was the first woman to win the Grand Slam with victories at the Australian Open, French Open, Wimbledon, and the U.S. Open and who is considered one of the most powerful and important stars in her sport in the twentieth century.

Connolly rose to tennis prominence from a broken home and an impoverished background. Her father, Martin Connolly, a naval officer, deserted her mother, Jassamine Wood Connolly, when their only daughter was four years old. Her

Maureen Connolly, 1952. ASSOCIATED PRESS AP

mother's second marriage, to August Berste, and another divorce added to the turbulence of Connolly's youth. Her mother pushed her to become a singer or dancer, without success. Although Connolly's first love was horses, the neighborhood tennis courts provided a more affordable sporting option. Connolly's first coach, Wilbur Folsom, recognized her talent and changed her left-handed stroke into a right-handed style. As she later recalled, "I became Folsom's shadow, a whirling dervish as a ball boy, the most eager pupil he ever had." She then moved on to work with Eleanor "Teach" Tennant, the most famous coach in the 1940s. Tennant instilled in her student the philosophy that a player had to hate her opponents to achieve tennis victories.

Connolly soon emerged as a top player in Southern California and won the national championship for girls eighteen and under in 1949. At age fifteen she was the youngest to accomplish the feat up to that time. She defended her title successfully in 1950. A sportswriter called the five-foot, four-inch athlete "Little Mo" after the famous battleship USS *Missouri,* labeled "Big Mo." The nickname stuck. In 1951 Connolly, a Roman Catholic, graduated from Cathedral High School in San Diego. With the determination that had become her trademark, she set out to become the best female tennis player in the world.

A few months later Connolly stood at the top of the tennis universe. At the United States National Championships on the grass courts of Forest Hills, New York, she bested Doris Hart, a longtime friend, in the semifinals, then carved out a thrilling victory in the finals, 6–3, 1–6, 6–4, over Shirley Fry. At age sixteen Connolly was the youngest women's champion in the history of the U.S. Open, a record that stood until 1979, when Tracy Austin won the title.

Sportswriters exclaimed over Connolly's ability to hit deadly accurate ground strokes from the baseline. Not blessed with a powerful serve and only adequate with her volleys, Connolly used her fear of losing and her precision off the ground to thwart her opponents. In 1952 she won both Wimbledon and the U.S. Open to establish herself as the best woman in the game. At Wimbledon she played through a slight shoulder injury despite the objections of her coach. In a press conference after her first-round match, she announced that Tennant was no longer her coach. The two women were never reconciled. At the end of the year Connolly began working with a new coach, Harry Hopman of Australia. To defeat her rivals, she relied less on the anger that Tennant had instilled in her and more on her natural talent for the game.

No woman had yet won the four major championships in a single year, and Connolly pursued that goal with steely determination throughout 1953. She roared through the Australian Open in January without the loss of a single set. She was almost as dominant in May at the French Open on the red clay of Roland Garros Stadium, dropping only

one set en route to the championship. Then, at Wimbledon, she and Doris Hart hooked up in an epic woman's final that Connolly won, 8–6, 7–5. Several months later she completed the Grand Slam by defeating Hart again in the U.S. Open finals, 6–2, 6–4.

Connolly continued her mastery of women's tennis in the first half of 1954 at the French Open and at Wimbledon. She was behind 5–2 in the second set against Louise Brough at Wimbledon when she reeled off five straight games and a 6–2, 7–5 triumph. A long and productive career seemed to lie ahead of her at age twenty. In 1989 veteran tennis reporter Bud Collins called her "possibly the greatest of all female players."

Tragedy ended her playing career on 20 July 1954. Connolly was riding her favorite horse, Colonel Merry Boy, near her home when a passing cement truck hit the animal. Connolly was thrown to the ground, her right leg seriously injured. After a four hour surgery, she embarked on an ambitious program of rehabilitation; however, Connolly realized that she could never regain her old form and retired from competitive tennis. In June 1955 she married Norman Brinker, a former member of the U.S. Equestrian team. They had two daughters, Cindy and Brenda.

In retirement, Connolly remained active in the tennis world. She reported on matches for newspapers and coached the British Wightman Cup team when it played in the United States. Promising young women tennis players often stayed at the Brinker household in Dallas to receive instruction from her. In cooperation with her husband and a friend, Nancy Jeffett, she established the Maureen Connolly Brinker Foundation to help the careers of young tennis players. The Foundation, "one of the largest private tennis foundations of its kind in the world," attests to her long-term legacy to the sport of tennis. Connolly was inducted into the Tennis Hall of Fame in 1968.

In 1966 Connolly felt the pain of the ovarian cancer that took her life. She fought the disease with her customary courage and the energy she had brought to the tennis court. She died in Dallas at age thirty-four and is buried there in Sparkman-Hillcrest Cemetery.

Although it is difficult to compare tennis players across eras, Connolly remains one of the top five athletes in her sport of all time. Only Steffi Graf in 1988 duplicated Connolly's Grand Slam, and Connolly's record of nine Grand Slam tournament victories in four years attests to her power and skill on the courts. For power, determination, and total commitment to her sport, Connolly had few equals in the world of twentieth-century women's tennis.

★

Connolly's letters and scrapbooks are in the possession of her family. She wrote two books, *Power Tennis* (1954) and *Forehand Drive* (1957), the second of which is more autobiographical. Cindy Brinker Simmons, one of Connolly's daughters, wrote, with Robert Darden, *Little Mo's Legacy: A Mother's Lesson's, A Daughter's Story* (2001), an informative and warm memoir. Doris Hart, *Tennis with Hart* (1955), offers the recollections of one of Connolly's opponents. Ted Tingling, *Love and Faults: Personalities Who Have Changed the History of Tennis in My Lifetime* (1979), offers a useful analysis of Connolly's career. Billie Jean King, writing with Cynthia Starr in *We Have Come a Long Way: The Story of Women's Tennis* (1988), comments perceptively on where Connolly stands in the history of women's tennis. Bud Collins, *My Life with the Pros* (1989), provides a more recent assessment of her standing in the sport. Allison Danzig, "The Little Girl with the Big Racquet," *New York Times* (23 Aug. 1953), looks at Connolly at the height of her career. An obituary is in the *New York Times* (22 June 1969).

KAREN GOULD

CONNORS, James Scott ("Jimmy") (*b.* 2 September 1952 in East St. Louis, Illinois), tennis champion who was one of the most dominant players from the mid-1970s through the mid-1980s and who won the U.S. Open on three different surfaces.

Connors was the son of James Connors, a tollbooth manager; his mother, Gloria, and his maternal grandmother,

Jimmy Connors at the 1992 French Open. AP/WIDE WORLD PHOTOS

Bertha Thompson, were both first-rate tennis players. They put a racquet in his hand as soon as he was able to hold it, and his mother later declared that he had a solid game at age five. Gloria Connors was her son's coach until he was sixteen; mother and son then moved to Los Angeles so he could receive special training from Pancho Segura, one of the most unorthodox and most effective players of the 1940s and 1950s. Under Segura's tutelage, Connors learned to make his two-handed backhand a fearsome weapon; Segura himself had been noted for using two hands on both the forehand and backhand side.

Connors attended the University of California, Los Angeles, and was All-American in tennis in 1971. He turned professional the following January but the sport he entered was in some disarray. The new Open era had begun in 1968, which meant that major tournaments like Wimbledon (England) and Forest Hills (New York City) were open to both amateurs and professionals. But a conflict between the All-England Championships at Wimbledon and the World Championship Tennis (WCT) circuit led to nearly all the big names boycotting Wimbledon in 1973. That boycott had negative implications for the careers of men like John Newcombe and Stan Smith, both serve-and-volley players and former Wimbledon champs. Into the opening created by the boycott came Connors and his new all-court game.

By 1974 Connors had developed a game that was both unorthodox and highly effective. He never had a powerful or intimidating serve but rather evolved into one of the best all-court players ever seen on the tour. His ground strokes were hit nearly flat, especially his two-handed backhand. Connors developed the best return of serve on the tour, often punishing taller, more elegant players with his sharp angles and use of flat shots. Even critics acknowledged that his was probably the second-best service return ever seen, after that of Don Budge, who had dominated tennis in the late 1930s. Connors had one of the best overheads in the game, but his volleys, while effective, were uninspired. Rather than any single weapon, his game depended on a relentless competitive spirit; between 1970 and 1990, no other player fought as hard for every point as did Connors.

His breakthrough came in 1974, when he won the Australian Open, Wimbledon, and the U.S Open. His victim in the finals at both Wimbledon and Forest Hills was the Australian player Ken Rosewall. The Wimbledon final was a devastating 6–1, 6–1, 6–4 performance. It was the most impressive rout achieved by any U.S. player in the professional era. In that magical year, Connors won 99 out of 103 matches played. Comparisons were soon made between him and the Australian champion Rod Laver, who had won the Grand Slam (with victories at Wimbledon and the Australian, French, and U.S. Opens) in 1962 and 1969, but Connors's combative spirit forbade any serious associations.

He always saw himself as an outsider, even when he was on top of the sport. Connors's victories were marred by his notoriously childlike behavior. He mocked Rosewall at times, and rather than shake hands at the end of a match, he displayed contempt for his opponent. For a generation of older U.S. players, men like Stan Smith, Bob Lutz, and Arthur Ashe, this behavior made all Americans seem unsportsmanlike and rude.

Connors refused to play in Davis Cup competition that year. Responding to this decision, Ashe declared that Connors was "seemingly unpatriotic." Connors filed a multimillion-dollar lawsuit against Ashe, whom he then faced in the Wimbledon finals of 1975.

Ashe was the underdog going into the final, but he had studied Connors's game at length and identified a few weaknesses that he managed to exploit. As ferocious as Connors's attack was, he had trouble scooping low forehands on his approach shots, and his second serve lacked punch. Ashe believed that if he could keep Connors guessing and prevent him from steamrolling the match, anything might happen. Happen it did. Ashe won the match by a lopsided 6–1, 6–1, 5–7, 6–4. While Connors remained number one in world rankings, the feeling that he was invincible died that July afternoon. Making matters worse, he lost to Manuel Orantes, a Spanish clay-court expert, at Forest Hills that fall. Keen observers began to question whether Connors had the right temperament to stay in competition.

Connors roared back, however. He won Forest Hills in 1976 and ran neck-and-neck with the Swedish player Bjorn Borg in the fight for number one. In the early summer of 1977, Connors seemed in his best form ever, which made his five-set loss to Borg at Wimbledon even more painful. Connors was down 4–0 in the fifth and final set when he found a remarkable reservoir of energy within; he raced back to even the match at four-all and clearly had the momentum. Just as he reached parity, though, Connors appeared to run out of gas. Borg swept the last two games and walked away with his second Wimbledon crown (he won five consecutive Wimbledons, 1976–1980).

That autumn Connors lost the U.S. Open final to Guillermo Vilas. Clay-court masters like Borg, Vilas, and others seemed to have found the weak point of Connors's game: low balls to his one-handed forehand.

Connors met Borg in the Wimbledon finals yet again in 1978. Connors won the first two games and then only five more in the entire match. He was humbled in a stunning 6–2, 6–2, 6–3 defeat. Borg had greatly improved his serve, while Connors was playing the same as he always had. That same year, Connors was threatened by the appearance of another American player, the brash John McEnroe. While Borg and Connors fought each other hard on the court, there was no real animosity between them.

Things were different with Connors and McEnroe. As commentator Bud Collins once put it, "They hated each other."

Connors lost to Borg in the 1979 semifinals at Wimbledon, and the Swede went on to his fourth consecutive title on the grass. The next year spelled the end of Connors's long run as either number one or number two. Borg won his fifth consecutive Wimbledon, McEnroe took the U.S. Open, and both players showed greater shotmaking skill than Connors, though perhaps not as much competitive spirit. When McEnroe ended Borg's string of Wimbledon victories in 1981, it seemed as if Connors had become a sideshow to the Borg-McEnroe rivalry.

As usual, Connors thwarted his critics to come back for another important win. In July 1982 he dueled with McEnroe for four hours and fourteen minutes in a thrilling five-setter at the Wimbledon finals. He showed the vintage Connors, complete with dazzling shots and outrageous behavior. The final score was in Connors's favor: 3–6, 6–3, 6–7, 7–6, 6–4. Anyone who thought that this victory was a fluke was convinced otherwise when Connors defeated Ivan Lendl in the final at the U.S. Open two months later: 6–3, 6–2, 4–6, 6–4. That year was Connors's comeback year; he seemed to have vindicated himself against the odds.

After 1983 Connors was still seen as a competitive threat, but as a man past his prime. Younger, stronger players like Stefan Edberg and then Boris Becker became known for their aggressive attack games, and Connors's all-court skill faded in people's minds. What remained though, was the competitive ferocity.

Connors won few tournaments after 1985, but he continued to compete. In one last blaze of glory, he reached the U.S. Open semifinals in 1991. To get there he fought an intense four-hour, forty-one-minute match with Aaron Krickstein on what happened to be his thirty-ninth birthday. The grueling match showed that Connors was still the best draw in the men's game. New York fans had always appreciated him more than Wimbledon or Australian fans did; now they applauded his vigorous effort. He reached the quarters, but lost there to a steady Jim Courier. Stefan Edberg, who won the tournament, called Connors "Mr. Open."

That was the last gasp. Connors retired from competition in 1993, citing a long list of injuries. He was by then a family man, having married former *Playboy* Playmate Patti McGuire in 1979. He worked for a time as a television broadcaster, but was never as effective in the role. By 2000 Connors was a thoroughly retired man.

In 1974 it had seemed as if Connors might have dominated the world of professional tennis for the next ten years. His demolition of an older generation of Australians like Ken Rosewall gave new excitement and energy to U.S. tennis. Connors's career was brilliant, but he was thwarted to some extent by the powerful combination of Bjorn Borg and John McEnroe. None of this contradicts the fact that Connors was one of the great American tennis champions, or that he won three U.S. Opens on three different surfaces (grass in 1974, clay in 1976, and Har-Tru in 1978, 1982, and 1983). Nor does it obscure the fact that Connors achieved his wins without reliance on any single weapon, such as Borg's serve, McEnroe's volleys, or Rosewall's slice backhand. To a great extent, Connors's game was invented, a contortion that worked well time and again.

★

Useful resources include "Jimmy Connors: The Hellion of Tennis," *Time* magazine cover story (28 Apr. 1975); Jack Kramer, with Frank Deford, *The Game: My Forty Years in Tennis* (1979); Barry Lorge, "Jimmy Connors: Star Spangled Hero or the Ugly American?" *World Tennis* (Jan. 1979); Bud Collins, *My Life with the Pros* (1989); and Curry Kirkpatrick, "Open and Shut," *Sports Illustrated* cover story (18 Sept. 1991).

SAMUEL WILLARD CROMPTON

COOPER, Cynthia (*b.* 14 April 1963 in Chicago, Illinois), basketball guard who played on the U.S. Olympic gold- and bronze-medal teams, led the Women's National Basketball Association (WNBA) Houston Comets to four championship titles, and was the league's Most Valuable Player (MVP) in 1997 and 1998.

Cooper was the fifth of eight children. Her family moved to Los Angeles when she was barely a year old and lived in Watts, an impoverished neighborhood plagued by drugs, gangs, and violence. Her mother, Mary Cobbs, raised the children by herself after divorcing Kenneth Cooper, a factory worker, when Cooper was about six years old. Cobbs was a custodian for the Los Angeles Rapid Transit Department. After their house burned down, the family went on welfare, and Cobbs had to work several jobs until she was able to buy another house. In her autobiography, *She Got Game* (1999), Cooper wrote that she was often hungry, living on potatoes and rice and begging for nickels with her younger brother Everett (called Ricky).

Cooper was a track star in junior high, winning the 400-meter race, and was Los Angeles City Champion of the 300-meter low hurdles. In 1978 she watched a female basketball player going in for a layup and knew she had found her niche. Although her junior high had no basketball team, she convinced high school coach Lucias Franklin to help her learn basketball that summer. Cooper excelled on the Locke High School varsity team, the Saints, who won the California 4A championship in 1981, her senior year. Averaging thirty-one points per game, Cooper was Marine League MVP and Los Angeles City Player of the Year. That

Cynthia Cooper. AP/WIDE WORLD PHOTOS

summer, Cooper went to Taiwan as the youngest member of America's Jones Cup team.

Recruited by coach Linda Sharp, Cooper received a scholarship to attend the University of Southern California (USC) in Los Angeles. She made the team, the Women of Troy, in her first year (1981–1982), averaging 14.6 points a game. Cooper wrote that her inner-city high school left her poorly prepared for college, and she became academically ineligible to play in the fall of 1983 and again in the 1984–1985 season.

In 1985, when her brother Ricky was stabbed and killed, Cooper left USC to work as a bank teller. After coach Sharp convinced Cooper that her basketball talent would help her escape a life of poverty, Cooper rejoined the team for the 1985–1986 season, averaging 17.2 points per game and earning the title "Comeback Kid" from the *Los Angeles Times.* Cooper left USC after the 1985–1986 season without finishing her degree to play basketball in Europe, the only professional option for female players. She tried out for the U.S. Olympic basketball team and was the only one of 300 applicants (those not invited to try out) to make the team. She played for the United States in the Goodwill Games (1986 and 1990), and for the gold-medal team in the Pan American games in 1987. Cooper spent the next several years in Europe, first in Valencia, Spain. She was named MVP of the European All-Star game in 1987.

Cooper was the third highest scorer on the U.S. gold-medal Olympic team in Seoul, Korea, in 1988. Four years later, she played on the bronze-medal team in Barcelona, Spain, and played in Parma, Italy, from 1987 to 1994. Wanting to return to the United States, Cooper became an assistant coach at the University of Houston in 1994. But she missed playing, and an offer from Alcamo in Sicily lured Cooper back to Europe. She played in Alcamo from 1994 to 1996, then in Parma in 1996 and 1997. During her years abroad, Cooper learned Spanish and became fluent in Italian. She brought several of her nieces and nephews to live and travel with her, hoping to give them a better education and more opportunity than she had while growing up in Watts.

In 1996 two women's basketball leagues were forming in the United States. The American Basketball League (ABL) required a $25 application fee, but Cooper believed her experience should speak for itself. She called the WNBA, where she was one of the top sixteen names already selected. All she had to do was sign a contract. After ten years abroad, the opportunity to play professional ball at home was a dream come true. She was assigned to the Houston Comets, who won the first WNBA championship in 1997, having lost only three of thirty games. They won the next three WNBA championships as well, and Cooper was the MVP of the championship series each year. She was on the WNBA All-Star team in each of the four seasons she played (the only unanimous choice in 1997), and led the Comets in points scored, free-throw percentage, assists, minutes played, and scoring average. Cooper retired from playing at the end of the 1999–2000 season, and the Phoenix Mercury hired her as head coach in 2001.

By the time Cooper's mother was diagnosed with breast cancer in March of 1997, Cooper had an endorsement deal with General Motors (GM) and an internship in their marketing department. With GM she developed Concept: Cure, an organization that raises funds for breast cancer research and promotes public awareness of the disease, a cause for which Cooper became a spokesperson. GM agreed to donate 50 cents to breast cancer research for each WNBA ticket sold, and almost $600,000 was donated in 1996, far exceeding expectations. Cooper was honored as *Ms.* magazine's Woman of the Year in 1998, for her combination of being a great athlete and role model who excelled despite much adversity.

Cooper credits her mother with teaching her to overcome adversity. Playing basketball enabled her to leave a poor and violent neighborhood and gave her the self-confidence she lacked growing up. She often attended her mother's chemotherapy treatments and then left the hospital to play in a game. Her mother died in February 1999, and she also lost her best friend and teammate, Kim Perrot, to cancer on 19 August that year, yet Cooper still led her

team to a WNBA championship. The five-foot, ten-inch, 150 pound Cooper won two NCAA championships with USC, led the European League in scoring eight times, and was the three-point champion twice. She was the all-time leading scorer in the WNBA when she retired and the first WNBA player to reach 300, 400, 500, 1,000, 2,000, and 2,500 points. She is in the top ten in most other WNBA statistical categories. In 2000 Cooper received her third ESPY award from ESPN, given to athletes who excel in their sport. Despite playing most of her career in obscurity, she became a marquee star of the WNBA for four years, and was called the league's "Michael Jordan" by New York Liberty coach Richie Adubato.

Cooper takes care of eight nieces and nephews in her home in Houston, Texas, and has adopted her nephew Tyquon. In 2000 she led a goodwill trip to Angola, Africa, delivering books and medical supplies. Cooper married Brian Dyke on 28 April 2001. She continues to be actively involved in community outreach programs, such as the Houston Public Library's interactive program to increase the reading skills of children in the Houston area, and in promoting sports for girls and African-American women.

★

Cooper's autobiography, *She Got Game: My Personal Odyssey* (1999), is the most comprehensive source for information. Most interviews, such as the one in *People Weekly* (22 June 1998), or *Working Woman* (Sept. 1999), contain much of the same information contained in the book. The 1998 *Current Biography Yearbook* has an entry on Cooper. In 1999 Cooper released the *Cynthia Cooper MVP Video Series*, three tapes with workout tips, motivational talks, and inspirational messages for girls "to succeed in sports and in life." The series was reviewed by the *Library Journal* 124, no. 18 (1 Nov. 1999).

JANE BRODSKY FITZPATRICK

CORBETT, James John (*b.* 1 September 1866 in San Francisco, California; *d.* 18 February 1933 in New York City), stylish boxer, renowned for his agility and scientific approach, who held the Heavyweight Champion of the World title from 1892 to 1897.

Corbett, one of twelve children, was the son of Irish immigrant parents. His father, Patrick Corbett, came from County Mayo, while his mother, Katherine McDonald Corbett, had her roots in Dublin. Corbett's father operated a livery stable in San Francisco while his mother raised their children, ten of whom lived to adulthood. As Corbett related in his memoirs, his family's home life was troubled. Corbett's father was prone to fits of depression; in August 1898 he shot his wife in the head as she lay sleeping before taking his own life as well.

James Corbett, 1894. © BETTMANN/CORBIS

Ambitious from an early age, Corbett disappointed his mother by refusing to study for the priesthood. Through his father, he found employment at the Nevada Bank in San Francisco, working his way up from messenger to assistant teller. During this time he began to cultivate the dapper, well-tailored look that would earn him the nickname "Gentleman Jim." His job at the bank did not distract him from his love of athletics. Corbett became an impressive sprinter and gymnast during his teenage years and considered pursuing professional baseball for a time. After taking boxing lessons from Walter Watson at San Francisco's Olympic Club, he decided to channel his abilities toward a career in the ring.

Corbett turned professional at age eighteen, gaining fame soon after by defeating Joe Choynski in a series of three bouts. His winning streak continued into 1890, when he won a four-round decision over Jake Kilrain. The following year, he fought Peter Jackson to a draw after a three-hour, sixty-one-round battle. By that time he had attained a nationwide reputation and acquired a manager, William A. Brady. Shamelessly aggressive in his promotion of Corbett, Brady would remain with the fighter for the rest of his career.

Corbett cultivated an image that emphasized his ring savvy and speed rather than sheer muscle. He championed

a "scientific" approach to boxing, emphasizing thorough physical conditioning. His was dubbed "the dancing master" because of his quickness. "From the time I began to box I made up my mind that footwork was half the game," he said later in life. "If I could always keep away where the other fellow couldn't hit me, and jump in and hit him when he did not expect it, it was only a question of how long he could last in front of me."

It was only a matter of time before Corbett sent out a challenge to heavyweight champion John L. Sullivan. After wearing the crown for ten years, Sullivan had become sluggish and complacent, his legendary brute strength diminished. Corbett warmed up to the task of dethroning Sullivan by sparring with him in a San Francisco exhibition in June 1891. Next, he challenged the champion to a real match, set for 7 September 1892 at the Olympic Club in New Orleans. Corbett slimmed down to 178 pounds for the fight and trained strenuously with Mike Donovan, a leading boxing coach. Meanwhile, Sullivan derided his opponent as a "young dude" and kept an indifferent training schedule.

Corbett exuded a flippant confidence as he met Sullivan in the ring, enraging the champion. It became evident early in the fight that the younger boxer's nimbleness, combined with a surprising punching force, put him in command of the contest.

Sullivan kept charging at Corbett but failed to land solid blows, while Corbett dodged and wove as he counterpunched with deadly accuracy. Bloodied but still standing, Sullivan held on until the twenty-first round, when he finally succumbed to a hard right to the jaw. The news that the mighty Sullivan had lost his title to the "young dude" made international headlines. In a gracious gesture, Corbett participated in a benefit sparring match with Sullivan at Madison Square Garden in New York City on 17 September to raise funds for the financially-strapped ex-champion.

In 1893 Corbett appeared in a touring stage show written in his honor. His fame helped draw crowds, though resentment from Sullivan partisans followed him as well. No one challenged him for the heavyweight title until British fighter Charley Mitchell met him in the ring on 25 January 1894 at the Jacksonville (Florida) Athletic Club. Corbett dispatched his opponent with a third-round knockout. On 17 September of that same year, his knockout victory over Peter Courtney became the first boxing match to be captured on film.

In the ring and on stage, Corbett carefully cultivated his image as a well-mannered professional athlete. His private life was more complicated, however. He married actress Olive Lake on 8 June 1886. They divorced on 2 August 1895. On 15 August 1895 he married Jessie Taylor, known as Vera Stanwood, of Omaha, Nebraska. He carried on a series of affairs, including one with actress Mae West. His relations with his second wife were stormy; at one point she publicly accused him of threatening to kill her. Despite such incidents, the couple remained married for thirty-eight years. Corbett had no children.

On 17 March 1897 Corbett defended his title against Bob "Ruby Robert" Fitzsimmons in Carson City, Nevada. The British-born challenger knocked out Corbett in the fourteenth round with his trademark punch to the solar plexus. On 11 May 1900 Corbett fought to regain the heavyweight belt from James J. Jeffries, a former sparring partner who had defeated Fitzsimmons the previous year. At first, Corbett's quickness and craft seemed to dominate; finally, Jeffries's superior power prevailed, and Corbett fell in the twenty-third round. Corbett defeated "Kid" McCoy three months after this fight, and on 14 August 1903, he faced Jeffries in a rematch. This time it took only ten rounds for Jeffries to beat him. It proved to be Corbett's last fight.

After his final loss, Corbett remained on the periphery of the boxing world, helping to train Jeffries in his ill-advised bout with Jack Johnson in 1910. He remained in the public eye as a stage performer and (largely inaccurate) newspaper boxing tipster. In 1925 he told a somewhat sanitized version of his life in an autobiography, *The Roar of the Crowd*. He died of liver cancer at age sixty-six at his modest home in Queens, New York, on a street later renamed Corbett Road. He is buried in Cypress Hills Cemetery in Brooklyn. His legend was revived by the film *Gentleman Jim* (1942) starring Errol Flynn. Corbett is remembered today as a technically gifted pugilist who helped to lift boxing out of its crude early period into a mainstream sport.

★

Corbett's autobiography, *The Roar of the Crowd: The True Tale of the Rise and Fall of a Champion* (1925), is entertaining but less than trustworthy, especially concerning his personal life. Nat Fleischer, *"Gentleman Jim": The Story of James J. Corbett* (1942), is also overly protective of the fighter's legend. Far better is Patrick Myler, *Gentleman Jim Corbett: The Truth Behind a Boxing Legend* (1998), a balanced and unflinching portrait of its subject's strengths and flaws. A good secondary source is Michael T. Isenberg's *John L. Sullivan and His America* (1988), which analyzes the 1892 Sullivan-Corbett match in considerable detail.

BARRY ALFONSO

CORDERO, Angel Tomas, Jr. (*b.* 8 November 1942 in Santurce, Puerto Rico), Thoroughbred jockey, trainer, and owner who rode to more than 7,000 career wins, including three Kentucky Derby victories, and amassed a multimillion-dollar personal fortune.

Cordero is the son of Angel T. Cordero, Sr., and Mercedes (Hernandez) Cordero. It is no surprise that he gravitated toward a career in the saddle, as his mother was the daughter of a jockey and a trainer, and he had some twenty uncles and cousins who also rode professionally. Cordero was first put on the back of a horse at the tender age of five months. By the time he was three years old he "rode" an old saddle on a fence and was adept at transferring his switch from one hand to the other.

Cordero studied at the Institute of Puerto Rico, otherwise known as Puerto Rico Junior College of Accounting. Although two years younger than Braulio Baeza (eventually a five-time top-earning jockey, elected to the National Museum of Racing Hall of Fame in 1976), Cordero shared many similarities with his Panamanian rival. Cordero, like Baeza, grew up in a subculture where the critical elements of daily life were horses, tracks, and racing.

He rode his first winner on 15 June 1960 at age eighteen, astride Celador at El Commandante Race Track in Puerto Rico. It would be easy to describe Cordero's long and successful career as simply a rags-to-riches saga. In reality, however, Cordero confronted a series of vagaries and challenges both physical and professional. For example, when he first raced in the United States in 1962 he was not able to replicate his successes in Puerto Rico. He rode regularly on a variety of New York State tracks—Aqueduct, Belmont Park, Saratoga—but he was a dismal failure. He recalls the experiences as disastrous. He had no networking skills with which to negotiate and facilitate contact with trainers and owners, and his English-language skills were negligible. After a few months he packed up his silks, saddles, and whips and returned home. In 1965 he was prevailed upon by fellow Puerto Rican jockey Eddie Belmonte to try again and thus returned to the New York racing scene. In a 1975 *New York Times* interview Cordero spelled out the tough-minded credo that was instrumental in seeing him survive his American apprenticeship: "You work, work, work and wait for something to happen."

This philosophy was critical to his eventual success because, while many riders sat out days when racing conditions were appalling, Cordero made it a point of honor to ride despite adverse elements or troubling health problems. In 1968 Cordero spoke of battling on and continuing to think competitively despite nose operations, an ankle injury, suspected pneumonia, racing handicaps, and seventy days of racing suspensions for overly aggressive riding.

At the end of the 1966 season Cordero was a top-ten rider at Aqueduct. A year later he was New York's most successful jockey of all time, with 277 wins. In 1968 he was North America's most successful jockey, with 345 wins. He bested his nearest rival, Alvaro Pineda, by a generous margin of sixteen victories.

In 1969 Cordero was again New York's premier jockey. One year later, in 1970, he finished in third place. Over the next four years he was in the runner-up position. Certainly

Angel Cordero, Jr., 1995. ASSOCIATED PRESS AP

his eager, enthusiastic—some would say excessively bois- terous—racing action affected his racing fortunes. He was repeatedly hauled in front of the stewards and his reputa- tion was increasingly that of a brilliant but dangerously aggressive rider.

The Kentucky Derby can claim to be the world's most famous horse race. In terms of prestige and equestrian his- tory it occupies a hallowed place. Cordero experienced one of the low points of his career when in May 1973 the racing authorities of Aqueduct gave him a ten-day racing suspen- sion. This meant that he could not ride his Derby mount My Gallant, which was a pre-race favorite. Moreover, his earlier career Derby mounts on Verbatim (1968), Corn Off the Cob (1970), and Jim French (1971) had all been un- successful. However, in the hundredth running of the Ken- tucky Derby, on 4 May 1974, Cordero, on Cannonade and clearly firing on all six cylinders, defeated Hudson County by two-and-one-quarter lengths. Commentators noted Cordero's facility at getting the best out of Cannonade by whipping the horse with a right-handed, and then a left- handed, technique. This, of course, was a skill taught to him when he was literally an infant.

During the 1970s Cordero maintained a successful pro- file despite his perennial problem of incurring racing sus- pensions. In 1974 he and Laffit Pincay became the first two jockeys to win more than $4 million in one racing season. A year later Cordero moved out of the sports pages and onto the front pages of major North American newspapers as a result of one sensational day of racing—12 March 1975—in which he won six races. Racing handicapper Pat Lynch helped explain the athletic genius of the extraordi- nary Puerto Rican rider, described as "a rider in full flower. . . . He's exuberant. . . . He doesn't walk, he jogs. . . . He bounces. Everything about the guy is quick, quick."

Toward the end of his career Cordero still maintained a grueling racing schedule. In 1991, at age forty-nine, he started 1,341 races, earning 238 first places, 212 seconds, 186 thirds, and $9,383,904. By the end of 1992 he had amassed 7,057 wins in 38,646 racing starts. His career earn- ings reached phenomenal proportions even in an era when baseball, basketball, football, tennis, and golf stars became multimillionaires. Cordero's career earnings have amounted to a staggering $164,571,847.

Cordero was inducted into the National Museum of Racing Hall of Fame on 11 August 1988, one year after becoming the sixth jockey to ride 6,000 winners. He at- tained this feat while guiding Lost Kitty to a first place at Monmouth Park in Oceanport, New Jersey. On 17 October 1991 Cordero joined Willie Shoemaker and Laffit Pincay, Jr., as the only Thoroughbred jockeys to have achieved 7,000 wins. When asked which of his victories had meant the most to him and why, Cordero replied, "The Kentucky Derby—winning it three times was special. It's everybody's dream." Cordero won aboard Cannonade in 1974, Bold Forbes in 1976, and Spend a Buck in 1985.

On 12 January 1992 Cordero, no stranger to serious in- jury, tumbled at the Aqueduct Race Track in Jamaica, New York. He suffered a broken elbow, three smashed ribs, and a damaged spleen. He consequently retired from Thor- oughbred racing to seek a trainer's license. His first triumph in this role came as trainer of Puchinito on 13 June 1992 at Belmont Park Race Track in Elmont, New York.

Cordero was genetically blessed in being comfortable at his racing weight. Most trainers expect jockeys to weigh 113 or 114 pounds. This results in the vast majority of jockeys having to strenuously diet, use diuretics, and fast. In Cor- dero's case, his five-foot, three-inch frame and his metab- olism kept him comfortably under the 113-pound ceiling.

Cordero and his first wife, Santa, had two children be- fore their divorce. Cordero's second wife, Marjorie, a former jockey and trainer, had one son and one daughter. Marjorie was killed by a hit-and-run driver in January 2001.

Cordero won acclaim for his fiercely competitive inten- sity and risk-taking. His numerous honors include earning Eclipse Awards as Jockey of the Year in 1982 and 1983 and being the leading jockey in earnings for 1976, 1982, and 1983. He remains a folk hero for the New York Puerto Rican community and was featured in the pop song "Cordero y Belmonte" by the Latino singer Ismael Rivera. Cordero's Hall of Fame citation and plaque opens with the words: "A fierce competitor, and a popular athlete with the racing public."

★

Current Biography (1975) contains a thorough narrative on Cordero's early years, including a series of evocative and illuminating excerpts from the *New York Post,* the *New York Times, Newsday,* and *Sport.* Short biographies are in the *Biographical Dictionary of American Sports* (1995) and the *Encyclopedia of Ethnicity and Sports in the United States* (2000). Tom Gilcoyne, an archival assistant at the National Museum of Racing and Hall of Fame in Saratoga Springs, New York, provides a useful Hall of Fame mini-biography of Cordero.

SCOTT A. G. M. CRAWFORD

COSELL, Howard (*b.* 25 March 1918 in Winston-Salem, North Carolina; *d.* 23 April 1995 in New York City), brash, egotistical sports journalist who inspired admiration and loathing from colleagues and sports fans alike in his zeal for "telling it like it is."

Cosell was born Howard William Cohen, the younger child of Isadore Martin Cohen, an accountant for a chain of clothing stores, and Nellie Rosenthal Cohen, a homemaker. His family moved to Brooklyn, New York, before he was three. He indulged his passion for athletics by serving as the sports editor of the newspaper at Alexander Hamilton High School. He enrolled in New York University in 1935 and studied liberal arts before switching at his parents' request to the law school. He obtained a law degree there in 1940.

Cohen enlisted in the U.S. Army Transportation Corps in 1942 and was stationed at the New York Port of Embarkation, where he rose to the rank of major and supervised all personnel. There he met Corporal Mary Edith "Emmy" Abrams, a pretty blonde whom it was against army regulations to date. Undaunted, he obtained written permission from a general for his courtship. The two married in 1944 and had two children. They remained devoted partners until Emmy Cosell's death in 1990.

At some point in his young adulthood Cohen legally changed his surname to Cosell. To those who viewed the change as a denial of his Jewish heritage, he replied that his family's name in Poland ("Kasell") was actually closer to "Cosell" than "Cohen" and had been mangled by the U.S. immigration authorities.

After the end of World War II, Cosell established his own law practice, continuing his lifelong interest in sports by numbering athletes among his clients. In 1951 he helped

Howard Cosell. ARCHIVE PHOTOS, INC.

to incorporate Little League baseball in the New York area, and in 1953 the restless lawyer found the opportunity he had been seeking, as the host of the ABC radio program *All-League Clubhouse,* in which Little Leaguers asked questions of major-league players. In 1956 ABC offered him a contract as a radio sports reporter, and he abandoned his law practice.

Cosell embraced radio eagerly, lugging around the heavy tape recorders of the period. He developed contacts in the sports world and earned a reputation for hard-hitting interviews. He slowly moved into television, becoming the nightly sports reporter for WABC-TV in New York in 1961 while continuing his radio work.

From 1959 on, Cosell covered boxing for ABC and finally achieved nationwide familiarity through his championing of the boxer Muhammad Ali in the 1960s. When the boxer abandoned the name Cassius Clay and converted to Islam, Cosell was the first broadcaster to use the new name. He also supported Ali in his battle to retain his heavyweight title and right to box in the United States, when officials penalized the boxer because he was a conscientious objector during the Vietnam War. Cosell loudly proclaimed Ali's persecutors racist and their arguments unconstitutional.

Cosell came into his full glory when Roone Arledge, president of ABC Sports, decided to court viewers in 1970 by expanding football telecasting beyond the weekend. *Monday Night Football,* a program in which Cosell was a fixture through 1983, gave him a forum for his athlete interviews, his three-dollar vocabulary, and his frankness.

He viewed himself as a maverick and a pioneer, a "hard" journalist in a field that had hitherto consisted of jocks and cheerleaders. Cosell took his mission to serve the U.S. public so seriously that in the mid-1970s he even considered running for the U.S. Senate. "That wasn't chutzpah," remarked the *Washington Post* sportswriter Shirley Povich of the sportscaster's political aspirations. "That was Cosell."

Cosell became a huge celebrity during his stint at *Monday Night Football.* He worked on a variety of sports broadcasts, including those of several Olympic Games and the famed 1973 tennis "Battle of the Sexes" between Billie Jean King and Bobby Riggs. He also appeared on television programs such as *The Odd Couple, The Dean Martin Show,* and *Rowan and Martin's Laugh-In.* His Brooklyn accent and middle-aged, toupee-enhanced appearance evoked instant familiarity.

He guest-hosted talk shows and even briefly hosted a variety show, *Saturday Night Live with Howard Cosell* (1975). Such was his cultural currency that the filmmaker Woody Allen employed him, most notably in *Bananas* (1971), in which Cosell rushed to interview an assassinated Latin American dictator on his deathbed and performed a play-by-play analysis of the consummation of a marriage.

Despite his visibility, Cosell was not universally popular. "Arrogant, pompous, obnoxious, vain, cruel, verbose, a show-off. I have been called all of these," he wrote in his book *Cosell* (1973). "Of course I am." Cosell expressed his opinions about sports and his life off the air in several other books: *Like It Is* (1974); *I Never Played the Game,* with Peter Bonventre (1985); and *What's Wrong with Sports,* with Shelby Whitfield (1991). Like his on-air commentary, his books made enemies. Of *I Never Played the Game,* Povich wrote, "Oh yes he did, and he played it spitefully and with self-promotion always in mind as he homed into the big story, this poseur of the public's right to know, who for years played his own game of How Great I Am and Don't You Forget It."

In 1982, after witnessing a particularly brutal fight, Cosell announced that he would no longer cover boxing; after he retired from *Monday Night Football* the next year he extended his disdain to that sport as well. He continued to perform radio sports commentary until 1992, although after the cancellation of his ABC program *SportsBeat* in 1985 he no longer appeared regularly on television. In 1991 Cosell underwent an operation for cancer, and a series of strokes left him weak and increasingly reclusive. He died of a heart embolism in New York City on 23 April 1995.

Cosell exerted considerable influence on sports journalism. Although he was not always the champion of the people he thought he was, he took a stand against racism in sports and fought for coverage of such difficult issues as drugs in the athletic world. He helped to make *Monday Night Football* an institution that changed network sports programming. In the final analysis, however, it was his loud personality rather than his subject matter that struck his audiences—so much that a 1978 poll found him both the nation's most liked and most hated broadcaster. In 1984 the *Washington Post* columnist Tony Kornheiser summed up Cosell's legacy: "Yes, he was contentious. Yes, he was controversial. But damn it, he was compelling."

★

Aside from his own works, the best book about Cosell is by the television producer Terry O'Neil, *The Game Behind the Game: High Pressure, High Stakes in Television Sports* (1989). Cosell inspired a number of profiles, including three in *TV Guide:* Saul Braun, "The Voice You Love to Hate" (28 Aug. 1971); Melvin Durslag, "Howard Cosell vs. the World" (27 Sept. 1975); and David Shaw, "Before You Boo Howard Cosell" (9 Feb. 1980). Also helpful are Harry Waters, "This Is Howard Cosell," *Newsweek* (2 Oct. 1972); Tony Kornheiser, "Cosell's Legacy," *Washington Post* (23 Aug. 1984); and Shirley Povich, "Cosell: What's a Low Punch Among Friends?," *Washington Post* (11 Oct. 1985). Obituaries are in the *New York Times* and *Washington Post* (both 24 Apr. 1995), and Povich's remembrance is in the *Washington Post* (2 May 1995).

TINKY "DAKOTA" WEISBLAT

COSTAS, Robert Quinlan ("Bob") (*b.* 22 March 1952 in Queens, New York), highly respected television and radio sports journalist and analyst.

First known as a play-by-play announcer for football, basketball, and baseball, Costas became NBC-TV's leading sports personality, hosting the network's seasonal coverage of the National Football League (NFL), the National Basketball Association (NBA), and Major League Baseball (MLB). He also anchors the network's presentation of prestige events, including the World Series, the Super Bowl, and the Olympic Games. His broadcast activities outside the sports arena have included his own daily interview series, appearances on entertainment shows, and regular contributions to NBC News programs.

A native New Yorker who grew up in suburban Long Island, Costas, the son of John George Costas, an electrical engineer, and Jayne Quinlan Costas, often went to baseball

Bob Costas, 1996. © WALLY McNAMEE/CORBIS

games at Yankee Stadium with his father. But listening to sports on the radio seemed to make a more lasting impression on him than a trip to the ballpark. "To me, a game wasn't a game unless an announcer was describing it," he told a reporter for *Inside Sports*. He recalls that even while *playing* ball as a child he would narrate games aloud, imitating such childhood idols as New York sportscasters Red Barber, Mel Allen, and Marty Glickman. "There was a mystique to radio broadcasting," he explained to a reporter. "I wanted to be one of those voices."

Following his graduation from Commack South High School in 1970, Costas enrolled at Syracuse University, where he studied communications and worked at WAER, the student-run radio station, in hopes of making his childhood dream real. His career progress gradually outstripped his progress toward a degree. By his junior year he had won a job in commercial broadcasting as play-by-play announcer at WSYR for the Syracuse Blazers of the American Hockey League. During the middle of his senior year Costas left college altogether to join the broadcast crew at KMOX, the CBS affiliate in St. Louis, the city he still calls home.

The busy sports lineup at KMOX put Costas at the microphone for University of Missouri Big Eight college basketball as well as for the pro games of the Spirit of St. Louis of the old American Basketball Association. Though still shy of his twenty-fifth birthday, his free-flowing mastery of the game and its vocabulary won the notice of CBS Sports bigwigs, who began to use him in spot assignments

for network television coverage of NBA and NFL games.

In 1980 Costas signed on as a network regular with NBC Sports. It was the beginning of a long and fruitful association that would lead him to media stardom. He became familiar to midwestern NFL fans as a member of the pool of regional announcing teams covering American Football Conference (AFC) games for NBC-TV. Costas advanced to the national spotlight in 1984 as anchor of the network's coast-to-coast wraparound program (known after various name changes as *NFL Live*). The show included predictions, interviews, highlights, and analysis each Sunday in pregame, halftime, and postgame segments.

A lover of baseball above all else in sports, Costas got his dream assignment in 1983 when he was named primary play-by-play announcer for NBC's *Game of the Week*. Teamed in the booth with former Yankee shortstop Tony Kubek, Costas redefined the art of the baseball broadcast during a six-season run. An acute student of the game with a photographic memory for faces and statistics, he cultivated an ability to deliver trenchant analytic commentary in a conversational, personable tone. His ability and willingness to break the smiley-face proscenium of broadcast sports for the well-deserved glib or even sarcastic remark made him a favorite of millions of viewers. A picture of Costas that appeared in the *New York Times* was appropriately captioned "Reverent and irreverent at the same time."

Working the World Series, the Super Bowl, the NBA playoffs, and whatever other major events the network won during the bidding wars of the 1980s, Costas became, in effect, the voice and face of NBC Sports. That status was affirmed when he was chosen to anchor NBC's coverage of the 1992 Summer Olympics in Barcelona, Spain. Working more than twelve hours a day during the seventeen-day event, he oversaw what many critics agree was the most comprehensive broadcast coverage ever of the Olympics. He won an Emmy Award and apparently a lock on the Olympic anchor position at NBC, hosting the Summer Games in 1996 (Atlanta) and 2000 (Sydney) and the 2002 Winter Olympics in Salt Lake City.

In an unusual move for a television network that had invested so much in promoting the image of Costas as the persona of its sports division, NBC granted him a general-interest Monday-through-Friday late-night talk show in 1988, *Later with Bob Costas*. Over the next six years Costas proved himself an able and eclectic raconteur, engaging the likes of such figures as Barry Goldwater, Little Richard, Oliver Stone, Paul McCartney, and Dr. Ruth Westheimer. The success of the show prompted speculation that he might pursue any number of lucrative opportunities, including the all-consuming anchor spot on NBC's *Today Show*. But while he has expanded his role at the network to become a contributor of sports stories to NBC News programs, Costas would not hear of leaving the sports beat. "Ten years from now," he told *Sport* magazine, "I don't know what I'll be doing, except one of the things will be baseball." Costas has similarly remained loyal to his first media romance, radio, continuing to broadcast his weekly syndicated program, *Costas Coast to Coast,* as a labor of love.

Bob Costas married Carol Randall "Randi" Krummenacher in 1983. The couple has two children, a son and a daughter, and they make their home in St. Louis, though Costas maintains an apartment in New York, the headquarters for most of his national television work. Asked about the unusual long-distance commuting arrangement, he replied, "I love St. Louis. It's a good place to raise a family." Costas has won a dozen Emmy Awards and been voted Broadcaster of the Year seven times by his professional colleagues. Recent projects include *On the Record with Bob Costas,* a wide-ranging sports interview program for HBO.

★

Costas received a great deal of media attention when he was first chosen to anchor NBC-TV's Olympic coverage, including the following useful print items: David Ellis, "America's Host," in *Time* (3 Aug. 1992); an interview with the sportswriter Bill Carter in the *New York Times* (22 July 1992); and a major article in *Current Biography Yearbook 1993.* William Taafe profiled Costas at an earlier stage of his career in "A Fun Guy, No Kidding," *Sports Illustrated* (12 May 1986). Costas wrote *Fair Ball: A Fan's Case for Baseball* (2000), which addresses the present and future of the major leagues in the age of television.

DAVID MARC

COUNSILMAN, James Edward ("Doc") (*b.* 28 December 1920 in Birmingham, Alabama), two-time coach of the U.S. Men's Olympic Swimming Team who led the Indiana University men's swim team to six consecutive National Collegiate Athletic Association (NCAA) championships and also authored an influential book based on motion studies that changed competitive swimming techniques.

Given his career as one of swimming's most successful coaches, it is surprising that Counsilman did not begin to swim competitively until he was almost twenty years old. Born in Birmingham to Joseph and Ottilia (Schamburg) Counsilman, the future coach attended high school in St. Louis, where he was an all-around athlete in football, basketball, track, and baseball. In addition to these activities, he also participated on his high school diving team. Employed as a telephone lineman after graduation, Counsilman took up swimming as a recreational pursuit at a local branch of the Young Men's Christian Association. However, after gaining the attention of the coach Ernie Vornbrock, Counsilman began to train in earnest as a competitive swimmer with the goal of entering the Amateur Athletic Union (AAU) competition to be held in St. Louis in August 1941.

Although Counsilman did not win his event, the 200-meter breaststroke, at the competition, his progress under Vornbrock earned him an offer of an athletic scholarship at Ohio State University (OSU) with the swim coach Mike Peppe. Entering college in the fall of 1941, Counsilman took the national AAU title for the 200-meter breaststroke in 1942 as part of the OSU team. His college career was interrupted, however, for military service in 1943; as a B-24 bomber pilot for the U.S. Army Air Forces in the European theater, his plane once ran out of fuel over Yugoslavia. Fortunately, the crew was rescued by friendly forces, who sheltered them until they could be ferried out of the country. Counsilman received the Distinguished Flying Cross and Air Medal with cluster for his military service.

At the conclusion of World War II, Counsilman resumed his studies at OSU and gained another national title in the 200-meter breaststroke event, and the OSU men's swim team earned two NCAA championships during his undergraduate days as the team's captain. Counsilman also started a family with his wife, the former Marjorie Scrafford; they were married on 15 June 1943 and the couple eventually had four children. Completing a B.S. degree in 1947, Counsilman and his family spent a year at the University of Illinois, where he earned an M.S. degree in science in 1948 while working as an assistant swimming coach. Continuing his studies at Iowa State University, Counsilman then pursued his doctorate in human performance, which he finished in 1951. From 1952 to 1957 Counsilman rose through the ranks at the State University of New York at Cortland (then Cortland State Teachers College), earning the rank of professor in his final year there. He was also a prolific author in leading athletic journals, publishing numerous articles that explored swimming as a science.

In 1957 Counsilman accepted a position as an assistant professor and coach of the men's swim team at Indiana University (IU) in Bloomington. Although the school's swimming program was not known as a strong one, Counsilman quickly built it into a national powerhouse. One of the key concepts behind his coaching style was building a sense of camaraderie among his athletes; in the early days at IU, he accomplished this on some of the long road trips that Counsilman and the team took to national meets. The coach also used various games during workout sessions to help his athletes release tension and refocus on their training.

In light of his reputation for team-building skills, Counsilman was appointed as the coach of the U.S. Olympic Men's Swimming Team for the 1964 games in Osaka, Japan. Of the twenty-one medals awarded in seven individual competitions, Counsilman's team won eleven, including

James Counsilman *(right)* and Olympic freestyle swimmer Alan Somers. AP/WIDE WORLD PHOTOS

four of seven gold medals. In addition, the U.S. team swept all three team events. With his team winning well over half the medals awarded in swimming events, Counsilman returned to IU as an Olympic hero. Further enhancing his reputation, Counsilman published the first edition of *The Science of Swimming* (1968), based on his motion studies of championship swimmers. Counsilman invoked the eighteenth-century fluid principle theories of the Swiss scientist Daniel Bernoulli to conclude that a propeller-like sculling stroke was more efficient than a stroke that went straight back. Based on his coaching experience, he also opened Counsilman, Hunsaker, and Associates, an aquatic design and consulting firm, in 1970.

While leading the IU men's swimming team to six straight NCAA championships from 1968 to 1973, Counsilman also trained Olympic athletes, including Mark Spitz and John Kinsella. In 1976 he served again as the U.S. Olympic Men's Swimming Team coach; the team astounded the swimming world by taking twenty-six of the thirty-three medals awarded for individual events and both gold medals for team events. U.S. swimmers took every gold medal in the swimming competition except one; in five events, they swept the field. Of the thirteen swimming events, the U.S. team set eleven new world records. Also in 1976 he was inducted into the International Swimming Hall of Fame.

In 1979 Counsilman took up a new challenge: swimming the English Channel. His completion of this daunt-ing task at the age of fifty-eight made him the oldest person to accomplish the feat. In the next decade, however, Counsilman faced other challenges; in addition to suffering from arthritis, the coach was diagnosed with Parkinson's disease in the 1980s. Admitting that his health problems were slowing him down, Counsilman retired as a professor of physical education and swimming coach from IU in 1990. In his retirement, Counsilman updated his classic book, which appeared as *The New Science of Swimming* in 1994, and he continued to work as a consultant on aquatic projects.

In all, Counsilman trained forty-eight Olympic athletes and served as a mentor to generations of swimmers at IU and elsewhere. In recognition of his contributions, IU established the Counsilman Center for the Science of Swimming. With his pioneering scientific studies and warm regard within the swimming community, Counsilman is assured a legacy as one of the leading coaches in the sport's history.

★

Counsilman authored three books on swimming: *The Science of Swimming* (1968), with the second edition retitled as *The New Science of Swimming* (1994); *The Complete Book of Swimming* (1977); and *Competitive Swimming Manual for Coaches and Swimmers* (1977). Profiles of Counsilman's career appeared in *Sports Illustrated* (4 Apr. 1990), and *Swim Magazine* (July/Aug. 1996). Anecdotes from athletes trained by the coach were posted on the Indiana University website (31 Aug. 2001), <http://www.indiana. edu/hplab/whatsupdoc.html>. Counsilman's innovations in the science of swimming were reviewed in an essay by Kim McDonald, *Washington Post* (11 Aug. 1999).

TIMOTHY BORDEN

COUSY, Robert ("Bob") (*b.* 9 August 1928 in New York City), premier guard for the National Basketball Association's (NBA) Boston Celtics, coach, radio commentator, and Basketball Hall of Fame inductee who was cited in the *Biographical History of Basketball* as one of the fifty greatest NBA players of all time.

Cousy was the only child of a cab driver whose full name is not known, and Juliet Corlet Cousy, a homemaker and occasional teacher of French. Cousy's parents arrived in the United States on a ship from France a few months before Cousy was born. He discovered in his twenties that he had a half sister, Blanche Pettuy, his father's daughter from a

Bob Cousy, 1953. ASSOCIATED PRESS FILES

202

previous marriage, sixteen years his senior and living in Nice, France. For the first five years of his life Cousy spoke only French. He lived a meager existence first on East Eighty-third Street, then on nearby East End Avenue in Manhattan, and his father often worked seven days a week. Cousy attended Saint Katherine's parochial school on East Eighty-sixth Street and Third Avenue. In the summer of 1939 the family, in a somewhat improved economic situation, moved to Saint Albans on Long Island, first renting, then buying a house. Cousy first attended the public school because the parochial school was filled, then he attended Andrew Jackson High School. From Morty Arkin, a local playground director, he learned how to properly hold and shoot a basketball, and in his enthusiasm he practiced noon and night. He played both for teams of the community leagues and for the junior varsity and the varsity of Andrew Jackson High School. In the summers he worked at the Tamarack Lodge in the Catskills and played in the basketball league there. He graduated from Andrew Jackson High School in 1946.

With his parents insisting he attend a Catholic college, Cousy enrolled at Holy Cross College in Worcester, Massachusetts, in 1946. He made the basketball team as an alternate, then he became a starter. Though he and coach Alvin "Doggie" Julian did not get along—Julian would not speak to him for long periods—the team enjoyed great success, winning the National Collegiate Athletic Association (NCAA) championship his junior year. In Cousy's senior year Julian left to coach the professional Boston Celtics, and the more affable Lester "Buster" Sheary took over as Holy Cross coach. The team reeled off twenty-six consecutive victories, though they faltered in the postseason tournament games. Cousy averaged 19.4 points a game and made most All-America team selections. In a Holy Cross game Cousy, hemmed in by opposing players, made his first behind-the-back pass. On 9 December 1950 Cousy married Marie "Missie" Ritterhisch, his high school sweetheart. They had four children.

Cousy, to his surprise, was not drafted by the Boston Celtics and its new coach Arnold "Red" Auerbach, who professed a disdain for the "local yokels" and chose instead Chuck Share, a tall center from Bowling Green. Cousy went to the Tri-Cities team in the Midwest at a salary, after hard negotiation, of $9,000 per year. He was promptly traded to the Chicago Stags, which folded before the opening of the season. The Stags players were distributed throughout the league. Auerbach and other coaches wanted Max Zaslofsky, and since the matter could not be settled, they agreed to draw slips from a hat. Boston drew Cousy's name, for that team a fortuitous turn of events.

Cousy played for the Celtics from 1950 to 1963, becoming a premier playmaking guard and initiator of the fast break as well as an ample scorer. He played a wide-open game featuring sleight-of-hand passes from all angles and behind-the-back dribbles. At first he was seen, with some justification, as a showboater, known as the "Houdini of the Hardwood," but he learned to control his antics for the betterment of the team. He amazed observers with his ability to find the open man when no opening seemed to exist. Cousy was by no means among the quickest players in the league, venturing in *Cousy on the Celtic Mystique* (1988), "I couldn't have beaten my grandmother down the court in a race." But he had, as he pointed out in *Basketball Is My Life* (1957), certain physical attributes that ensured his success, including "unusually long arms and sharply sloping ape-like shoulders . . . huge, ham-like hands . . . tremendously powerful thighs . . . unusual peripheral vision. I can see more than most people out of the corner of my eyes."

"Easy Ed" Macauley was Boston's capable center during the first half of Cousy's professional playing career. But when the Celtics acquired the rebounding and defensive star center Bill Russell, the team went on to greatness, winning National Basketball Association (NBA) championships every year from 1957 through 1966 except 1958. Other Cousy teammates included the sharp-shooting guard Bill Sharman, the forward Tommy Heinsohn, the rough-and-tumble rebounding forward "Jungle Jim" Luscutoff, and the versatile sixth man Frank Ramsey. Though standing only six feet, one inch, Cousy finished second to Neil Johnston in scoring in 1954. He led the Celtics in scoring from 1951 through 1955 and was the league leader in assists from 1953 through 1960. In 1957 he was voted the Most Valuable Player (MVP) in the league, and twice he was voted MVP in All-Star games. He finished his career with an 18.4 points-per-game scoring average and a 7.5 assists-per-game average, which he raised to 8.6 assists-per-game in 109 playoff games.

In 1953 Cousy came up with the idea for a players' union and became the driving force for its establishment against the hard opposition of Commissioner Maurice Podloff and even some players, particularly the Fort Wayne Pistons, who feared the retribution of their powerful owner, the wealthy industrialist Fred Zollner. Success finally came on 18 April 1957 with the signatures of the Board of Governors of the National Basketball Association. The agreement provided for, among other things, a limit on the number of exhibition games that could be scheduled and the establishment of a board of arbitration to settle player-owner disputes.

Cousy reached out beyond playing basketball to business ventures. In September 1951 he opened a gas station in Worcester, Massachusetts, with Frank Oftring, a fellow Holy Cross basketball player, and in the summer of 1952 he and a friend, Joe Sharry, set up for-profit basketball games in Hyannis on Cape Cod, Massachusetts. Neither of these ventures succeeded. Later in the 1950s Cousy en-

tered into a partnership and bought Camp Graylag, a boys' camp in Pittsfield, New Hampshire, which did well.

For a while Cousy was dogged by law enforcement authorities. When he was a Holy Cross player, he sold basketball tickets to a man and did not turn in the money to the appropriate officials. When college betting scandals broke out in 1951, Cousy was accused of collaborating with gamblers. In February 1953 Cousy was questioned and exonerated by the New York district attorney's office. It turned out that the man who bought the tickets was a gambler doing business with a bookie, who stood nearby to verify that contact was made with Cousy. Cousy did not know he was expected to "shave" points. When the score did not turn out as the bookie expected, Cousy was blamed, and his ticket-selling activity was exposed.

After his retirement as an active player in 1963, Cousy coached the basketball team at Boston College for six years. For the 1969–1970 season he coached the Cincinnati Royals. During his tenure he traded away the stars Oscar "the Big O" Robertson and Jerry Lucas to make room for young prospects. Cousy himself appeared in one game at age forty-one, thus becoming the oldest person to play in an NBA game. Cousy next became a radio broadcaster of Celtics games, beginning at WBZ in Boston.

In *Cousy on the Celtic Mystique* the retired player reflected on the quality of the current players. He felt that they were superbly talented and shot the ball better than the players of his day but that they did not "think" the game as well. They exhibited more dribbling, less passing, more turnovers, and less commitment to the good of the team. He praised Maurice Cheeks, the Philadelphia 76ers guard, and Norm van Lier, the Chicago Bulls guard, for passing to the right man and for their general good sense. He considered Larry Bird, the legendary Celtics forward, the ultimate basketball player. Bird, Cousy explained, was a playmaker despite the fact that he was a forward, was totally unselfish, and could play through pain.

Cousy was the epitome of the playmaking guard, paving the way for the likes of John Stockton of the Utah Jazz and "Magic" Johnson of the Los Angeles Lakers. Though the schedule in his day included fewer than eighty-two games, his 6,955 assists place him high on the all-time list.

★

Bob Cousy, as told to Al Hirshberg, *Basketball Is My Life* (1957), an autobiography written while Cousy was playing with the Celtics, is invaluable for information on his early years. Cousy, *Cousy on the Celtic Mystique* (1988), explains why the Celtics were both the most beloved and most hated team. See also Cousy and Frank G. Power, Jr., with additional material by William E. Warren, *Basketball, Concepts and Techniques* (1983); B. G. Kelly, "For the Love of the Game," *Boston* magazine (Feb. 1991); and Peter Bjarkman, *Biographical History of Basketball* (2000).

ABRAHAM A. DAVIDSON

CRABBE, Clarence Linden ("Buster") (*b.* 7 February 1908 in Oakland, California; *d.* 23 April 1983 in Scottsdale, Arizona), champion Olympic swimmer who broke five world records and earned more than fifty world and national championships; movie actor; and promoter of physical fitness and nutrition via the lecture circuit, television, and publications.

Financial circumstances compelled Crabbe's parents, Edward Clinton Simmons Crabbe, Jr., a real estate agent, and Agnes Lucy McNamara Crabbe, a homemaker, to move the family to Hawaii, home of Crabbe's paternal grandparents, when Crabbe was two years old. After attending local schools, he enrolled at Honolulu Military Academy, which, by the time he graduated in June 1927, had merged with Punahou High School. Crabbe and his younger brother Edward ("Buddy") learned to swim and surf at an early age. Crabbe also excelled in football, baseball, track, and horseback riding, and he earned sixteen sports letters (including three in swimming) in high school. When his father prohibited Buddy from traveling alone with a Honolulu swimming team to Japan, Crabbe qualified as another teammate.

Buster Crabbe as Tarzan, 1930s. Associated Press MOVIE STAR NEWS

As a freshman at the University of Hawaii, Crabbe qualified to compete on the U.S. swimming team (which included the Olympic swimming champ and film star Johnny Weissmuller) heading for Amsterdam for the summer Olympic Games in 1928. Crabbe won a bronze medal for the men's 1,500-meter freestyle at 20.28.8. One-tenth of a second prevented him from winning the bronze for the men's 400-meter freestyle.

On 22 August 1928 in Graz, Austria, Crabbe broke the world's record for the men's 300-meter backstroke. In 1929, he led the Outrigger Canoe Club of Honolulu, a team that included his brother, to victory in the national outdoors team championship, held for a second year at San Francisco; he won 21 of the 23 points for the team. Crabbe decided to transfer that year to a prelaw track with a major in political science at the University of Southern California; he graduated with a B.A. in June 1932. From 1927 through 1931 Crabbe held the one-mile swim title. He cautiously safeguarded his amateur status as he prepared for the 1932 Olympics in Los Angeles. Among other jobs, the six-foot athlete played an extra in a few Hollywood films as well as a stunt man (at no fee) for Joel McCrea in the motion picture *The Most Dangerous Game* (1932).

The American men's swimming team (this time without Weissmuller) was concerned about the powerful Japanese in the 1932 Olympic Games. During 1931 meets in Japan, the American team, with Crabbe as captain, placed fourth in the 400 meters and fifth in both the 800 and 1,500 meters. Crabbe proudly led the parade of 1932 Olympians. By this time officially known in competition as "Buster Crabbe," he became the only non-Japanese to win a 1932 gold medal in a major men's swimming event. He set a new Olympic record in the men's 400-meter freestyle at 4:48.4, as he defeated the world record holder, France's Jean Taris, who won the silver at 4:48.5. Crabbe acquired no medal for his final event when he placed fifth in the men's 1,500-meter freestyle. He soon retired from amateur sports. His fastest amateur time was said to have been 4:38 for the 400-meter freestyle.

From among two dozen athletes, Crabbe won the Paramount screen test search at the 1932 Olympics for a potentially new Weissmuller-type athlete–screen star; his contract was renewed until 1939. Crabbe's first starring role was in *King of the Jungle* (1933) as a Tarzan-like lead named Kaspa, the lion man. Crabbe married Adah Virginia Held on 13 April 1933, and they eventually had one son and two daughters. Two months after the wedding the studio lent him out to play the lead in a twelve-part serial entitled *Tarzan the Fearless*.

Paramount had presented Crabbe in so many westerns that a 1936 poll ranked him tenth among the most moneymaking western stars. But that year Universal borrowed Crabbe to star in what turned out to be his most popular series, the million-dollar, thirteen-part *Flash Gordon* (1936), one of the studio's biggest profitmakers.

Crabbe became the "king of the sound serials." His amateur swimming achievements highlighted his exceptionally masculine good looks and impressive physique so that he readily became a serial matinee idol in Hollywood; he represented a real-life American hero to many young people as he continued appearing in more feature films during the 1930s and 1940s and more serials during the 1950s and 1960s. Two final films, *The Comeback Trail* (1971) and *Swim Team* (1980), passed into oblivion.

Crabbe never let his swimming prowess fall into disuse. (There is even a color photograph of him swimming and looking robust just days before his death in 1983.) After Weissmuller's departure in October 1940, Crabbe joined Eleanor Holm in Billy Rose's *Aquacade* at New York's World's Fair, swimming in the specially constructed 275-foot pool at Flushing Meadows. Later, Crabbe and Weissmuller appeared together in two films: *Swamp Fire* (1946) and *Captive Girl* (1950). During World War II Crabbe toured the nation with his own *Buster Crabbe's Aquaparade;* during a three-month period at Fort Sill, Oklahoma, he and Al "Fuzzy" St. John (a comic costar in his later western features) made instructional field artillery films.

Television attracted Crabbe during the 1950s, and he and his wife presented a fifteen-minute weekday morning exercise show, *Figure Fashioning* (WOR-TV, New York). With a proper diet, regular workouts at the gym, and at least two days per week at the pool, he maintained his own weight close to that of his Olympic days, around 188 pounds. He also hosted an afternoon children's show, *The Buster Crabbe Show*, in which he presented some of his serials and feature films and responded to children's letters. From 1955 to 1957, Crabbe starred in the television series *Captain Gallant of the Foreign Legion.*

In addition, Crabbe appeared on top dramatic and comedy programs as well as talk shows, especially between 1952 and 1961. *Dial M for Murder* marked his 1955 stage debut, in Kennebunkport, Maine. During the mid-1960s he recorded a spoken-record album on Flash Gordon; New York's public television network aired his entire *Flash Gordon* serial in 1975.

In the summer of 1951 Crabbe relocated his family from California to Somerville, New Jersey, and for the next eighteen years he worked on available Saturdays as director of water sports at the Concord, a prominent Catskills resort hotel in Kiamesha Lake, New York. He was also a silent partner in the Shelton Hotel Health Club in New York City. He served as vice president and then executive direc-

tor of Cascade Industries in Edison, New Jersey, which was responsible for producing Buster Crabbe swimming pools. In 1952 he cofounded what became known as Buster Crabbe's Camp Menaga for Boys (it was coeducational the first three years) on Saranac Lake in the Adirondacks; he sold it in 1964. Crabbe was among the first honorees of the International Swimming Hall of Fame (ISHOF), in Fort Lauderdale, Florida, in 1965. Along with Weissmuller and Holm, he served as a guest commentator with Jack Whitaker for the first international meet sponsored by the ISHOF (*Sports Spectacular*, CBS) and joined Weissmuller on *The Ed Sullivan Show* to endorse the ISHOF in 1967.

Crabbe still competed, particularly during the 1970s, with the national AAU, and he won the men's 1,500-meter freestyle in the 60- to 65-year-old group in 1972. By the 1970s he was living in Scottsdale, Arizona. He and Weissmuller were feted at City Hall (10 September 1976) upon their election to the World Body Building Guild Hall of Fame. In an article for the *New York Times* (23 July 1979), Crabbe commented on the improvements in competitive swimming techniques, diet, and even the pools themselves since his Olympic days; he exclaimed that he "couldn't even match the girls" in current Olympic timing. He served on the Organizing Olympic Committee for the 1984 Olympics in Los Angeles and on 30 July 1982 he led into the Los Angeles Coliseum fellow athletes from the 1932 Olympics who were joining in the fiftieth anniversary celebration of those Los Angeles games. Crabbe died of a sudden heart attack at his home on 23 April 1983, before the games were played. His remains were cremated and given to his family.

Crabbe's positive, energetic, and earnest personality helped to convey at the pool and on the large and small screens his lifelong commitment to the importance of exercise and nutrition. When interviewed for sports fans, he was proud of and content with his amateur swimming achievements but never failed to conclude that each generation of swimmers outshone him in endurance, dedication, and speed—because that is the ever-progressive nature of the sport.

★

Crabbe authored two fitness books: *Energistics: The Simple Shape-Up Exercise Plan* (1976), and, with Raphael Cilento, M.D., *Buster Crabbe's Arthritis Exercise Book* (1980). James Robert Parish and William T. Leonard, *Hollywood Players, The Thirties* (1976) provides information about Crabbe's film career. Karl Whitezel, *Buster Crabbe: A Self-Portrait* (1997), was published fourteen years after Crabbe's death. Extensive interviews from the 1960s appear in Don Shay, *Conversations*, vol. 1 (1969). Interviews in the *New York Times* include Val Adams, "Children and Women Come First: Buster Crabbe Tries to Entertain One and Help the Other" (13 May 1951); and "Then and Now" (23 July 1979), with a brief discussion about competitive swimming. William Oscar Johnson, "A Star Was Born," *Sports Illustrated* 61 (18 July 1984) contains detailed text and stills. Obituaries are in the *Washington Post* and *Los Angeles Times* (both 24 Apr. 1983), and the *New York Times* and *Chicago Tribune* (both 25 Apr. 1983).

MADELINE SAPIENZA

CUNNINGHAM, Glenn (*b.* 4 August 1909 in Atlanta, Kansas; *d.* 10 March 1988 in Menifee, Arkansas), two-time U.S. Olympic track and field team member who set collegiate, national, and world records after overcoming serious physical challenges.

Cunningham was one of seven children born to Henry Clint and Rosa (Moore) Cunningham. In February 1917 he and an older brother, Floyd, started a fire in the potbellied stove at the Sunflower Schoolhouse, lighting what they thought was kerosene, and causing the building to became engulfed in flames. As Cunningham recalled, "Incredibly, both of us . . . ran two miles to our home after trying to put out the fire in our clothing. When we arrived, we took off Floyd's shoes and put them on a small sled outside the door, and the fire remaining consumed both the sled and the shoes."

The fuel can had actually contained gasoline. Floyd died nine days later, and flames left the younger Cunningham so badly injured that doctors recommended leg amputation. His parents didn't acquiesce, and when the bandages were removed, his right leg was nearly three inches shorter than the left. Both of his arches were damaged, and the toes were nearly burned off his left foot. Local folklore still recalls the boy's determination to walk, steadying himself on a plow as his mother watched from inside the house. "As long as you believe you can do things," Cunningham said in a 1970s interview, "they're not impossible. You place limits on yourself mentally, not physically."

Although the Cunningham family left Kansas to work melon and hay fields in Colorado, they returned to their home state in 1922. Cunningham attended high school in Elkhart, where he participated in football, basketball, and track, sang in the glee club, and studied the violin. He helped his mother take in washing and his father clean manure out of barns. Before each track meet, he required an extensive massage and an hour-long warm-up period; this pre-race routine continued throughout his entire track and field career.

As a high school senior Cunningham won one-mile runs, state-level outdoor races, and the National Interscholastic meet in Chicago, where, during his last high school race, he set a world prep record of 4:24.7 for the mile. At Kansas University he garnered six Big Six mile-run titles and two National Collegiate Athletic Association (NCAA)

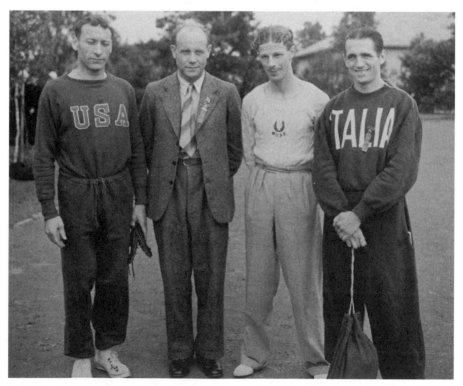

Glenn Cunningham (*left*) and fellow Olympic distance runners Paavo Nurmi, Jack Lovelock, and Louis Beccali, at the Berlin Olympics in 1936. ASSOCIATED PRESS AP

titles. He also earned ten Amateur Athletic Union (AAU) national titles throughout the 1930s, five of which were in the outdoor one-mile.

In 1932 Cunningham broke the American one-mile record (4:11.1), won the NCAA 1500-meter event, and placed fourth in the 1500-meter race at the Los Angeles Olympics. The following year, 1933, was a banner year; Cunningham won the coveted Sullivan Award as the country's top amateur athlete after winning the NCAA mile (4:09.8) and the AAU 800- and 1500-meter and setting a 4:06.7 world mile record at the Princeton Invitational Meet. Later that year the city of Elkhart celebrated Glenn Cunningham Day when he returned from Europe after winning eleven straight races. In 1934 Cunningham finished his B.A. in physical education at the University of Kansas.

Cunningham competed in the 1936 Olympics in Berlin, Germany, when 43 percent of the American population favored an Olympic boycott because of the Nazi leader Adolf Hitler's ideologies (Gallup Poll, 1935). Nevertheless, 384 Americans competed, including Jesse Owens, who won four gold track and field medals. Cunningham came home with a silver medal in the 1500-meter (3:48.4). He ran hard in the third lap, but Jack Loveland of New Zealand set a world record of 3:47.8. Cunningham was both disappointed and pleased with his silver medal: it was not gold, but he had broken the previous Olympic record. That same year he set an 800-meter world record of 1:49.7 and graduated from the University of Iowa with an M.A. in physical education.

In 1938 Cunningham boasted twelve of the fastest thirty-one track records, completed his Ph.D. in physical education at New York University, and was invited by Dartmouth College to test their new high-banked indoor track. There, he was described as "less the lissom runner, with his heavy stride and wide-thick shoulders, than a powerful blocking back or a nimble hodcarrier." Flanked by six Dartmouth runners, Cunningham completed his race at 4:04:4, "two full seconds faster than any other man had ever run the distance at any time," making the one-mile the "glamour event at indoor meets." While this race was unsanctioned, Cunningham's time wasn't surpassed until 1955.

After teaching physical education at Cornell University from 1940 to 1944, Cunningham joined the navy. There he attained the rank of lieutenant, established physical training programs at the Great Lakes and San Diego stations, and toured military hospitals to encourage the wounded. Cunningham had married Margaret Speir in August 1934 and they divorced in 1946; the following year, he married his second wife, Ruth Sheffield. Over the course of the two marriages Cunningham fathered twelve children.

He and Ruth helped thousands of troubled youth over a thirty-year span. They housed them at their 840-acre exotic animal ranch near Wichita, Kansas, and scrimped on personal expenses, going without a car for five years. At times they were almost close to broke but were eventually assisted by a nonprofit group called the Glenn Cunningham Youth Ranch. Cunningham went on lecture tours to raise money. He advocated discipline (errant teens got "backsides burned with [my] belt") along with love and warned others not to let "any pig-headed psychologist tell you different."

Cunningham donated land in Arkansas for another youth ranch, this one called Glenhaven in his honor. He died of a heart attack at the age of seventy-eight. Memorial services were conducted in Conway, Arkansas, and his body was cremated.

Cunningham, nicknamed "Iron Horse of Kansas," was inducted into the Kansas Sports Hall of Fame in 1961 and the National Track and Field Hall of Fame in Charleston, West Virginia, in 1974. He was named outstanding track performer of Madison Square Garden in New York City in 1978 and was inducted into the National Track and Field Hall of Fame and the Kansas State High School Athletic Association Hall of Fame in 1979 and 1983, respectively.

While Cunningham's track and field accomplishments, from the collegiate level to Olympian, were remarkable, his ability to overcome challenges was even more noteworthy. Besides being an outstanding athlete, he was well known for his principles and convictions. His status as role model and his contributions to the development of youth are considered among his finest achievements.

★

Cunningham's autobiography is *Never Quit* (1981). See also F. Glen Lloyd, "He Puts Kids on the Right Track," *Today's Health* 46, no. 12 (Dec. 1968) and "When Cunningham of Kansas Runs, He Clocks Himself by His Stride," the *Kansas City Times* (12 Mar. 1938). A front-page article serving as an obituary is in the *Tri-State News* (Elkhart, Kan., 17 March 1988).

KELLY BOYER SAGERT

CUNNINGHAM, William John ("Billy") (*b.* 3 June 1943 in Brooklyn, New York), professional basketball player known for his vertical leap who was a top scorer and rebounder in the 1960s and 1970s, and who later became a winning coach, television commentator, and team owner.

Cunningham grew up in Brooklyn and on his fifth birthday he received a basketball. He ran to the nearest school, three blocks away, and started shooting baskets. "I lived there that summer," he later recalled. "I can't put my finger on it exactly, but there was just something about the game. I loved it instantly." Cunningham attended Erasmus Hall

High School and became known as the Kangaroo Kid for his impressive jumping ability. In 1961, his senior year, Cunningham led his team to the city championship and was a high school All-American.

The University of North Carolina (UNC) coach Frank McGuire convinced Cunningham to enroll there. Cunningham arrived in Chapel Hill just as Dean Smith was taking over as the head basketball coach of the UNC Tar Heels. At six feet, seven inches tall and 220 pounds, Cunningham was a consistent scorer and fierce rebounder. During a game in 1963 against Clemson University, he grabbed a record twenty-seven rebounds. Against Tulane University on 10 December 1964, he set a UNC record by scoring forty-eight points. He was twice named an All-American during his collegiate years. In his final season, he was the Atlantic Coast Conference Player of the Year. For his college career he averaged 24.8 points per game and set a school record with 1,062 rebounds.

In 1965 Cunningham graduated from UNC and was selected by the Philadelphia 76ers in the first round of the National Basketball Association (NBA) draft. In his rookie season of 1965–1966 Cunningham was at first assigned to be a guard, then switched positions, becoming a small forward. Averaging 14.3 points per game, Cunningham was named to the league's All-Rookie team. In 1966 Cunning-

Billy Cunningham, c. 1975. AP/WIDE WORLD PHOTOS

ham married Sondra; they had two daughters.

In the 1966–1967 season the 76ers were a powerhouse, winning sixty-eight against only thirteen losses and beating the Boston Celtics and San Francisco in the playoffs to win the championship. Some have called the team the greatest of all time. Cunningham could not even crack the starting lineup—which included Wilt Chamberlain, Chet Walker, Lucious Jackson, Hal Greer, and Wally Jones—but he averaged 18.5 points and 7.3 rebounds per game coming off the bench.

The following season Philadelphia won sixty-two games and the Eastern Division title but lost to the Celtics in the playoffs. Cunningham scored 18.9 points per game. The next year he exploded for 24.8 points per game and 12.8 rebounds and he was named a first-team All-Star. In the 1969–1970 season he averaged a career high of 26.1 points, the fourth highest in the league, and was again selected as an All-Star. In the 1970–1971 season he again was an All-Star starter and finished ninth in the NBA with 23.0 points per game. The next season, the consistent Cunningham scored 23.3 points per game and was selected as an All-Star for the fourth time.

Cunningham played with visible enthusiasm. He was a tough, intense, competitive player who used his intelligence as much as his physical talents. "The beauty part of playing basketball," he once said, "is that your mind is occupied with playing basketball and nothing else, and you're having fun."

After the 1971–1972 season, Cunningham left Philadelphia and the NBA for the rival American Basketball Association (ABA), signing on with the (North) Carolina Cougars. The two teams waged a court battle, each claiming the rights to Cunningham, but the new league won. At Carolina, he was reunited with the coach Larry Brown, who had been a UNC teammate. The Cougars had finished last the previous season, but with Brown and Cunningham inspiring the team, the Cougars finished first. Cunningham led the league in steals with 216 and was fourth in scoring with a 24.1 points-per-game average. He was named Most Valuable Player in the ABA.

In his second season with Carolina, Cunningham was hampered by injuries, but he still managed a 20.5 average in 32 games. In 1974 Cunningham returned to the 76ers. In the twentieth game of the 1975–1976 season, Cunningham's career suddenly and inexplicably ended. While he was dribbling down the court, his knee exploded. He was finished as a player. "In a way the injury made things easy for me," he said later. "I never had to agonize over that decision all athletes face" about when to retire. For his eleven-year career, Cunningham averaged 21.2 points per game. He scored 16,310 points and pulled down nearly 8,000 rebounds. His jersey number "32" was later retired by Philadelphia.

Cunningham returned to Philadelphia in 1977 to become the coach of the 76ers, replacing Gene Shue. He inherited a team of underachievers led by Julius Erving. Knowing he was inexperienced, Cunningham assembled a group of veteran ex-coaches as assistants, including Chuck Daly, who later to become head coach of the Detroit Pistons. Under Cunningham, the team reached the Eastern Conference finals in 1978 and the NBA finals in 1980 and 1982. After acquiring the talented Moses Malone for the 1982–1983 season, Philadelphia won sixty-five regular season games and then the league championship, losing one of thirteen play-off games. They were a winning team the next two seasons but could not repeat as champions, and Cunningham retired after the 1984–1985 season.

Cunningham reached 200, 300, and 400 wins faster than any previous coach in NBA history. Fiery and volatile, he would pace the sidelines, driving his team relentlessly. During his eight seasons as the coach of the 76ers, Philadelphia won 454 regular season games and lost 196. His teams won sixty-six play-off games and lost twenty-nine. On 6 May 1986 Cunningham was elected into the NBA Hall of Fame, as one of its ten initial inductees. In 1996 he was voted one of the top fifty players at the NBA's fiftieth anniversary.

Cunningham was part of a group that helped to secure an NBA franchise for Miami in the late 1980s. He spent several years as one of the owners of the Miami Heat and the team quickly became a contender. In 1997 Cunningham became the expert commentator for the CBS television network's coverage of NBA games. He got kudos for his smooth-sounding, incisive work with the play-by-play announcer Dick Stockton.

Throughout his life, Cunningham excelled at all aspects of the game he loved. As a player, he was fiery yet consistent, pulling down rebounds and scoring points. He was a consummate team player, and he used the same unifying concept and enthusiasm to become a successful head coach. As an owner and commentator, he also made a favorable impression. "I don't know anything he has done that hasn't worked," said the Orlando, Florida, executive Pat Williams. "It's a remarkable life."

★

There is no full-length biography of Cunningham, but he is mentioned in most authoritative histories of basketball and in several magazine and online profiles. See, for example, Jan Hubbard, ed., *The Official NBA Basketball Encyclopedia,* 3d ed. (2000).

MICHAEL BETZOLD

D

D'AMATO, Constantine ("Cus") (*b*. 17 January 1908 in New York City; *d*. 4 November 1985 in New York City), professional boxing manager and trainer who opened his home to young, would-be fighters from the urban ghettos; several of these youths became world champions.

D'Amato was born in the Bronx, the seventh of eight sons of Italian immigrants Damiamo D'Amato, a coal and ice deliverer, and Elizabeth (Rosato) D'Amato, a homemaker. Tragically, only five of the eight children survived infancy; likewise, D'Amato's mother died when he was very young. He learned to box as a child from his father and an older brother. D'Amato's youthful matches usually took place on the city streets rather than in the ring. It was in the midst of such street fighting that D'Amato, at age twelve, received a severe blow to the head that put an end to his hopes of entering the professional boxing arena. The impact left him with one eye severely impaired and not long afterward, in another street fight, D'Amato tangled with a bona fide heavyweight fighter. He took another serious blow to the head, which left him dazed for several days. With lingering effects from both blows, D'Amato ultimately dropped out of high school and went to work in a mill. By age twenty-two his hair had turned gray, and he was nearly bald by his early thirties. Already color-blind, he faced the premature deterioration of his eyesight and senses of hearing, taste, and smell.

In 1930, following a brief stint working on the campaign of Fiorello La Guardia, the mayor of New York City, D'Amato entered into a partnership with Jack Barrow to establish the Empire Sports Club at the Gramercy Gym on Fourteenth Street near Manhattan's Union Square. D'Amato also served as a boxing coach in the U.S. Army during the late 1930s, but he was discharged before the United States entered World War II. After the war ended he returned to New York City and devoted all of his time to training young fighters; he lived and even slept at the Gramercy Gym. D'Amato took such a personal interest in each of his pupils that he reputedly refused to take his fair portion of the prize purses they won. He valued mental acuity over physical prowess and instructed his boxers accordingly. The troubled youths he took into his gym during the 1940s included the young Rocky Graziano, who became a middleweight champion in 1947 and a hall of fame boxer, and in 1952 D'Amato began training Floyd Patterson. In 1956, at age twenty-one, Patterson won the heavyweight championship, the youngest boxer to do so until Mike Tyson won the belt in 1986 at age twenty. D'Amato, who helped to train Tyson as well, died before his last protégé's victory.

The crime-riddled business of boxing during the 1950s was controlled by the International Boxing Club. D'Amato stood personally at odds with this alleged racketeering organization and was instrumental in breaking its hold on the sport. In the late 1950s, largely through D'Amato's efforts, the prizefight industry was opened up to support bout

Cus D'Amato, 1972. AP/WIDE WORLD PHOTOS

venues outside of Madison Square Garden, where the boxing monopoly at that time was centered. Perhaps in retaliation against D'Amato for his antagonistic stance toward the crime machine, New York City revoked his manager's license during the late 1950s, allegedly because of his associations with known underworld figures. He petitioned successfully for reinstatement of the license in 1959, but abandoned his New York City gym altogether in 1962.

With financial backing from two associates, Jim Jacobs and Bill Cayton, in 1962 D'Amato established a new gymnasium facility in Catskill, upstate New York, near the home of Camille Ewald. D'Amato and Ewald had met in the 1940s and eventually entered into a common-law relationship. Ewald supported D'Amato in his dedication to training socially challenged youths, and she allowed her home to function as a halfway house for D'Amato's pupils, often fulfilling the role of a mother figure to them. Most notably, D'Amato and Ewald, in anticipation of Tyson's future athletic success, established legal guardianship over the young man in an effort to protect him both personally and financially from the cutthroat boxing establishment.

D'Amato and Ewald never married, although their close friendship lasted for decades, until his death.

D'Amato was well known for giving away, reinvesting, and loaning out his money as quickly as it was acquired. According to his one-time pupil Patterson, D'Amato "gave money away like . . . water," because he "cared more about his fighters than money." Because of D'Amato's great generosity and despite his frugality, he was driven to bankruptcy in the early 1970s and was thereafter subsidized largely by Jacobs, his business partner. According to the journalist José Torres, a former Olympic boxer and light-heavyweight champion, D'Amato's distaste for money was intense; the trainer had "an aversion to opulence . . . [which] he felt was a creation of the devil."

D'Amato died from pneumonia on 4 November 1985, and was buried in Catskill. After his death, his friends and colleagues held a memorial service at the old Gramercy Gym. Many who knew D'Amato well continued to quote his wisdom years later, remembering him as a kindly trainer who was two parts philosopher and one part sportsman. As a former D'Amato protégé and a lifelong friend, Torres applauded his mentor's ability to nurture wayward boys toward respectability. "[Cus] understood the boy's defensive posture," Torres said of D'Amato's influence over Tyson, a particularly incorrigible youth. Tyson was "a remorseless predator. . . . Just the sort of challenge Cus savored."

★

Dave Anderson interviewed D'Amato for *In the Corner: Great Boxing Trainers Talk About Their Art* (1991). D'Amato is discussed in José Torres, *Fire and Fear: The Inside Story of Mike Tyson* (1989), and Ronald K. Fried, *Corner Men: The Great Boxing Trainers* (1991). For information on D'Amato's relationship with Tyson see "Pennies from Heaven," *Las Vegas Review-Journal* (12 Jan. 1999). An obituary is in the *New York Times Biographical Service* 16 (5 Nov. 1985).

GLORIA COOKSEY

DANDRIDGE, Ray(mond) Emmitt (*b.* 31 August 1913 in Richmond, Virginia; *d.* 12 February 1994 in Melbourne, Florida), National Baseball Hall of Fame third baseman known for his slick fielding and line-drive batting in the Negro Leagues.

Dandridge was the only son of Archie Dandridge, a textile worker and former semiprofessional catcher, and Alberta Thompson Dandridge. He learned to play baseball with makeshift equipment on a weedy field as a young boy. He was ten years old when he and his sisters moved to Buffalo, New York, to live with their mother.

Dandridge attended Buffalo's integrated schools and

participated in all sports before dropping out of Public School Twenty-eight after completing the ninth grade. For a while he attended a vocational school part time. At age eighteen he moved back to Richmond and began playing semiprofessional baseball there. A year later the squat five-foot, seven-inch, 170 pounder became a member of the Paramounts, who booked a game with the barnstorming Detroit Stars of the Negro National League (NNL). Dandridge had a good game against the Stars, hitting a home run and impressing the Stars manager Candy Jim Taylor, who offered him a spot on the team. Dandridge was reluctant to join Detroit, but Taylor persisted and Dandridge's father persuaded him to try to make a career in baseball.

Dandridge, known as "Hooks" or "Dandy," joined the Stars for $15 per week in 1933, in the depths of the Great Depression, and Taylor was unable to meet the payroll. The manager disbanded the team and sold its bus to raise cash to pay for the players' transportation back home. Dandridge finished the season with the Nashville (Tennessee) Elite Giants. The next year he joined the Newark (New Jersey) Dodgers and remained with them and their successors, the Newark Eagles, for much of his career. His batting average hovered around .350 in NNL play.

Dandridge was regarded as the finest third baseman of the 1930s Negro Leagues, if not of all time. Monte Irvin, his teammate on the Newark Eagles, said of Dandridge, "Once you saw him you'd never forget him because he was short and bowlegged. But he was quick as a cat and if the ball got to him real quick, he would always time it so his throw would just beat you. When he had to hurry it was the same way, the throw would just beat you. He was the best I've ever seen on a swinging bunt. Because he was already short and would come in full speed, take that ball, and toss it underhand and just get you. It was a thing of beauty just to see him come in and flip that ball underhand without even slowing down on it."

Dandridge used an oversized fielder's glove and swallowed ground balls like a vacuum cleaner. He was a clutch hitter who sprayed line drives in every direction. During the 1939 season Dandridge was lured to Latin America by the pleasant rustle of cash. He went first to Venezuela to play for the Caracas Vargas club. After the team won the Venezuelan League championship, Dandridge went to Mexico. He hit .347 to help the Veracruz Diablos take the Mexican title. Dandridge earned about $10,000 per season in baseball-mad Mexico. He received extra money for living expenses, and his first wife, Florence, was provided a maid. Dandridge and his wife had a daughter and two sons.

Mexico had another attraction besides good salaries for Negro Leaguers. African-American players were not segregated and were treated like first-class citizens. However in 1942 Dandridge returned to the United States and the Newark Eagles, joining two other future Hall of Famers—

Willie Wells and Larry Doby—in the infield. He batted .370 and led the NNL in hits, runs, and total bases. He was chosen for the annual Negro League All-Star game for the third time that year. He went back to Mexico in 1945 as the playing manager of the Mexico City Reds.

In 1948 Dandridge again came back to the United States to manage the New York Cubans. The next year he was signed by the New York Giants (later the San Francisco Giants), along with the Cubans pitcher Dave Barnhill. Both were assigned to the top Giants farm club, the Minneapolis Millers of the AAA American Association, and were the first African Americans on the team. Dandridge was thirty-six years old and past his baseball prime years, but he hit .362 in the 1949 season.

In 1950 Dandridge was joined on the Millers by the nineteen-year-old Willie Mays, a rising Giants star who had played for the Birmingham Black Barons for two years. Mays was called up to New York late in the 1951 season, leaving Dandridge forlorn in Minneapolis. Despite his disappointment at not joining Mays on the Giants, Dandridge had a fine year, batting .311 in 1950 and leading the league in hits. He was awarded the Silver Ball Award as the American Association's Most Valuable Player. Some sources speculate that Dandridge was not called to New York or sold to another major league club because Giants owner Horace Stoneham thought he was a big drawing card in Minneapolis.

Dandridge hit .324 in 1951, his third season with the Millers. The following year he batted .291, then left Minneapolis for a season in the Pacific Coast League with the Sacramento Solons and Oakland Oaks, both in California. That was his last year in the minors. He spent 1953 as a player-manager of the semiprofessional Bismarck (North Dakota) Bisons before hanging up his spikes for good.

Dandridge went home to Newark and worked for several years as a bartender and manager of a liquor store. He then joined the city's recreation department as a youth worker. Upon his retirement, the city council honored Dandridge with a resolution saluting him for "the immeasurable contribution he made as a pioneer in breaking down racial barriers for the many black athletes who followed in his footsteps." In 1985 a baseball field in Newark's West Side Park was named for him. Dandridge also scouted briefly for the San Francisco Giants.

The culminating honor of Dandridge's lifetime came in 1987, when he was elected to the National Baseball Hall of Fame in Cooperstown, New York. Dandridge concluded his touching speech after his induction by smiling and asking, "What took you so long?" In his day he had set the standard for third basemen until Brooks Robinson came along in 1955.

Dandridge and his second wife, Henrietta, had no children, and spent their retirement years in Palm Bay, Florida, which named an avenue for him. He died after a seven-year battle with prostate cancer and is buried at Fountain-head Memorial Park in Palm Bay.

★

The most complete summary of Dandridge's life is in James A. Riley, *Dandy, Day, and the Devil* (1987), which also has brief biographies of Leon Day and Willie Wells, two other African-American baseball stars. See also James A. Riley, *The Biographical Encyclopedia of the Negro Baseball Leagues* (1994), and Dick Clark and Larry Lester, *The Negro Leagues Book* (1994).

ROBERT W. PETERSON

DAVENPORT, Lindsay (*b.* 8 June 1976 in Palos Verdes, California), tennis player who was the first U.S.-born player to win the U.S. Open since Chris Evert.

Davenport grew up the youngest of three daughters in a family that was oriented toward volleyball. Her father, Wink, was a member of the 1968 U.S. Olympic men's volleyball team; her mother, Ann, played and coached the sport; and her two older siblings played on college teams. Despite all this, Davenport turned to tennis at an early age and used her height (she grew to six feet, two inches tall) and strength to advantage. What she lacked was a graceful presence on the court. When she approached Robert Lansdorp, the former coach of two-time U.S. Open champion

Lindsay Davenport. AP/WIDE WORLD PHOTOS

Tracy Austin, for lessons, he dismissed her at first and only later responded to her tearful requests. Lansdorp became an inspiration to his protégé, but even he commented on the discrepancy between her terrific shotmaking and her lack of athletic coordination.

Davenport was a shy and awkward teenager. Most of her fellow high school classmates in Murrieta, California, did not even know she was an active tennis player until she won both the singles and doubles titles at the U.S. Junior Open in 1992. A few months later she became a professional. Her first professional tournament was at Indian Wells, California. At her second tourney, the Virginia Slims of Florida, Davenport stunned observers with an upset victory over Argentina's Gabriela Sabatini. These early successes attracted considerable attention, but Davenport lost in the first round of the French Open that spring, and some commentators were inclined to see her as a one-season wonder.

Around the time that Davenport turned professional, an important and revealing book was published about the women's tour. Novelist and journalist Michael Mewshaw explored the good, bad, and ugly of women's tennis in *Ladies of the Court: Grace and Disgrace on the Women's Tennis Tour* (1993). After spending an entire year (1991) following the tour and conducting interviews, Mewshaw chronicled the numerous rivalries, the frenetic pace of competition, and the conflicts endured by young women who wanted to win on the court, but still wanted to appear feminine. Readers were inclined to think that the women's tour had disintegrated into a soulless quest for money and celebrity status.

But Davenport never fit into any of these stereotypes. While she struggled with an awkward presence and with her weight, she nearly always seemed the epitome of an unspoiled young woman with her head truly on her shoulders. Davenport did not get bogged down with clothing designers or endorsements; rather, she stuck to the business of playing tennis. Likewise, her family was most atypical. Because of the family emphasis on volleyball, Davenport was not pestered by her parents or her siblings over her shots or strategy. They applauded her successes but seemed genuinely busy in their own right, and her mother was not even present at some of Davenport's great successes (notably at Wimbledon in 1999). When questioned about this, Davenport replied that it was a great relief to have a family that had a life of its own.

Always cheerful and friendly, Davenport seldom seemed "let down" after losing a big match, and she claimed her parents never put pressure on her, whether to win the big events or anything else. Davenport moved up the ranks slowly and steadily. In 1995 she was ranked twelfth in the world, and in 1996 she rose to number nine and won the

Olympic gold medal in singles play at the summer games in Atlanta. In 1998 she reached the number-one spot.

Davenport's height and physical strength were complemented by a huge forehand, one of the most explosive strokes on the tour. While she was not an elegant volleyer, she had a terrific overhead, and physically she seemed reminiscent of Martina Navratilova in strength and capacity. Like Navratilova, Davenport struggled with weight problems. She was significantly overweight during most of her first five years on tour, leading some fellow players to dub her "Dump Truck." These cruel comments did not set Davenport back, but the strain of her parents' divorce in the late 1990s took a true toll.

In 1997, however, Davenport made a determined effort to improve her fitness, and breakthrough results soon followed. Her first big success came at the U.S. Open in 1998. She swept through the tournament without the loss of a set and was 69–15 overall that year. Nine months later she defeated Steffi Graf in the finals at Wimbledon; again, Davenport lost no sets in the tournament. One year later she reached the finals of Wimbledon and the semifinals of the U.S. Open but was beaten both times by Venus Williams, whose catlike quickness enabled her to outmaneuver Davenport on court.

Coached by Robert Van't Hof, Davenport made plans for a major move in 2001. She was hampered by leg injuries that kept her out of the French Open, but she returned in June and won at Eastbourne, the warm-up tournament for Wimbledon, in convincing fashion. The All-England Championships began well for Davenport. She did not lose a set as she cruised to the semifinals, where she met Venus Williams once again. Davenport fans were dismayed by her performance in the match. Williams played flawless tennis, while Davenport struggled with her serve and strokes. The end result, 6–1, 6–7, 6–1, convincingly demonstrated how dominant Williams could be when her game was "on." Despite the loss, Davenport remained just about the only player on tour who was seen as able to compete with Williams in the power department.

Jim Greer of *Sports Illustrated* came close to describing Davenport when he wrote: "She is, in a way, the Sandra Bullock of tennis." Like the actress Bullock, Davenport was unfailingly modest and unassuming in press interviews, and unlike many of her fellow players, she seemed to obtain a great deal of joy from the game itself. In that, she resembled a much earlier player, the Australian Evonne Goolagong, in the 1970s.

Whether Davenport will continue her solid success, or whether she will rise to greater heights, has yet to be seen. But in a sport that is known for prima donnas and posturing, she is a refreshing example of a "nice girl" who wins her matches.

★

Articles tracing Davenport's career throughout the 1990s include "Davenport, 16, Makes a Quick Start," *USA Today* (8 Apr. 1993); L. Jon Wertheim, "Lissome Lindsay," *Sports Illustrated* (24 Aug. 1998); *New York Times* (5 July 1999); Jim Greer, "The Nice Girl Who Finished First," *Tennis* (Sept. 1999); and Rick Reilly, "You Call This a Tennis Mom?" *Sports Illustrated* (13 Sept. 1999).

SAMUEL WILLARD CROMPTON

DAVIS, Al(len) (*b.* 4 July 1929 in Brockton, Massachusetts), football coach and executive who built the Oakland Raiders into one of the dominant National Football League (NFL) teams of the 1970s and 1980s.

Davis is one of two sons of Louis Davis, a businessman, and Rose Kirshenbaum Davis, a homemaker. The family moved to the Crown Heights neighborhood in Brooklyn, New York, when Davis was five, and he spent his youth playing sports in the public parks. At Erasmus Hall High School Davis played varsity basketball for coach Al Badain, his first major influence in sports with whom he retained a lifelong connection, and was named "Most Popular Boy." Davis enrolled at Wittenberg College in Ohio in January 1947, but after one semester transferred for the fall term to Syracuse University, where the six-foot-tall student played on the junior varsity basketball team. Seeking more playing time, Davis tried Hartwick College in New York for a month in the fall of 1948 before returning to Syracuse. Failing again to make the varsity basketball team, Davis drifted toward football. He studied intensely the new, innovative coach hired by Syracuse for the 1949 season, Ben Schwartzwalder, observing his practices and poring over playbooks borrowed from friends who were team members.

After graduating from Syracuse in 1950 with a B.A. in English, Davis was hired as a line coach at Adelphi College in Garden City, New York, and also served as head baseball coach. He began regularly attending coaching clinics; his first article, "Line Quarterbacking at Its Best," published in the May 1952 issue of *Scholastic Coach,* was followed by many others. Drafted into the U.S. army in 1952, Davis became the first private ever to be chosen head coach of a military football team, at Fort Belvoir, Virginia. His most notable victory came over the University of Maryland, the defending national champions. Davis left the army in 1954 and was hired by head coach Weeb Ewbank of the Baltimore Colts as a player-personnel scout, an area in which he excelled.

Davis married Carol Segall in the fall of 1954; they had one son. The following year, General Mark Clark at The Citadel in Charleston, South Carolina, hired him as head line coach and top recruiter. In 1956 Davis asked Clark to appoint him to fill the vacant head coaching slot, but when

Al Davis, 2000. © AFP/CORBIS

Clark refused his request due to his relative youth and rumors of excesses in recruiting, Davis left The Citadel. In 1957 he was named line coach at the University of Southern California (USC). At USC, Davis promoted his blocking system (two hits per block), known as "Go-Go-with-Oomph." He continued to recruit successfully and was named defensive coordinator for the 1959 season. The creation of the American Football League (AFL) in August 1959 opened up employment opportunities, and the ambitious Davis became offensive end coach for the Los Angeles Chargers in their inaugural 1960 season, remaining there for three years.

On 15 January 1963 Davis achieved his ambition to be a head coach when he was hired by the new Oakland Raiders (relocated from Minnesota), who also named him general manager with full control of the team. At age thirty-three, Davis was the youngest person ever to hold such posts in modern professional football. The franchise had fared poorly, having had three different head coaches in three years, gone .214 overall, and winning only one game in 1962. Davis changed the operation rapidly, choosing a black and silver color scheme with a pirate emblem on the helmet, and introducing a team motto, "Pride and Poise," to which was later added a second motto, "Commitment to Excellence." Davis's first Raiders team, half of whose members were rookies, went 10–4, and he was named Coach of the Year. He remained head coach for two more seasons before being hired as AFL commissioner on 8 April 1966. At his first press conference, Davis announced, "I have dictatorial powers," and warned that the league would "fight for players."

Davis favored an aggressive policy against the rival National Football League (NFL), focusing on signing star quarterbacks, but the NFL was interested in a merger, as were the AFL team owners, and Davis was at the heart of the negotiations. Davis resented the merger, which was announced on 6 June 1966 (to take full effect in 1970), because of the indemnities required of the AFL teams to "join" the NFL and the selection of Pete Rozelle as the sole commissioner of the newly merged NFL. Davis referred to the merger as "Yalta," recalling the 1945 Allied conference, and was uninterested in the newly created position of president of the AFL and returned to Oakland as a managing general partner (with 10 percent ownership) for the 1967 season.

The 1967 Oakland team earned the best record in AFL history, 13–1, but lost Super Bowl II to Vince Lombardi's Green Bay Packers, 33–14. Their first Super Bowl win came in Super Bowl XI on 9 January 1977, 32–14 over Minnesota. Davis was more of a trader than a drafter, favored size, and sometimes found castaways, notably quarterback Jim Plunkett, who, although supposedly over the hill, led the Raiders to victory over Philadelphia in the 1981 Super Bowl XV, the first wildcard team (or added team that was not champion of its division) to win the event. Between 1963 and 1996, the Raiders went .644, the best record of any professional sports franchise, enjoyed a streak of sixteen consecutive winning seasons (broken in 1981), and played in four Super Bowls, three of which they won: in 1977 and 1981, as the Oakland Raiders, and then in 1984 as the Los Angeles Raiders, with a score of 38–9 over the Washington Redskins.

The Raiders' mystique shone especially on the American Broadcasting Company's (ABC) *Monday Night Football,* an instant national institution that started on ABC television in 1970. That year the Raiders began their streak of appearing at least once every season on *Monday Night Football,* as the network favored "glamour" teams that, it hoped, would attract high ratings. The Raiders were 29–6–1 in their appearances on the show through 1990, which was the longest streak of any team. The only season in which the Raiders did not play on a Monday night was in 1998, and they continued to appear after this season, but the mystique of their "always-winning" reputation had vaporized after 1990.

When Davis learned in 1979 that the Los Angeles Rams were planning to abandon their home field at Memorial Coliseum to move to Anaheim, he began negotiations to move the Raiders to Los Angeles. In pursuing these negotiations, Davis ignored NFL rules regarding such propositions because he believed, correctly, that he would be opposed by both the Rams and the league office. Davis signed an agreement with the Coliseum on 1 March 1980, and the lawsuits began. A Los Angeles jury ruled in favor of Davis's antitrust arguments and the Raiders on 7 May 1982; a second jury on 13 April 1983 assessed $35 million in damages (upheld on appeal), which the NFL paid the team. Davis then signed a ten-year deal, and the Oakland Raiders were no more. After their 1984 Super Bowl win the team went into decline, with only three playoff appearances from 1986 to 1997, and the NFL blackout rule for nonsellouts, combined with Coliseum's 90,000 plus seating capacity, meant that few games were locally televised. Davis took the Raiders back to Oakland in 1995 to begin anew, but he was unable immediately to replicate his previous success. In 1996 Davis became the commissioner of the American Football League and gave up his coaching position.

Davis personified the AFL image—upstart, innovative, and individualistic. From his start with the Raiders he had no appearance or dress code for his players, then an unusual policy, and he favored the wide-open style of play. He gained for himself and his team an iconoclastic, outlaw reputation, which was epitomized in his familiar saying, "Just win, baby." Davis was the future of the NFL before it happened, and he helped make it happen. He was named to the Pro Football Hall of Fame in 1992.

★

Davis is profiled in Ira Simmons, *Black Knight: Al Davis and His Raiders* (1990); Glenn Dickey, *Just Win, Baby: Al Davis and His Raiders* (1991); and Mark Ribowsky, *Slick: The Silver and Black Life of Al Davis* (1991).

LAWSON BOWLING

Glenn Davis *(left)* and fellow Heisman Trophy winner Felix "Doc" Blanchard. ASSOCIATED PRESS UNITED STATES MILITARY ACADEMY

DAVIS, Glenn Woodward ("Junior") (*b.* 26 December 1924 in Claremont, California), collegiate and pro halfback who was dubbed "Mr. Outside" and is remembered for his dazzling speed on the field.

Little about Davis's life was ordinary. Born to Ralph and Irna Davis, he arrived just a few minutes after his twin brother and on their older sister's third birthday. Davis and his brother were inseparable. At Bonita High School in La Verne, California, the two boys played many sports together, including football, baseball, basketball, and track, and Davis won sixteen letters before graduating. With his brother as quarterback, Davis, the freshman fullback, ran for 1,028 yards in 144 attempts. In his senior year, he scored 236 points, a record in the Southern California Prep league. He was named the California Interscholastic Federation (CIF) Football Player of the Year, All-CIF center field in baseball in 1942, and won the Knute Rockne Track Trophy in 1943. Professional baseball teams courted him for his throwing ability; basketball coaches said he was a great shooter; and track experts said that he could be an Olympic

sprinter. The *Los Angeles Times* called him the best athlete ever developed in Southern California.

In 1943 the U.S. Military Academy at West Point, New York, offered Davis an appointment. He refused to accept unless his brother was also admitted. The two soon found themselves at the prestigious academy. As a plebe the 170-pound Davis won varsity letters in three different sports, and he could have done the same in track had he been interested.

Although Davis's athletic prowess astonished everyone, his academic performance left much to be desired. After being expelled from West Point in December of 1943, he spent six months studying math and won reappointment. His football coach, Earl "Red" Blaik, moved Davis to halfback in 1944, and Davis, along with fullback Felix "Doc" Blanchard, became national figures. Together they were known as the "Touchdown Twins," and "Mr. Inside and Mr. Outside." Blanchard busted up the middle between the tackles, while Davis had the speed and breakaway skills to run to the outside. Some sports critics have suggested they were the best backfield in the history of college football. Defenses who tried to bottle up Blanchard in the middle were torched by Davis running to the outside; if they managed to stop Davis, Blanchard plowed up the middle. Davis also had power and rarely ran out of bounds as he swept around ends. Instead, he knifed between defenders or hit them head on in the open field.

Blanchard and Davis became part of the best Army team ever, winning every game in three seasons from 1944 to 1946 except one: a 0–0 tie game against Notre Dame in 1946. In his first year Davis set various records, scoring twenty touchdowns and averaging 11.1 yards per carry. The 1944 game against Navy stands as Davis's greatest football memory. "We were on the threshold of the first unbeaten Army season since 1916," said Davis. "Navy was the only team standing in the way of our winning the intercollegiate football championship . . . and what an obstacle!" Army did win, 23–7, with Davis scoring his twentieth touchdown of the season and becoming the leading scorer in the country.

The next year Army defeated Notre Dame 48–0 and in the 1945 season finale beat Navy 32–13, with Blanchard and Davis scoring all five of Army's touchdowns. Blanchard received the Heisman Trophy that year; Davis came in second in the voting. Grantland Rice wrote in the *New York Sun* that "in a modern way Scylla and Charybdis are better known as Doc Blanchard and Davis of the Army team. If one doesn't wreck you, the other probably will." Some observers, however, suggested that since many good football players were serving overseas during the World War II years, the lack of top football talent made Davis look better than he really was. Nevertheless, 1946—a year many of those football players returned to the game—proved one of Davis's best years. He had a forty-yard touchdown run, threw a twenty-seven-yard touchdown pass, and had 265 yards of total offense in one game (against Navy). He won the Heisman Trophy that year, as well as the Maxwell Trophy and the Walter Camp Trophy, and was voted the 1946 Associated Press Athlete of the Year. That year Davis also broke the all-time military physical fitness efficiency test. The 1,000-point test measures overall agility, strength, and endurance, with test-takers at the time averaging in the mid-500s. Davis scored an astonishing 926.5 points. He was voted All-American three times and ended his college football career with 59 touchdowns, 2,957 yards rushing, and 4,129 total yards. Davis was inducted into the College Football Hall of Fame in 1961.

After Davis's graduation the Brooklyn Dodgers offered him a $75,000 contract to play baseball, but he chose instead to serve his military obligation in Korea. Upon his return to the game in 1950 he joined the Los Angeles Rams of the National Football League (NFL), helping them get to the title game against Cleveland. On the Rams' first play from scrimmage, Davis caught an eighty-two-yard touchdown pass from Bob Waterfield. Although the Rams went on to lose the game, Davis had a notable rookie season. Unfortunately, the next year was not as productive. Though Davis had avoided any serious injuries from playing sports, he had torn a knee ligament while filming the movie *The Spirit of West Point* (1947). The injury reoccurred in 1951, and he did not see much playing time during that season, which was the season when the Rams won the NFL title. Davis retired from football at the end of the year and married Harriet Lancaster. He took a position with the *Los Angeles Times* special events department. In 1987 the Glenn Davis Award for Outstanding Southern California Prep School Football Player was established, honoring the Southern California athlete. After retiring, Davis moved to LaQuinta, California, and married Yvonne Ameche, the widow of Baltimore Colts fullback Alan Ameche, on 12 July 1996. Davis was named to the College Football All-Century team in January 2000.

Davis was one of the finest athletes to play college football. Although he had a short tenure in the NFL, his spectacular performance at West Point makes him one of the greatest running backs in football history.

★

Murray Goodman and Leonard Lewin, *My Greatest Day in Football* (1948), records Davis's recollections of the 1944 game that pitted Army against Navy in the intercollegiate championship game. John McCallum and W. W. Heffelfinger, *This Was Football* (1954), recalls Davis's days at West Point, along with a number of anecdotes from coaches and teammates. Joe Horrigan and Bob Carroll, *Football Greats* (1998), details Davis's major accomplishments on the field. Grantland Rice, *Los Angeles Times* (8 Nov. 1945), contains a description of Davis's running abilities and athleticism during his 1945 season at Army.

MARKUS H. MCDOWELL

DAVIS, John Henry (*b.* 12 January 1921 in Smithtown, New York; *d.* 13 July 1984 in Albuquerque, New Mexico), amateur weight lifter who, as an Olympic and world champion, was the world's premier heavyweight lifter from 1940 to 1953.

Davis, named after the legendary African-American strongman John Henry, was brought up by his mother, Margaret Campbell Davis, and attended but did not graduate from public schools in Brooklyn, New York. He never knew his father, also named John Davis. An all-around athlete, he was especially proficient in handball and gymnastics (rings and horizontal bar) and once did a standing broad jump of nearly eleven feet. He started weight lifting in 1937 with a barbell owned by a friend and entered his first contest

John Davis at the 1948 Olympic Games in London. © BETTMANN/ CORBIS

that November at the French Sporting Club in New York City. As a light heavyweight he displayed remarkable natural ability by pressing 220 pounds, snatching 215 pounds, and cleaning and jerking 260 pounds.

Endowed with great pulling strength, Davis quickly reached the heights of national and international competition. In 1938, at age seventeen, he captured the junior national title, took second at the senior nationals, and won the world championships in Vienna, Austria, with a world-record press of 258.5 pounds, a snatch of 264 pounds, and a clean and jerk of 330 pounds. Davis earned two more national titles as a light heavyweight, then took the heavyweight crown in the next three years. At the 1941 senior national championships he became the first man in history to exceed a 1,000-pound total with a 320-pound press, a 315-pound snatch, and a 370-pound clean and jerk. Although his lifting career was interrupted by military service in World War II (during which he saw a tour of duty in the South Pacific with the 717th Medical Sanitary Company) and a bout of hemolytic jaundice, Davis returned to win five more world championships and Olympic gold medals in 1948 (London) and 1952 (Helsinki). In 1951, at the first Pan-American Games in Buenos Aires, he made his best lifts with a 336.25-pound press, a 330.5-pound snatch, and a 396.75-pound clean and jerk for a world-record 1,063.5-pound total. He was the brightest star and

most consistent performer of the U.S. international teams during the "golden age" of U.S. weight lifting in the late 1940s and early 1950s.

What was most intriguing to contemporaries was Davis's execution of magnificent feats of strength seemingly without effort and, at least until his later years, with much in reserve. Usually he lifted only enough to win and never tested his limits. Nevertheless he set nineteen world records in all four lifting categories at various times and became the first amateur to clean and jerk more than 400 pounds. Davis also lifted 500 pounds in the squat for ten repetitions and performed a 705-pound dead lift at a body weight of 193 pounds. Weighing even less, he bench pressed 310 pounds, one-hand snatched 215 pounds, and one-arm curled 103 pounds. Despite his small hand size, Davis possessed phenomenal gripping strength. In what was probably the greatest challenge of his career, he lifted the famous Apollon railway wheels in Paris, France, overhead in 1949. Although they weighed just 366 pounds, the wheels were mounted on a nonrevolving axle that was 1.93 inches in diameter. Because the axle was too wide to pull with a knuckles-forward grip, Davis had to use a reverse (dead lift) grip to get the weight off the floor and flip one hand in flight. After failing eight times, he became only the third man to master this challenge.

Coinciding with his great strength, Davis had one of the finest physiques of his era. At the 1942 Mr. America contest his weight-lifting coach thought his musculature was "as good as that of the winners," but Davis vowed never to enter such a contest because he believed "a Negro cannot win." Still, in 1941 he was the first African American to appear on the cover of a major bodybuilding magazine and, through the worldwide visibility he gained as a lifter, Davis did much to pave the way for other African Americans in the sport.

Davis possessed a deep, powerful baritone-bass voice and was especially fond of opera. He always brought sheet music on international trips and sang operatic duets with his teammate Pete George, a tenor-baritone, in their room. At the 1953 world championships in Stockholm, Sweden, a local reporter was so impressed with the quality of their singing that he secured a week's engagement for them at the China International Variety Theater. They received good reviews and the Swedish subsidiary of RCA recorded their performance. Davis also sang on the soundtrack for *The Strongest Man in the World* (1953), a film about his lifting career that was produced by Bud Greenspan. A chronic case of hiccups prevented him from pursuing an operatic career.

Modest, pleasant, and relaxed, Davis could be seen chewing gum as he prepared to lift record weights. His 1946 marriage to Louise Morton was childless and eventually resulted in separation and divorce. The real love of his life was Alyce Stagg Yarick, an early female weight lifter and the wife of a prominent gym operator in Oakland, California, with whom he had a son in 1954. They never married, but Davis bequeathed all his worldly possessions to her.

For twenty-five years Davis worked as a prison guard for the New York City Department of Corrections, including an assignment on Riker's Island, until his retirement in 1979. He moved first to Modesto, California, where he lived briefly, then to Albuquerque. A heavy smoker in later years, he developed lung cancer, which eventually spread to his entire body. He died at age sixty-three at the Saint Francis Gardens Nursing Home in Albuquerque and is buried in the Santa Fe National Cemetery in New Mexico.

For most of his lifting career Davis was regarded as invincible. He remained undefeated for fifteen of his nineteen competitive years. He was the first African American to win an Olympic weight-lifting title and the only one to become both an Olympic and world champion. By Hoffman formula body weight calculations, he often was rated as the world's best lifter. Davis became a member of both the U.S. Olympic Hall of Fame and the Weightlifting Hall of Fame.

★

The most extensive coverage of Davis's personal life and lifting career is available in Osmo Kiiha, "John Henry Davis, Jr.," *Iron Master* 11 (Apr. 1993). See also Bob Hoffman, "John Davis: World's Greatest Weightlifter," *Strength and Health* 19 (Oct. 1951); Jim Murray, "John Davis: Iron Game Immortal," *Strength and Health* 22 (June 1954); Charlie Shields, "John Davis: Portrait of a Champion," *Strength and Health* 42 (Jan. 1974); and Arthur Drechsler, "John Davis: Hero and Legend," *Weightlifting USA* 19 (winter 2000–2001).

JOHN D. FAIR

DEAN, Jay Hanna ("Dizzy") (*b.* 16 January 1910 in Lucas, Arkansas; *d.* 17 July 1974 in Reno, Nevada), Hall of Fame pitcher, broadcaster, raconteur, and unique baseball personality.

Dean, who also used the name Jerome Herman but was best known by his nickname Dizzy, was the second of three surviving children of Albert Monroe Dean and his wife, Alma Frances Nelson, who were sharecroppers. Dean's mother died of tuberculosis when he was eight, and after her death his school attendance was sporadic. Dean's father remarried, and the family lived in several places, including Chickalah, Arkansas, and Spaulding, Oklahoma.

Dean joined the U.S. Army at sixteen. He was incapable of following orders—hence his nickname—but he was a standout pitcher for the regimental team, as well as for several semiprofessional teams in and around San Antonio,

Dizzy Dean accepting the National League's Most Valuable Player Award for 1935. ASSOCIATED PRESS AP

Texas. Dean left the army in March 1929, and in May was signed to a contract by the St. Louis Cardinals organization.

Dean began his professional career in 1930 with the Class A St. Joseph Saints, was promoted to the Class AAA Houston Buffaloes, and pitched the final game of the season for the St. Louis Cardinals, defeating the Pittsburgh Pirates 3–1. During spring training in 1931, though, Dean was incorrigible. He ran up monumental bills and arrived late for practices. Two weeks into the season, he was optioned back to Houston. A month later, he announced that he was getting married.

Dean's intended was Patricia Nash, a department store clerk who was three years older than Dean and had been married twice before. The Cardinals did their best to talk Dean out of the marriage, but Dean refused to listen, and the couple married on 15 June 1931. To the shock of the Cardinals, the marriage turned out to be the best thing that could have happened to Dean. His wife, who also acted as his business manager, brought order to his chaotic life and put him on a strict savings plan. They had no children.

Dean was six feet, two inches tall, and weighed 180 pounds, but his weight frequently dropped twenty pounds during the course of a season. He threw right-handed, and had a great fast ball, curve ball, and change of pace, but what made Dean a spectacular pitcher was his control. He rarely walked opposing batters, and he placed his pitches beautifully over specific sections of the plate. He was also a good batter (a rarity among pitchers), a solid fielder, and a daring base runner. Dean had only two weaknesses—his love of extra challenges, such as trying to strike out batters with their favorite pitches, and his insistence on overwork.

Dean got his chance to pitch regularly in the major leagues in 1932. For the next five years, he dominated baseball with his stellar pitching, exuberant personality, and brash boasts ("It ain't bragging if you can back it up," he said). He finished the 1932 season with a record of 18–15 and led the National League in innings pitched (286) and strikeouts (191). The Cardinals, however, sank to sixth place and suffered losses of $100,000, so 1933 salaries were slashed. "This here Depression ain't my fault," Dean protested, but he had to settle for $3,000, the same salary that he received in 1932.

In 1933 Dean was the only reliable pitcher on the Cardinals staff. He finished the season with a record of 20–18, half his losses coming on days when he pitched with two days of rest or less. Dean's younger brother Paul joined the Cardinals in 1934, and Dean predicted that he and Paul would win forty-five games. They surpassed this outrageous forecast, winning forty-nine. The Cardinals clinched the pennant on the final day of the season, with Dean, who finished the season with a record of 30–7, pitching.

The Cardinals were first called the "Gas House Gang" during the 1934 World Series because of their aggressive, no-holds-barred play and their dirt-stained uniforms. Highlights of the series included Dean pitching Game 1 and defeating the Detroit Tigers 8–3; Dean entering Game 4 as a pinch runner and being knocked unconscious by a thrown ball when he ran into second base standing up to break up a double play; Dean pitching the next day ("You can't beat me hittin' me in the head"), but losing 3–2; Paul taking the must-win Game 6, 4–3; and Dean shutting out the Tigers on six hits in the final game, while Cardinal batters broke loose to coast to an 11–0 win. Over the winter, Dean was named the National League's Most Valuable Player.

The Cardinals were edged out for the pennant by the Chicago Cubs in 1935, but this was no fault of the Deans, who bore the brunt of the pitching duties and ended the season with a combined forty-seven wins. Dean had a record of 28–12.

Dean had another fine season in 1936, but Paul developed arm trouble. Dean took up some of the slack (on two occasions he pitched three straight days, two full games, and three innings of relief in between), but he could not do it all. He finished the year with a record of 25–13, and the Cardinals finished in a tie for second.

While Dean was pitching in the 1937 All-Star Game, a line drive broke his left toe. Two weeks later, Dean was

pitching again, but he was not pitching well; his delivery was altered, and he was limping. By late August, he had developed serious arm trouble. He finished the year with a record of 13–10.

Dean was traded to the Chicago Cubs in March 1938. He pitched well initially, although he was only able to use his fast ball sparingly, then was out from 3 May to 17 July with a sore arm. When Dean returned, it was obvious that he no longer had his fast ball, and he finished the season with a record of 7–1. Still, he won a crucial game at the end of the season to help the Cubs win the pennant, and he started the second game of the World Series. Dean managed to keep the New York Yankees off balance for seven innings with his control and changes of speed. But the Yankees took the lead in the eighth inning and won the game 6–3. They went on to complete a series sweep.

In 1939, pitching in pain, Dean had a 6–4 record. In 1940 he went to the minor leagues to experiment with his delivery. He won two games after he was called back, but was hit hard in his other outings and finished the year with a record of 3–3. Dean started just one game in 1941 and was knocked out in the first inning. On 14 May he announced his retirement. The Cubs immediately made him a coach.

One month later, however, the Falstaff Brewing Corporation offered Dean a job in St. Louis broadcasting home games of the Cardinals and the Browns, and he quickly accepted. It turned out that Dean, who loved to talk and had strong, if unorthodox, verbal skills, was a natural at broadcasting. He switched tenses and invented new verb conjugations (swang, throwed, slud), mispronounced even common names, and laced his broadcasts with malapropisms: batters walked "confidentially" to the plate; runners returned to their "respectable" bases. None of that mattered, since Dean had a sound knowledge of the game and knew how to communicate what was happening. He also knew how to entertain. When the going got slow, he might tell stories (he was a masterful story teller) or even sing his favorite song, "The Wabash Cannonball."

Dean helped to broadcast Yankee television games during the 1950 and 1951 seasons, returned to radio in 1952 to broadcast Mutual Radio's *Game of the Day,* then moved back to television in 1953 when a national *Game of the Week* began airing Saturday afternoons on the American Broadcasting System (ABC). Dean was also elected to baseball's Hall of Fame in 1953. "This is the greatest honor I ever received," he said in his induction speech, "and I wanna think the Lord for givin' me a good right arm, a strong back, and a weak mind."

Game of the Week moved to the Columbia Broadcasting System (CBS) in 1955. Although rival networks also offered Saturday-afternoon games, *Game of the Week* dominated the ratings. However, when the National Broadcasting System (NBC) acquired exclusive rights to a national Saturday game in 1966, Dean was not retained as an announcer. He did not need to work, since his wife had invested their money wisely, but he did regional broadcasts for the Atlanta Braves and continued to make personal appearances for Falstaff. Dean died from a heart attack and is buried in the Bond Cemetery in Bond, Mississippi, where the Deans had moved in the mid-1950s.

Dean's time of baseball greatness was relatively short, from 1932 through 1936, but during those five years he dominated baseball as few others have. Dean led the National League four consecutive years in both complete games (1933–1936) and strikeouts (1932–1935), and his lifetime winning percentage is an eye-popping .644. Although Dean's lifetime statistics fall short of those of most of baseball's other greats, his best five years compare favorably with the best five years of any pitcher who ever played. As a broadcaster, he is best remembered for his ability to entertain and for demonstrating that possessing a cookie-cutter personality is not a prerequisite for broadcasters. His stories gave fans a feeling of personal connection to baseball's lore, and as the lead broadcaster of *Game of the Week* he introduced an entire generation to the pleasures of major league baseball.

★

There is a file on Dean at the National Baseball Hall of Fame Library in Cooperstown, New York. Valuable biographies include Curt Smith, *America's Dizzy Dean* (1978); Robert Gregory, *Diz: Dizzy Dean and Baseball during the Great Depression* (1992); and Vince Staten, *Ol' Diz: A Biography of Dizzy Dean* (1992). For complete statistics on Dean's career, see *The Baseball Encyclopedia* (1996). An obituary is in the *New York Times* (18 Jul. 1974).

LYNN HOOGENBOOM

DEFORD, Frank (*b.* 16 December 1938 in Baltimore, Maryland), sportswriter known for the perceptiveness, wit, and compassion of his comments in magazines and books and on National Public Radio.

Deford was the eldest of three sons born to a middle-class couple, Benjamin Deford, a businessman, and Louise Deford. Looking back on his earliest years, he said, "For a writer, I had a terrible thing—a happy childhood." He decided at age ten that he could write. He enjoyed sports but was not as good at playing them as he was at writing. At Princeton University, from which he graduated in 1962 with an A.B. degree in history and sociology, Deford wrote for and edited the *Daily Princetonian* and also wrote two plays that were produced on campus. He had not intended to go into sportswriting, but when *Sports Illustrated* offered him a job after graduation, he took it. He began as a re-

porter but soon was assigned longer feature articles, which made his reputation. He married Carol Penner in 1965; the couple had three children.

In the 1970s Deford began publishing books. His first, *There She Is: The Life and Times of Miss America* (1971), dealt with a nonsports form of spectacle. He also served as a ghostwriter for books by the tennis stars Arthur Ashe, Jack Kramer, Billie Jean King, and Pam Shriver and told the sad story of the tennis great Bill Tilden, whose career was destroyed by the revelation of his homosexuality. The 1970s also brought Deford great sorrow. His second child, Alexandra, was born in 1971. As an infant she seemed sickly, and soon she was diagnosed with cystic fibrosis. The doctors said she might die in days, but she suffered through operations and painful treatments until 1980. Deford joined the Cystic Fibrosis Foundation, eventually becoming its chairman, and wrote a moving account of the experience, *Alex: The Life of a Child* (1983), which was made into a movie.

In 1980 Deford began a weekly sports commentary for National Public Radio (NPR), where he remained for more than twenty years. He gained recognition for his sportswriting, being voted the sportswriter of the year by the National Association of Sportswriters and Sportscasters every year from 1982 through 1988, but he still recognized the low estimation in which his field was held. In 1987 Deford published a collection of his best sports features and called it *The World's Tallest Midget,* his sarcastic view of the way the world perceived the "best sportswriter." The book showed the remarkable range of subjects that could be covered in just seventeen sports articles. It included studies of such famous sports personalities as the football pioneer George Halas and the Marquette University basketball coach Al McGuire, and an account of the well-known 1957 National Collegiate Athletic Association basketball championship. There was also a report of a boxing match between two unknowns that ended in death and the remarkable tale of "The Toughest Coach There Was," an otherwise forgotten Mississippi junior college coach.

By the late 1980s Deford was thinking of moving on to new career challenges. He had been with *Sports Illustrated* for a quarter of a century, and he was becoming tired of interviewing athletes much younger than himself. An opportunity presented itself in 1989, when the Mexican millionaire Emilio Azcarra set out to create the first American daily sports newspaper. He called it the *National* and hired Deford as its editor in chief. Deford said that it would show that Americans really buy the newspaper for the sports page. Whatever the merits of that theory, the *National* never was able to solve its distribution problems. It published its first issue in January 1990 and its last in June 1991.

When Deford left *Sports Illustrated* to work for the *National,* there was bitterness on both sides. Some people at

Frank Deford with the last issue of the *National*, 1991. ASSOCIATED PRESS AP

the magazine believed that the *National* was intended to compete with *Sports Illustrated,* a theory Deford denied. In 1992 he began writing commentary for *Newsweek* and signed a contract with *Vanity Fair* to produce three profiles per year. Deford also wanted to be a serious novelist. He already had turned out five light sports novels—*Cut 'n' Run* (1973), *The Owner* (1976), *Everybody's All-American* (1981), *The Spy in the Deuce Court* (1986), and *Casey on the Loose* (1989)—but he now grew more ambitious. After the demise of the *National,* he wrote *Love and Infamy,* a historical novel with no sports content that portrayed the World War II events at Pearl Harbor through the eyes of two best friends, one Japanese and one American. The novel was published in 1993 to a generally respectful critical response, but it did not become a best-seller.

In 1998 Deford and *Sports Illustrated* reconciled. He returned to writing for the magazine, and his NPR commentaries began appearing on their website. In 2000 he wrote the Home Box Office television special *Bill Russell: My Life, My Way,* and in 2001 he published *The Best of Frank Deford: I'm Just Getting Started,* which interspersed radio commentaries with longer essays on such figures as the Indiana University basketball coach Bob Knight and the famed basketball player Wilt Chamberlain.

Deford brought to his sportswriting a knowledge of the technicalities of the sport he was describing (and he wrote about most of them), a graceful prose style often brightened with wit, and, most of all, a compassionate understanding of the human realities of the story he was telling. In writing stature, he was far more than the world's tallest midget.

★

Deford has written little about himself, but there is some autobiographical detail in *Alex* (1983), and the two collections of his articles. He discusses his fiction-writing ambitions in Christopher Goodrich, *Publishers Weekly* (6 Dec. 1993), and reminisces about his NPR work in the "Listen" section of the *Durham Sun-Times* (Nov. 1999). In Johnette Howard, *Houston Chronicle* (18 June 2000), Deford is taken to task for his *Sports Illustrated* article on the sexy image of the tennis player Anna Kournikova. Noreen O'Leary admiringly summarized his career in *Mediaweek* (8 May 2000).

ARTHUR D. HLAVATY

DELVECCHIO, Alex Peter ("Fats") (*b.* 4 December 1932 in Fort William, Ontario, Canada), hockey player noted for his longevity, skill, consistency, durability, and gentlemanly play.

After a brief period in the minor leagues with the Fort William Rangers of the Thunder Bay Junior Hockey League, the Oshawa Generals of the Ontario Hockey Association, and the Indianapolis Capitals of the American Hockey League, Delvecchio joined the Detroit Red Wings prior to the 1951–1952 season. Playing in sixty-five games

Alex Delvecchio *(center, in dark jersey)* scoring a goal again Toronto, 1956. © BETTMANN/CORBIS

during his rookie campaign, he scored fifteen goals and added twenty-two assists.

When the Red Wing general manager Jack Adams traded team captain Sid Abel to the Chicago Blackhawks on 22 July 1952, Delvecchio united with Gordie Howe and Ted Lindsay to replace Abel on the famed "Production Line." The Red Wings never faltered, winning the Prince of Wales Trophy, which was at that time awarded to the team posting the best record during the regular season, for the fifth consecutive year. Although eclipsed by his more celebrated teammates, Delvecchio finished fifth in the league in scoring with fifty-nine points on sixteen goals and forty-three assists. His graceful skating, superb puck handling, and flawless passing contributed in no small measure to Howe's league-leading ninety-five points (forty-nine goals, forty-six assists) and to Lindsay's seventy-one (thirty-two, thirty-nine). For his efforts, Delvecchio was named a Second-Team All Star.

The Red Wings dominated the National Hockey League (NHL) during the early 1950s, and Delvecchio's name was inscribed on the Stanley Cup three times, in 1952, 1954, and 1955. On 14 April 1955, in the seventh game of the Stanley Cup Finals, Delvecchio scored twice to secure a 3–1 victory over the Montreal Canadiens, clinching what proved to be the Wings last championship in forty-two years. In the wake of this success, a series of

regrettable, and often inexplicable, trades, began to effect the gradual but steady decline of the team throughout the rest of Delvecchio's career. Although the Wings remained competitive, returning to the Stanley Cup Finals in 1956, 1961, 1963, 1964, and 1966, Detroit did not win another cup until nearly a quarter century after Delvecchio retired. In spite of his team's decline, Delvecchio maintained his own fine play.

With the departure of Lindsay in the summer of 1957, Delvecchio moved from center to left wing on a line with Howe and third-year center Norm Ullman. Adjusting effortlessly to his new position, Delvecchio prospered. During the 1957–1958 season, he matched his career high in points with fifty-nine, scoring twenty-one goals and recording thirty-eight assists while playing in all seventy of the Red Wings regular season games. The following season he again earned second-team All Star honors, this time as a left wing.

Throughout his long career, Delvecchio accumulated only 383 penalty minutes, and never totaled more than 37 Penalties in Minutes (PIM) in a single season. A testament to his restrained and judicious play, Delvecchio received the Lady Byng Trophy, awarded annually "to the player adjudged to have exhibited the best type of sportsmanship and gentlemanly conduct combined with a high standard of playing ability," in 1959, 1966, and 1969.

Statistically, Delvecchio's finest season came late in his career. In the 1968–1969 season, playing for a Red Wings squad that finished fifth in the six-team East Division and failed to make the playoffs for the third straight season, Delvecchio amassed eighty-three points on twenty-five goals and fifty-eight assists. His totals were good enough to rank him seventh in the league in scoring.

Delvecchio's amiable, rotund face earned him the nickname "Fats" early in his career, an epithet he never escaped. Yet the identification was no emblem of disrespect. On the contrary, teammates and opponents alike admired Delvecchio. As evidence of this respect, Delvecchio was elected captain of the Red Wings in 1962. He retained the position until his retirement on 9 November 1973, eleven games into the 1973–1974 season. At the time Delvecchio left hockey, only teammate Howe had enjoyed a longer tenure in the NHL or had played in more NHL games. Similarly, Delvecchio's 825 assists and 1,281 points ranked second only to Howe, while his 456 goals were sixth at that point in NHL history.

Delvecchio served as coach of the Red Wings from 1973 until 1975, and again for nine games during the 1975–1976 season. He compiled a rather dismal record of 82 wins, 131 losses, and 32 ties. As general manager between 1974 and 1977, he could do little to revive the once proud franchise, which by the early 1970s had tumbled into utter disarray. Finding it difficult to communicate with younger players who no longer gave automatic and unquestioned obedience to authority, Delvecchio was compelled to trade the talented but disgruntled Marcel Dionne to the Los Angeles Kings. He also quarreled with star right wing Mickey Redmond.

Injuries had forced Redmond to miss most of the 1974–1975 season and the final forty-three games in 1975–1976, a total equal to the number of games Delvecchio had missed during his entire career. Although Redmond had actually suffered nerve damage in his right leg severe enough to necessitate his retirement, Delvecchio considered him irresponsible and indolent, and suspended him before placing him on waivers. "He's no good to us," Delvecchio complained. "I'm tired of hearing players' excuses for mediocre work. I don't want to have such disruptive influences on my team." Delvecchio's association with the abysmal Red Wings of the 1970s was an unbecoming finale for a man who represented the glorious legacy of a bygone era.

An exemplary team player who labored in relative obscurity throughout his career, Delvecchio was inducted into the Hockey Hall of Fame in 1977. The Red Wings organization, which he served so proudly, so long, and so well, honored him by retiring his number 10 on 10 November 1991. A model of durability, consistency, and longevity, Delvecchio played 1,549 NHL games. During twenty-two full seasons with the Detroit Red Wings, he missed only forty-three games due to injury or illness. In thirteen of those seasons, he scored at least 20 goals, compiling a career total of 456 to accompany 825 assists. Delvecchio also netted 35 goals and registered 69 assists in 121 playoffs contests. Talented and intelligent, yet modest and unprepossessing, Delvecchio rarely made a mistake on the ice, and he personified the triumph of substance over style.

★

Delvecchio is mentioned in Stan Fischler, *Detroit Red Wings: Greatest Moments and Players* (2001); Paul R. Greenland, *Wings of Fire: The History of the Detroit Red Wings* (1997); Richard Bak, *The Detroit Red Wings: The Illustrated History* (1998); Bob Duff, "Franchise Histories: Detroit Red Wings," in *Total Hockey: The Official Encyclopedia of the National Hockey League,* 2d ed., by Dan Diamond (2000); and Brian McFarlane, *The Detroit Red Wings* (1999).

MARK MALVASI

DEMPSEY, William Harrison ("Jack") (*b.* 24 June 1895 in Manassa, Colorado; *d.* 31 May 1983 in New York City), heavyweight boxing champion, one of the most famous sports figures of the twentieth century, regarded by many sports historians as the best heavyweight prizefighter ever.

Dempsey was the ninth of eleven children born to a disreputable father, Hyrum Dempsey, and Celia Smoot Dempsey, a homemaker. At age sixteen he left home to hitch rides on railroad cars in a constant quest for work. He often offered to fight in exchange for a dollar, and he became legendary for taking on and beating all comers in bars. When manager Jack "Doc" Kearns of San Francisco undertook Dempsey's training, the fighter was a frightening figure. He was only six feet, three-quarters of an inch tall and weighed less than 190 pounds (he weighed 190 during his prime)—not particularly imposing statistics for a heavyweight prizefighter—but Dempsey moved like a cat, and he was always restless, constantly pacing like a caged animal. His agility was impressive, but it was his sheer savagery when boxing that frightened onlookers.

Dempsey made his professional debut on 17 August 1914 in a six-round bout against a journeyman boxer, Young Hancock, that ended in a tie. He boxed often, improving his skills from bout to bout. He is sometimes characterized as wild and even clumsy, but he was in fact an intelligent athlete who paid attention to his manager and who developed exceptional skills. On 26 April 1915 he knocked out the tough fighter Anamas Campbell. Dempsey fought Johnny Sudenberg to two draws the following May and June, but on 1 February 1916 he knocked Sudenberg out in the second round of their match.

Dempsey was a devastating puncher with either hand,

Jack Dempsey. ARCHIVE PHOTOS, INC.

and he disciplined his nervous energy into a relentless attack during which he never seemed to tire. Further, he had outstanding defensive skills; he picked off an opponent's blows with his forearms or slipped one way, then another, so that an opponent's punches found only air. There was no mercy in him; an opponent in trouble was an opponent doomed. Dempsey would stand over a fallen opponent to begin pummeling the man the moment he tried to stand.

Dempsey found himself making good money, and he overspent. Because of this, his career took a turn for the worse when he deliberately lost a bout on 16 February 1917 against Fireman Jim Flynn—a very good boxer, but someone Dempsey should have beaten. That he had been paid to take a fall was obvious to all observers because he dropped to the canvas on mystery punches. In a rematch on 14 February 1918, Dempsey knocked out Flynn in the first round.

Further tarnishing Dempsey's reputation was his trial for draft evasion during World War I, an accusation which made him look unpatriotic and cowardly. However, his fortunes took a turn for the better when one of the top boxing promoters of the day, Tex Rickard, took an interest in him and arranged high-paying matches for him. On 4 July 1919 Dempsey fought Jess Willard for the world heavyweight championship. Willard was huge at six feet, six

inches tall and 250 pounds, and he packed a terrific punch. Billed as the "Manassa Mauler," the much smaller Dempsey fulfilled his promise by mauling the giant Willard, knocking him out in the third round. Rickard almost instantly took to promoting Dempsey as "Jack the Giant Killer."

On 6 September 1920 Dempsey defended his title against Billy Miske, a skilled boxer who had given Dempsey trouble in previous bouts, but Miske was suffering from Bright's disease (an inflammation of the kidneys) and did not fare well. Dempsey knocked him out in the third round. On 14 December 1920 the stylish boxer Bill Brennan almost outfought Dempsey, losing by a knockout in the twelfth round. Rickard then arranged a match made in heaven (from a promoter's point of view) between Dempsey and Georges Carpentier, the world light-heavyweight champion and European heavyweight champion. Carpentier was a war hero, and Rickard's publicity portrayed Dempsey as the villain. The public responded by producing the first million-dollar gate in boxing history. Dempsey was faster, more skilled, and hit harder than Carpentier; he knocked Carpentier out in the fourth round.

The high life appealed to Dempsey, and he was a rich man after only a few title defenses. Even so, he was persuaded to defend his championship again, facing Tommy Gibbons on 4 July 1923 for another big payday. Gibbons was clever and a master of boxing skills, and he lasted a full fifteen rounds against Dempsey. This fight proved that Dempsey was much more than a savage brawler, because he outboxed one of the best boxers of the era, winning twelve of the fifteen rounds.

Dempsey had another big payday when he fought Luis Firpo of Argentina on 14 September 1923. Firpo weighed about 220 pounds and was noted for his ability to take punishment. He appeared to be the fighter who could defeat Dempsey. Dempsey knocked Firpo down seven times in the first round, but each time Firpo came up swinging. He eventually caught Dempsey with a crushing blow that sent him through the ropes and onto the typewriters of ringside journalists. Dempsey was dazed and wobbly but climbed back into the ring and survived the round. The second round was almost anticlimactic, with Dempsey giving Firpo a terrific beating to win by a knockout. This match brought about a change in boxing rules that later came to haunt Dempsey. The image of Dempsey standing over the fallen Firpo, ready to pound him the moment he stood, was unsettling, so boxing commissions around the United States created the rule that a fighter had to go to a neutral corner whenever he knocked his opponent down.

Dempsey did not defend his title for three years, during which he neglected himself. On 7 February 1925 he married actress Estelle Taylor, having been divorced from his first wife Maxine Cates Dempsey. Meanwhile, Gene Tunney, a stylish boxer from a good family and good schools, rose to prominence. Tunney regarded boxing as a sort of fencing match, a matter more of skill than brawn. He and Dempsey met on 23 September 1926 at Philadelphia's Sesquicentennial Stadium in front of a crowd of over 120,000 people. A boxer whose skills were almost without equal in any weight class, Tunney bobbed, wove, ducked, and slipped aside while hammering Dempsey with rapid punching combinations. By the match's end, Dempsey's face was swollen and one eye was entirely shut. When his wife, Estelle, asked him what happened, he said, "Honey, I forgot to duck." Tunney won the decision.

Dempsey, virtually a symbol of the freewheeling 1920s, had been beaten, and because of how he responded to his defeat, he became even more popular than before. He said that he was a lucky man to have been defeated by a gentleman, and he made no excuses.

On 21 July 1927 Dempsey fought contender Jack Sharkey in an effort to earn a rematch against Tunney. Sharkey won the early rounds with his sharp movement around the ring, but Dempsey wore him down, then knocked him out in the seventh round. It was a wonderful payday for Dempsey because the match was the first in history to draw a four-million-dollar gate.

In one of the most famous matches in history, Dempsey and Tunney met again at Chicago's Soldier Field on 22 September 1927. Dempsey was a good boxer, but Tunney was better, deflecting most of Dempsey's blows and proving that he could take a punch when Dempsey managed to hit him. To most observers, Tunney was winning the fight going into the seventh round. Then Dempsey finally outfoxed his opponent, feinting one way, then delivering a sharp punch to the head with the other, followed by several slashing blows. Tunney dropped like a sack of potatoes, shaking his head. Dempsey stood over him; the referee motioned Dempsey to a neutral corner. When Dempsey remembered the rule, he walked to the corner, but five seconds had elapsed, and then the referee began his count over Tunney. Prizefighters are taught to wait until the referee counts to nine before standing up, so whether or not Tunney could have gotten up after nine seconds elapsed is a mystery; by the time the referee counted to nine, fourteen seconds had actually elapsed. That is when Tunney stood. Tunney won the ten-round decision, defeating Dempsey for a second time. Dempsey unsuccessfully appealed the decision on the basis of the long count.

Dempsey retired, fighting only exhibition matches. He said that the long count turned out to be lucky for him because people sympathized with him, and it made him a topic of conversation long after his career was over. He opened a restaurant on the corner of Fiftieth Street and Eighth Avenue in New York, before moving it to Broadway. It became a popular tourist attraction, and Dempsey was usually on the premises, proving himself a gracious host. Dempsey also married his third wife, Hannah Williams Dempsey; they separated in 1940. In spite of the legend of the savage brawler, Dempsey became a beloved figure. But he had pride. To his dying day, he told anyone who asked that he was the best heavyweight prizefighter ever.

Dempsey died in New York of natural causes at age eighty-seven. He is buried on Long Island in Southampton Cemetery, Southampton, New York.

★

Dempsey wrote at least three autobiographies with the help of professional writers; the most revealing is probably Dempsey, Bob Considine, and Bill Slocum, *Dempsey: By the Man Himself* (1960). Dempsey also wrote a down-to-earth book, *Championship Fighting: Explosive Punching and Aggressive Defense* (1950). Randy Roberts, *Jack Dempsey: The Manassa Mauler* (1979), sets forth the essentials of Dempsey's life. A curious bit of history is Toby Smith, *Kid Blackie: Jack Dempsey's Colorado Days* (1987; variant title: *Kid Blackie: The Colorado Days of Jack Dempsey*); it offers details about Dempsey the brawler. Roger Kahn, *A Flame of Pure Fire: Jack Dempsey and the Roaring '20s* (2000), is breathtaking in its scope while discussing Dempsey as a cultural phenomenon. Mort Kamin, "Aging Bull," *Sports Illustrated* (17 April 1995), tells of Dempsey's life in 1940. William Knack, "The Long Count," *Sports Illustrated* (22 Sept. 1997), details the events surrounding the infamous "long count" in the second bout between Dempsey and Tunney. Tom Callahan, "Memories of a Heavyweight," *Time* (13 June 1983) is an obituary that focuses on Dempsey's character, and "Jack Dempsey, RIP," *National Review* (24 June 1983), is an obituary that summarizes Dempsey's boxing career.

KIRK H. BEETZ

DE VARONA, Donna (*b.* 20 April 1947 in San Diego, California), two-time Olympic gold medalist in swimming, founding member of the Women's Sports Foundation, and television sportscasting pioneer.

De Varona grew up in Lafayette, California, near San Francisco, with her parents, David de Varona, an insurance salesman, and Martha Smith de Varona, a retail sales associate, and three siblings. De Varona was an active, athletic child who participated in many sports. But she was frustrated that the Little League baseball enjoyed by her older brother did not allow girls to play. As an adult, she lamented in a magazine interview, "I spent all my money on bubble gum so I could bribe my way into the Little League, and I wound up with a uniform with number '0' on it. I picked up the bats." De Varona's frustration with gender inequality in sports led to her efforts later in life to change the system.

Donna de Varona. AP/WIDE WORLD PHOTOS

Her main sports focus as an adolescent became swimming. Her father, a celebrated rower and All-American football player at the University of California, was her first coach. She entered her first competitive swim meet at age nine. In 1960, at age thirteen, she qualified as an alternate on the U.S. Olympic swimming team. She participated in the 1960 Olympics in Rome, Italy, as the team's youngest member, a significant achievement even though her event was canceled.

Between the Rome games and the 1964 Olympics in Tokyo, Japan, de Varona also trained in the backstroke, butterfly, and freestyle, setting world records. At the 1964 games she won the first-ever 400-meter medley, in which competitors swam four laps (one each of the breaststroke, backstroke, butterfly, and freestyle), setting a world record. She was also a member of the gold-medal-winning team in the 400-meter freestyle relay. At age seventeen, after the 1964 Olympic Games, de Varona retired from competitive swimming. During her swimming career she won thirty-seven individual national titles and set eighteen national and world records.

De Varona is considered not only one of the fastest swimmers, but also one of the most versatile and best all-around swimmers. These thirty-seven individual national championships were won using three different strokes including freestyle, backstroke, and butterfly. In addition she set eight long-course (fifty-meter pool) world records and ten short-course (twenty-five-yard pool) American records.

De Varona graduated from Santa Clara High School in 1965. She began her broadcasting career at age seventeen, when she was hired to be a part of a live telecast for the Senior Men's National Swimming and Diving Championships. That year, as an undergraduate at the University of California, Los Angeles, the American Broadcasting Company (ABC) hired de Varona as the first female sportscaster on a television network (she would return to earn a B.S. in political science in 1986). She also appeared on ABC's *Wide World of Sports*. De Varona widened her scope by juggling roles as host, co-host, special reporter, and analyst during some of ABC's premiere events, and was the first woman to cover the Olympics on television, including six Olympic Summer Games from 1968 to 1996, and four Olympic Winter Games from 1980 to 1994. In addition, she served as the first female host of the 1980 Olympic coverage in Moscow, Russia. In 1998, she joined the TNT coverage at the Nagano Winter Olympics, hosting with Jim Lampley as they did at the 1984 Games. De Varona continued a successful career in broadcasting for the next twenty years, covering many sports and the Olympics for cable networks as well as for ABC and NBC. She won an Emmy Award in 1991 for her report on a Special Olympics athlete. De Varona also co-produced, wrote, and hosted "Keepers of the Flame," a one-hour ABC Olympic television special that was nominated for an Emmy Award.

In April 2000, de Varona sued ABC Sports, claiming an unlawful termination because of age and sex. She maintained that executives warned her that her advancing age was a detriment because ABC wanted to reach a younger market. Later that year, de Varona joined NBC's Olympic coverage at the Sydney, Australia, Olympics, marking the broadcast of her twelfth Olympic Games. Since 1998, de Varona has provided weekly commentary for Sporting News Radio, the nation's largest sports radio network. She received the Gracie Allen Award for excellence in broadcasting in 2000 and 2001.

Throughout her athletic and broadcasting careers de Varona always championed fairness and increasing opportunities for women. In 1974 she and tennis star Billie Jean King joined forces to found the Women's Sports Foundation, an organization dedicated to encouraging girls and women to participate in sports and demanding gender equality in sport. De Varona testified in 1972 in both the Senate and the House to help pass Title IX legislation, and she also supported the Amateur Sports Act of 1978. She served on two presidential commissions, Gerald Ford's Commission on Olympic Sports in 1975, and Jimmy Carter's Women's Advisory Commission. She also served five times on the President's Council on Physical Fitness and Sports.

De Varona married John Pinto, an investment banker, on 10 January 1987; they had two children. In 1996 de Varona was a recipient of the Flo Hyman Award at the Tenth Annual National Girls and Women in Sport Day. In 1999 she was named as the chair of the organizing committee for the women's World Cup soccer tournament. De Varona was inducted into the International Swimming

Hall of Fame in 1969, the International Women's Sports Hall of Fame, and the U.S. Olympic Hall of Fame in 1987. As an outstanding young athlete, a champion of equal rights for women in the sports arena, and a highly visible presence in the media, de Varona made a significant impact on the world of women's sports.

★

During her swimming career, de Varona appeared on the covers of *Life* (9 Oct. 1964), and several other national magazines. She wrote *Hydro-Aerobics* (1984), with Barry Tarshis. Several books highlight de Varona's accomplishments, including Anne Johnson, *Great Women in Sports* (1996), and K. Christensen, A. Guttman, and G. Pfister, *International Encyclopedia of Women and Sports* (2001). Three good online resources are the Women's Sports Foundation website at www.womensportsfoundation.org, the ISHOF website at www.ishof.org, and the Olympic Hall of Fame website at www.olympic-usa.org.

SHAWN LADDA

DICKERSON, Eric Demetric (*b.* 2 September 1960 in Sealy, Texas), one of the most prolific running backs in college and the National Football League (NFL) who, with his tremendous stamina and smooth running style, broke rushing records at Southern Methodist University and in the NFL with the Los Angeles Rams and Indianapolis Colts.

Dickerson was raised in the small town of Sealy by his great-aunt Viola and great-uncle Kary. He grew up in a loving and supportive home, believing they were his mother and father. When he was fifteen, however, he discovered that his birth mother was Mary, a woman he thought to be his older sister. Dickerson seems to have been relatively unaffected by these revelations. He maintained a close relationship with both Viola, whom he considered his true mother, and Kary, who died when Eric was seventeen.

At Sealy High School Dickerson ran for over 6,000 yards and was a Parade High School All-American. He ran the 100-yard dash in 9.4 seconds and held the record for the most yards in a Texas High School championship game at 296 yards—a record not broken until 1994 by another running back from Sealy. He was the nation's top prep school running back during his senior year.

Dickerson wanted to play for coach Barry Switzer at the University of Oklahoma, but his mother felt that Southern Methodist University (SMU) in Dallas was better for him—she didn't trust Switzer. Dickerson bowed to her wishes and entered SMU in 1978. His first year there was miserable because the older players resented the hype surrounding his high school play, and his injuries that year limited him to only 477 yards rushing on 115 carries. Returning for his sophomore year, his coaches implemented

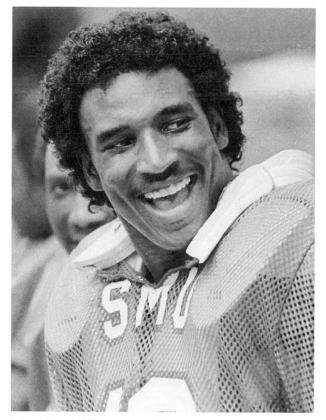

Eric Dickerson, 1982. ASSOCIATED PRESS AP

a strategy that had him and running back Craig James alternate as tailback. Though Dickerson rushed for 928 yards that season and averaged 7.9 yards per carry, he felt that the coaches weren't using him to his fullest ability.

Disheartened, he attempted to transfer to Oklahoma. But Switzer never received his phone message, and his mother's opinion of the coach hadn't changed. As a result, Dickerson returned to SMU for the remainder of his college career. Later, Dickerson wrote that he learned two things from this experience: "don't be so impatient" and "my mom has excellent advice." He went on to break Earl Campbell's Southwestern Conference rushing record with 4,450 yards and the SMU touchdown record with forty-seven. He averaged an astonishing 147 rushing yards per game and won All-American honors in his final two years. His running style was so smooth that it appeared he was running at half speed—until he broke into the secondary, and no one could catch him.

Dickerson's wish to play for the Los Angeles Rams came true when they chose him as the second overall choice in the 1982 draft, after the Colts chose John Elway as the number-one pick. That July the Los Angeles Express of the United States Football League offered Dickerson a contract substantially larger than that of the Rams. Dickerson turned to his mother for advice again. "Go with the NFL," she told him, noting that the NFL was better established.

Though the six-foot, three-inch, 220-pound Dickerson had poor eyesight and wore goggles on the field, he broke the rookie rushing record that year with 1,808 yards on 390 attempts and 18 rushing touchdowns. He was named Rookie of the Year by the Associated Press and was the NFC Player of the Year. His second year was even better: he rushed for 2,105 yards, breaking the single-season record from 1973 held by his idol, O. J. Simpson. He also broke Simpson's record for the most 100-yard rushing games in a season with twelve, as well as the record for the most yards from scrimmage in a single season with 2,244.

With Dickerson's help, the Rams made it to the playoffs in each of his first four years; he led the league in rushing three of them. His ability to run as hard at the end of the game as in the beginning earned him the nickname "Mr. Fourth Quarter." He holds the NFL record for yards rushing in a playoff game (285).

In 1985 Dickerson held out for more money and missed the first two games of the season. Nevertheless, he rushed for 1,234 yards that season and set a personal record of 248 yards rushing in a single game against the Cowboys. In 1986 he was named the Associated Press Offensive Player of the Year.

In the strike-shortened season of 1987, Dickerson's constant complaining and contract disputes led the Rams to trade him to the Indianapolis Colts in a three-team, ten-player deal. In only nine games with the Colts he rushed for 1,011 yards. He followed with two more 1,000-yard seasons, setting an NFL record with seven straight 1,000-yard seasons.

In 1990 the Colts accused Dickerson of exaggerating minor injuries, and others suggested that despite his speed, he was lazy, running out of bounds when it wasn't necessary. They suspended him for a number of games in the 1991 season for "conduct detrimental to the team." The next season the Colts traded Dickerson to the Los Angeles Raiders on draft day. After an unproductive season, the Raiders released him, and the Atlanta Falcons picked him up and tried to trade him to the Green Bay Packers. However, Dickerson failed a physical when the team doctors discovered a spinal injury. As a result, he retired on 20 October 1993.

Dickerson ended his career with 13,259 yards, ranking fourth in total yards behind Walter Payton, Barry Sanders, and Emmitt Smith. He was only the seventh running back to reach 10,000 yards rushing, but he reached it faster (ninety-one games) than any of the other seven. He was named to six Pro Bowls and was an All-Pro five times. In 1999 he was inducted into the NFL Hall of Fame.

After retiring, Dickerson devoted himself to public speaking and charity work, and was a college football analyst and sideline reporter. He also cohosted *In the Huddle*

for Fox Sports with his former SMU teammate Craig James. Beginning in 2000 he became the sideline reporter for ABC's *Monday Night Football*.

Dickerson's speed, fluid moves, and straight-up running style, coupled with his stamina and his record-setting rushing yardage, make him one of the premiere running backs in the annals of the NFL.

★

Eric Dickerson and Steve Delsohn, *On the Run* (1986), is an autobiographical story in which Dickerson gives numerous personal details and defends himself against some of the criticisms leveled at him. Two books written during his play with the Rams give brief biographies of Dickerson: Rich Roberts, *Eric Dickerson: Record-Breaking Rusher* (1985), and Nancy Neilson, *Eric Dickerson* (1988). *Football Greats* by Joe Horrigan and Bob Carroll (1998) details Dickerson's major accomplishments on the field and relates some anecdotes.

Markus H. McDowell

DICKEY, William Malcolm ("Bill") (*b.* 6 June 1907 in Bastrop, Louisiana; *d.* 12 November 1993 in Little Rock, Arkansas), National Baseball Hall of Fame enshrinee who posted a lifetime batting average of .313, was voted to the All-Star team eleven times, and served as a coach under New York Yankee manager Casey Stengel.

Dickey was one of six children born into the working-class family of John Dickey, a railroad worker, and Laura Dickey, a homemaker. Dickey graduated from Searcy High School in 1925 with an academic diploma. He attended Little Rock Junior College in Arkansas but dropped out after one year. In 1928 he married Violet Ann Arnold of Passaic, New Jersey; they had one daughter. While in college Dickey played semiprofessional baseball in Hot Springs, Arkansas, where he was signed in 1926 by the Little Rock team in the Southern Association. A number of major league teams displayed interest in the young catcher, who signed a contract with the New York Yankees in 1928, with the condition that he start the season with Little Rock. After hitting .300 in sixty games for the minor league team, Dickey was promoted to the Yankees, where he finished the season hitting .200 in ten games.

Dickey became the Yankees' regular catcher in 1929 and went on to catch at least 100 games a year in each of thirteen consecutive seasons (1929–1941), an enduring major league record. He was an integral part of the great Yankee teams managed by Joe McCarthy during the 1930s and early 1940s that included such stars as Lou Gehrig, Joe DiMaggio, Lefty Gomez, Red Ruffing, Joe Gordon, and Charlie Keller. In 1936 Dickey hit .362, his highest single-season batting average, and in 1943, his last full season, he batted .353 in eighty-five games. He spent the 1944 and 1945 seasons as

Bill Dickey, 1935. ASSOCIATED PRESS AP

a lieutenant in the U.S. Navy, and in this capacity organized recreational activities in the Pacific.

After the war Dickey returned to the Yankees in 1946 as an active player, but when McCarthy resigned as manager because of ill health, Dickey was named to replace him. He served in that capacity until September, when he resigned due to illness, and when it became obvious that the Yankees could not overtake the Boston Red Sox, who won the pennant that year. His record as interim manager was 57–48. He was succeeded for the remainder of the year by Johnny Neun.

Dickey returned to the Yankees in 1949 as a coach under Casey Stengel and served in that capacity until 1957. He is credited with tutoring Larry "Yogi" Berra in the basic skills of catching as well teaching Elston Howard, the Yankees' first African-American player, the ropes as a catcher. In 1954 Dickey was elected to the National Baseball Hall of Fame. He scouted for the Yankees from 1959 to 1960, then retired from baseball to sell securities as a representative for Stephens, Inc., a brokerage firm in Little Rock, an occupation he pursued until 1977, when he retired.

Dickey, who batted left-handed but threw right-handed, was the premier catcher of the 1930s and early 1940s. He was a lifetime .313 hitter who played in 1,789 games and made 1,969 hits, including 343 doubles, 72 triples, 202 home runs, 930 runs scored, and 1,209 runs batted in. He played in every inning of the 1938 World Series contest, in which the Yankees won. Dickey bridged the Babe Ruth, Lou Gehrig, and Joe DiMaggio eras as a player and the early Mickey Mantle years as a coach. His quiet demeanor belied his fiery approach to his job as catcher. For example, on 4 July 1932 he was suspended for thirty days and fined $1,000 for breaking the jaw of Washington Senator Carl Reynolds with a punch after a collision at home plate.

Dickey's career was filled with singular highlights. He hit three home runs in one game on 6 July 1939; he caught 125 games without a passed ball during the 1931 season; he was the first player to catch 100 or more games for thirteen seasons; and he was selected for eleven All-Star games. A close friend of Lou Gehrig and his roommate on the road, he was the first Yankee player to find out about Gehrig's illness and was the only active player to play himself in the movie *Pride of the Yankees* (1942). Asked by the sportswriter John P. Carmichael to recall his greatest day in baseball, Dickey chose game five of the 1943 World Series, when he hit a two-run home run off St. Louis Cardinal pitcher Mort Cooper in a 2–0 series-winning Yankee victory.

Dickey's Yankee jersey number 8, was retired in 1972 in honor of both him and Yogi Berra, who had worn the same number. In 1980 the Yankee foundation gave Dickey the Pride of the Yankees Award as well. Dickey died at age eighty-six of complications from a stroke in Little Rock. He is buried there in Roselawn Cemetery.

Dickey was unquestionably one of the baseball's greatest catchers. An expert handler of pitchers and the owner of a deadly accurate arm, in his day Dickey rivaled outstanding catchers such as Mickey Cochrane of the Philadelphia Athletics and Gabby Hartnett of the Chicago Cubs as baseball's best defensive receiver. Adding his extraordinary batting achievements to his top-notch defensive skills, Dickey must be rated among the best all-around catchers in the history of baseball.

★

There is no biography of Bill Dickey, but a great deal of information about him is included in books and anthologies on baseball. See Ray Robinson, *Iron Horse: Lou Gehrig in His Time* (1990); Lee Allen and Tom Meany, *King of the Diamond* (1965); and *My Greatest Day in Baseball, As Told to John P. Carmichael, Sports Editor of the Chicago Daily News, and Other Noted Sports Writers* (1945). An obituary is in the *New York Times* (14 Nov. 1993).

JACK FISCHEL

DIDRIKSON ZAHARIAS, Mildred Ella ("Babe") (*b.* 26 June 1911 in Port Arthur, Texas; *d.* 27 September 1956 in Galveston, Texas), accomplished multisport female athlete who was an Olympic gold medallist, a cofounder of the Ladies Professional Golf Association, a pioneer in women's sports, and a medical humanitarian.

Didrikson was the sixth of seven children born to Ole Didriksen, a seaman, furniture refinisher, and cabinetmaker, and Hannah Marie Olson, who took in wealthy neighbors' laundry for pay. An early error in Didrikson Zaharias's school records changed the spelling of her name from "Didriksen" to "Didrikson." She let the error go unchecked into adulthood because she thought the new spelling sounded less ethnic. Three of Didrikson's siblings were born in Norway. In 1905 her father immigrated to Port Arthur, Texas, and fulfilled immigration requirements by working for three years before bringing his family to join him.

Didrikson's nickname "Babe" originated from the Norwegian *baden,* meaning baby. For a short while Babe was the youngest, and her mother, never fluent in English, used a mixed Norwegian-English within the home. The adult Babe claimed her nickname's origin stemmed from childhood pals who dubbed her in honor of Babe Ruth, the legendary baseball slugger. Early on Didrikson learned the value of colorful and hyperbolic storytelling from her father, who frequently regaled the clan with exotic tales of his days at sea. Babe adopted his style and regularly distorted facts to entertain an audience.

In the gritty, seaport shipping town of Port Arthur, Didrikson was a natural leader among her peer group and managed to escape parental scrutiny to indulge in competitive games. She challenged any child, usually boys, to marble-shooting competitions, foot races, jumping contests,

Babe Didrikson Zaharias, 1947. ASSOCIATED PRESS

and throwing marathons. She loathed household chores, such as cleaning, cooking, and sewing, that were considered girls' proper domain. Her parents proudly encouraged her exceptional athleticism. Didrikson relished this supportive atmosphere and never felt parental judgment against her tomboyishness, which bordered on ruffian status. She unapologetically fought, cursed, and masterminded dangerous pranks. After a crushing hurricane forced her mother to insist that they move seventeen miles inland to Beaumont, Texas, Didrikson was quickly dubbed "the worst kid on Doucette Street." On this street she practiced her "hedge hopping," knee crooked, as she imagined Olympic glory.

First at David Crockett Junior High, then at Beaumont High, Didrikson distinguished herself as a stellar athlete. She excelled in baseball, basketball, tennis, golf, swimming, and diving. In high school she was charismatic, adored by some teammates and loathed by others. She shunned the stereotypical interests assigned to girls and consequently was an outsider to the daily activities of both boys and girls. The Beaumont-based sports writer "Tiny" Bill Scurlock wrote of Babe in these years that she was "flamboyant, down-to-earth, apparently gruff at times . . . but considerate, humorous friendly, warm-hearted and generous."

Her reputation on the basketball court lured Colonel M. J. McCombs from the Dallas-based Employer's Casualty Insurance Company (ECIC) to a Royal Purple high school game with an eye toward recruiting her for his company's industrial league team. Duly impressed with her aggressive play and scoring ability, he offered her a $75-per-month salary to work as a "secretary" and play ball for the company team. During the middle of the Great Depression, this was a terrific wage, and her parents agreed in part to encourage her athleticism but also to garner this fantastic salary for the family's betterment. Didrikson withdrew from Beaumont temporarily on 14 February 1930, to return in June for her diploma, and sent $45 home each month.

In reality Didrikson never sat behind a typewriter, but she led the Golden Cyclones to two national championships in 1930 and 1931. She was twice selected to the All-America team. She also honed her self-promotional skills while at ECIC. She insisted on wearing skin-tight orange satin shorts and tank tops that semiscandalized the fans but packed the house full. Her teammates quickly followed suit.

During the basketball off-season Didrikson competed on other ECIC teams. She was a feared slugger in softball and once falsely claimed she had hit thirteen home runs in a double header; and she was the star attraction of the diving team dubbed "Mildred Didrikson and Her Employer's Casualty Girls." The team members also gave golf lessons at the Dallas Country Club and in the summer competed in track and field at McCombs's behest. Her practice sessions became legendary. She pushed herself physically beyond all reasonable comfort, but the results were mighty. At an Amateur Athletic Union (AAU) sanctioned meet in June 1930, Didrikson, competing on a badly cut foot, set a U.S. record in the high jump and placed first in the shot put, baseball throw, and javelin. Her team won the meet, outscoring their nearest competitor 78 to 46. Didrikson scored 28. The Golden Cyclones won the AAU crown. This cemented Didrikson's determination to try for the 1932 Olympics, a dream she had harbored since her childhood. At the 1932 AAU championships in Evanston, Illinois, which doubled as the U.S. Olympic team tryouts, Babe competed as a one-woman team, a clever stunt concocted by McCombs, and she blew away her competition. She won six of the ten events in which she competed: the shot put, setting AAU and U.S. records of 39 feet 6.5 inches; the baseball throw, setting a world record of 272 feet 2 inches; the javelin throw, besting her own world record with 139 feet 3 inches; the 80-meter hurdles with 12.1 seconds; first place tie with Jean Shiley in the high jump with 5 feet 3/16 inches, setting an AAU record; and the broad jump with 17 feet 6 inches. She captured fourth in the discus. In the space of three hours Didrikson won six gold medals, broke four world records, and single-handedly earned thirty points. The second place team scored twenty-two points.

This stellar series of accomplishments catapulted Didrikson into the national headlines. Ironically, Olympic rules insisted that women compete in only three events per Olympic Games. They reasoned that women's frail physiology and childbearing capabilities would be damaged with greater exertion. Frustrated, Didrikson chose the javelin, the high jump, and the 80-meter hurdles. At the Los Angeles Games, Didrikson's stellar performances gained her international recognition as the undisputed female Olympic star. She set a world record in the javelin with a throw of 143 feet 4 inches. In the 80-meter hurdles she set world and Olympic records with a time of 11.7 seconds, which surpassed her previous mark set at Evanston. This victory, she quipped to an eager press corps, is where "all that hedge hopping on Doucette Street finally paid off." In her third event she was awarded a controversial tie for first with Jean Shiley, her steady rival in the high jump. Didrikson actually outjumped Shiley, but her unorthodox style provoked controversy. After a thirty-minute delay and numerous reviews of the visual tape, Didrikson was awarded a half-gold, half-silver medal, the only one of its kind. It symbolized in a clear way the controversy Didrikson embodied.

Following her Olympic triumphs, Didrikson parlayed her fame into paychecks through a brief stint as a stage entertainer in Chicago, where she sang, played the harmonica, and "performed" on a treadmill. She pitched for the all-male, all-bearded barnstorming baseball team of former big leaguers called the House of David, and she ar-

ranged one-on-one pitching outings against active big leaguers such as Jimmy Foxx, and Paul Dean, and Dizzy Dean. This vagabond existence was lonely and profitable, and it smacked of sideshow theatrics. From 1932 through 1934 Didrikson was hounded by cruel portrayals in the press, which cast her as neither female nor male but rather the premiere member of a "Third Sex" and, equally disparaging, a "muscle moll."

Didrikson sought two things, relief from the unkind speculation about her gender identity and a steady source of income that emanated from athletic talent, not circus-like antics. To this end she tackled golf with the same vehement devotion she had levied at track and field. Plagued with a series of amateur versus professional designations, Didrikson found her playing opportunities severely limited. She believed she was not of the ilk that women's golf sought to attract because she was working class, ethnic, loud, coarse, and self-aggrandizing. Under the gentle and humorous tutelage of Bertha Bowen, a higher-up in Dallas's women's golf scene, Didrikson successfully transformed herself into a "lady golfer" replete with makeup, toned-down language, and permed hair. While she flailed against this transition to "proper womanhood," she understood that any further economic success depended upon a transformed public image. During these years she practiced golf tirelessly, often driving 1,500 balls in a day until her hands bled.

In January 1938, still struggling to regain her amateur standing, Didrikson was paired with a professional wrestler, George "the Crying Greek from Cripple Creek [Colorado]" Zaharias, at a celebrity golf tournament in Los Angeles, California. After a swift courtship, they married on 3 January 1938 in St. Louis, and had no children. George Zaharias also became her manager, promoter, and biggest fan. Didrikson Zaharias liked to tell the press that Zaharias was originally a svelte and fit "Greek G-d" who later, through slothful eating habits and complete physical abandon, ballooned out to over 400 pounds. She then changed her estimation of her husband to "just another gawd-damned Greek." A laugh, Didrikson Zaharias believed, was worth any cost, even if at was at George's or her own expense. During these lean years Didrikson Zaharias engaged in one-on-one matches with great male golf professionals, including Gene Sarazen.

Restored to competitive status, Didrikson Zaharias dominated women's golf in the 1940s. She routinely hit 250- to 275-yard tee shots and sank 20-foot putts easily. She pandered to the gallery, performing outrageous trick shots while bantering saucy one-liners. These antics made her a thorn in the sides of some of her golf peers, Betty Hicks prime among them. But all golfers acknowledged that Didrikson Zaharias brought to their sport the flair and the box office so badly needed. Her staunchest ally and defender was Peggy Kirk Bell.

Didrikson Zaharias was overpowering her competition by 1945. She won her second Texas Women's Open, her third Western Open, and placed first over Betty Jameson in seventy-two-hole challenge matches at Los Angeles and San Antonio. For this she was named Woman Athlete of the Year in the annual Associated Press poll. She had won that award in 1932 for her track and field excellence, and she ultimately won it a total of six times in her life.

In 1946 Didrikson Zaharias began her phenomenal winning streak of thirteen consecutive tournaments. Most newsworthy was her capture of the British Women's Amateur Championship in 1947. She was the first American woman to win the coveted title. In matches Didrikson Zaharias often obliterated her nearest opponent by upwards of ten strokes. In other instances she eked out thrilling last-minute victories. This unparalleled record opened up new economic opportunities, including endorsements of sports equipment, a clothing line named after her, a ghostwriting stint as a golf columnist, and a position as saleswoman for batteries, watches, and other miscellaneous products. She became the first female athlete to earn over $100,000 in her career.

By 1950 Didrikson Zaharias was the undisputed queen of women's golf. She and George Zaharias helped found the Ladies Professional Golf Association (LPGA) from 1946 to 1947 that assured competitors of improved paydays. Yet their strong-armed tactics, reminiscent of Zaharias's "wrastlin' racket," alienated most of the league's other founders. Despite her stormy relationships with her golfing peers, Didrikson Zaharias was elected president of the LPGA three times.

By 1950 Didrikson Zaharias yearned for a permanent home and a less-grueling life. George Zaharias did not agree and ignored her mounting fatigue and the distance growing between them. At a tournament in San Antonio, Didrikson Zaharias met Betty Dodd, a much-ballyhooed young golfer, twenty years Didrikson Zaharias's junior, who became her travel companion, personal caretaker, intimate companion, and second lifelong mate. Throughout their six-year relationship, Didrikson Zaharias adamantly denied and hid their sexual intimacy. Zaharias, fully aware of the women's bond, chose to remain in residence at the various homes he grudgingly finally agreed to establish. He frequently took long solo road trips in their flamboyant pink Cadillac, leaving Didrikson Zaharias and Dodd alone to pursue the simple pleasures of home life and golf tournaments.

In April 1953 Didrikson Zaharias, who had been remarkably healthy throughout her life, was diagnosed with colon cancer. Once the colostomy was performed, she and Dodd entered a new phase of their relationship. Dodd be-

came the only medical caretaker Didrikson Zaharias fully trusted. Her physicians at the University of Texas Medical Branch in Galveston told Didrikson Zaharias she was cured of the disease, and she went public with her cancer as a self-help role model, an extremely brave action in the 1950s, when cancer was stigmatized and feared. Didrikson Zaharias appeared on behalf of the American Cancer Society, engaged in much-needed fund-raising, and started a series of Babe Zaharias Golf Tournaments to benefit cancer treatment and research. Her struggles took on Herculean dimensions in the press. She returned to competitive golf a mere fourteen weeks after her operation and regained championship form in February 1954.

Between 1953 and September 1956, when she finally succumbed to the disease, Didrikson Zaharias struggled through a series of debilitating hospitalizations, indeterminate diagnoses, and immense personal stress aggravated by the increasingly acrimonious relationship between Zaharias and Dodd. Upon her death Didrikson Zaharias was mourned by surviving kin, President Dwight D. Eisenhower, the European press, fans, peers, and her two partners. She is buried in Forest Park Cemetery in Beaumont.

The sports legacy of Didrikson Zaharias is unparalleled. She captured eighty-two golf tournament wins in her eighteen-year dominance of women's golf; she was inducted into seven sports halls of fame; she was named Female Athlete of the Half Century in 1950; and she held and broke hundreds of individual sports records. An impressive museum in her honor in Beaumont rotates her trophies twice yearly to allow each some "show time," so great are they in number. She also distinguished herself as a medical humanitarian through her efforts on behalf of cancer education and fund-raising.

At the close of the twentieth century, as the lists of greats were compiled, Didrikson Zaharias emerged as the top female athlete of the century chosen by the Associated Press and the ESPN Sports Network. Few would dispute her reign as the greatest all-sport athlete. Her own life foreshadowed the dilemmas and struggles faced by generations of women athletes. At the same time she greatly expanded the opportunities for all those who followed in the paths she blazed.

★

Didrikson Zaharias's personal papers are in the Special Collections of the John Gray Library at Lamar University, Beaumont, Texas, and newspaper clippings chronicle her illustrious career in the scrapbooks at the Babe Didrikson Zaharias Museum, Beaumont, Texas. See Babe Didrikson Zaharias as told to Harry Paxton, *This Life I've Led: My Autobiography* (1955). The most comprehensive biography is Susan E. Cayleff, *Babe: The Life and Legend of Babe Didrikson Zaharias* (1995). A young adult version also by Cayleff is *Babe Didrikson: The Greatest All-Sport Athlete of*

All Time (2000). Also of value is William Oscar Johnson and Nancy Williamson, *Whatta-Gal* (1975). An obituary is in the *New York Times* (27 Sept. 1956).

SUSAN E. CAYLEFF

DILLARD, Harrison   (*b.* 8 July 1923 in Cleveland, Ohio), Hall of Fame athlete and the only man in Olympic history to win gold medals as both a sprinter and a hurdler.

Dillard, whose father sold ice and coal door-to-door from a horse-drawn wagon, grew up in Cleveland. As skinny African-American boy of thirteen, he sat on a Cleveland curb in 1936 and watched a victory parade for Jesse Owens, who had just won four gold medals at the Olympics in Berlin; Dillard was filled with the desire to run and be an Olympic athlete like Owens. Dillard, whose nickname was "Bones," was taunted by friends saying that he was too scrawny to compete.

One key person, however, was encouraging: Owens, at an Ohio track meet, gave Dillard his Olympic running shoes and advised him to become a hurdler. Throughout his teen years Dillard and his friends used to take the seats out of abandoned cars, burn off the fabric, and use the spring frameworks as hurdles for their practice sessions. Dillard graduated from Cleveland's East Technical High School in 1941; its illustrious graduates included track and field stars Owens and Dave Albritton.

Dillard initially planned to attend Ohio State University, because Owens had gone there and Larry Snyder, Owens's coach, was still there. However, Ohio State was 140 miles from home. He eventually decided to train with Coach Eddie Finnegan at Baldwin-Wallace College in nearby Berea, Ohio.

In his first two years of college Dillard won four national collegiate titles in the high and low hurdles and fourteen Amateur Athletic Union (AAU) outdoor titles in the high and low hurdles. But he was in the U.S. military reserves while attending Baldwin-Wallace, and about a week before his sophomore year ended, Dillard's running career was interrupted when he was called to active duty. During basic training he and some friends got a three-day pass to run in the Ohio Conference championship. Dillard led his team to victory by winning both sprints, both hurdles, and the sprint relay.

While serving in Italy during World War II, Dillard was a member of a segregated troop made up entirely of African Americans, although the officers were white. They initially fought next to the 442nd Infantry Regiment, which was made up of young Japanese-American men. Dillard said, "I recall vividly seeing them walking through fire on the lowlands below. They were over there dying while their relatives were back home in detention camps." Dillard competed on military teams in the "GI Olympics," winning four gold medals and leading General George Patton to say, "He's the best goddamn athlete I've ever seen."

When the war ended Dillard went back to training and to college and by the spring of 1946 his talent was bloom-

Harrison Dillard (*front row, right*) and the 400-meter relay team, en route to the 1948 Olympics. ASSOCIATED PRESS AP

ing. Before his graduation in 1949, he won the National Collegiate Athletic Association (NCAA) and AAU 120-yard and 220-yard hurdles in both 1946 and 1947. With times of 22.3 seconds in the 220 in 1946 (Salt Lake City) and 13.6 seconds in the 120 in 1948 (Kansas Relays in Lawrence), Dillard tied world records in both events.

Part of Dillard's ability to win came from his physique and his personal style. At five feet, ten inches tall and a slender 150 pounds, he did not have the power to leap over hurdles. To compensate, he "drove" over them, clearing thirteen feet total: seven feet before the hurdle and six feet after, about two feet more than other hurdlers. In 1947 and 1948 he won eighty-two consecutive hurdle events and set world records.

Before the 1948 Olympics in London, Dillard said, "I want to clean up the way Jesse Owens did in Berlin." He hit a hurdle in the final trial, however, and did not place in the final for the 110-meter hurdles. But he did qualify for the 100-meter dash. Dillard and fellow American sprinter Barney Ewell hit the finish tape together. Officials had to look at photographs of the race to determine the winner—the first time that technique, now common, was used at an Olympics. Dillard was awarded the gold. He had fittingly tied the Olympic record of 10.3 seconds set by his idol, Owens. In 1948 Dillard also won gold as a member of the U.S. 400-meter relay team, but despite his gold medals for the sprints, he still wanted a gold in the hurdles. Four years later, at the 1952 Olympics in Helsinki, Finland, he hoped he would have his chance.

In 1949 Dillard was employed by the Cleveland Indians baseball club. He wrote promotional material and made public appearances, sometimes as many as a hundred a year. But he continued to run, and the ball club kept him on the payroll while he took time off to train for the 1952 Olympic trials. Winning both the national championship and the Olympic trials, Dillard was a favorite for a gold medal in the 110-meter hurdles.

In the final at Helsinki, he ran cleanly over the hurdles, while his competitor, the American John Davis, hit a hurdle toward the end and landed flatly. Dillard had the tiny lead he needed; the two reached the tape with identical times of 13.7 seconds, but Dillard was in front, winning the gold and fulfilling his promise. At the end of his track career, he was affectionately called "Old Bones" because of his age (twenty-nine).

Dillard was the first runner to win the 100-meter dash in one Olympics and the 110-meter hurdles in another. He also won a gold medal as a member of the U.S. 400-meter relay team in the 1952 Olympics, as he had in 1948, giving him a career gold medal total of four, equal to that of his hero, Owens.

Some innovations in hurdling resulted from Dillard's winning style. For example, modern sprinters look at the

ground when they get on their marks; in Dillard's time, they looked straight ahead. Dillard found that this position led him to look at the sky when he took off, so he began looking at the ground so his head would be aligned straight forward when he took off. In addition, he initiated a very high action with the trailing knee, a motion now used by many hurdlers. Dillard once commented, "I've always felt that sprinters, including me, are a dime a dozen. That's just running. But when you combine running with the gymnastic ability required in the hurdles, you have a high art in track and field athletics."

Later in life Dillard worked for the Cleveland school system, wrote a column for the *Cleveland Press,* and worked in public relations.

Dillard won the Sullivan Award for Amateur Athlete of the Year in 1953. Over the course of his career he won two consecutive double titles in the NCAA and AAU, as well as another AAU title. He won nine indoor AAU championships, set records in the high and low hurdles, and defeated some of the best sprinters in the world. Truly, Owens had passed on his spikes to the right athlete.

★

Cordner Nelson, *Track and Field: The Great Ones* (1970), and *Track's Greatest Champions* (1986), have lengthy chapters on Dillard's life and career. Also see John J. Fogerty, *Tales of Gold* (1987), and Neil Duncanson, *The Fastest Men on Earth: The 100m Olympic Champions* (1988). Informative websites are <http://www.usatf.org> and <http://www.hickoksports.com.>

KELLY WINTERS

DiMAGGIO, Joseph Paul ("Joe"; "The Yankee Clipper") (*b.* 25 November 1914 in Martinez, California; *d.* 8 March 1999 in Hollywood, Florida), one of baseball's greatest players whose varied skills, winning record, fifty-six consecutive-game hitting streak, and role in Marilyn Monroe's life made him a cultural hero.

DiMaggio's parents, Giuseppe Paolo DiMaggio and Rosalie (Mercurio) DiMaggio , were born near Palermo, Italy, probably in the poor Sicilian fishing village of Isola Delle Femmine, where they married. A fisherman, Giuseppe emigrated to the San Francisco area in 1898, and Rosalie and a daughter followed in 1902. In America they had three more girls and five boys, each with the middle name of Paul, after their father and his favorite saint. DiMaggio was born next to last. The big Italian-American family became a strand in the legend of DiMaggio's life, embodying the American dream of "immigrant to riches" success in arguably the most American of sports—baseball, the national pastime.

As a boy, DiMaggio seemed, like many a traditional

Joe DiMaggio, 1938. © BETTMANN/CORBIS

hero, an unlikely candidate for greatness. A quiet, moody, self-contained school dropout (from Galileo High School, San Francisco, in 1930) with no discernible ambition, he at first preferred playing tennis to baseball. His largely unassimilated father considered baseball a "bum's game," but several of DiMaggio's older brothers had shown proficiency at it, particularly Vincent, who in 1931, a low point of the Great Depression, placed on the family kitchen table $1,500 in cash he had earned from the Triple A Pacific Coast League San Francisco Seals. That softened Giuseppe's attitude. Vince and another brother, Dominic, would later become major leaguers.

A superb, seemingly natural and untutored hitter and hard thrower from the start, young DiMaggio earned recognition, merchandise, and money playing as a semiprofessional. Like a traditional hero, his narrative has many wonderful but untrue discovery stories. In one version the scout Spike Hennessey sees him peering through a knothole at the Seals' park looking for Vince. Hennessey tells DiMaggio, "Never stand on the outside, looking in, unless it's jail," and he hauls the frightened boy to an interview with the Seals' president Charlie Graham that ends with DiMaggio being offered a contract. In fact, his technically amateur exploits had often been observed by local scouts and written about frequently in area sports columns when Vince suggested in 1932 that his younger brother help the

Seals out and play shortstop for their last three games. Prophetically, DiMaggio tripled his first time at bat.

In 1933 the right-handed eighteen-year-old batted .340 and set a minor league record, hitting in sixty-one consecutive games. He hit .341 the next year and .398 in 1935. With DiMaggio in the lineup, attendance at Seals' games rose dramatically. He was especially popular among the coast region's numerous Italian Americans, who sought an authentic hero to highlight their increased presence and success as Americans. DiMaggio was the perfect antidote to the clownish, ersatz ex-heavyweight champion Primo Carnera and the un-American Fascist leader Benito Mussolini.

The New York Yankees bought DiMaggio's contract in 1934, gambling that he had recovered fully from a knee injury. Already in 1936 the rangy six foot, two inch rookie, so green he thought the "quote" a writer asked him for was something to drink, was heralded as Babe Ruth's successor in keeping the Yankees on top, a role the magnificent but somehow unspectacular Lou Gehrig had not been able to fulfill. DiMaggio delivered. He would win three Most Valuable Player awards. The Ruth Yankees (1920–1934) won seven pennants and four World Series. During DiMaggio's thirteen seasons (1936–1951; interrupted by army service 1943–1945), the Yankees won ten pennants and nine World Series. DiMaggio was the complete ballplayer: a clutch-hitting slugger and consistent hitter who rarely struck out, a brilliant and graceful center fielder with a great arm, an excellent base runner, and a team player who led by performance.

Prior to his service in the military during World War II, DiMaggio led the American League in batting average (twice), runs, runs batted in (RBI), triples, home runs, total bases, and slugging average. His most famous feat was his fifty-six consecutive-game hitting streak, begun in 1941 with a single against Edgar Smith of the Chicago White Sox on 15 May and ended in a night game 17 July by the Cleveland Indians' Al Smith and Jim Bagby, Jr., with a double-play grounder to Lou Boudreau. The streak has become a legendary achievement in American sport, an almost magical phenomenon that, like Babe Ruth's home run records, may fall but will forever remain a part of sports mythology. Further, like only a few sporting events (such as black Jack Johnson's defeat of white Jess Willard for the heavyweight championship on 4 July 1910), the streak has fostered continued analysis: countless attempts have been made to account for the national excitement it generated, and speculation abounds concerning its historic resonance at a time when post-depression America was being pulled into the trauma of World War II.

Although his dominating level of skill diminished following his return from the service, DiMaggio could still demonstrate his greatness. In 1947 he hit .315, and in the American League only Ted Williams had more runs batted or total bases or a higher slugging average. The Yankees won the World Series against Jackie Robinson's Brooklyn Dodgers, despite Al Gionfiddo's now legendary robbery of what should have been a game-tying DiMaggio home run. In 1948 he hit .320 (his lifetime average would be .325) and led the league in RBI and home runs.

The next year provided possibly the last epic chapter of DiMaggio's playing career. Injuries had prevented him from starting several seasons, including his first, but he had always come back to star as expected. The 1949 season reinforced his image as a wounded hero. In November 1948 he had an operation to eliminate a painful bone spur in his heel and limped through spring training, trying unsuccessfully to rehabilitate himself. Concurrently, the aging athlete and his team's new manager, Casey Stengel, were trying to adjust to each other. DiMaggio did not start the season and grew increasingly depressed and withdrawn. In early May 1949 he attended his father's funeral. In June the "hot" heel, which reportedly felt as though tacks were being driven into it, finally cooled, some accounts say overnight. He returned to the lineup in a critical away series in late June with arch rival Boston, leading what instantaneously became "his" team again to a three-game sweep, hitting five for eleven (.455), with nine RBI and four home runs. During Game 3 a small plane circled Fenway Park displaying a banner that read THE GREAT DiMAGGIO. *Life,* the country's most popular barometer of fame at the time, called him on 1 August a "national hero" whose comeback was achieved "in perfect, fairy-tale fashion." DiMaggio retired after the Yankees beat the New York Giants in the World Series of 1951, a season in which he hit .263. In 1955 he was voted into baseball's Hall of Fame.

DiMaggio had married Dorothy Arnold (Dorothy Arnoldine Olson), a former showgirl and starlet, in 1939. Their union produced a son, Joseph Paul DiMaggio, Jr., and lasted five on-and-off years. But the American movie star Marilyn Monroe came to be known as the great love of his life. The two met in 1952, married 14 January 1954, divorced 27 October the same year, and maintained an intermittently distant, angry, friendly, and intimate relationship until Monroe's shockingly bizarre death on 4 August 1962.

Episodes of the couple's intersecting lives form a grand, romantic, tragic narrative. On their honeymoon trip to Japan, Monroe entertained American troops in Korea and told DiMaggio breathlessly he had never experienced a reception like hers. He curtly replied that he had. DiMaggio was both angered and embarrassed when Monroe's skirt lifted high above her knees as she stood over a subway grating in New York while filming *The Seven Year Itch* (1955). And at her death DiMaggio took control and made the arrangements for a dignified funeral. For decades after, he sent roses to be placed each week at her crypt.

To an unusual extent, he became enshrined as a national symbol, an icon of individual attainment. DiMaggio personified Ernest Hemingway's famous concept of courage—"grace under pressure"—despite injury in his athletic career and ultimately in his relationship with Monroe. Hemingway had presented him as a worthy hero who would well understand an ordinary man's pain in *The Old Man and the Sea* (1952). While Cole Porter and Oscar Hammerstein II, among other lyricists, had previously alluded in popular songs to his skill and grace, the younger singer-songwriter Paul Simon (then of the duo Simon and Garfunkel) featured DiMaggio hauntingly in the song "Mrs. Robinson" (from the 1967 film *The Graduate*), embodying old, long-vanished American virtues, representing an entire generation's search for lost innocence.

Aging gracefully, DiMaggio kept sporadically before the public as the star attraction at old-timers' games, memorabilia signings, and in a variety of visible jobs, most famously as media spokesman in the 1970s for a bank and for the "Mr. Coffee" coffeemaker. He died at home on 8 March 1999, after a lengthy illness following removal of a cancerous tumor from his lung. The nation's deathwatch was protracted, but characteristically his funeral in San Francisco was private. He is buried in Holy Cross Cemetery in Colma, California.

The solid basis of DiMaggio's fame was his high and all-around ability, which earned him, according to a poll of sportswriters and fans during baseball's declared 1969 centennial, the title of "Greatest Living Player." At his best he seemed to play at once with no limit to his ability, yet gracefully within self-established but far-reaching bounds. He has been described as painfully shy, "deadpan," not greatly educated, a stereotypical "young man from the provinces" plunged into the world of the country's signature sport, in its biggest city, for sports' most publicized and successful franchise. Yet he negotiated with amazing success a dangerously high-powered, sometimes mutually exploitative, existence. DiMaggio helped carve out an image for himself that seemed on the surface purely spontaneous. He could be sulky, self-centered, cold, manipulative, and, not surprisingly for a child of the Great Depression, penurious. Through his great skill and grace and through the dignity of a nurtured image that he somehow projected as innate, DiMaggio became a nation's model of worthy, virtuous prowess. It could not have been easy, but he made it look as natural as his swing.

★

Lucky to Be a Yankee, which lists DiMaggio as author, was ghost-written by Tom Meany and published in three versions, the last two "with additional material" (1946, 1949, 1951). Michael Seidel, *Streak: Joe DiMaggio and the Summer of '41* (1988), is an excellent analysis of DiMaggio's single greatest attainment. Maury Allen, *Where Have You Gone, Joe DiMaggio? The Story of America's*

Last Hero (1975), is partisan but balanced, with many interviews. Jack B. Moore, *Joe DiMaggio, Baseball's Yankee Clipper* (1986), clarifies his biography, reviews the literature about him (updated in Richard Gilliam, ed., "Literature About Joe DiMaggio, 1987–Present," in *Joltin' Joe DiMaggio* [1999]), and analyzes his status as a cultural hero. *DiMaggio: An Illustrated Life* (1999), edited by Dick Johnson with text by Glen Stout, contains excellent photographs and a well-researched resume of DiMaggio's life and career. Richard Ben Cramer, *Joe DiMaggio: The Hero's Life* (2000), is extensive and iconoclastic but sometimes undocumented and therefore should be consulted with care. Gay Talese, "The Silent Season of a Hero," *Esquire* (July 1966), focuses on the dark side of DiMaggio's life after baseball and Monroe, and Roger Angell's *New Yorker* remembrance (22 Mar. 1999) is a lovely elegy. Special collections at the University of South Florida, Tampa, and the Cooperstown Baseball Hall of Fame contain some archival materials. "Joe DiMaggio: A Hero's Life" in *The American Experience* series is a good video with supplementary online aids. An obituary is in the *New York Times* (9 Mar. 1999).

JACK B. MOORE

DITKA, Mike (*b.* 18 October 1939 in Carnegie, Pennsylvania), Pro Football Hall of Famer who was known for his unwavering dedication, his intimidating offense, and his overall gutsiness, and who excelled as both player and coach.

Ditka's father, Mike, was an ex-marine, a retired railroader, and a longtime local union president; his mother, Charlotte, was a homemaker. His father taught him, his two brothers, and their sister that they could be the very best if they would fight as hard as they could at everything they tried. Ditka attended Aliquippa High School, where he lettered in football, baseball, and basketball. He weighed only 130 pounds when he first tried out for football as a sophomore. By his junior year he was much larger and played both an end on offense and corner linebacker on defense. Aliquippa did not lose a single game. In his senior year Ditka played fullback and attracted the attention of college scouts by the dozens. He seriously considered an offer from Notre Dame but, after his graduation in 1947, finally opted to attend the University of Pittsburgh.

With Pittsburgh's Panthers, Ditka had the opportunity to demonstrate his varied athletic skills. Defensively, he was exceptional at end and at linebacker. Offensively, as a standout tight end he was a superior blocker and a fine receiver. As the Panthers' captain, he demanded of himself and his teammates a maximum effort on every play. Ditka earned All-America honors in 1961 and ranked among the nation's top punters. He averaged forty yards a punt in his final three seasons.

A few credits shy of graduating from Pittsburgh, Ditka began his National Football League (NFL) career in 1961,

when the Chicago Bears made him their first-round selection. Until that year the prototype tight end in the NFL played close to the tackle, blocked most of the time, and occasionally would catch a pass for ten yards or so. Ditka changed that almost immediately. He still blocked, but he showed something else, too. In his first exhibition game he caught a button-hook pass for twelve yards. In the huddle, quarterback Bill Wade instructed him, "Hook now and take off when the safety man crowds you." The result was a seventy-yard catch and a run for a touchdown. "That play," Ditka recalls, "gave me the confidence to be a pro. I knew it wasn't impossible for me to outdo these guys." Ditka startled opponents with fifty-six catches for 1,076 yards and twelve touchdowns, earning NFL Rookie of the Year and All-NFL honors in the process. Defensive coaches were forced to devise new methods of combating this new offensive terror.

In the Associated Press Rookie of the Year balloting, Ditka received eighteen votes; runner-up Fran Tarkenton of the Minnesota Vikings received only six. Despite a knee injury suffered in the eleventh game that would have sidelined most, Ditka agreed to play in the Pro Bowl. He was subsequently picked for the next four Pro Bowls as he continued to ravage enemy defenses. He was named All-NFL again in 1962, 1963, and 1964. Ditka played five more seasons with the Bears, earning a Pro Bowl trip each year, before being traded to Philadelphia in 1967. After two years with the Philadelphia Eagles he played four more with the Dallas Cowboys, for whom he caught a touchdown pass from Roger Staubach in a 24–3 win over the Miami Dolphins in Super Bowl VI.

Ditka retired from playing following the 1972 season and was hired by the Cowboys' head coach, Tom Landry, as an offensive assistant and special teams coach. At this point Ditka—known by players as "Iron Mike"—reiterated his playing philosophy, which he intended to stress with his charges as a coach: "There's more to winning than wanting to. You have to prove yourself every Sunday. Just throwing your helmet on the field doesn't scare anyone." In Ditka's nine seasons as assistant coach, the Cowboys were in the playoffs eight times and won six division titles, three NFL championships, and the NFL crown following the 1977 campaign.

Prior to the 1982 season Ditka signed on as head coach of the Chicago Bears, taking over a team that had just two winning seasons in the previous nineteen years. Ditka was a coach with an unwillingness to lose with grace—an outgrowth of his father's demanding code. His own code word for teamwork was ACE: Attitude, Character, and Enthusiasm. He gave 110 percent to the game and expected the same of his team. He intended to build a championship team through the draft and in 1982 took Jim McMahon, a

Mike Ditka held aloft after his Chicago Bears won Super Bowl XX, 1986. ASSOCIATED PRESS AP

quarterback, as his first pick for the Bears. In 1983 the team began to take form.

At the end of the 1983 season the Bears had moved to .500. Ditka believed that "you need to try to hit the other guy before he hits you and if you hit hard enough, maybe he won't want to hit you back." He growled and seethed on the sidelines. The team took full shape in the 1984 draft. The Bears finished the season at 10–6 and for the first time since 1963 won a postseason game. They lost in the second round to San Francisco. In 1985 they destroyed the league en route to a 15–1 record. After winning only one playoff game in twenty-one years, the Bears shut out both the Giants and the Rams. Led by the charismatic quarterback McMahon and assisted by the 300-pound William "Refrigerator" Perry, Chicago then overpowered the New England Patriots, 46–10, in the most lopsided Super Bowl to date.

Ditka was awarded Coach of the Year honors in 1985 and 1988 by *The Sporting News,* the Associated Press, and pro football writers. After a 5–11 season in 1992, however, he was fired by the Bears' president, Mike McCaskey. Ditka then served as an analyst on NBC-TV's Sunday NFL news and highlights show, *NFL Live,* until January 1997, when he became the coach for the New Orleans Saints. Ditka, the twelfth head coach in New Orleans Saints' history, compiled a 127–101 record in fourteen seasons of coaching. After a disappointing season in 1999, however, he was fired the next year.

In 1988 Ditka was inducted into the Pro Football Hall of Fame. His 427 career receptions included 75 catches in 1964 and an NFL record for tight ends that was not exceeded until San Diego's Kellen Winslow broke it in 1980.

In 2001 Ditka still held four Chicago Bears records: consecutive games with a reception, touchdown receptions, most receptions by a rookie, and most touchdown catches by a rookie. He is one of only two coaches to have won a Super Bowl as a player, assistant coach, and head coach. He is also one of just four head coaches to record over 100 coaching victories in ten seasons.

Ditka is a television veteran. In addition to his four years as a regular NBC sports commentator, he has appeared in numerous commercials as well as in guest spots on *L.A. Law* and *Saturday Night Live.* In 1988, after Ditka had a heart attack, he became a spokesperson for American Heart Association heart disease campaigns. He was a guest analyst for NBC's *Super Bowl Live* pregame, halftime, and postgame shows in 1993. Outside of football, Ditka has helped raise money for many charitable organizations, including Misericordia, a residential facility for young people with developmental disabilities. He is highly sought after as a motivational speaker and television personality.

Ditka married his second wife, Diana, in 1977. They live in New Orleans. He had four children from his first marriage to Marge, whom he divorced in 1972.

"Success isn't measured by money or power or social rank," Ditka observed. "Success is measured by your discipline and inner peace. You're never a loser until you quit trying."

★

Ditka is the author of *Ditka: An Autobiography* (1987) *and Don't Get Me Wrong: Mike Ditka's Insights, Outbursts, Kudos, and Comebacks* (1988). See also Richard Whittingham, *The Bears: A*

75-Year Celebration (1994), and Gary D'Amato, *Mudbaths and Bloodbaths: The Inside Story of the Bears–Packers Rivalry* (1997).

REED B. MARKHAM

DOBY, Lawrence Eugene ("Larry") (*b.* 13 December 1924 in Camden, South Carolina), baseball player who became the first African American to play in the American League when he joined the Cleveland Indians in 1947.

Doby was the only child of David Doby, a stable hand and semiprofessional baseball player, and Etta Brooks, a domestic. Doby saw little of his father during his childhood because David Doby went north to work as a groom. His mother also went north, to Paterson, New Jersey, to work as a domestic, leaving her son in the care of his maternal grandmother and, later, his father's sister and her husband. Doby completed the eighth grade at Mather Academy, a Methodist mission school for African-American children, in 1938.

That summer he visited his mother in Paterson, and she insisted that he stay there and attend Eastside High School. Eastside was well regarded academically and had a strong sports program. Doby, a quiet, reserved young man, was one of about twenty-five African-American students in the

Larry Doby. ARCHIVE PHOTOS, INC.

school. As a superb athlete, he was popular with students of all races. In his four years at Eastside, Doby won eleven letters in baseball, football, basketball, and track and earned All-State honors in the first three sports. During high school Doby played basketball in a recreational league as well as on the school team. In summer he played with three semiprofessional baseball teams, including the well-known African-American team Smart Set. Among his teammates on the Smart Set was Monte Irvin, another African American who integrated organized baseball in the late 1940s.

Doby was offered a basketball scholarship at Long Island University in Brooklyn, New York, after his high-school graduation in 1942. He also signed to play professional baseball as an infielder with the Newark (New Jersey) Eagles, who finished in third place in the Negro National League (NNL) that year. To protect his amateur standing at Long Island University, he appeared with the Eagles as Larry Walker. Late in his freshman year, Doby transferred to Virginia Union College, an African-American institution in Richmond, and played on its basketball team. He rejoined the Eagles for the 1943 season but was drafted into the U.S. Navy in the spring. The United States had been plunged into World War II by a Japanese aerial assault on Pearl Harbor in December 1941, and young men were being called to serve in the segregated armed forces. Doby was assigned to the African-American boot camp at Great Lakes Naval Training Station near Chicago. After basic training, he became a physical training instructor and played on the baseball and basketball teams that represented the African-American sailors at Great Lakes.

As the end of World War II neared in the late summer of 1945, Doby was stationed on a tiny coral island in the South Pacific. There he heard a radio report that Branch Rickey, the president of the Brooklyn Dodgers (later the Los Angeles Dodgers), had signed an African-American player named Jackie Robinson to play with the Montreal Royals, the top Dodgers farm club, in 1946. "Then I felt I had a chance to play Major League baseball," Doby remembered. He was discharged from the navy in January 1946 and almost immediately went to Puerto Rico for two months of winter baseball. He rejoined the Newark Eagles as their second baseman and earned a place on the NNL's All-Star team. Doby, a power-hitting left-handed batter, posted a batting average of .341 as the Eagles easily won both halves of the NNL's pennant race and beat the Kansas City Monarchs of the Negro American League, four games to three, in the Negro World Series.

On 10 August 1946, Doby married his high school sweetheart, Helen Curvy, in Paterson. They had five children. Mrs. Doby died of cancer in July 2001.

In 1947 Doby had played only forty-one games with the Eagles when his rights were sold to the Cleveland Indians

241

and stepped over the color line, debuting as a big leaguer on 3 July, eleven weeks after Robinson had integrated the National League by joining the Dodgers. Bill Veeck, the colorful and innovative president of the Indians, paid Effa Manley, the co-owner of the Eagles, $10,000 for Doby plus an additional $10,000 if Doby made the team. He did, although he was not yet a star. The six-foot, one-inch, 180-pound Doby batted only .156 in thirty-two at bats as a pinch hitter and occasional infielder. Worse, only Joe Gordon, the Indians second baseman, went out of his way to welcome Doby to the club. Some teammates refused to shake hands with him. Opponents and fans booed and shouted insults at Doby. A shortstop spat on him as he slid into second base, and he was frequently the target of fast balls thrown at his head.

In 1948 the Hall of Famers Tris Speaker and Bill McKechnie converted Doby into a center fielder, and his considerable talent became evident. Doby batted .301 in 121 games with fourteen home runs. Over his thirteen-year career in the Major Leagues with the Indians, Chicago White Sox, and Detroit Tigers, he batted .283 and slugged 253 home runs. He led the American League twice for homers (with thirty-two both years) and once for runs batted in (126). He was named to the league's All-Star team six straight years (1949–1954).

After retiring from the Major Leagues at the age of thirty-seven, Doby played for two years with the Chunichi Dragons in Japan's Central League. Later he became a batting coach for the Montreal Expos and Chicago White Sox and was briefly the Sox manager in 1978. For several years he was the director of community relations for the New York Nets basketball team and special assistant to the American League president. In 1998 Doby was elected to the Baseball Hall of Fame. Doby's playing statistics did not match those of the game's top players, but his importance as a pioneer in the integration of baseball was rivaled only by that of Jackie Robinson. His old mentor Veeck had assessed Doby's career in 1962: "If Larry had come up just a little later, when things were just a little better, he might very well have become one of the greatest players of all time."

★

The best source on Doby is Joseph Thomas Moore, *Pride Against Prejudice: The Biography of Larry Doby* (1988). Doby is the subject of a chapter in Bill Veeck's entertaining memoir, written with Ed Linn, *Veeck—As in Wreck* (1962). His record in African-American baseball is covered in Dick Clark and Larry Lester, eds., *The Negro Leagues Book* (1994), and James A. Riley, *Biographical Encyclopedia of the Negro Baseball Leagues* (1994). Doby's record in the big leagues is cited in the fourth edition of *The Baseball Encyclopedia* (1979), and the John Thorn et al., eds., *Total Baseball,* 6th ed. (1999).

ROBERT W. PETERSON

DONOVAN, Anne Theresa (*b.* 1 November 1961 in Ridgewood, New Jersey), professional basketball player and coach, a three-time Kodak All-American and three-time Olympian known for her size, power, skill, dedication, and good nature.

Growing up in a close Irish-American family of eight, Donovan always had her family's support. She began playing basketball in her New Jersey driveway. When she entered Paramus Catholic High School in 1975 she was already six feet, one inch tall and towered above most of her teammates. With her height and skill Donovan had the potential to be a ruthless aggressor on the court, mean and threatening. That was not her style. In one high-school game her coach, Rose Battaglia, was using Donovan in a crushing full-court press. The other team could not even inbound the ball. During a time-out Donovan asked Battaglia if they could stop the press. The stunned coach asked Donovan why she wanted to abandon a press that was working so well. Donovan replied, "You're not the one looking into that poor girl's eyes."

Anne Donovan (*left*) as a high school player, c. 1979. © BETTMANN/CORBIS

Donovan's kind and easy nature did not prevent her from winning and setting records. During her junior and senior years she led Paramus to two consecutive undefeated seasons and two Group III state championships. Her individual awards also reflected her skill and ability. She was named to the First Team Parade All-America in 1978 and 1979. In her senior year she averaged thirty-five points and seventeen rebounds per game and was named the Dial Soap National High School Player of the Year. With 2,583 career points Donovan became the most recruited player in the country.

After graduating from Paramus in 1979, the now six-foot, eight-inch Donovan joined the Lady Monarchs at Old Dominion University (ODU) in Norfolk, Virginia, where she majored in leisure studies, and continued to shine on the court. As a first-year student Donovan led ODU to a 37–1 record and the Association of Intercollegiate Athletics for Women (AIAW) national championship victory. In her junior year ODU made an AIAW third-place finish and in her senior year a Final Four appearance. During Donovan's tenure ODU accumulated a 116–20 record.

Donovan's individual totals were equally impressive. She scored 2,719 points in 136 games for an average of 20 points per game, making her the team's all-time leading scorer. Donovan also amassed 1,976 rebounds and an incredible 801 blocked shots, a National Collegiate Athletic Association (NCAA) record. By the time she left ODU in 1983, she held twenty-five school records. From 1981 to 1983 Donovan was consistently named a First Team All-American by the Women's Basketball Coaches Association, American Women's Sports Foundation, and *Basketball Weekly*. She also held Most Valuable Player honors in the ODU Optimist Classic (1980–1983) and the Sun Belt Conference (1983). Donovan capped her college career with the Naismith and Champion Player of the Year awards in 1983.

Donovan was named to three Olympic teams; only four other basketball players held that distinction. The first squad fell victim to the U.S. boycott of the 1980 Moscow games, but in 1984 and 1988 the U.S. team won the gold medal. Donovan was also a member of twelve U.S. basketball teams. She collected medals on the first-place Olympic Festival East teams in 1978 and 1979; on the 1981 World University Games team that took silver; on the gold- and silver-winning Pan American Games squads; and on the World Champion team, winning a silver medal in 1983 and a gold medal in 1986. Out of eleven possible medals, Donovan was part of teams that won nine golds and two silvers.

With her amateur career over, Donovan was forced to look for professional leagues in other countries since there were no professional leagues in the U.S. She decided to play in Japan, although most other U.S. women players opted for European teams. Her parents were skeptical but

said Donovan could go as long as they got to visit. She spent five seasons (1983–1988) in Shizuoka, Japan, and one season (1988–1989) in Modena, Italy, before returning to the United States to coach.

Donovan's first coaching job brought her back to ODU, where she served as an assistant coach of the women's basketball team for six years (1990–1995). During her time on the ODU coaching staff the team won four Colonial Athletic Association (CAA) conference titles and made five NCAA tournament appearances. In 1995 Donovan accepted the head coach position at East Carolina University in Greenville, North Carolina. The Lady Pirates were struggling, having collected only ten wins during the previous two seasons. In just two years with Donovan as their coach, the Lady Pirates earned a CAA tournament championship appearance.

Donovan's extensive playing experience as well as her coaching experience contributed to her success in the international coaching arena. She was named the assistant coach for the 1997 U.S. Basketball Women's World Championship qualifying team. The team had a 4–2 record and earned the silver medal in Brazil, which qualified the United States for the Thirteenth World Championship. The U.S. squad also built a 12–1 record and claimed two tournament titles during a precompetition exhibition tour of Canada, Germany, and Slovakia.

Having coached college and international basketball, Donovan decided to try her hand at coaching professional women's basketball. In 1997 she became the head coach for the Philadelphia Rage in the American Basketball League (ABL). The ABL and the Women's National Basketball Association (WNBA) were created within three months of each other, and were the first efforts at a professional league for women since the Women's Basketball League (WBL) in the late 1970s. The WNBA, however, had the backing of the powerful NBA. Unable to compete with the financial and marketing strength of the NBA, the ABL folded after the 1988–1989 season. Undeterred, Donovan accepted a temporary position with the WNBA in October 1999. The Indiana Fever needed an interim head coach while Nell Fortner coached the national team for the 2000 Olympics. Fortner was grateful to have someone of Donovan's caliber coaching the Fever in her absence. Once Donovan's commitment to the Fever was complete, she was named the head coach of the Charlotte Sting, also a WNBA team, in March 2001.

Donovan was inducted into the Naismith Memorial Basketball Hall of Fame in 1995, the Women's Basketball Hall of Fame in 1999, and the New Jersey Sportswriters Association Hall of Fame in 2000. Continuously involved with women's basketball since 1975, Donovan demonstrated that women could be aggressive and remain in control both on and off the court. While her height gave Donovan an obvious advantage as a player, her work ethic and perseverance set her apart.

★

Information on Donovan comes primarily from current WNBA material and coverage from her college and Olympic career. "Donovan Having Fun Shooting for the Gold," *New York Times Biographical Service* (1987), provides information on her international play. A second article, "Anne Donovan," *Basketball Digest* (Mar. 2001), is about the 1988 Olympics in Seoul, while "A League of Her Own," *World of Hibernia* (autumn 2000), provides a brief biographical sketch. Information on Donovan as the head coach of the Sting can be found on the team's website at <http://www.wnba.com/sting>.

LISA A. ENNIS

DORSETT, Anthony Drew ("Tony") (*b.* 7 April 1954 in Rochester, Pennsylvania), outstanding running back and Pro Football Hall of Fame inductee who won the 1976 Heisman Trophy at the University of Pittsburgh and played in two Super Bowls with the Dallas Cowboys.

Dorsett, the son of West and Myrtle Dorsett, was born in Rochester, Pennsylvania. Playing two seasons for Hopewell High School in western Pennsylvania, he was a *Parade* magazine consensus All-American. His 212 yards gained in one game was a high school record that stood for twelve years.

Dorsett was five feet, eleven inches tall and weighed only 160 pounds when he started as a freshman running back at the University of Pittsburgh in 1973. He finished that year with 1,586 yards and twelve touchdowns in eleven games, on his way to his first selection as an All-American. His accomplishments included gaining 265 yards against Northwestern University.

The sophomore jinx saw his production drop to just over 1,000 yards and eleven touchdowns during the next season. Still, he averaged 4.6 yards per carry. In his third season Dorsett was back over 1,500 yards with an amazing average of 6.8 yards per carry. The highlight of that year was his 303 yards gained against Notre Dame in just twenty-three carries. He capped off his college career with a remarkable senior year in which he gained 1,948 yards while scoring twenty-two touchdowns. In the Sugar Bowl, he added another 202 yards to his totals. A candidate for the Heisman Trophy all four years, Dorsett earned that coveted award in 1976.

At the end of his college career, Dorsett had set more than a score of records at the university and national level. He helped the University of Pittsburgh win the national championship in 1976. He was a first-team All-American all four years.

Tony Dorsett at the Pro Football Hall of Fame, 1994. ASSOCIATED PRESS AP

Dorsett was the first player to gain more than 1,000 yards each of his four college seasons—his total was 6,082 yards rushing (he gained another 406 yards as a receiver and 127 on kick returns). His three seasons with more than 1,500 yards was another record. He tied Glenn Davis (of Army) with fifty-nine touchdowns, but set a record with 356 total career points. His average of 141.1 yards per game over a four-year career is still impressive. He tied Archie Griffin (of Ohio State University) with thirty-three (out of a total of forty-three games played) 100-yard games; eleven of his 100-yard games were accomplished in a single season, also a record.

Dorsett, whose weight by then had climbed to 189 pounds, was drafted by the Dallas Cowboys in the first round of the 1977 professional draft. He rewarded the Cowboys with a season of more than 1,000 yards gained and thirteen touchdowns scored; his running average was an impressive 4.8 yards per carry. The National Football League (NFL) recognized him as Rookie of the Year. In the playoffs, Dorsett scored two touchdowns in Dallas's 37–7 victory over the Chicago Bears. In the conference championship, he scored the final touchdown as the Cowboys beat the Minnesota Vikings 23–6. Though only a first season player, Dorsett got Dallas off to a lead with a three-yard touchdown run in the Super Bowl; Dallas defeated the Denver Broncos 27–10 as he carried fifteen times for sixty-six yards.

In his second season as a pro, Dorsett improved to over 1,300 yards gained on 290 carries. He added an additional 378 yards on thirty-seven receptions. Dallas again made it to the playoffs. Dorsett did not score in the Cowboys' 27–20 victory over the Atlanta Falcons, but had one touchdown in their 28–0 shutout of the Los Angeles Rams in the conference championship. Super Bowl XIII was against the powerful Pittsburgh Steelers. Pittsburgh edged Dallas 35–31 despite Dorsett's ninety-six yards gained on sixteen carries. He added another forty-four yards on four receptions.

In his first nine seasons with the Cowboys, Dorsett was over 1,000 yards each year except for the strike-shortened season of 1982. His best performance was in 1981 when he gained more than 1,600 yards on 342 carries. In three other years, he went over 1,300 yards rushing, though he never again scored more than the thirteen touchdowns of his rookie season.

In postseason play, Dorsett scored one touchdown running and one receiving in Dallas's 34–13 victory over the Rams in the 1980 wild card game. In the conference championship game, he scored the only Dallas touchdown against the Philadelphia Eagles, who won 20–7. The next year, he scored touchdowns in both playoff games, but after beating the Tampa Bay Buccaneers in the first round the Cowboys were edged 28–27 by the San Francisco 49ers.

Nagged by injuries, Dorsett's production deteriorated in the last three years of his career. He missed three full games in 1986 and four the next year. For his last season, 1988, he was traded to Denver. Though he played in all sixteen games, he fell below 4.0 yards per carry for only the third time in his career.

In twelve NFL seasons, Dorsett played in 173 games. He gained almost 1,300 yards, an average of 4.3 yards per carry putting him among the all-time leading rushers in NFL history. Adding the additional 3,500 yards on receptions, his all-purpose total was more than 16,000 yards. He scored ninety touchdowns, seventy-seven by rushing. In seventeen postseason contests, he added close to 1,400 yards rushing and more than 400 receiving. He played in five National Conference title games and two Super Bowls. He was picked for the Pro-Bowl on four different occasions.

Dorsett is married to Julie Dorsett. They have two children and reside in the Dallas area. Their son, Anthony, also played in the NFL.

Not big by the standards of his day for running backs, Dorsett was an elusive runner who excelled in changing speed and direction to find holes in the defense. In 1993, against Minnesota, he scored on a ninety-nine-yard run

from scrimmage. Under NFL rules, that is a record that can be tied but never broken. He was elected to the Pro Football Hall of Fame in 1994.

★

An article in the *Evening News* (Buffalo, New York) (30 Nov. 1976) summarizes Dorsett's college career. Other information can be found in Bob Caroll et al., *Total Football* (1997), David L. Porter, ed., *Biographical Dictionary of American Sport: Football* (1987), and the Pro Football Hall of Fame Archives in Canton, Ohio.

Art Barbeau

DREXLER, Clyde (*b.* 22 June 1962 in New Orleans, Louisiana), one of basketball's all-time great guards who was a ten-time National Basketball Association (NBA) All-Star, a member of the 1992 Olympic "Dream Team," and a dominant player during the 1980s and 1990s.

Drexler, the third of seven children, was four years old when his mother, Eunice Drexler Scott, moved the family to Houston. A single parent, she made sure that all of her children understood the importance of getting an education and that they always completed their schoolwork thoroughly and accurately. In the 1980s she established the successful Drexler's Barbecue restaurant near the campus of the University of Houston. Drexler's father, James, worked for the Carbon Black Chemical Company.

At six feet, seven inches tall and 222 pounds, Drexler acquired the nickname "The Glide" because of his smooth and effortless high-flying moves to the basketball hoop. His professional basketball career began on a junior high school playground in Houston, where he made his first dunk shot. However, Drexler's interest in sports began earlier, with Little League baseball and basketball. His fascination with the dunk began when he was fifteen years old and six feet, one inch tall. The first time Drexler made his magic dunk shot he towered over two other opponents as he went toward the rim, even though the basket was a foot higher than regulations required.

Drexler initially declined to try out for the high school basketball team because he felt it would take too much time away from his studies. In Drexler's junior year at Sterling High School, the basketball coach persuaded him and his mother that he should play. Drexler's hard work, dedication, and competitive spirit led to his consistent improvement during his two years at Sterling. By the end of his second year he had played every position on the team. As a senior, he was named the team's Most Valuable Player (MVP) and made the All-Houston Independent School District team. Drexler graduated from high school in 1980.

For college, Drexler decided to stay near home in familiar surroundings and attended the University of Hous

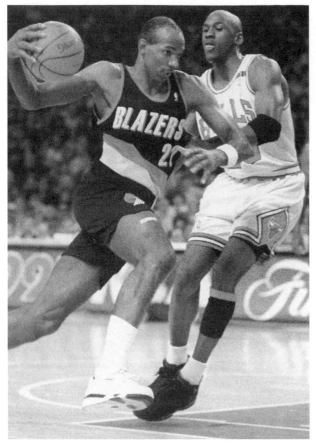

Clyde Drexler (left) with Michael Jordan, 1992. ASSOCIATED PRESS AP

ton, where he first played with the center Hakeem Olajuwon and with Larry Michaeux. They became known as the Fraternity Dunk. Drexler described his team's semifinal game against Louisville at the National Collegiate Athletic Association Final Four as the highlight of his college career. In 1983 the Houston Cougars made it to their second Final Four Championship tournament. The team ranked among the nation's dominant college teams and was called Phi Slamma Jama for their above-the-rim acrobatics. Also in 1983 Drexler was named the Southwest Conference Player of the Year.

According to the Houston coach Guy Lewis, Drexler developed into one of the nation's best two-way guards. His leaping ability and smooth moves to the basket brought him to national prominence. Lewis described Drexler as a superlative defensive player due to his quickness, good hands, and great anticipation. Drexler was the focal point of Houston's transition game, excelling more as a scorer than as a shooter. He scored and rebounded in double figures in forty-five games during his college career, becoming the first Houston player to score more than 1,000 points, grab over 900 rebounds, and collect over 300 assists. Drexler also finished as a record holder in career steals with 268.

In 1983 Drexler decided to forego his senior year in college and entered the professional NBA draft pool. He was chosen in the first round (fourteenth overall) by the Portland Trail Blazers. His first two seasons in Oregon were a time of orientation to the professional game. In the 1985–1986 season, Drexler's third with the Blazers, he became an NBA All-Star, repeating this honor for ten successive seasons thereafter. Drexler stayed with the Trail Blazers for more than eleven seasons, going to the playoffs each year. Portland sports fans felt that Drexler did not always get the recognition he deserved because he was a quiet star in a city removed from intense media hype.

In Drexler's early years with the Trail Blazers, the team usually lost early in the finals. They gradually acquired additional talent and became one of the NBA's powerhouses in the early 1990s. As Portland developed into a contender, recognition came to Drexler. The Blazers went to the NBA finals in 1990 and 1992 and the conference finals in 1991. In the 1990–1991 season Drexler earned All-NBA Second Team honors. The following season was his most memorable; he averaged twenty-five points (fourth in the league), became the second Trail Blazer in history to make the All-NBA First Team, and finished second to Michael Jordan in MVP balloting. The finale to his season was earning a gold medal at the 1992 Olympics in Barcelona, Spain, with the Dream Team.

In the next two NBA seasons Drexler was hampered by injuries and his production fell. In the 1994–1995 season he indicated that he wanted to be traded, and in February 1995 Drexler was reunited with his college teammate Olajuwon, joining the Houston Rockets. Working together, the two powered the Rockets to the 1995 NBA Championship. However, hampered by injuries, Drexler announced that the 1997–1998 season would be his last as a professional player. In four seasons with the Rockets, Drexler averaged 19 points, 6.1 rebounds, and 5.4 assists. He joined Calvin Murphy, Moses Malone, and the Rockets coach Rudy Tomjanovich as the only former Houston players to have their jersey numbers retired (Drexler was 22). In his fifteen-season NBA career, Drexler scored 22,195 points for eighteenth on the career list, with 6,677 rebounds and 6,125 assists.

In 1998 Drexler returned to the University of Houston as the head basketball coach. In 2000 he announced his retirement from that position, explaining he had "enjoyed coaching the Cougars in the past two seasons. It gave me the opportunity to give back to my alma mater. I like being involved with basketball on a daily basis, but I felt that I needed to step away and spend more time with my kids. Right now I want to concentrate on my family." Besides spending time with his wife, Gaynelle, whom he married in December 1988, and their four children, Drexler continued his community involvement after retirement. While in Portland he served as an honorary spokesman for the

Blazer Avia Scholastic Improvement Concepts Program, designed to encourage academic achievement. In Houston, he sponsored an inner-city youth summer basketball camp.

★

An extensive biography of Drexler is in *African-American Sports Greats* (1995). A complete NBA statistical record is posted at the website <http://www.nba.com/playerfile>.

JOHNNIEQUE B. LOVE

DRYSDALE, Don(ald) Scott (*b.* 23 July 1936 in Van Nuys, California; *d.* 3 July 1993 in Montreal, Quebec, Canada), Hall of Fame pitcher for the Brooklyn and Los Angeles Dodgers in 1950s and 1960s and baseball announcer.

Drysdale was one of two children born to Scott Sumner and Verna Ruth Ley. Drysdale's father, who worked as a repair supervisor for Pacific Telephone and Telegraph, was a former minor-league baseball player and nurtured his son's interest in the sport. Due to his father's fears that his son might suffer an arm injury, Drysdale played at second base for the Van Nuys high school team until his senior year, when he pitched ten winning games in eleven starts.

Although Drysdale was scouted by several major league clubs, the Brooklyn Dodgers, who had made Drysdale's

Don Drysdale, 1962. ASSOCIATED PRESS AP

father a part-time scout, had the inside track, signing Drysdale to a contract in June 1954. After agreeing to play with the Dodgers, Drysdale was dispatched to Bakersfield in the California League, where he won eight games and lost five. The following season Drysdale was promoted to Montreal of the International League, where he injured his hand and pitched ineffectively during the second half of the 1955 campaign.

The Dodgers pitching staff was short handed in 1956 due to injuries, so Drysdale was promoted to the parent club. Used as a spot starter, the young pitcher won five games and lost five, although his earned run average (ERA) of 2.64 was outstanding. Drysdale even made a relief appearance in the famous 1956 World Series, as the Dodgers lost to the New York Yankees. Improving in 1957, Drysdale won seventeen games with a 2.69 ERA.

The Dodgers deserted Brooklyn for the untapped market of Los Angeles following the 1957 season. Until Dodger Stadium could be constructed at Chavez Ravine, the Dodgers played in the Los Angeles Coliseum. Not built for baseball, the coliseum was renovated with a left-field screen that was only 251 feet from home plate. This short porch made it difficult for pitchers such as Drysdale, and his early Los Angeles statistics did not match his Brooklyn start. During the four years in which the Dodgers played at the Coliseum, Drysdale won fifty-seven games but had fifty losses. However, Los Angeles did defeat the Chicago White Sox in the 1959 World Series, and Drysdale won Game 3 of the series.

The Dodgers moved to Chavez Ravine in 1962, and Drysdale enjoyed one of his most successful seasons. The right-hander won twenty-five games, struck out 232 batters, and attained an ERA of 2.83. His accomplishments were acknowledged by his selection for the Cy Young award and as the Sporting News Major League Pitcher of the Year. During the 1962 season, Drysdale altered his delivery from a side arm motion, which intimidated right-handed batters, to more overhand style, making Drysdale more effective against left-handed hitters. The handsome Drysdale received numerous endorsement opportunities and made cameo appearances in Hollywood television productions. Drysdale married professional model Eula Eugenia "Ginger" Dubberly on 27 September 1958; they had one child.

Drysdale's winning percentage slipped to nineteen victories and seventeen losses in 1963, but his ERA was an impressive 2.63. Drysdale also won game three in the Dodgers World Series sweep of the New York Yankees that year. The Dodgers slumped into the second division in 1964, but Drysdale continued to pitch well, compiling eighteen victories with an ERA of 2.18. The Dodgers returned to their winning ways in 1965, and Drysdale contributed twenty-three victories and a World Series win over the Minnesota Twins.

In the spring of 1966 Drysdale and his pitching teammate Sandy Koufax evoked the wrath of Dodger management and received considerable media attention when the two held out in tandem, seeking three-year contracts. The two pitchers missed spring training before settling for more than $100,000 each. Although the Dodgers would not win another world championship with Drysdale, the right-hander posted thirteen victories in 1966 for a Los Angeles squad that was swept by the Baltimore Orioles in the World Series. The Dodgers failed to repeat as National League champions in 1967, but Drysdale pitched well with a 2.74 earned average and thirteen victories. Drysdale's 1968 season was one of his most remarkable, as the right-hander pitched six consecutive shutouts and hurled fifty-eight and two-thirds innings without allowing an earned run, a mark that remained unbroken until 1988 when it was bested by another Dodger pitcher. Drysdale suffered from arm problems in 1969, and after a poor performance against the Pittsburgh Pirates, the proud athlete announced his retirement from baseball. That same year he and Dubberley divorced.

In fourteen seasons with the Dodgers, Drysdale pitched 3,432 innings, won 209 games as opposed to 166 losses, struck out 2,486 batters, threw 49 shutouts, and compiled an ERA of 2.95. He also established a reputation for being unafraid to pitch inside, setting a major league record by hitting 154 batters. Of his intimidating reputation, Drysdale remarked, "I never hit anybody in the head in my life. But you have to move them off the plate, you have to get them out of there." An all-around athlete, Drysdale was a fine batter, who finished his career with twenty-nine home runs. He played in five World Series and made nine All-Star teams. Drysdale was inducted into the National Baseball Hall of Fame in 1984.

Following his playing days, Drysdale pursued a career in baseball broadcasting, working for the Montreal Expos, Texas Rangers, California Angels, and Chicago White Sox. From 1978 to 1987, Drysdale was a television sports commentator for the American Broadcasting Corporation (ABC), and while covering the "Superstars" competition for ABC in 1979, Drysdale met Ann Meyers, a four-time All-America basketball player. Drysdale and Meyers married on 1 November 1986; they had three children.

Drysdale teamed with Vin Scully to announce Dodger games in 1988. On 3 July 1993, while the Dodgers were visiting Montreal, Drysdale was found dead from a heart attack in his hotel room. He is buried at Forest Lawn Memorial Park in Glendale, California. Drysdale had established a competitive reputation with his Hall of Fame credentials. But in death, he was most remembered as a compassionate individual. Drysdale's Hall of Fame colleague and friend Sandy Koufax recalled, "I'll remember all the little things we shared as friends, things that will never be public. I'll remember his humor. He was just a warm friendly human being."

★

A player file on Drysdale is available in the National Baseball Hall of Fame, in Cooperstown, New York. For an autobiographical account of Drysdale's baseball career, see Don Drysdale and Bob Verdi, *Once a Bum, Always a Dodger* (1990). For Drysdale's relationship with his manager Walter Alston, see Walter Alston with Si Burick, *Alston and the Dodgers* (1966). For biographical profiles of Drysdale, see Huston Horn, "Ex-Bad Boy's Big Year," *Sports Illustrated* (20 Aug. 1962); Milton J. Schapiro, *The Don Drysdale Story* (1964); and "Departure of Big D," *Time* (22 Aug. 1969). Obituaries are in the *New York Times* and *Los Angeles Times* (both 4 July 1993).

RON BRILEY

DUNCAN, Timothy Theodore (*b.* 25 April 1976 in St. Croix, Virgin Islands), three-time National Association of Basketball Coaches defensive player of the year, National Basketball Association rookie of the year (1997–1998), and dominating power forward for the San Antonio Spurs.

Duncan, one of three children of William Duncan, a mason, and Ione Duncan, a midwife, became one of the dominating power forwards in the National Basketball Association (NBA). At age thirteen he was a top-ranked swimmer in his age group in the 400-meter freestyle; at the end of the twentieth century, he continued to hold records in the 50- and 100-meter freestyle for the Virgin Islands. Two major events, sad in different ways, followed these achievements within a year: Hurricane Hugo swept through the Caribbean in 1989, destroying the swimming complex where Duncan trained, and his mother died of breast cancer. In a change of focus, the swimmer turned his attention to basketball.

The six footer began playing basketball in the ninth grade at Saint Dunstan's Episcopal High School and soon became one of Saint Croix's top players. By his senior year he was six feet, ten inches tall and was averaging 25 points, 12 rebounds, and 5 blocked shots per game, but he did not attract the attention of college recruiters. Chris King, an NBA player promoting the league in the Caribbean, was impressed by Duncan's coverage against Alonzo Mourning in exhibition games. He urged Dave Odom, the head coach at Wake Forest University in Winston-Salem, North Carolina, to take a look at Duncan. After entering Wake Forest in the autumn of 1993, the shy, little-known freshman developed his basketball skills quickly to become a powerhouse on defense, setting the school record for blocked shots. His freshman performance earned him a spot on the college All-Star team in an exhibition game against the Dream Team II, the NBA squad of superstars.

Tim Duncan. AP/WIDE WORLD PHOTOS

During his sophomore year Duncan helped Wake Forest's Demon Deacons reach the sweet-sixteen round of the National Collegiate Athletic Association (NCAA) Division I postseason tournament. He became one of only two players in his conference to average a double double, meaning his per-game averages of points scored and number of rebounds were both in double digits. The National Association of Basketball Coaches (NABC) named Duncan as its national defensive player of the year for three consecutive years: 1995, 1996, and 1997. Considered a promising prospect for the NBA, Duncan could have secured a lucrative contract but opted to remain in school. His junior year earned Wake Forest its second Atlantic Coast Conference (ACC) Championship title, and the team advanced to the elite eight in the NCAA postseason tournament. Named as the Atlantic Coast Conference player of the year, he was again pursued for the NBA draft, and again Duncan chose to remain in school, keeping a promise to his mother that he would earn a college degree.

As a senior Duncan continued to develop his skills, im-

proving his strength and passing and honing the offensive moves that later became his trademark in the NBA. He led the NCAA Division I in rebounding, with 20.8 points per game. His superiority was so evident that he was named college basketball's player of the year for 1996–1997 by the Associated Press, U.S. Basketball Writers Association, NABC, *Sporting News*, and *Basketball Times*, and also won both the James A. Naismith Award and the John R. Wooden Award, which honor the nation's top collegiate basketball player. Duncan's statistics at Wake Forest included being the all-time leading shot blocker in ACC history, with 481 blocked shots. He was only the tenth player in NCAA Division I history to score at least 2,000 points and get at least 1,500 rebounds. This was quite a feat for a young man whose original sport was swimming. Coach Odom said of Duncan, "In thirty-one years of coaching, I've never met a more fierce competitor, a player who gives you more every day than Tim—in every challenge."

On 25 June 1997, after receiving a B.A. degree in psychology, Duncan made his long-awaited entrance into the NBA draft and was selected as the first overall pick by the San Antonio Spurs. Although starting as a power forward, his skills allowed him to excel as a center. Duncan and the Spurs center David Robinson, jointly called the Twin Towers, worked well together by combining their size, speed, and power. Duncan's rookie year was outstanding. He started in all eighty-two games and he was thirteenth in the NBA in scoring, with an average of 21.1 points per game; third in rebounding, with 11.9 rebounds per game; sixth in blocked shots, with 2.51 blocks per game; and fourth in field-goal percentage, with 54.9 percent. He was named the rookie of the month for all six months of the NBA regular season, only the third player to gain that honor, and he was the only rookie selected to participate in the 1998 NBA All-Star Game. Naturally, Duncan was named the NBA rookie of the year. The Spurs coach George Karl stated, "He's a quiet assassin who is skilled in all aspects of the game." During his second year as a professional, Duncan continued to be one of the league's most dominant players. Through the shortened season (because of a lockout of players by NBA team owners during contract disputes), the Spurs tied for the best record in the NBA. Duncan was named to the All-NBA First Team and the NBA All-Defensive First Team.

The hometown hero of the Virgin Islands did not escape the criticism that inevitably comes with being a professional athlete. Some critics said that Duncan was not physical enough in his game—he played with too much finesse. Others said that he seemed emotionless during games—he didn't pump his fists or thump his chest. Still others said that his placid expression, even during dramatic games, indicated that he did not play with intensity and thus did not care about winning. The critics, however, noted the intensity, still without the flashiness, with which Duncan played in the 1999 NBA playoffs against Kevin Garnett of the Minnesota Timberwolves, Shaquille O'Neal of the Los Angeles Lakers, and Rasheed Wallace of the Portland Trailblazers. The Spurs and Duncan then dominated the New York Knicks to capture their first NBA Championship title. Duncan was named the co-Most Valuable Player of the NBA finals and for the second straight season was named to both the All-NBA First Team and the All-Defense Team. During the 2000–2001 season he started in all eighty-two games and, for the third time, led the league in double doubles.

On 12 July 2001 Duncan married longtime girlfriend Amy Sherrill. He holds the annual Tim Duncan Charity Golf Classic to raise money for the Kids Sports Network, a nonprofit association that promotes sports and fitness for kids through coach education, special events, and regular networking with youth sports associations and agencies. He once explained his seeming aloofness by saying, "I've got a million things going on in my head at all times." A movie and video fan and a knife collector, the shy Duncan showed that an athlete does not have to be flamboyant to be successful.

★

Several full-length children's biographies have been written about Duncan. They are Mark Stewart, *Tim Duncan: Tower of Power* (1999); Jeremy Byman, *Tim Duncan* (2000); Kevin Kernan, *Tim Duncan: Slam Duncan* (2000); Ken Rappoport, *Tim Duncan: Star Forward* (2000); and Stew Thornley, *Super Sports Star Tim Duncan* (2001). General biographical sources include *Current Biography Yearbook* (1999); Geri Koeppel, "Tim Duncan," in *Newsmakers 2000,* edited by Aaron Oppliger (2000); and Ed Decker, "Tim Duncan," in *Contemporary Black Biography* (1999).

JOYCE K. THORNTON

DUNDEE, Angelo (*b.* 30 August 1922 in Philadelphia, Pennsylvania), boxing trainer and manager who handled heavyweight champion Muhammad Ali, as well as world champions Carmen Basilio, Sugar Ramos, Luis Rodriquez, Jose Napoles, Willie Pastrano, Ralph Dupas, and Sugar Ray Leonard.

Dundee is the son of Angelo Mirenda, an Italian immigrant railroad worker, and Philomena, a homemaker. Dundee's family lived in the Italian community of South Philadelphia; his mother never learned English and his father never learned to write it. Dundee had five brothers and three sisters, two of whom died as infants.

Dundee's oldest brother, Joseph, fought briefly as a professional boxer, adopting the last name of Italian-American champions Vince Dundee and Joseph Dundee. Dundee's second oldest brother, Chris, left home at the age of fifteen,

eventually becoming one of the most influential promoters in boxing under the name Chris Dundee.

Angelo Mirena, as Dundee was then known, graduated from South Philadelphia High School in 1938. He worked as an inspector in a naval aircraft factory until his induction into the Army Air Corps in October 1943. Trained in aircraft maintenance, Dundee was posted to Amiens, France, for the duration of the war and rose to staff sergeant.

Dundee worked briefly in the aircraft industry in Philadelphia following his discharge from the army. In 1947 he moved to New York City to work for his brother Chris, changing his name from Mirena to Dundee, which his family used in the boxing business. Dundee slept on a pull-out sofa in Chris's office, room 711 of the Capitol Hotel, directly across from Madison Square Garden, then located at Fiftieth Street and Eighth Avenue. In New York Dundee served an unofficial apprenticeship to the great boxing trainers and cut men of the day, including Charley Goldman, Ray Arcel, Chickie Ferrara, and other denizens of the legendary Stillman's Gym. "I never trained nobody up in New York City," Dundee said. "I just observed. I worked corners. What I did was keep my mouth shut and my eyes open."

In 1951 Dundee moved to Miami, Florida, to join his brother Chris, who had relocated his business there. The following year he married fashion model Helen Bolton; they had two children.

Soon Angelo Dundee was handling future champions Luis Rodriguez, Jose Napoles, Sugar Ramos, Ralph Dupas, and Willie Pastrano. In 1955 Dundee worked in Carmen Basilio's corner when Basilio defeated Joe Netro for the welterweight title. In 1963 two of Dundee's fighters won championships in one night: Luis Rodriguez defeated Emile Griffith for the welterweight title and Sugar Ramos defeated Davey Moore for the featherweight title. This feat was marred by tragedy when Moore collapsed and died following the bout.

Shortly after 1960 Olympic gold medallist Cassius Clay turned professional, he became disenchanted with his trainers, former light-heavyweight champion Archie Moore and veteran corner man Dick Saddler. The Louisville businessmen guiding Clay's career turned to Dundee. Dundee's celebrated role in Clay's 1963 victory over British contender Henry Cooper is a quintessential example of how a quick-thinking corner man can save a boxer's career. At the close of the fourth round, a powerful left hook from Cooper floored Clay, but he managed to stagger back to his corner. Thinking fast, Dundee used his finger to enlarge a small tear he had noticed in Clay's glove earlier in the fight and demanded that a new glove be found. The ensuing confusion bought Clay the time he needed to recuperate, and he scored a knockout in the next round. Dundee's poise again saved the day during Clay's 1964 Miami Beach title bout against heavyweight champion Sonny Liston. After

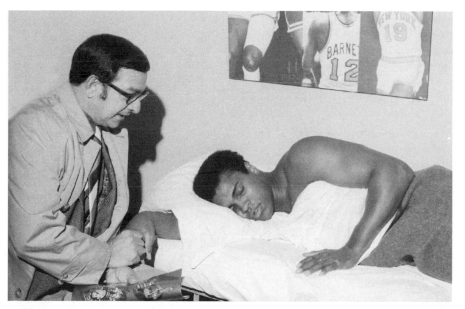

Angelo Dundee with Muhammad Ali, resting up for a bout with Joe Frazier, 8 March 1971. © BETTMANN/
CORBIS

the fifth round, Clay complained that a foreign substance in his eyes was blinding him and told Dundee to "cut the gloves off." Instead, Dundee calmed his fighter and washed out his eyes. "When the bell rang," Dundee recalled, "I shoved Clay off the stool." Liston quit in his corner before the start of the seventh round.

In his early days at Stillman's Gym, Dundee learned to accommodate his fighter's ego, or, as he put it, "blend into any kind of a scene." This habit served Dundee well when Clay joined the Nation of Islam, changed his name to Muhammad Ali, refused to be inducted into the army, and was banned from boxing for over three years. Dundee ignored the politics surrounding Ali and never became involved in Ali's personal life. In 1966 Ali hired Herbert Muhammad, son of Muslim leader Elijah Muhammad, as his manager, but Dundee stayed on as trainer.

Few experts picked Ali in his 1974 match against heavyweight champion George Foreman, but Dundee helped Ali devise a winning strategy. "I told my guy that he could feint Foreman," Dundee recalled after the fight, "that he could move him because in a clinch Foreman put both his feet together, he was off balance to be moved. . . . I saw those things and I told my guy about them. He [Ali] remembered because he knows that when I see things through my eyes, I see things." In 1987 Ali said, "Never told anybody, but I had doubts. After Frazier beat me, after Spinks beat me. He made me believe again. Angelo really had more confidence in me than I did."

In 1976 Olympic gold medalist Sugar Ray Leonard chose Dundee to be his manager and trainer. Dundee picked Leonard's early opponents so that, as Dundee said,

Leonard learned "how to handle height, how to handle a short guy, how to handle a quick guy, how to handle a tough guy." Though Leonard lost his welterweight title to Roberto Duran in June 1980, he was prepared for the return bout later that year. After the controversial "No Mas" ("no more") fight, which ended after Duran quit during the eighth round, Dundee told the press: "We took everything away from Duran. When he tried to box with us, Ray jabbed his head off. When he tried to muscle Ray on the ropes, my guy banged him to the body with both hands and spun him like a baby. We knew everything Duran was going to try, and we were ready for it." Perhaps Dundee's most famous moment in Leonard's corner came following the twelfth round of Leonard's fourteen-round 1981 welterweight championship victory over Thomas Hearns. With Leonard behind on points and his left eye practically closed, Dundee told Leonard, "You're blowing it, son. You're blowing it. This is what separates the men from the boys." Dundee was in Leonard's corner again for the fighter's 1987 upset win over Marvin Hagler for the middleweight title, a fight that prompted Dave Anderson of the *New York Times* to describe Dundee as a "Michelangelo" who had constructed another "boxing masterpiece." This was Dundee's last fight in Leonard's corner, owing to a contractual dispute. In 1994, Dundee worked in George Foreman's corner where Foreman became the oldest man in boxing history to win the heavyweight championship of the world. That same year, Dundee was inducted into the International Boxing Hall of Fame.

Compact, graceful, and tanned, Dundee is a modest, upbeat, and highly quotable man who avoids confrontations outside the ring. Complemented following one of Leonard's victories, Dundee replied, "Thanks, but Ray did the fighting." This self-effacing quality, along with immense powers of observation and presence of mind, has allowed Dundee to endure as, in his own words, a "psychologist, nurse-maid, and father figure" to his many fighters.

★

Dundee's informative autobiography is *I Only Talk Winning* (1985), written by Dundee with Mike Winters. Chapters devoted to Dundee are in Ronald K. Fried, *Corner Men: Great Boxing Trainers* (1991), and Dave Anderson, *In the Corner: Great Boxing Trainers Talk About Their Art* (1992). Valuable magazine profiles include Phil Berger's "Dundee: Champ of the Corner Men," *New York Times Magazine* (Nov. 1981), and Gary Smith's "The Corner Man," *Sports Illustrated* (2 Nov. 1987).

RONALD K. FRIED

DUROCHER, Leo Ernest   (*b.* 27 July 1905 in West Springfield, Massachusetts; *d.* 7 October 1991 in Palm Springs, California), Hall of Fame baseball player and manager who led the New York Giants to their come-from-behind 1951 pennant and became famous for saying, "Nice guys finish last."

Durocher was born in an industrial and railroad town ninety miles west of Boston, one of four sons of Clarinda Provost Durocher, a homemaker, and George Durocher, a railroad worker; his parents were of French Canadian heritage. As a young man, Durocher spent less time in the classroom—there are no records that he ever attended high school—than at the baseball field and pool halls. On the diamond, he was a slick-fielding, light-hitting shortstop; at the billiards table, he came in contact with hustlers and gamblers, the kind of men with whom he would associate all his life. By age sixteen Durocher was out of school, working for a living and playing semiprofessional ball. In 1925 he joined the Eastern League's Hartford Senators and caught the attention of the New York Yankees, who purchased the rights to him at the end of the season.

Durocher made his Major League debut at the end of the 1925 season, but it was 1928 before the five-foot, nine-inch shortstop caught on full-time in the Majors. He lasted two seasons with the Yankees, including their World Series–winning campaign of 1928, but he wore out his welcome with his teammates and was traded to the Cincinnati Reds in 1930. Before he left, none other than Babe Ruth dubbed Durocher as "the All-America out." After three seasons with the Reds, Durocher was dealt to the St. Louis Cardinals, where he became a key member of the Gas House Gang. Leo the Lip was just one character on a team full of them—the pitching Dean brothers, Paul and Dizzy; Pepper Martin; and the player-manager Frankie Frisch. The Cardinals won a World Series in 1934.

Leo Durocher, 1951. ASSOCIATED PRESS AP

Durocher was traded to the Brooklyn Dodgers after the 1937 season. He became the team's captain in 1938 and began his managing career in 1939, replacing Burleigh Grimes. (He served as a player-manager until 1945, when his playing career ended.) Durocher spent most of the next two decades, the prime of his career, at the heart of New York City baseball. Constantly battling, whether with umpires, fans, or baseball executives, Durocher remade the Dodgers, longtime losers, in his own fighting image and led them to a pennant in 1941, their first in twenty-one years. The Dodgers captured the National League pennant again in 1947, but without Durocher. The baseball commissioner A. B. ("Happy") Chandler suspended him for that season, for reasons that were never clearly stated. Chandler cited only an "accumulation of unpleasant incidents detrimental to baseball." The suspension came after Chandler warned Durocher to end his friendships with several known gamblers, including Bugsy Siegel and the actor George Raft, who had been investigated for running a crooked dice game at Durocher's apartment. In January 1947, Durocher made headlines by marrying the Hollywood actress Laraine Day in El Paso, Texas, on the same day she received a "quickie" divorce in Juárez, Mexico. The move drew outrage, since Day was in the midst of California's one-year waiting period for a divorce from Ray Hendricks. Durocher later claimed to have remarried Day in 1948, after the waiting period expired, making it "official." The marriage to Day, which lasted until 1960, was the third of Durocher's four marriages. Earlier, he had been married to Ruby Marie Hartley, who bore his only child, daughter Barbara, from 1930 and 1934, and to Grace Dozier from 1934 to 1943. In 1969 he would marry Lynne Walker Goldblatt; that marriage lasted until 1981.

Durocher's suspension was partly the responsibility of his former boss, Larry "Lee" MacPhail, the Dodger executive who gave Durocher his first managing job. MacPhail was fired by the team in 1942 and ended up running the Dodgers' crosstown rivals, the New York Yankees. Shortly after the scandal over Durocher's marriage to Day, as the Dodgers trained in Cuba for the 1947 season, Durocher and MacPhail became embroiled in a battle of words, after Durocher saw two men with gambling connections sitting in—or near—MacPhail's personal box at a spring training game. MacPhail complained to Chandler that Durocher had taken actions "detrimental to baseball," sparking a probe that resulted in Durocher's suspension.

Durocher's raucous, profane personality, his pool-hall roots, and the company he kept colored perceptions about the suspension, leading to the widespread belief that it was for gambling. It was never shown that Chandler had any evidence of Durocher's gambling. Almost as soon as Durocher was back on the Dodgers bench in 1948, he was gone—across the Brooklyn Bridge to Manhattan and the team's fierce National League rivals, the New York Giants. In a stunning midseason move, the Dodgers president Branch Rickey decided that he had had enough of Durocher and fired him at the same time that the Giants were firing their manager Mel Ott. The Giants replaced Ott with the man who, in discussing Ott and his team two years earlier, so memorably had told reporters, "Nice guys finish last."

Three years later Durocher had his revenge as the Giants came from thirteen and a half games behind the Dodgers in mid-August to tie them for the National League title. In the finale of a three-game playoff, the Giants player Bobby Thomson clubbed a three-run home run in the bottom of the ninth—the famous "shot heard 'round the world"—to give the Giants a 5–4 victory and the pennant. The Giants comeback, the so-called Little Miracle of Coogan's Bluff, may have been tainted in 2001, when many former players detailed in a *Wall Street Journal* story an elaborate scheme, rigged by Durocher, that allowed the Giants to steal opponents' signals during the last ten weeks of the 1951 season. The Giants fell to the Yankees in that year's World Series; three years later Durocher won his only world championship as a manager when the Giants swept the favored Cleveland Indians.

Durocher quit as the Giants manager after the 1955 season to become a television commentator. In 1961 he returned to the field as a coach with the Dodgers (who by then had moved to Los Angeles) and then as the manager of the Chicago Cubs in 1966. Again Durocher turned around a perennial loser, leading the Cubs out of the National League basement. But the team's highest finish under Durocher was second place. The most famous season of his Wrigley Field tenure was 1969, when his team blew a September lead and lost the National League East to the New York Mets. Fired midway through 1972, Durocher became the manager of the Houston Astros a month later. He stayed in Houston through the end of the 1973 season, after which he resigned, saying that he could not communicate with modern ball players. Although Durocher won 2,008 games as a manager, he was denied entry to the Baseball Hall of Fame during his lifetime, likely a result of the many enemies he had made in the game. He finally was inducted into the Hall of Fame in 1994. Durocher died at age eighty-six of natural causes at Desert Hospital in Palm Springs and is buried at Forest Lawn Memorial Park in Los Angeles.

Beloved by many of his own players and hated by the opposition, Durocher was the scourge of umpires and baseball executives alike, a hero when he was on your side and the embodiment of evil when he was not. His declaration that "nice guys finish last" came to embody the win-at-all-costs approach to U.S. sports.

★

Although nearly everything in it should be taken with a grain of salt, Durocher's memoir, written with Ed Linn, *Nice Guys Finish Last* (1975), is one of the most entertaining examples of the sports "as-told-to" genre ever published. After Durocher's death, the *New York Times* writer Gerald Eskenazi published *The Lip: A Biography of Leo Durocher* (1993), which does much to set the record straight about Durocher's controversial life. Durocher figures prominently in Peter Golenbock, *Bums: An Oral History of the Brooklyn Dodgers* (1984); Ray Robinson, *The Home Run Heard 'Round the World: The Dramatic Story of the 1951 Giants-Dodgers Pennant Race* (1991); and David Claerbaut, *Durocher's Cubs: The Greatest Team That Didn't Win* (2000). Jim Murray wrote a reminiscence for the *Los Angeles Times* (8 Oct. 1991), as did Hal Bock for the *Associated Press* (9 Oct. 1991). Obituaries are in the *New York Times* and *Chicago Tribune* (both 8 Oct. 1991).

TIM WHITMIRE

E

EARNHARDT, (Ralph) Dale (*b.* 29 April 1951 in Kannapolis, North Carolina; *d.* 18 February 2001 in Daytona, Florida), professional stock car racer who won a record-tying seven championships before his tragic death at the 2001 Daytona 500.

Earnhardt became familiar with the world of stock car racing at an early age. His father, the professional racing pioneer Ralph Lee Earnhardt, won more than 350 races during his twenty-three-year career and often took his son to the tracks. Earnhardt dreamed of following in his father's footsteps and began competing in area races at age fifteen. Two years later he got married (his first of three wives) and dropped out of school in the ninth grade to work full time. Although Earnhardt held a variety of jobs, he continued racing on weekends. He often borrowed money to maintain his vehicles and reimbursed creditors with his meager winnings. In 1973 his life changed forever when his father died while working on a race car. Earnhardt became even more committed to racing professionally and continued competing in local events while seeking greater opportunities. Two years later he made the most of his professional debut.

On 25 May 1975 Earnhardt drove in his first Winston Cup race, the Charlotte Motor Speedway's World 600. The Winston Cup series is National Association for Stock Car Auto Racing's (NASCAR) most prestigious annual series. Throughout the year, drivers participate in several races that constitute the series and accumulate points in each race based on their finishes. The annual championship goes to the driver with the most points earned that year. Earnhardt finished twenty-second in his first Winston Cup race and made eight more starts in the series during his first three years on the circuit.

In 1978 the California racing sponsor Rod Osterlund gave Earnhardt his first full-time Winston Cup contract, which proved the biggest opportunity of his racing career. On 1 April 1979 Earnhardt won his first race in sixteen starts on the prestigious NASCAR circuit at the Southeastern 500 in Bristol, Tennessee. He later won the 1979 NASCAR Rookie of the Year award and became the first driver to win more than $200,000 in his first full season. In 1980 Earnhardt captured NASCAR's season points title and the Winston Cup Championship, which made him the only driver to win rookie and cup honors in consecutive years.

Earnhardt's winning stalled when Osterlund sold his racing team to Jim Stacy in 1981. The disgruntled driver left Stacy after four races to drive for Bud Moore in 1982 and 1983, but won only three races. In 1984 Earnhardt joined Richard Childress and formed one of the most successful partnerships in NASCAR history. Earnhardt claimed his second Winston Cup in 1986. The following season he earned a career-high eleven wins and won a third championship. Three of his victories came after he bumped drivers out of his way to take the lead in close races. His aggressive style justified his "Ironhead" and "Intimidator"

Dale Earnhardt. GALE RESEARCH (DETROIT)

nicknames and earned him a warning from NASCAR's president to modify his reckless on-track behavior.

Reprimanded but undaunted, Earnhardt continued to win in the 1990s. He claimed his fourth, fifth, sixth, and seventh Winston Cup titles in 1990, 1991, 1993, and 1994, earning an average of more than $3 million each season. His seventh championship tied the NASCAR legend Richard Petty for most career titles. The only achievement that continued to elude Earnhardt was a victory in the Daytona 500, the NASCAR season's first and most prestigious race. In 1998 he won the event in his twentieth attempt. Following his victory, Earnhardt cut a memorable figure "3," his car number, in the raceway's grass infield as spectators and opponents alike celebrated with the self-proclaimed "Man in Black." Later the same year NASCAR honored Earnhardt and his father as two of the greatest fifty drivers in motorsports history.

The Earnhardt family's affair with racing grew in 2000, as Dale Earnhardt, Jr., joined his father on the Winston Cup series. Later that year, Earnhardt raced against his sons Dale, Jr., and Kerry in the Pepsi 400. Earnhardt and Lee Petty remain the only drivers to have competed against two sons in the same event. Racing with his sons seemed to rejuvenate the veteran Earnhardt, who finished second in the 2000 Winston Cup point standings. This intensified

the tragedy of 18 February 2001, when Earnhardt died after crashing into the wall as he entered the fourth and last turn of the Daytona 500's final lap. He is buried in Kannapolis, North Carolina.

Despite his untimely death, Earnhardt was one of the most successful drivers in NASCAR history. In 2001 he ranked first in top-ten Winston Cup annual point standing finishes (20), sixth in wins (76), seventh in races started (676), fourth in top-five performances (281), won a record $41 million, and finished in the top ten of 428 Winston Cup races. He was the only three-time winner of the Winston Select Series (1987, 1990, 1993); claimed four International Race of Champions wins (1990, 1995, 1999, 2000); earned National Motorsports Press Association Driver of the Year awards in 1980, 1986 (cohonoree), 1987, 1990, and 1994; and captured American Driver of the Year honors twice (1987 and 1994). Earnhardt's titles and accomplishments, however, were only one measure of his legacy. The response his death elicited from fans and fellow racers demonstrated an influence that extended far beyond Earnhardt's role as a NASCAR driver.

Earnhardt became the rare professional athlete with whom many racing fans identified. His aggressive driving style, sullen disposition, and mysterious persona reflected a fierce individualism that increased his popularity and infused the sport with an unprecedented level of passion. Loyalties intensified as Earnhardt became NASCAR's most marketed and recognized driver when the sport grew in national exposure and popularity during the 1990s. Fans most appreciated Earnhardt's toughness and love of racing. Events following his death revealed why the racing official H. A. Wheeler called Earnhardt "the Michael Jordan of our sport." In national telecasts of NASCAR races after the tragedy, broadcasters maintained a symbolic silence during third laps while spectators stood and raised three fingers, rituals that honored Earnhardt's famous racing number. On 10 July 2001, two days after Dale, Jr., won the first race at Daytona since his father's fatal crash, the North Carolina legislature passed a resolution praising Earnhardt and the contributions he made to his home state.

★

No adequate biography on Earnhardt existed upon his death, but several magazine and newspaper articles paid tribute to his life and accomplishments following the Daytona accident. For more on Earnhardt's life and career, see Rick Bragg, "Racer's Death Leaves Hole in Heart of His Hometown," *New York Times* (21 Feb. 2001); Mark Bechtel, "Crushing," *Sports Illustrated* (26 Feb. 2001); and Robert Sullivan, "The Last Lap," *Time* (5 Mar. 2001). In addition, the informative websites <http://www.daleearnhardt.net> and <http://www.daleearnhardt.com> chronicle Earnhardt's triumphs. An obituary is in the *Charlotte Observer* (19 Feb. 2001).

J. MICHAEL BUTLER

EDERLE, Gertrude Caroline ("Trudy") (*b.* 23 October 1906 in New York City), swimmer who, at age nineteen, became the first woman to swim across the English Channel, demolishing the previous record by nearly two hours.

Ederle was one of six children (four girls and two boys) of the German immigrants Henry Ederle and Gertrude Hazerstroh, who lived on the West Side of Manhattan and worked in the family's butcher shop. To escape the summer heat, the young Ederle learned to swim in the neighborhood pool. Swimming soon became her passion. At age thirteen she joined the Women's Swimming Association of New York so that she could swim all year round. Her sister, Margaret, got her into competitive swimming. "I liked to fool around in the water, but I didn't like being serious about it," recalled Ederle. "Meg's the one who wanted to make me a champion." In 1921 Ederle captured the first victory of her career, winning the Metropolitan New York junior 100-meter freestyle championship. Her first major international recognition came in 1924 at the Olympic Games in Paris. As the lead-off swimmer on the U.S. 400-meter freestyle relay team, Ederle won a gold medal and

Trudy Ederle. ARCHIVE PHOTOS, INC.

set a world record with her teammates Euphrasia Donnelly, Ethel Lackie, and Mariechen Wehselau. She also won two bronze medals in the 100-meter and 400-meter freestyle races. Ederle turned professional in 1925. By then she had set twenty-nine world and U.S. women's freestyle records.

Ederle's next goal was to conquer the English Channel. Before 1925 only five men had succeeded in their attempts to swim across the channel, all using the conventional breaststroke. At a time when the longest distance for women's swimming in the Olympics was 400 meters, the idea of a female swimming twenty-one miles using the crawl was unthinkable. The stroke was considered too strenuous for distance swimming, although earlier in 1925 Ederle had swum a similar distance between Manhattan's Battery and Sandy Hook, New Jersey, in seven hours. Her attempt at the English Channel in 1925 failed, however, not because of the rough seas but from a human error. After swimming for nearly nine hours, Ederle began to vomit the salt water she had swallowed. Someone in the attending boat grabbed her arm to assist, which led to her disqualification. "I was really mad," recalled Ederle, "because I knew I could make it." There was no stopping her a year later.

On 6 August 1926 at Cape Gris-Nez, France, Ederle donned a revolutionary two-piece bathing suit that her sister Margaret had designed and slipped on a red rubber cap and self-designed waterproof goggles; then she put on layers of grease, not only to keep her body warm in the sixty-one degree Fahrenheit water but to protect her from the jellyfish. Knowing that bookies in London had set five-to-one odds against her, Ederle looked at the gray sky and the gruff seas and said to herself, "Please God, help me." Then, shortly after 7:00 A.M., she waded into the water.

It is not hard to imagine the challenge Ederle was facing. Her fuel for the trip included cold chicken and beef broth, which had to be delivered to her by a net on a long pole, for her attempt would have been nullified if she had touched the accompanying boat. Her worst enemies were the turbulent waters and brutal tides, which pushed Ederle far off her planned course. When the weather became violent in late afternoon, those in the accompanying tugboat frequently asked, "Do you want to come out, Trudy?" She simply answered, "What for?" "What for" later became another nickname for Ederle. Finally at 9:40 P.M. Ederle touched the English shore at Kingsdown, miles north of Dover, her intended destination. She wound up swimming nearly 35 miles, 14 more than the 21-mile crossing. But Ederle completed her course in 14 hours, 31 minutes. Not only did she become the first woman to conquer the English Channel, she also obliterated the previous record of 16 hours, 23 minutes set in 1923 by an Italian man, Sebastian Tirabocchi.

Ederle received a hero's welcome when she returned to New York on a steamship three weeks later. As the vessel approached the city, she was asked to go to the upper deck. "The planes want to welcome you," Ederle recalled being told. "They want to drop flowers down." She went up there. It was not a joke. "The planes circled around and swooped down and dropped those bouquets," recounted Ederle. "They were just gorgeous. I never felt anything like that. I was proud, very, very proud." An estimated two million New Yorkers lined the parade route to heap their applause on their favorite daughter. The mayor James Walker equated her crossing to those of Moses, Caesar, and George Washington. President Calvin Coolidge called Ederle "America's best girl," and Charles Tobias and Al Sherman immortalized the heroine with their song "Trudy."

News of her success pushed the stories of the screen icon Rudolph Valentino's funeral and Jack Dempsey's training for his fight with Gene Tunney off many front pages. In at least one poll, Americans voted her the top athlete of 1926, ahead of the baseball player Babe Ruth. Ederle's swell of fame passed quickly, before she had much chance to capitalize on it. She made some money with a vaudeville act in which she demonstrated her crawl stroke in a specially built swimming tank. But mobility became a major problem for most of her adult life. In 1933 Ederle fractured her spine after toppling down a flight of stairs at her friends' home in Hempstead, New York. For the following four and a half years, she was in a cast and the pain never fully subsided. Also deafness, which some ascribed to her channel swim, plagued her for decades and made her rather reclusive. She never married. Ederle was inducted into the International Swimming Hall of Fame in 1965 and into the International Women's Sports Hall of Fame in 1980.

In an era when women were believed incapable of enduring strenuous physical activities and women's athletics were suppressed by the "anti-Olympics and antivarsity competition" movement led by women physical educators and sports leaders, Ederle's crossing of the English Channel helped to change perceptions of female athletes and inspired countless women and girls to take up swimming and various other sports. It also had a profound effect on others. "I would not have swapped my place in the tug this day," wrote a journalist who had spent fifteen hours in a little boat witnessing Ederle make history, "for a seat at the ringside of the greatest fight or at the arena of the greatest game in the world. For this, in my opinion, is the greatest sports story in the world."

★

Two good retrospective articles on Ederle's channel swim and her subsequent life are Kelli Anderson, "The Young Woman and the Sea," *Sports Illustrated* (29 Nov. 1999), and Elliot Denman, "A Pioneer Looks Back on Her Unforgettable Feat," *New York Times* (30 Apr. 2001). Biographical sketches may be found in Robert J. Condon, *Great Women Athletes of the Twentieth Century* (1991); Susan Ware, *Forgotten Heroes: Inspiring American Portraits from Our Leading Historians* (1998); and Janet Woolum, *Outstanding Women Athletes* (1998).

YING WUSHANLEY

EDWARDS, Teresa (*b.* 19 July 1964 in Cairo, Georgia), basketball player whose amateur and professional career covered a nineteen-year period, beginning with her freshman year at the University of Georgia in 1982 and ending with her retirement after the 2000 Olympics. Often called the Michael Jordan of women's basketball, she is a living basketball legend.

Edwards grew up in Cairo, Georgia, a small southern town in which everyone knew everyone else. She was the oldest child of Leroy Copeland and of Mildred Edwards, a single mother of five. To provide for her daughter and four sons, the elder Edwards labored in vegetable fields and worked at a syrup factory. Young Edwards was inspired by her mother's hard work and devotion to God. Motivated by her mother's words, "If you're not going to do it right—and do it hard—don't do it at all," she went on to become one of the greatest women basketball players of all time.

Teresa Edwards. AP/WIDE WORLD PHOTOS

Edwards grew up playing basketball with her four brothers. Her first hoop was a bicycle wheel rim nailed to a tree in the front yard. She learned that she had a real talent for the game when she made the middle school girls basketball team in the seventh grade. Edwards became a star of the Cairo High School team and was an All-American her senior year. Andy Landers, the coach at the University of Georgia, was so impressed with her high school play that he offered her a full scholarship.

At the University of Georgia, five foot, eleven inch Edwards played point guard, and in 1983 she was selected as a freshman All-American. She led the Lady Bulldogs to three Southeastern Conference (SEC) titles (1983, 1984, 1986), participated in four National Collegiate Athletic Association (NCAA) tournaments, and helped her team make it to two Final Four appearances (1983 and 1985). In her sophomore year Edwards was selected for the 1984 U.S. Olympic women's basketball team, which won a gold medal in Los Angeles. Back at school in Georgia, she averaged 15.5 points and 5.1 assists per game. In 2001 she remained the University of Georgia's all-time leader in as-

sists, at 653, and steals, at 342. To honor her accomplishments Georgia retired her number 5 jersey and named her to their All-Time Top Ten Female Athletes list.

As a member (and sometimes co-captain) of twenty-two power-packed American teams and a winner of twelve international medals, nine gold and three bronze, Edwards established herself as an unsurpassed international amateur. Aside from winning four Olympic gold medals in five Olympic Games (1984, 1988, 1992, 1996, and 2000), she was a member of the gold-medal-winning U. S. women's basketball teams that dominated the Goodwill Games, the World Championships, and the Pan-American Games between 1986 and 1990. In addition, Edwards led her teams to a bronze medal finish at the 1992 Olympic Games in Barcelona, the 1991 Pan-American Games, and the 1994 World Championships. Edwards is a three-time winner (1987, 1990, and 1996) of the prestigious USA Basketball's Female Athlete of the Year Award. Her hometown of Cairo honored her in 1988 by naming a street after her. In 1996 the Women's Sports Foundation named her Team Athlete of the Year.

When Edwards's basketball career at the University of Georgia ended in 1986, there were no opportunities for women to pursue a professional basketball career in the United States. So Edwards continued her career overseas. From 1987 through 1988 she played for S. P. Magenta in Vicenza, and Magenta, Italy. Back in the States, Edwards became the first member of her family to graduate from college, completing her degree in leisure studies in 1989 at the University of Georgia. Then, after graduation, she played for the Mitsubishi Electric Corporation in Nagoya, Japan, for four years, leading Mitsubishi to its first playoff games in 1993. While playing in Japan, Edwards averaged 27.7 points and twelve rebounds per game. Returning to Europe in 1994, she played for C. B. Dorna Basketball Club in Valencia, Spain, and for Tarbes Gespe Bigorre in Tarbes, France.

In 1996 Edwards was a founding member, marquee player, and coach for the American Basketball League (ABL), which remained in operation until December of 1998. She is credited with coining the league's slogan, "Little girls need big girls to look up to." Prior to the ABL's bankruptcy, Edwards was elected to the ABL board of directors, and Gary Cavalli, ABL chief executive officer, announced that she was his choice to eventually succeed him as CEO. Edwards played two years for the Atlanta Glory; in her second year she was the first player-coach in the ABL. At the end of the 1998 season she stepped down as coach and was traded to the Philadelphia Rage (for the 1998–1999 season, which ended prematurely when the league folded). During her three seasons Edwards was first in ABL scoring with an average of twenty-one points per game and fourth in assists with an average of 5.6 per game.

She set a record as the only player to score forty or more points in a game and accomplished this four times.

After the demise of the ABL, the Women's National Basketball Association (WNBA) offered Edwards a player position. She turned down the offer when they refused to pay her more than $65,000—considerably less than the $125,000 she had made as an ABL player.

Edwards retired from basketball after the 2000 Olympics. When Nell Fortner, the coach of the 2000 U.S. Olympic women's basketball team, was asked about Edwards, she said, "I have to put her in the category of one of the best, if not the best, players in the world." Edwards resides in Atlanta and works as a motivational speaker.

Edwards is the only American basketball player to have played in five Olympic Games. She co-captained the 1988, 1996 and 2000 U.S. Olympic women's basketball teams. In Olympic competition she earned four gold medals and one bronze. She was honored at the 1996 Olympics in Atlanta by being selected to recite the Olympic Oath at the Opening Ceremonies on behalf of all the Olympic athletes. At age twenty, she was the youngest member of the 1984 Olympic team and at age thirty-six, the oldest member of the 2000 Olympic team. An important part of women's basketball history, Edwards was truly instrumental in the rise of women's college and professional basketball.

★

There is no adult biography of Teresa Edwards. A number of children's books give a brief biography. Related books include Sara Corbet, *Venus to the Hoop* (1997); Christina Lessa, *Women Who Win* (1998); James Ponti, *WNBA Stars of Women's Basketball* (1999); and Tara VanDerveer, with Joan Ryan, *Shooting from the Outside: How a Coach and Her Olympic Team Transformed Women's Basketball* (1997). See also "100 Greatest Female Athletes: 22. Teresa Edwards, Basketball," *Sports Illustrated for Women* (winter 1999–2000, pullout section), and Robin Norwood, "Seven Days to the Sydney Olympics: Recognition Is at End of Road," *Los Angeles Times* (8 Sept. 2000). Good sources on the Internet are "Teresa's Bio," *Teresa Edwards,* http://www.teresaedwards.com, and "Teresa Edwards," *Official Site of USA Basketball,* http://usabasketball.com/usab/Women/edwards_bio.html.

GAI INGHAM BERLAGE

ELWAY, John Albert (*b.* 28 June 1960 in Port Angeles, Washington), quarterback who led the National Football League's (NFL) Denver Broncos to five Super Bowl face-offs, including two successive victories in 1998 and 1999.

Elway, both a twin and one of three children born to Jan and Jack Elway, was almost destined to play football. As the only male child of a successful high school and college coach, he was exposed to the game at an early age. His father had played quarterback for Washington State Uni-

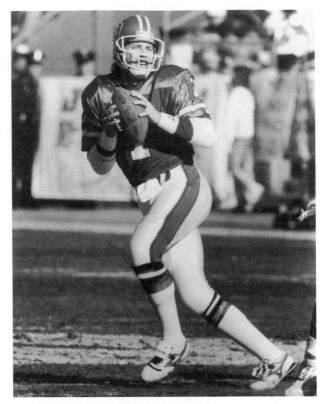

John Elway. AP/WIDE WORLD PHOTOS

versity before getting into coaching, and his paternal grandfather Harry Elway quarterbacked a team against the Carlisle Indians, including the legendary Jim Thorpe.

Elway's family moved around a good deal, as Elway's father jumped from one coaching job to another. Elway's first love was baseball, an interest that was encouraged by his father, who urged him to practice batting both left-handed and right-handed. At Granada Hills High School in Los Angeles, Elway batted .500 during his years on the baseball team. However, his interest in baseball did not keep him away from the family game of football. He started playing organized football in the sixth grade as a running back. As time went by, Elway's throwing arm began to develop, and by junior high his coaches encouraged him to make the switch from running back to quarterback.

During his football career at Granada Hills High School, Elway completed 60 percent of his passes for a total of 5,711 yards and 49 touchdowns. He led his high school team to the league championship and the state semifinals. Despite a knee injury that cut short play in his senior year, Elway managed to post a very impressive record, completing 129 of 200 passes for total yardage of 1,837 and 19 touchdowns. Elway credits his father for teaching him how to run and throw, abilities that gave the younger Elway "enormous confidence," according to high school coach Jack Neumeier. The Granada Hills coach told the *Los An-*

geles *Daily News,* "I don't think I ever coached a competitor like John Elway."

At Stanford University, Elway played on both the football and baseball teams. The Cardinals football team lost more games than they won, but Elway still managed to electrify college fans with some of his gridiron feats. In his freshman year, Elway completed 50 of 97 passes for 544 yards and 6 touchdowns, and the next year was the best in his college career. As a sophomore, Elway completed 248 of 379 passes—an incredible 65 percent completion rate—for 2,889 yards and 27 touchdowns. Over the four years of his college career, Elway completed 774 passes out of 1,246 attempts, for total yardage of 9,349 and 77 touchdowns. He also set a National College Athletic Association (NCAA) record for the lowest percentage of intercepted passes in a career and finished second to Herschel Walker of the University of Georgia in balloting for the 1982 Heisman award.

After graduating from Stanford with a bachelor's degree in economics, Elway came close to turning his back on football in favor of a baseball career. Drafted in April 1983 by the Baltimore Orioles, Elway made no secret of his unhappiness at the prospect of playing for the losing baseball team. He suggested that he would rather play baseball for the New York Yankees and football for the Baltimore Colts, though the Colts had finished last in the NFL standings during the previous season, and Elway did not particularly like Colts coach Frank Kush. Most important, Elway had expressed a strong preference for playing in the West. Fortunately the Denver Broncos jumped at the chance to trade for Elway.

Elway's rookie year with the Broncos was a tough one, but he managed to lead the team to a 9–7 record. However, Elway's personal statistics left a lot to be desired. He completed less than half of his passes, scoring seven touchdowns, but tossing fourteen interceptions. Despite Elway's somewhat wobbly start, Broncos coach Dan Reeves felt confident that he would in time improve and become a first-rate quarterback. Elway himself had his confidence shaken when unhappy fans began to boo him as he took the field.

After his rocky rookie season, Elway returned to California and married college sweetheart Janet. Back in Denver for his second season, Elway's performance improved. He raised his pass completion rate to 56 percent, throwing for eighteen touchdowns, and led his team to the American Football Conference (AFC) West division title. Unfortunately the Broncos were knocked off in the first round of the playoffs by the Pittsburgh Steelers, but the team and Elway had shown the football world that they were capable of great things. Elway truly came into his own during the 1985 season, ranking second in the NFL in pass completions and passing yards. However, even though the Broncos won eleven games, they did not make the playoffs.

Although Elway's personal performance faltered a bit during his fourth season, the Broncos won eleven games

and the AFC West division title. Taking down the New England Patriots and the Cleveland Browns in the playoffs, the team made it into Super Bowl XXI in 1987, facing off against the New York Giants. Despite a strong first half in which the Broncos led New York 10–9, in the end the Giants prevailed, defeating Denver 39–20. The following year the Broncos returned to the Super Bowl, but lost again, falling this time to the Washington Redskins 42–10.

Elway led the Broncos to the Super Bowl five times, becoming the first quarterback ever to start in five Super Bowls. However, it was not until Super Bowl XXXII in 1998 that the team finally tasted victory, defeating the Green Bay Packers 31–24. Next year the Broncos were back again, defeating the Atlanta Falcons 34–19 in Super Bowl XXXIII.

Elway quit the Broncos in 1999 after his second Super Bowl win. He finished his career ranked second all-time with 51,475 passing yards and third all-time with 300 touchdowns. Already a successful businessman in the Denver area, Elway sold his chain of auto dealerships for a reported $82.5 million in 1997. He has since become involved as an advisor for a number of commercial ventures, including MVP.com, SportsLine.com Inc., and Dreams Inc. Elway and his wife live in the Denver area with their four children, and spend much of their time operating the Elway Foundation, which works to prevent child abuse.

Elway's decision to bow out of professional football at the top of his game seemed to fit well with the image he had shaped for himself throughout his years in the game. Never shrinking from challenge, Elway was always persistent in his continuing quest for football's greatest glory. And when he had proved he could achieve his goal, he stayed around long enough to do it again, just to show that he could.

★

For information about Elway in his own words, see *Comeback Kid* (1997), written with Greg Brown, and *Elway* (1998). Books by others about Elway include Clay Latimer, *John Elway: Armed and Dangerous* (1998); Michael Silver, *John Elway: The Drive of a Champion* (1998); Denis Dougherty, *John Elway* (1999); and Matt Christopher, *In the Huddle with . . . John Elway* (1999).

DON AMERMAN

ERVING, Julius Winfield, II ("Dr. J.") (*b.* 22 February 1950 in Hempstead, New York), professional basketball player whose freestyle, dunking play led the New York Nets to two American Basketball Association (ABA) titles, revitalized the National Basketball Association (NBA) in the late 1970s, and spawned a generation of imitators.

Erving was the second of three children born to Julius Erving and Callie Erving. After his parents separated when he was three, Erving's mother worked as a domestic to

Julius Erving ("Dr. J."). AP/WIDE WORLD PHOTOS

championship, earning his second straight All-Conference selection. Erving also received the first half of his nickname from teammate Leon Saunders. "I used to call [Leon] Professor because he always wanted to argue," Erving recalled. "After that he started calling me The Doctor." The name stuck when the two attended college together.

College scouts had shown scant interest in Erving until his growth spurt and standout senior season. He considered scholarship offers from such local schools as St. John's and Hofstra but chose to attend the University of Massachusetts in Amherst, where the basketball coach, Jack Leaman, was an old friend of his high school coach, Ray Wilson. During the 1968–1969 season Erving grew to six feet, six inches, and he attracted sellout crowds to the Curry Hicks Cage, where he led the freshman team to an undefeated season. Erving joined the varsity squad in the 1969–1970 season and averaged 26.3 points and 20.2 rebounds per game over two seasons.

Despite his popularity in Amherst, Erving was relatively unknown nationally in April 1971, when he chose to forgo his final year of collegiate eligibility to sign a four-year, $500,000 free-agent contract with the Virginia Squires of the ABA. He scored 27.3 points per game as a rookie with the Squires and was selected for the All-ABA Second Team. In the 1972 NBA draft, he was selected by the Milwaukee Bucks but returned to Virginia following legal battles. In the 1972–1973 season he raised his scoring average by 3.9 points per game, earning the first of four consecutive All-ABA First Team selections. Though he gained recognition as a top talent, Erving was hampered by the small-market status of the Squires. In 1973 he began to emerge from relative obscurity when he was traded to the New York Nets. He averaged 27.4 points and 10.7 rebounds per game, leading the Nets to the 1974 ABA title and winning the first of three consecutive league Most Valuable Player (MVP) awards. In February 1974 Erving married Turquoise Brown; they had four children.

In one of the greatest individual performances ever by a basketball player in a championship series, Erving scored 226 points and grabbed 85 rebounds over six games as the Nets beat the Denver Nuggets to win the last-ever ABA championship in 1976. Erving finished his five-year ABA career with two championships, three scoring titles, and three MVP awards. Following the Nets' victory the franchise was absorbed into the NBA, as were the San Antonio Spurs, the Indiana Pacers, and Denver.

Locked in a salary dispute with the Nets, Erving was sold to the Philadelphia 76ers on the eve of the 1976–1977 NBA season when Philadelphia's general manager, Pat Williams, convinced the new owner, Eugene Dixon, to sign "the Babe Ruth of basketball." Erving became "the six-million-dollar man," referring to the $3 million it took to pry him from the Nets plus the $3-million contract he

support the family. They moved into a housing project in Hempstead, on Long Island, New York, overlooking Campbell Park, where Erving first played basketball. His long arms, large hands, and court sense impressed Park Director Andy Haggerty, who recommended Erving to Don Ryan, the director of the local Salvation Army center's basketball program. By 1961–1962, Erving was the second team's top scorer and most valuable player; the following year, he led the Hempstead Salvation Army squad to a 31–1 record. In 1964, when Erving was fourteen years old, his mother married Dan Lindsay, a sanitation worker, and the family moved into his house in Roosevelt, New York. Erving enrolled at Roosevelt High School that year but did not make the varsity team until his junior season.

Despite a reserve role as a junior, Erving still managed to lead Roosevelt in scoring and rebounding. The summer of 1967, between his junior and senior years of high school, his height hit six feet, three inches. He then became a starting player and led Roosevelt to a share of the conference

signed with Philadelphia. Nets season ticket holders, who had little interest in watching an Erving-less team, were offered a 10 percent rebate.

Erving was supposed to win a championship for Philadelphia, but each year brought disappointment. Hampered by tendinitis in his knees and the decision to downplay his high-flying act to fit in with his new team, Erving averaged 21.6 points per game his first year with Philadelphia, seven fewer than he had with the Nets. The Sixers reached the NBA Finals that year but blew a 2–0 lead against Bill Walton's Portland Trail Blazers, losing four straight games. The Washington Bullets dominated the eastern division the next two years, with Philadelphia taking a back seat to the team led by Wes Unseld.

Despite Washington's superiority, the Sixers were improving. Erving grew more comfortable in his surroundings, in 1980 becoming one of two active players to be named to the NBA's 35th Anniversary Team. Kareem Abdul-Jabbar of the Los Angeles Lakers was the other active player selected. The two faced off in the NBA Finals that year, with Erving making one of the most incredible shots in NBA history in Game 4. Erving drove past defender Mark Landsberger along the right baseline. He left his feet on that side of the basket, preparing to take a layup. When the seven-foot, two-inch Abdul-Jabbar blocked his path to the basket, Erving brought the ball down and hung in the air, floating behind the backboard. He reached the other side of the rim, where he extended back toward the court, gently flipping up an underhanded scoop for the basket. Erving's legendary baseline move was not enough to propel Philadelphia to victory. The Lakers won Game 5 and then, in Game 6, Magic Johnson filled in for the injured Abdul-Jabbar at center, scoring 42 points to bring Los Angeles to victory.

The following season, 1980–1981, Erving averaged 24.6 points per game and won the NBA's MVP award. But Philadelphia could not protect a 3–1 series lead against the Boston Celtics in the conference finals, losing to Larry Bird's club. In 1981–1982 Erving again averaged over 24 points per game, but one more time, the 76ers lost to the Lakers in the NBA Finals. Realizing they needed a powerful center to compete with Abdul-Jabbar, Williams traded for the Houston Rockets' Moses Malone. The tandem of Erving, who scored 21.4 points per game, and Malone, who averaged 24.5 points, combined to lead Philadelphia to a 65–17 regular season record. For the third time in six seasons the Lakers were the 76ers' opponent in the NBA Finals, but this time Philadelphia overpowered Los Angeles, sweeping the first four games to capture the 1983 championship.

Erving's career gradually declined as he drew more on guile and experience than on the unparalleled physical skills he enjoyed in earlier years. When Erving announced

he would retire after the 1986–1987 season, the entire year turned into a farewell tour. In city after city he was honored for his contributions to the game. Needing 36 points in his last home game to become only the third player to score 30,000 points, Erving, who had switched to shooting guard that year, reached the milestone in the first three periods in a performance reminiscent of his ABA days.

After retiring at the age of thirty-seven, Erving pursued various business interests. His Erving Group, established in 1979, flourished, investing in a Coca-Cola bottling plant in Philadelphia and in various television stations. In 1993 the television network NBC hired Erving as a studio analyst for its NBA telecasts. Four years later he joined the Orlando Magic as executive vice president, a position he still held in 2001.

Off the court, Erving has faced tragedy and controversy. In 1962 his father died in an automobile accident. In April 1969, during Erving's junior year at the University of Massachusetts, his younger brother, Marvin, died of lupus at the age of sixteen. In 1999, after published reports suggested he was the father of tennis star Alexandra Stevenson, Erving admitted to an extramarital affair with a Philadelphia sportswriter in 1980 that resulted in Stevenson's birth. The next year Erving's youngest son, Cory, disappeared in late May and was found dead in his car in a pool of water in July.

Erving was named an All-Star in each of his sixteen professional seasons and is the only player to be named MVP in both the NBA and the ABA. He was enshrined in the Naismith Memorial Basketball Hall of Fame in 1993 and was named to the NBA's 50th Anniversary Team in 1996. Erving redefined the forward position with his high-flying, extemporaneous style of play. He was like a jazz musician on the court, improvising in midair and transforming basketball into a form of innovative individual expression that spawned imitators like Dominique Wilkins and Michael Jordan. He popularized the slam dunk, showing that athleticism could soar above size. With his large hands, Erving also turned ball handling into an art form and popularized an open-court, fast-breaking game.

Erving not only transformed basketball, he changed the way people watched and enjoyed the game. When he entered the NBA, two-thirds of the franchises were on the brink of financial collapse and fans were losing interest in the game. "What he did," wrote Frank Deford upon Erving's retirement, "was to alter the perception of the game, and the way people appreciated it." At the same time he was inventing new shots above the rim, Erving was an ambassador for the game both on and off the court. He played basketball with elegance, but just as importantly, conducted himself with class. "There have been some better people off the court," said the former Laker coach, Pat Riley. "Like a few mothers and the pope. But there was only one Dr. J the player."

★

James Haskins, *Dr. J: A Biography of Julius Erving* (1975), is a look at Erving's life and early career. Marty Bell, *The Legend of Dr. J* (1981), examines Erving's influence on basketball. "Last Rounds for the Doctor: As Julius Erving Says Goodbye, Seven Writers Remember," *Sports Illustrated* (4 May 1987), is a collection of reminiscences on Erving's career. Don Cox, "The Erving Empire," *Business News* (2 Nov. 1988), looks at Erving's vast business interests. Joe Gergen, "Three of a Kind: Brown, Erving, Yaz Grew Up on Long Island, Then Grew into Legends" is an online article that traces Erving's roots on Long Island, paying specific attention to his early basketball development: www.lihistory.com/specspor/stars.htm.

DANNY MASSEY

ESPOSITO, Phil(ip) Anthony (*b.* 20 February 1942 in Sault Sainte Marie, Ontario, Canada), Hall of Fame hockey player particularly noted for his scoring abilities, and hockey entrepreneur who helped the National Hockey League (NHL) expand successfully into the southern United States.

A native Canadian who immigrated to the United States in 1962, Esposito was the older son of Patrick J. Esposito and Frances S. Dipietro. Hockey was the focus of Esposito's life (as it was also for his younger brother Tony) from a very early age. In fact, Esposito dropped out of high school to pursue a hockey career by playing in the minor leagues.

By 1961 he had turned professional, playing for the Saint Catherine's Teepees (Ontario Hockey Association) in 1961–1962, earning 71 points in 49 games (32 goals, 39 assists). The same year he appeared in six games for the Sault Sainte Marie Thunderbirds of the Eastern Pro Hockey League (EPHL). Esposito then joined the St. Louis Braves (EPHL) for the 1962–1963 season, during which he skated in 71 games and earned a total of 90 points (36 goals, 54 assists).

In the 1963–1964 season Esposito appeared with the St. Louis Braves and then the Chicago Blackhawks (NHL), where he remained for three more seasons. During his stint with the Braves, Esposito was in 43 games and scored 26 goals with 54 assists, giving him 80 points. The same year, in 27 games with the Blackhawks, Esposito scored 3 goals and added 2 assists, for a total of 5 points. Over the next three years, Esposito's annual point total averaged approximately 55 in the regular season.

In 1967 Esposito was traded to the Boston Bruins in a deal that included Ken Hodge and Fred Stanfield in exchange for Pit Martin, Jack Morris, and Giles Marotte. From the start Esposito was a phenomenal Bruin, and his productivity soared. In 1968–1969 he became the first NHL player to surpass 100 points in a single season, scoring 49 goals and 77 assists for a total of 126 points. He was to remain above 100 points per regular season throughout most of his career as a Boston Bruin (except for 84 points earned in his first year with the Bruins and 99 points in

Phil Esposito, 2000. ASSOCIATED PRESS AP

the 1969–1970 season). Evidence of Esposito's unprecedented contributions to the team and the game was his appearance on the NHL First All-Star team every year from 1969 through 1974 and on the NHL Second All-Star team in 1968 and 1975.

The single-season highlight of Esposito's professional career is the astonishing numbers he earned in the 1970–1971 season, which ended with 76 goals in 78 games and an additional 76 assists for a total of 152 points. Beginning with this year, Esposito led the NHL in points scored through the 1973–1974 season. These impressive scores resulted in Esposito earning the Art Ross Trophy (for the NHL scoring leader) five times—in 1969 and then again in each year from 1971 through 1974. Additionally, he earned the Hart Memorial Trophy as the NHL's Most Valuable Player (MVP) in 1969 and in 1974. In the 1970–1971 season and again in the 1973–1974 season, Esposito received the Lester B. Pearson Award after being selected by the NHL players themselves as the league's MVP.

Esposito and the Boston team flourished during these years as the center led the line, including Fred Stanfield and Bobby Orr. Despite his excellent beginning as a Bruin (the team reached the Stanley Cup playoffs in 1967–1968 for the first time since postseason play in 1959), Esposito and his teammates keenly felt the absence of ultimate proof of their dominance of the game, a Stanley Cup championship. Finally, the 1969–1970 season, in which Esposito scored 99 points, was followed by 14 postseason games during which Esposito racked up 27 points in 14 games; he produced 13 goals and 14 assists, and the Bruins won the Stanley Cup. The team won the cup again after the 1970–1971 season. Esposito married his wife, Donna, on 7 August 1976. He had two daughters from a previous marriage.

As the line aged and injuries began to mount, Esposito's production continued at an extremely high level, but the Bruins sought change and traded Esposito to the New York Rangers, where he played until his retirement during the 1980–1981 season. From the beginning of his six seasons with the Rangers, Esposito also began to feel the effects of various injuries, but his numbers remained impressive through the 1979–1980 season, his last full NHL year.

After his playing career ended, Esposito assumed a variety of managerial roles in the Rangers' organization. He became the general manager of the team in 1986; during the 1986–1987 season he replaced Coach Ted Sator with Tom Webber, whom he also fired. Just before the Stanley Cup playoffs, Esposito assumed the job of coach, but the Rangers lost in the first round. The following season, after again assuming the job of coach and general manager, Esposito lost these positions because the Rangers did not even qualify for postseason play.

Subsequently, Esposito became instrumental in developing the Tampa Bay Lightning, working in executive capacities for the organization from 1990 through 1998. His brother Tony, also a former NHL star and a 1988 Hall of Famer, also worked as an executive in the NHL.

Measuring six feet, one inch, weighing 205 pounds, and shooting left, Esposito played in the NHL for eighteen seasons, from 1963 to 1981. His development as a center began with a reputation for hanging around the net, where he could pick up so-called easy goals and points. However, by the time he hit his stride with the Boston Bruins, his prowess as a goal and assists scorer clearly benefited not only his own record-breaking scoring but also the team's fortune. To this day the single-season point total of 152 remains a significant record. Esposito's final numbers as a professional hockey center are truly impressive: in a total of 1,282 games, Esposito scored 717 goals and 873 assists for a total of 1,590 points. His postseason career numbers include play in 130 games, 61 goals, and 76 assists totaling 137 points. In 1984 Esposito was inducted into the Hockey Hall of Fame, and a few years later, the Bruins retired the number seven in his honor. In 2001 he still remained among the top twenty in the NHL in the number of points scored, goals, and assists in his career.

★

Esposito is the author of *The Brothers Esposito* (1972); with Gerald Eskenazi, *Hockey Is My Life* (1972); with Tony Esposito, *We Can Teach You How to Play Hockey* (1972); and with Dick Dew, *Phil Esposito's Winning Hockey for Beginners* (1976). Michael McKinley, *Etched in Ice: A Tribute to Hockey's Defining Moments* (1998); Al Strachan, *One Hundred Years of Hockey: Chronicle of a Century on Ice* (1999); and Chris Goyens et al., *Blades on Ice: A Century of Professional Hockey* (2000), all have profiles of Esposito. For an inside look at the 1972 eight-game showdown between the Soviet national team and Canadians drawn from the NHL, in which the Esposito brothers played a role, see "Coming of Age: Who Will Ever Forget THE GOAL?" *Maclean's* (1 July 1999).

JAMES J. SULLIVAN III

EVANS, Janet (*b.* 28 August 1971 in Placentia, California), first U.S. woman to win four Olympic gold medals in swimming and one of the best middle-distance swimmers in the history of the sport.

Evans grew up in suburban California with her father, Paul Evans, a veterinarian, her mother, Barbara, who served as her unofficial coach, and two siblings. She was comfortable in the water at age one, and by the time she was four she had joined Fullerton Aquatics team with Coach Bud McAllister and could swim all four strokes. At five she was already competing in the six-and-under age group. Evans set her first Orange County record and her first National Age Group record at ages six and ten, respectively. Her record-setting time (2:18.07), achieved in the 200-meter freestyle when she was ten years old, was not bettered for seven years. Although she was two years younger than the next youngest girl in the competition, she destroyed the field in the 1,500 freestyle at the Junior Nationals in San Jose, California, in 1984. At fifteen, Evans was ranked among the world's top ten swimmers in the 400- and 800-meter freestyle and the 400 individual medley (IM).

Evans's training schedule was grueling. Six days a week she was out of bed at 4:45 A.M. and trained at the Independence Park Pool in nearby Fullerton. After school she had another session, swimming a total of about ten miles a day plus working out at the gym regularly.

She stole the show at the 1987 Phillips 66 U.S. Swimming Long Course Championships, breaking two long-standing women's world records in the 800 freestyle and 1,500 freestyle, with victories in four events. Evans claimed the record for the 400 freestyle the following year. Based on exceptional performance as a high school swimmer, she won the Phillips Performance Award. She was also named Best American Swimmer in 1987 and emerged from the U.S. long-course championships as the best woman distance swimmer in the world.

At the Seoul Olympics in September 1988, Evans was a petite high school junior, who, at seventeen, was only slightly over five feet tall, with her weight hovering around 100 pounds. A *Sports Illustrated* Olympic preview article (14 Sept. 1988) by Jill Lieber explained Evans's success despite her small size: "Janet compensated for her size by taking more strokes than her competitors—36 to travel 25 yards and 62 to go 50 meters; a top female distance swimmer typically takes about 50 strokes for 50 meters." Spectators marveled at her strange stiff-armed, windmilling stroke. More records were shattered as she brought home the gold in the 400 freestyle (4:03.85, Olympic and world record), the 800 freestyle (8:20.20, Olympic record), and the 400 IM (4:37.76). She had actually set a new world record in the 800 freestyle (8:17.12) in 1987. The 1,500 freestyle was not offered as an Olympic event to women at that time because it was considered too strenuous, but Evans went on to become the first woman to break the sixteen-minute barrier in the event (at Orlando later in 1988) with a world-record time of 15:52:10. Her father gave her a red BMW convertible as a reward for her outstanding performance at Seoul.

The popular Evans, selected as homecoming queen, graduated from El Dorado High School in 1989, with a 3.5 grade point average. She began her college career at Stanford University in 1989 and trained under Richard Quick. At the 1989 Pan Pacific games, she bettered her world record in the 800 freestyle to 8:16.22 and also won the Amateur Athletic Union's annual James E. Sullivan Award as the best amateur athlete, only the fourth time a female swimmer was a recipient. She was also elected United States Olympic Committee (USOC) Sports Woman of the Year

Janet Evans. AP/WIDE WORLD PHOTOS

in 1989. Evans was respected by her teammates for her hard work and mental strength. She left Stanford and gave up two years of collegiate eligibility because of a National Collegiate Athletic Association (NCAA) rule limiting swimmers to twenty hours per week of practice time.

In 1991 Evans transferred to the University of Texas and began to train with Coach Mark Schubert. She was fond of a team shirt that sported the words "Tough and EXceptionally fASt" (capital letters spell Texas). At the 1992 Barcelona Olympics 1992, Evans won the gold medal in the 800 freestyle and the silver in the 400 freestyle, but neither she nor anyone else bettered her earlier record times. Disappointed by her performance, she quit swimming for four months. Soon after, Evans transferred to the University of Southern California (USC) and resumed training with Schubert, who had recently accepted the head coaching position there. She added an hour-long run to her conditioning routine, and her times improved from Barcelona but still did not match her world-record times. Evans graduated from USC in 1994 with a degree in communications.

Evans continued to train for the 1996 Olympics, which

were held in Atlanta, Georgia. Due to her extraordinary competitiveness, she made the team in the 400 and 800 freestyle. At the age of twenty-four, she was taller and heavier (now five feet, six inches tall and weighing 113 pounds) and not as fast as she was in her prime, but still the most successful female competitive swimmer in Olympic history. She carried the Olympic torch into the stadium in Atlanta, her third Olympics. She did not win a fifth gold medal and did not even reach the finals in the 400 freestyle; however, she had participated in three Olympics, an unusual accomplishment in swimming.

Evans retired from competitive swimming after Atlanta. She signed several lucrative endorsement contracts and toured the nation giving motivational speeches. She has served as a volunteer coach for the USC women's swim team and has commentated on ESPN and Fox for televised swimming events. The Janet Evans Invitational, part of the United States Swimming Grand Prix Series, is among the largest meets in the nation. In 2001 Evans's first team in Fullerton honored her with the dedication of the Janet Evans Swim Complex. Evans, who has a diabetic brother, is also active in charity work, where her principal focus is the American Diabetes Association.

With many of her records still intact and having won five Olympic medals from Seoul and Barcelona, Evans is listed among the best swimmers of the twentieth century. Additional statistics include seven world records, four world championship medals, four short-course championship gold medals, forty-five U.S. national championships, and seven NCAA national championships. She has been a model for many aspiring young athletes, and will be remembered as much for her humility and endearing smile as for her trademark bursts of speed and unique swimming style.

★

Biographical entries are in *Current Biography Yearbook* (1996), *Encyclopedia of Women and Sports in America* (1998), and Judy L. Hasday, *Extraordinary Women Athletes* (2000). Profiles appear in *Sports Illustrated* (26 Mar. 1990), *Time* (27 Jul. 1992), and the *Time* Summer Olympics Supplement (Summer 1996).

JEANNIE P. MILLER

EVERT, Christine Marie ("Chris") (*b.* 21 December 1954 in Fort Lauderdale, Florida), tennis player and sports commentator whose outstanding record and style of play contributed to the popularity of women's professional tennis in the 1970s and 1980s.

Evert is the daughter of James ("Jimmy") Evert and Colette Thompson. James was a former tennis player who became the teaching pro and manager at the Holiday Park tennis center in Fort Lauderdale; Colette was a homemaker active in local charities. Evert was the second of five children and

Chris Evert, 1987. AP/WIDE WORLD PHOTOS

the oldest of three daughters. A Roman Catholic, she graduated from Saint Thomas Aquinas High School in Fort Lauderdale in 1972.

Under her father's astute tutelage, along with her brothers and sisters, Evert started playing tennis at the Holiday Park courts. Her talent for the game was apparent at an early age. With her father's direction, she developed what became her signature stroke, the two-handed backhand. Because as a child she lacked the strength to hit the shot with only one hand on the racket, she relied on the two-handed stroke and stayed with it throughout her career. Evert also displayed the commitment to discipline and the willingness to practice that marked her game.

By her mid-teens Evert was gaining the notice of the top tennis players as a dangerous opponent. In the autumn of 1970 she defeated two top-ranked competitors at a tournament in Charlotte, North Carolina. One of her victims was Margaret Smith Court, then the number-one female player in the world. Evert lost in the final, but this event established her as one of the up-and-coming players in women's tennis. Her ascendancy continued during the first half of 1971, as she won the Virginia Slims Masters in Saint Petersburg, Florida, in April, and joined the winning American Wightman Cup team against Great Britain.

Evert burst upon the national sports consciousness at the U.S. Open that August. At the age of sixteen she won her first round match, survived a grueling three-set match in the second round against Mary Ann Eisel, and won two more matches before facing Billie Jean King in the semifinals. Although King won in straight sets, 6–3, 6–2, Evert impressed a national television audience with her poise and all-around game. She became the sensation of the tournament and established an enduring popularity as "Chris Evert," she of the devastating baseline game and the punishing two-handed backhand. Her consistency and calm demeanor on the court attracted fans, as did her respect for the game and her opponents. "I'm very glad that I came along when I did in the '70s," Evert wrote in a 1993 article for *USA Weekly*. "It was the emergence of big-time tennis. It was still fun; there was camaraderie on the tour." Over the next eighteen years Evert was a model of consistency at the highest level of women's tennis. From 1971 to 1983 she entered thirty-four Grand Slam tournaments and in each one she reached the semifinals or better. For thirteen consecutive years she won at least one Grand Slam tournament annually, a record that still stands and is not likely to be equaled or excelled in the near future. From August 1973 through May 1979 she triumphed in 125 straight matches on clay, the surface on which she was most comfortable. During her career, her ranking never dropped below fourth in the world, and her match record in singles was a sparkling 1309–146.

The Grand Slams were Evert's showcase. She won the Australian Open twice (1982, 1984) and was victorious at Wimbledon three times (1974, 1976, 1981). The grass courts at Wimbledon were not suited to her game, and the British press, which styled her the "Ice Maiden," often provided unwelcome distractions. In the French Open, Evert dominated her contemporaries. She garnered seven titles (1974, 1975, 1979, 1980, 1983, 1985, 1986) as the red clay of Roland Garros Stadium accentuated her consistency from the baseline and the patience and depth of her ground strokes. She also won the U.S. Open six times (1975, 1976, 1977, 1978, 1980, 1982), and her overall record of 101 match wins remained the best for both men and women players at the dawn of the twenty-first century. Evert earned over $8,000,000 in prize money during her career.

What made Evert such a popular athlete were her two stirring rivalries with major contemporaries in women's tennis and her fascinating personal life. On the court, her first major foe during the 1970s was the mercurial star Billie Jean King. She and Evert met often in decisive matches in the major tournaments. But it was her many duels with Martina Navratilova that became the stuff of enduring tennis legend. Part of it was the sheer stylistic contrast between the two women as tennis players. Navratilova, an immigrant from Czechoslovakia, had an athletic serve-and-volley game. For sheer power, no woman of the time could match Navratilova's attacking style. Evert's game rested on the precision of her ground strokes from the baseline. This contrast of styles and competitive approaches led to a fierce rivalry that kept their fans riveted throughout their heyday.

As Evert later conceded, the physical and mental challenge from Navratilova helped her lift her game to a higher level to meet the demands and give her a realistic chance of winning. Although Evert ended up with a losing record to her friend and rival, she won her share of decisive matches in the major tournaments. In the 1982 Australian Open final she outlasted Navratilova in a searing three-set match, 6–3, 2–6, 6–3. She also pulled out dramatic consecutive victories in the French Open over Navratilova in 1985 and 1986, in matches that had the Roland Garros stadium crowd at a fever pitch of excitement. Through all of the ups and downs of being competitors, Evert recalled in *USA Weekly* that the two women "used to hit with each other and after the match go to a movie." During the height of their rivalry, the two players became identified with each other. Tennis fans simply had to say "Chris and Martina" to invoke the memories of their great matches and the potential of another encounter in a tournament final.

Evert's private life attracted almost as much press attention as her performance on the court. She had a highly publicized romance with the male tennis star Jimmy Connors, a romance that ended in 1974. In the years that followed she dated movie star Burt Reynolds. Evert married the British tennis star John Lloyd on 17 April 1979. Their union lasted seven years before the pressures of professional tennis led to a divorce in 1986. Two years later, on 30 July 1988, she married Andy Mill, an Olympic skier for the United States. They have three sons, Alexander James, Nicholas Joseph, and Colton Jack, and the family lives in Aspen, Colorado, and Boca Raton, Florida.

By the late 1980s Evert's game showed signs of her advancing age in tennis terms. After an appearance at the U.S. Open in 1989, she retired from competition. "In the last few years, I was trying to get out of myself things that weren't there anymore—the motivation, the single-mindedness," she noted in 1993. Retirement from tennis did not mean that Evert stepped away from the game she loves. She is a tennis commentator with the National Broadcasting Company (NBC) for the French Open and Wimbledon. She operates a tennis academy in Boca Raton, and sponsors a charity tennis tournament. She remains an active leader in the Women's Tennis Association. Early in 2001 she became publisher of *Tennis Magazine* in what she described as a "partnership" with the popular periodical. Her goal, according to the publisher's letter in the March 2001 issue of the magazine, is "to help elevate our endeavor to a championship level." From this editorial platform, she is likely to retain her pervasive influence over her sport.

Evert is one of the most important figures in women's tennis history. During her playing career she was the most celebrated athlete in the sport. In 1985 the Women's Sports

Foundation designated her as the Greatest Woman Athlete of the quarter-century after 1960. Other polls have recognized her as the most famous female athlete in the nation. In some respects, Evert was an unlikely object of so much adoration. She did not express her emotions on the court and her demeanor was always businesslike. Nonetheless, her skill as a tennis player, her coolness under pressure, and her unrelenting will to win won over a legion of fans. In her 1982 autobiography *Chrissie,* she articulated her guiding philosophy: "I love tennis, I love the competition, the sheer challenge of playing to perfection." The extent to which Evert achieved her goals during her career accounted for her place in the affections of sports fans in the United States and around the world.

★

Evert's autobiography, with Neil Amdur, *Chrissie: My Own Story* (1982), traces her life through the midpoint of her tennis career. Her book with John Lloyd and Carol Thatcher, *Lloyd on Lloyd* (1985), can be read in light of the Lloyds' divorce a year later. Bud Collins, *My Life with the Pros* (1990), and John Feinstein, *Hard Courts: Real Life on the Professional Tennis Tours* (1991), assess Evert's place in the sport. "My Love Match with Andy," *Good Housekeeping* (Oct. 1990); "The Trouble with Tennis Today," *USA Weekly* (27–29 Aug. 1993); and "Publisher's Letter," *Tennis Magazine* (Mar. 2001), are examples of Evert's writings after retirement from competitive tennis.

KAREN GOULD

EWBANK, Wilbur Charles ("Weeb") (*b.* 6 May 1907 in Richmond, Indiana; *d.* 18 November 1998 in Oxford, Ohio), football coach noted for coaching three championship teams, two in the National Football League (NFL) and one in the American Football League (AFL), and for coaching teams in two of the most memorable football games in history.

Ewbank was born to a family of grocers in Richmond, Indiana. By 1916, at age nine, he was doing what many sons of grocers did in that era: driving a horse-drawn wagon to deliver groceries. That year he managed to find a ride to Dayton, Ohio, to watch Jim Thorpe and the Canton Bulldogs football team. He eventually attended the Oliver P. Morton High School, where he excelled in sports. There, he met his future wife, Lucy, and married her; they remained married for the rest of his life.

Ewbank played for the football and baseball teams of his college, Miami University of Ohio in Oxford. He became the captain of the baseball team and was a quarterback for the football team, backing up Paul Brown, who would later give Ewbank his chance to coach professional football.

After graduating from college in 1928, Ewbank took a coaching job at Van Wert High School in Ohio, earning

$2,000 per year. In 1930 he returned to Oxford to coach McGuffey High School. Oxford became his family's permanent home. His McGuffey teams won seventy-one games and lost twenty-one during his thirteen-year tenure. In 1936, in the middle of a winning streak that lasted a total of twenty-one games, his team was both undefeated and unscored upon.

In 1943 Ewbank joined the U.S. Navy and was stationed at the Great Lakes Naval Training Center, thirty miles northeast of Chicago in Great Lakes, Illinois, where his old friend Brown was coaching the base's football team. Ewbank became an assistant coach for Brown. In 1946, after leaving the navy, he joined the coaching staff of the Brown University football team and became the coach of the school's basketball team. In 1947 he went to St. Louis's Washington University, where he was head football coach for two years, winning fourteen games and losing four.

Meanwhile, Brown had become head coach of the Cleveland Browns of the All-America Football Conference (AAFC). He hired his friend Ewbank to coach the kickers and the linemen. Ewbank emphasized protecting the passer—the sort of protection he as a quarterback would have liked to have had. Cleveland won the All-America conference title in 1949. Then, in 1950, the Browns and other All-America teams were absorbed into the NFL. The first game of the season was a matchup between the Browns and the NFL champion Philadelphia Eagles, in which the Eagles were favored to defeat the Browns by at least three touchdowns. However, the Browns won, establishing the validity of the former All-America teams.

Ewbank coached for the Browns through 1953. In 1954 he took the head coaching job for the Baltimore Colts. At that time the Colts were a terrible team. Ewbank created a system of offense that kept the basics simple, making it easy to learn. Hall of Fame lineman Jim Parker remembered that Ewbank made pass blocking "a science."

The team needed a quarterback who could pass well, and in 1955 Ewbank found one in Johnny Unitas. Unitas, who had tried out for the Pittsburgh Steelers and had been cut from that team's roster, was playing semiprofessional football when he was brought to Ewbank's attention by a letter from someone who had seen him play. Ewbank gave Unitas a tryout and liked his toughness. He signed Unitas to the Colts and then redesigned his offense to emphasize Unitas's strengths: his sharp arm movements when passing, his quick movements from side to side, and his intelligence. It was typical of Ewbank to bring out in his players what others had given up on; Unitas became the most celebrated quarterback of his time.

In 1958 the Colts and the New York Giants played for the NFL championship. The hard-fought game was nationally telecast, and it electrified its audience. It is often called "The Greatest Game in History" because it marked

Weeb Ewbank, 1973. © BETTMANN/CORBIS

the emergence of professional football as a major television sport. The Colts won the game and captured the NFL championship again in 1959.

Ewbank was fired by the Colts in 1962, as team owner Carroll Rosenbloom was impatient with the team's 7–7 won-lost record of that year. In 1963 Ewbank became the head coach and general manager of a dismal team that had just escaped bankruptcy, the New York Jets of the AFL. He did for the Jets what he had done for the Colts, finding players for them that others had given up on, such as Johnny Sample, a defensive back cut by the Colts in 1966 who would become the captain of the defense for the Jets.

By 1967 the Jets were becoming a respectable team. The team's owner shelled out $400,000 to sign brash, difficult quarterback Joe Namath, and Ewbank designed an offense that emphasized Namath's fluid motion and quick passing release. In 1969 the Jets met the Colts in Super Bowl III. The Colts were expected to demolish the Jets, but Ewbank had designed a plan that took advantage of weaknesses in the Colts' defensive line, and his team executed the plan almost to perfection. This was the second of Ewbank's two most memorable games, because the Jets' victory ushered in the merger of the rival leagues by establishing that AFL teams could play on a par with the best the NFL had.

In 1973 Ewbank retired from coaching, and in 1974 he retired as general manager for the Jets. In 1978 he was elected to the Pro Football Hall of Fame. He never lost interest in football or in his former players and staff. He died at his home in Oxford at age ninety-one and is buried in Oxford Cemetery. Hundreds of people attended his funeral. He had three children, eight grandchildren, and sev-enteen great-grandchildren, but many of his former players said that he and his wife had been father and mother to them as well.

Ewbank stood five feet, seven inches tall and weighed 180 pounds while he was with the Baltimore Colts. His walk was usually described as a waddle. During games he seemed sometimes frantic on the sidelines and sometimes not there at all. His career professional football record as a head coach for regular season games was 130 wins and 129 losses, with seven ties, for a .502 winning percentage. Despite these unremarkable statistics, he was one of football's greatest coaches.

★

Goal to Go: The Greatest Football Games I Have Coached (1972), by Ewbank and Neil Roiter, offers a firsthand look at how Ewbank coached his teams. Paul Zimmerman, *The Last Season of Weeb Ewbank* (1974), offers an intimate behind-the-scenes look at Ewbank. Larry Fox, *Broadway Joe and His Super Jets* (1969), offers a history of the New York Jets franchise and how it was transformed from bankruptcy into a championship team. *The Game That Changed Pro Football* (1989), by Stephen Hanks, focuses on the Jets' Super Bowl victory.

KIRK H. BEETZ

EWELL, Henry Norwood ("Barney") (*b.* 25 February 1918 in Lancaster, Pennsylvania; *d.* 4 April 1996 in Lancaster, Pennsylvania), sprinter who tied the world record in the 100-meter race at the U.S. Olympic Trials in 1948, and won a gold medal in the 400-meter relay at the 1948 London Olympics at the age of thirty.

Born to a poor family in Lancaster, Pennsylvania, Ewell had strongly muscled legs, a "half-moon" smile, and a notably pleasant and easygoing personality. While still in high school in Lancaster, he won the U.S. junior sprint title for 1936, and followed this with a stellar career on the track team at Pennsylvania State University.

While at Penn State, Ewell was a nine-time All-American. He won the long jump and the 100- and 220-yard dashes in three consecutive years of the Intercollegiate Association of Amateur Athletes of America (IC4A) championships; no athlete before him had even won the events two years in a row. In 1940 and 1941 he won back-to-back National College Athletic Association (NCAA) championships in both the 100- and 200-meter races. He was the Amateur Athletic Union (AAU) outdoor 100-meter champion in 1941, 1945, and 1948, and the 200-meter champion in 1939, 1946, and 1947. From 1940 through 1942 he won the long jump at the IC4A outdoor meet; he also won the indoor long jump in 1940 and 1942, and the AAU indoor long jump in 1944 and 1945.

On the mostly white Penn State campus, the African-American Ewell stood out, but not only because of his race and his athletic talent. He was well known on campus for his friendly manner, personal charm, and sense of humor. John Lucas, an Olympic historian and professor of exercise and sport science who was a track and field coach for Penn State, said of Ewell, "He was as poor as a church mouse. He had not had any money and yet he was an upbeat, joy-filled guy."

When the 1940 and 1944 Olympics were canceled due to World War II, Ewell was forced to wait until he was well past his athletic prime to compete again. Most sprinters are in their prime in their twenties; Ewell won his Olympic medals at age thirty, a notable achievement that has made track fans wonder what he would have done if he could have competed at a world level earlier. The war also disrupted Ewell's education; he postponed his 1942 graduation from Penn State so that he could enlist in the U.S. Army in 1941. When asked what division of the army he wanted to be in, he said, joking, "Any one but the cavalry because if we get in trouble and have to run, I don't want the horses to get in my way." He served with distinction until 1945, and returned to competition and college when the war was over, eventually graduating from Penn State with a B.S. degree in 1947.

At the 1948 AAU championship, which was also the trial for the 1948 Olympics, Ewell tied the world record of 10.2 in the 100-meter dash. At the Olympics, in the 100-meter race, Ewell and sprinter Harrison Dillard sped across the finish line in a dead heat. Ewell, so convinced that he had won, jumped up and down, exulting. The officials, however, were not convinced, and had to study photos of the finish in order to determine who had won—the first time this technique, now common in sports, was used in the

Barney Ewell, 1942. ASSOCIATED PRESS AP

Olympics. When they awarded the win to Dillard, Ewell, with characteristic dignity, walked over and congratulated him. Three days later, in the 200-meter dash, Ewell and Mel Patton recorded identical 21.1-second times for the event. Again, the gold medal went to Patton, and Ewell again graciously congratulated the winner.

Ewell was not originally slated to run on the 400-meter relay team, but when member Ed Conwell became sick, he was chosen to fill in. The team won easily, but the changeover between Ewell and teammate Lorenzo Wright was ruled to have occurred out of the exchange zone, and the U.S. team was disqualified. The team protested, and the Olympic Jury of Appeal viewed a film of the changeover. They found that the baton pass was made correctly, the ruling was reversed, and Ewell finally received Olympic gold, to go along with his two silver medals.

In honor of his Olympic achievements, his hometown of Lancaster awarded Ewell a house and car. The track authorities said that acceptance of these gifts made Ewell a professional athlete, one who competed for pay. At the time, only amateur athletes, those who received no money from their sport, were allowed to compete, so Ewell was barred from further Olympic competition. After being barred, Ewell competed in Australia and New Zealand as a professional athlete. Later in his life, he worked for an electric company in Lancaster.

In the early 1990s, Ewell, who suffered from poor circulation, fought against increasing health problems. He lost several toes, and in 1993 had his right leg amputated below the knee after his veins became infected. In 1995 his left leg was amputated above the knee. At the time he was living in Conestoga View, a nursing home in Lancaster, and used a wheelchair or crutches to get around. Despite his health problems and limited mobility, he remained optimistic and often joked and laughed with visitors.

Herman Goffberg, a teammate of Ewell's while they were both at Penn State, visited Ewell in the early 1990s and was upset by Ewell's poverty. He organized a fund-raising effort that eventually brought in $16,000 from Ewell's friends and fans, money that allowed Ewell to live out the last years of his life in relative comfort and dignity.

Ewell died of complications from his amputations on 4 April 1996, and was buried in Lancaster. He was survived by his wife, Duella, and their four children.

If Ewell had been allowed to compete at the Olympic level as a younger athlete, there is no doubt that he would have been a favored contender for at least one gold medal in the sprint events. *U.S. Track and Field News* named Ewell one of the ten greatest sprinters of all time, and he was named to the Track and Field Hall of Fame in 1986. His lifetime achievements were honored at halftime during the Penn State-Wisconsin men's basketball game on 17 February 1995, and Goffberg has established a $25,000 scholarship in Ewell's name at Penn State. In addition, the Penn State Sports Hall of Fame will have a section named after Ewell.

★

There is no full-length biography of the running career of Ewell. Short articles on Ewell appear in R. L. Quercetani's *A World History of Track and Field Athletics, 1864–1964* (1964), Reid M. Hanley's *Who's Who in Track and Field* (1973), and Bill Mallon, Ian Buchanan, and Jeffrey Tishman's *Quest for Gold* (1984). Detailed material on Ewell's life and achievements is somewhat difficult to find; the best sources are articles published in the Penn State *Digital Collegian* (5 Apr. 1996 and 2 May 1997). An obituary by Kevin Gorman is in *Digital Collegian* (5 Apr. 1996).

KELLY WINTERS

EWING, Patrick Aloysius (*b.* 5 August 1962 in Kingston, Jamaica), basketball player who was a three-time All-American at Georgetown University before becoming the New York Knicks all-time leading scorer and one of the top pure-shooting centers in National Basketball Association history.

Ewing, the fifth of seven children born to Carl and Dorothy Ewing, played cricket and soccer as a child in Jamaica. With assistance from relatives in New York City, Dorothy Ewing left Jamaica for the United States in 1971 and settled in Cambridge, Massachusetts, where she worked in the cafeteria at Massachusetts General Hospital. Her husband, a heavy-duty mechanic in Jamaica, joined her two years later

Patrick Ewing. AP/WIDE WORLD PHOTOS

and found a job at a rubber company. The Ewing children followed, one or two at a time, with Patrick arriving in January 1975.

A six-foot, one-inch tall seventh grader, Ewing began his organized basketball career at the Achievement School, a remedial center for junior high school students in Cambridge. By eighth grade, he had grown to six feet, six inches, and was recruited by Head Coach Mike Jarvis to play at Rindge and Latin High School in Cambridge. Playing center, Ewing led the school to a 74–1 record over four years, including three state championships. The high schooler spoke with a heavy Jamaican accent and was often the target of racially motivated ridicule from opposing fans. The taunting did not affect Ewing's play, however. The center was so impressive, he was invited to the Olympic trials in the summer after his junior year, the first such invitation ever extended to a high school player. In his senior year, Ewing grew to seven feet and became the most heavily sought-after player in the nation. He chose Georgetown University in Washington, D.C., because he liked its coach, John Thompson.

At Georgetown, Ewing continued to be the target of racism. That hostility, along with his mother's death in 1983 and public criticism when he fathered a son out of wedlock in 1984, turned Ewing into an intensely private person. Sheltered by Thompson, Ewing rarely spoke with the media. But his actions on the court needed no explanation. He dominated defensively, becoming Georgetown's all-time leader in rebounding and blocked shots, earning the nickname Hoya Destroya. Ewing was the anchor of the Hoya Paranoia defense, so-called after its intimidating, relentless style of play that pressured opponents into turnovers.

As a freshman, Ewing led the Hoyas to the National Collegiate Athletic Association (NCAA) championship game, where they lost to Michael Jordan's North Carolina Tar Heels, 63–62. In the 1983–1984 season, during Ewing's junior year, he was elected the tournament's Most Valuable Player when the Hoyas won their first-ever national title, beating Hakeem Olajuwon's University of Houston Cougars 84–75. That summer, Ewing played for the U.S. Olympic team, which won a gold medal in Los Angeles. In his senior year, Ewing won the National Player of the Year award and the Hoyas reached the NCAA title game for the third time in four years; Villanova upset them 66–64. The three-time All-American finished his collegiate career as the Big East Conference's then all-time leading rebounder.

With Ewing the consensus first pick in the 1985 draft, the National Basketball Association (NBA) switched from a coin toss between the worst team in each conference to a lottery where the worst seven teams overall would have an equal chance to gain the first selection and land the superstar center. The Knicks won the sweepstakes, and on 18 June, as expected, selected Ewing with the first pick. He signed a ten-year contract worth $30 million, the most money ever given to an NBA rookie.

Knicks fans looked to Ewing as the savior of a franchise that had finished the previous season 24–58, third worst in the league. He arrived in New York, the pressure of rebuilding a team with a storied tradition placed squarely on his shoulders. Renowned for his intimidating defense in college, Ewing displayed a surprising offensive potency during his rookie season, averaging twenty points per game. He was an All-Star and earned Rookie of the Year honors, but the Knicks missed out on the playoffs in his first two years. In the 1987–1988 season, under new head coach Rick Pitino, the Knicks employed the pressing, trapping style of play that was the trademark of Ewing's Georgetown team, and the center got his first taste of playoff basketball in an opening round loss to the Boston Celtics.

In 1991 Pat Riley took over as head coach of the Knicks, ushering in a string of successes for the team. Ewing averaged twenty-four points and eleven rebounds per game over three years, culminating in a trip to the NBA Finals in 1994. But New York again came up short. In fact, Ewing's entire Knicks career was marred by the team's failure to win a championship. Because of Ewing's solid play,

many Knicks teams had chances to win NBA titles. But each year, injuries, missteps, or more talented teams got in the way.

The 1989 Eastern Conference semifinal series against the Chicago Bulls marked the beginning of a heated rivalry between the two teams that would bring great disappointment to Ewing. Over eight years, the Knicks and the Bulls played six playoff series, with Chicago winning five times. The only New York win came in the 1993–1994 season, when the legendary Chicago guard Michael Jordan was playing baseball. Jordan's Chicago Bulls stopped the Knicks in the playoffs from 1991 through 1993. In the 1992–1993 season, the Knicks won 60 games, were seeded first in the Eastern Conference and appeared set to knock off two-time defending champion Chicago. But Charles Smith's missed lay-ups in the final moments of game five of the conference finals doomed Ewing's team as it squandered a 2–0 series lead.

A year later, when the Knicks finally reached the NBA Finals, Hakeem Olajuwon blocked John Starks's potential series winning shot at the buzzer in game six. Despite Ewing's record-breaking 30 blocked shots in the series, Houston won when Starks shot 0–11 from three-point range in the final game. In 1995–1996, Ewing's finger roll at the buzzer hit the back of the rim and bounded away as the Knicks fell to the Pacers in seven games in the conference semifinals. Perhaps Ewing's greatest disappointment came when he was suspended, along with four other teammates, after leaving the bench during an altercation in game five of the 1996–1997 conference semifinals against the Miami Heat. That year, management had finally surrounded Ewing with other capable scorers, signing Allan Houston away from the Detroit Pistons and trading with the Charlotte Hornets for Larry Johnson. But with five key veterans excluded from play over two games, the Knicks blew a 3–1 series lead.

With his professional life marked by frustration at his team's failure to gain the elusive NBA championship that would cap his career, Ewing's personal life fell on hard times as well. He had married Rita Williams, whom he met while interning on Capitol Hill during his Georgetown years, in July 1990. They had two children together, but a 1998 affair, allegedly with a Knicks' City Dancer, resulted in divorce. Ewing's Knicks career also came to an end. Unwilling to give the aging center the two-year contract he desired, the Knicks traded him to the Seattle Supersonics in a three-team deal in July 2000. After a subpar season in Seattle, Ewing signed a free agent contract with the Orlando Magic in July 2001.

Hard work, an eternal optimism, and an inability to accept defeat marked Ewing's career. He annually proclaimed, "This is our year," backing up his predictions with supreme, warrior-like effort. Ewing parlayed that tireless work ethic into eleven All-Star appearances, a 1992 gold medal as part of the "Dream Team," and selection as one of the NBA's fifty greatest players ever. A defensive stopper in college, Ewing's fifteen-foot jump shot became virtually unstoppable in his years with the Knicks.

He left New York as the team's all-time leader in many statistical categories, including games played, points, rebounds, steals, and blocks. But, surrounded by inadequate talent early in his career and thwarted by injuries and bizarre mishaps in his later years, Ewing's championship predictions never came true. Although his career is often defined by the Knicks' inability to win a title, it was Ewing who put his team and its fans in position to believe that each year was going to be *the* year.

★

An interview with filmmaker Spike Lee, in *Interview* (May 1990), touches on Ewing's childhood in Cambridge. Ewing's peers offer their perceptions of the superstar in Michael Arace, "It's Easy to Understand Ewing's No. 1 Career Goal," *The Hartford Courant* (5 Nov. 1993). Jackie MacMullan, "Life Has Tried, but Failed to Make Ewing Lose His Hidden Smile," *Boston Globe* (2 May 1993), analyzes the impact of Ewing's harsh experiences growing up. Curtis Bunn, "Journey Recalls Racism for Ewing," *Daily News* (11 Sept. 1994), follows Ewing on a trip to South Africa, where he recounts the racism he faced in Cambridge and at Georgetown. An entertaining source of biographical information on Ewing, from childhood to NBA stardom, is NBA Entertainment's video "Standing Tall" (1994).

DANNY MASSEY

EWING, William ("Buck") (*b.* 17 October 1859 in Hoagland, Ohio; *d.* 20 October 1906 in Cincinnati, Ohio), baseball catcher whose potent bat and unsurpassed fielding earned him a reputation as one of the finest all-around players of the nineteenth century.

William Ewing was born the second of five children of Samuel and Martha Ewing in Hoagland, Ohio, a small community on the outskirts of Cincinnati. When William was still in his infancy, the family established residence in Cincinnati's East End, the railroad depot to a city known for its bustling hog market. But during William's childhood, Cincinnati may have been most famous for its baseball team. In 1869 the Cincinnati Red Stockings toured the country as the first openly professional team in history, and their success ushered in the game's professional era. Samuel Ewing supported his family as a teamster, but two of his sons would ultimately choose baseball as their profession. William's younger brother, John, would pitch in the major leagues for four seasons, once winning an ERA title, and William would become arguably the greatest all-around player of his generation, and unquestionably its greatest catcher.

Buck Ewing, from a Goodwin & Co. baseball card, c. 1887–1890. BASE-BALL CARDS FROM THE BENJAMIN K. EDWARDS COLLECTION/THE LIBRARY OF CONGRESS

In 1878 William supplemented his $10 per week job as a teamster for a distillery company by catching for the Mohawk Browns, one of Cincinnati's numerous sandlot teams. After playing two seasons with the Browns, and part of one season with the minor league Rochester Hop Bitters, Ewing joined the Troy Haymakers of the National League near the end of the 1880 season. Ewing batted just .178, but his catching abilities so impressed the club that in the offseason the youngster was signed to a $1,000 contract.

The confidence Troy displayed in Ewing would be vindicated in the years to come, as "Buck" (a childhood nickname that was picked up by reporters early in his career) all but revolutionized the catcher position. In an era when catchers wore little protective equipment, and consequently had to play well behind the batter to avoid injury, Ewing was one of the first to don a padded glove and crouch directly behind home plate. He was renowned for his rocket throwing arm, and often threw out baserunners directly from the crouching position.

Ewing played in an era when bunting and base stealing were the order of the day, so it is likely that he could have crafted a notable career on the merits of his defense alone. Nonetheless, when the Troy club disbanded following the 1882 season and Ewing's contract was awarded to the New York Giants, his offensive skills started to blossom. In 1883, he batted .303 and led the league with 10 home runs. Over the course of the next several seasons, Ewing displayed a degree of offensive consistency rarely seen from a catcher—from 1885 to 1893, he batted over .300 every season. Indeed, his offense was considered so integral to the New York attack that when not catching, Ewing played at third, short, or in the outfield. His versatility extended to the basepaths as well. From 1886 (the first season stolen base records were kept) until the end of his career, Ewing swiped 354 bases—the most ever recorded by a catcher. This inspired performance helped form the nucleus of a Giants team that included six future Hall-of-Famers in Ewing, John Ward, Mickey Welch, Tim Keefe, Roger Connor, and Jim O'Rourke.

Despite that impressive array of talent, New York often finished below expectations. When the Giants could do no better than fourth place in 1887, Ewing was installed as the team's captain—a position similar to the modern-day manager. Under his tutelage, the team catapulted to the top of the standings, winning back-to-back pennants in 1888 and 1889. In contrast to some of the more hardline managers of his time, Ewing's leadership style was marked by a jocular affability. As one writer later remarked, "If [Ewing] wanted to reprove a player . . . he voiced his remarks good-naturedly and never left a sting behind."

If Ewing's easygoing style brought him the respect of his fellow players, then his foray into the ill-fated Players League in 1890 damaged much of that reputation. Designed to rid the game of inequities such as the reserve clause, which bound a player to his team for the duration of his career, the Players League attracted hundreds of players for its inaugural 1890 season, including Ewing, who managed and played for the PL's New York entry. But Ewing had his doubts about the profitability of the new league, and when the venture began to hemorrhage money, he secretly met with National League officials to talk consolidation. Many players felt that Ewing's actions compromised the bargaining power of the fledgling circuit, and when the PL collapsed a few months after season's end,

Ewing was branded in some quarters as the "cunning traitor" of the thwarted revolution.

After the PL's demise, Ewing returned to the National League, where he played for New York for two more seasons before being traded to Cleveland. Though Ewing continued to contribute with his bat (in 1893, he batted in a career-best 122 runs), injuries limited his playing time and effectively ended his days as a catcher. In 1895 he returned to Cincinnati, where he managed and played out the remainder of his career for the hometown Reds. In five seasons at the Cincinnati helm, Ewing piloted the Reds to a winning record every year, though his teams never finished higher than third place. In 1900 he accepted a job managing for the New York Giants, but when the team won just 21 of its first 62 games, Ewing resigned.

He moved back to Cincinnati, where he lived with his wife, Anna Lawson McCaig, whom he married in 1889, and their two children. Though he lived comfortably, thanks to some wise investments in the real estate market, Ewing's health soon began to fail. After a prolonged illness, he died on 20 October 1906, a victim of Bright's disease. He is buried in Cincinnati's Mt. Washington Cemetery.

At first glance, Ewing's lifetime statistics indicate a good, but not necessarily extraordinary, career. In 1,315 games, Ewing posted a .307 batting average, collected 1,655 hits, and scored 1,129 runs—numbers not good enough to rank in the top 100 all-time players. But Ewing's true value cannot be accurately judged without considering that for most of his career, he played catcher, the most physically demanding position on the field, and played it in an era before modern protective equipment was available. Not only did he field this crucial position with remarkable skill, he also made an asset out of himself as a batter, baserunner, and team leader. To many of those who saw him play, Ewing was the nonpareil all-around ballplayer of his day, or as Francis Richter, the esteemed editor of the *Reach Guide*, wrote in 1919, "the greatest player of all time from the standpoint of supreme excellence in all departments . . . a player without a weakness of any kind, physical, mental, or temperamental."

★

There is no full-length biography of Ewing. A good amount of information on him is available in clipping files maintained by the National Baseball Hall of Fame Library and by the *Sporting News*. For a close look at Ewing's role in the demise of the Players League, see Bryan Di Salvatore, *A Clever Base-Ballist: The Life and Times of John Montgomery Ward* (1999). The definitive source for all baseball statistics is John Thorn, Pete Palmer, and Michael Gershman, eds., *Total Baseball*, 7th ed. (2001).

DAVID JONES

F

FAVRE, Brett Lorenzo (*b*. 10 October 1969 in Gulfport, Mississippi), quarterback for the Green Bay Packers best known for winning Super Bowl XXXI and for earning three National Football League (NFL) Most Valuable Player (MVP) honors.

Favre has always been bigger than life. He was nine pounds, fifteen ounces and twenty-one inches long at birth. Favre grew up in Kiln, Mississippi. His father, Irvin Favre, was a driver's education and physical education teacher as well as a baseball and football coach. His mother, Bonita French, was a special education teacher. "If you slapped him when he was little, he'd say it didn't hurt. He would never give in," said his mother about Favre.

Favre and his three siblings grew up immersed in sports. He attended Hancock North Central High School from 1983 to 1987, and his father coached him in baseball and football. In football he played quarterback, strong safety, place kicker, and punter. In baseball he was a pitcher and led the team in batting every year. Because Irvin Favre preferred a running game, Brett Favre ended his high school football career with just 800 passing yards. On the personal front Favre met Deanna Tynes when he was thirteen, and they dated throughout high school and college.

When Favre arrived at the University of Southern Mississippi (USM) in 1987, he was a seventh-string quarterback, but he worked his way up to starting quarterback in his freshman year. In his sophomore year (1988) Favre led his team to a 10–2 record, and they won the Independence Bowl, 38–18, over the University of Texas–El Paso (UTEP). On 6 February 1989 Tynes gave birth to their daughter. In Favre's junior year (1989) the football team went 5–6. In July 1990 a car accident threatened to end Favre's football career. His injuries included a fractured vertebra, a lacerated liver, and a bruised abdomen, and doctors removed thirty inches of his intestine. Favre made a miraculous recovery and led his team to an 8–2 record in his senior year (1990), but they lost to North Carolina State, 31–27, in the All American Bowl. Nevertheless Favre was the game's Most Valuable Player (MVP). He finished his career at USM with school records for yards (8,193), pass attempts (1,234), completions (656), completion percentage (53 percent), and touchdowns (55). Favre's major was special education, but he did not graduate.

The Atlanta Falcons selected Favre in the second round of the 1991 draft. In the 1991 season his total offense was five passes, and two were interceptions. Before the 1992 season he was traded to the Green Bay Packers. Favre replaced an injured Don Majikowski in the third game of the 1992 season, and he never relinquished the starting quarterback position. The Packers finished 9–7, and Favre went to the Pro Bowl. In 1993 Green Bay went 9–7 and became the first Packers team to make the playoffs in a nonstrike year since 1972. They beat Detroit 28–24 but lost to Dallas 27–17. Favre also played in the 1993 Pro Bowl. Although Favre had made great strides in his first two seasons at

Brett Favre. AP/WIDE WORLD PHOTOS

Green Bay, he was an inconsistent player. He threw thirty-seven touchdown passes, but he also threw thirty-nine interceptions.

In 1994 the Packers finished 9–7 and again made the playoffs. In a repeat of the 1993 season finale, they beat Detroit 16–12 but lost to Dallas. The year 1995 was a milestone for the team. Favre finished the season with a best in the National Football League (NFL) with 4,413 passing yards, he became the first player in team history to post 3,000 yards in 4 individual seasons, and he led the National Football Conference (NFC) with a 99.5 passing rating. He started in the Pro Bowl and won his first NFL MVP award. The Packers went 11–5 and won the NFC Central Division title. In the playoffs they beat Atlanta 37–20 and San Francisco 27–17, but again they lost to Dallas 38–27.

While everything was going well professionally for Favre, he had become addicted to Vicodin. He had taken the prescription drug on and off for years to manage pain, but it became an addiction in 1995. At one point he took up to fifteen pills a night. In 1995 he blacked out on the flight home after the Pro Bowl. He quit cold turkey soon after, but the saga did not end there. In February 1996 Favre had a seizure prior to surgery on his ankle, which his doctors reported to the NFL. At a meeting with NFL doctors, Favre admitted his addiction, and the NFL made him check into the Menninger Clinic in Topeka, Kansas. He was released from the clinic in June 1996. Changed by his stint in rehabilitation, Favre married his longtime girlfriend Tynes on 14 July 1996. They subsequently had another daughter.

The 1996 Packers went 13–3 in the regular season, won their division, and beat San Francisco 35–14 and Carolina 30–13 in the playoffs. Super Bowl XXXI was in New Orleans, where the Packers faced the New England Patriots. On the Packers' second play Favre audibled a risky play. He connected with the receiver Andre Rison on a twenty-yard pass that Rison ran in for the touchdown. The Packers went on to win the Super Bowl 35–21. Favre started in the Pro Bowl and won his second regular season MVP award.

In 1997 the Packers again went 13–3 in the regular season, and they beat Tampa Bay 21–7 and San Francisco 23–10 to advance to the Super Bowl. The game was a thriller, but Denver won 31–24. Favre went to another Pro Bowl, and he won his third consecutive MVP, sharing the award with Detroit's Barry Sanders. In 1998 the Packers were 11–5 in the regular season but lost to San Francisco 30–27 in the playoffs. Favre led the NFL in passing yards, and he made a tongue-in-cheek acting debut in the movie *There's Something About Mary* (1998).

During the 1999 and 2000 seasons the Packers hit a rough spot, finishing 8–8 and 9–7 respectively with no playoff berths. However, Favre continued to rack up personal achievements, including reaching 30,000 passing yards in 1999, having his third career 4,000-yard passing season in 1999, and setting an NFL record of starting in 141 consecutive regular season games in 2000.

In 1996 Favre founded the Brett Favre Forward Foundation, which donates money to charities, including Special Olympics, Make-A-Wish, and Boys and Girls Clubs. He established an annual golf tournament and softball game to generate money for his foundation. *The Sporting News* named him one of the "100 Good Guys" in sports in July 2000 in recognition of his philanthropy. Signed by the Packers to a ten-year contract in 2001, he splits his time between homes in Mississippi and Green Bay.

Favre said about his quarterbacking, "No one can change the part of me that attempts plays some quarterbacks shouldn't even attempt." Taking risks in football, he proved himself a quarterback for the ages. Loved by fans, feared by opponents, and a friend to people in need, he also exhibited his human side, beating an addiction and becoming a better person in the process. Perhaps that is his greatest victory.

★

Brett Favre with Chris Havel, *Favre: For the Record* (1997), is a full-length autobiography. Other comprehensive biographies are Steve Cameron, *Brett Favre: Huck Finn Grows Up* (1996), and Irv Favre, *Brett Favre* (1997). Valuable articles about Favre include Dan Dieffenbach, "I Think I'll Be in the Hall of Fame One Day," *Sport* (Nov. 1995); Ken Fuson, "Guts and Glory," *Esquire* (Oct. 1996); William Plummer, "Beating the Blitz," *People Weekly* (24 Oct. 1996); Steve Wulf, "Leaders of the Pack," *Time* (27 Jan. 1997); Dave Kindred, "He's Green Bay's Latest Starr," *Sporting*

News (3 Feb. 1997); Barry M. Bloom, "Born a Rebel," *Sport* (Aug. 1997); Bob Der, "Guts and Glory," *Sports Illustrated for Kids* (Sept. 1997); Richard Justice, "It's Superman," *Washington Post* (20 Jan. 1998); and Paul Attner, "A Wiser Brett Favre . . . Really," *Sporting News* (24 July 2000).

KRISTAN GINTHER

FEARS, Thomas Jesse ("Tom") (*b.* 3 December 1923 in Guadalajara, Mexico; *d.* 4 January 2000 in Palm Desert, California), Hall of Fame football player who for fifty years held the record for most receptions in a game.

If anyone deserves to be called a true Southern California sports hero, it is Fears. He grew up in Los Angeles, attended Southern California schools, and played and coached for the Los Angeles Rams. Fears attended Manual Arts High School in Los Angeles and played both offense and defense and won All-Southern California honors as tight end. During those years, he worked as an usher at the Los Angeles Coliseum, where he would later play for the Rams.

After graduating in 1941, he attended Santa Clara College and earned accolades and attention from the NFL as a receiver for his size and strength. After two years of college, Fears joined the Air Force in 1944 to serve in World War II. He was captain of the Second Air Force Super-

bombers team (1944–1945). When he returned, the Cleveland Rams drafted him as a future selection in the 1945 draft, not realizing he still had two years before eligibility. Fears transferred to UCLA, where he enjoyed two years as an All-American, lettering both years and graduating in 1948. He was part of the famous "mud bowl" of 1947, so called because of the weather and field conditions during the game, when UCLA won the bid to go to the Rose Bowl. Fears had a number of injuries that year, however, and UCLA was often without his services. Nevertheless, he was elected to the College Football Hall of Fame in 1976.

During the Rams' training camp in 1948, Fears practiced as a defensive back. In his first game he intercepted two passes and returned one for a touchdown. The Rams then switched him to offense, and he became the first rookie to lead the NFL in receiving honors, going on to lead the league in receptions for the next three seasons.

Along with his teammates Elroy "Crazylegs" Hirsch and Bob Boyd, the six-foot, two-inch, 215-pound Fears became part of the famous "three-end attack." From 1948 to 1950 he caught an amazing 212 passes for 2,827 yards and 20 touchdowns. He set the league record for receptions in a season with 77 in 1949 and then broke his own record the next year with 80 receptions. On his birthday in 1950, in a game against the Green Bay Packers, he set the record for the most receptions in a game with 18. He held this record for fifty years until 3 December 2000 when Terrell

Tom Fears *(right)* with teammate Norm Van Brocklin, 1951. ASSOCIATED PRESS AP

Owens of the 49ers made 20 receptions against the Bears. Also in 1950 he caught three touchdown passes to help the Rams win the Western Division title over the Chicago Bears. The Rams were down 7–3 in the third quarter but they scored 41 points in the fourth quarter to win the game, starting with a 68-yard touchdown pass to Fears.

Fears set the scoring record for a single game in a 70–27 win over the Colts in 1950 and was a major player for the Rams in 1951 when they set records in single-season scoring, passing yards per game, and average points per game (39). With quarterback Bob Waterfield and the three wideouts, the Rams of 1950 had one of the highest scoring offenses in history until they broke many of their own records in 2000 as the St. Louis Rams. Yet Fears always insisted that his skills did not match up to many other receivers. He credited his statistics to the Rams' highly innovative passing attack. His teammate, Elroy Hirsch, took exception to Fears's modesty when he said, "He was as fine a third-down receiver as anyone in the league."

The Rams went to the title game in 1950 but lost to Cleveland 30–28. In the title game the following year, however, Fears caught a 13-yard pass and ran 60 yards to score the winning touchdown in the fourth quarter and give the Rams their first NFL title since moving to the West Coast. Fears was named an All-NFL player twice (1949 and 1950).

The next six years of Fears's career included a number of injuries, and his performance suffered as a consequence. He retired after the 1956 season to spend more time with his wife, Luella, and their six children, ending his career with 5,397 yards and 38 touchdowns. He averaged 13.5 yards per catch in his career and was the first receiver to retire with 400 receptions. Fears also had two interceptions, one defensive touchdown, and kicked twelve extra points and one field goal. He was elected to the Hall of Fame in 1970.

In 1960 Fears became an assistant coach with the Los Angeles Rams, serving under head coach Bob Waterfield, his former quarterback. The two did not enjoy the same success at coaching as they had on the field, and they won just eight games in two seasons. At the end of the 1961 season, Fears joined the Green Bay Packers as an assistant coach and worked under the legendary Vince Lombardi. A new franchise begun in New Orleans in 1967 selected Fears as their first head coach. But the Saints replaced him in his third season after winning only one game of the first six that season.

Fears moved back to California, and in 1974 and 1975 he coached the Southern California Sun, a New World Football League team, for two years. After a long battle with Alzheimer's disease beginning in the 1990s, Fears died at age seventy-seven on 4 January 2000 in Palm Desert, California—just three weeks before the Rams, now in St. Louis, won the league title for the first time since Fears had helped them do so fifty years earlier.

Although Fears was not fast, his ability to run precise patterns and to use his size and strength well made him one of the most prolific receivers of all time.

★

Howard Roberts, *The Story of Pro Football* (1953), relates Fears's contributions to the Rams' winning seasons. For summaries and anecdotes of some of Fears's college achievements, see Allison Danzig, *The History of American Football: Its Great Teams, Players, and Coaches* (1956). Joe Horrigan and Bob Carroll, *Football Greats* (1998), details Fears's major accomplishments on the field and relates some anecdotes.

MARKUS H. McDOWELL

FELLER, Robert William Andrew ("Bob") (*b.* 3 November 1918 near Van Meter, Iowa), the dominant pitcher from 1936 to 1956, considered by many baseball writers to be the best pitcher of all, because of his three no-hit games and twelve one-hit games for the Cleveland Indians, while leading the American League in wins six times and strikeouts seven times.

Feller was one of two children of Lena Forrett, a school teacher, nurse, newspaper correspondent, and school board

Bob Feller, 1959. ASSOCIATED PRESS AP

member, and William Feller, a farmer. He was born and raised on his father's farm three miles from Van Meter, Iowa. By the time he was thirteen years old, Feller was the cleanup hitter on Van Meter's American Legion baseball team, playing against much older players. When he was fourteen, his father, who had been a semi-professional pitcher in his younger days, created a baseball diamond on the farm for him.

Major League Baseball had a rule against signing players who were still in high school, so the Cleveland Indians signed Feller to a club contract in 1935 secretly, when he was sixteen. Legend has it that Feller received a dollar and a baseball as his signing bonus. When Feller showed up in a Cleveland Indians uniform for spring training, the minor league Des Moines, Iowa, ball club of the Western League, with whom he had played for a short time, protested, claiming Feller should have to play for them. Although Cleveland's signing of Feller was plainly against the rules, Feller insisted on honoring his contract with them. Commissioner Kenesaw Mountain Landis let Cleveland keep him and fined Cleveland $7,500, a bargain for the Indians considering the bidding war for Feller's services was expected to exceed $100,000.

The Indians learned quickly, as did the American League, that Feller was the phenomenon that he seemed to be. He was six feet tall and 185 pounds, and had a motion that had him looking back toward third base before delivering his pitch. Feller seemed to regularly throw fastballs at over 100 miles per hour. It was frightening, and soon earned him the name "Rapid Robert." "I just reared back and let them go," he said, and they flew all over the place. "Where the ball went was up to heaven. Sometimes I threw the ball clean up into the stands," he later remarked. While leading the league in bases on balls in four different seasons, he had batters ready to duck and run.

He struck out fifteen St. Louis Browns batters in his first start on 23 August 1936. Later that season, he struck out seventeen Philadelphia Athletics batters in a game. He was only seventeen, and at the end of the season, he returned to Van Meter, Iowa, and finished high school, graduating in 1937.

In 1938 the Indians discovered that their young pitcher had star power. He drew fans just to see him pitch; in the later years of his career, the team estimated that when he pitched he drew an additional 10,000 fans beyond what would be normally expected. His 17 wins and 11 losses record for 1938 was good, but his striking out eighteen Detroit Tigers batters on 2 October 1938 was sensational, and a new record for a nine-inning ball game. Earlier, on 20 April of that year, he pitched the first of what would be twelve career one-hitters.

For 1939 he led the league with 24 wins, with only 9 losses. He also led the league with 14 wild pitches; batting

against him was not for the faint of heart. On opening day, 16 April 1940, he pitched a no-hitter against the Chicago White Sox, racking up 27 wins against 11 losses for the season. By this time, he was a complete pitcher, because he had a curveball that was as good as his fastball. In 1941, he had another record, with 25 wins and 11 losses, and he was one of the most celebrated players in baseball. He seemed destined to break numerous career records.

On 7 December 1941, the Empire of Japan bombed Pearl Harbor and America went to war, and on December 9 Feller enlisted in the United States Navy. Formally inducted on 6 January 1942, he was first sent to Norfolk, Virginia, for training, and then to the USS *Alabama* as an antiaircraft gunner. He would later joke, "Baseball in the navy always was much more fun than it had been in the major leagues," but he saw serious duty and battle, earning eight battle stars, as well as five campaign ribbons.

Two major league ballplayers had been killed in action, others were wounded, and for many their athletic careers were ruined. When Feller was discharged from the navy, near the end of the 1945 season, some observers thought he might have lost his fastball. But in 1946, he came back strong. On 30 April 1946, he pitched his second career no-hitter, this one against the New York Yankees, the team he admittedly most desired to defeat, beating them 1–0. That year, using a photographic test run by *Life* magazine, Feller's fastball was timed at nearly 100 miles per hour. Further, he struck out 348 batters for the season, then believed to be a new record (as it later turned out, however, Rube Waddell struck out 349 in 1904).

Feller signed a contract with the Indians for over $80,000 for the 1947. He responded with a 20–11 win-loss record, but after hurting his arm he slumped to merely above-average performances from 1948 to 1950. At the start of the 1950 season, at Feller's suggestion, he took a $20,000 pay cut, for a salary of $45,000. But the desire to win still burned strong in Feller, and in 1951 he had a spectacular season with 22 wins and 8 losses, for a .733 winning percentage, and he pitched his third no-hitter on 1 July, versus the Detroit Tigers, tying what was then the career record. The next season was a poor one, 9 wins and 13 losses, and the number of his starts diminished thereafter, although his 13 wins against 3 losses in 1954 contributed significantly to the Indians' winning that year's American League pennant.

In 1957, the year following his retirement, Feller's uniform number 19 was retired by the Indians, and in 1962 he became the first pitcher since Walter Johnson to be elected to the National Baseball Hall of Fame in his first year of eligibility. When professional baseball held its Centennial Celebration in 1969, he was named greatest living right-handed pitcher. Many writers before and since have insisted that he was the greatest pitcher of all, period.

He settled in Gates Mills, Ohio, with his second wife,

Anne Morris Giuiland, whom he married on 1 October 1974, and learned to fly airplanes. Feller became the Cleveland Indians' goodwill ambassador, traveling the United States to visit as many as fifty minor league games a year through the 1980s. A statue of him pitching was erected at Jacobs Field, the Indians' ballpark. In 1995, the Bob Feller Museum, designed by his son Steve, was opened in Van Meter, Iowa, becoming an instant tourist attraction. Feller never lost the magical connection he had with people, and was always loved by fans.

★

Feller has always been notable for his witty quips and pointed epithets, and his autobiography *Now Pitching, Bob Feller* (1990), written with Bill Gilbert, has plenty of these along with his insights into baseball of his era and how it has since changed. *Bob Feller's Little Black Book of Baseball Wisdom* (2001) by Feller and Burton Rocks is a delightful assortment of anecdotes, tales, and observations. Of Feller's instructional books, *Pitching to Win* (1952) probably offers the most insight into his approach to playing baseball. J. Ronald Oakley's *Baseball's Last Golden Age, 1946–1960* (1994) places Feller's career in the context of its era. "Bob Feller" in Donald Honig, *Baseball When the Grass Was Real* (1975) is an interview in which Feller discusses what he considers to be the highlights of his baseball career. Jerome Holtzmen, "An American Hero," *Baseball Digest* (Dec. 2000), is an account of Feller's service in the navy during World War II. In Van Meter, Iowa, the Bob Feller Museum displays uniforms, balls, bats, photographs, and other memorabilia related to Feller's career, and it is a major tourist attraction.

KIRK H. BEETZ

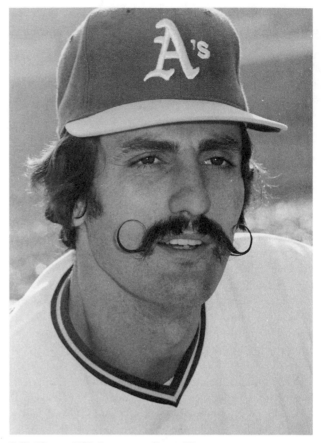

Rollie Fingers, 1973. ASSOCIATED PRESS AP

FINGERS, Roland Glen ("Rollie")   (*b.* 25 August 1946 in Steubenville, Ohio), Cy Young Award–winning relief pitcher who dominated batters in both major leagues in the 1970s and 1980s.

Fingers was raised in Upland, California, one of three children. His mother, Edna Pearl Stafford, was a third-grade teacher; his father, George Michael Fingers, a former minor league pitcher in the St. Louis Cardinals organization, worked for the California state government. Fingers excelled in golf and baseball as a young man and attended Upland High School from 1957 to 1961 and Chaffee Junior College in Rancho Cucamonga, California, from 1961 to 1963.

Fingers was signed as a free agent by the Kansas City Athletics on 24 December 1964 and began pitching in their minor league system in 1965. He was called up to the major league team in 1968 but only pitched in one game. The following spring, in 1969, he made it back to the major league club and pitched his first full year, entering sixty

games and posting a 6–7 record, with a 3.71 earned-run average. For the next three years, Fingers bounced between duties as a starting pitcher and reliever. Finally, in 1971 Athletics manager Dick Williams made Fingers strictly a reliever. That year the Athletics won the first of their five consecutive American League West titles.

The year 1972 was a defining one for Fingers. When outfielder Reggie Jackson showed up for spring training wearing a beard, several of his teammates, including Fingers, also grew facial hair. Thus was born Fingers's handlebar mustache, his trademark for the rest of his career. More important, in his first full year in the bullpen, Fingers had his best year to date, posting an 11–9 record with 21 saves and a 2.51 earned-run average.

Fingers soon developed into one of the most dominant closers in the game. Over the three-year period from 1972 to 1974, he averaged 20⅓ saves and a 2.36 earned-run average in an average sixty-seven appearances per year. The Athletics also dominated the major leagues, winning the World Series in 1972, 1973, and 1974.

In 1975 the Athletics (who had since moved to Oakland) won the Western Division title in the American League, but the loss of key players quickly eroded the once-dominant franchise. Fingers played out the option year of his contract in 1976 and was granted free agency that November. He signed with the San Diego Padres on 14 December 1976. The Padres had been gathering top free agents to bolster their chances in the National League, and Fingers was a key addition.

Moving into the National League did not seem to challenge Fingers's dominance on the mound, however. In his first year with the Padres, he led the league with seventy-eight appearances, finishing with an 8–9 record and a 3.00 earned-run average. He also led the league with thirty-five saves and was named the National League Fireman of the Year as best reliever by the *Sporting News*. He was equally dominant in 1978, again leading the league in saves and capturing the Fireman of the Year title. Teammate Gaylord Perry, who won the National League Cy Young Award as the best pitcher in the league, said, "Never in my sixteen seasons have I had the good fortune of having a pitcher like Fingers in my bullpen."

Fingers pitched for the Padres from 1977 to 1980, and although he remained one of the top relief pitchers in baseball, the Padres never finished higher than fourth place and eleven games out of first place. Finger was traded to the St. Louis Cardinals on 8 December 1980; four days later he was traded to the Milwaukee Brewers.

Back in the American League, Fingers was more dominant than he had ever been before. A labor strike broke up the 1981 baseball season, but it had no affect on Fingers. He finished the strike-shortened season with a 6–3 record, 28 saves, and a 1.04 earned-run average, while figuring in 55 percent of his team's victories. Although the Brewers made it into the postseason that year, they were knocked out in the first round. Fingers, however, made history when he became the first relief pitcher to win the Cy Young Award and the Most Valuable Player Award in the same year. Fingers returned to pitch in 1982, but endured pain in his arm for most of the season and was forced to sit out the World Series when the Brewers played the Cardinals. He attempted to return in 1983, but the pain returned, too; he ultimately underwent surgery and missed the entire season. Fingers contributed sparingly to the team over the next two years. When the Brewers released him on 14 November 1985, he retired. During his seventeen-year major league career, he had saved 341 games, more than anyone in history up until then.

Fingers maintained his San Diego residence for many years after his baseball career ended, but moved in 1998 with his wife, Lori, to Las Vegas, Nevada, to pursue business interests. He has three children from previous marriages.

Fingers was inducted into the Baseball Hall of Fame in 1992, only the second relief pitcher ever to be afforded the honor. During his career, he pitched in sixteen World Series games, finishing with a 2–2 record and a 1.35 earned-run average. He led the league in saves three times, twice led the league in games finished in relief, and was named Fireman of the Year by *The Sporting News* four times. Although his single-season and career-save totals have been topped since his retirement, it should be noted that by the late 1990s relief pitchers typically earned saves by pitching no more than one inning in an outing—as middle relievers, set-up pitchers, and closers—so Fingers, who averaged nearly two innings per outing, essentially did the work of two or three pitchers of recent years.

★

For information regarding Fingers's final statistics, awards, and career movements, post-1985 copies of *The Baseball Encyclopedia* are very useful. Stephen Hanks, *The Twentieth-Century Baseball Chronicle* (1991), presents a good chronological history of Fingers's influence in conjunction with the rest of major league baseball. The Ken Burns series, *Baseball* (1994), in video and book format, provides particularly interesting information on Fingers's years in Oakland and the personalities that made up the Athletics. Fingers's arm problems in Milwaukee are covered in an article by Steve Wulf, "Taking a Ride on the Handlebars," *Sports Illustrated* (June 1984).

TODD TOBIAS

FITZSIMMONS, James Edward ("Sunny Jim") (*b.* 23 July 1874 in Brooklyn, New York; *d.* 11 March 1966 in Miami, Florida), Thoroughbred racehorse trainer who trained some of the top horses from the 1930s through the 1950s.

Fitzsimmons was born in Sheepshead Bay, in south Brooklyn, on land that later became the site of a horse racing track. His father was George Fitzsimmons, a farmer, and his mother was Catherine (Murphy) Fitzsimmons. His education consisted of occasional attendance at a one-room school.

Young Fitzsimmons got his first look at a horse racing track when the old Sheepshead Bay oval was constructed around his family's homestead, and its inaugural race took place on 19 June 1880. It did not take him long to realize he could make more money stopping at the stables in the morning than he could by continuing through them on his way to school. He got his first steady racetrack job at age eleven as an errand boy for the Dwyer Brothers stable. It is purely coincidental that he later trained nine winners of the Dwyer Stakes.

In 1889, at the age of sixteen, Fitzsimmons began a short and unsuccessful career as a jockey. He worked as a jockey until 1901, when he switched to training. His own description of his skill as a jockey—"pretty mediocre"—explains why. He told this story to illustrate his point. "I was riding at Guttenberg [New Jersey] when they first held night rac-

Jim Fitzsimmons, 1956. AP/WIDE WORLD PHOTOS

ing under the lights. I hadn't had a winner in some time. When I got a chance to win one I was halfway down the stretch when I saw something coming at me and I went to a drive. I needed that winner. When we pulled up, I found out we had won by ten lengths. The other horse was my shadow chasing me. I know enough to outride my shadow." His last mount as a journeyman jockey was Agnes D., who ran fifth of five in the Tidal Stakes at Sheepshead Bay in 1901. A few races later the same horse became his first winner as a trainer.

Always a family man, Fitzsimmons married Jenny Harvey in June 1891; they eventually had five sons and one daughter. He became known as Mr. Fitz by everyone in racing and nicknamed Sunny Jim for his wonderful disposition and cheerful outlook on life and work. "My grandfather always had a good word for anybody who approached him, whether from the top or bottom of the racing fraternity," his grandson John J. Fitzsimmons, also a trainer, wrote. "He loved the fans—the $2 bettors—and always spoke out in their behalf."

His grandson also said that it was his grandfather's love of the sport that made him such a great trainer and person.

"How my grandfather loved racing! The people, the horses, the loser, the winner, everything about it. I'm surprised he didn't live to be 200, the way he always looked forward to next year and the new crop of two-year-olds. Any time anything got him down, he would always look forward to the new crop coming up."

Fitzsimmons had an instinctive feel for horses. In 1923 he got the break that launched his career with high-class horses. At that time, he took on the horses of the Belair Stud, owned by William Woodward. These included Triple Crown winners Gallant Fox and his son Omaha. Fitzsimmons trained horses for this stable until it closed in 1955. Later that decade, he took over the horses of the Wheatley Stable, owned by Ogden Mills and Mrs. Henry Carnegie Phipps. This association lasted until his retirement in 1963.

Fitzsimmons had many great qualities as a trainer, including the ability to bring a horse to a big race in peak condition. One of his many career high points came in the summer of 1955. After his horse Nashua lost to Swaps in the Kentucky Derby, a match race was arranged between the two horses at Chicago's Washington Park. Nashua defeated Swaps by over six lengths and became the leading money-winner by taking both the Preakness (in Pimlico, Maryland) and Belmont Stakes (in Belmont Park, New York).

For Belair, Fitzsimmons trained Gallant Fox in 1930 and Omaha in 1935; Horses of the Year Granville in 1936 and Nashua in 1955; and champions Vagrancy, champion three-year-old and Handicap Mare of 1942, Faireno, and Happy Gal. For Mrs. Phipps he trained 1957 Horse of the Year Bold Ruler (sire of Secretariat) and champions High Voltage, champion two-year-old Filly of 1952; Misty Morn, champion three-year-old and Handicap Mare in 1955; and Castle Forbes, Diabolo, and Dice. Other fine Thoroughbreds he developed were Dark Secret, Seabiscuit, Johnstown, Fenelon, and Busanda. He trained winners of six Belmonts, four Preaknesses, three Kentucky Derbys, five Suburbans, eight Wood Memorials, ten Saratoga Cups, seven Jockey Club Gold Cups, eight Alabamas, eight Lawrence Realizations, and nine Dweyer Stakes.

In assessing the relative gifts of the horses he trained, Fitzsimmons said, "It is difficult to select a best horse from so many fine ones, but I would lean toward Gallant Fox. He never went to the track without doing his best."

After leading all other trainers in winnings in 1936, 1939, and 1955, Fitzsimmons was inducted into the National Museum of Racing Hall of Fame in 1958 and later became the first president of the HBPAF (now the National Horsemen's Benevolent and Protective Association). Over his more than seventy years in racing Fitzsimmons trained 2,428 winners and five times (in 1930, 1932, 1936, 1939, and 1955) was the leading money-winning trainer. Active until he was almost ninety, he retired in 1963 and lived in the Miami area, continuing to visit the track almost daily up to the week of his death at age ninety-one.

Fitzsimmons died on 11 March 1966 in Cedars of Lebanon Hospital, Miami, a long way from the little cottage in Brooklyn where he was born. "His heart just gave out," said his son John, for many years his father's chief assistant, along with his brother Jimmy. Fitzsimmons is buried in the Holy Cross Cemetery, Brooklyn, New York.

Within the sport of racing, Fitzsimmons's fame was global. Horsemen and -women from Europe, South America, and elsewhere made it a point to meet him when they visited a track where he was training. In his sixth-grade handwriting it was difficult for him to sign autographs, but he tried to oblige the fans. Neophytes enjoying their first day at the races asked the more knowledgeable fans, "Which one is Sunny Jim?"

★

For further information see Jimmy Breslin, *Sunny Jim* (1962), the *Lincoln Library of Sports Champions* 4 (1974), and the National Turf Writers Association, *Members in the National Museum of Racing Hall of Fame* (Saratoga Springs, N.Y.). *Bloodhorse* magazine is a good source of articles about Fitzsimmons, especially "James Edward Fitzsimmons" (Mar. 1966). See also John J. Fitzsimmons, "Grandfather," in *Horseman's Journal* (Feb. 1976). An obituary is in the *New York Times* (12 Mar. 1966).

JOAN GOODBODY

FLEMING, Peggy Gale (*b.* 27 July 1948 in San Jose, California), figure skater who was the only American to have won a gold medal in the 1968 Olympics in Grenoble, France, and who was a five-time U.S. Figure Skating Champion and three-time World Champion.

Fleming was one of four daughters born to Albert Eugene Fleming, a newspaper pressman, and Doris Elizabeth Deal, a homemaker who designed and sewed her daughter's outfits for competitions. Fleming was an active child who enjoyed tree climbing, baseball, and surfing. When Fleming was nine years old, her father took employment with the *Cleveland Plains Dealer,* and the family settled in Cleveland. Fleming acquired her first pair of skates and began practicing at the Arena Figure Skating Club.

In order to enable their daughter to pursue figure skating competitively, Fleming's parents moved once again to California, where Fleming became so good at skating that she represented the Saint Moritz Ice Skating Club, passed the preliminaries and the first United States Figure Skating Association's (USFSA) tests, and won the Central Pacific Junior Girls Championship. By this time, the family had moved to Los Angeles, where Fleming's father had been employed by the *Los Angeles Times* and where Peggy's tal-

Peggy Fleming, 1970. © BETTMANN/CORBIS

ent for figure skating was readily apparent. She represented the Arctic Blades Figure Skating Club and was victorious at all four Southwest Pacific regional competitions (juvenile, novice, junior, and senior), as well as three out of four Pacific Coast sectional events (juvenile, novice, and senior) in consecutive years from 1960 to 1963.

In 1961 Fleming's coach, Will Kipp, and the entire U.S. national figure skating team were killed in a plane crash in Brussels, Belgium. After the devastating loss of the team on its way to the Prague World Championships, Fleming helped to revitalize the sport of figure skating in the United States. She won a silver medal in the Novice Ladies competition during the U.S. Championships, her first, in 1962, and a bronze in the Junior Ladies event in 1963. In 1964, after earning sixth place at the Olympic Winter Games at Innsbruck, Austria, she became America's youngest national champion in the Ladies event and achieved seventh place in her first World Championships tournament. The next year, she once again won the U.S. National Championships in Lake Placid, New York, an honor that she would hold for the next three years, and for a total of five consecutive years. In addition, she earned second place in the North American Championships and third in the World Championships. Fleming's family moved to Colorado Springs, Colorado, in order for her to train with the constant availability of ice at the Broadmoor Skating Club and with Carlo Fassi, former European champion and coach.

In 1966 in Davos, Switzerland, Fleming was victorious in the World Championships for the first time. Her father, who had held several jobs to permit her to follow her dream of becoming a world-class figure skater, died that same year.

Fleming was again a winner in the North American competition and at the World Championships in Vienna in 1967. Although she surpassed all competitors at the World Championships in Geneva the following year, Fleming will always be remembered for her performance at the 1968 Winter Olympics in Grenoble. She was the only American competitor to come home with a gold medal. Her free-skating program has been described as superb, and she finished 88.2 points ahead of her closest competitor in the first Olympics to be televised live and in color.

Six months after the event, Fleming starred in the first of five television specials entitled "Here's Peggy Fleming." Another of her specials won two Emmy Awards, and in 1973 her fourth special, filmed entirely in the Soviet Union, became the first joint television production by the United States and the Soviet Union.

In 1970 Fleming married dermatologist Greg Jenkins; they have two sons. Invited to the White House by four different presidents, in 1980 Fleming was the first skater ever asked to perform there.

Over the years, Fleming has been an on-air analyst for ABC Sports, hosted a Mutual of Omaha special about poaching in East Africa, served on the boards of numerous foundations, made many feature performances for Ice Follies and Holiday on Ice, and received numerous commercial endorsements, including one for Os-Cal. In January of 1998, on the thirtieth anniversary of her gold medal victory at Grenoble, Fleming was diagnosed with breast cancer. Since then, she has served as the national spokeswoman for Speak Out, a breast cancer awareness campaign that stresses the importance of early detection.

Fleming has received a variety of accolades, including the ABC Athlete of the Year Award in 1967; the Babe Didrikson Zaharias Award in 1968; the Sports Illustrated Fortieth Anniversary "40 for the Ages" honor in 1994; the U.S. Olympic Committee's Olympic Spirit Award in 1997; and the Sports Illustrated Twentieth Century Award in 1999, naming her one of an elite group of seven "Athletes Who Changed the Game."

Fleming was inducted into the U.S. Figure Skating Association Hall of Fame in 1976. She has also been inducted into the following honorary organizations: the U.S. Olympic Hall of Fame; the Women's Sports Foundation Hall of Fame; the International Women's Hall of Fame; and the World Figure Skating Hall of Fame.

Fleming's regal poise on the ice will always be what characterizes her image. Her elegance and courage under adverse circumstances combined with a "steel-like strength" have allowed her to capture the minds and hearts of people everywhere.

★

Fleming wrote *The Long Program: Skating Towards Life's Victories* (1999) with Peter Kaminsky. Biographical sketches are in Robert J. Condon, *Great Women Athletes of the Twentieth Century* (1991), and Christina Lessa, *Women Who Win: Stories of Triumph in Sport and in Life* (1998). For more information about Fleming, see her official website at <http://www.peggyfleming.net/>.

ADRIANA C. TOMASINO

FLOOD, Curt(is) Charles (*b.* 18 January 1938 in Houston, Texas; *d.* 20 January 1997 in Inglewood, California), outstanding outfielder in the 1960s who challenged the legality of baseball's reserve clause, laying the groundwork for player free agency.

Flood was the last of the six children of Herman Flood and Laura Flood. When Flood was two years old, his family moved to Oakland, California, his mother and father both worked at menial jobs in a hospital. His father often took a second job to supplement their income. At nine years old Flood joined a police-sponsored midget league baseball team coached by George Powles, a prominent Oakland baseball figure who also coached the baseball stars Frank Robinson, Vada Pinson, and Joe Morgan among others. Flood and Robinson were teammates on one of Powles's American Legion teams, and Flood followed Robinson into

Curt Flood, 1962. © BETTMANN/CORBIS

the Cincinnati Reds organization in 1956. Another school-age influence for Flood was Jim Chambers, an art teacher at Hoover Junior High School. Chambers instilled in Flood a lifelong love of art. Flood attended the College of Arts and Crafts in Oakland, California, and worked as a portrait artist during the off-seasons.

In February 1956 Flood began his baseball career with the Cincinnati organization and immediately met unfamiliar segregation when he arrived in Tampa, Florida, for spring training. Sent to the Class B Carolina League to play for High Point–Thomasville, he faced the full brunt of racial discrimination in the recently desegregated southern minor leagues. The following year Flood played for Savannah in the South Atlantic League. After two successful seasons in the Reds' system that included brief playing stints in Cincinnati both years, Flood was traded to the St. Louis Cardinals. Shortly thereafter, in February 1959, Flood married Beverly Collins; their union produced four children. They later divorced, and Flood married again.

With the Cardinals, Flood blossomed into one of the best center fielders in baseball during the 1960s. During the 1964 season Flood helped lead the Cardinals to the first of the three pennants they won in the 1960s (1964, 1967, and 1968) and the first of two World Series titles. While he registered a career batting average of .293 with 1,861 hits, his legacy as a player was cast in center field. The best defensive center fielder of his day, he won seven straight National League Gold Gloves, an award given for fielding excellence at each position, between 1963 and 1969. Flood set records by playing 223 consecutive games without an error and 568 consecutive fielding chances without an error.

After the 1968 season, when the Cardinals won the National League pennant but lost to the Detroit Tigers in the World Series, Flood was offered a salary of $77,500 for 1969. Seeking a larger salary, Flood held out during the beginning of spring training. He came to terms with the Cardinals, but his offense slipped a bit during the season as he batted .285 in 1969. On 7 October 1969 Flood was traded with the catcher Tim McCarver and two others to the Philadelphia Phillies in a blockbuster trade for the slugger Dick Allen, Cookie Rojas, and Jerry Johnson.

Flood had been with the Cardinals since 1958, had business interests in St. Louis, and did not particularly want to play in Philadelphia, where the team was a perennial second-division finisher and the fans were, in his opinion, hostile to African-American baseball players. Flood contacted the Major League Baseball Players Association director Marvin Miller about his legal rights in challenging the trade. Since the 1870s baseball had incorporated into the standard players contract the reserve clause, which bound the player for one year plus an option for the following season. When a player signed a contract, he was bound for that year and the year after. Miller wanted to

challenge this clause, but he was seeking to do so with a bench player who could claim that, by being bound to a team and not getting an opportunity to play, he was losing a chance to earn a livelihood. Instead, Miller ended up with one of the game's best stars issuing a challenge to that part of the contract.

Before taking the case, player representatives and union officials grilled Flood on his desire to pursue the case. Miller and others raised a concern that Flood could be perceived as using this case merely as a ploy to demand a higher salary. Flood insisted that was not the case, nor was he motivated by militancy. He simply desired to have a say in where he worked the following year. He wrote the Major League Baseball commissioner Bowie Kuhn in December 1969 to declare his desire to "consider offers from other clubs." The case, *Flood* v. *Kuhn* (1972), was a landmark case in the history of sports law. Flood sat out the 1970 season to reinforce his stand that he desired to select his place of employment.

The case was first heard in May 1970 in New York City. In August, Flood lost his case but started a series of appeals eventually heard by the U.S. Supreme Court. In 1972 the Court ruled against Flood (5–3) on the basis that baseball was exempt from the antitrust laws because it was a sport, not a business. While Major League Baseball won the day in court, the Players Association, led by Miller, obtained some major concessions, including arbitration that eventually led to player free agency in 1975. In November 1970 Flood was traded to the Washington Senators for three minor league players. Flood reported to camp and played twenty-four games for the Senators that season. He batted just .200 and did not feel that he could return to the skills that had earned him accolades as the best center fielder in baseball. He decided to retire at the age of thirty-three.

Flood's postbaseball career was symbolized by periodic returns to the baseball world. He broadcast games for the Oakland A's during the 1979 season and later worked as a recreation specialist for the city of Oakland until 1987. He served as the commissioner of two fringe baseball organizations called the Senior League and the Fantasy Major Slo-Pitch Softball League. Attempting to reproduce the popularity of the senior golf tour, the Senior League sought to field teams of former major and minor league players over the age of thirty-give for a winter league based in Florida. Many writers noted the irony that Flood was the commissioner of a baseball league. The Fantasy Major Slo-Pitch Softball League was formed in 1987 as an indoor league in Florissant, Missouri. As commissioner Flood recruited former major league players. Later Flood served with the administration of the United Baseball League, a major league competitor planned during the prolonged player strike of the 1994 season. When the strike ended in 1995, the plans for the league dissolved. Flood died of throat cancer and is buried in Inglewood Park Cemetery in Inglewood, California.

★

The National Baseball Hall of Fame Library in Cooperstown, New York, houses a file on Flood. See Flood with Richard Carter, *The Way It Is* (1971); Lee Lowenfish and Tony Lupien, *The Imperfect Diamond: The Story of Baseball's Reserve System and the Men Who Fought to Change It* (1980); and Marvin Miller, *A Whole Different Ball Game: The Inside Story of Baseball's New Deal* (1992).

COREY SEEMAN

FORD, Edward Charles ("Whitey") (*b*. 21 October 1928 in New York City), southpaw pitcher for the New York Yankees who holds the all-time World Series record for most consecutive scoreless innings pitched and most wins.

Ford was a true son of New York, a hometown boy, brash, irreverent, funny, and a thoroughly professional athlete whose World Series records seem unapproachable. He was born to John Ford, a bartender, and Edith Ford, a homemaker, in Manhattan, but the family soon moved across the river to Astoria, Queens. Ford said his Grandma Johnson knew more about baseball than anyone else in the family. Ford grew up playing sandlot ball with the Thirty-fourth Avenue Boys Club of Astoria.

When it came time to attend high school Ford chose to travel by subway to Manhattan each day rather than attend his local high school, which did not have a baseball team. He enrolled at Aviation Trades High School, although he had little interest in technical subjects, and played first base and pitched for the school's baseball team. After graduation Ford continued to pitch for the Boys Club and did well enough to attract the attention of scouts from the New York Yankees, the Brooklyn Dodgers, and the Boston Red Sox. Yankee scout Paul Kritchell paid special attention. The Yankees offered Ford $7,000 in 1946; he signed and spent the next several years in the Yankee farm system. Small for a baseball player, he stood five feet, ten inches and weighed 180 pounds.

In 1950, in the middle of the summer, with the Yankees battling the Detroit Tigers for the pennant, Ford was called up from Kansas City, Class AA. Ford's debut was not auspicious; he lost his first major-league game. He seemed confident, though, and the rest of the season was a triumph. Ford won nine games for the Yankees while losing only one as he helped the Bronx Bombers win the pennant. He also captured the first World Series win of his career in Game 4 against the Philadelphia Phillies.

Ford's baseball career was interrupted by a two-year stint in the U.S. Army at Fort Monmouth, New Jersey.

During a furlough on 14 April 1951 he married a girl from Astoria, Joan Foran, whom he had met in an ice cream parlor when she was just thirteen and he was sixteen. The entire Yankee team was invited to attend, but the shy Mickey Mantle just sat in the bus. The couple had three children.

Ford played very little baseball in the army, and he was concerned that his return to the majors would suffer because of it. He need not have worried. Back with the Yankees in 1953, Ford had an outstanding 18–6 season. In 1954 his record was 16–8, followed by 18–7 in 1955, and 19–6 in 1956.

Ted Williams called Ford one of the five toughest pitchers he ever faced (Eddie Lopat, Bob Lemon, Bob Feller, and Hoyt Wilhelm were the others). In addition to his fastball, Ford threw an excellent curve and a slider. He was especially effective sidearming lefties and helped win many of his own games with a good pickoff move and outstanding fielding.

Off the field, Ford was popular with the other Yankees, who enjoyed his quick wit and easy manner. Dubbed the "Yankee Quipper," Ford was best known as "Whitey," a name given to him by Lefty Gomez in reference to Ford's very fair hair. Elston Howard referred to Ford as "Chairman of the Board," and Mickey Mantle called him "the original city slicker." (*Slick* is the title of Ford's autobiography.)

Ford, who liked a good time, but never before he was scheduled to pitch, occasionally got into trouble, most notably at the Copacabana night club in New York City in 1957. At the Copa with teammates to celebrate Billy Martin's birthday, a fight with other patrons broke out. Six Yankees, including Ford, Mantle, and Yogi Berra were fined for breaking training. Ford has always denied wrongdoing by the Yankees.

On the field Ford was the consummate professional, totally focused on the game. Nevertheless, in 1957 he faltered because of arm and shoulder problems that scaled back his record to 11–5. His earned run average (ERA) was still only 2.01.

The pitching coach Johnny Sain was important to Ford's revival. While working on Ford's slider, Sain taught him to throw smoothly, placing less stress on the arm. Ford agreed to refrain from playing golf on days when he was scheduled to pitch a night game. When Ralph Houk replaced Casey Stengel as manager, he made sure to pitch Ford at least every four days. Longer periods of rest did not work well for the southpaw.

Year after year Ford chalked up outstanding win-loss records, but for nine seasons the magical twenty victories eluded him. In fact, he had only two years when he won twenty or more games, 1961 and 1962. Ford's best year in the majors was 1961, when he compiled a remarkable 25–4 record. Not surprisingly, he was named the Cy Young

Whitey Ford at the start of his twelfth World Series, 1964. ASSOCIATED PRESS AP

winner as the best pitcher of the year. Ford also added to his total of continuous shutout innings in World Series play. In 1960 he pitched two shutouts against the Pittsburgh Pirates, and followed that in 1961 against the Cincinnati Reds with another fourteen shutout innings, thirty-two in all. He had broken Babe Ruth's record; his own was still standing into the twenty-first century.

As the best Yankee pitcher on perhaps the best team in the history of baseball, Ford was modest about his winning, understanding that he played on extraordinary teams with the likes of Mantle, Roger Maris, Phil Rizzuto, and Berra. But he heaped special praise on the reliever from Puerto Rico, Luis Arroyo, who could usually be counted on to relieve Ford in the seventh or eighth innings to save the win. Ford said, "Arroyo deserved half of my salary." When Ford was honored with a Whitey Ford Day at Yankee Stadium (Ford joked that he lobbied hard for the day), Arroyo emerged from a huge LifeSaver package mounted on a truck.

Ford holds several World Series records, including most innings pitched (146), most strikeouts (94), most wins (10), and most losses (8). His total win-loss record is 236–106, a .690 percentage, and his lifetime ERA is 2.75.

Ford pitched his last major-league game in 1967; an overdeveloped muscle in his left arm was a factor in ending his career. In 1974 he was installed in the National Baseball Hall of Fame along with Mickey Mantle, whom he called the brother he never had. Ford's number 16 was retired by the Yankees in 1974, making Ford the only Yankee pitcher in history to have his number retired by the organization.

In his autobiography Ford admitted to pitching mud balls or dirt balls (dirt plus saliva) late in his career, something he learned from Lew Burdette of the Milwaukee Braves. He also revealed that he had a ring specially made that he used to scratch the ball.

Ford remained active with the Yankees as a coach and consultant in Florida and New York. In 2000 he was honored with a second Whitey Ford Day at Yankee Stadium in recognition of fifty years in the Yankee organization. Twice treated for brain cancer, Ford, an avid golfer, still looked fit in his seventies.

★

With Phil Pepe, Ford wrote *Slick* (1987), a revealing autobiography. Ford and Mickey Mantle, his closest friend, wrote a joint autobiography, *Whitey and Mickey* (1977), with Joseph Durso. Ken Young, *Cy Young Award Winners* (1994), has a chapter on Ford that includes his pitching records. Harvey Frommer, *The New York Yankee Encyclopedia* (1997), includes complete records. Phil

Rizzuto and Al Silverman, *The "Miracle" New York Yankees* (1962), provides insights from the Yankee shortstop. The entry on Ford in *Current Biography* (1962) covers his career through the 1961 season.

KAREN E. MARKOE

FOSBURY, Richard Douglas ("Dick") (*b.* 6 March 1947 in Portland, Oregon), high jumper who revolutionized the sport by inventing a new method of clearing the bar, known today as the "Fosbury Flop" and used by high jumpers around the world.

Fosbury never set out to invent a new method of high jumping. Until high school he used a traditional move called the "scissors," in which the jumper makes a curved approach to the bar, leaps over it sideways with the legs scissoring around it, and lands on the back and shoulders. Fosbury was tall and lanky, so he kept knocking off the bar. Another move, the straddle, or "belly roll," also defeated him.

At a meet in May 1963 at Grants Pass, Oregon, Fosbury changed his technique. Each time the bar was raised he lifted his hips a little higher, which made his shoulders drop back. He said, "My mind wanted me to get over the bar, and intuitively, it figured out what was the most efficient way." Technically, Fosbury's style was a modification of the scissor jump, whereby the jumper makes a curved approach to the bar. However, instead of leaping sideways

and legs first over the bar, Fosbury arched backwards over the bar, leading with his head and shoulders and slipping his legs and feet over last. He named the move the "Fosbury Flop" after reading a local newspaper headline that read "Fosbury Flops over the Bar."

At Oregon State University, where his jumping skill earned him a full scholarship, Coach Berny Wagner discouraged him from using the flop and urged him to use the traditional form. After a year without success he returned to his own move and broke the school record with a six-foot-ten-inch jump. Fosbury developed the jump so well that he won back-to-back National Collegiate Athletic Association (NCAA) championships during his college career. At the 1968 Olympic trials he was almost eliminated but then cleared a personal record height of seven feet, two inches on his first attempt.

The 1968 Olympics in Mexico City took place during the summer between Fosbury's junior and senior years at college. By the end of the first day of competition he had cleared every height on his first attempt. The 80,000 spectators were so fascinated by Fosbury's unusual technique that when the marathon leader entered the stadium for the final lap of his 26.2-mile race, he was hardly noticed. Fosbury proved the worth of his technique by setting an Olympic and American record of seven feet, four and a quarter inches and by winning the gold medal.

Some track and field observers were initially dismayed by the new technique. U.S. Olympic coach Payton Jordan said, "Kids imitate champions. If they try to imitate Fos-

Dick Fosbury, 1967. © BETTMANN/CORBIS

bury, he will wipe out an entire generation of high jumpers because they will all have broken necks." Although jumpers may appear to land on their necks, they actually land on their shoulders. The development and use of Fosbury's move was aided by the introduction of softer landing materials; instead of landing on sand, jumpers started landing on padded mats, which were introduced during Fosbury's career.

Fosbury said, "The problem with something revolutionary is that most of the elite athletes had invested so much time in their technique and movements that they didn't want to give it up, so they stuck with what they knew." It would be ten years before the majority of jumpers used Fosbury's technique. The first athletes to pick it up were, not surprisingly, the youngest ones.

As a result of his startling Olympic win, Fosbury received a huge amount of attention. He was interviewed on popular television shows, taught celebrities how to do the flop, and met presidents and kings. The attention was overwhelming, and Fosbury found it difficult to deal with. "You get out of control," he said, looking back. "You're put on a pedestal, and the public reaction is either overdone, or they tear you down. When you step down from that podium, they don't let you become human."

Fosbury's reaction was to live quietly and to drop out of competition for a while to give himself time to collect his thoughts. Although he did not make the 1972 U.S. Olympic team, many of the world's leading high jumpers used his technique that year at the Munich Olympic Games. Fosbury has maintained his lanky physique and is only ten pounds over his college weight. He has remained fit by hiking, in-line skating with his teenage son, mountain biking, and snowboarding. In 1973 he competed in the short-lived International Track Association professional circuit.

Fosbury now works as a city engineer in Ketchum, Idaho, and is co-owner of an engineering firm. He holds high jump clinics each summer at a track camp for young athletes.

In 1998 Fosbury competed at the World Masters competition in Eugene, Oregon, and won the bronze medal. He was pleased to be involved because he believes in the value of exercise and would like to be a role model of healthy living for his age group. He was elected to the United States Olympic Hall of Fame in 1992.

★

Roy Blount, Jr., "Being Backwards Gets Results," *Sports Illustrated* (10 Feb. 1969), provides a lengthy article on Fosbury's life and accomplishments up to that date. *The Lincoln Library of Sports Champions,* vol. 5 (1993), includes a detailed chapter on Fosbury. For details of his performance at the World Masters Games, see Kerry Eggers, "Fosbury Will Compete with No Fear of Flop," *Oregonian* (12 Aug. 1998). In an interview in the *Honolulu Star-Bulletin* (13 Feb. 1999), Fosbury describes how he came up with his innovative jumping technique.

KELLY WINTERS

FOSTER, Andrew ("Rube") (*b.* 17 September 1879 in Calvert, Texas; *d.* 9 December 1930 in Kankakee, Illinois), hulking founder of the Negro National League who, in three decades as a player, manager, and executive, became one of the most influential and visionary figures in baseball history.

Foster was raised in Calvert, a bustling cotton town and railroad hub in Texas that during his childhood was the one of the largest cities in the state. His mother, Sarah Foster, was a gospel singer and his father, Andrew Foster, was a minister in the African Methodist Episcopal church. (Both parents were likely former slaves.) Foster's mother died when he was a child, and his father remarried, giving Foster several half-siblings. In 1897 he enrolled in Tillotson College in Austin, Texas, where he briefly studied for the ministry and pitched for the school's baseball team. For several years afterward, he worked as a day laborer in Calvert and occasionally as a pitcher for the Waco Yellowjackets, a nearby black team.

Rube Foster (*left*) and Red Sox teammate Del Gainer, c. 1915. © CORBIS

In 1902 Foster left for Chicago to join the Union Giants, a powerful black team run by respected manager Frank Leland, at a salary of $40 per month. After one season there, he moved on to New York City, where he reportedly compiled a 58–1 record for the Cuban X Giants after mastering a new pitch called the fadeaway. (Today this pitch is known as the screwball.) Around this time, he is said to have taught the fadeaway to New York Giants pitcher Christy Mathewson at spring training in Hot Springs, Arkansas, although this claim remains unverified. From 1904 to 1906 Foster pitched for the powerful Philadelphia Giants, where he reportedly defeated the celebrated pitcher Rube Waddell in an exhibition game, thus earning the nickname he would carry for the rest of his life, Rube. In a much ballyhooed championship game in 1904, Foster defeated his ex-teammates, the Cuban X Giants, striking out eighteen batters and cementing his reputation as one of the best pitchers in baseball. By 1907 his renown was so great that when Sol White, his manager in Philadelphia, published a baseball manual, it was Foster who authored the section titled "How to Pitch."

In 1907, at age twenty-seven, Foster returned to Chicago and rejoined Leland, this time as player-manager. In 1910 the Foster-led Leland Giants were one of the most powerful teams in baseball history. In addition to Foster, their lineup included the unparalleled John Henry Lloyd at shortstop, left-handed slugger Pete Hill in center field, power hitter Grant "Home Run" Johnson at second base, and star defensive catcher Bruce Petway. Playing against all comers, the team posted a 123–6 record for the season. Foster decided to capitalize on this success by splitting with Leland to form a team of his own in 1911. With financial backing from a white businessman, John Schorling, Foster purchased South Side Park from the Chicago White Sox, who had vacated it in 1910 when Comiskey Park was built. Foster christened his new team the Chicago American Giants and paid generous salaries that induced many star African-American players to join his franchise.

Under Foster's guidance the American Giants pioneered the speedy, slashing style of play for which black baseball would become famous. With smarts that equaled their skills, Foster's players employed techniques like the hit-and-run, the sacrifice bunt, and the stolen base to become black baseball's dominant team of the 1910s. The American Giants were members of the formidable (and integrated) Chicago City League. During the winter months Foster frequently took them on tour, playing in locales including Havana, Cuba; Seattle, Washington; Portland, Oregon; and Butte, Montana. By 1917 Foster had retired as a player, instead devoting his time to the managerial and business aspects of the team.

In 1920, with black baseball plagued by scheduling difficulties among the various independent teams, Foster decided to create his own league. In a meeting at the Paseo YMCA in Kansas City on 13 February 1920, Foster and five other businessmen met to officially form the Negro National League. Earlier attempts to form African-American leagues had been unsuccessful, but Foster succeeded where others had failed. The league's founding coincided with the Great Migration of 1916 to 1921, when 500,000 blacks left the rural South to live and work in northern cities; they were often eager to attend a ball game after a day's work in a factory or slaughterhouse.

Foster was elected president and treasurer of the new organization, which included his own American Giants as well as teams in Chicago, Detroit, New York City, Kansas City, St. Louis, Indianapolis, and Dayton, Ohio. Foster envisioned his league as a rival to the white major leagues and worked tirelessly to gain the approval of both fans and the press. The league was a first-class operation—the American Giants traveled in their own private Pullman car—and its success led the *Chicago Defender* to label Foster "the most successful Colored man in baseball, the only one that has made it a business."

Foster ran his league with the same autocratic leadership style that characterized his counterpart in white baseball, Kenesaw Mountain Landis. He drew no salary as the league's president, but as its booking agent he kept 10 percent of all gate receipts. In addition to owning the American Giants, Foster was a part-owner of several other teams in the league and distributed players among them to ensure competitive balance. His high-handedness disenchanted some fellow executives, but his success as a businessman ensured their continued support.

Foster's league and team both enjoyed considerable success in the 1920s, as the American Giants captured the first three Negro National League titles. The team's top pitcher during the decade, and perhaps the best in black baseball, was Willie Foster, his half brother. Willie was twenty-five years younger than Foster and, having been raised by his grandparents in Mississippi, barely knew his famous brother before joining the American Giants. Though the brothers had their differences, the pitching skills of the one and the managing skills of the other kept the team competitive during the mid-1920s.

Foster married Sarah Watts on 29 October 1908; they had two children. In 1925 some acquaintances noticed that Foster's actions had suddenly become erratic and paranoid, and his family observed memory and recognition problems. On 11 February 1926, according to his son, Foster held a clandestine meeting with John McGraw and Ban Johnson, two of white baseball's most influential figures. Shortly thereafter he began exhibiting signs of mental illness, including barricading himself in a public rest room and, later, chasing imaginary fly balls in his front yard. Early in 1926, after a violent confrontation at their apartment on Chicago's Michigan Avenue, Foster's wife had him committed to Kankakee State Hospital, a state-run mental institution.

After four years there he was said to be gradually recovering when, on the evening of 9 December 1930, a nurse found Foster dead in his bed. The official cause of death was heart failure, and he was buried at Lincoln Cemetery in Chicago. The next summer, after having been without Foster's guidance for four years, the Negro National League folded. His contributions to baseball went largely unrecognized until 2 August 1981 when, more than half a century after his death, he was inducted into the National Baseball Hall of Fame.

Foster was famed for his commanding yet easygoing manner, smoking his ubiquitous pipe while addressing males and females alike as "darlin'" in his booming Texas drawl. A mythic figure in many ways, he was known for his generosity with money and for finding work for down-and-out ballplayers. Although only about six feet tall, he weighed more than 250 pounds at his heaviest and impressed most who met him as a gigantic man in every sense of the word. An organizational genius, Foster proved that segregated baseball could be a viable business for African-American entrepreneurs. As an outstanding player, innovative manager, and visionary businessman, he is arguably the most uniquely talented individual in baseball history.

★

Foster is the subject of a sketchy biography by Charles E. Whitehead, *A Man and His Diamonds* (1980). Better information can be found in the archives of the National Baseball Hall of Fame Library, which contain clippings, correspondence, and other materials. Considerable information on Foster's early playing career is in Jerry Malloy, ed., *Sol White's History of Colored Base Ball, with Other Documents on the Early Black Game* (1995). A detailed chapter on Foster appears in John Holway, *Blackball Stars: Negro League Pioneers* (1988). Notable articles were published in *Abbott's Monthly* (Nov. 1930), *Afro* magazine (5 Sept. 1953), and *Hue* magazine (Aug. 1957). An obituary is in the *Chicago Defender* (11 Dec. 1930).

ERIC ENDERS

FOX, Jacob Nelson ("Nellie") (*b.* 25 December 1927 in St. Thomas, Pennsylvania; *d.* 1 December 1975 in Baltimore, Maryland), twelve-time all-star second baseman for the Chicago White Sox in the 1950s and Most Valuable Player in the American League in 1959 who was renowned for his all-out style of hustle and his small size.

Fox was one of three sons born to Jacob Fox, a carpenter, and Mae (Foreman) Fox, a homemaker, in the small town that he called home his entire life. As a youngster he played both soccer and baseball, but he quit school at the age of

sixteen to play professional baseball in the Philadelphia A's organization.

The A's manager Connie Mack signed Fox in 1944 not only because he was a promising player but also because he was too young to be drafted into the military. Fox played professionally in Lancaster, Pennsylvania, and in Jamestown, New York, in 1944 and 1945. However, in 1946 he was drafted, and he spent the 1946 season in the U.S. army stationed with the occupational forces in Korea. He married Joanne Statler, also from St. Thomas, on 30 June 1947. They had two daughters. In 1947 and 1948 Fox split time between minor league assignments and the Philadelphia A's. He reached the major leagues permanently in 1949, but in 1950 he was sent to the Chicago White Sox in exchange for the catcher Joe Tipton, a trade recognized as one of the best in White Sox history.

With good fielding instruction from the White Sox coach Jimmy Adair and hitting instruction from the White Sox coach Roger "Doc" Cramer, Fox became a stellar second baseman and an excellent hitter. "Nellie" became most well known for his vigorous style of play. Marty Marion, one of his managers, remarked that the five-foot, nine-inch, 160-pound Fox had "the highest energy" of any player he had seen. Al Lopez, another White Sox manager, commented that Fox was the "hustlingest" player he ever managed, and Paul Richards noted that Fox had "the best attitude" of any ballplayer he knew.

In addition to his dynamic style of play, Fox developed significant talent. He was a twelve-time all-star, he won three Gold Glove awards for fielding excellence at second base, he led the major leagues in most fielding chances at second base for eight consecutive years, and he led second basemen in double plays for five seasons. He also set a major league record of 798 consecutive games played at second base. That record would have been 1,076 games had not Marion, manager of the White Sox in the mid-1950s, forced Fox to sit out one game so he could rest.

As a hitter Fox lacked power, hitting only thirty-five home runs in his career. His specialty was hitting the single and putting the ball in play. While most players had begun to use a narrow-handled bat to generate power by the 1950s, Cramer convinced Fox to use a "bottle shaped" bat with a thick handle that enabled him to make frequent contact. An excellent bunter, he picked up about twenty hits a year by bunting. In thirteen seasons he led either the American League or the National League with the fewest strikeouts, once going ninety-eight games without striking out. For seven consecutive years he led the American League in singles. His lifetime batting average was .288, hitting over .300 in six of his years with the White Sox.

The high point of Fox's career came in 1959, when he and the shortstop Luis Aparicio led the "Go-Go" White Sox to the American League pennant, interrupting a streak

Nellie Fox, 1953. ASSOCIATED PRESS AP

of Yankee pennants both before and after that year. Unlike the Yankees, who were a power-filled team, the White Sox team played low-scoring games marked with excitement, taking an extra base on a ball hit to the outfield, stealing bases more frequently, and hustling for every run. Fox was the leader of that team and became the most popular player in Chicago, boasting an enormous fan club. Fox, Aparicio, and the pitcher Early Wynn finished 1–2–3 in the voting for the American League Most Valuable Player that year. Although the White Sox lost the World Series to the Los Angeles Dodgers, Fox hit .375 in the six-game series.

Fox played four more successful seasons for the White Sox before being traded to the Houston Colt 45s before the 1964 season. He played two years for the Colt 45s, then he coached in Houston through the 1966 and 1967 seasons. During that time he helped prepare a young second baseman named Joe Morgan to break many of his own records for longevity, fielding prowess, and hitting. Morgan eventually landed in the Hall of Fame. From 1968 through 1971 Fox coached for the Washington Senators, and he moved with the Senators to Dallas, where he coached the Texas Rangers from 1971 to 1973.

Retiring from baseball after the 1973 season, Fox returned to St. Thomas, Pennsylvania. He managed the bowling alley, restaurant, and sporting goods businesses in nearby Chambersburg, Pennsylvania, that he had opened in 1956. Fox, whose trademark was a huge "chaw" of to-

bacco in his cheek whenever he played the game, was stricken with skin cancer on several parts of his body after his retirement. He died at the age of forty-seven from cancer in University Hospital in Baltimore, Maryland. He is buried at St. Thomas Cemetery in his hometown.

Fox was elected to the Baseball Hall of Fame posthumously in 1997. Chicago fans, baseball purists, and many former players had campaigned for years for his election to the Hall of Fame. However, not until 1997 did the Veterans Committee have sufficient votes for Fox's inclusion in the illustrious company of honorees at Cooperstown. Hall of Fame credentials for players often focus on power hitting and large numbers of runs batted in. Fielding prowess has less appeal to voters. Although the reason is unknown, baseball researchers and insiders believe that Lopez, Fox's manager of many years and a member of the Veterans Committee, was responsible for blocking Fox's earlier selection into the Hall of Fame.

★

The best sources on Fox include Richard C. Lindberg, *The White Sox Encyclopedia* (1997); Dave Condon, *The Go-Go White Sox* (1960); Roger Kahn, "Little Nellie's a Man Now," *Sport* (Apr. 1958); the files of the *Sporting News;* and Joseph L. Reichler, ed., *The Baseball Encyclopedia* (1990). An obituary is in the *New York Times* (2 Dec. 1975).

HARRY JEBSEN, JR.

FOXX, James Emory ("Jimmie") (*b.* 22 October 1907 in Sudlersville, Maryland; *d.* 21 July 1967 in Miami, Florida), baseball Hall-of-Famer, known as "Double X" who was the premier homerun hitter in the major leagues during the 1930s.

Foxx was one of two children of tenant farmers Samuel Dell "Dell" Foxx and Margaret "Mattie" Smith. Foxx's father was a star of town ball (an early form of baseball) for many years. Foxx gained his baseball knowledge and skills largely from his father's instruction and hours of practice, and much of his upper body strength from various chores he did on the farm. By age fourteen, Foxx was playing town ball (usually as catcher) with mostly older boys. He attended Sudlersville High School from 1921 to 1924 and starred in baseball, track and field, soccer, basketball, and volleyball.

Foxx won the 220-yard run and running high jump at the 1923 Maryland State Olympiad, prompting one Baltimore newspaper to call him the most promising young athlete in Maryland. He also starred in baseball in the spring of 1923 for Sudlersville High School and the Queen Anne's County All Stars (star players from that county's high schools). H. C. "Curley" Byrd, the baseball coach and athletic director at the University of Maryland at College Park, offered Foxx an athletic scholarship to attend school there. But Foxx apparently declined. His athletic career took off

Jimmie Foxx, 1935. ASSOCIATED PRESS AP

even faster in 1924, to the point that he did not finish his last month of school in tenth grade and only attended about one month of eleventh grade in the fall of 1924.

Foxx first played professional baseball in May 1924 at age sixteen with Frank "Homerun" Baker's Easton (Maryland) club in the Eastern Shore League. He started the season for Baker as catcher and had several major league scouts following him by midseason. By the end of July, Mike Drennan, a scout for the Philadelphia Athletics, purchased Foxx's contract for manager Connie Mack for the sum of $2,000. Baker and Mack agreed that Foxx would not report to the Athletics until the end of Easton's season. Baker's club finished last in the league standings, and the first-place Parksley (Virginia) Spuds club asked Foxx to play for the team in the Five States Series against Blue Ridge League champion, Martinsburg. With Mack's consent, Foxx played for Parksley. He slugged four homeruns and batted .391 as the Spuds defeated the Blue Sox, four games out of six.

Mack used Foxx sparingly in the Athletics lineup from 1925 to 1927, at catcher, outfield, and first base. Foxx played regularly in 1928, splitting his time between first base and third base. In 1929 Mack made Foxx his regular first baseman and Foxx created an early season sensation. Foxx was batting over .400 in early June and still leading the league in batting in July when he appeared on the cover of *Time* magazine, an honor denied to Babe Ruth and Lou Gehrig. Foxx finished fourth in the league in batting and starred for the Athletics in the 1929 World Series, slugging two homers. Foxx had married Helen Heite on 26 December 1928. They had two sons, one of whom, Jimmy, Jr., was born during the 1929 Series.

Foxx became a national celebrity, and baseball writers began calling him the "right-handed Ruth." In the early 1930s Foxx had unofficial records for longest homeruns for a right-handed batter in most American League parks, as did Ruth for a left-handed batter. Early in his career, the press gave Foxx nicknames such as the "Sudlersville Slugger" and the "Maryland Broadback." Later he received his more common nicknames of "Double X" and "The Beast."

Foxx's signature accomplishment occurred when he slugged fifty-eight homeruns in 1932, just two homeruns behind Babe Ruth's single season mark. In 1933 he led the AL in homers, runs batted in, and batting average, winning the Triple Crown. From then on, many boys picked Foxx as their favorite player over Ruth and Gehrig. Foxx wrote a booklet, *How I Bat,* released in May 1933. Foxx also looked the part of a homerun slugger. He cut off his uniform sleeves only a few inches down from his shoulders to gain more freedom of movement and show off his huge biceps.

Foxx made a trip to Japan in 1934 with the "All-Americans" baseball club (Ruth, Gehrig, Mack, and others), despite being beaned several weeks earlier while barnstorming in Canada after the regular season. The All-Americans were undefeated in Japan, Ruth being the main attraction. In one game Foxx played each of the nine positions on the field, one position per inning.

Due to financial losses, Connie Mack sold Foxx to Boston Red Sox owner Tom Yawkey in December 1935. Foxx played just over six years with the Red Sox before winding down his playing career with the Chicago Cubs and Philadelphia Phillies as a part-time player. Foxx enjoyed some outstanding seasons with the Red Sox, especially 1936, 1938, and 1939. He set single season homerun (50) and runs batted in (175) marks for the Red Sox in 1938 that still stood after the 2001 baseball season.

Foxx was not as boisterous and self-promoting in public as Babe Ruth, but he loved the adulation he received from fans and relished the camaraderie with other players and celebrities. Foxx had a winning smile and was very popular with teammates and opposing players. His trademark was his generosity, and some friends even felt he was generous to the point he did not watch out for himself. Apparently, he was never ejected from a baseball game. He enjoyed the night life and was always a big tipper. Foxx loved hunting, mostly for small game in the off-season, and often played golf. He suffered from sinus conditions from 1931 through the end of his playing career. At times his vision was severely impaired and eventually it contributed in part to the decline of his batting.

Foxx and his wife divorced in 1943 and he married Dorothy Anderson Yard on 18 June that same year. They had one son, James Emory Foxx III, and Foxx was very close to Dorothy's son John and her daughter Nanci. Foxx had great difficulty in securing any long-term employment after baseball and gained jobs mostly as a sales representative for various industries.

Foxx was inducted into the National Baseball Hall-of-Fame in 1951. He managed the Fort Wayne Daisies of the All American Girls Professional Baseball League to a pennant in his only season as a manager in 1952. He also coached for the University of Miami in 1956 and 1957, and briefly for the Minneapolis Millers in 1958. He fell short of his ambition to manage a major league club. Foxx died from asphyxiation after choking on a piece of meat lodged in his throat. He is buried in Flagler Memorial Park in Miami, Florida.

Foxx won three American League Most Valuable Player awards (1932, 1933, and 1938), led his league in batting average twice, led in homeruns four times, and hit thirty or more homeruns in twelve consecutive seasons (a major league record). He was versatile in the field and a team player. His lifetime .609 slugging average is fourth best ever. Foxx batted .344 (22 for 64) in 18 World Series games from

1929 to 1931. The *Sporting News* named Foxx the fifteenth Greatest Major Leaguer of the Twentieth Century in 1997. Ted Williams said, "I saw only one other player [other than Foxx] who made the bat and baseball sound like it did when he really hit one, and that guy was Mickey Mantle."

The town of Sudlersville paid Foxx the ultimate tribute in 1997 when they dedicated a life-size bronze statue of him in the center of town. John Steadman, a longtime sportswriter and baseball historian, spoke during the ceremony and said, "With apologies to Hank Aaron, Willie Mays, Ralph Kiner and others, Jimmie Foxx was (and still is) the greatest right-handed slugger of all time."

★

A rare booklet written by Foxx called *How I Bat* (1933), describes his approach to batting. Biographies on Foxx include one for children, Norman Macht, *Jimmie Foxx* (1991); and full-length biographies Bob Gorman, *Double X: The Story of Jimmie Foxx—Baseball's Forgotten Hero* (1990); W. Harrison Daniel, *Jimmie Foxx: The Life and Times of a Baseball Hall-of-Famer* (1996); and Mark Millikin, *Jimmie Foxx: The Pride of Sudlersville* (1998). Fred Lieb wrote a detailed article on Foxx that serves as an obituary in the *Sporting News* (5 Aug. 1967). Obituaries are in the *New York Times* and the *Baltimore Sun* (22 July 1967).

MARK R. MILLIKIN

FOYT, A(nthony) J(oseph), Jr. (*b.* 16 January 1935 in Houston, Texas), professional race car driver who between 1957 and 1992 won seven United States Auto Club championships, four Indianapolis 500 races, and France's premier race, the Twenty-four Hours of Le Mans.

Foyt was one of three children born to Anthony "Tony" Joseph Foyt, Sr., a mechanic, garage owner, and well-known builder of racing engines, and Elizabeth (Emma Evelyn) Monk, a homemaker. Unbelievably, Foyt climbed behind the wheel at the tender age of three, driving a gas-powered miniature racer that his father built for him. By age eleven he was racing midget cars. He dropped out of high school in the eleventh grade to work as a mechanic in his father's garage, the Burton and Foyt Garage. While he was working in the family's shop, Foyt learned lessons that served him well in his later career. Not only was he given the opportunity to pursue his love of racing, but he also gained valuable firsthand knowledge of the inner workings of automobiles, especially the engines. By 1953 he was a well known figure on the midget and stock car circuits. During his early career on dirt tracks, Foyt's friends gave him the moniker "Fancy Pants" because he commonly wore freshly laundered and starched white pants, silk shirts, and cowboy boots.

Foyt married Lucy Zarr in 1955; they had two sons and

A. J. Foyt, 1992. ASSOCIATED PRESS AP

one daughter. Two years after his marriage, Foyt began racing professionally.

Foyt is best remembered for his appearances at the Indianapolis 500, qualifying at Indy thirty-five consecutive times between 1958 and 1992. During his career at Indianapolis, he electrified racing fans with his driving abilities, but one of his most memorable moments at America's most prominent race was in 1961. From the beginning, this race proved sensational. Jim Hurtubise, a young driver participating in his first race at the sacred Brickyard, led the field for the first thirty-five laps until engine trouble forced him out of the race. Once Hurtubise was out of the race, Rufus Parnell "Parnelli" Jones took the lead position. Jones maintained his lead for the first seventy-five miles despite being struck in the forehead by loose debris left on the track from an earlier wreck. Even though Jones could barely see through his blood-drenched goggles, it was engine trouble that forced him from the race.

The new frontrunner was now Eddie Sachs, and following close behind him was Foyt, pushing the new leader for first place. As the race unfolded, the two men swapped the lead position ten times, Sachs outrunning Foyt in the straightaways and Foyt catching him in the turns. With thirty miles left to go in the race, both men made what they calculated to be their final pit stop. Both pit crews serviced their respective cars and had their drivers back on the track in record time. Foyt immediately noticed his car was running unusually fast. He was able to pass Sachs and built a measurable lead over him.

Just as Foyt began to visualize his first victory at Indy, a member of his racing team flashed him a sign that read "Fuel Low." During his last stop, an undetected clogged fuel line had prevented his crew from refueling his car with enough gas to finish the race. This had in essence made the car lighter, thus accounting for the car's ability to run faster than before. All seemed lost. Another pit stop meant Sachs would win the race, but if Foyt ran out of gas he would lose the race for sure. Cussing his crew, Foyt pulled into the pit area and refueled. But he did not give up, a character trait that served him well throughout his career. Back on the track, the frustrated Foyt pushed his car harder than before, but Sachs maintained his lead.

However, Foyt's persistence paid off. With five laps left in the race, Sachs began to experience tire trouble. It seemed evident that if Sachs continued to push his car, the result would be a crash-causing blowout. Sachs was forced to pull into the pit area and change his worn tires. Foyt roared into the lead for the final time, winning his first Indianapolis 500. That same year, he won eighteen more United States Auto Club—sponsored races and his second consecutive national championship.

Foyt was now well on his way to becoming a racing legend. He won a third national championship in 1963, winning three races and not finishing lower than eighth in any event. The next year, he exceeded his prior accomplishments by winning the Indy 500 for a second time, winning the Daytona Firecracker 400 stock car race, breaking the record for most career wins in an Indy car, and winning his fourth USAC National championship. Foyt won his fifth national championship in 1967. He also won his third Indianapolis 500, finishing more than two laps ahead of the second-place driver, Al Unser, Sr. Just over one week after his victory at the Indianapolis 500, Foyt and fellow team member Dan Gurney took first at France's premier race, the Twenty-four Hours of Le Mans. Foyt became the first driver to win both the Indy 500 and the Le Mans. In 1972 he won the Daytona 500, the most important race sponsored by the National Association for Stock Car Auto Racing.

In the 1970s Foyt remained at the top of his profession. In 1975 and again in 1979 he won his sixth and seventh USAC national championships. He won the Indy 500 for the fourth time in 1977. In the 1980s Foyt was still competitive, and his biggest win of the decade came in 1985, when he won the Twelve Hours of Sebring, America's oldest endurance race. The 1990s brought an end to Foyt's career behind the wheel. He qualified for the Indy 500 again in 1991 and 1992. He showed up at Indianapolis in 1993, but shocked the crowd on the first day of qualifying by announcing his retirement. He raced in one more professional race following his retirement. In 1994 he drove in the first NASCAR event held at the Indianapolis Motor Speedway, the Brickyard 400, but failed to win.

Foyt runs A. J. Foyt Enterprises, a race car shop that has been based in Houston since 1965, and he also serves on the board of directors of Riverway Bank and Service Corporation International, one of the nation's largest funeral chains. Foyt has remained active in the sport that he loves by fielding racing teams and sponsoring promising young drivers.

Foyt will forever remain a legend in the world of auto racing. No one has come close to matching his career of winning sixty-seven Indy car events and seven USAC season championships. Also, he remains the only driver to have won the Indy 500, NASCAR's Daytona 500, and the Twenty-four Hours of Le Mans. From day one, Foyt was a man of conviction, believing in the American dream and in himself as well. It was only fitting that he was inducted into the Motor Sports Hall of Fame in 1989.

★

Foyt and William Neely, a sports writer, chronicle most of Foyt's racing career in *A. J.: My Life as America's Greatest Race Car Driver* (1983). This work gives insight into Foyt's perspective and experience both on and off the race track. Bill Libby, *Foyt* (1974), is a biographical work that offers a balanced view of Foyt's early career. For a general history of the first seventy-five years of the Indianapolis 500 race, see Rich Taylor, *Indy: Seventy-Five Years of Auto Racing's Greatest Spectacle* (1991). Numerous magazine and newspaper articles cover Foyt's life and professional career. Among the more informative are John McGill, "Last Tango at Indy?," *Sporting News* 211 (27 May 1991): 39–40; William Nack, "Twilight of a Titan," *Sports Illustrated* (30 Sept. 1991); Malcolm Moran, "Defying the Odds at Indy," *New York Times* (25 May 1986); and Ken Denlinger, "Foyt Faces New Turns at Indy 500; 58-Year-Old Racing Legend No Longer Behind the Wheel," *Washington Post* (27 May 1993).

KENNETH WAYNE HOWELL

FRANCE, William Henry Getty, Sr. ("Bill") (*b.* 26 September 1909 in Horse Pasture, Virginia; *d.* 7 June 1992 in Ormand Beach, Florida), stock-car race executive and key founder of the National Association for Stock Car Auto Racing (NASCAR).

The patron saint of NASCAR, Bill France came from humble origins. One of three children of William H. France

Bill France, 1984. ASSOCIATED PRESS AP

and Emma Graham, he grew up on a farm and relished rural life. His passion was playing and tinkering with all sorts of cars and motorcycles. At six feet, five inches tall and 230 pounds, France was of imposing stature and a dominating presence. He was an outstanding basketball player at Washington Central High; his size and build clearly helped him to be an impact performer on the court. France married Anne Bledsoe in North Carolina in June 1931, and they had two sons. Both sons have played important roles in sustaining the France legend and dynasty and in making NASCAR America's premier auto-racing form at the start of the twenty-first century.

During the autumn of 1934, the Frances decided to move their home base to Miami. However, their car broke down in Daytona Beach, Florida, and the France family settled there instead. Daytona Beach is today a symbolic home of NASCAR. It is the site of NASCAR's Hall of Fame, and the Winston Cup series begins its ten-month annual circuit with the February running of the Daytona 500, arguably NASCAR's most famous and prestigious race.

Eventually, France got a bank loan, opened a garage and service station, and began his lifelong fascination with stock cars as an innovative mechanic willing to experiment with new designs and unusual devices. He combined driving and engine tuning to good effect and, at the wheel of a 1935 Ford Mustang, earned a fifth place finish in a Daytona Beach race on a course that was more sandy beach than tarmacadam road. In 1938 he and a friend took over the promotion, organization, and publicity of the many Daytona Beach area stock-car races. In the space of only a few months, France and restaurateur Charlie Reese made a profit of more than $4,000, a considerable amount of money at a time when America was slowly escaping the economic quagmire of the depression. During World War II France worked for the Daytona Beach Boat Works and helped build motor torpedo boats.

Brad Herzog described the manner in which France's sense of vision and his sharp management acumen pointed stock-car racing in the right direction: France "saw a need to regulate promoters and assure collection of prize money, to form a standard set of rules and specifications for all drivers and automobiles, to inaugurate a national championship and then a point system, to provide insurance for the drivers, and to create a central headquarters."

As a result of France's savoir faire and his remarkable ability to avoid confrontation and achieve consensus, a meeting of Southeastern race promoters was convened by France, and on 12 December 1947 NASCAR came into being. Months later, in February 1948, NASCAR was incorporated. France possessed P. T. Barnum's critical grasp of the all-importance of staging, promotion, and publicity as strategies to establish a viable marketplace for a fledgling form of public theater.

An important feature undergirding NASCAR's eventual success was France's commitment to his dream of transforming a rough, informal, redneck activity into a structured, formal sport. As early as 1944 France restarted stock racing at Daytona Beach and then inaugurated races in North Carolina, South Carolina, and Georgia.

According to Richard Pillsbury, the very first "strictly stock race" was a long distance 150-mile race held in North Carolina on Charlotte's three-quarter-mile dirt oval on 19 June 1948. "The race, which featured a purse of $5,000 was open to all comers who owned a full-size American car."

From the outset France was determined that his racing philosophy—strictly regulated, equal competition to create a "level playing field"—should be embraced by all NASCAR competitors. At NASCAR's first Grand National Championship held in Charlotte on 19 June 1949, the winner, Glenn Dunnaway, was disqualified by France. Dunnaway had used a piece of illegal equipment, and France was determined to hold to the moral high ground. Dunnaway's car owner objected and took NASCAR to court. France's court victory affirmed NASCAR's authority to set and uphold stringent standards regarding the development of stock cars. This central tenet of the France "doctrine" has been the major reason that NASCAR races, like great horse races, are won by fractions of a second and portions of a "body length" rather than by the larger, less exciting margins that have lessened the spectator appeal for Formula One Grand Prix racing.

In 1959 France supervised the opening of the Daytona International Speedway. The *Biographical Dictionary of American Sports* highlights some of the challenges faced by France during the 1950s when he had to carve and create race tracks out of beach terrain, a friendly site for promenading and bathing but ill textured for feisty stock cars. "France faced the unenviable task of giving order and structure to the various beach races. France had to determine in advance on what days the tide would be low at the right time to allow races to be held. Handling traffic when the tide was coming in was another tricky problem. Another problem was controlling admissions around a four-mile unfenced race track."

With the Daytona International Speedway, France transformed a dusty oval of less than a mile long into a modern amphitheater with thousands of open-air seats and a totally unobstructed view of the whole circuit, a thirty-one degree banking, and a configuration that allowed drivers to race side by side. The track was designed for high speeds and heightened drama.

France followed his Daytona success with the creation, a decade later, of the Alabama International Motor Speedway near Talladega. Talladega was longer and steeper than Daytona. Furman Bisher said of France that he "took the car off the streets and turned it into a sport as national as the National Football League." A 1978 *Sports Illustrated* article noted that France "made stock-car racing a huge success by building speedways in swamps, keeping corporations guessing and unions at bay. Here is the man who brought you . . . bumper-to-bumper competition."

France was not always a beloved figure. In 1961 he prevented NASCAR drivers from joining the Teamsters Union, and in 1969, when the Professional Drivers Association boycotted Talladega because of safety concerns, France brought in replacement drivers, drove demonstration laps himself at 176 miles per hour, and "the show went on." Although France passed control of NASCAR to his son Bill France, Jr., in 1972, the two defining factors for France and NASCAR took place earlier. These were the creation of a genuine folk hero who came in the form of NASCAR's greatest ever driver—Richard Petty, who had won 200 races by 1984—and the setting up, in 1971, of NASCAR's Grand National Circuit, which eventually came to be known as the Winston Cup Series. In 1990 France was inducted into the Motorsports Hall of Fame of America and the International Motor Hall of Fame. He died of natural causes and is buried in Hillside Cemetery, Ormond Beach, Florida.

At his death, France, as the father figure of NASCAR, must have taken huge pleasure in a sport that was marked by extraordinary growth. A backwoods, regional, noisy "bump and grind" chase had metamorphosed into—via the Winston Cup—thirty-one races in nineteen states with four million spectators and prize money of $25 million. France might have rubbed his eyes in disbelief had he been alive in 2000. In 1999 seventeen of the top twenty attended sporting events in the United States were NASCAR races, and NASCAR was worth $2.8 billion in television rights.

★

Richard Pillsbury is the doyen of NASCAR essayists and his "Stock Car Racing" in the *Encyclopedia of World Sport,* vol. 3 (1996) provides a factual overview of the sport. His writing on stock-car racing in *The Theater of Sport* (1995) is glorious. Other useful sources are Furman Bisher's piece in *Sky* (June 1980), Brock Yates's *Sports Illustrated* profile (June 1978), and an entry on France in David L. Porter, ed., *Biographical Dictionary of American Sports* (1995). For a graphic, journalistic account of France's life and career see Brad Herzog, *The 100 Most Important People in American Sport History* (1995). Mark D. Howell, *From Moonshine to Madison Avenue* (1997), provides a well-constructed social history of NASCAR.

SCOTT A. G. M. CRAWFORD

FRASER, Gretchen Claudia (*b.* 11 February 1919 in Tacoma, Washington; *d.* 18 February 1994 in Sun Valley, Idaho), first U.S. skier—male or female—to win an Olympic medal and an Olympic gold medal.

Born Gretchen Claudia Kunigk and raised in the shadow of Mt. Rainier's slopes—her family owned a resort in the area—Fraser did not begin skiing until she was a teenager, much to the dismay of her Norwegian-born, ski-loving mother, who had campaigned for the development of public skiing on Mount Rainier.

Fraser finally ventured out to the slopes on a sightseeing tour and was instantly hooked. While she honed her skiing skills, she met a young man named Donald Fraser, a member of the 1936 Olympic ski team. He was impressed with her—he found her form awkward yet promising. They married in 1939 and spent their time training for the upcoming Olympic tryouts. They each made the team, but the 1940 Olympic Games were canceled because of World War II.

Fraser continued skiing and in 1940 won the first ever Diamond Sun event, held in Sun Valley, Idaho. She won the race again in 1941, beating out men's skiing ace Dick Durrance. That year she also won the national alpine com-

Gretchen Fraser, 1948. ASSOCIATED PRESS AP

bined and downhill titles. In 1942 she skied her way to the national slalom championship. Fraser also worked as a movie double for numerous stars in ski pictures, appearing in *Thin Ice* (1937) and *Sun Valley Serenade* (1941).

Meanwhile, Don Fraser spent several years as an aerial gunner in the U.S. Navy. Fraser retired from skiing but kept active by giving swimming, riding, and skiing lessons to veterans in U.S. Army hospitals. With her husband at war, Fraser was lonely. She took flying lessons, earned a pilot's license, and joined the Ninety-niners, an international women's flying organization.

When World War II ended and Don Fraser came home, the couple opened a oil and gasoline distribution business based in Vancouver, Washington. It was a team operation; Don Fraser drove the trucks, and Gretchen Fraser kept the books.

As their lives settled down, Don Fraser encouraged his wife to start skiing again. He wanted her to try out for the 1948 Olympic Games. Running their own business kept them busy, and Fraser did not have much time to practice, but the twenty-eight-year-old underdog nevertheless handily made the Olympic team and headed for the 1948 Winter Games at St. Moritz, Switzerland.

Fraser won two medals at the Winter Olympics, breaking the U.S. ski drought—they were the first medals ever won by any U.S. skier. Her achievement is especially impressive given that the women's ski team did not have a coach. Female skiers of Fraser's day received very little support because during the 1940s there was still debate as to whether or not ski competitions were "ladylike." Thus when Fraser and the other women skiers gathered in Europe to prepare for the Games, their only training was that every day a different skier from the men's team came to coach them. Three weeks before the Games, the women's manager Alice Kiaer was so fed up she used her own money to hire Walter Haensli to coach the U.S. women skiers. Haensli, a Swiss who had almost made the Swiss Olympic team, worked out a regular training regimen for the women.

Fraser pulled through for the United States and won a silver medal in the alpine combined—a downhill racing and slalom event that has since been discontinued. A few days later, on 5 February 1948, she made history by winning a gold medal in the giant slalom despite adverse circumstances. The first problem was that she wore bib No. 1, generally a bad starting position. The slalom is a timed downhill race where skiers zigzag through a course of flags or gates. Because she skied first, Fraser broke in the course and did not have the benefit of watching others go before her to see where the slick spots were.

Fraser stood in first place after the first run of the two that make up the race. Before her second run, there were technical difficulties with the gates, and she was forced wait in starting position for more than ten minutes while technicians fixed a glitch in the telephone line. For most skiers, the delay would have killed their concentration, but not Fraser. When she got the signal to go, she zigzagged down the course with reckless abandon at nearly sixty miles per hour, ultimately winning the gold.

Newspapers loved the story of the unknown, pigtailed homemaker who had won the gold. Fraser, later seen on the front of the Wheaties cereal box in 1951, was an inspiration to all. She proved that years of coaching were not necessary to become an international star.

Although Fraser left competition after the Games, her tireless promotion of the sport never ended. During the 1952 Winter Games in Oslo, Norway, she served as manager of the U.S. women's ski team. In 1960 she was inducted into the U.S. National Ski Hall of Fame.

Fraser's yearning for adventure and the outdoors never left her. She and her husband spent a portion of their lives training field dogs. Along with their son, they spent long stretches of time on hunting and fishing trips in the Washington wilderness. The couple also owned a seaplane and flew to the Canadian lake region. One year the world traveler and news personality Lowell Thomas invited the Frasers to join him on Alaska's Juneau Ice Cap to film one of his *High Adventure* television episodes.

Even into her sixties, Fraser remained an active promoter of skiing. She raised funds for the national team and served on the Sun Valley Ski Education Foundation. She also helped found a ski club for amputees and helped with the Idaho Special Olympics.

Women athletes of Fraser's period received little attention. As late as 1982 an article in the *Washington Post* overlooked Fraser's medals when it reported that "Jimmie Heuga was twenty years old when he won an Olympic bronze medal on a snow-covered Australian alp. It was 1964, and the United States had never before won an Olympic medal in skiing." Never mind that Fraser had won an Olympic medal sixteen years before, when Heuga was a small child.

Fraser had heart bypass surgery in 1986, but she continued skiing nearly every day until her death. She died at the age of seventy-five, just five weeks after her husband.

★

Several books contain short chapters on Fraser's life. Among them are Phyllis Hollander, *American Women in Sports* (1972); Al J. Stump, *Champions Against Odds* (1952); and Joe Layden, *Women in Sports* (1997); although many of the books, written in the 1950s and 1970s, are sexist in their depictions of female athletes and tend to brush over their abilities. For a more recent biography, see Luanne Pfeifer, *Gretchen's Gold: The Life of Gretchen Fraser, America's First Gold Medalist* (1996). Newspaper articles to consult include "Buried Gold," *Washington Post* (24 Feb. 1982); "3 Gold Medalists' Words of Advice," the *New York Times* (5 Feb. 1984); and "First Lady of Skiing Blazed Trail For Others," the *Idaho Statesman* (9 Feb. 2001).

LISA FRICK

FRAZIER, Joe (*b.* 12 January 1944 in Beaufort, South Carolina), boxer who won the 1964 Olympic gold medal and was world heavyweight champion from 1970 to 1973; he fought nemesis Muhammad Ali three times and won once in 1971.

Frazier was one of thirteen children of Rubin and Dolly Frazier. He grew up in rural poverty, the youngest of seven sons. Frazier credits his success to a strong work ethic and solid values established early in life. Working in the fields alongside his siblings, Frazier picked vegetables grown by the wealthy white landowners of Beaufort, South Carolina, earning fifteen cents per filled crate. Frazier's father, a sharecropper, woodcutter, and junk dealer, lost an arm in a car accident shortly before young Frazier was born, yet served as a model of strength. Frazier's father, to whom he was very close, built the family's house while engaging his children in farm and domestic labor.

For recreation, Frazier tied homemade heavy bags to tree branches and pretended to be boxing legends Joe Louis, Ezzard Charles, or Archie Moore. He attended a segregated high school until dropping out in the tenth grade at age fourteen. After marrying Florence Smith in 1959, Frazier

Joe Frazier, 1968. © BETTMANN/CORBIS

"Smokin" was Frazier's term for this style, which led to his nickname of "Smokin' Joe."

When Muhammad Ali was stripped of his title for refusing induction into the U.S. Army due to religious reasons in 1967, the professional heavyweight division was in disarray. An opportunistic Frazier defeated nemesis Buster Mathis for the New York State world title 4 March 1968 at Madison Square Garden, a title bout sponsored by the World Boxing Association (WBA). He made six defenses of his title, including a unification fight in which he knocked out WBA titleholder Jimmy Ellis in the fifth round on 16 February 1970, achieving widespread recognition as world champion.

In the summer of 1970, former champ Ali was granted a license to fight again, and public demand for a showdown between the former champion and the reigning titleholder surfaced. Thus began a mostly adversarial link between the two men that lasted for years. Ali promoted the upcoming fight by relying on his trademark rhetoric and insulting banter. Frazier, who had generally been supportive of Ali in the past, including lending him money months earlier, reacted with frustration and anger. Ali labeled Frazier an "Uncle Tom," an odd assertion for a man born into a middle-class family in Louisville, Kentucky, to make about the earnest Frazier, who grew up dirt poor in South Carolina. Frazier retorted by alleging Ali's Muslim religion was "a front," and he referred to Ali by his birth name, Cassius Clay, in a show of disrespect. Although both men were Olympic champions during the same decade, and children of the South, both they and the media saw the two as very different.

The unprecedented meeting of two undefeated heavyweight champions, called by boxing experts the most anticipated heavyweight title fight since the Joe Louis versus Billy Conn rematch of 1946, occurred on 8 March 1971. Each fighter received a record sum of $2.5 million and the bout was broadcast worldwide on closed-circuit television to an audience of about 300 million viewers. The sellout crowd at Madison Square Garden was treated to an epic battle, resulting in a unanimous decision for Frazier after fifteen grueling rounds. Even after the victory solidified Frazier as undisputed champion of the world, he was not well received by some critics. *Boxing Illustrated* published a story by Bryant Gumbel titled: "Is Joe Frazier a White Champion in a Black Skin?"

Frazier's reign as champion ended in January 1973, against George Foreman in Kingston, Jamaica. Foreman dropped the uncompromising Frazier six times before the fight was stopped in the second round. But Frazier then defeated Joe Bugner in his next fight, setting up a rubber match with Ali, who had beaten Foreman and regained the heavyweight title. In suffocating heat just outside the Philippines capital of Manila on 1 October 1975, the two aging

migrated north seeking opportunity after running into trouble with the owners of the farm on which he was working. After a brief stay with relatives in New York, he moved to Philadelphia, where he found work in a kosher slaughterhouse and sent money home to his wife, who had given birth to their first of seven children. In 1961, seeking to lose weight, he began working out at a Police Athletic League gym, where he was spotted by Yancey "Yank" Durham, a veteran Philadelphia fight trainer. Durham noticed the stocky Frazier could throw a tremendous punch and immediately recruited him to organized boxing.

After enjoying immediate success in the amateur ranks, where he earned the 1962 Philadelphia Golden Gloves novice heavyweight title and won the Middle Atlantic Golden Gloves heavyweight championships in 1962, 1963, and 1964, Frazier competed at the 1964 Olympic trials. Buster Mathis outpointed him, but he was chosen as an alternate, and when Mathis broke his thumb before the international competition he replaced him on the team. Frazier won a gold medal in heavyweight competition at the 1964 Olympics in Tokyo, Japan, and then returned to Philadelphia, still poor. He continued to win handily, even after turning professional in 1965. The unrelenting Frazier displayed a strong jaw, good punching power, and a nonstop attack that gave adversaries little time to think or maneuver.

warriors dueled for fourteen rounds in a contest Ali dubbed the "Thrilla in Manila." Frazier's ferocious body blows appeared to stun Ali during the middle rounds, but the champion surfaced as the aggressor late in the fight. By the end of the fourteenth round, Frazier's eyes were badly swollen, and his corner stopped the bout. Ali later said, "It was the closest I've come to death." Boxing experts rate the contest one of the greatest heavyweight championship fights in history. Nine months later, Frazier lost a rematch against Foreman and retired after the fight. In December 1981 he launched a one-bout comeback, but drew with journeyman Floyd "Jumbo" Cummings.

On 14 March 2001 Ali publicly apologized for calling Frazier an "Uncle Tom" and "too ugly to be the champ," before their first fight in 1971. Frazier embraced the apology, ending their public feud. In retirement, Frazier trained boxers and became a professional singer. His ensemble group, aptly named the "Smokin' Joe and the Knockouts," performed rock and gospel music in nightclubs and recorded for Capitol Records. Frazier was inducted into *Ring Magazine*'s Boxing Hall of Fame in 1980 and the International Boxing Hall of Fame in 1990. He has made several public appearances at Joe Frazier's Gym in Philadelphia. Of his seven children, two have followed him into boxing. His son, Marvis Frazier, fought for the heavyweight championship twice in the 1980s, losing to both Larry Holmes and Mike Tyson. Daughter Jacqui-Frazier Lyde is a lawyer, women's professional boxer, and promoter.

★

Frazier collaborated with Phil Berger to produce *Smokin' Joe* (1996), a good source of biographical information. Several articles in the popular press capture major events in Frazier's life. One worth consulting is Dave Anderson, "Beaufort, S.C., Loves Frazier," *New York Times* (10 Apr. 1971). Richard Sandomir, "No Floating, No Stinging: Ali Extends Hand to Frazier," *New York Times* (15 Mar. 2001), describes the end of the Ali and Frazier feud. Jeffrey Sammons, *Beyond the Ring: The Role of Boxing in American Society* (1988), is a good source of information about several boxers, including Frazier. Bert Randolph Sugar, ed., *The Great Fights* (1981), presents Frazier's major bouts in detail in this rich history. David Remnick, *King of the World* (1998), describes the major cultural changes that swept boxing and much of America in the 1960s and early 1970s. His account also describes the fascinating link between Ali and Frazier.

R. Jake Sudderth

FRAZIER, Walt, II ("Clyde") (*b.* 29 March 1945 in Atlanta, Georgia), professional basketball player whose quick hands and unflappable demeanor led the New York Knicks to two world championships in the 1970s and earned him entry to the Naismith Memorial Basketball Hall of Fame.

Frazier was the oldest of nine children born to Walt Frazier, Sr., and Eula Frazier. Walt, Sr., a hustler, was not around much for his children, forcing Frazier to become a surrogate father to his seven sisters and one brother. He grew up in a modest duplex in segregated Atlanta, playing basketball on dirt playgrounds with older children. Frazier attended Howard High School, captaining the baseball, basketball, and football teams. He was an All-City player on the basketball court, but it was his ability to throw a football sixty yards on the fly with pinpoint accuracy that most attracted the college scouts. He declined several scholarship offers because they came without the assurance that he would play quarterback. "There wasn't a big market for black quarterbacks," explained Frazier, so he chose basketball and, on the advice of a man he knew from church, attended Southern Illinois University at Carbondale on a scholarship.

After averaging twenty-five points per game for the Salukis during his freshman year (1963–1964), Frazier feuded with the basketball coach Jack Hartman during his sophomore season. Despite being benched for much of the latter part of the year, he earned Division II All-America honors for the second consecutive year. Frazier's schoolwork began to suffer, and he stopped going to classes and considered dropping out of college. In the summer of 1965 he married

Walt Frazier (*left*) accepting the Most Valuable Player trophy for the 1971 ABA-NBA All-Star Game. Associated Press

his college girlfriend, Marsha; they had a son. The marriage lasted one and a half years. Frazier never remarried.

Frazier's poor academic record precluded him from playing basketball in the 1965–1966 season. While studying to restore his eligibility, Frazier was allowed to practice with the Salukis. There was one caveat: Coach Hartman forbade Frazier to touch the ball on offense. "I had to play defense every day," recalled Frazier. He learned that playing strong defense required more than just quickness, reflexes, and instinct. Frazier later noted, "You had to be smart to play defense. You had to watch your man, see what he does." Frazier resumed playing for the team in the 1966–1967 season. He averaged 18.2 points per game and was named as a Division I All-American. He also was chosen as the Most Valuable Player of the then-prestigious National Invitation Tournament when Southern Illinois defeated Marquette University at Madison Square Garden to gain the championship.

Months later Frazier was selected as the fifth pick in the first round of the 1967 professional basketball draft by the New York Knicks. Forgoing his final year of collegiate eligibility, the six-foot, four-inch guard signed a three-year, $100,000 contract with New York. Frazier started slowly, but was energized when the coach William "Red" Holzman took over for Dick McGuire midway through the 1967–1968 season. Holzman's emphasis on an aggressive defense and penetrating guard play utilized Frazier's strengths as a player, and his court time and confidence soared.

Frazier became the anchor of a Knicks team that included the future Hall of Famers Willis Reed, Bill Bradley, and Dave DeBusschere. "The Knicks were the first team where everybody played defense, and played it all over the court," recalled Frazier. With hands described by an opponent as "quicker than a lizard's tongue," Frazier captured his first of seven consecutive selections to the National Basketball Association (NBA) All-Defensive First Team in 1968–1969. "The flies have heard about me, and don't come around anymore," said Frazier, referring to opposing guards who adjusted their game when facing him. "They had to think about where I was and change the way they operated."

On the strength of their team defense, the Knicks reached the Eastern Conference finals in 1968–1969 and the NBA finals in 1969–1970. In the latter season, they won eighteen straight games, setting an NBA record. New York finished the season with the NBA's best record (60–22), despite ranking only ninth in the league in scoring. They allowed just 105.9 points per game, nearly six points fewer than their closest competitor. It was during that year that Madison Square Garden fans initiated the popular roar "Dee-fense, Dee-fense." With 36 points, 19 assists, 7 rebounds, and 5 steals in game seven of the 1970 finals

against the Los Angeles Lakers, Frazier led the Knicks to their first-ever championship. Although his play was somewhat overshadowed by that of his injured teammate Willis Reed, who limped onto the court during warm-ups and scored the game's first two baskets, Frazier gave one of the best performances ever in a championship game.

Knicks fans not only admired Frazier's defense and penetrating drives—they loved his cool, calm on-court demeanor. He never argued with officials and, according to his teammate Bill Bradley, the guard played with a "smooth and effortless grace, as if he were a dancer revealing the beauty of a body in movement." Off the court, Frazier was also the embodiment of cool. He became well known for his after-hours partying, Rolls-Royce car, and stylish, eye-catching wardrobe, which included expensive furs and wide-brimmed hats. After the movie *Bonnie and Clyde* came out in 1967, Frazier's affinity for outlandish headwear led the team trainer Danny Whelan to nickname him "Clyde."

Frazier blossomed into a major scoring threat in the 1970–1971 season, averaging 21.7 points per game, his highest scoring output as a Knick. In the middle of the 1971–1972 season, the Knicks traded for Frazier's longtime rival, the guard Earl Monroe. Many thought the two could not coexist, but the Knicks returned to the NBA finals that season (where they lost to the Lakers). The next year, Frazier continued to flourish offensively, notching a career-high 23.2 points per game. With Frazier and Monroe in the backcourt for a full season, the Knicks beat the Boston Celtics in the Eastern Conference finals and then defeated the Lakers to capture the 1973 NBA title.

Although Frazier continued to excel, earning three straight All-Star selections, the Knicks declined, missing the play-offs in 1975 and 1976. On the eve of the 1977–1978 season, Frazier was traded to the Cleveland Cavaliers as compensation for the signing of the guard Jim Cleamons. The flamboyant guard who had fallen in love with New York City was devastated by the move. Hobbled by a chronic foot injury, Frazier suffered through two subpar years with the Cavaliers before being released just three games into the 1979–1980 season. Frazier retired, and in December 1979 the Knicks raised his number 10 jersey to the rafters at Madison Square Garden.

Based in Atlanta, Frazier worked as a player agent before moving back to New York to serve as the host of an upscale sports bar. He spent much of his retirement in tranquil Saint Croix in the Virgin Islands, purchasing a house and a thirty-eight-foot trimaran and earning his captain's license. In 1989 Frazier was hired as an analyst on Knicks broadcasts. The colorful commentator delighted fans with a stream of creative, often rhyming phrases. To Frazier, a Patrick Ewing basket became a "Ewing doing"; a guard driving toward the hoop was "orchestrating and penetrating"; and a team that scored after an unselfish possession was "swishing and dishing." Frazier remained an active sports broadcaster into the new century, and vividly described his love of language in *Word Jam: An Electrifying, Mesmerizing, Gravity-Defying Guide to a Powerful and Awesome Vocabulary* (2001).

Frazier was elected to the Naismith Memorial Basketball Hall of Fame in 1987 and was named as one of the NBA's fifty greatest players in 1996. He brought the role of the guard into prominence both on the offensive and defensive ends of the court. An excellent defender, a fine scorer, and a solid rebounder, he also possessed the unselfish ability to make his teammates better players. But when the situation demanded it, Frazier knew how to take control. After scoring forty-three points in a 1970 game he said, "I always look for the open man and tonight I was the open man." As always, Frazier's personal and professional personas were one and the same—cool.

★

An early look into Frazier's persona on and off the court, including an inventory of his wardrobe, is his own *Rockin' Steady: A Guide to Basketball and Cool* (1974). His autobiography is *Walt Frazier: One Magic Season and a Basketball Life* (1988). For details of the magical 1969–1970 Knicks season see *Knicks: New York's 1970 NBA Champion* (2000), a collection of articles from the *New York Daily News*. Stan Isaacs, "The Voice of Rhyme and Reason," *Newsday* (4 Mar. 1990), looks at Frazier's emergence as a colorful radio and television analyst. Bob Raissman, "Clyde's Mentors Won't Be Forgotten," *Daily News* (20 Nov. 1998), describes Frazier's relationships with Red Holzman and Jack Hartman.

DANNY MASSEY

FRICK, Ford Christopher (*b.* 19 December 1894 near Wawaka, Indiana; *d.* 8 April 1978 in Bronxville, New York), sportswriter, radio broadcaster, and baseball executive who first served as president of the National League and from 1951 to 1965 as national commissioner of baseball.

Frick, born on a farm near the town of Wawaka, was one of five children (and the only son) of Jacob and Emma (Prickett) Frick. After graduating from high school in 1910 he worked for a year on the Ft. Wayne, Indiana, *Gazette* before enrolling at DePauw University. He worked his way through college writing sports for papers in Indiana and in Chicago. As a boy, Frick had wanted to be a ballplayer and at DePauw was on both the baseball and track teams. The summer after receiving his B.A. in 1915, he played first base with the Walsenburg, Colorado, semiprofessional team; in the fall of that year he turned to teaching business English at the Walsenburg high school, then at Colorado College in Colorado Springs. Frick married Eleanor Cowing on 15 September 1916; they had one son. A year's stint as a re-

Ford Frick, 1941. ASSOCIATED PRESS AP

porter on the Colorado Springs *Gazette* followed in 1917, but during World War I he worked for the Veterans Bureau in Denver. With the war's end, Frick went back to reporting, joining the staff of the Denver *Rocky Mountain News,* and later in 1919 returned to the Colorado Springs paper as a columnist. His work came to the attention of Arthur Brisbane, editor of the New York *Evening Journal,* a Hearst newspaper, and in 1922 Frick was offered a job on the other New York newspaper, the *American;* in 1923 he transferred to the New York *Evening Journal.*

For the next eleven years Frick wrote a daily sports column combining news and commentary in the enthusiastic, hero-worshipping style made popular by his near contemporary, the sportswriter Grantland Rice. In addition, between 1924 and 1933 Frick, who generally covered the New York Yankees, was a ghostwriter for articles by Babe Ruth, Lou Gehrig, and the Yankees manager Miller Huggins. Concurrently, between 1930 and 1934 Frick did a daily sports broadcast in New York, including the first radio coverage of Brooklyn Dodgers home games in 1931 and programs devoted to the New York Giants — Dodgers games. These programs won him the friendship of Giants manager John McGraw, which proved instrumental in changing the course of Frick's career.

With McGraw's backing, Frick was appointed the publicity director for the National League in 1934, and later that year was elected president. In the seventeen years he served in that position, Frick took the league through the challenges of the Great Depression, World War II player shortages, and the bitter struggle over racial integration of the game. At first his fellow baseball writers were skeptical of Frick's executive skills (especially criticizing his indecision in arbitrating confrontations between feisty players like Dizzy Dean and Leo Durocher and the umpires) and accused him of being a front man for the baseball club owners. By 1951, however, Frick had racked up a number of executive accomplishments: putting several teams on better financial footing; overcoming resistance to night games, thereby greatly increasing attendance; adding to the number of players on each team; increasing players' salaries; and defending the entry of the first black player in the major leagues (Jackie Robinson, who played for the Dodgers) in 1947. When the St. Louis Cardinals threatened to strike rather than play against Robinson, Frick announced that strikers would be suspended, stating, "This is the United States of America, and one citizen has as much right to play as another. The National League will go down the line with Robinson whatever the consequence." Frick himself was proudest of being one of the originators of the idea for a baseball museum and library in Cooperstown, New York. The National Baseball Hall of Fame and Museum was established in 1939; Frick was later chairman of the board.

When baseball commissioner Kenesaw Mountain Landis died in 1944, Frick was the choice of many club owners to succeed him, but he lost out to Albert ("Happy") Chandler, a former U.S. senator from Kentucky. Chandler was not reelected as commissioner in 1951, and this time Frick was chosen for the post, becoming the third national commissioner and first baseball insider to hold the position. In the fourteen years he served, he increased revenues by pushing for the construction of all-weather, all-purpose stadiums and television coverage of games, and he presided over the expansion of the American and National Leagues with teams from coast to coast. Refusing to intervene when the Giants and the Dodgers decided to leave New York for California, his only comment was, "It's a league matter, not for the commissioner's office." Another of his controversial positions was upholding baseball's exemption from federal antitrust laws. Frick defended the reserve clause in players' contracts, which prohibited players from acting as free agents and prevented them from accepting offers from other teams before their contracts expired. Frick was called to Washington, D.C., seventeen times to testify before congressional committees on this issue. Once again, sportswriters accused him of passivity and acting in the owners' interests. Nor was his popularity among fans enhanced by an alleged remark in 1961 (which he later denied making) to the effect that if Roger Maris broke Babe Ruth's season home run record, the statistic should be entered in the record books with an asterisk. (Ruth had hit 60 homers in a season of 154 games; Maris ended 1961 having homered 61 times but in the course of an expanded season of 162 games. No asterisk is in the record books.)

In 1970, five years after he retired from office, Frick's contributions to baseball were recognized by his election to the National Baseball Hall of Fame. He died in Lawrence Hospital in Bronxville, having been in ill health for several years as a result of a series of strokes. He was interred at Christ Church (Episcopal) in Bronxville.

The baseball commissioner with the dignified, low-key manner contrasted with the passionate fan Frick had always been and the man who considered himself "still a newspaperman at heart" and missed the excitement of the press box. Being commissioner was "a lonely job," Frick admitted. But his remark on being elected to the Hall of Fame summarizes him best: "I've always been a lucky guy. I've always been at the right place at the right time."

★

Frick's papers are housed in the National Baseball Library, part of the National Baseball Hall of Fame in Cooperstown, New York. He was the ghostwriter of *Babe Ruth's Own Book of Baseball* (1978). His *Games, Asterisks* [an allusion to his alleged remark on the Maris-Ruth home run record controversy], *and People: Memoirs of a Lucky Fan* (1973), include both a defense of his positions as commissioner and chapters on his early days as a reporter, the color-line issue, and baseball's nationwide expansion. Further information on Frick's early career is found in *Current Biography* (1954), and in Jerome Holtzman, *No Cheering in the Press Box* (1974), which gives a full account of the founding of the National Baseball Hall of Fame and provides an update of Frick's career in his own words. Background information on the issues Frick faced can be found in *The Imperfect Diamond: The Story of Baseball's Reserve System and the Men Who Fought to Change It* (1980), by Lee Lowenfish and Tony Lupien; and *American Baseball* 3: *From Postwar Expansion to the Electronic Age* (1983), by David Voigt. Obituaries are in the *New York Times* (10 Apr. 1978), and the *Sporting News* (22 Apr. 1978).

ELEANOR F. WEDGE

FRISCH, Frank Francis ("Frankie") (*b.* 9 September 1898 in Queens, New York; *d.* 12 March 1973 in Wilmington, Delaware), baseball second baseman for the New York Giants and St. Louis Cardinals; manager for the Cardinals, Pittsburgh Pirates, and Chicago Cubs; broadcaster for the Boston Braves and New York Giants; and Baseball Hall of Fame inductee.

Frisch was the second of four sons of Franz Frisch, a wealthy lace linen manufacturer, and Katherine Stahl, a homemaker. After graduating from Fordham Preparatory School in 1916, Frisch attended Fordham University,

Frankie Frisch, 1934. ASSOCIATED PRESS AP

where he was a sprinter on the track team and captained the basketball, baseball, and football teams, earning the halfback's position on Walter Camp's All-American second team in 1918. After his sophomore year in 1919, Frisch signed with the New York Giants, managed by John Mc-Graw, a strict disciplinarian and fiery leader who was a future Hall of Fame member. McGraw liked Frisch's scrappy play and taught his protege the physical skills, mental toughness, and strategies that would contribute to Frisch's success as a player and manager.

The Giants won four consecutive National League pennants between 1921 and 1924, and the World Series Championships in 1921 and 1922, in large part because of Frisch's hitting, base running, and fielding. In 1921 Frisch hit .341, led the National League with 49 stolen bases, and batted .300 in the Giants' World Series victory over the New York Yankees. In 1922 he hit .327 against the league and .471 against Yankee pitchers as the Giants again captured the World Series. Frisch enjoyed one of his best offensive seasons in 1923, leading the league in hits (223) and total bases (311) and reaching career highs in batting average (.348) and home runs (12). In 1924 Frisch hit .328 and tied for the league lead with 121 runs while serving as captain and receiving a team-high salary of $17,500.

Although Frisch, who threw right-handed, played third

base and shortstop, second base was his main position. Despite permanent injuries to his right hand, Frisch, who stood five feet, eleven inches tall and weighed 165 pounds, displayed the quickness and range that made him one of the finest defensive second basemen of his era, attaining the highest fielding percentage for National League second basemen in four seasons. Dubbed the "Fordham Flash" by sportswriters, Frisch stole 419 bases in his career. A natural left-sided batter, Frisch used an awkward cross-handed grip when batting from the right side, but McGraw worked with him to adopt the traditional hand-over-hand grip. Frisch became one of the finest switch hitters in baseball history, hitting .300 or above in thirteen seasons.

Frisch hit a respectable .331 in 1925, but the Giants slipped to a distant second-place finish behind the Pittsburgh Pirates. Although the highest-paid Giant player for three consecutive years, Frisch, who suffered financial losses when the Florida land boom collapsed, held out for more money, reporting late to spring training in 1926. The unsuccessful holdout and the Giants' poor season probably contributed to the strained relationship between Frisch and McGraw. After the 1926 season the Giants traded Frisch, who hit .314, to the St. Louis Cardinals for Rogers Hornsby, a future Hall of Fame second baseman, who had also fallen out of favor with management.

Though the Hornsby trade angered St. Louis fans, Frisch won them over with his fiery, competitive play in 1927. He led National League second basemen in fielding percentage and assists and set a major-league record for second basemen by handling 1,059 chances. Offensively, he hit .337, led the league with 48 stolen bases, and struck out only 10 times in 617 at bats, setting the major-league record for fewest strikeouts in a season by a switch hitter. The Cardinals won National League pennants in 1928 and 1930. In 1931 Frisch was named the league's most valuable player, leading the league with twenty-eight stolen bases and the Cardinals to the World Series championship. He considered this the best team of his career. Frisch became manager in 1933 and continued to play second base. In 1934 he led the hard-playing, colorful players known as the "Gas House Gang" to a World Series championship. He managed the Cardinals through 1938, followed by stints with Pittsburgh (1940–1946), and the Chicago Cubs (1949–1951), but never managed another World Series winner.

Frisch worked as a baseball radio announcer in Boston in 1939, a radio announcer for the New York Giants from 1947 to 1948, and a radio and television announcer from 1952 to 1956. His wife, Ada E. Lucy, whom he had married in 1923, died in 1971. They had no children. In June 1972 he married Augusta Kass. Frisch, an avid gardener who listened to classical music, died from critical injuries suffered in an automobile accident. He is buried in the Woodlawn Cemetery in the Bronx, New York.

During his nineteen-year career Frisch's competitive nature and well-rounded play contributed to his teams' winning eight National League pennants and four World Series championships. Known as a clutch hitter capable of putting the ball into play, Frisch achieved a career batting average of .316 and was one of the most difficult batters to strike out in baseball history, fanning only 272 times in 9,112 plate appearances—an average of one strike out every 33.5 at-bats. Considered one of the best second basemen of his era, Frisch led the National League in stolen bases three times and was selected the league's Most Valuable Player in 1931. Frisch played in the first two All-Star games in 1933 and 1934, stroking the National League's first home run in each contest. He was inducted into the National Baseball Hall of Fame in 1947.

★

The National Baseball Hall of Fame in Cooperstown, New York, has a file on Frisch containing clippings and original documents. Frisch's autobiography, *Frank Frisch: The Fordham Flash* (1962), covers his long career as a player and manager. Bob Broeg, *The Pilot Light and the Gas House Gang* (1980), provides stories and anecdotes about Frisch and baseball players, managers, and executives who influenced his career. Leonard Koppett, *The Man in the Dugout: Baseball's Top Managers and How They Got That Way* (1993), discusses Frisch's managerial style. Obituaries are in the *New York Times* (13 Mar. 1973), and the *Sporting News* (24 Mar. 1973).

PAUL A. FRISCH

FULKS, Joseph Franklin ("Joe") (*b.* 26 October 1921 in Birmingham, Kentucky; *d.* 21 March 1976 in Eddyville, Kentucky), one of the most prolific scorers in professional basketball. He held the single-game National Basketball Association scoring record of sixty-three points for nearly ten years.

Fulks was born in a farmhouse outside Birmingham, Kentucky, and began playing basketball before he was ten. From an early age he loved shooting, which would be true throughout his career. He began his high school years at Birmingham High, where he stayed only three years before transferring to Kuttawa High School when the family moved. His high school coach at Birmingham wanted to alter his shooting style because Fulks shot in an unorthodox manner that emphasized his great leaping ability (and emulated the style of a Birmingham High player whom Fulks had idolized when he was in grade school). The coach at Kuttawa was more tolerant of the young man, who had grown from a six-foot-tall freshman to nearly six feet, five inches by the time of his junior year in high school. That year (1938) Fulks led his team to the Kentucky State Tournament semifinals as he broke the state scoring record and was voted All-State.

Joe Fulks, 1949. AP/WIDE WORLD PHOTOS

Following graduation Fulks enrolled in Millsaps College in Jackson, Mississippi, in the fall of 1940, but he soon transferred to Murray State Teachers College in Kentucky, where he met his future wife, Mary Sue Gillespie. Fulks averaged 13.2 points per game in forty-seven games for Murray State and was later elected to the National Association of Intercollegiate Athletics Basketball Hall of Fame (1952). He also was selected as a Kentucky Intercollegiate Athletic Conference All-Star. Fulks's college career was cut short when he enlisted in the Marines in 1943; he served in the South Pacific during World War II in addition to playing with a Marine All-Star team.

Following the war Fulks remained with the Marines, playing for the All-Star Leathernecks, who toured the United States. Fulks left the Marines in 1946 at the rank of sergeant. His great shooting attracted bidders from both the National Basketball League (NBL) and the newly formed Basketball Association of America (BAA), though most had never seen him play and were relying on second-hand accounts of his basketball prowess. Fulks turned down a one-year $5,000 contract offer from Eddie Gottlieb, the owner of the Philadelphia Warriors of the BAA, who then upped the offer to $8,000 for the year plus a new car. It was a good deal for both men. During his first year in the BAA (1946–1947) Fulks played forward and scored

1,389 points, an average of 23.2 points per game, which led the league. He also led the league in field goals made and attempted as well as free throws made and attempted. The Warriors team was the first champion of the BAA, defeating the Chicago Stags four games to one in the league playoffs.

During the next two years Fulks led and finished second in the league (to George Mikan) in scoring; he was named All-BAA for three years. The Warriors lost in the BAA finals in 1947–1948. In February of 1949 Fulks scored sixty-three points against the Indianapolis Jets, a professional record for points in one game that stood for ten years, until the Los Angeles Lakers' Elgin Baylor scored sixty-four points in 1959. Amazingly Fulks's record, set in a 108–87 victory, came before 1954, when the National Basketball Association (NBA) introduced the twenty-four-second clock, which speeded up play and increased scoring. Before 1954 teams averaged about eighty points per game (the highest-scoring team averaged eighty-four points per game) and shot about thirty percent from the field. In his record-setting game Fulks made twenty-seven of fifty-six shots and solidified his shooting reputation nationally. Many basketball observers saw this as one of the greatest factors in the success of professional basketball at that time. Fulks was one of the first players to popularize the jump shot, and he acquired the nickname "Jumpin' Joe" for that reason.

In 1949 the BAA and the NBL merged to form the NBA, with an unwieldy seventeen teams. Fulks and the Warriors both performed poorly, but the next year (1950–1951) both returned to prominence, with the Warriors winning the regular season title in the Eastern Division of the NBA and Fulks becoming the scoring leader on the team with an average of 18.7 points per game. In the 1951–1952 and 1952–1953 seasons Fulks and the Warriors declined. He was no longer the team scoring leader, having yielded that distinction to Paul Arizin and then to Neil Johnston, but he still averaged 15.1 and 11.9 points per game, respectively,

in those years. In his last season (1953–1954), Fulks averaged 2.5 points per game. He had never been particularly fast or a good defender, so his lack of scoring indicated to everyone that his career was at an end. He retired at the age of thirty-two. At the time of his retirement Fulks was the second-highest career average scorer in the NBA (behind George Mikan), with an average of 16.4 points per game. He was selected All-BAA First Team in the 1947–1948 and 1948–1949 seasons and to the NBA All-Star Game in 1951 and 1952.

After his retirement Fulks worked in various jobs, most notably as a production supervisor for GAF Corporation in Calvert City, Kentucky. He and his wife had four children. In 1970 he was named to the NBA's Silver Anniversary Team, and in 1978 he was elected posthumously to the Naismith Memorial Basketball Hall of Fame. Shortly after being hired as athletic director at Kentucky State Penitentiary, Fulks was murdered at age fifty-four in an argument (supposedly over a gun). At the time he was estranged from his wife and living with his parents in Benton, Kentucky. He is buried in Birmingham Cemetery.

Fulks was considered by many to be the first professional shooting star, displaying an ability to make a variety of shots. Over time he changed from a two-handed to a one-handed shooter. Called "the greatest basketball player in the country" by *Sporting News* in 1949 after his record-setting scoring, he electrified fans with his outside shooting.

★

There is no biography of Fulks and few chapters in any books or articles that are particularly informative regarding his life. His death was noted in a short *New York Times* article (22 Mar. 1976), but there was no formal obituary. The Joe Fulks file at the Naismith Memorial Basketball Hall of Fame has clippings and accounts of games, but because it was compiled posthumously there are gaps in information.

MURRY R. NELSON

G

GABLE, Dan(iel) (*b.* 25 October 1948 in Waterloo, Iowa), the greatest amateur wrestler and wrestling coach in United States history.

Born and raised in Waterloo, Iowa, Gable was the only son and second child of Mack, a blue-collar worker at the local John Deere plant, and Katie Gable. At age four, Gable became active in the Waterloo Young Men's Christian Association (YMCA) and participated actively in their programs until he was fourteen. On several occasions Gable credited his YMCA experiences for their positive role in helping to shape both his values and his athletic career. When he was eight and nine years old, Gable was on the Waterloo YMCA swimming team. He was an intense, fearless, and determined competitor who had a strong will to win. This attitude, toughness, and relentless work ethic would define the rest of his life. In the 1958–1959 season he was undefeated in the backstroke and was on the eighty-yard medley relay team that won the event in the State YMCA Midget Division Championships. On his tenth birthday his parents gave him a set of weights, which—after some prodding from his mother—he used to his advantage. The tragic murder of his older sister when Gable was fifteen years old also had a profound influence on his life. His parents wanted to move, but Gable said no criminal was going to drive him out of his house and hometown.

Iowa and amateur wrestling (not to be confused with entertainment-oriented television wrestling) enjoy a special relationship. Amateur wrestling is important in Iowa, where duel meets frequently draw more than 5,000 fans. To watch an Iowa wrestler compete is to witness a private war fought in public between two finely honed combatants. Like a school-yard fight, it's whip or be whipped. Gable's wrestling career started at Waterloo West High School in the ninety-five-pound weight category. Gable was a four-time state champion and undefeated in high school wrestling (64–0). His college record was 118–1 at Iowa State University. He won 117 matches in a row, losing only to Larry Owings in the 1970 National Collegiate Athletic Association (NCAA) Championships. Gable was NCAA champion in 1968 and 1969; and the tournament's Most Valuable Player in 1969 at 137 pounds. He was selected the nation's outstanding wrestler by the Amateur Athletic Union (AAU) in 1970, and the United States Wrestling Federation in 1971. Gable was the *Amateur Wrestling News* "Man of the Year" in 1970.

Gable won the world lightweight freestyle championship in Sofia, Bulgaria, in August 1971 and at 150 pounds was the only U.S. wrestler to defeat the Soviets in a freestyle wrestling meet in Moscow on 10 February 1972. Gable was unscored on in his six-match march to a gold medal in the Munich Olympic games in 1972, the only wrestler in Olympic history to achieve that degree of success. The day after winning the Olympic gold medal, he resumed his training routine by running four miles.

Dan Gable *(left)* wrestling Stephanos Ionidis, 1972. AP/WIDE WORLD PHOTOS

When he returned from Munich, Gable took a job as assistant wrestling coach at the University of Iowa. As a coach, he continued his pursuit of excellence. He was named head coach in 1977. He won NCAA "Rookie Coach of the Year" honors when the Hawkeyes went 17–1–1, and placed third in the NCAA Championships. He went on to coach the University of Iowa to nine straight NCAA titles from 1978 to 1986. In his twenty years as the head wrestling coach at the University of Iowa, his teams won every Big Ten Championship and earned fifteen NCAA national team titles. During that time he coached 152 All-Americans, 106 Big Ten individual champions, and forty-five individual national champions, on eleven scholarships per year. Gable pioneered the use of video in coaching wrestling. His Hawkeye wrestlers had a duel meet record of 355 wins, twenty-one losses, and five ties. In addition to being consistent Big Ten winners, they never lost a meet in Iowa City, their home venue.

Gable was the Olympic head wrestling coach in 1980 and 1984, co-coach in 2000, and was the U.S. freestyle coach for the 1976 and 1988 Olympics. He also was head coach for five World teams, ten World Cup teams, the 1986 Goodwill Games, and several All-Star teams sent to Europe and the Soviet Union. In 1984 he turned down an offer of nearly $3 million to coach at Oklahoma State University. Gable did not even consider the offer, claiming, "Everything I like to do is in this state. I've been loyal to Iowa. I've represented it to people all over the world. I'm not money driven." In January 1997 the bespectacled and balding Gable underwent hip replacement surgery at University Hospital in Iowa City, Iowa. The following March, five of

Iowa's six finalists in the NCAA tournament won individual titles, equaling a feat his team achieved first in 1986. After the 1997 season he took a one-year leave of absence, and in January 1998 had his second hip replaced. In March 1998 Iowa won another NCAA wrestling championship.

In 1980 Gable was named to the National Wrestling Hall of Fame, and to the U.S. Olympic Hall of Fame in 1985. He and his wife, Kathy, have four girls. At the beginning of the twenty-first century, he was serving as assistant to the athletic director of the University of Iowa, promoting amateur wrestling all over the world, coaching potential Olympic wrestlers in the local sports club, and being considered as a possible Republican candidate for governor of Iowa.

Gable dominated his sport as few others ever have. Only a handful of athletes, which might include Jim Thorpe, Johnny Weissmuller, Mildred "Babe" Didrikson, Wayne Gretzky, and Tiger Woods have ever been as controlling in their sport, and few, if any, coaches have comparable records of success.

★

Dan Gable, *Coaching Wrestling Successfully* (1998), contains biographical information. There are three biographies: Stephen T. Holland's *Takin' Dan Gable* (1983), Russ Smith's *Dan Gable: "The" Wrestler* (1983), and Nolan Zavoral's *A Season on the Mat: Dan Gable and the Pursuit of Perfection* (1998). Zavoral's biography is the best. A considerable section of Michael Chapman's *A History of Wrestling in Iowa: From Gotch to Gable* (1981), is about Gable. Two magazine articles about Gable are excellent: John Irving's "Gorgeous Dan," *Esquire* (Apr. 1973), and particularly Scott Raab's "Nasty Dan and His Wrestling Empire," *Sport* (Apr. 1988). Finally, University of Iowa Sports Information and the *New York Times* (31 Aug. 1971; 11 Feb. 1972; 22 Mar. 1988; 24 Jan. 1997; 24 Mar. 1997; 15 July 1997; 9 Jan. 1998; and 15 July 2001) are indispensable.

KEITH MCCLELLAN

GAINES, Clarence Edward, Sr. ("Bighouse") (*b.* 21 May 1923 in Paducah, Kentucky), Hall of Fame college basketball coach and leading African-American sports figure who spent forty-seven seasons at Winston-Salem State University, North Carolina, amassing 828 career wins.

Gaines was the son of Lester and Olivia Bolen Gaines. An all-around student at Lincoln High School in Paducah, he played the trumpet in the school band, excelled in football as an offensive lineman, making the All-State team, and also played for the basketball team. Gaines graduated from Lincoln in 1941 as the class salutatorian. Given the segregated state of southern education at the time, it was virtually inevitable that he would attend an African-American college. The family's doctor suggested Morgan State University in Baltimore, Maryland, his alma mater, where the football coach Eddie Hurt was his friend. Oral tradition has it that shortly after Gaines's arrival at Morgan State he attained his famous moniker "Bighouse." The business manager, observing Gaines's six-foot, two-inch, 250-pound physique, declared, "Boy, I never seen anything bigger than you but a house." Intending to become a dentist, Gaines majored in chemistry, graduating with a B.S. in 1945. At Morgan, football was his principal sport—he was named as an All-American—but he also participated in basketball and track.

At Hurt's suggestion, Gaines decided to spend a year as an assistant football coach at Winston-Salem Teachers College. Arriving in North Carolina, Gaines found a school with a total enrollment of under six hundred and a male enrollment, largely due to the wartime situation, of fewer than one hundred. Winston-Salem's football coach Brutus Wilson was a fellow Morgan State graduate who coached all sports at the tiny college; thus, when Wilson decided to move to nearby Shaw University, he literally took the athletic department with him. This left Gaines, at the age of twenty-three, in charge as the athletic director, athletic trainer, ticket manager, head football coach, and head basketball coach. Gaines coached the Winston-Salem Teachers College Rams football team for three seasons (1947–1949), compiling a record of 20–12–4 and being named the Central Intercollegiate Athletic Association (CIAA) Coach of the Year in 1948, when Winston-Salem finished 8–1. With veterans flooding into colleges under the GI Bill, Winston-Salem's enrollment and revenue grew, permitting Gaines in 1949 to give up football in order to concentrate on basketball. He also remained as the athletic director.

In 1950 Gaines married Clara Berry, a Latin teacher in Winston-Salem's public school system; they had a daughter and a son. Clarence Edward Gaines, Jr., eventually worked for the Chicago Bulls as a scout. Also in 1950, Gaines completed an M.A. in education from Teachers College, Columbia University, New York City.

Basketball at the historically African-American colleges in the South was growing in the 1940s under the influence of John McLendon, with whom Gaines developed a long-lasting professional and personal relationship and whose up-tempo playing style he followed. McLendon had learned basketball from the game's inventor, James Naismith, while a student at the University of Kansas, although he was not allowed to play on the segregated team. He began coaching in Durham, North Carolina, at North Carolina College (later North Carolina Central University) in 1940, remaining there until 1951. McLendon's teams ran, blocked shots, and pressed; their exploits, reported almost exclusively in the African-American press, were mostly unknown to whites but avidly followed by African Americans. As Gaines later recalled of his own athletes, "You couldn't get their name in the paper half the time." Regarding road trips, Gaines recalled that when his team traveled to Baltimore to play Morgan State, they stayed in an African American hotel in Richmond, not stopping along the way, because "Virginia was full of rebels." The segregated setup meant, however, that Gaines had an ironic recruiting advantage: "We picked up a lot of the top kids because there was no place for them to go." Colleges outside the segregated region of the southern and border states did not follow a rigid color line, but integrated teams were rare throughout the country.

In 1949 African-American college coaches organized the National Athletic Steering Committee, whose goal was to integrate postseason tournaments. In 1953 the National Association of Intercollegiate Athletics (NAIA), with its small-college membership, opened its Kansas City tournament to the African-American schools. Gaines's Winston-Salem teams went 80–55 in his first five seasons. The Rams ultimately won eight CIAA titles under his tutelage and won at least twenty games during eighteen of his seasons. Gaines was the recipient of the CIAA Basketball Tournament Outstanding Coach of the Year Award for the first time in 1953 and won that award on seven more occasions; six times he was named the CIAA Coach of the Year for basketball. In 1957 the National Collegiate Athletic Association (NCAA) created the College Division tournament, which was open to African-American schools. Nashville's Tennessee State College, now coached by Gaines's confidant McLendon, won the NAIA championship that year, the first all-African-American team and the first team from an African-American college to win a national championship tournament.

Gaines's 1961 team, his best yet, went 26–5, won the CIAA, and was led by the player Cleo Hill, who, when drafted by the St. Louis Hawks, became the first player from an African-American college to be selected first in the National Basketball Association (NBA) draft. In 1963 Gaines recruited his greatest player, Vernon Earl "The Pearl" Monroe, out of Philadelphia, Pennsylvania, where he had starred for John Bartram High School. Monroe found Gaines to be a strict disciplinarian who would call the parents if he were experiencing a problem with a player. Gaines counseled Monroe, as he did others, on the need for self-control, limiting "flamboyance" as one tried to fit into the greater world outside of the African-American community. Monroe's dramatic spin moves on the basketball court, however, were encouraged by his coach. The Rams won more than twenty games in each of Monroe's four seasons at Winston-Salem, but his senior year proved to be the climax. The Pearl averaged 41.5 points per game and scored 1,329 total points for the season (with three-point goals not yet in the rules), still the fourth-highest scoring college player in a season as of 2001. In 1967 the Rams won the NCAA College Division (later Division II) national championship, 77–74, over Southwest Missouri State. They were the first African-American college team to win an NCAA basketball title, and Gaines became the first African-American coach to be named the College Division National Coach of the Year. Monroe, selected by the Baltimore Bullets in the first round of the 1967 NBA draft, was selected as the Rookie of the Year in 1968.

By 1967 even the Atlantic Coast and Southeastern Conferences had integrated their student bodies and athletic teams, changing the recruiting situation immensely. Outstanding African-American student-athletes had far more options. Now widely known because of his national championship and Monroe's success, Gaines chose to remain at Winston-Salem, piling up victories, shaping lives, encouraging what he called the "development of a complete person" in his players, and participating in his profession. He became one of the most respected and frequently honored citizens of Winston-Salem. He served as the president of the CIAA (1970–1974), was a member of the U.S. Olympic Committee (1973–1976), belonged to the board of the Naismith Memorial Basketball Hall of Fame (1980–1990), and was the president of the National Association of Basketball Coaches (1989). Upon his retirement in 1993, his record stood at 828–446. At the time, he was college basketball's second-winningest coach. His position slipped to third place in 1997.

Gaines's forty-seven-year basketball coaching career at Winston-Salem State University (1946–1993) spanned the eras of African-American college basketball, from relative obscurity in segregation to growing recognition in the beginning stages of integration, to renewed relative obscurity. His greatest season, 1967, was an ironic climax to the world of African-American college athletics as it stood on the cusp of large-scale integration. He was inducted into the Naismith Memorial Basketball Hall of Fame in 1982.

★

Winston-Salem State University's "'Bighouse' Gaines Collection," donated by Gaines in 1997, is the repository of his career, and may be found on the website <http://www.wssu.edu/athletics/menbball/bighouse.htm>. The history of African-American college basketball, focusing on McLendon and Gaines, is treated in the eighth chapter of Billy Packer with Roland Lezenby, *The Golden Game* (1991). Gaines's relationship with Earl Monroe is described in Nelson George, *Elevating the Game: Black Men and Basketball* (1992). For a profile of Gaines, see Ralph Wiley, "College Basketball Preview 1990–1991: Bighouse," *Sports Illustrated* (19 Nov. 1990).

LAWSON BOWLING

GARCIAPARRA, (Anthony) Nomar (*b*. 23 July 1973 in Whittier, California), Red Sox shortstop who in 1997 recorded one of the best rookie seasons in baseball history, including a thirty-game hitting streak (an American League rookie record), a major league record for most RBI by a leadoff man (ninety-eight), and another for home runs by a rookie shortstop (thirty).

Garciaparra, the oldest of four children born to Ramon and Sylvia Garciaparra, grew up in southern California playing baseball, soccer, and football under the direction of his sports-infatuated father.

Garciaparra was named after the University of Southern California (USC) football star running back Anthony Davis. Garciaparra's mother was a USC fan who grew fond of the name Anthony after repeatedly hearing it over the loudspeaker. Garciaparra's Mexican-born father added the middle name Nomar—it's his own name spelled backward. During his youngest days, Garciaparra went by Anthony. When he started school and realized there were other Anthonys, he decided to go by Nomar.

From the time Garciaparra began playing T-ball at age six, he was so serious about the game that the other children's parents nicknamed him "No-Nonsense Nomar," a moniker that is still fitting. In his youth Garciaparra ex-

Nomar Garciaparra. AP/WIDE WORLD PHOTOS

celled at baseball and soccer and was a place kicker on his high school football team. Though he enjoyed all sports, baseball was his favorite, and his father forced him to learn every position so he'd respect them all.

"I never had a baseball hero or anything like that," Garciaparra told *Sports Illustrated*. "I loved the game just for the sake of playing it. I'd tell my dad from the time I was five or six, 'Teach me that. Don't tell me about who plays the game in the majors. Tell me how to play it.' I wanted to learn as much as I could about every position."

At the dinner table, father and son discussed strategy and outlined plays on napkins. The pair spent many afternoons honing Garciaparra's baseball skills. To motivate his son to become a hitter, Ramon paid him twenty-five cents for each hit but fined him double each time he swung but failed to make contact. Ramon hated to see his son strike out, especially by not swinging and risking a strikeout by just standing still. Garciaparra consequently learned to swing at nearly every pitch, and the system turned him into a formidable hitter unafraid to attack the ball.

In 1991 Garciaparra graduated from Saint John Bosco High School in Bellflower, California. The Milwaukee Brewers drafted him in the fifth round, though he never signed. Several colleges courted him as well, offering him scholarships in baseball, soccer, and/or football. Garciaparra chose to play baseball at the Georgia Institute of Technology.

In 1992 Garciaparra played with future professionals when he made the U.S. Olympic baseball team, which made it to the semifinals. He treated his Olympic experience as an opportunity to study baseball from a new angle and returned to college with renewed intensity. He specifically watched the other U.S. Olympic team shortstops, including Chris Gomez (who went on to play for the Padres). The Olympic team also played exhibition games before the start of major league games; seeing the pros in the dugout and watching them play inspired him to try harder. The season he returned, his junior year, Garciaparra helped lead Georgia Tech to the College World Series. Though the team lost the championship game, Garciaparra's performance earned him All-Tournament honors.

Garciaparra decided to forgo his senior year after the Boston Red Sox picked him in the first round of the June 1994 draft. He moved quickly through the ranks of the Boston minor league organization and in 1996 played Triple-A ball for the Pawtucket (Rhode Island) Red Sox. He proved himself a steady hitter, batting .343 in 43 games with 16 home runs and 46 RBI, though he was hampered by a hamstring tear and a sprained ankle. His teammates nominated him player of the year. Boston called Garciaparra up to the majors in late August 1996. His first major league hit was a home run. That year he played in twenty-four games, batting .241. He also smacked 4 home runs and had 16 RBI.

During 1997, his first full season in the majors, Garciaparra took the league by storm. Between 26 July and 29 August he had a thirty-game hitting streak, breaking the American League's rookie hitting streak record of twenty-six, set in 1943. Garciaparra led the AL in hits with 209 and in triples with eleven. He was named AL rookie of the year.

Garciaparra has become known for more than just his statistics; his eccentric rituals are also widely discussed. During the season Garciaparra never changes or washes his cap. He wears the same underwear to each game. He walks into the dugout toddler-style, placing both feet on every step—one foot, then the other. He tugs on his batting gloves before every pitch and taps his toes in the dirt. On the infield, he spits into his glove after nearly every pitch. Though many make fun of his fidgeting and call Garciaparra superstitious, he defends his quirks, brushing them off as routines that make him comfortable on the ballfield. While his skills on the diamond keep fans watching, Garciaparra's chiseled Hollywood features and bulging forearms keep the teenage girls swooning. *People* magazine named him one of the most eligible bachelors in the United States.

But Garciaparra is where he is today because of his devotion to baseball. During practice he fields with a child-size glove to make sure he doesn't get sloppy. Also, he has improved his batting average each season. He started at .241 during his twenty-four-game stint in 1996. In 1997 he batted .306 and steadily increased to .372 in 2000.

Part of the reason for his increase in average is his increase in size. Over the years Garciaparra has morphed from the 135 pounds he weighed in high school into 190 pounds of explosive muscle. During the off-season he is dedicated to strenuous muscle-building workouts. He first tried this approach after his 1995 season in the minors, which wore him out. He gained fifteen pounds in three months and discovered the next year that he had the power to hit homers. Garciaparra's workout regimen includes abdominal crunches and resistance training—fielding balls while tied to a bungee—and he does it every day from 9:00 A.M. to 4:30 P.M.

"I saw him at Georgia Tech," former Red Sox teammate Aaron Sele told *Sports Illustrated*. "He was a rail, just a skinny old shortstop. As I watched him develop, I knew why it happened. He's got an incredible desire. I don't know anybody who's more driven."

Since his rookie season, Garciaparra has been compared to legendary New York Yankees player Joe DiMaggio. He is, after all, the only right-hander in more than sixty years to hit as high as .372 since DiMaggio hit .381 in 1939.

Some baseball pundits predict that Garciaparra will be the first player in more than sixty years to hit .400. Baseball agent Scott Boras conducted a statistical study that shows that if Garciaparra keeps on pace, by age forty he will have tallied 513 home runs and 3,581 hits and have a career batting average of .336.

A potential barrier to these achievements is Garciaparra's likelihood of injury, given his high-intensity play; he spent much of the 2001 season out of commission following wrist surgery. If he does get back on track, it may be time to say, "Move over, DiMaggio."

★

For a synopsis of Garciaparra's career, see James Buckley, Jr., *Super Shortstops: Jeter, Nomar, and A-Rod* (2001). Among the more informative journal articles about Garciaparra are *Sports Illustrated* (1 Sept. 1997); *Sport* (Sept. 1998); and *Sports Illustrated* (5 Mar. 2001). Among newspaper articles, see the *Boston Globe* (11 Apr. 2001).

LISA FRICK

GARLITS, Don(ald) (*b.* 14 January 1932 in Tampa, Florida), legendary drag racer who won the American Hot Rod Association (AHRA) Championship fourteen times and the National Hot Rod Association (NHRA) Championship three times, and is also known for his work to make drag racing a safer sport.

Garlits's father, Edward Garlits, was a Westinghouse engineer in the 1920s. In collaboration with others in his laboratory, he invented both the electric fan and the electric iron. When his health began to fail, he left Pittsburgh for El Paso, Texas, then later opened a health food store and restaurant in New Jersey. As part of his newfound health food religion, he divorced his first wife around 1925 and married Helen Lorenz, a sixteen year old who worked in his store. They moved to Tampa, Florida, where Garlits was born.

Like his father, Garlits had a knack for tinkering with machines. When he was fourteen, he pulled engines out of cars and worked on them with his friends. Garlits graduated from a Tampa public high school in 1948, and his grades were good enough to get him a position in a bookkeeping office. But Garlits was not meant to be a bookkeeper. After only six months, he walked out of the office, never to return.

From there, he returned to his first love, working on cars. He worked for body shops, then for a radiator shop, but Garlits seem to have hit on something when he began working as a race car mechanic. Rather than enthusiastically embracing drag racing, he began doing it because it was the thing to do. Beginning in 1952, Garlits raced others on Tampa's deserted back roads, using a souped up 1927 Model T. Later he switched to a 1940 maroon Ford convertible with a Cadillac V-8 engine.

Taking a break from racing in 1952, he met Pat Bieger, an eighteen year old from Kentucky, while waterskiing. While courting her, Garlits left racing, going to work for American Can Company. They were married on 20 February 1953. His passion for racing could not be cooled, though. When he began accumulating speeding tickets from illegal races, his wife first dismissed them as his sowing wild oats, but that all changed when he told her he was going to upgrade the camshaft in their new Ford. Out for a Sunday drive one month after they were married, Garlits "inadvertently" passed the Lake Wales Drag Strip. He promised they would only watch. By the end of the day, Garlits had won his first trophy, an eight-inch plastic model with an angel perched on top. It was the first of many to come.

At the urging of Wally Parks, *Hot Rod* magazine editor, Garlits entered legal drag racing contests in the Tampa area and began winning races. By the late 1950s Garlits had built his first dragster, *Swamp Rat I.* Because it was not as well built as some of the cars used by his competitors, he earned the nickname Don Garbage. That attribution soon faded; it was replaced by the nickname Big Daddy, given to him by a track announcer in 1962. His dragster soon bested any competitor and broke records, racing a quarter mile in 12.1 seconds at 108.17 mph and in 1957 at a record speed of 176.4 mph.

Garlits dominated the East Coast in the late 1950s, but racers on the West Coast refused to believe that he could best their precision-built dragsters. They charged that he ran, according to Tony Sakkis, on "backwoods tracks with inferior timing devices." They even went so far as to his ignore his speed record of 180.00 mph in 8.90 seconds, achieved on 8 December 1958, because it happened in the East. Garlits went West and challenged his detractors at the track. His repeated wins showed them that his records were legitimate. Further evidence of his skill came on 1 August 1964 at a race in Great Meadows, New Jersey, when he became the first racer to break the 200-mph-speed barrier, twice. After that, very few disputed his prowess.

The secret to Garlits's wins was simple—large fuel lines. Bigger fuel lines produce more speed. To keep others from stealing his innovation, he concealed the lines along the rail frames of the car. Each successor to his original *Swamp Rat* contained improvements that made Garlits a winner in many of his races. Version six, with its improved engine, was the car that allowed him to break the 200-mph-speed barrier; in version fourteen he moved the engine to better protect the driver; version twenty-two, with an even larger engine, allowed him to break the 250-mph-speed barrier; and version thirty included a bubble canopy and Kevlar wheels (later replaced with thirteen-inch airplane tires). Garlits later donated number thirty to the Smithsonian Institution in Washington, D.C.

But all of these improvements and innovations did not come without cost. Version one's supercharger blew up, badly burning Garlits's hands; version thirteen's transmission exploded, taking off part of his right foot; a broken back resulted when one of his dragster's parachutes failed to open; and another time his dragster's opening parachutes jerked the car violently, resulting in a serious bladder injury for Garlits. Each time, Garlits, supported by his wife and three daughters, bounced back and redesigned his car to make it safer. In the process, he made the whole profession a little safer because other racers imitated his cars.

The man who helped mold the sport of drag racing wanted to make sure the history of drag racing and the efforts of its legendary drivers were preserved. Garlits opened his Museum of Drag Racing in Ocala in 1984. The museum contains fifty-five history-making drag racers, including his first hot rod and the first version of *Swamp Rat*.

Garlits continued racing until 1994. In 1986 he had experienced a hair-raising incident at Englishtown, New Jersey, in which *Swamp Rat 30* lifted its front wheels off the ground, spun around, and headed toward the rear staging area. Only because he accidentally applied the throttle did the car reverse itself and head back toward the raceway where he shut her down. Garlits stayed on the sidelines for the 1988 season but came back in 1989 for a limited engagement with his longtime friend and rival Shirley Muldowney. Three years later, in 1992, Garlits came back to racing with the thirty-second version of *Swamp Rat* in an effort to break the 300-mph-speed barrier, but during a practice run his deploying parachute caused a detached retina. Following the advice of doctors, Garlits elected to scale back his racing, doing only exhibitions with Muldowney and acting as curator for his museum. Still, the man known for inventing the Top Fuel dragster and a more fire-resistant driving suit continued to race, impressing the audience during his occasional performances. On 2 September 2001, at age sixty-nine, he drove over 300 mph at the U.S. Nationals at Indianapolis—the oldest driver to accomplish this feat.

★

Garlits wrote two books about his life experiences: *King of the Dragsters: The Story of Big Daddy "Don" Garlits* (1967), with Brock W. Yates, and *Close Calls* (1984), with Darryl E. Hicks. Tony Sakkis, *Drag Racing Legends* (1996), offers biographical material on Garlits; information about Garlits is also in *Sports Illustrated* (13 Aug. 1964, 27 July 1970, and 29 Sept. 1986).

BRIAN B. CARPENTER

GEHRIG, (Henry) Lou(is) (*b.* 19 June 1903 in New York City; *d.* 2 June 1941 in New York City), baseball player who, as a key member of the New York Yankee teams of the 1920s and 1930s, ranks among the greatest first basemen of all time.

Gehrig was born Heinrich Ludwig Gehrig to a German immigrant family in the Yorkville neighborhood of New York City. His three siblings all died in infancy, so he was raised as an only child in a household where his Danish-born mother, Christina Fack, earned the only reliable salary. There is an ongoing dispute as to the character and habits of his father, Heinrich Gehrig, a day laborer. Some accounts portray Heinrich as a man prone to drinking bouts and a failure at finding steady employment. However, Heinrich was defended by Lou Gehrig's wife, Eleanor, who claimed the experience of her father-in-law was much more typical than the Horatio Alger immigrant tales that dogged the public imagination. She also offered an atypical evaluation of his drinking habits, pointing out that taverns were part of respectable socializing in German culture and that Heinrich was more interested in companionship than intoxication in his tavern visits.

What is certain is that Gehrig developed an intense work ethic and a belief that success in sports was the key to his acceptance in American society. He worked hard to overcome the anti-German prejudice he encountered during World War I and starred on both the football and baseball teams at Manhattan's High School of Commerce. Over the objections of his mother, he traveled to Chicago to play in a game against their top school team. He hit a game-

Lou Gehrig. AP/WIDE WORLD PHOTOS

winning grand slam and received his first mention in newspapers.

In his senior year, Gehrig was recruited to play football at Columbia University, where his mother worked as a housekeeper for a fraternity. The summer before college, he played twelve games for the Hartford, Connecticut, farm team of the New York Giants, using the name Lou Lewis, as college athletes are forbidden from playing professional sports. College authorities discovered what Gehrig had done, and he was ruled ineligible for football for one year and lost two years of baseball eligibility.

Gehrig began his college football career playing running back and defensive end on a team that compiled a 4–4 record. His one year of college baseball produced more impressive results. Yankee scout Paul Krichell signed him for a $1,500 bonus, and Gehrig spent 1923 and 1924 playing in the minors with brief stints with the Yankees.

In both college and his early baseball years, Gehrig was perceived as aloof. Gehrig in turn resented the social snobbery he encountered at Columbia and the difficulty of gaining acceptance from the veterans of the Yankee team. A poignant example of the latter occurred when the Yankees headed to New Orleans for spring training in 1925. He was spotted by a coach glumly walking the streets in search of a moonlighting job, since his first paycheck would not be issued until the regular season began. The coach got Gehrig to request a salary advance and arranged for him to move in with three teammates to reduce his expenses. The move helped, but his teammates viewed Gehrig as unsociable for not joining the team for carousing that he could ill afford.

On 1 June 1925 Yankee first baseman Wally Pipp left a game complaining of a headache. Gehrig stepped in, and he did not relinquish that position for 2,130 games. Nicknamed the "Iron Horse" for his resilience, he played through many injuries, including at least seventeen wrist, hand, and finger fractures. Gehrig, who hit for both average and power, would have been the marquee player on any team except the Yankees, where he played his early years in the shadow of Babe Ruth and his later years in that of Joe DiMaggio.

Gehrig played at a time when he was compared with Hall of Fame first basemen such as Jimmie Foxx and Hank Greenberg, but his career statistics are so impressive their recitation can be almost numbing. His career total of 493 home runs and lifetime .340 batting average are a tribute to his rare combination of power and a selective eye. In seven seasons he was able to drive in 150 runs or more. In a game against Connie Mack's Philadelphia Athletics in 1932, Gehrig hit four consecutive home runs, setting an American League single-game record. He was chosen as the Most Valuable Player in the American League in 1927, 1931, 1934, and 1936, and he started at first base in the annual All-Star game from 1933, the first year the contest was held, until his final full season in 1938. In addition to his offensive contributions, Gehrig compiled a .991 fielding percentage that belied the common perception that he lacked agility. Gehrig was tall and stocky and frequently portrayed as a lumbering power hitter.

Gehrig was a complete player on the field, but his public image was hampered by his reticent manner and his preference for keeping his life private off the field. Detroit Tiger manager Mickey Cochrane once quipped that Gehrig said "Hello" on opening day, "Goodbye" on closing day, and very little in between. Even his marriage to the vivacious Eleanor Grace Twitchell in 1933 resulted in her settling down instead of Gehrig becoming more gregarious.

One source of frequent speculation was the rumor of a personality clash between Babe Ruth and Gehrig. Certainly the two teammates were very different in their approach to baseball, and life in general. Gehrig was quiet, workmanlike, and uneasy in the spotlight. Ruth took his talent for granted, led a frantic social life, and loved public attention. Yet there is very little evidence that these differences caused friction between the two.

A rift was created, but it started at the dinner table, not the ballpark. In 1934 Ruth and his daughter were having dinner at the house of Gehrig's parents. Christina Gehrig, a woman renowned for her sharp tongue, criticized the way Ruth's beloved daughter was dressed. Reportedly the Babe grew furious, and as a result refused to speak to his teammate until his retirement ceremony in 1939. The insult to his child was likely the spark that set afire Ruth's smoldering resentment that Gehrig was reaching the prime of his career at a time when his own skills had started to deteriorate. It is a testimony to the stubbornness and pride of both men that they remained silent so long.

Evaluating the career of Gehrig is problematic. He played in an era with just sixteen teams, when hitters with a .300 lifetime batting average wound up sitting on the bench, and hit against pitching staffs untouched by the ravages of expansion, so it is difficult to compare his career with those of players after 1962. Certainly his consistency was outstanding. Gehrig's balanced offensive and defensive contributions are equally exceptional. The fact that he compiled such impressive RBI totals batting behind Babe Ruth during much of his career is perhaps his most impressive career statistic.

But more impressive than any individual statistic is Gehrig's key position in the legendary Yankee dynasty. From Ruth, Gehrig, and DiMaggio to Mickey Mantle and Reggie Jackson, the Yankees boasted many of the dominant ballplayers over a fifty-year span. As a result, the team moved beyond regional popularity to develop a national following.

Sadly, Gehrig is as well known for the tragic illness that led to his early death as he is for his athletic achievements.

During 1938 he began to experience bouts of dizziness and difficulty moving his legs. Repeated medical examinations were inconclusive, so he finally traveled to the Mayo Clinic in Rochester, Minnesota, after playing his last game on 30 April 1939. Doctors diagnosed Gehrig with amyotrophic lateral sclerosis (ALS), a neuromuscular disease that is incurable. The Yankees responded by declaring 4 July 1939 "Lou Gehrig Day." At his ceremony, tired but proud, Gehrig said the legendary words that proved the depth of his quiet courage: "Fans, for the past two weeks you have been reading about a bad break I got. Yet today I consider myself the luckiest man on the face of the earth."

Later that year Gehrig accepted an honorary position with the New York City Parole Commission. He did this as he had played baseball—quietly, with no wish for publicity. His one public campaign was his battle with the New York tabloids, which exploited the medical ignorance of the time by claiming ALS was contagious and that Gehrig had infected his teammates. Only his close circle of friends realized how ill he was, and the nation was shocked to hear of his death in 1941. He is buried in Kensico Cemetery in Valhalla, New York.

In an era when flamboyance counted, Gehrig's quiet approach kept him from the accolades he deserved. His record of 2,130 straight games was broken by Cal Ripken, Jr., in 1995. His monument in Yankee Stadium is a tribute to his talent and character, but is now one among many Yankee monuments. Gehrig did not project the glamour of some of his contemporaries, but it is his accomplishments that are a testimony to this remarkable athlete.

★

Paul Gallico, *Pride of the Yankees* (1941), is a biography published at the time of Gehrig's death. For a more recent profile, see Ray Robinson, *Iron Horse: Lou Gehrig in His Time* (1990). Gehrig's wife, Eleanor, published a memoir with Joseph Durso, *My Luke and I* (1976). An obituary is in the *New York Times* (3 June 1941).

MICHAEL POLLEY

GEHRINGER, Charles Leonard ("Charlie") (*b.* 11 May 1903 in Fowlerville, Michigan; *d.* 21 January 1993 in Bloomfield Hills, Michigan), baseball player who starred for the Detroit Tigers between 1926 and 1942. Known for his consistency and durability, Gehringer helped the Tigers win American League pennants in 1934 and 1940 and a World Series in 1935.

Gehringer was born on a farm about sixty miles north of Detroit. Perhaps because he anticipated a future milking cows, slopping hogs, and plowing fields, Gehringer became enamored with baseball at an early age. Although his parents objected, Gehringer and his brother Al laid out a diamond on the farm. "I was born and raised on a Michigan

Charlie Gehringer, 1934. ASSOCIATED PRESS AP

farm," Gehringer recalled, "and knowing first hand how much back-breaking work that involved, I decided pretty early what I *didn't* want. I figured maybe baseball would have shorter hours and easier work, so I figured I'd go after that."

Detroit Tigers outfielder Bobby Veach hunted pheasant in the vicinity of the Gehringer farm and, on one of his trips, heard about the five-foot, eleven-inch, 185-pound Gehringer from a local hunter. Veach recommended that Detroit give Gehringer a tryout under the supervision of the legendary Tigers manager, Ty Cobb. Rumors persist that Cobb doubted Gehringer's ability to hit major league pitching, but Cobb remembered the occasion differently. "I knew Charlie would hit," he explained, "and I was so anxious to sign him that I didn't even take the time to change out of my uniform before rushing him into the front office to sign a contract." Thus in 1924, after completing his freshman year at the University of Michigan, Gehringer signed with the Tigers' London, Ontario, Canada, farm club in the Class B Michigan-Ontario League. He received no signing bonus, just "some free advice from Cobb on stock market investments, which didn't do me much good because I didn't have any money to invest."

After a full season in Toronto with the Class AA International League (IL), during which he batted .325, slammed 25 home runs, drove in 108 runs, and led IL second basemen in fielding, Gehringer was called up to Detroit for the final eight games of the 1925 season. He played five games and batted .462 with 6 hits in 13 at bats.

In 1926 he became a mainstay of the Tigers infield, a fixture at second base until 1942.

Gehringer, first baseman Hank Greenberg, and outfielder Leon Allen "Goose" Goslin were dubbed the "G-Men" and led the Tigers to a pair of American League (AL) championships during the 1930s, and in 1935 to a World Series victory over the Chicago Cubs. In twenty World Series contests, the "Mechanical Man," as Gehringer was nicknamed for his incredible consistency, hit .321. Appearing in six consecutive All-Star games, including the first Mid-Summer Classic in 1933, Gehringer batted .500.

Gehringer played in 2,323 games during his career. He scored 1,774 runs, collected 2,839 hits, and stroked 574 doubles, 146 triples, and 184 home runs. He also drove in 1,427 runs, stole 182 bases, and compiled a lifetime batting average of .320 to accompany an on-base percentage of .404. After hitting .277 during his rookie season in 1926, Gehringer hit an impressive .317 in 1927 and .320 in 1928. His first truly great season, however, came in 1929 when he batted .339 and led the AL in hits (215), runs scored (131), doubles (45), and triples (19). His finest year statistically was 1937 when, as Most Valuable Player, he won the AL batting title with a .371 average.

Taciturn and diffident, Gehringer was uncommonly articulate with glove and bat. The incomparable grace and ease with which he fielded his position enabled him to lead AL second basemen in fielding percentage nine times, in assists seven times, and in putouts three times. Yet, if he made few errors, he also rarely made a spectacular play. Relying on his encyclopedic knowledge of AL hitters, Gehringer seemed always to be in the right place at the right time so that even the most challenging play seemed routine. Baseball historian H. G. Salsinger wrote that Gehringer "lacks showmanship, but he has polish that no other second baseman, with the exception of the great Napoleon Lajoie, ever had."

Gehringer batted over .300 in 13 of his 19 seasons with the Detroit Tigers. He scored 100 runs 12 times and had more than 100 runs batted in and 200 hits 7 times. Only once between 1927 and 1940 did Gehringer's batting average fall below .300 for a season. In 1932 he hit .298 with 44 doubles, 11 triples, 19 home runs, and 107 runs batted in. "I went for distance," he later admitted. "Got off to a great start. . . . I had eight homers when [Babe] Ruth had only three or four. I believe I still had eight when he hit his thirty-fourth. But I kept going for distance. Wound up under .300."

When his batting average dipped to a career low of .220, Gehringer announced his retirement following the 1941 season. Tigers management convinced him to postpone his departure for one year to help counter the shortage of players resulting from the U.S. entry into World War II. Gehringer obliged, then retired in 1942 and enlisted in the U.S. Navy at age thirty-nine. He spent three years as a naval fitness instructor, attaining the rank of lieutenant commander.

Returning to civilian life, Gehringer, who had never earned more than $35,000 a year playing baseball, became a partner in Gehringer and Forsyth, a lucrative automobile parts and accessories business from which he grew wealthy. Between August 1951 and October 1953 Gehringer also served as Tigers general manager, remaining with the organization as vice president until 1959.

Gehringer died at age eighty-nine after suffering a stroke, and is buried at Holy Sepulchre Cemetery in Southfield, Michigan. He was survived by his wife Josephine, to whom he had been married for forty-three years. The couple had no children.

Inducted into the Baseball Hall of Fame in 1949, Gehringer was its oldest living member at the time of his death. Stylish, elegant, and accomplished, yet modest, unassuming, and reserved, Gehringer long enjoyed the respect and admiration of his peers. "He says hello on opening day and goodbye on closing day," said teammate and manager Mickey Cochrane, "and in between he hits .350." Doc Cramer, a Tigers outfielder, added that "You wind him up on opening day and forget about him." "All I know," remarked Yankees pitcher Lefty Gomez, "is that whenever I'm pitching, he's on base." Gehringer credited Gomez with giving him the nickname the "Mechanical Man" in recognition of his consistently stellar play game after game, season after season. Bob Feller, a Cleveland Indians pitcher who faced him many times, put it most succinctly. Gehringer was, Feller wrote, "a gentleman and a great second baseman."

★

For information about Gehringer and his career, see Martin Appel and Burt Goldblatt, *Baseball's Best: The Hall of Fame Gallery* (1977); Anthony J. Connor, ed., *Voices from Cooperstown: Baseball's Hall of Famers Tell It Like It Was* (1998); Morris A. Eckhouse, "Detroit Tigers: The Cornerstone of Detroit Baseball Is Stability," in *Encyclopedia of Major League Baseball Team Histories: American League,* edited by Peter C. Bjarkman (1991); Bob Feller with Burton Rocks, *Bob Feller's Little Black Book of Baseball Wisdom* (2001); John McCallister, *The Tigers and Their Den: The Official Story of the Detroit Tigers* (1999); and David Pietrusza et al., *Baseball: The Biographical Encyclopedia* (2000). An obituary is in the *New York Times* (23 Jan. 1993).

MARK G. MALVASI

GIAMATTI, A(ngelo) Bartlett ("Bart") (*b.* 4 April 1938 in Boston, Massachusetts; *d.* 1 September 1989 in Oak Bluffs, Martha's Vineyard, Massachusetts), president of Yale University, president of baseball's National League, and commissioner of Major League Baseball for five months before suffering a fatal heart attack; he is recognized by many as the game's poet laureate and the ultimate protector of its integrity.

One of the three children of Mount Holyoke College literature and Italian language professor Valentine Giamatti and Mary Claybaugh Walton Giamatti, Giamatti grew up in South Hadley, Massachusetts, where he learned to love Dante, the art of conversation, and the Boston Red Sox. Val Giamatti was the most influential person in his son's life, teaching him the joys of literature, scholarship, and baseball. Unfortunately, he also smoked four packs of cigarettes a day—and his son would grow up to do the same.

As a boy, Giamatti possessed no real baseball playing skills. He felt such a deep passion for the game, however, that his high school coach made a place for him on the squad as the team's manager. This allowed him to demonstrate his organizational skills as a baseball administrator for the first time.

After graduating from Andover, Giamatti entered Yale College in 1956. He became an academic and social star, the close friend of classmate Dick Cavett (who later became a television celebrity), and the recipient of a student's highest honor, being chosen to give the class oration at his 1960 graduation. In that speech, which set the tone for the rest of his life, Giamatti encouraged his peers to be "creative and humane men in society. Let us not seek always a sedative, in one form or another, for what ails us, but let us seek a cure."

Giamatti received his doctorate in comparative literature from Yale in 1964, choosing for his dissertation thesis the role of the garden in Renaissance literature. (Years later he would proclaim the baseball field America's most important "garden.") He began his teaching career at Princeton University, returning to Yale in 1966. His theatrical presentation style, passion for learning, and ability to draw parallels from Renaissance literature to contemporary American life soon electrified the campus. A former student observed that Giamatti "read Dante's original Italian as a maestro reads music—with love."

Before reaching his fortieth birthday, Giamatti was named the nineteenth president of Yale University. Never bashful about his idealism, on his first day in office he issued a memo to the entire Yale community, stating that "henceforth, as a matter of university policy, evil is abolished and paradise is restored. I trust all of us will do whatever possible to achieve this policy objective." But he also told his colleagues, "All I ever wanted to be president of was the American League."

During his eight years at Yale's helm, Giamatti imposed a balanced budget on the university, made significant inroads in restoring the campus's physical plant, proved himself a major-league fund-raiser, and began to raise his national baseball profile. His passion for the Boston Red Sox asserted itself even in his contract negotiations, when he demanded that the university install cable television into his residence so he could watch more ball games. Walking around the campus, he wore his Red Sox cap and jacket.

Bart Giamatti announcing his decision to ban Pete Rose from baseball, 1989. ASSOCIATED PRESS AP

Most important, he started publishing articles about the national pastime.

First came his classic essay "The Green Fields of the Mind," a paean to baseball published in the *Yale Alumni Magazine* shortly after Giamatti was named president. Next came a prize-winning article in *Harper's Magazine,* where Giamatti expressed his outrage that the New York Mets had traded star pitcher Tom Seaver to Cincinnati. Finally, when major league players went on strike in 1981, he wrote a *New York Times* editorial blasting everyone involved: "The people of America care about baseball, not about your squalid little squabbles." By 1983 Giamatti was on the short list of candidates for commissioner. Pressured by high-powered Yale alumni, however, he withdrew his name from consideration, and Peter Ueberroth, after his highly acclaimed leadership of the 1984 Olympics, was chosen instead.

When baseball's leaders offered Giamatti the presidency of the National League in 1986, however, he said yes. At the press conference announcing his acceptance of the job, Giamatti justified his decision in the context of his academic background, saying, "Men of letters have always gravitated to sports. I've always found baseball the most satisfying and nourishing pursuit outside literature."

From his first day as league president to his final days as commissioner, Giamatti believed that he had only one real constituency—the fan—and one goal—to make sure the integrity of the game remained pure. When the Cincinnati skipper Pete Rose pushed the umpire Dave Pallone in a game, Rose was suspended for thirty days and fined $10,000. When Billy Hatcher of the Astros got caught with a corked bat, and the Dodgers' Jay Howell and the Phillies' Kevin Gross put pine tar on and sandpaper in their respective gloves, Giamatti imposed the stiffest penalties ever assessed for such acts of cheating.

Ueberroth stepped down three years later, and Giamatti became the game's seventh commissioner. His brief tenure was most notable for his handling of the scandal surrounding allegations that Reds manager Rose had bet on baseball. The dispute, which went to court, was a sensation in the media. Finally, on 24 August 1989 a settlement was reached. Although the agreement failed to specify that the Cincinnati legend had definitively wagered on the game, it did provide that Rose be banished from baseball for life. He would, however, eventually be able to petition for reinstatement. In announcing the agreement, Commissioner Giamatti displayed his passion for integrity, saying, "The matter of Mr. Rose is now closed. It will be debated and discussed. Let no one think that it did not hurt baseball. That hurt will pass, however, as the great glory of the game asserts itself and a resilient institution goes forward. Let it also be clear that no individual is superior to the game."

Exactly one week later, while preparing for a Labor Day weekend at his Martha's Vineyard home, Giamatti suffered a massive heart attack and died at the age of fifty-one. He is buried in Grove Street Cemetery, New Haven, Connecticut, and is survived by his wife, Toni, and their three children.

Immediately following his death, tributes rang out. The most memorable observation published throughout the media came from Roger Angell of the *New Yorker*. In researching an exhaustive article about Giamatti in 1988, the journalist came across his subject's own words from a book *Exile and Change in Renaissance Literature* written years ago by the then Yale professor to describe a fifteenth-century Italian poet named Matteo Boiardo. Angell determined that in summarizing the essence of Boiardo, Giamatti had probably been trying to make a statement about his own personal quest. The similarities between the poet and the baseball executive following in his footsteps five centuries later captivated Angell, and, in the aftermath of his sudden death, now rang true for the late commissioner's millions of admirers. In this context, Roger Angell closed his article and defined the final legacy of A. Bartlett Giamatti:

Boiardo's deepest desire [is] to conserve something of purpose in a world of confusion. He knows that chivalry is an outmoded system, but he wants to keep something of its value, its respect for grace and noble behavior, even while he relinquishes its forms and structures. Boiardo wants to check the urge to dissolution . . . that time seems inevitably to embody. He does not want to turn back the clock and regain the old world, but he does want to recapture the sense of control of oneself, if nothing else, that marked life under the old system. He wants to be able to praise something other than the giddy headlong rush.

★

The most complete biography of Giamatti is James Reston, Jr., *Collision at Home Plate: The Lives of Pete Rose and Bart Giamatti* (1991). Probably the best compilation of the late commissioner's quotations on the game can be found in Anthony Valerio, *Bart: A Life of A. Bartlett Giamatti, by Him and About Him* (1991). The two leading articles about Giamatti are Roger Angell, "The Sporting Scene: Celebration," *New Yorker* (22 Aug. 1988), and Frank Deford, "A Gentleman and a Scholar," *Sports Illustrated* (17 Apr. 1989).

TALMAGE BOSTON

GIBBS, Joe Jackson (b. 25 November 1940 in Mocksville, North Carolina), head coach of the Washington Redskins football team from 1981 to 1993 who brought that team to 140 victories in twelve years, including three Super Bowl championships.

Born in Mocksville, North Carolina, Gibbs was one of two children born to J. C. and Winnie Gibbs. Gibbs's father was employed in various capacities as an officer of the peace, including as a sheriff's deputy, until he eventually moved the family to Santa Fe Springs, California, and thereafter worked in a bank. Gibbs's mother worked for the telephone company. As the family moved, Gibbs spent his early boyhood in Mocksville, Asheville, and Sand Hill, North Carolina, where he enjoyed basketball, hunting, and football. Later, in California, he attended Santa Fe Springs High School and then Cerritos Junior College in Norwalk, California, before enrolling at California State University in San Diego in 1961. At San Diego State he earned a B.S. degree in physical education in 1964 and an M.S. degree in 1966.

Gibbs's innate interest in sports was evident throughout his college career. As an undergraduate at San Diego State he played tight end, linebacker, and guard for the Aztecs under coach Don Coryell. Gibbs later served as a graduate assistant, coaching the offensive line for Coryell from 1964 to 1966. In 1967 and 1968, Gibbs served as the offensive line coach for the Florida State Seminoles, and there he focused on a pass-oriented offense that contributed to that team's 15–4–2 record during those years. At the University of Southern California (USC)—again coaching the offen-

Joe Gibbs, 1992. ASSOCIATED PRESS AP

sive line—Gibbs worked under head coach John McKay and contributed to the Trojans' 15–4–1 record for the two-year period from 1969 to 1970. Gibbs then spent two additional years of college-level coaching as an assistant coach with the University of Arkansas Razorbacks in the 1971–1972 season before going to the National Football League (NFL) in 1973.

In his first position in the NFL, Gibbs was hired by Coryell to coach the offensive backfield of the St. Louis Cardinals. Gibbs left the Cardinals in 1977 with a 42–27–1 record, including two National Football Conference (NFC) Eastern Division titles. He then stepped into the role of offensive coordinator for the Tampa Bay Buccaneers under former USC coach McKay, but in 1979 Gibbs moved to San Diego as offensive coordinator for the Chargers—again under Coryell. Gibbs remained with the Chargers through 1980, and the team took Western Division American Football Conference (AFC) titles both years.

On 13 January 1981, after fifteen years of assistant coaching, Gibbs entered into a series of negotiations with Washington Redskins owner Jack Kent Cooke and emerged as the head coach of the Redskins, replacing Jack Pardee. Gibbs set off precariously, with no wins in his first five games. However, the team regrouped for a spectacular finale, completing the 1981 season with a 27–17 victory

against the Miami Dolphins in Super Bowl XVII. The Super Bowl win proved in retrospect to be not only the culmination of a championship season but also a prologue to eleven winning seasons during Gibbs's twelve-year tenure as Washington's head coach. The Redskins took the NFC Eastern Division Title for three consecutive years from 1982 to 1984, including NFC titles in 1982 and 1983, and Gibbs received Associated Press Coach of the Year honors for those same two years. Although Gibbs's team set a record for most points scored during a season (541) during the regular 1983 season, the Redskins failed to capture a second consecutive championship, losing to the Los Angeles Raiders in Super Bowl XVIII in January 1984.

Gibbs, a quiet-spoken yet hard-working and dedicated head coach, had by 1986 established his abilities in achieving four consecutive seasons of ten victories each. He added subsequent NFL championships, beginning in 1988 with a 42–10 win against the Denver Broncos in Super Bowl XXII, and again in 1992 against the Buffalo Bills. *Sporting News* cited Gibbs as Coach of the Year after the 1991 season. With the Redskins' 37–24 victory against the Bills in Super Bowl XXVI in 1992, Gibbs became one of only three NFL coaches to win three Super Bowls. Observers credited Gibbs generously because he overcame the disadvantage of persistent player turnover during the course of his coaching career with the Washington, D.C., team. Most notably, Gibbs generated his Super Bowl triumphs using a succession of different quarterbacks, beginning with Joe Theismann in 1982, Doug Williams in 1988, and Mark Rypien in 1992.

In the heyday of his winning leadership, Gibbs stunned the sporting public on 5 March 1993 by announcing his resignation as head coach of the Washington Redskins. Disregarding the two years remaining on his contract—which were valued at an estimated $2.5 million—Gibbs cited his desire to spend more time with his wife, the former Pat Escobar, and two sons. Gibbs's assistant, Richie Petitbon, stepped in as a replacement head coach. In retirement Gibbs turned his interest to a second career in NASCAR Winston Cup racing, purchasing a NASCAR team in August 1991 and founding Joe Gibbs Racing.

In 1991 Gibbs penned an autobiography with Jerry Jenkins. In his book Gibbs spoke out with brutal honesty regarding his financial failings, his born-again Christian faith, and other personal matters. Hard-working and forthright, Gibbs showed that he could coach without being histrionic or using profanity. He was named to the Pro Football Hall of Fame in Canton, Ohio, on 26 January 1996.

★

Gibbs's autobiography, written with Jerry Jenkins, is *Joe Gibbs: Fourth and One* (1991). Gibbs is featured in *New York Times Bio-*

graphical Service, vols. 14 (1983) and 15 (1984). See also David L. Porter, ed., *Biographical Dictionary of American Sports: Football* (1987), and *Current Biography Yearbook,* 53d Annual (1992). A brief, but insightful, critique appeared on the occasion of his retirement, in *Sports Illustrated* (15 Mar. 1993).

GLORIA COOKSEY

GIBSON, Althea (*b.* 25 August 1927 in Silver, South Carolina), tennis champion, golf professional, state official, and the first African American to compete in major tennis championships.

Gibson, the eldest of five children of Daniel Gibson and Anna Washington Gibson, sharecroppers, moved with her family from South Carolina to Harlem, New York City, in 1929. She grew up on West 135th Street and was what can only be described as a problem child. She played hooky from school and remembers riding the subways for hours at a time rather than return home to face her parents' wrath. Tall, strong, and athletic, Gibson played paddle tennis on New York City streets before switching to lawn tennis in the 1940s. Recognizing her athletic talent, her father attempted to teach his headstrong daughter how to box. After she knocked him down, he allowed her to pursue her own dreams of tennis.

She won the National Negro girls' championship twice and was tutored by Dr. Robert Johnson of Lynchburg, Virginia. The African-American physician recognized her tal-

Althea Gibson at Wimbledon, 1957. AP/WIDE WORLD PHOTOS

ent and practically adopted her while training her in the style and etiquette of lawn tennis. She entered Florida Agricultural and Mechanical University in 1949 on a tennis scholarship. She played for the school on the tennis and basketball teams and graduated in 1953 with a B.S. degree.

That seemed to be the summit of Gibson's ambitions, as African Americans simply did not play lawn tennis in the first fifty years of the sport. Lawn tennis establishments refused membership and play time to African Americans, who therefore could not obtain the points and ranking needed to play in major championships like Forest Hills and Wimbledon. Even well-meaning white Americans did not understand the pervasive discrimination that prevented African-American athletes from attaining their potential—not until 1950, when Gibson applied to play at the U.S. Championships at Forest Hills.

Gibson was ready for lawn tennis, but lawn tennis was not ready for an African-American player. She was not invited to any event until the former champion Alice Marble wrote a stinging editorial in *American Lawn Tennis* in July 1950. Marble pointed out that black talent could not be denied, that tennis would eventually open its doors as the U.S. armed forces had recently done. Rather than wait, Marble urged, the tennis establishment should embrace African-American players.

Largely because of Marble's essay, Gibson entered the courts at Forest Hills on 28 August 1950, the first African American to do so. Later Gibson recalled, "There was a terrible thunderstorm during my first match at Forest Hills. One of those eagles [concrete eagles adorning the upper level of the stadium] was struck by lightning. I couldn't believe it. The eagle fell to the ground, and luckily nobody was killed. It may have been an omen that times were changing."

Gibson won her first match in convincing fashion. In the second round she faced Louise Brough, the tournament's third seed. Rain delays spread the match over two days, and though she held a significant lead, Gibson was ultimately defeated. It was a match that showed the importance of battle seasoning; while she was a remarkable athlete, Gibson had not yet fully matured. The following year (1951) she became the first black person to play in the All-England Tennis Championships at Wimbledon.

The maturity and the seasoning took such a long time that around 1955 Gibson was ready to give up on tennis altogether. She was dissuaded from giving up by an invitation to play exhibition matches on a goodwill tour in Southeast Asia. Perhaps because she was away from the United States—and racial pressures—she shone on the tour, defeating all her rivals. So Gibson was back in tennis, but was yet to prove herself ready for the big-time matches—the Grand Slam events.

Gibson's first win in the majors came at Roland Garros

in 1956. She won the French Championship, defeating Angela Mortimer, 6–0, 12–10. Gibson was the first African American ever to win one of the "Grand Slam" events, which are the Australian, French, English, and U.S. championships. Considering that Gibson had grown up playing paddle tennis and on hard courts, her win on the soft clay was remarkable and presaged greater things to come.

Gibson lost at the finals of the U.S. National Championship at Forest Hills that autumn, but the coming year, 1957, was to be all hers. She defeated fellow American Darlene Hard at Wimbledon by the lopsided score of 6–3, 6–2. Minutes later came a historic event; Gibson received the Wimbledon Cup from the hand of Queen Elizabeth II. Not only the first African American in tennis, she was now the first to win the All-England Championships.

Glory led to further glory. Gibson was welcomed back to New York City that summer by a ticker-tape parade. This was a huge moment for African-American pride, as had been the success of Jackie Robinson, the first African-American player in baseball's major leagues, a few years earlier. Gibson had broken the color barrier in tennis, and done so with panache.

That September, Gibson won the U.S. National Championship at Forest Hills. She creamed Louise Brough, 6–3, 6–2. Minutes later she received congratulations and the cup from Vice President Richard Nixon. It was another historic moment, one that would not be equaled in intensity until Arthur Ashe won the same tournament in 1968.

Ten days before Gibson won at Forest Hills, she appeared on the cover of *Time* magazine, perhaps the first African-American woman to achieve that distinction. The accompanying *Time* article, "That Gibson Girl," chronicled Gibson's long struggle to achieve a place on the court and to mature into the great player she had become. In 1957 Gibson stood among those who publicly represented the pride and dignity of African Americans. Jackie Robinson, who had just retired from baseball, and Marian Anderson, who in 1955 had been the first African American to perform at New York's Metropolitan Opera, were others. Also in 1957 Gibson became the number-one ranked female tennis player in the world and the Associated Press named her the Female Athlete of the Year.

Gibson repeated her successes in 1958. She defeated Angela Mortimer at Wimbledon, 8–6, 6–2, and Darlene Hard at Forest Hills, 3–6, 6–1, 6–2. There was no doubt that after years of poverty, obscurity, and difficulties, Gibson was the number-one player in the world. She was truly tennis queen that year.

Like most players of that time, Gibson turned professional after her triumphs. She went to pro status in 1958 and played exhibition matches before and at intervals between Harlem Globetrotter games. She also found time to appear in a John Wayne movie, *The Horse Soldiers* (1958).

Life on the professional circuit proved less rewarding psychologically than Gibson's years as an amateur. She retired from tennis rather early and looked for another challenge, which she found in the newly expanding Ladies Professional Golf Association (LPGA). She entered golf in 1964 and competed in a number of tournaments over the next few years. Her height and arm strength proved an asset, but she had taken up the game too late to make a powerful impact. Even so, she was the first African-American woman to hold an LPGA player card; once again, she led the way.

Gibson married William Darben in 1965 and Sidney Llewellyn in 1983. She retired from golf in 1967 and spent many years as a tennis teacher. She was inducted into the International Tennis Hall of Fame in 1971 and the International Women's Sports Hall of Fame in 1980. Gibson became special consultant to the New Jersey Governor's Council on Physical Fitness and Sport in 1988.

Sadly, circumstances took Gibson down financially. She suffered a stroke in 1995, then two years later her former doubles partner Angela Buxton revealed that the Gibson was financially destitute; medical bills and investments gone sour had ruined her finances. The Althea Gibson Foundation raised approximately $100,000 to rescue Gibson from her plight. In 1999 the Althea Gibson Early Childhood Education Academy opened in East Orange, New Jersey, where she had lived since 1970.

Gibson was a terrific tennis player, a tough competitor, and wonderful role model. At her best, she was among the top dozen women players between 1950 and 2000.

★

Informative books include *Women's Tennis: A Historical Documentary of the Players and Their Game*, by Angela Lumpkin (1981), and Gibson's own books: *I Always Wanted to Be Somebody* (1958), edited by Ed Fitzgerald, and *So Much to Live For* (1968). Relevant articles about Gibson include "That Gibson Girl," *Time* (26 Aug. 1957); and Ken Kamlet, "Going It Alone," *Tennis* (Sept. 1999).

SAMUEL WILLARD CROMPTON

GIBSON, Josh(ua) (*b.* 21 December 1911 in Buena Vista, Georgia; *d.* 20 January 1947 in Pittsburgh, Pennsylvania), professional baseball player considered the Negro Leagues' greatest home run hitter, enshrinee of the National Baseball Hall of Fame.

Gibson, the eldest of three children of Mark and Nancey Woodlock Gibson, was born in Buena Vista, Georgia, where his father farmed a tiny bit of acreage, barely enough to support the family. When Gibson was about twelve years old, his father headed north alone in search of a better life, eventually settling in Pittsburgh, where he found a job working for the Carnegie-Illinois Steel Company. After

Josh Gibson. AP/WIDE WORLD PHOTOS

about a year, he sent for his family and settled them into a modest home in Pleasant Valley, a black neighborhood on Pittsburgh's north side.

It was in this Pittsburgh neighborhood that Gibson was first introduced to sports. He showed particular talent for swimming and baseball, proving a natural hitter. At age sixteen Gibson joined his first formal baseball team, an all-black, company-sponsored amateur club known as Gimbel's A. C. that played throughout the Pittsburgh metropolitan area. Shortly after completing the ninth grade he dropped out of school and took a job with Westinghouse Air Brake, playing catcher for the company's baseball team in his spare time.

Although he was blessed with an extraordinary talent for baseball, Gibson grew up in an era when the major leagues were off limits—on a de facto basis, as no written prohibition existed—to black players. This meant that Gibson could hope for nothing more than winning a position with one of the teams of the Negro Leagues. The Negro League teams were rich in talent, producing such great ballplayers as Satchel Paige and Jackie Robinson, but they were uniformly poor in terms of financial resources, which meant they could not compete with the salaries of major league teams. However, Gibson soon decided that

he'd rather be playing ball than working in a factory. In his late teens Gibson was discovered by the manager of the Pittsburgh Crawfords, a local professional team, and quickly signed to a contract. Shortly afterward he met Helen Mason, and the two were married on 7 March 1929. The newlyweds moved in with Helen's parents. When Gibson wasn't playing ball for the Crawfords, he operated an elevator for Gimbel's Department Store in Pittsburgh.

In late July 1930 Gibson left the Crawfords and signed as a catcher with the Homestead Grays, Pittsburgh's professional Negro League team. The Grays were attracted to his powerful hitting rather than his catching skills. Shortly thereafter Gibson suffered a stunning personal loss when Helen died giving birth to twins. Lost without his beloved wife, Gibson took little interest in the fraternal twins, who were named Josh and Helen and raised by Helen's parents.

In his first full year with the Grays, Gibson managed to knock in seventy-five home runs as the team traveled through Pennsylvania, Ohio, New York, and West Virginia, playing against other black teams and a handful of white semiprofessional teams. Early in his career Gibson became known as the Black Babe Ruth and among the players of the Negro Leagues was second only to Satchel Paige in terms of popularity. In February 1932 Gibson again signed with the Grays, only to renege on the contract a day later when the owner of the Crawfords offered him $250 a month to play for that team. Despite threats from the Grays, Gibson reported to the Crawford spring training camp. Felled by an appendicitis attack, he missed the first three weeks of the season but returned to the team when it opened its new stadium in Pittsburgh on 30 April 1932. For the team's first game in its new stadium, Satchel Paige pitched and Gibson played behind the plate. The duo was unable to prevent a 1–0 loss. However, Paige and Gibson developed a close friendship, and Gibson began to accompany Satchel occasionally when he moonlighted for other teams.

In 1933 Gibson enjoyed another winning season and was tapped to appear in the first Negro League All-Star game. He also found love once again when he met Hattie Jones, with whom he soon was sharing a home. Gibson played the 1934 season for the Crawfords, but he and Paige drew far greater attention after the season when they traveled the country playing against an all-white, All-Star team that included pitcher Dizzy Dean. Dean was so frustrated when Gibson hit a huge home run off him that he decided to abandon the mound and play outfield for the rest of the game.

Paige left the Crawfords at the beginning of the 1935 season over a pay dispute, but the team won the Negro National League pennant anyway, thanks in no small part to the power of Gibson's bat. Although Gibson returned to the team in 1936, the Crawfords were unable to duplicate the success of 1935. For Gibson, however, 1936 was a banner year; he batted .457 and smashed in fourteen home runs. In 1937 he refused to play for the Crawfords when the team wouldn't pay him what he demanded. In late March of that year he was traded back to the Homestead Grays. Midway through the season he left the Grays to play in the Dominican Republic with other players from the Negro League.

When the political climate in the Dominican Republic began to deteriorate, Gibson returned to the Grays late in 1937. However, he began to encounter significant problems with alcohol abuse and, by 1940, marijuana use. That year Gibson played the season in Mexico and Venezuela, in part to escape his disintegrating relationship with Jones. The following year he reneged on his contract with the Grays to play for a club in Mexico, and the Grays owner asked the court to force Gibson to return. This led to an agreement from Gibson to return to the Grays for the 1942 season.

Gibson played for the Grays in 1942, leading the team to a face-off with the Kansas City Monarchs—led by Satchel Paige—in the Negro League World Series. However, the glories from early in the season were soon forgotten as Paige easily dominated Gibson throughout the series, at one point striking him out on three straight pitches. It was clear that his abuse of alcohol had taken a terrible toll.

Felled by a seizure on New Year's Day 1943, Gibson was rushed to a hospital, where he was diagnosed with a brain tumor. The ballplayer declined to have the tumor removed, and he failed to inform the Grays management of his condition. A few months later he started the season in fine form, turning in a strong performance for the whole year and leading his team to a Negro League World Series victory over the Birmingham Black Barons. But his alcohol problem continued to worsen, and his behavior was at times erratic. His decline seemed to accelerate in 1944, particularly following the start of a relationship with Grace Fournier, who was rumored to be a drug addict. Although the Grays once again bested the Black Barons in the Negro League World Series, Gibson's performance was but a shadow of the previous year's.

In 1945 Gibson turned in a very impressive batting average of .393 but managed to swat in only four home runs. The following year, in what was to be his final season playing ball, his hitting remained strong, but he began to show dramatic signs of the toll that alcohol was taking on his body. Near the end of 1946 Gibson was no longer able to care for himself, and he moved into his mother's home in Pittsburgh. He died there of a stroke at age thirty-five, and is buried in Pittsburgh in the Allegheny Cemetery.

One of the greatest ballplayers of all time, Gibson's talent was eventually recognized in 1972 when he was inducted posthumously into the National Baseball Hall of Fame. It would be difficult to find a more tragic figure in

professional baseball than Gibson. A shining star of baseball's Negro Leagues, he died only three months before Jackie Robinson became the first black player in the major leagues.

With a lifetime batting average of .347, Gibson was widely considered the best hitter in the Negro Leagues. Equally impressive are the 800 to 900 home runs he hit in his seventeen years of playing ball. Walter Johnson, who pitched for the Washington Senators, said of Gibson, "He hits the ball a mile." Paige, who played with Gibson on the Pittsburgh Crawfords and later pitched for the Cleveland Indians, declared Gibson "the greatest hitter who ever lived."

★

The most comprehensive account of Gibson's life and baseball career is in Mark Ribowsky, *The Power and the Darkness: The Life of Josh Gibson in the Shadows of the Game* (1996). Other useful books include William Brashler, *Josh Gibson: A Life in the Negro Leagues* (1978); and John B. Holway, *Josh Gibson* (1999). For an overview of the history of Negro League baseball in the United States, see Robert Peterson, *Only the Ball Was White* (1970).

DON AMERMAN

GIBSON, Pack Robert ("Bob") (*b.* 9 November 1935 in Omaha, Nebraska), baseball pitcher, winner of two Cy Young Awards and one National League Most Valuable Player Award, holder of the modern record for best earned run average in a season, and a model of fierce competition and devotion to winning.

Gibson was the youngest of seven children. Gibson's father, Pack Gibson, died months before his birth, and his mother, Victoria Brown Gibson, worked at the Omaha Lace Factory and cleaned in homes and hospitals to support her family. Both parents had moved from Louisiana to Nebraska during the Great Depression, but work was scarce for Pack, a cabinetmaker. The family lived in a subsidized housing project, which Gibson described in interviews as a training ground for his physical and mental toughness. Many of Gibson's convictions about racial intolerance as well as his ferocity on the athletic field were instilled during his childhood and youth in Omaha's Logan Fontelle projects. In the absence of a father, and in light of conflicts between the adolescent Gibson and his stepfather, the formative influence on his athletic and character development was his eldest brother, Leroy ("Josh"). This brother returned from World War II "profoundly disillusioned" but earned a master's degree in social work and devoted countless hours to coaching his brothers and other neighborhood youth in baseball and basketball. Gibson recalls with pleasure victories over more affluent, well-equipped teams in both sports.

Bob Gibson, 1967. AP/WIDE WORLD PHOTOS

As a child, Gibson had obvious talent and intense desire, but he suffered from heart problems and severe asthma. His mother at times feared for his survival. After his major league years, he appeared in a commercial for a pharmaceutical product, and announced that his career was not hindered by asthma. He also developed childhood rickets, a bone disease that may have contributed to his developing an arthritic elbow in his pitching arm at the height of his career. As Gibson learned to cope with his illnesses, however, he was honing his skills and determination to succeed in professional basketball. After playing on Nebraska's state baseball championship team at age fifteen and being named to Omaha's American Legion All-City team as a switch-hitting shortstop and outfielder, Gibson expected to compete for the varsity at Omaha Technical High School, where he starred in basketball and track. He blames the coach's cutting him on an unspoken policy limiting the number of black players on each school team. With a new coach, Gibson distinguished himself in his senior year, winning a basketball scholarship to Creighton University. He told an interviewer in 1981, upon his election to the National Baseball Hall of Fame, "I grew up fighting a lot of things. I was the first black student ever to play baseball and basketball at Creighton University. I went through some tough times." These involved resistance among coaches, fellow athletes, and fans to integration at the university. Other tough times occurred on road trips to towns less enlightened than Omaha, where Gibson endured discrimination in housing, food services, and personal facili-

ties. He suffered these indignities even more intensely during the year he played for the Columbus (Georgia) Foxes, a Cardinal minor league team, and again during the Cardinals' spring training in St. Petersburg, Florida, to which he traveled in segregated railroad cars, then was not permitted to stay in the hotel with his white teammates.

As a result of these instances of discrimination, Gibson felt profoundly the growing pains of American baseball during the decades after Robinson joined the Dodgers. He felt that his first opportunity to pitch at the major league level came despite the hostility of Cardinal manager Solly Hemus. Hemus was succeeded in 1961 by Johnny Keane, and under Keane's management, Gibson, Curt Flood, Bill White, and other black players initiated an era of goodwill among team members. The team addressed racism internally, and a St. Petersburg businessman bought two motels into which Cardinal players, led by superstars Stan Musial and Ken Boyer, moved their families in what first baseman White later called "our own little civil rights movement."

With manager and team working harmoniously to address issues of race and justice, the Cardinals prospered, and Gibson's career took off. The wildness that plagued his early career abated. By 1964 he led the team to a world championship, then was named the World Series Most Valuable Player. Always a clutch performer, Gibson's concentration intensified under the pressure of championship games. He appeared in three World Series, was named Most Valuable Player in two (1964 and 1967). After losing his first World Series start in 1964, Gibson won seven in a row before losing his final Series appearance, partly because of a misplayed fly ball. In all his World Series appearances, he posted an earned run average of 1.89, with 92 strikeouts in 81 innings—all this against the best the American League had to offer. Twice (1964 and 1967) he won the decisive seventh game of the World Series.

A celebrated incident that illustrates Gibson's competitiveness and intensity occurred on 15 July 1967. Pittsburgh's Roberto Clemente hit a fierce line drive off the pitcher's shin for the Pirates' first hit. After facing two batters, Gibson collapsed while pitching to the next one. His fibula had broken above the ankle. Amazingly, he returned to action, beating the Mets on 7 September. He shut out the Phillies a week later to clinch the pennant, then had what may be the most outstanding World Series pitching performance ever against Boston. He held the Red Sox to three runs and fourteen hits, winning three complete games and striking out twenty-six batters in twenty-seven innings. He had stopped walking on crutches in August. In 2000 he recalled Boston fans telling him, "Gibson, you broke my haaht."

Despite these honors, Gibson's home life was deteriorating. Gibson and his first wife, Charlene, whom he married in 1958 and with whom he had two daughters, faced discrimination in purchasing a home, and the couple was moving toward an eventual divorce. Gibson's 1968 season, however, was one for the ages. He was National League Most Valuable Player and won the first of two Cy Young Awards. His earned run average, 1.12 (over 8 weeks at midseason it was 0.19!), was the best since 1914, during the dead ball era. No pitcher in modern times has approached that level of excellence, one not mirrored in his won-lost record, 22–9. In the nine games Gibson lost, the Cardinals scored only twelve runs. His twenty-eight complete games included thirteen shutouts and five 1–0 losses. A comparable achievement was evolving in the American League, where Tiger Denny McLain became the first pitcher since 1934 to win more than thirty games.

When Gibson and McLain faced one another in game four of the 1968 World Series, Gibson won, striking out ten. In the first game, Gibson broke Sandy Koufax's record by striking out seventeen batters in a Series game. Catcher Tim McCarver recalls gesturing toward the scoreboard after Gibson struck out his sixteenth Tiger, but Gibson snarled in competitive fury, "Gimme the goddam ball!" McCarver pointed again toward the scoreboard, and Gibson did not quite smile, but "looked less fierce"—for a moment. In twenty-seven innings he struck out thirty-five Tigers, but the Tigers won game seven, when Gibson's friend Curt Flood misplayed a line drive into a triple.

After McLain's and Gibson's heroics, as well as Don Drysdale's record of fifty-seven and two-thirds consecutive scoreless innings, major league baseball lowered the mound from fifteen to ten inches to encourage offense, thereby to appeal to fans. Some call this change the Gibson Rule. Gibson pitched his only no-hitter against the Pirates in 1971. He remained an intimidating force in the National League during the early 1970s, winning another Cy Young Award with his 23–7 record in 1970. By 1973, however, Gibson's earned run average was rising while his winning percentage was dropping, to .545 in 1973 and .458 in 1974. By 1975 it was clear that asthma, a rheumatic heart, and arthritis had diminished Gibson's effectiveness. The man who had ceased playing basketball for the Harlem Globetrotters in 1957 because the competition was not sufficiently intense retired during a 3–10 season with a lifetime earned run average of 2.91 and 3,117 strikeouts. This record was second only to Walter Johnson's, whose record was subsequently broken by Steve Carlton and Nolan Ryan.

In 1981, Gibson's first year of eligibility, he was voted into the Hall of Fame, receiving 337 of 401 first-place votes. Appropriately, he was inducted with Cardinal old-timer Johnny Mize and the late Rube Foster, founder of the Negro Leagues. He was selected as the fifth pitcher on the All-Century team in 1999.

Gibson married Wendy Nelson in 1981 (they have one son) and has since operated several businesses in Omaha. His friend Joe Torre hired him in 1981 as "attitude coach" of the Mets, and he has occasionally worked as an analyst for major league games. The title he chose for his 1994 autobiography, *Stranger to the Game,* suggests Gibson's disappointment that major league teams, especially the Cardinals, have not sought his counsel as a coach or an executive. But since the autobiography came out, he has served as the Cardinals' bullpen coach (1995) and subsequently as a pitching instructor for the Cardinals during spring training. He has also worked as both a television analyst and a consultant to former American League president Gene Budig.

Gibson's legacy remains that of a magnificent pitcher who perfected the art of intimidating the batter by pitching inside, then painting the outside corner with a vicious slider. Gibson once said, "I seldom threw at a batter. When I did, I always hit him." Modern baseball has seen few pitchers of Gibson's talent, his determination, or his ferocity. He was a complete player; he won nine consecutive Gold Gloves and hit twenty-four career home runs. In 2000 he characterized himself to Gordon Edes as a "glowering black man who wouldn't make small talk or apologize for pitching inside."

★

Books about Gibson and his career include Gibson's own *Stranger to the Game* (1994), written with Lonnie Wheeler; and Geoffrey C. Ward and Ken Burns, "The Eighth Inning: A Whole New Ball Game," in *Baseball: An Illustrated History* (1994). Relevant articles include James Buckey, Jr., "1967: Bob Gibson," in a special advertising section produced by the Editorial Projects Department of *Sports Illustrated* (7 Oct. 1991); Steve Rushin, "The Season of High Heat," *Sports Illustrated* (19 July 1993); and Gordon Edes, "A Hitter's Nightmare," *Baseball Digest* (6 Sept. 2000).

DAVID C. DOUGHERTY

GIFFORD, Frank Newton (*b.* 16 August 1930 in Santa Monica, California), famed as a multipurpose running back for the New York Giants as well as a broadcaster for football games and other sports; member of both the College Football Hall of Fame and the Pro Football Hall of Fame.

Gifford is often portrayed as a "golden boy" who starred at the University of Southern California (USC) in Los Angeles, California, and soared on to become a great player in the National Football League (NFL). This is a fable; Gifford was no pampered southern California golden boy. As one of three children of frequently unemployed Weldon Wayne and Lola Mae Hawkins, he had a hard life. His father struggled to support the family throughout the Great Depression, working on oil rigs when he could. During this time, they moved through forty-seven towns—sometimes two in a day—living in their automobile or in parks before finding affordable housing.

By the time he reached Bakersfield High School, in Bakersfield, California, Gifford's grades were poor, and he may have been a disciplinary problem. But even as a transfer student, he made the football team as a quarterback. He credited his high school football coach with straightening him out during his junior year by showing him how he could escape the life his father had lived. Thereafter, he took his schoolwork seriously in hopes of earning an athletic scholarship to USC. When his grades were still not good enough for USC, he attended Bakersfield Junior College from 1948 to 1949 and earned the grades he needed. Meanwhile, he was honored as a Junior College All-American in football, and his good grades enabled him to receive his scholarship to USC.

In the first game of 1949, versus the United States Naval Academy, USC lost one of its starting safeties to injury and Gifford replaced him. Gifford intercepted two passes in the game, and thus one of the greatest careers in college football was begun. In 1951 a new coach, Jess Hill, made Gifford a running back, becoming the prototype for the modern tailback. On options, he completed thirty-two passes for 303 yards and two touchdowns, while rushing for 841 yards and seven touchdowns. That year, Gifford was named college All-American.

On 13 January 1952 Gifford married his girlfriend, Maxine Avis Ewart, and the New York Giants drafted him in the first round, eleventh overall. Gifford wanted to focus

Frank Gifford, 1997. © MITCHELL GERBER/CORBIS

on playing only one position, but NFL teams had only thirty players at the time, and some had to play "both ways" (offense and defense). Gifford's versatility meant that he played defensive back and offensive back, and he returned punts, but when Vince Lombardi became defensive coach in 1954, he made Gifford a full-time running back.

Gifford said that his real professional football career began then. He became an All Pro at halfback; he would be selected seven times for the Pro Bowl not only as a halfback but as a flanker and a defensive back. By the time he retired from football, he had passed for fourteen touchdowns, run for 3,609 yards and thirty-four touchdowns, received 367 passes for 5,434 yards and forty-three touchdowns, and returned an interception for a touchdown. He still holds the New York Giants team records for average yards per carry (4.3) and total touchdowns. In 1956 the United Press International named him NFL Most Valuable Player (MVP) of the Year.

On 28 December 1958 Gifford played in the NFL championship game against the Baltimore Colts. The game was to become legendary, often called the "Greatest Game Ever Played," because it electrified a large television audience and helped make football into a popular television sport. Though Gifford had a difficult day, fumbling twice in the first quarter, he went on to rush for a touchdown, eventually to carry the Giants to within inches of victory. However, a disputed play, in which officials may have mis-spotted the ball just short of a first down, created a fourth down on which the Giants punted. The Colts then tied the game and won it in overtime.

In 1959 Gifford was named MVP in the Pro Bowl, but he would soon fall on hard times. On 20 November 1960, in a game against the Philadelphia Eagles, Gifford caught a pass and stepped to turn up field when Eagles linebacker Chuck Bednarik stopped him cold with a ferocious hit. Gifford was hospitalized with a severe concussion for ten days, and he missed the rest of the season. Because his severe injury seemed to make a return to playing football impossible, Gifford announced his retirement.

Yet he returned to the Giants for the 1961 season, becoming a flanker. His exceptional versatility was shown to advantage in this role as sometime runner, sometime receiver, and sometime passer, and he returned to the Pro Bowl. By the time he had retired in 1964, he had been working as a television broadcaster for six years. In 1962 he had become a sports reporter for WCBS-TV in New York. In 1965 he joined CBS full time, covering not only football, but golf and basketball as well.

He was a broadcaster for the first Monday night NFL game to be broadcast on television, in 1966 on CBS. In 1971 he was hired by ABC to join Howard Cosell and former Dallas Cowboys quarterback Don Meredith in the broadcast booth for the second year of *ABC's Monday Night Football*. He was to be the play-by-play man while Meredith provided analysis and Cosell provided color commentary. The show was a great success, and Gifford's broadcasting career boomed; he remained with the show in various positions until 1998. ABC included him in its Olympic Games coverage for the Summer Games of 1972, 1976, and 1984, and the Winter Games of 1976, 1980, 1984, and 1988, during which Gifford earned praise for his work covering skiing events.

In 1976 Gifford was elected to the College Football Hall of Fame. In 1977 he was enshrined in the Pro Football Hall of Fame, and he also won an Emmy Award for his sports broadcasting. He formed an enduring relationship with the Special Olympics and won a Christopher Award in 1984 for his work on the 1983 International Special Olympics. He also became heavily involved in the March of Dimes and the National Society for Multiple Sclerosis, of which he was a member of the board of directors from 1973 to 1978.

While Gifford's career transitions went smoothly, his personal life did not fare as well. His first marriage, during which he had three children, ended in divorce, and his second marriage to Astrid Narss in 1978, ended in divorce

as well, in 1986. On 18 October 1986, he married for the third time, to Kathie Lee Johnson, whom he had met in 1984 and who was a rising television star, becoming the cohost of *Live with Regis and Kathie Lee*. It seemed a marriage made in heaven, between the upright sports hero and an American sweetheart, and together they had two children. But in 1997 a grocery store tabloid, the *Globe,* paid $75,000 to a Gifford acquaintance to seduce him in a hotel, tarnishing his reputation and jeopardizing his marriage. Gifford retired in 1998 and decided to focus on his personal life. His marriage survived and Gifford continued to be a valued worker for charities, particularly two he and his wife founded together in honor of their children, Cody's House and Cassidy's Place.

★

In *Gifford on Courage* (1976), by Gifford and Charles Mangel, Gifford examines the lives of athletes to explain the nature of courage in sports. In *Gifford: The Whole Ten Yards* (1993; also published as *The Whole Ten Yards*), written with Harry Waters, Gifford tells about his years playing football, his years as a sports broadcaster, and his marriage to television star Kathie Lee Gifford. William N. Wallace's *Frank Gifford* (1969) predates Gifford's success on *ABC's Monday Night Football* but covers his playing career. Jerry Izenberg, *New York Giants: Seventy-five Years* (1999), and Victoria J. Parillo, *The New York Giants: 75 Years of Football Memories* (1999), profile Gifford in the context of his career with the Giants.

KIRK H. BEETZ

GILLMAN, Sid(ney) (*b.* 26 October 1911 in Minneapolis, Minnesota), football coach best known for his influence on offensive strategy and tactics.

Gillman, the father of football's modern passing offense, was born into a Jewish family in Minneapolis. His father, David Gillman, owned several movie theaters; his mother, Sarah Dickerson Gillman, was a housewife. Gillman became passionate about football and film at an early age. He was a star end on the North (Minneapolis) High School football team and, cutting football highlights out of the newsreels shown in his father's theater, he made primitive game films from spliced footage.

From 1931 to 1933, Gillman played football at Ohio State University (OSU). In his senior year he was named co-captain of the Buckeye team and won honorable mention All-America honors. After graduating from OSU with a B.A. in English, he worked as a graduate assistant for the Buckeye football team. In 1935 he married Esther Berg; the couple had a son and three daughters. He also became an assistant coach at Denison University in 1935. The following year he played professional football for the Cleveland

Sid Gillman, 1960s. ASSOCIATED PRESS AP

Gillman left Cincinnati in 1955 to become head coach of the Los Angeles Rams, marking his debut as a National Football League (NFL) coach. In his rookie year, the Rams played in the league's championship game for the first time in three years, losing to the Cleveland Browns 38–14. Gillman also started the league's first film exchange program. He managed only one other winning season with the Rams, resigning after a 2–10 campaign in 1959 with an overall record of 28–32–1. He achieved greater success as the head coach and general manager of the Los Angeles (after 1960, San Diego) Chargers of the new American Football League. The Chargers became a model of success for the rest of the league, winning five Western Conference championships in the league's first six seasons. Although the Chargers lost consecutive title games to the Houston Oilers (1960 and 1961) and the Buffalo Bills (1964 and 1965), they won the 1963 championship in spectacular fashion, amassing 610 yards of total offense in a 51–10 victory over the Boston Patriots. Gillman's overall record with the Chargers was 87–57–6.

As coach and general manager, Gillman was a tough, driven perfectionist. Charger coaches' meetings featured loud, heated arguments, usually at Gillman's instigation. After the Chargers posted a 4–10 season in 1962, he held the team's next training camp at Rough Acres Ranch, a grassless patch of desert that had to be cleared of rattlesnakes before each practice. He was just as assertive with his fellow head coaches. His pregame ritual with Kansas City head coach Hank Stram included throwing Stram's game plan on the ground and stepping on it. He also continued the take-no-prisoners attitude that had characterized his college coaching career. During a 56–10 trouncing of Denver, whose head coach, Jack Faulkner, was Gillman's former assistant, Gillman went for a superfluous two-point conversion in the game's waning moments. Gillman was also tough on himself, working longer hours than any coach in the professional ranks. He displayed limitless enthusiasm, and he thrived on the strategies of the game.

The innovative offense Gillman installed as the Chargers' head coach remains his greatest legacy. The Chargers became the first team to regularly use all five eligible receivers in pass patterns, and they were also the first team to send a receiver deep on almost every play. Gillman's aggressive passing offense attacked every part of the field, stretching defenses vertically with long bombs to wide receivers and deep passes to tight ends, and stretching defenses horizontally with quick strikes to the sidelines. Reversing a popular axiom, he stated that the Chargers "passed to set up the run." Yet Gillman was also obsessed with stretching the defense with the running game. He pulled tackles to lead sweeps for all-league running backs Keith Lincoln and Paul Lowe, with Hall of Fame tackle Ron Mix usually leading the play.

Rams of the American Football League (AFL) while coaching at Denison.

Gillman's college coaching career included assistant coaching positions at Denison from 1935 to 1937 and also in 1941, Ohio State University from 1938 to 1940, Miami University of Ohio from 1942 to 1943, and for the U.S. Military Academy in 1948.

He was head coach at Miami of Ohio from 1944 to 1947 (with a record of 31–16–1) and at Cincinnati from 1949 to 1954 (with a record of 50–13–1). As a head coach, Gillman was known for producing winning teams, running up scores on inferior opponents, and pioneering or adopting coaching innovations. An early advocate of the platoon system, he also won recognition as an expert on option blocking, a simplified blocking scheme that allowed backs to run through holes as they developed. An outspoken proponent of using film as a coaching tool, he became the first coach to film practice sessions. His reliance on film reached new heights at Cincinnati. When he rushed first-quarter game film to a studio so that he could review it with his team at halftime, however, the National Collegiate Athletic Association (NCAA) ruled that this use of film constituted an unfair advantage. The NCAA also placed Cincinnati on probation for recruiting violations in 1955.

After 1965 the Chargers fell to a perennial third-place finish in the AFL West. Resigning as head coach in 1969 because of a perforated ulcer, Gillman was employed as the team's general manager when the NFL and the AFL merged in 1970. He returned as head coach for ten games in 1971. Despite repeated "retirements," he continued coaching for sixteen years. As the head coach of the Houston Oilers from 1973 to 1974 (with a record of 8–15), he ended an eighteen-game losing streak and won AFC Coach of the Year honors in 1974. He also worked as an assistant coach with the Dallas Cowboys (1972), Chicago Bears (1977), Philadelphia Eagles (1979–1980, 1982), and the Los Angeles Express of the United States Football League (USFL) in 1984. He spent four months as the head coach and athletic director of United States International University (1979) and helped as a volunteer assistant coach at the University of Pittsburgh (1987). Public recognition of Gillman's accomplishments increased as his coaching career neared its end. Elected to the Professional Football Hall of Fame in 1983, his selection as a member of the College Football Hall of Fame in 1989 made him the only coach enshrined in both. He was also enshrined in the International Jewish Sports Hall of Fame in 1991.

Gillman remains an important figure in the history of football for several reasons. Few of his peers matched his .814 career winning percentage (81–19–2) as a college head coach. As a professional head coach, his record was 123–104–7. Gillman was also an influential figure in the early development of the AFL, the only league that successfully challenged the NFL. His many innovations overshadow these accomplishments, however. While Paul Brown, Tom Landry, and Bill Walsh were more successful than Gillman at winning championships, Gillman deserves to be rated with them as one of the game's greatest innovators.

★

Todd Tobias, *A Bolt from the Past: Sid Gillman as Head Coach in the American Football League* (1999), a master's thesis published at the University of San Diego, provides a full-length account of Gillman's coaching career in the AFL. Bob Curran, *The $400,000 Quarterback* (1965), includes a more succinct account of Gillman's influence during the AFL's first five years. David L. Porter, ed., *Biographical Dictionary of American Sports: Football* (1987), contains a biography of Gillman. Bob Carroll et al., eds., *Total Football: The Official Encyclopedia of the National Football League* (1999), provides an account of Gillman's coaching career. Valuable articles include Earl Lawson, "Football's Man Without Mercy," *Saturday Evening Post* (8 Oct. 1955); Paul Zimmerman, "When Sid Was Caesar," *Sports Illustrated* (1 Feb. 1988), and "Screen Gem," *Sports Illustrated* (2 Sept. 1991); and Bob Wolf, "Under Sid Gillman, the Charger Era Came to Pass," *Los Angeles Times* (16 Aug. 1989).

THOMAS SCHAFFER

GLICKMAN, Martin Irving ("Marty") (*b.* 14 August 1917 in New York City; *d.* 3 January 2001 in New York City), collegiate sports star at Syracuse University and a member of the 1936 U.S. Olympic track team who became the voice of New York City sports for half a century as a play-by-play radio commentator.

Born in the Bronx to Romanian-Jewish immigrant parents, Harry and Molly Glickman, Marty Glickman became a track star at James Madison High School in Brooklyn, where he held national prep titles in both the indoor and the outdoor 100-yard dashes. The pervasive anti-Semitism of American amateur sports in the 1930s, however, stood in the way of the many athletic scholarships he might otherwise have been offered. He was, however, able to enroll at Syracuse University in 1935 due to the efforts of a group of Jewish alumni who, wanting to bring a Jewish athlete to the upstate New York campus, offered to pay his tuition.

Glickman excelled as a running back for the Orangemen football team as well as a short-distance sprinter on the track team. He capped off a brilliant freshman year by winning a berth in the 400-meter relay event on the 1936 U.S. Olympic team. The 1936 games, however, were held in Nazi Berlin, and when Adolph Hitler let it be known that he was displeased by the presence of a Jewish athlete, the American coaches, though under no obligation to do so, benched Glickman and a Jewish teammate, Sam Stoller. Sixty-two years later the U.S. Olympic Committee honored Glickman with its first General Douglas MacArthur Award for "service to the Olympic cause," an event widely interpreted as an acknowledgment of the wrong that had been done to him.

Glickman's career as a sportscaster began while he was still a student. Following a two-touchdown performance in Syracuse's 1937 upset of nationally ranked Cornell University, the owner of a local men's clothing store offered Glickman $15 per show to write and host a weekly sports roundup on the radio station WSYR. Upon graduation with a B.A. degree in history in 1939, Glickman returned to New York City, intent on making a career in sports radio. He worked at a clothing store and played minor league football for the Jersey City Giants on weekends to support himself while volunteering to work as an all-purpose gopher at the radio station WHN. "I worked there for one solid year without getting paid a dime. It was the Depression, and that's what you did in those days to get a foothold," he wrote in his autobiography.

After Glickman was hired full-time by WHN in 1940, his duties at the station included play-by-play announcing for New York City's two National Hockey League (NHL) teams, the Rangers and the Americans, and hosting his own daily program, *Baseball Today,* during which he used wire

Marty Glickman, 1980. He holds a photograph of Jesse Owens in the 1936 Berlin Olympics, from which Glickman was excluded because he was Jewish. ASSOCIATED PRESS AP

service copy as a framework for dramatic verbal recreations of the day's big league baseball highlights. In 1943 he called the play-by-play of the first-known broadcast of a basketball game, an all-star benefit for the American Red Cross at Madison Square Garden in New York City. (Previously, the industry wisdom had been that basketball was too difficult a game for radio listeners to follow.) Later that year, he joined the U.S. Marine Corps, serving in the Marshall Islands during World War II as an air traffic controller. He was discharged with the rank of first lieutenant in 1946.

After the war, Glickman returned to WHN as sports director and continued to pioneer basketball broadcasting. College competition dominated the sport, and he was at the microphone for dozens of games between the national powers that played in Madison Square Garden doubleheaders. At the same time, unlike many of his contemporaries, he saw the possibilities of professional basketball and secured radio rights for WHN to carry the newly formed New York Knicks when they commenced play in 1946.

"Unlike football and baseball," he told an interviewer, "basketball is a fluid game and there's constant change. I

spread the terminology of the city game: the top of the key, the elbow of the foul line, one-handed jump, two-handed set, and so on. I spoke in the *vox populi*. I developed a technique—the style of 'following the ball.' I could always speak rapidly and I knew the game. It was easy for me and I enjoyed doing it." Sportscaster Bob Costas, a Glickman protégé, credits Glickman with "laying out the geography of the court."

As in all mass communication, technical knowledge needs to be packaged in showmanship, and here too Glickman excelled. When a basket was scored, he would call out, "Good!" and, pausing a breath, add, "like Nedick's," a reference to the chain of New York City hot dog and orange-drink stands that sponsored the Knicks for many years. This became a household phrase in New York City. Another Glickman original was the call of "Swishhhhhhhhhhh . . ." when a ball went through the hoop without touching the rim or backboard. He chalked up another milestone in 1949 when he called the first televised basketball game.

College football, which had a long radio history, had a spectacular breakout into popularity as a professional game during the 1950s, and Marty Glickman was a part of this development as well. In 1948 he began a twenty-three-year run as the play-by-play voice of the New York Giants on the radio station WNEW. When the National Football League (NFL) began appearing on television in the mid-1950s, the league maintained a policy of local television blackouts for games that were not sold out. Not only did hundreds of thousands of New York City fans depend on Glickman's radio broadcasts for blacked-out games, but many chose to turn off the sound when games were televised, preferring to tune their radios in to Glickman and partner Al DeRogatis. "When I broadcast a game," Glickman said, "I want people to be able to see the game. You paint a word-picture. What I try to do is not only have them see the game, but I try to have listeners feel the game. That was the important thing."

Though clearly a favorite of New York fans, Glickman was never offered a national network television contract for NBA basketball or NFL football. It is generally believed that network executives feared that his distinctive accent—alternately described as "too New York," "too Jewish," and "too lower class"—would simply not play throughout the country. However, this did not prevent NBC, ESPN, and other television sports operations from hiring Glickman to coach their announcers.

In 1971, despite a long record of quality work and fan loyalty, Glickman was unceremoniously let go from the Giants broadcast team in favor of a younger man. After sitting out a season, he bounced back, as was his character, and took over play-by-play duties for the rival New York Jets. When the Jets' radio rights changed hands in 1979,

Glickman again found himself without a professional football job. In 1988 yet another station bought the broadcast rights. It surprised no one and delighted many when seventy-one-year-old Glickman returned as the voice of the New York Jets for another five years. George Vecsey of the *New York Times* greeted the return, writing, "The master will be on WCBS radio with that crisp sidewalk-flavored cadence that always put you alongside the 50-yard line. For some of us, the game of football was never as perfect in person as when Glickman was describing it for our ears."

Glickman's list of sportscasting firsts extended into the cable era. When HBO went on line on 8 November 1972, its premier cablecast was a New York Rangers–Vancouver Canucks hockey game from Madison Square Garden with Glickman calling the action. He served as sports adviser to the fledgling operation during the 1970s and was instrumental in establishing HBO as a primary venue for professional boxing.

The dean of New York City sportscasters died of complications from heart bypass surgery at age eighty-three. He was survived by Marjorie Dorman, his wife of sixty years, and their four children. His remains were cremated.

Although a series of slights had peppered his career as athlete and broadcaster, Glickman repeatedly brushed these off and moved on to new achievements. A generation of sportscasters, including stars of the profession such as Bob Costas, Len Berman, Dick Enberg, and Marv Albert, readily acknowledge him as mentor and teacher. Over the years, Glickman was inducted into the Basketball Hall of Fame, the Sportscasters Hall of Fame, and the New York Jewish Sports Hall of Fame, all of which memorialize his life and accomplishments.

★

An autobiography written with Stan Isaacs, *The Fastest Kid on the Block*, was published in 1996. An audiotape and transcription of a two-hour interview recorded in 1999 are among the oral history holdings of the Center for the Study of Popular Television at Syracuse University. Obituaries are in the *New York Times* and New York *Newsday* (both 4 Jan. 2001) and in the *Boston Globe* and *Los Angeles Times* (both 5 Jan. 2001).

DAVID MARC

GOMEZ, Vernon Louis ("Lefty")   (*b.* 26 November 1909 in Rodeo, California; *d.* 17 February 1989 in Larkspur, California), quick-witted, left-handed Yankee pitcher of the 1930s and one of the top World Series pitchers of all time.

Gomez was of Irish-Spanish extraction and descended from the early settlers of California. His father, Manuel Gomez, was probably a dairy farmer; his mother's name is listed in sources as both Mary and Elizabeth. Gomez grew

Lefty Gomez, 1936. AP/WIDE WORLD PHOTOS

to be a six-foot, two-inch string bean with a throwing arm that attracted scouts by the time he was sixteen and pitching for semiprofessional teams near San Francisco. Nick Williams, the manager of the Pacific Coast League's San Francisco Seals, signed him to a professional contract and sent him to Salt Lake City of the Utah-Idaho League in 1928. Promoted to the Seals in 1929 at age nineteen, he put together an 18–11 record in 267 innings, prompting the Yankees to purchase him at the end of the year for a reported $35,000. Although he made the Yankees out of spring training in 1930, the manager Bob Shawkey sent him to the American Association's Saint Paul team for more seasoning and to put on weight after his first fifteen appearances with the big club produced a disappointing 2–5 record. With Saint Paul, Gomez won eight while losing four.

Gomez made the Yankees again in 1931 and quickly became one of the top pitchers in the American League, winning twenty-one games and losing only nine in 243 innings. His 2.63 earned run average was second in the league to the great Lefty Grove. When Cy Perkins, a long-time catcher with the Philadelphia Athletics, joined the Yankees as a coach, he turned Gomez into the team's ace, helping him harness his wildness. The following year Gomez led the Yankees to the World Series with a 24–7 record, defeating the thrice-defending champion Athletics seven times on the way to the pennant. He began his World Series dominance that year, defeating the Chicago Cubs 5–2 in game two as the Yankees swept the series.

In 1933 Gomez was the American League starting and winning pitcher in the first All-Star game. During his career he started five All-Star games, winning three and losing one. He finished 16–10 as the Yankees failed to repeat, finishing seven games behind the Washington Senators. On 26 February of that year he married the Broadway star June O'Dea. Although they had a well-publicized breakup in the early years of their marriage, they reconciled, were married fifty-five years, and had four children together.

The newly married Gomez pitched brilliantly in 1934, winning twenty-six games while losing just five. He led the league in seven major categories including wins, winning percentage (.839), earned run average (2.33), complete games (25), innings (282), strikeouts (158), and shutouts (tied with 6). After a mediocre 1935 the Yankees, bolstered by the rookie Joe DiMaggio, returned to the World Series in 1936, aided significantly by Gomez's 13–7 record. Gomez won game two (18–4) and game six (13–5) of the series as the Yankees defeated the New York Giants four games to two.

Gomez's on-field antics were legendary and earned him the nicknames "El Goofy," the "Gay Caballero," and the "Singular Castilian." It was during the second game of the 1936 World Series that he stood on the mound and watched an airplane fly overhead, delaying the game. He had a quirky personality off the field as well. One rainy day he tried to call Johannesburg, South Africa, just to talk to someone there. On another occasion he came up with the idea of a revolving goldfish bowl "to make life easier for the older goldfish."

Gomez roomed with DiMaggio for several years and was his closest friend on the team. It was to DiMaggio that he mainly referred when asked to what he attributed his success. "Clean living and a fast outfield," was his classic reply. Another time after an inning in which three hits were run down and caught by his outfielders, he quipped, "I'd rather be lucky than good."

In 1937 Gomez reentered the twenty-win circle, putting together a 21–11 record to lead the Yankees to their second straight pennant. He again led the league in wins, earned run average (2.33), strikeouts (194), and shutouts (6). The Yankees again defeated the cross-river Giants in the World Series, this time four games to one, as Gomez opened and closed the series with victories in game one (8–1) and game five (4–2). Both of his wins were complete games and his earned run average for the series was a sparkling 1.50.

The following year, the Yanks won their third consec-utive pennant as Gomez went 18–12. In 1938 they again swept the Chicago Cubs and Gomez won his sixth World Series game without a defeat, winning the second game 6–3 in come-from-behind fashion. Down three to two, he escaped a bases-loaded jam; then in the top of the eighth he left for a pinch hitter still trailing in the game. But the Yankees rallied to win, thanks to a two-run homer by the light-hitting Frankie Crosetti; the reliever Johnny Murphy saved the victory for Gomez. In the latter years of Gomez's career, Murphy became almost his appendage, saving countless ball games for him. Gomez was appreciative and used his wonderful wit to show it. Once when asked how long he planned to pitch, he answered, "As long as Murphy's arm holds out."

Gomez struggled with various ailments during the last years of his career, managing to post a 12–8 record in 1939 despite a pulled muscle and stiff neck. After a sore arm almost completely sidelined him in 1940, he came back with a 15–5 record in 1941. The problem returned in 1942 when he threw only eighty innings on his way to a 6–4 record. During that year a sportswriter asked Gomez about the manager Joe McCarthy: "Smart manager, isn't he Lefty?" Quick as a wink, Gomez replied, "He must be. He hasn't asked me to pitch in over a month."

Gomez finished his active playing career in 1942 by pitching and losing one game with the Washington Senators. For his career he compiled 189 wins against 102 losses for an outstanding .649 winning percentage. He won twenty more games four times and opponents could manage only a .242 batting average against him overall.

He never lost his quick wit. Shortly after his retirement from baseball, he was called upon to fill out a job application form. In the "reason for leaving last employment" blank, Gomez wrote, "Couldn't get anybody out." He managed Yankee farm clubs for several years, lending his humor to the enterprise. Once while coaching third base for the Binghamton Triplets, his team had runners on first and second when the batter singled to center. The lead runner rounded third, then hesitated and came sliding back into the base just as the runner from first slid into third from the other side. Gomez let out a loud whoop and joined them with a slide into third from the coach's box.

He worked for many years for the Wilson Sporting Goods Company before retiring to the banquet circuit, where current events gave him new material. When Neil Armstrong first walked on the moon, he and other scientists from the National Aeronautics and Space Administration were puzzled by an unidentified white object on the surface. Gomez quipped that he immediately knew what it was, "A home-run ball Jimmie Foxx hit off me in 1937."

Gomez kept his sense of humor to the end of his life. He suffered from congestive heart failure and, about a week before his death, a doctor leaned over his hospital bed and asked him, "Lefty, picture yourself on the mound and rate the pain from one to ten." Gomez looked at the doctor and replied, "Who's hitting, Doc?" Gomez died on 17 February 1989 and is buried in Mount Tamalpais Cemetery in San Rafael, California.

Lefty Gomez was one of the finest clutch pitchers of his generation and the ace of many of the great New York Yankee teams of the 1930s. Most notable in addition to his prowess on the mound was his legendary sense of humor, most often aimed at himself. He was one of the great wits in the history of sports.

★

No full-scale biography of Gomez exists, but the National Baseball Library in Cooperstown, New York, houses material on his career. See also chapters on Gomez in Arthur Daley, *Times at Bat: A Half Century of Baseball* (1950); Tom Meany, *Baseball's Greatest Pitchers* (1951); and Tom Meany, *The Greatest Yankees of Them All* (1969). A more recent article focusing on Gomez's wit is "Lefty Gomez: The Life of the Party," *Elysian Fields Quarterly* 18, no. 1 (2001).

C. PAUL ROGERS III

GONZALES, Richard Alonzo ("Pancho") (*b.* 9 May 1928 in Los Angeles, California; *d.* 3 July 1995 in Las Vegas, Nevada), tennis champion who was the first Hispanic player to achieve outstanding success in tennis, and one of the most graceful athletes ever seen on the tennis court.

Born in southern California to a Mexican-American working-class family, Gonzales was the son of Manuel Gonzales, a furniture fitter and set painter, and Carmen Gonzales, a seamstress. Gonzales never had a formal tennis lesson but practiced with other local boys, playing on the Har-Tru courts that made California tennis distinctive. He quit school at the age of fifteen to begin his tennis career.

For most of its early years, the men's tennis tour had been seen as an elite institution, dominated by young white men who could afford to play for years without remuneration. While there were some exceptions to the general rule, there were few minority players in the game until the emergence of Gonzales. Two attributes distinguished him from the start: he had natural, graceful strokes—especially his overhead and serve, which became classics of their type—and he was a ferocious competitor, always trying to gain the net and put away the point. Unlike many serve-and-volley players of the 1980s and 1990s, Gonzales had terrific ground strokes as well as an aggressive attack, and his cat-like quickness earned him nicknames like "The Tiger."

What he most lacked was a sense of humor. Given his struggle to make it in tennis, Gonzales was completely unable to laugh at himself, to shrug off a bad match or a bad

Pancho Gonzales, 1949. AP/WIDE WORLD PHOTOS

day. He never became a regular member of the tour's social scene. Much as this isolation may have served his competitive spirit, it ill-served his attempt to be an ambassador for minorities in the game.

When Gonzales won the U.S. National Championship at Forest Hills in 1948 and 1949, he decided to turn professional. Older players, Don Budge and Bobby Riggs among them, tried to dissuade him, urging him to stay amateur for a few additional years to continue his development. Not surprisingly, Gonzales could not resist the $85,000 offered if he would go head-to-head with Jack Kramer in a series of exhibition matches.

Kramer was the best in the game. While tennis aficionados did—and still do—debate the virtues of their favorite players, it seems fair to say that Gonzales had the greater natural talent but that Kramer had both the strategy and determination to outlast him. In his autobiography, Kramer emphasized the importance of diet and nutrition and hinted that Gonzales's fondness for soft drinks and fast food were part of the reason Kramer bested him in the yearlong competition.

In retrospect, it is clear that the decision to turn professional was disastrous for Gonzales's career. Until 1968, when the "Open Tennis" era began, there was a strict delineation between amateur and professional competition in tennis. It was customary to turn professional in order to make money after winning Wimbledon and Forest Hills in the same year. Gonzales had won Forest Hills twice, but he turned professional at a young age and would long be remembered as "the greatest player who never won Wimbledon." Kramer later estimated that Gonzales might have won as many as seven Wimbledons had he remained an amateur through the 1950s.

Gonzales dominated the professional tour from 1954 until 1962. He faced and defeated a string of worthy opponents, among them Tony Trabert, Frank Sedgman, and Ken Rosewall. Only once during these eight years was Gonzales overmatched, and that time fortune smiled upon him.

Rosewall and Lew Hoad had burst onto the tennis scene in 1952. Young Australians who had been raised on grass courts, they brought an incredible zest for the game and increased crowds wherever they went. They could not have been more different. Rosewall was small, trim, dignified, and played an elegant game. Hoad was large, strong, brash, and utterly lovable. Even Gonzales, who seldom tried to make friends, liked Hoad, and came to admire him for this uncanny shotmaking.

In 1958 Gonzales went on tour against Hoad, who had recently turned professional. For those who witnessed the matches, it was among the most memorable of all rivalries. Gonzales had the more elegant strokes and probably covered the court better, but Hoad had immense physical strength and could turn baseline shots into surprise winners. By late in the year, Gonzales had fallen behind; as in 1949, he seemed destined to become the victim of another prodigy. Instead, Hoad's back began to give him serious trouble. He pulled out of the competition and was never the same again as far as tennis was concerned. Gonzales remained the king of professional tennis. His competitors called him "Gorgo," meaning "gorilla."

Professional success did not mellow Gonzales. He remained feisty, fiery, and continually suspicious both of his rivals and the tour, which he believed paid him less than he deserved. Following a dispute with Kramer (who was by then the tour's preeminent promoter and organizer), Gonzales retired abruptly in 1963.

Five years later, tennis became "open" for the first time. The major tournaments were thus open to both amateurs and professionals. Hungering for the Wimbledon title he had never won, as well as a last burst of glory, Gonzales entered Wimbledon in 1968. In the first round he drew Charlie Pasarell, a young American player. Gonzales was forty-one, and a grandfather, but he was not yet ready to step aside.

The match was one of the best ever seen at Wimbledon. It took five hours and twelve minutes and spanned two days. Gonzales emerged the victor, 22–24, 1–6, 16–14, 6–3, 11–9. Tennis no longer sees matches like this because of the twelve-game tiebreaker, instituted in 1970. Today's fans, who grew up watching tennis on television, applaud the tiebreak rule, which makes for swifter, more decisive tennis. Purists, however, lament the days when a match took as long as necessary to declare a winner. Gonzales was among the purists. He had won (and lost) many such titanic matches and believed they called for a higher level of play.

The match with Pasarell was the last hurrah. Gonzales played off and on for another two years, but the magic was gone. He had slowed noticeably, and his still elegant game could not contend with the faster variety played by Stan Smith, John Newcombe, and later by Jimmy Connors. Gonzales retired yet again.

He wrote two books outlining his classic tennis style. Tennis fans still find it hard to comprehend that Gonzales never had formal lessons; he seemed to develop tennis strokes in the way that others learn to walk. In 1968 he was elected to the International Tennis Hall of Fame. Gonzales died in Las Vegas, Nevada, in 1995. He was sixty-seven and had been battling stomach cancer.

Gonzales's personal life was at least as stormy as his career. He married a total of six times, twice to the same woman: Madelyn Darrow. His last marriage was to Rita Agassi, sister of tennis great Andre Agassi. Gonzales was survived by seven children.

One of the great questions is, How does Gonzales compare to other great champions? He had one of the most fluid games of any time period; only Pete Sampras could rival him in that category. He was a ferocious competitor, an artist on the court. It is sad that the division between professional and amateur tennis cost him so dearly. One measure of his greatness is that he competed on nearly equal terms with Hoad, who, most keen observers believe, had the most natural talent and the strongest game that tennis has ever seen. Gonzales's career was marred by his decision to turn professional; Hoad's was ruined by back trouble. Such are the vicissitudes of tennis at its highest level.

★

Gonzales's life is chronicled in *Man with a Racket: The Autobiography of Pancho Gonzales, as Told to Cy Rice* (1959). See also Pancho Gonzales and Dick Hawk, *Tennis* (1962), edited by Gladys Heldman. Other references to his career can be found in Bud Collins, *My Life with the Pros* (1989), and Jack Kramer, with Frank Deford, *The Game: My 40 Years in Tennis* (1979). Gonzales's career statistics are listed in the *Official Encyclopedia of Tennis* (1962). The match with Hoad is reported in "Hoad vs. Gonzales," *Sports Illustrated* (16 June 1958). An obituary is in the *New York Times* (5 July 1995).

SAMUEL WILLARD CROMPTON

GORDON, Jeff (*b.* 4 August 1971 in Vallejo, California), champion National Association for Stock Car Auto Racing (NASCAR) driver.

Gordon is the stepson of John Bickford, Sr., the owner of a manufacturing company specializing in auto parts, and Carol, who devoted much of her time to her son's racing career; he has two siblings. The writer Mark Bechtel, in George Tiedemann's *Trading Paint* (2001), summarized Gordon's upbringing as being "groomed to race cars," and as a result Gordon emerged as "a prodigious talent." At age four Gordon was a fiercely competitive BMX (mountain bike) rider, but when he was five his mother put a stop to high-speed biking because she felt it was too dangerous. However, at that time Gordon's stepfather bought him a six-foot, quarter-midget racing car. Gordon's stepfather was instrumental in steering Gordon toward racing. Bickford admitted: "I was living my dreams through Jeff. His being small made it obvious he'd never be a football player. So I taught him the only thing I knew, how to race." Bickford revealed the importance of focus, discipline, and intensity in Gordon's upbringing: "I approached it from a professional standpoint. This wasn't about having fun. If we want to have fun we'll go to Disney World." By age eight Gordon and his stepfather had a "stable" of eight cars, and the young Gordon was racing every week of the year.

In 1979 Gordon won his first national quarter-midget

Jeff Gordon. AP/WIDE WORLD PHOTOS

championship, and in 1982 he won his second national quarter-midget championship. From 1979 to 1982 he also raced go-karts and frequently bested rivals many years his senior. In 1986 Bickford moved the family from California to Pittsboro, Indiana, to allow Gordon more opportunities to race cars. Although only a village of 1,000 inhabitants, Pittsboro is a mere fifteen miles from the famous Indianapolis Motor Speedway. In 1989 Gordon won his first midget race, and in 1990, as a nineteen year old, he won the U.S. Automobile Club (USAC) full midget championship. Gordon was featured several times on ESPN's racing program *Thursday Night Thunder.* His good looks and extraordinary driving transformed the 1989 Pittsboro High School prom king into a genuine all-American folk hero. Immediately following graduation, Gordon enrolled in a driving school run by stock car legend Buck Baker in Rockingham, North Carolina.

Despite Gordon's "Indy" locale, his parents urged him to try the NASCAR circuit. Many drivers must slowly serve their apprenticeships by graduating through the ranks of the Craftsman Truck series and the Busch Circuit before venturing onto the NASCAR stage. With Gordon the 1990s were a blur as he rewrote the record books and quickly established himself as the "boy wonder" of auto racing. His achievements in the period 1990 to 2000 were considerable. In 1994 he won the inaugural Brickyard 400 at the Indianapolis Motor Speedway. The five-foot, seven-inch, 150-pound Chevrolet driver won Winston Cup championships in 1995, 1997, and 1998 and was runner-up to Terry Labonte in 1996. In 1995 Gordon became the youngest Winston Cup Series champion in NASCAR's modern era to that date in only his third full season. Gordon became the youngest driver to win the Daytona 500 twice and the youngest driver in Winston Cup history to achieve fifty career wins with his victory in the 2000 running of the Die Hard 500 at Talladega Superspeedway. By the end of 2000 Gordon's racing credentials were, by any yardstick, astonishing. In 257 starts he secured 52 wins, 122 top five finishes, and 159 top ten finishes, and his prize money totaled $29,570,670.

During his rookie season Gordon met Brooke Sealey, a Miss Winston model, and they married in November 1994, following the conclusion of Gordon's second NASCAR racing season. His wife, a born-again Christian with a strong commitment to Bible study, church attendance, and a teetotal lifestyle, had a profound impact on Gordon. A famous NASCAR awards photograph shows Dale Earnhardt and Gordon toasting one another. The former is consuming hard liquor, the later is quaffing milk. Gordon's credo is simple, God first, family next, and racing third.

Gordon's fan support, while considerable, stands in stark contrast to significant groups of race aficionados who have felt alienated and resentful about the seeming ease of Gordon's ascendancy. His racing team, known for their bright colors as the Rainbow Warriors, "composed of hired guns, athletes trained to come in one race day to get him in and out of the pits in a hurry," has been unsettling for some. In the tough macho world of snarling engines and 200-mile-per-hour stock cars, the "unthreatening" manner of Gordon's "sunny aura" has nourished public antipathies that seem more in keeping with professional wrestling or ice hockey. At NASCAR races it is not unusual to see spectators waving placards that read "Anybody but Gordon." His fellow NASCAR driver and regular rival Dale Jarrett said about Gordon, "He shouldn't be allowed to be that young, that talented, that experienced, and that good looking."

The year 2001 was difficult and trying for both NASCAR and Gordon. The tragedy of Dale Earnhardt's death at the conclusion of the Daytona 500 in February cast a mantle of gloom and doom over not just NASCAR but American race fans in general. While Earnhardt and Gordon were not close friends, indeed the media portrayed them as adversaries, they respected one another. Their many competitive duels resulted in mutual success. Between 1990 and 2000 Earnhardt and Gordon won seven out of ten driver championships and combined for eighty-seven wins.

Gordon and his wife, who have no children, settled near Charlotte, North Carolina. Gordon keeps fit by playing racquetball, water skiing, and snow skiing and relaxes with video games. He is active in many charities, including the Leukemia Society and Make-a-Wish Foundation.

★

For an excellent photographic study of Gordon supported by a chatty journalistic narrative, see Frank Moriarty, *Jeff Gordon* (1999). Bob McCullough, *My Greatest Day in NASCAR* (2000), features a transcribed interview with Gordon, and George Tiedemann, *Trading Paint: Dale Earnhardt v. Jeff Gordon* (2001), includes pieces by Mark Bechtel with in-depth profiles of Gordon. *Current Biography Yearbook* (2000) contains a detailed, richly layered minibiography of Gordon. Bill Center, *Ultimate Stock Car* (2000), is a good overview of NASCAR with informative segments on Gordon. Richard Pillsbury, "Stock Car Racing," in *The Theater of Sport,* edited by Karl B. Raiz (1995), is a superb essay. The *Gastonia, North Carolina, Gaston Gazette* runs a weekly column, written primarily by Monte Dutton, on NASCAR that is syndicated across the United States.

SCOTT A. G. M. CRAWFORD

GOTCH, Frank Alvin (*b.* 27 April 1878 near Humboldt, Iowa; *d.* 17 December 1917 in Humboldt, Iowa), professional freestyle wrestling champion considered one of the greatest in the history of the sport.

Gotch was the last of nine children born to Frederich Rudolph and Amelia Gotch. His parents were farmers who were married in 1855 and moved to the United States from Germany in 1863. Gotch attended a one-room schoolhouse in north-central Iowa, but like most children of the day he spent much of his time working on the farm. Gotch gained a reputation wrestling against other farm boys; his big break came when he was twenty-one years old.

In those days, big-name professional wrestlers would travel from town to town challenging local tough guys to matches. They would take bets on the outcome and pocket the winnings. On 18 June 1899 Dan McLeod, once considered the heavyweight champion of the United States, came to Luverne, Iowa, and challenged Gotch. There were no formal sanctioning bodies for wrestling, so champions were declared by newspapers, and title matches were arranged by promoters. Gotch accepted McLeod's challenge, and the two wrestled on a cinder track for nearly two hours before McLeod prevailed.

McLeod arranged for Gotch to meet Martin "Farmer" Burns, a smaller wrestler who was a master of holds and considered to be the top wrestling coach of the time. Burns decided he could turn Gotch into a champion. After training with Burns, Gotch traveled to Alaska to compete in the booming mining towns. He wrestled under the name Frank Kennedy and became the champion of the Klondike. Gotch earned $30,000 in his six-month stint in Alaska, an enormous sum in those days.

Gotch returned to Iowa to prepare for a bout for the U.S. championship with Tom Jenkins, and resumed the use of his given name. Jenkins had been recognized as champion since 1899 when Gotch met him in a match in 1903. Jenkins won the 1903 match, but Gotch eventually defeated Jenkins for the title on 8 January 1904 in Bellingham, Washington. The two met a total of eight times, with Gotch winning five of the matches.

Gotch's next challenge was George Hackenschmidt, an Estonian who held the world championship. Hackenschmidt was a former weightlifter who switched to wrestling at age twenty because it offered greater earning potential. He was a major star in Europe and had defeated Jenkins twice, once in Europe under Greco-Roman rules, a traditional style that allowed holds above the waist only, and once in the United States under freestyle rules.

Gotch met Hackenschmidt in a freestyle match on 3 April 1908 at the Dexter Park Pavilion in Chicago. Gotch, age twenty-nine, was five feet, eleven inches tall, and weighed 196 pounds; he had a forty-four-inch chest and a thirty-five-inch waist. Hackenschmidt, also twenty-nine, was five feet, nine inches tall, and weighed 218 pounds; he had a fifty-two-inch chest and a thirty-five-inch waist. Hackenschmidt's reputation was so great that President

Theodore Roosevelt, a wrestling fan, was quoted as saying, "If I couldn't be president, I'd want to be George Hackenschmidt."

Gotch's training regimen had included running to improve his stamina. In front of 8,000 spectators he wore down Hackenschmidt to win the title after a two-hour best-of-three fall match. Hackenschmidt conceded the first fall and refused to lock up for the second, quitting the match. He later accused Gotch of oiling himself so he would be difficult to hold on to.

A rematch was scheduled for 4 September 1911 in Comiskey Park. The heavily hyped rematch drew 33,000 fans and plenty of controversy. Gotch won the match relatively easily, winning the first fall in twenty-seven minutes and the second fall in just six minutes. It was rumored that Hackenschmidt had suffered a serious knee injury in training and that he went into the ring with no chance of winning. It is still debated whether Hackenschmidt used the injury as an excuse for the loss, or if a training partner was paid by gamblers to injure him, or whether he threw the match. Hackenschmidt denied this accusation and even as an old man would get angry at the mere mention of Gotch's name.

The speculation was also a product of the times. Wrestling had a carnival background, and rigged matches had already soiled the reputation of the sport. But Gotch was largely free of question because of his dominance, and continued to defend his title through 1914. He won eighty-eight consecutive matches to end his career, finishing with a record of 154–6. In 1915 he also wrestled hundreds of exhibition matches without a loss, offering his opponents $100 if they lasted more than fifteen minutes.

Soon after Gotch's retirement, the nature of wrestling changed. Promoters had grown impatient with the long and sometimes overly technical matches and desired both greater control over champions and the opportunity to earn larger purses. The result was a sport in which the outcome of each match was entirely predetermined.

In 1916 Gotch became ill and started losing weight. Despite rumors that he had syphilis, his official death certificate indicated his condition as kidney failure. A year later Gotch died at age thirty-nine at his home in Humboldt, just three years after his retirement.

Gotch was one of the first sports heroes to cross over into show business. He starred in a play that toured the world and wrestled in front of President Roosevelt in the White House. Gotch was married to Gladys Oestrich; they had one son.

★

A biography of Gotch is Mike Chapman, *Gotch: An American Hero* (1999). Bob Kurson, "Real Mayhem," in *Chicago* (Sept.

1999), is a story about the Gotch-Hackenschmidt matches. The most complete audiovisual collection on Gotch is at the International Wrestling Institute and Museum in Newton, Iowa.

RAY KRUEGER

GOWDY, Curt(is) (*b.* 31 July 1919 in Green River, Wyoming), Hall of Fame sports broadcaster and businessman.

Gowdy was the son of Edward Gowdy, a dispatcher for the Union Pacific Railroad, and Ruth Smith, a homemaker. He was educated in the Cheyenne, Wyoming, public schools and graduated in 1938 from Cheyenne High School. An outstanding high-school basketball player, Gowdy also showed his father's enthusiasm for the outdoors and began fly-fishing for trout in Wyoming streams at the age of eight. He attended the University of Wyoming in Laramie, where he played forward for the basketball team. In his junior year, he was part of a Wyoming team that reached the National Collegiate Athletic Association (NCAA) tournament, then a select group of just eight teams from throughout the nation. He also played tennis, winning three varsity letters. In 1942 Gowdy graduated from Wyoming with an M.S. degree in business.

After a brief stint in the U.S. Army Air Corps, Gowdy was discharged for medical reasons and returned to Cheyenne. While recuperating from back surgery at home, he accepted a five-dollar offer to broadcast a local high-school football game. In November 1943, before about a dozen freezing fans, he made his broadcasting debut sitting on an orange crate while doing play-by-play of a six-person football game for the Cheyenne radio station KSBC. Gowdy stayed with the station for two years and began broadcasting local basketball as well as football games. He also wrote and served as editor for the *Cheyenne Eagle* from 1943 to 1945.

In 1945 Gowdy caught the attention of Ken Brown, the station manager of KOMA radio in Oklahoma City, and obtained a job as KOMA's sports director. From 1946 through 1949 he announced the play-by-play for the University of Oklahoma, Norman, football team, which gained national prominence under the leadership of Bud Wilkenson, the school's new young coach. The success of Oklahoma's football program provided Gowdy with several opportunities to broadcast to national audiences. Basketball games at Oklahoma State University in Stillwater also gave Gowdy national exposure, as the Stillwater teams competed for national championships. Meanwhile, he spent his summers broadcasting Texas League baseball games in Oklahoma City for KOCY. On 24 June 1949 Gowdy married Jerre Dawkins, a student at the University of Oklahoma; they had three children.

Curt Gowdy, 2000. ASSOCIATED PRESS AP

In 1949 Gowdy secured the number-two play-by-play position for the New York Yankees, alongside Mel Allen on WINS in New York City. He was one of almost 300 competitors for the prestigious position. During the off-season in New York, he announced basketball games from Madison Square Garden and other sports events in Boston and New York. In 1951 Gowdy landed the head radio position for the Boston Red Sox baseball franchise on WHDH. His tenure with the Red Sox lasted until 1966. While he was with the Red Sox, Gowdy continued to announce college and professional football events for the American Broadcasting Company (ABC) during the autumn and winter seasons. Working during the early 1960s with the television producer Roone Arledge, the man who revolutionized football coverage for the budding television market, Gowdy developed the idea for a worldwide sports show for television and in 1964 began hosting ABC's *Wide World of Sports.*

Following the success of the *Wide World of Sports,* Gowdy became the lead host in ABC's *American Sportsman* in 1964. The four-time Emmy Award–winning show dedicated to outdoor hunting and fishing took him around the world and featured such guests as the entertainers Bing Crosby and Phil Harris and the baseball great Ted Williams, a close friend. In 1966 Gowdy joined the National

Broadcasting Company and became the lead football and baseball announcer for the television network, providing play-by-play for American Football Conference games and Major League Baseball's *Game of the Week* on Saturday afternoons. In 1976 he moved on to the Columbia Broadcasting System until his retirement in 1979. Even in retirement Gowdy maintained his presence in television and radio with the *American Sportsman* and other ventures, such as Home Box Office's *Inside the NFL.*

During the 1960s and 1970s Gowdy was one of the most recognizable voices in U.S. sports, and by the end of his career he had covered the gamut of sports, broadcasting for every major television network. Known for his familiar style, accurate and knowledgeable reporting, and pleasant manner, Gowdy earned a place as an icon in sportscasting. During his career he announced sixteen World Series, twelve Rose Bowls, eight Super Bowls, eight Olympic Games, and twenty-two NCAA Final Four championships in college basketball. Throughout his tenure on television and radio Gowdy earned seven awards from various national organizations. He was named as the Sportscaster of the Year three times, and in 1970 he was the first sports broadcaster to receive the George Foster Peabody Award for excellence in reporting. In 1984 Gowdy also received the Ford C. Frick Award at the National Baseball Hall of Fame, and the following year, he was inducted into the American Sportscasters Association Hall of Fame.

In 1957 Gowdy took a year off from broadcasting because of persistent back problems. Concerned that his broadcasting career might soon end, he began buying local radio stations and purchased operations in Wyoming, Massachusetts, and Florida. These investments proved to be highly successful. Gowdy wrote two books based on his broadcasting experiences, *Cowboy at the Mike* (1966), with Al Hirshberg, and *Seasons to Remember: The Way It Was in American Sports, 1945–1960* (1993), with John Powers. An avid conservationist, Gowdy served on the boards of Trout Unlimited and the International Game Fish Association. Recognizing that sport fishermen could no longer fish the streams as he had done in his youth, when trout limits were twenty per day, Gowdy became an advocate for "catch and release" as the best way to protect the waters and fish for future generations.

With respect to his well-informed, yet relaxed style at the microphone, Gowdy once explained, "I tried to pretend that I was sitting in the stands with a buddy watching the game—poking him in the ribs when something exciting happened. I never took myself too seriously. An announcer is only as good as yesterday's performance."

★

For a discussion of Gowdy's radio career, see Curt Smith, *Of Mikes and Men: From Ray Scott to Curt Gowdy—Broadcast Tales from the Pro Football Booth* (1998). See also Curt Smith, *The Storytellers: From Mel Allen to Bob Costas, Sixty Years of Baseball Tales from the Broadcast Booth* (1995).

MICHAEL J. DEVINE

GRAHAM, Otto Everett, Jr. (*b.* 6 December 1921 in Waukegan, Illinois), quarterback who led the Cleveland Browns to ten straight division or league crowns.

Graham was one of four sons of Otto Everett Graham and Cordonna Hayes, who both taught music in the public schools in Waukegan. Graham was born making records. His birth weight of fourteen pounds, twelve ounces, still stands as a record for the state of Illinois. Graham excelled in sports and music during his high school years at Waukegan High School. He became the Illinois French horn champion at age sixteen and also played the violin, piano, and coronet. As a senior, Graham played in his high school's National Champion brass sextet. An all-around athlete, he played football, basketball, and baseball, and was a member of Illinois All-State squads in basketball (1937) and football (1938).

Graham, who stood six feet, one inch tall, entered Northwestern University in 1941 on a basketball scholarship, majoring in education with a minor in music. In his sophomore year he ended up playing football as well, the result of being discovered playing in an intramural game by "Pappy" Waldorf, the coach at Northwestern. Graham set a Big Ten record in 1942, his junior year, by completing 89 of 182 passes for 1,092 yards. As a senior he was an All-American in both football and basketball. Graham picked up his nickname, "Automatic Otto," from his basketball playing; he was the team captain and the second leading Big Ten scorer. In football he was named Big Ten Most Valuable Player (MVP), and he was named Wildcat basketball MVP in 1943. Graham also held Northwestern's third highest batting average, and he was third in balloting in 1943 for the Heisman Trophy as a result of his football playing.

After graduating from Northwestern in 1944 with a major in education, Graham spent two years in the Navy's V-5 carrier program. He married his college sweetheart Beverly Collinge in 1945; they had three children. Following preflight training Graham went to the University of North Carolina at Chapel Hill, where he became a cadet regimental commander. At Chapel Hill Graham learned the T-formation and, with coach Paul Brown, began to develop a style of quarterbacking that featured his throwing ability and established passing as an essential offensive strategy. After World War II ended, Graham played a season of basketball with the Rochester Royals, the team that won the National Basketball League championship in 1946. He then switched to football, signing with the Cleveland Browns, a new team in the upstart All-America Football Conference (AAFC).

The AAFC, founded in June 1944, began its first season in September 1946. The Browns were the new kids on the block. The newcomers, as Graham recalled, were looked on with disdain: "Oh, the derogatory comments that were

Otto Graham, 1954. ASSOCIATED PRESS AP

being made by the NFL owners, players, coaches, you name it. They said the worst team in the NFL could beat our best team [from the AAFC]."

Graham's performance and the Browns' success over the four years that the AAFC existed surely made believers of many. The Browns dominated the conference in 1946 and 1947, went undefeated in 1948, and won their fourth title in 1949, shattering records for attendance at professional football games along the way. Graham passed for a total of 86 touchdowns during the four seasons, and the Browns were 52–4–3. Graham was named the league's MVP in 1947, 1948, and 1949.

Whatever skepticism remained concerning Graham's talents and the Browns' ability to win games disappeared when the Browns joined the National Football League (NFL) in 1950 and played against the Philadelphia Eagles, the NFL champions for two years running. The Eagles, so the current wisdom had it, were to teach the Browns how the game was played. It did not work out quite that way. Graham threw three touchdown passes and the Browns manhandled the Eagles, posting a final score of 35–10. "It was the highlight of my career," Graham later said. The Browns lost only twice during the season and went on to win the championship against the Los Angeles Rams, a team that had defected from Cleveland in 1945. Graham was named the NFL's MVP, the first of three such awards.

The Browns were runners-up in title games for the next three years, once against the Rams, twice against the Lions. They won it all in 1954, with Graham putting on a bravura performance against the Lions. He threw three touchdown passes and ran for three more as the Browns crushed the Lions 56–10. Graham wanted to retire at the end of the 1954 season, but Paul Brown convinced him to play one more year and win one more NFL title, this time against the Rams. Graham threw for two touchdowns and ran for two more, and the Browns won 38–14.

Graham was thirty-three years old when he retired from the Browns in 1944. In 1955 he received the Rae Hickock Belt as the best athlete in the United States–All Sports for having led his team to ten straight championship games and winning seven, four in the AAFC and three in the NFL. Graham was the first football player to receive this honor. The Browns retired his number 14 jersey, the first jersey retired by the team. Graham's jersey and his Hickcock Belt are now in the Professional Football Hall of Fame. Graham was inducted into the Pro Football Hall of Fame in 1965, the first year of his eligibility, and in 1994 he was named along with Sammy Baugh, Johnny Unitas, and Joe Montana to the NFL's seventy-fifth anniversary all-time team.

In 1959 Graham became the athletic director and football coach at the United States Coast Guard Academy in New London, Connecticut, a position he left briefly to be the head coach and general manager of the Washington Redskins from 1966 to 1968. He returned to the Academy after being replaced by Vince Lombardi and remained its athletic director and coach until his retirement in 1985. Graham also coached ten All-Star squads, with wins over the Detroit Lions in 1958 and the Green Bay Packers in 1963.

An enormously gifted athlete, Graham is one of those players who shaped and defined the modern game of football. He was an able captain who led by conveying his belief in the talents and capabilities of his teammates. He was not boisterous and did not show off or berate his teammates for lapses; he was a consummate craftsman and a joy to watch.

★

Biographical material about Graham's life and career is scattered among a myriad of books about the Browns and professional football. Helpful books are John Keim, *Legends by the Lake: The Cleveland Browns at Municipal Stadium* (1999); Peter King, *Greatest Quarterbacks* (1999); and Richard Shmelter, *The Browns: Cleveland's Team* (1999).

ROBERT B. CAREY

GRANGE, Harold Edward ("Red") (*b.* 13 June 1903 in Forksville, Pennsylvania; *d.* 28 January 1991 in Lake Wales, Florida), red-haired football idol during the Jazz Age of the 1920s whose astounding feats as a college and professional player helped popularize pro football as a viable commercial enterprise.

Born the third of four children of Lyle and Sadie (Sherman) Grange, Grange experienced a difficult childhood. His mother died when he was only five, prompting his father, a lumberjack foreman, to move from Pennsylvania to Wheaton, Illinois, a town west of Chicago. There he had relatives who could help raise his daughters and sons. The family moved sporadically until the elder Grange's appointment as police chief provided some stability. Young Grange spent a year working on his uncle's nearby farm and delivered huge blocks of ice to homes during the summer months, later earning him the sobriquet the "Wheaton Iceman."

Inheriting size, strength, speed, and a genuine sense of humility from his father, Grange soon excelled in sports. Though not big by modern football standards, the 180-lb., five-foot, ten inch-tall Grange earned sixteen letters at Wheaton Community High School, competing in football, basketball, baseball, and track. As a sophomore running back Grange showed his early promise by scoring fifteen touchdowns in only seven games and winning selection to the all-county team. The following year he accounted for

Red Grange, 1925. ASSOCIATED PRESS

thirty-six touchdowns and thirty extra points, twice scoring more than fifty points in a game. His senior year proved only slightly less impressive, with twenty-six touchdowns and thirty-four points after touchdowns (PATs). He added all-sectional honors in basketball and state track championships in the 100- and 220-yard dashes as well as the long jump to his list of incredible accomplishments during his high school career.

Grange enrolled at the University of Illinois in 1922, when freshmen were ineligible for varsity competition. He emerged as a star the following year, however, as Illinois vied with other midwestern schools for regional honors and national publicity. College football teams began winning acclaim for their institutions in the late nineteenth century, and by the 1920s college football enjoyed a national following. Its widespread popularity spawned the construction of massive stadiums on college campuses to maximize revenues as sports became commercialized enterprises linked to higher education. Newspapers, magazines, and the new technology of radio provided extensive coverage of games, promoting teams, coaches, and individual players.

Within that era of ballyhoo, the "Four Horsemen" of Notre Dame garnered fame as a well-oiled machine, guided by the coaching genius of Knute Rockne, but Grange's gridiron feats emerged as the catalyst for individual stardom. Grange's accomplishments, combined with a shy, reserved, and humble demeanor, produced the qualities expected of heroes, further endearing him to a multitude of fans.

Grange gained fame for his long, dazzling runs through the opposition and for turning short pass plays into long gains. He clearly made his mark in his first varsity game (against the University of Nebraska in 1923), rushing for more than 200 yards and scoring three touchdowns, two on long runs. He scored the winning touchdown against Iowa, defending conference champion, and gained 247 yards against Northwestern. Grange tallied the winning scores against Chicago, Wisconsin, and Ohio State, amassing 1,260 yards and leading the league in scoring en route to an undefeated season, the conference cochampionship, and All-American honors.

The following year ensured his football immortality. Coach Bob Zuppke switched Grange to the tailback position in the single wing formation to make better use of his multiple talents, and his versatility soon became evident.

The University of Illinois had erected a massive stadium for its campus, accommodating more than 60,000 eager patrons. Deemed Memorial Stadium to honor the Illinois students who had made the ultimate sacrifice during World War I, the arena symbolically linked football with patriotism, and regional rival Michigan had been scheduled for the dedication game (1924), ensuring widespread media coverage.

Grange struck like lightning, returning the opening kickoff 95 yards for a touchdown. He quickly scored three more times within the first twelve minutes of the contest on runs of sixty-seven, fifty-six, and forty-four yards. After resting throughout the second quarter, he returned in the third period to score yet again, then passed for another touchdown in the final stanza. He had run for more than 400 yards and passed in excess of 60 to ensure the Illinois victory. The performance won Grange instant celebrity status. Newspaper and magazine articles raised him to heroic proportions by emphasizing not only his prodigious athletic abilities but his humility, work ethic, and reputed poverty in small-town America. Such qualities resonated with American perceptions of the past and the egalitarian promise of democracy as citizens wrestled with rapid societal changes wrought by urbanization, industrialization, and commercialization. Grange represented traditional values yet proved to be a transitional figure in the new economy.

Despite such recognition the eastern media still perceived "western" football as substandard and Grange's exploits as dubious. Grange erased their doubts in the 1925 season. After a disappointing start, Illinois traveled to Philadelphia to meet Penn, the best of the eastern teams the previous year and undefeated in 1925. Before the suspect eyes of the eastern sportswriters and on a muddy field, Grange ran for 363 yards and scored three touchdowns to humiliate Penn 24–2.

More than 100 reporters and over 85,000 fans watched Grange's last collegiate game at Ohio State. Although he passed for only one touchdown, Grange created a bigger stir and a burgeoning scandal after the game when he announced he would leave college to join the professional football ranks with the Chicago Bears. His decision and lucrative contract, engineered by agent C. C. Pyle, caused collegiate coaches to ostracize their professional counterparts for meddling and led to a change in National Football League (NFL) policy to prohibit recruitment before graduation.

Pyle had struck a favorable deal with the Bears, providing Grange with 50 percent of the gate receipts. Pyle himself would receive 40 percent of Grange's take. Both the Bears and Pyle wanted to cash in on Grange's celebrity status, and the young football star soon took the field for a Thanksgiving Day game in Chicago against the first-place Cardinals. More than 36,000 fans filled Cubs Park and thousands more were turned away, but the game proved anticlimactic. Disappointed spectators, there to see Grange run, booed Cardinal punter Paddy Driscoll, who continually negated Grange's chances by kicking the ball away from him in a scoreless tie.

The Bears sold out again the following week against a weak team from Columbus, Ohio, and Grange played well in a narrow victory. Thereafter, the Bears embarked on barnstorming tours that capitalized on the Grange phenomenon. In addition to the Bears' regularly scheduled league games, Pyle added contests in several large cities. After an easy win in St. Louis, the Bears turned eastward, playing before 35,000 in Philadelphia and more than 70,000 in New York, where Grange was accorded a bodyguard of fifty policemen for the largest crowd to witness a pro game up to that time. Grange's stellar play and Pyle's promotional abilities engendered numerous endorsement contracts as Grange, bestowed with the nickname "Galloping

Ghost" by sportswriter Grantland Rice, assumed the modern role of athletic huckster.

The tour continued through Washington, Boston, and Pittsburgh, with Grange becoming a marked man by opponents. The scheduled tour called for eight games in twelve days, but an injury to Grange caused him to miss two games, and the Bears canceled a final appearance at Cleveland. After a two-week hiatus, a southern and western tour resumed the day after Christmas and lasted through January 1926. Grange returned to the field for three games in Florida, one in New Orleans, and three in California, where 75,000 spectators paid to see the game in Los Angeles. The tour concluded with games in Portland and Seattle.

Spurred by the tour's success, Pyle sought part ownership of the Bears' franchise for himself and his client. Denied and unable to secure another franchise in the NFL, Pyle organized a rival organization to exploit Grange's fame for the 1926 season. Hastily established and victimized by bad weather that limited attendance, the alternative American Football League struggled through one season before expiring. Grange still drew fans, however, and the NFL welcomed his return as he and Pyle managed the New York Yankees' franchise.

Midway through the 1927 season Grange suffered a serious knee injury in a game against the Bears that sidelined him for four weeks and greatly limited his effectiveness thereafter. Reinjured in a postseason barnstorming tour, Grange sat out the 1928 football season engaged in a vaudeville tour and a Hollywood movie. Pyle committed him to appear in *One Minute to Play* and *The Racing Romeo,* and Grange also appeared in a profitable movie serial called *The Galloping Ghost.* After terminating his partnership with Pyle, Grange returned to the Chicago Bears for the 1929 season, where he joined his younger brother Garland. Although football fans continued to throng to Grange appearances, a dislocated shoulder further hampered his offensive abilities.

Grange had greater success during the 1930 football season, and he gained more than 1,000 yards, played stellar defense, and won selection to the all-NFL team. He reclaimed that honor the following year, although his offensive production had declined. Grange continued to play well defensively in 1932, and he won additional fame for his winning touchdown catch while lying on his back during the championship playoff game with the Portsmouth, Ohio, Spartans. This memorable night game was played indoors at the Chicago Stadium on an abbreviated field due to inclement weather. In the 1933 title game Grange made the game-saving tackle as time expired against the New York Giants.

The 1934 season began with the Bears opposing a college all-star team before more than 79,000 at Soldier Field in Chicago. Grange had helped publicize the event, which remained a popular preseason spectacle for more than four decades. The initial scoreless tie failed to settle the debate over the merits of collegiate versus professional players. The Bears completed an undefeated season but lost the championship game to the Giants, who had donned gym shoes in the famous "sneakers" game played on a frozen field at the Polo Grounds. Grange retired after another postseason tour.

Grange remained with the Bears as an assistant coach through the 1937 season and parlayed his fame into other opportunities. He had written football commentaries for newspapers as early as the 1920s and became a regular contributor to the *Saturday Evening Post* in 1932. His articles further established the credibility of professional football by extolling its players' predominance in comparison to the college game. Grange began announcing football games in 1934 and continued his broadcasting career with the CBS radio network thereafter, providing observation and analysis periodically during the fall.

In 1937 Grange relinquished his coaching duties in favor of a sales manager position with the Hinckley & Schmitt water company. During that year he also contributed to a biography of Bob Zuppke, his former coach at Illinois.

Grange married Margaret Hazelberg, an airline stewardess, on 13 October 1941 in Crown Point, Indiana. She is credited with bringing financial stability to the football star's previously spendthrift lifestyle, and in 1942 he started his own insurance business in Chicago.

In 1944 Grange accepted the presidency of a new professional football league, but he resigned before play commenced to ensure the success of his insurance brokerage. He became a public relations representative for the Falstaff Brewing Company, and he continued his radio commentaries, which expanded to television broadcasts in the years following World War II. Grange covered the Bears' games until his retirement from that role in 1963, and he reported on college contests until 1969.

In 1950 Illinois Republicans, attracted by Grange's conservative political views, elected him a trustee of the University of Illinois. He served in that role for five years, despite suffering a heart attack in 1951. In 1954 the Granges left Chicago for Florida, residing in Miami for five years until they built a house near Lake Wales in central Florida, where Grange pursued boating, fishing, and golfing.

Despite that secluded location, Grange remained in demand. In 1957 Congress summoned his testimony in its investigation of professional football's adherence to antitrust laws. He furthered his political involvement in 1960 as a member of a Republican national organizing committee.

Although Grange tried to maintain a low profile throughout the remainder of his life, his fame followed

him. The National Collegiate Hall of Fame had already inducted him when the Pro Football Hall of Fame made him a charter member in 1963. The Helms Athletic Foundation offered additional laurels, and the Football Writers Association named him the only unanimous choice for its all-time All-America team in 1969. His own career had been a model for professional athletes, drawing comparisons to the superstars of the 1960s who enjoyed remunerative contracts and endorsements, yet his courteous, reserved, and modest behavior offered ample contrast to their boisterous and flamboyant individuality.

Age and old football injuries slowed Grange in the 1980s. He was diagnosed with Parkinson's disease in 1990 and died on 28 January 1991 of pneumonia in Lake Wales Hospital in Florida.

The longevity of Grange's mark on football and American culture is undeniable. It took sixty-five years before another player surpassed his scoring records at Illinois, and Howard Griffith did so with much less fanfare. Grange is often credited with bringing credibility and popularity to professional football, perhaps attributing too much credit to a singular individual. Societal processes, economic conditions, and media attention certainly provided the environment for hero worship, as they did for Babe Ruth in baseball or Jack Dempsey in boxing, but Grange's legendary football feats surely catapulted him to national celebrity status, forever linking his name with the sport.

★

The Red Grange Story: An Autobiography (1953), was written with Ira Morton almost forty years before Grange's death. *Halas by Halas: The Autobiography of George Halas* (1979), provides substantial coverage of Grange's pro football career. John Carroll's award-winning biography *Red Grange and the Rise of Modern Football* (1999) is the most complete account of Grange's life, and John Sayle Watterson, *College Football: History, Spectacle, Controversy* (2000), presents a brief summary of the player's college exploits. *The Coffin Corner* (19:1, 1997), the official magazine of the Progressive Football Researchers Association, gives a detailed evolution of the "Grange League" of 1926. An obituary is in the *New York Times* (29 Jan. 1991).

GERALD R. GEMS

GRAZIANO, Rocky (*b.* 6 June 1922 in New York City; *d.* 22 May 1990 in New York City), middleweight boxing champion who won his title in a 1947 rematch with Tony Zale and went on to become a successful author and television personality.

Graziano was born Thomas Rocco Barbella, the fifth child of Nick and Ida Scinto Barbella. He grew up on the Lower East Side of Manhattan in a tough neighborhood where

Rocky Graziano, 1947. ASSOCIATED PRESS AP

his father, a former boxer, struggled to support the family. Graziano's father had a drinking problem and was prone to violence, while his mother developed mental and emotional problems that required hospitalization. Growing up angry and rebellious, Graziano dropped out of sixth grade and was arrested for breaking into a vending machine at age twelve. A downward spiral of petty criminal acts led to three terms in reform school over the next several years. Among his more comical exploits in his early teens was an attempt to dig up the grave of New York Dutch colonial governor Peter Stuyvesant in search of his gold watch and silver peg leg.

In his childhood, Graziano was forced to spar with his older brother Joe, whom his father saw as professional boxer material. He hated the experience and vowed never to follow his father into the ring. As a street fighter, though, Graziano did not hesitate to battle all comers. In 1939 he began to channel his rage into bouts at New York's famed Stillman's Gym. His first real fight there was against Antonio Fernandez, a professional who whipped him soundly. Two months later he tried again, this time adopting the name of his sister's boyfriend, Rocky Graziano, as his boxing moniker. He won the contest and was awarded a medal by the Metropolitan Amateur Athletic Union, which he promptly hocked for $15.

Graziano's budding career was interrupted in 1940 when a parole violation sent him first to a New York City reform school, then to the city jail on Riker's Island. Shortly after his release, he was drafted into the U.S. Army. While stationed at Fort Dix in New Jersey, he knocked out a captain and went AWOL, which eventually led to a nine-month sentence in Leavenworth Federal Penitentiary in Kansas. He kept in shape as a member of the prison boxing squad while serving his time.

Once freed, Graziano decided to change his ways and pursue boxing in earnest. He quickly established himself as a brawler with real brute power, if not great finesse. He fought between the welterweight and middleweight divisions, trudging through years of mixed victories and defeats from 1942 through 1944. His luck began to change on 9 March 1945, when he took on the highly regarded welterweight Billy Arnold at Madison Square Garden. Graziano had lost two consecutive bouts to Harold Green at the end of 1944 and was not expected to prevail against Arnold. But Graziano scored an upset by knocking out his opponent in the third round. He went on to beat Al "Bummy" Davis on 25 May 1945 and to knock out Freddie Cochrane in two consecutive matches—29 June and 24 August 1945—the second of which *Ring* magazine declared the Fight of the Year for 1945.

More than anything, it was Graziano's savagery in the ring that caught the attention of boxing professionals and sportswriters. His uncontrollable fury was on display when he scored a knock-out win over Marty Servo at Madison Square Garden on 29 March 1946. The bout climaxed in the second round, as Graziano smashed Servo repeatedly in the head with his punishing right as he held his opponent's chin up with his left, pounding until Servo fell senseless.

The bout with Servo served as a warm-up for the first of Graziano's three famous fights with Tony Zale for the world middleweight title. The first of these was held at New York's Yankee Stadium on 27 September 1946 and is remembered as an especially ferocious match; *Ring* magazine proclaimed it Fight of the Year. In the sixth round, Zale rallied from Graziano's near-knockout blows to deliver a shot to his opponent's solar plexus. Graziano crumbled, nearly paralyzed with pain, and went down for the count. His chance for a rematch was delayed when his New York boxing license was suspended for three months on the charge of failing to report a $100,000 bribe. Banned from New York, he met Zale instead at Chicago Stadium on 16 July 1947, where he endured blood loss and badly swollen eyes to knock out Zale in the sixth round. He continued to pummel his fallen opponent until the referee pulled him off. At the end of the fight, which *Ring* declared as Fight of the Year, Graziano took the microphone and said, "Hey, Ma, your bad boy done it. . . ." I told you somebody up there likes me." This went on to become the fighter's trademark line.

The third and final match between Graziano and Zale took place at Roosevelt Stadium in Jersey City, New Jersey, on 10 June 1948. The defending champion seemed to lack some of his old fire, and was knocked out by a left hook from Zale in the third round. He had held the world heavyweight title for just eleven months. Years later, Graziano saw this defeat as a positive turning point in his life. "The last of Rocco Barbella had been knocked out of me," he said. "The wild kid was gone forever. . . ."

By that time Graziano had been married happily for nearly five years to Norma Unger, whom he married on 10 August 1943, and was the father of two daughters. His days as a juvenile delinquent were long behind him and the rage that drove him to fight was fading. He continued to box after losing his title, going undefeated in his next twenty-one fights. His 19 September 1951 match with Tony Janiro was considered especially memorable, showing flashes of Graziano's old brawler style. On 16 April 1952 he went up against Sugar Ray Robinson for his last shot at the middleweight title at Chicago Stadium. When he knocked Robinson to the floor in the third round, hopes rose that the former champion would regain his crown. These proved premature when Robinson revived and knocked out Graziano in the same round. Five months later, he lost to Chuck Davey in a ten-round bout. With that, Graziano retired with few regrets, and a lifetime record of sixty-seven wins, ten losses, and sixty-two draws, with fifty-two knockouts.

With his lovably battered face and thick New York ac-

cent, Graziano became a popular television performer. He cohosted a variety show with comedienne Martha Raye in the 1950s and later appeared in commercials for dog food, auto transmissions, and yogurt. This last television spot led to his recording a comedy album, *The Maharisi Yogurt,* for R.I.C. Records. Graziano's best-selling 1955 autobiography *Somebody Up There Likes Me* was made into a film starring Paul Newman the following year. He appeared as himself in several movies, including *Mr. Rock and Roll* (1957) and *Country Music Holiday* (1958). Graziano went on to write or coauthor other books, including *The Rocky Road to Physical Fitness* (1968) and *Somebody Down Here Likes Me, Too* (1979).

After suffering declining health for a number of years, Graziano died of cardiopulmonary failure at New York Hospital in 1990. Tributes appeared in the press that stressed his generous, humble nature as much as his fighting prowess. His crude ring technique kept him from being considered a truly front-rank champion. Rather, it was his inspiring up-from-the-streets story and the resilient optimism of his later years that guaranteed him an enduring place in sports history.

★

Graziano's *Somebody Up There Likes Me* (1955), written with Rowland Baker, is a captivating memoir, though its dates are not always reliable. *Somebody Down Here Likes Me, Too* (1979), written with Ralph Corsel, continues in a similar vein. Don Dunphy's *Don Dunphy at Ringside* (1988) provides detailed coverage of Graziano's fights with Zale and Arnold, and Peter Walsh's *Men of Steel* (1993) is reliable for biographical information. Obituaries are in the *New York Times* (23 May 1990), and *Newsday* (24 May 1990), both of which provide well-researched overviews of his life and career.

BARRY ALFONSO

GREB, Edward Henry ("Harry") (*b.* 6 June 1894 in Pittsburgh, Pennsylvania; *d.* 22 October 1926 in Atlantic City, New Jersey), professional boxer who won both the world middleweight and American light heavyweight titles in the 1920s.

Greb was born Edward Henry Berg to Pious and Anne Berg in a Pittsburgh street car on the corner of Fitch and Dauphin Streets. Legend has it that he was a fighter from the start, giving his mother an inadvertent black eye when he was just a day old. He grew up in a strict household to parents who, according to record, never went to see him fight in the ring.

After winning his first five amateur bouts, Berg was signed to a professional boxing contract by James M. "Red" Mason. He fought his first pro match under the name Harry Greb (reversing the letters of his last name) on 29 May 1913, a six-round no-decision against Frank Kirkwood.

Harry Greb. ARCHIVE PHOTOS, INC.

history. Not known for his punching power, he overwhelmed opponents with quick, accurate punches thrown from a variety of angles, earning him the nickname the Human Windmill. Greb fought so often he rarely needed extensive training for his bouts. His ring endurance remains virtually unmatched in boxing history.

Greb's 299 career bouts included a record forty-four fights in one year, and he fought more bouts than Jim Corbett, Jim Jeffries, Gene Tunney, Joe Louis, Rocky Marciano, and Muhammad Ali combined. His ring record includes many of the most famous fighters in history, including Gene Tunney, Mickey Walker, Battling Levinsky, Tommy Loughran, Mike Gibbons, Jack Dillon, Al McCoy, Tiger Flowers, and Gunboat Smith.

Greb's greatest boxing ambition was to fight Jack Dempsey for the heavyweight title. He was considered a serious challenger to Dempsey's crown in 1922, sparring with him twice that year. Both times, however, he was thrown out of the champion's camp by Dempsey's manager, Jack "Doc" Kearns, who accused Greb of being "too rough with my fighter." Asked in 1925 how he would have fared had he fought Dempsey, Greb remarked, "If I didn't blind him by the sixth round, he would have killed me in the seventh."

Sportswriters of the time labeled Greb one of the dirtiest fighters they had seen, accusing him of biting, butting, gouging, and thumbing his opponents. Boxing writer W. O. McGeehan described Greb's ring style as "the manly art of modified murder." Greb laughed off such accusations but did acknowledge that his style was less than refined. "Prize fighting ain't the noblest of arts," he said, "and I ain't its noblest artist."

Despite his reputation for roughness, Greb lost only one fight via disqualification—to Kid Norfolk on 19 April 1924—and it is generally accepted that it was against Norfolk three years earlier, on 29 August, that he permanently lost the sight in his right eye due to an errant thumbing. (Other accounts have Greb losing his sight following a head butt against Jeff Smith on 1 February 1922.) Greb also had poor vision in his left eye. Though unable to see clearly as far as across the ring, he passed pre-fight physicals by memorizing eye charts.

In contrast to his rough style in the ring, Greb kept himself impeccably groomed. He slicked his hair down with Vaseline prior to each fight and was said by close friend and stablemate Cuddy DeMarco to get angrier about getting his hair mussed during fights than he was about getting punched.

Greb engaged in the most memorable bout of his career on 23 May 1922. Then under the tutelage of manager George Engel, he challenged undefeated light heavyweight champion Gene Tunney. Though Tunney was more than two inches taller and twelve pounds heavier than Greb, the

Greb's first pro victory came in his next bout, a second-round technical knockout of "Battling" Murphy on 19 July. He followed with a first-round knockout of Lloyd Crutcher in Punxatawney, Pennsylvania, on 13 August, Greb's first fight outside his native Pittsburgh. Three six-round no-decision bouts followed before Greb suffered his first pro defeat, a second-round knockout, to Joe Chip on 29 November.

In 1914 and 1915, Greb fought thirty-one straight no-decision bouts. Standing five-foot-eight, his career weight varied between 142 and 173 pounds, but his relatively small size was never a limitation. "Big guys don't bother me," Greb said. "They just get in their own way." His willingness to take on all comers resulted in bouts against such luminaries as Jack Blackburn, a lightweight who later earned fame as the principal trainer of heavyweight champion Joe Louis; former middleweight champion George "Chip" Chipolunis; and Tommy Gibbons, who would later fight Jack Dempsey for the world heavyweight title.

From 1916 to 1920 Greb battled his way through the middleweight ranks. He fought 152 times and earned wins over middleweight great Mike Gibbons and former light heavyweight champion Jack Dillon. In time, Greb earned a reputation as one of the more colorful fighters in ring

challenger battered him for fifteen rounds to win the title. Tunney's beating was so severe he lost two quarts of blood during the bout and spent the week after the fight in a hospital. This fight was the first of a five-bout series between Greb and Tunney. Of the remaining four contests, Tunney won two and two resulted in no-decisions.

After reuniting with his original manager, Red Mason, Greb lost his title to Tunney in their first rematch, a fifteen-round decision on 23 February 1923 in New York City. Tunney had enlisted the help of world lightweight champion Benny Leonard, a master boxer who showed him ways to combat Greb's hard-charging style, namely through punches under the heart to slow Greb down. The strategy worked, but six months later Greb won the world middleweight championship when he defeated Johnny Wilson on 31 August. He defended his title six times, including a famous fifteen-round decision over Mickey Walker in New York on 2 July 1925. Legend has it that Greb and Walker continued their contest outside a New York nightclub later that same evening. Two weeks later, the irrepressible Greb boxed future light heavyweight champion "Slapsie" Maxie Rosenbloom to a ten-round no-decision in a nontitle bout.

Greb lost the middleweight title on a split decision to Tiger Flowers on 26 February 1926. The two rematched six months later, and when Greb lost a controversial decision, the Madison Square Garden crowd rioted.

Greb announced his retirement following this bout. He was thirty-two years old, married, and had one daughter, whom he loved dearly. Shortly after retiring, Greb was involved in an auto accident that left his nose broken and both legs injured. A bone fragment was hampering his breathing, and since he was contemplating a ring comeback, he decided to undergo surgery to have his nose fixed and a cataract removed from his eye. On 21 October 1926 Greb underwent surgery in Atlantic City, New Jersey, during which he was given ether mixed with nitrous oxide and oxygen. He slipped into a coma and the next day died of heart failure induced by shock from the operation.

Greb's career record was 115–8–3, with one no-contest and 178 no-decisions. His 299 career fights ranks third in ring history. He was the American light heavyweight champion from 1922 to 1923 and the world middleweight champion from 1923 to 1926. An inductee of the International Boxing Hall of Fame, Greb is remembered by ring historians as one of the great fighters of all time. While he is said to have lived the high life outside the ring, friends who knew him discount those stories as exaggerated segments of the Greb legend.

★

Greb's colorful career is documented in James R. Fair, *Give Him to the Angels: The Story of Harry Greb* (1945), the only full-

length account of his life. Biographical accounts appear in Gilbert Odd, *Boxing: The Great Champions* (1974); James B. Roberts and Alex Skutt, *The Boxing Register* (1999); and Bert Randolph Sugar, *The 100 Greatest Boxers of All Time* (1984).

EDWARD GRUVER

GREENBERG, Henry Benjamin ("Hank") (*b.* 1 January 1911 in New York City; *d.* 4 September 1986 in Beverly Hills, California), first Jewish baseball player enshrined in the National Baseball Hall of Fame and two-time American League (AL) Most Valuable Player (MVP) who was widely acclaimed for his hitting ability and respected for his good sportsmanship.

Greenberg was the third of four children of David Greenberg and Sarah Schwartz, both immigrants from Romania. The family lived in Manhattan where Greenberg's father owned the Acme Textile Shrinking Works and his mother was a homemaker. Orthodox Jews, the Greenbergs kept a kosher home in which both English and Yiddish were spoken.

In his autobiography, Greenberg recalled that, when the family moved to the Bronx when he was six or seven, "it was also the turning point of my life because of Crotona Park, its large athletic field, and school sports." A tall, ungainly youth who eventually attained a height of six feet, four inches, Greenberg's love of sports developed early, much to the dismay of his parents, who prized education and envisioned professional careers for their children. He spent countless hours playing baseball, basketball, and even, at James Monroe High School, a little football; baseball, however, was always his major obsession.

With a determination to excel that continued throughout his career, Greenberg practiced long hours, honing his skills and taming the awkwardness that came with his large body and flat feet. During his years in the major leagues, he would hire peanut vendors and park attendants to shag balls for him as he practiced before games. Celebrated sportswriter Red Smith wrote that Greenberg "earned all the honors that came to him."

In the interim between graduation from high school in February 1929 and commencement of fall classes at New York University (NYU), where he had been awarded an athletic scholarship, Greenberg played semiprofessional baseball in the Blackstone Valley League in Massachusetts. During his stint with the East Douglas team, several major league scouts expressed interest, but it was the Detroit Tigers that eventually signed Greenberg to a contract. Subsequently, he completed one semester at NYU, but then dropped out to concentrate on baseball; his father, who viewed the sport as merely a game, conceded it was an

Hank Greenberg *(left)* with Phil Cavarretta of the Chicago Cubs, 1945. AP/WIDE WORLD PHOTOS

acceptable business after learning of his son's $9,000 salary offer.

Greenberg's career with the Tigers did not begin auspiciously. Assigned first to a Triple-A team, as provided in his contract, he saw rapid demotions to lower-level leagues as his batting and fielding skills failed to live up to promise. It was not until 1932, while playing in the Texas League, that he began to emerge as a power hitter and competent first baseman; that year, he was voted MVP in the league. In 1933 he was called up to the Tigers.

In his long career with the Tigers, Greenberg brought glory to himself as well as to his team. In addition to his athletic feats, he won the respect of the fans, writers, and other players by remaining dignified in the face of rampant anti-Semitism. With the Tigers fighting for the pennant in 1934, Greenberg was faced with the dilemma of playing on Rosh Hashanah, the Jewish New Year—should he betray his heritage or let down his teammates? A last-minute dispensation from Detroit's chief rabbi led to two home runs and a win for the Tigers. Greenberg's father, however, laid down the law with regard to his son playing on Yom Kippur, the holiest of Jewish holidays, and Greenberg declined to play that day. This courageous act was memorialized in a poem by Edgar Guest in the Detroit *Free Press* ending with, "We shall miss him on the infield and shall miss him at the bat. But he's true to his religion—and I honor him for that!"

Greenberg was named the American League's MVP in 1935 and 1940. In 1938 he hit fifty-eight home runs, coming close to matching Babe Ruth's (at that time) record. There were rumors, which Greenberg discounted, that pitchers deliberately walked him in the last few games of the season because they did not want a Jew breaking Ruth's record. Although he did not surpass Ruth, he led the American League in home runs in 1935, 1938, 1940, and 1946; was first in RBI in 1935, 1937, 1940, and 1946; and played in four World Series. To accommodate the team's needs, he switched from first base to left field in 1940 and excelled at that position as well.

Drafted into the U.S. Army in May 1941, Greenberg was discharged because of age just days before the Japanese attacked Pearl Harbor. Placing duty to his country ahead of personal glory, he immediately enlisted in the U.S. Army Air Corps and rose to the rank of captain, serving as commander of a B-29; he did not play baseball again until 1 July 1945.

He came back to the Tigers in grand style, winning the pennant for them by hitting a grand slam home run in the ninth inning on the last day of the season. However, the war years and age were beginning to take their toll on his ability to hit. In what Greenberg considered an act of betrayal, the Tigers sold him to the Pittsburgh Pirates in 1947. He retired as an active player after one season with the National League team. Continuing in the sport he loved, he spent the years 1948 to 1957 as general manager of the Cleveland Indians; from 1959 to 1961 he was vice president of the Chicago White Sox. Greenberg was inducted into the Hall of Fame in 1956.

Focused on baseball, Greenberg avoided the drinking and carousing typical of players during his era. His work ethic left little time for socialization or other activities, although later in life he enjoyed tennis and squash. His marriage in 1946, when he was described as baseball's most eligible bachelor, to department store heiress Caral Gimbel ended in divorce in 1958; they had three children.

Astute financially, Greenberg brokered lucrative contracts for himself and was steadfast and creative in his monetary demands from team owners. When he was drafted into the army, he was commanding a salary second only to Babe Ruth in his prime. In 1947 the Pittsburgh Pirates paid him the then-astounding sum of $100,000. After his retirement from baseball, Greenberg pursued a successful career as an investor.

Greenberg died at age seventy-five at his home after a long struggle with cancer, a battle he kept from public knowledge. He was survived by his wife, the former Mary Jo DiCicco (née Tarola). Interment was at Hillside Memorial Park, Los Angeles.

Stories about Greenberg extol not only his athleticism but also his hard work and dedication to the sport of baseball. Having endured prejudice himself, he provided moral support to Jackie Robinson when he became the first African American in the major leagues. Greenberg is remembered as a player whose demeanor made him a role model for fans and players alike.

★

Greenberg contemplated writing his autobiography but died before completing the task. Ira Berkow was asked by the family to write the book, which he did by using tapes dictated by Greenberg and through much additional research. Berkow wished to present the book as an autobiography, and it is written in the first person: *Hank Greenberg, The Story of My Life,* edited and with an introduction by Ira Berkow (1989). A documentary film, *The Life and Times of Hank Greenberg* (2000), examines his career from the standpoint of his Jewishness. The film was reviewed by Lawrence Van Gelder in the *New York Times* (12 Jan. 2000). Red Smith, "Hating to See Hank Go," New York *Herald Tribune* (17 Aug. 1946), is an essay on Greenberg's rumored impending retirement. Steve Rushin discusses Greenberg's patriotism in an article in *Sports Illustrated* (16 July 2001). An obituary is in the *New York Times* (5 Sept. 1986).

MYRNA W. MERRON

GREENE, Charles Edward ("Mean Joe") (*b.* 24 September 1946 in Temple, Texas), football player who was the heart and soul of one of the best defensive units, "the Steel Curtain," as a member of the Pittsburgh Steelers' 1970s Super Bowl dynasty.

Greene is a sensitive and private person, so full details of his family background are sketchy. Given the nickname "Joe" by an aunt when he was young, Greene is the oldest of four children. His father was a carpenter who "just went somewhere" when Greene was about ten years old. Greene's mother worked as a domestic to keep the family together after that time. Greene said: "We never felt deprived growing up. We always had clothes and they were clean. I don't ever recall being on welfare."

As the oldest Greene looked after his younger siblings after school, and he retained that fatherly attitude toward his younger teammates as a college and pro football player. To help support his brothers and sisters, he earned money as a laborer but vowed to find a better way of life. Football was his ticket to that life. Eventually reaching 6 feet 4 inches and 275 pounds, Greene, like many other Texas youngsters, found football a natural calling. He began to play at Temple's Dunbar High School but was not recruited by the power schools of the still-segregated Southwest Conference (SWC).

After his high school graduation in 1965, Greene chose North Texas State (now the University of North Texas) over Texas A&I (now Texas A&M at Kingsville), New Mexico State, and the University of Houston. While at North Texas (1965–1969), he was converted from his high school position of linebacker to defensive tackle. Greene earned some All-America mention as a junior, and as a senior in

Mean Joe Greene. AP/WIDE WORLD PHOTOS

1968 he was a consensus All-America though still relatively unknown. As a member of the North Texas Eagles, Greene acquired the foundation for his "Mean Joe" nickname if not the actual nickname. The wife of the North Texas sports information director, Sidney Sue Graham, thought the outstanding Eagles defense should have a catchy nickname. Since the school's colors were green and white, "the Mean Green" caught on as a collective nickname. Eventually Greene became "Mean Joe," but he never liked the sobriquet. He once told a writer, "My friends just call me 'Joe.'" Greene married Agnes Craft while they were both students at North Texas. The couple had three children.

The Pittsburgh Steelers of the National Football League (NFL), who needed help at many positions, shocked much of the football world by making Greene, a little-known player from a little-known school, their first-round draft choice as opposed to heralded Notre Dame quarterback Terry Hanratty, a Pittsburgh-area native. But the new Steelers coach Chuck Noll had scouted Greene as a college player and was convinced he could be the cornerstone of a great defensive unit. Not only was the well-versed Noll correct about Greene, he also secured Hanratty in the second round of the 1969 draft. This did not keep the Pittsburgh media from blaring banner headlines asking, "Joe Who?"

Although the Steelers were several years away from the dynasty years, Greene made an immediate impact and impression. At the time NFL rookies were hazed by veteran players. Greene was not about to do a veteran's bidding, and he said so. He also invoked the wrath of the seasoned players by "holding out" for twenty-three days of training camp before reporting. When he finally got to the Steelers camp, the veterans were prepared to teach him the ways of the NFL. However, Greene did the teaching. In a drill called "the meatgrinder," Greene faced two established Steelers veterans, the starting center Ray Mansfield and the Pro Bowl guard Bruce VanDyke. Relating what happened, Mansfield said, "He [Greene] grabbed Bruce by the shoulder pads and me by the neck and threw both of us away like we were ragdogs." Mansfield continued: "Suddenly we had a player who was better than the other guys. It was like having a big brother show up when the class bully was chasing you."

Greene's aggressive play in his first year, when the Steelers won their first game and lost the next thirteen, got him ejected from several games. But it also got the attention of the rest of the NFL, and he was named the Associated Press (AP) NFL Defensive Rookie of the Year. He also was named to play in the Pro Bowl, an honor he gained nine more times before his storied career ended after the 1981 season.

By 1972 the Steelers were contenders, but before they won their first championship of any kind, Greene needed to perform at a near superhuman level. On 10 December 1972 Pittsburgh played the Houston Oilers (now the Tennessee Titans). With the score tied 3–3, the starting quarterback, the Professional Football Hall of Famer Terry Bradshaw, was injured. Greene, by now the unquestioned leader of the team, told his defensive mates, "We can't let 'em score a point." He then led by example. He sacked the Houston quarterback Dan Pastorini five times, blocked a field goal attempt, and fought through three blockers to strip an Oilers runner of the ball and recovered the fumble. The Steelers won the game 9–3 on two more field goals set up by the good field position established by the outstanding play of Greene and the other Steel Curtain defenders. Said Noll, a Pro Football Hall of Fame inductee as a four-time undefeated Super Bowl coach: "It was just an unbelievable performance and effort. I've watched the film a dozen times and I still can't believe it."

Greene performed similarly throughout the Steelers' Super Bowl reign, which saw them capture the coveted Vince Lombardi Trophy (as Super Bowl champions) after Super Bowls IX, X, XIII, and XIV, an unprecedented run of four titles in a six-year span. Green was named the NFL Defensive Player of the Year in 1972 and 1974. He was also All-Pro many times before he retired. Television endorsements beckoned the charismatic Greene. He starred in a spot in which an exhausted Greene accepts a postgame Coca-Cola from a young fan. A scowling Greene downs the entire Coke in one continuous gulp and says nothing. The discouraged youngster begins walking away but is stopped when a menacing-looking Greene calls out, "Hey, kid, here." Greene then throws the elated youngster his game jersey. The music swells and all is well. Those who know him best contend this depicts the real Mean Joe Greene. So successful was the television spot that it spawned a made-for-TV movie, "The Steeler and the Pittsburgh Kid."

A chronic back problem hastened Greene's retirement in 1981, and Greene became an NFL defensive line coach first with the Steelers, next with the Miami Dolphins, and then with the Arizona Cardinals. Noll called Greene, "The best I've ever seen—there'll never be another Joe Greene." While his offensive teammates Bradshaw, Franco Harris, Lynn Swann, and John Stallworth won more accolades, Greene captured the fancy of Pittsburgh's blue-collar fans and redefined how his position, defensive tackle, is played. Greene was elected into the Professional Football Hall of Fame in 1987.

★

Greene's life and career are discussed in Roy Blount, Jr., *About Three Bricks Shy of a Load* (1974); Ray Didinger, *Great Teams*

Great Years—The Pittsburgh Steelers (1974); and Larry Fox, *Mean Joe Greene and the Steelers' Front Four* (1975).

JIM CAMPBELL

GREGG, (Alvis) Forrest (*b.* 18 October 1933 in Birthright, Texas), football player who was an All-Pro offensive tackle for the Green Bay Packers of the National Football League (NFL) and who joined eleven Packers teammates in the Pro Football Hall of Fame.

Gregg, known from his earliest days by his middle name, moved with his family to Sulphur Springs, Texas, about seventy-five miles east of Dallas, as an adolescent. His father, David Boyd Gregg, who also went by his middle name, was a farmer. His mother, Josephine Shirley, was a homemaker. Gregg was one of eleven children. He showed athletic ability at an early age, and by the time he reached Sulphur Springs High School, he was talented enough to take part in basketball, baseball, and track and field in addition to starring in football. Gregg earned a football grant-in-aid to attend Southern Methodist University (SMU) in Dallas, enrolling in the fall of 1952. Freshmen were not eligible for varsity play at that time, but Gregg made an impact as a sophomore. By his senior year he had the respect of his Mustang coaches and teammates. He was elected captain of the team and was a two-time All-Southwest Conference (SWC) choice. Gregg was also named an All-America as a senior.

Gregg's size—six feet, four inches and 230 pounds—attracted Green Bay Packers scouts, and that team made him their second-round draft choice for 1956. Gregg, who played offense and defense at SMU, projected himself as a defensive tackle but soon ended up on offense. Although light at his weight, he held his own as a rookie. A Reserve Officer Training Corps (ROTC) member in college, Gregg postponed his military obligation until after his first NFL season. His twenty-one-month "hitch" caused him to miss the entire 1957 season, but he was back in the Packers uniform for 1958. He fashioned a then-record streak of 188 consecutive games played before he retired. The only serious injury Gregg suffered in his long and highly decorated career was a broken arm as a high school sophomore.

Green Bay had a reputation as the NFL's "Siberia" in the 1950s. The team's glory days were a distant memory at that time. However, Gregg and a group of talented young players, including Jim Taylor, Jim Ringo, Bart Starr, and Ray Nitschke, all future members of the Pro Football Hall of Fame, were on hand, waiting for direction and leadership. Coach Vince Lombardi arrived and showed the way. From a 1–10–1 record in 1958, Lombardi guided the

Packers to a 7–5 mark in 1959, his first year at the helm. Also in 1959 Gregg, unlike many pro players, returned to SMU and completed his degree work, graduating with a B.S. in physical education. In 1960 the Packers played for the NFL championship. Although Green Bay lost to the Philadelphia Eagles that year, they reigned as NFL champions in 1961 and 1962. Gregg had an especially gratifying year in 1961. Because the guard Jerry Kramer suffered injuries, Gregg was forced to move from tackle to guard. He was just as effective in that position, and he was again selected to play in the Pro Bowl and was named to the All-Pro teams. During his career Gregg played in nine Pro Bowls and was an All-Pro eight times. On 12 July 1960 Gregg married Barbara Sue Dedek; they had two children. Gregg's son, Forrest Gregg, Jr., followed his father to SMU and into coaching.

Gregg was a keen student of the game. He soaked up every word and every instruction that Lombardi had to offer. He supplemented this by studying miles and miles of game film. By studying so much film Gregg knew exactly what his opponent would do when they met on the field. He was never surprised. He also honed his skills by practicing daily against the Hall of Fame defensive end Willie Davis. Said Gregg: "After Willie, nearly everything else was easy. He kept me sharp and taught me a lot about what to expect from other defensive ends." Gregg continued: "I watched all the film I could of Jim Parker and Roosevelt Brown [acknowledged masters of the tackle position], especially when I first came into the league. That's the only way a fellow with a little ability can become a good tackle, that and a lot of hard work." Gregg's durability also attested to his superior conditioning. With Gregg, the Packers won Super Bowls I and II.

Several times Gregg attempted to retire and go into coaching. He actually accepted a position on the University of Tennessee staff in 1963 only to be persuaded by Lombardi, who called Gregg "the finest football player I ever coached," to continue playing. In 1965 injuries again hit the Packers guards, and Gregg again played guard as well as tackle. His play was of such a high caliber that the Associated Press (AP) named him as a guard to its All-Pro team, while the United Press International (UPI) selected him as a tackle. Twice more, in 1969 and 1970, Gregg attempted to retire. Although he was set to coach in each of those seasons, when the whistle sounded for the opening kickoff, Gregg was back playing his familiar right tackle position. Finally the thirty-eight-year-old Gregg was released by the Packers in 1971. Tom Landry, however, coaxed Gregg to sign with the Dallas Cowboys as a player. Gregg helped the Cowboys to its first Super Bowl championship and his third.

Gregg at last began his coaching career as an assistant

with the San Diego Chargers in 1972. He moved to Cleveland for the 1974 season and was head coach of the Browns in 1975. He was voted NFL Coach of the Year in 1976 for improving the Browns from 3–11 in 1975 to 9–5 in 1976. In his final Browns season, 1977, Gregg was inducted into the Pro Football Hall of Fame. After a stint in the Canadian Football League (CFL) with the Toronto Argonauts, Gregg returned to the NFL as the head coach of the Cincinnati Bengals in 1980. In his second season he had the Bengals in Super Bowl XVI. His team lost to the budding San Francisco dynasty, but Gregg became the first Super Bowl player to take a team to the Super Bowl as a head coach. In 1984 he returned to Green Bay determined to return the Packers to the glory days he had experienced as a part of the dynasty with championships in 1961, 1962, 1965, 1966, and 1967. He compiled a 25–37–1 record in Green Bay, then left the Packers after the 1987 season to return to his college alma mater. SMU was coming off of a two-year "death penalty" (no football) imposed by the National Collegiate Athletic Association (NCAA) for illegal payments to players. Gregg reestablished the once proud program, then in 1991 he moved into the athletics director's position, where he remained until he retired in the mid-1990s.

Gregg was dependable, durable, and versatile. He studied the game of football and was greatly influenced by Lombardi. He used the lessons he learned from his mentor to become a successful coach but is best remembered as an elite player. Said the late coach George Allen: "My teams avoided him as much as possible. At other times, we double-teamed him. But I don't think I ever saw Forrest Gregg play anything other than an outstanding football game." Lombardi commented: "He keeps trying to improve himself all the time. That's what makes Gregg such a fine offensive tackle. He is never satisfied with anything less than a top grade on every play." Many years after his playing career, Gregg remained a popular choice for an offensive tackle position on any NFL all-time team.

★

Gregg's life and career are discussed in Vince Lombardi with W. C. Heinz, *Run to Daylight!* (1963); Chuck Johnson, *The Greatest Packers* (1968); George Allen with Ben Olan, *Pro Football's 100 Greatest Players* (1982); Ritter Collett, *Super Stripes* (1982); and Rick Korch, *The Truly Great* (1993).

JIM CAMPBELL

GRETZKY, Wayne Douglas ("The Great One") (b. 26 January 1961 in Brantford, Ontario, Canada), ice hockey player widely considered the best of all time who was instrumental in increasing the sport's popularity in the United States.

Gretzky was born and raised in the city of Brantford, approximately sixty-five miles southwest of Toronto. His father, Walter Gretzky, was the son of Polish and Russian immigrants and worked for Bell Canada; his mother, Phyllis, was a homemaker. He had one sister and three younger brothers. By the age of two, he had begun playing a version of hockey indoors on the hardwood floors of his grandparents' house, using a rubber ball and a Chicago Black Hawks souvenir hockey stick, with his grandmother acting as the goaltender. As a toddler he learned to skate on the nearby Nith River in Canning, Ontario, and his father commenced an annual winter ritual of turning the family's backyard on Varadi Avenue into an ice rink, where his eldest son quickly developed his playing skills. Although the youngest division in the local minor hockey program was for ten year olds,

Wayne Gretzky. AP/WIDE WORLD PHOTOS

he made the team at age six and scored once during his first season of organized hockey. It was at this time that Gretzky's trademark practice of tucking in his hockey jersey on one side arose, as he was forced to wear a uniform designed for much older and larger players.

That first season was followed by seasons of 27, 104, and 196 goals, followed by an astounding 378 goals in 69 games as a four-foot, four-inch-tall ten year old. The following year Gretzky was the subject of an article in *Canadian Magazine* and became a celebrity, as he also excelled at other sports including lacrosse and baseball. However, the attention he received for his scoring exploits was not well received by all of Brantford's 70,000 citizens, particularly the parents of his teammates and opponents. Gretzky was slight for his age and, playing in higher age groups, his early success was not expected to last.

As pressures mounted in his hometown and a need for stronger competition arose, Gretzky relocated to the metropolitan Toronto area at the age of fourteen. He played two seasons of junior "B" hockey for the Toronto Young Nationals organization—weighing 135 pounds and competing against men as old as twenty—and was drafted third overall by the Sault Sainte Marie Greyhounds of the Ontario Hockey Association (OHA). When he arrived to play for that team, his playing number "9" (worn in honor of his idol Gordie Howe) was already taken. He opted for "99" at his coach's suggestion, a number that would become synonymous with excellence in the sport. Gretzky scored seventy goals and was designated the OHA's rookie of the year, in addition to being named the circuit's most gentlemanly player, although skepticism about his hockey future remained because of his slight build and awkward skating style. He finished the academic year at Sir James Dunn High School, as his hockey commitments would later preclude him from finishing high school.

The following season Gretzky took advantage of the underage hiring practices of the professional World Hockey Association (WHA) and joined the Indianapolis Racers in the fall of 1978 at age seventeen, signing a personal services contract with the team owner Nelson Skalbania. After eight games the financially ailing team traded the 155-pound center to the Edmonton Oilers, where he led the team in scoring and won more rookie honors. The following season the Oilers joined the National Hockey League (NHL), and Gretzky tied for the league lead in scoring, was awarded the Hart Trophy as the league's Most Valuable Player (MVP), and captured the Lady Byng Trophy for sportsmanship. However, he was deemed ineligible for rookie-of-the-year honors as he had played in the WHA.

From the time he entered the NHL in 1979, Gretzky dominated professional hockey in a manner matched by few, if any, in other sports. He won the league's MVP award nine times in his first ten seasons, was the league-scoring champion a total of ten times, and led the Oilers to four Stanley Cup victories in a five-year stretch between 1984 and 1988. In two of those seasons, he was also awarded the Conn Smythe Trophy as the MVP during the play-offs. This was in spite of routinely having the poorest results on team fitness tests and boasting only a 140-pound bench press. In Canada, Gretzky became a cultural icon, a symbol to Canadians of hard work, fair play, and humility. However, some concerns were raised when he began dating American model-actress Janet Jones, and the Canadian press suggested that Gretzky's controversial trade to Los Angeles was partially orchestrated by Jones's desire to move to the U.S. The couple eventually married on 16 July 1988, in what was dubbed "Canada's Royal Wedding." They had a daughter and three sons.

Despite the Oilers' success on the ice, the team owner Peter Pocklington was in financial trouble. He hoped to take the team public in order to raise money, but his scheme was complicated by the fact that his prized asset, Gretzky, was under a personal services contract and also eligible for free agency in 1992. The new Los Angeles Kings team owner Bruce McNall courted Pocklington and offered players, draft picks, and $15 million cash for Gretzky. Hockey was not popular in the U.S. Sunbelt and lagged behind the other three major professional team sports. McNall (and the rest of the NHL) hoped that Gretzky's presence in the second-largest U.S. market would help to increase the sport's prominence in the nation, which became possible after Gretzky requested a trade.

In August 1988 Gretzky was traded to the Kings. McNall renegotiated his contract, setting a standard that would ripple down through the NHL and affect salaries for years to come. His impact on the ice was felt immediately, as the Kings improved to fourth overall in the league, winning twelve more games in 1988–1989 than the previous year, and the Los Angeles Forum began to sell out. After losing the league's MVP award to Mario Lemieux the season before, Gretzky won the award again and, in an emotional seven-game series, defeated the Oilers during the 1989 play-offs. That year he passed his idol Gordie Howe's all-time point record of 1,850. Although the team did not win the Stanley Cup during Gretzky's tenure with the Kings, the 1989 play-off year raised interest in the sport in southern California. According to Gretzky, "People who used to think that ice was only good for making daiquiris were driving around with Kings pennants on their Jaguar antennas."

Gretzky led the Kings to the Stanley Cup finals in 1993, but that remained the closest he got to winning the cup again. He did, however, raise hockey's profile in the United States and, in the wake of a surge in popularity, the NHL expanded or relocated to a number of warm-weather cities, including San Jose, Anaheim, Miami, Tampa, and Phoenix.

During the 1995–1996 campaign Gretzky was traded to the St. Louis Blues, and the following season he signed with the New York Rangers. He played three seasons there to finish out his career in 1999, retiring as the leader in most of the NHL's career statistical categories, and holding or sharing more than sixty NHL records. The Hockey Hall of Fame waived its waiting period for retired players and he was enshrined in the fall of 1999, in the presence of his family. The Great One also was named the greatest hockey player of all time by *Hockey News* and North America's fifth-greatest athlete by ESPN *Sports Century*. He continued to be involved in hockey, as the executive director and general manager of the Canadian team for the 2002 Olympic Games, and became a minority owner and the director of hockey operations for the NHL's Phoenix Coyotes.

Although Gretzky's exploits on the ice merit his inclusion on the list of the greatest athletes of all time, his impact off the ice and the manner in which he carried himself also deserve recognition. According to his former teammate and fellow superstar Mark Messier, "He basically took the league on his shoulders and carried them to a place that nobody twenty years ago would have ever thought hockey would be right now." The U.S. Hockey Hall of Fame created the Wayne Gretzky Award, to be given to those who have made significant contributions to the growth of U.S. hockey.

Gretzky succeeded through skill and hard work, despite being considered by many to be too small, weak, and awkward. When asked about the secrets to his success, he said, "Maybe what separated me is that I had passion for the game. Secondly, I was dedicated to it. I prepared for every game and I always felt like I hadn't done enough." Off the ice, Gretzky was a soft-spoken, articulate, thoughtful individual who would occasionally speak out on issues he felt were harming the image of the sport, such as fighting. If anything, he was criticized for avoiding controversy. In all, Gretzky changed the sport immeasurably. From a playing perspective he led a movement toward a more fluid, creative, fast-moving game, while as hockey's goodwill ambassador he significantly increased the status of his sport.

★

Gretzky recounts his career through his transition to Los Angeles in *Gretzky: An Autobiography* (1990), with R. Reilly. There have been numerous biographies of Gretzky, but a particularly interesting view comes from his father in Walter Gretzky with J. Taylor, *Gretzky* (1984). A fascinating account of the early years of the Edmonton Oilers is given by P. Gzowski, who traveled with the team for a year to write *The Game of Our Lives* (1981). For a discussion of the impact on Canada of Gretzky's trade to the Kings, see S. Jackson, "Gretzky, Crisis, and Canadian Identity in 1988: Rearticulating the Americanization of Culture Debate," *Sociology of Sport Journal* 11 (1994).

DANIEL S. MASON

GRIFFEY, (George) Ken(neth), Jr. (*b.* 21 November 1969 in Donora, Pennsylvania), baseball player considered one of the most productive hitters and gifted outfielders of his generation.

Griffey was born to play baseball. George Kenneth Griffey, Sr., his father, was drafted by the Cincinnati Reds the year Griffey, Jr., was born. In 1973 Griffey, Sr., was called up by the major league club and the family moved to Cincinnati, where Griffey was raised. The elder Griffey enjoyed a nineteen-year career playing for the Reds, New York Yankees, Atlanta Braves, and Seattle Mariners. He was a crucial part of the Cincinnati "Big Red Machine" that won consecutive World Series titles in 1975 and 1976. Griffey, Jr., grew up in that clubhouse, soaking in the atmosphere of professional baseball and success.

Griffey attended Moeller High School in Cincinnati, the same school that produced the baseball players Barry Larkin and Buddy Bell. A standout athlete in several sports, Griffey was especially successful playing baseball, setting a school mark (later broken) of eleven home runs in a season. In 1987 the Seattle Mariners made the seventeen-year-old

Ken Griffey, Jr. AP/WIDE WORLD PHOTOS

Griffey the first player selected in the amateur draft and signed him for a $160,000 bonus. He got off to a fast start, hitting .313 with fourteen homers and forty runs batted in (RBI) during his first year in the minors. It was a tough year, however. In 1992 Griffey revealed to a newspaper reporter that after his first season in Seattle he swallowed more than 270 aspirin in a failed suicide attempt and wound up in intensive care.

Griffey's time in the minors was limited. He started the 1988 season with the Class A San Bernardino, California, team and was promoted to Class AA in Vermont in August. Determined to make the major league roster, Griffey had a phenomenal spring in 1989, hitting .359 while collecting twenty-one RBI. He effectively forced the Mariners to make him a part of the club, and at age nineteen he became the youngest player in the majors that year. When Griffey, Sr., signed a one-year deal with the Mariners, the Griffeys became the first father-son duo to play in the major leagues in the same season. By July 1989 Griffey, Jr., was hitting about .300. He was a front-runner as the Rookie of the Year until he broke his hand. He returned in August but wound up hitting only .181 over the remainder of the year. His season average was .264.

Griffey improved with time. In 1990 he batted .300 with twenty-two home runs and was selected to the American League All-Star team. Matching the accomplishment of his father, in 1992 he was named the All-Star game Most Valuable Player (MVP), hitting three for four with a home run. In 1994 Griffey challenged Roger Maris's record of sixty-one home runs by hitting twenty-two by the end of May. The chase was interrupted in August, when the major league players went on strike and did not return. By the time the season ended he was on a pace to hit fifty-eight home runs.

Griffey became known for his fluid and graceful defense as well as for his hitting; he won ten consecutive gold gloves between 1990 and 1999. At times, however, his aggressive defensive play had a cost. In 1995 he slammed into a wall and fractured his wrist in fifteen places. The injury required surgery, a metal plate, and screws to stabilize the wrist. After Griffey returned to playing that year, Seattle gathered steam in August and charged from behind to overtake the California Angels from thirteen games back, finishing the year tied for the division title. Seattle won a single-game playoff (9–1) to advance to the divisional championship series. In the 1995 playoffs against the New York Yankees, Griffey tied Reggie Jackson's record of five home runs and six RBI in five playoff games. He also scored the run that sent Seattle to its first-ever American League Championship series, against the Cleveland Indians, who won the series in six games.

Before the 1996 season Griffey was briefly the highest-paid player in baseball, signing a four-year deal worth $34 million. His fan appeal was unmistakable, as that season the twenty-six year old was the top vote-getter in the All-Star balloting and was a serious contender for MVP honors, along with his twenty-one-year-old rookie teammate Alex Rodriguez. Griffey came in fourth in the balloting.

In 1997 Griffey was healthy the entire season and tried again to break Maris's record. By 4 July he had thirty home runs and seemed within striking distance of the record. A slight hamstring injury and a death in the family slowed his pace, but Griffey still hit .304 with fifty-six home runs, his best season since joining the majors. He was the unanimous choice as the American League MVP, the thirteenth player in history to receive all first-place votes, and was voted as the Player of the Year by his fellow major leaguers.

In 1998, while Mark McGwire and Sammy Sosa pursued Maris's record and eventually surpassed it, Griffey had another magnificent season, hitting fifty-six home runs for the second consecutive year with 146 RBI. He was elected to his ninth consecutive All-Star game and again received the most votes of any player.

After the 1999 season Griffey decided he wanted out of Seattle. After playing there for eleven seasons, he turned down the team's offer of a $135 million contract and demanded a trade. He cited a variety of reasons for his decision, including a desire to be closer to his home and family in Orlando, Florida. A number of teams at first appeared in the running for Griffey's services, but eventually the Mariners struck a deal with the Cincinnati Reds, with Bret Tomko, Mike Cameron, and others going to Seattle in return for Griffey.

Griffey signed a nine-year, $112.5 million deal with Cincinnati. At the time, the contract was the richest ever in the history of baseball, although Griffey's annual salary was the sport's seventh highest. Fifty-seven percent of the contract was spread out over sixteen years of deferred payments. The Reds, who had won ninety-six games in 1999 but lost a one-game playoff to the New York Mets, appeared poised to make the push to the World Series. The Reds general manager Jim Bowden was acutely aware of the need to have a genuine superstar on the Reds roster as the team prepared to move into a new stadium in the 2003 season.

Griffey's results with the Reds were disappointing as the team entered the new century. He struggled immediately upon entering the Cincinnati lineup, hitting about .200 in the first two months of the season. Back and hamstring problems kept him out of the daily lineup for extended stretches. Nevertheless, he remained one of the marquee players of his era, with his magnetic personality charming fans and corporate sponsors alike. He was named to the All-Century team in 1999, a month shy of his thirtieth birthday, along with the likes of Hank Aaron, Pete Rose, and Ted Williams.

★

Griffey's autobiography, edited by Mark Vancil, is *Junior: Griffey on Griffey* (1997). "Ken Griffey, Jr.," in *Contemporary Black Biography,* vol. 12 (1996), provides an in-depth profile of his career achievements. See also an interview, Michael Kinsley, "The Griffey Dilemma," and Thomas Stinson, "Tale of Two Griffeys," in *Sporting News* (20 Dec. 1999 and 12 Mar. 2001). Walter Leavy, "Is Ken Griffey . . . Baseball's Best Ever?" is in *Ebony* (May 1998). Gary Smith, "Home Run Fever," is a cover story in *Sports Illustrated* (3 Aug. 1998), and Bill Madden, "That Kid Could Break My Record," is a cover story in *Sport* (June 1998).

PHILIP NAPOLI

GRIFFITH, Clark Calvin (*b.* 20 November 1869 in Clear Creek, Missouri; *d.* 27 October 1955 in Washington, D.C.), baseball player, manager, and owner best known for his long association with the Washington Senators.

Griffith was one of five children born to Isaiah Griffith, a commercial hunter and trapper, and Sarah Wright. Not long after Griffith's birth, his father was killed in a deer-hunting accident, and his mother went to work with her sons on the family farm. As a youngster Griffith lived in a log cabin on the prairie in western Missouri. He became a professional trapper by age ten and shared work responsibilities on the family farm. When he was thirteen Griffith contracted malaria, and in search of a healthier climate, his

mother moved the family to Bloomington, Illinois, in 1883, where she ran a boarding house. Due to his poor health in Missouri, Griffith missed much of his elementary schooling, but he attended Normal High School in Bloomington from 1883–1887.

In Bloomington, Griffith made the acquaintance of the pitching great Charles "Old Hoss" Radbourne, who shared his baseball expertise with the aspiring teenager. Griffith developed a six-pitch repertory, which he used with such acumen that he earned the nickname "the Old Fox" at an early stage of his professional career.

At age seventeen Griffith pitched for a local semiprofessional team, and he signed his first pro contract with Bloomington of the Central Interstate League in 1888. He then spent three years with Milwaukee of the Western League, from the second half of the 1888 season through 1890. In 1891 he jumped to the newly formed American Association, splitting the year with the St. Louis Browns and the Boston Reds. Griffith pitched for Tacoma, Washington, of the Pacific Northwest League in 1892. Joining the Oakland Oaks of the Pacific Coast League in 1893, Griffith was 30–18, but he led a strike against the team owner for back pay. While on strike he worked as an actor in San Francisco's Barbary Coast district. Late in the season Cap Anson signed Griffith for the Chicago Colts of the National League.

Beginning in 1894 Griffith won more than twenty games for six straight seasons. The string was broken in

Clark Griffith *(far left)* with Chuck Stobbs and Bob Porterfield of the Washington Senators, 1953. ASSOCIATED PRESS AP

1900, when he led an uprising against the league, demanding an increase in the salary ceiling to $3,000. This provided players the opportunity to jump to the newly formed American League, and Griffith was among the first to go. As a reward for his assistance in getting some established players to move to the new league, Griffith's old friend Charles Comiskey appointed him playing manager of the Chicago White Stockings. Griffith responded immediately as he posted a 24–7 record, the league's top winning percentage, to lead the team to the inaugural American League pennant in 1901.

In 1903 Griffith was transferred to the New York Highlanders, a new franchise in a hostile New York Giants environment. But Griffith arranged for the chiefs of Tammany Hall, a political machine, to invest in his club, and these political connections helped him secure a foothold in the city. During his five seasons in New York, Griffith felt he was not treated fairly by the owners, press, or fans, the beginning of a lifelong enmity toward the franchise. In 1909 he began a three-year stint as manager of the Cincinnati Reds before he took the opportunity that determined the direction of the rest of his life.

In 1912 the Washington Senators, a troubled franchise, hired Griffith as manager. He mortgaged his Montana ranch, bought 10 percent of the Senators stock, and was elected to the board of directors. That season he invited President Taft to the pitcher's mound, and initiated the practice of inviting the president to throw out the ceremonial first pitch on opening day of each new season.

In 1920 Griffith bought a controlling percentage of the franchise stock, resigned as manager, and became the club president, a post he held until he died. In 1924 and 1925 the Senators won successive pennants, capturing the World Series in 1924. The team's success on the field was not matched financially. Despite the monetary limitations, Griffith negotiated some astute trades and built another pennant winner in 1933. However, this was his last.

During the Senators' lean times, Griffith showed he was an innovator. He introduced the element of entertainment to the game when he used Al Schact and Nick Altrock as baseball comedians to attract larger crowds. Former ballplayers, the duo had developed various slapstick routines performed before games or between innings. Griffith also led the call for a rules change to ban the spitball to make the game safer. During both World War I and World War II, Griffith raised money to provide baseball equipment for servicemen overseas. He expanded the major league talent pool when he signed the first Cuban, Armando Marsans, in 1910. Griffith explored an even greater reservoir of baseball talent when he discussed with the Homestead Grays sluggers Josh Gibson and Buck Leonard the possibility of playing for the Senators. If Gibson and Leonard had been signed to a major league contract, it would have opened the door to African Americans, before the era of Jackie Rob-

inson. Griffith did not sign either of them in the end. The Old Fox received baseball's highest honor in 1946, when he was inducted into the National Baseball Hall of Fame at Cooperstown, New York.

Griffith married Addie Ann Robertson on 12 December 1900. They had no children. When Addie's brother died, she and Griffith reared his seven children and informally adopted two, Calvin and Thelma, who officially changed their names to Griffith. Calvin Robertson Griffith, Sr., became a baseball executive and eventually replaced his adoptive father as president of the Washington Senators. Thelma Griffith married the Senators star Joe Cronin, who later managed the Senators and became president of the American League.

Griffith learned to use political connections to further his baseball endeavors. He was friends with eight presidents, and he became baseball's liaison to President Franklin Delano Roosevelt. His access to the White House was instrumental in ensuring that baseball continued through two world wars. When Griffith died of a massive stomach hemorrhage a few months short of his eighty-sixth birthday, he was considered one of the most influential men in Washington. Griffith kept a sign on his desk that read: "Long life. Sleep plenty, eat moderately, and keep your conscience clean." That was the credo by which he lived, and his life was the American dream come true. Beginning as an impoverished, fatherless boy and working his way up to become the owner of a major league ball club, he commanded the respect and admiration of those around him. His personal work ethic was a legacy to his family, and his pioneering presence, both as a player and an owner, helped baseball evolve for the better.

★

Calvin Robertson Griffith's authorized biography, *Calvin: Baseball's Last Dinosaur* (1990), provides some insight about his father. David Porter, ed., *Dictionary of American Sports: Baseball* (1987); Mike Shatzkin, ed., *The Ballplayers* (1990); and Lowell Reidenbough, *Baseball's Hall of Fame: Cooperstown* (1997), are helpful sources of information. Paul MacFarlanc, ed., *Daguerreotypes* (1981), and John Thorn et al., eds., *Total Baseball* (1997), contain useful statistical data. A two-page article, "Baseball Man," appears in *Sports Illustrated* (7 Nov. 1955). "In His Debt" is brief obituary in *Newsweek* (7 Nov. 1955).

JAMES A. RILEY

GRIFFITH, Emile Alphonse (*b.* 3 February 1938 in St. Thomas, Virgin Islands), one of the greatest boxers of all time, and only the third in history to earn both the welterweight and middleweight titles during a career that included 112 bouts and spanned nineteen years.

One of eight children born to mechanic Emile Griffith and his wife Emelda, Griffith left the Virgin Islands for New

Emile Griffith, 1965. AP/WIDE WORLD PHOTOS

York City sometime between 1954 and 1957, taking a job as a stock boy in the millinery factory where his mother already worked. Boxing manager Howard Albert, whose father owned the factory, encouraged Griffith to try boxing and sent him to legendary trainer Gil Clancy's Times Square Gym. Together Albert and Clancy managed Griffith's career, guiding him to fifty-one victories in fifty-three amateur bouts and to the New York, Eastern, and Intercity Golden Gloves championships in the 147-pound division.

Under the tutelage of Clancy and Albert, Griffith turned professional in 1958 and enjoyed quick success as a welterweight (141–147 pounds). Winning seventeen of his first nineteen fights, he lost only to Randy Sandy and Denny Moyer. Subsequent victories over Jorge Fernandez, Florentino Fernandez, Willie Toweel, and Luis Rodriguez raised Griffith's record to twenty-four wins against only two losses, and brought him a shot at the welterweight title then held by the rugged but erratic Benny "Kid" Paret of Cuba.

In their first fight, at the Miami Beach Convention Hall on 1 April 1961, Paret was ahead on points until the thirteenth round when Griffith stunned him with a left hook and followed with swift right that dropped Paret to the canvas. Griffith successfully defended his welterweight title against Gaspar Ortega on 3 June 1961 and won a nontitle fight against Yama Bahama before a rematch with Paret.

In a controversial split decision, Paret regained the welterweight championship on 30 September 1961.

A genuine animosity existed between Griffith and Paret. At the weigh-in before their third meeting, scheduled to take place at Madison Square Garden on 24 March 1962, Paret intensified this rancor by calling Griffith a *maricon,* Spanish slang for homosexual. Griffith vowed revenge, and from the opening bell the fight was a savage brawl. A right from Paret floored Griffith near the end of the sixth round, but he rallied and took control of the proceedings. In the twelfth Griffith trapped Paret along the ropes and administered a fearful beating. The helpless Paret absorbed more than twenty blows before referee Ruby Goldstein intervened to stop the fight. Rushed to Roosevelt Hospital, Paret, who had not fully recovered from injuries sustained in his previous fight with Gene Fullmer, underwent emergency brain surgery but never regained consciousness. He lapsed into a coma and died on 3 April 1962.

The clamor to abolish boxing rose to a crescendo in the wake of Paret's death. Millions of Americans had watched the fatal bout on the *Gillette Fight of the Week.* "Apparently," explained ringside announcer Don Dunphy, "people were calling friends and telling them to tune in, that a guy was getting beaten to death on the TV." When he learned of Paret's condition, Griffith tried to visit him in the hospital, but Paret's family refused to permit it. A distraught Griffith nearly retired. "I would have quit," he recalled in an interview, "but I didn't know how to do anything else. . . . I've never stopped anybody since then, really."

Griffith resumed his career, defeating Ralph DuPas on 13 July 1962 to retain the welterweight title he had taken from Paret. On 21 March 1963 Griffith lost his welterweight title to Luis Rodriguez, but reclaimed the crown seventy-nine days later, on 8 June, with a fifteen-round decision.

In a disastrous nontitle fight on 20 December 1963, Rubin "Hurricane" Carter knocked Griffith out for the first time in his career. Yet Griffith returned to the ring in February 1964, again vanquishing DuPas before defending his welterweight crown against Luis Rodriguez, Brian Curvis, Jose Stable, and Manuel Gonzalez. On 20 August 1965 Griffith lost a unanimous decision to Don Fullmer for the vacant World Boxing Association (WBA) middleweight title, but in April 1966 he faced Nigerian Dick Tiger for the world middleweight (155–160 pounds) championship.

Griffith bested Tiger for the title in a disputed fifteen-round judgment, then survived two exacting title defenses against Joey Archer in July 1966 and January 1967. In a raucous contest with Italian Giovanni "Nino" Benvenuti, Griffith lost the middleweight championship on 17 April 1967 only to recapture it five months later, pummeling Benvenuti in what was one of the best fights of his career.

Benvenuti, however, prevailed in their third encounter on 4 March 1968 to retake the middleweight title.

At thirty, Griffith apparently gave no thought to retirement. After falling to Benvenuti, he returned to the welterweight division and, on 18 October 1969, fought Cuban Jose Napoles who inflicted a decisive beating. Following the fight with Napoles, however, Griffith put together an impressive string of ten consecutive victories that earned him another shot at the middleweight title, this time against Argentinean Carlos Monzon who had wrested it from Benvenuti. In their first engagement on 25 September 1971, Monzon scored a technical knockout in the fourteenth round. Two years later in June 1973, Griffith punished Monzon, who barely escaped with the victory. Spectators at ringside greeted the announcement of Monzon's triumph with boos and catcalls; Gil Clancy alleged that officials had falsified their scorecards to Monzon's advantage.

Griffith finally stepped out of the ring in 1977 at the age of thirty-nine. His last title fight, for the World Boxing Commission (WBC) light middleweight crown, came in Berlin against Eckhard Dagge on 18 September 1976. He lost a split decision.

Having squandered most of the purses he had won, Griffith worked as a juvenile officer in Jersey City, New Jersey, but often took jobs as a bouncer at assorted New York night clubs to support his wife, Sadie Mae, whom he had married in 1971, and his large extended family. In 1992 a gang of thugs beat Griffith senseless with a baseball bat and robbed him of $800 outside a bar on Forty-second Street. He recovered only after several months in intensive care.

Criticized throughout his nineteen-year career for lacking the "killer instinct," Griffith used a blend of speed, truculence, and courage to post eighty-five victories. Although not blessed with a devastating punch (he recorded only 23 knockouts in 112 professional bouts), Emile Griffith was a consummate fighter. He used his fists briskly and intelligently and could alter his tactics to suit his opponent. Five times a world champion in two separate weight divisions, Griffith battled through 339 rounds in 22 sanctioned title bouts, more than any other boxer in history. By the 1980s he had begun to impart the wisdom of his experience to a new generation of fighters, including such hopefuls as Wilfred Benitez, Simon Brown, Juan LaPorte, and James "Bonecrusher" Smith. A sage of the "sweet science," Griffith was inducted into the International Boxing Hall of Fame in 1990.

★

Books that contain information on Griffith include Gilbert Odd, *Boxing: The Great Champions* (1974); Nigel Collins, *Boxing Babylon* (1990); Peter Walsh, *Men of Steel: The Lives and Times of Boxing's Middleweight Champions* (1993); and James B. Roberts and Alexander G. Skutt, *The Boxing Register: International Boxing Hall of Fame Official Record Book* (1998). Magazine articles include Chandler Brossard, "A Most Unusual Champion," *Look* (18 Apr. 1967); Milton Gross, "Camping out with the Champ," *Sports Illustrated* (7 Nov. 1966); and Bruce Benderson, "A Champion of Times Square," *Village Voice* 42, no. 31 (5 Aug. 1997): 118.

Mark G. Malvasi

GRIFFITH JOYNER, Florence Delorez ("Flo Jo") (*b.* 21 December 1959 in Los Angeles, California; *d.* 21 September 1998 in Mission Viejo, California), flamboyant track athlete and champion sprinter who was the first American woman to win four medals in one Olympics.

The seventh of eleven children, Griffith Joyner was four when her parents, Robert, an electronics technician and Florence, a seamstress, divorced. Mother and children moved from the Mojave Desert, where the Griffith family had been living, to the Jordan Downs housing project in the Watts section of Los Angeles. Griffith Joyner began running track at age seven at the 92nd Street Elementary School. She said that she ran because she could just "get in the wind" and because it helped her to stand out from her siblings. When visiting her father in the Mojave Desert,

Florence Griffith Joyner, c. 1992. © Neal Preston/Corbis

she chased jackrabbits to improve her speed. In elementary and junior high school, Griffith Joyner competed in the 50- and 70-meter dashes at events held by the Sugar Ray Robinson Youth Foundation for disadvantaged youth. When she was fourteen, she won first place for two consecutive years at the annual Jesse Owens National Youth Games. Graduating from Jordan High School in 1978, not only had she set school records in sprinting and the long jump, but she had begun to forge her own unique colorful style in clothing, hairstyles, and fingernail decorations.

Griffith Joyner entered California State University at Northridge in 1978, dropping out after her freshman year. Bob Kersee, her track coach, encouraged her to return to school and helped her secure financial aid. In 1980 she followed Kersee to University of California at Los Angeles (UCLA) to pursue a track career. Competing against top American runners, Griffith Joyner won the National Collegiate Athletic Association (NCAA) championship in the 200 meters in 1982 and the 400 meters in 1983. Upset after winning only a silver medal in the 200 meters in the Los Angeles Olympics in 1984, she stopped competing and became a customer service representative for the Union Bank in Los Angeles during the day and a beautician at night. With her training schedule severely cut, she gained weight. In 1987 she sought the help of Kersee to train for the 1988 Olympic Trials. She married Al Joyner on 10 October 1987; they had one daughter. In preparation for the 1988 Olympics, following a strict training regimen, Griffith Joyner got her weight back to 130 pounds. At the 1987 World Championship Games in Rome, she won a silver medal and popularized the hooded running uniform, which was later incorporated into the 1988 U.S. Olympic Team uniform.

Second best was not good enough for Griffith Joyner. To improve her performance, she stepped up her daily regimen to include sprint workouts and 3.7-mile runs, and, four days a week, weight-training sessions and partial squats with 320-pound weights on her shoulders. She left her bank job to work part-time in employee relations for Anheuser-Busch so that she would have more time to train. Griffith Joyner prepared for the Olympics by participating in four races at the U.S. Olympic Trials at Indiana University-Purdue University–Indianapolis in July 1988. There she ran the four fastest 100 meters in women's track history. She attributed her success to the discovery that she could attain greater speed by relaxing more as well as to her track outfits, with their high-cut legs and low-cut tops, that gave her freer movement. A few weeks after the Olympic trials, Griffith Joyner fired Kersee and replaced him as trainer with her husband. She said that she needed full-time attention, and, in addition, Kersee's percentage of her earnings was too high.

In the Olympics in Seoul, South Korea, in September 1988, Griffith Joyner continued to rewrite the track and field record books; she set an Olympic record for the 100 meters, winning the gold medal; she broke the world record twice in the 200 meters, winning the gold medal in 21.34 seconds. She won her third gold medal running the third leg of the 400-meter relay and a silver medal in the 1600-meter relay. After the Olympics, there was a rumor that Griffith Joyner might be using steroids—a rumor she vehemently denied, vowing that she was opposed to the use of performance-enhancing drugs. She never failed a drug test.

After the Olympics, Joyner appeared on television talk shows and on the covers of national and international magazines; she was also a commentator for various sports events. She appeared in one film, *The Chaser,* and had a recurring role on the television drama *Santa Barbara.* Her commercial endorsements included soft drinks, several Japanese products, and the marketing of a "Flo Jo" doll. She also designed uniforms for the National Basketball Association's Indiana Pacers. On 25 February 1989 Joyner announced that she was retiring from track to spend time writing, acting, and coaching her husband. There was some speculation that she wanted to avoid the mandatory spot drug testing that would start in 1989.

In 1988 Griffith Joyner was named French Sportswoman of the Year, Athlete of the Year by TASS, the Soviet press agency, and recipient of both the Jesse Owens Award and the Sullivan Award as the top American amateur athlete. In 1989 she received the U.S. Olympic Committee Award, the Golden Camera Award in Berlin, and the Harvard Foundation Award. She became spokeswoman for the American Cancer Society, the Multiple Sclerosis Foundation, and Project Eco-School.

In 1993 Griffith Joyner became the first woman to cochair the President's Council on Physical Fitness and Sports. She also served as an honorary board member of the National Osteoporosis Foundation. In 1994 she and her husband coestablished the Griffith Joyner Foundation for disadvantaged youth. Griffith Joyner was inducted into the USA Track and Field Hall of Fame in 1995. At age thirty-eight, she died of an epileptic seizure. She is buried at El Toro Memorial Park in Lake Forest, California.

Still the world record holder of the 100- and 200-meter dashes, the glamorous and athletic Joyner was a role model for young women in sports. Although her dazzling speed, captivating style, and multiple talents elevated her to the top in the world of sports, she never forgot where she came from and devoted significant time and resources toward helping children make the most of their abilities. USA Track and Field media information officer Pete Cava said, "It is not so much the incredible performances, but Griffith Joyner the person—the person who cared about young people, the person who was involved so much in her community [that is her legacy]." Griffith Joyner said that her "mother taught us all that nothing is going to be handed to you—you have to make things happen," and Griffith Joyner, the groundbreaker who set standards of speed and demonstrated her flair as a fashion maverick, did just that.

★

Joyner made several videocassettes on health-related issues. She coauthored *Running for Dummies,* a guide to the basics and benefits of running, which includes sixteen full-color photographs of Griffith Joyner. There are several full-length juvenile biographies. They include Rob Kirkpatrick, *Florence Griffith Joyner: Olympic Runner* (2001); Alan Venable, *Flo Jo: The Story of Florence Griffith Joyner* (1999); Mark Stewart, *Florence Griffith Joyner* (1996), April Koral, *Florence Griffith Joyner: Track and Field Star* (1992); and Nathan Aaseng, *Florence Griffith Joyner: Dazzling Olympian* (1989). Biographical sources for the reader/researcher include the entry in Martha Plowden, *Olympic Black Women* (1996); Nagueyalti Warren, in *Notable Black American Women, Book II* (1996), edited by Jessie Carney Smith; Rob Nagel, "The Joyners," in *Epic Lives—One Hundred Black Women Who Made a Difference* (1993), edited by Jessie Carney Smith; *Current Biography Yearbook* (1989); and Joe LaPointe, "Florence Griffith Joyner," in *Newsmakers* (1989). Obituaries are in the *New York Times* and *Los Angeles Times* (both 22 Sept. 1998).

JOYCE K. THORNTON

GROVE, Robert Moses ("Lefty") (*b.* 6 March 1900 in Lonaconing, Maryland; *d.* 22 May 1975 in Norwalk, Ohio), baseball player who won an unprecedented nine earned-run-average (ERA) and five winning-percentage titles and is considered by many the greatest pitcher of all time.

Grove, one of eight children born to miner John Groves and homemaker Emma Beeman in the Maryland panhandle, stayed in school only through the eighth grade before taking on a series of jobs. Like all his male siblings, he spent time in the mines, but after two weeks he resigned, announcing to his father, "Dad, I didn't put that coal in here, and I hope I don't have to take no more of her out."

Adding the nickname "Lefty" and dropping the "s" from his last name along the way, Grove began playing organized baseball at the late age of seventeen. He pitched for town teams in Midland and Cumberland, and at age twenty signed with the Martinsburg, West Virginia, team of the Class C Blue Ridge League. After he struck out sixty batters over fifty-nine innings in just a month, he was signed by the Double-A, International League Baltimore Orioles. What followed was perhaps the most enjoyable part of Grove's career. During four and a half relaxing seasons with the Orioles, probably history's greatest minor league team, he won 108 games, lost thirty-six, pitched .750 ball, and fanned a minor league record of 1,108 batters.

Lefty Grove, 1925. © BETTMANN/CORBIS

Why did Grove remain in the minors until age twenty-five? Because there was no major league draft from the International League at the time, and Baltimore owner Jack Dunn had a meal ticket in his star left-hander.

Following the 1924 season, Dunn sold Grove to the A's for a record $100,600, the last $600 thrown in to make it the richest signing of a minor leaguer in history and $600 more than the down payment the Yankees parted with for Babe Ruth. After a shaky 10–12 rookie season, Grove took wing. He won 195 games, one Most Valuable Player award, and the undisputed title of baseball's best pitcher by the end of his nine years in Philadelphia.

A teammate once described Grove as a man with "a fastball and a mean disposition." The description fit perfectly for much of his career. While pitching for the Philadelphia Athletics from 1925 to 1933, he threw a high fastball that seemed to rise as it approached the hitter. In baseball argot, it "handcuffed" them. He pitched differently for the Boston Red Sox from 1934 to 1941, but the depiction lingered. A small-town guy who could be generous with his friends, Grove grew defensive and uncooperative in big cities. He often refused to sign autographs or conduct interviews and berated everything from inanimate objects to teammates.

The quintessential moment of his career was 23 August

1931, in St. Louis, Missouri. En route to his greatest (31–4) season, Grove stood at the peak of his powers. He had won twenty-five games, losing only two, and tied the American League record with sixteen consecutive wins. His opponents that afternoon were the St. Louis Browns. After the Browns' Fritz Schulte reached base on a two-out single in the third inning, Oscar (Ski) Mellilo hit a line drive directly at the left fielder. Unfortunately, the regular left fielder, Al Simmons, was in Milwaukee getting treatment for an ailing ankle. His substitute, a rookie named Handsome Jimmy Moore, misjudged the drive, which tipped off his glove for a run-scoring double. Grove allowed no more St. Louis runs, but his obscure mound opponent, Dick Coffman, shut down the Athletics completely.

Following the 1–0 loss, the A's headed for a grubby clubhouse with peeling paint and wooden lockers to await Grove's inevitable tantrum. He responded with perhaps the most complete clubhouse demolition in history. Raging at Simmons for his absence and at manager Connie Mack for not insisting that Simmons play, Grove attempted to tear off the clubhouse door, shredded the wooden partitions between lockers, and ripped off his uniform with both hands, the buttons flying three lockers down. "Threw everything I could get my hands on—bats, balls, shoes, gloves, benches, water buckets, whatever was handy," Grove proudly told author Donald Honig.

Claiming he was strapped for cash, Mack, who doubled as A's owner, sold Grove to the Boston Red Sox after the 1933 season. As any woebegone Red Sox fan could have predicted, Grove immediately hurt his arm and wasted the 1934 season. Dismissed as a "lemon," he rebuilt his arm and refashioned his repertoire in perhaps the greatest resurrection of any pitcher ever. Spotting his fastball and relying on what he called "curve and control," Grove won four ERA titles between the ages of thirty-five and thirty-nine. He also granted enough interviews, signed enough autographs, and showed enough good humor to rebuild his reputation. Alas, Grove's retirement was lost in the news from Pearl Harbor, costing him the tribute he deserved.

Back home in Lonaconing, Maryland, and later near his son Bobby in Norwalk, Ohio, Grove had a bittersweet retirement. He had an affair, divorced his wife Ethel (Gardner)—an act both partners later regretted, according to relatives—had a distant relationship with his daughter Doris, and endured the death of his son. Despite this personal turmoil, Grove enjoyed gardening and golf and coached an integrated youth team. Grove died peacefully in a rocking chair while watching a soap opera at his daughter-in-law's house.

His teammates never protested Grove's antics. For one thing, they knew his rage fueled an uncompromising will to win. For another, they knew he was a winner. While starring for three pennant winners and two world champions, he had a 300–141 record for an otherworldly .680 winning percentage, won seven straight strikeout titles, and eight times won twenty or more games, all during a "lively ball" period more friendly to hitters than pitchers. In an epoch when all starters were expected to relieve, he pitched better out of the bullpen than any of his peers. Though other pitchers won more often and fanned more batters, baseball historians like Bill James and Daniel Okrent consider Grove the greatest ever. They reason that because pitching statistics vary by era, the only true standard for excellence is dominance. Grove's nine ERA and five winning-percentage titles are unmatched, and *Total Baseball* rated his "adjusted" ERA of 148 points first on the all-time list.

★

The only full-length biography is *Lefty Grove: American Original* (2000) by Jim Kaplan. Statistical information and a brief biography are in all editions of *Total Baseball*. Harold Kaese's 1942 article in the *Saturday Evening Post* provides an excellent short profile. Obituaries are in the *Philadelphia Inquirer* and *Boston Globe* (both 23 May 1975).

JIM KAPLAN

GROZA, Lou (*b.* 25 January 1924 in Martin's Ferry, Ohio; *d.* 29 November 2000 in Middleburg Heights, Ohio), tackle and placekicker with the Cleveland Browns, the team's career scoring leader and one of the game's all-time great placekickers.

Lou Groza was born above Groza's Tavern in Martin's Ferry, Ohio, into a very athletic family. His father was a tavern-keeper and his mother a homemaker. At six foot three, he was the smallest of three sons, but very much an athlete. He played baseball, football, and basketball in high school and was known as the "Big Chief" because he was the captain of each of his teams.

After high school Groza went to Ohio State University, where he tried out for the freshman football team. It was there that Paul Brown, then a coach at Ohio State, saw him display the ability to placekick a football through the goalpost uprights from forty, fifty, even fifty-five yards away. An extraordinary skill then and now, it was one that would earn Groza the nickname "The Toe." It was something he had learned growing up trailing after his brother Frank. "I used to get a kick out of kicking the ball over the telephone wires when we would play touch football in the street," he recalled. "I liked to see how far I could make it go." Very far, it turned out.

Groza did not go to Ohio State as a placekicking specialist, but as a tackle. He would play only three games on the freshman squad before entering the U.S. Army during

Lou Groza, 1961. He had just set the NFL record for total points scored in a season (826). ASSOCIATED PRESS

World War II. He served as a surgical technician in the Philippines, usually some five miles behind the front lines, assisting doctors as they helped the wounded. When he had time, he kept his football skills sharp as he and his buddies scrimmaged with footballs sent by Paul Brown. After his discharge from the service in February 1946, Groza returned, at age twenty-two, to Ohio State, but instead of finishing his degree he followed Brown to Cleveland. Brown was putting together the Cleveland Browns, a new franchise in the equally new All-America Football Conference (AAFC). Groza would eventually return to Ohio State to complete his degree work.

The man who would become the Toe started with the Browns as a tackle, a position he played from 1946 to 1959, first in the AAFC and after 1950, in the National Football League (NFL). Though weighing 255 pounds, he was fast—he could run the forty-yard dash in 4.8 seconds. During that time Groza earned All-NFL tackle honors six times and was named NFL Player of the Year in 1954. Even when playing tackle, his kicking ability gave Cleveland great tactical range. As Paul Brown recalled, "He was always a great potential weapon when we were inside an opponent's 49 yard line." In 1953 Groza made 88.5 percent of his field goals, at a time when 53 percent was the average. That mark remained as the best in professional football until 1982, when Mark Moseley of the Washington Redskins made 95.2 percent of his kicks. The numbers still impress; they were achieved at a time when playing and field conditions were considerably more demanding than they have become. Poor playing surfaces and wider hash

marks meant harsh angles to the uprights, and defenders could be hoisted up on their teammates' shoulders to try to block the kick.

Groza's career as a tackle ended in 1960 because of a back injury, but he was coaxed back to the Browns as a kicking specialist, making his foot a target for his opponents. He said, "Guys would yell out, 'Step on Groza's foot.' We were playing the Lions once and the guy I was playing against came over and stomped on my foot in the huddle and ran back to the line of scrimmage laughing." Groza used a square-toed shoe—he wore it even when he played tackle—and would kick straight on after taking exactly two and a half steps toward the ball.

Probably the most famous of all of Groza's kicks, the one that resulted in a friend's bronzing the square-toed shoe he wore to accomplish it, was the field goal he kicked against the Los Angeles Rams in the 1950 championship game, with twenty-eight seconds left in the game. Here were the upstart Browns, recently brought into the NFL from the now-defunct AAFC that they had dominated during the Conference's four years of existence, playing the Rams, a team that had left Cleveland five years before. The unthinkable possibility, that the Cleveland Browns—wearing sneakers because of the condition of the field—could win the NFL Championship their first year in the League came down to Groza's making a field goal.

As Groza later recalled the moment, "What made it tough was that I have a tennis shoe on my left foot and football shoe on my right, and I took the cleats off the bottom of it so it had a flat sole. I felt like a cat where you put paper on his paws and he's trying to walk around. It was a funny sensation." Groza and his teammates would be the only ones to savor the quirkiness of the arrangement as the Rams failed in a last attempt to score. The Browns had scaled the heights, booted there in no small measure by the Toe.

Also in 1950 Groza married his wife, Jackie, and started a family. They had a daughter and three sons, whom they raised in Berea, Ohio, where Groza had his insurance business and was active in civic affairs. Berea honored him as the twenty-fifth winner of the Grindstone Award and as Berea's Outstanding Citizen for 1990.

Groza retired in 1967, the last of the original Browns to do so. He remained a Browns booster to the end of his life. He was the franchise's career scoring leader and was inducted into the Hall of Fame in 1974. Cleveland retired his number, 76. Groza was seventy-six when he died at Southwest General Health Center of an apparent heart attack; his health had been failing for some time before his death.

For many Browns fans, Groza was what the team was about. He was the only Brown to play in all twelve of their championship games—four in the AAFC and eight in the NFL. He was also the only Brown to play with every one of Cleveland's other twelve Hall of Famers. Groza gave the word *reliable* new meaning. College football's top place-kicker each year is honored with the Lou Groza Award.

★

Groza collaborated on his biography with Mark Hodermarsky, *The Toe: The Lou Groza Story* (1995). His career is discussed in John Keim, *Legends by the Lake: The Cleveland Browns at Municipal Stadium* (1999), and Richard Shmelter, *The Browns: Cleveland's Team* (1999). Obituaries are in the *Akron Beacon Journal* (30 Nov. 2000) and in *Time* and *Sports Illustrated* (both 11 Dec. 2000).

ROBERT B. COREY

GURNEY, Dan(iel) Sexton (*b.* 13 April 1931 in Port Jefferson, Long Island, New York), outstanding multifaceted auto driver who had an equally illustrious second career as a race car manufacturer and team owner.

Gurney is the son of John Gurney, a Metropolitan Opera star with a bravura singing style who shaped his son's larger-than-life personality, and Roma Sexton, who enjoyed entertaining and traveling. Gurney attended high school on Long Island, New York, and following his graduation his family relocated to Riverside, California. There he developed his racing skills by twisting, turning, and "gun-ning" his way through the orange groves of Southern California. Gurney attended and graduated from Menlo Junior College. Establishing his competitive persona, he successfully drag raced in California during his college years. After graduation he served for two years, 1952–1954, with the U.S. Army, spending much of that time in Korea.

Gurney began his racing career at the relatively advanced age of twenty-four. As befits someone who was buoyed by racing internationally, his first official road-racing vehicle (1955) was not an American racer but a quintessentially British roadster produced by Triumph in England known as the TR2. Following his initial U.S. race victory in 1958, Gurney signed a contract to drive sports cars for the famous Italian race firm Ferrari. He then joined the giant German automobile manufacturer Porsche and enjoyed a sensational 1961 season. He was runner-up in the 1961 World Driver's Championship. The following year Gurney again drove for Porsche. While it was a disappointing season for Porsche, the company's solitary shining moment was Gurney's victory in the French Grand Prix.

In the 1960s Gurney finished in the top five in the World Driving Championship on four occasions. However, the fact that he drove himself and his engines in an unforgiving manner undoubtedly caused engines to blow up, and mechanical problems plagued his career. He alternately sparkled and struggled in European Formula One racing, and his Indianapolis 500 resumé from 1962 to 1970 expe-

Dan Gurney with some items in his auto racing collection. ASSOCIATED PRESS AP

rienced similar vicissitudes. In 1968, 1969, and 1970 he finished second, second, and third at Indy. However, on five other occasions, he failed to finish the race.

Even during this period, the 1960s and the early 1970s, Gurney had a considerable impact on auto racing's technical side. His competitive Indianapolis 500 finishes were in racing cars he designed. His conviction that rear-engine automobiles could and would win at Indy inspired Ford Motor Company to invest heavily in developing the then radical and controversial rear-engine Lotus Fords. As a result of Gurney's vigor and vision, these same Lotus Fords, sadly not driven by Gurney, won the big race five times between 1965 and 1973.

Not content with establishing himself as America's best-known Formula One driver, Gurney returned to Riverside and took up stock car racing. He had a nearly perfect sequence of Motor Trend 500 race triumphs from 1963 to 1968. The year 1967 was especially memorable for Gurney. He designed his own race car, the Eagle. He won the Race of Champions, the Belgian Grand Prix (driving his Eagle), and the Le Mans twenty-four-hour race with the legendary A. J. Foyt, and Gurney triumphed in his initial U.S. Automobile Club (USAC) championship race. G. N. Georgano, the editor of *Encyclopedia of Motor Sport* (1971), underscored Gurney's astonishing versatility when he wrote that Gurney was the "first driver to win championship races in all four major categories: Formula One, Sports cars, Stock cars and Indianapolis cars."

By the time Gurney retired from active racing in 1970, the depth and range of his racing achievements marked him as one of America's greatest auto racers. The *Michigan Motorsport Hall of Fame* celebrates a driver with a fifteen-year career who "raced in 303 events in 20 countries with 25 different makes of cars, winning 48 races and finishing on the podium an additional 41 times! . . . He claimed 32 career poles and started on the front row of the grid an additional and astonishing 58 times!"

Ralph Hickok, in *A Who's Who of Sporting Champions* (1995), described Gurney as "a sort of renaissance man of American auto racing." In 1964 Gurney entered the world of auto racing design and management when he and Carroll Shelby founded All-American Racers. Gurney became sole owner in 1967, and a year later Gurney's Eagle racing cars were first, second, and fourth in the Indianapolis 500. Gurney was one of the original founders of Championship Auto Racing Teams (CART), and he coined the acronym. At Le Mans in 1967 he became the first winning driver to shake a champagne bottle and spray spectators and fellow drivers with "victory fizz." In 1971 he invented the Gurney Flap, a wickerbill, and he pioneered the use of a full-face helmet for Indy and Grand Prix driving. He was a cofounder of the Long Beach Grand Prix in California in 1974, and he served on its board of directors for twenty-four years.

An avid reader of political and military history, Gurney also delights in opera, good cigars, and old movies. He had four children in his first marriage. In 1970 he married Evi. They had two children and settled in Newport Beach, California. Gurney was inducted into the Indianapolis Speedway Hall of Fame. Traditionally stellar American drivers have stayed within the borders of the United States. Gurney's passion for racing made him unequivocally at the time America's most cosmopolitan driver. He loved to race both in the United States and overseas. The international racetrack was his home. Gurney was lionized for his gregarious personality, his driving persona, and his racing style that took cars to their technical limits.

★

The Michigan Motorsports Hall of Fame in Novi is an excellent source of updated Web pages and other publicity source materials concerning Dan Gurney; one of the best websites is <http://www.allamericanracers.com/bio.html>. John L. Evers contributed a meticulous entry on Gurney in David L. Porter, *Biographical Dictionary of American Sports* (1988). G. N. Georgano, *Encyclopedia of Motor Sport* (1971), includes a thorough accounting of Gurney's driving career. Shorter pieces on Gurney are in John Arlott, *Oxford Companion to World Sports and Games* (1975); Sporting News, *The Chronicle of Twentieth Century Sport* (1992); and Ralph Hickock, *A Who's Who of Sporting Champions* (1995). A photograph of Gurney shaking a bottle of Moët et Chandon at the 1967 Le Mans is in *Sports Illustrated* (25 June 2001).

SCOTT A. G. M. CRAWFORD

GWYNN, Anthony Keith ("Tony") (*b*. 9 May 1960 in Los Angeles, California), baseball player who won eight National League batting titles as an outfielder with the San Diego Padres.

Gwynn, the second of three sons of Charles A. Gwynn, a warehouse manager, and Vandella Douglas Gwynn, a postal worker, grew up in Long Beach, California. His brothers Charles Gwynn, Jr., and Chris Gwynn played professional baseball also. Gwynn graduated in 1977 from Polytechnic High School in Long Beach and entered San Diego State University on a basketball scholarship. He starred as a point guard in basketball and set the Aztecs' career assist record. He also hit over .400 in baseball during his junior and senior seasons and became the first Western Athletic Conference athlete to make all-conference in both sports. In June 1981, though Gwynn had not graduated from San Diego State, the San Diego Clippers of the National Basketball Association selected him in the tenth round of its amateur draft, and the San Diego Padres baseball club drafted him in the third round. Gwynn married Alicea Cureton in 1981. They had two children and made their home in Poway, California.

Tony Gwynn. AP/WIDE WORLD PHOTOS

Gwynn's professional baseball career began in 1981 at Walla Walla, Washington, where he led the Northwest League with a .331 batting average. Gwynn finished 1981 with Amarillo, Texas, of the Texas League and began 1982 with Hawaii of the Pacific Coast League. He spent parts of 1982 and 1983 with the San Diego Padres, quickly blossoming into a National League star. The 5-foot, 11-inch, 200-pound Gwynn, batting and throwing left-handed, led the senior circuit with a .351 batting average and 213 hits in 1984. He batted .368 to help San Diego defeat the Chicago Cubs in the 1984 National League Championship Series but only hit .263 against the Detroit Tigers in the World Series, as the Padres lost, 4 games to 1.

Gwynn continually ranked among National League batting leaders. In 1986 he paced the senior circuit with 218 hits and 107 runs scored. His .370 batting average led the major leagues in 1987, while his 218 hits topped the National League. Gwynn repeated as National League batting champion with a .313 mark in 1988 and with .336 in 1989, when he led the senior circuit with 203 hits. After batting .309 with 177 hits in 1990, he in 1991 ranked third with a .317 batting average and again hit .317 in 1992. Gwynn won four Gold Glove awards for defensive excellence in 1986, 1987, 1989, and 1990.

In 1993 Gwynn's superb .358 batting average trailed only Andres Galarraga in the National League. On 4 August Gwynn collected six hits in a game against the San Francisco Giants. In the strike-shortened 1994 season Gwynn set a club record batting a National League best and a career high .394 with 165 hits and 64 runs batted in (RBI). His batting average marked the highest in the senior circuit since Bill Terry hit .401 in 1930 and the best in the major leagues since Ted Williams attained .406 in 1941. Gwynn won another National League batting title in 1995 with a major league best at .368, becoming the first player to hit over .350 in three consecutive seasons since Joe Medwick in the 1930s. He shared the National League lead with 197 hits.

Gwynn batted .353 in 1996 to become only the seventh major leaguer to win three straight hitting crowns and joined Ty Cobb as the only players to compile two separate streaks of three consecutive batting titles. He hit .308 against the St. Louis Cardinals in the National League Division Series after playing 1,648 regular season games between the two postseason appearances. Gwynn in 1997 enjoyed the most spectacular season of his illustrious career, winning his eighth batting title with a major league best .372 to tie Honus Wagner for the most National League batting crowns in a career to that date. Cobb earned twelve in the American League. The only major leaguer to win four batting titles in two separate decades, Gwynn joined Wagner, Rod Carew, and Wade Boggs with four consecutive batting titles. He also established career highs with 17 home runs and 119 RBI, shattered club records with 220 hits and 49 doubles, posted personal bests with 68 extra-base hits and 324 total bases, and paced the National League with 67 multi-hit games.

Gwynn helped San Diego post its best record in franchise history in 1998 with a .321 batting average, 16 home runs, and 69 RBI, and he hit a team best .500 with 8 hits, a home run, and 3 RBI in the World Series sweep by the New York Yankees. In 1999 he batted .338 and on 6 August became the twenty-second major leaguer to reach the 3,000-hit pinnacle with a first-inning single off Dan Smith of the Montreal Expos. Gwynn hit .323 in limited 2000 action, surpassing .300 for the eighteenth consecutive season to break Wagner's National League record. Cobb topped .300 for 23 straight American League campaigns. In 2001 Gwynn became the seventeenth major leaguer to play at least twenty major league seasons and spend his entire career with one team. Gwynn announced he would retire at the conclusion of the 2001 season and, along with the retiring Baltimore Oriole Cal Ripken, Jr., was honored with the Commissioner's Award at the All-Star Game in Seattle.

Using an unusually small bat, Gwynn led the Padres in career batting average (.338), runs scored (1,383), hits (3,141), doubles (543), triples (85), RBI (1,138), stolen bases (319), walks (790), and games played (2,440). He stood second in on-base percentage (.388) and ranked third in home runs (135) and slugging percentage (.459). Besides pacing all active players in batting average and hits, Gwynn ranked second in doubles, fourth in total bases, and fifth in runs. Gwynn led the National League a record 7 times in singles and shared the record with Pete Rose for pacing the senior circuit 7 times in hits. In 9,288 career at bats, he struck out only 434 times. The likable Gwynn, admired for his work ethic, combined video technology with hours of extra drill to augment his natural batting talent.

Gwynn was named to the National League All-Star team fifteen times and started eleven times. He made the *Sporting News* Silver Slugger team seven times (1984, 1986, 1987, 1989, 1994, 1995, 1997) and the *Sporting News* All-Star team five times (1984, 1986, 1987, 1989, 1994). He earned Padres Most Valuable Player honors seven times (1984, 1986, 1987, 1988, 1994, 1995, 1997), won Rawlings Gold Glove awards five times (1986, 1987, 1989, 1990, 1991), and garnered National League Player of the Month accolades five times. In 1995 he won the Branch Rickey Award for outstanding community service and the inaugural Chairman's Award for best exemplifying the community spirit of the family of the Padres owner John Moore. In 1999 Gwynn received the Roberto Clemente Man of the Year award for best combining sportsmanship and community involvement with excellence on the field and was inducted into the World Sports Humanitarian Hall of Fame. The Tony and Alicia Gwynn Foundation funds many organizations supporting needy children. In 2001, Gwynn decided to serve as volunteer hitting and outfield coach at San Diego State University in 2002 and succeed Jim Dietz as head baseball coach.

★

Gwynn's file is at the National Baseball Library in Cooperstown, New York. For his early career see Tony Gwynn and Jim Geschke, *Tony!* (1986), and Gwynn and Jim Rosenthal, *Total Baseball Player* (1992). His hitting philosophy is in Gwynn and Roger Vaughan, *The Art of Hitting* (1998). *The San Diego Padres 2001 Media Guide* outlines his personal and career baseball highlights and records. See also *Current Biography* (1996) and *Contemporary Black Biography,* vol. 18 (1998). Pertinent articles include Ivan Maisel, "He's a Hefty Problem for Pitchers," *Sports Illustrated* (14 May 1984); Ron Fimrite, "Small Stick, Tall Stats," *Sports Illustrated* (14 Apr. 1986); Danny Knobler, "Psst . . . Heard About Tony Gwynn," *Newsweek* (Aug. 1989); Cary S. Miller, "Tony Has Swung a Hot Bat Throughout His Entire Career," *Sports Collectors Digest* (3 Nov. 1989); Tim Kurkjian, "Beginning Again," *Sports Illustrated* (11 Mar. 1991); Kevin Kernan, "The Sport Q & A: Tony Gwynn," *Sport* (July 1991); Barry Bloom, "Tony Gwynn," *Sport* (Sept. 1994); and Richard Hoffer, "Fear of Failure," *Sports Illustrated* (18 Sept. 1995).

DAVID L. PORTER

H

HAGEN, Walter C. (*b.* 21 December 1892 in Rochester, New York; *d.* 6 October 1969 in Traverse City, Michigan), first professional touring golfer, winner of eleven major championship titles, including the British Open, which he was the first American-born golfer to win.

Hagen was the second of five children born to William Hagen, a millwright and blacksmith, and Louise Balko, a homemaker. He grew up in the town of Brighton, a satellite of Rochester, in a small two-story home his father built. Never interested in formal education, Hagen dropped out of school in the middle grades so that he could devote more time to athletics, especially golf.

As the son of working-class German immigrants, Hagen was not a likely candidate for golf, an elite sport. In 1895, however, the wealthy citizens of Rochester organized one of the country's first golf clubs and constructed their course within blocks of the Hagen homestead. Before his ninth birthday, Hagen had secured a job as caddie at the Country Club of Rochester. (CCR).

Hagen became a favorite at the club, where his enthusiasm caught the eye of the local professional, Andrew Christie. In 1907 Christie promoted Hagen to assistant professional. Through hours of practice and occasional rounds with Christie, Hagen sharpened his competitive skill. He entered the Canadian Open in 1912 and finished in twelfth place. Also that year Christie resigned his post at the CCR, and Hagen was his logical successor. In 1913 Hagen played

in his first major championship, the U.S. Open at Brookline, Massachusetts. There he watched as a young American amateur, Francis Ouimet, stunned the golf world by defeating two British professionals in an eighteen-hole play-off. If overshadowed by Ouimet's feat, Hagen played well, finishing in a tie for fourth place.

The next season Hagen broke through by winning the U.S. Open at the Midlothian Country Club in Chicago. That victory was quickly followed by others in such important events as the Western and Metropolitan Opens. Although he did not serve in the military during World War I, the war brought some important changes for Hagen. The cancellation of tournaments and the rise of war relief matches showed the savvy golfer that exhibition tour golf was viable. On 29 January 1917 Hagen married Margaret Johnson, and within a year his only child, a son, was born. In 1918 they moved to Detroit, where Hagen became the first professional of the Oakland Hills Country Club.

By the time he relocated to Michigan, Hagen was a handsome, famous athlete. He stood just under six feet tall, weighed about 170 pounds, had dark blue eyes and neatly trimmed black hair, and was always impeccably dressed. Before moving from Rochester, Hagen was a modest, unassuming young man who did not drink or smoke. In Detroit, however, he discovered the nightlife, blossoming into the hedonistic, self-confident "Sir Walter Hagen." Whatever the cause of his metamorphosis, it took a toll on his marriage; he and his wife divorced on 18 May 1921.

Walter Hagen *(second from right)* with *(from left)* Johnny Parnell, Bobby Jones, and Gene Sarazen. ASSO-CIATED PRESS AP

Meanwhile, Hagen thrived professionally. After winning his second (and last) U.S. Open in 1919, he announced his resignation from Oakland Hills and his plan to become the first "unattached" professional touring golfer. He played hundreds of exhibitions nationwide between the dozen or so competitive events on the golf calendar. In 1921 he hired Robert Harlow to book events, negotiate endorsement contracts, and generally work as his full-time manager and agent.

Hagen took his first trip abroad in 1920 but performed dismally in the British Open, finishing in fifty-second place. Undaunted, he returned the following year and improved to sixth place. Then in 1922, at England's Royal St. George's links, Hagen made golf history when he became the first American-born professional to win the British Open. The victory began a three-year period during which he was unquestionably the world's top golfer. He lost the British Open by one stroke in 1923, but won it again in 1924, prompting the *New York Times* to declare Hagen "the greatest competitive golfer who ever lived—bar none." Hagen also picked up his second Professional Golfers' Association (PGA) championship in 1924, the first of four consecutive victories in that event. With his career reaching its

zenith, Hagen made a second attempt at marriage; on 30 April 1923 he married Edna Straus, but within four years the couple was separated, and on 26 June 1937 they divorced.

In 1926 Hagen defeated the great Atlanta amateur Bobby Jones, twelve and eleven, in a highly publicized exhibition. The lopsided victory was ironic, though, because Jones would go on from that match to dominate the sport in the late 1920s. Yet if not the world's best, Hagen continued to display flashes of brilliance. He won two more British Opens in 1928 and 1929, along with his PGA championships. Hagen was also pivotal to the early success of the Ryder Cup competition, serving as captain for the first six U.S. squads (he captained a seventh squad, but unofficially). He captured his last tournament, the Gasparilla Open, in 1935 and also finished third place that year in the U.S. Open. In all, Hagen won some forty-five tournaments worldwide, including two U.S. Opens, four British Opens, five PGA championships, and five Western Opens.

By World War II, Hagen was finished with competitive golf. Always something of a golf vagabond since leaving Oakland Hills in 1919, he finally bought his first house in 1953, a twenty-acre estate on Long Lake, near Traverse

City, Michigan. He spent his final years there alone, except for a housekeeper, and in surprising obscurity for a man who had once been declared "the greatest golfer ever." Hagen died quietly in his cabin on Long Lake in the fall of 1969 following a long bout with cancer of the larynx. He was interred at the Holy Sepulcher Cemetery in Birmingham, Michigan.

Hagen's eleven major championship victories ranks third all-time, behind Jack Nicklaus and Bobby Jones. Yet his significance to golf history runs much deeper than his competitive record. Most important, Hagen was the first successful "unattached" professional golfer—the first to make a living through exhibiting his skill for profit instead of through giving lessons and selling equipment. His efforts laid the groundwork for a regular golf tour that began to emerge by 1930. Beyond that, Hagen was a star with a humble background in an elite sport. Like Arnold Palmer and Tiger Woods, he democratized golf and considerably widened its public appeal. In sum, he belongs on a short list of athletes—including Babe Ruth, Red Grange, and Jack Dempsey—who established modern professional sports in the early part of the twentieth century.

★

Hagen's autobiography, *The Walter Hagen Story* (1956), written with Margaret Seaton Heck, provides entertaining but disorganized and incomplete coverage of Hagen's life and career. The only full-scale biographical treatment of Hagen is Stephen R. Lowe, *Sir Walter and Mr. Jones: Walter Hagen, Bobby Jones, and the Rise of American Golf* (2000). A tribute to Hagen by Arthur Daley appeared in the *New York Times* (5 Nov. 1969). Obituaries are in the *Detroit News* (6 Oct. 1969) and the *New York Times* and London *Times* (both 7 Oct. 1969).

STEPHEN R. LOWE

HAGLER, Marvin Nathaniel (*b.* 23 May 1954 in Newark, New Jersey), boxer who was the undisputed middleweight champion of the world from 1980 to 1987.

Born in Newark, New Jersey, Hagler was raised in Rocky Marciano's hometown, Brockton, Massachusetts. In Brockton he met the Petronelli brothers, Goody and Pat. Hagler worked at their construction company during the day and trained at their boxing gym at night. The Petronellis trained and managed Hagler for most of his career.

Hagler, known for his incredible physique and his powerful left hand, stood five feet, nine inches tall and weighed 160 pounds. Early on, Hagler clearly understood that what he did in the gym translated to victories inside the ring. In an interview with CBS in the 1990s Hagler commented, "For me, I loved the training. That was the easiest part about the fight game because I loved being in shape, and

I loved training. . . . The main thing is not trying to leave all your fight in the gym." His training and work ethic permitted him to achieve a record of fifty-seven amateur triumphs. After he was awarded the Amateur Athletic Union (AAU) middleweight title in 1973, he turned professional.

Hagler won his first professional fight, a second-round technical knockout of Terry Ryan, in 1973. As his career progressed he frequently traveled to other fighters' hometowns for bouts. Many of his pre-title competitions took place in Philadelphia, Pennsylvania. There he met contenders such as Bobby Watts, Willie "The Worm" Monroe, Eugene "Cyclone" Hart, and Vinnie Briscoe. After one fight, Briscoe—a world ranked contender—encouraged Hagler, telling him "You're going to be champion."

After six years in the ring, Hagler was ready for his first title fight. In 1979 he boxed world middleweight champion Vito Antuofermo to a fifteen-round draw. Nearly a year later, on 27 September 1980, Hagler finally took the world title from Great Britain's Alan Minter in a third-round knockout. Racial tension loomed over the fight, as both Minter, a white fighter, and Hagler, an African American, were reported to have made derogatory racial statements prior to the bout. Both men fought hard, but the referee stopped the fight when Minter was bleeding badly from a cut over the eye and a bloody nose. British fans reacted angrily to the decision, throwing bottles into the ring. Hagler exited with a police escort.

Hagler went on to defend the title twelve times from 1981 through 1987. His victims included names from all across the spectrum of middleweight fighters. Antuofermo, who had denied Hagler's first title attempt, fell in five rounds. With his shaved head and sculpted body, Hagler was all business in the ring. In 1982 he knocked out William "Caveman" Lee in sixty-seven seconds. He won a rematch with Obelmeijas, ending it in the fifth round. Early in 1983 he knocked out Tony Sibson and Wilford Scypion, in the sixth and fourth rounds, respectively. He scored a unanimous decision over Roberto "Hands of Steel" Duran to retain his crown on 10 November 1983. This bout was held before nearly 15,000 fans in the outdoor arena at Caesars Palace in Las Vegas, Nevada, as were many of his fights, due to Hagler's burgeoning popularity.

While Hagler was on top of his game, his success was not without controversy. On 19 October 1984 Hagler scored a third-round technical knockout of Mustapha Hamsho. The bout was scheduled for fifteen rounds, an illegal length, for the World Boxing Council had previously restricted title bouts to twelve rounds. Hagler was stripped of his crown on 20 October. Undeterred, Hagler regained his championship with a ten-round knockout of Juan Roldan on 30 March 1985 in Las Vegas.

Regarded as "one of the most exciting fights of all time,"

Marvin Hagler. AP/WIDE WORLD PHOTOS

Hagler retained his title when the referee stopped his fight against Thomas Hearns on 15 April 1985 in Las Vegas. The match saw both fighters fight ferociously from the opening bell. In the third round, the ringside physician was called to examine cuts above and below Hagler's eye. The doctor determined that the champion could continue. When the brawl recommenced, Hagler used two of his famous rights to put the contender on his back. According to the trainer, Angelo Dundee, the combatants, "fighting like the end of the world, managed to compress fifteen rounds into three."

Hearns had previously only lost to Sugar Ray Leonard; Hagler, the undisputed middleweight champion, would also succumb to Leonard. Before meeting Leonard, however, Hagler retained his title for the twelfth time in an eleventh-round knockout of John "The Beast" Mugabi. The Ugandan-born Mugabi had won twenty-six fights, all by knockout, before falling to Hagler.

Hagler's last fight was on 6 April 1987: the long awaited showdown with Sugar Ray Leonard. Leonard, who came out of retirement for the match, out-boxed Hagler. It was an intense fight in which each man landed over 100 punches. The fight went twelve rounds and the decision went to Leonard. Hagler was adamant that he deserved a chance to regain his title from Leonard, but unable to secure a rematch, Hagler retired in 1987.

After retirement, Hagler pursued an acting career and appeared in several films. He moved to Milan, Italy, and pursued acting with the same determination that he gave to boxing. He was inducted into the International Boxing Hall of Fame in Canastota, New York, in 1992.

Disciplined and fierce, Hagler represented his adopted hometown well. He felt it was important to bring the wins home to Brockton, Massachusetts—a town otherwise known only for the manufacture of shoes. Following in Rocky Marciano's steps, Hagler was the second world champion from this otherwise lackluster suburb of Boston. Despite his self-anointed title of "Marvelous"—he legally changed his name to Marvelous Marvin Hagler in 1982—and his local heroics, Hagler maintained a concise philosophy, "I always took one fight at a time." That attitude produced a record of 62–3–2, with fifty-two knockouts, and estimated earnings of $30 million.

★

For further information about Hagler, see *Jet* (8 Feb. 1993). An announcement of Hagler's induction to the Boxing Hall of Fame is in *Forbes* (6 Apr. 1987), and Carolyn Gloeckner and Howard Schroeder, *Marvelous Marvin Hagler* (1985), covers Hagler's fight with Leonard.

MOLLY BOYLE

HALAS, George Stanley   (*b.* 2 February 1895 in Chicago, Illinois; *d.* 31 October 1983 in Chicago, Illinois), one of the founders and prime movers of the National Football League (NFL) and for sixty-three years the owner of its Chicago Bears, for which he was known as "Papa Bear."

George Stanley Halas was born in Pilsen, a Czech community on Chicago's West Side, the youngest of eight children of Frank Halas, an immigrant tailor from Pilsen, Bohemia, and Barbara Poledna, who ran a grocery store. Four of the children died in infancy. Frank Halas cleaned and repaired rented apartments to earn additional money. He also reported for a Bohemian-language newspaper.

Halas's earliest memories were of playing seventeen-inch softball with his two older brothers, using manhole covers and sewer grills as bases. Life centered on the Sunday mass at the Saint Vitus Church and the Pilsen social center, the Sokol, where the Halas brothers led neighborhood boys in indoor baseball. By the time he was ten he had become an avid fan of the Chicago Cubs, who then played only a mile from the Halas home. He fought the Fourteenth Street gang to get to the games before learning to outrun them. His persistence paid off; first baseman Frank Chance frequently took "the Kid" to the game through the pass-gate.

Halas learned the value of hard work and a dollar at an early age. He toted coal for the family's nickel-plated stoves, rode a horse-drawn wagon to the South Water Street vegetable market, stopped at the rail station for fresh milk from suburban farms, and then delivered his morning newspapers on foot. Critics later claimed he "threw dollars around as though they were manhole covers," and Halas admitted as much. Though weighing only 120 pounds, Halas played baseball, basketball, and lightweight football at Crane Technical High School, patterning himself after the fictional Frank Merriwell. When he was fifteen his father died, and his mother increased his weekly allowance to seventy-five cents while urging him "to save heavily for college." He graduated from Crane Tech in 1913, worked for a year in the payroll department of Western Electric, and began dating a neighborhood girl named Wilhelmina Bushing, whom he called Min, who also worked there.

In the fall of 1914 Halas enrolled at the University of Illinois. He majored in civil engineering and, at 140 pounds, played reserve halfback. That summer he worked for Western Electric. By the next fall, having shot up to six feet and 170 pounds, he made Bob Zuppke's varsity team as backup wide receiver and sustained a broken jaw. As a junior Halas started before breaking a leg, and also won letters in baseball and basketball. On crutches, he took careful notes on how Zuppke prepared his team. He enlisted in the U.S. Navy in 1918 and was assigned to the Great Lakes Naval Training Station, where he played for the Great Lakes Bluejackets. Halas was voted the Most Valuable Player when he caught two touchdown passes and returned an interception seventy-seven yards, pacing the Bluejackets to a 17–0 win over the Mare Island Marines in the 1919 Rose Bowl. After graduating from college, Halas, a switch hitter, played eleven games with the New York Yankees, "full of spirit" but "unable to hit the curve ball." He injured his hip in a slide at third and later observed that he was replaced in right field by Babe Ruth.

After the baseball season Halas took a $55-a-week job in the bridge design department of the Chicago, Burlington, and Quincy Railroad, but he longed to play football. He played on the fourteen-man, semipro Hammond, Indiana, Bulldogs for $100 a game. Halas's team defeated Jim Thorpe's Canton Bulldogs for the championship after a six-game season. A. E. Staley, owner of the Staley Starch Works, paid Halas to come to Decatur, Illinois, in March 1920 to coach the company's football team. Halas liked players with great desire—he called it "mental heat"—and recruited former Notre Dame center George Trafton, Great Lakes halfback Jimmy Conzelman, Canton end Guy Chamberlin, and Illinois teammate Edward "Dutch" Sternaman to star on the Decatur Staleys.

Over the objections of Amos Alonzo Stagg and other college coaches who decried athletes who played for money, Halas aggressively lobbied for a professional league that would charge for tickets and pay its players. Ralph Hay, manager of the Canton Bulldogs, shared his enthusiasm. Representatives from twelve teams met in Hay's Hupmobile dealership on the evening of 17 September 1920

George Halas, 1933. ASSOCIATED PRESS AP

Within two hours the American Professional Football Association was formed, and Jim Thorpe was elected its president without pay. Franchises from Cleveland to Rock Island were awarded for $100 apiece.

At twenty-five Halas coached, scheduled, wrote press releases, played end, collected gate receipts, and paid salaries for the Decatur Staleys in their inaugural season. They breezed past the Moline Tractors 20–0 and the Kewanee Walworths 27–0 en route to a 10–1–1 season that climaxed with a 10–0 win over the Chicago Cardinals before a crowd of 8,500 at Wrigley Field. A championship game against the undefeated Akron Indians at Wrigley ended in a scoreless tie and drew 10,800, at fifty cents apiece. Halas earned $2,322.77 that year, enough to give Min a $250 engagement ring he had bought in a pawnshop.

The Staleys opened the 1921 season with convincing wins over Waukegan and Rock Island, but it was not enough to persuade their owner to field the team a third week. Staley felt he could no longer afford the expensive burden of pro football. On 6 October he gave Halas $5,000 in seed money to move the team to Chicago on condition that it still be called the Staleys. Halas took Sternaman in as a 50-50 partner and agreed to give Bill Veeck, president of the Chicago Cubs, 15 percent of the gate receipts and concessions for the use of Cubs Park. Halas and Sternaman publicized the team at meetings with Chicago sports editors and by leafleting in the Loop. Eight thousand spectators paid a dollar apiece to see the Staleys defeat the Rochester (New York) Jeffersons 16–13 on 16 October 1921. A condensed version of Halas's own account of the game appeared in the press the following day. The Staleys finished the season 10–1–1, claimed the league championship, and showed a $7 profit for the year.

The Chicago Bears were incorporated at a league meeting on 28 January 1922. They boasted Illinois's colors of navy blue and burnt orange and were called the Bears because of Halas's passion for the Cubs. Halas married Min on 18 February 1922; they had a daughter in 1923 and a son in 1925. The name National Football League was suggested by Halas at an association meeting in June 1922. The Bears were the league's most successful franchise, winning seventy-five games, losing twenty-nine, and tieing seventeen during the 1920s. Halas's ninety-eight-yard run for a touchdown of a Jim Thorpe fumble in 1922 put him in the record books. His signing Harold "Red" Grange, the "Galloping Ghost" from the University of Illinois, in 1925 to a nineteen-city barnstorming tour drew 360,000 fans and gave the Bears their first sellout game at Wrigley Field. The excitement peaked in a Polo Grounds battle against the New York Giants that set a league attendance record of 73,561 and helped to establish pro football as a national sport.

In 1930 Halas retired as both a player and a coach. His determination and IOU's were needed to carry the Bears through the worst years of the depression. By 1932 only eight teams remained of the thirty-three that had played in the league during the 1920s. Halas borrowed money to buy out Sternaman's interest in the team. With Zuppke's former assistant Ralph Jones, he refined the T formation and added a man-in-motion, which opened up the game and increased scoring and attendance. The football became streamlined to improve passing. Competition was created through Eastern and Western Divisions. After a three-year sabbatical, Halas returned to coaching in 1933. The Bears were 23–2–1 behind the backfield tandem of Bronko Nagurski, perhaps the greatest blocker in NFL history, and Beattie Feathers, the league's first 1,000-yard runner, and appeared in two championship games, winning one.

Halas understood that the viability of the National Football League depended on strengthening its weakest franchises and equalizing their access to college talent. In 1936 he worked with league president Joe Carr to create the first college football draft. Halas chose future Hall of Fame tackle Joe Stydahar and guard Dan Fortmann in that draft. They joined veteran end Bill Hewitt and guard-tackle George Musso, future Hall of Famers as well, in establishing the backbone of a team as hard-nosed and competitive as its coach and owner. Columbia quarterback Sid Luckman joined the team in 1939, followed by running back George McAfee, center Clyde "Bulldog" Turner, and ends Ken Kavanaugh and Hampton Pool a year later. When Washington owner and Halas rival George Preston Marshall called the Bears "crybabies" after their disputed early-season loss to the Redskins, the "Monsters of the Midway" responded by annihilating the Skins 73–0 in the 1940 championship game, going on to win the league title in two of the following three years, while posting a record of 40–6–1.

In 1942 Halas, then forty-six, began a thirty-nine-month enlistment in the U.S. Navy, where he used his background in engineering to train aircraft mechanics. He returned to coach the Bears to another championship in 1946. The following year he became one of the first owners to televise all his home games, and set up a twenty-five-station radio network to carry the games. Later he would successfully argue that all television rights be assigned to the league and that revenues be shared equally by both small- and large-market teams.

The Bears finished second in six of nine seasons through the mid-1950s, frustrating Halas and forcing him, at his wife's insistence, to temporarily retire from coaching. At the start of the 1958 season, however, Halas was back on the field again, determined at age sixty-three to win another championship. But by 1960 his hat-throwing and referee-baiting sideline tantrums during a 5–6–1 season convinced critics that the game had passed the irascible field commander by. "My body was on the sidelines," he later explained, "but my spirit was right there with my players." Each loss was "an agony" that would only "dissipate through victory." Halas painstakingly rebuilt his Bears through the college draft and on defense and was ready by 1963 to challenge Vince Lombardi's Green Bay Packers for league dominance. The Bears beat the Packers twice that year, 10–3 at Lambeau Field and 26–7 in Chicago, and won the NFL championship for the first time in seventeen years by defeating the New York Giants, 14–10, in a moment of personal triumph for the sixty-eight-year-old coach.

Halas's arthritic hip and the sudden death of Min, "the Bears' most avid fan," on Valentine's Day, 1966, led to his retirement from coaching on 27 May 1968. In forty years he had amassed 321 coaching victories, the most in league history, and was inducted as a charter member into the NFL Hall of Fame. He made his son, George Stanley ("Mugs") Halas, Jr., president of the Bears and gave him day-to-day management of the team.

Halas strongly encouraged the merger of the NFL with the competing American Football League. This helped to create the ultimate televised sporting event on fall Sundays and Monday nights, eventually boosting the value of franchises into the hundreds of millions of dollars. The Bears, however, struggled on the field. In 1974, after several losing seasons, Halas hired Jim Finks to become the team's executive vice president and general manager. The sudden death of his son, Mugs, on 16 December 1979 deeply saddened Halas. In January 1982 he brought in Mike Ditka, a star of the 1963 championship team, "to return the Bears to our former glory." It happened in January 1986, when the Bears blasted the New England Patriots in an international sports spectacle, Super Bowl XX, 46–10, that led to a tumultuous civic celebration in Chicago. Halas didn't live to see it. His death at age eighty-eight following a variety of illnesses saw him memorialized by longtime NFL Commissioner Pete Rozelle for helping to invent a game "very much like George himself—full of wisdom and creativity, vitality and endurance, and above all, intensely competitive." Halas is buried in Chicago.

During Halas's four separate ten-year tenures as head coach, the Bears were 321–148–31 and won seven championships. During that time, Halas helped to transform professional football from a small city, Midwestern sandlot sport to an entertainment industry worth billions. It was Pete Rozelle who observed that "George Halas was the National Football League."

★

Biographical material on the life and career of George Halas is kept at Halas Hall, the Chicago Bears' administrative headquarters in Lake Forest, Illinois, and at the Pro Football League Hall of Fame in Canton, Ohio. Halas wrote an autobiography

with Gwen Morgan and Arthur Veysey, *Halas by Halas* (1979). Biographical treatments of his life are included in Howard Roberts, *The Chicago Bears* (1947); George Vass, *George Halas and the Chicago Bears* (1971); Richard Whittingham, *The Chicago Bears: From George Halas to Super Bowl XX, An Illustrated History* (1979); Cooper Rollow, *Cooper Rollow's Bears Football Book* (1985); Larry R. Gerlach, "George Stanley Halas," in David L. Porter, ed., *Biographical Dictionary of American Sports* (1987); and Richard Whittingham, *The Bears: A Seventy-Five-Year Celebration* (1994). An obituary is in the *New York Times*, and an appreciation of his contribution to professional football is in the *Chicago Tribune* (both 1 Nov. 1983).

BRUCE J. EVENSEN

HALL, Glenn Henry (*b.* 3 October 1931 in Humbolt, Saskatchewan, Canada), star National Hockey League goaltender who holds the record for most consecutive games played by an NHL netminder.

Glenn Hall, the second son of Henry ("Hank") Hall and Agnes Cruickshank, was born in the tiny village of Humbolt, seventy-five miles from Saskatoon. His father, a Canadian National Railways engineer for more than thirty years, was a serious hockey fan and encouraged him in his

Glenn Hall, 1962. AP/WIDE WORLD PHOTOS

pursuit of Canada's national pastime. Hall attended local schools and completed high school, but his real focus was on hockey.

Although Hall made his mark in sports tending goal, he played forward until he was twelve years old. He was captain of his team, and if the coach did not show up for a game he was in charge of designating the position each skater was to play. On one such occasion, he decided to experiment playing in net. Because his was a poor team, there was plenty of action for the goalie, and he liked it. He played the position until his retirement in 1971.

Hall's official hockey records begin with his two seasons as goalie for his hometown Humbolt Indians, of the Saskatchewan Junior Hockey League. From there he moved to the Windsor, Ontario, Spitfires, the Junior team sponsored by the Detroit Red Wings. During his stint in the Ontario Hockey Association he began his collection of significant awards, being voted the winner of the "Red" Tilson Trophy, the equivalent of Most Valuable Player in the circuit. His next stop was with the Indianapolis Capitols of the American League, where he received rave notices for his outstanding performances.

Although both Detroit management and the rest of the National Hockey League (NHL) were impressed when Hall filled in for the injured Terry Sawchuck in 1952–1953 (his Goals Against Average was a stingy 1.67 during those six games), the Wings were not about to oust the game's number-one goaltender by replacing him, especially with an untried rookie. The result was his assignment to their apprenticeship club, the Edmonton Flyers of the Western Hockey League, for two seasons. Hall's contention is that during all of those fledgling years he was never specifically coached in his position. "You learned by watching, and trial and error," he recalled. "If you were not paying attention you fell by the wayside!"

The bombastic Jack Adams, manager of the parent Motor City sextet, was seldom satisfied with the status quo, even after championship seasons. During the summer of 1955 he traded his All-Star goalie, Sawchuck, to the Boston Bruins and promoted Hall to the world's premier loop. As the 1955–1956 schedule began, the man who was to become known as "Mr. Goalie" commenced his streak of 502 regular-season games. He soon made his employers forget their former netminder: earning twelve shutouts, registering an amazing 2.11 Goals Against Average, being awarded the Calder Trophy as Rookie of the Year, and being selected Second All Star Goalie. Despite surpassing his first-year successes the following campaign by being chosen First All-Star backstop, Hall's differences with the Red Wing bosses saw him shipped off to Chicago after the 1956–1957 season.

For ten consecutive seasons Hall anchored the defensive system of the Blackhawks, his Goals Against Average never exceeding 3.00 and dipping to a sensational 2.30 the first

year he won the Vezina Trophy, the circuit's top goalie award. During his tenure in the Windy City he was voted to either the first or second All Star team eight times, and repeated as number-one netminder again in 1966–1967. It was there that Hall earned his long-lasting nickname. The public address announcer made it a habit of introducing him as "Number one, Mr. Goalie."

As talented as he was, life as a professional guardian of the nets brought little pleasure Hall's way during the passing years. He said, "I'd sometimes ask myself, what on earth am I doing in hockey? If I could support my four kids any other way, you can bet I wouldn't be playing goal! If I had to start over again, I wouldn't have been a hockey player. I'd have worked in the post office!"

He had very good reason to make those comments. Hall's passion to excel affected his nerves to the degree that he was nauseous before games began. One year, near the end of his career, he was so distraught about the stress he was feeling that he was ready to quit. Hall was allergic to leather, making it necessary for him always to wear white cotton gloves under his hockey gauntlets. Because he was unable to adjust to wearing a protective facemask, he became more and more vulnerable to injury caused by the erratic shooting associated with the slapshot. On one occasion a screened drive caught him full in the mouth, knocking him unconscious. Hall was taken to the infirmary, where a doctor administered multiple stitches without anaesthetic. After an hour of torturous facial repairs, he picked up his stick and mitts and returned to action.

Because of his reticence about standing in the goal crease while forwards and defensemen fired the puck his way at speeds up to one hundred miles per hour, Hall often held out for more money as an incentive to return to the hockey battleground. This fostered a legend that grew with the passing of time. When it came time to renew his contract each fall, it was said that Hall was late reporting to training camp because he was "painting the barn" on his 160-acre farm near Edmonton, Alberta. This came to the fore when, in 1967, the expansion St. Louis Blues made him a part of their drafted roster. Hall had made the decision to retire that spring, but the Missouri franchise was determined to solidify their new team with solid netminding. When the barn-painting theme came up, manager Murray Patrick said he was willing to help him paint it if he would just put his name on the dotted line. He finally did, for an unprecedented $47,500 per year.

Hall's finest hour came during the 1968 NHL Stanley Cup finals. Although the much weaker St. Louis sextet was no match for the Eastern Division Champion Montreal Canadiens, "Mr. Goalie" was at his acrobatic best, fending off shot after shot in a losing cause. As one journalist described it, "He defended the St. Louis goal with the agile ferocity of the entire Green Bay football club!" Hall's extraordinary performance earned him the Conn Smythe Trophy, awarded to the Most Valuable Player of the play-offs.

Teamed with the aging Jacques Plante, Hall's name was once again engraved on the Vezina Trophy in 1968–1969. His contribution to that joint honor was recognized by his once more being voted the first All-Star goalie of the twelve-team league. Two years later Hall hung up his pads once and for all.

Hall's avocation had always been farming. Even though he coached briefly at the Junior level and was a goaltending consultant for the Colorado Rockies and then the Calgary Flames, he has retired to do, in his own words, "the things I like to do." At this writing he lives on his Stoney Plain, Alberta, farm with Pauline, his wife of forty-seven years, enjoying their four children and grandchildren, who live nearby.

★

Hall's life and career are considered in Richard Beddoes, Stan Fischler, and Ira Gitler, *Hockey* (1973); Trent Frayne, *The Mad Men of Hockey* (1974); Dick Irvin, *In the Crease* (1995); Brian McFalone, *Over the Glass and Into the Crowd* (1997); and Total Sports Publishing, *Total Hockey* (2000). There is as yet no full-length published biography of Hall.

GLEN R. GOODHAND

HAMILL, Dorothy Stuart (*b*. 26 July 1956 in Chicago, Illinois), Winter Olympic and World Figure Skating champion turned professional skater whose career earned her lasting international popularity.

One of three children born to Chalmers Hamill, a businessman, and Carol Clough, a homemaker, Dorothy Hamill grew up in Riverside, Connecticut. At the age of eight she discovered a battered pair of ice skates, tried her wings on Morse's Pond behind her grandparents' Massachusetts home, and became enchanted with skating. Her parents encouraged her dreams by providing private lessons at Playland in Rye, New York, and her mother scouted "practice patches" throughout the area. The neophyte quickly mastered elementary moves, including skating backward.

At various times, mother and daughter moved to different cities in search of the best coaches. Otto Gold, a strong disciplinarian, changed Hamill's technique and taught her figures. He encouraged the energetic ten-year-old to join the United States Figure Skating Association to qualify for regional competition. She studied summers with Gold at Lake Placid, but missed her friends. Hamill described this time as "a wall closing around me and [I] experienced my first taste of the essential loneliness of a life dominated by a single goal. . . . I was skating for the long haul, no matter

Dorothy Hamill, 1976. AP/WIDE WORLD PHOTOS

what the cost, no matter where it took me. I already knew it was worth it." Hamill passed her initial qualifying tests in 1966, prompting one of her peers, Cynthia Van Valkenburg, to suggest they were ready for pairs competition. Despite Gold's opposition, they competed, but came in last.

Hamill won her first gold medal in 1967 at the Wollman Open. Now under coach Gustave Lussi's firm guidance, her free-skating techniques progressed substantially. He worked with her to develop "the Hamill Camel," a spin combination using a flying layover and a sit spin finale. Lussi's most important advice was, "You have to believe you can do it. You have to have guts to be a great skater. . . . If you hesitate, you are lost." On Hamill's eleventh birthday her friends gave her pierced earrings—thirteen pairs in all. The youngster then bargained with her parents to get her ears pierced if she won her next competition. By summer's end, the victor was sporting pierced earrings.

From 1968 to 1976 Hamill continued to train and compete in regional and national events under a succession of trainers including Barbara Taplan, Sonya Klopfer Dunfield, Ellen Burka, Brian Foley, and Carlo Fassi. For luck, she traveled with her collection of stuffed animals. Because of nearsightedness, she was dubbed "Squint." By 1970 Hamill qualified to enter international senior competition. Along the way she acquired many friends, enhanced her figure- and free-skating styles through ballet, and endured "constant butterflies" and some injuries. She scored first in free skating at the Boston Eastern Regionals.

Hamill's schoolwork had been suffering as her training intensified. Occasionally, when she and her mother traveled to other cities to perfect her techniques, her mother hired private tutors. She moved with her mother to New York, where she enrolled in flexible academic classes at the Yoder School between skating sessions. After finishing fifth at the Nationals in 1972, Hamill was invited to Sapporo, Japan, for the North American championships, where she won the silver medal. Chosen to represent the National Figure Skating Association, Hamill captured the French St. Gervais and German Nebelhorn trophies.

Renowned coach Carlo Fassi was impressed with Hamill's potential and had trained her in the summer of 1971 at his training camp in Tulsa, Oklahoma; in 1972 Hamill trained part-time at his new rink in Denver, Colorado, while finishing her high-school requirements. Fassi advised Hamill, "Concentrate, focus, make your mind into a tunnel and look to the other end where the light is shining." In Toronto that summer, Hamill worked with Ellen Burka on the double axel, a jump with two and a half turns in the air. Every week there were theater-on-ice classes, where students played a role mimed to music and projected to an audience. Hamill represented the United States in 1972, placing first at the Richmond Trophy in London, and performing for Queen Elizabeth at a gala televised ice show. Her father flew with her to Bratislava, Czechoslovakia, for Skate Prague, where she won the short program and the Prague Trophy. While behind the Iron Curtain the police confiscated the Hamill passports for a time, but they recovered them and continued to Vienna. Hamill won her first National Senior title in 1974 at Providence, Rhode Island, and placed second in the World Championship in Figure Skating at Munich, Germany. She was chosen to join the International Skating Union tour, a group that provided excellent opportunities for performers to gain self-confidence. Hamill graduated from the Colorado Academy in 1974.

In 1975, still with Fassi, she began final rigorous training for the 1976 Olympics. In January 1976 Hamill won first place in the Colorado Springs Nationals. Suga, a famous hair stylist, created the "Hamill Cut," a distinctive wedge cut, for the Olympics. *Time* magazine and ABC-TV featured the young skater in cover stories. At the 1976 Winter Olympics at Innsbruck, Austria, Hamill earned high artistic and technical scores to win the Gold Medal. Thrilled, she kept the prize under her pillow. The graceful young American represented the hopes and dreams of thousands of people. She had achieving her dreams by win-

ning the National, Olympic, and World titles. After she won the World Championship in Göteborg, Sweden, colleague Dick Button asked, "What's next?" Hamill answered impishly, "I'm going to smoke a cigar."

Hamill turned professional following her Olympic victory, joining the Ice Capades in 1977, and starring in television specials and skating exhibitions. Boyfriends came and went until she met singer Dean Martin, Jr.; they married on 8 January 1982 and divorced in 1984. Hamill married sports physician Kenneth Forsythe in 1987; they had a daughter in 1989, and later divorced.

When the Ice Capades went bankrupt in the early 1990s, Hamill purchased and revamped the show. Hamill announced her retirement from touring in 1995, but she used her celebrity to promote charitable causes and continued to make special appearances as late as 1998. She has served as National Chairperson for the American Cancer Society, on the President's Council on Physical Fitness and Sports, on the International Special Olympics, and at Ronald McDonald House, often working with handicapped children through skating clinics.

Hamill was inducted into the Olympic Hall of Fame in 1991, and into the United States Figure Skating Association Hall of Fame in 1992. Honors include a plaque at Morse's Pond in Massachusetts; Dorothy Hamill Rink in Greenwich, Connecticut; and an honorary diploma from Greenwich High School, which she attended before moving to New York. Named an "Outstanding Young American," her portrait is hung in the National Art Museum of Sport. The *Ladies Home Journal* named Hamill the "most trusted woman in America." In 1984 she earned an Emmy for her performance in *Romeo and Juliet* on CBS-TV. Although diagnosed with osteoarthritis, Hamill continued to skate and has joined fellow Olympian Bruce Jenner in a program to alert the public to the disease. Hamill has truly realized her personal and professional goals, as well as contributed to her community.

★

Biographies of Hamill include Elizabeth van Steenwyk, *Dorothy Hamill: Olympic Champion* (1976), and Edward F. Dolan, Jr., and Richard B. Lyttle, *Dorothy Hamill, Olympic Skating Champion* (1979). Hamill cowrote an autobiography with Elva Clairmont, *On and Off the Ice* (1983). Her career is also chronicled in various series on sports stars, including Miranda Smith, "Dorothy Hamill," *Superstars* (1977), and William R. Sanford and Carl R. Green, "Dorothy Hamill," *Sports Immortals* (1993).

JOAN LIZZIO

HAMILTON, Scott Scovell (*b*. 28 September 1958 in Toledo, Ohio), figure skater who was a four-time world champion from 1981 to 1984 and won a gold medal at the 1984 Winter Olympics.

Hamilton was adopted by Dorothy McIntosh and Ernest Hamilton, both descendants of famous colonial Americans, John Adams and Alexander Hamilton, respectively. Both parents also became college professors, Dorothy in the field of home economics and family relations and Ernest in plant ecology. Hamilton has a sister and an adopted brother.

At the age of four Hamilton stopped growing, a condition doctors tentatively attributed to an inability to absorb nutrients. He also evidenced respiratory problems, and until age nine was subjected to constant medical reevaluations and varied treatments. When he began skating he was short and underweight, and appeared on the ice with a feeding tube extending from his nose. But for the first time in his life, Hamilton felt equal to everyone else because, as he put it, "I didn't have so far to fall." He soon began to grow and gain weight, possibly from the challenge of the exercise itself. Hamilton simply stated, "The more I gave to skating, the more it gave back in the form of emotional and physical strength."

From the beginning of his career, Hamilton was primarily attracted to two aspects of figure skating: the athleticism necessary for speed and jumps, and the art of entertaining an audience. However, to be competitive he also needed to perfect the technique of inscribing figures in the

Scott Hamilton, 1997. AP/WIDE WORLD PHOTOS

ice, patterns used to demonstrate the skater's control, position, and balance.

In 1972, at the beginning of his high school years, Hamilton left home to train with Pierre Brunet in Illinois. At that point he showed promise as a skater, but he lacked motivation and self-discipline. Two important events provided the impetus he needed. First, an anonymous couple agreed to sponsor Hamilton as a potential Olympic athlete. He left his studies at Bowling Green High School to pursue his career full time. Second, he witnessed his mother's unstinting emotional support while she herself was fighting cancer; she died of the disease in 1977. Up to that point Hamilton had done reasonably well, with a first at the U.S. Men's Junior Championship while under the tutorage of coach Carlo Fassi, and a ninth in his first senior Nationals. But in 1978, with newfound inner strength and a technical breakthrough triple Lutz/double-toe combination, he placed third in the Nationals and a respectable eleventh in the Worlds.

Aided by the expertise of his new coach, Don Laws, Hamilton finished third in the 1980 Nationals, earning him a place on the upcoming United States Olympic team. Ironically, just as his reputation was extending beyond national limits, one international figure-skating judge made the comment that Hamilton had no chance to succeed because the five-foot, three-inch, 115-pound skater wasn't big enough to create a strong impression on the ice. His Olympic teammates felt differently, however. Seeing him as an athlete who exemplified Olympic courage, they voted him honorary flag-bearer in the opening ceremonies. At the competition itself, he finished fifth and received a standing ovation from the audience.

In 1981, with a program that included challenging jumps and intricate footwork and spins, Hamilton again received a standing ovation, this time as national champion. Between the years 1982 and 1984, Hamilton maintained both the national and world championship titles despite challenges from other superior technicians, such as Brian Boitano, and the psychological pressure of maintaining excellence. Hamilton's creativity helped. In the 1982 Worlds, his flair for comedy emerged and proved successful with both judges and audience. Likewise, in 1983, he discarded the ballet-like skating outfits traditionally worn by male skaters and replaced them with a speed skating suit. The innovation proved successful, and Hamilton left Helsinki a three-time world champion.

Hamilton's Olympic dream was finally realized in 1984 at Sarajevo. Together with Laws, he planned a program that exploited his strengths—speed, footwork, a big opening triple Lutz, and an athletic resolution. However, through the three phases of the competition his performance was adversely affected by an inner ear imbalance. Sheer athletic stamina held the long program together, but because of his illness it suffered from lack of precision. "They didn't see me at my best today," he wrote, "but they saw the best I had in me." In the end, it was enough. On the basis of the three scores, Hamilton received the gold medal and became the 1984 Olympic champion.

Rather than ending his amateur career with a less-than-ideal performance, Hamilton seized one more opportunity for an unqualified win by brilliantly defending his world title in 1984. Shortly thereafter, he announced his plans to skate professionally with Ice Capades, and two years later he cofounded Stars on Ice, a highly successful touring company. "Stars on Ice came at a time when people were becoming more sophisticated to what skating is all about," he later observed. Hamilton also competed in World Professional Championships, and in 1987 began an alternate career on television as a figure skating analyst for CBS. In 1988 he received the Jacques Favert Award, the International Skating Union's highest recognition of merit.

In March 1997 Hamilton was diagnosed with testicular cancer and underwent a rigorous combination treatment of chemotherapy and surgery. "With my own belief that the only disability in life is a bad attitude, I feel 100 percent confident that I can overcome this disease," he told reporters. He was right. With his cancer in remission, he began skating to fund ongoing cancer research and a program of support for patients and their families. In 2001 Hamilton retired from the highly successful Stars on Ice. He was inducted into both the United States Olympic Hall of Fame and the World Skating Hall of Fame in 1990.

Throughout his skating career, Hamilton turned formidable challenges to his personal advantage. He compensated for his small stature by developing impressive jumping techniques, extended lines, intricate footwork, and the ability to entertain an audience. However, his place in the history of figure skating was assured by solid achievements, including eight consecutive national and world titles. Hamilton also extended the dimensions of ice entertainment as cofounder, performer, and producer of Stars on Ice. Finally, through grappling with a devastating disease and aiding others similarly afflicted, Hamilton once again seized a seemingly insurmountable obstacle as an opportunity for positive gain.

★

Hamilton's autobiography, *Landing It, My Life On and Off the Ice* (1999), contains pertinent details, personal reflections, and observations of contemporary figure skaters. Articles on Hamilton include "Figure Skating; Hamilton Has Cancer," *New York Times* (20 Mar. 1997), and Barry Wilner, "Hamilton Hanging Up Tour Skates, Heading for Other Challenges," Associated Press, Sports News (15 Dec. 2000).

JUDITH HAWKINS

HAMM, Mariel Margaret ("Mia") (*b.* 17 March 1972 in Selma, Alabama), considered the best all-around female soccer player in the world and one of America's most recognizable athletes.

Hamm was born in 1972, the same year that the federal Title IX law prohibiting discrimination against female athletes took effect. Many have pointed to her career as evidence that the law has made a difference. Her father was a colonel in the U.S. Air Force, and his career meant that her childhood was filled with frequent moves to such places as California, Italy, Virginia, and Texas. She was the fourth of sixth children born to Bill and Stephanie Hamm. The last to join the family was her older brother Garrett, adopted at age eight when Mia was five.

In a book on soccer she authored in 1999, Hamm recalls first playing the sport at age six when her brother Garrett could run circles around her. By age ten, she had joined an eleven-year-old boys' team and eventually led them in scoring. While playing on an Olympic development team in Texas at age fourteen, she drew the attention of the coach of the U.S. National Team, Anson Dorrance. He told the *New York Times* when he saw her play that she was "this skinny brunette (who) took off like she had been shot out

Mia Hamm, 1999. ARCHIVE PHOTOS, INC.

of a cannon." At age fifteen she became the youngest player, male or female, ever to join the national team.

In 1989 Hamm followed Dorrance to the University of North Carolina at Chapel Hill where he was coaching. Because her parents moved to Italy that year, Dorrance was declared her legal guardian and remains one of the most influential figures in her life. At the university, she led her team to four National Collegiate Athletic Association (NCAA) soccer championships. Also while there, she met Christiaan Corry in a class covering the collapse of the Soviet Union. The marine pilot would become her husband in 1995.

In 1991 she joined the U.S. Team for the first-ever Women's World Cup in China. At nineteen she was the team's youngest player. The team's victory opened the door for women's soccer in the United States and marked the beginning of an unprecedented wave of popularity of the sport among young girls. But at the time, the team returned to the United States in virtual anonymity. Hamm wrote the following in her book:

> There were no TV crews or fans waiting for us at the airport when we returned, just several friends and U.S. Soccer Federation Representatives. *Sports Illustrated* chose to note the historic victory with a tiny mention in its scorecard section, and newspapers across the country buried the story next to the tire ads in the back. No one offered us endorsements, money or fame, and while we enjoy those things now, it's not why we play. Look back at the pictures of all the young faces on that 1991 team, awash with smiles, the glow of a world championship, and athletic glory in its purest form, and it becomes obvious why we play.

After her graduation from UNC in 1994 with a degree in political science, the university retired her No. 19 jersey. That year was the first of five consecutive times she was named the U.S. Soccer Federation's Female Athlete of the Year. In 1995 she returned to the Women's World Cup, where the team took the bronze as Norway won the gold. In 1996 she helped lead the U.S. Olympic team to the first-ever gold medal awarded in women's soccer, which catapulted Hamm to a new level of fame. She acknowledged her role as a pioneer in the sport but accepted the accompanying celebrity reluctantly, sometimes expressing doubt in her own abilities. After her coach and others called her the world's best female soccer player, Hamm responded in her book, "They're wrong. I have the potential, maybe, but I'm still not there. But because I can't believe what they say, because I'm not yet satisfied, someday I may prove them right."

In 1997 Hamm was named to *People* magazine's "50 Most Beautiful People" list and ranked No. 14 on the "Soccer Business International" list of most influential people in the sport. But the year would be a dark period for her.

Hamm's brother Garrett died at twenty-eight from complications from aplastic anemia, a bone marrow disease. Two years later, she formed the Mia Hamm Foundation to raise money and awareness for two causes close to her heart: bone marrow disease research and creating opportunities for young women in sports.

By 1999 the Women's World Cup had come a long way from the virtual media blackout Hamm described in 1991. Television, magazines, and newspapers everywhere were filled with images of Hamm and her teammates celebrating their dramatic victory. She appeared in a commercial with Michael Jordan in which she flipped him over in a judo maneuver as Irving Berlin's music declared, "Anything you can do, I can do better." The Nike Corporation named a building after her. That year, with her 108th goal, she surpassed the previous international women's goal-scoring record of 107 goals.

In 2000 the U.S. Olympic women's soccer team was unable to defend its gold, taking the silver in a heartbreaking loss to Norway in Sydney, Australia. But Hamm's profile remained high as she became one of nineteen players with an ownership stake in the new WUSA, the first world-class women's professional soccer league. The league was formed with the backing of five cable industry corporations.

The league launched in early 2001, quickly surpassing its attendance goal of 7,500 fans per game (as of July 2001, the average was close to 8,500 a game). Several times Hamm's presence on the field was credited with swelling crowds beyond 30,000 fans. But the career travel demands of both Hamm and her husband took a toll. In July 2001 she confirmed that she was beginning divorce proceedings with Corry after six years of marriage.

At the same time, Hamm declared to the *New York Times* that she had "loved every minute" of her soccer career. She was looking forward to the conclusion of her inaugural professional season, and even further ahead than that. She said she intended to play on the 2003 Women's World Cup team in China and the 2004 Athens Olympics, seeking more gold medals to add symmetry to her remarkable career.

★

Hamm wrote *Go for the Goal: A Champion's Guide to Winning in Soccer and Life* in 1999. She was on the cover of *Sports Illustrated for Women* (Mar./Apr. 2001). She has been profiled in the *New York Times* (11 June 1999 and 10 July 2001).

LEIGH DYER

HANNAH, John Allen (*b.* 4 April 1951 in Canton, Georgia), three-sport letterman at the University of Alabama and member of the Pro Football Hall of Fame, considered perhaps the greatest offensive lineman in the history of the game.

Hannah was born into a football family, one of three sons of Herbert ("Herb") Hannah and Geneva ("Coupe") Watkins, a homemaker. At birth Hannah weighed ten and a half pounds, and it was jokingly said that he was fed hamburger instead of baby food. By the time he was in the eighth grade, his thighs measured thirty-three inches. After a five-year stint in the navy, his father went to college through a football scholarship. In 1947, at age twenty-six, Herb Hannah entered the University of Alabama and began a football tradition that came to include his brother and all three of his sons.

When he finished school, he signed a one-year contract with the New York Giants, becoming the oldest rookie in National Football League (NFL) history. The elder Hannah retired after one year, feeling the need to focus on his family. Herb Hannah moved the family to Georgia, where he coached high school football for four years, and then returned to Albertville to go into the agricultural business.

John Hannah attended Baylor School for Boys (which later became the co-ed Baylor School) in Chattanooga, Tennessee, for four years. He decided to return to Albertville for his senior year at Albertville High School. By that time he was six feet, three inches tall and weighed 265 pounds, but speed was no problem for him. Hannah's size and ability impressed college scouts. Although both Notre

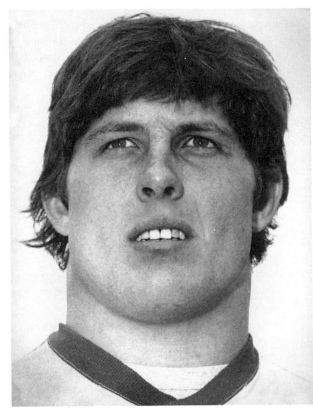

John Hannah, 1983. AP/WIDE WORLD PHOTOS

Dame and the University of Southern California recruited him, Alabama was his first choice. He entered the University of Alabama in 1969, becoming the heaviest player that Coach Paul ("Bear") Bryant had ever recruited. He lettered in wrestling in his freshman year but in the spring switched to track and field. In 1970 Hannah won the Southeastern Intercollegiate wrestling championship and the Southeastern Conference (SEC) shot put (sixty-one feet, five inches) and discus (177 feet, one inch) championships.

In 1971 Hannah became part of what was known as the "Dream Team." Bear Bryant had begun scheduling the games for that season two years earlier, not knowing the strength of the opposition. It turned out to be the most challenging schedule any contender for a national championship ever had. Six of the teams were ranked in the top twenty of the Associated Press poll, and five would play in postseason bowls. Alabama beat them all. Coach Bryant was named National Coach of the Year, and Alabama was ranked number two. On 1 January 1972 Alabama met top-ranked Nebraska in the Orange Bowl in Miami. Hannah and his teammates lost to the Nebraska Cornhuskers 38–6 and remained at number two in the rankings. In the summer of 1972, after his sophomore year, Hannah married his high school sweetheart, Page Pickens, an Alabama cheerleader. Less than two years later they separated. Hannah had always had a wild side, and the separation from his wife accentuated it. He began to frequent bars and nightclubs and to run with a crowd that frightened his father, who was fearful that he would let alcohol or drugs ruin his life. Early in 1973 he turned his life around, reuniting with his wife and becoming an active member of the Fellowship of Christian Athletes.

At Alabama, Hannah lettered in three sports (football, wrestling, and track and field). The three-time All-SEC gridiron choice twice made All-American (1971–1972). In 1972 Hannah was selected Offensive Lineman of the Year by the Touchdown Club of Washington, D.C., among many others. He was one of four finalists for the Lombardi Award and received the Jacobs Award as the best SEC blocker. He played in the Astro Bluebonnet (1970), Orange (1972), and Cotton (1973) Bowls as well as the College All-Star game (1972) and Hula Bowl (1973). As a senior, he was eleventh in the Heisman Trophy voting, an almost unheard-of ranking for an offensive lineman.

With his impressive record, professional football scouts were interested in recruiting Hannah. Early in 1973 he was drafted in the first round by the New England Patriots. Inexperienced in contract negotiating, Hannah acquired an agent, who negotiated a contract for four years playing for very little money. At the same time the Patriot owners were boasting that they had the greatest offensive lineman in football. During his rookie season in 1973, Hannah was a consensus choice on the NFL All-Rookie team, and in 1974 he was named to the All-AFC (American Football Conference) honor squad. At the beginning of 1976 he was chosen All-Pro guard for that year and every year for the remainder of his career. His overpowering blocking during the 1978 season made it possible for the Patriots to set what was then an NFL record of 3,165 yards rushing. Over a period of two seasons (1982 and 1983), the Patriots' total rushing record of 3,952 yards was the best in the entire NFL.

Hannah had not been happy with the Patriots' management and considered retirement in 1983, but he played two more years. In 1985 the Patriots won the AFC championship, becoming the only wild-card playoff team ever to win a trip to the Super Bowl, in this case Super Bowl XX in New Orleans. In the playoffs Hannah and his brother Charley, who played with the Los Angeles Raiders, met on the gridiron, both wearing number 73 and both playing guard. The Patriots won a 26–17 victory. A Patriots victory over the Chicago Bears would have provided a perfect ending for Hannah's career, but they lost 46–10. Hannah played in Super Bowl XX with two torn rotator cuffs and a knee in which the bones were wasting away. Even in a great deal of pain, he had held his own against stellar Bears defensive lineman William ("Refrigerator") Perry. Hannah underwent surgery on both shoulders in February 1986 and knee surgery the following May. In his thirteen years with the Patriots, he missed only five games out of 191.

Hannah retired on 30 June 1986. He remained in Boston, where his son and daughter attended school, and continued to be a part of the family business until his father retired and sold it. Hannah and his wife divorced in 1993. In 1988 he was named to the Alabama Sports Hall of Fame. Three years later he was elected to the Pro Football Hall of Fame, the first year of his eligibility. He was the first Patriot and second offensive guard to receive this honor.

Experts on football have trouble agreeing who is the best quarterback or running back or receiver in the NFL, but when it comes to offensive linemen, Hannah is without peer. His success and football greatness can be attributed to the fact that he truly loved football and always gave it his very best. He earned the title of "greatest offensive lineman of all time."

★

Player scrapbooks from the 1892 to the present, containing clippings, video footage of the football games, books, photographs, and correspondence, are available from the research library of the Paul W. Bryant Museum, University of Alabama, Tuscaloosa. The Hall of Fame presentation and acceptance speech can be heard at the website of the Pro Football Hall of Fame, <http://www.profootballhof.com>. Articles about Hannah's career are Paul Zimmerman, "The Maturing of John Hannah," *Football Digest* (Dec. 1975) and "John Hannah Doesn't Fiddle Around," *Sports Illustrated* (3 Aug. 1981); and Jimmy Bryan, "John Hannah Was Born to Football Greatness," *Birmingham News* (23 June 1991). See also Thomas C. Ford, *Alabama's Family Tides* (1988), and Lars Anderson, "Catching Up with John Hannah," *Time* (14 Feb. 2000).

BETTY B. VINSON

HARMON, Thomas Dudley ("Tom") (*b.* 28 September 1919 in Gary, Indiana; *d.* 15 March 1990 in Los Angeles, California), football player and sports broadcaster who was one of the most talented and exciting halfbacks in college football history.

Harmon was one of four sons born to Louis A. Harmon, a Gary policeman, and Rose Harmon, a homemaker. Harmon attended Horace Mann High School in Gary and starred in football, basketball, baseball, and track, winning fourteen varsity letters there. Though he was an outstanding baseball pitcher and was captain of the basketball team, football and track garnered Harmon's greatest prep fame. A four-year member of Horace Mann's varsity football team, he was named high school football's national scoring champion in 1936 after tallying 150 points. He was selected to the Indiana All-State football team for two years. Harmon also won state track championships for the 100-yard dash and the 220-yard low hurdles.

Harmon was interested in attending Dartmouth or Notre Dame, the latter a favorite of his Irish-Catholic parents. But his high school coach, Doug Kerr, a Michigan man, encouraged Harmon to attend his alma mater. The University of Michigan's beautiful campus and reputation as a good academic school finally convinced Harmon to enroll there in the fall of 1937, after he had graduated from Horace Mann.

Harmon, wearing jersey number 98 and starting at tailback, made a big splash at Michigan as a junior in 1939. His highlights included scoring 3 touchdowns and rushing for 206 yards against Yale; scoring 4 touchdowns, including a 95-yard interception return, against Iowa; and rushing for 202 yards, scoring 2 touchdowns and passing for another, in a thrilling 19–17 win over Pennsylvania. In the third quarter against Pennsylvania, deep in Michigan territory, Harmon started off on a sweep around left end but reversed direction and circled back toward his goal line. Changing direction again, Harmon finally broke loose for a 63-yard touchdown gallop down the left sideline. He easily ran twice that 63-yard distance, the greatest play of his career, in the game Harmon later described as the most exciting he ever experienced. For the 1939 season Harmon scored 14 touchdowns and tallied 102 points, both the highest marks in the nation. In addition he rushed for 868

Tom Harmon, 1946. AP/WIDE WORLD PHOTOS

yards on 129 carries and completed 37 of 94 passes for 488 yards and 6 touchdowns. He was named a consensus All-American halfback and finished second in the Heisman Trophy balloting to Iowa's Nile Kinnick.

In 1940 Harmon, at six feet, two inches and two hundred pounds, was again at tailback for a Michigan team that ranked among the best in the country. His season highlights included 4 touchdown runs, 94, 70, 86, and 7 yards respectively, against California, and 3 touchdown games against Michigan State, Harvard, and Ohio State. The California game produced the most remembered play of Harmon's career. A fan named Bud Brennan came out of the grandstands and attempted to tackle Harmon near the end of his third long touchdown gallop, but Harmon narrowly avoided him at the goal line. Against Ohio State in his final college game Harmon broke Red Grange's Big Ten Conference career touchdown record, his final tally coming with thirty-eight seconds left to play.

For 1940 Harmon had 844 rushing yards on 186 carries, he completed forty-two of ninety-three passes for 502 yards and seven touchdowns, and he scored 16 touchdowns and 117 points, again leading the nation in points scored. He was named unanimous All-American halfback for 1940, and his host of awards included the Heisman Trophy, the Maxwell Trophy, and the Associated Press Male Athlete of the Year. Yet Harmon always remained disappointed about

the 1940 season, as Minnesota had handed Michigan a 7–6 upset defeat that cost the Wolverines the national championship on a day Harmon described as the "most frustrating" of his life.

Harmon played in the Shrine All-Star Game in January 1941, and while on the West Coast he appeared on Bing Crosby's radio show, where he met his future wife Elyse Knox, a movie actress. That summer, after graduating with majors in speech and English, he starred in a movie entitled *Harmon of Michigan.* He was voted into the starting lineup for the College All-Stars and threw a touchdown pass against the Chicago Bears in the annual charity game in Chicago. The Bears selected Harmon in the first round of the 1941 National Football League (NFL) draft, but he instead accepted a broadcasting job that included covering Michigan football games. He played one game for the New York Americans of the American Football League. Harmon enlisted in the U.S. Army Air Corps on 5 November 1941 and was accepted for flying school.

In April 1943 Harmon was the only survivor when his B-25 bomber crashed in the jungle of Dutch Guiana (Suriname) while on a routine mission. After a grueling six-day hike through the swampy jungle, he finally stumbled into a native settlement. After rehabilitation he was trained as a fighter pilot and sent to the Asian theater. On 30 October 1943 Harmon's plane was shot down over China, and with his legs and hands severely burned in a cockpit explosion, he parachuted into a lake. Rescued by Chinese guerrillas, Harmon was guided on a perilous journey through Japanese-held territory and reached an American base. For his ordeals as Lieutenant he was awarded the Silver Star and the Purple Heart.

Harmon and Elyse Knox were married on 26 August 1944 in a chapel on the University of Michigan campus. Discharged from the Army Air Force on 12 August 1945, Harmon played again for the College All-Stars later that month. He signed a contract with the Los Angeles Rams for the 1946–1947 seasons, but the wartime injuries to Harmon's legs had robbed him of much of his former speed. He retired from pro football after two seasons.

Harmon then returned to broadcasting, while he and Elyse began raising a family of three children, Christie, Kelly, and Mark, the last a noted movie actor. In the early 1950s Harmon began doing the nightly sports report on Channel 2 in Los Angeles, moving to KTLA television from 1958 to 1964. In 1961 he also started a long-running nightly sports radio show for ABC. In the late 1960s Harmon returned to KTLA to broadcast University of California, Los Angeles (UCLA) football, moving in 1974 to the Hughes Television Network. He spent his final years hosting a popular show, *Raider Playbook,* after the NFL's Oakland Raiders moved to Los Angeles in 1982. He died of a heart attack at age seventy. He is buried in Los Angeles.

Harmon was one of the greatest all-around players in college football history, a top headliner in an era of exceptional players. He combined sprinter speed, line-smashing power, and an excellent passing touch to lead Michigan football back to its earlier glory days. In his college career Harmon scored 237 points, including 33 touchdowns, while gaining 2,134 yards on 398 carries and completing 101 of 233 passes for 1,399 yards and 16 touchdowns. He was inducted into the College Football Hall of Fame in 1954.

★

Among the best sources on Harmon's football career are Mervin D. Hyman and Gordon S. White, Jr., *Big Ten Football: Its Life and Times, Great Coaches, Players, and Games* (1977); and Dave Newhouse, *After the Glory—Heisman* (1985). Also notable is Richard M. Cohen, Jordan A. Deutsch, and David S. Neft, *The University of Michigan Football Scrapbook* (1978), which includes a well-written forward by Harmon. Obituaries are in the *Los Angeles Times* (16 Mar. 1990) and the *New York Times* (17 Mar. 1990).

RAYMOND SCHMIDT

HARRIS, Franco (*b.* 7 March 1950 in Fort Dix, New Jersey), premier running back for the Pittsburgh Steelers through four Super Bowl victories; he was inducted into the Pro Football Hall of Fame in 1990.

The son of Chad Harris, a career army officer, and Gina Parenti Harris, his Italian-born wife, Harris graduated from Rancocas Valley Regional High School, in Mount Holly, New Jersey, in 1968 and then went to Pennsylvania State University. He graduated in 1972 with a degree in hotel and restaurant management. By that time he had already established himself as a good running back. Though considered a backup to Lydell Mitchell, in three years Harris carried the ball 380 times for 2,002 yards.

Harris was drafted by a team of perennial losers, the Pittsburgh Steelers, in the first round of the 1972 draft and began his long career under the legendary coach Chuck Noll. In his debut season, however, Harris started only two of his first seven games. Nevertheless, his performance was good enough to make him only the fifth rookie in National Football League (NFL) history to gain over 1,000 yards. His longest run from scrimmage was seventy-five yards.

For the first time in its history, the Steelers made it to the playoffs in 1972, in which they fought a titanic defensive battle with the Oakland Raiders. Leading 6–0 on two field goals by Roy Gerela, an Oakland touchdown by Ken Stabler suddenly put the Steelers behind with only 1:13 left in the game. As time ran down, the Steelers faced a fourth and ten from their own forty-yard line. Quarterback Terry Bradshaw's pass to "Frenchy" Fuqua bounced off defensive back Jack Tatum. Harris caught the rebound off his shoetops at the Oakland forty-two yard line and carried it in for the winning score as time expired, a catch immortalized as the "immaculate reception." The Steelers advanced to the American Football Conference (AFC) championship game only to be edged 21–17 by the Miami Dolphins on their way to a perfect season.

The 1974 season was a glory year for the Steelers. In the first round of the playoffs against Buffalo, Harris broke the game open in the second quarter, capping a sixty-six-yard

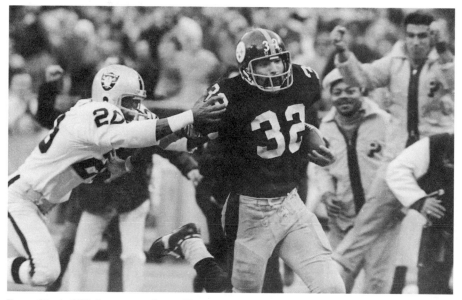

Franco Harris, 1972. ASSOCIATED PRESS AP

drive by diving in from the one-yard line. After linebacker Jack Ham recovered a Buffalo fumble on the first play, Harris ended another drive with a four-yard burst. Buffalo never recovered and the Steelers emerged victorious at 32–14. Trailing Oakland in the AFC championships, Harris scored twice in the fourth quarter, tying the game with an eight-yard run. Following a Lynn Swann touchdown and a field goal by Oakland, Harris ensured the 24–13 victory for the Steelers with a twenty-one-yard run late in the game. This gave the Steelers their first Super Bowl appearance, playing against the Minnesota Vikings. The only first-half score in this game was a safety for the Steelers, but Harris gave them their margin of victory with a nine-yard run in the third quarter as Pittsburgh went on to a 16–6 victory. On thirty-four carries, Harris gained 158 yards; both were highs for a Super Bowl. He was named Most Valuable Player of Super Bowl IX.

The following year again pitted Pittsburgh against Oakland in the playoffs. On an icy field, with the score 3–0 going into the fourth quarter, Harris scored the Steelers' first touchdown in their 16–10 victory. Against Baltimore in the conference championship game, Harris started the Steeler scoring with a three-yard run in the opening quarter, as Pittsburgh prevailed 28–10. The Steelers trailed Dallas in Super Bowl X but came back to win 21–17 with two fourth-quarter touchdowns. Harris carried the ball twenty-seven times for eighty-two yards in the game.

In 1976 the Steelers set a playoff record with a total of 526 offensive yards against Baltimore in a 40–14 win. Facing Oakland, with Harris out of the lineup in the conference championship game, Pittsburgh lost 24–7. The following year the Steelers dropped the playoff opener 34–21 to the Denver Broncos, though Harris scored on a one-yard dive.

The Steelers got their revenge against Denver in the opening round of the 1978 playoffs as Harris scored the game's first two touchdowns on a one-yard dive and an eighteen-yard run, leading to a final score of 33–10. The famed "Steel Curtain" defense showed its mettle in the AFC championship game, allowing Houston only a field goal and a safety. Harris got the offense started with a seven-yard run; the Steelers won, 34–5. Super Bowl XIII again pitted Pittsburgh against Dallas. Harris, who carried twenty times for sixty-eight yards, scored a fourth-quarter touchdown to give the Steelers a narrow 35–31 victory. With that win the Steelers became the first team to win three Super Bowls.

In the 1979 playoffs Harris scored the last Pittsburgh touchdown in their opening win over Miami, 34–14. They continued their defensive mastery in the conference championship with a 27–13 thumping of Houston. Super Bowl XIV, however, was a struggle. Harris scored Pittsburgh's first touchdown in the second quarter, but the Los Angeles Rams led 19–17 at the end of the third quarter. In the final period the Steelers took the lead, 24–19, but a Rams' drive threatened to end the Steeler run. After linebacker Jack Lambert intercepted a pass at the Pittsburgh fourteen-yard line, Harris capped the long drive by diving in from the one. Pittsburgh repeated as Super Bowl champions and captured their fourth title of the decade, then an NFL record.

Harris played thirteen seasons in the NFL: twelve with the Steelers and one, his last, with Seattle. In 173 games he carried the ball 2,949 times, gaining 12,120 yards. He rushed for over 1,000 yards eight times, gaining 1,246 yards in the 1975 season. He averaged 4.1 yards per carry and scored ninety-one touchdowns. As a receiver he caught 307 passes for 2,287 additional yards and nine more touchdowns. He earned four Super Bowl rings.

Following his retirement Harris lived on Pittsburgh's North Side with his wife, Dana Dokmanovich Harris, and son, Franco Dokmanovich "Dok" Harris. Committed to community service, he worked for Children's Hospital and a number of other charities. In 1982 he was awarded the Whizzer White Humanitarian Award.

At six feet, two inches tall and 230 pounds, Harris earned his reputation as a durable power back. He played intelligently, however, avoiding unnecessary punishment by sliding out of bounds when he felt he had gained as much yardage as possible. As a result, he missed only nine games in thirteen years. He was the leading rusher in thirteen of the nineteen postseason games in which he played and was selected to the Pro Bowl nine times. At the time of his retirement, only Walter Payton and Jimmy Brown had gained more yardage on the ground. *College and Pro Football Newsweekly* named him their player of the decade of the 1970s. Yet despite his many accomplishments, Harris is best remembered for one play in his rookie season, the "immaculate reception" that brought the Steelers their first-ever playoff victory.

★

Articles about Franco Harris can be found in David L. Porter, ed., Biographical Dictionary of American Sports: Football (1987), and Bob Carroll et al., Total Football: The Official Encyclopedia of the National Football League (1997). Magazine coverage includes Rich Emert, "The Play of a Lifetime," Tribune-Review (21 Dec. 1997). Further information can be found in the National Pro Football Hall of Fame archives in Canton, Ohio.

ART BARBEAU

HARTACK, William J. ("Bill") (*b.* 9 December 1932 in Edensburg, Pennsylvania), jockey of uncompromising honesty and great skill who won five Kentucky Derbys and three Preaknesses; one of the most successful riders of the twentieth century.

Hartack was named for his father, a Slavic immigrant who became a Pennsylvania coal miner. He was raised on his widowed father's farm north of Belsano, Pennsylvania. In 1949 he graduated as valedictorian from the Black Lick Township High School near Johnstown, Pennsylvania.

Hartack did not embark on a riding career until after graduation from high school. He won his first race at Waterford Park in West Virginia on 14 October 1952 on a horse that had cost just $100.

In 1953 he rode 328 winners (28 percent) as an apprentice most of the season. In 1955 he led all other jockeys with 417 victories. The next year he passed jockeys in money earned with $2,343,955 in purses. By this time Hartack was riding the best horses from the renowned Calumet Farm stable. In his first Kentucky Derby, in 1956, Hartack finished second at the mile-and-a-quarter track with Calumet's Fabius. Two weeks later he avenged his Kentucky Derby defeat by winning the Preakness, a slightly shorter race at 1 3/16 mile, aboard the same horse, the first of three times he won that race. Later the same year Hartack rode Barbizon, another Calumet horse, to a thrilling victory in the two-year-old Garden State Stakes.

Bill Hartack, 1964. AP/WIDE WORLD PHOTOS

In 1957 Hartack became the first jockey to win over $3 million in a single year. This amazing earnings record stood until 1967. Also in 1957 he set another record that lasted eleven years; he had sixty-two wins at Hialeah (Florida) in forty days. Incredibly, he also won forty-three stakes that year, setting another record. In the 1957 Kentucky Derby, Hartack rode Iron Liege (who was trained by Jimmy Jones), one of three favored horses. He took Iron Liege to the front at the head of the stretch and held off Gallant Man to win by a nose. Willie Shoemaker, the jockey aboard Gallant Man, supposedly misjudged the finish line by standing up in the stirrups momentarily, thus costing his horse the victory.

Hartack and Shoemaker demonstrated contrasting riding styles. Shoemaker generally sat quietly on a horse, even when coming from behind in a rush, while Hartack preferred to lead from the outset and pumped, scrubbed, whipped, and urged his horse forward. Hartack described his riding style as "looking like a sack of manure on a horse." But this did not deter him from winning all types of races, including the little ones.

Hartack was known for his difficult personality; he antagonized racing stewards, trainers, owners, and journalists alike. His blazing desire to win made him angry with anything less than his best. His blunt honesty and frequent displays of temper were familiar in the racing world. In late 1958 a temper tantrum caused Calumet Farm to terminate its connection with Hartack. Nevertheless, his brilliant riding kept him on the best horses. He won five Kentucky Derbys: Iron Liege, 1953; Venetian Way, 1960; Decidedly, 1962; Northern Dancer, 1964; and Majestic Prince, 1969. Only Eddie Arcaro has won as many Derbys. One of Hartack's agents, Chick Lang, said with a smile after the 1969 Derby, "Bill rides this race like he invented it."

Hartack did not want to retire in the early 1970s, so he seized an opportunity to race in Hong Kong. He raced there for three seasons, riding many top horses, including Silver Lining, Hong Kong's Horse of the Year for 1978.

Hartack's racing record at his retirement speaks for itself. From 1953 to 1974 in the United States, he rode a total of 21,535 mounts with 4,272 wins, a 19.8 percent win record. He was the leading jockey in races won in 1955, 1956, 1957, and 1960, and the leading jockey in purse moneys in 1956 and 1957. In addition to his five Kentucky Derby wins (out of nine tries), his classic successes include winning the Preakness three times (1956, 1964, and 1969) and the Belmont (1960). He was inducted into the National Museum of Racing Hall of Fame in 1959.

Since 1981 he has served as a racing official, ABC television commentator, and technical adviser for racing movies. He resides in Florida.

Hartack was acclaimed as an intelligent, knowledgeable rider with a keen desire to win and a deft skill at transmitting that desire to his mounts. When he was thirty-nine he became the fifth jockey in history to win more than 4,000 races. His $25,878,063 in total purses set a record at the time. His consistent winning percentage has been topped by few riders. He rode a number of Hall of Fame horses but identified his best mount as 1957 Florida Derby winner Gen. Duke and his best two-year-old mount as Ridan.

★

The National Museum of Racing and Hall of Fame maintains files on Hartack. Articles of interest are in *The Blood-Horse, The Daily Racing Form, Turf and Sport Digest,* the *New York Times,* and *The Horsemen's Journal.*

JOAN GOODBODY

HASKINS, Donald Lee (*b.* 14 March 1930 in Enid, Oklahoma), gruff, principled basketball coach who broke racial barriers by guiding Texas Western College to the 1966 NCAA championship and who went on to become one of the most successful coaches in college basketball history.

Haskins was born at the beginning of the Great Depression on the outskirts of the region soon to become known as the Dust Bowl. His parents were Paul Haskins, a truck driver and semipro baseball player, and Opal Richey Haskins, a homemaker. Haskins's father instilled a love of sports and hunting in his two sons. Haskins's first love was baseball, but by his freshman year in high school he was determined to become a basketball player, devoting so much time to the sport that, as he later wrote, "On the night of the junior-senior prom, while people were dancing, I was shooting baskets." He matriculated at Oklahoma A&M University (now Oklahoma State) in 1948, where he joined the basketball team and earned pocket money by hustling pool. At first Haskins resented the grueling tactics of Henry "Hank" Iba, A&M's legendary coach, but he eventually gained respect for Iba's toughness and insistence on team play—traits that would later come to characterize Haskins's own teams. Haskins was a good, but not great, player, earning second team all-conference honors in 1951–1952, his senior season. With Haskins playing guard and forward, Oklahoma A&M was national runner-up in 1948–1949 and placed fourth in 1950–1951.

In 1951 Haskins married Mary Louise Gorman. Their marriage lasted more than fifty years and produced four sons. Haskins left college in 1954, twelve hours short of graduation, to play semipro basketball with the Artesia (New Mexico) Travelers. (He would complete his degree at West Texas State College in 1958.) In 1956 he took a high school coaching job in Benjamin, Texas—population 300—where he coached the football team and boys' and girls' basketball teams in addition to driving the school bus.

After a year there, he moved on to similar jobs in Hedley, Texas, where he stayed four years, and Dumas, Texas, where he remained for a year.

In 1961 Haskins was named head basketball coach at Texas Western College in El Paso, Texas, a job he would hold for the next thirty-eight years. El Paso, isolated from the rest of Texas both culturally and geographically, proved a haven for African-American student-athletes who were attracted by the community's relative lack of racism. In 1956 Texas Western had been the first college in a southern state to integrate its basketball team, and when Haskins arrived, he inherited a star African-American player, native El Pasoan Nolan Richardson. Haskins was an immediate success at Texas Western, posting winning records in each of his first fifteen seasons. His best players in those years included Jim "Bad News" Barnes, a dominating center who became the first overall pick in the 1964 NBA draft, and Hall of Fame point guard Nate "Tiny" Archibald.

By the 1965–1966 season, Haskins's fifth, Texas Western had become a force to be reckoned with. The team's six best players were African Americans, and Haskins played them all, successfully resisting an edict from Texas Western's president to play only three black players at a time. Led by center David Lattin and point guard Bobby Joe Hill, the Miners won their first twenty-three games and ended the regular season ranked third nationally with a 23–1 record. A tough, smart, and defense-minded team, Texas Western was an unknown quantity to most of the country as they won their first three games in the NCAA Tournament to reach the Final Four. On 18 March 1966 they defeated Utah to reach the championship game against a heavily favored—and all-white—team from the University of Kentucky. Though little remarked upon at the time, the racial issues at stake were clear. African-American players were still unofficially banned from the Southeast, Southwest, and Atlantic Coast Conferences. It was the first time an all-black starting lineup had appeared in the championship game, shattering the myth that any squad lacking a white player would inevitably degenerate into chaos. The statement was underscored by the fact that the Miners were facing Kentucky, a bastion of segregation whose coach, Adolph Rupp, had privately vowed never to recruit blacks, and who referred to the Texas Western men as "a bunch of coons" during a halftime speech to his players.

Texas Western quickly took control of the game. Near the end of the first half, back-to-back steals by Hill turned the tide in the Miners' favor, and they led the rest of the way, winning 72–65. Although the championship made Haskins an instant hero in El Paso, the victory quickly became tinged with racial bitterness, as hate letters from nonblacks poured in from across the country. But some blacks criticized Haskins too. On one hand, the black radical scholar Harry Edwards accused him of exploiting Af-

Don Haskins (*right*) and Orsten Artis. AP/WIDE WORLD PHOTOS

rican-American athletes, while on the other, the white author James Michener attacked Haskins's team with a racist harangue in his book *Sports in America*. "That next year was about the saddest and toughest of my life," Haskins later recalled. "A lot of days I wished we had finished second."

After the 1966 season schools with greater prestige and resources than Texas Western (which was renamed the University of Texas at El Paso [UTEP] in 1967) often tried to lure Haskins away. But he found that he liked El Paso's laid-back attitude—and its proximity to good hunting and fishing—too much to move. In 1969 he accepted an offer from the University of Detroit to triple his $20,000 salary, but after just one day in Michigan, he grew homesick, changed his mind, and returned to UTEP.

In 1972 Haskins was briefly reunited with his mentor, Iba, when he served as Iba's assistant on the U.S. Olympic basketball team. The 1980s, meanwhile, saw Haskins's Miners dominate the Western Athletic Conference, winning an average of twenty-three games per year while collecting five conference titles and seven consecutive NCAA Tournament appearances. The 1988–1989 squad, led by future NBA all-stars Tim Hardaway and Antonio Davis, went 26–7. But as the 1990s approached, Haskins seemed to lose his recruiting touch, and finding players became increasingly difficult after 1993, when some minor rules violations resulted in NCAA sanctions against UTEP. In addition, top athletes were increasingly reluctant to commit to an aging, disciplinarian, and defense-minded coach at a desert school in the middle of nowhere.

But Haskins kept coaching, putting his players through relentless defensive drills with a gruff demeanor that earned him the nickname "The Bear." On 20 January 1996 he suffered a heart attack during halftime of a game and, after undergoing triple bypass surgery, sat out the rest of the season. He came back the next season, and in September 1997 UTEP's basketball arena was renamed the Don Haskins Center. Later that month, on 29 September, Haskins received his sport's highest honor when he was inducted into the Basketball Hall of Fame in Springfield, Massachusetts. A year later, on 24 August 1998, he announced his retirement from coaching.

Haskins finished his thirty-eight-year career at UTEP with a 719–353 record, ranking as the tenth winningest coach in Division I history. Although the Miners played in fourteen NCAA tournaments during Haskins's tenure, they compiled a mediocre 14–13 tournament record, and were able to advance past the second round only once after the 1966 championship season. In the 1992 tournament—Haskins's last—his underdog team surprised top-seeded Kansas in the second round to advance to the Sweet Sixteen.

Haskins was famed as a teacher of young coaches, serving as a mentor for such future coaches as Richardson and Tim Floyd, and is one of the foremost defensive coaches in the history of the college game. His lasting legacy, however, is the 1966 championship game. As time passed Texas Western's victory came to be regarded by many as the most significant game in college basketball history. After 1966 college basketball integrated at light speed, and even Kentucky had an African-American player by 1969. Dozens of prominent basketball figures, including Bob McAdoo, Rick

Majerus, Tubby Smith, and Pat Riley (a member of the losing 1966 Kentucky team), have cited the 1966 championship game as an inspiration to their careers. Haskins, for his part, always maintained that race played no part in choosing his lineup that night. "I played my five best players, who happened to be black," he said. "If it advanced opportunities for blacks and showed the world what they could do, well and good."

★

Haskins wrote an autobiography, *Haskins: The Bear Facts* (1987, as told to Ray Sanchez). Two books describe the 1966 championship season in great detail: Ray Sanchez, *Basketball's Biggest Upset* (1991); and Frank Fitzpatrick, *And the Walls Came Tumbling Down* (1999). Haskins was featured frequently in *Sports Illustrated,* including major articles on 28 Mar. 1966, 15 July 1968, 21 Mar. 1991, and 1 Mar. 1999. Significant articles also appear in *Texas Parade* (Jan. 1967), the *Austin American-Statesman* (1 Mar. 1997), and the *El Paso Times* (4 Feb. 1997, 25 Aug. 1999, and 18 Mar. 2001). Finally, the UTEP men's basketball media guide, published annually by the school's athletic department, contains an exhaustive amount of information about Haskins, his teams, and his players.

ERIC ENDERS

HAVLICEK, John Joseph (*b.* 8 April 1940 in Martins Ferry, Ohio), basketball player who played his entire sixteen-year career with the Boston Celtics and retired as one of the greatest players in National Basketball Association (NBA) history.

Havlicek, the youngest of Frank and Amanda Havlicek's three children, was born in Martins Ferry, Ohio, but spent his childhood in Lansing, Ohio. Many of Lansing's 700 residents were employed in nearby coal mines and steel mills. Havlicek's father came to the United States from Czechoslovakia at age eleven and his mother was of Croatian decent. His parents owned a grocery store in nearby Dillonsville, where Havlicek helped out on the weekends.

When Havlicek was six years old, he discovered a talent for running and would run nonstop between mileposts along the highway. Running became his passion, and his stamina and conditioning would become his trademark during his career.

Havlicek attended Bridgeport High School, where he was a teammate and neighbor of future Hall of Fame baseball pitcher Phil Niekro. An outstanding athlete, Havlicek was an all-state selection in basketball, football, and baseball. Known as the "Bridgeport H-Bomb," Havlicek set a state scoring record by tallying forty points in a single basketball game. Although he averaged nearly thirty points a game, Havlicek was better known for his defensive ability.

John Havlicek. ARCHIVE PHOTOS, INC.

His outstanding high school athletic career produced nearly eighty college scholarship offers, most of them for football, at which he excelled as quarterback.

After a brilliant high school career, Havlicek enrolled at Ohio State University, where he was the centerpiece of that school's greatest era of basketball success. Playing under Hall of Fame coach Fred Taylor and with teammates (and future Hall of Famers) Jerry Lucas and Bob Knight, the Buckeyes compiled a three-year record of 78–6 and won three Big Ten titles from 1960 to 1962.

During that three-year span, the Buckeyes reached the National Collegiate Athletic Association (NCAA) championship game each year, winning the title in 1960 and finishing as runner-up in 1961 and 1962. In his first college season, Havlicek led Ohio State to a 25–3 record and the NCAA championship with a victory over Cincinnati. An All-American and team captain in 1962, Havlicek led the Buckeyes to a 26–2 record and a third consecutive trip to the NCAA championship game.

After college, Havlicek was a first-round draft selection in 1962 for the Boston Celtics. He was also chosen in the seventh round of the National Football League draft as a wide receiver by the Cleveland Browns despite never having played college football. Havlicek remained on the Browns' roster until the final cut.

Havlicek began his career with the Celtics as a reserve player even though he was one of the best players on the team. At six-feet, five-inches tall and 205 pounds, he entered the league as a defensive standout and was the heir to Frank Ramsey as the Celtics' sixth man. For years he was the first player off the bench and soon became recognized as the NBA's best sixth man. In the years since, he has become the standard by which all such players are measured.

Throughout his career, "Hondo" (as Havlicek was known) was highly regarded for his nonstop motion, tremendous all-around basketball skills, and knowledge of the game. Havlicek was a thirteen-time All-Star from 1966 to 1978, and helped lead the Celtics to eight NBA championships in sixteen years. He was a four-time All-NBA first-team selection and a seven-time All-NBA second-team selection. His defensive ability earned him five NBA All-Defensive first team spots and three NBA All-Defensive second team berths. He was named to the NBA's thirty-fifth anniversary All-Time Team in 1980 and the NBA's fiftieth anniversary All-Time Team in 1996.

Havlicek increased his all-around performance during the playoffs, where he bolstered his scoring average from 20.8 points to 22.0 points per game in 172 playoff appearances. He matched the NBA Finals single-game record for most points scored in an overtime period (nine) on 10 May 1974 against the Milwaukee Bucks. He also shared the single-game playoff record for most field goals made (twenty-four) on 1 April 1973 against the Atlanta Hawks. In addition, he was named the Most Valuable Player of the 1974 NBA Finals in Boston's victory over the Milwaukee Bucks.

Despite his statistical records, Havlicek may best be remembered for his defensive steal in the 1965 Eastern Conference Finals against the Philadelphia 76ers. In the decisive final game, Havlicek stole an inbound pass thrown by Hall of Famer Hal Greer under the Philadelphia basket with five seconds remaining to preserve the Celtics' 110–109 victory. The play, which set off a celebration by the crowd, became immortalized by legendary Celtics' broadcaster Johnny Most, who shouted on the radio "Havlicek stole the ball."

Havlicek retired from the Celtics on 9 April 1978 after sixteen brilliant seasons. During his career, Havlicek rewrote the record books, becoming one of the greatest basketball players the sport has ever seen. He recorded sixteen straight seasons as a 1,000-point scorer and retired as the NBA's third all-time leading scorer (26,395 points) behind Wilt Chamberlain and Oscar Robertson. Upon retirement, he ranked first in most games played (1,270), second in most field goals made (10,531), first in most field goals attempted (23,930), second in most minutes played

(46,471), eighth in most free throws made (5,369), ninth in most free throws attempted (6,589), sixth in most assists (6,114), and seventh in most personal fouls (3,281). Havlicek still ranks as the leading scorer in Celtic history.

In 1983 Havlicek was inducted into the Naismith Memorial Basketball Hall of Fame along with fellow Celtic teammate Sam Jones. Havlicek is also a member of the 1987 Class of the National High School Sports Hall of Fame.

Since his playing days, Havlicek has become a very successful businessman and is a franchisee for Wendy's, a fast-food chain. He has also done promotional work for RJR Nabisco and the Garycorp Company in Leominster, Massachusetts, and makes appearances as a corporate speaker. He and his wife, Beth Evans Havlicek, whom he married on 17 June 1967, are the parents of two children.

★

The best single-volume book on Havlicek is *Hondo: Celtic Man in Motion* (1977), written by Havlicek and *Boston Globe* writer Bob Ryan. Two other books offer a comprehensive history of the Boston Celtics and discuss Havlicek and his role on the team: Bob Ryan, *The Boston Celtics: The History, Legends and Images of America's Most Celebrated Team* (1989), and Peter C. Bjarkman, *Boston Celtics Encyclopedia* (1999). Two magazine articles, Frank Deford, "Some Old Pros Refuse to Die," *Sports Illustrated* (9 May 1966), and Mark Engel, "John Havlicek: Man of the Year," *Basketball Weekly* (4 Jan. 1979), offer particularly good discussion of Havlicek at different points of his career. Additional information is available from Havlicek's file at the Basketball Hall of Fame.

DOUGLAS A. STARK

HAWKINS, Cornelius L. ("Connie") (*b.* 17 July 1942 in New York City), professional basketball player who was blacklisted by the National Basketball Association (NBA) due to false allegations about his involvement in a point-shaving scandal; star performer for the Harlem Globetrotters, the Pittsburgh/Minnesota Pipers, and the Phoenix Suns.

Hawkins was one of six children born to Isaiah Hawkins, a day laborer, and Dorothy Hawkins. Hawkins's father abandoned the family when Hawkins was about ten years old, and his mother supported her children as a cook in a day nursery, despite suffering from glaucoma that eventually produced blindness. The family lived in a run-down flat near an elevated railroad line in the Bedford-Stuyvesant section of Brooklyn, New York City, a neighborhood in the process of becoming one of the most notorious slums in the United States. As a youth Hawkins survived on the streets, heeding his mother's stern admonishment to avoid street gangs and criminal behavior. Instead he thrived on public playgrounds, becoming one of the city's legendary street basketball players (he is generally considered to be

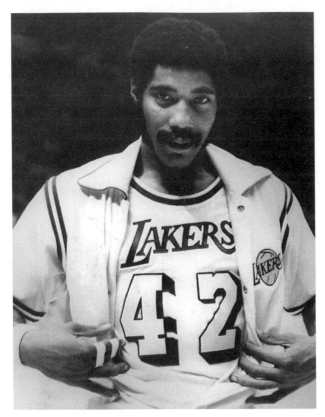

Connie Hawkins, 1973. AP/WIDE WORLD PHOTOS

one of the greatest playground players in city history). Hawkins dunked his first basketball at age eleven as a star at Boys' High in Brooklyn, and was named to *Parade Magazine*'s High School All-American first team in 1960.

Standing a lithe six foot, eight inches tall at 215 pounds, with enormous hands attached to long arms, Hawkins possessed great jumping ability, extreme quickness, and excellent peripheral vision, and he was one of the nation's most highly recruited high school players in the spring of 1960. Because his academic record was extremely poor (standardized tests showed he had an IQ of less than 75 and the reading skills of a seventh grader), Hawkins received a certificate of attendance from Boys' High indicating that he had attended for four years but had not met the academic requirements for a regular diploma. After much deliberation, Hawkins opted to attend the University of Iowa where a lucrative deal arranged by athletic officials with a local booster seemed most attractive.

When he entered Iowa in 1960, Hawkins starred for the freshman team and attracted unusually large crowds by putting on a dazzling show during warm-ups, when he would simultaneously palm two balls and in one leap slam-dunk them both. However, unusual circumstances prevented him from ever playing at the college varsity level. In April of his freshman year Hawkins was implicated in an unfolding point-shaving scandal being investigated by the New York City police under the supervision of crusading District Attorney Frank Hogan. Gamblers who were pressured to produce names in return for prosecutorial leniency named Hawkins as one of the players involved. He was held in custody and grilled for fourteen days without the benefit of legal counsel, all the while protesting his innocence. The naive nineteen-year-old eventually agreed to confess, he later said, because "I'd never get out if I kept telling the truth." Ultimately, he was not charged in this major scandal, but his name was mentioned in the indictments of others as an alleged intermediary between other players and gamblers. The University of Iowa swiftly dismissed him from school.

Eventually it came to light that Hawkins had been identified because he had accepted a $200 gift from the notorious fixer Jack Molinas to pay for an airline ticket to Iowa City. At the time, Hawkins did not know of Molinas's unsavory character or his record of having been booted out of the NBA in 1954 for betting on the games of his own team, the Fort Wayne Zollner (now Detroit) Pistons. Hawkins simply remembered Molinas as "a nice person," not unlike the many hangers-on who were part of the New York City playground basketball scene. From prison, Molinas released a signed affidavit stating that although he had intended to use Hawkins in future point-shaving schemes, he never had done so, and that Hawkins was unaware of his plans.

Formally barred from college basketball and blacklisted by the NBA, Hawkins entered an eight-year period of wandering in basketball's wilderness. He played for the Pittsburgh Rens in the ill-fated American Basketball League (ABL) for two years (1962–1963) and then joined the Harlem Globetrotters. In 1967 he joined the Pittsburgh Pipers of the new American Basketball Association (ABA). Despite a painful knee injury, Hawkins averaged twenty-six points per game, led the Pipers to the league title in its inaugural season, and was named the ABA's Most Valuable Player. The following year, the Pipers moved to Minneapolis where Hawkins played for one season. In both 1964 and 1965 Hawkins made himself available to the NBA draft, but no team selected him. When the NBA formally barred him in 1966 for his involvement in the Molinas case, he filed an antitrust suit against the league, and the suit slowly made its way through the federal court system. Finally, in June of 1969, the NBA offered Hawkins a $1.3 million settlement and agreed to drop its ban against him.

Hawkins began his "rookie" season in the NBA in 1969 with the Phoenix Suns, who won his contractual rights in a flip of a coin with Seattle. He quickly became one of the league's outstanding players. Fans appreciated his flamboyant style of play, and many youngsters attempted to grow huge sideburns that became part of his NBA persona.

Hawkins played five seasons with the Suns and was the first member of the expansion team to be named to the All-NBA First Team (1970). He played with the Los Angeles Lakers from 1973 to 1975 and retired in 1976 after one season with the Atlanta Hawks. During his NBA career, Hawkins averaged sixteen points and eight rebounds per game.

Hawkins and his wife, Nancy, who married in the late 1960s, raised two children and settled in Phoenix, where he worked for the Suns as a community relations representative and continued to live once he retired. The Suns retired his number 42 in 1976, and in 1992 Hawkins was inducted into the Naismith Memorial Basketball Hall of Fame in Springfield, Massachusetts.

With a playing style that often included enormous swoops to the rim followed by a monstrous slam dunk, Hawkins brought the "above the rim" game to modern basketball, paving the way for such later stars as Julius Erving and Michael Jordan.

★

Much of the Hawkins saga can be found in the excellent journalistic account by David Wolf, *Foul!* (1972). See also an extended segment on Hawkins in Richard O. Davies, *America's Obsession: Sports and Society Since 1945* (1994); and Randy Roberts and James Olson, *Winning Is the Only Thing* (1989).

RICHARD O. DAVIES

Elvin Hayes *(center)*, 1978. ASSOCIATED PRESS AP

HAYES, Elvin Ernest (*b.* 17 November 1945 in Rayville, Louisiana), one of the most talented forwards in the history of the National Basketball Association (NBA), noted for his trademark turnaround jump shot.

Hayes was the youngest of six children born to Christopher Hayes and Savannah Hayes, cotton mill workers in the small, poverty-stricken town of Rayville, Louisiana. To escape the prejudice and violence against African Americans he witnessed daily, Hayes played baseball, his favorite sport. Beginning a career in basketball was completely unintentional. Although he was an honor student throughout high school, Hayes was often suspended for class pranks. In an attempt to steer him away from the dangerous turn his life was taking, the Reverend John Calvin, a teacher and coach at Eula D. Britton High School, arranged to place Hayes on the basketball team. Clumsy at first, Hayes practiced, and in his junior year he perfected his signature shot, the turnaround jumper. Hayes believed his outside shooting was inadequate, so he developed the turnaround jumper to neutralize taller opponents. He led his team to fifty-four straight wins and a state championship while averaging thirty-five points per game. He was named to the All-Conference, All-State, and All-America teams and in 1964, his

senior year, he was voted the team's Most Valuable Player (MVP).

More than 100 colleges and universities recruited Hayes. He entered the University of Houston in 1964, where he and Don Chaney were the first African-American athletes to join the basketball program. Hayes credited Coach Guy Lewis for his development, saying Coach Lewis and his assistant Harvey Pate "were like fathers to us (Elvin's father died when he [Elvin] was seventeen), showing us respect and treating every one of us the same—black or white." Hayes established many records at the University of Houston, including 2,884 points, 1,602 rebounds, and a 31-points-per-game average. He led his team in scoring every year he played. Hayes carried Houston to three straight National Collegiate Athletic Association (NCAA) tournament appearances and held the NCAA record for most field goals at 1,215. He was named First Team All-America two times and was College Player of the Year in 1968.

Perhaps the most memorable event of Hayes's college years was competing in the "game of the century" against the University of California at Los Angeles (UCLA) led by Lew Alcindor (Kareem Abdul-Jabbar). In January 1968 Hayes and the University of Houston Cougars ended the UCLA Bruins' forty-seven-game winning streak in the first nationally televised college basketball game, played at the Houston Astrodome in front of the largest attendance at a college basketball game to that date. Hayes broke a 69–69 tie with 28 seconds left by making 2 free throws. A *Houston Post* writer saw a parallel between the U.S. Navy's aircraft carrier *Enterprise*, called "the big E," and Hayes, thus coining the nickname "the Big E" that stayed with Hayes throughout his career. Prior to his senior year, Hayes married a fellow student Erna; they have four children.

Hayes was already a formidable player before he began his professional career, and he had not yet reached his full height of six feet nine inches. The San Diego Rockets chose him as the first overall pick in the 1968 NBA draft, and Hayes continued to set records his rookie year. He averaged twenty-eight points per game, leading all players, and was named to the All-Rookie Team. Hayes followed the Rockets to Houston (1971–1972) but later was traded to the Baltimore Bullets (1972–1973). He remained with the Bullets during their stint as the Capitol Bullets (1973–1974) and finally as the Washington Bullets (1974–1981). During his tenure with the Bullets, Hayes established himself as one of the greatest players in basketball history. He was named to the All-NBA first team in three years and was an All-Star for twelve straight years. The Bullets progressed to the NBA finals three times and were victorious in 1978. Named the Most Valuable Player of the series, Hayes finally overcame the stigma of "never winning the big one." Fittingly he finished his basketball career where he had developed his tremendous talent when he returned to Houston to join the Rockets in 1981.

When Hayes retired in 1984 he was among the top in many NBA statistical categories, including third in scoring (27,313 points), third in rebounds (16,279), third in blocked shots (1,743), and first in minutes played (nearly 50,000). Incredibly he missed only 9 games in 16 seasons and ranked third in most games played (1,303). Hayes's achievements earned him selection to the Naismith Memorial Basketball Hall of Fame in 1990. In 1996 Hayes was selected to the NBA's Fiftieth Anniversary All-Time Team.

Hayes completed his education at the University of Houston in 1986, graduating with a B.A. in recreation and speech. He entered into several business ventures, including raising cattle on his ranch near Brenham, Texas, and acquiring a car dealership in Houston.

Enjoying the time he spent with children, Hayes became involved with numerous charitable organizations, including the United Way, the Special Olympics, and the District of Columbia Society for Crippled Children among others. Perhaps most important to him was developing a "real relationship with God." Throughout the NBA, Hayes was well known for his religious conviction, and it was not unusual for him to give a speech at a church while he was on the road.

★

Hayes's autobiography, *They Call Me the "Big E"* (1978), co-written with Bill Gilbert, gives many insights into Hayes's character but contains little specific personal information. Scott Crawford, "Elvin Hayes," in *African American Sports Greats* (1999), edited by David Porter, is a good source for biographical information. S. H. Burchard, *Sports Star Elvin Hayes* (1980), is a good juvenile book on Hayes. David Llores, "No Back Seat for Elvin," *Ebony* (Mar. 1968), gives some family information not available elsewhere. John Papanek, "The Big E Wants an MVP," *Sports Illustrated* (16 Oct. 1978), is an excellent assessment of Hayes's career. Information can also be found at the NBA History website: <www.nba.com/history/Elvin_Hayes.html>.

RACHENETTA V. STIMAGE

HAYES, Robert ("Bob"; "Bullet") (*b.* 20 December 1942 in Jacksonville, Florida), world-record sprinter, Olympic champion, and football player for the Dallas Cowboys who is the only person ever to win both an Olympic gold medal and a Super Bowl ring.

Hayes grew up in the ghetto on the east side of Jacksonville, Florida, the youngest of three children of a poor African-American family. His family's poverty increased when his father returned from World War II in a wheelchair, as their main source of income became his father's disability pension. Hayes, who spent much of his childhood skipping school and roaming the streets with friends, escaped much of his father's military-style discipline and once recalled, "Being the youngest in the family I kinda got everything I wanted." He also noted that he did not apply himself to earning good grades.

One of the fastest runners of all time, Hayes, known as "Bullet" to his fans, began sprinting at age sixteen. He was more interested in football at the time, but when the track coach saw him running in gym class, wearing ordinary street shoes and outstripping everyone in the class, he convinced him to join the track team. At his first meet, Hayes entered seven events—the 100, 220, 440, and 880 yards, as well as the sprint relay, long jump, and high jump. He won them all. His friends, seeing an opportunity to cash in, began setting him up to race against the older boys in the school and taking bets on the action. It was a sure thing: he always won.

Despite his success on the track, he was still more interested in football and won a football scholarship to Florida A&M University in Tallahassee. However, he did not stay on the football field long. Track coach Robert (Pete) Griffin became a mentor and father figure to the young runner and helped him improve his speed on the track. They worked together, and Hayes steadily improved.

Bob Hayes, 1964. © BETTMANN/CORBIS

In 1961 Hayes repaid Griffin's interest when he became the thirteenth person to tie the then world record, set by Mel Patton, of 9.3 seconds for the 100-yard dash. In that same season, he was only a tenth of a second behind the world record for the straight 220-yard run, with a time of 20.1 seconds.

Strongly built and a "power runner," Hayes was described as looking more like a boxer than a sprinter. One sportswriter commented, "When he ran, he seemed to roll from side to side as he pawed his way down the track." He was one of the heaviest sprinters on the track, weighing over 190 pounds, with broad shoulders and pigeon toes. Still, no matter what his appearance or style, it clearly worked for him. He once told some onlookers who criticized his appearance, "They don't take pictures at the start, only at the finish."

On 17 February 1962 Hayes tied the new world record, set by Frank Budd, at 9.2 seconds for 100 yards—but the Amateur Athletic Union (AAU) did not accept the heat because a .22 caliber gun, rather than .32 caliber, was used. In 1963 he beat the world record with a time of 9.1 seconds on an almost windless course in St. Louis. That same year,

he tied the world records for the 200 meters and 220-yard (turn course) sprints. He showed the true intensity of his speed in a relay in Hanover, Germany, in 1963, where he made up four yards in his leg of the relay. Later calculations revealed that he had run faster than twenty-six miles per hour that day.

In 1964 he became the first man to break 6 seconds for the indoor sixty yards, with a time of 5.9 seconds. In the same year, at the Olympic Games in Tokyo, he won with a wind-assisted time of 9.9 seconds in the 100-meter semifinal, but in the final, set a legal time of 10.0 seconds and won by two yards, the widest margin in the history of the Olympic 100-meter event. Six days later, in the anchor leg of the 4 × 100-meter relay, he turned a two-meter deficit into a three-meter lead, bringing the U.S. team to a world-record time. It was one of the most impressive performances in the annals of international track competition.

After the Olympics, Hayes signed a contract with the Dallas Cowboys and proved to be as outstanding on the football field as he was on the track. A rookie sensation, he soon intimidated opponents with his world-class speed. Zone defenses were created specifically to try to cope with his threat. Speed became a requisite for other National Football League (NFL) receivers. Hayes's average yards per catch was 21.8, he made 50-yard touchdowns at least once a season, and he was an excellent punt returner. He was only the second rookie with a record of more than 1,000 yards receiving.

During his second season, Hayes had a league-best record of thirteen touchdown catches, with a career high 1,232 yards and sixty-four receptions. In his last big season, 1971, he again led the NFL with twenty-four yards per catch and eight touchdowns, and that year the Cowboys won the Super Bowl.

In 1974 Hayes was traded to the San Francisco 49ers, but only stayed with the team for a few months. Troubled times followed, during which his marriage broke up. He had abused drugs and alcohol and served eighteen months in prison for drug trafficking. He underwent rehabilitation for drug and alcohol problems several times and later became involved in programs to discourage young people from using drugs. Some observers have speculated that his troubles began as a result of Hayes's depression about the impending end of his athletic career.

Over Hayes's entire football career, he had 365 catches for 7,414 yards and seventy-one career touchdowns, one of which was a 95-yarder. He still holds team records for season average (20.8 yards) and career average (11.1 yards). He is also the only athlete in history to win both an Olympic gold medal and a Super Bowl ring. In 2001, the Cowboys inducted Hayes into their Ring of Honor and was elected to the USA Track and Field Hall of Fame in 1976. Known as "The Fastest Human in the World," Hayes had a phenomenal career and was a versatile and enormously gifted athlete with great natural speed. Very few have equaled his top performance in two different sports.

★

Neil Duncanson's *The Fastest Men on Earth* (1988) has a lengthy chapter on Hayes's entire career, from sprinter to ex–football player, and discusses his running style and personal life. In the *1984 Olympic Handbook* (1984), Norman Giller sums up his track achievements. An article in the *Detroit News* (11 May 2001) describes his football career and announced his induction into the Ring of Honor.

KELLY WINTERS

HAYES, Wayne Woodrow ("Woody") (*b.* 14 February 1913 in Clifton, Ohio; *d.* 12 March 1987 in Upper Arlington, Ohio), college football coach who led the Ohio State Buckeyes to three national championships and developed dozens of outstanding players yet tarnished his reputation with his explosive temper.

Hayes was the youngest of three children born to Wayne Benton Hayes, a teacher and public school superintendent in Newcomerstown, Ohio, and Effie Jane Hupp Hayes, a homemaker. Hayes's father instilled in him a love of learning and books, and Hayes's sixth- and seventh-grade teacher fanned his interest in history and English. He came to appreciate sports by doing small chores for the retired pitching great Denton "Cy" Young, manager of the town baseball team. Hayes and his brother also liked boxing and often staged exhibition bouts against their parents' wishes. At Newcomerstown High School, Hayes played basketball and football, starting in football at tackle and captaining that team as a senior in 1931.

A good player, Hayes developed a reputation as a smart athlete contemptuous of defeat. He earned three football letters at Denison College, from which he graduated in 1935 with a B.A. in history and English. Unable to afford law school, his preference, he took a job as a seventh-grade teacher and assistant football coach at Mingo Junction (Ohio) High School in 1935. The next summer he began graduate work in educational administration at Ohio State University, where he received a master's degree in 1948. He moved to New Philadelphia (Ohio) High School in 1937 and became head football coach the following year. In the summer of 1941 he enlisted in the navy and rose to command a patrol boat and a destroyer escort in the Pacific theater. He married Anne Gross of New Philadelphia in 1942. They had one son.

After being discharged as a lieutenant commander in 1946, Hayes returned to Denison as head football coach. His first season was a disaster. But in 1947 and 1948 he

Woody Hayes, 1971. ASSOCIATED PRESS AP

pushed his players hard, and the Denison Big Red went undefeated. Miami (Ohio) University hired Hayes as head coach in 1949. His first team finished 5–4, but in 1950 the Miami Redskins won all but their first game and upset Arizona State in the Salad Bowl, 35–21. Hayes's success as a recruiter and his near-obsessive devotion to conditioning and discipline made him attractive to Ohio State, which was searching for a coach for the third time in seven years. However, his lack of major college experience made Hayes a controversial choice. The Buckeye players did not take to his hard-nosed approach either. They locked him out of the dressing room prior to the game against Illinois and a week later lost to their arch-rival Michigan, 7–0, to end the season at 4–3–2. Hayes weathered this storm and the public's discontent that accompanied it. His 1952 team finished 6–3, and victories over Illinois and Michigan probably saved his job.

Hayes dismissed his critics two years later, when the Buckeyes went undefeated and beat Southern California in the Rose Bowl. The Associated Press (AP) named the Buckeyes national champions. In 1957 they won a second national championship, this time from United Press International (UPI), for a 9–1 season that included a Rose Bowl win over Oregon. The American Football Coaches' Association gave Hayes its Coach of the Year award, further cementing his status. In 1968 Hayes won a third national title, this time from both wire service polls, as the Buckeyes went 10–0 and defeated Southern California in the Rose Bowl again. By this time Hayes was regarded as one of the best.

Hayes coached a style of football often described as "three yards and a cloud of dust." It relied on sound execution of fundamentals, strong and punishing defense, and relentless, conservative offense that eschewed passing. He and his assistants devoted long hours to preparation, and even in the off-season his mind was never far from football. Hayes likened the game to warfare and read military history to reinforce this viewpoint. He adopted George Patton as his hero and frequently referred to his naval experience for ways to solve problems. His intensely competitive attitude made many games memorable, especially when Ohio State played Michigan. Hayes refused to call the Michigan team anything but "that team up north," and his yearly battles against the Wolverine coach Glen "Bo" Schembechler, one of Hayes's protégés, for supremacy in the Big Ten transformed the conference for a while into the "Big Two and the Little Eight."

Hayes possessed a great deal of personal charm. He was a polished public speaker with a fine sense of humor. *The Woody Hayes Show,* a half-hour of live television that ran throughout his career, was required viewing for many Buckeye fans. More importantly Hayes was extremely loyal to his players and his assistant coaches, and he even titled the third of his three books *You Win with People* (1973). Stories about his devotion to those who played for him are legion, and many centered on his insistence that they earn a degree no matter how long it might take. While Hayes lived a modest life, he made sure his coaches were well paid. He worked them hard and trained them well. As a result eighteen of his forty-two assistants became head coaches. His affection for Ohio State University was unbounded. When student demonstrators forced the university to close in the wake of the National Guard shootings at Kent State in May 1970, Hayes prowled the campus, listening to the protesters' speeches and urging everyone to remain calm.

Hayes's inability to harness his own temper, though, proved his undoing. His career was marred by sporadic outbursts aimed at game officials and members of the media. When a Clemson linebacker intercepted a pass in front of the Ohio State bench to ensure a Buckeye loss in the 1978 Gator Bowl, Hayes lost control and punched the player in the face. The university fired him the next morning. Hayes's record at Ohio State over 28 years was 205–68–10, and his 241 victories overall ranked him third all-time when he was terminated. His teams won or shared thirteen Big Ten championships and appeared in eight Rose Bowls.

In retirement Hayes gradually came to terms with the reason for his dismissal and his mixed legacy. He continued to speak at athletic banquets and a variety of other functions, as he had throughout his career. He delivered the 1986 winter commencement address at Ohio State, during which he freely expressed his love for the university. He died at home of a heart attack, and is buried in Union Cemetery in Columbus.

★

Hayes wrote three books, *Football at Ohio State* (1957), *Hot Line to Victory* (1969), and *You Win with People* (1973). While most books on Hayes are quite laudatory, Paul Hornung, *Woody Hayes: A Reflection* (1991), is balanced; and Robert Vare, *Buckeye: A Study of Coach Woody Hayes and the Ohio State Football Machine* (1974), is even critical. An obituary is in *The Sporting News* (23 Mar. 1987).

STEVEN P. GIETSCHIER

HAYNES, Marques Oreole (*b.* 3 October 1926 in Sand Springs, Oklahoma), star basketball player for the Harlem Globetrotters and the first member of the well-known African-American team elected to the Naismith Memorial Basketball Hall of Fame.

The youngest of four children of Matthew and Hattie Haynes of Tulsa, Oklahoma, Haynes focused on sports at an early age. His father, a domestic worker, left the family when Haynes was only four years old. After this loss, he concentrated heavily on competing in sports with his older siblings. He starred in basketball at Booker T. Washington

Marques Haynes, 1951. ASSOCIATED PRESS AP

High School, leading the team to a state championship in 1942. That same year Haynes entered Oklahoma's Langston University, an African-American college. Between 1942 and 1946 he was a four-time All-State, All-Conference, and team Most Valuable Player selection. Haynes led Langston in scoring all four years, during which time the team compiled a 112–3 record that included a fifty-nine-game winning streak. Haynes earned a bachelor's degree in industrial education in 1946.

With his amazing blend of quickness and guile, the six-foot, 160-pound athlete caught the attention of the Harlem (New York) Globetrotters owner Abe Saperstein in 1946 when Langston defeated the Globetrotters 74–70. After his graduation Haynes hitchhiked from his home in Sand Springs to Saperstein's apartment in Chicago, arriving at the team owner's door at 2:30 A.M. to request a tryout. The tired owner asked him to display his skills, and Haynes obliged by providing a spectacular dribbling exhibition in the hallway of the building. After signing and playing with the Kansas City Stars, an affiliate of the Globetrotters, in 1946, Haynes was promoted to the main squad in 1947.

When Haynes joined the Globetrotters he immediately embarked on one of the most prolific travel schedules in sports history. The game schedule was particularly draining because air travel was not prevalent during this era. In 1949 the Globetrotters played fourteen games in five days during a tour in Alaska. In 1950 the squad toured Western Europe and North Africa, playing games and giving exhibitions. A year later they played in Central and South America; in Rio de Janeiro, Brazil, they drew a crowd of 50,000 for one game.

Haynes likened the Globetrotters to basketball's version of baseball's Negro Leagues, which featured outstanding players who were not fully appreciated during their playing days. In the 1940s, before the National Basketball Association (NBA) realized commercial success, the league staged doubleheaders with the Globetrotters out of financial necessity. The New York Rens and the Globetrotters helped to popularize the game to the masses. When the Globetrotters defeated the NBA's championship team, the Minneapolis Lakers, in 1948 and 1949 and won eleven of eighteen games during a barnstorming tour in 1950, a "World Series of Basketball," NBA owners took notice.

Three years later, upon learning that Saperstein was trying to sell him to the Philadelphia Warriors, Haynes objected and asked for a bump in salary instead. When Saperstein refused, Haynes left to found the Harlem Magicians, who in 1955 recruited the Globetrotter Reece "Goose" Tatum to join him. Before widespread integration, most Globetrotters found themselves at a disadvantage in salary negotiations. With few available options for employment, players were forced to take what Saperstein offered them. Haynes became a symbolic and powerful figure

when he launched the Magicians. Proving that an African American could own, operate, and market a major sports organization, he and the team prospered. His contemporaries respected Haynes's ambition and success in creating his own form of opportunity.

On the court Haynes was considered by many observers to be the greatest dribbler ever to play basketball. He often infuriated and baffled opponents with his moves. With one knee on the court, or even lying down, he could maneuver the ball between his legs and behind his back to evade defenders at will, moves that influenced future professional basketball players like Earvin "Magic" Johnson of the Los Angeles Lakers. His ability to keep the ball away from defenders on the court was a potent weapon. During contests with the Minneapolis Lakers in 1948 and 1949, Haynes's ability to nurse a lead at the end of the game with his dribbling was a key to victory. (There was no shot clock in those days.)

Haynes's long and distinguished association with basketball lasted five decades. After his first tour with the Globetrotters (1946–1953), he played for the Magicians (1953–1972). Haynes returned to the Globetrotters as a player and coach after Saperstein's death, working with the squad from 1972 to 1979. He joined Meadowlark Lemon's traveling Bucketeers (1979–1981) before finishing his career with the Magicians. Overall, Haynes played in more than 12,000 games and traveled more than 4 million miles. He visited nearly 100 countries, including Germany, where in summer 1950 the Globies entertained a crowd of 75,000, the largest basketball audience in history at the time. The game was held to ease anti-American feelings in post–World War II Europe and the venue was Berlin's Olympic Stadium, where fourteen years earlier Adolf Hitler had ignored the exploits of great African-American Olympians like the track star Jesse Owens. The basketball event became a sign of American goodwill for thousands around the globe and a source of pride for Haynes and his teammates.

Haynes was enshrined in the National Association of Intercollegiate Athletics Hall of Fame in 1985, the Oklahoma Hall of Fame in 1990, and the East Hartford, Connecticut, Hall of Fame in 1992. In 1993 he was inducted into the Jim Thorpe Memorial Hall of Fame, and a twelve-mile section of Oklahoma State Highway 97 was renamed the Marques Haynes Highway one year later. Haynes also was enshrined in the Langston University Hall of Fame in 1995 and the Naismith Memorial Basketball Hall of Fame in 1998. At the twilight of the twentieth century, he joined Wilt Chamberlain and Meadowlark Lemon as the only three players in the history of the Harlem Globetrotters to have their jerseys retired.

After his basketball career was over, Haynes became a full-time resident of Dallas, Texas, where he owned and managed a water filtration company and was a respected member of the local business community. He and his wife, Joan, have two daughters.

★

Although there is no full-length biography of Haynes, several books describe events during the era in which he played and the impact of the Globetrotters on the professional growth of basketball. Extremely valuable are George Vecsey, *Harlem Globetrotters* (1973), and Josh Wilker, *The Harlem Globetrotters* (1997). Several additional works focus on the racist nature of basketball's early institutional management; Robert W. Peterson, *Only the Ball Was White* (1970), and his *Cages to Jump Shots: Pro Basketball's Early Years* (1990), contain little personal information on Haynes but provide helpful context when analyzing his career. See also Nelson George, *Elevating the Game: Black Men and Basketball* (1992). For a summary of Haynes's career highlights, see David L. Porter, ed., *Biographical Dictionary of American Sports: Basketball and Other Indoor Sports* (1989).

R. JAKE SUDDERTH

HEARNS, Thomas (*b.* 18 October 1958 in Memphis, Tennessee), one of boxing's most versatile and fearless fighters and the only man to win world championship belts in six different weight divisions.

Young Hearns lived with his mother's father, Henry Tallie, on a farm near Grand Junction, Tennessee, until he was four years old. He grew tall and taciturn, like his grandfather, whom he would often visit and work with in the fields. In 1963 John Hearns, Hearns's father, took the family to Detroit. Three years later, John Hearns left home.

Hearns's mother, Lois, worked in a bank by day and as a hairdresser in her home by night to make ends meet. The family lived in a small apartment in a poor section of the city.

When he was sixteen, Hearns wandered into the Kronk Recreation Center, where a boxing trainer named Emanuel Steward was trying to groom young talent. John Hearns, who kept in touch with his children by phone, begged his former wife not to let Hearns fight. But Steward took Hearns under his wing and became a longtime mentor. Hearns dropped out of high school in the eleventh grade and quickly became an amateur boxing sensation. After winning 155 amateur bouts and losing only eight, Hearns turned professional on 25 November 1977, knocking out Jerome Hill in two rounds. In his first year as a pro, Hearns won all thirteen of his bouts by knockouts in three rounds or less.

Solemn and brooding, with heavily lidded eyes, Hearns, nicknamed the "Hit Man," was extremely aggressive in the ring. At six feet, one inch, though his left hand was not as strong and he held it down by his side, Hearns had a powerful, lightning-quick right jab.

John Hearns was getting ready to leave his home in Memphis to see his son fight for the World Boxing Association (WBA) welterweight title in 1980 when he collapsed and died of a heart attack. In the fight, on August 2, Hearns crushed Pipino Cuevas with a second-round knockout. He retained the title by defeating three boxers over the next ten months.

On 16 September 1981 Hearns, undefeated in thirty-two matches, faced Sugar Ray Leonard in a memorable fight in Las Vegas. Hearns was a favorite and by the twelfth

Thomas Hearns *(right)* after delivering a knockout blow to Jay Snyder, 1998. ASSOCIATED PRESS AP

round was leading on all three judges' cards. But Leonard fought back furiously and won on a technical knockout in the fourteenth round. It was Hearns's first loss, and one he would never forget.

Moving to a different weight division, Hearns beat Wilfred Benitez on 3 December 1982 for the World Boxing Council (WBC) junior middleweight title. He successfully defended that title three times, including a celebrated second-round knockout of Roberto Duran in June 1984.

On 15 April 1985, Marvin Hagler and Hearns battled in a middleweight fight. It was a chaotic, reckless melee that ended when Hagler won on a technical knockout in the third round. Hagler would never agree to a rematch. Though Hearns lost the match, he cemented his reputation as the fearsome "Hit Man." "He has no fear," Steward said once. "Sometimes I wish he was a little scared." Hearns said he had the capacity to be afraid: "Anything that walks or moves, I don't fear. But I have a great fear of flying. I'm terrified of it."

At the height of his fame, Hearns, by nature a reticent man, hired a tutor to sharpen his speaking and writing abilities. "I don't feel comfortable with strangers," he told boxing photographer Arlene Schulman. Between bouts, he would often play benefit celebrity basketball games with National Basketball Association stars like Julius Erving. In his hometown of Detroit, he was a godlike figure.

In March 1987, Hearns beat Dennis Andries to win the WBC light heavyweight title. That October, he became the first man to win titles in four weight classes when he decked Juan Domingo Roldan for the WBC middleweight belt. But on 6 June 1988, Hearns unexpectedly lost the middleweight title. Hearns was winning a typical bloody slugfest when Iran Barkley suddenly downed him in the third round. Barkley won the bout but ended up in the hospital. That November, Hearns won his fifth division title, beating James Kinchen to win the World Boxing Organization (WBO)'s super middleweight belt.

Hearns finally got his rematch with Leonard on 12 June 1989 in Las Vegas. "I've never gotten over that loss [in 1981]," Hearns said before the fight. "I think about it every day. . . . You have no idea how that man has weighed on my mind." Hearns, a 3-to-1 underdog, dropped Leonard to the canvas twice—in the third and eleventh rounds. But Leonard fought back viciously, and by the end of the fifteen-round match, Hearns could barely stand. It ended in a controversial draw. "I thought I won, everybody thought I won," Hearns said.

In April 1990, Hearns beat Michael Olajide in Atlantic City to retain his WBO super middleweight championship. After the fight, Hearns and Steward parted ways, and Alex Sherer took over as Hearns's manager-trainer. Sherer tried to add a left hook to his repertoire.

The next target was a sixth weight division. On 3 June 1991, Hearns was a 2-to-1 underdog against unbeaten WBA light heavyweight champion Virgil Hill. Hearns's surprising use of his left hand made the difference. He broke Hill's nose in the second round and won the match in a unanimous decision. Nine months later, Hearns again faced Barkley, the much younger fighter. Two of the three referees gave the fight to Barkley by the slimmest of margins. It was the first time Hearns had ever lost by decision.

On the downside of his career, Hearns fought mostly unknowns in little-noticed bouts. In 2000, Hearns, age forty-one, lost a fight to an aging, mediocre boxer, Uriah Grant, at Detroit's Joe Louis Arena. Hearns sprained his ankle and was unable to come out of his corner for the third round. Before the fight, he had announced he would finally retire and become a promoter.

Hearns finished his career with fifty-nine wins, five losses, and one draw. He was one of the greatest fighters ever, at least for the first three rounds of a match. Never a complete boxer, Hearns was a knockout artist, using his deadly right hand with frightening efficiency. Sometimes he seemed to lose his concentration if his opponent was still standing after a few rounds. Hearns, always the aggressor, was a crowd favorite—his matches were never dull. Even in defeat, he was intimidating.

★

Vignettes about Hearns appear in Arlene Schulman, *The Prizefighters: An Intimate Look at Champions* and *Contenders* (1994). There are several profiles in *Sports Illustrated* (9 Nov. 1987; 5 June 1989; 19 June 1989; 7 May 1990; 17 June 1991; 30 Mar. 1992; and 17 Apr. 2000). Websites with Hearns's record are <http://www.kronkgym.com/fighters/hearns.html> and <http://www.cyberboxingzone.com/boxing/thearns.htm>.

MICHAEL BETZOLD

HEFFELFINGER, William Walter ("Pudge") (*b*. 20 December 1867 in Minneapolis, Minnesota; *d*. 2 April 1954 in Blessing, Texas), football player who was the first significant star of the collegiate game and the first professional football player.

Heffelfinger was the son of Christopher B. Heffelfinger, a shoe manufacturer, and Mary Ellen Totton, a homemaker, in a family with three sons and four daughters. Nicknamed "Pudge" for his size, which was huge by the standards of the day, he played four years of baseball at Minneapolis Central High. He helped organize and served as captain (when captains served as coaches) for the school's first football team. After graduating from Central, Heffelfinger entered Yale University in the fall of 1888, a time when the teams coached by Walter Camp dominated intercollegiate football. At Yale he weighed 188 pounds his freshman year

Pudge Heffelfinger, c. 1890. AP/WIDE WORLD PHOTOS

and 205 pounds by the time he was a senior. At six feet, three inches he towered over his teammates.

In his four years as a college player Heffelfinger, called "Heff" by his teammates, helped lead Yale to its apogee of football glory. The 1888 team went 13–0 and outscored the opposition 698 points to 0. Yale's 1889 record was 15–1, with a loss to Princeton. The 1890 record was 13–1, with a loss to Harvard. The 1891 team is considered one of Yale's greatest. Heffelfinger teamed with the famed wiry tackler Frank Hinkey to produce a 13–0 record, piling up 478 points to 0 for the opposition. Walter Camp named Heffelfinger to his inaugural All-American team in 1889 and included him twice more, in 1890 and 1891. Thereafter Heffelfinger was routinely named to all-time American teams.

Dominant as both an offensive and a defensive player, Heffelfinger was the most formidable player of his era, when his size, speed, and ferocity of attack were highly valued. Typically players were drawn up into tightly held formations, and they violently crashed their unprotected bodies into one another to grind out small increments of yardage. Against Princeton's infamous wedge, whereby blockers tightly formed into a V formation around the advancing ball carrier, Heffelfinger devised a new tactic. He doubled up his knees and leaped into the lead blocker, causing "the wedge to shiver and collapse," he said in his book of reminiscences.

Heffelfinger developed an offensive blocking maneuver called the "pulling guard" play. Starting from left guard, he pulled out of the offensive line and led interference for the ball carrier, making him the first guard to run interference. Said Heffelfinger: "I've never claimed to be the greatest guard of my generation, let alone of all time. But when it comes to running interference, I won't take a back seat to anybody."

Football was not Heffelfinger's only athletic endeavor. He also made time at Yale for baseball, boxing, crew, and weight throwing. He only felt truly passionate about football, however. Heffelfinger received a bachelor's degree from Yale's Sheffield Scientific School in 1891.

While pursuing a career after graduation, Heffelfinger continued his participation in football. He reportedly played on a few semiprofessional teams in the fall of 1891 while studying law and railroad economics at Yale. Heffelfinger is generally credited by football historians with giving birth to pro football when he became the first professional player by signing a contract for $500 to play for the Allegheny Athletic Association football team in a game against the Pittsburgh Athletic Club team on 12 November 1892. Prior to that game Heffelfinger contended he had been paid only in silver pocket watches. In 1892 he also played for the Chicago Athletic Club, appearing in six games in twelve days.

In 1893 Heffelfinger found a job with the Great Northern Railroad, but he quickly gave that up when he was hired as head coach by the University of California to teach "Yale football" to the school's team. This was followed by head coaching stints at Lehigh University (1894) and the University of Minnesota (1895). From 1896 through 1910 he served as the volunteer line coach for the Minnesota team.

Upon his return to Minnesota in 1894, Heffelfinger entered his father's shoe business, and in 1904 he became the company's vice president and general manager. Heffelfinger married Grace Harriet Pierce in 1901; they had one son and two daughters. When the shoe company went out of business in 1907, Heffelfinger found success as a building contractor. Entering politics, he served as a Hennepin County commissioner from 1924 to 1948.

Heffelfinger helped fuel the growing legends that portrayed him as a larger than life figure. In 1916, helping Coach Tad Jones work with the Yale team, Heffelfinger scrimmaged against the varsity and supposedly roughed up three of his star players so badly that Jones had to pull the 48-year-old veteran out of the contest. In 1922, at the age of fifty-four, Heffelfinger played in a charity game pitting veteran players against a team of recent Ohio State graduates and held his own for fifty-five minutes. In 1933, at the age of sixty-nine, the old veteran was talked into participating in a charity game, but he was injured within nine minutes and had to leave.

In 1933 Heffelfinger founded Heffelfinger Publications, which put out guides and promotional booklets on football and baseball. His *Football Facts* guide became a standard resource in the sport after he established the publication in the 1930s. Heffelfinger was a founding member of the New York Touchdown Club in 1933, an organization of former football players dedicated to the promotion of the game and to honoring players of the past. In 1937 his fellow members named Heffelfinger the greatest player of all time. In 1951 he was elected in the inaugural class of fifty-one notables to the National Collegiate Football Hall of Fame. He also was named a member of the Helms Athletic Hall of Fame. He died at the family home at the age of eighty-six in Blessing, Texas.

Heffelfinger was a large man by the standards of early football, but he only became bigger as football prospered and grew from its infant days. He eventually became an icon of college football's rough and tumble era, representing the almost superhuman toughness and ferocity of the players who played the game out zest for competition and for the glory of their schools. His lifelong advocacy of a game he dearly loved helped connect Americans to the rich heritage of collegiate football and its traditions. He was America's first football hero.

★

Heffelfinger's years at Yale are detailed in the Walter Camp papers at Yale University. His reminiscences are W. W. (Pudge) Heffelfinger with George Trevor, "Nobody Put Me on My Back," *Saturday Evening Post* (15 Oct. 1938), and "Football's Golden Era," *Saturday Evening Post* (29 Oct. 1938). W. W. "Pudge" Heffelfinger, *This Was Football* (1954), is a collaboration with John McCallum that derives a good part of its material from the *Saturday Evening Post* articles. An obituary is in the *New York Times* (3 Apr. 1954).

ROBERT PRUTER

HEIDEN, Eric Arthur (*b.* 14 June 1958 in Madison, Wisconsin), Olympic speed skater who was the first U.S. world speed skating champion and the first athlete to win five gold medals in a single Olympics.

Eric Heiden was born into a family who provided the resources for his mastery of speed skating, while also inher-

Eric Heiden. AP/WIDE WORLD PHOTOS

iting humility in the bargain. His father, Jack Heiden, is an orthopedic surgeon and his mother, Nancy Heiden, dedicated to her children, is independently employed. As a child Heiden participated in speed skating with his sister, Beth, but did not begin to skate seriously until 1972, at the age of fourteen. With Beth as his training partner and competitive ally, he progressed, training five hours a day.

At age seventeen Heiden competed in the 1976 Olympic Games at Innsbruck, Austria, where he began an exceptionally successful winning career, placing seventh in the 1,500-meter race and nineteenth in the 5,000-meter event. Though his early success was thought by many to be a fluke, the next year Heiden took the competition by surprise, gaining the overall title at the World Championships, the first U.S. speed skater to do so. He showed these wins were no accident by repeating in 1978, 1979, and 1980.

By February 1980, at the Winter Games in Lake Placid, New York, Heiden was the skater to beat. On 17 February he won the gold medal in the Olympic speed skating 500-meter race. At six-foot-one and 185 pounds, with a 32-inch waist and 27-inch thighs, Heiden combined physical strength with an intense competitive drive. He continued his extraordinary streak at Lake Placid by winning the 5,000-meter, 1,000-meter, 1,500-meter, and 10,000-meter competitions, setting a record in each event. Heiden was the first athlete to win five gold medals in a single Winter Olympics.

This accomplishment gained Heiden worldwide recognition. He received the 1980 Sullivan award for the country's best amateur athlete and the 1980 U.S. Olympic committee's Athlete of the Year award. He might have stayed in speed skating if he could have, in his own words, been "obscure in an obscure sport." But with such performances it was impossible to stay obscure, and he announced his plan to retire from skating at the end of the season. However, the competitive drive was not gone. Heiden for years had trained for speed skating by cycling in the off-season. Teamed with his sister, Beth, an Olympic bronze medalist in 1980, he knew that cycling demanded aerobic capacity and leg strength, which paralleled and supported his speed skating training. He turned to competitive cycling.

In the 1980 Summer Olympics, Heiden was an alternate on the U.S. Olympic Cycling Road Team. Though he never raced in an Olympics, he continued to compete in professional cycling and won two notable competitions in 1985: the Hot Spot Sprints in the Tour of Italy and the Corestates USPro Road title in Philadelphia. He was a member of the first U.S. team (7-Eleven) to compete in the Tour de France in 1986. Unfortunately, fate caught up with Heiden as he crashed on the famed L'Alpe d'Huez mountain leg of the race. He received a concussion from the accident and withdrew from the event.

A year later Heiden rode in his last race, a criterium in Dallas. "I'd flatted and was working my way to the pit for repairs," he recalled. "But I hit a cement planter, crashed and fell into a bed of flowers. That was that, I ended my career by landing in a flower bed."

Heiden was remarkable in that he maintained an intense training schedule while attending school. Humble about his achievements, he was able to sustain his passion for athletics without losing sight of his educational goals or his dream of being a physician like his father. Heiden stayed registered for classes at the University of Wisconsin while he speed skated at the Olympic games, and was a student at Stanford Medical School while he cycled. Upon completing his medical degree he did his residency in orthopedics, specializing in sports medicine.

Currently Heiden is an assistant professor of arthroscopy and sports medicine at the University of California–Davis. Beginning in 1999 he also has joined several UC–Davis Medical Center professionals who serve as the team physicians for the Sacramento Kings of the National Basketball Association (NBA) and the Sacramento Monarchs of the Women's National Basketball Association (WNBA). Heiden's fondness for working with sports teams has expanded to hockey, in which he serves as physician for several international junior hockey teams.

As an assistant team physician with the Kings, Heiden has performed diagnosis and surgery on many professional athletes. Since 1984 Heiden has periodically served as a television analyst for several networks during the Winter Olympics. With his sister, he is actively involved with the Special Olympics.

The awards and rewards for Heiden's accomplishments have been continual since the gold medals he won in 1980. In 2000 he traveled to Europe and received several millennium honors. He received a Skater of the Century designation in Holland and was also named to the century's one hundred top athletes list by several organizations and publications. He has also been elected to be in the Cycling Hall of Fame.

Sportsmanship and humility have always been hallmarks of Heiden's athletic career. He did not compete for admiration of the public; he competed for the love of the sport. His family was also a factor in his humility. When million-dollar offers came in for both him and Beth, their parents immediately hired an attorney to muddle through the offers and to underscore the belief that the wins were not to be thoughtlessly commercialized. There is life after sports. "I think most people, when they look back at the things they've accomplished, it's the one's they've had to work the hardest at that mean the most to them," Heiden said. "To me, it's the fact that I'm here, an orthopedic surgeon. I've had to work pretty hard to get to this point in my career."

Now married to Karen Drews, also a physician and marathon runner, Heiden maintains his fitness by sometimes cycling to work. Despite retiring from professional sports in 1987, he still feels he could compete and perhaps coach. In 2001 the Heidens had their first child, a daughter.

★

Newspaper articles on Heiden include Dave Kindred, "Heiden's View of His Success: What's the Fuss?" *Washington Post* (24 Feb. 1980). Among magazine articles on Heiden are L. Jon Wertheim, "Still Handy with the Blade: Not That Long Ago Self-effacing Surgeon Eric Heiden was an Olympic Hero," *Sports Illustrated* (Nov. 1988). The U.S. Olympic Committee's website <http://www.usoc.org/news> features several articles on Heiden, including Lindsay DeWall, "Where Are They Now?" Another web article is Larry Schwartz, "Eric Heiden Was a Reluctant Hero," <http://espn.go.com/sportscentury/features>.

SHARON KAY STOLL

HEIN, Mel(vin) John (*b*. 22 August 1909 in Redding, California; *d*. 31 January 1992 in San Clemente, California), center who was one of the greatest stars in professional football during the first half of the twentieth century.

Hein began his football career at Burlington High School in the northwest corner of Washington State, near the Ca-

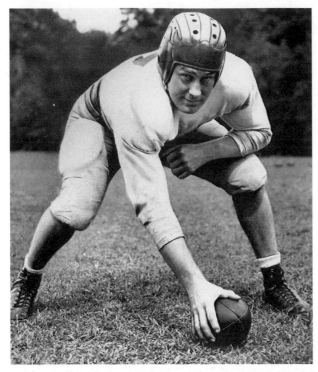

Mel Hein, 1940. AP/WIDE WORLD PHOTOS

nadian border. He played college football at Washington State University (WSU), where he teamed with Turk Edwards to propel the Cougars to an undefeated season in 1930 and a berth in the 1931 Rose Bowl. The versatile Hein played every position on the line (center, guard, and tackle) in college, and even started on WSU's 1930 basketball team. After earning All-America status with the Cougars, Hein sought to play professional football.

The strapping young player wrote to three teams in 1931, seeking employment. The Providence Steamrollers responded first, offering him a $125-per-game contract. Hein signed the document and mailed it back, but the next day a better offer ($150 per game) arrived from the New York Giants. Hein immediately wired the postmaster in Providence, pleading with him to intercept the Steamroller contract and return it to his possession. Good fortune followed both the Giants and Hein as the postal official granted his request, thus beginning one of the greatest associations between a player and an organization in the history of professional football.

Hein played like his nickname, "Old Indestructible." His powerful six-foot, three-inch, 225-pound frame was nearly unstoppable on the field. He captained Giants teams that won seven division titles and two league championships in the 1930s and 1940s. On defense, he played linebacker and was known for his bone-crushing tackles and skilled pass coverage. When the Giants had the ball, Hein played center and snapped the ball unerringly. His skill in blocking and ability to devise unique methods on the field reached legendary status. Hein revolutionized his position on the offensive line through a number of strategic enhancements. He was the first professional center to pull from the line to lead blocking on running plays, and he helped pioneer the strategy of dropping back to pass block for the quarterback. The Giants even made use of Hein's athletic talents to employ a "center sneak," a special trick play. After taking the snap from Hein, the Giants quarterback would flip the ball back to him and fake a handoff to a back as Hein bulled his way downfield.

Hein was always on the field. During his fifteen years with the Giants, he played both sides of the ball and never missed a game. He was injured only once, during the 1938 championship game against the Green Bay Packers. Despite losing consciousness briefly and suffering a broken nose, Hein returned a few minutes later to help the Giants win the game. He usually played all sixty minutes in the more than 200 contests of his career. A team leader off the field as well as on, Hein was credited with ending a brutal Giants tradition of hazing young players by using his influence with squad veterans. In time, his perfection on the field was so respected that he served as almost as a player-coach. During the last four years of Hein's career, Giants head coach Steve Owen allowed him to limit his practices to one day a week because Hein was commuting from Schenectady while serving as head coach at Union College. Hein was well compensated with a salary of $5,000 a year, making him the highest-paid lineman in the National Football League (NFL).

After retiring as a player, Hein was an assistant coach with the Los Angeles Dons of the All-America Football League in 1947 and 1948, the New York Football Yankees in 1949, and the Los Angeles Rams of the NFL in 1950. He began coaching college football in 1951 at the University of Southern California (USC), where he stayed for fifteen years. Hein was also named supervisor of officials for the American Football League (AFL) in 1966, a position he continued to fill for the American Football Conference after the AFL merged with the NFL. Hein retired in 1974.

Over the years, Hein's reputation made him a legendary figure among New York sports fans. Giants owner Wellington Mara, who grew up awed by the great 1930s teams of his youth, once called Hein the best player of the team's first fifty years. Al Davis, legendary Raiders owner and former coach, who worked alongside Hein when both were assistants at USC in the 1950s, called him "one of the greatest football players who ever lived." Sports columnist Dave Anderson of the *New York Times* once picked the top twenty-five players ever to perform for New York football teams. Every position was worthy of debate except center.

Anderson argued that no other candidate could compare to Hein.

In addition to being named All-Pro eight straight seasons, Hein is the only offensive lineman ever to win the NFL's Most Valuable Player award (1938). He received charter membership in the College Football Hall of Fame in 1954. When the Pro Football Hall of Fame opened its doors in 1963, Hein was a charter member, the first center to be enshrined. In 1983 he was the first athlete honored with the Washington State University Distinguished Alumnus Award. He was also recognized on the NFL's 75th Anniversary team in 1994, two years after his death. He was named to the Walter Camp All-Century Football Team on 28 December 1999. When retired coaches, sports information directors, and media selected the eighty-three-player Walter Camp squad, Hein was one of only three centers recognized. The *Sporting News* named Hein one of the top 100 football players of all time during the same year.

Hein died from complications of stomach cancer. He was survived by his wife Florance, a son and daughter, and four grandchildren.

★

The Pro Football Hall of Fame in Canton, Ohio, provides good background information about Hein and his career with the Giants. Some of the most voluminous material about Hein's football career has been produced by the Professional Football Researchers Association (PFRA) in Huntingdon, Pennsylvania. PFRA Executive Director Bob Carroll wrote an excellent biography of Hein in the group's journal, the *Coffin Corner*, V (1983). An obituary is in the *New York Times* (2 Feb. 1992). Washington State University houses some excellent resources specific to Hein's college career. Of particular interest are historical photographs of Hein available from the Hutchinson Studio Photographs of Washington State and Pullman, Washington, 1927–1973, available at the Manuscripts, Archives, and Special Collections section of the WSU library system.

R. JAKE SUDDERTH

HEINZ, Wilfred Charles ("Bill") (*b.* 11 January 1915 in Mount Vernon, New York), sportswriter, sports columnist, reporter, war correspondent, novelist, coauthor with Vince Lombardi of *Run to Daylight!*, and leading American sportswriter for nearly half a century.

Heinz was the only child of Frederick Louis Sylvester Heinz, a salesman, and Elizabeth Thielke Heinz. Growing up in a New York City suburb, he played childhood sports and followed the exploits of the athletic heroes of the day. Heinz dreamed of a career in sport but possessed only modest athletic talents. He developed a love for reading and literature and would aspire to a journalistic career.

Heinz attended Middlebury College in Middlebury, Vermont, where he was sports editor of the college newspaper and yearbook. After graduating with a B.A. degree in political science in 1937, Heinz landed a job as a messenger boy with the *New York Sun*. By 1939 he had become a copy boy and had begun to contribute short pieces for the newspaper. Placed on staff as a city reporter, he gradually learned his craft as a reporter, rewrite man, and feature writer. On 18 January 1941, Heinz married Elizabeth Bailey, whom he had met when they were college students. They had two daughters.

During World War II, Heinz became the *Sun's* junior war correspondent in 1943. In April 1944 he was sent to London to report on Allied preparations for the invasion of Europe. After covering the naval bombardment of Normandy, Heinz replaced the *Sun's* senior war correspondent in August 1944, covering the advance of the First Army across France and Germany through the final days of the war in Europe. In a 1961 interview, Heinz would recall the war years as the time during which he truly learned to write. In his European wartime dispatches, Heinz cut to the essence of the story. In simple, stark, effective language, he conveyed the brutal reality of war—the chaos, devastation, and emotional turmoil, devoid of excess verbiage and artifice.

Heinz returned to New York in June 1945, shortly after V-E Day. He was rewarded with a $1,000 bonus and a three-month vacation. The *Sun* had assigned him to their Washington bureau, but he wanted to write sports instead. When Heinz returned from vacation that September, he was assigned to the sports department where he would remain until the newspaper published its last edition on 4 January 1950.

Heinz quickly developed as one of the finest sportswriters in the field. He wrote features, general assignments, atmospheric essays, and portraits of athletes and teams preparing for upcoming contests. Although capably covering all sports, he wrote most perceptively and movingly about boxing, baseball, and horse racing. He became a denizen of Manhattan's Stillman's Gym, a Midtown boxing locale that was the focus of the sport's thriving activity in the immediate postwar years. On 10 January 1949 he began his own sports column, "The Sport Scene," which appeared five times weekly. His columns included sketches of sporting personalities, atmospheric pieces often centered around his favorite sporting venues, and conversation pieces in which the writer replicates blocks of conversation with a delicate touch for the subject's voice.

During the 1940s, Heinz began to contribute freelance articles and short stories to some of the leading magazines of the time. For a month in the summer of 1950, he was guest columnist for the *New York Daily News*. He rejected the offer of a regular column with the *News* to pursue freelance work. In the late 1940s and throughout the 1950s, Heinz did some of his best magazine writing and would win five E. P. Dutton Awards between 1948 and 1959 for best magazine sports story. He also worked in television sports writing and promotion during this period and would continue to do so in the following decade.

Heinz's growing literary reputation during the 1950s commanded increasingly higher fees for his magazine work. After receiving a substantial sum for a two-part *Look* magazine profile of jockey Eddie Arcaro in 1956, he worked for eleven months to produce his first book, the novel *The Professional* (1958). *The Professional* tells the story of a middleweight boxing contender and his manager, preparing for a title bout, as seen through the eyes of sportswriter Frank Hughes, an alter ego for Heinz. The book was highly praised by reviewers and even lauded by Ernest Hemingway. It encapsulates Heinz's style and credo: careful attention to detail, authentic dialogue, a sensitivity and understanding of fighters and the fight game coupled with pointed criticism of inept dilettantes, crass commercialism, and sensationalism that Heinz saw engulfing much of contemporary society.

In 1961 Heinz compiled and edited *The Fireside Book of Boxing,* an anthology of boxing pieces. For a time, his literary interests gravitated towards medicine. A 20 January 1961 *Life* magazine piece on an innovative chest operation led to *The Surgeon* (1963), a fictional account of eight hours in the working life of a thoracic surgeon. In 1962 Heinz began a collaboration with Green Bay Packers football coach Vince Lombardi that would lead to *Run to Daylight!* (1963). This seminal work, the first of many such books linking author with coach to reveal the inner workings that precede the game, was related through Lombardi's perspective and voice and became a best-seller, widely praised and often imitated.

Several years later, Heinz teamed with Dr. H. Richard Hornberger, a Korean War U.S. Army doctor who, as Richard Hooker, produced the seriocomic novel *M*A*S*H* (1968). The result was a fast-paced, episodic account of the 4077th Mobile Army Surgical Hospital (MASH) that was the basis for the 1970 film and the long-running (1972–1983) television series. Heinz's final novel was *Emergency!* (1974), an account of a county medical center emergency room.

In the 1970s, Heinz revisited some of the sports personalities he had written about years earlier. The result was *Once They Heard the Cheers* (1979), an effective blend of then and now that incorporated some of the best of his previous work, reconfigured to update the lives of yesterday's heroes. *American Mirror* (1982) was a collection of thirteen of his best magazine and newspaper pieces with brief updates. Both books were received well critically.

After many years of semi-retirement, living with his wife in Dorset, Vermont, Heinz belatedly was rediscovered by both print and electronic journalism, both for the quality of his writing and the clarity of his insights. In *The Best American Sportswriting of the Century* (1999), editor David Halberstam selected three Heinz pieces for inclusion. In 1999 Heinz was coeditor with Nathan Ward of *The Book of Boxing,* a revised and expanded version of the 1961 work. In 2001 a second, expanded anthology of Heinz's work was published (*What a Time It Was: The Best of W. C. Heinz on Sports*).

Heinz is the final member of the mid-twentieth-century sportswriting coterie that included Red Smith, Frank Graham, and Jimmy Cannon who, through idiosyncratic methods and stylistic breakthroughs, shattered the stereotyped conventions that had encumbered their profession since sport's so-called Golden Age in the 1920s.

Heinz was, and remains, a purist and a traditionalist in the best sense—an introspective writer who displayed a sensitivity for the struggles of athletes and their wives, who viewed sport at its highest level as the purest form of self-expression reflecting the result of science, practice, invention, and adaptation, and who retained an abiding respect for professionalism, physical courage, quiet competence, and the honest workmen who plied their trades both in and out of sport.

★

There is no full-length biography of Heinz. He provided some biographical material in the introductory chapter of W. C. Heinz, *Once They Heard the Cheers* (1970). His literary career is analyzed in detail by Edward J. Tassinari, *Dictionary of Literary Biography: Twentieth-Century American Sportswriters* 171 (1996): 132–144. David Halberstam has been instrumental in reviving interest in Heinz's work. See the introduction in Halberstam, ed., *The Best American Sports Writing, 1991* (1991); Halberstam, ed., *The Best American Sports Writing of the Century* (1999); and Halberstam's foreword in *What a Time It Was: The Best of W. C. Heinz on Sports* (2001). Heinz was one of many New York City sportswriters whose writing was critiqued by A. J. Liebling in "The Scribes of Destiny," *New Yorker* 22 (28 Sept. 1946). A brief interview with Heinz is in "Out of the Ring," *Newsweek* 58 (9 Oct. 1961). His role, together with that of Jimmy Cannon, in the flowering of a more personal sportswriting style is found in Jack Newfield, "Journalism: Old, New and Corporate," *Dutton Review* 1 (1970): 151–156. The most complete account of his life is Jeff MacGregor, "Heavyweight Champion of the Word," *Sports Illustrated* 93 (25 Sept. 2000).

EDWARD J. TASSINARI

HEISMAN, John William ("Johnny") (*b.* 23 October 1869 in Cleveland, Ohio; *d.* 3 October 1936 in New York City), one of the early innovators in college football coaching who is memorialized by the Heisman Memorial Trophy, emblematic of college football's "outstanding player," presented annually by the Downtown Athletic Club of New York.

Heisman's grandfather, Baron von Bogart, was a nobleman in Germany. The baron's son, Heisman's father, John M. von Bogart, had a rebellious streak, and against his father's wishes he married a peasant girl. So enraged was the baron that he disinherited his son. So defiant was the son that he and his bride, Sarah Lehr Heisman, sailed for America and settled in Cleveland, Ohio. The baron's son also took his wife's maiden name as his own last name. The baron later relented and asked the young couple to return to Germany, but they liked the United States and chose to stay.

Johann Wilhelm Heisman was born two weeks before Princeton and Rutgers played what is considered the first intercollegiate football game in New Brunswick, New Jersey. His father was a cooper or barrel maker, and his mother was a homemaker. In the 1870s the family moved to Titusville, Pennsylvania, where the nation's first oil boom was taking place. After graduating from Titusville High School in 1887, Heisman matriculated at Brown University that year. He played football and baseball there, but the football was not "varsity," as Brown had dropped intercollegiate football. It was reinstated in 1889, but by that time Heisman had transferred to the University of Pennsylvania. While with the Quakers, Heisman and his teammates played a game indoors at Madison Square Garden. During this game the Garden's chemically produced, direct-current electrical lighting system damaged Heisman's eyes.

This drastically changed Heisman's career path and perhaps the face of college football. Instead of using the law degree he took from Penn in the spring of 1892, Heisman

Johnny Heisman, 1920. © BETTMANN/CORBIS

became the first football coach at the progressive Oberlin College in Ohio. Under the rules of the day Heisman, because he was enrolled as a graduate student in art, could play on the team he coached. He and the team were successful immediately, going undefeated and scoring 262 points to their opponents' 30. Among Oberlin's 7 victories were 40–0 and 50–0 whitewashings of Ohio State. It was not uncommon in the early days of college football for schools to play nearby rivals more than once in a season. *Harper's Weekly* magazine termed Oberlin's Yeomen "one of the three strongest teams west of the Alleghenies."

The next season (1893) found Heisman at another small Ohio school, Buchtel, now the University of Akron. The highlight of that season was a game at the state fair in Columbus against Ohio State. Once again a Heisman team defeated the Buckeyes, 12–6. Heisman was back at Oberlin for the 1894 season, but he went south in 1895 to Alabama Polytechnic Institute, now Auburn University. In a three-game season Heisman's team lost to Vanderbilt (9–6) but stunned Alabama (48–0) and Georgia (16–6). During this time Heisman saw an illegal forward pass play and thought if it were legal "it would scatter the mob." Football at the time was massed formations with often brutal tactics. Heisman wrote to Walter Camp, "the Father of American Football" and the sport's rules guru, asking him to legalize the forward pass. Camp never replied, but the game became so barbaric, with twenty-three on-field deaths in 1905, that President Theodore Roosevelt issued an edict: "Clean up football or it will be banned." Camp and the rules committee legalized the forward pass for the 1906 season.

As the nineteenth century played out, Heisman built a solid reputation at Auburn. He was considered part of an elite coaching triumvirate that included Amos Alonzo Stagg and Glenn S. "Pop" Warner. Heisman moved on to Clemson in 1900. His first season gave Clemson its first undefeated season. Heisman, who always enjoyed outfoxing an opponent, was at his best in 1902. For a game with Georgia Tech in Atlanta, he sent a group of his "scrubs," substitute players posing as the varsity, into Atlanta the day before the game. They checked into a hotel that evening and then, at the behest of the locals, stayed out all night partying. Atlantans bet heavily on the hometown Tech after word of Clemson's carousing got around. The Clemson varsity had actually spent the night—well rested—in a small village just outside the city. To the surprise of many in the crowd at the field where the game was played, the Clemson starters arrived for the game fresh and ready to play. Heisman's Clemson team destroyed Georgia Tech 44–5. After his team embarrassed Tech again in 1903, 73–0, the Atlanta university enticed Heisman to come and coach them in 1904.

At Georgia Tech, Heisman had his greatest success, a record of 102–29–7 through 1919. While there Heisman also took part in "summer stock" theater. He was especially fond of Shakespearean roles. In 1903 he married a fellow thespian, Evelyn McCollum Cox.

Heisman was a stern taskmaster and a devout believer in fundamentals. He often addressed his team as if he were emoting from a theatrical stage, once saying, as he held up a football: "Gentlemen, what is this? It is a prolate spheroid, an elongated sphere, in which the outer casing is drawn tightly over a somewhat smaller rubber bladder. Better to have died as a small boy than to *fumble* this football."

Perhaps nothing in Heisman's early years at Tech foretold what would happen in 1916. He and other coaches of his era often coached more than one sport. Stung in the spring by a 22–0 baseball loss to little Cumberland College, who used players from the Nashville team of the professional Southern Association, Heisman was bent on revenge. He offered Cumberland $500 to play a football game that fall. When Cumberland later tried to back out, citing a lack of players, Heisman threatened to sue for breach of contract. The Cumberland team forced to play that fateful football game was really a group of inexperienced fraternity boys (Kappa Sigma).

In the historic game neither team made a first down. Cumberland could not, and Georgia Tech did not have to. It never took Tech more than three plays to score one of its thirty-two touchdowns that day. Tech led at the halftime intermission 126–0. Between the halves Heisman told his team: "Gentlemen, you're doing all right. You've got them on the run. We're ahead, but don't let up. You can never tell what these tricky Cumberland players have up their sleeves. Be alert." Despite a second half with shortened third and fourth quarters, the final score was 220–0. Heisman had his revenge ten sweet times over. The score has remained for decades the most lopsided game in the history of intercollegiate football.

Heisman's 1916 team was voted the mythical national champion. They outscored their opponents 421–20. Only three teams, Washington and Lee (7), Auburn (7), and North Carolina (6), scored on them. By this time the pioneer coach had devised the "Heisman shift," in which before a play only the center was at the line of scrimmage. The rest of the team was several yards back and in a single line. The players went in motion right before the snap of the ball. As one southern writer described it, "The team deployed with the suddenness of a J. E. B. Stuart cavalry raid."

While at Tech in 1919, Heisman and his wife shocked their friends when they announced they were getting a divorce. Heisman simply said: "There are no hard feelings. I have agreed that wherever Mrs. Heisman wishes to live, I will live in another place." Mrs. Heisman chose to remain in Atlanta. Heisman returned to his alma mater Penn for three years and then moved on to Washington and Jefferson College in Washington, Pennsylvania. In 1924 Heisman,

now married to Edith Maora Cole, took the head coaching job at Rice. Heisman and Maora, the name she was known by, were sweethearts when she was a student and he was coach at Buchtel years before, but when she was diagnosed with tuberculosis, they had decided not to marry. Heisman coached four seasons at Rice, bringing the small Southwest Conference school respectability. After the 1927 season Heisman retired from active coaching, moved to New York City, where he had a thriving sporting goods business, and became athletics director at the Downtown Athletic Club.

In 1935 Willard Price, the founder and editor of the *Downtown Athletic Club Journal,* proposed a trophy "for the outstanding college player east of the Mississippi." Heisman at first was opposed to "singling out one man from a team sport." But when he mentioned it casually and saw the enthusiasm of former players and writers, he changed his stance. Thus the Downtown Athletic Club Trophy came into being in 1935.

In October 1936 Heisman died after a brief bout with bronchial pneumonia. He is buried in Forest Home Cemetery in Rhinelander, Wisconsin, the home of his second wife where he often spent his summers. On 10 December 1936 the Downtown Athletic Club awarded its second trophy. This time it had a new name, the John W. Heisman Memorial Trophy, which became the most recognized award in college sports.

Heisman, a true innovator and a successful pioneer coach, was one of the driving forces behind the acceptance of college football in the United States. A somewhat austere and formal man to most, he could "let his hair down" with those close to him. He allowed the famed sportswriter Grantland Rice to call him "Jack" and his wife Maora to call him "Jackie."

★

Heisman wrote a technical book, *Principles of Football* (1922). His life and career are discussed in John T. Brady, *The Heisman: A Symbol of Excellence* (1984); Bert Randolph Sugar, *The Southeastern Conference* (1979); Allison Danzig, *The History of American Football* (1956); and Edwin Pope, *Football's Greatest Coaches* (1955). An obituary is in the *New York Times* (4 Oct. 1936).

JIM CAMPBELL

HEISS JENKINS, Carol Elizabeth (*b.* 20 January 1940 in New York City), gold medal figure skater at the 1960 Winter Olympics who also won the silver medal in 1956 and five consecutive world championships.

Heiss, the oldest of the three children born to Edward Heiss and Marie Gademann Heiss, grew up in the working-class area of Ozone Park, Queens, in New York City. Her father, who was a baker, and her mother, a freelance textile de-

Carol Heiss. AP/WIDE WORLD PHOTOS

signer, had emigrated separately from Germany in the 1920s and met in the United States. Although the family was never financially affluent, Heiss's parents supported her pursuits in the expensive sport of figure skating, and her brother Bruce Heiss and her sister Nancy Heiss also became accomplished skaters. Carol received her first pair of ice skates for Christmas when she was four years old and, displaying talent at the sport, soon began to take lessons. She rose early each morning to skate at the Iceland Rink atop Madison Square Garden, where she was coached by the former Olympic pairs champions Andrée Brunet and Pierre Brunet.

At the age of eleven Heiss won her first national title, the National Novice Championship. Just two years later she placed second at the 1953 National Championship behind Tenley Albright, as she did for the next three years. She also finished in fourth place at the 1953 World Championship. In 1954 a collision with her sister during practice resulted in a severed tendon that prevented her from competing at the world competition that year. She returned to the ice for the 1955 World Championship, but she was unable to beat Albright once again and had to settle for the silver medal.

At the 1956 Winter Olympics in Cortina d'Ampezzo, Italy, Heiss distinguished herself as the first woman to complete a double axel jump. Despite this achievement, the gold medal went to Albright by a narrow margin, 169.6 points to Heiss's 168.1 points, which secured her the silver medal. Rumors held that a feud transpired between the two skaters when it appeared that Heiss would not pose for photos with her rival or congratulate her, and later at the World Championship Heiss stayed at a different hotel from the rest of the skating team. Both women denied these charges, asserting their friendship.

At the World Championship in Garmisch-Partenkirchen, Germany, following the Olympics, Heiss finally dethroned her chief competitor after a near-perfect performance of compulsory ("school") figures, which at that time counted for 60 percent of the score. She also executed a free program that included two double axels, a double flip, double loops, and a flying sit spin. Awarded six first and three second places from the nine judges, the petite sixteen-year-old skater, distinguished by her blonde ponytail hairdo that resembled a propeller when she spun around the ice, became the youngest to win this title since Sonja Henie had won at the age of fifteen. At the National Championship that followed, however, Heiss once again had to settle for second place behind Albright, who retired after that competition.

In October 1956 Heiss's mother died of cancer, and the teenager took over running the household and caring for her two younger siblings. In 1957, after graduating from the Professional Children's School, she enrolled in New York University on a full scholarship to study English while continuing her training. She won five consecutive World Championships beginning in 1956 and four consecutive national titles from 1957 to 1960.

The only title that eluded Heiss was that of Olympic gold medalist, but the 1960 Winter Olympics in Squaw Valley, California, offered her a second chance. At the opening ceremonies she took the Olympic Oath on behalf of all the participating athletes, the first woman to perform this honor. Her free program, which included such difficult moves as the Axel Paulsen, the spread eagle, and the arabesque spin, was far more intricate than that of any of her competitors, who this time did not include Albright. The nine judges unanimously awarded Heiss first place, and she won the gold medal by a wide margin.

Following her Olympic victory, Heiss asserted that she would not become a professional skater. She added one more World Championship to her list of credits and then changed her mind, going on to do product endorsements and show skating. She also starred in a B movie, *Snow White and the Three Stooges,* released in 1961, for which she earned $100,000. She used the money to pay college tuitions for her brother and sister as well as her own debt for back lessons.

On 30 April 1960 Heiss, who came from a family of skaters, married into another family of skaters when she wed Hayes Alan Jenkins, the 1956 men's figure skating gold medalist whose brother was the Olympic champion in 1960. She moved to his home in Akron, Ohio, where he worked as a lawyer following his graduation from Harvard Law School. After retiring from her career as a figure skater around 1961, Carol Heiss Jenkins raised one son and two daughters.

In 1973 Heiss Jenkins was inducted into the Ice Skating Hall of Fame in Akron, Ohio, and in 1976 she was inducted into the U.S. Figure Skating Association Hall of Fame. In 1978, when an indoor ice rink was built in Akron, she began her coaching career. Later she went to the Winterhurst Ice Rink in Lakewood, Ohio, where she coached top national and international skaters, including Timothy Goebel, Tonia Kwiatkowski, Lisa Ervin, and Aren Nielsen.

Heiss Jenkins's figure skating style combined grace and strength, as demonstrated in such difficult moves as the double axel. During the era in which she competed, figure skating experienced a transition from its focus on artistry to a mixture of art and athleticism, and she embodied this change. Her rivalry with Albright added drama to the skating scene of the mid-1950s. During her skating career Heiss Jenkins was considered by some experts as the best American female figure skater of all time, notable because of the young age at which she became a world-class skater.

★

A biographical sketch of Heiss in *Current Biography* (1959) covers her life until 1959. Another contemporary view of her life is J. K. Lagemann's essay, "Meet the Champion," *Reader's Digest* (Apr. 1959). For a detailed description of her performance in the 1956 Olympics, see the *New York Times* (3 Feb. 1956); for an account of her World Championship upset victory, see the *New York Times* (19 Feb. 1956); and for her 1960 Olympic win, see the *New York Times* (24 Feb. 1960). Amy Rosewater, "Olympic Dream Revisited," *Cleveland Plain Dealer* (9 Feb. 2000), provides an in-depth look at her activities as a coach.

ARLENE R. QUARATIELLO

HENDERSON, Rickey (*b.* 25 December 1958 in Chicago, Illinois), professional baseball player who is considered by many the best leadoff batter as well as one of the most colorful characters in the game's history.

Henderson was born Rickey Henley en route to the hospital in the back seat of Bobbie and John Henley's Oldsmobile. In his autobiography Henderson attributes his premature entry into the world to his great speed: "I've always been fast, from the minute I was born." Henderson was the fourth of Bobbie's seven children. When he was two his father, a truck driver, abandoned his wife and family and was never heard from again. After her husband left, Bobbie

Rickey Henderson, 1982. © BETTMANN/CORBIS

moved her family to her mother's farm in Pine Bluff, Arkansas. When Henderson was ten his mother moved the family to Oakland, California, where she married Paul Henderson. Bobbie's new husband adopted the children, changing their name to Henderson; he and Bobbie had two children of their own. Eventually, however, they separated, and Bobbie raised the children alone. Henderson recalls, "Most of my life, there was no man in the house. Grandma raised us in Arkansas, and Momma raised us in Oakland." Bobbie supported the family by working as a registered nurse.

Henderson attended Oakland Technical High School, where he met Pamela Palmer, the future mother of his two daughters. In high school Henderson excelled in baseball, football, and basketball. Football was Henderson's first love. As a high school All-America running back, he rushed for 1,100 yards during his senior year and received more than twenty football scholarship offers. Excelling equally in baseball, Henderson batted .716 as a high school junior and .465 as a senior. He graduated from high school in 1976.

In the June 1976 draft Henderson was chosen in the fourth round by the Oakland Athletics, largely at the urging of Jim Guinn, a Berkeley, California, police officer and part-time Athletics' scout. Yet Henderson's baseball career owes less to Guinn than to his mother. If the choice had been Henderson's, he would have accepted a football scholarship. Instead, he left the decision to his mother; she chose baseball, believing that her son would have a healthier and longer career in that sport.

After signing with the Athletics, Henderson was sent to their rookie farm team in Boise, Idaho. He started his professional baseball career on a high note, batting .336 and stealing 29 bases in 36 attempts. The following year, in 1977, while playing for the Athletics' Class-A California League in Modesto, Henderson batted .345 and set a league record in stolen bases with ninety-five. On 26 May 1977 he stole seven bases in one game, becoming only the fourth player in professional baseball to accomplish this feat. The Athletics continued to promote Henderson, and on 23 June 1979 he was in the starting lineup for the parent team.

Henderson's professional baseball career has been impressive. Since beginning in the major leagues he has hit over .300 in eight seasons (he also hit over .300 in his four years in the minors). Between 1980 and 1991 he was an All-Star player in all but one season. In 1981 he won the Gold Glove award for fielding, and in 1990 he received the Most Valuable Player (MVP) award. His record of stolen bases, though, is his most notable achievement in baseball. On 30 September 1980 he became only the third player in major league history to steal at least 100 bases in one season; he repeated this accomplishment in 1982 and 1983. On 26 August 1982 he stole four bases in a game against Milwaukee, thus passing Lou Brock's one-year record of 118. Henderson ended the 1982 season with 130 stolen bases in 149 games. On 4 June 1988, playing for the New York Yankees, Henderson stole his 249th base, breaking Hal Chase's lifetime record of 248. In 1989, again playing for Oakland, Henderson was named the American League Championship Series MVP. He reached base 14 times in 5 games and set a new record of 8 stolen bases in a postseason series.

His impressive numbers notwithstanding, Henderson has often been labeled a liability for baseball teams. Although he has spent most of his career in an Athletics uniform, he has been traded among various ball clubs, including the Yankees, the New York Mets, the Toronto Blue Jays, the San Diego Padres, and the Seattle Mariners. Complaining frequently about his salary, Henderson often has had conflicts with management. He has been accused of milking injuries and playing below his ability. As the Mets' general manager, Steve Phillips, said in May of 2000, "No matter how much talent you have, if you continue to create problems and situations, you wear out your welcome." At the same time Henderson generally is liked by his fellow players.

Still, Henderson has also been frequently criticized for seeking publicity at inappropriate moments, often waving to the fans and posing for their cameras during games. Having fun with the fans loosens Henderson up, as he is the first to admit. In fact, the first sentence in his autobiography is "Yes, I am a hot dog." Then he follows with

"Ever hear of a hot dog who couldn't play?" Henderson takes pride in doing things out of the ordinary, such as jogging slowly around the bases after a home run, taking his time in the batter's box, and moving slowly to first base after a walk. "But that's just me," he says. "I'm just trying to have fun and approach the game the same way I've always approached it. . . . [T]hat's the way I've been able to show the fans a good time. Call it Rickey Time."

Henderson, regardless of whether one finds him entertaining or annoying, has produced numbers that rank him among the best baseball players of all time. At five feet, ten inches tall and 190 pounds, Henderson has always taken excellent care of his health. This, along with his confident attitude and obvious talent, has contributed to his success over a long career. As *Newsweek*'s George F. Will writes, "Baseball's history is written largely in numbers, and numbers say Henderson's may have been the most impressive all-round career in the last quarter century."

★

Henderson's autobiography, *Off Base: Confessions of a Thief* (1992), was edited by John Shea. Children's biographies include Paul Schleicher, *Rickey Henderson: Sports Personalities*; Ann Bauleke, *Rickey Henderson: Record Stealer* (1991); and Mitsuko Herrera, *Rickey Henderson*. Articles about Henderson appear in books such as *Baseball's Top 100: The Best Individual Seasons of All Time* (1996).

CANDICE MANCINI KNIGHT

HENIE, Sonja (*b.* 8 April 1912 in Oslo, Norway; *d.* 12 October 1969 on a Paris-to-Oslo plane flight), champion figure skater who won three consecutive Olympic gold medals and most Norwegian, European, and world figure skating championships.

In her autobiography, *Wings on My Feet*, Henie explained that the primary factor facilitating her being so "lucky" in achieving her skating goals was her family's wealth. Her father, Hans Wilhelm Henie, was a successful fur trader and amateur athlete, and her mother, Selma Lochman Nielsen, inherited her family's wealth. Henie's first love was dancing, and she began to study ballet at age four; the ballet element in her later skating, both as champion amateur and professional, was always evident.

At age seven Henie learned to skate from her elder and only brother, Leif. Already exposed to Norway's favorite sport, skiing, Henie preferred figure skating; she loved the "whirling" sensation of ice-skating and the resulting "sense of power" over distance and gravity. Hjordis Olsen, an amateur skater at a private club, drilled Henie in mastering the mandatory school figures. At the same time, Henie studied ballet in Oslo.

Sonja Henie. AP/WIDE WORLD PHOTOS

In 1921, at Oslo's Frogner Stadium, Henie competed in and won Norway's highest junior level of competition. She no longer attended school but studied at home with tutors. The result of her first entry into the national championship at Frogner, in 1922, was to win second place. When she returned the following year, she secured the women's national championship title and, as part of her record-making legacy, would come back the subsequent six years to retain that title. Oscar Holte, the outstanding Norwegian skating coach, supervised much of her training in Oslo and at St. Moritz, Switzerland, as she prepared to enter the International Winter Sports Week at Chamonix, France; retroactively, this special "week" became an official part of the first Winter Olympics in 1924.

Frogner Stadium was the site of the 1927 Women's World Figure Skating Championship. Dressed in a white velvet, bell-skirted dress designed by her mother, Henie won over Austria's Herma Planck-Szabo. Henie secured the subsequent nine consecutive world titles, fostering suspicion among the Austrians, who complained that three of the five judges had been Norwegians; soon each country would be allowed only one judge per event.

In the summer of 1927 Henie had the thrill of seeing her idol, Russian dancer Anna Pavlova, on stage in London, which inspired her to adapt Pavlova's *Dying Swan* to figure skating. This adaptation formed the basis for Henie's free-skating program at the 1928 Olympics at St. Moritz, where the blonde-haired, five-foot, two-inch Henie, at 104 pounds, presented flawless figures and a free-skating program that included a combination of double "Axel Paulsens" (as the double axel was then called) and nineteen spins, twirls, and jumps. In January 1930, after additional success in winning Norway's skating doubles championship three times, she impressed her first New York City audience of 15,000 at the amateur Ice Carnival exhibition at Madison Square Garden. A 1930 *New York Times* article dubbed Henie a "Pavlova on Ice" and stressed her athletic prowess.

A dynamic athlete, Henie ranked third among Norway's female tennis players and was "a daring equestrienne." In August 1931 her Chrysler roadster came in second in an amateur automobile race in Stockholm, and she became runner-up in the Norwegian national tennis tournament in 1932. In recognition of her skating and other athletic accomplishments, she became the first woman to receive a medal from the Norwegian government for versatility and achievement in sports.

Henie returned to the United States in 1932 for more exhibitions and for the third Winter Olympic Games at Lake Placid, New York. There, Henie won her second gold medal in figure skating, with 2,302.5 points. Her free-skating program, with its musical medley of stage songs, received a standing ovation. From 1931 through 1936, Henie competed in and won six consecutive women's European Figure Skating Championships

In 1936 Henie won her third and final gold medal at the fourth Winter Olympic Games at Garmisch-Partenkirchen, Germany, by earning 2,971.4 points. During the twentieth century no competitor was able to match Henie's three consecutive Olympic gold medals in women's figure skating. After Henie won the world championship one last time in 1936, she prepared to retire from amateur sports and enter professional skating. She also planned to become a Hollywood actress and to accomplish on screen for ice-skating what Fred Astaire had done for dancing. *Sonja Henie's Night,* an exhibition that played before and during the intermission of ice hockey games at Madison Square Garden during March 1936, was a success. Her skating built on the innovative styles of Jackson Haines and Hilda Holowsky. Later programs included her famous hula sketch. Five thousand potential ticket-buyers had to be turned away when she returned to Madison Square Garden in 1937 with the start of her *Hollywood Ice Revue.* In December 1937 Henie was received into Norway's Knightly Order of St. Olaf.

Henie was also successful in Hollywood. Though Metro-Goldwin-Mayer (MGM) had expressed interest in her after the 1936 Olympics, when she arrived in the United States Henie and her father planned a gala skating exhibition to be attended by top motion-picture stars and executives, including Twentieth Century–Fox's Darryl F. Zanuck, who signed Henie up for a first-time appearance on the American screen as a leading star. Her first American film, *One in a Million* (1936), starring Don Ameche and Adolphe Menjou, opened in New York in 1936 and quickly grossed $2 million. According to various polls, by the end of 1937 Henie ranked among the top ten Hollywood earners; by 1938 she was among Twentieth Century–Fox's top female stars, which included Shirley Temple, Alice Faye, and Loretta Young; and by 1939 she ranked as the third most popular screen actor after Shirley Temple and Clark Gable. *Sun Valley Serenade* (1941), with John Payne and Glenn Miller and His Orchestra, received three Academy Award nominations for best cinematography, best music, and best song ("Chattanooga Choo Choo"), but her two releases in 1942 and 1943 marked the end of her contract with Twentieth Century–Fox. Her final two Hollywood films, released in 1945 by RKO and in 1948 by Universal, no longer enthralled postwar audiences, who preferred more sophisticated scripts. Her last film, *Hello London* (1958), received only limited showings in parts of England. She earned at least $25 million from her lucrative motion-picture career.

Henie married Daniel Reid Topping, an American sports investor from Greenwich, Connecticut, on 4 July 1940; they divorced in 1946. She became a United States citizen in 1941. On 15 September 1949 she married Winthrop Gardiner, Jr., a business executive; he divorced her on 14 May 1956 for "desertion and mental cruelty." Her third and final marriage was to fellow Norwegian Niels Onstad, a shipping magnate, on 9 June 1956. She had no children.

Henie kept her Hollywood home in Holmby Hills and enjoyed her Grundholtet villa in Norway and apartment in Lausanne, Switzerland. Onstad transformed her art collecting interest from traditional masters to contemporary works; they donated 250 paintings and millions of dollars to Norway and in 1968 completed the Henie-Onstad Museum near Oslo to house the collection and, after Henie's death, her career memorabilia.

In the fall of 1968 Henie was diagnosed with leukemia. While traveling with her husband in Europe, she became uncomfortably ill in Paris. Her husband chartered a plane to convey her from Paris to Oslo to see her doctor, but she died onboard in her sleep. Norway's king and queen attended the funeral service. A horizontal boulder forms her grave mark, which is located on Henie-Onstad Museum property.

Henie was the greatest of all women figure skaters from the 1920s to the 1940s, and perhaps of the entire twentieth century. It was not just the sheer quantity of her titles and awards or profits from skating in revues and from motion pictures that distinguished her, but rather the unique quality of her skating, her innovative influence on the development of women's competitive skating, and her overall creative artistry and ingenuity, for which she has secured a unique niche in the history of figure skating.

★

Henie's autobiography, written with Janet Owen, is *Wings on My Feet* (1940). Henie's brother speaks of her extremely violent temper in Raymond Strait and Leif Henie, *Queen of Ice, Queen of Shadows: The Unsuspected Life of Sonja Henie* (1985). An excellent book that devotes much attention to Henie in the context of the development of skating is Nigel Brown, *Ice-Skating: A History* (1959). John Axe, *Collectible Sonja Henie* (1979), includes covers and programs of some of the revues, in addition to brief text and photographs of dolls and skates. Entries on Henie, many with further bibliographies, appear in Barbara Sicherman and Carol Hurd Green, eds., *Notable American Women: The Modern Period: A Biographical Dictionary* (1980); Robert J. Condon, *The Fifty Finest Athletes of the 20th Century: A Worldwide Reference* (1990); and Robert Markel, ed., *The Women's Sports Encyclopedia* (1997). For emphasis on Henie's film career, see entries in David Shipman, *The Great Movie Stars: The Golden Years* (1970; rev. ed. 1974); James Robert Parish, *The Fox Girls* (1971); and James Vinson, ed., *The International Dictionary of Films and Filmmakers*, vol. 3, *Actors and Actresses* (1986). An obituary is in the *New York Times* (13 Oct. 1969). An excellent video documentary directed and produced by Edvard Hambro is entitled *Sonja Henie: Queen of the Ice* (1993).

MADELINE SAPIENZA

HIRSCH, Elroy Leon ("Crazylegs") (*b.* 17 June 1923 in Wausau, Wisconsin), receiver who was the first player to hold the flanker position in the National Football league (NFL), he revolutionized the position in the 1940s and 1950s with his unorthodox running style.

Hirsch was the son of Otto Peter Hirsch and Mayme Sabena Magnusen. His interest in football began early when, as a boy, he often made the trip to Green Bay to watch his hero, Don Hutson, play for the Green Bay Packers.

At Wausau High School, where he attended from 1937 to 1942, Hirsch was an extremely fast athlete who lettered in football, basketball, baseball, and track despite his unorthodox running style. His strange, flailing form often deceived opponents as to his speed. After a game at Soldier Field in Chicago in 1943, when Hirsch was a sophomore halfback at the University of Wisconsin, a sportswriter for the *Chicago Daily News* wrote, "Hirsch ran like a demented duck. His crazy legs were gyrating in six different directions all at the same time during a 61-yard touchdown that solidified the win." The description stuck, and Hirsch was known thereafter as "Crazylegs" Hirsch. He won All-American honors that year and helped his team win the national championship. Years later, his coach Harry Stuhldreher of the University of Wisconsin at Madison would say that Hirsch was one of the best athletes he had ever seen—fast, smart, and hard to tackle.

Hirsch transferred to Michigan State in 1944 as part of a U.S. Army training program and had similar success on the field. After an interruption of his college football career by naval service in World War II, Hirsch returned to finish his career by playing in a special game that pitted the College All-Stars against the NFL's Cleveland Rams in 1946. Hirsch scored on a 68-yard run and caught a 35-yard touchdown pass that enabled the All-Stars to upset the Rams 16–0. Hirsch was named the Most Valuable Player of the game.

The Los Angeles Rams drafted Hirsch in the first round of the 1945 draft as a future pick, but he decided instead to join the Chicago Rockets in the newly formed All-America Football Conference (AAFC). The AAFC hoped to rival the NFL by signing young stars such as Hirsch to play in the league. Unfortunately, Hirsch had a number of injuries in the three years he played for the Rockets, including a life-threatening skull fracture. Although doctors said Hirsch could never play football again, he refused to accept that diagnosis and worked hard to regain his full strength and abilities.

Hirsch joined the Rams in 1949. Coach Joe Stydahar moved him to tight end where he excelled as part of the Rams' revolutionary "three-end" offense. Along with receivers Tom Fears and Bob Shaw, Hirsch revolutionized the position of receiver. For most teams at that time, rushing was the staple of offensive football; passing was used either for variety to enhance the running game or as a last resort in long yardage situations. Hirsch and the rest of the Rams' offense made the passing attack a primary force in football for decades to come.

In order to accommodate Hirsch in the wide receiver formation, the Rams created a new position they called "flanker." At six foot, two inches tall, and 190 pounds, Hirsch was the first receiving end to move out closer to the sideline, away from the line of scrimmage. Hirsch's speed and athleticism made him a devastating long threat. He became one of the best at catching long passes over his shoulder without breaking stride, and it is largely because of Hirsch that the word "bomb" came to refer to a long, arcing pass. That year, Hirsch caught touchdown passes of 34, 33, 46, 53, 72, 76, 79, and 81 yards, and he was also a major player when the Rams won the Western Division title in 1949, 1950, and 1951. Hirsch led the NFL in receiving and scoring in 1951, with 66 catches for 1,495 yards and 17 touchdowns. These statistics have since been surpassed, but Hirsch did it in a 12-game season. He averaged

Elroy "Crazylegs" Hirsch, 1953. AP/WIDE WORLD PHOTOS

an astonishing 22.7 yards-per-catch in 1951, a year in which he helped the Rams win the NFL title, defeating the Cleveland Browns 24–17. After the game, Hirsch characteristically played down his own stunning contributions and praised his teammates for their role in the win.

Hirsch became a superstar in Los Angeles with his own radio and television shows, and even played himself in a 1953 film about his life, *Crazylegs, All-American.* The following year he also starred in *Unchained,* another football film. As an example of Hirsch's growing fame, after one game in 1954, a swarm of fans accosted him and stripped him of most of his gear as souvenirs.

Hirsch retired in 1957 with 343 receptions, 6,299 receiving yards, and 53 touchdowns. But retirement did not end Hirsch's involvement in football or athletics. For two years (1958–1960) he was the sports director for Union Oil Company of California, and he replaced Pete Rozelle as the general manager of the Rams in 1960. In 1969 Hirsch moved back to Wisconsin to become athletic director for his alma mater, the University of Wisconsin at Madison, where he spent the next eighteen years. Hirsch had two children with his wife, Ruth Katherine Stahmer, whom he had married in 1946. He remained in Madison after retiring from the University of Wisconsin Athletic Department in 1987.

As the first flanker in football, "Crazylegs" Hirsch revolutionized the position of wide receiver with his deep-threat ability, speed, and athleticism. Hirsch's happy-go-lucky demeanor, quick quips, and refreshing humility about his own abilities made him a success both on and off the field. Hirsch's 18.4 yards-per-catch career average is still one of the best in the NFL. He also caught touchdown passes in eleven straight games, a record since surpassed only by San Francisco 49er Jerry Rice in 1987. Hirsch joined his boyhood hero, Don Hutson, on the NFL 50th-anniversary All-Time Team in 1969. He was inducted into the NFL Hall of Fame in 1968 and the College Football Hall of Fame in 1974.

★

John McCallum and W. W. Heffelfinger, *This Was Football* (1954), details Hirsch's abilities with a number of game summaries and anecdotes from his days at Wisconsin and Michigan State. Joe Horrigan and Bob Carroll, *Football Greats* (1998), describes Hirsch's major accomplishments on the field. Summaries and anecdotes of some of Hirsch's college and NFL achievements are found in Allison Danzig, *The History of American Football* (1956).

MARKUS H. McDOWELL

HITCHCOCK, Thomas, Jr. ("Tommy") (*b.* 1900 in Aiken, South Carolina; *d.* 12 April 1944 in Salisbury, England), charismatic and highly successful polo player; youngest ten-goaler in polo history in his day and for eighty years thereafter; member of five unbeaten Westchester cup teams; and four-time U.S. Open championship winner.

Hitchcock, the son of Thomas Hitchcock and Louise Corcoran Eustis, was born at Mon Repos, his family's winter home in Aiken, South Carolina. Both his parents had strong equestrian interests. His father was a ten-goal polo player who played in the first international match on record, against England in 1886 in Newport, Rhode Island. His mother was a well-known rider to hounds, polo coach, and mentor of many youngsters who under her tutelage were known as the Meadow Larks and who went on to distinguished careers on the polo field. Under these circumstances, it is no surprise that Hitchcock began to ride at an early age. Attendance at Saint Paul's School did not prevent him from winning both the Junior Championship at age sixteen and the Senior Championship three years later, both coveted prizes in that era.

In 1917 the United States entered World War I. Hitchcock tried to enlist in the armed forces but was turned down because he was too young. Through family connections with the former president Theodore Roosevelt, he was posted to the Escadrille Lafayette, a French unit composed of American volunteers. After undergoing combat training at Bourges, France, Hitchcock saw action at the Western Front and shot down some German planes before being brought down himself and taken as a prisoner of war. Typically indomitable, while being transferred from one POW

camp to another he escaped from a train and found his way to neutral Switzerland, trudging along for eight nights on foot. He returned to the United States toward the end of the war and enrolled at Harvard, studying chemical engineering. An indifferent student, after a few years Hitchcock went to Oxford University in England, following his father's footsteps.

While in England Hitchcock was on the team that won the 1921 Hurlingham Club's Champion Cup, the most important British polo tournament. Always recognized as an outstanding polo player, his international career began with the 1921 American challenge for the Westchester Cup, a United States–England contest. Still a student at Oxford, Hitchcock played in the number two position on the team that took the Cup back to the United States with ease.

After that successful outing, Hitchcock's handicap was raised to the maximum rating of ten goals, making him the youngest player to achieve that summit. Only Adolfo Cambiaso, the Argentine phenomenon, has broken that record, which stood unchallenged for almost eighty years. Hitchcock held his ten-goal handicap until his retirement from the game at the onset of World War II. There was one exception: in 1935 he was lowered to nine goals following a serious fall in an East-West match in Chicago, an injury-plagued series in which he was captain of the East squad.

The 1924 Olympic Games were held in Paris, France. The countries entered in the polo competition were Argentina, Great Britain, Spain, France, and the United States. Hitchcock led the American team, which included the tall Californian Elmer J. Boeseke, Rodman Wanamaker, and Fred Roe from Pennsylvania. In a round-robin format, the U.S. and Argentine teams easily disposed of the others, so the decisive game came down to those two. The match, played in a light rain, was tied until the final seconds, when Jack Nelson managed to score, making the final tally Argentina 6, United States 5. This was Argentina's first-ever Olympic gold medal.

Hitchcock's successes on the polo grounds and in the business world—he was a partner in Lehman Brothers—were complemented by a happy family life. In the late 1920s he married Margaret Mellon Laughlin, a young widow with an infant son. Avoiding a church wedding, as he was Catholic and she Presbyterian, they were married at the Plaza Hotel in New York City. They had four children, two daughters and twin sons.

Hitchcock fired the American imagination more than any other polo player. It was commonly said that when he stormed onto the field, polo became a national sport. His presence drew crowds of enthusiasts to the Meadow Brook Club on Long Island, New York, for the U.S. Open Championship and the international series with Argentina and England. His famous piebald pony, Tobiano, became an icon and a great favorite of the polo crowd. An inspirational leader and a relentless player, Hitchcock was also a shrewd strategist of the game. His *Rules and Tactics*, issued to his teammates prior to the 1930 international series, has been reprinted several times and remains current today.

Most of Hitchcock's career in polo took place during what has been called the golden era of American sport. His name was as well known in his day as were the names Babe Ruth, Bill Tilden, and Bobby Jones. No other polo player, before or since, has projected his charisma and been as instantly recognizable. Hitchcock was a member of five unbeaten Westchester Cup teams—in 1921, 1924, 1927, 1930, and 1936. All but the first played at Meadow Brook. He also was on the 1928 Cup of the Americas winning team; in this series the Argentines managed to take one of the three matches, finally beating the Americans in the 1936 contest. Business commitments prevented him from participating in the 1932 Cup of the Americas in Buenos Aires and the 1936 Westchester Cup, played at Hurlingham Club in London. His record in the U.S. Open stands at four championships (1923, 1927, 1935, and 1936).

Hitchcock also pursued a lifelong interest in aviation. His first airplane purchase was a Fairchild seaplane; he owned two other airplanes as well. He started the American Export Airline Company and later purchased TACA, a Latin-American air carrier. All this brought him into direct competition with the all-powerful Juan Trippe's Pan Am airline. Before much more could be accomplished, World War II started in Europe. Hitchcock's polo career came to an end, but not before he led the first forty-goal team ever—four ten-goalers, the absolute maximum—in a handicap match against a visiting British side.

Hitchcock enlisted as a pilot when the United States entered World War II. On 12 April 1944 he was killed when the Mustang fighter plane he was test-flying crashed near the ancient cathedral city of Salisbury in southern England. He was forty-four years old. His death was reported on the first page of the *New York Times*. An unidentified reporter wrote, "He was intelligent, personable, humorous, of superb physical equipment and wholly devoid of pretense . . . The best of America was in his veins—not the nonsense of any social class, but the country's intellect and character."

★

For further information, see Nelson Aldrich, *Tommy Hitchcock: An American Hero* (1985); Grantland Rice, *The Tumult and the Shouting* (1954); and David L. Porter, *Biographical Dictionary of American Sports: Outdoor Sports* (1998).

HORACE A. LAFFAYE

HOGAN, (William) Ben (*b.* 13 August 1912 in Stephenville, Texas; *d.* 25 July 1997 in Fort Worth, Texas), legendary golfer with sixty-three career wins, including all four of golf's major championships.

Hogan, the youngest of three children, was born into a hard-working, poor family. His father, Chester C. Hogan, was a blacksmith and mechanic; his mother was Clara (Williams) Hogan. Hogan's father committed suicide in 1922, when Hogan was nine, and his mother, who had been a homemaker, went to work as a seamstress at Cheney's, a small dress shop on Main Street in Fort Worth. The family had moved by then to Fort Worth, Texas, where Hogan attended public school. He quit Central High School before graduation. Schoolmates remembered him as bitter, taciturn, and aloof.

Hogan assumed responsibility for his family, selling newspapers at Fort Worth's Union Station, but at age twelve, he discovered he could earn more, 65 cents a round, as a caddie. He began his golfing career, walking seventeen miles to work as a shop boy at Forth Worth's Glen Garden Country Club. Hogan was driven by three needs: "I didn't want to be a burden to my mother. Two, I needed to put food on the table. Three, I needed a place to sleep." The caddie yard was like reform school. Newcomers were bullied, and skinny little Hogan was stuffed in a barrel and pushed down a hill. As he said later, "For a new caddie to break in, he had to win a fistfight with one of the older, bigger caddies. So they threw me in against one of those fellas, and I got the better of him."

Hogan was left-handed but, unable to afford left-handed clubs, mastered a right-handed grip. He turned pro

Ben Hogan, 1940. © BETTMANN/CORBIS

in 1929 at age seventeen, and joined the tour two years later. He spent sixteen years overcoming a pull hook, replacing it with a slight fade by gripping with his right hand on top with the V pointing to his chin. These changes resulted in a higher, straighter ball flight than the leftward hook, and allowed a more consistent high fade. Hogan got distance by the use of his body and favorable hand action at the moment of impact. He weighed only 137 pounds, yet became one of the longest hitters the game has ever known.

Hogan married his hometown sweetheart Valerie Fox on 14 April 1935; they had no children. The couple traveled together to tournaments on such a limited food budget that they once lived on purloined oranges for two weeks. Hogan finally started winning in 1938, and by 1940 was considered a serious contender. He placed second in six consecutive tournaments and won Pinehurst's North and South Open. He was golf's leading moneymaker in 1940 ($10,656); in 1941 ($18,358); in 1942 ($13,143); and earned a gross income of almost $90,000 in 1943.

At the peak of his form, Hogan served in the Army Air Corps for two and a half years, from 1943 to 1945, and was stationed in the United States. During the war, Bobby Jones played with Hogan in a Chicago tournament. He said, "Ben Hogan is the hardest worker I've ever seen. . . . He thinks only in terms of birdies. His goal is never the green. It's the cup."

After an honorable discharge as an Army Air Force lieutenant, Hogan returned to the Professional Golfers Association (PGA) tournament schedule. He shortened his backswing and adopted "the Hogan stance." He won the Portland Open in 1946 with a 27-under-par, 72-hole score of 261. Averaging 65 strokes over 18 holes, Hogan set a PGA record. Fred Corcoran, PGA director, called this round "golf's masterpiece." Hogan again was the tour's leading moneymaker for 1946 and 1948. In 1947, while walking out to the practice tee in Fort Worth, he suddenly realized, "I've learned to play golf."

Before Hogan came on the scene, professional golfers rarely practiced between tournaments. Hogan putted on hotel rugs for practice and examined grass blades on greens to improve his putts. He worked for "the tempo" with calloused hands that sometimes bled. Someone compared Hogan's golf drive to a machine stamping out bottle caps. Golfers emulated Hogan's golfing style and mimicked his professional attire of white linen caps, beige shirts, beige and gray cardigans, and neatly pressed slacks.

At Norwood Hills, St. Louis, the site of the 1948 PGA title tournament, Hogan suffering with a sore back, complained about the year-round PGA schedule, "I want to die an old man, not a young one." He rallied, picked up a $3,500 winning check, took one day's rest, and rushed off to Fort Worth to play the 72 hole Colonial National Invitation Tournament.

After wins for Hogan in 1947 and 1948 at the U.S. Open Riviera in Los Angeles, caddies named the course, "Hogan's Alley." Hogan scored 276, chopping 5 strokes off the U.S. Open record, broken by Gene Sarazen 26 years earlier. Although Riviera was his, Hogan claimed, "There's no such thing as a course that fits a man's playing style."

Hogan's mystique was limitless. Jimmy Demaret, a fellow golfer, observed, "Nobody gets close to Ben Hogan." Hogan attracted curious onlookers—from champion golfers to weekend duffers. Annoyed by spectators, he said, "The change-jinglers always wait until you reach the top of your backswing, then there's a silence like a kitchen clock stopping."

Hogan was a golfing legend and a hero to nongolfers. On 2 February 1949, while returning home to Fort Worth, he and his wife were involved in a near-fatal car accident. Hogan bravely threw himself across his wife, Valerie, sparing her from death. Hogan's heroic act, life-threatening injury, miraculous return to golf on bandaged legs, and triumphal championship wins following the accident, were immortalized in the movie, *Follow the Sun* (1951).

Sixteen months after the accident, Hogan won the 1950 U.S. Open at Merion, Pennsylvania. With a 36-hole final, he delivered a memorable one-iron shot, forcing a three-way playoff. In a four-stroke victory, Hogan shot 69 to defeat Lloyd Mangrum and George Fazio.

Hogan's best season was in 1953, at age forty-one. He won five of six 72-hole tournaments, and three major championships—his first and only British Open at Carnoustie, the Masters, and the U.S. Open. Before the modern Grand Slam, Hogan chose the Open over the USPGA, which finished the day before the Open. On his return to the United States after his British Open championship, he received a ticker-tape parade on Broadway, the first given to a golfer since the 1930 parade for Bobby Jones.

Hogan was the author of *Power Golf* (1948), and of *Five Lessons: The Modern Fundamentals of Golf* (1957), aimed at improving the games of golfers, especially those shooting 85–90 who want to shoot 75. Hogan wrote, "Contrary to anything you may have read on the subject, there is no such individual as a born golfer. Some have more natural ability than others, but they've all been made."

In the 1946 National Open Championship at Canterbury Country Club in Cleveland, Ohio, Hogan's nine iron was lost or stolen. "I've never been able to find a nine iron since which 'feels' as good to me as my old one," he said later. In 1947 he broke his favorite driver of ten years. Interested in superior clubs, he designed golf equipment, manufactured by the Ben Hogan Company. Future champion Gary Player once called Hogan for golf tips. "Mr. Hogan, I wonder if I could ask you for some advice?" Hogan asked Player, "Do you play Ben Hogan clubs, son?" "No, I play Dunlop clubs, sir." "Well, then," Hogan quipped, "call Mr. Dunlop."

Hogan approached life and golf with the same determined spirit. His drive for excellence, analytical devotion to practice, and dedicated seriousness altered the game of golf and how golfers would view it forever. His steel-gray eyes seemed foreboding. He received several nicknames—"Bantam Ben," "The Hawk," and "Wee Ice Mon"—but no one dared call him "Ben." He was simply "Hogan."

Hogan concentrated on improvement throughout his golfing career. He shunned praise and considered golf a job to get done and do well. When golf enthusiasts touted his natural swing, Hogan muttered, "There's nothing natural about the golf swing." In the 1967 Masters, at age fifty-four Hogan set a record by shooting the back nine in 30 strokes, a gratifying moment in his career. Hard work and practice were the earmarks of Hogan's success, with daily sessions at the range well into his seventies. Hogan told *Golf Digest* in 1978, "There is not enough daylight in a day to practice all the shots you ought to be practicing." Hogan had colon cancer surgery in 1995, suffered from Alzheimer's disease, and died of a stroke in his Fort Worth home at age eighty-four. He is buried in Fort Worth's Greenwood Mausoleum.

Between 1940 and 1956 Hogan played in thirty majors and placed in the top five twenty-two times. From 1940 through 1960, Hogan scored in the top ten in the U.S. Open. He was Masters runner-up four times—never less than seventh from 1941 though 1956. In all, Hogan won a total of nine major championships: two Masters (1951, 1953); four U.S. Opens (1948, 1950, 1951, 1953); two PGAs (1946, 1948); one British Open (1953, breaking the course record); and ended his career with sixty-three victories, third behind Sam Snead (81) and Jack Nicklaus (70). Hogan has been lauded as the greatest golfer of all time, greater even than Harry Vardon and Bobby Jones. A humble perfectionist, Hogan once remarked, "I'm the sole judge of my standards."

★

Curt Sampson, *Hogan* (1996), is the definitive biography on Hogan's life. David Leadbetter, *The Fundamentals of Hogan* (2000), reviews Hogan's practice habits. Some of the best magazine articles about Hogan's early years are: "The Weary Hogan," *Newsweek* (7 June 1948) and "Down Hogan's Ailey [*sic*]," *Time* (21 June 1948). Tributes to Hogan's life are "The Pain in Perfection," *The New York Times Book Review* (4 Jan. 1998); "The Mystique Lives On," *Sports Illustrated* (4 Aug. 1997); "Eulogies: The Master," *Time* (4 Aug. 1997); and "Ben Hogan," *Golf Magazine* (Oct. 1997). An obituary is in the *New York Times* (26 July 1997).

SANDRA REDMOND PETERS

HOLDSCLAW, Chamique Shaunta (*b.* 9 August 1977 in Flushing, New York), four-time All-American and professional basketball player known for her grace and style on and off the court.

Holdsclaw grew up playing basketball on the cement courts outside of her grandmother's housing project, Astoria Houses, in Queens. Holdsclaw is the eldest child of Bonita Holdsclaw, a data entry clerk, and Willie Johnson, a car mechanic. Her parents' struggle with alcohol often left Holdsclaw caring for her younger brother, Davon. The children would often steal money from their parents in order to buy dinner. Holdsclaw always had to be strong and driven.

When Holdsclaw was eleven years old her unmarried parents split, her mother entered treatment for alcoholism, and she and Davon went to live with their grandmother June. Although Astoria Houses was a tough and sometimes violent neighborhood of twenty different buildings, her grandmother gave Holdsclaw the structure and security she

Chamique Holdsclaw. AP/WIDE WORLD PHOTOS

had never had with her parents. After catching Holdsclaw skipping school, her grandmother placed her in Queens Lutheran, a small private school, and enrolled her in ballet and jazz classes. Grandmother Holdsclaw also made certain that homework was completed right after school and took the children to church every Sunday. Eventually, Davon went back to live with Bonita, but Chamique chose to stay with her grandmother.

Holdsclaw's uncle Thurman introduced her to basketball when she was nine, but she did not play regularly until moving to her grandmother's. Under the watchful eye of her grandmother, Holdsclaw began playing ball with neighborhood boys. Soon she was hooked and earned the nickname "Flat Out" because she would flat out quit anything to play basketball. Between basketball, her grandmother, and good friends she avoided the pitfalls of inner-city life.

Holdsclaw's experience with organized basketball began at Christ the King High School, from which she graduated as the all-time school leader in scoring (2,118 points) and rebounds (1,532). Coach Vinny Cannizzaro already had one of the top basketball programs when Tyrone Green, Astoria House after-school program director, told him he needed to see Holdsclaw play. Cannizzaro expected to see Holdsclaw playing with other girls and was shocked to find her the only girl on the court. Within just a few minutes he knew he had to recruit Holdsclaw.

She led the team to four state titles and a record of 106–4 by her graduation in 1995. Averaging 24.8 points and 15.9 rebounds per game during her senior year, she became the school's all-time scoring leader. She also earned New York's Miss Basketball title three times and the Naismith Award for the best female high school player in the United States (1995). Holdsclaw received a good deal of national exposure during her high school career. Cannizzaro ran the Amateur Athletic Union (AAU) program for girls during the summer. These teams traveled and competed in tournaments to showcase players for college coaches.

Fiercely recruited—by the time she was a junior she was getting upwards of twenty letters a day—Holdsclaw chose the University of Tennessee–Knoxville and Pat Summitt's Lady Vols. Tennessee was not the initial frontrunner; even Coach Summitt doubted whether a big city girl would come to live in Tennessee. In the end Holdsclaw was impressed with Tennessee's graduation rate, its stress on academics, and the overall structure and discipline of the program. She was also influenced by her grandmother, June Holdsclaw, who liked Pat Summitt and believed that Chamique would benefit from going to a southern school. The University of Tennessee was her second college visit; she did not go on any others.

Her college career was nothing less than spectacular. Earning a starting position her freshman year, Holdsclaw led the team in scoring and rebounding as well as to the National Collegiate Athletic Association (NCAA) championship. In her first week of play she was named Southeastern Conference Player of the Week, averaging nearly thirteen points per game over her first three games. She was also the only freshman named to the All-America first team. Also her freshman year, ESPN named her the College Basketball Player of the Week, the first time a woman had been so honored.

Holdsclaw's sophomore season was much tougher. That year the team lost ten games, more than any other Lady Vol squad. Individually, however, Holdsclaw was having a good season, scoring an average of 20.2 points a game. Despite regular season difficulties the Lady Vols took home a second national championship, making them the second women's team to win consecutive national titles. During Holdsclaw's junior year she led the Lady Vols to their third consecutive NCAA title and a perfect 39–0 season, the best record in either women's or men's basketball. Her performance earned her the Final Four Most Valuable Player Award. A fourth national title, however, eluded the Lady Vols in 1999. This was the first time Holdsclaw had not taken home a championship title since junior high.

Overall Holdsclaw boasted an amazing college record. She led her team to three consecutive titles, a total record of 131–17; she set NCAA tournament and university records for scoring, with 3,025 career points, and rebounding, with 1,295 rebounds. She became the first female basketball player to win the James E. Sullivan Memorial Award given to the nation's top amateur athlete. Holdsclaw graduated in 1999 with a B.A. degree in political science. Always a solid student, Holdsclaw opted to remain in school when the Women's National Basketball Association (WNBA) was organized and finish her degree, honoring a promise she had made to her grandmother. The University recognized her contribution to the sport and school by naming a campus street for her, and she is one of the few Lady Vols players who have had their jerseys retired. During her first three collegiate seasons, Holdsclaw earned All-American honors and All-America from 1996–1997 to 1998–1999. In June 1998 Holdsclaw was awarded the Honda-Broderick Cup, given annually to the nation's most outstanding female collegiate athlete.

Holdsclaw's collegiate career also included international play. During summers she played on the U.S. National Women's Basketball Team. The youngest and only college player on the national team, Holdsclaw led her professional and Olympic teammates in scoring and rebounding in 1997 and became USA Basketball's Female Athlete of the Year.

Holdsclaw began her professional career when she was chosen as the first-round draft pick by the Washington Mystics in the WNBA draft. She was the only rookie voted onto the WNBA All Star team during the inaugural year

(1999) for the WNBA All-Star game. While the Mystics still struggle on the court, their record has improved with Holdsclaw's help. In her first year with the Mystics, Holdsclaw averaged 16.9 points per game and started thirty-one of thirty-two games. Holdsclaw received the 1999 WNBA Rookie of the Year award for her first year with the Mystics, and she continues to play strong and influence the game. In 2000 she was given the Naismith Award for women's player of the century.

Holdsclaw revolutionized the world of women's basketball, taking it to a new level of intensity. Her versatility and skill set her apart from past players. She can elevate above male adversaries and dominate the game. Throughout all her hardship and success, Holdsclaw has remained humble and ever thankful. An issue of *SLAM,* a magazine for NBA fans, states, "Holdsclaw should be overdosing on attitude. But she isn't. Never has."

More insight can be found in her first advertising commercial. She told Nike she wanted her first commercial to be personal. They came up with several options, and she chose the one in which she recites part of Psalm 23, which is also why she wears jersey 23. Her grandmother instilled in her a strong faith in God. Her faith and her character make her an outstanding role model for young players, especially girls. Holdsclaw lives in Alexandria, Virginia, with her boyfriend, Larry Williams. The couple met during Holdsclaw's freshman year at UTK.

★

With Jennifer Frey, Holdsclaw wrote *Chamique: On Family, Focus, and Basketball* (2000), in which she discusses growing up in New York, her grandmother, and her first impressions of Tennessee. Pat Head Summitt with Sally Jenkins, *Raise the Roof: The Inspiring Story of the Tennessee Lady Vols' Undefeated 1997–1998 Season* (1998), gives an account of the Lady Vols' undefeated season. HBO did an excellent documentary on the Lady Vols during Holdsclaw's sophomore season called *A Cinderella Season: The Lady Vols Fight Back* (1998). There are numerous articles written about Holdsclaw; two of the most interesting are "Chamique Holdsclaw" in *Biography Today* (Sept. 2000) and "Is Chamique Holdsclaw Ready for the NBA?" in *SLAM* (Oct. 1998).

LISA A. ENNIS

HOLMAN, Nathan ("Nat") (*b.* 19 October 1896 in New York City; *d.* 12 February 1995 in New York City), professional basketball player, college coach, member of the original Celtics, and recipient of many awards for playing professionally and for coaching at City College of New York (CCNY).

Holman was the son of the Russian Jewish immigrants Louis Holman, who operated a grocery store, and Mary Goldman Holman. Holman's interest in basketball, football, baseball, and soccer began in New York's Seward Park and the Educational Alliance and Henry Street Settlement. With six brothers and three sisters, he ascribed the development of his athletic prowess in four sports to the influence of his brothers, who were heavily involved in athletics. Contemporaries described Holman's basketball play as characterized by a tantalizing and deceptive change of pace, flawless dribbling and passing with an uncanny eye for spotting an open teammate. He was capable of accurate shooting from the outside or on a dead run, and he possessed excellent defensive skills, including an inherent ability to anticipate every move of his teammates and opponents on the floor. Upon graduating from New York's Commerce High in 1913, Holman matriculated to the Savage School of Physical Education while simultaneously signing to play with the professional Knickerbocker Big Five.

Holman received a B.S. degree in 1917 and accepted appointment as instructor of hygiene and coach of soccer and freshman basketball at City College of New York (CCNY). After serving a year in the U.S. Navy during World War I, he returned to CCNY and was named head basketball coach for the 1919–1920 season. His selection made him the youngest head coach in the country at twenty-three years old and simultaneously marked the completion of his master's degree at New York University (NYU).

Holman played on twelve additional professional teams, including a stint in 1917–1918 with independent teams in and around New York City when professional leagues suspended play during World War I. From the time he was selected as CCNY's head coach until 1930, Holman played a tortuous schedule of professional games. This was possible because collegiate teams played primarily on Saturday nights, and the entire season schedule ranged from thirteen to seventeen games. Also the ease of travel by railroad on the East Coast allowed Holman and other professionals to play six and seven nights a week, often finishing up with two on Sunday.

Before embarking on an illustrious career with the original Celtics, Holman played for the New York Whirlwinds, a new team organized by the boxing promoter Ted Rickard, who challenged the original Celtics to a three-game series during the spring of 1921. The first game, won by the Whirlwinds 40–27, was played before a crowd of 11,000 in New York City's Seventy-first Regiment Armory. The second contest drew a crowd of 8,000 in the Sixty-ninth Regiment Armory, where the Celtics prevailed in a tight game, 26–24. The third game was not played, and the *Reach Guide* (1921) explained the reasons for its cancellation: "The series created so much interest that certain gamblers tried to connect in the fixing of one of the games. Thanks to two of the games' star players, a basketball Black Sox Scandal

Nat Holman waves from atop his CCNY players, which had just won the 1950 NCAA tournament. ASSO-
CIATED PRESS AP

was averted." (The reference was to baseball's 1919 World Series, in which eight Chicago White Sox players dumped the series to Cincinnati.) Since gambling on professional basketball was not uncommon among owners, players, spectators, and referees, the *Reach Guide* explanation appears the most plausible among a litany of reasons presented by writers.

Holman played exclusively for the original Celtics from 1921 to 1928 and established himself as one of the premier professional players of the era. The Celtics' owners, James A. Furey and his brother Thomas Furey, prevented players from switching teams by signing them to exclusive contracts with generous salaries for that time. Scheduling as many as 200 games in a season, the team compiled a winning percentage of .900 and became one of the first four teams voted into the Naismith Basketball Hall of Fame. After the Celtics disbanded, Holman played two more professional seasons.

His playing exploits are best exemplified by his numerous awards. He was inducted into the Naismith Memorial Hall of Fame and the Helms Hall of Fame, was named as the third greatest player of the half-century, was chosen by *Sport Magazine* to the All-Time College All-America second team, and was chosen for Ed Wachter's All-Pro first team in 1941. He married Ruth Jackson in 1945; she died in 1967.

Holman's CCNY teams played within a team concept—short passes, set shooting, a tenacious switching man-to-man defense, an offense revolving around several

pivot plays, and continual movement without the ball. This style of play led to several outstanding seasons, including 1923 (12–1), 1924 (12–1), 1932 (16–1), 1933 (13–1), and 1934 (14–1), and an overall record of 422 wins and 188 losses (.692). Of course the 1950–1951 team, the only team to win the National Invitational Tournament (NIT) and the National Collegiate Athletic Association (NCAA) Tournament in the same season, was Holman's best because it was number one in the country. But during the 1951–1952 season events began to unfold that washed away most of the luster garnered by the "grand slam" team. Seven team members had been doing business with gamblers, and CCNY was heavily implicated in the first major gambling scandal in college basketball's history.

Despite Holman's self-serving pronouncements of innocence after the scandals were exposed, a thorough investigation by the governing body of public colleges in New York City uncovered a number of athletic abuses in the CCNY program. These included forging of transcripts, matriculation of unqualified students, failure by Holman to report to higher authorities an incidence of a bribe attempt, and Holman's sanctioning of an exhibition basketball trip by CCNY players to South America, where they received a kickback from local promoters. Holman was also excoriated by Judge Saul S. Streit, who believed the pronouncements by Holman and other coaches of their naïveté regarding illegal gambling on college basketball "was comical." Holman was dismissed by the New York City Board of Higher

Education, but he appealed the decision to the New York State commissioner of education, who rescinded the board's action and reinstated Holman as the CCNY head coach for the 1954–1955 season. After retiring in 1960, Holman continued to operate his basketball camp and promoted basketball in Israel. He granted interviews to writers selectively because of his reluctance to discuss the 1951 scandal.

★

Holman's two books, *Scientific Basketball* (1922) and *Holman on Basketball* (1950), are primarily treatises on his coaching strategies. Three of the best sources describing Holman's career as a basketball player are Bernard Postal, Jesse Silver, and Roy Silver, *Encyclopedia of Jews in Sports* (1955); Robert W. Peterson, *Cages to Jump Shots: Pro Basketball's Early Years* (1990); and Murray Nelson, *The Original Celtics: The New York Celtics Invent Modern Basketball* (1999). Holman's role in the 1951 scandals is objectively recounted in Charles Rosen, *Scandals of '51: How the Gamblers Almost Killed College Basketball* (1979); Stanley Cohen, *The Game They Played* (1977); and Albert Figone, "Gambling and College Basketball: The Scandal of 1951," *Journal of Sport History* 16, no. 1 (spring 1989). An obituary is in the *New York Times* (13 Feb. 1995).

AL FIGONE

HORNSBY, Rogers ("Rajah") (*b.* 27 April 1896 near Winters, Texas; *d.* 5 January 1963 in Chicago, Illinois), baseball player whose .358 lifetime batting average in the major leagues is the highest ever compiled by a right-handed batter and second only to Ty Cobb's among all players.

Hornsby was the youngest of five children born to Aaron Edward Hornsby, a farmer and rancher, and Mary Dallas Rogers, a homemaker. When he was two years old, his father died, and his mother moved the family from their small farm in Runnels County in west-central Texas back eastward to Travis County, where both father and mother had grown up. A few years later the Hornsbys moved to Fort Worth, a thriving meat-packing center. At Fort Worth, Hornsby attended school through the tenth grade, worked as a checker at the stockyards, and developed his skills as a baseball player on stockyard and city-league teams.

Hornsby began his professional baseball career in 1914 at the bottom of the minor leagues at Hugo, Oklahoma. That summer and the next season, which he spent at Denison, Texas, in the Western Association, Hornsby batted only .232 and .277 and, playing shortstop most of the time, erred frequently. However, a scout for the St. Louis Cardinals of the National League (NL) liked what he saw in the youngster, who stood just under six feet tall but weighed only 135 pounds. Lacking the finances to purchase proven players from the higher minor leagues, the Cardinals paid Denison $500 for Hornsby's contract. During one month of the 1915 season with the St. Louis team, Hornsby could manage only fourteen hits in eighteen games.

Although he had done little to impress Cardinal manager Miller Huggins, Hornsby was determined to stick in the major leagues. He spent the off-season at his uncle's farm at Lockhart, Texas, eating heartily and gaining at least thirty pounds. When he reported for spring training with the Cardinals at San Antonio, he was bigger and stronger. Standing as far back in the batter's box and as far away from home plate as possible and holding his 36-inch, 38-ounce bat at its end, he repeatedly sent the ball to the far distances of the outfield. Kept on the St. Louis roster when the season began, Hornsby established himself as a big-leaguer, batting .313, which was the fourth-best mark in the league. Although the financially strapped Cardinals remained a run-of-the-mill team, Hornsby emerged as a full-fledged star, averaging .327 in 1917, slumping to .281 in the war-shortened 1918 season, climbing back to .318 in 1919, and then, in 1920, winning his first batting title at .370 and also leading the NL with 98 runs batted in.

For the next five seasons, Hornsby led the NL in batting. After .397, .401, and .384 seasons, the Texan reached his peak with a .424 average in 1924, the highest batting average for any major-leaguer in the twentieth century, and came back to hit .405 the next season. He also became the NL's foremost power hitter in a decade when the baseball was livelier, the spitball and other "trick pitches" had been made illegal, and increasing numbers of players were emulating the free-swinging style of Babe Ruth in the American League (AL). Hornsby's forty-two home runs in 1922 and thirty-nine in 1925 were more than anyone other than Ruth had hit up to then.

Settling at second base by 1921, Hornsby was never more than passable as a fielder, but no one doubted his greatness as a hitter. In 1926 he struggled most of the season with a back injury and batted only .317, but as player-manager, he led the Cardinals to their first NL pennant and then to an upset of Ruth and the mighty New York Yankees in a legendary seven-game 1926 World Series.

Hornsby read little and rarely attended motion pictures, convinced that both reading and moviegoing were bad for a hitter's eyesight. He lived by the admonitions of his widowed mother (who died in 1926): shun tobacco and liquor, and always tell the truth. However admirable in principle strict truthfulness may be, Hornsby frequently came across as caustic, insufferably tactless, and totally insensitive to the opinions and feelings of others. He did indulge in one major vice—gambling on horse races. Although he made some of the biggest salaries of his time, he lost substantially, ran up debts to bookmakers and other players, and repeat-

Rogers Hornsby, 1927. ASSOCIATED PRESS AP

his teams won pennants in the Texas League and Pacific Coast League in 1950 and 1951, he returned to the majors as manager of the Browns. There he lasted only fifty games before he was fired by Bill Veeck, the equally headstrong president of the struggling franchise. Later in that 1952 season, Hornsby signed to manage the NL's Cincinnati Reds; that job lasted only until September 1953, when he was fired again—for the last time. From then on, Hornsby worked in youth baseball clinics in Chicago and as a batting coach for the Cubs and the expansion-franchise New York Mets. He was still employed by the Mets when he died of a heart attack following cataract surgery, and his body was buried in the Hornsby family cemetery near Austin, Texas.

Hornsby was married three times. He wed Sarah Martin in 1918, but that marriage ended in 1922 as a consequence of his well-publicized affair with Mary Jeannette Pennington Hine, a St. Louis divorcee. Married in 1924, Hornsby and his second wife were estranged for several years before her death in 1956. The next year he married Marjorie Bernice Frederick Porter, a Chicago widow, and they were married until Hornsby's death. He was the father of two sons, the first with Martin, and the second with Hine.

Hornsby was a great baseball player, but he never learned much about human relations. "I have never been a yes man," he boasted a few years before his death. Baseball was his life; he cared for little else—except which horse looked good that day. Asked what he had gotten out of life, he said simply, "I wore a big-league uniform, and I had the best equipment, and I traveled in style, and I could play baseball every day. What else is there?"

★

The National Baseball Library in Cooperstown, New York, and the *Sporting News* archives in St. Louis have substantial collections relating to Hornsby. The only full-fledged biographical treatment is Charles C. Alexander, *Rogers Hornsby: A Biography* (1995). Two books were published under his name: *My Kind of Baseball* (1953), with J. Roy Stockton; and *My War with Baseball* (1953), with Bill Surface (1953). For Hornsby's career records, see Craig Carter, ed., *Daguerreotypes* (1990).

CHARLES C. ALEXANDER

edly antagonized club officials and Kenesaw Mountain Landis, baseball's dictatorial commissioner.

After the brilliant 1926 World Series triumph, Hornsby quarreled with Cardinal business manager Branch Rickey and owner Sam Breadon and was traded to the New York Giants. He played one season with the Giants for the legendary John McGraw, then was traded to the lowly Boston Braves, where he managed the team for most of the 1928 season and won his seventh and last batting title. Traded yet again, Hornsby helped power the Chicago Cubs to the 1929 NL pennant, and at the end of the following season, succeeded Joe McCarthy as Cubs manager. His chronic horse-playing and plainspoken ways got him fired midway through the 1932 season. After a brief stint as a player back with the Cardinals, Hornsby took over managership of the woeful St. Louis Browns in the AL. A desultory four years with the Browns ended in July 1937, when he was fired again.

For the next fifteen years Hornsby was a baseball vagabond, managing in the minor leagues and even briefly in Mexico, and working in radio and television. Finally, after

HORNUNG, Paul Vernon (*b.* 23 December 1935 in Louisville, Kentucky), Heisman Trophy winner and Pro Football Hall of Fame halfback who is recognized as the premier all-purpose back of the 1960s.

Hornung was an only child of Paul and Loretta Hornung. His father, an insurance agent, separated from his mother when Hornung was three. His mother worked in the personnel section of the Louisville Army Medical Depot.

A star athlete at Louisville's Flaget High School, a Cath-

Paul Hornung with his Heisman Trophy, 1956. ASSOCIATED PRESS AP

olic institution, Hornung scored a school record thirty-two points in one game and averaged just under twenty points per game as a senior. He was a standout pitcher on the school's baseball team and the starting quarterback and placekicker in football. His senior season, Hornung was named All-City, All-State and All-Catholic school quarterback while maintaining an A average. He received scholarship offers from nearly fifty major universities and surprised many observers by turning down Kentucky football coach Paul "Bear" Bryant to attend Notre Dame.

Hornung played his first game for the Notre Dame varsity as a sophomore in the 1954 season opener against Texas, handling the placekicking duties in a 21–0 victory. He saw his first action at offensive and defensive halfback against Navy in the fifth game of the season and later played quarterback for the first time as a collegian, completing five passes in a backup role in a 42–13 win over North Carolina.

Hornung also played basketball for the Fighting Irish in his sophomore year, scoring sixty-one points in ten games. Hornung became a varsity starter at quarterback his junior season, gaining 1,215 total yards to rank fourth in the country and lead Notre Dame to an 8–2 record. At the end of the 1955 season, he was named to four All-America teams. As a senior, Hornung led Notre Dame in nine statistical categories and on 4 December 1956 became the only

player to win a Heisman Trophy as a member of a losing team, the Irish having gone 2–8.

Using their bonus choice, the Green Bay Packers made Hornung the top pick in the 1957 NFL draft, and on 9 January 1957 Hornung agreed to a three-year contract at $16,000 per season. During his first two seasons with the Packers, the team went 4–19–1 under two different head coaches. Hornung's career turnaround began in 1959, when the Packers hired Vince Lombardi as head coach and general manager, and Lombardi made Hornung the team's starting left halfback.

Finally secure in knowing he would no longer be shuttled from one position to another, Hornung blossomed under Lombardi. The left halfback position was key in Lombardi's offense, and the six-foot, two-inch, 220-pound Hornung immediately established himself as a triple threat who could run, throw the option, or block for fullback Jim Taylor. Hornung and Taylor became the NFL's version of "Mr. Inside and Mr. Outside," and the Packers enjoyed a winning campaign in Lombardi's first year, finishing 7–5 in 1959. Hornung led the Packers in rushing with 681 yards and the league in scoring with 94 points on 7 touchdowns, 7 field goals, and 31 point-after conversions.

Hornung's breakthrough season came in 1960. Displaying his talents as a runner, passer, pass receiver, blocker, and placekicker, Hornung scored an NFL record 176 points to lead the Packers to an 8–4 record and the Western Conference title. He was the NFL's dominant player, rushing for thirteen touchdowns, scoring twice on pass receptions, converting fifteen of twenty-eight field goal attempts, and making forty-one straight point-after conversions.

In the 1960 NFL championship game against the Eagles in Philadelphia, Hornung suffered a third-quarter neck injury that would hinder his career, and Green Bay lost 17–13. He was drafted into the U.S. Army during the Berlin crisis and missed part of the 1961 regular season, when the Packers went 11–3 during the regular season to repeat as Western Conference champions. Hornung did score a personal-best four touchdowns and a team-record 33 points in a 45–21 win over the Baltimore Colts on 8 October. He finished the season with 146 points.

Hornung was on Christmas leave from the army when the Packers met the New York Giants in the NFL title game on 31 December 1961 in Green Bay's City Stadium. Scoring a playoff-record 19 points, Hornung enhanced his reputation as a clutch player and was named most valuable player as the Packers defeated the Giants 37–0.

Hornung opened the 1962 season in style, scoring twenty-eight points in a 34–7 win over the Minnesota Vikings on 16 September. A knee injury suffered four weeks later in a rematch against the Vikings hampered his performance and caused him to miss six games, but the Packers still rolled to another Western Conference title with a 13–1 record. In the 1962 NFL championship game, which was played against the Giants amid bitter cold and wind in Yankee Stadium on 30 December, Hornung set up the Packers' only touchdown of the game with a long completion on a halfback option pass. Green Bay won 16–7, to repeat as NFL champions.

Hollywood handsome with curly blond hair and blue eyes, Hornung gained fame as pro football's "Golden Boy." He was the NFL's most eligible bachelor and a noted playboy. But his career endured a serious setback on 17 April 1963 when NFL commissioner Pete Rozelle suspended Hornung and Detroit Lions defensive tackle Alex Karras for betting on pro football games. Hornung was contrite—he admitted he had bet on NFL games but never against the Packers.

Hornung was reinstated on 16 March 1964, but a year's absence had dulled his skills. He missed five straight field goals against Baltimore and an extra point in another game that meant the difference for the Packers between a loss and a tie. He finished the 1964 season with 107 points but converted just 12 of 38 field goal attempts.

Hornung's struggles continued in the 1965 season, and he was benched by Lombardi for three games. Reinstated for a 12 December showdown with the Colts in Baltimore, Hornung ran through a thick fog to score a new personal-best five touchdowns. Totaling 61 yards rushing and 115 receiving, Hornung starred in Green Bay's 42–27 win over the Colts. Two weeks later, the Packers and Colts met in Lambeau Field in a one-game playoff to decide the Western Conference title. Playing with an injured knee, swollen wrist, and bruised chest, Hornung scored Green Bay's lone touchdown in a 13–10 overtime victory. On 2 January 1966 the Packers faced the defending NFL champion Cleveland Browns for the NFL title. Amid ice, snow, and frozen mud, Hornung carried the ball eighteen times for a game-high 105 yards. He scored the game-clinching touchdown on a thirteen-yard sweep in the third quarter to give the Packers an eventual 23–12 victory.

Hornung was slowed in the 1966 season by the recurrence of a painful pinched nerve in his size-eighteen neck, and he missed the Packers' post-season victories over Dallas in the NFL championship game and Kansas City in the first AFL-NFL World Championship Game. Still plagued by injury, Hornung decided to retire in July 1967 rather than risk severe injury.

Hornung played the game of football with flair and skill. During his nine-year career, he rushed for 3,711 yards, scored 760 points, owned a 4.2 yards-per-carry average, and ran for 50 touchdowns. He gained an additional 1,480 yards receiving and finished his career with a total of 62 touchdowns. Hornung was famous for his good looks and clutch play, and he is generally considered one of the best big-game players and goal-line runners in NFL history.

In retirement, Hornung became a sports commentator and an analyst for Notre Dame football and enjoyed success as a businessman and real estate investor. He was inducted into the Pro Football Hall of Fame in 1986 and is also a member of the Packers' Hall of Fame.

★

There are two books about Hornung. The first is Dick Schaap, *Paul Hornung: Pro Football Golden Boy* (1962), the second, an autobiography, is *Football and the Single Man,* as told to Al Silverman (1965). Hornung's life and career are chronicled in Jack Hand, *Great Running Backs of the NFL* (1966), and Lud Duroska, *Great Pro Running Backs* (1973).

EDWARD GRUVER

HOWE, Gordon ("Gordie") (*b.* 31 March 1928 in Floral, Saskatchewan, Canada), National Hockey League superstar who was named Canada's Athlete of the Year in 1963 and elected to the Hockey Hall of Fame in 1972.

Howe was one of nine children of Albert Howe, a mechanic, laborer, and construction worker, and Katherine Schultz Howe, a homemaker. Howe's first skates were discovered in a "grab bag," which his mother had traded for a few cents to a neighbor who needed milk for her baby. When Howe outgrew them, he played goal, because it was one position on his school team he could manage without blades. Although he was diagnosed as having a calcium deficiency in his backbone and warned that a severe blow might easily break his back, Howe continued to skate. Howe's natural hockey skills earned him All-Star standing in school and in minor hockey leagues, and eventually a berth on the local "Senior" team. A scout for the New York Rangers spotted the talented fifteen-year-old, and he was invited to the Rangers' training camp in Winnipeg in 1943. Howe had never had full equipment available before, and he avoided embarrassment by watching other players put on their gear, piece by piece. Lonely and homesick, he left camp prematurely and returned to Saskatoon; and Rangers' manager Lester Patrick declared Howe was not NHL (National Hockey League) material.

Fortunately, Fred Pinkney, a scout for the Detroit Red Wings, did not give up as quickly on this fine professional prospect. Assured that other players from his home area would accompany him to the Red Wings training camp in Windsor, Ontario, Howe agreed to go. He immediately impressed Coach Jack Adams. "Jolly Jawn," as Adams was affectionately known, was especially taken with the teenager's ability to shoot either from the right or left side, a trait that enhanced his wizardry in scoring for years to come. Howe was assigned to Detroit's junior squad in Galt, Ontario, and the following season signed his first professional contract with Omaha Knights of the United States League.

Success did not come immediately for Howe, who would eventually be called "Mr. Hockey." He rode the bench for the first part of the 1946 season with the Omaha farm sextet and scored only seven goals in his first full campaign with the parent club. But as the 1947–1948 season got under way, Howe was teamed with veteran Sid Abel and a belligerent left winger named Ted Lindsay. The famous "Production Line" was born, and Howe's personal career took off. The milestones soon began to add up. Howe scored his 100th goal on 17 February 1951; his 200th almost two years later to the day; his 300th on 7 February 1956; his 400th on 13 December 1958; and his 500th on 14 March 1962. The next rung on his ladder to NHL scoring supremacy was goal number 545 on 19 November 1963, a scoring total which surpassed that of the retired Maurice "Rocket" Richard and launched Howe into first place in league history. Howe ultimately achieved a record-setting 801 goals in regular season play over his professional career and established several other NHL records, including most seasons played (26), most regular-season games (1,767), and most selections to NHL all-star teams (21 selections— 12 times to the first team, 9 to the second). Howe's other

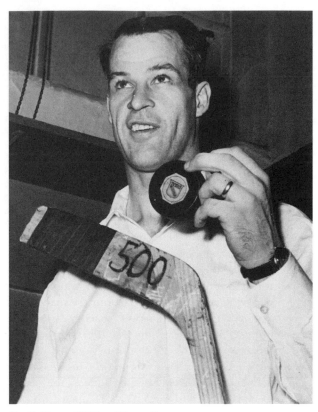

Gordie Howe. AP/WIDE WORLD PHOTOS

NHL records include most winning goals (122), most games including playoffs (1,924), and most career points by a right winger (1,850). Howe spent twenty-five NHL seasons with Detroit and one with Hartford.

Howe married Colleen Joffa in 1953. They had four children, two of whom, Mark and Marty, followed their father into the NHL. When the Houston Aeros of the fledgling World Hockey Association (WHA) ignored the age limit for drafting junior players and claimed the Howe brothers in the summer of 1973, the Texas management invited their forty-five-year-old father, who had retired from the Red Wings two years earlier, to join the team as well. When the trio skated out on the ice for the first scheduled game, a precedent was set—the first father-son combination in a professional hockey game. The three appeared on the ice together again in the 1979–1980 season when the Howes were playing for the New England Whalers in Hartford, and Howe became the first grandfather to play professional hockey.

Howe's trophy room abounds with awards and plaques. He won both the Art Ross Trophy (leading scorer) and the Hart Memorial Trophy (Most Valuable Player) six times, the last time at the age of thirty-eight. He was selected as Canada's Athlete of the Year in 1963 and chosen to receive the Lester Patrick Trophy for outstanding service to U.S.

hockey in 1967. He received the Order of Canada medal in 1971.

There is no record of Howe ever losing a fight in the major leagues. He often had to defend himself against illegal tactics that opponents used to stop him, but he maintained, "I come to play hockey, not to fight!" Although many skaters insisted he was liberal with the use of his elbows, Hall of Famer Bobby Hull disagreed: "If you want to play hockey, he'll play; but if guys want to fool around, they always come out second best!"

Howe has been showered with countless tributes. In 1959 "Gordie Howe Night" was staged at the Detroit Olympia; in 1966 the city of Saskatoon gave him a "day" and named a sports complex for him; in March 1971 Toronto held a formal reception for him at City Hall; and on Labor Day that same year, the City of Detroit honored him in like fashion. Former Canadian Prime Minister Lester B. Pearson summarized the spirit of all the tributes: "Both on the ice and off, Gordie Howe's conduct has demonstrated a high quality of sportsmanship and competence that is an example to us all. He has earned the title: Mr. Hockey."

Howe survived many injuries (including one that threatened his life), a kidney stone, surgery on his arthritic wrist, a death threat, and three hundred stitches, on his way to playing more major-league (NHL and WHA combined) games (2,186) and scoring more regular-season goals (975) than any other player in history. In 1998 Howe participated in a game with the International Hockey League's Detroit Vipers, becoming the first hockey player to appear in a professional game in each of six decades.

★

Biographical works include Jim Vipond, *Gordie Howe, Number 9* (1971); Gordon Howe and Colleen Howe, *After the Applause* (1990), written with Charles Wilkins; Gordon Howe and Colleen Howe, *And Howe* (1995), written with Tom Delisle; and Frank Conron, *Gordie Howe: My Hockey Memories* (1999). See also *The Total Hockey Encyclopedia* (2000).

GLEN GOODHEAD

HUBBARD, (Robert) Cal (*b.* 31 October 1900 in Keytesville, Missouri; *d.* 17 October 1977 in Saint Petersburg, Florida), college and professional football player and major league baseball umpire who was one of the greatest linemen in football history and was named to the college football, professional football, and baseball Halls of Fame.

Hubbard was one of five children born to Robert P. Hubbard, a farmer, and Sally Ford, a homemaker. Raised in north-central Missouri, Hubbard attended Glasgow High School, where he participated in football and track, and eventually transferred to Keytesville High School, from

Cal Hubbard, 1932. © BETTMANN/CORBIS

which he graduated in 1919. He then attended a business college in Chillicothe, Missouri, while working at a variety of odd jobs.

Hubbard enrolled in 1922 at Centenary College in Shreveport, Louisiana, so that he could play football under the direction of the coach Alvin "Bo" McMillin. With good size and speed, Hubbard was a standout at guard and tackle for three seasons as Centenary compiled an overall record of 26–3–0 from 1922 to 1924. He was selected as a Second-Team All-American for 1924 by the sportswriter Lawrence Perry.

When McMillin moved to Geneva College in Beaver Falls, Pennsylvania, in 1925, Hubbard also transferred and, after sitting out one season of ineligibility, took over as an end for Geneva in 1926. Again a standout, he received a First-Team All-America selection from the *New York World* and a third-team berth from the International News Service (INS), as Geneva posted a record of 8–2–0 that included a 16–7 upset win over Harvard University. Hubbard graduated from Geneva in 1927 with a B.A. and, after being pursued by three professional football teams, decided to sign with the New York Giants of the National Football League (NFL) as a linebacker and offensive tackle for $150 per game. He married Ruth Frishkorn on 27 November 1927; the couple had two sons.

Hubbard was an agile lineman and had good lateral movement, which, combined with his speed (100-yard dash in eleven seconds), allowed him to overtake and tackle ball carriers. He also was very strong and one of the larger players (six feet, two inches and 253 pounds) in the NFL, and he was regarded as a rugged "straight-ahead" tackler and a devastating blocker. An easygoing and even-tempered man off the field, his physical capabilities usually brought him the role of team "policeman" in dealing with overaggressive opposition players.

With Hubbard sparking a defense that allowed just twenty points in thirteen games, the Giants won the NFL championship in 1927 with an 11–1–1 record. But on a road trip to Green Bay, Wisconsin, in 1928, Hubbard was greatly impressed by the small-town atmosphere and soon demanded that he be traded to the Packers. Along with Hubbard, Green Bay also acquired several other key players, and the Packers proceeded to field the NFL's first dynasty. With Hubbard missing just three games in three years and playing tackle, linebacker, and occasionally offensive end, Green Bay rolled to the NFL championship in 1929 (12–0–1), 1930 (10–3–1), and 1931 (12–2–0).

His years with Green Bay were the best of his professional football career, and when the NFL began selecting an annual All-Pro team in 1931, Hubbard was recognized as a starting tackle for the seasons of 1931 to 1933. He took a break from professional football and served as an assistant line coach at Texas A&M University in College Station in 1934, before returning to Green Bay for the 1935 season. Hubbard closed out his NFL career in 1936 playing for the New York Giants and the Pittsburgh Pirates. He returned to football briefly in 1942 as the head coach at Geneva College, where he compiled a record of 6–3–0. Hubbard's place as one of the gridiron sport's greatest names was confirmed with his election to the College Football Hall of Fame in 1962 and the Pro Football Hall of Fame in 1963.

Early in his professional football career, Hubbard had considered shaping a second career as a baseball umpire during football's off-seasons, and so he had written a letter expressing his interest to Judge William G. Bramham, an executive in minor league baseball's National Association. This initiative resulted in Hubbard's assignment as an umpire in the Piedmont League in 1928, beginning an eight-year run (1928–1935) in various minor leagues that included the prestigious International League (1931–1935).

In 1936 Hubbard was promoted to an umpire in the American League, a position he held for sixteen seasons. He became known as one of the finest umpires in major league baseball. While working as an umpire, Hubbard's eyes were once examined by the Boston Optical Laboratory, and it was determined that he had twenty-ten vision. During his career as an umpire he worked four World Series (1938, 1942, 1946, 1949) and three All-Star games (1939, 1944, 1949).

Hunting had always been an off-season pastime that Hubbard enjoyed, but when he was accidentally struck in the eye by a shotgun pellet in late 1951, his umpiring career

was ended. He was hired by the American League as an assistant supervisor of umpires in 1952, and two years later he was named the league's supervisor of umpires—a position he held for sixteen years until his retirement in late 1969. While serving as the league's umpiring supervisor, he was a strong advocate for better pay and working conditions for umpires, and also campaigned unsuccessfully for the legalization of the spitball. Hubbard was elected to the Baseball Hall of Fame in 1976 by the Veteran's Committee, making him the first individual honored by three major Halls of Fame.

A physically imposing man, Hubbard was known for his down-to-earth personality. Considered to be an outstanding duplicate-bridge player, he also enjoyed chess and music. After the death of his first wife in 1962, he married Mildred Sykes in 1963. Following his retirement from baseball, the couple lived in Milan, Missouri, on their 300-acre farm and then in Saint Petersburg, Florida, where Hubbard died at age seventy-six after a lengthy struggle with cancer. He is buried in Oakwood Cemetery in Milan.

Hubbard, recognized by many as the greatest tackle in professional football history, was named to the NFL's Fiftieth Anniversary All-Time squad. Coach McMillin described him as "the greatest football player of all time," and the coaches George Halas and Curly Lambeau called Hubbard "the best lineman" they had ever seen in professional football. An intelligent and aggressive player known for his speed and athleticism, Hubbard became a prototype for the football linebackers of the late twentieth century.

★

Accounts of Hubbard's gridiron career appear in most works on professional football history, including Alexander M. Weyand, *Football Immortals* (1962); George Sullivan, *Pro Football's All-Time Greats* (1968); and Denis J. Harrington, *The Pro Football Hall of Fame* (1991). Coverage of his baseball career is in Martin Appel and Burt Goldblatt, *Baseball's Best: The Hall of Fame Gallery* (1977). Obituaries are in the *New York Times* (18 Oct. 1977) and *Sporting News* (5 Nov. 1977).

RAYMOND SCHMIDT

HUBBELL, Carl Owen (*b.* 22 June 1903 near Carthage, Missouri; *d.* 21 November 1988 in Scottsdale, Arizona), left-handed star baseball pitcher for the New York Giants in the 1930s, who was known affectionately as "The Meal Ticket" or "King Carl," and specialized in the "screwball" pitch.

Hubbell was one of seven children born to George Owen (G. O.) Hubbell, a farmer, and Margaret Dell (Maggie) Upp Hubbell. Hubbell's father sharecropped on a rented cotton farm from 1896 to 1908 near what was then Red Oak, Missouri, outside Carthage. He also played catcher

Carl Hubbell, 1932. ASSOCIATED PRESS AP

for a local team. The family moved in 1908 to a farm near Stroud, Oklahoma, and then in 1918 to a farm outside Meeker, Oklahoma. Carl and his siblings attended Meeker High School. Some years later, this town of three hundred would announce itself as the "Home of Carl Hubbell," and the front lawn of the high school would display a sandstone statue of Hubbell hurling a baseball.

After graduation, Carl worked for an oil company as a roustabout. Playing on the firm's baseball team encouraged him to be a professional. He was destined to spend five discouraging years in the minors, beginning with Cushing in the Class D Oklahoma State League in 1923. From there he went first to the Western Association and then to the Western League, where he pitched successfully for Oklahoma City in 1925. Hubbell attended spring training with the Detroit Tigers in 1926 and 1927, who he paid $20,000 for his contract, but he did not make the team. In 1926 with Toronto in the International League, he won seven games and lost seven; the following year, playing with Decatur in the Three-I League, he won fourteen games.

The Tigers sold Hubbell in 1928 to Beaumont in the Texas League without putting him into a game. Now twenty-five years old, Hubbell made up his mind to quit baseball if he did not make it to the majors. Luck turned his way. A part-time scout for the New York Giants, Dick Kinsella, in Houston as a delegate to the Democratic presidential convention, saw Hubbell pitch a brilliant game against the Houston Buffs. He called John McGraw, the

fiery, long-term manager of the New York Giants, and urged him to acquire the skinny southpaw who stood six feet tall and weighed 170 pounds. The Giants, with whom Hubbell would spend his entire major league career, paid Beaumont a record $40,000 for him.

Hubbell was already experimenting with a "screwball," reminiscent of the "fadeaway" made famous by former Giants star Christy Mathewson. Hubbell's pitch was a curveball thrown by snapping the wrist inward so that the ball sped toward the plate away from a right-handed batter, and then, when it reached home plate, dropped to the left or right as if it had rolled off a table. Hubbell's sharp curve and good speed helped make him as effective against left-handed hitters as against right-handed ones. The screwball is hard on the elbow, and Hubbell was warned that it was going to damage his. In fact, his arm was eventually twisted so badly that the palm of his hand faced outward.

Hubbell won twenty games or more in a season five years in a row (1933–1937). His best year was 1933 when he won twenty-three games and lost twelve and was named the National League's Most Valuable Player. His earned run average, 1.66, remains the lowest ever recorded for a left-handed hurler, and he registered 156 strikeouts in 308⅔ innings. In a never-to-be-forgotten game on 6 July he pitched an eighteen-inning 1–0 shutout of the St. Louis Cardinals, allowing only six hits and striking out twelve. From 12 July to 1 August, he hurled 46⅓ scoreless innings, a record that stood for a generation when it was surpassed by Don Drysdale and Orel Hershisher. He recorded ten shutouts during the season. In the World Series against the Washington Senators, he led the Giants to victory in five games, winning game one by 4–2 and game four by 2–1, in eleven innings. His effectiveness was prodigious: he struck out the first three Senators who faced him and pitched twenty consecutive innings without yielding an earned run. In 1936, when he won his second Most Valuable Player award, Hubbell went 26 and 6, winning the last 16 in a row. He started the next season by winning his first eight decisions, his first loss not coming until Memorial Day. His streak of twenty-four consecutive wins must be measured against the old National League record of nineteen established by "Rube" Marquard also of the Giants in 1912. In his awesome sixteen-year career, Hubbell registered 253 wins against 154 losses, and in 535 games compiled a 2.98 earned run average. He was elected to the Baseball Hall of Fame in Cooperstown, New York, in 1947. The Giants retired his number 11.

Hubbell was selected as the starting pitcher for the National League in the second All-Star Game, played on 10 July 1934 at the Polo Grounds in New York, his home field. The format, showcasing the premier players of the two major leagues, was still a baseball novelty, and the public's interest was keen. In the event, the contest placed Carl Hubbell as a superstar in baseball folklore.

On that hot afternoon, the first batter for the American League, Charlie Gehringer, the star second baseman of the Detroit Tigers, singled; then Heinie Manush of the Washington Senators, the league's leading batter, walked. Both base runners shortly advanced on a double steal. At this juncture, relying chiefly on his patented pitch, with which the American League batters were mostly unfamiliar, Hubbard proceeded to strike out in succession three of the most feared sluggers baseball has known: Babe Ruth, who was called out on a screwball after going to one ball and two strikes; Lou Gehrig, who went down swinging on a three-and-two pitch; and Jimmie Foxx, who also fanned swinging. The thunderous ovation given to the Giants' ace by the throng of almost 50,000 fans was so deafening and prolonged that the ballpark appeared to shiver on its foundations. Hubbell started the second inning by striking out Al Simmons, a power-hitting outfielder of the Philadelphia Athletics; then Joe Cronin, the player-manager of the American League team, who was at shortstop. The string was finally broken when Bill Dickey, the peerless catcher of the New York Yankees, struck a single. After Hubbell and Willis Hudlin of the Cleveland Indians, the American League starter, had departed, the game became a slugfest, and the American Leaguers eventually won 9–7.

Hubbell pitched a no-hitter against the Pittsburgh Pirates on 8 May 1929. Although Hubbell's skill declined as bone chips crippled his left elbow, on Memorial Day 1940

he held the Brooklyn Dodgers to one hit and faced only twenty-seven batters (the sole base runner having been erased in a double play) in what he considered his best game ever. Only two balls had been hit to the outfield.

Hubbell married Lucille Herrington on 25 January 1930; they had two sons. After Herrington's death in 1964, Hubbell married Julia Stanfield. Hubbell became the farm director and chief of player development for the Giants following his retirement after the 1943 season. When the team moved to San Francisco in 1958, he went with them. Hubbell suffered a stroke in 1977 and afterward served as a part-time scout for the club.

The highest salary Hubbell earned in one year was $21,000, and he was living on Social Security checks at the time of his death, which followed severe head and chest injuries sustained on 19 November 1988 in an automobile crash about a mile from his home in Mesa, Arizona. Hubbell died two days later at Scottsdale Memorial Hospital and is buried in Meeker-Newhope Cemetery in Meeker.

★

Files on Carl Hubbell are in the National Baseball Library at Cooperstown, New York. His memorabilia, presented by Hubbell on his seventy-fifth birthday, are in the Carl Hubbell Museum located in Meeker City Hall. Quiet and reserved on and off the field, Hubbell was never an alluring subject for a full biography. The facts of his baseball achievements are found piecemeal in many books, whose titles speak to his standing in the history of the game. The books include Tom Meany, *Baseball's Greatest Players* (1953); Red Reeder, *On the Mound: Three Great Pitchers* (1966); Robert H. Shoemaker, *The Best in Baseball* (1974); and Donald Honig, *The Greatest Pitchers of All Time* (1988). For a description of Hubbell's most famous strikeout feat, see Donald Honig, *All-Star Game: A Pictorial History, 1933 to the Present* (1987). For Hubbell's place among his teammates, see Peter Williams, *Bill Terry and the Golden Age of New York Baseball* (1999). An obituary is in the *New York Times* (22 Nov. 1988); an appreciation by Shirley Povich is in the *Washington Post* (23 Nov. 1988).

HENRY F. GRAFF

HUGGINS, Miller James (*b.* 27 March 1879 in Cincinnati, Ohio; *d.* 25 September 1929 in New York City), National Baseball Hall of Fame manager (1964), also a fine second baseman, who led the New York Yankees to six American League pennants and three World Series championships.

Huggins grew up in the Fourth Ward of Cincinnati, then a very run-down, violent neighborhood. It was there that the short Huggins learned to stand up to people bigger than himself. He had a brother and a sister, both of whom remained close to him all his life, with his sister living with him until he died. As a teenager, Huggins played second

Miller Huggins, 1928. ASSOCIATED PRESS AP

was especially good at tracking down ground balls hit far to his right and far to his left. He led the National League in assists twice (1905 and 1906), in putouts once (1907), and in double plays twice (1905 and 1906).

Huggins's exceptional intelligence became evident during his years with Cincinnati, and he was a team leader. During the off-season he attended Cincinnati Law School and became a lawyer, although he never practiced law. In 1910 he was traded to the National League's St. Louis franchise. In 1913 he was named the player-manager of the ball club; in 1917 he retired as a player to become a full-time manager. At the end of that year he led a group of investors in an effort to buy the St. Louis club, but he was rebuffed, and he quit the team.

Huggins's record as a manager at St. Louis was not impressive. His team had only two winning seasons out the five he managed, but Ban Johnson, the president of the American League, urged the New York Yankees to hire him to manage their club, which they did. The team he took over was pathetic, but he instilled discipline in them, and they finished third in their league in 1919 and 1920. It was in 1920 that the Yankees began purchasing contracts from the Boston Red Sox, still notorious in Boston, including the contract of star pitcher and part-time outfielder Babe Ruth.

In the World Series in both 1921 and 1922, Huggins was outmanaged by the New York Giants' John McGraw, whose team hammered the Yankees. Indeed, Huggins seemed desperate, taking gambles on players who failed to perform well, even starting the marginal pitcher Harry Harper (4 wins, 3 losses for the season) in game six of the 1921 World Series. Yet, in 1923 Huggins made all the right moves, and with outstanding performances by his pitchers, he and the Yankees finally beat the Giants in the World Series.

After this triumph Huggins faced the greatest trials of his career. Ruth and other Yankee players had let their discipline decline, ignoring curfews and carousing at all hours, and while playing their minds were not on the game. The Yankees finished second in 1924 to the Washington Senators, a fine ball club led by an exceptional pitching staff, but in the next year the team slumped horribly. When Ruth showed up late for practice and hung over on 29 August 1925, Huggins fined him $5,000, by far the most any major leaguer had ever been fined. Ruth exploded in rage. Jake Ruppert, owner of the Yankees, backed Huggins all the way against Ruth, and Ruth had to apologize to Huggins and the team.

It was on that day that Huggins began his most important feat, turning a group of talented boys into men. Much is made of Ruth's wild behavior, but rarely is it pointed out that after 1925, with Huggins's guidance, he became more

base for the Shamrocks, a semipro team in Cincinnati. In 1900 he played for the St. Paul team of the American Association.

Huggins began his major league career with a young ballplayer's dream: he was signed by his hometown ball club, the Cincinnati Reds. He was twenty-five years old and to many observers too small—he was five feet, six inches tall and weighed about 140 pounds—but he played in 140 games during his rookie season, 1904, and he scored ninety-six runs, earning the starting job as the team's second baseman. Thereafter, he became one of the best lead-off hitters of his time. He was very good at getting on base, using his small strike zone for many bases on balls. Because of this, his on-base percentage was always high, even though he was not a great hitter. But he was not paid to hit but to score runs, and he scored over 100 runs three times, in 1905, 1910, and 1911, with a career high of 117 in 1905. He was a master base runner when base running was crucial; during the "dead ball" era, teams scraped and schemed just to score one run at a time.

In addition to being an excellent lead-off hitter, Huggins was an outstanding fielder. In an era of fine second basemen, Huggins was a standout, fielding for nearly all of his playing career better than most of his contemporaries. He disciplined, keeping in shape during the off-season and paying attention when he was supposed to.

The Yankees of 1926, 1927, and 1928 may have been the greatest dynasty ever, winning pennants each season and the World Series in four-game sweeps in 1927 and 1928 (they lost to the St. Louis Cardinals in 1926). During these years Huggins had to contend with several prima donnas. His number-three (Ruth) and number-four (Lou Gehrig) hitters often did not speak to each other over some slight or another, and others on the team bickered and complained as well. However, Huggins held the team together with diplomacy, a paternal caring for players with problems, and firm discipline with enough flexibility in it for his players' expansive personalities to be expressed.

On 22 September 1929 Huggins felt unwell, and he made coach Art Fletcher the team's substitute manager. He was taken to Saint Vincent Hospital in New York, where on 25 September he died of blood poisoning. His funeral in Cincinnati was attended by many ballplayers, and the American League cancelled all the day's games in his honor. He is buried in Spring Grove Cemetery, Cincinnati, Ohio.

On 30 May 1932 a monument in Huggins's honor was placed in center field in Yankee Stadium. It was eventually joined by monuments to Ruth, Gehrig, and Joe DiMaggio. In 1964 Huggins was named to the National Baseball Hall of Fame for his managerial career by the Special Veterans Committee. In his time Huggins was regarded as one of baseball's best minds, and he was a prototype for the modern manager, who has to be part diplomat to manage teams populated by big egos and big paychecks. He may be fairly credited with saving Ruth's career when Ruth lost all self-discipline and became ill in 1925; he nurtured the shy Gehrig into a star; and he helped his often fractious players think and play as a team.

★

Harvey Frommer, "Miller Huggins," in his *Baseball's Greatest Managers* (1985); Hank Nuwer, "Miller Huggins: The Mighty Mite," in his *Strategies of the Great Baseball Managers* (1988); and William Mead, *The Inside Game: Baseball's Master Strategists* (1991), explain the importance of Huggins's contributions as a manager. Leo Trachtenberg, *The Wonder Team: The True Story of the Incomparable 1927 New York Yankees* (1995), describes how Huggins interacted with his team. "Miller Huggins Dies" in the *New York Times* (26 Sept. 1929) is an obituary that discusses his career and the reaction to his death.

KIRK H. BEETZ

HULL, Brett (*b.* 8 August 1964 in Belleville, Ontario, Canada), one of professional hockey's most feared offensive players, who surpassed his own father, the legendary Bobby Hull, in scoring goals.

Hull, the son of Bobby Hull, a hockey player, and Joanne McKay, a figure skater, was born on his father's cattle farm in Belleville, Ontario, and grew up in Chicago and Winnipeg, Ontario, where his dad played hockey. By age three, Brett was already showing a skating talent he had inherited from both of his parents. Hull said his father "never taught me anything directly. He just said, 'Watch me.' " Brett Hull proved a quick study, especially at picking up his father's famous slap shot.

When Hull was twelve, his parents went through an ugly, well-publicized divorce. Hull and his three brothers and one sister went to live with his mother in Vancouver, British Columbia. After the divorce, Hull rarely saw his father until he started his own hockey career. As a teenager, he was too overweight to attract the interests of hockey scouts, even though he had a deadly shot. At five foot, nine inches, and 220 pounds, Hull was in poor physical condition. He quit playing hockey at age eighteen, but his mother talked him into playing again.

In 1983 Hull joined a second-tier junior team in Penticton, British Columbia, where he scored 105 goals in 56

Brett Hull. AP/WIDE WORLD PHOTOS

games. That earned him a scholarship to the University of Minnesota–Duluth. In his sophomore year, Hull scored fifty-two goals in forty-two games and was a finalist for the Hobey Baker Award as the best college player in the United States. He also played for the U.S. team in the 1986 world championships in Moscow and led the team in scoring.

Hull left college after his sophomore year to sign with the Calgary Flames of the National Hockey League. After making his pro debut in the Stanley Cup finals, Hull was sent to the minors. Scoring fifty goals for the Moncton (New Brunswick) Wildcats, he made the American Hockey League all-star team, and the Flames promoted him to the National Hockey League (NHL) for the 1987–1988 season.

Hull did not fit in with Calgary, a veteran team. A right winger, Hull was known as a "sniper," a player who lay in wait for a goal-scoring opportunity but was otherwise largely uninvolved in the game. Calgary traded him to the St. Louis Blues late in the 1988 season.

Hull made the all-star team in his first full year with the Blues, scoring forty-one goals. After the season, St. Louis coach Brian Sutter advised Hull to get in better shape and work on his overall game. Hull began working out and reported to camp the next fall ten pounds lighter. In the 1989–1990 season, Hull scored seventy-two goals, a new league record for a winger. He had only ten penalty minutes all season and, like his father, earned a Lady Byng trophy for good sportsmanship. After that season, which he finished by scoring twelve more goals in the playoffs, Hull signed a four-year contract for $8.3 million. It was a dizzying rise to stardom.

The next season, 1990–1991, Hull scored eighty-six goals, six short of Wayne Gretzky's single-season record. That year, he won the Hart Memorial Trophy as the league's most valuable player. In the Stanley Cup finals, the Minnesota North Stars beat St. Louis largely because they had two players relentlessly guarding Hull.

Hull again led the league in scoring in the 1991–1992 season with seventy goals. After the season, however, Hull was upset because St. Louis traded away his friend, center Adam Oates, who had set up many of his goals. Though disgruntled, Hull still scored fifty-four goals in the 1992–1993 season and fifty-seven the following year.

Unlike his father, Hull was not known for his skating ability, his toughness, or his visibility. His strategy was to lie low and await a scoring opportunity. "My whole game is based on deception," he said. "I don't do a lot because I don't want to be noticed." Hull excelled at finding gaps in defensive coverage. He would come out of nowhere, take a pass, and quickly shoot. Many considered him to have the quickest release in the game, and his shots had deadly accuracy.

Hull conceded that he employed more mental energy than physical energy, and described himself as "the laziest man alive." Scoring goals was easy for him, but he admitted that playing hockey was hard, and he did not seem to take the sport too seriously. Carefree, talkative, and gregarious, Hull obviously enjoyed himself both on and off the ice.

Hull's stay in St. Louis turned that city, first and foremost a baseball town, into a hotbed of enthusiasm for hockey. Although the Blues often got close, they never won the Stanley Cup during Hull's tenure. Hull was traded to Dallas before the 1998–1999 season.

In his first year with Dallas, the Stars made it to the Stanley Cup finals against the Buffalo Sabres, and Hull scored a controversial goal that won the championship. But during his three seasons with Dallas, Hall clashed frequently with coach Ken Hitchcock. Hockey's era of big offense was suddenly over, and like many teams, Dallas emphasized defense and team play. Hull went along reluctantly, showing he could be a more complete player. But for him, scoring ninety-five goals in three seasons was a letdown. He said scoring "is the one thing I love to do, and it's almost like you are not allowed to do it anymore."

At the beginning of the 2000–2001 season, Hull surpassed his father on the all time goals list, but he insisted he was not his equal. "I have more goals and more points, but I'm certainly not going to consider myself one of the top five greatest players ever," he said. Through the 2000–2001 season, Hull had 649 goals, seventh on the all-time list. He ranked fifth in career playoff goals with eighty-six, including twenty game winners. After Dallas lost in the Stanley Cup playoffs, Hull signed a two-year contract in August 2001 with the Detroit Red Wings, a perennial contender.

Hull's career trajectory mirrored that of his father. Bobby Hull changed the game from a defensive struggle to a high-scoring sport, and when Brett Hull entered the NHL, he became the foremost practitioner of all-out offense. In the latter part of his career, Hull found his skills to be increasingly incompatible with the latest fashion in hockey philosophy. He was not nearly the complete player his father was, but he was the most frightening opponent many goalies ever encountered.

★

Hull's autobiography, written with Kevin Allen, is *Brett* (1996). Juvenile biographies include Margaret J. Goldstein, *Brett Hull: Hockey's Top Gun* (1992); Mark Stewart, *Brett Hull: The Incredible Hull* (1998); and Lou Friedman, *Brett Hull* (1999). A profile and interview are in *Hockey Digest* 29 (summer 2001).

MICHAEL BETZOLD

HULL, Robert Marvin, Jr. ("Bobby") (*b.* 3 January 1939 in Point Anne, Ontario, Canada), hockey player whose offensive prowess, matinee-idol looks, and electrifying play greatly increased the game's popularity during the period of the National Hockey League's greatest expansion (1967–1981).

Hull's father, Robert M. Hull, Sr., dreamed of playing professional hockey. Instead, he started a family at a young age and needed a steady income. While he and his wife raised eleven children, he worked at a cement plant in Point Anne, a town in southeastern Ontario. He bought his oldest son, Robert Jr., a pair of ice skates for Christmas when the boy was three years old, and by the end of that day, the child was skating unaided. By age five, he was getting up daily at 5:00 A.M. to skate on Lake Ontario's Bay of Quinte near his home. He played hockey constantly, often with his sisters and brothers.

By the time he was twelve, Hull was playing with his father in an amateur league. That same year (1951), Bob Wilson, chief scout for the Chicago Blackhawks, saw Hull play in a bantam game in nearby Belleville, Ontario, and claimed rights to the young left-handed shooter. Under the existing National Hockey League (NHL) rules, no other team could sign him.

After the Blackhawks convinced Hull's mother to let him leave home, they sent him to Hesperer, Ontario, to play on a juvenile team. The next season (1952–1953), Hull led the Woodstock team to a Junior B hockey championship, and at age fifteen he was playing for the St. Catharines Junior A team in the top amateur league in Canada. Hull

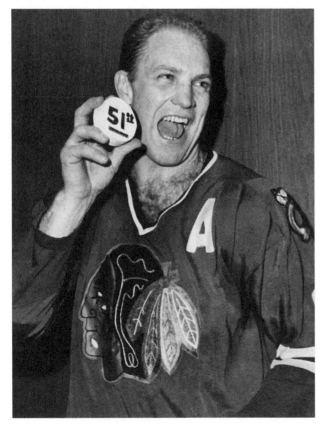

Bobby Hull. AP/WIDE WORLD PHOTOS

was a headstrong teenager, and when coach Rudy Pilous shifted him from center to left wing, he quit for four games, mistakenly believing it was a demotion. He returned only when Pilous agreed to let him remain at center.

After high school football practice one afternoon in 1956, Hull was told to report to a Blackhawks exhibition game in St. Catharines, where he scored two goals against the New York Rangers. Chicago, for years one of the National Hockey League's doormats, was eager to get Hull into its lineup. Hull joined the club at age eighteen, and soon after that Pilous became head coach. Pilous again switched Hull to left wing, this time without resistance, as Hull understood that was where he was best suited to play.

In his third season (1959–1960), Hull became the second-youngest player ever to win an NHL scoring championship. The following year, he led the Blackhawks to their first Stanley Cup since 1938. In the 1961–1962 season, Hull scored two goals in the final game to become the third player in hockey history to reach fifty goals in a season. Thanks largely to their magnetic young star, the Blackhawks became a perennial powerhouse and the league's richest franchise.

With his blond hair and muscular good looks, Hull, nicknamed the "Golden Jet," became hockey's top drawing card. He combined the graceful, gliding moves of a figure skater with a reckless, all-out style of play that electrified fans. Hull would carry the puck, skating with long strides down the ice, and then unleash his devastating slap shot. The fastest skater in the league, Hull was once clocked at twenty-nine miles per hour. But he was by no means a one-dimensional goal scorer. He played tough defense, was a superb stick handler, frequently killed penalties, and excelled on power plays. At five foot, ten inches and 195 pounds, Hull was tough and displayed incredible endurance, often logging the most playing time on his squad. "Unless you stop him in his own end of the rink, you don't have a chance," said rival star player Andy Bathgate of the Toronto Maple Leafs. "He's too big and strong."

In the 1964–1965 season, after scoring twenty-seven goals in his first twenty-seven games, Hull attracted widespread attention for another assault on the fifty-goal record, but a late-season injury and a slump that followed it derailed his chances. That year, he won the Hart Trophy as the league's most valuable player (MVP) and also the Lady Byng Trophy as the most sportsmanlike—a rare combination. Though often harassed and double-teamed by opponents, Hull seldom fought back. "When you hit back, it's just for your own self-satisfaction," Hull said. "I get mine from putting the puck in the net."

Although Bathgate and Montreal's Bernie Geoffrion are credited with inventing the slap shot, Hull made it the modern game's most feared weapon. His slap shot was clocked at 119 miles per hour—so fast that the puck often would sail right in and then out of a goalie's gloved hand. With teammate Stan Mikita, Hull also discovered and perfected the curved hockey stick, or "banana blade," and made it such a dangerous offensive tool that the NHL passed a rule to limit the degree of curvature.

Hull was the focus of intense publicity in the 1965–1966 season until he finally broke the hallowed fifty-goal standard in his sixty-first game before a sell-out crowd at Chicago Stadium. Finishing with fifty-four goals, he was named the league's MVP for the second consecutive year. Over the following three seasons, Hull led the league in scoring each year. In 1968 he became the first hockey player to earn $100,000 a year. In the 1968–1969 season, he increased his own record to fifty-eight goals.

By 1972 Hull had been the league's top goal scorer seven times and was a ten-time all-star. Thanks largely to his fame, the popularity of hockey was expanding into cities far from the Canadian border. Seeking to capitalize on the hockey craze, a rival league, the World Hockey Association (WHA), began play in 1972. The WHA scored its biggest coup when its Winnipeg Jets signed Hull to a $1.75 million contract. The NHL sued to stop Hull from jumping leagues but lost in court. Because of Hull, the WHA gained instant respectability and the Jets became the new league's main attraction.

Hull starred for Winnipeg during the WHA's entire seven seasons of existence. He was named the league's MVP in the 1972–1973 season and again in 1974–1975, when he scored a phenomenal seventy-seven goals for yet another new professional record. When the NHL absorbed the WHA and its teams at the start of the 1979–1980 season, Hull returned to play in his old league and was traded to the Hartford Whalers. It was his final season. He tried to come back with the New York Rangers in 1981, but did not make the team.

Hull was only a teenager when he married Judy Learie, and they had one child before divorcing. Hull then married Joanne McKay, a professional skater. They had five children. Hull wanted his sons Bobby Jr., Blake, and Brett to have the same opportunity for skating as he did when he was young, and would frequently take them with him to team practices and let them skate. Before the start of the 1965–1966 season the Hull boys were becoming such a distraction that the Blackhawks banned children from team workouts. Hull staged a brief walkout and said he wanted to be traded. It was one of the few rifts he had with management during his career.

Hull's brother Dennis played with him on the Blackhawks for a brief time. Hull's son Brett went on to enjoy his own phenomenal hockey career, outdoing many of his father's scoring records, but he could not hope to match his father's impact on the sport.

In a career of 23 seasons, Hull scored 913 goals and made 895 assists for a total of 1,808 points, a mark eclipsed at the time only by Wayne Gretzky and Gordie Howe. Including playoff games, Hull scored 1,018 goals—the most by any left wing in hockey history. But it was Hull's charisma, even more than his productivity, that made him the sport's top ambassador. More than any other player, the handsome, gregarious Hull was responsible for hockey transcending its reputation as a provincial Canadian sport and becoming a big attraction in the United States. The rapid expansion of the NHL from six teams to thirty owed much to Hull's leadership in transforming the game from a slow, defensive battle to a wide-open, high-scoring, crowd-pleasing show. In many respects, Hull was the Babe Ruth of hockey.

By the time Hull retired from hockey, the game was much different than when he had entered the NHL. No longer were players vying to break the record of fifty goals in a season, they were shooting for eighty. No longer were there six teams, all of them in or near Canada. Instead the league had about thirty teams, including those in places like Los Angeles and Dallas. Hockey had a national television contract in the United States. Hull played a major role in all of these changes. By popularizing the slap shot and the curved stick, Hull gave the sport an offensive boost. His flamboyant style of play and accessibility to the media made him the game's first truly modern star. And his role as hockey's ambassador and chief promoter helped attract millions of new fans and players.

★

Several biographies of Hull are informative, including Julian May, *Bobby Hull: Hockey's Golden Jet* (1974); Ted Zalewski, *Bobby Hull: The Golden Jet* (1974); and Scott Young, *Bobby Hull, Superstar* (1974). Another biography, Jim Hunt, *Bobby Hull* (1966), was written during the early part of Hull's career.

MICHAEL BETZOLD

HUNT, Lamar (*b.* 2 August 1932 in El Dorado, Arkansas), founder of the American Football League, professional sports promoter, and founder and owner of the Kansas City Chiefs who was elected to the Pro Football Hall of Fame in 1972, the National Soccer Hall of Fame in 1982, and the International Tennis Hall of Fame in 1993.

Hunt was one of six children born to Harold Lafayette "June" Hunt, Jr., an oil executive, and Lyda Bunker Hunt, a homemaker. The family moved to Tyler, Texas, in late 1933 and in 1938 relocated to Dallas, Texas, where Hunt's father established the offices of the Hunt Oil Company. As a youngster Hunt and his older brother Bunker Hunt read the newspaper and digested the sports page by discussing the box scores and attendance numbers of various sporting events. Lamar Hunt received his high school education at the Hill School in Pottstown, Pennsylvania, where he played halfback and served as captain of the varsity team during his senior year.

In 1952, after his high school graduation, Hunt returned to Dallas and entered Southern Methodist University, where he majored in geology. He continued his interest in sports when he joined the Southern Methodist University football team and played for four years at the wide receiver position. Short and thin (under six feet tall), Hunt played sparingly and never lettered in the sport.

While Hunt was at Southern Methodist he began to dabble in the sports business. As an undergraduate he built a batting cage, where he charged individuals a quarter to bat ten balls. The batting cage was a successful venture, and he soon added a watermelon concession stand. Later he opened a miniature golf course, but that venture failed.

In 1956 Hunt graduated from Southern Methodist University with a degree in geology. Shortly after his graduation he married Rose Mary Carr, but the couple, who had no children, divorced in 1962. In August 1959 Hunt became frustrated because he could not acquire a National Football League (NFL) franchise team for the city of Dallas. He created a rival league, the American Football League (AFL), financed by the Hunt family oil wealth. Hunt formed the Dallas Texans to play in the league, and over the next few months six more teams across the country affiliated with the AFL.

The newly created league and team faced stiff competition from the National Football League, which also established a Dallas franchise. In May 1963 Hunt moved the Dallas Texans to Kansas City, where no other professional football team operated, and the Dallas Texans became the Kansas City Chiefs. A year later Hunt married Norma Lynn Knobel. They had four children. The two football conferences continued to battle each other for supremacy, and finally in the spring of 1966 the two leagues merged. Hunt, who figured prominently in the merger negotiations, served as the AFL representative in talks with the Dallas Cowboy owner Tex Schramm and the NFL commissioner Pete Rozelle. Hunt was also instrumental in negotiating the first football television contract for the AFL teams. In 1970 Hunt's Kansas City Chiefs captured a Super Bowl victory for their owner.

Hunt did not limit his interest in investing and promoting professional sports to football. In 1966 he purchased an 11.25 percent interest in the Chicago Bulls basketball team and founded the Dallas Tornado, a North American Soccer League franchise. A year later, in 1967, he founded the World Championship Tennis tour.

Prior to 1967 the International Lawn Tennis Federation supervised the sport of tennis. Lamar's competing organization, the World Championship Tennis Tour, signed to professional contracts players who played on a newly cre-

Lamar Hunt, 2001. ASSOCIATED PRESS AP

ated professional tennis circuit. Hunt originally envisioned a circuit of linked tennis tournaments that would culminate in one final playoff tournament of the world's best players. Unfortunately the World Championship Tennis tour ended in 1989 because Hunt's circuit increasingly faced competition from other promoters who wished to manage and promote their own tennis events. When the Association of Tennis Professionals reorganized the men's tour in 1990, they left out the World Championship Tennis circuit, which led to its demise. Despite Hunt's critics, he was inducted to the International Tennis Hall of Fame in 1993 for his tireless effort to support and promote professional tennis.

Another of Hunt's lasting contributions to sports promotion came with his support of professional soccer in the United States. In 1967 the Dallas Tornado, a professional soccer team owned by Hunt, took the field as an inaugural member of the North American Soccer League (NASL). The Tornado won the NASL soccer championship in 1971. Unfortunately the team folded in 1982, which left Hunt without a professional soccer team to support. Ironically, the same year the Tornado folded Hunt was inducted into the National Soccer Hall of Fame for promoting the sport.

Hunt's interest and promotion of sports outside of football did not sit well with his fellow professional football franchise owners. Some owners wanted Hunt to divest himself of all his holdings even though the league allowed its owners to have minority interests in other professional sports franchises. Hunt refused to comply and continued to promote professional sports outside of football.

In 1996 Hunt once again promoted and invested in professional soccer by becoming the owner of two teams, the Columbus Crew and the Kansas City Wizards, in the newly organized Major League Soccer (MLS) circuit. The Crew played for its first three years in Ohio State University's football stadium, but Hunt realized the team needed its own facility. At a cost of $28.5 million he bankrolled a 22,485-seat stadium that opened to the public in 1999. The Wizards played in Arrowhead Stadium, home to Hunt's Kansas City Chiefs. In the 2000 Major League Soccer Championship game, the Wizards defeated the Chicago Fire to win their first MLS title.

Hunt, best known as the founder of the American Football League and the owner of the Kansas City Chiefs, is also remembered for tirelessly promoting professional soccer and tennis. His induction into the football, soccer, and tennis halls of fame validates his success as a professional sports promoter.

★

Biographical data and information regarding Hunt's role in founding the American Football League and the Kansas City Chiefs is in Joe McGuff, *Winning It All: The Chiefs of the AFL* (1970); Don Kowet, *The Rich Who Own Sports* (1977); Harry Hurt III, *Texas Rich: The Hunt Dynasty from the Early Oil Days Through the Silver Crash* (1981); and David Harris, *The League: The Rise and Decline of the NFL* (1986). Information concerning Hunt's role in the World Championship Tennis Tour is in Peter Bodo, "When April Wasn't the Cruelest Month," *Tennis* (Apr. 1995). Hunt's interest in professional soccer is discussed in Ian Thomsen and Kevin Cook, "Taking Out a Mortgage on the Future," *Sports Illustrated* (31 May 1999).

JON E. TAYLOR

HUNTER, James Augustus ("Catfish"; "Jim") (*b.* 8 April 1946 in Hertford, North Carolina; *d.* 9 September 1999 in Hertford, North Carolina), standout major league pitcher who played on World Series–winning teams for the Oakland A's and New York Yankees, and earned election to the National Baseball Hall of Fame.

Hunter, the son of Abbott and Lillie Harrell Hunter, dominated high school competition with a powerful right arm that drew the attention of many major league scouts. Unfortunately, a hunting accident, in which his brother inadvertently fired shots into his foot, sidetracked his career.

The incident left a series of shotgun pellets in his foot and curtailed his fastball by limiting his ability to push off the mound. Although most scouts no longer considered Hunter one of the best high school pitchers in the country, Kansas City A's scout Clyde Kluttz and team owner Charlie Finley maintained their loyalty. Finley paid for Hunter's foot operation and signed him to a 1964 contract that included a $75,000 bonus. Finley also fitted Hunter with the nickname of "Catfish," concocting a fabricated story to accompany the origin of his new identity.

The following spring, the A's planned to send the nineteen-year-old to the minor leagues, but his surprising maturity convinced management that he should remain with Kansas City. "Here's a kid right out of high school who goes on the major league mound and pitches as if he were a veteran," said Jack Aker, a reliever for the A's. "Catfish never showed a bit of fear or nervousness. He just picked up on major league baseball like it was another day back at his high school in Hertford, North Carolina."

With no minor league training, Hunter showed flashes of stardom in his first three seasons, but it wasn't until 1968 (with the A's franchise by then relocated to Oakland, California) that he started to gain national recognition. On 8 May Hunter pitched a perfect game against the hard-hitting Minnesota Twins. Afterwards, Hunter exhibited his typical modesty, refusing an attempt by teammates to lift him onto their shoulders. "I just wanted to get out of there as quickly as possible," Hunter told *Sport* magazine. "I was too embarrassed."

As much as Hunter made an impression with his growing pitching talent, he impressed the veteran A's players even more with his demeanor, both on the pitching mound and in the clubhouse. Hunter was reserved, but his shyness eventually gave way to a subtle confidence, allowing him to become a team leader. "Catfish was a jokester, one of the guys, and very unassuming," said A's captain Sal Bando. "He was liked by everybody."

Hunter's teammates enjoyed his practical jokes, even if his managers did not. Early in 1971 the A's found themselves playing poorly, which did not please their new skipper, Dick Williams. Prior to boarding the team bus at the Milwaukee airport, one of the players decided to steal a battery-operated megaphone from the team airplane. Williams angrily lectured his players, demanding the megaphone be returned immediately. As an irritated Williams continued his diatribe, one of the players—none other than Hunter—dropped the megaphone from the bus onto the sidewalk.

On the field, Hunter played a large part in the A's' 101-win season in 1971—marking their first trip to the postseason under Finley. Hunter's emergence as a star in 1971 was even more impressive, considering his starts were often pushed back so that the A's could start Vida Blue—on his

Catfish Hunter, 1974. © BETTMANN/CORBIS

way to the Most Valuable Player (MVP) and Cy Young awards—at home as often as possible. Yet Hunter never publicly complained and continued to pitch well, reaching the twenty-win plateau for the first time.

Hunter relied on tenacity and competitiveness to compensate for his lack of a feared fastball—a shortcoming often noted by opponents. When a reporter approached Cincinnati Reds left fielder Pete Rose during the 1972 World Series and asked him if he would characterize Hunter as a great pitcher, Rose responded tersely: "No, I wouldn't. He's a good pitcher, but hell, I'm not gonna make him out to be a super pitcher because he's not." Unshaken by such uncomplimentary words, Hunter won two games and posted a 2.81 ERA in helping the A's defeat the Reds.

In spite of his success, which included three consecutive twenty-one-win seasons and a twenty-five-win campaign, Hunter remained modest—and good-hearted with teammates. One day in 1974 Hunter presented a greeting card to little-known infielder John Donaldson, who was about to complete his fourth year of service, making him eligible for a Major League Baseball (MLB) pension. The card, signed by the Hunter family, read as follows: "From the four of us for your fourth." The gesture left Donaldson overwhelmed. "That shows what kind of class Hunter has," Donaldson told the *Sporting News.*

Hunter's popularity with teammates was reaffirmed when he became a free agent after the A's won their third consecutive World Series in 1974. Finley's failure to make an insurance payment as part of the pitcher's contract triggered his departure, with the timing proving especially

good for Hunter, the American League's Cy Young Award winner. After all but two teams made him offers, Hunter elected to sign a five-year, $3.75 million contract with the New York Yankees. "With Catfish, we were world champions," A's outfielder Reggie Jackson told *Sport* magazine. "Without him, we have to struggle to win the division." Without Hunter, the A's did manage to win the American League West, but went no further, losing the playoffs in three straight games.

Despite a fifth consecutive twenty-win season in 1975, Hunter's Yankees didn't make the post-season. Nonetheless, the Yankees soon replaced the A's as the elite team in the league. In 1976 the Yankees won the American League pennant, followed by World Series titles in 1977 and 1978. Hunter thus enjoyed an incredible stretch of five world championships in seven years.

The 1978 season, however, proved bittersweet for Hunter. While the Yankees won their second straight championship, Hunter discovered that he was suffering from diabetes. The disease forced him to take regular medication for the rest of his life.

Although Hunter's five-year contract with the Yankees expired, he returned for one more season in the Bronx, but struggled badly, winning just two of eleven decisions. Still relatively young at thirty-three, he decided to retire in order to spend more time with his family. In 1987 Hunter won election to the National Baseball Hall of Fame.

Hunter's post-playing days did not treat him kindly. In addition to battling diabetes, he noticed problems holding a shotgun in his hand while hunting near his farm in 1998. A visit to Johns Hopkins Hospital resulted in a diagnosis of amyotrophic lateral sclerosis—or ALS—a fatal disease that had previously claimed the life of Yankee great Lou Gehrig. Over the next year and a half, Hunter courageously battled ALS, refusing to publicly complain about his fate. During the summer of 1999 he fell while trying to climb steps and suffered severe head injuries. The fall—the direct result of the effects of ALS—ultimately contributed to his death at the age of fifty-three. Hunter left behind a wife, Helen, and three children. He is buried in Cedarwood Cemetery in Hertford, North Carolina.

Although his career was nearly short-circuited as a youth, Hunter maximized his success as a pitcher, becoming an integral part of two of the game's most dominant franchises of the 1970s. He also maintained his down-to-earth nature, making him one of baseball's most well-loved and respected players. In addition, he worked with friends to form the Jim "Catfish" Hunter ALS Foundation, an organization dedicated to bringing an end to the fatal disease.

★

For additional information on Hunter, see Jim "Catfish" Hunter and Armen Keteyian, *Catfish: My Life in Baseball* (1988); Bruce Markusen, *Baseball's Last Dynasty: Charlie Finley's Oakland A's* (1998); and clippings files for Jim "Catfish" Hunter at the National Baseball Hall of Fame Library, Cooperstown, N.Y.

BRUCE MARKUSEN

HUTSON, Don(ald) Montgomery (*b.* 31 January 1913 in Pine Bluff, Arkansas; *d.* 26 June 1997 in Rancho Mirage, California), football player credited with revolutionizing the running of pass patterns and generally considered to be the best wide receiver in football history.

Hutson was one of three sons born to Roy B. Hutson, a conductor on the Cotton Belt Railroad, and his wife, Mabel Clark, a homemaker. As a student Hutson achieved the rank of Eagle Scout and attended Pine Bluff High School. Pine Bluff fielded formal athletic teams only for football and basketball, and Hutson played both sports, although he played football only as a senior. Graduating in 1931, Hutson was invited to attend the University of Alabama with his highly recruited friend Bob Seawall.

During his sophomore and junior football seasons (1932 and 1933) at Alabama, Hutson saw little playing time until late in the 1933 season, and for the two seasons he compiled a total of just seven pass receptions for seventy-eight yards. Meanwhile, he was also playing centerfield for Alabama's baseball team and running for the track team; competing in the 100 yard and 220 yard dash. In 1934 Alabama fielded a football powerhouse and was considered one of the best teams in the history of Southern football. Hutson caught

Don Hutson *(right)* and Alabama teammate Dixie Howell, both All-Americans, 1935. © BETTMANN/CORBIS

19 passes for 326 yards and 3 touchdowns, and was named a consensus All-America end.

In the postseason during his last year at Alabama, Hutson and his team bombed Stanford 29–13 in the Rose Bowl game on 1 January 1935. In the game, Hutson exploded with six pass receptions for 165 yards and 2 touchdowns that covered 54 and 61 yards. In the aftermath of his Rose Bowl performance, Hutson was contacted by many professional football teams, and he signed contracts for $175 per game with both the Green Bay Packers and the Brooklyn Dodgers of the National Football League (NFL). President Joe Carr awarded Hutson to Green Bay on the basis of its contract being postmarked minutes earlier than the contract with Brooklyn, and in later years Hutson always considered himself fortunate to have gone with the pass-oriented Packers.

Hutson's NFL career started impressively as he and the Packers played the Chicago Bears in their second game of the season in October 1935. On the first play from scrimmage, Hutson outmaneuvered and then outran Beattie Feathers of the Bears to haul in a long touchdown pass on an eighty-three-yard scoring play for the only tally of the day. When the two teams met again later that season, Hutson caught two touchdown passes, including another game-winner. Hutson finished his rookie season of 1935 with 18 receptions for 420 yards, and on 14 December 1935 he married Julia Richards; the couple later had three daughters. In 1936 Hutson became recognized as one of the league's premier receivers as he led the NFL in receptions and was named to the All-Pro team. The Packers rolled to the 1936 league championship with a 21–6 win over the Boston Redskins as Hutson scored on a forty-three-yard pass.

Hutson, nicknamed "Alabama Antelope," was six feet, one inches tall, 180 pounds, and played wearing small shoulder pads and no hip pads. He had the speed of a sprinter—9.7 seconds for the 100-yard dash. He ran effortlessly while leaning well forward, and had great deception and maneuverability at full speed. Hutson is usually credited with being the first wide receiver to run pass patterns with sharp cutting angles while feinting continuously. Opposing teams attempted to cover Hutson with two and sometimes three defenders, but the techniques he brought to his position, along with a great pair of hands, made him nearly unstoppable. It was said that if he could touch the ball he would make the catch. Hutson also played defensive safety, totaling thirty career interceptions, while also handling Green Bay's placekicking duties from 1940 to 1945.

The 1937 season witnessed the start of one Hutson streak, as he registered pass receptions in ninety-five consecutive games between 1937 and 1945, and in 1938 he began a run of eight consecutive seasons as an All-Pro selection. Statistically, Hutson's greatest season was 1942 when he tallied 74 pass receptions for 1,211 yards and 17 touchdowns—the first time a receiver had exceeded 1,000 yards—although, admittedly, the quality of play in the NFL was down because so many players were away during World War II. His 1942 season was highlighted by three-touchdown performances against the Cleveland Rams and Chicago Cardinals, and 8 receptions for 147 yards against the Bears.

Hutson's 1941 and 1944 seasons were equally impressive. He logged 58 catches for 738 yards and 10 touchdowns in 1941; in 1944 he added another 58 receptions that were good for 866 yards and 9 touchdowns. Also in 1941, Hutson notched a brilliant three-touchdown effort in a come-from-behind win over Washington that propelled the Packers into a Western Division playoff game.

In 1944 Green Bay won its third NFL championship during Hutson's eleven-year career, and represented professional football in the 1945 College All-Star Game in Chicago. Hutson had been a member of the College All-Stars in the 1935 game, before turning in three sparkling appearances in the annual classic for the Packers (1937, 1940, and 1935). In the 1940 game Hutson had three touchdown receptions (eighty-one, thirty-five, and thirty yards) against the collegians, and he capped things off in the 1945 game with an eighty-five-yard interception return for a touchdown. The 1945 season was Hutson's last in professional football, and his final campaign was highlighted on 7 October 1945 as he logged four touchdown receptions and a total of twenty-nine points in the second quarter against the Detroit Lions.

Hutson retired after the 1945 season and then served two years as an assistant coach for the Packers. He left football in 1948 and turned his attentions to his bowling establishment in Green Bay. In 1950 Hutson and his family moved to Racine, Wisconsin, where he opened a Chevrolet and Cadillac automobile dealership. He retired from business in 1984. Hutson died at Rancho Mirage, California, where he had lived during his retirement years.

When Don Hutson retired from professional football, his personal league records required nearly a full page in the NFL guide, and many were still standing more than a half-century later. One of the greatest players in pro football history, Hutson was an innovator who transformed his position, and he remains the prototype wide receiver against whom all others are measured. Hutson finished his NFL career with 488 pass receptions that were good for 7,991 yards and 99 touchdowns; while he led the NFL eight times in receptions, pass-receiving yards seven times, touchdowns eight times, total scoring five times, and was named to the All-Pro team nine times. Among his many honors, Hutson was named to the College Football Hall of Fame in 1951, the Pro Football Hall of Fame in 1963, and to the NFL seventy-fifth anniversary team in 1994. In 1994 the Packers named their new indoor practice facility after Hutson.

★

Accounts of Hutson's exploits appear in most works on professional football history, including interviews that appeared in George Sullivan, *Pro Football's All-Time Greats: The Immortals in Pro Football's Hall of Fame* (1968); Myron Cope, *The Game That Was: The Early Days of Pro Football* (1970); and Richard Whittingham, *What a Game They Played: Stories of the Early Days of Pro Football by Those Who Were There* (1984). For a detailed review of Hutson's pro seasons, see Larry D. Names, *The History of the Green Bay Packers, Book II: The Lambeau Years Part Two* (1989). Obituaries are in the *Milwaukee Journal* and the *New York Times* (both 27 June 1997).

RAYMOND SCHMIDT

I

IBA, Henry Payne ("Hank") (*b.* 6 August 1904 in Easton, Missouri; *d.* 15 January 1993 in Stillwater, Oklahoma), pioneering collegiate basketball coach famous for his patterned offense and tenacious defensive style of play.

Iba was the son of Henry Burkey Iba, a department store salesman, and Zylfa Dell Payne Iba, a homemaker. He had one sister and three brothers, two of whom, Clarence and Earl, would coach basketball at the college level. Iba attended local schools, graduating from Easton High School in 1923, and he grew to six feet, two inches tall and 185 pounds. While at Westminster College in Fulton, Missouri, which he attended from 1923 through 1927, Iba participated in a wide range of sports, including football, basketball, baseball, and track. He finished his schooling at Maryville State Teachers College in Missouri, obtaining a B.S. in physical education in 1928.

In 1927 Iba began his coaching career at Classen High School in Oklahoma City; in his second year, the team won the state basketball championship. He moved to Maryville State to coach from 1929 to 1933, then to the University of Colorado for the 1933–1934 season. He then went to Oklahoma A&M College in Stillwater as a basketball coach for the Cowboys from 1934 until his retirement in 1970. He also coached the baseball team from 1934 to 1941, persuading the future major league pitcher Allie Reynolds to give baseball a try. In the midst of these early coaching years Iba married Doyne Williams on 25 August 1930. They had

one son, Henry Williams "Moe" Iba, who played for his father (1958–1962) and went on to coach basketball at the college level.

Iba employed seminal coaching schemes with his basketball teams. His "motion offense" relied on a thoroughly practiced passing game to spread the opposing defense. The team ran play after play until the opponent made a mistake, allowing an A&M Cowboy to streak to the basket for an easy score. Iba responded to critics of his ball-control tactics by saying, "I want my boys to shoot. I love my boys to shoot. But, glory be, make it a good shot." His defense tactics had an even more lasting influence. The coach schooled his teams to play a physical half-court, man-to-man defense, characterized by players helping out their teammates. Fans often heard Iba's hoarse voice bellowing, "Help! Help! Help!" to keep the opposing offense at the perimeter.

Iba made it clear from the beginning that he was in control and devoted to discipline. After swishing a shot in practice a player asked the first-year coach, "Is that the way to shoot that shot, Hank?" The thirty-year-old coach responded, "You don't know me well enough to call me Hank, son." From then on it was "Mr. Iba" to all but his close friends, who called him Henry. Mr. Iba would not tolerate mistakes, especially mental mistakes. Players heard, "Cut that out!" roared from the sideline at a misstep in practice or a game. Iba was an advocate of hard work, scheduling a total of nine hours of practice on Christmas

Hank Iba receiving a trophy for winning the NCAA championship game for Texas A&M, 1948. ASSOCIATED PRESS AP

Day or New Year's Day to instill the discipline needed to run both an offense and a defense dependent on teamwork and close timing. Although he was gruff and demanding, Iba was known as a gentleman off the court, and his former players regarded him as a close friend for life.

The Cowboys were in back-to-back National Collegiate Athletic Association (NCAA) championships in 1945 and 1946. These accomplishments were products of Iba's discipline, but also reflected his ability to teach. Bob Kurland, at nearly seven feet, enrolled in the Cowboys program in 1943. He was gangly, not particularly coordinated, and lacked stamina—an unlikely prospect for basketball success. Yet Iba pushed him to develop physically, and redesigned the A&M offense and defense, stationing Kurland under the basket to take advantage of his height. In response to Iba's tactics, goal tending became illegal after the 1943–1944 season. Iba not only endorsed the new ruling but reworked his defense again to allow Kurland to continue to exert a commanding presence.

Henry G. Bennett, the president of Oklahoma A&M, appointed Iba as the athletic director in 1935 to put the university on the map athletically. Iba responded. By 1967 Oklahoma State University (the name changed in 1957) was second only to the University of Southern California in NCAA team championships. The basketball team did much to add to A&M's renown. In addition to winning two national championships, the Cowboys played in the 1949 NCAA final game, losing to Kentucky 46–36. They played in the inaugural National Invitational Tournament (1938) and three others (1940, 1944, and 1956).

Iba was the head coach of an unprecedented three Olympic basketball teams (1964, 1968, and 1972). Only his 1972 team failed to win a gold medal, in one of the most controversial contests in Olympic history. The U.S. team appeared to have defeated the Soviet Union's team by one point, but a courtside Olympic official twice ordered three seconds to be put back on the clock. The U.S.S.R. made a disputed basket during the third playing of the last seconds and won the gold. The U.S. team, with Iba's approval, boycotted the medal ceremony.

The final decade of the Iba era was not as illustrious as his earlier coaching years. Critics claimed, with some justification, that the game had passed him by. The principal problem was Iba's aversion to recruiting. Before the NCAA banned the practice, he selected his players from regional tryouts. Iba found having to coax young men into his program distasteful. Equally loathsome to him was the increasingly popular up-tempo style of basketball. Nonetheless, fourteen Missouri Valley Conference titles, a Big Eight Championship in 1965, and an overall record of 767 collegiate victories against 338 losses testified to his coaching prowess. The records of the men he taught to coach—Don Haskins (University of Texas at El Paso), Jack Hartman (Kansas State), Eddie Sutton (Oklahoma State)—demonstrated that the Iba style, especially his defensive approach, could be successfully incorporated into a faster game. Sutton and Haskins sought Iba's advice up to his death at age eighty eight from heart failure. He is buried in Stillwater's Fairlawn Cemetery.

Iba's honors were extensive: National Coach of the Year in 1945 and 1946, Basketball Hall of Fame, Olympic Hall of Fame, and Missouri and Oklahoma Halls of Fame. The tributes were well deserved. Iba was an influential tactician and exceptional coach. When he had good, but not great, players he molded them into a smoothly working team that could dictate the tempo of a game and usually win. When he had or developed exceptional players, such as Kurland, Iba was flexible enough to tailor his style to the talents of his team and defeat anyone.

★

John Paul Bischoff, *Mr. Iba: Basketball's Aggie Iron Duke* (1980), thoroughly covers Iba's life and career through the 1972 Olympics. In a sparkling overview of Iba's career, Michael McKenzie presents vignettes and anecdotes in *Oklahoma State University: History-Making Basketball* (1992). For a more workmanlike treatment, see Doris Dellinger, *A History of the Oklahoma State University Intercollegiate Athletics* (1987), which furnishes a year-by-year review of Iba's basketball seasons and adds details on his role as the athletic director. Obituaries are in the *New York Times* (16 Jan. 1993) and the *Daily Oklahoman* (16 and 17 Jan. 1993).

WILLIAM H. MULLINS

INKSTER, Juli Simpson (*b.* 24 June 1960 in Santa Cruz, California), one of the top players of the Ladies Professional Golf Association (LPGA) and a member of its Hall of Fame.

Inkster was born Juli Simpson, the youngest of four children of Jack Simpson, a fireman, and Carole Simpson. Her childhood home was near the fourteenth hole at Pasatiempo Golf Club in Santa Cruz, California, and she took up the sport at the age of fifteen. At sixteen she began taking lessons at Pasatiempo from Brian Inkster, from whom she learned her signature swing; they married four years later, on 26 July 1980, and had two daughters.

Inkster attended San Jose State University on a golf scholarship, where she was a collegiate All-American all four years. In 1978, while still in college, she qualified for the U.S. Women's Open as an amateur, and in 1980 she won her first U.S. Amateur title; she repeated the win the following year, becoming only the ninth player to accomplish this feat.

In 1982 Inkster became the first woman since 1934 to win the title in three consecutive years. She was a member of the 1980 and 1982 World Cup teams and the U.S. Curtis Cup team in 1982. She won numerous honors in her early years, including the 1981 California Amateur of the Year and 1982 Bay Area Athlete of the Year titles. *Golf Digest* named her the 1981 and 1982 number-one-ranked amateur, and the following year the magazine named her Rookie of the Year.

In 1983 Inkster joined the Ladies Professional Golf Association (LPGA) tour, and in 1984 she won the fifth tournament she entered, the Safeco Classic. The same year she became the first rookie to win two major championships, the Nabisco Dinah Shore and the du Maurier, Ltd. Classic, which she won in a sudden-death playoff with another former Rookie of the Year, Pat Bradley. Inkster posted more victories in 1986, 1987, and 1989, the year she won both the Nabisco Dinah Shore and the Crestar Classic for the second time.

In 1990 Inkster cut back her participation because of the birth of her first daughter, managing only a fifth-place finish in the Plantation Pat Bradley International Tournament. She returned to competition when her daughter was only seven weeks old but had difficulty concentrating, and went twenty-seven months without a victory before winning the 1991 Bay State Classic. Between 1991 and 1994 she won two tournaments and was in the playoffs of two major championships. With the birth of her second daughter in 1994, Inkster played in only sixteen events, and her best finish was a tie for second in the Ping Welch's Championship held in Boston. She posted only second- and fourth-place finishes during 1995 and 1996 and considered retiring from golf, but instead recommitted herself to the game and began working with a new coach, Mike McGetrick. Inkster got a second wind in 1998, when she recorded her seventeenth career LPGA victory in defending her Samsung World Championship title, as well as shooting a career first hole-in-one and tying a career low of sixty-four during the second round of another tournament. Catching fire in 1999, Inkster won five tournaments. With her twenty-second victory, at the Safeway LPGA Championship, she joined Pat Bradley as the second woman to complete the modern career grand slam (then comprising the du Maurier Classic, U.S. Women's Open, Nabisco Dinah Shore Championship, and the McDonald's LPGA Championship), along with the earlier grand slam winners Louise Suggs and Mickey Wright. Inkster had won all four major championships on the LPGA tour, including the U.S. Open and two Professional Golf Association (PGA) championships.

At five feet, seven inches and slim, Inkster is considered diminutive compared to other golfers competing in the LPGA tour. However, her powerful drive averages 255 yards, making her one of the longest hitters in the women's golf game. Inkster manages her game with a consistency in all areas of play, such as greens hit and putts per round. In

Juli Inkster. AP/WIDE WORLD PHOTOS

the past four years she has maintained a stroke average of seventy.

Inkster won the $800,000 Safeway LPGA Golf Championship on 26 September 1999 by six strokes, assuring her entry into the LPGA Hall of Fame as its seventeenth member. She won $120,000 with this victory and celebrated by being showered with champagne by her friends and competitors on the tour. She celebrated her fortieth birthday on the Friday of the tournament. Inkster also was honored in October 1999 by the Women's Sports Foundation as a Sportswoman of the Year.

Considered the most difficult Hall of Fame in all sports to break into, the forty-eight-year-old LPGA Hall of Fame changed its criteria to Inkster's benefit shortly before her induction. Because of its stringent requirements, only seventeen women golfers had entered the LPGA Hall of Fame in nearly half a century. Nothing would compare, however, with the celebratory champagne shower Inkster enjoyed while still an active player. In late 2001 she was the only Hall of Fame golfer still active on the tour.

Inkster continues to blaze a trail in the annals of the LPGA, earning more than $6 million in career wins. She has won back-to-back victories in the McDonalds LPGA Championship, the Long Drugs Championship, and a third career Samsung World Championship title.

"I realized I could be a mom and play golf," she said. "It's a fine balance. I have a lot of support at home. It's not easy, but I am doing what I love to do."

★

There is no full-length published biography of Inkster at this time. Articles on Inkster include Alan Shipnuck, "Better than Ever: Winning Majors Never Gets Old for Juli Inkster," *Sports Illustrated* (3 July 2000), and an article in *Golfweek* (1 July 2000).

ROSEMARIE S. CARDOSO

IVERSON, Allen Ezail (*b.* 7 June 1975 in Hampton, Virginia), professional basketball player regarded as one of the most dynamic players in the National Basketball Association.

Iverson was raised by his mother, Ann Iverson, who was just sixteen and living with her grandmother when Iverson was born. Iverson's biological father, Allen Broughton, disappeared before Iverson's birth. The family gave him the nickname "Bubbachuck" after two uncles.

When Iverson was still a baby, Ann moved in with Michael Freeman, who worked as a welder for the Newport News Shipyard and Dry Dock Company. He and Ann later had two children together. Freeman lost his job after a car accident in 1988. In 1991 and again in 1994, Freeman was arrested and convicted for selling drugs. This meant that Iverson grew up in severe poverty in an apartment that sometimes had no electricity or hot water. To make ends meet, Ann worked for Amway, at a convenience store, on an assembly line at Avon Fashions, as a secretary at Langley Air Force Base, and as a welder at the shipyard. They moved from one poor neighborhood to another around Hampton and Newport News, Virginia.

When Iverson was eight years old, Ann introduced him to basketball. Ann herself had been a varsity player on the women's basketball team at Bethel High School in Hampton in the 1970s. She taught Iverson ball handling, shooting, and crossover dribble, the move Iverson would become known for later in his basketball career. Gary Moore, Iverson's elementary school football coach, recognized the boy's gift and helped him become a tough player. Moore would eventually become Iverson's personal manager when he played with the Philadelphia 76ers.

During his junior year of high school, Iverson led the Bethel High School football team to the Virginia State Class AAA championship. He also led the basketball team to a state championship by averaging 31.6 points per game. He was named Virginia High School Player of the Year in both football and basketball by the Associated Press in 1992. In that year, *Parade* magazine named him the National High School Basketball Player of the Year and among the top ten football players in the nation. His performances earned him the nickname "The Answer."

On 14 February 1993 Iverson was involved in a racially motivated brawl at the Circle Lanes bowling alley. Iverson and three other African-American teenagers were arrested and charged with "maiming by mob." Iverson was convicted and sentenced to five years in jail. The conviction drew national attention because of Iverson's athletic fame and the nature of the case. After serving four months at the Newport News City Farm, Iverson was granted conditional clemency by Virginia governor Douglas Wilder. The state court of appeals overturned the conviction in 1995 because of insufficient evidence.

During that period, Ann contacted Georgetown University's basketball coach, John Thompson, who had a reputation for helping talented but troubled young athletes. Iverson finished high school at Richard M. Milburn, an alternative high school for at-risk youth located in Virginia Beach, and received his diploma. In 1994 Iverson arrived at Georgetown University in Washington, D.C.

During his two seasons with the Georgetown Hoyas, Iverson averaged twenty-three points per game. He was selected Big East Rookie of the Year in 1995, Freshman of the Year by *Basketball Weekly* in 1995, and Big East Defensive Player of the Year in 1995 and 1996. He was named All-American First Team by Associated Press in 1996. He also led the United States to the gold medal in the 1995 World University Games in Japan.

In May 1996 Iverson announced he was turning professional. Iverson's decision to enter the 1996 National Basketball Association (NBA) draft before he graduated from college was made mainly because of his family's financial problems. On 26 June 1996 Iverson was the first round number-one pick by the Philadelphia 76ers. Iverson was the first point-guard to be drafted number-one since Earvin "Magic" Johnson in 1979 and the smallest, at six feet tall and 165 pounds, number-one pick ever.

Iverson quickly established himself as one of the most promising players in the NBA. He scored thirty points in

Allen Iverson. AP/WIDE WORLD PHOTOS

his first NBA game against the Milwaukee Bucks. His lightning-quick crossover dribble confused defenders. He broke the NBA rookie record by scoring 40 or more points in five consecutive games. During his first season Iverson averaged 23.5 points per game. He was named NBA All-Rookie First Team and in 1997 was Shick Rookie of the Year.

During the off-season, Iverson was arrested when Virginia police found a handgun and marijuana in a speeding car he was riding in. He was given two years probation with monthly drug tests and a hundred hours of community service.

The 76ers started the 1997–1998 season with Larry Brown, a veteran coach who had experience with young teams. Iverson and Brown argued on and off the court. During the 1998–1999 season, Brown switched Iverson from point guard to shooting guard. The result was that Iverson led the NBA in scoring with 26.8 points per game and was named to the All-NBA First Team.

Before the 1999–2000 season, Iverson signed a six-year, $70.9 million contract with the 76ers, the largest contract ever in the team's history. However, in the summer of 2000 Iverson's habitual tardiness and disrespect for Coach Brown prompted management to initiate a trade that would send him to the hapless Los Angeles Clippers. The trade did not go through for a technical reason, but it served as a wake-up call to Iverson, who did not want to leave Philadelphia. Iverson entered the 2000–2001 season a changed man. Disciplinary action became unnecessary; in fact, at his request he was named co-captain. He led the team to a 10–0 season start. Iverson's 31.1 points per game made him the first player to average more than 30 points since Michael Jordan in the 1995–1996 season. Brown praised Iverson for his work ethic and commitment to the game. In the NBA All-Star game in February 2001, he was named Most Valuable Player (MVP). The 76ers faced the Los Angeles Lakers for the NBA national title.

The Lakers had just racked up a 15–0 postseason record, and their superstars, Shaquille O'Neal and Kobe Bryant, were healthy. But the 76ers had just finished a seven-game series against the Toronto Raptors and the Milwaukee Bucks, and almost every 76er played with injuries. To "Answer" the challenge, Iverson scored forty-eight points in the finals opener, and the 76ers stunned the world by beating the Lakers 107–101. It was the Lakers first defeat in sixty-seven days, breaking the Lakers' expectation of becoming the first undefeated champion in the NBA history. Individually, the 76ers swept all important NBA season awards. Larry Brown earned his first NBA Coach of the Year honor, Dikembe Mutombo grabbed Defensive Player of the Year, Aaron McKie won Sixth Man of the Year, and Iverson won Most Valuable Player. He was the smallest player ever to win the regular season MVP award.

Besides basketball, family and friends are the most important things in Iverson's life. He has financially supported about a dozen relatives and several longtime friends. He sent his stepfather to a substance-abuse rehabilitation clinic. Iverson and Tawanna Turner have two children, and Iverson married Turner on 23 August 2001.

Iverson's physical appearance, which often flouts NBA standards, featured cornrows, tattoos, heavy jewelry, and long baggy shorts. The league and the 76ers' management also have questioned his choice of friends, a group known as the Iverson Posse. He recorded a controversial rap CD titled *Forty Bars,* which drew criticism from several civil rights groups for its harsh words toward gays and women.

Quick, fearless, and tough are the words usually used to describe Iverson. He is so quick on the court that he makes the best defenders look slow. Despite his small frame, Iverson is fearless navigating among taller players and making acrobatic shots and creative passes. He ignores injuries and plays tough. Iverson has established himself as one of professional sports' most exciting athletes.

★

There are several book-length biographies available, including Charles E. Schmidt, Jr., *Allen Iverson* (1998); Mark Stewart, *Allen Iverson: Motion and Emotion* (2001); and Stew Thornley, *Allen Iverson: Star Guard* (2001). Biographical essays can be found in *Sports Stars* (1994–1998) and in *Contemporary Black Biography,* vol. 24 (2000). Phil Taylor, "Courted and Convicted," *Sports Illustrated* (26 July 1993), details the bowling alley incident and Iverson's troubled past. Other extensive biographical articles include Bill Brubaker, "Iverson in Transition: Troubled Past to NBA Future," *Washington Post* (16 June 1996); Mark Heisler, "76ers' Brash Rookie Allen Iverson Does It His Way as He Takes the NBA by Storm," *Los Angeles Times* (29 Dec. 1996); Rick Reilly, "Counter Point," *Sports Illustrated* (9 Mar. 1998); Charles Pierce, "Iverson, Allen," *Esquire* (Nov. 1999); Gary Smith, "Mama's Boys," *Sports Illustrated* (23 Apr. 2001); and K. C. Johnson, "Changing Direction: Iverson's Growth Has Pushed 76ers to New Heights," *Dallas Morning News* (11 June 2001).

DI SU

J

JACKSON, Joseph Jefferson Wofford ("Shoeless Joe") (*b.* 16 July 1888 in Pickens County, South Carolina; *d.* 5 December 1951 in Greenville, South Carolina), major-league baseball player and third leading all-time hitter, barred from professional baseball because of his participation in a scandal involving eight Chicago White Sox players who conspired with gamblers to lose the 1919 World Series to the Cincinnati Reds.

Jackson was the oldest of eight children of George Elmore Jackson, a sharecropper, farmer, and mill hand, and Martha, a housewife. Jackson received no formal education and began working in cotton mills before he was thirteen years old. In 1908, at the age of twenty, he married fifteen-year-old Katie Wynn. They had no children.

Jackson began playing baseball for the Brandon Mills team when he was thirteen, earning $2.50 per game. By the time he was twenty he signed to play for the Greenville Spinners. It was there that he earned the nickname "Shoeless Joe" after playing a game without shoes because of bad blisters caused by a new pair of spikes. In August 1908 he signed with the Philadelphia A's and played there sporadically in September 1908 and again late in 1909. In 1910 he was traded to the Cleveland Indians, and in the middle of the 1915 season he was traded to the Chicago White Sox.

A gifted hitter, Jackson was described by his contemporaries as having the most natural hitting stroke in the game. His .356 career batting average trails only Ty Cobb and Rogers Hornsby in best lifetime averages. Jackson's career statistics are more significant because he seldom played in his first three years and in 1918 he worked in a war industry most of the season. In his nine full seasons he had 1,774 hits, drove in 785 runs, and scored 873 runs. He batted .408 in 1911, losing the championship to Ty Cobb, who hit .420. In the troubled 1920 season, Jackson hit .382, drove in 121 runs and scored 105 while striking out only fourteen times.

The Black Sox scandal of 1919 blemished Jackson's reputation forever. Jackson was the most notable of eight White Sox players involved in a conspiracy to lose the 1919 World Series to the Cincinnati Reds. Gamblers Arnold Rothstein, Abe Attell, and Sport Sullivan offered $20,000 to each of the eight players in exchange for fixing the games. The signal that the players had accepted the offer centered on the first batter of Game One of the World Series. Ed Cicotte, the White Sox pitcher, was to hit the first batter, which he did.

The origins of the scandal are traced to the penurious manner in which White Sox owner Charles Comiskey managed his players. He paid just $3 a day for meals while most teams gave players $4, and charged his players twenty-five cents to launder their uniforms. With such a small allotment for laundry, players refused to wash their uniforms, and the team became known as the Black Sox. Furthermore, the salaries Comiskey paid to notable players such as Jackson, Cicotte, Eddie Collins, and Buck Weaver were far below those paid for high-quality players on other

Shoeless Joe Jackson. ASSOCIATED PRESS AP

teams. Adding to the money issues were the cliques on the White Sox team; members were divided into those who had a college education and those who did not.

Jackson batted .375 during the series, but the extent of his role has never been fully clarified. Like many of the eight, Jackson never received the promised $20,000. At most he received $5,000, left in his room by a fellow player, for his part in throwing the series. Though Jackson did report the money to the White Sox, Comiskey did not report this information to baseball authorities.

Rumors of the scandal circulated immediately, but it was not until late in the next season that details surfaced as reporters dug into the story, which broke in August 1920. By September a grand jury was chosen to investigate the matter. Comiskey immediately suspended the eight suspected players, and the White Sox fell out of the 1920 pennant chase.

Jackson and the seven other players appeared before the grand jury. By the end of October the jury filed nine counts of fraud and conspiracy against the indicted players. The trial took place in Chicago in June 1921. The circumstances of the trial were bizarre. Documents disappeared; baseball was in turmoil with the election of Kenesaw Mountain Landis as the commissioner on 11 November 1920, replacing the three-member commission that had governed the game since 1903; and charges about the duplicitous role of Comiskey persisted. The jury eventually found the players and gamblers innocent. Commissioner Landis, however, ruling "in the best interest of the game," barred all eight players from the game for life. This action was taken to remove the stigma of fixed games that had arisen as early as the 1910s and reached its apogee with the Black Sox scandal.

With no education, a drinking problem, and few resources to rely on, Jackson played semiprofessional baseball, first in the Midwest and then in the South. While playing for the White Sox, he had opened a poolroom in Greenville, South Carolina. With his wife as manager, he became a small businessman, running a Greenville dry-cleaning business, a barbecue restaurant, and finally a liquor store. He frequently coached teams and continued through the 1930s to play baseball wherever he could. In 1934, at the age of forty-five, Jackson applied for reinstatement to baseball so that he could play in the minor leagues, but Landis refused his request.

Jackson died of a heart attack caused by arteriosclerosis and cirrhosis of the liver in 1951. He is buried at Woodlawn Memorial Park in Greenville.

In the 1990s Jackson became a cult figure. A strong campaign to reinstate Jackson and to allow his election to the National Baseball Hall of Fame began after the publication of W. P. Kinsella's *Shoeless Joe* (1982) and its film adaptation *Field of Dreams* (1989).

Players, notably Bob Feller, Ted Williams, and Pete Rose, supported Jackson's inclusion in the Hall of Fame. Politicians from South Carolina and Iowa (the location of the Field of Dreams—the baseball field in the middle of a cornfield in Dyersville that was used in the filming of the movie) also voiced support for Jackson's election. The city of Greenville and the Jackson family have profited from his notoriety. An automated auction of his memorabilia, including his famous bat, "Black Betsy," sold in August 2001 for $577,610.

★

The best sources on the life of Jackson include Warren Brown, *The Chicago White Sox* (1952); Eliot Asinoff, *Eight Men Out* (1963); Bill Veeck and Edward Linn, *The Hustler's Handbook* (1965); Harvey Frommer, *Shoeless Joe and Ragtime Baseball* (1992); Donald Gropman, *Say It Ain't So, Joe!* (1999); and David Fleitz, *Shoeless: The Life and Times of Joe Jackson* (2001).

HARRY JEBSEN, JR.

JACKSON, Philip Douglas ("Phil") (*b.* 17 September 1945 in Deer Lodge, Montana), National Basketball Association player noted for his eccentricities who later coached eight NBA championship teams.

Phil Jackson's parents were Pentecostal ministers, and they seem to have instilled in him a great respect for spirituality, one of the characteristics that contributed to his becoming a great basketball coach. Early in life, Jackson found an outlet in playing sports, and in high school he played not only basketball but football and baseball.

From 1963 to 1967, he attended the University of North Dakota and played basketball under Coach Bill Fitch. He was six feet, eight inches tall, thin, and seemingly all angles and elbows. His aggressive defense and high scoring led to his twice being named an All-American. While in college, he pursued his spiritual interests, and when he graduated he was a Buddhist.

Had he played in the 1980s or later, Jackson would probably have been a first-round draft choice and a starter in the National Basketball Association (NBA), but in 1967 there were far fewer NBA teams, and he was a second round choice, seventeenth overall. He then had some tough choices to make. In general, NBA players were not paid as well as baseball and football players, and many college stars chose to take jobs with corporations, playing for corporate teams or in amateur ball, meanwhile building careers in

Phil Jackson. AP/WIDE WORLD PHOTOS

business. Jackson had to decide between an $11,000 per year offer from the Phillips 66 Oilers, with a business career, or a $13,500 offer from the New York Knicks. He chose the Knicks.

He wore his hair long and followed spiritual practices that, in those days, were out of the mainstream. Yet, this seeming rebel learned Coach Red Holzman's unselfish style of play, and he became the team's "sixth man." He proved to be a fine defensive player; his jerky movements, shoulder twitches, and ever-moving hands annoyed opposing players and threw them off balance. He suffered several injuries while with the Knicks and had spinal-fusion surgery in 1969, causing him to miss the 1969–1970 season. He came back to be a pivotal reserve player who made the most of his opportunities, and he was important in the Knicks's 1972–1973 NBA championship season. By then, his antics and tough rebounding had made him a fan favorite.

Jackson was traded to the New Jersey Nets in 1978, and he retired in 1980, finishing with 3,454 rebounds, 898 assists, 199 blocks, and a 6.7 points per game average in 807 games—very good marks for a reserve player.

In 1982 he became coach of the Albany Patroons in the Continental Basketball Association. In five years of coaching the Patroons he compiled 117 wins and 90 losses, was named CBA Coach of the Year, and won the 1984 CBA championship. This experience led to his being hired as an assistant coach for Doug Collins of the Chicago Bulls.

On 17 December 1988 Collins was ejected early from a game, and Jackson took over. He spoke only briefly with the players, tinkering a bit with team strategy, and set the players loose. "It was like we were let out of a cage," said team forward Horace Grant. The team won. Even though the Bulls made it to the conference finals, where they lost, in 1989, Collins was fired, and Jackson was named to replace him. At the time, he seemed an odd leader for a high-energy sport. He was calm during games, kept his talks with his players during breaks to about thirty seconds, spread sweet grass in the locker room in Lakota-inspired ceremonies to drive out evil spirits and encourage good ones, and meditated thirty minutes a day with burning incense. During games, he treated his players as intelligent men who knew what they were supposed to do, but it was in practices that they learned what was expected of them. Throughout his coaching career, Jackson has insisted that practices are his chief pleasure in coaching, knowing that if twelve men worked hard as a team to master skills, they would be able to play as one.

The Bulls offense had focused on getting the ball to Michael Jordan, the scoring star, and Jordan had turned in magnificent seasons, but Jackson created a different pattern using the Triangle Offense, which emphasized ball handling, passing, and team play. Once Jackson sold Jordan and the other players on this idea, Jordan's scoring went down a little, but the team won championships, with NBA titles in 1991, 1992, and 1993. When Jordan's father was murdered in 1993, the superstar retired from basketball, later to play minor league baseball. The Bulls won 55 and lost 27 in 1993–1994—a fine record—but they slumped to 47–35 the next season.

When Jordan ended his retirement and returned, he made it clear that he would play only for Jackson. The Bulls won three consecutive NBA championships in 1996, 1997, and 1998, and Jackson was voted NBA Coach of the Year in 1996. Jackson's 1995–1996 season was the most spectacular of his career. The Bulls won seventy-two and lost only ten games, setting an NBA record for wins and for winning percentage. The Bulls went on to win fifteen games while losing only three in the playoffs, winning the NBA championship. Yet not all was happy in the offices of the Bulls. After the 1998 championship, several Bulls players were to become free agents, and Jackson had frequent, loud disagreements with general manager Jerry Krause over what to do about them; Jackson was forced out of his coaching job and retired. Jordan, true to his word, retired as well.

After a year off, during which Jackson enjoyed himself at his Montana home, the Los Angeles Lakers, with some urging from their star center Shaquille O'Neal, offered Jackson their head coaching position. When Jackson accepted the job, his wife June of twenty-five years left him over the issue of how much time he spent on coaching (twenty-four hours a day, he has said).

In an astonishing feat of coaching, Jackson convinced a team of independent stars to play his brand of unselfish basketball, and the Lakers won consecutive championships in 2000 and 2001. Jackson attributed some of his success to living every moment for itself, even while visualizing long-term goals, as well as to psychologically supporting his players, to being "in touch with them."

★

Jackson had earned some fame for his independent views with *Maverick: More Than a Game* (1975), coauthored with Charley Rosen. Pulled together from interviews conducted by Rosen with Jackson, this book was updated considerably for *More Than a Game* (2001) because Jackson had become more than an eccentric—he had become the coach with the second-most championships in NBA history. Another thoughtful book is *Mindgames: Phil Jackson's Long Strange Journey* (2000) by Roland Lazenby, an in-depth study of the man. *Sacred Hoops: Spiritual Lessons of a Hardwood Warrior* (1996) by Jackson and Hugh Delehenty offers insight into how Jackson applies his beliefs to managing basketball players, as well as to his life. Fun to read is *The Gospel According to Phil: The Words and Wisdom of Chicago Bulls Coach Phil Jackson; An Unauthorized Collection* (1997) by David Whitaker, a short

gathering of remarks from one of the most quotable people in sports.

KIRK H. BEETZ

JACKSON, Reginald Martinez ("Reggie") (*b.* 18 May 1946 in Wyncote, Pennsylvania), outspoken and flamboyant Baseball Hall of Fame outfielder and designated hitter famed for his "tape measure" home runs and nicknamed "Mr. October" for his incredible postseason feats.

Jackson was one of six children of Martinez Jackson, a tailor and former Negro League player, and Clara Jackson. Clara Jackson moved out of the household with the three youngest children when Reggie was seven. Jackson was a football star at Cheltenham High School, and in 1964 he received an athletic scholarship to Arizona State University, also a top baseball school. In the 1966 baseball draft Charles Finley of the Kansas City Athletics (also known as the A's) chose Jackson and offered him an $85,000 signing bonus, which Jackson accepted.

Jackson moved rapidly up in the A's minor league system, reaching the highest minor league level in Birmingham, Alabama, by 1967, when he was chosen as the league's Player of the Year. Fourteen months after signing, he was called to the majors. On 8 July 1968 Jackson married his college sweetheart, Juanita Campos, known as "Jennie." The couple divorced in February 1973.

Reggie Jackson. AP/WIDE WORLD PHOTOS

By this time the A's had moved from Kansas City to Oakland, California, where Jackson proved expert in gaining media attention. "It was as if the power of the earth and the sky and the sands and the waters were in these hands," he once said of one of his home runs. In 1969 Jackson was on a pace to break the single-season home run record of sixty-one. The mounting pressure, however, caused a nervous stomach, eye twitches, and rashes, and he ended the season with forty-seven home runs.

The boisterous Oakland A's, an extremely talented group, were known as "the mustache gang," the first team in the modern era to feature facial hair. In 1972, as the team charged to the pennant, Jackson tore his hamstring in a daring steal of home. He was forced to watch Oakland's World Series victory on crutches. In 1973, however, he came back to become the unanimous winner of the American League Most Valuable Player (MVP) award, and as the key figure in the team's second straight World Series victory, he won the series MVP award as well. Despite struggles with Finley over salaries, the team won its third straight World Series victory in 1974, and Jackson was featured on the covers of both *Time* and *Sports Illustrated* in a two-week period. The irrepressible Jackson began his 1975 autobiography writing, "My name is Reggie Jackson and I am the best in baseball."

After another salary dispute, Finley called Jackson to say: "Reggie, this is Charlie. We've traded you to Baltimore. Good luck." In 1976 baseball instituted its first free agent reentry draft. Jackson's availability led to a price war won by the Yankee owner George Steinbrenner, who combined $3 million for five years with the possibilities of playing in America's media capital to lure Jackson to the Big Apple.

Billy Martin, the pugnacious Yankee manager, opposed Jackson's signing, and the Yankee players resented Jackson's ostentatious lifestyle and what they saw as his phoniness and arrogance. "I'm a nigger to them," Jackson noted. "I don't know how to be subservient." The team leader, the catcher Thurman Munson, seethed at an article in which Jackson declared, "This team, it all flows from me. . . . I'm the straw that stirs the drink." Jackson claimed the quote was taken out of context, that he meant that he was the last piece of the puzzle that would lead the Yankees to a championship.

On 18 June 1977 a national television audience watched a confrontation between Jackson and Martin, who had removed Jackson from a game in Boston for lackadaisical play in the outfield. Nevertheless Jackson was in his usual postseason form in the 1977 World Series, hitting .450 with 5 home runs. In a feat described by one writer as the greatest single-day individual athletic achievement of the century, Jackson hit three consecutive first-pitch home runs off three different pitchers in the decisive game of the series. It had

been fifteen years since the Yankees had won a World Series. An elated Jackson commented, "You win a World Series and then you win in New York, and it isn't until then that you understand the difference."

Jackson had said, "If I played in New York, they'd name a candy bar after me." In 1978 they did. On opening day a candy company gave away a free Reggie bar to each fan. Later in the season an embittered Martin suspended Jackson for five days in a dispute over a bunt sign. Martin's resentment grew over Jackson's close relationship with Steinbrenner. Finally Martin told reporters, "The two of them deserve each other, one's a born liar and the other is convicted." He was fired as manager and replaced with the more amenable Bob Lemon.

In 1982, as a free agent, Jackson signed a four-year deal with the California Angels for the then astounding sum of nearly $1 million a year. When he returned to Yankee Stadium in an Angels uniform, the crowd roared, "Reg-gie, Reg-gie, Reg-gie," and he responded by hitting a home run. He led the Angels to one division title and continued to hit his patented home runs, passing Mickey Mantle's career total of 536 in 1986. In 1987 Jackson returned to the Oakland A's for a grand farewell tour, after which he retired.

In 1993, his first year of eligibility, Jackson was the only person selected to the Baseball Hall of Fame. "If Cooperstown didn't exist, Reggie Jackson would have invented it, just so he would have a place to go this summer and make a speech about himself," commented the *Sporting News*. Jackson later remarked that he was picked on the first ballot only because of his postseason exploits, since he was only a lifetime .262 hitter and set the major league record of 2,597 strikeouts. He was, however, at the time of his retirement sixth on the list of home runs with 563 and one of only 4 people who hit 500 home runs and stole 200 bases. He was picked for the All-Star team fourteen times. In twenty-one major league seasons Jackson had justified the title "Mr. October." He played on eleven division winners, six pennant winners, and five world champions. He had a .357 lifetime World Series average and at the time the best World Series slugging average of .755.

After his retirement Jackson parlayed his fame into a variety of activities and businesses. In a continuation of his roller coaster relationship with Steinbrenner, Jackson was hired as a "special adviser" to the Yankees, resigned over a $14,000 travel expense dispute in 1999, and was rehired the following year. He built a "one-man conglomerate" that included software sales, real estate, a multimillion-dollar classic car collection, insurance, sports memorabilia, and autograph shows. In 1999 *Forbes* magazine estimated his net worth at $20 million. Jackson also funds a charity called the Mr. October Foundation for Kids.

Jackson once remarked rather humbly that he would

settle for being "one half the player Willie Mays was." Jackson did have an enormous impact on the game. He was the first great October player, and he was, in the words of the *Sporting News,* "the first African American major leaguer to make flamboyance fashionable. Jackie Robinson broke the color barrier. Reggie Jackson broke the hot-doggism barrier." Jackson's teams almost always won. He had "it," a difficult-to-define star quality. A psychiatrist noted: "Reggie would be successful in any endeavor he tries. If he were a brain surgeon, he'd be the best. . . . Some people just have that aura." Jackson summarized his career: "I've been picked off, picked on and picked myself back up. Live big, die big. That's my way."

★

A good biography is Maury Allen, *Mr. October: The Reggie Jackson Story* (1980), but it only covers up to 1980. Among the several biographies for children is Andrew Woods, *Young Reggie: Hall of Fame Champion* (1996).

LOUISE A. MAYO

JACOBS, Helen Hull (*b*. 6 August 1908 in Globe, Arizona; *d*. 2 June 1997 in East Hampton, New York), the greatest runner-up in women's tennis and beloved underdog, known for her trademark poise and perseverance in the face of defeat. Her controversial rivalry with champion Helen Wills, dubbed "The Battle of the Two Helens," thrilled and captivated media and fans of the 1930s.

Jacobs and her parents, Roland H. Jacobs and Eula Hull Jacobs, moved from Globe, Arizona, to San Francisco in 1914. Her father, an engineer and investor in copper mines, sought new employment in the Bay Area when the value of his investments began to decline. He relocated his family to Berkeley, where he leased the former home of the Wills family, whose daughter Helen had become a tennis champion as a teenager. Jacobs occupied Helen Wills's old room.

Other coincidences set the stage for Jacobs to follow in the shadow of Wills. In 1922 Roland Jacobs bought his daughter a tennis racket and encouraged her to play, if only for exercise. When she regularly began beating him as well as winning local tournaments, she attracted enough attention for a match to be arranged between the two Helens at the Berkeley Tennis Club where Wills trained. Jacobs was fourteen; Wills was seventeen and had already won the national junior championships. They played one practice set, and Wills crushed Jacobs 6–0 in seven minutes. Jacobs showed the determination that would become her trademark when she asked Wills for another set. Wills flatly declined, but a flame seemed to have been lit in Jacobs.

Jacobs's tenacity impressed William "Pop" Fuller, the renowned tennis coach who was then training Helen Wills.

Helen Jacobs, 1929. © BETTMANN/CORBIS

Although Jacobs did not yet dream of becoming a professional tennis player, she agreed to become Fuller's student. In 1924 and 1925 she won the junior national championship and at age eighteen began her twelve-year tenure playing in America's Wightman Cup, an annual tournament between British and American women's teams. After graduating from Berkeley High School, she entered the University of California at Berkeley in 1926 and eventually dropped out to devote all her time to tennis. She then rose to the finals of Grand Slam tournaments, only to lose each time, and badly, to Helen Wills: at the U.S. Open in 1928, she lost 6–2, 6–1, and at Wimbledon in 1929, she lost 6–1, 6–2. She also lost championships to Wills at the French and U.S. Opens in 1930, and at Wimbledon in 1932. But by 1928 Jacobs had broken into the top ten and would remain in those ranks through 1940.

Sportswriters and the media called the growing rivalry between Jacobs and Wills the "Battle of the Two Helens," dramatizing their opposing personalities and playing styles and igniting an interest in their matches. Despite their similarities in background, Wills and Jacobs were radically different players. Wills had earned the nicknames "Little Miss Poker Face" and the "Ice Queen" for her beauty and stoicism; Jacobs was known for her friendliness and sense of humor. She rejected the era's traditional expectations of femininity by wearing a hair net on the court and no makeup or nail polish. She was also a chain smoker. At Wimbledon in 1933, Jacobs played one match in shorts instead of a skirt—the first woman to do so—adding a spirit of rebelliousness to her famed self-reliance. She did not intend to make a political statement, however, and later said only, "It seemed the sensible thing to do."

Jacobs's attitude, rather than her skill, defined her as a player. Through her defeats in final after final, she won a devoted following for her sterling sportsmanship and unwavering courage. Alice Marble, a contemporary who defeated Jacobs in the U.S. Open finals in 1936, 1939, and 1940 said, "She had more will to win, more drive and guts than anyone else. . . . She never gave up." When compared with Wills and Marble, Jacobs's backhand was lackluster and her forehand was weak; she depended heavily on an unremarkable but reliable forehand slice. Although quick and dexterous at the net, her volleying paled in comparison to the greats of her time. Regardless, Jacobs's unyielding rallies and inexhaustible spirit often led her to victory.

In 1933 Jacobs appeared ready to finally penetrate Wills's domination over the women's game. On August 26, in front of 8,000 fans expecting a typical blowout, they met again in the U.S. final. The media further stirred excitement by branding their rivalry a "feud" and a "cat fight." But Jacobs had won the U.S. title the previous year and at age 25 was at the top of her game. She took the first set, 8–6. It was the first set she had ever won against Wills.

The match ended with a strange and unexpected anticlimax. Wills won the second set 6–3, but double-faulted to open the third set. This blunder seemed to offer up the game to Jacobs, who climbed to a 3–0 lead. At that point, Wills confounded her opponent and the fans. She walked to the umpire, gathered her sweater, and retired from the match. Jacobs rushed to Wills, begging her to continue and suggesting a break, but Wills retrieved her rackets and left the court. Jacobs had technically won, but Wills's sudden and unexplained withdrawal tainted the outcome. It is still debated whether Wills had injured her back or leg, or if she simply refused to face the humiliation of losing to Jacobs.

A Wimbledon final on 5 July 1935 presented Jacobs the match point against Wills she had longed for her entire career. In a Centre Court stadium packed with 19,000 mesmerized fans, Wills served an ace to close out the first set 6–3. Jacobs retaliated with strong, low forehand slices and claimed the second set 6–3. Everyone in the stadium rose to their feet during the changeover before the third set and cheered wildly. Wills came out strong with blazing passing shots, but then slowed and fell behind 4–2. Jacobs seized the opportunity and surged ahead 5–2. At match point the stadium again thundered with applause. Jacobs, fierce and focused, drove Wills off the court with powerful slices and

charged the net with a deep approach shot. Wills struggled to reach the ball and offered up a feeble lob, looping the ball high into the air. Catching a breeze, the ball hung in the sky, and Jacobs, unable to find position for an easy overhead smash to at last conquer her rival, was now dangerously off-balance. Stooping awkwardly as the ball fell, she swung in desperation—and hit the ball directly into the net. Stunned and devastated by her mistake, Jacobs never recovered. She lost the third set 7–5, and, more importantly, the chance to end the fifteen-year era of being second place to Wills.

Jacobs remained undeterred by this heartbreaking loss. She went on to win the U.S. title later that year (her fourth consecutive win in that tournament) and won Wimbledon in 1936, a year in which she was ranked number one. She continued to represent the United States in the Wightman Cup until 1938. At the conclusion of her career, Jacobs had won a total of nine Grand Slam titles, and had been ranked in the top 10 twelve straight times from 1928. In 1962 she was inducted into the International Tennis Hall of Fame.

After retiring from tennis in 1947, Jacobs became a commander in the U.S. Navy, one of only five women to achieve this ranking. Never having given up her childhood dream of writing, she published nineteen books, including an autobiography, children's books, historical novels, and several books on tennis. She also ran a small farm on Long Island, and lived with her partner Virginia Gurnee. Jacobs died of a heart attack at her home in East Hampton.

For nearly twenty-five years, Jacobs was a crowd favorite, not loved for her wins, but instead for the inexhaustible spirit and graciousness she brought to the game. She transcended the spectacle surrounding her rivalry with Wills with unforgettable dignity, compassion, and optimism.

★

Jacobs's autobiography, *Beyond the Game: An Autobiography* (1936), was written under the pseudonym H. Braxton Hill. Larry Engelmann, *The Goddess and the American Girl* (1998), describes the rivalry between Jacobs and Wills and their matches in dramatic detail. Victoria Sherrow, *The Encyclopedia of Women and Sports* (1996); Bud Collins and Zander Hollander, *The Encyclopedia of Tennis* (1997); and Joe Layden, *Women in Sports* (1997), all provide background, career highlights, and statistics. Jacobs appears in a cover story in *Time* (14 Sept. 1936). An obituary is in the *New York Times* (4 June 1997).

SARAH FEEHAN

JACOBS, Hirsch (*b.* 8 April 1904 in New York City; *d.* 13 February 1970 in Miami, Florida), Thoroughbred trainer and owner-breeder who won more races than any other trainer.

Jacobs's father, an immigrant Jewish tailor who worked for twenty-eight years at Arnheim's on Broadway, and his

Hirsch Jacobs, 1948. AP/WIDE WORLD PHOTOS

mother raised ten children. The family moved from Manhattan to Brooklyn, where, at age eight, Jacobs began raising and racing pigeons. He graduated, at thirteen years old, from public school in 1917 and became a steamfitter's assistant. In 1920 his boss's brother, Charlie Ferraro, and Jacobs formed a partnership for racing pigeons. With Jacobs training the birds, the two won most of the major Atlantic seaboard pigeon-racing sweepstakes. In 1923, Jacobs served as racing secretary for the Brooklyn, East New York, and Queensborough Concourse pigeon-racing clubs.

In 1924 Ferraro invited Jacobs to vacation with him in Havana. There, at Oriental Park, Ferraro used $1,500 of wager winnings to purchase a horse named Demijohn in a claiming race and asked Jacobs to be his trainer. Working with claimed horses, Jacobs and Ferraro won twenty-eight races and $27,515 in 1926 and fifty-nine races and $51,580 in 1927. In 1928 Jacobs left Ferraro and trained for Johnny Mascia and Louie Sylvestri before forming a partnership with lifetime friend and financial backer Isidor Bieber.

Jacobs had some unusual training and racing philosophies. He carefully examined his horses each day for soundness of body and behavior and often raced his horses into shape. "Why run a horse five furlongs at 6 A.M. for laughs when you can run him six furlongs at 3 P.M. for $10,000," he reasoned. Studying his horses and learning their personalities and individual conditions, he made a special point of daily examining their legs and devising a variety of remedies for their ailments. He also used innovative training methods and once exercised his horses by having them swim in the ocean over a two-week period.

On 28 October 1926, he claimed Reveillon, his first Thoroughbred, for $1,500. Jacobs raced him sixteen times in thirty-eight days. Reveillon finally won the thirteenth race on 29 December. In the spring of 1930, Jacobs claimed Sun Mission for $6,000. That horse won nineteen races, including Jacobs's first stakes victories, the 1930 Marianoa Handicap and Melrose Claiming Stakes, and $29,425.

Jacobs made a reputation for developing winners when he purchased Action, a lame steeplechase horse with a bowed tendon, for $1,000 in 1936. Action won eleven, and took one second, in thirteen starts and earned $22,435. His wins included the Woodmere Claiming Stakes, and the Aqueduct, Edgemere, and Manhattan Handicaps. Jacobs's reputation was enhanced in 1943 when he claimed the two-year-old Stymie in his third race for $1,500. Stymie won for the first time in his fourteenth race. He raced 131 times, won thirty-five races and a then record $918,485 for Jacobs. These winnings enabled Jacobs and Bieber to buy Stymie Manor near Monkton, Maryland. This farm became their breeding headquarters, and their mares are in the bloodlines of Seattle Slew, Sunday Silence, Skip Away, Spectacular Bid, Hail to Reason, and Personality. Another of Jacobs's successes was Searching, a mare with problem feet purchased for $15,000. Jacobs experimented with different shoes to protect her thin hoof walls. The future Hall of Famer won twenty-five races and $327,381. Her offspring, Affectionately, Admiring, and Priceless Gem, earned Jacobs and Bieber more than $2,000,000.

Jacobs, a stocky, blue-eyed redhead, married Ethel Dushock, the daughter of a Yonkers manufacturer, in 1933; they had three children. The older son, John, was Jacobs's principal assistant from 1963 to 1969. After his father's death, he won the Preakness Stakes with the 1970 three-year-old champion, Personality, and the 1970 Belmont Stakes with High Echelon. Starting in 1959, Jacobs listed his daughter, Patrice, as the owner of several of his horses. On 30 December 1972, she married Louis Wolfson of Harbor View Farm. They raised and raced Affirmed. Ethel Jacobs, who had been listed as the owner of some of the Jacobs's horses starting in 1936, led American owners in victories in 1936, 1937, and 1943. Several other members of the Jacobs family were involved in this business. Jacobs's father, after retiring from the garment business, was the stable foreman, three of his brothers trained horses, and another brother managed Stymie Manor.

Jacobs suffered a stroke in 1966 and sold over half of his stable through public auctions and private sales. At least fifty-five horses plus two shares of Hail to Reason sold for a total of $2,260,700. Jacobs died at age sixty-five of a cerebral hemorrhage during the 1970 Hialeah race meeting and is buried at Valhalla, New York.

Known for claiming inexpensive horses and developing them into winners, Jacobs trained horses that won a record 3,596 races, including 49 stakes races, earning a total $15,340,354. He also developed five great champions in his forty-five-year career: 1945 Handicap Horse and Hall of Famer, Stymie; 1960 Two-Year-Old Colt and the leading sire of 1970, Hail to Reason; Hall of Famer and 1965 Sprinter, Affectionately; 1966 Two-Year-Old Filly, Regal Gleam; and 1967 Handicap Mare Straight Deal.

Jacobs led all trainers in victories a record eleven times (1933–1939, 1941–1944), set a record in 1936 winning 177 races, and led trainers in earnings three times (1946, 1960, and 1965). The breeding partnership of Bieber and Jacobs led all breeders in earnings from 1964 to 1967 and won 3,513 races and $18,311,412. The Jacobs family and Bieber as owners won 2,947 races and $15,800,545. In 1958 the National Turf Writers elected Jacobs to the National Racing Hall of Fame. Pimlico honored him with the Hirsch Jacobs Stakes in 1975.

★

G. F. T. Ryall's "Profiles: Pigeon Man's Progress," *New Yorker* (5 Aug. 1939), describes Jacobs's life before Stymie. Howard M. Tuckner describes Jacobs's training philosophy and some of his success stories in "Man with Horse Sense," *New York Times Magazine* (21 May 1961). Gerald Holland focuses on the partnership of Jacobs and Isidor Bieber in "Sex, Slaughter, and Smoke," *Sports Illustrated* (26 June 1961). There are obituaries in *Blood-Horse* (21 Mar. 1970), *Bloodstock Breeders' Annual Review* (1970), *New York Times* (14 Feb. 1970), and one by Arnold Kirkpatrick that was reprinted in William Robertson and Dan Farley's *Hoofprints of the Century* (1976).

STEVEN P. SAVAGE

JAGR, Jaromir (*b.* 15 February 1972 in Kladno, Czechoslovakia [now Czech Republic]), hockey player who was the National Hockey League (NHL) leading scorer four times and the league's 1998–1999 Most Valuable Player (MVP).

Jagr, born only four years after the unsuccessful 1968 Prague Spring uprising against Communist rule, grew up in Czechoslovakia under the shadow of the Soviet dictatorship. His mother, Anna Jagr, and his father, Jaromir Jagr, worked on a farm and at a local factory, while his grandmother took care of him and his older sister Jitka Jagr. Prior to the Soviet Red Army's entry into Prague at the end of World War II, Jagr's grandparents had been wealthy landowners. "When the Communists came, they took it

Jaromir Jagr, 2000. ASSOCIATED PRESS AP

all," Jagr said with bitterness. "So much land. So much land." His grandfather died a political prisoner in 1968.

Jagr began skating at the age of three. When Jagr was six his father enrolled him in a youth hockey league so he could get as much practice and competition as possible. He excelled in the game. When asked why he decided to play professional hockey, he explained that "in Kladno, if you wanted to earn money, the best chance was to play hockey. And the Communists gave you everything for hockey until age 18—the ice time, the equipment, and everything else." In 1985 thirteen-year-old Jagr attended the World Junior Championships held in Prague. There he saw the nineteen-year-old Canadian sensation Mario Lemieux, whom Jagr adopted as his role model and five years later joined as a teammate in the National Hockey League (NHL).

Invited to play for the Czech national team, Jagr told the team's coaches he would not play for them unless he was permitted to wear number 68 in honor of his grandfather. Jagr also found other ways to rebel against the oppressive Communist regime in which he lived. He carried a picture of Ronald Reagan in his wallet, which was illegal. When Reagan learned that a Czech hockey player was risking jail to carry his photograph, the former president phoned Jagr to thank him. Jagr, taking the call, initially thought teammates were playing a practical joke on him. "This is President Reagan?" Jagr responded. "Sure, and I am George Bush."

In 1990 the Pittsburgh Penguins selected Jagr in that year's league draft. He was the fifth pick overall. To that point all the Czech players in the NHL had had to defect; Jagr became the first one not to have to do so. At six feet, two inches and more than 220 pounds, he sported long, dark, curly hair as a final act of rebellion against the Czech system, which had forbidden players to wear long hair. During his rookie season with the Penguins, Jagr scored 27 goals and 30 assists for 57 total points. These contributions helped Lemieux and the rest of the Penguins win their first-ever Stanley Cup championship. The Penguins won the Stanley Cup again the following season. During that year's playoffs, Jagr scored 11 goals and 24 total points in 21 games.

In the 1994–1995 strike-shortened season, Jagr became the first European-trained player to win the Art Ross Trophy awarded annually to the NHL's leading scorer. He finished second to Eric Lindros of the Philadelphia Flyers for the Hart Trophy, the league's Most Valuable Player (MVP) award. In 1995–1996 Jagr scored 62 goals and had 87 assists, and his 149 total points ranked second in the NHL. That year he broke single-season records for scoring by a European player and for combined goals and assists by a right wing. Jagr also became the first Czech player ever to reach the 50-goal mark in the NHL.

In 1997–1998 Jagr inherited Lemieux's role as the Penguins' leader. That year Jagr led the NHL with 35 goals and 102 overall points, the lowest total for an Art Ross winner in a nonshortened NHL season since 1967–1968. In 1998–1999 Jagr won another Art Ross Trophy. He also collected a Hart Trophy and the Lester B. Pearson Trophy, awarded to the MVP as chosen by the NHL players themselves. "I've said before, this means so much to me because it is voted on by the players," Jagr said.

The following season Jagr stunned his adoring fans by trimming his trademark curly locks. Despite missing 19 games because of injuries, he still scored 96 points, good enough to win another Art Ross Trophy. He also won the Pearson Trophy again and came within one point of winning another Hart Trophy. In 2000–2001 he took home another Art Ross Trophy, scoring 121 total points for the season.

Jagr's on-ice heroics have not been confined to the NHL. He played for the Czech Republic in the 1990, 1994, and 1996 World Championships and in the 1991 Canada Cup. In 1998 he played on the Czech Republic team that won the gold medal at the Nagano Olympics, defeating the Russians. Jagr, recalling 1968 and other horrors inflicted on his native land, was overjoyed. "It's different people now," he realized. "It's not their fault. But I'm glad we beat their team."

In July 2001 the Penguins management, for financial reasons, traded Jagr to the Washington Capitals. Additionally some sports writers and even some Penguins fans suspected that Jagr exaggerated his injuries. Jagr was happy about the trade. "I want to prove to everybody that I'm a great player," he said "I know what I can do. I know I didn't play my best last year, it was more up and down."

Jagr's place among the hockey greats is assured. "Jaromir is as close to the best player as there is, if not the best," said Kevin Constantine, the former coach of the Penguins. Wayne Gretzky, whom most hockey fans regard as among the top players in NHL history, also has praised Jagr: "He's smart, he's a good skater, and, most important in my opinion, he has great size and knows how to use it. He's the kind of guy who only comes along once in a while." Fittingly, in Gretzky's final NHL game with the New York Rangers, Jagr led his Penguins to victory over the Rangers by scoring a goal in overtime. Recognizing the symbolic significance of how the game ended, hockey writers described Jagr's goal as his "inheriting the throne from the Great One."

★

Information on Jagr can be found in Glenn Weir, Jeff Chapman, and Travis Weir, *Ultimate Hockey* (1999); Dan Diamond, ed., *Total Hockey: The Official Encyclopedia of the National Hockey League*, 2d ed. (2000); Eric Duhatschek, *Starforce Hockey: The Greatest Players of Today and Tomorrow* (2000); and Gary Mason and Barbara Gunn, *The Coolest Guys 2: Featuring Thirty-five of the Top Players from the Coolest Game on Earth* (2000).

IRINA BELENKY

JANSEN, Dan (*b.* 17 June 1965 in Milwaukee, Wisconsin), champion U.S. speed skater who competed in four consecutive Winter Olympic Games before striking gold in his final Olympic event.

Jansen, who began skating at age four, set his sights on Olympic gold while still in his early teens. It was no accident that Jansen got into speed skating. The youngest of nine children of Harry Jansen, a police officer, and Gerry Jansen, a nurse, he was born into a family of speed skaters. Jansen grew up in West Allis, Wisconsin, only a block from the rink that hosts the annual North American Speed Skating Championships. Because his parents could not afford a babysitter, they took him along to the rink, where his older brothers and sisters practiced. Before long it attracted

Dan Jansen. CORBIS CORPORATION (NEW YORK)

his interest, and by age four he had begun to skate. In Jansen's early years of skating, his father told *People,* Jansen was "no better than anyone else in the family. He had real wobbly ankles and had to work very hard on them."

It took a few years, but all that hard work paid off for Jansen, who had begun to win regional competitions by the time he was eight. While attending public schools in West Allis, he won his first national competition at age twelve. In 1984, at age eighteen, he competed in his first Winter Olympics, skating to fourth place in the 500 meters and sixteenth in the 1,000 meters. Thrilled at having come so close to taking the bronze in the 500-meter race, Jansen returned home to find that competitors who finish out of the medals do not get much respect, particularly from the media. "That's when I started to feel [that too big a deal is made out of] medals," he told *People.*

The preparation for Jansen's next shot at gold in the Winter Olympics of 1988 was marred by the diagnosis of one of his sisters, Jane Bere, with leukemia. The doctors told her that her only hope for survival was a bone marrow transplant. The only family members with compatible marrow were Jansen and his other sister, Joanne Jansen. Dan was fully prepared to be a donor, even though it likely would have spelled an end to his skating career. Bere, however, rejected his offer and instead accepted the marrow from Joanne. Bere appeared to be doing well immediately after the transplant surgery in September 1987, but only three months later she was forced to reenter the hospital.

Despite the gravity of his sister's illness, Jansen in February 1988 traveled to Calgary, Alberta, Canada, for the opening of the Olympics. "It hurt to leave her," he told *Sporting News* shortly after his arrival in the Olympic Village. "It makes all this [skating] seem unimportant. I want to go out there and do well for her because she's fought so hard." On the morning of his 500-meter speed skating competition, one of his brothers called to say that Bere was dying and wanted to say goodbye. Jansen spoke to her, but Bere's oxygen mask made it impossible for her to respond. An hour later she died. Considered a favorite for gold in the 500-meter event, Jansen vowed to dedicate the medal to his sister if he won. Sadly, only seconds into his race he fell and slid across the ice, taking another skater out of action in the process. Jansen had never before fallen in a race. Four days later he fell again after skating the first 800 meters of his 1,000-meter event at a record-setting pace.

America's heart went out to Jansen. Millions had seen his heartbreaking falls in Calgary in the wake of his sister's death. He received thousands of letters from fans upon his return to the United States. President Ronald Reagan invited him to the White House, and the U.S. Olympic Committee honored him with its Olympic Spirit Award. Jansen told *Rolling Stone:* "At that time I was more concerned about my sister than I was about skating. But now it's time for me to look ahead."

And look ahead he did. He won the World Sprint Championships, a combination of 500-meter and 1,000-meter races, later in 1988 and the overall men's title at the 1990 U.S. International Speed Skating Association championships. He accumulated a string of impressive victories, some at record paces, in the period leading up to the 1992 Winter Olympics at Albertville, France. In April 1990 Jansen married Robin Wicker, a hotel personnel director. They had two daughters, and later divorced in 1997. At the Olympics Jansen faltered, placing fourth, just out of the medals, in the 500-meter, his best event, and a dismal twenty-sixth in the 1,000-meter race. Many of the same Americans who had rooted for Jansen in 1988 and again in 1992 began to wonder if he really had what it took to finish in the medals.

A juggling of Olympics schedules, intended to stagger the summer and winter games by two years, meant that the next Winter Olympics was held in early 1994, only two years after Jansen's disappointments at Albertville. Despite his less than stellar record on Olympic ice, Jansen was considered a clear favorite in the 500-meter event at Lillehammer, Norway. His personal Olympic jinx, however, struck again, and he finished in eighth place after slipping and touching his hand to the ice, significantly slowing his pace. In what was to be his final Olympic event, the 1,000-meter,

Jansen amazed even himself with a record-breaking time of 1:12.43, despite a slight slip near the end of the race. His quest for Olympic gold had finally succeeded. Overcome with emotion, Jansen had difficulty singing the national anthem during the medals presentation. When the ceremony was over, he had begun to skate a victory lap when he was handed his infant daughter Jane, named for his sister. Holding her aloft, Jansen completed his long-awaited victory lap to the cheers of thousands.

With the Olympics behind him and the elusive gold medal finally hanging around his neck, Jansen announced his retirement from skating. From 1994 until 1998 he worked as a commentator for CBS Sports, and he continues to deliver motivational messages across the nation.

Undeterred by great personal tragedy and a string of stinging disappointments that surely would have broken a lesser man, Jansen persisted in his quest until he finally achieved his goal in a storybook ending that stirred the souls of all Americans. John Teaford, the former U.S. speed skating coach, perhaps summed it up best when he said of Jansen: "With someone like Dan, it's a comfort to see that there really are heroes; that America's family members are out there winning. No drugs, no big salaries, no scandals; just kids you'd like to see your sons and daughters marry."

★

After his gold medal performance in his final Olympic event, Jansen wrote, with Jack McCallum, *Full Circle: An Olympic Champion Shares His Breakthrough Story* (1994), the skater's own account of how he finally banished his demons and grabbed the gold. A biography of Jansen suitable for younger readers is Bob Italia, *Dan Jansen: Olympic Speedskating Champion* (1994). For fascinating insight into the training program that the sports psychologist Jim Loehr employed to bring Jansen and other sports stars to the peak of their games, see Jim Loehr, *The New Toughness Training for Sports* (1995).

DON AMERMAN

JEFFRIES, James Jackson (*b.* 15 April 1875 in Carroll, Ohio; *d.* 3 March 1953 in Burbank, California), heavyweight boxer considered one of the best champions of all time, but better known as the "Great White Hope" who lost to Jack Johnson in 1910.

Born in rural Ohio, Jeffries was the child of minister and farmer Alexis Jeffries and Rebecca Boyer Jeffries. The family, which grew to include five sons and three daughters, moved to Los Angeles in 1882. At age sixteen Jeffries had already reached six feet, two inches in height and was displaying the exceptional strength and agility that would mark him as a fighter. He found work as a boilermaker in Los Angeles during his teenage years, and tried his hand

James Jeffries. AP/WIDE WORLD PHOTOS

at mining in nearby Temecula as well. His youthful feats included killing a large deer on a hunting expedition, then carrying it nine miles on his shoulders to his camp without stopping to rest.

Jeffries began boxing at Los Angeles's East Side Athletic Club, knocking out his first five opponents. Heading for San Francisco, he won a series of bouts and, in 1897, became the sparring partner for heavyweight champion James J. "Jim" Corbett. Learning from Corbett's skill and agility, Jeffries took on experienced fighters Joe Choynksi and Gus Ruhlin, battling both to a draw. On 22 March 1898 he knocked out Peter Jackson, who had gone undefeated for fourteen years. Two months later he scored a twenty-round decision win over "Sailor" Tom Sharkey.

All these early matches took place in San Francisco. Jeffries did not fight outside of California until he defeated Bob Armstrong on 5 August 1898 in New York City. Observers marveled at his ability to throw bone-breaking punches and to absorb punishment without weakening. In prime condition Jeffries weighed between 205 and 227 pounds, but for a fighter of his size and weight he was remarkably quick on his feet. Author Jack London spoke for many when he called Jeffries physique "a perfection of symmetry that is the fruit of the highest organic development." An avid outdoorsman all his adult life, he was known for his sober, health-conscious habits.

Under the management and guidance of William A. Brady, Jeffries challenged Bob Fitzsimmons for the world heavyweight championship. Fitzsimmons was considered the favorite on the eve of the match, held 9 June 1899 at the Seaside Athletic Club on Coney Island. But an upset appeared in the making by the second round, as Jeffries managed to avoid Fitzsimmons's blows and dropped the champion with a left hook. Throughout the match, Jeffries came at Fitzsimmons in a crouch that allowed him to land repeated blows to his torso and head. The sturdy champion managed to hang on into the fifteenth round, when Jeffries finally knocked him out with a right uppercut.

Jeffries wore the heavyweight champion's crown with a remarkable lack of arrogance. He returned to the Seaside Athletic Club to defend his title against Tom Sharkey on 3 November 1899. After twenty-five bloody rounds, Jeffries was declared the winner as a battered Sharkey was taken to the hospital. Next, he easily bested Jack Finnegan in the first round of a 6 April 1900 match-up, then took on his old sparring partner Jim Corbett on 11 May of that year. Back again at the Seaside Athletic Club, Jeffries overcame the ex-champion's still-formidable footwork and punching tactics to knock him down in the twenty-third round.

Notable bouts the following year included a 15 November rematch with Gus Ruhlin in San Francisco that resulted in a fifth round knockout win. In the same city on 25 July 1902, Jeffries once again faced Fitzsimmons, still a formidable foe at age thirty-nine. The champion took a fierce mauling from the man he had beaten two years earlier, but hung on to knock out Fitzsimmons in the tenth round with a right to the stomach.

Following his second victory over Fitzsimmons, Jeffries starred as Davy Crockett in a touring stage show. These performances were followed by an exhibition match where the heavyweight champion boxed a few rounds with a sparring partner. In 1903, he and Fitzsimmons were paired in a series of exhibition matches as well. Jeffries was finding it hard to attract opponents worthy of his mettle. A third match with Corbett held 14 August 1903 in San Francisco was an unequal contest; Jeffries dispatched the now-faded Gentleman Jim in the tenth round.

After knocking out Jack Monroe in the second round of a 26 August 1904 match in San Francisco, Jeffries decided he'd had enough. Later that year, the undefeated world heavyweight champion bought 107 acres in Burbank, California, gave up boxing and became an alfalfa farmer. He and his new bride Freida (family name unknown) settled down to a comfortable life, raising their daughter Mary in seclusion. Jeffries did take time out to referee the elimination bout between his would-be successors, Marvin Hart and Jack Root. Over the next few years, he put on excessive weight and vowed never to fight again.

Against his better judgment, Jeffries was swept up in the hysteria over Jack Johnson's streak of ring victories. Many white Americans couldn't stand the idea that an African-American boxer kept defeating Caucasian opponents. Searching for a "Great White Hope," they settled on Jeffries, who finally agreed to fight for a $100,000 purse offered by promoter Tex Rickard. Enlisting Jim Corbett as his trainer, the ex-champ slimmed down to 227 pounds and brushed up his rusty ring skills. Expectations leading up to the 4 July 1910 bout, which was dubbed "The Fight of the Century," were enormous. Once the two contenders entered the ring in Reno, Nevada, it became clear that Jeffries was in no condition to take on Johnson. Taunting his opponent, Johnson evaded Jeffries's blows easily while slowly beating him into submission. Jeffries, exhausted, was counted out in the fifteenth round.

Despite his ignominious defeat, Jeffries was warmly regarded in his remaining years. He returned to his farm, where in later years he trained boxers and promoted bouts at his barn. He died peacefully on 3 March 1953. He is buried at Inglewood Park Cemetery, Los Angeles County. Considered one of the greatest heavyweight champions, he was also remembered as a kind, decent man. Jeffries's ill-advised comeback fight against Johnson was a false move in a largely exemplary boxing career.

★

Jeffries lacks a definitive modern biography. He is treated at length in several books on Jack Johnson, including Randy Roberts, *Papa Jack* (1986), and Finis Farr, *Black Champion* (1969). Veteran sportswriter William Inglis's *Champions off Guard* (1932) includes an insightful chapter of Jeffries. An obituary is in the *New York Times* (4 Mar. 1953).

BARRY ALFONSO

JENKINS, Carol Heiss. *See* Heiss Jenkins, Carol Elizabeth.

JENKINS, David Wilkinson (*b.* 29 June 1936 in Akron, Ohio), three-time world champion figure skater and Olympic gold medallist.

Jenkins was the third child of Hayes R. Jenkins, a lawyer and tire company executive, and Sarah Wilkinson Jenkins, a homemaker and judge for skating events. All three Jenkins offspring enjoyed skating as children, but the two brothers, David and Hayes, became the most successful siblings in figure skating history. Together they dominated the sport between 1953 and 1960. Hayes Jenkins won the gold medal at the 1956 Olympic Games, Jenkins won gold at the 1960 Olympic Games.

David Jenkins *(far right)* with Ronald Robertson *(left)* and Jenkins's older brother, Hayes Jenkins *(center)*.
ASSOCIATED PRESS AP

Jenkins was about six when he followed his older brother and sister to the Akron skating rink. He was a fearless youngster who loved to jump, sometimes with unfortunate results. At nine he invented what his then teacher Walter Arian called the Jenkins "forehead flop," knocking himself out for a considerable time. This setback did not diminish Jenkins's love of the sport. In 1953, five years after his brother had won the title, Jenkins became the U.S. junior champion. A few months later he joined his brother as part of the U.S. team and competed in his first world championship. His older brother won and Jenkins came fourth.

Neither brother would have reached this level if their talent had not been recognized by others. As Jenkins explained, "Skating was very expensive and the money dried up. We could not have continued without support from the Broadmoor Club in Colorado Springs." The two brothers and their mother had moved to Colorado in 1952 to take advantage of the club's sponsorship offer. In the 1950s, when athletes had to show they were not being paid to compete in order to retain their amateur status, the offer was both limited and controversial.

When his brother retired after winning Olympic gold and his fourth world crown in 1956, Jenkins took over his place at the top. As a skater Jenkins was nurtured by his brother, but because their skating styles were so different their abilities were not really compared. While Hayes was respected for his artistry, David was known for his athleticism, performing as many as three different types of triple rotation jumps—the flip, loop and salchow—in a single

routine, fifteen years before this became the norm. Jenkins finished fourth in the 1956 Olympic Games and won the bronze medal in the 1956 world championships, but he was never beaten again.

The governing body of figure skating, the International Skating Union, did not rule that championships must be held indoors until after 1967, and in Europe events mostly took place outdoors. European skaters referred to American competitors as "hot house plants" because of their inexperience with skating in bad weather. At the 1956 world championship, there was one place on the rink where the ice level suddenly dropped six inches, and Jenkins fell four times in the free skating because the brittle ice broke up under his skates. Even so, he managed to finish third and fell in competition only once more in the next four years. At other times, skaters in outdoor competitions were knocked over by the wind and drenched by the rain. The world championships were held in the United States in 1957, the first time since 1930, and only the second time ever. Under ideal conditions, and skating on home ice at the Broadmoor Club, Jenkins won the first of three successive world titles. All nine judges placed him first in both the school figures and the free-skating sections, a very rare occurrence.

Jenkins was unbeatable in the next years despite carrying a full academic load, first at Colorado College, where he earned a B.A. degree in 1958, and then at Western Reserve School of Medicine in Cleveland, where he earned an M.D. in 1963. As on the rink, Jenkins showed a stubborn streak in his determination to succeed in his medical studies, and his student draft deferment only gave him a greater incentive to succeed in both arenas. Amazingly, from 1954 on he skated in a back brace because of a weight lifting injury, and is probably the only person to manage triple jumps in that condition. Jenkins was also one of the first to try a triple axel jump in which the skater makes three and a half rotations in the air. Jenkins said of his attempts, "In practice I was landing it about thirty percent of the time. I gave up trying because I didn't need it and there was too much risk of injury." The jump was not accomplished in a world championship until 1978.

Jenkins's greatest glory came at the 1960 Winter Olympic Games in Squaw Valley, California, where he won the gold medal. The 1960 games were the first to be televised. Jenkins, who was relatively unknown to the general public before the games, was thrust into the limelight, although his fame did not match that accorded to today's star athletes. Jenkins describes the experience of winning gold as a profound one: "There are very few things in life that you can complete, take to the limit and say, 'That's it, I accomplished all that was possible. I can now set it aside.'"

Jenkins did not compete in the 1960 world championships, held a short time after the Olympics, because he felt he had lost too much study time to altitude training for the Squaw Valley Olympics. He retired to concentrate on his medical studies, taking a year off (1961–1962) to perform in an ice show to help pay for medical school. Jenkins graduated with an M.D. in 1963 and immediately after served two years in the U.S. Air Force. In June of 1965 he married Barbara Ruth Boling and settled in Tulsa, where he became a gastroenterologist. Neither his wife nor his three children skate.

★

Information about Jenkins's career can be found in Benjamin T. Wright's *Reader's Guide to Figure Skating's Hall of Fame* (1978); the International Skating Union's *75 years (1892–1967) of European and World's Championships in Figure Skating* (1970); and *The Official Book of Figure Skating* (1998), produced by the United States Figure Skating Association (USFSA). Various issues of *Skating,* the official magazine of the USFSA, contain articles on Jenkins, including Theresa Weld Blanchard's "Meet the Champions" (June 1953); Theodore G. Patterson's report "World Championships" (Apr. 1955); Blanchard's report "The World Championships" (May 1956); Blanchard's and Edith Ray's "The Championships of the World" (May 1957); and a further article on Jenkins by Blanchard, "David W. Jenkins" (June 1957). The report on the 1958 world championships is credited to "several U.S. observers" (Apr. 1958), and there is a further review of Jenkins's 1958 successes in Ray, "Meet the United States Champions" (June 1958).

SANDRA STEVENSON

JENKINS, Hayes Alan (*b.* 23 March 1933 in Akron, Ohio), figure skater who won four world championship gold medals and a gold medal at the 1956 Olympics.

Jenkins was eight when he and his eleven-year-old sister, Nancy Sue, began skating at the Akron Ice Land Arena. Their mother, Sarah Wilkinson, was a homemaker, and their father, Hayes Ray Jenkins, was a lawyer and tire company executive. The enthusiasm the children showed for skating led the family to look for more advanced coaching and ice time and they began commuting the thirty miles to Cleveland either before or after school and at weekends. Jenkins's younger brother, David, was dragged along and their mother eventually began judging skating events.

Before long Nancy Sue found competing as a single was too nerve-wracking, so she persuaded her brother Hayes to join her in the pairs and ice dance competitions. They achieved some success between 1945 and 1948 before Nancy Sue went off to college. Jenkins believed that the ice dancing improved his later work as a singles skater, by instilling the discipline of paying attention to the music. He also enjoyed the challenge of the "school figures," where skaters traced slow figure eights on the ice and were awarded points for accuracy and smoothness. At that time sixty percent of the marks for skating events were given to the school figures, which have not been part of the sport since 1990, and only forty percent went for the spins and jumps.

In 1948 Jenkins won the U.S. junior championship and was selected to go to Paris, France, for the 1949 world championships. With very little money available, and with corporate sponsorship strictly limited for amateurs, Jenkins went to Paris alone. The U.S. Figure Skating Association provided no financial support to participants, and only the senior champion got a portion of his fare paid to the worlds. Jenkins finished sixth, and was amazed by the sport's popularity in Europe as compared to the United States. The following year, in 1950, while still attending Buchtel High School, he won the world bronze medal.

In June 1951 Jenkins graduated from Buchtel and began studying economics at Northwestern University in Evanston, Illinois. In 1952 he made the Olympic team. In Oslo, Norway, Dick Button won his second consecutive Olympic gold medal and Jenkins finished fourth. He was the first from that school ever to take part in a Winter Olympics.

Jenkins had expected to stop skating in 1952. The time-consuming commute between his studies at Evanston and his training in downtown Chicago was starting to wear thin. However Jenkins and later his brother were offered scholarships at Colorado College, and they moved with their mother to Colorado Springs in the summer of 1952. By winning the 1953 world championships in Davos, Switzerland, Jenkins proved he had made the right decision.

Hayes Jenkins and Tenley Albright at the 1953 U.S. figure skating championships. ASSOCIATED PRESS AP

After winning the world title he was never beaten again. As world champion, Jenkins wanted to show that "I wasn't a flash in the pan. I didn't realize how hard it would be. Winning is totally different to defending a title. It's a different mind-set and it's much harder."

Shortly after his world win, Jenkins and the women's champion Tenley Albright were flown to Japan for several weeks, where they gave exhibitions and clinics to help Japanese skaters. In 1954 both Jenkins and his brother made the world championship team; Jenkins retained the title and David finished fourth. After winning his third world title in 1955, Jenkins went into the 1956 Olympic Games held in Cortina d'Ampezzo, Italy, as the favorite for gold. He was even featured with Tenley Albright on the cover of *Sports Illustrated*. Jenkins did not disappoint. He brought home the gold medal after staying in Europe for a few more weeks to win his fourth world championship.

In 1956 Jenkins graduated from Colorado College with a B.A. degree in economics. He appeared briefly in the summer of 1956 with *Holiday on Ice* to help finance his studies at Harvard Law School in Cambridge, Massachusetts, then hung up his skates. In 1959 he graduated from Harvard Law and passed the Ohio bar exam. On 30 April 1960 he married the figure skater Carol Heiss, shortly after she won an Olympic gold in Squaw Valley, California. Heiss won five world championships to Jenkins's four, a

fact which, her husband claimed, she never let him forget. The couple had three children.

Jenkins began a career as a lawyer, specializing in corporate and private international law. He joined the Goodyear Tire and Rubber Company in 1963, and retired as the firm's legal counsel on 1 January 1997. Jenkins was only the second U.S. male figure skater (after Dick Button) to win an Olympic gold medal. Together, the Jenkins brothers won eight consecutive annual U.S. championships, seven world titles, and two Olympic gold medals to dominate their sport completely between 1953 and 1960. They also won gold medals at the North American championships, a dual-country event between Canada and the United States that no longer exists.

Jenkins is referred to as "the complete skater." Figure skating and free skating demand very different skills, but Jenkins was equally admired for his solid technical mastery while slowly tracing geometrically perfect figure eights and for his artistry and musicality in free skating.

★

Information about Jenkins's career can be found in Benjamin T. Wright, *Reader's Guide to Figure Skating's Hall of Fame,* ed. Gregory R. Smith (1978); International Skating Union, *Seventy-five Years (1892–1967) of European and World Championships in Figure Skating* (1970); and U.S. Figure Skating Association, *The*

Official Book of Figure Skating (1998). Jenkins also features in Dick Button, *Dick Button on Skates* (1955). *Skating* magazine, the official publication of the U.S. Figure Skating Association, has featured many articles on Jenkins, especially at the height of his fame. Among the most informative are Theresa Weld Blanchard, *Skating* (Apr. 1952, Apr. 1953, June 1953, Apr. 1955, and June 1956). See also Theodore G. Patterson, *Skating* (May 1956).

SANDRA STEVENSON

JENNER, (William) Bruce (*b.* 28 October 1949 in Mount Kisco, New York), decathlete who won the gold medal at the 1976 Olympics in Montreal, Canada.

Jenner was the second of four children born to William Jenner, a tree surgeon, and Estelle Jenner, a homemaker. He spent his early childhood in Mount Kisco; when he was in his early teens, the family moved to Newton, Connecticut. Jenner came from a long line of athletes, and it seemed only natural that he would one day become an Olympic hero. His father had won the silver medal in the 100-yard dash at the U.S. Army Olympics in Nuremberg, Germany, in 1945, and his grandfather had run the Boston Marathon several times. While Jenner excelled at sports, he struggled with academics. An undiagnosed dyslexic, he had great difficulty learning to read and was ridiculed by his classmates. But things changed for him in the fifth grade when it was discovered that he was a fast runner. He quickly became popular and gained the respect of his peers.

Jenner attended Newton High School where he participated in basketball, football, and track. He won numerous trophies, including awards from the Eastern States water-ski competition and New York State's pole-vault and high-jump championships. Despite his poor grades, he received a football scholarship to Graceland College in Lamoni, Iowa. His days on the gridiron ended early in his freshman year after he suffered an injury to his knee, tearing his medial collateral ligament. Although he could no longer play football, he was still able to play on the school's basketball and track teams. It was track, however, that captured his heart. Jenner enjoyed the grueling demands of the sport as well as the personal challenges it presented. In track and field, unlike team sports, he relied solely on himself to win competitions. He competed in his first decathlon in 1970 and not only won the event but also broke the school's record.

Jenner decided to focus on the decathlon and set his goals for the 1972 Olympic Games in Munich, Germany. Only three decathletes would represent the United States at the games. After one year of training, Jenner arrived at the Olympic tryouts as a virtual unknown. He had difficulty on the first day of competition and finished in eleventh place. On the second day of the trials he inched up the rankings, and by the time he completed his pole vault and javelin throw, he had moved up to fifth place. His dream of competing at the Olympics depended on his performance in the last event, the 1,500-meter run. In order to secure a spot on the U.S. team, he needed to beat the person in third place by eighteen seconds. Jenner not only overcame the third-place athlete to make the U.S. team, he won the competition by twenty-one seconds. After a disappointing performance at the Olympics in Munich, where

Bruce Jenner. AP/WIDE WORLD PHOTOS

he finished in tenth place, Jenner returned to the United States determined to win the gold medal in the 1976 summer games in Montreal, Canada.

On 16 December 1972 Jenner married his college sweetheart, Chrystie Crownover; they had two children. Crownover worked as a flight attendant to support her husband while he prepared for the Olympic Games. Training became Jenner's main occupation, and he often worked out for eight hours a day, five days a week. He also worked part-time as an insurance salesman to help support his family, and in 1973 he graduated from Graceland College.

Jenner's hard work and dedication paid off in 1975 when he secured a spot on the U.S. Olympic team by winning the decathlon at the Pan-American Games in Mexico City. By the time the Olympic Games arrived, Jenner was favored to win the gold medal. After the first day of competition, Jenner trailed West Germany's Guido Kratschmer by thirty-five points, but on the second day, he competed in his stronger events: the 110-meter hurdles, discus, pole vault javelin, and 1,500-meter run. By the end of the eighth event, he had a giant lead. He set a personal record in the 1,500-meter, and also set a new world record with 8,618 points, in addition to taking home the gold medal and the title of world's greatest athlete. He retired from the sport that same day, feeling that he had accomplished his goal and that he had given up too much in life in order to win the gold medal. He made his point by leaving his vault poles at the Olympic stadium.

Jenner's achievement made him an instant celebrity. His story was featured in newspapers and magazines throughout the United States and he was sought after for public appearances and offered endorsement deals. Jenner received many accolades; he was named as the Associated Press Athlete of the Year and received the Sullivan Award as the best amateur athlete in the United States. His newfound fame and popularity landed him several acting roles, including cameo appearances on television shows and small roles in movies. He also worked as a sportscaster for ABC Sports, as guest host and special correspondent from 1976 to 1988, and was ABC's official representative to the 1988 Winter Games in Calgary. He also worked with NBC between 1976 and 1980 and anchored one of their pay-per-view channels during the 1992 summer games in Barcelona. Jenner also authored *Decathlon Challenge: Bruce Jenner's Story* (1977), an autobiography describing his road to the Olympics, and *Bruce and Chrystie Jenner's Guide to Family Fitness* (1978).

While Jenner's professional life thrived, his personal life underwent some major changes. After eight years, his marriage to Crownover ended in a high-profile divorce in 1980. One year later, Jenner married Linda Thompson, a former beauty queen and the ex-girlfriend of the singer Elvis Presley. They had two children before divorcing in 1986. Jenner met Kris Kardashian on a blind date in 1990, and the two

married five months later. Combined, the couple raised ten children, including those from their previous marriages. They had two daughters together, and live with their children in Hidden Hills, California.

Jenner credited Kardashian for being the mastermind behind their lucrative business ventures, which included infomercials, videotapes, a women's self-defense and fitness program, and a line of exercise equipment. Jenner also worked as a lecturer and was sought by major corporations for his motivational speeches. More than two decades after winning the Olympic decathlon, Jenner was still associated with the sport and was the subject of the CD-ROM game *Bruce Jenner's World-Class Decathlon* (1996). He was named to the Olympic Hall of Fame in 1986.

Twenty-five years after capturing the gold medal, Jenner is still revered as a champion. An athlete, sportscaster, motivational speaker, entrepreneur, and family man, Jenner's work ethic and indomitable spirit have enabled him to overcome obstacles on and off the track field and succeed in life.

★

Jenner has written several books, including with Phillip Finch, *Decathlon Challenge: Bruce Jenner's Story* (1977); *Bruce and Chrystie Jenner's Guide to Family Fitness* (1978); with Marc Abraham, *Bruce Jenner's Guide to the Olympics* (1979); with R. Smith Kiliper, *The Olympics and Me* (1980); with Bill Dobbins, *Bruce Jenner's The Athletic Body: A Complete Fitness Guide for Teenagers—Sports, Strength, Health, Agility* (1984); with Marc Abraham, *Bruce Jenner's Viewers Guide to the 1984 Summer Olympics* (1984); and with Mark Seal, *Finding the Champion Within: A Step-by-Step Plan for Reaching Your Full Potential* (1996). His life story and accomplishments also appear in *Current Biography Yearbook* (1977); *Sport* (July 1976, Nov. 1976); *Sports Illustrated* (9 Aug. 1976); and *People Weekly* (11 Apr. 1977, 15 July 1996).

SABINE LOUISSAINT

JETER, Derek Sanderson (*b.* 26 June 1974 in Pequannock, New Jersey), baseball player for the New York Yankees who in 2000 was the Most Valuable Player in the All-Star game and the World Series.

Jeter was the older of two children born to Charles Jeter, a drug and alcohol counselor, and Dorothy (Connors) Jeter, who worked in an accountancy firm. The family moved to Kalamazoo, Michigan, in 1979. Both Jeter and his sister were keen baseball fans as children, and their parents attended many school baseball and softball games. In the eighth grade Jeter predicted that he would be in a New York Yankees uniform within ten years. He played basketball and baseball at school, performing well at both, but his exceptional ability at baseball was evident from the time he joined the Westwood Little League team in Kalamazoo.

During high school Jeter played ball for the Kalamazoo

Derek Jeter, 2001. ASSOCIATED PRESS AP

Central High School team. In his junior year his batting average was an impressive .557, followed by a senior-year average of .508. In 1992 he was named the American Baseball Coaches Association High School Player of the Year. That summer, serious recruitment efforts on the part of Major League Baseball teams began in earnest. It seemed likely that Jeter would be signed by the Cincinnati Reds, when the call from the Yankees finally arrived. Despite the interest from other teams, Jeter was the first pick of the New York Yankees in the 1992 draft.

For the next four years the young shortstop played in the Yankees minor league system, beginning with the Tampa Yankees in 1992. His initial contract was for $700,000. By 2000 this had grown to a staggering $10 million for his fifth full major league season. However, Jeter struggled at first in the minor leagues. He was homesick in Tampa and hit just .200 as well as making twenty-eight errors in only fifty-eight games. In spring 1993 the Yankees moved him to the Greensboro Hornets, a Class A team in North Carolina, hoping to work on his skills with a lower-class team. Although his defense remained poor, Jeter's batting earned him the title of Most Outstanding Major League Prospect.

The 1994 season saw a dramatic shift in Jeter's fortunes as his playing merited a rapid rise to the Class AA Albany team in upstate New York, and then to the Class AAA

Columbus Clippers, the Yankees farm team in Ohio. During this period both the Yankees manager Joe Torre and the owner George Steinbrenner had opportunities to watch Jeter play, and helped him to move up quickly through the ranks. His record for the season was a .344 batting average with 5 home runs, 68 runs batted in (RBI), and 50 stolen bases. In 1994 Jeter was named the Minor League Player of the Year by *USA Today, Baseball America, Sporting News,* and *Baseball Weekly.* In the wake of Bernie Williams's absence, Jeter was called up to the Yankees briefly in September 1995. His appearance included an important hit that made possible a strong-looking finish to the team's season. Jeter returned to the minor leagues, only to find himself designated soon after as the starting shortstop for his beloved Yankees for the 1996 season.

When he was drafted at age eighteen, Jeter weighed just 160 pounds. He gradually raised his weight over the years, and during winter training in Tampa in 1995 he managed to add ten pounds in muscle to his slight six-foot, three-inch frame, reaching a more powerful 195 pounds. The extra bulk paid off. When he joined the Yankees in 1996, he was the first rookie in thirty-four years to start as a shortstop, and won the Rookie of the Year honor with an impressive 183 hits, 78 RBI, and 10 home runs in a season that saw the Yankees win their first World Series since 1981.

Jeter's performance in the late 1990s continued to be impressive, and he joined the ranks of several outstanding contemporary shortstops, including Alex Rodriguez of the Seattle Mariners and Nomar Garciaparra of the Boston Red Sox. These three players spearheaded a renewed interest in the shortstop's role in the game. Jeter became increasingly important to his team's success, and by 2001 he occupied a central place in the Yankees's lineup, earning four World Championship rings in his first six major league seasons. Jeter's performance earned him the awards of Most Valuable Player for both the All-Star game and the World Series in the 2000 season.

Called "E. P." or "Elvis Presley" because of the wild behavior he has inspired in female fans, Jeter has managed to keep his head despite the pressures of fame and vast wealth. He lives in both Manhattan's Upper East Side and Tampa, while maintaining close ties to his family. Jeter started his own foundation, Turn 2, to help youngsters in Kalamazoo and New York City deal with alcohol and drug-abuse problems. The foundation is managed on a day-to-day basis by his father.

As a baseball player, Jeter is known for his cool, hard-working professionalism. He begins his preseason training regimen almost immediately after the season ends and practices and works out regularly throughout the winter months in preparation for spring training. Few ball players have been this dedicated to the game. As a key member of the outstanding Yankees teams of the late 1990s, Jeter's hitting, fielding, and running appear set to continue to improve as he matures.

★

Jeter has been profiled in magazines from *Sports Illustrated* to *Vogue*. Articles of note include a profile in the *New York Times Magazine* (19 July 1998) and *Jet* (8 Mar. 1999). Further information about Jeter is available in a book he wrote with Jack Curry, *The Life You Imagine: Life Lessons for Achieving Your Dreams* (2000).

JAMES J. SULLIVAN III

JOBSON, Gary (*b.* 17 July 1950 in Hackensack, New Jersey), professional sailor, author, and television commentator who built a unique international career by participating in and documenting top-level amateur and professional sailboat racing and the diversity of sailing since the mid-1970s.

Jobson has exhibited an infectious enthusiasm for all forms of sailing since early childhood crewing in small boats on Barnegat Bay in New Jersey. His talent blossomed at New York Maritime College where he was on the water almost every day and kept a written record of how each of hundreds of races played out. His concerted practice and racing performance earned him All-American sailor titles three times, and he was named College Sailor of the Year in 1972 and 1973, the year he graduated. Jobson has been quoted as saying, "You are never a better sailor than the day you graduate from college sailing." He applied the experience to coaching at the United States Merchant Marine Academy for four years and then moved to the coaching staff of the U.S. Naval Academy.

Jobson took time off from coaching when he was recruited by the businessman, philanthropist, and yachtsman Ted Turner to be tactician in the 1977 America's Cup, which was still an august amateur event. On board the Twelve Meter Class sloop *Courageous,* Jobson's job was to provide critical strategy and tactics to Turner at the helm and help with crew coordination during practice. Turner's characteristic brash behavior played favorably with the press although less so with the yachting establishment. Nevertheless, *Courageous* beat the Australian challenger in four straight races, and the Cup stayed with the New York Yacht Club.

At twenty-six years old, Jobson had applied his racing experience and his coaching skills of communication and tactical analysis toward the success of what had been the underdog boat in the U.S. elimination rounds and then to winning the premiere event of international match racing. Turner helped motivate him by predicting, "Jobson, you will be a household name when this is over."

Jobson has always made a point of sharing what he

Gary Jobson after winning the Liberty Cup, 1988. AP/WIDE WORLD PHOTOS

knows with a wider audience. Turner and Jobson followed up their victory with a book on sailing tactics, *The Racing Edge,* which gave detailed advice for around-the-buoy racing in identical boats and for longer offshore races where the challenge is to beat a variety of boats evenly handicapped by rating formulas. Sometimes, an ocean race becomes a matter of survival as well as a competition, as in the infamous 1979 Fastnet Race when a storm savaged the fleet in the Irish Sea. Twenty-four boats were abandoned at sea, their crews saved by helicopters or rescue vessels. Fifteen people died. Jobson was with Turner's yacht *Tenacious,* which sailed the 605 miles through the disastrous tumult to win the race. He addressed the lessons learned from Fastnet and other incidents in his book *Storm Sailing.* Jobson has built an unprecedented career of lecturing and writing about sailing events around the world, based on his own experience and his insight into the many forms of sailing. Along with his book projects, he has contributed monthly columns to *Cruising World* and *Sailing World* magazines in his capacity of editor-at-large.

Most sailors excel in a particular type of boat or type of competition, although they may be intrigued by other sailing events. Jobson has made a point of experiencing all the diversity a wind-driven boat can offer, from small to large and from common designs to exotic feats of technology. "I have gone for the broad range of sailing as opposed to specializing in one particular area of the sport," Jobson said, "whether sailing a dinghy single-handed against one hundred boats, match racing a twelve meter, skipping across an ocean at thirty knots on a megamaran, or coordinating the efforts of twenty-six crew on a maxiyacht."

Since the 1980s, Jobson has added video production and television commentary to his accomplishments. He joined ESPN in 1985, and his coverage of sailing at the 1988 Olympic Games won an Emmy. He has produced thirty shows a year and produced or narrated forty home videos. Jobson uses innovative techniques of onboard cameras and computer animation to create exciting programs for sailors and non-sailors alike. His projects have involved extensive travel from his home in Annapolis, Maryland. The America's Cup competition, which moved to New Zealand in 1997, for example, has grown into a lavish, professional event with live commentary through the weeks of elimination rounds and the final match. Jobson has also given the public an appreciation of the strain and exhilaration felt by the pros sailing the Whitbread Round the World Race, a 32,000-mile, nine-month, ocean marathon.

For a change of pace, Jobson has tackled the adverse conditions of the Arctic and Antarctic on specialized sailboats built for such icy adventures. In his time off, he cruises Chesapeake Bay with his wife and three daughters. While rising to be a respected authority, he continued to find sailing fun, and as Turner predicted, became a household name.

Jobson has been generous with his time in encouraging sailing programs and raising money for charity. He has been the National Regatta chairman for the Leukemia and Lymphoma Society, and he helped start the first sailing team at Hampton University. For the total of his professional and personal contribution to sailing, the United States Sailing Association gave him their highest award in 1999, the Nathanael G. Herreshoff Trophy.

Jobson has excelled in promoting sailing to a broad audience, even while the sport itself was rapidly evolving through technological advancements and benefiting from the spectacles of professional events and corporate sponsorship—encouraged, not coincidentally, by successful media coverage.

★

Jobson has written for the novice, the expert, and the armchair sailor. *Sailing Fundamentals* is a fine introduction to sailing skills, and *Championship Tactics* burnishes the skills of those who think they know almost everything. *World Class Sailing* is a memoir of Jobson's views of some of the people, places, and yachts that have helped define his career. His videos capture the sights and sounds of sailing at its most challenging. "Caution to the Wind" is the essence of the 1997/1998 Whitbread Race, and "Expedition Antarctica" heads beyond normal recreational cruising grounds.

SHEILA MCCURDY

JOHNSON, Earvin, Jr. ("Magic") (*b.* 14 August 1959 in Lansing, Michigan), star basketball player who led the Los Angeles Lakers to several National Basketball Association championships, successful businessman, and AIDS activist.

Johnson was the sixth of ten children born to Earvin Johnson, Sr., an autoworker, and Christine Johnson, a cafeteria worker. His trademark nickname of "Magic" dates back to his years of playing ball at Lansing's Everett High School. Impressed by Johnson's smiling demeanor and his high-energy, quick-footed style on the basketball court, a local sportswriter dubbed him "Magic" after a game in which he scored thirty-six points, with sixteen rebounds and sixteen assists. The name stuck. In his senior year at Everett, Johnson averaged 28.8 points and 16.8 rebounds per game, leading the team to a 27–1 record of wins and losses and the state championship.

Hopping across town from high school in Lansing to Michigan State University in East Lansing, Johnson proved a real phenomenon. While still a freshman, he tapped those

Magic Johnson. AP/WIDE WORLD PHOTOS

magical playing skills to lead the university's Spartans to their first Big Ten title in nineteen years. When Johnson was a sophomore, Michigan State clinched the National Collegiate Athletic Association title, bringing an offer from the Los Angeles Lakers to turn professional at the end of his second year of college. In a preview of a rivalry that would emerge during his years of playing pro ball, Johnson led his MSU team to victory over Larry Bird and the rest of the Indiana University team in clinching the NCAA title. Unsure what to do, he sought the advice of one of his idols, Julius ("Dr. J") Erving, a star player with the Philadelphia 76ers and a man whom Johnson had never met. Not only did Erving offer his counsel to Johnson, but he also invited the twenty-year-old to Philadelphia to watch the National Basketball Association (NBA) playoffs. In the end, Johnson decided to pass up the last two years of his college eligibility and enter the 1979 NBA draft. He was tapped by the Lakers as the first pick overall.

Johnson's exuberant play helped transform the Lakers from the lackluster team of its earlier years into a major attraction in Los Angeles, luring thousands of enthusiastic fans to watch the team's winning ways. Among his teammates on the Lakers, Kareem Abdul-Jabbar served as Johnson's mentor, and together they developed a lively and entertaining style of play that came to be known as "showtime." In 1980 Johnson became the first rookie ever to win the NBA finals Most Valuable Player (MVP) award. He won the award twice more, in 1982 and 1987. Despite his brilliance on the court, Johnson experienced increasing tension with his teammates in the locker room, set off in large part by a 1981 contract that made him the highest-paid player in the history of professional basketball. Many of his teammates worried that Johnson would gain a de facto role in the management of the team by virtue of his astronomical salary. Their fears appeared to be well founded. Clashing with the Lakers coach, Paul Westhead, over the team's playing style, Johnson publicly requested that he be traded rather than being forced to play in a manner the was working for neither him nor the team as a whole. Instead of butting heads with the powerful Johnson, Westhead quit the team, and Johnson took heat from fans for this display of his clout. The criticism quickly dried up, however, when the Lakers started winning again.

During Johnson's years with the Lakers, the team won five championships, in 1980, 1982, 1985, 1987, and 1988. Along the way Johnson , who was six feet, nine inches tall and weighed 215 pounds, also played in a dozen All-Star games, twice winning the MVP award (in 1990 and 1992). By the time he reached the age of thirty, Johnson had turned out two books. The first, an autobiography entitled *Magic* (1983), combined anecdotal recollections of Johnson's childhood and college years with a journal-like profile recording the events of the 1981–1982 NBA season. Johnson's second book, *Magic's Touch: From Fast Break to Fundamentals with Basketball's Most Exciting Player* (1989), is essentially a guide to the game of basketball, although it does contain some autobiographical passages.

One of the great rivalries in NBA history developed between Johnson and Larry Bird of the Boston Celtics. From 1983 until 1988, the Lakers and Celtics dominated the NBA, with either Boston or Los Angeles walking away with the championship every year. During the 1983–1984 season, Magic led the NBA in assists, averaging 13.1 per game, a career high. The Lakers and the Celtics faced off in the NBA finals, but Boston, led by Bird, narrowly won the championship, four games to three. Los Angeles turned the tables the following year, beating the Celtics four games to two. The Lakers failed to make the finals in 1985–1986, but their East Coast rivals won the championship. The 1986–1987 season began with both Bird and Johnson at the top of their form. Johnson, in particular, had taken his game to a new level, averaging 23.9 points per game and leading the NBA in assists with 12.2 per game. Johnson led the Lakers to the NBA's best record with sixty-five wins. At the end of the regular season, he finally won what many considered a long-overdue NBA MVP award. To make this winning season even sweeter, Johnson led the Lakers to victory over the Celtics in the finals, four games to two, winning another MVP award when he was recognized as the outstanding player in the finals. Alex Ward, writing in the *New York Times Magazine,* offered this assessment of Johnson's amazing abilities on the basketball court: "Johnson is a point guard, the basketball equivalent of a quarterback. He brings the ball upcourt, sets up the plays, runs the fast breaks. His height gives him an advantage over other guards, and his ability to determine in an instant how a play might develop—by now it's a reflex—allows him to take maximum advantage of his teammates' extraordinary quickness."

In November 1991 Johnson stunned the entire nation when he announced publicly that he was retiring from basketball because he had contracted HIV (human immunodeficiency virus), the virus that causes AIDS (acquired immunodeficiency syndrome). At the same time he vowed to work to help educate young people about the dangers of HIV infection, a promise he has worked conscientiously to keep. The year following his startling revelation, Johnson published *My Life,* another installment in his continuing autobiography, which brings his life up to date and includes the discovery that he had contracted HIV. Johnson followed *My Life* with a book for teenagers entitled *What You Can Do to Avoid AIDS* (1992), a straightforward guide to safer sex. The book, with explicit illustrations about what teens can do to avoid infection, came under fire from a number of quarters, the most important of which were a group of three major booksellers who refused to stock it in their stores. Jackson leaped to the defense of his book, explaining that its purpose was to be "real—about everything" in an effort to save the lives of young people who might otherwise expose themselves to unnecessary risks.

Although Johnson's immediate reaction to his HIV diagnosis in 1991 was to retire from basketball, he was back on the court the following year when he agreed to join the 1992 U.S. Olympic "Dream Team." Some of the biggest stars in professional basketball played with Johnson on the gold medal–winning team, including Larry Bird, Clyde Drexler, Patrick Ewing, and Michael Jordan. Referring to the excitement generated by the formation of the All-Star team, Johnson told *Sports Illustrated:* "We have grabbed the world in a way that won't happen again. The excitement of the fans, the excitement of the other players who don't care how bad you beat them as long as they get a picture." During the 1992–1993 basketball season, Johnson returned briefly to the ranks of the Lakers and then signed on with NBC as a commentator for the remainder of the season. Two years later he returned to the Lakers as head coach. Still not willing to turn his back on the game, he rejoined the Lakers team to play thirty-two games of the 1995–1996 season.

A successful businessman who owns a number of movie theaters and shopping malls, Johnson also operates the Magic Johnson Foundation, which not only is involved with HIV/AIDS issues but also works hard to send underprivileged minority young people to college. He lives in the Los Angeles area with his wife Earleatha ("Cookie") Kelley, whom he married in September 1991. The couple has three children: Earvin III; Andre, Johnson's son from a previous relationship; and Elisa, who was adopted. Both Johnson and his wife believe that he was divinely selected to contract HIV—"God needed someone, and He picked me," he told *Sports Illustrated.* At first blush, Johnson's claim can seem brash and arrogant, but he has carried himself well in the years since the diagnosis. As *Sports Illustrated* put it, "Magic, like thousands of others, was a dead man walking, and now he is very much alive. That is a blessing and something close to a miracle."

In a performance almost as impressive as his fancy footwork, no-look passes, and shooting skills on the basketball court, Johnson has been playing a winning game against HIV since the early 1990s. He has experienced virtually no ill effects from the infection, and some medical professionals consider it unlikely that he will ever show signs of full-blown AIDS. In the years to come Johnson will be remembered best for his brilliance as a basketball player.

★

An excellent profile of Johnson's early life and career is in his autobiography *Magic* (1983), written with Richard Levin. With

Roy S. Johnson, Magic Johnson compiled a volume of his thoughts about basketball strategy entitled *Magic's Touch: From Fast Break to Fundamentals with Basketball's Most Exciting Player* (1989). In *My Life* (1992), written with William Novak, Johnson brings readers up to date on his life and career, including the diagnosis of HIV. Johnson's primer on safe sex, *What You Can Do to Avoid AIDS* (1992), also was written with William Novak. A lengthy biographical profile of Johnson is in *Newsmakers '88* (1989).

DON AMERMAN

JOHNSON, John Arthur ("Jack") (*b.* 31 March 1878 in Galveston, Texas; *d.* 10 June 1946 in Raleigh, North Carolina), first African American to hold the heavyweight boxing championship who was considered by many to be the greatest heavyweight of all time.

Johnson was the son of Henry Johnson, a former slave and a school janitor, and his wife Tiny, who had six children, of whom Johnson was the third. The boy's formal schooling ended after the fifth grade when he left Texas to roam the United States, riding the rails. Returning to Galveston in the mid-1890s, Johnson held back-breaking, muscle-building jobs, picking cotton and working as a stevedore on the rough-and-tumble waterfront. It was here that he honed his self-defense skills, participating in the notorious "battle royals," brutal competitions where groups of African-American youths, blindfolded and often naked, engaged in no-holds-barred brawls, while white southerners mockingly tossed pennies. The last standing contestant, often Johnson, was rewarded by being allowed to keep the change.

In 1897 or 1898 Johnson married Mary Austin, the first of his four wives and the only African American; they permanently separated in 1901 after she tired of her husband's repeated marital infidelity. Johnson never had children. He became a professional boxer with a third-round knockout of Jim Rocks in 1897. Prizefighting was then illegal in Texas, so he left to seek bouts up north. After returning home a few years later, he fought the older, more experienced veteran Joe Choynski, a Polish Jewish immigrant, who had earlier earned a draw against James J. Jeffries, the undefeated heavyweight champion. Johnson was knocked out by Choynski on 25 February 1901, and both were locked up after the illegal bout was raided by the Texas Rangers. Incarcerated together for a month, Choynski taught Johnson the tricks of the boxing trade.

After his release from prison, Johnson once again left Texas and lived the life of a hobo, traversing the western states from 1901 to 1903. In Los Angeles on 3 February 1903 he beat "Denver Ed" Martin to capture the "colored" heavyweight crown via a twenty-round decision. A defen-

Jack Johnson. The Library of Congress

compared to Johnson's 192 pounds and six feet, one inches, and believed the myth that African Americans had hard heads and weak stomachs. Thus Burns concentrated on hitting Johnson's body.

In front of 20,000 spectators Johnson hit Burns at will, dropping him in the first round and breaking his nose in the second; the champion's face was soon covered in blood, with his eyes swollen shut. Johnson displayed no urgency to end the slaughter. Finally, in the fourteenth round, he smashed Burns to the canvas and a new champion was crowned. Johnson was the first African American to win the world's heavyweight championship and became the seventh champion in the gloved era.

Within a year, Johnson successfully defended his title five times, all versus white boxers, including a victory over the future film star Victor McLaglen. White fans openly called for Johnson's dethronement and began a search for the "Great White Hope" who could beat him in the ring. Johnson, displaying a supremely arrogant demeanor, openly defied societal norms, enraging many white Americans. An enormous hero to the African-American community, he nevertheless worried the African-American bourgeoisie who viewed him as an impediment to racial progress. The conservative African-American leader Booker T. Washington urged him to act in a less brazen way. At times, Johnson affected a British accent, wore attire of clashing colors, sported a trademark shaved head, and filled his mouth with gold teeth. He paraded with a pet leopard and drove open-air roadsters, often in the company of white women.

In 1909 he defended his title against Stanley Ketchel, known as the Michigan Assassin and a great middleweight champ. Johnson weighed 205 pounds compared to Ketchel's 170 pounds, and the Colma, California, fight included a backroom deal to extend it for the benefit of motion-picture cameras. Johnson carried Ketchel into the twelfth round and then ended it with a knockout. Leading the continued call for a "white hope" was the journalist Jack London, who beseeched Jeffries to come out of retirement; the ex-champ, who had ballooned to more than 300 pounds, was eventually persuaded to return. The famed promoter George "Tex" Rickard's attempts to stage this "fight of the century" in California were stymied by the state's antiboxing forces, so he shifted the fight's locale to the dusty mining town of Reno, Nevada.

The fight was held on 4 July 1910 in Reno's sweltering heat. Jeffries, who had shed eighty pounds, was now thirty-seven and well past his fighting prime. Johnson, in contrast, was at the very apex of his powers. The media built up the event as much more than a mere athletic competition. The white press saw it as a racial struggle, opining confidently that Jeffries had "Runnymede and Agincourt behind him, while his black opponent had nothing but the jungle." The

sive specialist, Johnson won fifty-seven bouts between 1902 and 1907, mostly against other African-American fighters. Johnson's style was a lethal combination of strength, speed, and skill. He was practically unhittable at times. He possessed an uncanny ability to avoid punches and demonstrated two-fisted knockout power. A classic counterpuncher, his specialty was a rapier-like left jab, followed by what has been called the all-time greatest right uppercut. In addition, he was a master of repartee, often taunting and abusing opponents. He loved to dare slower opponents to hit his exposed body, dropping his gloves low, teasing, and, all the while, chatting with ringside spectators. Extremely articulate, he was also a master of ring psychology.

Johnson issued several challenges to Jeffries, the world champion. But sensing little to gain and much to lose, the Caucasian Jeffries maintained the boxing color line, refusing Johnson a title shot and retiring undefeated in 1904. Johnson soon began to stalk the new champion, Tommy Burns, seeking a title shot. Burns ducked Johnson, but the promoter Hugh J. "Huge Deal" McIntosh finally arranged a bout between the two at Ruschcutter's Bay in Sydney, Australia, on 26 December 1908. Burns, a defender of white supremacy, charged that Johnson was "yellow." He was guaranteed the unheard sum of 6,000 pounds sterling, the equivalent of $30,000, to Johnson's $5,000. Burns, actually a fattened-up middleweight, was an undersized 168 pounds

Chicago Defender, a leading African-American journal, wrote that Johnson would be battling "race hatred, prejudice, Negro persecution. . . . the future welfare of his people forms a part of the stake." With the fear of racial violence, alcohol was banned and handguns were checked at the gate.

The bout started slowly, but the second round decided the outcome. A Johnson left hook to Jeffries's left eye caused what was later deemed "irreparable damage to his eye and psyche." Johnson beat Jeffries to a bloody pulp—his face was a mass of pink welts and his eyes swollen shut. In the twelfth round, openly gasping for air, Jeffries spit out a huge wad of blood. After fifty-six minutes the Galveston Giant emerged victorious. Raucous celebrations erupted in many African-American communities, while inconsolable white mobs rampaged and race riots ensued, especially in the American South. Eleven blacks were murdered. Johnson made a cross-country victory tour via train back to Chicago. In Cheyenne, Wyoming, the U.S. Army's African-American Ninth Calvary, the celebrated Buffalo Soldiers, turned out en masse to honor and salute their warrior. At Chicago's Northwest Station, throngs of African Americans welcomed him home, making the event an unofficial holiday.

But Johnson faced new challenges outside the ring. In an attempt to crack down on commercialized vice and to calm the hysteria generated by the white slave trade, the U.S. Congress in 1910 passed the Mann Act, making it a felony to transport women across state lines "for the purposes of prostitution, debauchery, or any other immoral purposes." Johnson, who continued to defy the racial and sexual taboos of the era, openly traveled with white consorts and habitually boasted of his sexual conquests. In 1911 he married Etta Terry Duryea, a recently divorced Long Island socialite. Duryea subsequently was ostracized by her friends and suffered from depression; she committed suicide at Johnson's Chicago jazz club, the Café du Champions, in 1912.

When Johnson began to travel with Lucille Cameron, his eighteen-year-old private secretary, her mother leveled charges that he had abducted the young lady. The furor caused by the scandal resulted in his nightclub's loss of its liquor license and Johnson's indictment for violation of the Mann Act. While the charges were true in a technical sense, Cameron refused to corroborate them or to testify against her lover, and they married on 4 December 1912. After Johnson's acquittal, he was indicted a second time on similar charges.

Belle Schreiber, a well-known prostitute from Chicago's Everleigh Club, was the prosecution's star witness; she had suffered physical violence from Johnson's hand, and he had paid her travel expenses from Pittsburgh to Chicago for "immoral purposes." Convicted by an all-white jury in May 1913, Johnson was fined $1,000 and sentenced to a year and a day at the federal penitentiary at Joliet, Illinois. Out on bail and disguised as a member of an African-American baseball club, he fled the country. Accompanied by Cameron, he escaped to Canada and then to France. For the next seven years Johnson lived in exile, claiming his only crime was beating a white hero, Jeffries.

In Paris, Johnson defended his title three times. During the summer of 1914 he left Europe at the outbreak of hostilities between France and Germany. Traveling to Buenos Aires, Argentina, he performed in farcical wrestling matches, lived in Mexico, then relocated to neutral Spain, where he resided from 1915 to 1919. Having squandered his considerable fortune on a lavish lifestyle, he struggled financially. He was desperate for cash and wished to return to his homeland, so another "white hope" match was arranged. Jess Willard, a six-foot, six-inch Kansan known as the Pottawottamie Giant, was scheduled to fight Johnson at the Havana, Cuba, Oriente Racetrack in a forty-five-round bout. In scorching heat of 103 degrees Fahrenheit, Johnson, now thirty-seven and under the mistaken impression that charges would be dropped against him if he lost, appeared out of shape. The slow and lumbering Willard tried to hold on and wear down the older champion. In the twenty-sixth round Johnson fell to the ring floor and was counted out by the referee Jack Welch. Boxing historians have forever debated whether he took a dive; contemporary accounts varied.

After the Willard episode Johnson's skills clearly deteriorated. In 1919 he was befriended by the Mexican president Venustiano Carranza and opened a thriving saloon in Tijuana. After Carranza's 1920 assassination, now without a local protector, he decided to end his seven-year exile. Surrendering to federal authorities at the U.S. border, he served nine months at Leavenworth Prison in Kansas. A model prisoner, he was made the athletic director and fought five exhibitions at the jail. He continued to fight until 1928, but also earned a living with a unique vaudeville routine: dancing, juggling, and playing the bass fiddle while giving lectures. In 1924 he divorced Cameron and married Irene Marie Pineau, his fourth wife. At the 1933 Chicago World's Fair he was a human punching bag; youngsters sparred with him for a dollar.

In the late 1930s Johnson began a decade-long association with Hubert's Museum in New York City, a famous Times Square penny arcade, sideshow, and flea circus. There he regaled customers with tales of his life story, often adding to and fictionalizing his already glamorous past. During the years of World War II, he encouraged African Americans to enlist, and in 1945 he staged boxing exhibitions at New York City bond rallies. Always consumed by speed and a lifelong reckless driver, Johnson met his death on the road in June 1946. Driving eighty miles per hour, he attempted to avoid a truck, swerved, and hit a tree on Route 1 near Franklinton, North Carolina. He died of massive internal injuries at Raleigh's Saint Agnes Hospital. He is buried in Chicago's Graceland Cemetery.

In 1954 Johnson was a charter inductee in the Boxing Hall of Fame. While he always insisted on his personal right to equality, he showed no apparent concern for the plight of his race. Nat Fleischer, a boxing expert and the longtime publisher of *Ring Magazine*, wrote, "After years devoted to the study of heavyweight fighters, I have no hesitation in naming Jack Johnson the greatest of them all." While Johnson's exact ring record is cloudy, between 1897 and 1928 he had at least 114 recorded bouts, winning 80, with 45 by knockout.

★

The literature on Johnson's life and career is voluminous, but must be studied with caution as much myth and fiction has melded with fact. Johnson's two memoirs, *Mes Combats* (1914), written in French while he was in exile, and *Jack Johnson—In the Ring and Out* (1927), republished as *Jack Johnson Is a Dandy* (1969), are notoriously unreliable as factual documents. The lucid and detailed biography by Randy Roberts, *Papa Jack: Jack Johnson and the Era of White Hopes* (1985), is authoritative and contains an excellent annotated bibliography. An informative account of the Jeffries fight and the race issue is Lerone Bennett, "Jack Johnson and the Great White Hope," *Ebony* (Apr. 1994). For analysis of Johnson's national impact and context among other African-American athletes, see also Rex Lardner, *The Legendary Champions* (1972); Nat Fleischer, *An Illustrated History of Boxing* (1975, 1997); Lawrence Levine, *Black Culture and Black Consciousness: Afro-American Folk Thought from Slavery to Freedom* (1977); and Joe Dorinson, "Black Heroes in Sport," *Journal of Popular Culture* (winter 1997): 115–135. An obituary is in the *New York Times* (11 June 1946).

JEFFREY S. ROSEN

JOHNSON, Michael (*b.* 13 September 1967 in Dallas, Texas), track and field short-distance runner who was considered the fastest man in the world after his world record–shattering 200-meter and 400-meter races in the 1996 Atlanta Olympics.

Johnson was the youngest of five children of Paul Johnson, Sr., a truck driver, and Ruby Johnson, an elementary school teacher. The Johnsons enjoyed a comfortable, though not affluent, lifestyle in Dallas and emphasized education and religion in their family life. Throughout his primary and secondary schooling, Johnson took classes for the gifted, excelling in academics. At Skyline High School in Dallas, Johnson participated in sports, playing football in junior high and running track all through junior and senior high.

Michael Johnson. ARCHIVE PHOTOS, INC.

Upon his graduation in 1986 he was recruited by several colleges and chose to attend Baylor University, an hour's drive south in Waco, Texas, because of its strong Baptist heritage and its track and field coach, Clyde Hart.

Hart and Johnson immediately began an intense training regimen, which often culminated in Johnson's physical and mental exhaustion after practice. However, Johnson never once missed a scheduled day of training with Hart. Once the coach canceled practice due to bad weather; the team took the afternoon off, and Hart worked at his office, occasionally glancing out at the stormy weather pounding the track. He noticed a figure sprinting laps and discovered Johnson running his usual routine. Hart questioned the athlete, only to have Johnson reply that you never know when you might have to compete in the rain.

Johnson continued to excel in academics and majored in business, reasoning that he would need a career after his racing days were behind him. He ran competitively, winning five National Collegiate Athletic Association titles in the 200-meter dash and the 1,600-meter relay. Several of his school records still stand at Baylor, including his time of 20.41 seconds in the 200-meter dash in his first collegiate meet (in 1990, Johnson reset this record at a meet in Edinburgh, Scotland, with a time of 19.85). The following year, in 1988, he placed seventh in the 400-meter heats at the Olympic trials. That same year he broke his fibula in the NCAA Outdoor 200-meter race. In spite of his broken leg, *Track and Field News* ranked Johnson seventh overall in the United States. The next year, 1989, Johnson won the NCAA Indoor 200 meters and placed second in the 400 meters. In his senior year, he won the 400-meter USA Indoors and the 200-meter USA Indoors and Outdoors.

Johnson graduated from Baylor in 1990 with a degree in business and opted to continue training with Hart. The two had developed not only Johnson's peculiar upright running style—characterized by a perfectly straight back, thrown-out shoulders, and pounding arms and legs moving in synchronicity—but also his "danger zone" stare and the tunnel vision that helped him focus on both the track and professional athletic advancement.

Johnson won a gold medal in at the World Championships in 1991 in the 200 meters with a time of 20.01 into a headwind; his margin of 0.33 seconds was the largest in that race since Jesse Owens's in 1936. He repeated his wins at the USA Indoor and Outdoor 400 meters and 200 meters and was ranked the best in the world at both of those events by *Track and Field News*. At the 1992 Olympics in Barcelona, Johnson suffered a bout of food poisoning, placing only sixth in the 200-meter semifinals, but still managed to compete on the U.S. gold medal–winning 4 × 400–meter relay team. His ranking dropped to third and fifth in the world in the 200 meters and 400 meters, but rebounded to first the following year for the 400 meter. At the World Championships Johnson anchored the gold medal–winning 4 × 400–meter relay with the fastest relay leg in history. By 1995 Johnson had been ranked the fastest runner in the world nine times since 1990 in either the 400 meters and the 200 meters. Between 1989 and 1997 he had fifty-eight wins in the 400 meters.

He was untouchable, although his racing rivals were vocal in their dismissal of his talents. Carl Lewis, the running champion of the 1980s, publicly declaring that Johnson would not make the 1992 Olympic team. Johnson lashed back, stating that Lewis was trying to be the premier athlete in track and field and that he should "step down from there." Johnson announced his arrival at the 1996 Atlanta Olympics with a pair of sparkling gold Nike running shoes, specially designed for his finals. The eyes of the world were focused on his flying feet as he won gold in the 400 meters in 43.49 seconds, an Olympic record. He stunned the world later by winning the 200 meters in a world record–shattering 19.32 seconds. Of that dash, Johnson said, "I don't think that I can't break 19.32, because I know that race wasn't perfect." Though not perfect in his own eyes, Johnson nonetheless became the first man to win both the 200 meters and the 400 meters in the same Olympics.

Johnson raced during the next four years in anticipation of the 2000 Sydney Olympics, setting new world records as

he ran. *Track and Fields News* continued to rank him first in the world in the 400 meters. In 1997 Johnson and the Canadian sprinter Donovan Bailey engaged in a much-publicized 150-meter race, the winner of which would be declared the fastest man on Earth, but Johnson pulled up injured during the race. He was injured again a year later in the 2000 Olympic trials in the 200 meters and did not compete in that event. Johnson won another two gold medals, however, in the 400 meters and as the fourth leg in the 4 × 400–meter relay. At the end of that year he was again ranked first in the world in the 400 meters. Though seemingly invincible on the racetrack, Johnson announced plans to retire in 2001.

Johnson lives in Will Valley, California, with his wife, Kerry Doyen, whom he married on 3 October 1998, and their son.

Recognition of Johnson's excellence in track and field is often eclipsed in media stories by discussion of his intense devotion to his craft and of his unique upright running style. Nevertheless, Johnson's jaw-dropping performance at the Atlanta Olympics in the 200 meters will be remembered for years to come, and he is inarguably the greatest 400-meter runner who ever lived. Johnson was the first man to win both those races in the same Olympics and the first to successfully defend his 400 meters in the next. He also ran on two gold-medal 4 × 400–meter Olympic relay teams and won multiple world and U.S. championships. Along with Jesse Owens and Carl Lewis, Johnson will be marked as one of the twentieth century's greatest runners.

★

Johnson wrote *Slaying the Dragon* (1996), which combined business advice with autobiographical details about his early childhood, college life, and adult training. Two informative databases are *USA Track & Field* (2000) and *Cool Running* (2000). The former gives a detailed history of his career highlights; the latter focuses on his personality. Todd Copeland's "Frequent Flier" profile in the *Baylor Line* (summer 2000) offers insights into Johnson's perceptions of his wins and losses.

JUDITH A. PARKER

JOHNSON, Rafer Lewis (*b.* 18 August 1935 in Hillsboro, Texas), 1960 Olympic decathlon gold medalist and three-time world record holder who became one of America's finest sports ambassadors.

Johnson was the oldest of five children of Lewis Johnson, a day laborer and handyman, and Alma (Gibson) Johnson, a domestic and homemaker. In 1945 Lewis Johnson moved his family from Dallas to Kingsburg, California (located about twenty miles south of Fresno in the San Joaquin valley), where the family, for one year, made their home in

Rafer Johnson at the 1960 Olympics in Rome. ASSOCIATED PRESS AP

In the summer of 1952 Murl Dodson, Kingsburg's track coach, drove his sophomore star to nearby Tulare, California, to watch the U.S. Olympic Trials, a meet in which Bob Mathias broke the world decathlon record. Returning home Johnson told his coach, "I could have beaten most of the guys in the meet." From that day on Johnson was primarily a decathlete.

The decathlon event is a mini track meet that tests speed, strength, spring, stamina, and spirit. Over two days the athlete must contest ten basic events: 100 meters, long jump, shot put, high jump, and 400 meters on the first day, followed by 110-meter hurdles, discus throw, pole vault, javelin throw, and 1,500 meters on the second day. Scoring tables evaluate each performance and individual event scores are totaled to determine the overall victor. Decathlon champions are known as the world's top all-around athletes.

Johnson won a pair of modified high-school decathlons in 1952 and 1953, and then tried the standard version at the 1954 national Amateur Athletic Union (AAU) meet after graduating from Kingsburg High. He placed third. Ironically it was the lowest placing of his career. That summer, after being highly recruited as an athlete by two dozen universities, he decided to enroll at the University of California, Los Angeles (UCLA). He chose UCLA because of its long-standing commitment to racial equality; offers of academic, not athletic, scholarships for "A" students; and exceptional track coach Elvin "Ducky" Drake. Johnson set aside football and dabbled at basketball at UCLA where, as a junior, he was a backcourt starter for the coach John Wooden. But he primarily concentrated on the decathlon, and his success was meteoric. As a nineteen-year-old freshman he won the Pan-American Games crown, then rewarded his family and friends by breaking Bob Mathias's world record in a June 1955 meet in Kingsburg.

Johnson won the 1956 U.S. Olympic Trials decathlon and also made the U.S. team in the long-jump event. A knee injury slowed him down at the Melbourne (Australia) Olympic Games. But he offered no excuses. Johnson said of the winner Milt Campbell, "I lost to a good man." His college classmates elected him as the president of the UCLA student body in 1958. By then he was training with his UCLA Bruin teammate C. K. Yang of Formosa. Drake realized that he was coaching perhaps the world's two best athletes, and matched Johnson and Yang in daily training sessions with an eye on the 1960 Olympic Games in Rome. In 1958 Johnson again broke the world record with 8,302 (1950 tables) points at a dual meet against the Soviets in Moscow, Russia. In 1959, the year of his graduation from UCLA with a B.S. degree in physical education, he suffered a debilitating auto accident. Unable to run for the better part of a year, he headed to the weight room and built himself up for the throwing events. He recovered in time

a railroad boxcar. As a child Johnson loved to play and compete. "Maybe I was simply born that way. I wanted to be the fastest kid . . . to say I did not like losing is an understatement," he said years later. Competitiveness and sports talent ran in the family; Johnson's younger brother Jimmy became a defensive back for the San Francisco Forty-niners and was inducted into the Pro Football Hall of Fame.

At Kingsburg Joint Union High School, Johnson had a remarkable athletic career, distinguishing himself in football (as a halfback averaging nine yards per carry), basketball (averaging seventeen points per game), and baseball (where he hit over .400). But track and field was his strong suit. His strength, speed, and agility made him a natural for the decathlon event. Johnson was handicapped by numerous injuries before and during his athletic career. At age twelve he caught his left foot in a cannery belt, which required twenty-three stitches, crutches, and rehabilitation.

for the 1960 U.S. Olympic Trials /AAU meet where, against the ever-improving Yang, he set a third world record (8,683 points).

The Johnson-Yang decathlon battle in Rome was the stuff of legends. Not only was it the first Olympic decathlon ever televised, it was an incredibly close finish. After nine events, with Johnson holding a minuscule lead, the Bruin teammates had stopped helping one another. Yang, with far superior 1,500-meter skills, pushed the early pace. Yet lap after lap, in the darkness of Rome's Estadio Olympico, Johnson gamely hung on to C. K.'s shoulder, and he finished with a lifetime best, just 1.2 seconds behind Yang. Years later Johnson revealed, "I knew I had an advantage since that was the last race of my life, and there was no reason to hold anything back." Yang marginally won seven of the ten events head-to-head. Yet Johnson, with far superior efforts in the weight events, won the gold medal. The difference was only fifty-eight points. Drake walked to the infield, proclaiming, "Give them both the gold medal, give them both the gold medal."

At age twenty-five Johnson retired from amateur athletics and was able to claim three world records, two Olympic medals (one gold, one silver), three national AAU titles, and nine wins in an eleven-meet decathlon career. He was awarded the 1960 James P. Sullivan Award as the nation's top amateur athlete. That same year he was honored as the Associated Press Athlete of the Year. He also was elected to the National Track and Field Hall of Fame (1974) and to the Olympic Hall of Fame (1983).

Following his athletic career Johnson recruited for the Peace Corps, was a television sports analyst, and appeared in several dozen Hollywood films. He became a vice president of Continental Telephone. Johnson's life touched those of many well-known people. He was romantically linked with the feminist Gloria Steinem and played an active role in the 1968 presidential campaign of Robert F. Kennedy. On 5 June 1968, when Kennedy was assassinated at the Ambassador Hotel in Los Angeles, Johnson wrestled the assassin, Sirhan Sirhan, to the ground and pried the gun from his hand.

Johnson devoted countless hours to the mentally and physically handicapped. He became involved with the Special Olympics movement at its inception and served as the president of the California Special Olympics beginning in 1969. In 1984, to the surprise and delight of 100,000 spectators, he was the final torchbearer at the opening ceremonies of the Los Angeles Olympic Games. He served on many boards and committees in the areas of sports, business, and community services.

Johnson married Betsy Thorsen on 18 December 1971. Their two children, without parental urging, became world-class athletes. Josh was a two-time National Collegiate Athletic Association (NCAA) All-American in the javelin while at UCLA, and Jenny was the captain of UCLA's women's volleyball team and became a professional on the beach volleyball circuit.

A role model for all ages, Johnson won numerous awards for his athletic ability and community service. His uncommon poise and dignity made him one of the nation's most undervalued and underpublicized sports heroes, and he preferred it that way.

★

Johnson, in collaboration with Philip Goldberg, produced a straight-up autobiography, *The Best That I Can Be* (1999). Cordner Nelson, *Track and Field: The Great Ones* (1970), provides an expert's view of Johnson's athletic career and stature. For decathlon facts and a summary of Johnson's career the best source is Frank Zarnowski, *Decathlon: A Colorful History of Track and Field's Most Challenging Event* (1989). Bud Greenspan's popular television series *Olympiad* (beginning 1972) includes an hour-long video on the history of the Olympic decathlon, with particular emphasis on the Johnson-Yang struggle in Rome, and is the best source of video clips of Johnson's Olympic success.

FRANK ZARNOWSKI

JOHNSON, Randall David ("Randy") (*b.* 10 September 1963 in Walnut Creek, California), major league baseball pitcher who won one American League and three National League Cy Young Awards while becoming one of baseball's most dominant strikeout pitchers.

Johnson was the youngest of six children of Rollin "Bud" Johnson, a police officer, and Carol Johnson, a homemaker. He attended Livermore High School in California, where he played baseball and basketball. Graduating in 1982, Johnson drew notice by pitching a perfect game in his final high-school baseball start. The Atlanta Braves selected Johnson in the third round of the June 1982 major league baseball draft. He declined the team's offer, choosing instead to attend college at the University of Southern California, where he received a baseball/basketball scholarship. After his sophomore season, Johnson left the basketball program and concentrated on baseball. In 1985 Johnson entered the major league draft after his junior year of college. The Montreal Expos selected him as the second overall choice.

Johnson made his major league debut for the Expos on 15 September 1988, defeating the Pittsburgh Pirates. With his debut Johnson became (at six feet, ten inches) the tallest man ever to play major league baseball, a record he later shared with the pitcher Eric Hillman. In 1989 Johnson was traded to the Seattle Mariners where, in the next season, he became a staple in the pitching rotation, finishing with a 14–11 won-lost record, 3.65 earned run average, and 194

Randy Johnson. ARCHIVE PHOTOS, INC.

strikeouts, although he did lead the league by walking 120 batters. Johnson also recorded a no-hitter on 2 June 1990 against the Detroit Tigers.

In 1991 and 1992 Johnson continued both to strike out and walk a high number of batters, finishing with more than 200 strikeouts each year, but also leading the league in walks allowed each year. On 25 December 1992, as Johnson was flying to California to join his family for Christmas, his father died. Johnson considered ending his baseball career, but chose to use his father's death as an inspiration for success. He became a born-again Christian and began a practice of giving 10 percent of his earnings to charity.

Another event earlier that year also made a difference in Johnson's baseball career. Late in the 1992 season, while Johnson helped the all-time major league strikeout leader Nolan Ryan and the Texas Ranger pitching coach Tom House with an instructional video, the trio discovered a flaw in Johnson's mechanics that, when corrected, allowed him to add a few miles per hour to his fast ball while gaining a higher level of control over the location of his pitches. The next season, Johnson decreased his walk total while striking out over 300 batters for the first time in his career. He also established new career highs for wins, innings pitched, complete games, and shutouts, along with

posting a 3.24 earned run average. In November of that year, Johnson married Lisa, with whom he had four children.

In 1995 Johnson became the first Mariner to win the American League Cy Young Award. His statistics included an 18–2 won-lost record that set a record for the best winning percentage in a season for a starting pitcher with at least twenty decisions. His season also included a complete game win in a one-game play-off against the California Angels on 2 October that decided the American League West championship and put the Mariners into the postseason for the first time in franchise history. The Mariners defeated the New York Yankees in an American League divisional series, but lost to the Cleveland Indians in the American League championship series.

On 31 July 1998 the Seattle Mariners traded Johnson to the Houston Astros. While Johnson experienced a mediocre half-season in Seattle, with Houston he went 10–1 with a 1.28 earned run average. Again Johnson appeared in the postseason, but the Astros were beaten by the San Diego Padres in a National League divisional series.

On 30 November 1998 Johnson signed a four-year, $52.4 million contract with the Arizona Diamondbacks, which allowed him to play home games near his own home in the Phoenix suburb of Glendale, Arizona. In his first season with the Diamondbacks, Johnson won the National League Cy Young Award. He also helped the Diamondbacks make the playoffs in only their second season, which set a record for quickest playoff appearance by an expansion team. Johnson became one of only three pitchers to win a Cy Young Award in each league, following Gaylord Perry and accomplishing the feat concurrently with Pedro Martinez of the Boston Red Sox. But for the second season in a row, Johnson's team lost in an NL divisional series as the New York Mets beat the Diamondbacks in four games. Johnson also won the NL Cy Young Awards in 2000 and 2001. On 10 September 2000, he became the twelfth pitcher in major league history to record 3,000 strikeouts. The following year, on 8 May 2001, Johnson tied a major league record by striking out twenty batters in the first nine innings of a ball game.

During his career Johnson was active in a number of charities, including the Cystic Fibrosis Foundation, Salvation Army, and Make-a-Wish Foundation. An avid photographer, Johnson showed his work at the 1990 Art Expo in Los Angeles. He also maintained an active interest in hard rock music, including playing drums with Geddy Lee of the band Rush and members of the band Queensryche.

When Johnson first arrived to the major leagues he was considered an oddity because of his height and his reputation for dominance both in striking hitters out and lack of control in walking them. Even his nickname "The Big Unit" evoked an image of strangeness. But as the wins mounted, Johnson's image changed to reflect his pitching prowess and he became recognized as one of the most dominant strikeout pitchers in major league history.

★

Insights into Johnson's life and career can be found in Richard Hoffer, "Picture Perfect Pitcher," *Sports Illustrated* (4 May 1992); Rick Weinberg, "King of K," *Sport* (June 1994); Tom Verducci, "The Intimidator," *Sports Illustrated* (26 June 1995); and Nick Charles and Miro Cernetig, "The Amazing Randy," *People Weekly* (6 Oct. 1997).

RAYMOND I. SCHUCK

JOHNSON, Robert Glenn, Jr. ("Junior") (*b.* 28 June 1931 in Ingles Hollow, North Carolina), race-car driver who discovered drafting, obtained sponsorship for the sport from the R. J. Reynolds tobacco company, and won six National Association of Stock Car Automobile Racing (NASCAR) championships as a car owner.

Born to Robert Glenn Johnson and Lora Belle Johnson, Junior Johnson was the fourth of seven children. He started driving his father's truck around the family farm at age eight, several years before he was eligible to apply for a driver's license. Growing up during the Great Depression in rural North Carolina with his parents, Johnson and his family had to struggle to survive. His father was a farmer and saw mill operator, neither of which provided much income. Johnson's father turned to the only other option he felt that he had, the production and distribution of

Junior Johnson, 1964. AP PHOTO/STR/XN

moonshine whiskey. During the Great Depression, the production of moonshine was the best way to generate income, even though the federal government considered it to be a criminal activity. This illegally made whiskey was delivered by the light of the moon in the trunks of specially built cars. To be successful and not be caught by the federal agents, the delivery driver had to have nerves of steel to drive as fast as possible on the winding country roads with only moonlight to light the way. Junior was considered one of the best.

Johnson competed in his first race in the summer of 1949 at the newly constructed North Wilkesboro speedway in North Carolina. His brother L. P. had returned home early from the race to convince Junior to race his moonshine car in a preliminary race to warm up the fans for the main event. Johnson finished second in a race that included future racing champions Ned Jarrett and Ralph Earnhardt.

On Labor Day 1953 Johnson competed in his first NASCAR event at Darlington Raceway in Darlington, South Carolina. He qualified twenty-sixth and finished thirty-eighth. The next year Johnson competed in four NASCAR races. His first Grand National win came on 7 May 1955, at the Hickory Motor Speedway in Hickory, North Carolina. After qualifying second behind the car owned by Carl Kiekhaefer and driven by NASCAR racing legend Tim Flock, the battle for the lead was fierce between the two drivers. Johnson was racing so hard that twice he spun out while in the lead. After each spin Johnson regained control of his car and once again charged past Flock. After the race, Kiekhaefer was outraged that his car had lost. "Kiekhaefer was so mad I thought he was goin' to blow a gasket," said Johnson. Immediately after the race, Kiekhaefer filed a protest over its outcome, claiming that Johnson had cheated. Kiekhaefer was yelling, "No one can outrun my cars! No one can outrun my cars!" Johnson became irritated about Kiekhaefer's comments and responded, "That's a bunch of shit, 'cause I just did." NASCAR inspected the car and found nothing illegal, then encountered difficulty in reassembling the car. "NASCAR made Kiekhaefer pay to fix the car," commented Johnson, "That really tickled me."

Johnson went on to win five races that year. He was not as successful in 1956, as he spent eleven months and three days in a federal prison in Chillocothe, Ohio, for running moonshine for his father.

After a bounty of $10,000 was placed on his head by the local authorities in 1960, Johnson decided it was time to retire from the moonshine business and concentrate fully on racing. Driving an old underpowered Chevrolet against a field of more powerful Pontiacs at the Daytona raceway, Johnson discovered a phenomenon that forever changed the face of racing. During practice for the race, Johnson's engine topped out at 6,000 rpm. When he pulled in behind the Pontiac of Fireball Roberts during the race, he noticed that his car was now running at 7,000 rpm and had picked up speed. Drafting, as the technique was later called, created a vacuum behind the lead car that pulled the second car around the track and both cars went faster than they normally would. Johnson used this new technique to defeat Bobby Johns for the 1960 Daytona win. Johnson retired from driving six years later, but racing was still in his blood. He formed his own racing team and hired fellow North Carolinian Bobby Issac as his driver.

By 1970 the major automobile manufacturers were unsure about their commitment to NASCAR, and Johnson and many car owners were having difficulty funding their racing teams for the fifty-one NASCAR races. They needed sponsors. Johnson contacted the R. J. Reynolds tobacco company, which had recently been banned from advertising on television by the federal government, to discuss a team sponsorship. R. J. Reynolds had more than enough advertising money to sponsor one team; they wanted to sponsor the entire sport. Johnson contacted NASCAR owner Bill France, Sr., and in 1971, R. J. Reynolds became the title sponsor of NASCAR through its Winston brand of cigarettes. A few years later, in 1975, Johnson married his first wife, Flossie, in Las Vegas; they divorced on 27 October 1992. He married his second wife, Lias Day, on 11 November 1992.

Because of his felony conviction and the time he spent in federal prison in 1956, Johnson lived without many of his basic civil rights, including the right to vote. He was also prevented from being inducted into the North Carolina Motor Sports Hall of Fame because the chairman of the induction committee considered him nothing more than a common criminal. As a Christmas present in 1985, President Ronald W. Reagan signed a full presidential pardon, a request that had been pending since 1981. With this pardon came Johnson's induction into the North Carolina Motor Sports Hall of Fame in 1982. Johnson was also inducted in the National Motor Sports Press Association's Hall of Fame (1973), the International Motor Sports Hall of Fame (1990), Charlotte Motor Speedway's Court of Legends (1996), and Bristol Motor Speedway's Heroes of Bristol Hall of Fame (1997).

On 22 November 1995 Johnson sold his racing team to driver Brett Bodine and retired from the sport he had helped to build. During his racing career, Johnson started 313 races consisting of 51,988 laps and 38,054 miles. He won 50 races and led 12,651 laps. Even though his great success as a driver earned him the honor of being named the Greatest NASCAR Driver of All Time by *Sports Illustrated* in 1998, Johnson's greatest success came as a car owner. His drivers won 119 races and 6 NASCAR championships in 10 years. Johnson lives with his wife, Lisa, and two children on a 300-acre farm in Yadkin County, North Carolina.

★

Johnson's biography is Tom Higgins and Steve Waid, *Junior Johnson, Brave in Life* (1999). Tom Wolfe, "The Last American Hero Is Junior Johnson, Yes!" *Esquire* (1965), details the exploits of Johnson's early life. An article by Juliet Macur, "Junior Johnson: Racing Dull Compared to Running Moonshine," *Orlando Sentinel* (4 July 1998), discusses the legends and folklore surrounding Johnson.

JEROMY L. RUNION

JOHNSON, Walter Perry ("The Big Train") (*b.* 6 November 1887 in Coffeyville, Kansas; *d.* 11 December 1946 in Washington, D.C.), one of the greatest pitchers in baseball history, who was elected to the National Baseball Hall of Fame in Cooperstown, New York, in 1936.

Johnson was the second of six children, and the first of four sons, born into a farming family that hoped to improve

Walter Johnson, 1924. AP/WIDE WORLD PHOTOS

their lot by moving to California's new oil fields. His parents, Frank Edwin Johnson and Minnie (Perry) Johnson, had traveled to Kansas from Pennsylvania by wagon train, and moved to California the same way in 1901. Johnson attended Orange County's Fullerton High School, where he played on the baseball team. He also played baseball in Tacoma, Washington, before moving to Weiser, Idaho, to work for the telephone company.

In Weiser, Johnson knocked about playing semiprofessional baseball and became a local celebrity with his fastball. He was discovered as a sports talent when a traveling salesman saw him pitch in 1906. The salesman wrote to Joe Cantillon, the manager of the Washington Senators. Cantillon ignored the letters that kept coming about Johnson, even though the Senators needed players. He decided to send a catcher on his disabled list to check on an outfielder named Clyde Milan then playing in the Western Association, and while there take a look at Johnson. After receiving a favorable report on Johnson, the Senators offered him a $100 bonus, plus $350 per month and $9 for train fare to Washington, D.C.

Johnson's definitive nickname was "The Big Train," to distinguish his lashing, overpowering, sidearm fastballs that froze hitters and gave him 417 victories and a winning percentage of .599 in a twenty-one-year career with the Senators. Over that time, the winning percentage for the entire team was only .462. Johnson could have come from central casting for any baseball novel or motion picture. In appearance he was a gangly, raw-boned country boy, all natural talent and no guile, who could humble the best hitters and the best teams on almost any day he pitched.

Yet Johnson's first three seasons with the Senators were mediocre. Inexperience, a last-place team, and problems fielding the bunt all made his fastball less formidable. But he was durable, providing a lot of innings in a lot of games, for example going 13–25 in 1909. He could pitch with few rest days and was willing to start and relieve throughout his career. In 1908 he shut out the New York Highlanders (later known as the Yankees) three times in four days. His ascendancy as a dominating pitcher of his era began in 1910 when he won 25 games, followed by 23 in 1911, 32 in 1912, peaking in 1913 with a 36–7 won-to-lost record. In the 1913 season he also had an earned run average (ERA) of 1.09 and a string of fifty-six scoreless innings, a record that lasted for sixty-five years. On 24 June 1914 Johnson married Hazel Lee Roberts, the daughter of a Nevada congressman.

If baseball is immortal because of statistics, Johnson's career was a shrine to the game. His ERA was less than 2.0 in eleven years and 2.17 in his lifetime. In 1925 at the age of thirty-eight he was a twenty-game winner. He ranked first in shutouts with 110, second in wins with 417 (but with fewer losses than Cy Young), and third in innings pitched with 5,923, and he had a lifetime winning percentage of .599, all of which were achieved with substandard teams through most of his career. He led his league in wins six times, strikeouts twelve times, shutouts seven times, and ERA five times. Of his 279 losses, twenty-seven games were one to nothing and sixty-five were shutouts. Johnson was one of the first five players to be elected to the Baseball Hall of Fame, and the sports television conglomerate ESPN made him "60" in its top 100 athletes of the century in 1999.

Opponent hitters often decided to take a day off when they were scheduled to face Johnson, but the Big Train was not a headhunter. He did not as a rule throw at a hitter, although in his 5,923 innings he compiled a record of 206 hit batters. Instead he relied on raw speed and the ball's natural movement as it rocketed across the strike zone. "Sounding like a strike" was more than a one-line description of a Johnson fastball. In the 1924 World Series, Johnson's first, against the New York Giants, the umpire Bill Dineen told the Washington catcher Muddy Ruel that Johnson's pitching was so fast that he was doing some lively guessing as to where the ball crossed or didn't cross the plate. Ruel said he didn't tell Dineen to keep his eyes open since he himself was having trouble with Johnson's fastball.

For speed, Johnson himself believed "Smokey" Joe Wood was the fastest, claiming that no man alive could throw any harder than he could. Wood once said, "I threw so hard I thought my arm would fly right off my body." However, Wood won less than one-third of Johnson's total and, despite a stellar career with Boston and Cleveland, did not make the Hall of Fame. None of Johnson's contemporaries equaled his numbers. Nolan Ryan and Steve Carlton of the late twentieth century surpassed Johnson's strikeout totals, but Johnson's total record made him the greatest right-handed pitcher in baseball history.

It was unfortunate that the Senators did not become a contending team until Johnson was in his declining years. By 1923 the new owner Calvin Griffith had made some good trades and purchases and had made Bucky Harris the manager. Harris molded the Senators into a pennant winner in 1924 and 1925. Johnson became instrumental in the deciding seventh game in 1924 when he pitched four brilliant innings in relief in a twelve-inning game, and gained the victory when the Giants defense broke down. This was small recompense for his two losses as a starter in that series. In 1925 against Pittsburgh, Johnson was a decisive winner in his first two starts, but in the deciding seventh game on a rainy day, he couldn't hold a lead through the eighth inning and took a 9–7 loss. The gallant old master pitched two more seasons, finishing with 15–16 in 35 appearances in 1926 and 5–6 in 26 appearances in 1927.

In 1929 Johnson was made a manager for the Senators and had a mediocre three years. He then managed Cleveland from 1933 to 1935. Although his teams had a winning percentage, he was regarded as too easygoing. Under Joe Cronin as the manager, Washington again won a pennant in 1933, but lost to the Giants in the World Series. They fell to seventh place the next year and had only four winning seasons in the next twenty-six years.

Johnson slipped easily into retirement, a hero to baseball generally and to Washington, D.C., fans in particular. In 1936, to commemorate George Washington's birthday, he accommodated fans by throwing a silver dollar across the Rappahannock River, a distance of 272 feet (he abashedly commented, "The river was probably wider when George Washington threw his dollar"). In the same year Johnson followed Ty Cobb, Babe Ruth, Christy Mathewson, and Honus Wagner as one of the first five inductees into the National Baseball Hall of Fame. He owned a 550-acre dairy farm in Maryland that he shared with his five children, three boys and two girls (another daughter died in 1921). By then he was a widower, his wife, Hazel, having died in 1930. Johnson became involved in the Republican Party after serving as the president of the Association of Professional Baseball Players from 1936 to 1938. In 1938 he was elected to the board of commissioners of Montgomery County, Maryland, but in a run for the sixth congressional seat in 1940, he lost. He also served as an announcer at Washington Senators games and during World War II attended fund-raisers for the war effort.

Always physically fit at six feet, one inch and 200 pounds, Johnson died of a brain tumor at Georgetown Hospital on 11 December 1946. He is buried in Rockville Union Cemetery, Rockville, Maryland. Throughout his playing career and retirement years, Johnson remained the friendly, mild, modest man who had come to Washington, D.C., in 1907. Back then he had been so green that he believed a stranger who told him that he was already so famous they had named the Johnson Hotel after him. It was typical of Johnson that he enjoyed telling that story on himself.

★

Books about Johnson include Hy Turkin and S. C. Thompson, *The Official Encyclopedia of Baseball* (1977); Lawrence Ritter and Donald Honig, *The Image of Their Greatness: An Illustrated History of Baseball from 1900 to the Present* (1979); Joseph Reichler, *The Great All-Time Baseball Record Book: The Unique Sourcebook of Facts, Feats, and Figures* (1993); Jack Kavanaugh, *Walter Johnson: A Life* (1995); and Henry Thomas, *Baseball's Big Train* (1998). An obituary is in the *New York Times* (11 Dec. 1946).

JACK J. CARDOSO

JOHNSON, William D. ("Bill") (*b.* 1961 in Los Angeles, California), U.S. skiing champion, who in 1984 became the first American to win an Olympic gold medal in the men's downhill event.

Johnson was the son of Wallace Johnson, a computer analyst, and D. B. Johnson, a former office manager. When he was quite young, the family moved to Brightwood, Oregon, where Johnson and his three older siblings all became involved in skiing. Johnson showed a genuine talent for the sport from the very start. His daredevil streak surfaced early when, at age four, he was barely prevented by his grandmother from jumping off a rooftop. His parents were short of money and made substantial sacrifices to ensure that Johnson and his siblings had opportunities to ski, shuttling the family to ski meets in a station wagon that was on its last legs and sometimes sleeping in parking lots.

A bright student, Johnson turned his back on academics to focus all of his energies on skiing. He quit junior college to concentrate on training for the World Cup downhill races. Determined to mount a credible challenge to the European skiers, who up until that time had dominated the sport, Johnson won both the 1983 and 1984 U.S. downhill championships in the run-up to the 1984 Olympics in Sarajevo, Yugoslavia.

At the Olympics, Johnson irritated just about everybody in the skiing establishment with his cocky barrage of predictions that he would handily defeat all comers to win gold in the men's downhill. Although his predictions of victory won him a high profile, few knowledgeable observers considered him a real factor in the downhill race. His

Bill Johnson, 1984. ASSOCIATED PRESS AP

brashness was in no way diminished by the chorus of experts who confidently predicted he didn't have a chance. Up until the day of the race, he told anybody who would listen, "Everyone else can fight for second [place]." Then the brash Californian confounded everybody—particularly his fellow competitors Peter Mueller of Switzerland and Franz Klammer of Austria—by racing to victory by just over a quarter of a second, a respectable margin.

Although the naysayers were quick to dismiss Johnson as "just a glider," suggesting that his waxing technician had engineered the skier's amazing feat with a perfect waxing combination, Johnson refused to rein in his cockiness. After his wins at the International Ski Federation's World Cup competitions in 1984, he turned on the critics and declared, "I won three World Cups and the Olympics—I must've made a few good turns." Sadly, Johnson's glory of that year was not to be repeated. Two years later, skiing the downhill course at Val Gardena in Italy, he badly tore his knee ligaments in a savage crash on the notorious "camel bumps" near the bottom. Johnson continued skiing for the rest of the decade, but a lack of adequate training and persistent injuries, including back problems, marred his career, forcing him to retire from competitive skiing in 1990.

In 1987 he had married Gina Ricci. After leaving skiing, he concentrated first on real estate—building, renovating, and selling homes. His next venture was an unsuccessful assault on professional golf, which quickly faded after he failed to make the professional circuit. He tried his hand at a number of other ventures, including financial day trading and working as an electrician, but he had a short attention span and quickly lost interest in these endeavors. His mother explained, "He was always restless. Always looking for something else."

In 1991 tragedy struck when Johnson's one-year-old son drowned in the family's hot tub in Lake Tahoe, Nevada. Gina later gave birth to two more sons, but the marriage foundered over Johnson's inability to settle down and find steady work. Troubled by her husband's increasingly nomadic ways, Gina took their sons and moved to Sonoma, California, in 1999. The couple divorced in 2000.

For a few years Johnson operated a ski-racing camp at Crested Butte in Colorado, but when Salt Lake City, Utah, won the International Olympic Committee's nod to host the 2002 Winter Olympics, he decided it was time to dust off his skis and see if he still had the skills to make the U.S. downhill team. Johnson's ill-fated attempt to stage a skiing comeback was also a last-ditch effort to try to win back his ex-wife and sons, by returning to the only career at which he had been successful.

The head coach Bill Egan encouraged the long-idle Johnson to give it a try, saying, "It's a long shot, but go for it. If he can do it, more power to him." Less encouraging for Johnson was advice from his former coach Erik Stein-

berg. Although Steinberg acknowledged that Johnson's comeback effort could succeed, saying, "He's got the talent—anything's possible if he gets into bomb-proof shape," the coach warned that there was a good reason why few skiers attempted a comeback at age forty. "Mark Spitz tries a comeback, and what's the worst that can happen to him? In our sport, people can kill themselves."

Steinberg's warning proved hauntingly prophetic. On 22 March 2001 Johnson nearly killed himself in a horrific crash during a practice run at Big Mountain, near Whitefish, Montana. Catching an edge as he hurtled down the treacherous corkscrew course at more than fifty miles per hour, Johnson crashed face first into the icy slope. Tumbling through two safety nets, he nearly bit through his tongue. His ex-wife, at home in Sonoma, was told by authorities at Kalispell Regional Medical Center that Johnson had only a 25 percent chance of surviving. Johnson beat those grim odds; after coming out of a weeks-long coma, he faced a long and arduous course of rehabilitation to get back on his feet.

Johnson is lucky to have survived his injuries, which surely have ended his competitive skiing career. He will be remembered, however, as a gutsy, fearless competitor who managed to come through time and again when just about everyone else had counted him out.

★

The tragic ending to Johnson's comeback attempt is thoroughly explored in a number of articles, including E. M. Swift, "Last Run," *Sports Illustrated* (16 Apr. 2001); "Broken Dream: His Gold Medal Glory Behind Him, Bill Johnson Hoped a Return to Skiing Would Help Win Back His Family," *People* (14 May 2001); and Paula Parrish, "Downhill King," *Rocky Mountain News* (2 June 2001).

DON AMERMAN

JOHNSON, William Julius ("Judy") (*b.* 26 October 1900 in Snow Hill, Maryland; *d.* 15 June 1989 in Wilmington, Delaware), star third baseman in the old segregated Negro Leagues and later a major-league scout.

Johnson was the son of William Henry Johnson, a sailor, boxing coach, and athletic director of the Negro Settlement House in Wilmington, Delaware, and his wife, Annie Lee Johnson, a homemaker. As a boy, Johnson was taught how to box by his older sister Emma, but he preferred the baseball and football he played on integrated teams in Wilmington.

Johnson quit school after his freshman year at Howard High School in Wilmington and became a stevedore on the loading docks at Deep Water Port, New Jersey. He was not yet eighteen years old when he first played baseball for pay in 1918, earning $5 a game with the Bacharach Giants of

Atlantic City. In 1919 Johnson had a tryout with the Hilldale Club in Darby, Pennsylvania, a suburb of Philadelphia. Hilldale was one of the best African-American teams of that era, and Johnson, a five-foot, eleven-inch, 150-pounder, was deemed too small by its manager. He began playing with the semiprofessional Madison Stars in Philadelphia, and in 1920 the Stars sold him to Hilldale for $100.

As a rookie, Johnson earned $135 a month with Hilldale. Manager Billy Francis was the third baseman, so Johnson played shortstop for a time. He had the strong arm but not the foot speed required of a good shortstop, and he blossomed when he was shifted to third base. Johnson, who batted right-handed, was one of the team's leading hitters, posting averages not much under .400 as Hilldale won the first three pennants in the Eastern Colored League in 1923, 1924, and 1925. In the first Negro World Series in 1924, Johnson led his team in hitting with a .341 average , but Hilldale lost 5 games to 4 to the Kansas City Monarchs of the Negro National League. In the 1925 World Series, again against the Monarchs, Hilldale won 5 games to 1, but Johnson's batting slipped to .300.

Johnson was a sure-handed fielder with an excellent arm. He credited John Henry (Pop) Lloyd, one of the game's greatest shortstops, with giving him the skills. "He was a great man and a great teacher," said Johnson of Lloyd, who managed Hilldale in 1923. "He put the confidence in you and you had to do it—you just had to do it. I think that was one of the best years I ever had in baseball." Like many other Negro League stars, Johnson spent some winters on the diamond. He played in Cuba during six winters and spent one winter in Palm Beach, Florida, in the "Hotel League." Players, both black and white, were waiters in resort hotels and entertained the guests on the ballfield.

Johnson stayed with Hilldale through 1929 and then spent the next season as player-manager of the Homestead Grays in Pittsburgh. He rejoined the Hilldale club in 1931 and was player-manager during the team's two final years. It was tough going for African-American teams during the Great Depression. Salaries went unpaid, and the players agreed to divide what was left after expenses. Johnson told historian John B. Holway, "We used to play two games every Thursday, two on Saturday, and three on Sunday. I recall times when we'd go to New York to play a doubleheader and then a night game. We'd leave Coney Island at one o'clock at night, ride all night on the bus, and get into Pittsburgh for a twilight game on Monday."

Johnson went back to Pittsburgh in 1932, this time to play third base for the year-old Pittsburgh Crawfords. The Crawfords already boasted such stars as Josh Gibson, Satchel Paige, Oscar Charleston, and Cool Papa Bell, all future Hall of Famers. Over the next four seasons until his retirement in 1936, Johnson is credited with batting averages of .332, .333, .367, and .306.

Before leaving the Crawfords for good, Johnson went to Mexico with the team to play a series of games against major leaguers, including such stars as Rogers Hornsby and Jimmie Foxx. In twenty games against the big leaguers, Johnson batted .263.

Following his retirement from baseball, Johnson coached a semiprofessional basketball team in Delaware and drove a taxicab for the Continental Cab Company in Wilmington. After Jackie Robinson broke the color line in the major leagues in 1947, Johnson was hired as a scout by the Philadelphia (now Oakland) Athletics. One day he asked the Athletics's venerable owner Connie Mack why he had never hired black players. Mack told him, "Well, Judy, if you want to know the truth, there were just too many of you to go in." Johnson explained that Mack was saying, "It would take too many jobs away from the other (white) boys."

Johnson later scouted for the Philadelphia Phillies and Milwaukee (now Atlanta) Braves, and is credited with signing slugger Richie Allen and star outfielder Billy Bruton, who married Johnson's only child, Loretta.

Johnson was an enthusiastic teacher. He could analyze a young player's strengths and faults and make useful suggestions. His Pittsburgh Crawfords teammate Ted Page said, "He had the ability to see the qualities, the faults, of ballplayers and have the correction for them. Judy could have done the major leagues a lot more good as somebody who could help develop young players. He should have been in the majors . . . years ago as a coach. I always thought Judy would have made a perfect major league manager." Near the end of his life, Johnson was still a teacher, coaching sandlotters in Wilmington.

Johnson was elected to the National Baseball Hall of Fame in 1975, the sixth Negro Leaguer so honored. Subsequently, a city park in Wilmington was named for him, and his statue was erected at a baseball park. Johnson's wife of sixty-three years, Anita, a former schoolteacher, died in 1986. Three years later, Johnson suffered a stroke and died at the age of eighty-eight. He is buried at Silverbrook Cemetery in Wilmington.

★

Negro baseball historian John B. Holway devotes a chapter of *Blackball Stars* (1987), to Johnson's life and baseball career. Other useful sources are the biographical sketches of Johnson in Robert W. Peterson, *Only the Ball Was White* (1970); Dick Clark and Larry Lester, eds., *The Negro Leagues Book* (1994); and James A. Riley, *Biographical Encyclopedia of the Negro Baseball Leagues* (1994).

ROBERT W. PETERSON

JONES, David ("Deacon") (*b.* 9 December 1938 in Eatonville, Florida), Hall of Fame football player who was one of the first fast, hard-hitting defensive linemen and who perfected the head slap and coined the term "sack" for tackling the quarterback behind the line of scrimmage.

From his early childhood in Eatonville, Jones was determined and headstrong. Ishmael, his father, was a handyman, and Mattie, his mother, was a homemaker who helped the family in the fields during harvest seasons. His parents raised Jones, his two brothers, and his five sisters to be disciplined and hardworking as they struggled in their poor African-American town. His early experiences with poverty and discrimination led Jones to fight against injustice all of his life. He played basketball and baseball in the local schools, but football was the sport that he hoped would get him out of Eatonville. Playing both offense and defense for Hungerford High, Jones earned awards and high praise but received no inquiries from college teams. He graduated from Hungerford in 1956, and was convinced that his outspokenness led one of his coaches to squelch the interest of any college recruiters.

Jones worked in the fields and played semiprofessional basketball in an African-American Florida league until 1957, when a coach from the African-American South Carolina State College heard some stories about Jones's football skills. With his speed, power, and determination, Jones quickly won the South Carolina starting tackle position from the current All-Conference lineman and won the All-Conference Tackle honors himself in 1958. Although the likelihood of an African-American lineman at a small school getting noticed by the National Football League (NFL) was slim, his chance came when South Carolina played Florida Agricultural and Mechanical (A&M) University. A scout from the Los Angeles Rams was present to observe the A&M players, but most of his resulting notes concerned the six-foot, five-inch, 265-pound South Carolina offensive and defensive tackle who was all over the field, often chasing down running backs and receivers with his unusual speed.

In 1960 South Carolina revoked Jones's scholarship and expelled him, because of his failure to meet academic standards and his difficulties with the police after participating in civil rights protests. He briefly attended Mississippi Vocational (1960–1961) but was kicked out of the state by police who didn't want any "black troublemakers" in town. Not long after moving to New Orleans to live with his brother, he learned that the Los Angeles Rams had selected him in the fourteenth round of the NFL draft.

A fellow passenger on Jones's flight to Los Angeles remarked that no one would ever remember a football player named "David Jones." At his rookie press conference Jones told the reporters, "My name is Deacon Jones . . . and I've come to preach the gospel of winning football to the good people of Los Angeles." The Rams converted him to a defensive end, and Jones worked hard to make the team. Meanwhile, he discovered the unwritten NFL rule: no team had more than four African-American players. The Rams had been one of the first teams to accept any African-American players; this time they chose eight. In 1961, during training camp of his first year, Jones's speed, toughness, and determination ensured him a spot on the roster.

The Rams struggled during Jones's first two years under the head coach and former Rams quarterback Bob Waterfield, but Jones drew attention. Opposing teams had never seen a defensive end as fast as Jones, and even the celebrated offense of the Green Bay Packers led by Bart Starr struggled against him. While the Rams had a losing season, Jones was named the Rams Rookie of the Year in 1961 and was awarded a new contract. The Rams failed to improve from 1962 to 1964, when Harland Svare replaced Waterfield, but Jones and the Rams defense dominated the league. Svare, not fond of Jones's outspoken ways, suggested that he "settle down" and get married. Jones did so, but his marriage to Iretha Oberton in 1963 soon foundered.

Deacon Jones, 1969. ASSOCIATED PRESS AP

Although Jones was not faithful, he refused to divorce Oberton.

Jones was named to his first Pro Bowl in 1964. He and his fellow linemen Merlin Olsen, Roosevelt Grier, and Lamar Lundy became known as the Fearsome Foursome. Fortunes changed for the Rams in 1965 when George Allen became the coach, and the team then enjoyed five winning seasons and a number of playoff appearances. Always looking for an edge, Jones perfected the "head slap" after watching the boxer Muhammad Ali. Banned by the NFL after Jones retired, this crushing blow to the helmet, coupled with Jones's blazing speed, earned him more sacks and tackles than anyone in the league. Jones also coined the term "sack" to describe bringing the quarterback down behind the line of scrimmage. He said the move was "like sacking a great city like Rome or Troy."

The Rams owner Dan Reeves fired Allen in 1972. Reeves had tried to fire Allen before, but Jones and other players had rallied together and forced his reinstatement. This time, the coach was gone. A year later Jones was traded to the San Diego Chargers. His season ended bitterly as the NFL, wracked by criticism for allowing the widespread use of amphetamines and other drugs, singled out the Chargers and Jones (Jones was never convicted for illegal drug use). Fined by the league and disheartened, Jones considered retiring but he was traded to the Washington Redskins in 1974 and was reunited with Allen, his former coach. He played mainly on third-down passing situations, still performing admirably, and even kicking a field goal in his final regular season game. Jones retired after his 1974–1975 season with the Redskins.

During his fourteen years in the NFL, Jones was the Outstanding Defensive Player twice, went to eight Pro Bowls, and was named All–NFL/National Football Conference (NFC) six times (1965–1970). Although the NFL did not keep sack records during his career, unofficially Jones ranked second behind Reggie White with 180.5 and, as of 2001, he still held the single-season sack record of twenty-six in a fourteen-game season. He held the unofficial record for most solo tackles (753) and was named to the league's Team of the Seventies and to the All-Time Seventy-fifth Anniversary Team. In 1980 Jones was inducted into the Pro Football Hall of Fame.

During his time in Los Angeles, Jones began singing and recording with various bands. He also worked as a bodyguard for the candidate Robert F. Kennedy during the 1968 presidential campaign, but he was not present when Kennedy was assassinated, a tragedy that haunted him for years. After his retirement Jones continued singing and appearing in commercials and movies. He started the Deacon Jones Foundation, of which his second wife Elizabeth is chief operating and financial officer, to help inner-city students find scholarships and programs. In July 2001 Jones, along with Boomer Esiason, became an analyst for the Fox Sports Network's *NFL This Morning,* a live, Sunday-morning pregame show.

Jones's career statistics in sacks and solo tackles were astounding. In addition, his outspoken crusade against injustice off the field paved the way for a more fair and open NFL. Jones became known as the Secretary of Defense, a fitting epithet for a man who was not only the game's first star defensive lineman, but quite possibly the best pass-rusher in football history.

★

For an insightful and lively narrative of Jones's life from childhood to retirement, see his book with John Klawitter, *Headslap: The Life and Times of Deacon Jones* (1996). A second book by both men is *The Book of Deacon: The Wit and Wisdom of Deacon Jones* (2001), a collection of stories and sayings that underscores the player's toughness, determination, and outspokenness. A biography written about Jones at the peak of his NFL career is Bill Libby, *Life in the Pit: The Deacon Jones Story* (1970).

MARKUS H. MCDOWELL

JONES, Jerral Wayne ("Jerry") (*b.* 13 October 1942 in Los Angeles, California), college football player and owner of the Dallas Cowboys of the National Football League (NFL).

Jones was one of three children of J. W. "Pat" Jones, a future supermarket owner and insurance company founder, and Arminta Pearl Clark, a homemaker. Pat Jones, like many others, had moved the family from North Little Rock, Arkansas, to Los Angeles to work temporarily in the aircraft industry during World War II. Shortly after Jerry's birth the family returned to Arkansas.

Jones grew up in the Rose City section of North Little Rock. He was first introduced to organized football in junior high school. He made an impression on his coach, who used a psychological ploy to get the 120-pound Jones to tackle a 200-pounder. Once that was accomplished, Jones was fearless on the football field. Coach Jim Bohanan said of Jones: "He would run through a brick wall, and if you didn't tell him to stop, he'd do it again—and again. He was the fiercest competitor we *ever* had."

Jones was a hard-running and tough fullback for the North Little Rock High School Wildcats. The team was quite successful, defeating the more powerful team from Little Rock Central for the first time in years. But a loss cost North Little Rock a state championship. Nevertheless Jones was what Frank Broyles at the University of Arkansas was looking for, players who were smallish, quick, smart, and above all tough. Jones met the criteria and was recruited to play for the Razorbacks.

While on the Fayetteville campus, Jones met the fellow

Jerry Jones *(left)*, 2000. Associated Press AP

Razorback guard Jimmy Johnson and the freshman coach Barry Switzer, whose paths all crossed years later. The bright Jones was a good enough student that he graduated with his entering class (B.S., 1964), and because of a "red shirt" year, a season when he was in school but did not play, he took graduate courses and earned an M.B.A. degree during his fifth year at Arkansas.

Jones, while far from the Razorbacks' best player, was the unquestioned leader and was co-captain of the team. Jones received credit from his teammates for motivating Arkansas for their Cotton Bowl game with Nebraska in January 1965. The 10–7 win over the Cornhuskers left Arkansas, in the eyes of many, atop the intercollegiate football world.

Jones married Eugenia Carol "Gene" Chambers, a former Arkansas Poultry Princess, on 26 January 1963, while both were students at Arkansas. The couple had three children, one of whom, Stephen Jones, played linebacker at Arkansas and became chief operating officer and executive vice president of player personnel with the Dallas Cowboys. Following graduation Jones was ready to succeed. As the writer Jim Dent said: "Those who knew him, knew Jerry Jones was going places. They just couldn't imagine the altitude or the speed at which he would travel."

Actually Jones launched his business career during his last year in college, when he spent time on the road selling for the insurance company his father founded, Modern Security Life. Jones was executive vice president after he graduated, from 1965 to 1969. Coach Broyles, traveling throughout Arkansas giving speeches and recruiting, often bumped into Jones. Broyles said: "Shoot! He was wearin' new clothes, drivin' a new Cadillac El Dorado, and carryin' around a brief case. None of my other players was doin' that."

In 1970 Jones formed Arkoma Exploration, an independent oil and gas concern. The firm was phenomenally successful, establishing offices in Fort Smith, Arkansas, and Calgary, Alberta, Canada. Jones also became involved in banking, real estate, insurance, shipping, manufacturing, and even Arkansas Talents, a boxing promotions organization.

The considerable fortune Jones amassed allowed him to purchase the Dallas Cowboys on 25 February 1989 for a reported $234 million. Jones immediately irked some when he enthusiastically announced the hiring of his college teammate and road-game roommate Johnson. Perhaps Jones's enthusiasm masked from him the fact that he was firing the coaching legend Tom Landry, until then the only coach the Cowboys ever had.

Jones, who was also the team's general manager, and Johnson were subject to much criticism and ridicule when the Cowboys turned in a 1–15 record in the first season (1989) of Jones's ownership and Johnson's coaching. But by trading the star runner Herschel Walker for a host of draft choices, the Cowboys formed the nucleus of the team, including the quarterback Troy Aikman, the running back Emmitt Smith, and the wide receiver Michael Irvin, that won three Super Bowls (1993, 1994, and 1996) in four years. Johnson, however, was only around for the first two.

In what some observers called "a clash of Texas-size

egos," Jones and Johnson agreed to part company in 1994. Jones, it was said, bristled at Johnson's getting and taking too much credit. Before the parting Jones said, "There are five hundred people who can coach the Cowboys." Some wondered if Jones, who often stalked the sidelines talking to coaches and players, included himself.

"No. 500" was Switzer, who had great success at Oklahoma after leaving Arkansas. Switzer won the last Cowboys Super Bowl, but it could be argued that he did it with the talent assembled by Johnson. Switzer, too, fell out of favor, mainly because the Cowboys lacked discipline on and off the field, getting called for needless penalties and suffering drug arrests and run-ins with the law. Chan Gailey and Dave Campo subsequently were unable to reverse the team's downward spiral. Johnson's astute player evaluations were missed, as evidenced by the Cowboys' mediocre drafts when the core group began to age and retire. From 1997 to 2000 Dallas compiled a 29–35 record.

Jones has always been considered a maverick owner. He has never subscribed to the NFL's "League think" mindset, whereby all team owners put aside what was best for their individual franchises and did what was best for "the League." When Jones and the Cowboys were winning, his moves were considered innovative, and he enjoyed considerable attention and a considerable following. With the team in imminent danger of not holding onto its "America's Team" image, fewer and fewer team owners were willing to march to his drumbeat.

Jones has been active in many charities, perhaps none more so than the Salvation Army. The Cowboys' annual Thanksgiving game is the kickoff of the Salvation Army's Kettle Drive. Jones and his wife have been honored as the Salvation Army's Partners of the Year for their extensive involvement. With a seven-figure gift, they established the Gene and Jerry Jones Family Center for Children in Dallas. The couple also contributed heavily to the Library of Congress's restoration of the Thomas Jefferson Library. Another major gift, in conjunction with Jones's teammate Jim Lindsey, funded the University of Arkansas Hall of Champions, named in their honor.

Jones is controversial, but like so many other controversial figures, he has supporters as well as detractors. He counterbalances perceived transgressions with acts of altruism.

★

Jim Dent wrote a biography of Jones, *King of the Cowboys: The Life and Times of Jerry Jones* (1995). Jones's life and career are also discussed in Skip Bayless, *The 'Boys* (1993); Mike Fisher, *Stars and Strife* (1993); and Jimmy Johnson as told to Ed Hinton, *Turning the Thing Around* (1993).

JIM CAMPBELL

JONES, K. C. (*b.* 25 May 1932 in Taylor, Texas), defensive standout as a basketball guard for the Boston Celtics and as a coach for the Celtics and others.

Born into poverty, Jones, who, like his father, was named after the fabled railroad engineer, grew up to take on a legendary status of his own. Jones's years in Texas were hard as his father, a factory worker and cook, drifted from job to job during the depression. When his parents divorced in the early 1940s, the nine-year-old Jones moved with his mother, Eula, and two siblings to San Francisco. Jones was an athletic child and took up several sports. At San Francisco's Commerce High School he was a standout in both basketball and football before graduating in 1951. Jones's tenacious defense as a schoolboy player caught the eye of Phil Woolpert, the head coach for the University of San Francisco (USF). Woolpert was rebuilding USF's basketball program and recruited Jones and another gangly

K. C. Jones, 1994. ASSOCIATED PRESS NBA

schoolboy named Bill Russell, who became Jones's teammate for almost two decades and his friend for life. Although Jones had to sit out almost all of the 1953–1954 season due to a burst appendix, he and Russell led the USF Dons to the National Collegiate Athletic Association (NCAA) Championship in their junior and senior years, for the 1954–1955 and 1955–1956 seasons. Jones was named All-American his senior year and after receiving his B.A., he was selected with Russell for the gold-medal-winning 1956 U.S. Olympic basketball squad.

Russell's shot-blocking and rebounding drew the attention of the Boston Celtics coach Red Auerbach, who also became enamored with the hustle and tenacity of the scrappy Dons guard. Auerbach drafted Russell in the first round of the 1956 National Basketball Association (NBA) draft and called Jones's name in the second round. Jones doubted that he could crack the already-powerful Celtics lineup, however, and opted for a two-year stint in the U.S. Army instead. After his tour ended in 1958, Jones turned to football, playing in a few pre-season exhibition games with the Los Angeles Rams before finally accepting a spot with the Celtics and his old college roommate Russell, for the 1958–1959 season.

Jones saw limited playing time as a Celtics rookie, but was an able backup to the team's powerful backcourt of the All-Star guard Bill Sharman and the Hall of Famer Bob Cousy. For four years Jones supplied valuable minutes off the bench for four straight championship squads. Jones married Beverly Cain in 1960 at the end of the basketball season, and the couple had five children before divorcing in 1978.

In 1963, after Cousy's retirement, he stepped into the starting job as a point guard for the defending champions, along with his fellow guard Sam Jones. Although he was never an offensive standout, Jones excelled on the other side of the ball, closing down high-flying offensive players. With Jones now running the point, the Celtics continued their dominance over the NBA until 1967, when they finally relinquished their hold over the title after losing the Eastern Conference final, four games to one, against the Philadelphia 76ers. Jones retired after the 1967 season; his final campaign was the only one without a championship. The Celtics promptly retired his jersey, raising number 25 to the rafters of the old Boston Garden on 12 February 1967. For his days as a player, Jones was elected to the Naismith Memorial Basketball Hall of Fame in 1989.

His playing days behind him, Jones turned to coaching, first for Brandeis University in Waltham, Massachusetts, in 1970. The following year he repeated his role as a backup to Sharman, who was now the head coach of the Los Angeles Lakers. The Lakers took the championship that win-

ter and Jones, as the assistant coach, took home his ninth NBA Championship ring. The San Diego Conquistadors of the upstart American Basketball Association (ABA) wooed Jones away in 1973, and for the first time he was a head coach in the pros. He returned to the NBA a year later, as the coach of the Bullets, who had recently relocated from Baltimore to Washington, D.C. In only his second season, Jones took the Bullets to the finals, where they were swept by the Golden State Warriors. Jones was fired a year later, in 1976, and returned to an assistant position, first with Milwaukee and then again with the Celtics. In 1980, he married his second wife, Ellen.

When the Celtics head coach position opened up in 1983, Auerbach again put his faith in the quiet guard from USF, naming Jones to lead another generation of powerful Boston teams. Jones remained popular with his players, and his laid-back coaching style fit well with the creative play of a Celtics squad that included Larry Bird, Kevin McHale, and Robert Parrish. The first year under Jones (1983–1984) saw the team go 62–20 and won Jones yet another championship, his first as a head coach and his tenth overall. His .751 winning percentage as the Celtics skipper was the best of any coach in the franchise's history.

Jones left the Celtics after the 1988 season and moved on to another position as the assistant coach with the Seattle Supersonics. He became the Sonics head coach two years later, a position he held until 1992. In 1994 he began a two-year stint as an assistant for the Detroit Pistons. Jones returned to coaching in 1997, this time for the New England Blizzard of the American Basketball League (ABL), a women's professional league. He coached the Blizzard until the ABL collapsed in 1999, with the advent of the Women's National Basketball Association (WNBA). Afterward, Jones returned to college coaching, first for the University of Rhode Island in Kingston and then for the University of Hartford in Connecticut.

In his nine-year playing career as a point guard for the Boston Celtics, the six-foot, one-inch Jones averaged only .387 from the floor and .647 from the free throw line. However, Jones's soft-spoken personality and mediocre statistics belied his competitive fire and reputation as a defensive standout. Wherever Jones went, both as a player and as a coach, he seemed to bring victory with him. Two NCAA championships, an Olympic gold medal in 1956, eight NBA championships as a player, another two NBA championships as a head coach, and another two as an assistant added up to an unparalleled basketball career.

★

Jones has been the subject of numerous magazine profiles. He wrote, with Jack Warner, *Rebound: The Autobiography of K. C. Jones and an Inside Look at the Champion Boston Celtics* (1986).

His friendship with Bill Russell is discussed in Russell's two autobiographies, *Go Up for the Glory* (written with William McSweeney, 1966), and *Second Wind: The Memoirs of an Opinionated Man* (written with Taylor Branch, 1979). Jones is featured in *On and Off the Court* (1985) by Joe Fitzgerald and Celtics coach and owner Red Auerbach. Jones is also discussed in the many histories of the Celtics, including Joe Fitzgerald, *That Championship Feeling* (1974); Jeff Greenfield, *The World's Greatest Team: A Portrait of the Boston Celtics, 1957–1969* (1979); Bob Ryan, *The Boston Celtics* (1989); and Dan Shaughnessy, *Ever Green: The Boston Celtics* (1990). An in-depth discussion of the Celtics' championship season with Jones as coach (1985–1986) is in Peter May, *In the Last Banner* (1996).

MATTHEW TAYLOR RAFFETY

JONES, Marion Lois (*b*. 12 October 1975 in Los Angeles, California), basketball champion and sprinter widely considered to be the fastest woman in the world.

Jones is the daughter of George Jones and Marion Toler. When Jones was a child, her father abandoned the family. Later, her parents divorced. Her mother, who had emigrated from Belize to the United States, worked as a medical and legal transcriber and raised Jones and her older brother Albert.

An active child, Jones was exposed to various sports and excelled in all of them. She played T-ball, basketball, and softball, participated in gymnastics, and took ballet and tap dancing lessons. At the age of five Jones began running track and first played organized basketball when she was eleven. Impressed by the way Jones played basketball, the track coach Jack Dawson invited her to join his middle-school track club. She quickly dominated the competitions and won a national high school title in eighth grade. "I felt confident that she could be an Olympian," said Dawson. At the age of twelve Jones was competing internationally.

Before her ninth-grade year, the family relocated again to Camarillo in Ventura County, and Jones attended Rio Mesa High School, an ethnically mixed school in Oxnard. There she attracted national attention in basketball and track. In 1989 Jones was the first freshman in history to win California's state high school championship in the 100- and 200-meter dash. She won both events again in 1990. At the 1991 U.S. championships, Jones ran the 200 meters in 22.87 seconds, the fourth-fastest time recorded that year in the United States. In 1992, before her junior year, Toler moved the family once again to Thousand Oaks so that her daughter could attend the mostly white Thousand Oaks High School, where she had more opportunities for basketball. At Thousand Oaks High School she continued to dominate the track.

In the 1992 U.S. Olympic Trials in New Orleans, Jones set a national high school record in the 200 meters that still stood through 1999, and she qualified as an alternate in the 4 × 100–meter relay in Barcelona but turned down the opportunity to run the relay. Jones finished sixth in the 100

Marion Jones. ARCHIVE PHOTOS, INC.

meters and fourth in the 200, missing a spot on the team by .07 of a second. Her record at the time was the ninth fastest by a woman and the fastest for a woman under the age of eighteen. Jones's winning long jump of twenty-two-and-a-half feet was the second longest in history by a high-school competitor. In the 1992 world junior championships, she placed fifth in the 100 meters and seventh in the 200, and secured the second-runner spot on the U.S. 4 × 100–meter relay team, an accomplishment Jones called "the highlight of her track career." In June 1993 she won three events, the 100- and 200-meter dash, and the long jump, and was the first person to win nine California state titles at the California state high school track meet.

Celebrated as the greatest American female high school track and field athlete, Jones was also California's best female high school basketball player. She averaged 22.8 points in her final season and led Thousand Oaks to two state championship games, winning the title in 1992. By the time she graduated in 1993, Jones had won three consecutive Gatorade Circle of Champions National High School Girls Track and Field Athlete of the Year Awards. Jones is the only athlete to have won the award more than once. It was the first time in fifty years that a woman had won three national titles.

In the fall of 1993 Jones enrolled at the University of North Carolina at Chapel Hill (UNC), and her legend continued to grow. A forward in high school basketball, Jones was moved to point guard in her fourth collegiate game. In 1994 she led the Lady Tar Heels to the National Collegiate Athletic Association (NCAA) Division I title, the first ever for UNC and the first for an Atlantic Coast Conference (ACC) school. Jones became the leader of the team, averaging 14.1 points per game. Her speed earned her the nickname "Flash." By her second year of college, Jones became the first female sophomore in UNC's basketball history to score more than 1,000 career points. She was named to the ACC's first All-Star team, and she earned All-America honors. The team finished with a record of 30–5 but lost to Stanford University in the NCAA tournament.

Injuries forced Jones to miss her junior year, and the Lady Tar Heels went 13–14. Jones resumed her basketball career in 1996 and helped return the Tar Heels to the elite of women's college basketball. "It's unbelievable how big a factor Marion is," her teammate, Jessica Gaspar, told *USA Today*. Jones finished as one of the five finalists for the Naismith Award (presented annually to the male and female college players of the year) and was named All-America third team. She concluded the 1996–1997 season with an average of 18.1 points per game. During her three years playing at UNC, Jones averaged 16.8 points and scored 1,716 points. In spring 1997 she graduated from UNC with a B.A. in journalism and communications.

That April, she also began training with Trevor Graham, a silver medalist in the 4 × 400–meter relay. Jones won the 100-meter dash and the long jump at the 1997 U.S. national championships, then two gold medals in the 100 and the 4 × 100 relay at the world championship in Athens. Jones's winning jump was the longest by a woman that year.

At the 1998 U.S. Nationals in New Orleans, Jones won three titles and placed first in three events: the 100- and 200-meter dash and the long jump. That same year at the Goodwill Games in New York, she again won the 100 and 200 meters. Jones finished the year ranked number one in the world in those two events and in the long jump. Her miracle season continued at the World Cup in September 1998 in Johannesburg, South Africa, where she won the 200-meter dash and was the third fastest and fourth fastest in the 100 meters. Jones's thirty-seven consecutive wins ended in Johannesburg, where she finished second in the long jump.

On 3 October 1998 Jones married C. J. Hunter, the world shot-put champion, whom she had met two years earlier in the UNC weight room, and who inspired her to give up basketball and pursue a professional career in track and field. The following year she won the 100 meters and the long jump at the World Championships in Seville, Spain, but suffered a back injury and withdrew from the 200-meter final. Jones came back during the July 1999 U.S. trials and won her three main events, which qualified her for the Olympics in Sydney, Australia.

At the age of twenty-four, Jones became the world's highest profiled female athlete for pursuing five gold medals during the 2000 Olympic Games. In spite of the drug scandal that surrounded her husband and challenged her athletic dream in Sydney (Hunter had tested positive for steroids and was not allowed to compete in the Games), Jones proved to the world that she was a true competitor when she won three gold and two bronze medals.

In June 2001 Jones announced her separation from Hunter. The following month, the triple-time Olympic star went on to reaffirm her status as the top female sprinter in the world at the Goodwill Games in Brisbane, Australia, winning the 100-meter dash in 11.04 seconds.

Jones, "America's Golden Girl," is considered to be one of the most celebrated athletes in the world. Besides competing in sports, Jones speaks to youth groups about hard work and staying in school, and is a courtside reporter for NBC coverage of the Women's National Basketball Association (WNBA). Her unfailing determination and relentless competitiveness made her the most decorated female sprinter at a single Olympics. Only three other athletes, Jesse Owens, Carl Lewis, and Fanny Blankerskoen, have won four gold medals in a single Olympics. Nike recognized Jones's achievements and made a shoe for her. The five-foot-ten athlete is ranked as one of the greatest stars in U.S. track history.

★

There is one biography of Jones, Ron Rapoport, *See How She Runs: Marion Jones and the Making of a Champion* (2000). *Current Biography Yearbook* (1998) has useful information on Jones's career. John Brant, "Sight Set on Sydney," *Runners World* (Sept. 1998), has invaluable information about her career. Bennett Kinnon, "Marion Jones: America's Golden Girl," *Ebony* (Mar. 2001), discusses the controversy surrounding Jones's husband and about her life in the fast lane.

NJOKI-WA-KINYATTI

JONES, Robert Tyre, Jr. ("Bobby")   (*b.* 17 March 1902 in Atlanta, Georgia; *d.* 18 December 1971 in Atlanta, Georgia), considered the greatest amateur golfer ever, known for winning thirteen major championships, including the Grand Slam in 1930, and for cofounding the Augusta National Golf Club and the Masters Tournament.

Jones was the only child of Robert Purmedus Jones, a lawyer, and Clara Thomas, a homemaker. He was born and raised in Atlanta, where he excelled in school. Following a

Bobby Jones. AP/WIDE WORLD PHOTOS

successful career at Tech High School, where he graduated in 1918, Jones enrolled at the Georgia School of Technology. In 1922 he graduated with a degree in mechanical engineering. Jones then attended Harvard College in Cambridge, Massachusetts, where he received a B.A. in English literature in 1924. After working for two years in real estate, Jones entered Emory University's law program in Atlanta. In his third semester, he took the bar exam and passed. Jones joined his father's law firm in early 1928 and spent the rest of his life practicing both law and golf. On 17 June 1924 he married Mary Malone; they had three children.

Jones may have been the most intellectually well-rounded athlete ever, but despite all of his academic achievements, his primary arena was competitive golf. Although he was not born into a wealthy family, Jones had a relatively privileged upbringing, which was made possible by the social standing of his grandfather Robert Tyre Jones. That man's lasting influence meant his grandson and namesake was allowed access to the Atlanta Athletic Club (AAC) and its exclusive East Lake Country Club golf course. Jones was a sickly toddler and, from the age of five, he was taken each summer to East Lake in the hope that fresh air and exercise would help him to gain strength. From the beginning he was fascinated with the sport of golf and learned to play on the country club's course. East Lake's professional, Stewart Maiden, possessed a classic swing and it became a model for the young, impressionable Jones.

By the time he was nine, "Little Bob" was competing in local junior tournaments, even winning the 1911 AAC Junior Championship by defeating a sixteen-year-old opponent in the final match. Spurred on by the AAC's other talented youngsters, such as Perry Adair and Alexa Stirling, Jones continued to develop his competitive skill. After he fired a 68 in 1916 to tie East Lake's course record, the *New York Times* announced, "Georgia Has Golf Marvel!"

Jones's father determined his fourteen-year-old son was ready to taste national competition. In the fall of 1916 an overconfident Bobby Jones traveled to Philadelphia's Merion Cricket Club, the site of the U.S. Amateur Championship. After an exciting performance in the medal-qualifying rounds, Jones defeated the 1906 champion in the first round and the reigning Pennsylvania state champion in the second round. Those victories set up a third-round match with the defending national champion, Robert Gardner. Jones fought hard but eventually succumbed to Gardner's experience. Still, until he was eliminated, Jones was the biggest story of the week. Within a few days, he gained international fame and became the nation's number-one golf prodigy.

The 1916 U.S. Amateur Championship began a fifteen-year golf career for Jones. O. B. Keeler, Jones's good friend and biographer, liked to write that Jones really had two careers: seven lean years (1916–1922), followed by eight fat years (1923–1930). Actually, although he failed to win a major tournament, the first seven years of Jones's competitive record were not too lean. From 1916 to 1922 Jones steadily gained experience, physical strength, and emotional maturity. He particularly needed the latter, having developed a reputation as a club-throwing hothead. In 1919 he was the runner-up in the national amateur. Jones entered his first U.S. Open in 1920, finishing a solid eighth, and within two years he had improved to runner-up in that event.

By 1923 Jones was ready to break through. He finally won his first major title, claiming the U.S. Open in an exciting play-off with Bobby Cruickshank. This major victory was the first of thirteen overall; Jones won four U.S. Opens (1923, 1926, 1929, 1930), five U.S. Amateurs (1924, 1925, 1927, 1928, 1930), three British Opens (1926, 1927, 1930), and one British Amateur (1930). Jones also played on the first U.S. Walker Cup teams, serving as the captain in 1928 and 1930. Having accomplished the unprecedented feat of winning the Grand Slam—all four major crowns in one season—Jones retired from competitive golf late in 1930.

The 1930 Grand Slam win was often heralded as Jones's finest achievement, but his career U.S. Open record was equally impressive. In eleven starts between 1920 and 1930, Jones compiled four wins and four runners-up, losing twice in a play-off; he finished out of the top ten only once (eleventh in 1927). For a decade, Jones dominated the world's toughest medal tournament. Following the 1926 season, in which he won both the U.S. and British Opens, Jones was unquestionably the world's number-one golfer, a designation he held until his retirement.

With the exception of Babe Ruth, no sports star was more popular in the 1920s than Jones. Part of his appeal was based on his outstanding skill. Another part was based on his amateurism, personality, and handsome appearance. Jones was a model of sportsmanship; he never disrespected his opponents and became famous for calling penalty strokes on himself, even when it cost him a major tournament, as it did in the 1925 U.S. Open. By the time he started winning major championships, Jones had subdued his fiery temper and had learned to conduct himself with decorum and modesty. Finally, Jones looked like a matinee idol; he was five feet, seven inches tall, weighed about 165 pounds, and had light-brown hair, dark eyes, and a deep voice marked by a syrupy southern accent.

During his competitive years, the simon-pure Jones steadfastly abided by the amateur regulations of the U.S. Golf Association. He never, for example, accepted prize money in open events. Free from such strictures in retirement, Jones traded on his spotless image and unprecedented golf record in a handful of commercial projects. The

day he retired, Jones also revealed that he had signed a motion-picture contract with Warner Brothers to star in a series of golf instructional shorts entitled *How I Play Golf* (1931). They were so successful that Warner Brothers exercised its option to have Jones do another series, *How to Break Ninety* (1933). The movie deal brought Jones an estimated $250,000. Beyond that, Jones signed with A. G. Spalding and Brothers to design a new line of golf equipment bearing his name. Finally, Jones pursued a lifelong dream of building his own golf course. Joining forces with the New York financier Clifford Roberts and the renowned architect Alister MacKenzie, Jones created the Augusta National Golf Club in Georgia. In 1934 Jones and Roberts organized the Augusta National Invitational, soon renamed the Masters Tournament.

The years of the Great Depression were probably the best of Jones's life. Out of the limelight, he had more time to spend with his wife and three children, while reaping the benefits of his golf career. Although he was past the draft age when World War II erupted, Jones felt a duty to serve his country. Stationed by the U.S. Army in Europe in 1942, he worked as an intelligence officer, first helping to plan the invasion of Normandy and then taking part in it himself, landing in France on D-Day plus two. By the time he was discharged late in 1944, Jones had been promoted from captain to lieutenant colonel.

In 1948 Jones's life took a tragic turn. Experiencing pain in his back and insensitivity in his limbs, Jones submitted to several operations before being diagnosed with the rare, congenital spinal disorder syringomyelia. He played his last round of golf that year and soon went from walking with crutches to sitting in a wheelchair. It was a cruel fate for anyone, much less a former top athlete. Yet Jones remained as active as possible throughout the next two decades. He campaigned tirelessly for Dwight D. Eisenhower's 1952 and 1956 presidential campaigns, developing a deep friendship with the general. Jones also watched as Eisenhower, Roberts, and the exploits of Arnold Palmer helped to make his Masters Tournament a "major" event, the fourth leg of a modern professional Grand Slam: Eisenhower brought the club immense status by vacationing in Augusta numerous times during his presidency, Roberts skillfully negotiated contracts with CBS and helped the Masters to become a pioneer in televised golf, and Palmer won the tournament several times in the late 1950s and early 1960s in a dramatic style. By 1960, there was a consensus among golf writers that the Masters was a legitimate fourth "major" event of the year. Jones's annual involvement in presenting the tournament champion with a green jacket was a springtime highlight for all golf fans until 1968.

Through all of his pain and misfortune, Jones maintained a steady temper and personal charm. He not only remained popular, but was also widely revered. In December 1971 the sixty-nine-year-old Jones died of a heart aneurysm, a complication of his spinal disease. Never a religious man and always a nominal Protestant, Jones converted to Catholicism, his wife's faith, days before his death. He is buried in a secluded section of Atlanta's Oakland Cemetery.

Jones was the greatest amateur golfer of the twentieth century and a superstar of the Golden Age of Sports. His thirteen major championship victories ranked number two all-time, exceeded only by Jack Nicklaus, and no player has ever amassed so many major wins in such a short period. The fact that he compiled his record as an amateur was not only unique but historically significant because, in the 1920s, U.S. sports became increasingly professionalized. Jones's greatest legacy may be the Augusta National and the Masters Tournament. Whatever their virtues and shortcomings, those institutions have grown in importance and serve as an annual reminder of Jones's contributions to the game.

★

A collection of Jones's personal papers is housed at the U.S. Golf Association in Far Hills, New Jersey. A smaller file consisting mostly of newspaper clippings exists at the Robert W. Woodruff Library, Emory University, Atlanta, Georgia. Jones authored hundreds of articles and instructional works; his two autobiographies are *Down the Fairway* (1927), and *Golf Is My Game* (1960). For a full-scale biographical treatment of Jones, see Stephen R. Lowe, *Sir Walter and Mr. Jones: Walter Hagen, Bobby Jones, and the Rise of American Golf* (2000). Other useful biographical works include Richard Miller, *Triumphant Journey: The Saga of Bobby Jones and the Grand Slam of Golf* (1980), Sidney Matthew, *Portrait of a Gentleman: The Life and Times of Bobby Jones* (1995), and Stephen R. Lowe, "Demarbleizing Bobby Jones," *Georgia Historical Quarterly* (winter 1999). Obituaries are in the *New York Times* (19 Dec. 1971), and the *Atlanta Journal and Constitution* (19–20 Dec. 1971).

STEPHEN R. LOWE

JORDAN, Michael Jeffrey ("Air") (*b.* 17 February 1963 in Brooklyn, New York), basketball player who won a college national championship, two Olympic gold medals, and six National Basketball Association titles, making an impact that both defined and transcended his sport.

Jordan is one of the five children of Deloris Jordan and James Jordan. When Michael was still young, the family moved to Wilmington, North Carolina, where his father worked for General Electric and his mother worked for a bank. At the age of seven Jordan almost drowned in an incident that killed a friend. Otherwise Jordan's childhood was relatively typical. Nothing foreshadowed his eventual athletic exploits, although he excelled at youth baseball and played a lot of backyard basketball against his older brother Larry Jordan. "If I could beat him, I felt I could beat anybody," Michael Jordan said years later.

Michael Jordan, 1993. © SCOTT WACHTER/CORBIS

In time Jordan could beat his brother and just about anyone else, but not before he swallowed a dose of humility from his high school basketball coach. As a sophomore at Laney High School in Wilmington, Jordan was cut from the varsity squad. From then on his life seemingly became a quest to meet challenges and to prove himself. Jordan is quoted by Bob Greene in *Hang Time* (1992) as saying: "It made me know what disappointment felt like. And I knew that I didn't want to have that feeling ever again." He soon grew taller than everyone in his family, and he made the varsity team as a junior. By his senior year Jordan was almost six feet, six inches tall and was recruited by some of the country's top college basketball programs. He chose the University of North Carolina at Chapel Hill.

For the 1981–1982 season North Carolina started four players from a team that had advanced to the national championship game the previous spring. In an uncharacteristic move, legendary coach Dean Smith made the freshman Jordan his fifth starter. The newcomer did not disappoint, averaging 13.5 points per contest and hitting the winning shot against Georgetown University in the national championship game on 29 March 1982. Jordan claimed he had dreamed about such an ending a few hours before and later said, "I think that shot really put me on the map." By the end of his junior season in 1984, he was a unanimous choice for college Player of the Year.

With Smith's blessing, Jordan decided to forgo his senior season at North Carolina to enter the National Basketball Association (NBA) draft. He was selected third overall by the Chicago Bulls, behind Hakeem Olajuwon and Sam Bowie. But before he began his professional career, Jordan played on the 1984 U.S. Olympic team that won a gold medal in Los Angeles, and he paced the squad in scoring. When Jordan did take to the NBA hardwood, he was dynamic. Averaging 28.2 points per game, he led the previously hapless Bulls to the playoffs in the 1984–1985 season. He was an All-Star guard and won the league's Rookie of the Year award.

As his thrilling moves, spectacular dunks, and winning personality captivated America, Jordan began to reach an audience beyond traditional basketball fans. Nike's new Air Jordan basketball shoes sold fast, and before long people used the phrase "Air Jordan" to refer to both the sneakers and the player himself. His closely cropped hair and, when he played, protruding tongue also became popular trademarks.

The phenomenon was briefly halted early in the 1985–1986 season, when Jordan broke a bone in his foot. He missed sixty-four games, and the Bulls management wanted him to sit out the entire year. But Jordan undertook a rigorous rehabilitation regimen and insisted on returning to the lineup in time for the playoffs. Once there he was unstoppable, scoring forty-nine points in the first game of Chicago's opening-round series against the Boston Celtics. He set a postseason record of sixty-three points in a double-overtime loss in game two that mesmerized a nationwide television audience. Boston swept the series, but Larry Bird of the Celtics called his opponent "God disguised as Michael Jordan."

Jordan's legend grew from there. In 1986–1987 Jordan won the first of his record number of ten scoring titles, averaging 37.1 points per game. He followed that by scoring 35 points per contest in 1987–1988 and capturing the league's Most Valuable Player (MVP) and Defensive Player of the Year honors. He also won the NBA's slam-dunk competition during both seasons and was the All-Star game MVP in the latter season. In 1988–1989, Jordan averaged 32.5 points and achieved career bests of eight rebounds and eight assists per game.

The Bulls were labeled a one-man team that could not win a championship with Jordan dominating the action. His critics said he was good enough to make Chicago a playoff team and to win a series or two, but not good enough to carry the Bulls past a deep team like the Detroit Pistons. Despite the addition of the budding stars Scottie Pippen and Horace Grant, Chicago fell to Detroit in the 1988 and 1989 playoffs. The 1989 loss in the Eastern Conference finals was especially disheartening since it followed the exhilaration of a last-second, series-winning shot by Jordan that had eliminated the Cleveland Cavaliers in round one.

Surprising many, the Bulls management fired head coach Doug Collins and replaced him with Phil Jackson. Jackson installed a "triangle" offense to get other players on the team more involved. "In the beginning, I fought the triangle," Jordan admitted in his book *For the Love of the Game* (1998). But he soon realized its effectiveness and used it to his and the team's advantage. Jordan still averaged 33.6 points per game during the 1989–1990 season, the best of the league, and he tallied career highs of 69 points and 18 rebounds against Cleveland on 28 March 1990. However, the Bulls again lost to the Pistons in the conference finals, four games to three, and the critics remained.

The 1990–1991 season marked Chicago's breakthrough. Jordan again led the NBA in scoring, but Pippen was becoming one of the league's best players. The Bulls won sixty-one games and finally got past Detroit in the conference finals, four games to none. Playing for the championship against Magic Johnson and the Los Angeles Lakers, Chicago dropped the first game of the series but won the next four to take the trophy. Jordan added the MVP honors for the finals to his second league MVP award. One shot Jordan made in game two, after switching the ball from his right hand to his left in midair, may be the most memorable moment of a career filled with the spectacular.

As defending champions, the Bulls were even better. Chicago won sixty-seven games in 1991–1992, and Jordan again took home the league and finals MVP hardware along with his customary scoring title. The Bulls victimized Clyde Drexler and the Portland Trail Blazers in the championship series this time, four games to two. Jordan's moment of glory came during game one, when he made six three-point shots in the first half and looked as surprised as the audience witnessing the outburst. "The rim seemed like a big old huge bucket," he explained afterward.

During the summer of 1992 Jordan played on the U.S. Olympic "Dream Team" in Barcelona, Spain. It was the first time American professionals were allowed to participate in the Olympics, and Jordan collected a second gold medal. Pippen was also on the squad, and when he and Jordan returned to Chicago for the 1992–1993 season, they appeared tired. Nevertheless the Bulls won their division, and after Jordan eliminated Cleveland from the playoffs with another series-winning shot and helped the team overcome a two-game deficit to defeat the New York Knicks in the conference finals, they were back playing for another title. Chicago beat the Phoenix Suns in six games to win a third consecutive championship. Jordan averaged a record forty-one points per contest in the series and again was named MVP of the finals.

Although it may have seemed like Jordan's success could go on forever, he was exhausted, both physically and mentally. His popularity was such that he could not go anywhere without being mobbed. Furthermore he was criticized in Sam Smith's controversial book *The Jordan Rules* (1992) for treating teammates poorly, and he did not join them at a White House championship ceremony. His gambling habits were questioned, as he reportedly lost large sums of money betting on golf matches and took a late night trip to Atlantic City with his father during the playoffs. When his father was murdered in the summer of 1993, Jordan was devastated. "He was my best friend and knew everything about me," wrote Jordan in *For the Love of the Game*. On 6 October 1993 Jordan retired from basketball saying he had nothing left to prove. But undoubtedly he was motivated by more than that.

A few months later Jordan decided to give professional baseball a try, something he had previously discussed with his father. He signed a contract with the Chicago White Sox, owned by Jerry Reinsdorf, who also owned the Bulls, and was assigned to the minor league Birmingham Barons. Jordan batted .202, knocked in 51 runs, and stole 30 bases in 127 games with the Barons in 1994 before joining the Scottsdale Scorpions of the Arizona Fall League, where he hit .252 in 35 games. However, thirty-one-year-old rookie outfielders who have not played since their teenage years have never been in much demand in the major leagues. When a labor dispute threatened spring training games in 1995, Jordan chose to return to basketball, issuing a statement that simply said, "I'm back."

Jordan played seventeen regular-season games with the Bulls wearing uniform number 45 instead of his normal, retired number 23. Regardless, it did not take him long to shake off any rust. In his first week back he hit a shot at the buzzer to beat the Atlanta Hawks, and on 28 March 1995 he scored fifty-five points against the Knicks. However, Chicago lost its second-round playoff series to the Orlando Magic. Jordan returned to wearing number 23 and promised he would be better prepared for another championship run the next season. He went as far as to have a special basketball court set up on the Warner Brothers lot while he filmed the animated movie *Space Jam* (1996) over the summer.

Thus began the second act of Jordan's NBA dominance. During the off-season the Bulls acquired the rebounding ace and notorious bad boy Dennis Rodman to complement the duo of Jordan and Pippen. In 1995–1996, Chicago set a league record with seventy-two wins and defeated the Seattle Super Sonics in the finals, four games to two. Coincidentally, the series clincher occurred on Father's Day, and Jordan wept openly afterward.

In 1996–1997 the Bulls won sixty-nine more games and beat the Utah Jazz for the championship. In game one of the finals Jordan hit another winning shot at the buzzer, and in a game five victory he scored thirty-eight points while noticeably weakened by a stomach virus. "There were times in the third and fourth quarters that I felt like I was

going to pass out," recalled Jordan. Utah was again victimized in the finals the next season. In the closing moments of game six Jordan stripped the ball from the Jazz star Karl Malone and subsequently swished a jump shot to win the series. "It was like I was watching everything unfold in slow motion on television," described Jordan. "I had no intention of passing the ball under any circumstances. I figured I stole the ball and it was my opportunity to win or lose the game."

When the ball went through the net, it was also Jordan's opportunity to leave basketball in storybook fashion. On 13 January 1999, after an NBA labor dispute was settled, the thirty-five-year-old did just that, announcing his retirement for a second time. His return had produced three more scoring titles, NBA championships, and finals MVP awards and two more league and All-Star MVP trophies. That gave him career totals of ten scoring titles, six NBA championships, six finals MVP awards, five league MVP trophies, three All-Star MVP trophies, two Olympic gold medals, and one college national championship. In December 1999 ESPN-TV named Jordan the greatest North American athlete of the twentieth century. No one else was pictured on as many *Sports Illustrated* magazine covers.

In terms of societal impact, Jordan single-handedly boosted television ratings and the sales of the products he promoted. He made hundreds of millions from basketball and endorsements, yet few accused him of being overpaid because he generated far more. Despite occasional criticism that Jordan has not used his money and influence to effect needed social change, he is more often praised for his charitable endeavors and traditional values. He returned to North Carolina and earned his degree in geography in 1986. On 2 September 1989 he married Juanita Vanoy; they have three children.

Contradicting earlier claims he was not interested in owning a team, Jordan became a part owner of the NBA's Washington Wizards in 2000. In 2001 he relinquished his ownership to return to court for the Wizards at the age of thirty-eight, despite having said he was 99.9 percent sure he would never play again when he retired in 1999. From his hobby of golf to his vocation of basketball, the ultimate competitor still seeks challenges. "To compete to win, that's all I live for really."

★

Jordan wrote *Rare Air* (1993) and *For the Love of the Game* (1998). Information about Jordan's career is in Bob Greene's biography *Hang Time* (1992). Sam Smith criticized him in *The Jordan Rules* (1992). Quotes and career highlights are in NBA videos about Jordan, including *Come Fly with Me* (1990), *On and Off the Court* (1993), *Above and Beyond* (1996), and *His Airness* (1999). Other details are in the Jordan career retrospective at <http://www.NBA.com>.

JACK STYCZYNSKI

JOYNER, Florence Delorez Griffith ("Flo Jo"). *See* Griffith Joyner, Florence Delorez ("Flo Jo").

JOYNER-KERSEE, Jacqueline ("Jackie") (*b.* 3 March 1962 in East St. Louis, Illinois), track and basketball star who is known as America's best all-around female athlete and the greatest ever heptathlete.

Alfred Joyner, a construction worker and railroad switch operator, and Mary Joyner, a nurse's aide, were teenagers when they had their daughter Jackie, the second of their four children. Jackie was born in the same house as her father, at 1433 Piggott Avenue, in the impoverished city of East St. Louis.

It was evident early on that Joyner-Kersee would emerge as a talented athlete. She began competing and winning in track at nine years old. At first her parents wanted her to quit, although her father had been a hurdler and football player in high school. When Joyner-Kersee was able to do the "long jump" at more than seventeen feet at age twelve, however, her parents encouraged her to continue with her athletic pursuits. She even became a role model for her older brother, Alfred junior, who in 1984 became an Olympic gold medal winner in the triple jump.

Several incidents occurred in Joyner-Kersee's childhood that left lasting impressions: her dance instructor was murdered, she witnessed a man being shot near her home, and her grandfather killed his wife with a shotgun. Through it all Joyner-Kersee exhibited exceptional courage and determination. She attributes her steadfastness to her mother's many lessons. She was also inspired by a television movie about the American track star Mildred "Babe" Didrikson she had seen in 1975.

Joyner-Kersee attended Lincoln High School, where she was a good student despite her hectic athletic schedule. At age fourteen she won the first of four National Junior Pentathlon Championships, and during her junior year she set a state high school record in the long jump. She also began to play volleyball and basketball. She became so good at basketball that she was offered a basketball scholarship (in addition to a track scholarship) to attend the University of California, Los Angeles (UCLA). She accepted the basketball scholarship and became an All-American forward for the Bruins.

In 1980, just before starting at UCLA as a history major, Joyner-Kersee sought to earn a place on the U.S. team for the 1980 Moscow Olympics. Even though she qualified, the United States boycotted the games that year to protest the Soviet Union's invasion of Afghanistan, and she was unable to compete.

Joyner-Kersee's freshman year at UCLA was plagued by two major setbacks. She had been diagnosed with asthma, and her mother died of meningitis in January 1981. Joyner-Kersee and her brother Al were forced to remove their mother from life support, something their father could not bring himself to do. During this time Joyner-Kersee met her future husband, UCLA assistant track coach Bob Kersee. Kersee agreed with Joyner-Kersee's former coach George Ward that she would be a formidable competitor in multiple-event competitions. Joyner and Kersee married on 11 January 1986. (Kersee also coached Florence Griffith Joyner, Joyner-Kersee's future sister-in-law, until the summer of 1988, when her husband Al became her coach.)

In 1982 Joyner-Kersee won the National Collegiate Athletic Association (NCAA) Heptathlon Championship (the heptathlon, a two-day competition, consists of the 100-meter hurdles, the high jump, the shot put, and the 200-meter dash on the first day, and the long jump, the javelin, and the 800-meter race on the second day). The next year, both Joyner-Kersee and her brother were named to the U.S. Track and Field World Championships team for the competition in Helsinki, Finland. However, a pulled hamstring muscle prevented Joyner-Kersee from fulfilling her long-awaited goal.

Although Joyner-Kersee broke a U.S. heptathlon record with a score of 6,520 points in the trials for the 1984 Olympics in Los Angeles, she was injured again. Amazingly she managed to win a silver medal, missing the gold by only one-third of a second. Her brother, who had been a long shot for the triple jump, won the gold that year. In 1985 Joyner-Kersee also set a U.S. long jump record.

In 1986, after having graduated from UCLA with a B.A. in history, Joyner-Kersee decided to stop playing basketball and focus her attention on track. Her decision paid off that year during the Goodwill Games in Moscow; she broke the U.S. record for the 100-meter hurdles and the heptathlon record for the long jump. At the end of that two-day meet, Joyner-Kersee became the first woman from the United States since Babe Didrikson (who had set a triathlon record in 1936) to establish a multiple-event world record by earning a score of 7,148 in the heptathlon. Twenty-six days later she broke world heptathlon records at the U.S. Olympic Festival in Houston. As a result, Joyner-Kersee became the only athlete worldwide ever to have earned an average of over 7,000 points a year for the heptathlon.

In 1987 Joyner-Kersee won gold medals in both the long jump and heptathlon at the indoor and outdoor track-and-field championships in the United States, the Pan-American Games in Indianapolis, and the World Championships in Rome. She also set U.S., world, and Olympic records for the heptathlon at the 1988 Olympics in Seoul, South Korea, as well as the Olympic record for the long jump.

At age thirty, Joyner-Kersee once again proved to be the best in the heptathlon at the 1992 Olympics in Barcelona,

Jackie Joyner-Kersee. AP/WIDE WORLD PHOTOS

Spain, where she placed third in the long jump. The following year she earned a gold medal in the heptathlon at the World Championships in Stuttgart, Germany. In 1994 Joyner-Kersee was also victorious in the heptathlon competition at the Goodwill Games in St. Petersburg, Russia. She continued to compete in multiple events until 1988, when she retired following her win in the heptathlon at the Goodwill Games in Atlanta.

In retirement, Joyner-Kersee became a motivational speaker and a sports marketing agent. She founded the Jackie Joyner-Kersee Community Foundation in 1988, an organization dedicated to raising money for athletic, cultural, and educational programs for disadvantaged youth. Her message for children is this: "I remember where I came from. If young girls see the environment I grew up in, and my dreams and goals came true, they will realize that their dreams and goals might also come true." In 1997 her organization became known as the Jackie Joyner-Kersee Youth Center Foundation after merging with the East St. Louis Youth Center. On 1 March 2000 her dream of opening a youth center in her hometown had come true.

In July 2000 Joyner-Kersee emerged from retirement to compete in the long jump. Although she qualified for her fifth Olympic team, she eventually lost to newcomer Marion Jones. That year, however, Joyner-Kersee was selected as the *Sports Illustrated for Women*'s Greatest Female Athlete of the 20th Century. Joyner-Kersee's many years as an outstanding athlete who had to overcome remarkable odds was rewarded many times, and she has received many awards, including the Broderick Cup (1985); the James E. Sullivan Award (1986); the Sportsman of the Year Award, presented by the U.S. Olympic Committee (1986); the Jesse Owens Memorial Award (1986 and 1987); and the Associated Press Female Athlete of the Year Award (1987). She was the first woman to win the *Sporting News* Athlete of the Year Award in 1988.

Joyner-Kersee's "three D's"—determination, dedication, and desire—are her most valuable assets and were taught by her mother early on in life. In addition, her grandmother named her Jacqueline after former first lady Jacqueline Kennedy, because "Someday this girl will be the first lady of something." Her grandmother did not realize how right she would prove to be.

★

Joyner-Kersee's autobiography, written with Sonja Steptoe, is *A Kind of Grace: The Autobiography of the World's Greatest Female Athlete* (1997). A biographical sketch is in Jessie Carney Smith, ed., *Epic Lives: One Hundred Black Women Who Made a Difference* (1993). *A Kind of Grace: The Autobiography of the World's Greatest Female Athlete* is also available as a Time Warner AudioBook. See also Neil Cohen, *Jackie Joyner-Kersee* (1992), Lisa Burby, *Jackie Joyner-Kersee: Record-Breaking Runner* (1997), and Richard Rambeck, *Jackie Joyner Kersee* (1996). Articles include Michele Kort, "Go Jackie, Go," *Ms.* magazine (17 Oct. 1988); Renee D. Turner, "My Happiest Moment," *Ebony* 43 (Mar. 1988); and Kenny Moore, "Quest for New Conquests," *Sports Illustrated* 70 (5 June 1989).

ADRIANA C. TOMASINO

K

KAHANAMOKU, Duke (*b.* 24 August 1890 in Honolulu, Hawaii; *d.* 22 January 1968 in Honolulu, Hawaii), five-time Olympic medalist in swimming who also popularized the sport of surfing on his way to his becoming one of Hawaii's greatest athletes.

A descendent of Hawaii's royal family, Kahanamoku was born Duke Paoa Kahinu Mokoe Hulikohola Kahanamoku, Jr., one of six sons and three daughters of Duke Kahanamoku and Julia Paakonia Lonokahikini. The elder Kahanamoku worked as a police captain in Honolulu, where the family made its home near Waikiki Beach, later the site of many resort hotels. In 1893 business interests led by pineapple grower Sanford Dole overthrew the royal government. With the support of U.S. troops, Dole established a republic on the island in 1894 as an American protectorate, and in 1900 all native Hawaiians were granted U.S. citizenship.

Leaving school after the eleventh grade (around 1907), the six-foot, 190-pound Kahanamoku gained recognition for his natural abilities as an athlete as he grew into adulthood. An avid canoeist, surfer, and swimmer, Kahanamoku first made his mark as a freestyle swimmer. Aided by his size thirteen feet—which he used for a flutter kick in his freestyle adaptation of the Australian crawl—Kahanamoku astounded swimming officials of the Amateur Athletic Union (AAU) at the first tournament held in Hawaii in August 1911. Kahanamoku's 55.4-second performance in

the 100-yard freestyle event broke the existing world record by 4.6 seconds, but AAU officials measured the course several times before declaring Kahanamoku the winner.

Despite his victory, Kahanamoku still faced skepticism in the AAU over the validity of his performance. Determined to prove his critics wrong, Kahanamoku entered the trials for the 1912 Stockholm Olympics. In a series of competitions held in Philadelphia and New Jersey, he qualified in the 100-meter freestyle and 800-meter freestyle relay events, setting a new world record for his leg in the latter attempt. Kahanamoku set another record in a preliminary heat for the 100-meter finals in Stockholm, Sweden. He almost missed out on the finals, however; U.S. team officials had to scramble to find him just before the event because he had fallen asleep under a bridge. Quickly putting on his suit and diving into the water, Kahanamoku took the gold medal in the event with a time of 1:03.4. The new champion also left the games with a silver medal for his part on the relay team, which placed second to the Australians.

Along with Jim Thorpe, Kahanamoku emerged as one of the best-known athletes from the 1912 Olympics and embarked on a series of swimming exhibitions and AAU competitions around the United States over the next several years. Kahanamoku also gave numerous demonstrations of his surfing skills to oceanside audiences from Coney Island, New York, to Long Beach, California. It was his December 1914 appearance in Australia, however, that eventually gave

Duke Kahanamoku *(left)* with President Calvin Coolidge. INTERNATIONAL SWIMMING HALL OF FAME

rise to Kahanamoku's reputation as "the father of modern surfing."

Like other Polynesian groups, indigenous Hawaiians suffered many cultural changes since the arrival of European explorers in the eighteenth century. However, the traditional sport of surfing remained a popular pastime during Kahanamoku's youth. With boards of varying lengths and widths made out of native woods, many Hawaiians continued to fashion their own surfboards, which were prized personal possessions among the islands' surfers. Along with the handcrafted boards, traditional chants and folklore wove the sport into Hawaiian culture as a vital link with the past. Intrigued by the sport, some Australians had tried to make their own surfboards, but it was not until Kahanamoku's surfing exhibition during a visit for a swimming competition in Sydney that the sport had its true introduction. Constructing an eight-foot, six-inch-long board out of sugar pine, Kahanamoku took to Freshwater Beach in February 1915 and surfed the waves for a two-and-a-half hour exhibition. The demonstration kick-started a surfing craze in Australia that made it one of the country's most popular sports, and Kahanamoku was elevated to legendary status.

With the 1916 Olympics canceled by World War I, Kahanamoku had to wait until the 1920 Antwerp games in Belgium to defend his gold medal in the 100-meter freestyle. Although he was now thirty years old, Kahanamoku reached his peak performance in the games, with a world-record 1:01.4 gold-medal final in the 100-meter freestyle and the anchor leg in the U.S. team's record-setting 800-meter freestyle relay. Kahanamoku's final Olympic appearance, at the 1924 Paris games, added another silver medal to his collection in the 100-meter freestyle; this time, he was beaten by Johnny Weismuller of the U.S. team. Kahanamoku won five Olympic medals during his amateur career and served as an alternate on the U.S. water polo team for the 1932 Los Angeles Olympics.

Kahanamoku also gained attention for his exploits outside of sports. In 1925 he dove three times into a pounding surf off Corona del Mar, California, to save the lives of eight passengers from a capsized boat; the tragedy took the lives of seventeen other passengers. Kahanamoku appeared in several movies from the 1920s onward, playing supporting roles that ranged from pirates to princes; his best-known movie is the John Wayne adventure picture *Wake of the Red Witch* (1948), in which he played Ua Nuke, a Polynesian chief. In 1955 he had a bit part in the film version of *Mister Roberts,* again playing a chief. Kahanamoku also made a living by operating two gas stations in Hawaii, an income that he supplemented by his post as Honolulu's sheriff. First elected in 1936, Kahanamoku held the position for twenty-six years.

Kahanamoku was recognized as the personification of Hawaii's warm and genial spirit, as well as a superior athletic competitor, and remained a celebrity long after his Olympic days. He was inducted into the International Swimming Hall of Fame in 1965. After a series of illnesses that included a heart attack in 1955 and a cerebral blood clot in 1962, Kahanamoku died of a heart attack. His wife, Nadine Kahanamoku, whom he married on 2 August 1940, survived her husband by almost thirty years. Under her guidance, the surfing legend was commemorated with a landmark statue on Waikiki Beach. Dedicated in July 1990, the nine-foot statue shows Kahanamoku with a twelve-foot surf board and outstretched arms.

★

Biographies of Kahanamoku include Sandra K. Hall and Greg Ambrose, *Memories of Duke: The Legend Comes to Life* (1995), and Joe Brennan, *Duke Kahanamoku: Hawaii's Golden Man* (1974). Kahanamoku's life and career are also recounted in detail in Leonard Lueras, *Surfing: The Ultimate* (1984), and Drew Kampion, *Stoked: A History of Surf Culture* (1997). A tribute to Kahanamoku is in *Sports Illustrated* (17 Sept. 1990). An obituary is in the *New York Times* (23 Jan. 1968).

TIMOTHY BORDEN

KALINE, Al(bert) William (*b.* 19 December 1934 in Baltimore, Maryland), baseball player for the Detroit Tigers who became the youngest player to win a batting title.

Kaline, of German-Irish descent and raised as a devout Methodist, was one of three children born into a baseball family. His father, Nicholas Kaline, his two uncles Bib Kaline and Fred Kaline, and his paternal grandfather, Philip Kaline, were catchers for numerous semiprofessional teams that played in the Eastern Shore leagues of Maryland. Times were hard, and Kaline's father's meager income as a broom maker was supplemented by the income provided by his mother, Naomi Morgan, who did housework. Kaline was encouraged to play baseball on the local sandlots even before he reached school age. His youthful promise was threatened at the age of eight by osteomyelitis, which required that surgeons remove two inches of bone from his left foot, but he quickly recovered. With a family full of catchers, it was natural for Kaline's first ambition to be a pitcher. Blessed with an excellent right arm, he set the Baltimore elementary school record while attending Westport Grammar School by tossing a softball 173 feet 6 inches.

At Southern High School, Kaline moved to the outfield; hit over .400 in his sophomore, junior, and senior years; and was named to the All-Maryland high school team for four years. While all the major league teams showed interest in the young Kaline, Detroit's Ed Katalinas signed him with a $15,000 bonus plus a first-year contract of another $15,000 that promptly paid off the family mortgage and allowed Kaline's mother to undergo the surgery that saved her failing eyesight. Under league rules at the time a "bonus baby" had to stay with the major league team for two years, so Kaline never played in the minors. Following his graduation from high school in 1953, Kaline joined the

Al Kaline. AP/WIDE WORLD PHOTOS

Tigers on 24 June 1953 and saw limited playing time in only 30 games, hitting a meager .250. He played 138 games in 1954 with a .276 batting average, but he showed stellar promise as an outfielder when, in one game against the White Sox, he threw out runners at second, third, and home in successive innings. At the end of the season that year, on 16 October 1954, Kaline married his high school sweetheart, Louise Hamilton, in Baltimore, and the family moved to Michigan, where they raised two sons.

On 14 April 1955 Kaline displayed his potential for the coming year by hitting three home runs in a game, two of them in a single inning. Only twenty years of age, he became the youngest player to win a batting title to that date, hitting .340 and leading the league in total bases. He was voted starting right fielder for his first of sixteen All-Star games and finished second in the balloting for the Most Valuable Player (MVP) award behind Yogi Berra. The year ended with Kaline named American League Player of the Year by the *Sporting News.*

In the field Kaline sparkled as a defensive player and won ten Gold Gloves over an eleven-year span from 1957 to 1967. From 1970 to 1972 he played in 242 consecutive games without an error, leading the league in 1971 with a perfect 1.00 fielding average. Kaline's first venture into postseason play came during the 1968 World Series. After the Cardinals won three of the first four contests and were ahead 3–2 in the fifth game, Kaline's clutch, bases-loaded hit in the seventh inning drove in the game-winning run. His World Series batting average of .379 with 2 home runs and 8 runs batted in (RBI) helped the Tigers sweep the remainder of the games and win their first world championship since 1945. Kaline's team leadership and professionalism that year won him the Lou Gehrig Memorial Award, given annually to the individual in the game who best exemplifies the skills and integrity of the legendary Yankee first baseman.

Kaline continued to win awards and honors. On 2 August 1970 the Tigers held an Al Kaline Day attended by over 40,000 spectators at Tiger Stadium. Kaline, always community spirited, requested that all money donated that day be used to buy baseball equipment for Detroit's underprivileged children. In 1971 he became the first Detroit Tiger to make $100,000 a year, but he returned $8,000 to the management after a lackluster season, claiming he had not earned it. The next season, although he continued to struggle with injury and age in his twentieth season, he recovered in September to hit .316 and almost singlehandedly to lift the Tigers into the 1972 playoffs. The Tigers lost the American League Championship Series to Oakland.

Kaline began the 1974 season as the Tigers' designated hitter and on 24 September cracked his 3,000th hit. The line-drive double made him the first American League player to reach that plateau since Eddie Collins and Tris

Speaker in 1925 and the first player to do it as a designated hitter. Kaline finished the season with 3,007 hits, good for eleventh on the all-time list to that date. He became the Tiger leader in games played, home runs, walks, and put-outs, and only Ty Cobb had more hits and runs batted in. So respected was Kaline's consistency and professionalism that in 1980 the sportswriters of America made him only the tenth player elected into the Hall of Fame in his first year of eligibility. That year the Detroit Tigers made him the first Tiger to have his uniform, number 6, retired. In 1976 Kaline teamed with another former Tiger great, George Kell, to work as a color commentator for Detroit Tiger television broadcasts. He maintained that job until his retirement in June 2001. He subsequently became assistant to the vice president for team affairs.

Throughout Kaline's career the Detroit management tried to encourage him to be more colorful, hoping it would attract fans to the ballpark, but that was not his style of play. Some critics claimed Kaline never lived up to his early potential. He never won another batting crown, never led the league in home runs or in RBI, was never named the league's Most Valuable Player. But for twenty-two years he was the model of reliability in a professional ball player. He averaged almost 150 hits a year, hit 20 or more home runs 9 times, and hit .300 or better 8 times. In 1959 he led the league in slugging (.530) and in 1963 was again named the *Sporting News* Player of the Year. He retired among the all-time leaders in games played, at bats, hits, home runs, and total bases.

★

The two major biographies of Kaline are Al Hirshberg, *The Al Kaline Story* (1965), and Hal Butler, *Kaline* (1974). Kaline is a major figure in Butler, *Sports Heroes Who Wouldn't Quit* (1973); Cynthia J. Wilbur, *For the Love of the Game: Baseball Memories from the Men Who Were There* (1992); and Detroit News, *They Earned Their Stripes: The Detroit Tiger All-Time Team* (2000). Particularly informative is Patricia Zacharias, "Al Kaline—The Detroit Tigers' 'Mr. Perfection,'" *Detroit News* (10 Aug. 2001). Kaline is also in *The Baseball Register* (1969), *Current Biography* (1970), and *Total Baseball* (1995).

PATRICK A. TRIMBLE

KAROLYI, Béla (*b.* 13 September 1942 in Cluj, Romania), gymnastics coach who over a thirty-year career has coached nine Olympic champions, fifteen European medalists, and six U.S. National champions.

Karolyi's parents, Nandor, a civil engineer, and Iren, an accountant and homemaker, also had a daughter Maria, Béla's older sister. Unlike his sister, who earned a civil engineering degree by the age of twenty-one, Karolyi was an

Béla Karolyi. ARCHIVE PHOTOS, INC.

indifferent student, often in trouble, whose only interests were in animals and sports. At the age of fourteen he was coached by a local hammer thrower who encouraged him to build strength through weight training. In his teens Karolyi set a Romanian national record in this event.

At seventeen Karolyi found a job at the local slaughterhouse, was coached in boxing, fought in local matches, and continued to train for track and field events. Hard work, training, and success in the boxing ring won him the opportunity to compete in both national boxing and track and field events. He won the Junior National Boxing Championship. Unfortunately, training for two sports on top of working to earn a living took its toll, and Karolyi became ill. He returned home to his family, took a chance on a late admission to college, and started college in 1959 at Cluj Technical College.

Arriving five weeks after the start of classes, Karolyi was helped to catch up by a fellow student, Marta Eross, whom he married on 28 November 1963. Karolyi was on the handball and rugby teams, but gymnastics was always a struggle for him. He was a large, muscular young man, weighing in at 286 pounds, and the agility needed to pass the practical exam in gymnastics seemed out of his reach. He would fall and crash into the equipment. Dogged determination kept him practicing day after day on his own, finally asking for help from an assistant coach. In exchange for spotting for the gymnastics team during practice, he was given enough help to be able to pass the exam. Karolyi finally became skilled enough to compete with the gymnastic team, but after he broke his arm his competitive days were over and his focus changed to coaching.

Karolyi graduated in 1963 with a degree in physical education, and afterwards was obliged to serve three months in the Romanian army. Arriving late in the evening, the recruit was given whatever military uniform was left. The big man lined up for the early morning review holding boots six sizes too small, and wearing pants held together with rope and a shirt with sleeves just below his elbows. Although his cap fitted properly, Karolyi thumbed his nose at the military by wearing it sideways.

Marta, who had graduated first in their class, and Karolyi, who graduated second, both took teaching jobs close to one another in a poor, rural coal mining region of Romania. The Romanian education ministry eventually asked the Karolyis to be part of the first gymnastics school in the town of Onesti. In 1972 the first competitive team from Onesti, made up of ten-year-olds, competed in the Friendship Cup in Bulgaria. Nadia Comaneci won the all-around gold and the Romanians won the silver, beating the older teens from East Germany and the Soviet Union. One of Karolyi's contributions to gymnastics was his realization that girls as young as seven could be trained to perform complex athletic routines. In 1976, as the Karolyi-coached team won the right to compete in the upcoming Olympics, the official Olympic roster included four gymnasts from the Dinamo team, the government-supported secret police club. Supported by a high-ranking official, Karolyi was able to plead his case and was named as coach of the Romanian national and Olympic teams.

Karolyi's elfin pigtailed girls from Romania made their entrance to the world arena at the Montreal Olympics in 1976. Up against the powerful Soviet team and Eastern Bloc judges with political reasons for not wanting to upset the Soviet Union, the little girls flew through their routines. Nadia Comaneci made history, scoring six perfect tens and winning the overall gold medal. Karolyi's Romanian team changed the face of international gymnastics by showing that young girls could perform well at the highest level, and by taking an athletic approach to a sport that had always been seen as an aesthetic exercise. Romania welcomed the gymnasts and the Karolyis back with awards and celebrations all over the country. Karolyi himself was awarded the Romanian Labor Union Medal. However, everyone did not welcome Karolyi's success, and he began a long struggle with the bureaucracy and petty jealousies of the Romanian Gymnastics Federation.

Marta is known for her self-control and well-ordered consistency. Béla is known for his enthusiasm, forceful personality, and aggressiveness. Nowhere were these characteristics more evident than at the 1980 Moscow Olympics, which the United States boycotted because of the Soviet Union's invasion of Afghanistan. Believing that the Soviet judges had cheated to give their gymnast, Yelena Davydova, the gold over Comaneci, Karolyi argued with the appeals judge, knocked down the scoreboard twice, and created a forty-minute incident that stopped the competition. Worse yet, he criticized the Soviets to the ABC television reporter. Karolyi was called before the Romanian Central Committee for humiliating the Soviets and criticizing the games before the Western press. He was even threatened with prison. Shortly thereafter all funding to their gymnastics school was stopped, and the school almost closed. But the Romanian government realized it needed Karolyi. In 1981 the Karolyis, along with their friend and choreographer Geza Pozar, were given two weeks to prepare a team for an exhibition tour of the United States guaranteed to bring in $180,000 for the Romanian Gymnastics Federation. They were accompanied to the United States by the director of the Gymnastics Federation and several Romanian security officers.

At the conclusion of the tour the group was ready to return to Romania when the director of the Romanian federation, embarrassed by Karolyi's criticism of the Soviets' judging and probably wearing an electronic listening device, tried to trap the Karolyis and Pozar into admitting they were planning to defect (which they were not). Given the circumstances surrounding this accusation, if they returned to Romania they would go to prison. If they defected, the Karolyis risked losing their six-year-old daughter, and Pozar would be in danger of losing contact with his wife and children in Romania. Putting their faith in the International Immigration Law that allowed defecting individuals to keep their families together, the group remained in the United States. On the streets of New York, with just $300 among them, and unable to speak English, the three defectors faced a grim and frightening future. Over the next six months their introduction to the United States was difficult and frustrating.

Karolyi's reputation was well-known in the American gymnastics community, however, and eventually, after a short spell coaching at the University of Oklahoma, Karolyi was invited to Houston to develop a gymnastics center. Unfortunately, Karolyi's backers pulled out, but the Karolyis managed to find financing and founded Karolyi's Gymnastics in Houston in 1982. Pozar found a position with a gym in California, and a Texas congressman successfully pressured the Romanian government to reunite the families. The Karolyis' daughter Andrea joined them soon afterward. Béla Karolyi became an American citizen on 1 May 1990.

Diane Durham and Mary Lou Retton were the first of

many elite U.S. gymnasts who started the climb to international competition under Karolyi's coaching. Many of the young athletes were shocked by the tough training Karolyi put them through, but he also inspired them to reach new levels of athleticism and skill. At the 1984 Los Angeles Olympics Retton became the first gymnast from the United States to win the all-around champion's medal, as she had accumulated the most points from all four events (vault, beam, uneven bars, and floor exercise). Her success triggered a gymnastics craze that brought over a thousand gymnasts to Karolyi's gym, and to other gyms around the country. But unfortunately, as in Romania, resentment and jealousy were building within the U.S. gymnastic coaching ranks. Karolyi's own assertive and combative attitude did not help. Some criticized what they viewed as the harsh regime his gymnasts endured, while others attacked him as an attention-seeker who was always on the lookout for the next opportunity for publicity.

After the disappointing 1992 Olympics in Barcelona, with its professional athletes, politics, and money-driven concerns, the Karolyis became disillusioned with elite gymnastics coaching and withdrew from their position with the U.S. Olympic team. Their gymnastics center in Houston was thriving. Also, the gymnastics summer camp they had begun on their New Waverly, Texas, ranch in 1989 was succeeding beyond expectations. The camp, running from June 15 to August 15, began to draw more than 2,000 gymnasts each summer. Despite his disillusionment, Karolyi was persuaded in the late 1990s to return to training at a national level. He was appointed national coordinator for the U.S. women's team on 12 September 2001 and started training for the next Olympics.

In the 1970s and 1980s Karolyi's brand of "power gymnastics" based on strength training, conditioning, technique, and intensive practice became a benchmark for gymnastics coaches around the world. In the dedication of his autobiography, *Feel No Fear*, Karolyi credits his wife for having the mental strength and organizational skills to see them through difficulties both in Romania and the United States. It is important to note that both Karolyis coach the gymnasts, although the press pays the most attention to the quotable, charismatic, and flamboyant Béla.

★

The best, if not the most impartial, source of information on Karolyi is his autobiography written with Nancy Richardson, *Feel No Fear: The Power, Passion and Politics of a Life in Gymnastics* (1994). See also Nadia Comaneci and Graham Buxton Smither (photographer), *Nadia: The Autobiography of Nadia Comaneci* (1981); Mary Lou Retton and Béla Karolyi with John Powers, *Mary Lou: Creating an Olympic Champion* (1986); and Kerri Strug with John Lopez, *Landing on My Feet: A Diary of Dreams* (1997).

ROSEMARIE S. CARDOSO

KEELER, William Henry (*b.* 3 March 1872 in New York City; *d.* 1 January 1923 in New York City), Hall of Fame outfielder who had a batting average of .432 in 1897 and a lifetime major league batting average of .341. Keeler is regarded as the greatest bat handler who has ever lived.

Keeler, known as "Wee Willie," is one of the most famous and most mysterious stars in the history of baseball, with his major league career celebrated and his private life largely unknown. He was a very unlikely star when he joined the New York Giants in 1892, for he never played in the minor leagues. He was only five feet, four inches tall, and weighed only 140 pounds, and he was a left-handed third baseman. All these factors would keep most players out of the major leagues, but Keeler played third base as well as a right-hander. He was smart, and he was a wonder with a baseball bat.

Although Keeler would play third base, second base, and even a couple of games at shortstop in his career, playing mostly in the infield for the Giants, manager Ned Hanlon of his second team, the Baltimore Orioles (a National

Wee Willie Keeler. ASSOCIATED PRESS AP

League franchise) moved him to right field in 1894. Teammate John McGraw, a great third baseman who would become the game's greatest manager, said that the greatest catch he ever saw was made by Keeler in right field, leaping high into a barbed wire fence to make the catch. In general, however, Keeler's range in the outfield was below that of most of his contemporaries, although a quick release on balls he fielded made his arm above average.

The Baltimore clubs that Keeler played for from 1894 through 1898 were the greatest of their era and among the best ever, and Keeler was an important part of their success, for his clever, highly controlled hitting contributed to an attack that overwhelmed opposing pitchers. During this period, he became famous and much loved. He spoke in a Brooklyn accent with endearingly subpar grammar. Journalists loved quotes such as "Learn what pitch you can hit good; then wait for that pitch." Behind Keeler's "aw shucks" modesty and fractured English was a keenly intelligent mind that made the most his physical talents.

Keeler became one of baseball's biggest draws, with fans buying tickets just for the chance to see the seeming miracles he worked with his bat. His bat was light and short—only 30.5 inches—and he held it with his upper hand (the left) separated from his lower hand by several inches. His grip could shift according to the situation and what sort of pitch he saw coming his way, as could his batting stance, which usually began open but could close in an instant. Keeler could bunt perfectly down each baseline and past either side of a pitcher, so even when opposing infields were sure he was going to bunt, they had to guess where he was going to bunt or he would still drop the ball out of their reach. Further, Keeler would pop the ball over the heads of the infielders and in front of the outfielders for hits. When outfielders played shallow, Keeler whacked line drives over their heads. In one such situation, he hit a line drive past left fielder Ed Delahanty of Philadelphia for an inside-the-park grand-slam home run.

In the 1890s foul balls did not count as strikes, and a brilliant place-hitter like Keeler could foul off several pitches while looking for the one he wanted. However, in the dawn of the twentieth century the rule changed, with the first two foul balls becoming strikes. The rule had to be further refined because of Keeler. He was such a fine bunter that he would bunt foul several consecutive pitches while waiting for the pitch he favored, so foul *bunts* were made to count as third strikes. A further change was in the baseball itself, which became the notorious "dead ball" of 1900–1920 (the ball's hard core was wrapped more loosely than before by yarn and stitched loosely as well; this softness caused titanic swings to result in the ball just dribbling on the ground, until a harder, bouncier ball was introduced in 1921). Power-hitting teams had to adjust to a new era of playing just to get one or two runs in a game. The Ori-

oles themselves disappeared in 1899 when the National League reorganized and teams that were in financial trouble were eliminated.

In spite of these changes, Keeler thrived, adjusting his style of play to the new era. It was his good fortune to go to his hometown Brooklyn Superbas that year, where his popularity grew even greater. Hitting balls deep to drive in runners was no longer the best way to play the game, and base running—always important—increased in value; Keeler's quickness served him well. He was an opportunistic runner who, once on first base, was a master at taking an extra base, and he was a fine base stealer.

Keeler shifted leagues in 1903, joining the New York Highlanders of the American League. His fans from Brooklyn followed him to his new team and helped to save it from the financial trouble that threatened its existence. When a journalist suggested that Keeler write about how to hit, he responded with one of baseball's most enduring remarks: "I keep my eyes clear and I hit 'em where they ain't," he said, insisting he had little more to tell. He continued to follow his own advice as a starter through 1909, but his quickness was leaving him, and his batting averages dropped. He retired from the major leagues after the 1910 season, played some minor league games in 1911, then quit playing for good.

Keeler, the friendly, modest ballplayer who had talked to reporters in the dialect of a poor boy from the streets of Brooklyn, proved to be a shrewd investor. He put his earnings into real estate and became a rich man. In private, he was a tough man who would not be bullied; once, tormented by John McGraw, he brawled with McGraw in the showers of the locker room.

When Keeler unexpectedly died of heart disease, he was still beloved by fans. He was one of the wonders of sports, and in 1939 the Baseball Writers of America elected him to the Hall of Fame. Few players have been more deserving. Ted Williams, possibly the best all-around hitter ever, named Keeler to his list of the twenty best hitters. Keeler's ability to advance runners already on base may be unsurpassed, and his ability to disrupt defenses rivals that of Ty Cobb, Oscar Charleston, and Willie Mays. He is buried in Calvary Cemetery, Queens, New York, and his grave is a frequent stopping place for baseball fans.

★

The title of Burt Solomon, *Where They Ain't: The Fabled Life and Untimely Death of the Original Baltimore Orioles, the Team That Gave Birth to Modern Baseball* (1999), is inspired by Keeler's famous remark. The Baltimore Oriole teams of the late 1890s were some of the best teams in history, and Solomon does a good job of recalling the way baseball was played in those years. Charles F. Faber, *Baseball Pioneers: Ratings of Nineteenth Century Players* (1997), puts Keeler in the context of his era and suggests how

Keeler might measure up against later ballplayers. Leo Trachtenberg, "Wee Willie Keeler: Fame and Failure" in the *National Pastime* 13 (1993), discusses Keeler's achievements.

KIRK H. BEETZ

KELLY, John Brendan, Sr. ("Jack")   (*b.* 4 October 1889 in Philadelphia, Pennsylvania; *d.* 20 June 1960 in Philadelphia, Pennsylvania), a leading American oarsman after World War I who won two Olympic gold medals in 1920 and one in 1924.

Kelly, the youngest of ten children, emerged from his modest background to become a wealthy business owner and the holder of three Olympic gold medals. His parents, John Henry Kelly, a wool mill worker, and Mary Ann Costello, emigrated from Ireland. Kelly attended elementary school in Philadelphia but dropped out in the eighth grade to work, like his father, at a local wool mill. In 1907 he went to work at his brother Patrick Kelly's brick-contracting firm, starting as a water boy and eventually becoming a superintendent. He also attended night classes at Spring Garden Institute, where he learned architectural drawing. During his free time he participated in football, baseball, basketball, and boxing.

Kelly devoted his athletic skill most seriously to sculling, a hobby he pursued so tirelessly that his mother worried he was neglecting other parts of his life. By the age of seventeen he began rising each morning at 6:00 A.M. to practice rowing on the Schuylkill River. He then worked from 7:00 A.M. to 5:00 P.M. before returning to the river, where he practiced until dark. He trained all day on Sunday. Kelly began entering amateur sporting events and won his first competition in 1909. He excelled in single-oared competitions and as a partner with his cousin, Paul Costello, in double-oared competitions. He became a leading oarsman in the years before World War I, winning the American Henley in 1913 along with eight other races that year, and the National Association of Amateur Oarsmen's (NAAO) singles in 1914. He captured an impressive sixteen victories in 1916.

In 1918 Kelly entered the U.S. Army and was stationed in France, eventually rising to the rank of lieutenant. He boxed to keep in shape, defeating twelve opponents in a heavyweight boxing tournament, but missed the opportunity to fight Gene Tunney because of a broken ankle. Kelly was determined to escape the Irish ghetto of his youth. Released from the service in 1919, he borrowed $7,000 from his brothers, the playwright George Kelly and the vaudeville performer Walter Kelly, to start a bricklaying business that ultimately made him a millionaire. He returned to rowing competitions in 1919, winning the national title. He also won the NAAO singles in 1919 and 1920 along with a series of other titles.

In 1920 Kelly bought a new shell for the Diamond Sculls at Henley, a prestigious English competition he planned to enter. He was preparing to depart for England when he received a telegram rejecting his entry. Kelly later recalled being devastated; he read the cable over and over, feeling

Jack Kelly, 1941. ASSOCIATED PRESS AP

that he had been rejected because he worked with his hands. While sportswriters often repeated the story, adding to Kelly's fame and mystique, the reason for his rejection was more complicated. Kelly admitted years later that the competition disallowed manual laborers because they would have an unfair advantage over "gentlemen." As a businessman, though, he probably still would have qualified. The problem ran deeper. A long-standing animosity existed between Kelly's rowing club, Vesper, and the Henley stewards over what constituted professionalism in rowing. Because the Vesper Rowing Club offered some financial support to its members, Henley considered them a semiprofessional outfit. Kelly's disqualification had more to do with a disagreement over the proper nature of the sport than class.

Nonetheless, Kelly sought to answer the slight, and his chance came in Antwerp, Belgium, at the 1920 Olympics. He had wanted to enter the games as early as 1912, a daunting feat for someone who lacked the experience of competing on a college team. The 1916 games were canceled due to World War I. In 1920 he tried out for the American Olympic rowing and sculling team, and to everyone's surprise except his own, he was chosen as a member. The press enjoyed the matchup between Kelly and Jack Beresford in the singles competition, presenting it as a contest between a down-to-earth American worker and an elite British rower. When Kelly won, most saw it as a vindication for his being passed over at Henley, though most papers failed to mention that Beresford, originally named Wiszniewski, was a first-generation Pole who also came from a working-class background. Kelly also won the double-sculls competition with Costello, an even more impressive feat considering that Kelly had only one hour to rest between events. When he returned to Philadelphia after the games, 100,000 people turned out to cheer him.

Upon his return Kelly began extensive training for the 1924 games, leading his fiancée to note that she could not compete with his boat for his affection. After he and Costello defended their double-sculls title in the Paris Olympics in 1924, Kelly returned to Philadelphia to concentrate on his bricklaying business and to start a family. He married Margaret Majer on 30 January 1924. They had four children, including the actress and princess Grace Kelly. John Kelly placed his greatest hope, however, in John Kelly junior, called "Kell." He pushed his son from the age of seven to practice rowing, leaving Kell little time for other activities. The younger Kelly eventually won the Diamond Sculls competition in 1947, the U.S. single-sculls championship eight times, and a bronze medal in the 1956 Olympics. The elder Kelly retired from competing in 1926, but he remained involved as a patron and as a coach.

Kelly became involved in Philadelphia Democratic politics in the 1930s, serving as the chairman to the Democratic City Committee. He lost a close mayoral race in 1935 and a close Senate race in 1936. He served as Pennsylvania's secretary of revenue in 1936 and 1937 and remained active in Democratic politics through the 1950s. In 1952 he became the vice president of the Fairmount Park Commission, and in 1958 he became the organization's president. Kelly died from intestinal cancer in the East Falls section of Philadelphia, and is buried in Holy Sepulchre Cemetery near that city.

Kelly won 126 competitions between 1909 and 1926, making him a legend within the sculling world. His feat of winning two gold medals, for single- and double-sculls, in one day was unprecedented. He promoted physical fitness for youngsters throughout his life, serving as chairman for the Federal Security Agency's Committee on Physical Fitness during World War II and establishing the John B. Kelly Award in 1945. He was elected into the National Rowing Foundation Hall of Fame in 1956 and was elected into the U.S. Olympic Hall of Fame in 1990.

★

Anne Edwards, *The Grimaldis of Monaco* (1992), provides a good overview of Kelly's early life. Benjamin Ivry, *Regatta: A Celebration of Oarsmanship* (1988), retells the story of Kelly's rejection by the Henley stewards in 1920; and David L. Porter, ed., *Biographical Dictionary of American Sports: Outdoor Sports* (1988), includes a short entry outlining Kelly's sports career. Obituaries are in the *New York Times* (21 June 1960) and *Time* (11 July 1960).

RONNIE D. LANKFORD, JR.

KELLY, Michael Joseph ("King") (*b.* 31 December 1857 in Troy, New York; *d.* 8 November 1894 in Boston, Massachusetts), popular baseball player in the 1880s and the 1890s who won batting titles in 1884 and 1886 and was elected to the National Baseball Hall of Fame in 1945.

Kelly began his life as a poor, first-generation Irish American and became one of the most popular baseball players of the late nineteenth century. He was the son of Michael Kelly, a papermaker who had emigrated from Ireland, and Catherine Kelly. Kelly moved to Paterson, New Jersey, with his mother after his father's death. He dropped out of public school at an early age to work as a bobbin boy at a textile factory. In 1873, at the age of fifteen, he played organized baseball for the first time with the Troy Haymakers. In 1875 he played his first professional game with the Olympics of Paterson, and in 1878 he played a portion of the season for the Buckeye team in Columbus, Ohio.

In 1878 Manager Cal McVey recruited Kelly for the Cincinnati Red Stockings, where he played for two seasons. Although Kelly hit .348 during his second season and developed a reputation as a successful base stealer, McVey was not overly impressed. Cap Anson, believing the young man was only "green," brought him to the Chicago White Stockings in 1880. Anson, six feet tall and weighing 220 pounds, was an imposing figure and a difficult taskmaster. The undisciplined Kelly immediately realized that Anson's ideas about conditioning and training were much more arduous than he had been accustomed to. Nevertheless Kelly and his teammates persevered, forming a seasoned crew that dominated the National League throughout the 1880s.

Kelly quickly became a star player, partly because of his ability but also because of his good looks and exuberant personality. He stood nearly six feet tall, weighed 190 pounds, and was full of self-confidence. Responding to his flamboyance on the field, fans cheered, "Slide, Kelly, Slide!" when he stole bases. A song with that name became a popular hit. Kelly occasionally bent the rules. At a game against Boston in 1881, he took advantage of the early league's reliance on one umpire. Running from second base, he missed third base by ten to fifteen feet in his eagerness to reach home. Since the umpire was occupied with a play at first base, the earned run stood. He also developed a reputation as a drinker, and Anson, a teetotaler who demanded sober players, hired detectives to follow his wayward star. In one instance Anson hired agents to follow seven errant players, and the detectives eventually turned in a comprehensive report on their nocturnal wanderings. Kelly took objection to only one statement in the report. A detective claimed that Kelly drank a glass of lemonade late one night. The unrepentant ball player declared he had never drunk lemonade at that late hour, it was straight whiskey.

In Kelly's seven years with Chicago the team won five pennants. Although he had been recruited to play right field and to catch, he played infield and even pitched on several occasions. Kelly was a good hitter, but his specialty as a player was stealing bases. The league may have had faster runners and Kelly was often handicapped by bruises from catching because he did not wear shin pads, but his intelligence and daring led him to outdo all rivals. Studying a pitcher, taking a long lead, and twisting his feet to arrive at the base from an angle, he perfected the art of stealing bases. Despite the success of these years, Kelly was less than happy with his salary. He was paid $2,500 in 1886, a great deal of money at the time, but both Dan Brouthers and Hoss Radbourn made $4,000. He was also occasionally fined for drinking, and Kelly believed he should get this money back.

In 1887 Chicago sold Kelly to the Boston Beaneaters for the unheard of sum of $10,000, leading fans to refer to him as the "$10,000 Beauty." Although some believed the team sold him because he was a difficult player to work with, Anson said he sold him because the price was right and he wanted to help balance the teams within the league. At first

Michael "King" Kelly, from a Goodwin & Co. baseball card, c. 1887–1890. BASEBALL CARDS FROM THE BENJAMIN K. EDWARDS COLLECTION/THE LIBRARY OF CONGRESS

Kelly continued to play well. He stole eighty-four bases during his first year with Boston and became one of only ten players to steal six bases in one game in that era. In 1889 he stole sixty-eight bases and led the league in doubles with forty-one. During Kelly's time in Boston, though, his play began to diminish because of his drinking and his lack of self-control. His popularity, however, continued to grow, especially with Irish immigrants, who worshipped him.

In 1890 Kelly's career began to unravel. The National League offered him a $10,000 bribe to prevent him from joining the Players League revolt that year. When he turned it down, his market value dropped. He joined the rebel league in 1890 as player-manager and won the league's championship with an 81–48 record. In 1891 Kelly managed Kelly's Killers in Cincinnati, Ohio, a team created to fill the void when the Reds jumped to the National League. He returned to the Beaneaters in 1891, though his batting average dropped to .189 the next year. In 1893 he played twenty games for the New York Giants and drifted into the minors. He finally retired in 1894 after sixteen seasons.

Kelly appeared on vaudeville in Ernest L. Thayer's *Casey at the Bat* and opened a saloon in New York. In early November, while sailing from New York to Boston for a theatrical performance, Kelly contracted pneumonia. Three days later he was taken to Boston Emergency Hospital, where he died on 8 November 1894. His fans had not forgotten him. Over 5,000 Bostonians filed past his coffin in Elks Hall. Kelly is buried in Boston.

Kelly's lifetime statistics are impressive. He won the batting title twice, first in 1884 (.354) and then in 1886 (.388), and he led in runs scored between 1884 and 1886. Stolen base statistics were not kept until 1885, but in the late 1880s he averaged 62 stolen bases per year. His composite average was .308, and he collected 1,357 runs and 1,813 hits in 1,455 games. In 1945 Kelly was elected into the National Baseball Hall of Fame. He also is credited with either inventing or helping to popularize a number of innovations in baseball, including exchanging signals with pitchers and infielders and the "Chicago slide," sliding on his hip while keeping his body low to avoid the baseman's tag. Kelly's fame, large personality, and destructive lifestyle made him a prototype for later players like Babe Ruth and Mickey Mantle.

★

Stephen Fox, *Big Leagues: Professional Baseball, Football, and Basketball in National Memory* (1994), devotes a number of pages to Kelly's meteoric career. David Quentin Voigt, *Baseball: An Illustrated History* (1987), and Mike Shatzkin, ed., *The Ballplayers: Baseball's Ultimate Biographical Reference* (1990), offer sketches of Kelly's baseball career. Obituaries are in the *Chicago Tribune,* the *Chicago Daily News,* the *Boston Globe,* and the *New York Times* (all 9 Nov. 1894).

RONNIE D. LANKFORD, JR.

KETCHEL, Stanley (*b.* 14 September 1886 in Grand Rapids, Michigan; *d.* 15 October 1910 near Conway, Missouri), middleweight champion and Hall of Fame boxer.

Ketchel was born Stanislaus Kiecal, the son of Polish immigrants Thomas Kiecal and Julia Oblinsky, who were farmers. Growing up on the family farm, Ketchel was a restless youth who yearned for adventure and idolized the outlaws of the American West. He left home at fifteen to ride the rails and survived by living in hobo jungles and working at occasional jobs, such as quartz miner and field hand. The young Ketchel eventually drifted into Butte, Montana, a rough-and-tumble mining town, where he found work as a bellhop before becoming a saloon bouncer. A natural brawler with a passion for fisticuffs, he fought for money in unsanctioned bouts whenever possible and soon found work at Butte's Casino Theater taking on all comers for $20 a week. Ketchel engaged in more than 250

of these brutal affairs while honing his trade. He also worked as a sparring partner for the talented local fighter "Cyclone" Maurice Thompson to improve his technique. Thompson befriended Ketchel, taught him the tricks of the trade, and as legend has it, convinced the young boxer to Americanize his name.

Ketchel made his "professional" debut on 2 May 1904 at the Casino Theater, knocking out the local champion Kid Tracy in one round. Ketchel continued fighting in and around Butte throughout 1906, winning most of his bouts and knocking out thirty-five of forty opponents. "I used to hit them so hard," Ketchel boasted, "they used to fall over the footlights and land in the people's lap." His nonstop aggression and punching prowess coupled with the speed and alacrity with which he dispatched opponents made him a favorite with the rowdy fans and prompted a now-forgotten sportswriter to dub him the "Michigan Assassin."

In 1907 Ketchel caught a freight train to California, then a hotbed of boxing, but had difficulty finding fights until he knocked out the promising middleweight Mike McClure. Ketchel also fought the middleweight contender Joe Thomas three times. The first bout ended in a disappointing draw. The rematch proved to be a vicious brawl, in which a bloodied Ketchel rose from the canvas more than once and eventually knocked out his more experienced opponent. Ketchel won the third dustup via a thirty-round decision. He next demolished Mike "Twin" Sullivan in one round. On 9 May 1908 Ketchel won the middleweight championship from Mike Sullivan's twin brother Jack "Twin" Sullivan, knocking him out in twenty rounds in Colma, California.

Ketchel was an active champion, putting his title on the line four times in as many months. In June he decisioned Billy Papke in ten rounds, in July he knocked out Hugo Kelly in three rounds, and in August he knocked out his old nemesis Thomas in two rounds. He again faced Papke, who was to become his most bitter rival, on 7 September 1908 in Vernon, California. At the outset of the bout, as Ketchel raised his arms to touch gloves, Papke unleashed a solid blow to Ketchel's head, knocking him to the canvas. A bewildered Ketchel never recovered and absorbed a terrible beating before being knocked out in the twelfth round. On 26 November, however, Ketchel knocked out Papke in the eleventh round of another classic brawl to become the first man to regain the middleweight championship.

Although he could be quite amiable outside the ring, the ruggedly handsome Ketchel, or "Steve" as he was known, remained wild and untamed, a lover of fast cars and faster women. He was known to tote a revolver and once shot an unfortunate trainer in the leg for waking him too early before a fight. In 1909 Ketchel and his wily manager Willus Britt traveled to the East Coast to enhance Ketchel's growing popularity. Ketchel met the New York

Stanley Ketchel. © BETTMANN/CORBIS

press in full cowboy regalia to exploit his wild west image and rode down Fifth Avenue in an open car wearing an outlandish pink dressing gown and tossing peanuts to a cheering crowd. He told Nat Fleischer, the founder of *Ring* magazine, that he expected to "go out like a light . . . with an automobile engine jammed through my wishbone." On 26 March 1909 Ketchel fought the crafty light-heavyweight Philadelphia Jack O'Brien in New York City. Out-boxed and badly cut going into the tenth and final round, Ketchel unleashed a furious onslaught that ended with O'Brien out cold but saved by the bell. In a rematch three months later, Ketchel easily disposed of O'Brien in three rounds. Ketchel next met Papke in their fourth and final bout on 5 July. Fought during a raging storm in Colma, it was the most thrilling of their brutal encounters, and Ketchel won a twenty-round decision to retain the crown.

On 16 October 1909 Ketchel challenged the legendary Jack Johnson for the heavyweight championship, also fought in Colma. The bout was to be filmed, and both men allegedly agreed to fight to a draw, with Johnson "going easy" on Ketchel, to ensure a profit and possibly set up a lucrative rematch. With his superior height, reach, and defensive ability, Johnson easily dominated the early rounds. In the eleventh, however, Ketchel, overwhelmed by the desire to win, let loose a barrage of punches that stunned the champion. At the beginning of the twelfth, Ketchel raced across the ring and landed a wild right hand that knocked Johnson down. Johnson, seemingly more angry than hurt, quickly rose and, as Ketchel rushed in to resume his assault, connected with a crushing right hand that knocked out Ketchel.

Ketchel returned to the East Coast and engaged in five more bouts during 1910, including a no-decision affair with the ring great Sam Langford. Britt died after the Johnson fight, and the noted wit and Broadway hustler Wilson Mizner became Ketchel's manager and confidant. Under Mizner's tutelage Ketchel's wild lifestyle spun out of control, and although he kept winning, his strength and skills diminished. In October 1910 Ketchel traveled to a ranch owned by his friend R. P. Dickerson outside of Conway, Missouri, to resume serious training. Unfortunately he soon wrangled with the ranch hand Walter Dipley over the latter's mistreatment of a horse. The jealous Dipley suspected Ketchel of "having his way with" his common-law wife Goldie Smith, who was also the ranch cook. On 15 October Dipley shot Ketchel in the back while the champion was eating breakfast. Ketchel's body was returned to Grand Rapids, Michigan, and buried in Holy Cross Cemetery.

Ketchel, five feet, nine inches and 154 pounds of pure fury, is generally considered one of the best middleweights of all time and a true boxing legend. He emerged from the hobo jungles, honky-tonks, and mining towns of the American West to capture the middleweight championship at the age of twenty-one. During his reign he tore through the division, laying waste to all worthy contenders. Although a natural middleweight, Ketchel's strength, stamina, and ability to absorb punches made him a formidable opponent for boxers in the heavier divisions, including the great Johnson. Ketchel's two-fisted, swarming style, devastating blows, and devil-may-care attitude captured the imaginations of Americans and made him a wildly popular champ. His official record is 64 bouts, 52 wins, 4 losses, 4 draws, and 4 no-decisions with 49 knockouts. Ketchel was inducted into the Boxing Hall of Fame in 1954 and into the International Boxing Hall of Fame in 1990.

★

A full-length biography of Ketchel is Nat Fleischer, *The Michigan Assassin* (1946), a colorful though perhaps fanciful chronicle.

John D. McCallum, *The Encyclopedia of World Boxing Champions* (1975), includes a solid account of the boxer's tumultuous life both inside and outside the ring, as does Nigel Collins, *Boxing Babylon* (1990), which concentrates especially on the events leading up to Ketchel's death. A profile of Ketchel is in Bert Randolph Sugar, *The 100 Greatest Boxers of All Time* (1984). A news account of the Ketchel shooting and a capsule summary of his career is in the *New York Times* (16 Oct. 1910).

MICHAEL MCLEAN

KIDD, William Winston ("Billy") (*b.* 13 April 1943 in Burlington, Vermont), first American male to win Olympic medals in alpine skiing (1964), as well as the first person to win both amateur and professional ski titles in the same year (1970).

Kidd is the oldest of three children of innkeepers Elizabeth Hart and William Garrett Kidd, a descendant of the famous British pirate. Kidd began skiing on Mount Mansfield in Stowe, Vermont, mastering the New England

Billy Kidd. AP/WIDE WORLD PHOTOS

slopes to make the U.S. Eastern team at age fourteen and take second in the Junior National Championship at age seventeen. After graduating from Stowe High School in 1961, he skied on international circuits with the International Federation of Skiing (FIS), gaining a broad education from travel.

Kidd then attended the University of Colorado at Boulder from 1964 to 1969, graduating with a B.S. in economics, by which time he had switched his allegiance to the West. An early and chronic ankle injury affected Kidd's skiing style throughout his career; a thoughtful skier, he "had to figure out how to ski race without falling." He participated in both the FIS slalom and giant slalom World Cup races in 1962. Then, after recovering from a major injury, Kidd became the first American male to win Olympic medals in alpine skiing by taking the silver in the slalom (in 2:11:27) and the bronze in the combined (calculated on a point system) at the 1964 Olympics in Innsbruck, Austria. Validating the claims of the Olympic coach Bob Beattie that the Americans would succeed in heretofore European-won events, Kidd found Austria's steep icy slopes similar to those of the U.S. Northeast where he had grown up. That same banner year, he took third place in the FIS World Championship Hahnenkamm race, won the U.S. giant slalom in a blinding snowstorm, was named the athlete of the year by U.S. skiers, and took the Roche Cup (which he won again the following year).

In 1966, the year Kidd switched from wood to fiberglass skis, he was awarded a silver bowl at the Northeast Ski Council's annual sports conference for his contributions to northeastern skiing. Also, despite shattering his right leg and American hopes in Portillo, Chile (1966), and reinjuring his ankle (1967), Kidd snared many victories around the world. Several of these wins were against the Frenchman Jean-Claude Killy and his own teammate and rival Jimmie Heuga, who had come in third behind him in their first Olympics in 1964. After winning the World Cup slalom in both 1968 and 1969 and placing fifth in the 1968 Olympics in Grenoble, France, Kidd had another record-breaking year in 1970. He became the first American to take a World Cup championship (alpine combined at Val Gardena, Italy) and, turning pro, the International Ski Racing Association (ISRA) alpine combined and giant slalom. This was a triple achievement—the World Cup, the ISRA, and the first person to win both in the same year. Kidd also injured his back and ankle in 1970, influencing his decision to retire from racing in 1972.

During President Richard Nixon's administration, Kidd served as a member of the President's Council on Physical Fitness. Another outgrowth of Kidd's racing years was his long-lasting friendship with his younger teammate Heuga. They were, according to Heuga, "different beasts"—a quieter easterner and a more outgoing westerner. When Heuga developed multiple sclerosis and then fought the disease with exercise, he created the Jimmie Heuga Center for the Reanimation of the Physically Challenged in Edwards, Colorado. Kidd, a board member, supported his friend and helped to establish the Jimmie Heuga Ski Express, an annual fund-raising event for the center.

Kidd coauthored two books, *Ski in Six Days* (1975), a well-illustrated instructional guide, and *Billy Kidd's Ski Racing Book* (1984). Maintaining that ski racing "teaches you to organize and make the best use of your time . . . [as well as helping] improved concentration," Kidd covered all aspects of racing. Elected to both the National and Colorado Ski Halls of Fame, Kidd also won the 1987 AT&T award for commitment to excellence and dedication to skiing. *Ski Magazine* named him one of the top ten skiers of the century in 1999. After retiring from racing, he worked as a television commentator (including at the 1994 Olympics), ski team coach, and contributing editor of *Skiing*. Kidd deliberately only endorsed two major projects, the Special Olympics and Colorado's Steamboat Ski and Resort.

Started in 1968 by Eunice Kennedy Shriver, the Special Olympics gives individuals with mental retardation the chance to train and compete to develop confidence and self-esteem. Kidd was instrumental in holding the first International Winter Special Olympics in Steamboat Springs, Colorado, in 1977. A one-time board member of the nonprofit Special Olympics, Inc., he continues to provide financial and coaching support. For his volunteerism, Kidd received the Texaco Star Award with $2,500 (for a charity of his choice) as the Intermountain Regional Finalist in 2000, the same year the *Denver Post* named him the skier of the century. As the director of skiing at the Steamboat Ski and Resort since 1970, he continues to run the Billy Kidd Performance Center. This coaching program focuses on technical development, but Kidd does more than teach—he encourages and publicizes the sport.

At five feet, eight inches tall and approximately 155 pounds, the record-breaking Kidd has been associated with strategic skiing, many injuries, and a devotion to skiing and causes that support it. He has three children from his marriage with Kristin Day Kremer Fripp, whom he married in 1976 and divorced in 1988. Inspired by the skiers Buddy Werner and Heuga, the easterner from Stowe who became linked to Steamboat in the West now serves as an inspiration to others. In his signature Stetson, the 1964 Olympic champion and world-class ski racer symbolizes American achievement in skiing.

★

Kidd's two instructional books are *Ski in Six Days* (1975), with Douglas Kent Hall, and *Billy Kidd's Ski Racing Book* (1984), with the coauthor Bill Grout. In addition to technique, the latter contains material from Kidd's life and comments from other ski experts. The article by Chris Dufresne, "Their Medals Still Glisten," *Los Angeles Times* (26 Dec. 1993), discusses his friendship with Heuga. *Ski Magazine* and the *New York Times* have regularly recorded Kidd's activities and records.

RACHEL SHOR

KILLEBREW, Harmon Clayton (*b.* 29 June 1936 in Payette, Idaho), member of the National Baseball Hall of Fame whose home run total of 573 ranked sixth in major league history at the beginning of the twenty-first century.

Killebrew was one of four children born to H. C. Killebrew and Katherine Pearl May Killebrew. His father was a former college football player and professional wrestler who moved to Payette from Illinois in 1922. While Killebrew was growing up in Payette, his father served as sheriff and made his living painting houses, a task in which the son often aided his father. The younger Killebrew, however, was best known for his endeavors on the athletic field. At Payette High School he lettered in baseball, basketball, and football. When he graduated from high school in 1953, Killebrew's high school jersey number was retired. Although he was offered an athletic scholarship by the University of Oregon, Killebrew choose to attend the College of Idaho, where he enrolled for one semester.

In the summer of 1954 Killebrew played in the semiprofessional Idaho-Oregon Border League, where he hit an astounding .847 average and drew the attention of major league scouts. Senator Herman Welker of Idaho, a native of Payette, urged Clark Griffith, the owner of the Washington Senators, to investigate the young slugger. Ossie Bluege, the director of the Senators' farm system, signed Killebrew to a $30,000 contract—$6,000 a year for three years with a $12,000 bonus.

Under major league baseball's so-called "bonus baby" rule in place at the time, Killebrew had to spend two years with the Senators before he could be optioned to the minor leagues, where he could polish his hitting and work on defensive skills. Like most "bonus babies," he saw little playing time during his first two seasons with the Senators. In 1954 he had four hits in thirteen at bats with no home runs. The following season Killebrew managed eighty plate appearances with sixteen hits, four of which were home runs. He played mostly at third base, but his defensive skills were hardly at a major league level. In 1955 Killebrew married Elaine Roberts, his childhood sweetheart. They had five children.

From 1956 to 1958 Killebrew shuttled between Washington and the Senators' minor league affiliates in Chat-

Harmon Killebrew. ASSOCIATED PRESS AP

tanooga, Tennessee, and Indianapolis, Indiana. While some were ready to give up on Killebrew, Calvin R. Griffith, who had taken over the Senators following his uncle's death in 1955, traded the incumbent third baseman Eddie Yost to the Detroit Tigers. The club owner then ordered the manager Cookie Lavagetto to insert Killebrew in the starting lineup at third base for the 1959 season.

While he still struggled defensively, Killebrew rewarded Griffith's confidence by hitting twenty-eight home runs by the season's midpoint and was selected for the All-Star team. He slumped somewhat during the second half of the season but finished with forty-two home runs, tying Cleveland's Rocky Calavito for the American League lead. In 1960 Killebrew's home run total dipped to thirty-one. Killebrew's career really took off when Griffith, seeking greater revenue, moved the Washington franchise to Minnesota following the 1960 season. In 1961 Killebrew hit for a .288 average and slugged forty-six home runs, but with the media hoopla surrounding Roger Maris's assault on Babe Ruth's season home run mark of sixty, Killebrew's accomplishments were overshadowed.

However, Killebrew was not ignored for long. From 1962 to 1964 he led the American League in home runs, amassing totals of forty-eight, forty-five, and forty-nine. In 1965 the Minnesota Twins won the American League pennant and met the Los Angeles Dodgers in the World Series. Killebrew's home runs dropped to twenty-five as he missed

a good portion of that season due to a dislocated left elbow. He returned for the series, but the Twins lost to the Dodgers.

Shifted to first base, Killebrew improved his defensive play and continued to be a dominant player for the Twins throughout the late 1960s and the early 1970s. In 1967 he led the league with 44 home runs and 131 runs batted in. The Twins won the division championship in 1969, and Killebrew, who amassed 49 homers and 140 runs driven in, was selected as the league Most Valuable Player.

Though the Twins repeated as division champions in 1970, the club's record declined during the decade, as the tightfisted Griffith found it increasingly difficult to compete with accelerating player salaries. The production figures for an aging Killebrew also began to decline. In 1974, his last season with the Twins, Killebrew batted only .222 with 13 home runs. He was traded to the Kansas City Royals, where he completed his final campaign with 14 home runs and a batting average under .200.

Following the 1975 season Killebrew retired from major league baseball. During his twenty-two years in the big leagues, he slugged 573 home runs, sixth on the all-time list at the beginning of the twenty-first century; drove in 1,584 runs; and posted a slugging percentage of .509. He averaged a home run every 14.22 at bats, the fourth best percentage in major league history to his time. Although his career batting average was only .242, Killebrew had 2,086 hits and 1,559 walks. Selected for thirteen All-Star games, Killebrew was inducted into the National Baseball Hall of Fame in 1984.

As a baseball player Killebrew was noted for his power, but as a person he is quiet and reserved. A devout Mormon, he neither smokes nor drinks. His favorite recreation is hunting. His modest nature is evident in his wife's comment: "He doesn't say much about the ball game when he gets home, but I can tell when he has hit another home run. He always comes into the house looking sheepish."

Following his playing career, Killebrew worked as a baseball announcer for the Twins, the Oakland A's, and the California Angels. He resides in Scottsdale, Arizona, but maintains an interest in a Boise, Idaho, insurance and securities firm. As home run hitters such as Mark McGwire, Barry Bonds, and Ken Griffey, Jr., have challenged lifetime home run marks, the achievements of the modest Killebrew have been rediscovered by baseball fans.

★

A file on Killebrew is at the National Baseball Hall of Fame in Cooperstown, New York. For a laudatory sports biography, see Wayne J. Anderson, *Harmon Killebrew: Baseball's Superstar* (1965). For the Minnesota Twins and Killebrew, see Dave Mona and Dave Jarzyna, *Twenty-five Seasons* (1986). For journalistic accounts of Killebrew's baseball career, see Shirley Povich, "Strong

Boy of the Twins," *Saturday Evening Post* (15 Sept. 1962); and "The Nuclear Bomber," *Time* (14 Aug. 1964).

RON BRILEY

KINER, Ralph McPherran (*b.* 27 October 1922 in Santa Rita, New Mexico), professional baseball player and sports broadcaster, Hall of Famer, and the only player to lead his league or tie for leadership in home runs seven years in a row.

Kiner was the sole child of Ralph Macklin Kiner, a baker and steam shovel operator, and Beatrice Grayson, a registered nurse. Kiner's father died when he was four, and he and his mother moved to Alhambra, California, east of Los Angeles, where his mother secured a job with the Southern Pacific Railroad. Growing up during the Great Depression, Kiner attended Fremont Grammar School and held a magazine delivery route to earn extra money. His love for baseball, however, led him to concoct an elaborate scheme. Rather than going door-to-door delivering magazines, Kiner discovered he could make more money mowing lawns and still have time to play baseball with his friends. The system worked, until his mother found the accruing magazines buried in the backyard. The foiled plan earned him

Ralph Kiner, 1947. AP/WIDE WORLD PHOTOS

a six-month stint at Long Beach Military School. He went on to attend Alhambra High School and Pasadena Junior College (later Pasadena City College).

Actively sought by the New York Yankees, Kiner was only eighteen when Hollis "Sloppy" Thurston, a scout for the Pittsburgh Pirates, successfully signed him, sealing the deal with a novel $3,000 bonus offer. In 1941 Kiner reported to the Pirates spring training camp in San Bernardino, California. He made his professional baseball debut on 23 April 1941, starting as a left fielder for New York's Eastern League Class A Albany Senators (in the 1940s "A" was the third-highest minor-league level in baseball). As Kiner later told the *Albany Times Union,* however, playing in a lower-class league didn't make the game easy. "It was a really tough league," he remarked in June 2000. "It was a pitcher's league, and my second year I led the league in home runs with fourteen." The club won the 1942 Eastern League pennant and, after spending two seasons in Albany, Kiner was promoted to Toronto, Canada's AAA team in the International League.

Kiner played forty-three games in 1943 before being called up by the navy on a World War II enlistment. U.S. Navy Air Cadet Kiner began his military career on 8 June 1943. He served in training outfits at Saint Mary's College, Corpus Christi, Texas, and California Poly Tech in San Francisco, before becoming a commissioned officer. He served as a bomber pilot in the Pacific Theater from 1 July 1945 to 19 November 1945.

When Kiner returned to U.S. civilian life and baseball he moved up to the majors, winning a berth with the Pittsburgh Pirates. He played his first postwar game on 16 April 1946 before a St. Louis crowd of 14,000, going one for four in a 6–4 Pirates win over the Cardinals. Two days later, Kiner got his first major-league home run off Howie Pollet. In his rookie season, he belted twenty-three homers to beat Johnny Mize of the New York Giants for the National League (NL) home-run title, becoming the first NL rookie in forty years to top the conference in home runs. From 1946 to 1952, Kiner's first seven years in the majors, the six-foot, two-inch, 195-pound outfielder led the league or tied for leadership in home runs, the only player to do so for seven years in a row.

In 1947 the Steel City franchise obtained Hank Greenberg from the Detroit Tigers. Kiner attributed his continued hitting success to Greenberg's guidance. Greenberg adjusted the right-handed Kiner's batting stance and tutored him in a finer judgment of the strike zone. By moving his batting position closer to the plate and placing his feet twenty-seven to twenty-eight inches apart, Kiner was able to take a six-inch stride into the ball. The result was fifty-one home runs for 1947. On 13 October 1951, with Greenberg as his best man, Kiner married the tennis star Nancy

Chaffee in Santa Barbara, California. They had three children.

The post–World War II Pirates were a struggling second-division squad. Although Kiner was only a fair fielder, his keen ability to slug home runs made him the team's star. The author Bob Smizik noted, "Ralph Kiner drew enough people to Forbes Field during the grim years after World War II to enable the franchise to survive." His teammate Frankie Gustine said, "It was amazing. If Ralph batted in the eighth it seemed like the whole place would get up and leave. But if there was a chance he would bat in the ninth, no one left."

Still, the Pittsburgh general manager Branch Rickey viewed Kiner as a one-dimensional player. Rickey's dislike for Kiner dated to the player's bachelor days, when he squired Elizabeth Taylor, Janet Leigh, and other Hollywood starlets. Kiner further irked Rickey by working with the Players Association and demanding a high salary. In heated contract negotiations Rickey told Kiner that "the Pirates could finish last without him as easily as with him." Finally on 4 June 1953, a day Kiner called "one of the darkest moments of my life," Rickey sent Kiner, along with Joe Garagiola, Howie Pollet, and George Metkovich, to the Chicago Cubs for Toby Atwell, Bob Schultz, Preston Ward, George Freese, Bob Addis, Gene Hermanski, and $100,000.

During the 1953 season in Chicago, Kiner injured his back. The following year he was traded on 16 November 1954 to the Cleveland Indians for Sam Jones, Gale Wade, and $60,000. Still nagged by injury, he was released in October 1955. That same month Kiner became the general manager of the San Diego Padres, then in the Pacific Coast League. Five years later Kiner, Greenberg, and other business associates tried unsuccessfully to buy a West Coast expansion club from the American League. He jumped from the front office to the broadcast booth in 1961, joining Bill Veeck's Chicago White Sox. In 1962 he moved to an expansion club, the New York Mets, where he initially served as a play-by-play announcer. He continued his broadcasting association with the team into the 2000 season.

Kiner and his first wife divorced in 1968, and he married Barbara Ann Batcheldor on 6 March 1969. They had two children during nearly twelve years together, but divorced in 1981. He was married for the third time on 5 December 1982 to DiAnn Shugart.

Kiner was inducted into the National Baseball Hall of Fame by a narrow margin on 18 August 1975, his fifteenth and final year of eligibility. He needed 272 votes to be elected; he got 273. On 19 September 1987, in an evening ballpark ceremony, the Pittsburgh Pirates officially retired Kiner's number "4."

Kiner was a one-man home-run hitting crew. For every 100 at bats, he averaged 7.1 home runs, a percentage second only to Babe Ruth's. Over his ten-year playing career, Kiner averaged .279, with 37 home runs and over 100 runs batted in (RBIs) a season. He belted 369 career home runs and 1,015 RBIs. He led the NL in slugging percentage three times (1947, 1949, and 1951) and in bases on balls three times (1949, 1951, and 1952). He was the only player to hit home runs in three consecutive All-Star games (1949, 1950, and 1951), and was the first NL player to seek a $100,000 salary. Perhaps most enduringly, he was baseball's greatest home-run producer for seven years.

★

Kiner and Joe Gergen cowrote *Kiner's Korner: At Bat and on the Air—My Forty Years in Baseball* (1987), in which Kiner discusses both his playing career and his years in broadcasting. Biographical entries on Kiner can be found in Michael L. LaBlanc, ed., *Professional Sports Team Histories: Baseball* (1994); Donald Dewey and Nicholas Acocella, *The Biographical History of Baseball* (1995); and John C. Skipper, *A Biographical Dictionary of the Baseball Hall of Fame* (2000). See also Al Stump, "Mr. Home Run," *Sport* (June 1952); Marino Amoruso, "Ralph Kiner," *Sport Collectors Digest* (3 Feb. 1984); and Douglas T. Branch, "Kiner Got His Start in Albany," *Albany Times Union* (25 June 2000).

JOHN VORPERIAN

KING, Billie Jean Moffit (*b.* 22 November 1943 in Long Beach, California), tennis player who became a symbol of American feminism through her "Battle of the Sexes" match with Bobby Riggs, her advocacy of women's sports, and her push for gender equity.

King was the only daughter and the older of the two children of Willis B. Moffit, an engineer with the Long Beach fire department, and Betty Jerman Moffit, who worked as a medical receptionist. The family lived modestly during King's childhood. Randall "Randy" Moffit, her brother, later pitched in the major leagues for the San Francisco Giants.

King was a natural athlete from the start, and began playing tennis at age eleven; she quickly developed a passion for the sport on the public courts of Long Beach. Coached by tennis great Alice Marble, who called her student "short, fat, and aggressive," King perfected an attacking style that became her trademark. From the outset of her career, she chafed at the aristocratic side of tennis; "I was always uncomfortable in snooty private clubs," she said later. She won her first tournament at age fourteen. In 1961 at age eighteen, she and her partner, Karen Hantze, won the Wimbledon doubles title; they repeated the feat in 1962. While her tennis career soared, she attended Los Angeles State College of Applied Arts and Sciences from 1961 to 1966. She married Larry W. King on 17 September 1965.

Billy Jean King. ARCHIVE PHOTOS, INC.

By that time her success on the court had made her the number-one-ranked woman player in the United States. At five feet, four-and-a-half inches in height, she contended with uncertain knees that several times required surgery.

In 1966 King won the first of six Wimbledon singles titles; she successfully defended her title a year later. She also won the U.S. Open in 1967. During the next decade and a half, King won seventy-two tournaments and earned nearly $2 million in prize money. Along the way, she racked up many groundbreaking accolades: in 1971 she was the first female athlete to win more than $100,000 in a single year; in 1973 she became the first woman named as *Sports Illustrated*'s "Sportsperson of the Year"; and in 1976 *Time* magazine named her "Woman of the Year." In the early 1970s she founded several businesses to advance her personal interests: a practice called "team tennis," in which local franchises compete against one another in an arena setting; *WomenSports* magazine (now *Women's Sports and Fitness* magazine), cofounded with her husband in 1974; and a women's professional softball league in 1975, using her tennis earnings to sponsor a franchise.

In 1975 King announced a partial retirement from professional tennis (due to knee problems) in order to take a position as sports commentator on the ABC television network. King retired from competitive tennis in 1984 as one of the preeminent women to ever play the sport. During her career, she secured a dozen Grand Slam singles titles

and amassed twenty Wimbledon crowns in singles, doubles, and mixed doubles. Her slashing approach to the game, her constant verbal exhortations to herself, and her dogged will to win made her a crowd favorite. Always concerned with issues of equity for women players, King was a founding member of the Women's Tennis Association and presided over the organization from 1973 to 1975 and 1980 to 1981.

The event that made Billie Jean King a world figure was her celebrated match with self-proclaimed tennis hustler Bobby Riggs in the Houston Astrodome on 20 September 1973 before 31,000 fans and a worldwide television audience of 40 million. Riggs had beaten another excellent woman player, Margaret Smith Court, early in the year, and he boasted that at age fifty-five he could defeat any of the top-ranked women in tennis. "No broad can beat me," Riggs said. Billie Jean King accepted the challenge and proved him wrong. In a circus-like atmosphere that included her being carried in on a litter by four muscular men, King won an easy three-set victory, 6–4, 6–3, 6–3. The aging Riggs was outclassed in every phase of the game by the athletic King, and after the opening moments it was clear that Riggs had no weapons that could dent Billie Jean's superiority. The blowout triumph established King as one of the most famous athletes in the world. It also signaled a greater acceptance of women in sports and came to be seen as one of the shaping events for the emergence of feminism in the 1970s. As King observed in 1998, "that wasn't about tennis, it was about social change."

King's personal life kept her in the headlines. In 1972 she revealed that she had had an abortion in 1971, lest motherhood interfere with her career. Behind the scenes, her marriage was in trouble, and she had embarked on a romantic affair with Marilyn Barnett, a Beverly Hills hairdresser who later became King's personal assistant. The liaison ended in 1974, and in 1981 Barnett sued King for expenses and a house they had shared during their relationship. King admitted the affair but did not acknowledge that she was gay. The highly publicized "galimony" suit cost King an estimated $1.5 million in lost advertising endorsements and stereotyped her as a lesbian in much of American society. She and Larry King were divorced in the late 1980s once the suit had been resolved.

Another controversial aspect of King's career was her personal and financial involvement with the tobacco brands, such as Virginia Slims and its parent company, Phillip Morris, which sponsored women's tennis in the 1970s and 1980s. Appreciative of the monetary backing that sustained her profession, King accepted money for her promotional work for the companies and defended them against charges that cigarettes were dangerous to the health of everyone. When criticized for this stance in 1993, she responded that "we are proud of our relationship with an enlightened company like Philip Morris."

In the late 1990s King "came out" publicly about her status as a gay athlete and lent her prestige to "gay pride" events. She remained active as the coach of the U.S. Olympic Team and the American team in the Federation Cup competition; was inducted to the National Women's Hall of Fame in 1990; and became involved with "Discovery Zone," indoor planned play centers for children, as part of her goal of advocating coeducational team sports. Because of her impact on tennis and her drive to promote gender equity, King is a landmark figure in twentieth-century American sports. Still, she recognizes the controversies that have marked her sporting career, and she sums up her life in and out of tennis simply: "People don't feel safe with people who stretch them."

★

King's autobiography *Billie Jean,* with Kim Chapin (1974), is an account of her early career; a later autobiography, *Billie Jean,* with Frank Deford (1982), delves more into her personal life after the 1981 lawsuit. King also wrote *Tennis to Win,* with Kim Chapin (1970), an instructional book, and *We HAVE Come a Long Way: The Story of Women's Tennis,* with Cynthia Starr (1988), which is often revealing about its author. See also King, "Woman Tennis Pros Are Not 'Being Used' to Promote Smoking," *New York Times* (2 Dec. 1993). Bud Collins, *My Life with the Pros* (1989), and Alice Marble with Dale Leatherman, *Courting Danger* (1991), have insights into King's development. Useful articles about King include Mark Asher, "Tennis Ace Billie Jean King Reveals She Had Abortion," *Philadelphia Inquirer* (23 Feb. 1972); Anna Quindlen, "Billie Jean King Talks Comeback and Other Battles," *New York Times* (9 Jan. 1978); Neil Amdur, "Mrs. King Offers to Quit as W.T.A. Head, So Not to Hurt Players," *New York Times* (3 May 1981); and Robert Lipsyte, "Helping Others Before Helping Herself," *New York Times* (12 July 1998). King discussed her sexuality in an interview with *The Advocate* (18 Aug. 1998). The ABC network aired a made-for-television movie, "When Billie Beat Bobby," starring Holly Hunter as King (16 Apr. 2001).

KAREN GOULD

KING, Don(ald) (*b.* 20 August 1931 in Cleveland, Ohio), wild, wily sports impresario of unprecedented charisma who came to prominence in the 1970s, and for more than two decades was the unchallenged ruler of professional boxing.

King was the son of Clarence and Hattie King. After his father, a steelworker, died in an industrial accident, King lived with his mother and six siblings in a modest middle-class neighborhood where the family sold peanuts and homemade pies to make ends meet. King, who failed physical education at Audubon Junior High School, fared no

Don King, 1975. ASSOCIATED PRESS

better at John Adams High School, where he competed at 108 pounds as a flyweight fighter during his volatile academic career. Ironically he attained an imposing stature in adulthood, weighing 240 pounds.

From his earliest profession in the 1950s, as the kingpin of an illegal Cleveland-based numbers racket, King capitalized on an innate sales ability and a flair for persuasion. Within fifteen years he was grossing an estimated $15,000 per day from illicit street operations while working under the cover of a second, legitimate organization as the proprietor of the New Corner Tavern. King, who boasted a lengthy rap sheet, was the trigger man in a 1954 shooting, but escaped a murder indictment on the grounds of justifiable homicide. On a separate occasion he took a bullet in the head and survived.

King's luck ran out in 1966 when he was arrested for aggravated assault. Unlike the 1954 affair, he was convicted this time for manslaughter in the first degree after the victim died. A subsequent stint in Ohio's Marion Correctional Institute led King to a new appreciation of his own civil liberties and, amid rumors that he had paid off witnesses and otherwise obstructed justice, he served what critics have described as an inappropriately brief incarceration totaling three years and eleven months. He later received a full pardon from Governor James Rhodes of Ohio in 1983.

After his release from prison in 1971, King embarked on a lucrative career in the fight promotion game and was associated for a time with Video Technologies, a satellite broadcaster of boxing events. In 1973 he appeared at a heavyweight title match in Kingston, Jamaica, with the contingency for titleholder Joe Frazier. After that fight, in which the challenger George Foreman emerged as the new champion, King neatly switched sides and became Foreman's confidant. King then contracted Foreman to fight the contender Ken Norton before securing rights for Video Technologies to broadcast a title match between Foreman and the former champion Muhammad Ali. King reportedly obtained Foreman's signature for the Ali match on a blank sheet of paper and added the contract specifics after the fact.

The Foreman-Ali fight, billed as the "Rumble in the Jungle," became a springboard for King's career. It was the first of seven title contests involving Ali that his organization, Don King Productions, would promote. King negotiated an historic $11 million payoff for the bout, which was held on 30 October 1974 in Kinshasa, Zaire (later the Democratic Republic of the Congo). He also cofounded the Festival in Zaire (FIZ) corporation to organize several days of prefight festivities, turning the event into a media extravaganza.

In 1975 King organized a spectacular title bout between Ali and Frazier, the "Thrilla in Manila"—one of the most famous fights of all time—for which Ali was paid $6 million. Other fighters who competed in bouts promoted by King during the late twentieth century include Ernie Shavers, Jeff "Candy Slim" Merritt, Sugar Ray Leonard, Roberto Duran, and Mike Tyson. King also took over management of the heavyweight Larry Holmes after Holmes took the title from Ali.

King married Luvenia Mitchell in 1950; they had one daughter, born in 1955. King also had a son born out of wedlock. After his first marriage ended in divorce, he married Henrietta Renwick, the widow of one of his associates, in 1962 and adopted her young son, John Carl Renwick. While still a prison inmate, King finagled the purchase of a forty-acre farm on 26 March 1971, giving the title to his adopted son, who was fourteen years old at the time. The boy, later known as Carl King, became a boxing manager who reportedly collaborated with his stepfather to keep as much as 50 percent of each prize purse for the fights they handled.

Because of his larger-than-life audacity, King was suspected of numerous irregularities in his professional dealings. As a matter of record, his colleagues filed more than 100 lawsuits against him between 1974 and 1994. Beginning in 1977 the federal government targeted him for income tax transgressions and racketeering. Accusations aside, in 1999 a London court gave King a $12 million judgment against the promoter Frank Warren during a dispute over ending their business partnership.

King was elected to the International Boxing Hall of Fame in 1997 and received an honorary doctorate of human letters from North Carolina's Shaw University in 1998. A crafty and flamboyant publicist, King was one of the more colorful and intriguing personalities in modern sports history. Easily recognizable by his trademark outrageous hair, which stood almost straight up, he was known for both his ruthless tactics and his powers of persuasion. When he entered professional boxing in the 1970s the United States was smoldering in the wake of the civil rights movement, and African-American fighters dominated the lucrative heavyweight boxing division following the retirement of the Caucasian heavyweight champion Rocky Marciano in 1956. King capitalized not only on his identity as an African American but also on the unregulated boxing business to wield his clout and increase his influence. By 2001 he had promoted more than 300 fights in a career that spanned over a quarter of a century.

★

For an informative biography of King, see Jack Newfield, *Only in America: The Life and Crimes of Don King* (1995). Essay-length pieces on King appear in *Newsmakers* (1989), *Contemporary Black Biography,* vol. 14 (1997), and *Jet* (17 Nov. 1997).

GLORIA COOKSEY

KIPHUTH, Robert John Herman ("Bob") (*b.* 17 November 1890 in Tonawanda, New York; *d.* 7 January 1967 in New Haven, Connecticut), swim coach at Yale University, advocate of physical fitness, and innovator in training techniques who made Yale the dominant powerhouse in American collegiate swimming for forty years and who coached five U.S. Olympic swim teams.

Kiphuth was the eldest of the six children of John Kiphuth, a lumber-mill hand, and Mary Benin, who taught him to fear God and work hard. A member of the Evangelical Church, he neither smoked nor drank throughout his life. As a boy, he became involved in athletics at the YMCA and in 1910, at a stocky five-and-a-half feet, he was hired as its director of physical education. At the "Y," he met Louise DeLaney, of Buffalo, New York, who shared his interest in fitness. In 1914, as a result of her acquaintance with a former Yale official, Kiphuth was offered the position of assistant instructor of physical education at the university and he moved to New Haven. Kiphuth and DeLaney were married on 7 June 1917. They had one son, DeLaney Kiphuth.

In 1917 Kiphuth was asked to oversee the Carnegie Pool

Bob Kiphuth *(receiving trophy at right)* with the Yale swim team, 1953. AP/WIDE WORLD PHOTOS

at Yale because its superintendent had fallen ill. The next year Kiphuth was appointed swim coach, and he hurriedly learned as much as he could about the sport. Since the Carnegie Pool was too small to accommodate the entire Yale team, he put a group of second-line swimmers through a special set of land exercises that he devised from his knowledge of physical conditioning. The group subsequently excelled in the pool. He turned the experiment into a regular training program of what some dubbed "muscles and mileage"—having his swimmers undertake two months of calisthenics and work with weights and pulleys before they plunged into lengthy workouts in the water. The innovation helped produce a record of competitive success unequalled in collegiate swimming before or since. From 1918 to 1958, when Kiphuth retired, his Yale teams won 528 dual meets and lost only twelve, the last in 1945.

Kiphuth coached the U.S. Olympic Women's Swim Team in 1928 (Amsterdam), and the Men's Swim Team in 1932 (Los Angeles), 1936 (Berlin), 1948 (London), and 1952 (Helsinki). At the London Games, the American swimmers won all eight swimming and diving events, an unprecedented feat. But for Kiphuth, the most thrilling moment in his coaching career came in 1942 against the University of Michigan in its home pool. Michigan was strong, the water seemed rough, and the Yale swimmers were jittery. However, they crushed Michigan 70–16, winning every race while setting either a world's record, an American record, a Michigan record, or a Yale record.

Kiphuth held that a coach should behave like a stern but understanding father, declaring, "The boys of strong character and topflight ability will like him; the shirkers and crybabies will not. This is as it should be." Practicing what he preached, he might yell at laggard swimmers, "If you want to take a bath, get a cake of soap"; or chide even a victorious swimmer after a race for underperforming. But he chastised gently, and on swim-team trips he would chat with the team members, cheering and calming them. He was careful to encourage second-rank swimmers as well as champions, taking as much pride in their improvement as in that of his speedsters.

Even though he was a tough taskmaster, Kiphuth was held in high affection by Yale students, many of whom he knew because the university required that all its graduates know how to swim. It was long rumored that Kiphuth himself could not swim; he put the rumors to rest in 1948 before a large crowd at the fiftieth anniversary of Yale swimming by diving fully clothed into the water and paddling across the pool. In 1946 he was named director of athletics, a post that he relinquished in 1949 after suffering a heart attack and that was then filled by his son, DeLaney. In 1950 he was promoted to full professor of physical education at Yale. A student of physical education since his days at the YMCA, Kiphuth continued to explore training and swimming techniques. He spent many summers between the world wars studying physical education in England, France, Germany, and Japan. An evangelist of swimming and fitness, he published magazine articles and wrote or coauthored several books on both subjects, including

Swimming (with A. S. Barnes, 1942) and *Basic Swimming* (1950). His *How to Be Fit,* first published in 1942 for young men headed into the military, was reissued in 1950 in a revised edition addressed to women as well as men. Many men and women today, he wrote, "need to take special care of their bodies and train their muscles in order to overcome the enervating effects of present-day living, the softening that results from riding to school or job instead of walking, from spending hours at sedentary work."

Although formally educated only through high school, Kiphuth was a cultivated man. He audited courses at Yale, read avidly, and developed a range of literary and artistic interests. His absorption with body mechanics made him a devotee of ballet. His suite in Timothy Dwight College, where he was a fellow, contained some 4,000 books, including a number of first or rare editions. Art was the subject of many of the volumes. Oil paintings and water colors adorned the walls, sculptures occupied the niches, and the cabinets housed numerous recordings of classical music.

In 1967 Kiphuth died after watching the Yale swim team beat West Point. He is buried at Evergreen Cemetery in Hartford, Connecticut.

Kiphuth achieved international renown in the world of competitive swimming. His emphasis on conditioning and technique transformed the sport and helped foster an affluent society's emerging devotion to fitness. Swimmers came from around the world to train with him, and in the 1950s and early 1960s, he conducted swimming clinics in a number of countries, including Germany, Iceland, South Africa, Israel, India, Japan, and Mexico. In 1963 he received the Presidential Medal of Freedom for his role as a "continuing spokesman for physical fitness and development throughout the United States."

★

The principal sources of information about Kiphuth are a folder of clippings, articles, and press releases in the athletics department of Yale University; and an entry in *Current Biography* (1957). An obituary is in the *New York Times* (9 Jan. 1967).

DANIEL J. KEVLES

KIRALY, Karch (*b.* 30 November 1960 in Jackson, Michigan), three-time Olympic gold-medal winner—including for the first beach volleyball competition in the 1996 Olympics—recognized as the most famous and successful indoor and beach volleyball player in the sport's history.

Kiraly was born in Jackson, Michigan, an unlikely site for a future beach volleyball champion. His father, Laszlo Kiraly, was a refugee who fled his native Hungary after the Soviet invasion of 1956. While attending medical school at the University of Michigan, Laszlo met his wife, Toni Iffland; the family subsequently spent most of Kiraly's youth

Karch Kiraly, 1996. AP/WIDE WORLD PHOTOS

in Michigan while his father finished his medical education. A move to Santa Barbara, California, to complete Laszlo's medical internship permanently relocated the family to Southern California, where the father and son soon took up beach volleyball as a family activity.

For Laszlo, who had been a member of the Hungarian junior national volleyball team, this was no mere pastime. From the age of six, the young Kiraly was drilled in the basic skills that the sport demanded: serving, passing, setting, spiking, blocking, and digging. In a few years, Kiraly was playing in beach volleyball doubles matches; at the age of eleven he entered his first tournament at Corona del Mar, California, playing doubles with his father. The Kiralys lost both games in their first outing, but it was the last time they lost two matches in a row.

Later, Kiraly reminisced nostalgically about the 1970s beach volleyball scene, when he first entered tournaments with his father. Invented by William Morgan in 1895, volleyball was known primarily as an indoor sport played on a hard court, although its popularity as a beach game grew in the twentieth century. Southern Californians played the game in informal matches that grew into organized tournaments by the 1950s. A spirit of camaraderie ruled, as Kiraly later recalled, with losing players having to referee the next game. Tournament prizes usually amounted to nothing more than a trophy and bragging rights, although prize money became a more serious consideration with corporate sponsorships in the 1970s.

A prodigy on the beach volleyball circuit in Southern California, Kiraly first demonstrated the depth of his talent as a key member of the Santa Barbara High School indoor volleyball squad, which attained a record of eighty-three straight winning matches during his high-school career. For his efforts, Kiraly was named California's Most Valuable Player (MVP) in 1978, the same year the squad went undefeated. The following year Kiraly entered the University of California, Los Angeles (UCLA), where he earned a B.S. degree in biochemistry. He compiled an impressive collegiate career as a setter and hitter on the UCLA team, with the Bruins winning National Collegiate Athletic Association (NCAA) championships three out of his four years on the lineup. Kiraly also met his wife, Janna Miller, in 1983; like Kiraly, she was on the volleyball team at nearby Pepperdine University. The couple married in December 1986 and subsequently had two sons.

Although Kiraly had continued to play beach volleyball as a standout UCLA player under the coach Al Scates, he almost had to abandon the sport while he trained with the U.S. national team for the 1984 Olympics under the coach Doug Beal. Like many indoor volleyball coaches, Beal thought that beach volleyball weakened the skills that indoor volleyball demanded. Although beach volleyball—with teams of two players—made for a better all-around player, indoor volleyball—with teams of six players—forced each individual to work more precisely as part of a team strategy. Kiraly played in just one beach volleyball tournament while training for the 1984 Olympics.

The rigorous dedication to indoor volleyball paid off, as Kiraly and the U.S. national team won the gold medal at the Los Angeles Olympics, followed by a series of wins at the 1985 World Cup, 1986 World Championship, and 1987 Pan-American Games. Named as the U.S. team captain in 1985, Kiraly also earned World's Best Volleyball Player honors from the Fédération Internationale de Volleyball (FIVB) in 1986 as well as the MVP award at the 1985 World Cup. At the 1988 Olympics in Seoul, South Korea, the U.S. squad repeated its gold-medal performance at the first nonboycotted Olympics since 1976.

After playing indoor volleyball with Italy's Il Messaggero team in 1991, Kiraly decided to forego another stint on the U.S. national team for the 1992 Olympics. In addition to the rigors of training, he was reluctant to take on an extensive travel schedule that would keep him away from his San Clemente, California, home with his wife and two young sons. Fortunately, the growing interest in beach vol-

leyball presented him with a ready-made career on the beach volleyball circuit. From 1991 to 1996 Kiraly compiled a record of eighty open wins, most of them with the partner Kent Steffes. The two capped their careers by winning the gold medal in the first appearance of beach volleyball as an Olympic sport in Atlanta in 1996. On their way to the championship round, Kiraly and Steffes played one of the most exciting beach volleyball matches in the sport's history, narrowly edging out their rivals Christopher St. John "Sinjin" Smith and Carl Henkel in the quarterfinal match by a score of 17–15.

Kiraly was the all-time leader in prize winnings from beach volleyball, a figure approaching $3 million in 2000. With his perpetually tanned and toned six-foot, two-inch frame, Kiraly also snared a number of endorsement deals with companies including Coppertone suntan lotion, Speedo swimsuits, Revo sunglasses, and Swatch watches. He took a leadership role in the Association of Volleyball Professionals (AVP), a group organized by players to oversee the professional tour. Kiraly criticized the FIVB's efforts to exert more control over the sport, particularly its determination of the eligibility process for Olympic teams and its requirement that players wear more revealing uniforms while competing. Although Kiraly hoped to compete in his fourth Olympic games in Sydney, Australia, in 2000, an injury to his right shoulder in August 2000 put him out of competition for the rest of the season.

As a three-time gold medalist in indoor and beach volleyball, Kiraly was recognized as the preeminent volleyball player of his generation for his impressive record. As the first great Olympic champion in the sport of volleyball, however, Kiraly's stature among his colleagues and growing number of fans was already assured.

★

Kiraly published an account of his life and career with the cowriter Byron Shewman, *Sandman: An Autobiography* (1999). Kiraly also produced two volleyball guides with Shewman, *Karch Kiraly's Championship Volleyball* (1990), and *Beach Volleyball: Techniques, Training, and Tactics from the Game's Greatest Player* (1999). Shewman covered the history of the sport in *Volleyball Centennial: The First 100 Years* (1995). Coverage of Kiraly's 1996 gold-medal performance at the Atlanta Olympics appeared in *Sports Illustrated* (5 Aug. 1996). Kiraly's career has also been covered extensively in the sports pages of the *Los Angeles Times*.

TIMOTHY BORDEN

KLEM, William Joseph ("Bill") (*b.* 22 February 1874 in Rochester, New York; *d.* 16 September 1951 in Coral Gables, Florida), National League umpire from 1905 until 1940, and one of eight umpires selected to the National Baseball Hall of Fame. His ingenuity and dedication shaped the profession more than any other individual.

Klem (originally "Klimm") was born to German parents, Michael Klimm, a cooper, and Elizabeth Ehrmentraut. He grew up in the town of Rochester, and in his teens, he played semiprofessional baseball around Rochester as a first baseman or a catcher. In 1898 arm trouble forced him to give up the game he so loved. He continued to play in the sandlots and took up umpiring. He moved up quickly and first umpired professionally in the Connecticut State League in 1902. He proceeded through the ranks in the New York State League (1903) and the American Association (1904). His friend, major league umpire Silk O'Loughlin, warned him, "Stay away from it. Umpiring is a lousy business." Bill was not discouraged and made his debut as a National League umpire in 1905.

Umpiring has always been a thankless profession. Since the inception of the first professional baseball league in 1876, umpires have been subjected to the taunts of fans, the abuse of managers, and the disrespect of players. Klem came into the profession at a dangerous time. It was not uncommon for umpires to be beaten on the field by angry managers or chased by enraged mobs of fans after the game. Hall of Famer John Ward was said to have gained great respect by "punching the face of the man who dared make a bad call." In 1907 the old adage, "Kill the umpire," almost came true when Billy Evans lay near death for several days as the result of a bottle being thrown by a fan. The constant abuse made for a difficult life for umpires, often leading to alcoholism and depression.

Bill Klem, 1944. AP/WIDE WORLD PHOTOS

It is questionable whether the quality of umpiring was not deserving of the derision it received. Umpires were little more than ex-ballplayers or citizens who were down on their luck. They had little interest in improving their situation or doing a good job on the field. The low pay (as little as $5 per game) did not attract respectable people to the profession and often left them open to the persuasions of gamblers. Klem's tough-nosed nature and appreciation for the sport helped to change many of the problems with umpiring. His work resulted in better locker facilities and higher wages for all umpires. He was famous for "drawing a line" in the dirt that enraged players and managers were not to cross. Most importantly, his claim to have never missed a call in his heart added a dignity that had been missing in umpiring.

This is not to say he was never surrounded by controversy. Klem's confident nature often irritated those who were on the wrong side of his calls. One archenemy was the great New York Giant manager, John McGraw. After being tossed by Klem from a 1905 game, McGraw attempted to get Klem banished from the National League. Klem replied, "Mr. Manager, if it's possible for you to take my job away from me, I don't want the job." At times Klem's antics on the field bordered on egotism. He was given the nickname of "Catfish" due to some particular facial features. According to catcher Chief Meyers, "All you had to do was call him Catfish and out of the game you'd go. Maybe it was because he had rather prominent lips, and when he'd call a ball or a strike he'd let fly a rather fine spray from his mouth. Sort of gave the general impression of a catfish, you know."

Klem's ingenuity also developed many of the standards of the way umpiring is practiced today. He was the first umpire to institute hand signals so those outside of earshot knew exactly what his call was. He was also the first to use the inside chest protector. Klem said it gave him a better look at the strike zone because it allowed him to get closer to the catcher. The inside chest protector was the standard in the National League for most of the twentieth century and is now mandatory in both leagues.

Klem's record on the field is a testament to his supreme skill as an umpire and the respect he demanded around the league. He umpired strictly behind the plate for sixteen consecutive years due to his natural talent for judging balls and strikes and handling a game professionally. He also umpired in a record eighteen World Series, including five straight from 1911 to 1915. He worked the first All-Star game in 1933. His skill and respect earned him the nickname "The Old Arbitrator."

At a game in 1940, after a difficult call, Klem questioned his own ability. Not willing to continue on past his peak, Klem retired that afternoon. He was so valuable to baseball, however, that from 1941 until his death he served as the National League chief of umpires.

Klem married Marie Kranz in 1910. She traveled everywhere with her husband during his career in order to help banish the loneliness of the road. The two were childless, and they remained married until Klem died of a heart attack in 1951. He is buried in Graceland Memorial Park in Coral Gables.

Klem's hard work, honesty, and confidence helped to make baseball a better game for all involved. At a ceremony to honor Klem at New York's Polo Grounds on 2 September 1949, he professed, "Baseball to me is not a game; it is a religion."

★

No complete biography of Klem has been written. A great series of articles written by Klem with William J. Slocum appeared in *Collier's Magazine* in 1951. An excerpt is included in Charles Einstein, ed., *The Fireside Book of Baseball* (1956). A personal portrait of Klem and a reflection on how he was viewed by other umpires is evident in Jocko Conlan with Robert Creamer, *Jocko* (1967). Klem's clipping and photo files at the National Baseball Hall of Fame Library in Cooperstown, New York, are valuable sources of information. Some motion picture clips of Klem are also available at the library. See Klem in action in a film entitled *The Hall of Famers: Reel #2*, produced by the Hall of Fame. An obituary is in the *Sporting News* (26 Sept. 1951).

JEREMY JONES

KNIGHT, Robert Montgomery ("Bob") (*b.* 25 October 1940 in Massillon, Ohio), college basketball coach who won three national championships during his twenty-nine seasons at Indiana University while gaining notoriety for his misconduct on and off the court.

Knight, the only child of Carroll "Pat" Knight, a railroad man, and Hazel Menthorne Knight, a homemaker, grew up in Orrville, Ohio. Early on he excelled in sports, playing little league baseball and then, from the sixth grade on, basketball. He was six feet, one inch tall by the eighth grade, and although he also played football and baseball at Orrville High School, his real love was basketball. He made the varsity team as a freshman and was the captain his senior year. He averaged twenty-four points per game and, now at six feet, four inches tall, was named the school's best male athlete. He was also an excellent student, intellectually curious and inquisitive, although he was sometimes outspoken—a conflict with his coach resulted in a one-game suspension his senior year. Knight's marriage to Nancy Falk, a classmate at Orrville High, produced two sons, one of whom later played for him at Indiana University.

Bob Knight, 1998. © REUTERS NEWMEDIA INC./CORBIS

Graduating eighth in a class of eighty in 1958, Knight was attracted to Ohio State University (OSU) in Columbus by its tremendous basketball program under the coach Fred Taylor. OSU's team featured such stars as John Havlicek and Jerry Lucas. Knight, who played forward, was a good shooter but comparatively slow and prone to foul trouble. He started only a few games during his junior and senior seasons but was nonetheless named to the 1960 National Collegiate Athletic Association (NCAA) championship team. Perhaps his best moment as a college player came in the 1961 NCAA title game, when he scored his only basket, tying the game in the last minute, although Cincinnati went on to win in overtime.

As a student at OSU, Knight gravitated toward the subject of history, which remained a lifelong interest. Havlicek called him the smartest player on the team and Taylor, who admitted that Knight certainly was a character, used a less complimentary description, calling him "the brat from Orrville." After graduating with a B.S. in education and a minor in history and government in 1962, Knight was hired as a teacher and junior varsity basketball coach at Cuyahoga Falls (Ohio) High School. His famous temper began to show itself almost immediately, when he broke a clipboard in frustration during his first game there.

The following year Taylor, who remained a lifelong mentor and friend, got wind of an opening on the coaching staff at the U.S. Military Academy at West Point, New York, and informed Knight, who joined the staff in 1963 under the coach Tates Locke. In 1965, at age twenty-four, Knight became the youngest head coach in Division I basketball and proceeded to create the most successful era of basketball in Army history. His teams made four National Invitation Tournament (NIT) appearances during his six years as the coach, never lost to their arch rivals from the U.S. Naval Academy, led the nation in team defense, and earned a 22–6 record and their first-ever national ranking (sixteenth) in 1970—all this with a height limitation of six feet, six inches as well as a mandatory military commitment of five years of service upon graduation. The West Point authorities were displeased with Knight's volatile behavior during games, but this attracted little attention outside the academy.

During his time in New York, Knight studied the coaching philosophies and writings of the legendary West Point football coach Red Blaik and made contacts that developed into relationships with several of the older generation of football and basketball coaches, most notably Pete Newell, the retired coach of the 1959 NCAA championship team from the University of California. The two met in 1969 at the Cable Car Classic in San Francisco; Knight regarded Newell as the game's greatest coach and they collaborated regularly.

Knight returned to his Big Ten Conference roots in 1971 when he was named as the head coach at Indiana University (IU) in Bloomington. In Knight's second season, the IU Hoosiers won twenty games, gained the Big Ten title, and made the Final Four, losing to the University of California, Los Angeles (UCLA) in the semifinals. Knight's next team won another Big Ten crown and finished 23–5. His 1974–1975 team attracted the greatest attention yet, going 31–0 and gaining a number-one ranking before losing its regional final to the University of Kentucky, 92–90.

The Hoosiers were undefeated national champions in 1976, a feat not to be repeated in the rest of the twentieth century, with a team featuring Kent Benson, Tom Abernathy, and Scott May, all of whom went on to play for at least five years in the National Basketball Association (NBA). Indiana again won the NCAA title in 1981, led by the sophomore guard and future NBA star Isiah Thomas. In 1987 Knight won his third NCAA title with a team led by the Indiana high-school basketball legend and future college coach Steve Alford.

Knight stressed preparation, especially for big games, man-to-man defensive pressure, and the motion offense; he also used film and video to teach his players. He was known for getting the most out of his players, on whom he put great and constant pressure. Upon their graduation, former players were grateful for the caring and loyalty Knight expressed toward them. He closely adhered to the NCAA rules, recruiting only athletes willing to be students, monitored class attendance, and achieved a graduation rate of over 90 percent among those who stayed with the Indiana program.

Nicknamed "the general," Knight became a successful and entertaining speaker on the lecture circuit during the 1970s, both within and outside the coaching world, as well as a spokesman for academic values in college sports. He denounced gambling, complained about late weeknight games scheduled to accommodate television broadcasts, and publicly suggested that classroom teachers were grading their students far too easily and demanding far too little from them. He long resisted recruiting junior college players, but in the mid-1980s, deciding he had to change with the times, he began doing so, also adding some zone defenses to his trademark man-to-man. He coached the U.S. teams to gold medals at the 1979 Pan-American Games in San Juan, Puerto Rico, and the 1984 Olympics in Los Angeles. His fame became international when a Brazilian student named Jamar Themoteo Silva wrote his master's thesis about Knight's coaching methods.

At San Juan in 1979 Knight was arrested and fined in a minor incident with a police officer, following his expulsion from a game for berating an official. The incident attracted great attention, sowing the seeds for the eventual end of his IU coaching career. Even casual sports fans began to know Knight as the coach who, when frustrated by officials' calls, threw a chair onto the Assembly Hall court in Bloomington during a 1985 game with Purdue University (he apologized the next day); the video of this incident dogged him for years. From then on he was a marked man by elements in the national media. His fall came in 2000 after the discovery of a three-year-old video showing him choking the player Neil Reed for over two seconds. This was too much for IU's trustees and he was suspended with the warning that no further outbursts would be tolerated. Four months later, on 10 September 2000, Knight was fired after he roughly grabbed a student by the arm. The IU president Myles Brand cited Knight's "pattern of unacceptable behavior" as the basis for his dismissal. On 23 March 2001 Knight was hired to coach at Texas Technological University in Lubbock.

Knight's coaching record was extraordinary. His 1976 Hoosier team was the only undefeated Division I men's team in the post–John Wooden era (33–0). He was one of only three coaches to win NCAA, NIT, and Olympic titles. His overall coaching record through the year 2000 was 763–290, a .725 winning percentage. Sixteen of his assistant coaches became head college coaches and his most famous player at West Point, Mike Krzyzewski, went on to become a successful coach at Duke University in North Carolina. Knight's highly publicized lack of self-control, however, gave him an unsavory reputation despite an enviable record. He was voted into the Naismith Memorial Basketball Hall of Fame in 1991.

★

For details about Knight and his teams, see John Feinstein, *A Season on the Brink: A Year with Bob Knight and the Indiana Hoosiers* (1986), and Joan Mellen, *Bob Knight: His Own Man* (1988). Steve Alford gives a player's perspective in his memoir, written with John Garrity, *Playing for Knight: My Six Seasons with Coach Knight* (1989). Knight's dismissal from Indiana University is chronicled in Phil Berger, *Knight Fall: Bobby Knight: The Truth Behind America's Most Controversial Coach* (2000), which includes an appendix with Knight's complete public statement of 9 September 1979 regarding the San Juan incident. Knight's relationship with Pete Newell, among other things, is included in Bruce Jenkins, *A Good Man: The Pete Newell Story* (1999).

LAWSON BOWLING

KONO, Tommy Tamio (*b.* 27 June 1930 in Sacramento, California), amateur weightlifter who, as Olympic and world champion from 1952 to 1959, is widely acknowledged as one of the greatest strength athletes of all time.

Kono was the youngest of four sons of Kanichi Kono and Ichimi Ohata, both of whom worked in a Sacramento fruit cannery. Afflicted with asthma, Tommy weighed only seventy-four pounds at age eleven and missed a third of his schooling owing to illness. When his family was moved with other Japanese Americans during World War II to the Tule Lake Detention Camp in June 1942 in California, Kono discovered that the desert air relieved his breathing. By this time he had learned about bodybuilding from a Charles Atlas "ninety-seven-pound weakling" advertisement, and two Nisei (a person born and raised in the United States whose parents came from Japan) friends, Ben Hara and Tad Fujioka, assured him that a regular weight-training program would make him big and strong. Aboard a Greyhound bus, the family left the detention camp and returned to Sacramento on 3 December 1945.

Initially only able to bench press sixty-five pounds, Kono soon overcame his weakness and, as a high school senior in Sacramento, entered his first competition in 1948 in San Jose, California. He placed second as a lightweight with a 175-pound press, 185-pound snatch, and a 225-pound clean-and-jerk. Employing a routine of heavy squats for high repetitions, Kono quickly improved his basic strength. In 1949 he became Pacific Coast champion and won the outstanding lifter award, and in his first senior nationals in 1950 in Philadelphia, he nearly upset reigning champion Joe Pitman.

Kono was inducted into the U.S. Army in 1952 and sent to Camp Stillman in California in preparation to enter the Korean War. Friends who knew of his skill intervened, however, and he was transferred to Fort Mason in San Francisco so he could be near Oakland, then the center of American weightlifting. The army paid for his training, and

Tommy Kono, 1958. AP/WIDE WORLD PHOTOS

at the Olympics held in Helsinki in 1952 he achieved a world-record 259-pound snatch on his way to winning a gold medal in the lightweight class. Kono moved to Hawaii in 1955, and during the next several years, under the guidance of physician Richard You, he dominated the middling classes in world competition. As a middleweight, he won world championships in 1953, 1957, 1958, and 1959, and a silver medal at the 1960 Olympics in Rome. As a light heavyweight, he captured world titles in 1954 and 1955, and a gold medal in the 1956 Olympics in Melbourne with a world record 986-pound (three-lift) total. Always the linchpin for American teams in the 1950s, Kono excelled as a clutch performer.

An essential ingredient to Kono's success, derived from training alone in the basement of his home in his early years, was his ability to concentrate. Weightlifting, he contends, is possibly the closest of all the sports to Zen—a form of Buddhism involving an intense state of meditation rather than adherence to scripture or doctrine. Complete mastery of mind over body enabled him to lift very heavy weights when it counted most. Nowhere was this trait more evident than during his later career. Though plagued by knee injuries, he set world records in the press in 1961 in competitions in Moscow and Tokyo and held off a determined effort by Louisiana champion Lou Riecke to upset him at the national championships in the same year. In one of the most memorable moments in the annals of American weightlifting, Kono again beat Riecke with a superhuman 375-pound clean-and-jerk at the 1963 senior nationals, thereby earning him the best lifter award for the seventh time. For Kono, however, the most dramatic moment of his career was his victory at the 1957 world championships in Tehran. After twice failing to clear 358 pounds, he "shook, shivered, and quivered" under his final attempt in the clean-and-jerk to defeat his Russian adversary, Fyodor Bogdanovsky, on bodyweight. With only a skeleton American contingent present, he was seized by elated Iranians who carried him off the platform, almost as if he was their national hero.

By the time of his retirement in 1965, Kono had become an enduring icon in national and international lifting circles. He officially established seven Olympic, thirty-seven American, eight Pan American, and twenty-six world records. Extremely versatile, he is the only weightlifter to win medals in three different Olympiads in three different weight classes. He is also the only lifter to set world records in four separate weight classifications. Though known chiefly for his mental lifting and mastery of technique, Kono's feats of raw strength were prodigious. At a bodyweight of 152, he performed six sets of squats with 340 pounds for twelve repetitions in less than a half-hour. As a light heavyweight he did a front squat with 451 pounds and pressed a pair of 112.5-pound dumbbells for ten repe-

titions. Though standards in the press were becoming increasingly lax in the late 1950s, Kono displayed real strength by executing this lift in relatively strict style and continuing to set world records in it. By no means the least significant aspect of his accomplishments is that they preceded the introduction of anabolic steroids into the sport.

Kono always exuded a quiet and unassuming demeanor. He kept a cool head and was extremely helpful to teammates during training and competition. He repeatedly captained American teams abroad and, as a photography buff, frequently took pictures at meets. Kono, who believed that brides and barbells do not mix, delayed marriage until 4 May 1962. He met his wife, Florence Rodrigues, in December 1956, and they had three children. Following retirement from competition, Kono served as national weightlifting coach for Mexico, West Germany, and the United States for the 1968, 1972, and 1976 Olympics, respectively, and from 1987 until 1989 he coached the U.S. Women's World Team. During the 1980s and 1990s he worked for the city and county of Honolulu, Hawaii, as a recreation specialist. He also continued to officiate at national and international competitions, to serve on the board of the U.S. Weightlifting Federation, and to conduct weightlifting seminars throughout the Western Hemisphere.

Although weightlifting is his only sport, the versatile Kono won the Mr. World physique title in 1954 and Mr. Universe titles in 1955, 1957, and 1961—all held in conjunction with world weightlifting championships. In 1959 he was honored by a resolution passed by the House of Representatives of Hawaii's first legislative session for his "great achievements and contributions to the State of Hawaii." In 1990 he was inducted to the U.S. Olympic Hall of Fame, and in 1991 to the International Weightlifting Federation Hall of Fame. A particularly proud moment was in 1996, when Kono was invited as one of the "100 Golden Olympians" to be a special guest to the Centennial Olympic Games in Atlanta. No weightlifter has won the prestigious Sullivan Award of the Amateur Athletic Union, but Kono was runner-up four times. In a 1982 poll conducted by Hungarian Ferenc Fejer for the official magazine of the International Weightlifting Federation, Tommy Kono was rated the greatest weightlifter of all time.

★

A complete chronicle of Kono's lifting career is available in Osmo Kiiha, "The Incredible Tommy Kono," *The Iron Master* (5 Dec. 1990). Other useful portraits include A. Grove Day, "America's Mightiest Little Man," *Coronet* (July 1960); Harry McLaughlin, "Real Life Story of Tommy Kono," *Strength and Health* 32 (May 1964); Bill Kwon, "He's the Greatest, That's All," *Honolulu Star-Bulletin* (6 Aug. 1982); and Kwon, "Kono in U.S. Olympic Hall of Fame," *Honolulu Star-Bulletin* (5 July 1990). In addition to many training articles, the most complete rendering of Kono's own thoughts on the sport is available in his book *Weightlifting, Olympic Style* (2001).

JOHN D. FAIR

KOUFAX, Sanford ("Sandy") (*b*. 30 December 1935 in Brooklyn, New York), left-handed pitcher for the Brooklyn Dodgers and the Los Angeles Dodgers. In a five-year span of excellence, he led the National League in strikeouts for four years, threw a then-record four no-hitters, including a perfect game, and earned three Cy Young awards.

Koufax was the son of Jack and Evelyn Braun. His parents divorced when he was three years old, and his mother remarried six years later to Irving Koufax, a New York attorney. Adopted by his stepfather, Koufax attended Lafayette High School, where he starred as a guard on the basketball team and was a starting first baseman and backup pitcher on the baseball team. His basketball skills earned him a scholarship to the University of Cincinnati, where he majored in architecture his freshman year.

Koufax started as a forward on the Bearcats' freshman basketball team and decided to try out for the baseball team when he learned of the team's travel plans to New Orleans. Despite being an uncontrollably wild pitcher at times, Koufax impressed major league scouts with the speed of his

Sandy Koufax, 1962. © BETTMANN/CORBIS

fastball, which allowed him to strike out 51 batters in 32 innings.

On 14 December 1954 the eighteen-year-old Koufax was signed to a major league contract by Brooklyn Dodgers team president Walter O'Malley. Because he had received a substantial $14,000 signing bonus, Koufax was kept on the Dodgers' twenty-five-man major league roster and never pitched in the minor leagues. From 1955 to 1958 he pitched sporadically, and because he had pitched sparingly in high school and during his lone season at the University of Cincinnati, Koufax was placed in the unenviable position of having to learn his craft against major league hitters.

His rising fastball, estimated by scouts to range between 95 and 100 miles per hour, allowed him to post impressive strikeout totals even in his formative seasons. But his wildness also led to high walk and hit totals, and his inconsistency in his early years is best reflected by his mediocre winning percentage. When the Dodgers moved from Brooklyn to Los Angeles in 1958, Koufax responded to the change in scenery by going 8–6 in 1959 and registering 173 strikeouts in 153.1 innings, an average of 10 strikeouts per 9 innings. On 31 August Koufax struck out 18 San Francisco Giants to tie Bob Feller's major league record, helping the Dodgers to the World Series against the Chicago White Sox.

In 1961, on the advice of Dodgers catcher Norm Sherry, Koufax altered his mental approach to pitching by not trying to overthrow and strike out every hitter. He also fine-tuned his pitching mechanics, working with Dodgers pitching coach Joe Becker and scout Kenny Meyers to tighten his delivery to get a better view of home plate. Koufax responded to this coaching by going 18–13 in 1961 and leading the National League in strikeouts with 269. He was named to the National League's All-Star Team for the first time, beginning a span of six straight seasons he would be so honored.

In 1962 Koufax threw his first no-hitter, a 5–0 win over the New York Mets on 30 June, and the 1963 season saw Koufax become the dominant pitcher in baseball. Relying on a rising fastball and sweeping curveball, he led the National League with a 25–5 record, a 1.88 earned run average (ERA), and 306 strikeouts in 311 innings. On 11 May he threw his second no-hitter when he beat the San Francisco Giants 8–0. Koufax earned his first Cy Young award that season, as the best pitcher in both leagues. Leading the Dodgers to the National League pennant, Koufax was named the game one starter in the World Series against the two-time defending world champion New York Yankees. Opposing Yankees ace Edward "Whitey" Ford in Yankee Stadium, Koufax established a then-Series record with 15 strikeouts in a 5–2 victory. Koufax also beat Ford in game four, allowing the Dodgers to sweep the Yankees and earning himself Most Valuable Player (MVP) honors in the process. At the end of the season, Koufax was named Male Athlete of the Year by the Associated Press and baseball's Player of the Year by the *Sporting News.*

In 1964 injury kept Koufax from winning twenty games for the second time in three seasons, but despite the onset of arthritis in his pitching arm, he threw his third no-hitter, a 3–0 win in Philadelphia on 4 June. In 1965 Koufax embarked on one of the greatest pitching campaigns in major league history, when he went 26–8 with a 2.04 ERA and a National League record of 382 strikeouts in 335.2 innings. He threw a perfect game on 9 September against the Cubs, winning 1–0. Teamed with right-handed ace Don Drysdale in a one-two pitching combination unmatched in major league history, Koufax helped carry the Dodgers to another National League pennant.

Koufax made national headlines when he refused to pitch game one of the 1965 World Series against the Minnesota Twins due to his observance of the Jewish holiday, Yom Kippur. Koufax's religious stand transformed him in the eyes of many from a great pitcher to a great man. After losing game two, Koufax recorded shutout wins in games five and seven, leading the Dodgers to their second Series win in three years and again earning himself the World Series MVP award. He was also named the Associated Press Male Athlete of the Year, Sportsman of the Year by *Sports Illustrated,* and baseball's Player of the Year by the *Sporting News.* Koufax continued this mound dominance in 1966. Ignoring his increasingly painful arthritis, he posted career-best marks with 27 wins and a 1.73 ERA. Both marks were again league bests, and he led the National League in strikeouts for the fifth straight time, posting 317. He was voted the Cy Young Award winner for the second time in three seasons and the third time since 1963.

With Drysdale suffering a subpar season, Koufax shouldered the burden of leading the light-hitting Dodgers to a second straight league pennant and into another World Series. No one knew at the time, but game two of the series, on 6 October 1966, marked Koufax's final mound appearance in the major leagues. He was scheduled to start game five in Baltimore, but the Orioles swept the Dodgers in four straight.

On 18 November Koufax stunned the sports world by announcing his retirement due to arthritis. Over his final five seasons, he had gone 111–34 with 100 complete games and 33 shutouts, and pitched 4 no-hitters, including a perfect game. He became the first pitcher to strike out 300 batters in three different seasons and twice struck out 18 hitters in a game. He set another major league record by leading the league in ERA for five straight seasons. Despite the presence of such all-time greats as Willie Mays, Mickey Mantle, and Roberto Clemente, Koufax was named Player of the Decade in the 1960s.

Koufax celebrated his thirty-first birthday by signing a lucrative ten-year contract to serve as a major league base-

ball analyst for NBC. After years as one of pro sports' most eligible bachelors, the thirty-three-year-old Koufax married twenty-three-year-old Anne Widmark, the daughter of actor Richard Widmark, on New Year's Day, 1969. The couple moved from Los Angeles to a farmhouse in North Ellsworth, Maine. (They were divorced in the 1980s, and Koufax subsequently married and divorced a second time.) Koufax left NBC following the 1972 season but returned to baseball in 1979 as a pitching coach for the Dodgers. He remained with the Dodgers through 1982 and then left the team to serve as a volunteer coach in various major league camps.

Shy and retiring, Koufax avoided the media glare in his retirement years. Rarely granting interviews, he developed an aura of mystery and intrigue. In 1972 he became the youngest man ever elected to the Baseball Hall of Fame when he was inducted at the age of thirty-six. That same year he was honored at Dodger Stadium in a special ceremony retiring his uniform number, thirty-two. In 1999 Koufax was named to baseball's All-Century Team as one of the 100 greatest players in major league history. Koufax was also named by ESPN as one of the top fifty athletes of the century, the only baseball pitcher to be so honored.

★

Koufax teamed with author Ed Linn to write his autobiography, *Koufax* (1966). Koufax's life and career has also been the subject of several books: Arnold Hano, *Sandy Koufax: Strikeout King* (1964); George Vecsey, *The Baseball Life of Sandy Koufax* (1968); and Ed Gruver, *Koufax* (2000). Some magazine articles featuring Koufax are *Sports Illustrated* (4 Jan., 4 Apr., and 28 Nov. 1966); *Newsweek* (28 Mar., 8 Aug., and 28 Nov. 1966); *Life* (1 Apr. 1966); and *Time* (9 Sept. and 25 Nov. 1966). Of particular help in understanding Koufax is Tom Verducci, "The Left Arm of God," *Sports Illustrated* (12 July 1999).

EDWARD GRUVER

KRAMER, John Albert ("Jack") (*b.* 1 August 1921 in Las Vegas, Nevada), tennis champion, tennis promoter, and proponent of percentage tennis.

Kramer was born in Las Vegas, the son of David Kramer, a locomotive engineer. The family moved to Montebello, California, a Los Angeles suburb, so that Kramer could benefit from the top-notch tennis instructors there. After studying at Montebello High School, he spent one semester at the University of Southern California in Los Angeles, then one year at Rollins College in Winter Park, Florida, which was then one of the magnet schools for top tennis talent. He served in the U.S. Coast Guard during World War II, and then was ready to devote himself to the game of tennis.

The sport of tennis had suffered during the war. Some

Jack Kramer. AP/WIDE WORLD PHOTOS

Kramer had his first big success at the U.S. National Singles Championships at Forest Hills, New York, in 1946. He went on to win the Wimbledon tournament in England in 1947, repeated his victory at Forest Hills, and then turned professional. In the late 1940s there was still a distinct separation between the amateur and professional games; "open" tennis, meaning tournaments that were open to both amateurs and professionals, did not begin until 1968.

Kramer shone as a professional. He embarked on year-long odysseys in which he faced the same opponent, night after night, in different cities and towns. Two of his most memorable challenges were from Riggs in 1947 and Pancho Gonzales in 1949. Kramer smothered both of them, defeating Riggs by 81–20 and Gonzales by 96–27, as measured by their "one-on-one" tour totals. When questioned years later, Kramer often asserted that both Riggs and Gonzales were better players technically than he was, but that he had learned the knack of winning on the grueling tour and they had not.

Years of injuries eventually took their toll, and Kramer retired from playing tennis in 1952. He quickly began directing and managing tennis stars and events, in the style of an impresario. Kramer became the manager for the men's professional tour, which, in the words of the tennis commentator Bud Collins, was "four guys and a canvas court. They jaunted wherever the schedule, made up by their boss, Jack Kramer, carried them."

The 1950s were a time when great champions played for relatively small purses. Tennis players who wanted to earn some type of a living had to turn professional, and by doing so excluded themselves from the four big events of the Australian, French, English, and U.S. championships. This was a stiff price to pay, but nearly all of Kramer's sports contemporaries turned professional: Gonzales in 1949; Tony Trabert in 1956; and Ken Rosewall and Lew Hoad, the Australian boy wonders, in 1957. These formidable men, with egos to match, were subsequently managed and directed by Kramer, who decided on a schedule and sent his men and their canvas court around the world.

In his autobiography *The Game: My Forty Years in Tennis* (1979), Kramer said that he never missed playing, and that directing the tour was a wonderful new challenge. Still, professional tennis languished during the early 1960s, and talented athletes like Gonzales and Rod Laver played for even less money than they had previously. Fortunately, most of them were saved by the inauguration of open tennis in the spring of 1968. It was too late for Kramer as a player, but he took advantage of the new open tournaments by directing world championship tennis for several years. He also worked as a television broadcaster for NBC until he made some derogatory comments about the women's side of the game, for which he was fired. Kramer found another

major championships had not been held, no big new players had emerged, and the tennis world was caught between nostalgia for the earlier heyday of Donald Budge and the new tennis exemplified by Bobby Riggs. Into this mixture came the young Kramer, who soon showed his competitive spirit and heart. Known as the Hard Luck Kid, Kramer had to withdraw from several competitions and lost others due to injuries and illnesses including appendicitis, blisters, and tennis elbow. Whether these were simply run-of-the-mill ailments or whether they were brought on by his intense style cannot be determined. Regardless, Kramer changed men's tennis.

Even the greatest earlier champions, William Tilden and Budge among them, essentially had been all-court players, men who could play equally well in almost any location of the court. Kramer eschewed this approach, concentrating on what he called "percentage tennis" and what his admirers called the "big game." Kramer took the net each and every time it was possible, and used the "serve-volley" style of tennis to blast opponents off the court. While this style was intimidating, Kramer always claimed he employed it because he followed the percentages. It took far less energy, he argued, to follow a serve or approach shot to the net than it did to run back and forth around the baseline, in an ongoing duel.

audience when he and Frank Deford published *The Game*. As someone who had watched Ellsworth Vines and played the greats from Budge to Riggs, Kramer was uniquely able to comment on the sport's progression and retrogression, both as a sportscaster and as an author. Never one to hold back, he let his opinions fly in a manner that reminded some of his serves and volleys from thirty years earlier.

According to Kramer, Budge was the best player, day in and day out, that tennis had ever seen. But on an individual, one-day-at-a-time basis, Kramer rated Vines as the deadliest player ever to hit a serve. Kramer surprised many fans by placing Laver in the tier of "second greats," despite his sweeps of the four championships in 1962 and 1969, and by asserting that Riggs at his best would have beaten most of the other top players, including Gonzales. Most interesting was Kramer's alternative list of champions— his conjecture on who would have triumphed at Wimbledon and Forest Hills had the open tennis era begun in 1940 instead of 1968. Kramer speculated that he would have won five Wimbledons (instead of one) and five times at Forest Hills (instead of once). He also theorized that Gonzales would have won six Wimbledons (instead of none) and seven Forest Hills championships (instead of two).

In *The Game*, Kramer also addressed a question that perplexed fans and specialists alike: How would the greats of the 1930s and 1940s have fared against those of the 1970s? For example, what might have been the result of a match between Budge at his best and Bjorn Borg at his? Kramer asserted that the players of the 1930s and 1940s were better, both physically and mentally. Playing for peanuts as they did, they had to keep more finely toned and engaged in marathons of 100 matches per season. By contrast, Kramer opined that when big money came into the game after 1970 it hindered the development of many players whose talents were wasted in highly profitable exhibition matches. Kramer praised both Jimmy Connors and Borg for their technical skills, but placed them both in his second-rank tier of greats (with the possibility of moving up to the highest level). Because *The Game* was published in 1979, Kramer could not comment on Borg's eventual five Wimbledon victories or on the emergence of another prodigy, John McEnroe.

Often controversial and admired by many, Kramer exemplified the clean-cut U.S. look of the decade immediately following World War II. His remarkable tennis play, his dogged promotion of the professional tennis tour, and his keen insights made him one of the sport's most important commentators. Kramer did not make the big money that came in the open era, but like many of his contemporaries he claimed he had more fun than the money-driven players of the 1970s and later. For all this and more, Collins created an apt nickname for Kramer—the Magnet.

★

Kramer and Frank Deford coauthored *The Game: My Forty Years in Tennis* (1979). More information can be found in Bud Collins, *My Life with the Pros* (1989). See also "Jack Kramer," *Time* (1 Sept. 1947), an issue in which he also appeared on the cover; and Will Grimsley, *Tennis: Its History, People, and Events* (1971).

SAMUEL WILLARD CROMPTON

KRONE, Julieanne Louise ("Julie") (*b.* 24 July 1963 in Benton Harbor, Michigan), jockey best known as the first woman to win a Triple Crown race and the first woman to be inducted into the Thoroughbred Racing Hall of Fame.

Krone is the second child and only daughter of Judi Krone, a prizewinning show rider and breeder of horses, and Don Krone, an art teacher at Benton Harbor High School, who moonlighted as an instructor of art and photography at Lake Michigan College. Krone grew up on a farm near Eau Claire, Michigan, and began riding horses at the age of two. At age five she won the Berrien County Youth Fair horse show in the twenty-one-and-under division. By the time Krone was fifteen, her parents had separated. She almost joined a circus, after she impressed the owner with her ability to perform with horses, but decided to become a jockey instead.

In 1979 Krone obtained a job at Churchill Downs in Louisville, Kentucky, as a groom and exercise rider; she had not yet reached the legal working age of sixteen, but her mother, who had driven with her from Michigan, changed the month on her birth certificate from July to April. She lived with a trainer, Clarence Picou, and his wife, Donna. Krone dropped out of high school in her senior year and flew to Tampa, Florida, to live with her grandparents and race at the Tampa Bay Downs.

As a result of Krone's short stature (she was four feet, eight-and-a-half inches tall at the time), she was initially mistaken for a lost child by the wife of a trainer. Five weeks later, on 12 February 1981, Krone demonstrated her expertise as a rider and was in the winner's circle at the Tampa Bay Downs with a gelding named Lord Farckle. On 25 August 1981, for her first time, Krone won three races in the same day.

Also that year, Krone's brother moved to Maryland, and her mother, no longer on speaking terms with her, moved to Florida. Krone's ties with her past had been broken: the family farm and Krone's favorite horse, Ralph, had been sold, and her best friend from childhood had been killed in a motorcycle accident.

Soon after, Krone was given a sixty-day suspension from the track after police found marijuana in her car, and she had to attend a drug rehabilitation class. Her riding ability

Julie Krone. AP/WIDE WORLD PHOTOS

did not suffer from her lack of practice, however. On her first day back in competition, Krone won both of her assigned races. In 1982, at nineteen, she won the riding title at the Atlantic City, New Jersey, track, as the jockey with the most wins at that track that year. Unfortunately, after falling off a horse during a workout at Laurel Park in Maryland, Krone broke her back and was off the tracks for four months.

Five years after winning her first riding title at the Atlantic City track, Krone was the leading winner in 1987 at both Monmouth and the Meadowlands, in New Jersey. The next year Krone led in jockey standings for much of the winter meet at the Aqueduct in New York before finishing second. By 1989 she was the nation's third leading rider with 368 wins.

Krone became a fixture on the New York circuit in 1991, which was her most successful year in terms of earnings. During the 1992–1993 season she became the number-one jockey at Florida's Gulfstream Park. On 5 June 1993 Krone once again made history as the first woman to win a Triple Crown race, a feat she achieved at the Belmont Stakes; she was aboard the thirteen-to-one long shot Colonial Affair. On 20 August 1993 she became the third jockey in history to win five races in one day at Saratoga.

Her happiness was short-lived, however, because ten days later she suffered serious injuries after being kicked in the chest by a horse, resulting in a cardiac contusion, a fractured right ankle, and a wounded elbow. Krone married Matt Muzikar in 1995 and continued riding, only to become injured once again on 13 January 1996 when she broke both of her hands.

After this injury Krone suffered from depression and was diagnosed with post-traumatic stress disorder. She began seeing a psychiatrist for help in the healing process of both mind and body. As a result of her experience as an athlete suffering from a psychological disorder, Krone became a spokesperson for the Pfizer and Women's Sports Foundation—Minds in Motion Depression Awareness Campaign. She also became involved with the American Psychiatric Association's Annual Meeting in 2000, sponsored by the International Society of Sport Psychiatry.

On 23 March 1998 Krone was one of three athletes honored at the Nassau County Sports Commission Awards Dinner in New York. She was also a guest at the Franciscan Games Dinner on 19 September 1998. The following year was a difficult one for Krone: her mother died after battling cancer, she divorced her husband and moved to California, and she announced her retirement at the Aqueduct racetrack.

Since then Krone has served as a racing analyst for TVG in Los Angeles and is currently taking psychology courses to become a therapist. In 2000 she became the first female jockey inducted into the Thoroughbred Racing Hall of Fame, and in 2001 she became Gulfstream Park's official spokesperson. She married Jay Hovdey, a columnist for *The Daily Racing Forum,* on 27 May 2001.

Krone's enthusiasm and tenacity have served her well in the fast-paced world of horse racing. Her win at Belmont in 1993 is described as "the most significant victory in the history of sport by a female athlete against male competition." Her place in history is assured with a total of more than 3,500 winning races and earnings exceeding $81 million. She has overcome great odds and emerged victorious in a sport formerly dominated by men.

★

For information about Krone, see Julie Krone with Nancy Richardson, *Riding for My Life* (1995). A biographical sketch is in Christina Lessa, *Women Who Win: Stories of Triumph in Sport and in Life* (1998). An article pertaining to Krone's depression is Robert Lipsyte, "Backtalk: Julie Krone's Race Against Depression," *New York Times* (21 May 2000).

ADRIANA C. TOMASINO

KRZYZEWSKI, Michael William ("Mike")   (*b.* 13 February 1947 in Chicago, Illinois), college basketball coach who was a three-time Naismith National Coach of the Year (1989, 1992, 1999) and was inducted into the Naismith Memorial Basketball Hall of Fame in 2001.

Krzyzewski was the younger son of William Krzyzewski, an elevator operator, and Emily Pituch, a house cleaner. He grew up in Chicago and attended Weber High School, where he was a top student and athlete. From 1965 to 1969 he attended the U.S. Military Academy at West Point, New York, where he was a starting guard on the Army basketball team coached by Bobby Knight. Krzyzewski was a team captain in 1969, the same year he was named to the second-team All-National Invitation Tournament (NIT). After receiving a B.S. in psychology in 1969, he served in the military from 1969 to 1974, resigning with the rank of captain. Much of his time in the army was spent coaching basketball, including a stint as the head basketball coach at the U.S. Military Academy Preparatory School at Fort Belvoir, Virginia (1972–1974). Krzyzewski married Carol "Mickie" Marsh on 4 June 1969; they had three daughters.

By the time Krzyzewski left the military, Knight had become the head basketball coach at Indiana University in Bloomington. Krzyzewski spent the 1975 season at Indiana as a graduate assistant, leaving to become the head coach at his alma mater for the 1976 season. He coached the Army team to the 1978 NIT, compiling a 73–59 record in five seasons. Following the 1980 season the thirty-three-year-old Krzyzewski, highly recommended by Knight, was the surprise choice to become the head coach at Duke University in Durham, North Carolina, taking the position made vacant when Bill Foster left to head the University of South Carolina's basketball program.

At first Krzyzewski struggled at Duke, an academically elite, private institution, which played in the competitive Atlantic Coast Conference (ACC). His first Duke team went to the 1981 NIT, while his next two set school records for losses with seventeen apiece. After three seasons at Duke, Krzyzewski had a 38–47 record and critics wondered

Mike Krzyzewski. GARY CAMERON/REUTERS/HULTON|ARCHIVE

whether he was the right man for the job. His breakthrough season was 1984, when Duke went 24–10 and was invited to the National Collegiate Athletic Association (NCAA) tournament. By this time, the hallmarks of Krzyzewski basketball had been established: an aggressive, confrontational, man-to-man defense that challenged every pass, dribble, and shot. Duke rarely played a zone defense; on offense, the team emphasized mobility and versatility.

Krzyzewski became an especially effective recruiter, consistently signing the nation's top high-school players. By spring 2001 thirty-one of his recruits had been named to the prestigious McDonald's High School All-America team. He excelled as a motivator and a tactician, demonstrating a disciplined attention to detail and an ability to fine-tune each team to best take advantage of the players' particular skills.

In 1986 Duke began a nine-year period of basketball dominance in which they compiled a won-lost record of 264–59 through 1994. The 1986 team won thirty-seven games, equaling an NCAA record. Duke advanced to the NCAA tournament Final Four in 1986, 1988 through 1992, and 1994. Their record of five consecutive Final Four appearances (1988–1992) was surpassed only by the University of California, Los Angeles (UCLA), who appeared nine consecutive times (1967–1975). Duke lost in the 1986 national finals to the University of Louisville and in 1990 to the University of Nevada, Las Vegas (UNLV), but broke through in 1991, upsetting the defending champion and prohibitive favorite UNLV by 79–77 in the national semifinals and defeating Kansas University by 72–65 for the NCAA title. The following year Duke defended its national title, becoming the first team to do so since UCLA's run of seven straight championships from 1967 to 1973. During this nine-year period Krzyzewski had six Associated Press All-Americans, and three of his players—Johnny Dawkins (1986), Danny Ferry (1989), Christian Laettner (1992)—were voted as national players of the year.

Krzyzewski underwent back surgery prior to the 1995 season. He returned to coaching too quickly and was forced to take a leave of absence midway through the season. His team slumped in his absence, falling from 9–3 when he left to a final won-lost mark of 13–18, which ended Duke's streak of eleven consecutive NCAA tournament appearances. Fully recovered for the 1996 season, Krzyzewski led Duke back to the tournament but with a relatively mediocre 18–13.

Duke began a second period of dominance in the 1997 season, as a revitalized Krzyzewski resumed his peerless recruiting. Duke captured the ACC regular-season title in 1997 through 2000 and tied for first in 2001. Prior to this period no ACC school had ever won more than three straight regular-season crowns. Duke won the ACC tournament in 1999, 2000, and 2001. The 1999 team, led by the national player-of-the-year Elton Brand, won thirty-seven games but lost in the national finals to the University of Connecticut. In 2001 Krzyzewski won his third NCAA crown when Duke defeated the University of Arizona by 82–72 in the finals. That same year Shane Battier was the national player of the year.

Through the 2001 season Krzyzewski had compiled a 533–164 record at Duke and an overall mark of 606–223. His NCAA tournament history of 56–14 included nine appearances in the Final Four. His many honors included being named the ACC Coach of the Year six times (1984, 1986, 1987, 1997, 1999, 2000). Krzyzewski was named the National Association of Basketball Coaches (NABC) National Coach of the Year in 1991 and 1999, and the Naismith National Coach of the Year in 1989, 1992, and 1999. He was the head coach of the U.S. teams at the 1987 World University Games and the 1990 World Championships. Krzyzewski also served as the president of the NABC (1998–1999). In 2001 he was inducted into the Naismith Memorial Basketball Hall of Fame.

Krzyzewski has been highly successful at winning games and championships, while maintaining Duke's reputation for running a spotless program. His players have graduated at a high rate and, under his tenure, Duke frequently has been cited as a model college-basketball program. The *Sporting News* named Krzyzewski as its sports-

man of the year in 1992, writing, "On the court and off, Krzyzewski is a family man first, a teacher second, a basketball coach third, and a winner at all three. He is what's right about sports."

★

Krzyzewski's philosophy is summed up in Mike Krzyzewski with Donald T. Phillips, *Leading with the Heart: Coach K's Successful Strategies for Basketball, Business, and Life* (2000), and for further reading see also Mike Krzyzewski with Donald T. Phillips, *Five Point Play: Duke's Journey to the 2001 National Championships* (2001). Also useful are Bill Brill, *Duke Basketball: An Illustrated History* (1986); Bill Brill with Mike Krzyzewski, *A Season Is a Lifetime: The Inside Story of the Duke Blue Devils and Their Championship Seasons* (1993); and Gregg Doyel, *Coach K: Building the Duke Dynasty: The Story of Mike Krzyzewski and the Winning Tradition at Duke University* (1999).

JIM L. SUMNER

KURLAND, Robert ("Bob") (*b.* 23 December 1924 in St. Louis), college basketball player who led Oklahoma Agricultural and Mechanical College (A&M) to unprecedented back-to-back National Collegiate Athletic Association (NCAA) basketball championships in 1945 and 1946. His unusual height and shot-blocking methods helped lead to the adoption of the rule against goaltending.

Kurland, already six-feet, six-inches tall at age thirteen, was recruited for the school basketball team at Jennings High School in suburban St. Louis. He played for four years on the team, where his height gained him the nickname "the Jennings Giant," and he twice made the Class B state tournament. Kurland also won the Missouri high school high-jump championship in his senior year. He reached six feet, nine inches, at age seventeen, but his awkwardness on the court kept him from being recruited by college basketball programs—that is, until his high school coach informed him that coach Henry Iba of the Aggies at Oklahoma A&M University (now Oklahoma State University), who virtually never traveled to recruit, wanted to have dinner with him.

When they met in 1941, Iba invited Kurland to Stillwater, Oklahoma, for a tryout, as was the practice then, stressing that there were no guarantees of acceptance. After three days of workouts, Iba offered Kurland a scholarship and a part-time campus job, promising to try to teach him how to play at the college level. Kurland was attracted by the engineering program at A&M and decided to enroll, graduating in the fall of 1942. Like other young men over six-feet, six-inches tall, Kurland's height made him ineligible for military service.

Iba's teams were famous for their defense, and while the coach originally saw Kurland primarily as a defensive

Bob Kurland (right). AP/WIDE WORLD PHOTOS

player, he patiently encouraged him, through endless repetition, to develop a hook shot and improve his footwork. He also put Kurland on a jump-rope regimen and made him practice as much as four hours a day. As a collegian Kurland grew to weigh 225 pounds and stood just a shade under seven feet tall. This was a shocking height at that time, making Kurland subject to predictable abuse. University of Kansas coach Forrest "Phog" Allen called him a "glandular, mezzanine-peeping goon," and Kurland even referred to himself as a "strange giant." The University of Oklahoma (OU), A&M's cross-state rival, sent a man on stilts onto the court during warm-ups and had its shortest guard face Kurland for the initial jump ball; the Aggies' publicist came up with the nickname "Foothills." After playing sparingly in his freshman year, Kurland became a starter for the 1943–1944 season, averaging thirteen points per game and being named an All-American.

Kurland made his mark as a defender, blocking and batting away shots even as they were on their downward arc, as was then legal (no interference was permitted when the ball was in the imaginary cylinder directly above the basket). This was Iba's deliberate strategy and Kurland executed it with increasing dexterity. "Goaltending," as it came to be called, had not been an issue before, but now Phog Allen called for the basket to be raised from ten feet to twelve. Coach Bruce Drake at OU complained that the Sooners had lost to the Aggies because Kurland had taken over twenty shots out of the basket. Fans from rival schools booed when Kurland goaltended, and OU's Drake argued

in print that it was "practically impossible to beat a team whose giant raises his defensive umbrella over your goal."

As Drake was chairman of the National Collegiate Athletic Association (NCAA) rules committee, he was in a position to do more than whine—he arranged for an NCAA official to come to Norman, Oklahoma, for the OU–A&M game. Sitting on a platform set up behind the basket, the official observed Kurland's play to determine if his hands were over the cylinder when he blocked, and they were (the Aggies won the game, 14–11). The three-second rule had been adopted in 1936 to prevent players from camping out directly under the basket and waiting to be fed a pass, but as the lane was only six feet wide when Kurland played, his spectacular size meant that he was still close to the hoop.

Rival coaches managed to outlaw goaltending by the time Kurland started his junior season in fall 1944, but the rule change failed to slow him down in any way. The Aggies finished with a record of 26–4 (all losses to military teams) and won the 1945 NCAA title 49–45 over local favorite New York University at Madison Square Garden in a very physical contest. Kurland dominated on defense and offense with his inside game, scoring 22 points (of a team total of 49) before a record championship crowd of 18,035, and was the obvious choice for the Most Valuable Player (MVP) award.

In a postseason Red Cross charity event called the "Champion of Champions" game, A&M was matched with National Invitation Tournament champion DePaul University of Chicago, which had its own big man—six-foot, ten-inch George Mikan. Kurland and Mikan had faced each other twice before in their college careers, but this third matchup, inelegantly called the "battle of the goons," was far better publicized. Mikan got in foul trouble early, thanks largely to the efforts of A&M's defense, and the Aggies prevailed 52–44, with DePaul missing 80 of 96 shots attempted.

Kurland's senior year in 1945 was more of the same all around: he led the nation in scoring with an average 19 points per game, while his team earned a 28–3 record and another NCAA championship. This impressive record led Curt Gowdy, then an employee of Oklahoma City radio station KOMA, to suggest that A&M's (and OU's) games be broadcast for the first time, with Gowdy calling the games for both schools. Kurland scored a career high fifty-eight points in the last regular-season game of the year despite being guarded by "Easy" Ed Macauley of Saint Louis University, a future National Basketball Association (NBA) star with the Celtics and Hawks.

Kurland's continued rivalry with Mikan began to attract attention. In December 1945 A&M lost its first home game in two years to DePaul and Mikan, who outscored Kurland twenty-five to eighteen. The Aggies, however, won a rematch with the Blue Demons 46–38 before 12,000 fans at

Chicago Stadium, although Mikan again outscored Kurland nineteen to ten. A&M lost the next night to Bowling Green State University, but finished the year with fifteen straight wins and a second consecutive NCAA championship, becoming the first team to repeat.

For the first time the Final Four teams gathered at the championship site, Madison Square Garden in New York City, before a new record crowd of 18,479. In other firsts, the title game was televised, a filmed version was produced, and gate receipts topped the $100,000 mark. Kurland was named MVP for the second straight year as the Aggies defeated the University of North Carolina 43–40. He scored twenty-three points and assisted on all but four of A&M's other field goals, becoming the only player to score more than half of his team's points in the championship game.

Kurland turned down offers from the NBA's forerunner, the Basketball Association of America (BBA), accepting instead a job with Phillips Petroleum in Bartlesville, Oklahoma, as a part-time executive and full-time player on the company's Amateur Athletic Union (AAU) team, the Phillips 66ers. He played for the 66ers for six seasons (1946 to 1952), during which they won three AAU national championships (1947, 1948, 1950). He also played on the gold medal U.S. Olympic teams of 1948 and 1952, the first player to be a team member twice. Kurland enjoyed the greatest success of any big man in college basketball history up to his time and, with George Mikan, created the first famous rivalry between big men. A three-time All-American (in 1944, 1945, and 1946), Kurland was named Helms Foundation National Player of the Year in 1946 (an award won by Mikan the previous two years). He was elected to the Naismith Memorial Basketball Hall of Fame in 1961.

★

A lengthy interview with Bob Kurland is recorded in Billy Packer with Roland Lazenby, *Fifty Years of the Final Four: Golden Moments of the NCAA Basketball Tournament* (1987). Some information is available in Eric Nadel, *The Night Wilt Scored 100: Tales from Basketball's Past* (1990). Curt Gowdy and coauthor John Powers discuss Kurland at length in *Seasons to Remember: The Way It Was in American Sports, 1945–1960* (1991).

LAWSON BOWLING

KWAN, Michelle Wing (*b.* 7 July 1980 in Torrance, California), figure skater who in 1996 became the youngest world champion in U.S. history and in 1998 was winner of the Olympic silver medal in Nagano, Japan.

Kwan was the third of three children born to Daniel Kwan, a restaurant owner from Canton (now Guangzhou), China, and Estella Wing, a former nurse and television news anchor from Hong Kong. The couple had moved to

Michelle Kwan. ARCHIVE PHOTOS, INC.

the United States in 1974, where they ran a restaurant in Torrance, California, until their retirement in the 1990s. Gymnastics was Kwan's first sport, but her adored brother Ron's affinity for ice hockey soon had Michelle and her older sister clamoring to learn how to skate. At age five, Michelle began taking lessons at a rink in a mall near her home. In her autobiography, she wrote: "I got my first taste of what it's like to fly." In 1988, at age seven, Kwan watched on television as U.S. skater Brian Boitano won the men's gold medal at the Winter Olympic Games. Her dream was born, and she vowed to compete in the Olympics someday.

The Kwan family struggled financially to pay for the lessons, skates, and clothes required for both Michelle and her sister, Karen, also a competitive skater and ultimately a three-time top-ten finisher in the nationals. In 1991 the sisters won scholarships to Ice Castle International Training Center in Lake Arrowhead, California. There, Kwan met her future coach, Frank Carroll. Already a regional and sectional medalist at the junior level, Kwan turned to Carroll to prepare for her first junior nationals, which were then three weeks away. She placed ninth, below her expectations, but was no less determined to advance to the top level. While her coach was away at a conference, she persuaded her father to take her to the test which advanced her to the status of senior skater. Carroll was initially furious at the move. She placed sixth in the 1993 senior nationals (which Nancy Kerrigan won), and soon won a gold medal at the Olympic Festival in San Antonio.

The next year brought an unprecedented level of attention to women's figure skating and unexpectedly thrust Kwan into the national media spotlight. Just before the 1994 nationals, Kwan shared practice time with Kerrigan. As the two left the ice together, Kwan saw Kerrigan walk behind a curtain area backstage, then heard Kerrigan scream. She had been struck in the knee by an acquaintance of the husband of Kerrigan's chief rival, Tonya Harding. Kwan finished second behind Harding at the competition, and briefly won a spot on the U.S. Olympic team. The U.S. Figure Skating Association ruled that Kerrigan could skate in the Olympics, but ordered Kwan to travel to Norway as an alternate. Soon she was overwhelmed by a swarm of reporters clamoring to interview the pony-tailed adolescent. She did not get to compete, but enjoyed the small taste of her Olympic dream. A few months later she placed eighth in her first world championship.

In 1995 Kwan finished second in the U.S. Nationals and was elated by her two flawlessly performed programs at the world championship. But despite mistakes by other skaters, she placed fourth when Chinese skater Lu Chen won first place. She realized that judges and others perceived her as a "kid skater" and resolved to mature her style and develop the artistic side of her skating.

What followed was a breakthrough year for Kwan. Her choreographer, Lori Nichol, chose music from *Salome*, Richard Strauss's musical drama based on the New Testament story in which Salome performed the dance of the seven veils to earn the head of John the Baptist on a platter. At first, fifteen-year-old Kwan was shocked when she learned the story, but she warmed to the role. It led her to first-place victories at the 1996 nationals and made her at the time the youngest U.S. skater to win the world championship. But she would only briefly hold that distinction, as Tara Lipinski, an even younger skater, was moving up through the ranks of skating.

The following year, Kwan delivered a disastrous performance at the 1997 nationals, falling three times. In her autobiography, she wrote "I was so busy trying not to fall that I forgot to feel what was in my heart. I'd forgotten about my love of skating." At the world championship, she stumbled during her short program. But other events—including the diagnosis of her friend and fellow skater Scott Hamilton with testicular cancer—helped her put her mistakes into perspective. She rebounded with a beautiful long program performance and took the silver medal behind Lipinski.

Kwan and Lipinski were well-publicized rivals as they headed into the 1998 Olympics. Kwan was favored, having bested Lipinski in the 1998 U.S. Nationals with scores that included fifteen of a possible eighteen perfect 6.0 scores for artistry. But Kwan had been hampered by a stress fracture in her left foot. At the Olympics, she felt she skated well, but her performance could not match fifteen-year-old Lipinski's, and Kwan took the silver medal. As reported in *People* magazine, Kwan's coach told her: "You were wonderful, but it was not your greatest performance. It wasn't exciting." Kwan then "roared back," winning the world championship two months later (a victory marred by the absence of Lipinski, who had turned professional). By the time of the Goodwill Games that summer, the *New York Times* wrote, "her graciousness in defeat may even have made her more popular than she would have been in victory."

At the 1999 world championship, mistakes caused the favored Kwan to claim the silver behind the Russian skater Maria Butyrskaya. That fall, Kwan decided to enter the University of California at Los Angeles, the first time she had attended classes since eighth grade (she finished her secondary schooling with a tutor). She pushed ahead, winning gold medals at both the national and world championships in 2000 and being named that spring one of *People* magazine's "Fifty Most Beautiful People." The honor marked her transformation into a "svelte sophisticate" who experimented with new hairstyles, makeup, and clothes on her petite frame.

In 2001 Kwan was once again on top, successfully defending her title at both the national and world championships. But over the past two years she had endured some behind-the-scenes criticisms for a lack of freshness in her skating, and in June 2001 she announced the end of her eight-year collaboration with choreographer Nichol. She said she was searching for a new direction as she headed toward the 2002 Winter Olympics in Salt Lake City, Utah.

When at her top form, Kwan had earned the title of the greatest women's figure skater in the world, distinguished by her mix of artistry, athleticism, and drive. Her career since becoming a senior skater at age twelve in 1993 had been marked by a series of highs and lows, but she always distinguished herself with the poise and determination she showed in pulling herself back from unexpected losses or below-par performances. She had said in news conferences that she would only be twenty-five years old at the time of the 2006 Winter Olympics in Turin, Italy, and would be in no hurry to retire from competitive skating, anticipating, as a master of quick turnarounds, many victories to come in her career.

★

Kwan's autobiography is *Michelle Kwan: Heart of a Champion*, with Laura James (1997). The *Los Angeles Times* wrote about her at the beginning of her career (14 May 1993), and she has been profiled repeatedly since by the *New York Times* (4 Jan. 1998; 1 Feb. 1998; 20 Feb. 1998; 29 July 1998); the *Washington Post* (28 Mar. 1999); *People* (29 Mar. 1999); and the *Chicago Tribune* (14 June 2001).

LEIGH DYER

ISBN 0-684-31224-7

90000

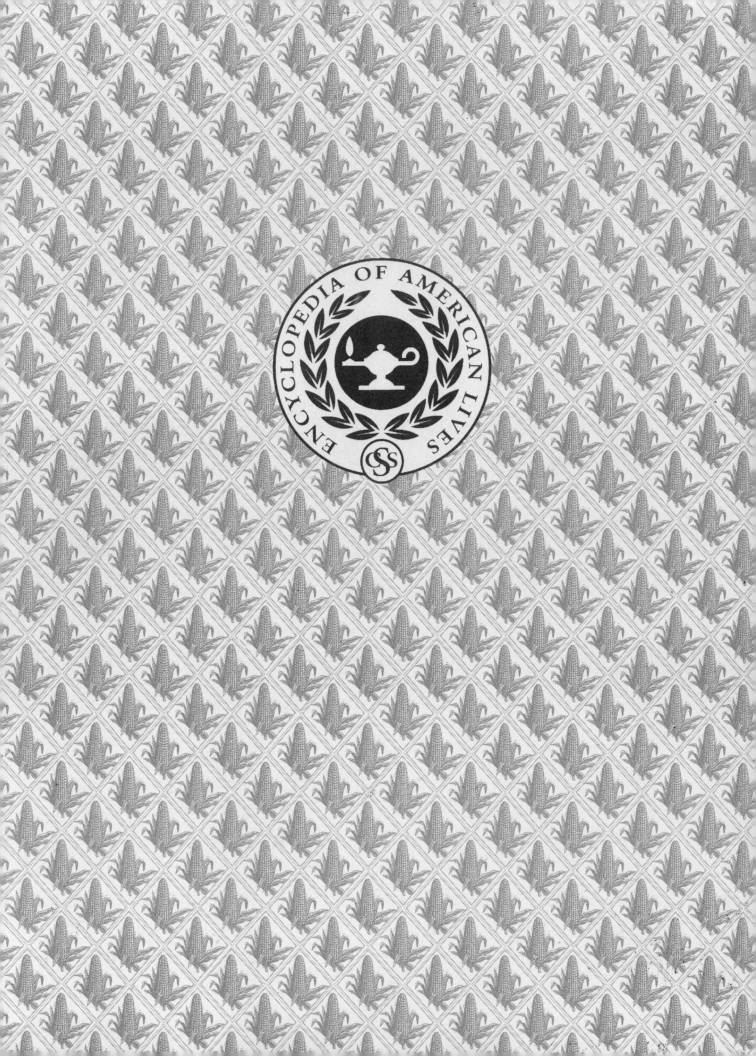

ENCYCLOPEDIA OF AMERICAN LIVES